W9-BPP-978

DATE DUE

Encyclopedia of Women and World Religion

Encyclopedia of Women and World Religion

Edited by

Serinity Young

Volume 1

Macmillan Reference USA
New York

Macmillan Reference USA
1633 Broadway, New York, NY 10019-6785

Printed in the United States of America

Printing Number

2 3 4 5 6 7 8 9 10

Library of Congress Cataloging-in-Publications Data

Encyclopedia of women and world religion / Serinity Young, editor in
    chief.
        p. cm.
        Includes bibliographical references and index.
        ISBN 0-02-964608-8 (set). — ISBN 0-02-864859-5 (vol. 1). — ISBN
    0-02-864860-9 (vol. 2)
        1. Women and religion—Encyclopedias.   I. Young, Serinity.
    BL458.E53   1998
    200′.82—dc21   98–39292
                                                                        CIP

This paper meets the requirements of ANSI-NISO Z39.48-1992 (Permanence of Paper).

Contents

Editorial and Production Staff

Project Editors
Nancy Wright
Sarah Cunningham

Editorial Assistant
Anthony Coloneri

Manuscript Editors
Jonathan Aretakis
Jessica Evans
Laura Rubin

Proofreaders
Nancy Gratton
Laura Rubin
Helen Wallace

Illustrations Editors
Hélène Potter
Toni Ann Scaramuzzo

Indexer
AEIOU, Inc.

Production Manager
Rose Capozzelli

MACMILLAN REFERENCE USA

Elly Dickason, *Publisher*
Toni Ann Scaramuzzo, *Managing Editor*

Introduction

The last twenty years have seen a magnificent flowering of scholarship on women and world religion that has permanently altered the way we look at religion. Much of this work, however, is not readily accessible to scholars and students working in disparate traditions and disciplines. This encyclopedia endeavors to represent this burgeoning field by serving as a culturally and historically comprehensive reference work that reflects contemporary approaches to women's history and experience in world religion from the beginning of time to the present.

Such a monumental project required taking a broad view that begins with the diverse composition of the editorial board—each member is an expert in a particular religious tradition, methodology, or geographical region. We have not always agreed, and the ensuing discussions have enriched and broadened this work. Individually, board members have discussed the project with colleagues and within various scholarly groups, drawing as much input as possible from the larger community. Additional scholars made important contributions as consultants, helping us to refine our choices of topics and to find contributors. Individual contributors sometimes challenged our approach to a topic or suggested additional topics, and more often than not their suggestions were incorporated.

Further, the editorial board made a conscious effort to avoid the domination of a Western viewpoint by actively seeking contributions from non-Western scholars. An important goal has been to include as many voices as possible and certainly not to seek unanimity of opinion. And, while the names of many contributors will be familiar to students of religion and women's studies as prominent figures in those disciplines, these scholars have agreed to explore their subjects in light of the special commitments of this work. In addition, a new and exciting generation of scholars, including male scholars, have analyzed and contextualized the contri-butions of their intellectual forebears through the prism of emerging approaches to the study of religion, history, and society. Articles such as "Women's Suffrage Movement" look with gratitude to the past while "Men's Spirituality Movement" acknowledges the impact of women's studies and women's knowledge on men's religious lives. Wherever possible, bibliographies have been designed to represent the range of opinion on a topic and thus are an invaluable source of recent scholarship from around the world. Finally, we have encouraged authors to include filmographies for articles. Special thanks go to Dr. Elaine Charnoff of the American Museum of Natural History in New York City for assisting many of our authors in this regard as well as for her own article, "Film and Video: Documentary Films and Videos."

All the world's religions are addressed here, but the broadest coverage is given to the major religions of the world through a series of interrelated articles. Each has an introductory overview article followed by articles on either specific historical periods or regional variations. Within these composite entries are articles entitled "Religious Rites and Practices" that attend to the all-important domestic rites associated with women, those entitled "History of Study" recover the lost voices of women scholars who did ground-breaking work in the past and analyze how the study of women has reshaped our understanding of these traditions. A special feature of this work is the inclusion of articles on subjects specifically identified with women or of particular relevance to women's religious life—for instance, "Eucharist" and "Compassion"—which are also listed in the cross-references that accompany the historical and geographical articles. Many of these are central terms within particular religious traditions; these articles both explore the terms from the point of view of women's religious participation and provide bibliographies that highlight recent, innovative scholarship.

By its very nature this work assumes the validity of the comparative method in both the study of religion and the study of women. Pursuing that method on so far-reaching a project has brought out both the uniqueness of the world's religions (in articles on the history of individual religions and their regional variations) and the similarities of the human spiritual quest and of women's religious experience (in articles on "Mysticism," "Asceticism," "Monasticism"). Certain comparative topics, such as "Eve" and "Monotheism" are relevant particularly or only to the monotheistic traditions of Judaism, Christianity, and Islam. In other cases, such as "Alchemy." "Wisdom," "Spirituality," and "Visions," topics have relevance to a broader range of religious traditions. Of special significance to the study of women in world religion is the series of articles on the "Body" itself, as well as its parts (e.g., "Breast," "Hair," "Womb," Vagina," "Yoni"). Related articles deal with what one does with the body—"Mutilation," "Asceticism," "Fasting"—and how we cover it—"Clothing," Ornamentation," "Cross-dressing."

Some articles bring out the ironies of women's religious life. For example, "Silence" contrasts its importance as a voluntary spiritual practice to the compulsory silencing of women by their religions. This and articles such as "Leadership" and "Possession" bring out significant differences between women's and men's religious experience. Some articles grapple with the skewering of women on the twin prongs of racism and sexism in particular traditions, such as "Oceanic Religions: Australia," which contrasts women's religious and social experience before and after colonialism; others explore these and related issues from specific theoretical perspectives ("Racism," "Sexism," "Androcentrism," "Ethnicity," "Colonialism and Postcolonialism").

Of particular interest for the comparative emphasis of this work is the category of transreligional terms such as "Nature," "Desire," and "Blood." Since it is a rare scholar who can command a truly representative range of the world religions, many of these articles take a case-study approach, focusing on the author's area of expertise while alluding to other traditions and, where possible, using the bibliographies to direct the reader to further examples. Thus, the index is an essential tool for locating additional information on a particular tradition, and it is also meant to encourage readers to explore this work at their leisure. Cross-references have the same goal: to offer the reader more detailed information on a particular topic or to suggest relevant relationships between different terms. In this regard, we have often employed a friendly redundancy, which permits the same topic to be covered from different perspectives. For instance, the work of classics scholar

Jane Harrison is covered in a biographical article that discusses her work, but she is also discussed in articles about topics she influenced, such as the study of Goddesses. Again, the index will prove helpful in uncovering these connections.

Because of space limitations most of the editors chose to limit the number of biographical and theagraphical entries by representing individuals in overview articles or within discussions of particular movements, such as "Bhakti" or the series of articles on "Goddess." The biographical entries are of necessity all short pieces (though supplemented by bibliographies), but they give powerful glimpses of women living highly diverse religious lives (e.g., "Jonas, Regina," "Ānandamayī Mā [Ananda Ma]," "Lenshina, Alice"). Within particular traditions there is no singular template followed by all women. Our choices for inclusion were based on presenting as wide a range of women's lives as possible. It is highly recommended that the reader explore these articles, especially those on women the reader may never have heard about, as a quick and easy way to access an unfamiliar religious tradition. These articles are readily accessible through the synoptic outline, which groups all the biographical entries together.

Women's religious status and experience are not necessarily static; frequently they are altered at various stages of life ("Rites of Passage"). Hence the inclusion of articles such as "Marriage and Singleness," "Wives," "Widows," "Motherhood and Grandmotherhood," "Virginity," and on practices such as "Celibacy," "Asceticism," "Mysticism," and "Witchcraft." By means of these articles and the series of "Religious Rites and Practices" articles, we have tried to balance the representation of extraordinary women within a tradition by offering a picture of women's day-to-day lives.

This work both challenges academic expertise and broadens its purview. Many of the articles reveal all too clearly the pernicious influence of sexism, which denied, and sadly often continues to deny, women full human status in their religions. This same sexism has afflicted scholarship on religion; more than just compensating for that fault, this encyclopedia is a celebration of the extraordinary amount of innovative and superior scholarship that has been accomplished in recent years. Several articles address this directly, such as "History of Religions," "Women's Studies," "Gender Studies," and "Women and Religion." Further theoretical issues surrounding the study of women and world religion are discussed in articles on particular academic disciplines, such as "History," "Anthropology of Religion," and "Psychology of Religion." Our agenda has been feminist in as broad a sense as contributors from various religious traditions, nationalities, sexual orientations, races, ethnicities, classes, ages, politics, and methodologies could make it. Some are people of faith, others atheist or agnostic. Most are scholars, many of whom blend social activism with their work, whereas others are social activists who utilize scholarship. All the authors have met the challenge of this project, which while maintaining scholarly standards of excellence for the interest of professional academics, remains accessible to the reading level of interested high school students and appealing to the general reader.

It is with pleasure that I acknowledge my debt to Paul Bernabeo, the original managing editor of this project, who grasped the significance of such a work and offered his patient assistance and unflagging support. Thanks are also due to our original publisher, Charles E. Smith. I deeply regret that he did not live to see it completed. We were in agreement as to who should be on the board, and once we were all assembled, a truly amazing feeling of camaraderie and collegiality characterized the meetings that generated the outline of this work, descriptions of articles, and a list of contributors. We have all been enriched by this exchange of ideas.

Essentially within the limitations of word allotments and certain patterning for the sake of continuity among traditions, each editor was autonomous in her specialty, though we all discussed each area and offered suggestions. (The overall organizational format of this encyclopedia is covered in the systematic outline of contents.) In this regard a special acknowledgment goes to Lawrence E. Sullivan, whose ideas and suggestions were so formative in the planning stages of this project, especially in shaping coverage of the microhistorical traditions. Among the editorial board, Caroline Walker Bynum made significant contributions to the overall plan of this work until other responsibilities limited her participation. E. Ann Matter then became the editor for the Christianity section. Francisca Cho handled East Asia; Naomi Goldenberg's main area was methodology (with the assistance of Ann Matter and myself); Susannah Heschel formulated Ancient Near Eastern and Israelite Religion as well as the Judaism section; Jane Smith shaped the Islam entries. The South, North, and Central Asian sections, as well as the Buddhism, Indo-European, Transreligional Phenomena, and Religion and Culture sections, fell under my purview, though especially with the help of Ann Mater on the last two. At the same time, each editor contributed to the development of other sections of the encyclopedia; and all were helpful in finding contributors for and shaping the content of articles in the Transreligional section.

My heartfelt thanks go to the members of the Macmillan staff who continued to support this project. My final word of gratitude, though, goes to the contributors who gave so generously of their time and expertise.

This project has received support form two additional sources—first from Meredith Davis and Stratford Sherman, and second from the University Seminars of Columbia University in the preparation of the manuscript for publication. Some of the ideas presented herein have benefited from discussions in the University Seminar on Buddhist Studies. This aid was deeply appreciated and is gratefully acknowledged.

Serinity Young

List of Articles

A

Abortion
June O'Connor

Adultery
Trevor M. Wade

African American Churches
Cheryl Townsend Gilkes

African Religions
Laura Grillo

Afro-Atlantic Religions
Ina Johanna Fandrich

Afterlife
Karen Lee Anderson

Agricultural Rituals
Jacob Olupona

'Ā'ishah
Riffat Hassan

Ala
Robert M. Baum

Alchemy
David White

Alinesitoué
Robert M. Baum

Almsgiving
Ellison Banks Findly

Amaterasu
Mary Evelyn Tucker

Amazons
Daniella Reinhard

Amulets
Rebecca Lesses

Ānandamayī Mā (Ananda Ma)
Karen Pechilis Prentiss

Ancestor Worship
Eliza F. Kent

Ancient Egyptian Religions
Barbara S. Lesko

Androcentrism
Rita M. Gross

Androgyny
Janice D. Willis

Angela of Foligno
Catherine M. Mooney

Animals
E. Ann Pearson

Anonymous
Lorine M. Getz

Antal
Vidya Dehejia

Anthropology
Rubina Ramji

Anthropology of Religion
Elizabeth Fuller Collins

Antisemitism and Jewish Identity
Marilyn Reizbaum

Aphrodite (Venus)
Sarah Iles Johnston

Apsāras
Annapurna Garimella

Archaeology
Beth Alpert Nakhai

Architecture: Overview
Juan E. Campo

Architecture: Nomadic or Seasonal
Labelle Prussin

Arctic Religions: In Asia
Piers Vitebsky

Arctic Religions: In North America
Bernard Saladin d'Anglure

Art
Diane Apostolos-Cappadona

Artemis (Diana)
Sarah Iles Johnston

Asceticism
Gail Corrington Streete

Asherah
Carole R. Fontaine

Asian and Asian American Traditions
Jung Ha Kim

Astrology
Serinity Young

Athena (Minerva)
Jenifer Neils

Athletics
Amy Hollywood

Auspicious and Inauspicious
Vivian-Lee Nyitray

Authority
Matthew Bagger

Autobiography and Biography: An Overview
Kim Knott

Autobiography and Biography: In Asian Religions
Vivian-Lee Nyitray

Autobiography and Biography: In Monotheistic Traditions
E. Ann Matter

List of Contributors

Anne Llewellyn Barstow
New York, NY
  Wicca

Tessa Bartholomeusz
Florida State University
  Buddhism: Southeast Asian
    Buddhism
  Saṅghamittā

Elizabeth Ann Bartlett
University of Minnesota
  Transcendentalism

Judith R. Baskin
State University of New York, Albany
  Judaism: In the Middle Ages
  Lilith

Leora Batnitzky
Princeton University
  Language

Janet L. Bauer
Trinity College, Hartford, CT
  Islam: In Iran and Turkey

Robert M. Baum
Iowa State University
  Ala
  Alinesitoué
  Witchcraft: Witchcraft in Africa

Lois Beck
Washington University
  Islam: Religious Rites and Practices

Mary Farrell Bednarowski
*United Theological Seminary of the
    Twin Cities, New Brighton, MN*
  Eddy, Mary Baker

Diane Bell
Leicester, MA
  Oceanic Religions: Australia

Elisabeth Benard
University of Puget Sound
  Shrines
  Yoginīs

Catherine Benton
Lake Forest College
  Boundaries
  Egg

Nadine Berardi
New York, NY
  Sarasvatī

Doris Bergen
University of Notre Dame
  Judaism: The Holocaust

Emilie L. Bergmann
University of California, Berkeley
  Juana Inés de la Cruz

Michael Berkowitz
University College, London
  Judaism: Modern Movements

Donna Berman
Elmont, NY
  Ethics: Feminist Ethics

Phillip Berryman
Philadelphia, PA
  Menchú, Rigoberta

Jodi Bilinkoff
*University of North Carolina,
    Greensboro*
  María de Santo Domingo
  Teresa of Avila

Khalid Yahya Blankinship
Philadelphia, PA
  Revelation

George Bond
Teachers College, Columbia University
  Lenshina, Alice

Elizabeth M. Bounds
Blacksburg, VA
  Political Science

Erika Bourguignon
Ohio State University
  Possession

Charlotte W. Boynton
Oxford, England
  Manfreda, Sister

Brenda E. Brasher
Mount Union College
  Couples

Jan N. Bremmer
Groningen, The Netherlands
  Castration
  Widows

Joanne Carlson Brown
First United Methodist Church, Seattle
  Protestantism

Judith K. Brown
Rochester, MI
  Menopause

Allaire Brumfield
Towson University
  Cybele

Marie-Florine Bruneau
University of Southern California
  Guyon, Jeanne Marie Bouvier de la
    Motte

Jorunn Jacobeson Buckley
Eastham, MA
  Mandaean Religion
  Sophia

Denise Kimber Buell
Williams College
  Heterosexism

Kelly Bulkeley
Kensington, CA
  Home
  Sacred Marriage

Grace G. Burford
Prescott College
  Buddhism: Buddhism In the West
  Buddhism: History of Study
  Desire

Caroline Walker Bynum
Columbia University
  Mechtild of Magdeburg

Suzanne Cahill
University of California, San Diego
  Queen Mother of the West

Juan E. Campo
University of California, Santa Barbara
  Architecture: Overview

Katie Cannon
Temple University
  Classism
  Hurston, Zora Neale

Francine Cardman
*Weston Jesuit School of Theology,
    Cambridge, MA*
  Christianity: Historical Overview
    from 300 to 1800
  Ministry
  Perpetua and Felicity

Robert T. Carpenter
University of California, Santa Barbara
  New Religions: In South America

Victoria Cass
University of Colorado, Boulder
  East Asian Religions: An Overview

Tina Chanter
University of Memphis
  Philosophy: In the West

Elaine Charnov
*American Museum of Natural History,
New York, NY*
Film and Video: Documentary Films
and Videos

Francisca Cho
Georgetown University
Confucianism: Politics and Authority
in the Confucian System
Literature: In the East

Carol P. Christ
Ariadne Institute, Athens, Greece
Goddess: Contemporary Goddess
Movement
Graves, Robert Ranke
Harrison, Jane Ellen
Religious Experience
Sappho
Thealogy

Mary C. Churchill
University of Colorado, Boulder
Lesbianism: In Microhistorical
Traditions
New Religions: In Native American
Traditions

Julia Clancy-Smith
University of Arizona
Islam: In Africa

Anne L. Clark
University of Vermont
Elisabeth of Schönau
Virgin Mary

L. Clarke
University of Pennsylvania
Prophecy

J. Shannon Clarkson
Guilford, CT
Sexism

Bradley S. Clough
Bard College
Disciples
Salvation

Thomas B. Coburn
St. Lawrence University
Prakriti

Alan Cole
Lewis and Clark College
Breasts
Buddhism: Religious Rites and
Practices

Susan Guettel Cole
State University New York, Buffalo
Demeter and Persephone

Elizabeth Fuller Collins
Ohio University
Anthropology of Religion
Divinity: Divinity and Humanity
New Religions: In Southeast Asia

Beth A. Conklin
Vanderbilt University
South American Religions: In the
Lowlands

Joann Wolski Conn
Neumann College
Thérèse of Lisieux

Paula M. Cooey
Trinity University, San Antonio, TX
Nature

miriam cooke
Duke University
War

Kate Cooper
University of Manchester, England
Martyrdom

Cathy Lynne Costin
California State University, Northridge
Material Culture

Laurie Cozad
University of Chicago Divinity School
Motherhood and Grandmotherhood
Spirits

Toni Craven
Fort Worth, TX
Images of Women: In the Apocrypha

Mary Rose D'Angelo
University of Notre Dame
Christianity: New Testament Canon
Hermaphrodite
Mary and Martha

Helen Damico
University of New Mexico
Freyja

Sheila Davaney
Iliff School of Theology, Denver
Essentialism
Theology: An Overview

Marlene Dobkin de Rios
Placentia, CA
Intoxicants and Hallucinogens

Jacqueline de Weever
Brooklyn, NY
Literature: In the West

Andrea Deagon
*University of North Carolina,
Wilmington*
Festivals

Vidya Dehejia
*Smithsonian Institution, South Asian
Art*
Antal
Māhadēviyakka

Valerie DeMarinis
Uppsala University, Sweden
Scandinavian Religions

Tirdad Derakhshani
Philadelphia, PA
Phenomenology of Religion

Laura S. Desmond
Chicago, IL
Hierarchy

Pam A. Detrixhe
Sharon Hill, PA
Moon

Miriam Robbins Dexter
Antioch University
Goddess: Prehistoric Goddesses

Debra Diamond
New York, NY
Iconography: In the East

Christine Downing
Eastbound, WA
Juno
Lesbianism: A Classical View
Mythology: Feminist Uses of
Mythology about Goddesses

Marymay Downing
University of Ottawa, Canada
Incest

Ellen M. Driscoll
University of Prince Edward Island
Twelve-Step Programs

Jill Dubisch
Northern Arizona University
Pilgrimage

Lucie DuFresne
University of Ottawa, Canada
Craft: In Monotheistic Traditions
Occultism

Jennifer Dumpert
Graduate Theological Union, San Francisco
Benten
Femininity
Sun
Witchcraft: Contemporary Witchcraft Movement

Ingrid Edlund-Berry
University of Texas, Austin
Etruscan and Roman Religion

Mary Edwardsen
Claremont, CA
Romanticism

Cynthia Eller
South Orange, NJ
Goddess: History of Study
Immanence and Transcendence
Matriarchy
Neopaganism

Kaspar Elm
Freie Universität, Berlin
Elizabeth of Hungary

Kathleen M. Erndl
Florida State University
Pārvatī
Yoni

Nancy A. Evans
Wheaton College
Delphi
Mystery Religions

Nancy Auer Falk
Western Michigan University
Karma
Sacred, The

Ina Johanna Fandrich
Philadelphia, PA
Afro-Atlantic Religions

Susan A. Farrell
Kingsborough Community College, Brooklyn, NY
Social Action

C. Anne Feldhaus
Arizona State University
Hinduism: Religious Rites and Practices

Julia Winder Fey
University of Central Arkansas
Secret Societies

Ellison Banks Findly
Trinity College, Hartford, CT
Almsgiving
Hinduism: An Overview

Naomi Finkelstein
Columbia University
Furies

Joyce Burkhalter Flueckiger
Emory University
Oral Tradition

Carole R. Fontaine
Andover-Newton Theological School, Newton Centre, MA
Asherah
Images of Women: In the Hebrew Bible
Wisdom: An Overview
Wisdom: In Ancient Near East and Israelite Religion

Geraldine Forbes
State University of New York, Oswego
Hinduism: Modern Movements

Pamela Frese
Wooster, OH
Food

Esther Fuchs
University of Arizona
Hermeneutics: Feminist Hermeneutics

Kirsten Stammer Fury
Jersey City, NJ
Performance Art

Eugene V. Gallagher
Connecticut College
Cults
Family
Rationality
Secularization
Sorcery
Utopian Communities
Witchcraft: History of Study
Yemaya

Annapurna Garimella
Columbia University
Apsāras

Frances M. Garrett
Portland, OR
Meditation in Asian Traditions

Barbara Geller
Wellesley College
Judaism: Roman, Byzantine, and Sassanian Judaism

Erica C. Gelser
University of Pennsylvania
Hildegard of Bingen

Mary Gerhart
Hobart and William Smith Colleges
Genre and Gender

Senta C. German
Columbia University
Minoan (Cretan) Religion

Lorine M. Getz
University of North Carolina, Charlotte
Anonymous
Irrationality
Solitude

Edmund T. Gilday
Grinnell College
Shintoism

Cheryl Townsend Gilkes
Colby College
African American Churches
Sociology

Ann Grodzins Gold
Syracuse University
Maya

Ellen Goldberg
Queen's University, Canada
Mahāprajāpatī
Philosophy: In the East
Yoga

Naomi R. Goldenberg
University of Ottawa, Canada
Jung, Carl

Karla Goldman
Hebrew Union College
Judaism: Contemporary Jewish Life

Barbara Gombach
Columbia University
Draupadī

Deirdre Good
General Theological Seminary, New York, NY
Christianity: Apocrypha
Christianity: Gnostic Writings

Felicitas Goodman
Cuyamungue Institute, Columbus, OH
Body Postures and Trance

Jean Graybeal
New York University
Feminine, The

June-Ann Greeley
Sacred Heart University, Fairfield,
Westport, CT
Clothing
Pregnancy

Miranda Aldhouse Green
University of Wales College, Newport,
England
Celtic Religions

Tamara M. Green
City University of New York, Hunter
College
Greek Religion
Iranian Religions
Muses
Priestess

Laura Grillo
Chicago, IL
African Religions
Body: In Microhistorical Societies
Circle
Purification

John Grim
Bucknell University
Couvade

Alexandra F. Griswold
University of Pennsylvania
McPherson, Aimee Semple

Rita M. Gross
University of Wisconsin, Eau Claire
Androcentrism
Comparative Religion
Eliade, Mircea

Jessica G. Gugino
Newton, MA
Media and Religion

Janet Gyatso
Amherst College
Machig Labdron

Bonna Devora Haberman
Harvard University Divinity School
Voice

Yvonne Haddad
Bloomfield, CT
Islam: In North America

Shelley P. Haley
Hamilton College
Hypatia

Nancy A. Hardesty
Clemson University
Evangelical, Holiness, Pentecostal,
and Fundamentalist Christianity

Lindsey Harlan
Connecticut College
Kama

Riffat Hassan
Louisville, KY
'Ā'ishah
Fāṭimah
Khadija
Rabi'a

Mervat F. Hatem
Howard University
Islam: Islamist Modern Movements
Women and Religion: Monotheistic
Traditions and Orientalism

Judith Hauptman
Jewish Theological Seminary, New
York, NY
Judaism: Religious Rites and
Practices
Ordination: In Judaism

Natalie Maxwell Hauptman
Manhattan School of Music
Compassion

John Stratton Hawley
Barnard College
Fundamentalism

Glen Alexander Hayes
Bloomfield College
Blood
Geography, Sacred
Shaktism
Time, Sacred

Kelly E. Hayes
University of Chicago Divinity School
Mutilation
Taboos

Mary Elaine Hegland
Santa Clara University
Domestic Rites
Ritual

Dorothy Helly
City University of New York, Hunter
College
Colonialism and Postcolonialism

Susan E. Henking
Hobart and William Smith Colleges
Lesbianism: In the West

Marcia K. Hermansen
Rutgers University, New Brunswick
Conversion

Rachel Monika Herweg
Berlin, Germany
Jonas, Regina

Susannah Heschel
National Humanities Center, Research
Triangle Park, NC
Judaism: An Overview
Judaism: Modern Era
Judaism: History of Study

Marsha Aileen Hewitt
Trinity College, Toronto
Critical Theory
Gimbutas, Marija
Ideology
Postmodernism

Teresia Mbari Hinga
DePaul University
Christianity: In Africa

Valerie J. Hoffman
University of Illinois
Ghazali, Zaynab al-

Barbara A. Holdrege
University of California, Santa Barbara
Sacred Literature

Susan Tower Hollis
Syracuse, NY
Isis
Neith

Amy Hollywood
Dartmouth College
Athletics
Beauvoir, Simone de
Body: In the West

Gail Holst-Warhaft
Cornell University
Mourning and Death Rites

Nancy R. Howell
Pacific Lutheran University
Science, Religion, and Women
Theism

Herbert Bardwell Huffmon
Drew University
Hebrew Bible: Prophets and Judges

Cynthia Ann Humes
Claremont McKenna College
Witchcraft: Witchcraft in Asia

Jean M. Humez
University of Massachusetts, Boston
Lee, Ann

Mary E. Hunt
Women's Alliance for Theology, Ethics and Ritual, Silver Spring, MD
Friendship

Anne Marie Hunter
Boston Justice Ministries
Rape

Massimo Introvigne
Torino, Italy
New Religions: An Overview

Ada María Isasi-Díaz
New York, NY
Mujerista Tradition
Theology: Women-Centered Theology

Sylvia Jacobs
North Carolina Central University
Christianity: In North America: American Protestant Women's Foreign Missionary Activity

Susan Pertel Jain
Barnard College
Dance and Drama: In Asian Traditions

Janet R. Jakobsen
University of Arizona
Cultural Studies
Feminisms
Gender Studies

Katherine Ludwig Jansen
Catholic University of America
Mary Magdalene

Chris Jochim
San Jose State University
Confucianism: An Overview
Confucianism: Modern Movements

Sarah Iles Johnston
Ohio State University
Aphrodite (Venus)
Artemis (Diana)
Hecate

Diane Jonte-Pace
Santa Clara University
Psychology of Religion

Morny Joy
University of Calgary
Deconstruction

Marion A. Kaplan
City University of New York, Queens College
Pappenheim, Bertha

Eileen F. Kearney
Saint Xavier University
Heloise

Laurel D. Kearns
Drew University
Spiritualism

Rosemary Skinner Keller
Union Theological Seminary, New York, NY
Christianity: In North America: United States

Laurel Kendall
American Museum of Natural History, New York, NY
East Asian Religions: Religious Rites and Practices
Shamans
Superstition

Eliza F. Kent
Chennai, India
Ancestor Worship

Kathy Kern
Lexington, KY
Blackwell, Antoinette Louisa

Flora Keshgegian
Brown University
Memory

Alan Kilpatrick
San Diego State University
Witchcraft: Witchcraft in Native America

Jung Ha Kim
Georgia State University
Asian and Asian-American Traditions

Ursula King
University of Bristol, England
Education: Education and Literacy
History of Religions
Interreligious Dialogue
Religion
Spirituality

David Kinsley
McMaster University
Kundalinī

Russell Kirkland
University of Georgia
Native American Religions
Taoism: An Overview

Ingrid Klass
San Francisco, CA
Ordination: In Buddhism

Anne Klein
Rice University
Self
Wisdom: Prajñā and Prajñāparamitā

Kim Knott
University of Leeds, England
Autobiography and Biography: An Overview

Jennifer Wright Knust
Columbia University
Sociology of Religion

Dorothy Ko
Rutgers University
Body: Female Body as Text in Imperial China

Richard Kohn
Kensington, CA
Buddhism: Himalyan Buddhism

Maureen Korp
Ottawa, Canada
Craft: In Microhistorical Traditions
Prehistoric Religions: Preagricultural Peoples

Ross S. Kraemer
University of Pennsylvania
Images of Women: In the New Testament
Judaism: From the Babylonian Exile Through the Second Temple
Maenads

Björn Krondorfer
St. Mary's College of Maryland
Dance and Drama: In Monotheistic Traditions

Maggie Kruesi
University of Pennsylvania
Ghosts

Ida Kummer
Paris, France
Film and Video: Feature Films and Videos

Linda Gordon Kuzmack
Kensington, MD
Szold, Henrietta

Linda L. Lam-Easton
California State University, Northridge
Emotion
Temptation and Seduction

Amy Paris Langenberg
Hanover, NH
Birth and Rebirth

Fate
Sex Change

Amy Lavine
New York, NY
Fertility and Barrenness
Sexuality

Anne Dutton Lazrove
Yale University
Mugai Nyodai

Bonnie Lee
Ottawa, Canada
Performance Theory

Mary Joan Winn Leith
Stonehill College
Mesopotamian Religions

Michelle Lelwica
Oakland, CA
Nudity

Lucia Lermond
City University of New York, Queens College
Diotima

Barbara S. Lesko
Brown University
Ancient Egyptian Religions

Rebecca Lesses
New York, NY
Amulets

Miriam Levering
Knoxville, TN
Buddhism: East Asian Buddhism
Monasticism: In the East

Laura Levitt
Philadelphia, PA
Theology: Feminist Theology

Carroll Lewin
University of Vermont
Islam: In Asia

Vasiliki Limberis
Temple University
Orthodox Christianity

Bruce Lincoln
University of Chicago Divinity School
Divination
Indo-European Religions
Initiation

Carla Locatelli
Milan, Italy
Epistemology
Semiotics

Timothy Lubin
University of Virginia
Rites of Passage

Philip Lutgendorf
University of Iowa
Sītā

Nancy C. Lutkehaus
University of Southern California
Benedict, Ruth
Mead, Margaret

Mary N. MacDonald
Le Moyne College
Marriage and Singleness: In Microhistorical Traditions

Carol Cornwall Madsen
Brigham Young University
Mormons

Armando Maggi
University of Pennsylvania
Pazzi, Maria Maddalena de'

Irena S. M. Makarushka
Portland, ME
Dualism

Patricia Malarcher
Surface Design Journal, Englewood, NJ
Weaving

Christel J. Manning
Sacred Heart University
New Religions: In Europe and the United States

Sylvia Marcos
Cuernavaca, Mexico
Mesoamerican Religions
New Religions: In Mexico

Judith G. Martin
University of Dayton
Education: Teaching Women and World Religions

Nancy R. Martin
Chapman University
Mirabai

E. Ann Matter
University of Pennsylvania
Autobiography and Biography: Monotheistic Traditions
Christianity: History of Study
Eucharist
Jackson, Rebecca Cox
Woman's Bible, The
Underhill, Evelyn

James McBride
New York, NY
Economics
Marxism

Rachel Fell McDermott
Barnard College
Durgā and Kālī

M. Carmel McEnroy
Lexington Theological Seminary, Lexington, KY
Christianity: In Europe

Bernard McGinn
University of Chicago Divinity School
Visionaries in Medieval Europe

Catherine McHale
Columbia University
Tricksters

Jo Ann Kay McNamara
City University of New York, Hunter College
Monasticism: In the West

Ruth I. Meserve
Indiana University, Bloomington
Inner Asian Religions of Nomadic Peoples

Rebekah L. Miles
Brite Divinity School, Texas Christian University
Morality

Margaret Mills
Delaware, PA
Folklore

Pamela J. Milne
University of Windsor, Canada
Gender Conflict

Patricia Monaghan
DePaul University
Images of Women: Myths and Symbols
Mythology: An Overview

Marit Monteiro
Nijmegen, The Netherlands
van Schurman, Anna Maria

Beverly Moon
New York University
Love
Psyche
Womb

Catherine M. Mooney
Virginia Commonwealth University
Angela of Foligno
Catherine of Genoa
Christianity: Apostolic Religious
Orders and Communities
Clare of Assisi

Sue Morgan
*University College Chichestor,
England*
History

Joseph M. Murphy
Georgetown University
Possession Cults

Beth Alpert Nakhai
University of Arizona
Archaeology

Vasudha Narayanan
University of Florida, Gainesville
Hinduism: In the West
Lakṣmī
Venkamamba, Tarigonda

Vanessa Nash
University of Pennsylvania
Mother Teresa

Jenifer Neils
Case Western Reserve University
Athena (Minerva)

Sarah Milledge Nelson
University of Denver
Prehistoric Religions:
Agriculturalists

Eva Neumaier-Dargyay
University of Alberta, Canada
Tārā

Lesley A. Northup
Florida International University
Liturgy

Vivian-Lee Nyitray
University of California, Riverside
Auspicious and Inauspicious
Autobiography and Biography: Asian
Religions
Mazu (Tianhou)
Virtue
Yin/Yang Polarity

June O'Connor
University of California, Riverside
Abortion

Kathleen O'Grady
University of Cambridge
Catherine of Siena

Contraception
Hermeneutics: An Overview
Menstruation
Ritual Studies

Mary R. O'Neil
University of Washington
Witchcraft: Witchcraft in European
Traditions

Maura O'Neill
Rancho Cucamonga, CA
Celibacy
Community

Jennifer Oldstone-Moore
Augustana College
East Asian Religions: History of
Study
Miaoshan
Nugua
Seidel, Anna

Jacob Olupona
University of California, Davis
Agricultural Rituals

Margaret Orbell
Ponsoby, New Zealand
Hina
Oceanic Religions: Polynesia and
Micronesia
Pele

Claudia Orenstein
Barnard College
Dance and Drama: An Overview

Gloria F. Orenstein
Los Angeles, CA
Women's Contemporary Spirituality
Movement

Leslie C. Orr
Concordia University
Laity

Jordan Paper
York University, Canada
Menarche

Jacqueline Pastis
La Salle University
Christianity: Paul and the Pauline
Tradition

Laurie Louise Patton
Emory University
Goddess: Historical Goddesses
Inspiration

E. Ann Pearson
Westmount, Canada
Animals

Women as Heroines
Vagina

Aracelia Pearson-Brok
New York, NY
Freud, Sigmund

Ann Pellegrini
Harvard University
Cultural Studies
Feminisms
Gender Studies

Michelene Pesantubbee
University of Colorado, Boulder
New Religions: In Native American
Traditions

Indira Viswanathan Peterson
Mount Holyoke College
Bhakti

Jane Marie Pinzino
University of Puget Sound
Joan of Arc

Wioleta Polinska
Evansville, IN
Creation and Recreation

Riv-Ellen Prell
University of Minnesota, Twin Cities
Myerhoff, Barbara

Karen Pechilis Prentiss
Drew University
Ānandamayī Mā (Ananda Ma)
Body: In the East
Craft: In Asian Traditions
Gender Roles
Kāraikkāl Ammaiyār
Music: Instruments and Voices

Cathy Preston
University of Colorado, Boulder
Cross-dressing

Leonard Norman Primiano
Cabrini College
Cabrini, Frances Xavier
Day, Dorothy
Goretti, Maria
Mother Divine
Seton, Elizabeth Ann

Labelle Prussin
Pomona, NY
Architecture: Nomadic or Seasonal

Kwok Pui-Lan
*Episcopal Divinity School, Cambridge,
MA*
Christianity: In Asia
Liberation Theologies

Kelley Ann Raab
Nebraska Wesleyan University
Women's Studies

Habibeh Rahim
Hofstra University
Divorce
Fasting
Hospitality
Infanticide

Rubina Ramji
University of Ottawa, Canada
Anthropology

Jane C. Redmont
Graduate Theological Union, Berkeley
Roman Catholicism

Ruth Anne Reese
Beverly, MA
Bible as Literature, The

Daniella Reinhard
University of Chicago
Amazons
Hera

Marilyn Reizbaum
Bowdoin College
Antisemitism and Jewish Identity

Robin G. Rinehart
Lafayette College
Hagiography

Catherine M. Roach
Harvard University
Environmentalism

Marian Ronan
Berkeley, CA
Theology: Feminist Theology

Jean E. Rosenfeld
Tarzana, CA
Space, Sacred

Guenther Roth
Columbia University
Weber, Max

Kate Ruby
New York, NY
Iconography: In the West

Rosemary Radford Ruether
*Garrett Theological Seminary,
    Evanston, IL*
Monotheism
Women's Suffrage Movement

Carol Schreier Rupprecht
Hamilton College
Literary Theory and Criticism

Letty M. Russell
Guilford, CT
Patriarchy

Jennifer Rycenga
San Jose State University
Crossroads
Music: An Overview
Seclusion
Silence

Bernard Saladin d'Anglure
Cité University, Quebec, Canada
Arctic Religions: In North America

M. Asha Samad
New York, NY
Mutilation, Genital

Andrew Sanders
*University of Ulster at Coleraine,
    Northern Ireland*
Witchcraft: An Overview

Kathleen M. Sands
University of Massachusetts, Boston
Humor
Sin

Mei-Mei Sanford
New York, NY
Osun

Jack M. Sasson
*University of North Carolina, Chapel
    Hill*
CanaanPhoenicia, Religions of
Inanna

Elizabeth A. Say
California State University, Northridge
Wives

Louisa Schein
Rutgers University, New Brunswick
Orientalism

Claudia Schippert
Temple University
Queer Theory

Barbara R. von Schlegell
University of Pennsylvania
Hagar

Peggy Schmeiser
University of Ottawa, Canada
Social Change

Jo Ann Scurlock
Chicago, IL
Witchcraft: Witchcraft and Magic in
    the Ancient Near East and the
    Bible

Naomi Seidman
*Graduate Theological Union, Berkeley,
    CA*
Gluckl of Hameln

Susan Starr Sered
Bar Ilan University, Israel
Places, Sacred
Women's Religions

Susan M. Setta
Northeastern University
Founders

Lynda Sexson
Montana State University
Lying and Dissimulation

Arvind Sharma
McGill University, Canada
Polytheism

Diane M. Sharon
*Jewish Theological Seminary of
    America, New York, NY*
Eve
Ishtar and Anat
Marriage and Singleness: In
    Judaism, Christianity, and
    Islam

Miranda Shaw
Richmond, VA
Vajrayoginī

Irene Silverblatt
Duke University
South American Religions: In the
    Andes

Nikky-Guininder Kaur Singh
Colby College
Dharma
Saints
Sikhism

Jane I. Smith
Hartford Seminary, Hartford, CT
Hawwa' (Eve)
Islam: In North America
Maryam (Mary)
Paradise
Sa'dawi, Nawal al-

Mary Carroll Smith
Centerville, MA
Warriors

Stuart Smithers
University of Puget Sound
Esotericism
Soul
Yates, Frances A.

Tamara Sonn
University of South Florida
Islam: An Overview
Islam: In the Arab Middle East

Gina Soter
Kalamazoo College
Hestia and Vesta

Denise A. Spellberg
University of Texas, Austin
Qur'an and Hadith

Nancy Stalker
Stanford University
New Religions: In East Asia

Eleanor Stebner
University of Winnipeg
Christianity: In North America:
Canada

Anthony M. Stevens-Arroyo
City University of New York, Brooklyn College
Caribbean Religions

Kay F. Stone
University of Winnipeg
Riddle

Mary Storm
Mill Valley, CA
Death
Hāritī
Suicide

Gail Corrington Streete
Rhodes College
Asceticism

Sharon A. Suh
South Pasadena, CA
Emptiness

Gopal Sukhu
New York, NY
Taoism: Images of the Tao

Winnifred Fallers Sullivan
Washington & Lee University
Law

Ines M. Talamantez
University of California, Santa Barbara
Dance and Drama: In
Microhistorical Traditions

L. J. "Tess" Tessier
Youngstown State University
Misogyny
Sister
Violence

John Thornton
Rockville, MD
Dona Beatriz

Francis V. Tiso
Isernia, Italy
Confession and Penitence
Divine Child

Diane Treacy-Cole
University of Bristol, England
Gnosticism
Heterodoxy and Orthodoxy
Patronage

Gary A. Tubb
Columbia University
Truth

Mary Evelyn Tucker
Bucknell University
Amaterasu
Pan Ch'ao

Janet H. Tulloch
University of Ottawa, Canada
Craft: An Overview
Female Personifications
Photography
Visual Arts

Edith Turner
University of Virginia
Food

Victoria Kennwick Urubshurow
George Washington University
Ḍākinīs

Lourens P. van den Bosch
Groningen, The Netherlands
Castration
Widows

Penny van Esterik
York University, Canada
Southeast Asian Religions

Piers Vitebsky
University of Cambridge, England
Arctic Religions: In Asia

Cornelia Vogelsanger
University of Zurich, Switzerland
Images of Women: Visual Images of
Human and Divine Women

Trevor M. Wade
Palo Alto, CA
Adultery
Chastity

Amina Wadud
Virginia Commonwealth University
Prayer

Sally Roesch Wagner
Aberdeen, SD
Gage, Matilda Joslyn

Henry J. Walker
Saints

James C. Waller
New School for Social Research, New York City
Men's Spirituality Movement
Shape-Shifting
Speech
Weil, Simone

Wiebke Walther
Bingen, Germany
Islam: In Europe
Islam: History of Study

Joanne C. Watkins
Truckee, CA
Himalayan Religions

Paul Watt
DePauw University
East Asian Religions: New Buddhist
Movements

Christian Wedemeyer
Columbia University
Vows

Judith Romney Wegner
Providence, RI
Islamic Law

Catherine Wessinger
Loyola University
Charisma
Leadership
Ordination: In Christianity
Theosophy

Carol Wayne White
Bucknell University
Lesbian Studies

David White
University of California, Santa Barbara
Alchemy

Ulrike Wiethaus
Wake Forest University
Hadewijch of Brabant
Visions

Delores S. Williams
Union Theological Seminary, New York, NY
  Womanist Traditions

Janice D. Willis
Wesleyan University
  Androgyny
  Buddhas, Bodhisattvas, and Arhats

Liz Wilson
Miami University, Oxford, OH
  Hinduism: History of Study
  Lands, Mythic
  Virginity

Elliot R. Wolfson
New York University
  Divinity: In Judaism
  Torah

Terry Woo
University of Toronto
  Philosophy: In the East

Nancy C. Wright
New York, NY
  Mammy Wata

Donna Marie Wulff
Brown University
  Rādhā

Katherine K. Young
McGill University, Canada
  Women and Religion: In the East

Serinity Young
Columbia University
  Astrology
  Buddhism: An Overview
  Dreams
  Magic
  Tantra
  Weather

Chunfang Yu
Rutgers University, New Brunswick
  Kuan Yin (Kannon)

Eleanor Zelliot
Randolph, MN
  Buddhism: Modern Movements
  Ordination: In Buddhism

Judith P. Zinsser
Miami University, Oxford, OH
  Periodization

Laurie Zoloth-Dorfman
Berkeley, CA
  Ethics: An Overview

Joyce Zonana
New Orleans, LA
  Images of Women: Literary Images
    of Human and Divine Women

Abortion

The world's religions, as cross-cultural symbol-systems that communicate meanings and values, offer resources for thinking about abortion and for deciding what reasons justify it. Since abortion is an act in which embryonic or fetal life is killed, concerns about the importance of life and its protection are at issue.

Contemporary critiques of sexism, patriarchy, and sexual abuse in religions and societies have expanded the frame through which abortion is viewed. Many strongly argue that a crisis pregnancy no longer be construed simply as an individual problem for a pregnant woman but that it also be viewed as a social matter for which many parties bear responsibility.

Although religious communities tend not to advocate or celebrate abortion, they do tolerate it for morally compelling reasons. Discussions within and among religious communities display differing interpretations about how best to identify the conceptus or fetus (as biological tissue, potential human life, human being, person-in-process, and so on), about how to assess the pregnant woman's responsibilities and rights, and about what are regarded as morally sound reasons that justify abortion. The traditions examined here—Judaism, Christianity, Islam, and Buddhism—share the broad claim that the destruction of embryonic or fetal life requires moral justification.

Judaism's traditional esteem for procreation and the value of progeny has been reaffirmed in the twentieth century in the face of the deaths of millions of Jews in the Nazi Holocaust. Sustaining and protecting life in the Jewish community is at the heart of Jewish values; gratitude for life is at the heart of Jewish devotion. Yet combined with these beliefs and affections is a primary interest in the pregnant mother's welfare and a judgment that the fetus is not considered a person with legal rights until the moment of birth. Traditional Judaism has reluctantly permitted or approved abortion under select circumstances, such as threat to the mother's health and cases of rape (Feldman, 1975). Although halakhic and rabbinic writings exhibit wide-ranging differences of judgment, some agreement is discernible: an unwanted pregnancy is insufficient cause for abortion, as is the motivation to limit family size or prevent the inconvenience and suffering of giving birth and raising children. The right to self-preservation, however, does permit abortion when the life of the mother is at stake. Strict interpretation of this right supports abortion only when the fetus threatens the mother's physical life; more lenient interpretations also justify abortion in the face of mental anguish, social disgrace, and other forms of pain (Biale, 1984; Lubarsky, 1995).

Catholic and Protestant Christianity each have a history of opposing abortion as a morally unacceptable taking of innocent human life. As in Judaism, exceptions are allowed. In recent centuries the Catholic tradition has formally identified two contexts that constitute compelling cause: a pregnancy where the uterus is cancerous and an ectopic (tubal) pregnancy. In both cases, surgery to save the life of the mother that has the secondary effect of terminating the pregnancy is seen as acceptable according to the moral principle of indirect effect. In the Roman Catholic tradition, only direct, intended abortions are absolutely prohibited by the official church (Connery, 1977). Catholics who disagree with official teaching, such as the organization Catholics for a Free Choice, offer additional reasons, such as rape and health factors for mother or fetus, as

1

sufficient cause; these views foster disagreement and debate.

Protestant Christianity has many varieties: fundamentalist and evangelical Protestantisms, which largely oppose abortion, and liberal and liberationist Protestantisms, which, though not advocating abortion, nonetheless treat with leniency those who undergo or effect abortion. Those supporting access to abortion commonly cite rape, incest, and threat to physical life and health of the mother. Additional reasons such as age, fetal health, and deprivation of socioeconomic resources, are added by some as relevant criteria for considering abortion (Harrison, 1983).

Because Islam envisions life as a gift from God, placing high priority on procreation, it has discouraged abortion. Nonetheless, abortions are tolerated for juridically valid reasons without criminal sanction. Historical reasons justifying abortion include threat to the health of the mother and the dependence of nursing infants on their mother's milk when wet nurses were not available. Some hold that abortion should be permitted up to the 120th day of gestation, when ensoulment is believed to occur and the fetus achieves the status of a person. Others argue that precedents against abortion should be maintained even before the fetus achieves the status of a person, because the fetus is in the process of becoming a person (Kelsay, 1994). Current discussions on birth control and family planning, reproductive technologies and risks, and sexual violence affect thinking about abortion. An open debate on abortion in the Muslim community is in its early stages (Ebrahim, 1989).

The Buddhist principle of not-killing makes abortion a prohibited practice, according to Buddhist texts. Abortion in Buddhist countries is widespread, however, indicating that concessions and exceptions abound. Some Buddhists justify abortion on the grounds that it is the nature of reality that some life forms be sacrificed so that others might live. Acceptance of abortion is prevalent in Japan and is vividly displayed in the popular ritual of *mizuko kuyo*, through which a woman and her family recognize the aborted fetus for having sacrificed its life for the good of others. The prayers and offerings (*kuyo*) of the ritual are enacted to assist the grief, guilt, and gratitude of the family as well as appease the water-child (*mizuko*) or fetus, who, it is believed, will be born at a later date (LaFleur, 1992). Given the Buddhist proscription against abortion, many Buddhists and non-Buddhists alike question whether this practice is authentic Buddhism (Keown, 1995).

These religious perspectives on abortion advise restraint. Yet even as each tradition resists abortion as the destruction of developing human life, each accepts abortion for what are regarded as morally sound reasons. The differences among traditions and among persons within the same tradition center around differences of judgment regarding what are considered morally acceptable reasons.

BIBLIOGRAPHY

Biale, Rachel. *Women and Jewish Law: An Exploration of Women's Issues in Halakhic Sources.* 1984. Chapter 9 on abortion displays a range of halakhic views.

Callahan, Daniel, and Sidney Callahan, eds. *Abortion: Understanding Differences.* 1984. An excellent collection of essays discussing the differing worldviews, assumptions, and hopes of the pro-life and pro-choice perspectives on abortion in the United States.

Connery, John. *Abortion: the Development of the Roman Catholic Perspective.* 1977. An important historical study.

Ebrahim, Abul Fadl Mohsin. *Abortion, Birth Control, and Surrogate Parenting: An Islamic Perspective.* 1989. This call for further research outlines Islamic textual sources and schools of thought that hold promise for illuminating contemporary medical ethical issues. The book's weakness is its brevity, given its wide-ranging agenda, and its frequent use of quotations in place of reasoned argument.

Feldman, David. *Marital Relations, Birth Control, and Abortion in Jewish Law.* 1975. A widely cited source.

Glendon, Mary Ann. *Abortion and Divorce in Western Law.* 1987. An excellent comparative study in Western law and public policy.

Harrison, Beverly Wildung. *Our Right to Choose: Toward a New Ethic of Abortion.* 1983. A feminist defense of elective abortion.

Jung, Patricia Beattie, and Thomas A. Shannon. *Abortion and Catholicism: The American Debate.* 1988. Displays a diversity of positions and analyses within American Catholicism.

Kelsay, John. "Islam and Medical Ethics." In *Religious Methods and Resources in Bioethics.* Edited by Paul F. Camenisch. 1994. Offers brief but illuminating insight on abortion in Islam.

Keown, Damien. *Buddhism and Bioethics.* 1995. An informative philosophical analysis.

LaFleur, William R. *Liquid Life: Abortion and Buddhism in Japan.* 1992. A fascinating study of the *mizuko kuyo* ritual recognition of abortion together with objections against it among contemporary Japanese Buddhists.

Lubarsky, Sandra B. "Judaism and the Justification of Abortion for Nonmedical Reasons." In *Contemporary Jewish Ethics and Morality.* Edited by Elliot N.

Dorff and Louis E. Newman. 1995. A philosophical examination of assumptions about abortion in rabbinic teachings and their relationship to halakhic claims.

Smith, Jane I. "The Experience of Muslim Women: Considerations of Power and Authority." In *The Islamic Impact.* Edited by Yvonne Yazbeck Haddad, Byron Haines, and Ellison Findly. 1984. This discussion contextualizes the abortion issue in terms of women's agency in society and culture.

JUNE O'CONNOR

Adultery

The threat of adultery has troubled religious authorities for centuries, most dramatically in patriarchal traditions such as Hinduism, Islam, Judaism, and Christianity, where marriage is valorized and viewed as a means to properly channel women's reproductive capacity and maintain patrilineal succession. In such traditions, where legitimate paternity and continuity of pure lineage, class, or caste are central tenets of religious observance, adultery is understood as a severe disruption of social and religious order. Hindu scriptures, for example, meticulously describe how adultery induces the dissolution of cosmic order, and the Jewish Talmud urges Jews to martyr themselves rather than commit adultery. Punishments include death, flogging, stoning, excommunication, enforced exile, and public trials of humiliation. Despite its general condemnation, adultery has been treated consistently as a far greater crime when committed by women than by men. Women are found guilty of adultery more frequently and punished more severely than their male counterparts, whose sexual lapses tend to be indulged, ignored, or tolerated. Indeed, whereas women are permitted sexual intimacy with a single partner, a husband, men have periodically received sanction to acquire multiple wives, concubines, harems, and to engage in sexual intercourse with slaves and prostitutes.

Part of this inequity stems from the way adultery is defined. Most religious texts consider a woman who has sexual relations with any man other than her husband to be an adulteress. In contrast, a man is generally deemed an adulterer only if he engages in sexual intercourse with a married woman (other than his wife). For instance, according to ancient Jewish law, a husband who suspects his wife of adultery can subject her to the Rite of the Water of Bitterness, a trial by a temple priest. It is the only trial of ordeal rather than due process found in Jewish scripture, and it applies only to a wife. There is no corresponding trial for a husband, implying that adultery can only be committed by a wife against a husband, not a husband against a wife.

Maintaining chastity is repeatedly declared a primary religious duty of women. In order to fulfill religious injunctions, a woman must usually marry and loyally serve her husband. Her sexual fidelity is seen as a measure of her faith, and her adultery likened to heresy, apostasy, or idolatry. Moreover, a woman's chastity is often tied to her male relatives' honor. If she acts with impropriety she defiles her entire lineage. Religious discourses frequently characterize women as lascivious, seductive, and adulterous by nature and do not trust them to maintain their own chastity. An extreme practice for ensuring women's chastity is genital mutilation, performed in parts of Africa, which ranges from the removal of the clitoris to sewing closed the labia of the vagina. Male relatives are licensed to control women's mobility, dress, and social interaction and to punish them for immodest behavior. Even minor transgres-

An illustration of a woman accused of infidelity walking over white-hot plowshare in an attempt to prove her innocence (Corbis-Bettmann).

OLD-TIME ORDEALS AND PUNISHMENTS.—ORDEAL BY FIRE—A WOMAN WALKING OVER HOT PLOWSHARES.

sions can arouse instant suspicion and retribution. In cases of adultery, male relatives have the right, even the duty, to beat or kill a woman in order to expunge the intolerable disgrace she has brought upon their lineage.

Men are the traditional authors and enforcers of laws concerning adultery. In addition, women generally hold lesser legal rights and standing and rarely possess the economic and social resources necessary to adequately defend themselves. Islamic courts, for example, demand the testimony of four adult males to convict individuals of adultery, deeming women unqualified to serve as witnesses. Furthermore, women who have become pregnant through rape are open to punishment for adultery if they cannot produce sufficient witnesses, while men are left unpunished for lack of evidence. The Hindu Laws of Manu decry an adulteress to be the only type of sinner never to be expiated for her crime; she forsakes all opportunity for salvation. As punishment, she should be devoured by dogs in a public place and will be reborn in the womb of a jackal and tormented by disease. Buddhist Jataka stories recommend that her ears and nose be cut off, thereby indelibly marking her transgression.

Adultery committed by a woman can be understood as a breach of her religious duty, an act of insubordination to the men on whom she is dependent, a threat to the legitimacy of her husband's lineage, and a deed that dishonors her entire kinship group. Social repercussions facing male adultery are usually inconsequential, whereas those imposed on adulterous women can be devastating, leading some women merely suspected of adultery to commit suicide, even when innocent.

BIBLIOGRAPHY

Abu-Lughod, Lila. *Veiled Sentiments.* 1988.

Ahmed, Leila. *Women and Gender in Islam: Historical Roots of a Modern Debate.* 1992.

Biale, Rachel. *Women and Jewish Law: An Exploration of Women's Issues in Halakhic Sources.* 1984.

Chakravarti, Uma. "Conceptualizing Brahmanical Patriarchy in Early India: Gender, Caste, Class and State." *Economic and Political Weekly* (April 3, 1993): 579–585.

El Sadaawi, Nawal. "Women and Islam." *Women's Studies International Forum* 5, no. 2 (1975): 193–206.

Kumari, Ranjana. *Female Sexuality in Hinduism.* Delhi, 1988.

Narayanan, Vasudha. "Hindu Perceptions of Auspiciousness and Sexuality." In *Women, Religion, and Sexuality: Studies on the Impact of Religious Teachings on Women.* Edited by Jeanne Becher. 1990.

Wegner, Judith Romney. *Chattel or Person? The Status of Women in the Mishnah.* 1988.

See also **Chastity**; **Marriage and Singleness**; **Sexuality**; **Virtue**.

TREVOR WADE

African American Churches

Originating in the eighteenth century, predominantly black denominations, black congregations in predominantly white denominations, and numerous independent black congregations have existed in small houses, megachurches with over ten thousand members, small rural buildings, urban storefronts of varying sizes, former synagogues, and rented spaces in hotels, theaters, and stadiums. These churches continue to shape and affirm the identities of black Americans and to foster a variety of social action strategies. The encounter between black and white people in the United States figures significantly in American religious history and in the stories of every African American denomination and congregation.

Historians and sociologists such as W. E. B. Du Bois, Carter Woodson, E. Franklin Frazier, James Melvin Washington, Evelyn Brooks Higginbotham, C. Eric Lincoln, and Lawrence Mamiya point to the centrality of the church as the organizational center and public sphere of the black community. The convocations of the black denominations and the transdenominational national conferences involving deacons, ushers, singers, musicians, women's groups, and ministers all serve to constitute a sense of national membership in the church and the larger black community. The interaction between these national religious groups and black secular organizations intensifies the prominent and important role of African American churches in defining racial-ethnic identity, constituting and actualizing a sense of shared fate and community, and resisting oppression and injustice.

An emphasis on the person and operation of the Holy Spirit ("Holy Ghost," in the more-favored King James Version) distinguishes black churches (including those not formally holiness or pentecostal) from their white counterparts. This is largely a consequence of women's spirituality. Women are the majority, ranging from sixty percent of the membership in larger churches with explicitly masculinist outreach to over ninety-five percent in the Sanctified Church (predominantly black holiness and pentecostal denominations and congregations). While exact membership figures are elusive, the general estimate is that women make up seventy-five percent of congregations.

An elderly African-American woman was taught how to vote at a church in Greene County. Rural Alabama churches held classes to make sure ballots would not be thrown out for improper markings by hostile white officials (Flip Schulke/Corbis).

Conventional wisdom recognizes that women, although subject to militant discrimination as ordained ministers, represent "the backbone" of the church because they are largely responsible for the organizational integrity of the church. African American churches depend upon an elaborate, historically derived womanist infrastructure that consists of missionary societies; women's conventions; an infinite variety of organizations largely staffed by women; and women's congregational and denominational services as teachers, superintendents, missionaries, evangelists, trustees, deaconesses, stewardesses, church mothers, ushers, singers, musicians, secretaries, clerks, accountants, treasurers, parliamentarians, committee members, pastors' wives, and organizers of annual church programs, especially Women's Day celebrations. Where women are ordained, they serve as pastors, assistant pastors, stewards, deacons, and, occasionally, bishops. In the historical records of most congregations and a few denominations women are among the church founders.

National Baptists and the Church of God in Christ do not support the ordination of women. Nevertheless, these two denominations influence the roles of women throughout African American churches. Although Baptist congregations and associations occasionally cooperate to ordain women, the majority of the members of the National Baptist Convention remain opposed. Baptist women sought ordination in the late nineteenth century and when this was militantly denied them, the women formed an auxiliary convention in 1901 and, under the leadership of Nannie Helen Burroughs, created an event in 1906 called "Women's Day." Women's Day spread to every black denomination and congregation and became, according to Miss Burroughs, "the principal 'money raising day' in Negro churches throughout America." Not only do Women's Days raise substantial portions—as much as one-third—of church annual budgets, but women, by virtue of their demographic advantage and long tradition of paid employment, provide the bulk of other church financing.

Many preaching women found roles as evangelists "speaking" and "teaching" in denominations that denied them ordination. The Church of God in Christ developed the strongest tradition of women evangelists, powerfully influencing clergywomen in other traditions. As ordination opportunities opened for women in the late twentieth century, women from the Church of God in Christ served as chaplains in the military and crossed over into the United Methodist Church, the African Methodist Episcopal Church, and other Protestant denominations to serve as clergy.

Women's traditions throughout African American churches emphasize the importance of the Holy Spirit or "Holy Ghost" for corporate worship and individual spirituality. Historically this religion of the spirit has depended upon the ability of women to organize and manage autonomous worship experiences in local congregations, national church convocations, and secular organizations such as women's clubs, fraternal organizations (for example, Eastern Star), and sororities (for example, Delta Sigma Theta, Inc.). These practices have their antecedents in African societies where women served as priestesses, healers, mediums, and worship leaders and, during slavery, in prayer groups and other worship services within the women's network.

The conflicts that characterize gender relations in African American churches have their roots in this history of spiritual leadership. Sparked by the *zeitgeist* of the civil rights movement when the roles of black women as community leaders, organizational officers, organizers, strategists, activists, teachers, and administrators were overshadowed by the leadership of male preachers and pastors, black women analyzed and challenged their exclusions from pastoral and other forms of official leadership. In the wake of the women's movement, black churchwomen–scholars utilized the ideas of Alice Walker who coined the term *womanist* to account for black women's distinctive history, preferences, and practices, most especially black women's "love" of "the Spirit." They described women's roles and practices in African American churches, generating black feminist critiques, sociocultural analyses, and constructive womanist perspectives in the areas of theology, ethics, and biblical studies.

BIBLIOGRAPHY

Cone, James H., and Gayraud Wilmore, eds. *Black Theology: A Documentary History.* Vol. 2. 1993.

Dodson, Jualyne E., and Cheryl Townsend Gilkes. "Something Within: Social Change and Collective Endurance in the Sacred World of Black Christian Women." *Women and Religion in America. Vol. 3, The Twentieth Century.* Edited by Rosemary Radford Ruether and Rosemary Skinner Keller. 1986.

Gilkes, Cheryl Townsend. " 'Together and in Harness': Women's Traditions in the Sanctified Church." *Signs: Journal of Women in Culture and Society* 11, no. 4 (1985): 678–699.

Higginbotham, Evelyn Brooks. *Righteous Discontent: The Women's Movement in the Black Baptist Church, 1880–1920.* 1993.

Lincoln, C. Eric, and Lawrence H. Mamiya. *The Black Church in the African American Experience.* 1990.

Townes, Emilie M., ed. *A Troubling in My Soul: Womanist Perspectives on Evil and Suffering.* 1993.

———. *Embracing the Spirit: Womanist Perspectives on Hope, Transformation and Salvation.* 1997.

Walker, Alice. *In Search of Our Mothers' Gardens: Womanist Prose.* 1983.

White, Deborah Gray. *Ar'n't I A Woman: Female Slaves in the Plantation South.* 1985.

See also Womanist Traditions.

CHERYL TOWNSEND GILKES

African Religions

A study of the indigenous religions of sub-Saharan Africa poses unique problems for Western scholarship. The idea of "religion" as a separate entity or as a disembodied system of belief is a Western idea and a relatively modern invention. While the academy has privileged the study of sacred texts as the authoritative articulation of religious doctrine, many African philosophies are mostly oral traditions inscribed in visual iconography and transmitted primarily through ritual. Also, scholarship has largely categorized indigenous African religions as "traditional," postulating that their worldviews, beliefs, and practices are circumscribed by ethnic identity, and contrasted them to "world religions," those to which one can supposedly subscribe without regard to social status or historical situation. The term *traditional* also connotes something ancient, pure (unadulterated by outside cultural influences) and suggests an unchanging way of life persisting to the present. In reality, African religions must be understood to encompass both continuity with the past, adaptation to historical events and social circumstance, and innovation. Finally, the phrase *African Religions* risks implying that there is homogeneity among all African cultures, whereas Africa is a vast continent encompassing tremendous geographic variation and cultural diversity.

CHARACTERISTIC FEATURES ACROSS AFRICAN RELIGIONS

General Worldview

While no single orthodox body of concepts and practices can properly be identified as characterizing African religions, generally these traditions articulate a common view that the fundamental human condition is imperfect, and suffering, sickness, and death can be alleviated and controlled through ritual action. The focus is not on salvation, with a promise of reward in the afterlife, but on the renewal of human affairs in this world: the reparation of social ruptures and corresponding spiritual dissonance as antecedents for physical healing, the promotion of moral values, and the perpetuation of the community. Increasing depth of knowledge about the nature and use of sacred power is transmitted through initiation. A characteristic focus is ritual, not as a mere rote conformity to established patterns of behavior, but as a reflexive strategy for addressing the contingencies of life: ensuring fecundity, eliciting healing, and guiding the passage through the stages of human life.

Conceptions of Divinity and the Spiritual Hierarchy

African religions conceive of a spiritual hierarchy where secondary divinities, spirits, and ancestors provide measured access to sacred power. However, they uphold the existence of one God, maker of a dynamic universe. In some cases, it appears that the supreme being is directly involved in everyday life and attended to in ritual, but closer examination reveals that such a creator god stands above the kind of reciprocal relationships more readily assumed by secondary divinities, mediating spirits, and ancestors. Among the Ashanti of Ghana, elders regularly pour libations and offer prayers to Nyame, the creator, giving thanks and asking for blessing. However, the veneration of matrilineal ancestors has pride of place in ritual life, for they are considered the foundation of the moral order. According to the mythology of the Dogon of Mali, the word of Amma caused a vibration that mixed the elements and so initiated the creation of the world, and the Dogon do erect altars to this being. However, the principal cult is not to Amma but to the *nommo*, primordial beings and first ancestors whose actions allowed the world to evolve. Furthermore, they seek guidance and mediation in human affairs through divination, bestowed on humanity by one of the *nommo*, a trickster called Ogo. Among the Yoruba of Nigeria the almighty creator, Olodumare (Olurun), reigns over a pantheon of secondary divinities, *orisha*. While this Yoruba deity has neither priests not cult group, the cult of the *orisha* is active and widespread. The transcendent God does not depend upon the reciprocal relationship to human beings that cultic activity articulates and reinforces. In the Great Lake region of East Africa, Mulungu, though omnipresent, is only sought in prayer as a last resort; among the Dinka and Nuer, Nilotic peoples of the Sudan, God is addressed in prayer, but clan divinities are nearer to the world of human concerns. In southern Africa, the Khoisan cosmological myths indicate that after an initial order was established, the creator's role diminished, while another being serves as administrator. Considered capricious and prone to blunder, this being is the divinity who actively intercedes in human affairs, from childbirth to trade.

A close identification of the creator with an archdivinity, charged with the affairs of the world, make conceptions of the gender of deity more inclusive. The earth goddess "Ala, the archdivinity among the Igbo of Nigeria, is variously described as the wife or the daughter, and more firmly, the terrestrial expression of Chukwu," the supreme being (Idowu, 1973, p. 171). In the Fon tradition in Benin, the supreme being, Mawu-Lisa governs as a twin force with dual gender. Mawu, as the "mother of the gods" and the gentle female principle, is more beloved than her male twin and spouse, Lisa (Pelton, 1980, p. 103). Amma is alternatively presented by Dogon myths as a sky god mating with the female earth, or as having a womb. Among the Yoruba, the secondary divinities, the *orisha*, and their devotees have a mutually intimate relationship of service and protection, sometimes expressed in terms of a marriage in which the gender of the two "spouses" is considered fluid.

The secondary divinities are most intimately involved in human concerns. For example, rather than supplicating the "high god" with prayers of petition or sacrificial offerings, the Akan turn to the *abosom*, who serve the supreme being as messengers and intermediaries, and to the ancestors. The divinities are alternately represented as deputies, monitors, or messengers of the supreme being, and sometimes as God's "children." At the deepest levels of some religious teachings, initiates are taught that they are refractions of the divine essence, deriving their attributes from deity.

Secondary divinities give mythic form to sacred power present in the elements. For example, the fiery personality of Shango, a Yoruba *orisha* who has both female

The priestess of the spirits is helped by her assistants as she dances the Ahoe-Komy and enters a trance possessed by spirits (Marc Garanger/Corbis).

and male manifestations, reflects the transformative and revelatory power of thunder and lightning. The Yoruba honor the earth as a sacred being, called Oduduwa, sometimes presented as a female deity and as the wife of Olurun, associated with the heavens. Among the Dogon, the cultivation of agricultural fields sacralizes the body of the earth, the first mother. The river Ogu is considered both the sanctuary and embodiment of the Yoruba female deity, Yemoja. In Ghana, Tano is the deity associated with fresh waters, while in Côte d'Ivoire it is Bia. Faro is the Bambara water spirit who is responsible for fecundity. Mami Wata, a water divinity worshipped widely across West and Central Africa, is regarded by her devotees as non-African in origin (Drewal, 1988, p. 38). Inspired by mermaids and portraits of hindu snake charmers, Mami Wata appears as a light-skinned woman with long dark tresses, surrounded by snakes. The naturalism of her representation is unique in African iconography of such spirits, but her association with the snake is suggestive of the ubiquitous rainbow serpent who unites the waters of heaven and earth. "There is in all of this . . . a metaphoric capture of the moral potentiality inherent in certain powers of the natural world" (Thompson, 1983, p. 93).

Ancestors also serve to some degree as mediators, providing access to spiritual guidance and power. Only those who lived a full measure of life, who cultivated moral values and achieved social standing can become ancestors, and are honored by their decendants after death with libations and sacrifices and implored for blessing and assistance. As the guardians of the moral order, ancestors reprimand those who neglect or breach normative prescriptions by bringing illness or misfortune to their errant descendants. The ancestors, in turn, may eventually return to earth, reborn as children within their lineage. The ancestors can take precedence over the divinities. A prevalent Akan myth relates that when the Creator, Odomankoma first roamed the earth, he met women already settled there, and so points to the fact that the veneration of matrilineal ancestors is most fundamental to Akan religiosity.

The Primacy of Ritual

The principal vision that all African religions share is that humans must vigilantly maintain a harmonious relationship with the divine powers of the cosmos in order to prosper. Ritual is the way to negotiate a responsible relationship in the community, with the ancestors, spiritual forces within nature, and the gods. Blood sacrifice, the most important of rituals, expresses the reciprocal bond between divinity and devotee. The life force of blood "feeds" the gods even as it channels their animating energy. A devotee must not forsake the ritual duties that sustain this relationship, for the divinities, while supportive, are also demanding and can trouble a negligent devotee by causing illness or chronic misfortune.

The most dramatic and intimate contact between devotee and divinity occurs through possession trance. In most cases, possession is actively sought, induced by inhaling vapors of a medicinal leaf or through techniques facilitating altered states of consciousness: rhythmic chanting, drumming, and dance. Sometimes only a priest is susceptible, but among the vodun (Benin), all initiates are receptacles of the gods. The possessed are called horsemen because they are mounted by the spirits and submit to their control. Once embodied, the presiding divinity interacts with the participating congregation.

Contact with the divinities is not always so direct. Mediators between the human and divine realms are often necessary. Specialists range from a simple offi-

ciant at a family altar to prophets and sacred kings. Diviners are such mediators, ritual specialists who master a technique of reading the visual signs through which the divinities are believed to communicate. More than mere fortune-telling, divination is a form of diagnosis, a technique for determining the cause of suffering and misfortune. Through the manipulation of divinatory apparatus and the interpretation of the random patterns it elicits, diviners situate clients in a cosmic context, help them deliberate their options in light of social conventions and sacred ideals, and solicit spiritual favor. The Yoruba system of divination, Ifa, is also practiced by the Igbo, the Ewe of Togo and Ghana, and the Fon of Benin, and is at the core of African-American religions of Santeria and Candomblé. Sandogo is a women's divination society of the Senufo of Côte d'Ivoire. Composed of members of every matrilineage segment in the village, this society safeguards their succession (Hackett, 1996, p. 122). In contrast with public displays that are characteristic of their male counterparts, Sandogo consultations are private.

Mythological themes: Creation and Transformation

African myths embody profound philosophical reflections, express ultimate values, and identify moral standards. African myths are neither recounted as a single narrative story nor are they completely related through an established anthology. The mythology of oral culture is embedded within ritual practice. Their deeper meanings are revealed only by processes of initiation. For example, a cosmogonic myth that recounts the sacrifice of a primordial being as the act that established order at the beginning of time can provide the model for a ritual sacrifice that aims at restoring social harmony.

African mythology and ritual commonly depict the cosmos as an anthropomorphic entity. The human body is a microcosm and incorporates the same primordial elements and essential forces that make up the universe. Therefore, cosmogonic myths explain the origins of creation and at the same time address the question of human existence. According to one Dogon myth, the primordial human being was a smith, able to transform the elements of earth and fire into tools. There were other beings before the smith, but he was the first human. When he fell to earth from the heavens, his amorphous body was broken into joints, giving him permanent shape and definition. Amma, the creator, gave human beings joints as well. The elbow symbolizes the human capacity to work so that, like the divinities, we too are fashioners of the world. Human labors, especially agriculture, bind the elements in harmonious conjunction and maintain the world as a dynamic, fecund creation. The human being is therefore a co-creator, and work is an ethical duty of cosmic proportion.

The trickster is a type of mythic character prevalent in African mythology who also represents transformation. An ambiguous character, the trickster introduces disorder and confusion into the original divine plan, but in so doing paves the way for a new, more dynamic order. Legba, a Fon trickster, is a notorious troublemaker. His lawlessness and unbridled sexuality is shameless (Pelton, p. 88). He is nevertheless not the incarnation of evil, for while Legba is disruptive and unpredictable, he is ultimately a creative agent and a revered transformer. Like other such trickster figures, Legba presides over divination; he is the linguist who translates the message and purpose of Mawu, the supreme deity. Myths about the Dogon trickster, Ogo, show him to be equally restless and rebellious, tearing away from the primordial womb of Amma to pursue a world of his own making. But like Legba, Ogo mediates between human and divine realms through divination. Such African myths communicate an important paradox: the cosmos, grounded in a fundamental divine order, is characterized by constant change and renewal.

It is noteworthy that the existential situation of God's distance from humans' mundane concerns is often attributed to an offense committed by women. Akan mythology, for example, relates that Onyame, the creator, once inhabited the world, but this original intimate association was severed because women, while pounding yam, continually struck Onyame with their pestles. There is irony and humor in portraying a petty annoyance as the catalyst for God's retreat from the immediate human realm. Such levity mitigates any dramatic sense of crisis that this predicament might imply. A strikingly similar myth of the Dinka of Sudan relates that when the first woman lifted her pestle to pound millet, she struck the sky, causing the supreme being to withdraw. While this is thought to have introduced toil, sickness, and death to the human condition, it also freed humans from the prohibitively narrow margin of life under God's immediate control.

THE CONSTRUCTION OF GENDER IN MYTH AND RITUAL

Complementarity of Male and Female

A widespread African ideal is the complementarity between men and women, a theme articulated in myth, recapitulated in ritual, and reiterated in the distinct social roles assigned to the sexes. Given the disproportionate creative power of women—the ability to bring forth life—a balance between domains of production and reproduction is symbolically restored by excluding women from certain creative enterprises, notably ironworking and carving.

Men typically claim the exclusive right to create human figurines, and sometimes carvers are subjected to prohibitions that resemble those ritually imposed on a pregnant woman: isolation and dietary and sexual restrictions (Adams 1980, pp. 163–167). For this reason, women are never smiths or smelters; the ironworking process is a transformative enterprise reserved for men. The analogies between working the furnace and bellows to forge ore, and the process of copulation and gestation is made visually evident in both symbol and ritual surrounding ironworking. In much of the Bantu-speaking region of Central Africa, furnaces are gynecomorphic, adorned with breasts and other female appurtenances, including female body scarification patterns (Herbert, 1993, p. 32). In Angola the Chokwe word for furnace, *lutengo,* also means vulva, while the block of iron produced in this "womb" is called the son of woman. The action of the bellows extends the sexual metaphor. The Njanja of Zimbabwe see them explicitly as the male organ penetrating the female body of the furnace. The symbolic parallel between smithing and gestation is reinforced among the Mande where smiths' wives becomes their counterparts, midwives. In Zaire, the smith, having assumed the procreative role, works in isolation. A woman who violates the prohibition against approaching a furnace is thought to risk sterility.

Gender identities and domains are painstakingly established in myths, ritual, and social role. But the idea that gender can be situational, transitional, or even androgynous is also readily accepted in African worldviews. For example, postmenopausal women are admitted to the Mende male secret society, Poro, where they occupy critical offices.

The Play of Gender: Female Virtues and Religious Ideals

The *gelede* masquerades of the Yoruba of Nigeria and Benin are lavish spectacles designed to represent and honor the Great Mothers and to celebrate the power they wield. The Great Mothers, known as witches, are primarily elder women who possess extraordinary but ambivalent powers. They can be beneficent, bringing wealth and fertility, or they can impel the forces of disaster: disease, famine, and barrenness. Their power to intercede makes them as commanding a force as the ancestors or the divinities, and so they are called the "owners of the world." *Gelede* is executed to assuage the innate power of women and marshal their secret resources for the benefit of society.

Gelede is performed in the marketplace, a domain controlled by women. The two masks depicting the Great Mothers are the bearded women (Iyanala) or a bird of the night (Eye Oro). Both forms represent aspects of spiritual power and the capacity for transformation. Facial hair on a woman indicates a witch whose powers cannot be contained by a single gender. The Great Mothers straddle the complementary realms of male and female, binding the sexes with overarching power. Therefore, they are called "owners of two bodies." The bird is a mediator, traversing the realms of earth and sky, but the mask also recalls beliefs that the Mothers transform themselves into night birds to attack the souls of their enemies. Its protruding beak is red, as if stained with blood, alluding to the cruel capacities of the witches. The bloody beak also points to *ase*, the life force. The shedding of blood in ritual sacrifice releases this sustaining vital force and precedes most ritual ceremonies in which the ancestors, divinities, or Mothers are called upon for blessing.

Initiation and the Construction of Gender

The progression of birth, growth, illness, and death shows that the entire human career shares in the fundamental dynamic of the universe: transformation. Rituals marks these natural occasions, lending to them religious meaning. Initiation is a rite of passage that enables adolescents to assume a new social role by indoctrinating novices into the religious significance of their new status, revealing how social life and moral order are in keeping with the patterns of the cosmos.

Initiation rites for girls are not as common or elaborate as those for boys. *Chisungu*, a female initiation rite among the Bemba of Zambia, conveys the ideals of womanhood through images constructed in pottery, a medium exclusive to women (Richards, 1956). It is initiation into the religious meaning of their reproductive powers that allows girls to achieve their full cultural status as women. The Chewa people of Zambia and Malawi used to perform similar female initiation ceremonies. In the *cinamwali* ceremonies pubescent girls were secluded in the shrine of a medium of the python spirit, believed to control fertility. There they would be given instruction in sex and childrearing, and would make clay figures or *vilengo:* python, tortoise, hare, and a human couple. These were vessels that would channel the reincarnation of ancestral spirits into the wombs of new brides (Hackett, 1996, pp. 110–111).

Clitoridectomy is a common rite of female initiation. While the surgical removal of the clitoris and parts of the labia minora is more radical than male circumcision and more dangerous, both widespread practices of genital mutilation are understood to be important means by which gender is culturally defined. All vestiges of androgyny are eliminated as the anatomical parts perceived to be correlating with the opposite sex are cut away. The surgery dramatizes the role of culture in constructing womanhood and ensuring reproduction.

From the perspective of participants, such blood rituals reinforce interpersonal bonds and establish strong female ties, and so can be seen as a reaction against male domination, especially in patriarchal and virilocal cultures. Clitoridectomy also serves to dissociate sexual function from reproduction, enhancing the value of maternity while suppressing sexual response. In this way the status of women is reduced to motherhood which is culturally esteemed (Sered, 1994, p. 128).

Ritual Healing: Gynecology and the Power of Gender

Women's social status is enhanced with motherhood, and much women's ritual is organized to celebrate and protect female reproductive power or to restore fecundity. For the Yaka of Zaire, infertility is more than a personal crisis; it is a tear in the very fabric of the cosmos. The Yaka healing cult, *khita*, aims at "gynecology" in a broad sense, that is, it purports to heal women's reproductive ailments by activating the primal womb to which every woman is connected. *Khita* "celebrates and arouses *ngoongu,* . . . the uterus of the world" as a resource for regeneration (Devisch, 1993, p. 213).

At the apex of the *khita* ritual the female initiate who suffers from gynecological dysfunction is led to identify herself with death in the expectation of a return to life. She is "turned upside down comparable to a bat or like an animal killed in the hunt and brought home suspended from a pole" (p. 183). Then she is placed in seclusion, " to assimilate in her experience the means of . . . the fetal condition" (p. 196). Identifying herself with an androgynous embryo enclosed in the womb, the patient undergoes a self-generated transformation, and reconstitutes her physical integrity. This therapeutic ritual is effective because it "focuses on the initiate's life-bearing capacity in concert with the same capacity in the cosmos" (p. 213).

Inclusion and Exclusion of Women: Establishing Domains of Power

Masking societies are religious institutions that visually represent the cosmic order and the dynamics of the world system, or embody the ancestors who preside over the moral comportment of the living. Although most masking societies are exclusively male, the discovery of masks by women is a common mythic theme. According to most accounts, women drew the original masks and the power invested in them from the ground or fished them from the water. Women are considered the first owners of a number of other important sacred and ritual objects (totemic emblems, bull-roarers, ceremonial songs and dances, etc.) as well as the source of cultural institutions and phenomena that formed the world (Pernet, 1992, p. 140). Nevertheless, the myths typically go on to recount how women lost their prerogative over the masks and their associated institutions to men who tricked or robbed them. The accounts of their transfer to men allow male identity to be established in distinction from the primal female powers of reproduction, serve to demarcate the cultural boundaries and hierarchies established between the sexes, and legitimate the exclusion of women from this ritual sphere.

While in principle, the excluded women are ignorant of the true nature of the masks and fear them, in practice women both support the custom of mask-making and maintain the conventions of ritual by expression requisite emotions of terror and grief. For example, in Owo (Nigeria) when a procession of masks from one quarter of town enters a neighboring ward, the women of the "invaded" territory run screaming into their houses, barring doors and windows behind them. These enactments, in most cases, are "an essential and obligatory part of the rite itself" (Pernet, 1992, p. 157). Reacting to and interacting with the mask according to the accepted norms, the "excluded" women cannot truly be interpreted as mere spectators. They take an active part in the ritual.

Female Virtues

The Sande secret society, on the other hand, is unique in that masks are made and controlled by women and play a central role in the initiation of its exclusively female members. Sande is ubiquitous among the Mande-speaking peoples, and its religious vision and political power extend across Liberia, Sierra Leone, Côte d'Ivoire, and Guinea. The sacred Sande mask, Sowei, incarnates the spirit of society and communicates through its iconography the ideals of womanhood and female power. The Sowei helmet-style mask, completely encompassing the head, and the smooth distended forehead of its face are reminiscent of the swollen belly of a pregnant woman. The analogy between pregnant woman and mask makes clear the mythic theme of woman as controller of the original "mask," the womb.

The Sande mask is understood to represent divine origins of both women and their masks. The best pieces are said to be sculpted by the water spirits in the "abode of heaven, under water (where) miracles of delicacy are the norm" (Boone, 1986, p. 161). Like the birth of an infant breaking from the waters of woman, the mask is understood to emerge from the hidden depths. Among the mask's most striking features are the coils of flesh at the neck, representing the concentric rings of water formed as the head breaks from the surface. Iconographically, the neck coils function as does a halo in Western art, signifying women as human in form, but divine in essence (Boone, 1986, p. 170).

The elaborately plated coiffure is another essential feature of this classic mask. Analogous to the flora of the earth, the female coiffure reinforces the identification of woman with Great Mother Earth. In Yoruba art, too, the head is unusually large and elaborately decorated, with special attention to the coiffure. Detailed plaiting renders homage to the river goddess, Osun. Believed to have power to influence the destinies of both humans and gods, this goddess's preeminence enhances the status of women who are also seen as originators of life (Hackett, 1996, p. 74). In Sande, the plaiting is, moreover, likened to the weaving of the fetus in the womb.

The crest at the crown of the coiffure is typically comprised of three or five segmented petals spread like an exotic, open flower. It is likely a representation of the female genitalia, the celebrated locus of creation. Protruding unabashedly like the spread labia inviting conception, giving birth, or undergoing ritual transformation in clitoridectomy, the female sex is glorified in icon as that most secret revealed as most sacred, the source of power and being.

THE IMPACT OF SCHOLARSHIP BY WOMEN

Androcentrism has dominated the anthropological accounts of African religions. There are few studies that elicit women's constructs of the world. Since the complementarity between the sexes is such a ubiquitous theme, it stands to reason that the portrait of both women's and men's situations is distorted by studies based on male informants alone (Pernet, 1992, p. 155).

Anthropologists and historians of religions have begun to challenge the prevailing consensus of universal male dominance and to describe more complex gender arrangements (Sanday and Goodenough, 1990, p. 4). Alternatives to the view of male supremacy are warranted, especially in the study of Africa, where gender ideologies appear to be somewhat fluid and accommodating.

BIBLIOGRAPHY

Adams, Marie Jeanne [Monni]. "Afterword: Spheres of Men's and Women's Creativity." *Ethnologische Zeitschrift Zuerich.* 1980.

Ben-Amos, Paula. "In Honor of Queen Mothers." In *The Art of Power: The Power of Art.* Edited by Paula Ben-Amos and Arnold Rubin. 1983.

Boddy, Janice. *Wombs and Alien Spirits: Women, Men and the Zar Cult in Northern Sudan.* 1989.

Boone, Sylvia. *Radiance from the Waters: Ideals of Feminine Beauty in Mende Art.* 1986.

Devisch, R. *Se recréer femme: manipulation sémantique d'une situation d'infécondité chez les yaka du Zaire.* Berlin, 1984.

Devish, René. *Weaving the Threads of Life: The Khita Gyn-Eco-Logical Healing Cult Among the Yaka.* 1993.

Dieterlen, Germaine. *Essai sur la religion bambara.* Paris, 1951.

Douglas, Mary. *Natural Symbols: Explorations in Cosmology.* London, 1970.

Drewal, Henry, and Margaret Thompson Drewal. *Gelede: Art and Female Power among the Yoruba.* 1983.

Drewal, Margaret Thompson. *Yoruba Ritual: Performers, Play, Agency.* African Systems of Thought. Charles S. Bird and Ivan Karp, General Editors. 1992.

Glaze, Anita. *Art and Death in a Senufo Village.* 1981.

Griaule, Marcel et Germaine Dieterlen. *Le Renard Pale.* Paris, 1965.

Hackett, Rosalind I. J. *Art and Religion in Africa.* Religion in the Arts Series. London, 1996.

Herbert, Eugenia W. *Iron, Gender and Power: Rituals of Transformation in African Society.* 1984.

Idowu, E. Bolaju. *African Traditional Religion: A Definition.* London, 1973.

Jackson, Michael. *Paths Toward a Clearing: Radical Empiricism and Ethnographic Inquiry.* 1989.

Jacobson-Widding, Anita, ed. *Body and Space: Symbolic Models of Unity and Division in African Cosmology and Experience.* Acta Universitatis Upsliensis, Uppsala Studies in Cultural Anthropology. 1991.

MacCormack, Carol. "Sande: The Public Face of a Secret Society." In *The New Religions of Africa.* Edited by Benetta Jules-Rosette. 1979.

Peek, Philip, ed. *African Divination Systems: Ways of Knowing.* 1991.

Pelton, Robert D. *The Trickster in West Africa: A Study of Mythic Irony and Sacred Delight.* 1980.

Pernet, Henry. *Ritual Masks: Deceptions and Revelations.* Trans. from the French by Laura Grillo. 1992.

Phillips, Ruth. "Masking in Mende Sande Society Initiation Rituals," *International African Institute* 48, no. 3 (1978): 265–276.

Piault, Marc-Henry. "Négro-Africaines (Religions)." In *Encyclopaedia Universalis,* Corpus 12. Paris, 1988.

Richards, Audrey. *Chisungu: A Girl's Initiation Ceremony among the Bemba of Northern Rhodesia.* London, 1956.

Ryan, Patrick J. " 'Arise, O God!': The Problem of 'Gods' in West Africa." *Journal of Religion in Africa* 11 , no. 3 (1980).

Sanday, Peggy Reeves, and Ruth Gallagher Goodenough, eds. *Beyond the Second Sex: New Directions in the Anthropology of Gender.* 1990.

Sered, Susan Starr. *Priestess, Mother, Sacred Sister: Religions Dominated by Women.* 1994.

Shaw, Rosalind. "The Invention of African Traditional Religion.' " *Religion* 20, no. 4 (October 1990): 339–354.

Thompson, Robert Farris. *Flash of the Spirit: African & Afro-American Art and Philosophy.* 1983.

Turner, Victor. *The Drums of Affliction.* 1968.

Wilmsen, Edwin N. "Khoi and San Religion." In *The Encyclopedia of Religion.* Edited by Mircea Elaide. 1987.

Zahan, Dominique. *Sociétés d'initiation bambara.* Paris, 1960.

LAURA GRILLO

Afro-Atlantic Religions

The formation of African-based New World religions took place within the past five hundred years throughout the Americas and the Caribbean. These neo-African faith traditions are very diverse because of their informal, nondogmatic structure and their unique history. Membership is based on initiation into a line of devotees organized in small family-like worship communities called "houses" and a wide range of societies. Since affiliating with these religious traditions is usually kept secret to the general public, it is impossible to determine exactly how many people are participating in these groups. Today, there must be at least 50 million members dispersed throughout the Americas, in Brazil alone more than 25 million. During the last two decades their numbers have been rising exponentially especially in the large urban centers from New York to Rio de Janeiro. Although African-based religions appeal particularly to Black Protestant and Liberation activists, they have attracted people from all walks of life, transcending racial, gender, and class boundaries. Because of their holistic, sensual practices, their gender-inclusive theologies and mythologies, and the considerable opportunities for female power and leadership these traditions have been particularly attractive to women.

African-based New World religions are profoundly pragmatic and ingeniously syncretistic and thus difficult to assess. The majority of their faithful initiates are simultaneously members of a major Christian denomination, especially the Roman Catholic Church. In undivided devotion they proudly celebrate the African spirit world while embracing Christianity. While for the devotees there is little or no contradiction between serving the spirits and going to church, such flexible and inclusive religious identity is generally unthinkable according to Western Christian doctrine, which separates "pure" Christian faith (meaning established Christian standards developed by European or Euro-American church officials) from what is sometimes condemned as African "heathendom" or "witchcraft."

HISTORICAL OVERVIEW

The history of African diaspora beliefs has its origin in the Atlantic slave trade, the Middle Passage. After Christopher Columbus' arrival in the Caribbean in 1492, European conquerors began a massive genocide among the native population. The soon-decimated indigenous people were not able to carry out the ambitious mining and agriculture projects in the vast, newly-taken territories. Hence, "free" labor from Africa was shipped across the Atlantic Ocean under the most dehumanizing of circumstances to meet the high demand. The enslaved men, women, and children were deported from hundreds of different ethnic groups in Western and Central Africa stretching from the Senegambia region to Angola. Among them were the Fon people from Dahomey (Benin), the Yoruba from Nigeria, and the Bakongo from the Congo region, whose cultural heritage became prominent in the formation of African-based New World religions (Thompson, 1983).

Though transformed and modified under the trauma of violent separation from their homelands and hindered by brutal oppression under slavery, African cultural traditions and religious beliefs persisted in their new environment. To assert African cultural and religious identity vis-à-vis extreme humiliation and abuse became a powerful strategy of resistance. Elements of African religious practices and faith survived on the large-scale New World plantations in the seventeenth and eighteenth century and developed by the nineteenth century into cohesive African-based New World religions such as Vodun in Haiti, Santeria in Cuba, Espiritualismo in Puerto Rico, Candomblé and Umbanda in Brazil, and many more. Others grew out of the maroon communities and free African settlements, as for instance the Kumina tradition in Jamaica and the Shango religion in Trinidad. The leadership of African religious professionals (priests, priestesses, diviners, healers) and intense worship sessions (with ecstatic sacred singing, dancing, and drumming) were at the core of almost every slave uprising including the Haitian revolution. Given their turbulent genesis, African diaspora religions are creative amalgamations of multiple African faith traditions that also absorbed elements of Christianity, the religious system imposed on them by the colonial rulers, and aspects of the religious traditions of the indigenous American population, often their allies in the underground resistance, as well as the spiritist teachings of the French esoteric thinker Allan

Priestess Yaffa heats the tip of spear in a candle light to perform her ceremony as Vodou Queen in New Orleans, Louisiana (Phillip Gould/Corbis).

Kardec whose notion of the living dead was akin to their own. Yet, despite enforced and voluntary syncretistic alterations, these traditions remained essentially African in their basic patterns of beliefs and practices, at times preserving religious customs of the eighteenth and nineteenth century that no longer exist in their African homelands. The single most successful surviving trans-Atlantic African tradition is probably the Orisha religion of the Yoruba people, which spread in vibrantly thriving New World forms such as Cuban Santeria and Brazilian Candomble and Umbanda.

As more and more people of African descent poured from the plantations into the booming cities they brought their religious heritage with them. This change from rural to urban environment is significant regarding gender relations. While in the rural context the patriarchal structures of their African homelands prevail, the urban subculture with its predominantly female domestic work force triggered in many places a thorough feminization of the African-based religious traditions. For instance, Vodou in New Orleans, Candomblé in Salvador de Bahia, and Umbanda in Rio de Janeiro became primarily women's religions with powerful female leaders such as the legendary Marie Laveaux (Landes, 1947; Bastide, 1978; Fandrich, 1994). More recently, migrations from areas in the Caribbean and Latin America into the northern industrialized countries have spread African diaspora religions in North America and Europe even among people without any genetic or cultural African heritage. African diaspora religions have thus truly reached the status of world religions.

BELIEF SYSTEMS, RITUAL PRACTICES, AND RELIGIOUS LEADERSHIP

African diaspora religions are largely based on oral traditions, which only in recent history have been written down. Their complex cosmologies and mythologies explain the origin, purpose, and meaning of everything in the universe and teach appropriate moral behavior. As mentioned above there are no dogmas, sacred scriptures, or formal institutions in these traditions and therefore no overarching hierarchy that separates orthodoxy from heresies. Yet, this general openness does not mean anarchy. Traditions are meticulously observed and carefully handed down from one generation to the next. The names and particularities of the sacred stories and theologies vary regionally. Nevertheless, a basic religious system can be identified as characteristic throughout the African diaspora.

As in Western monotheistic religions there is the belief in one supreme being, the creator of the universe who is both androgenous and beyond gender categories. Yet, God Almighty is generally not worshiped. In addition there is a pantheon of spiritual beings who personify symbolically natural elements and principles of behavior such as love or war. In the Yoruba religion these spiritual beings are called *orisha,* in Haitian Vodun as the *lwa.* Since there is no exact European equivalent for this concept they have been translated as "deities" or "divinities," "spirits," "saints," "mysteries," or "angels." Unlike the supreme being, the orisha-type spiritual beings permeate eery aspect of life. Their existence is thus closely intertwined with human fate. Hence, they require careful devotion in ritual, prayer, and sacrifice. They have distinct, gendered personalities with clearly distinguishable character traits. These personal characteristics are praised and welcomed in ceremonies by a certain set of rhythms, dance movements, and songs dedicated to each of them. Each *orisha* or *lwa* is also symbolized by a certain color, or combination of colors, carries certain sacred objects representing the force personified in the divinity, and

has very specific appetites determining the sacred foods and libation beverages to be offered to them. For example, "Ezili-Freda," the Haitian *lwa* of love and beauty, covers her face with white powder, speaks with a high-pitched, sweet voice, carries a fan, likes to wear pink dresses, and loves honey and sweets. Finally, there are the spirits of the ancestors who also need to be respected, revered, and literally fed with sacrificial offerings and libations just like the *orishas* for the dead are presumed to dwell among the living as long as they are remembered. Hence the living are thought to exist in constant interaction not only with one another but also with the orishas and the spirits of the dead in a complex web of meaning. Powerful ancestors can gain the status of an orisha over time.

Another commonality throughout the African diaspora is the belief in a predetermined fate and reincarnation. Elaborate systems of divination serve to discern one's calling in life and how to secure the support of the divine forces through good and bad times. A "reading" of a trained diviner also indicates which sacrifices or ritual practices have to be made to satisfy the spirit world and thus to reestablish harmony and balance in the universe.

The sacrifices are often connected with spirit feasts called *bembe* in Yoruba, which can be described as dramatic dance-song-music-food performance-ritual-feasts. A crucial part of such events are the ubiquitously present sacred drums. They represent the heart beat of life and invoke the sacred rhythms attributed to the individual divinities. The ritual feasts culminate in spirit mediumship—the ecstatic manifestation of divine energy in the human body of a distinguished devotee. This process has often been labeled "spirit possession." However, according to Western imagination and terminology the idea of spirit possession is usually associated with the involuntary invasion of an evil entity that needs to be exorcized in order to insure the well-being of the "possessed" individual. To the contrary, spirit mediumship in the African context represents the highest form of devotion: mystical union with the divine. It is an honor, a blessing, and a privilege, not a curse to be "possessed." Hence, African spirit mediumship is a form of service to the divine and to the worship community. It enables the spirits to express their love, concern, humor, and sometimes criticism and rage to their devotees; and vice versa, it allows the worship community to show their love and respect to the divinities. Both in Africa and the New World diaspora the majority of spirit mediums are women. *Bembe*-type celebrations take place within the privacy of a "house" or *ile* in Yoruba. In addition, there are also public festivals and pilgrimages.

Since dealing with the spirits is considered to be dangerous business, it requires the assistance of qualified religious professionals who know the particular rituals, dances, songs, rhythms, and foods needed when approaching the spirit world in order to secure their support. A senior priest or priestess officiates at the core of every "house." He or she initiates and trains the members of his/her "house." The relationship between the initiated and their leaders usually constitutes a mutual life-long commitment similar to that between parents and their children. The training for the priesthood ("taking *ocha*" in Yoruba) takes place in several stages of initiation and may last many years. Leaders of a "house" and their disciples also have the responsibility to serve the general public with advice, counseling, and healing when requested. There is no hierarchy among such leaders. However, their influence and following varies greatly depending on their personal charisma and "knowledge" and hence the effectiveness of their spiritual work. "Knowledge" means in this context spiritual power, the intuitive capacity to read the human psyche, and competence in holistic healing. Depending on the number of followers and the reputation of their "knowledge," such religious leaders, male or female, can be very influential within their community and even far beyond it.

WOMEN AND FEMALE CONCEPTS OF THE DIVINE

To asses the role of women in the ritual context and the female gendered aspects of the divine in the African diaspora traditions is complicated for two reasons: (1) African-based New World religions inherited the complex ambiguity of African notions of gender. (2) The history of slavery and the subsequent pervasive social reality of racism and sexism created a peculiar affinity between women and African-based religions.

The manner in which we conceptualize reality and thus our belief system is significantly shaped by the structure of our language. Different from European languages, West and Central African languages have no notion of gender in their grammatical classifications of nouns. Hence, while these languages do have ways of expressing gender differences, their very grammatical structure expresses a gender flexibility literally inconceivable in European languages. Thus, West and Central African languages provide ways to conceive of social roles in a more flexible manner than the highly gender-specific Western languages do.

Corresponding to the linguistic flexibility, gender is in the African context not a biological given, but has always been understood as socially constructed (Matory, 1994), thus preceding by centuries Western modern post-structuralist insights. Personhood, male or female, does not come "naturally." It evolves over the life cycle and must be achieved through the intervention of relevant groups, including divinities and ancestral spirits, whose intervention can determine prescriptions for gender behavior. Therefore, throughout Africa and the African diaspora, gender roles seem to be legitimated by corresponding mythology.

According to the sacred narratives, on one level, the *orishas* or *lwas* have indisputably gendered identities: Eshu-Elegba, Ogun, Shango, and Obatala like their Haitian counterparts Papa Legba, Papa Ogou, and Dambalah-Wedo are envisioned as male characters such as trickster and divine messenger, male warrior, just king, and divine father; while Oshun and Yemaja as their Haitian equivalents the Ezili figures (Ezili-Freda and Ezili-Danto) are viewed as female personae, as "goddess" of love and beauty and as archetypes of divine motherhood.

However, on another level, the same divinities embody forces that transcend these gender classifications generally assigned to them. Essentially they are androgenous and ultimately beyond gender. This androgenous potential in all living things including the spirit entities explains why cross-sex impersonations and role changes during rituals are not unusual. Male divinities can manifest themselves in female devotees and, vice versa. It also provides explanation for the syncretic amalgamations between Catholic saints and African divinities with changed gender identification. For instance, St. Barbara, a female saint, represents the force of Shango, a male figure in the Yoruba pantheon, because of her fiery death depicted on the lithographs reminded the enslaved Africans of the thunder and lightning power of their divine king.

These ambiguities offer women possibilities to see themselves mirrored in divine images that are entirely lacking in Western Christianity and Judaism. For instance, the image of a major storm representing the anger of Oya (the female *orisha* who rules the winds and is nick named "patron saint of feminists" in Brazil) though fearsome can have an enormously empowering effect on a woman who identifies with this divinity. She can relate to her rage as a justified divine energy of which to be proud (Gleason, 1987). There is no reason for her to suppress, or as is common among Western women, to feel guilty about such an emotion.

Besides the possibility for female priesthood, African cultures have created another social institution that is salient regarding women's empowerment: In many parts of West and Central Africa there are strictly gender-separated secret societies. Their primary purpose is to initiate the youth into the proper behavior of adult life with all its duties and responsibilities. But, beyond this function they are also custodians of the "correct" traditions. They enforce the ethical norms and values to be observed in the community in order to guard communal harmony and well-being. Moral standards of gender-specific roles and duties are defined and implemented by them. In many cases to be a member of such a society defines even the ethnic identity of a group. With few exceptions the institution of female secret societies did not survive the Middle Passage. Nevertheless, the African traditions of strong female bonding persisted in the religions of the diaspora. It continued to promote female power, self-esteem, and leadership, thus yielding effective avenues to counteract the multiple sources of women's oppression: economic exploitation, racism, and sexism.

The surviving African continuities are more pronounced among women than among men, not because women are more traditional than men or more sentimentally attached to the past. Instead, women are motivated to hold on to their African traditions because they seek the protection of their ancestral spirit world in order to escape the degradation of a male dominated society. As sanctified divine mediums they can hold to the supernatural world against male power and can draw lines that a man cannot cross: limits to his sexuality (the body of the devotee has to be pure, not contaminated by sexual activity), limits to his authority (the woman escapes, according to her age, the domination of her father, or of her husband for the entire time of her initiation apprenticeship and leaves him at each feast for the divinity that she incarnates), and revenge against his tyranny (deities can ask for jewelry, dresses, money, etc., for their medium; Bastide, 1978).

It is the affirmation of female power, female self-esteem, and female bonding that draws women from all walks of life, even well-to-do white women, into the circles of these African-based religions.

AFRO-CARIBBEAN TRADITIONS: *SANTERÍA*

Also known as *la regla de ocha* or *lucumí* Santería (meaning "the way of the saints") is the unofficial national religion of Cuba. It combines popular Spanish Catholicism and the religion of the Yoruba people. It also shows significant Congo influences in the *palo* rites. *Ocha* (initiation into the priesthood) is equally open to males and females then called *babalorisha* or *padrino* ("godfather") and *iyalorisha* or *madrina* ("godmother"). Their godchildren can be male or female. However, women are not allowed to become *babalaos* (highly esteemed, specially trained divination priests). They are also excluded from

playing the sacred *bata* ritual drums, although the drums themselves have female attributes.

Vodun

Contrary to popular beliefs Vodun, also known as Vodou, is not a vicious form of witchcraft but a highly sophisticated African-based mystical religion, the non-official national faith of Haiti. The name derived from the word *vodu* in the Fon language, meaning "divine force or mystery." The Vodun religion consists of two basic rites: the more delicate Rada rites based on traditions from Dahomey and the more ferocious Petrwo rites displaying Congo heritage. Each set of rites has a key female character: the white "Ezili-Freda," a sweet love goddess who adores upper-class luxuries, and the dark-skinned "Ezili-Dantò," fearless divine soldier of liberation and symbol of divine motherhood and strength. Vodun is organized in small sanctuary societies (*ounfo*) around a charismatic spiritual leader, a *manbo* ("priestess") or *oungan* ("priest"). There is no hierarchy among *mambos* and *oungans*. A *manbo* like an *oungan* accepts both male and female apprentices (*ounsi*).

AFRO-BRAZILIAN TRADITIONS: CANDOMBLÉ AND UMBANDA

Two main types of African-based mediumistic religions exist in Brazil; in both female members predominate. Candomblé appeared in the predominantly black northern state Bahia as the religion of primarily poor people and claims to be the more authentically African. The more widespread Umbanda (sometimes called Macumba) type grew out of the huge urban centers of Rio de Janeiro and Sao Paulo and has successfully established itself not only among the black poorest of the poor but also in the racially mixed middle-class and even among the ranks of the almost exclusively white upper class. Umbanda (meaning "the art of curing") is today the fastest growing religion in Brazil, rivaled only by the Pentecostal movement. Rituals are held in small sanctuaries called *centros, terreros,* or *tendas*. The highest ranking religious leader of such centers is either a female *mai de santo* ("mother of the saints") or a male *pai de santo* ("father of the saints") and has undisputed authority of the *filhas* and *filhos* ("daughters" and "sons of the saints"), initiated aspiring mediums in training.

POLITICAL RELIGIOUS MOVEMENTS: RASTAFARIAN RELIGION

Unlike the above-discussed traditions Rastafarianism is not a mediumistic religion, but rather a sociopolitical protest movement with religious undercurrents. Antiestablishment protest groups in Jamaica aligned themselves with the pan-African Ethiopianism movement and the teachings of Marcus Garvey early in the twentieth century. Their identification with Ethiopia is based on biblical symbolism. After the enthronement of Ras ("Prince") Tafari as emperor Haile Selassie of Ethiopia in 1930 they called themselves Rastafarians. They believe Selassie to be the returned messiah who will deliver the black race from bondage in "Babylon" (America). They seek ultimately repatriation with "Zion" (Africa). Rastas have a distinct life style (e.g., dread locks, vegetarianism, *ganja* smoking, reggae music), which reinforces patriarchal rule with strict subordination of women (Clark, 1986).

BIBLIOGRAPHY

BOOKS

Arroyo, Anthony Stephens, and Andrés Perez y Mena. *Enigmatic Powers: Syncretism with African and Indigenous Peoples' Religions among Latinos.* 1995.

Badejo, Diedre. *Òṣun Ṣẹ̀ẹ̀gèsí. The Elegant Deity of Wealth, Power, and Femininity.* 1996.

Barnes, Sandra T., ed. *Africa's Ogun: Old World and New.* 1989.

Bastide, Roger. *The African Religions of Brazil.* Translated by Helen Sebba. 1978.

Brandon, George Edward. *Santeria from Africa to the New World: The Dead Sell Memories.* 1993.

Brown, Karen McCarthy. *Mama Lola.* 1991.

Clark, Peter. *Black Paradise: The Rastafarian Movement.* 1986.

Curry, Mary Cuthrell. *Making the Gods in New York: The Yoruba Community in the African American Community.* 1997.

Deren, Maya. *Divine Horsemen: The Living Gods of Haiti.* 1953, Reprint, 1970.

Fandrich, Ina. "The Mysterious Voodoo Queen Marie Laveaux: A Study of Power and Religious Leadership in Nineteenth-Century New Orleans." Ph.D. diss., Temple University, 1994.

Gleason, Judith. *Oya: In Praise of the Goddess.* 1987.

Iwashita, Pedro. *Maria e Iemanja: Analise de um sincretismo.* Recife, Brazil, 1989.

Landes, Ruth. *The City of Women.* 1947.

Matory, Lorand. *Sex and the Empire That Is No More: Gender and the Politics of Metaphor in Oyo Yoruba Religion.* 1994.

Métraux, Alfred. *Voodoo in Haiti.* 1972.

Murphy, Joseph. *Working the Spirits: An African Religion in America.* 1994.

Thompson, Robert Farris. *Flash and the Spirit: African and Afro-American Art and Philosophy.* 1983.

Rey, Terry Edward. "Classes of Mary in the Haitian Religious Field: A Theoretical Analysis of the Effects of Socioeconomic Class on the Perception and Uses of a Religious Symbol." Ph.D. diss., Temple University, 1996.

Teish, Luisah. *Jambalaya.* 1985.

ARTICLES

Apter, Andrew, "The Embodiment of Paradox: Yoruba Kingship and Female Power." *Cultural Anthropology* 6 (May 1991): 212–229.

Klein, Herbert S. "African Women in the Atlantic Slave Trade." In *Women and Slavery in Africa.* Edited by Claire Robertson and Martin A. Klein. 1983.

Perez y Mena, Andrés. "Cuban Santería, Haitian Vodun, Puerto Rican Spiritualism: A Multiculturalist Inquiry into Syncretism." *Journal for the Scientific Study of Religion* 37, no. 1 (March 1998): 15–27.

INA JOHANNA FANDRICH

Afterlife

Religious imagination of life continuing after death is a discourse that domesticates the future, expanding life beyond the boundaries of human existence. It claims the afterlife as potentially more important than life and—because human actions have repercussions beyond human witness—induces society to conform to religious models of social behavior. Afterlife narratives commonly construct morality in terms of future pain and pleasure, as if suffering and joy were supernatural consequences of previous human actions. Doctrines of the afterlife portray continuity between the cosmic and social orders, showing the cosmos or deity as having the power to punish and reward social behavior; in conforming to idealized social order one conforms to divine order. Religious discourse on women's afterlife commonly portrays women as punished or rewarded after death according to the same criteria by which they are judged in life; pious, subordinate earthly wives are promised a future as pious, subordinate heavenly wives.

DEATH, REBIRTH, RESURRECTION, AND REINCARNATION

In many religions the afterlife is a new life, in which the dead acquire new or renewed bodies appropriate to their destination. In his treatise the *City of God*, the Christian theologian Augustine airs debate over whether women will retain their sex in the resurrection. Some argue, he says, that women will be resurrected in male bodies as men. In his view women will be resurrected in female bodies because there will be no lust and no childbirth; because women will have no sexuality, they

A funerary papyrus from ancient Thebes in Egypt depicts the afterlife judgement of Princess Entiu-ny. Anubis weighs the heart of the princess in the balance against a statuette of the goddess of truth (The Metropolitan Museum of Art).

may be saved as women (Bk. 22, ch. 17). Buddhist treatises, such as the *Sukhāvatīvyūha Sutra*, on enlightenment through rebirth in the Western Paradise, claim that no one is born as a woman there, because being female is an obstacle to enlightenment; women may become reborn there as men if they practice despising their own gender and meditating on manhood. Islamic eschatology imagines a day of final judgment when all souls must attempt to cross a narrow bridge: the unfaithful fall into the fire below but the faithful cross into a heavenly garden, with bodies resurrected from their graves, renewed and purified. Eternal virgins await the faithful males, who become capable of one hundred times their earthly sexual power. These doctrines idealize a future in which male bodies are the iconic standard while women's bodies are desexed or entirely absent.

Numerous soteriologies envision that those who die are reborn again among the living, in a cycle of transmigration. Hindus and Buddhists consider this cycle as the vehicle of human suffering, because although the most meritorious persons may avoid hell, until they escape this cycle they will be perpetually reborn to potential suffering. In each life such persons will suffer the torment of gestating in the body of a woman, which is itself a place of hell—the fetus, conscious, remembering its past lives, is inundated with the mother's repulsive body fluids just as the dead in hell swim in rivers of blood. Eskimos and Alaskan Athabaskans hope that, through rebirth, the dead will return to their families; women perform mortuary rituals to enable this. According to anthropologist Sergei Kan, among the nineteenth-century Alaskan Tlingit, a woman who wanted to give birth to a recently deceased relative would keep fingernails, hair, and other substances from

the corpse in her belt; while the body was being cremated, she would circumambulate the pyre eight times, then sketch a short path from it and urinate while calling the spirit to return. Hindus, Buddhists, and Native Americans believe that reincarnating souls can change gender; Hindu myths show that gender changes in rebirth, though possible, are uncommon.

WOMEN IN HEAVEN AND HELL

According to Brahmanic Hinduism, traditional Islamic hadith doctrine, and the Zoroastrian vision narrative *Ardā Wirāz Nāmag*, women attain heaven through a combination of piety and chastity, though a woman's religious practice is not salvific when it conflicts with her husband's domestic desires. Hinduism guarantees heaven to women who are immolated on their husbands' funeral pyres; Norse, Muslim, and Aztec women who die in childbirth are assured heaven. Islamic heaven, populated with nymphs, promises exquisite sexual pleasure to men. The Qur'an mentions (suras 44:54, 52:20, 55:72, and 56:22; see also 56:35–38, 78:33, and 37:48–49), and tradition expands upon, the wondrous *houri* maidens awarded for male virtue. *Houris* are women, but not earthly: their bodies are made of saffron, musk, amber, and camphor; they do not sleep, menstruate, spit, express mucous, get pregnant, or get sick; they do not lose their virginity in sexual intercourse; and they are exclusively dedicated to one man. In Islam heaven is where many *houris* and resurrected earthly wives will attend one man who will come and go as he pleases while women wait patiently, without jealousy or anger. Brahmanic Hinduism likewise promises heavens where families are reunited and women's virtue is rewarded with attendance to husbands and children, while men's virtue is rewarded with the sexual favors of nymphs. Narratives of heaven show serving men as women's natural happiness.

Judaism contains no normative instructions concerning the afterlife. Heaven and hell are barely alluded to in biblical writings, although later apocalyptic literature includess visionary tours of hell. Pious Jewish women as well as men are expected to live in paradise after death, although most Jewish images of heaven depict a patriarchal world in which men study holy texts and women are the footstools of their husbands. Reincarnation, which appears in some esoteric Jewish teachings, presents a male soul's incarnation into the body of a woman (or an animal) as a punishment for sin.

Visionary narratives elaborate women's damnation more explicitly than women's salvation, locating more women in hell than in heaven and explaining the sins for which women are sent to hell as relating especially to marriage and sexuality. According to the Islamicist

Jane I. Smith, traditional narratives of Muhammad's narrative of ascent say that he witnessed the fire of judgment and saw that its inhabitants were mostly women, damned because of sexual infidelity, disobedience, deception, and ingratitude toward their husbands, and because of the restrictions on menstruating women's performing all the religious obligations. Women in Zoroastrian hell, according to Wirāz's vision, were damned primarily for three types of sins: adultery, poor treatment of children (including abortion), and lack of subservience toward their husbands (including not consenting to sex whenever their husbands wanted it). In the visionary Italian poet Dante Alighieri's *Divine Comedy*, more women appear in the *Inferno* than anywhere else in his cosmos. Dante identifies women with body, lust, and sin, and populates the *Inferno*'s Circle of Lust with a majority of women, defining that sin as feminine—as if to be female is to be essentially sexual, and essentially sinful.

END OF TIME AS INVERSION

Apocalyptic narratives envision an end-time, where historical time and cosmic time merge, and where the dead join the living in a collective afterlife of judgment, redemption, and inversion. Islamic eschatology suggests that after the day of judgment, natural order will become reversed: not only will the seas boil and the sun rise in the west, but men will have to work for women to earn their living, husbands will have to obey their wives, the population of women will outnumber men, religious knowledge will decline, and ignorance will prevail, as life becomes a kind of living hell. By associating the reversal of gender order with death and the termination of society, these images equate women's social power with men's demise, as if women's power were an inherent threat to religion and society.

Narratives of life beyond human existence establish that time, cosmic space, and all living beings are organized by cosmic rather than human will, such that gender roles of the living are supernaturally ordained: in past, present, and future, and throughout the cosmic realms, women who are subservient to men, deity, and social system are happy and blessed, while insubordinate women are tormented and damned. Indeed, women's subordination is the foundation for social and religious order.

BIBLIOGRAPHY

Although the afterlife, in general, is the focus of significant scholarship, analyses that focus specifically on religious portrayals of women in the afterlife are relatively limited. The following sources address the issue directly, although in some cases with only modest elaboration; they provide useful source information that could direct further research.

Bynum, Caroline Walker. *The Resurrection of the Body in Western Christianity, 200–1336.* 1995.

Duyvendak, J. J. L. *A Chinese "Divina Commedia."* Leiden, 1952.

Jordan, David K. *Gods, Ghosts, and Ancestors: The Folk Religion of a Taiwanese Village.* 1972.

Kan, Sergei. *Symbolic Immortality: The Tlingit Potlatch of the Nineteenth Century.* 1989.

Kirkham, Victoria. "A Canon of Women in Dante's *Commedia.*" *Annali D'Italianistica* 7 (1989): 15–41.

Kohn, Livia. *Early Chinese Mysticism: Philosophy and Soteriology in the Taoist Tradition.* 1992. See esp. chap. 5, "Ecstatic Exploration of the Otherworld."

Law, Bimala Charan. *Heaven and Hell in Buddhist Perspective.* 1925.

Perrin, Michel. *The Way of Dead Indians: Goajiro Myths and Symbols.* Translated by Michael Fineberg. 1987.

Smith, Jane I. and Yvonne Y. Haddad. "Women and the Afterlife: The Islamic View as Seen from the Qur'ān and Tradition." *Journal of the American Academy of Religion* 43 (1975): 39–50.

Sullivan, Thelma D. "Pregnancy, Childbirth, and the Deification of the Women Who Died in Childbirth." *Estudios de Cultura Náhuatl* 6 (1966): 65–95.

Teiser, Stephen. *The Scripture on the Ten Kings and the Making of Purgatory in Medieval Chinese Buddhism.* 1994.

Tibetan Book of the Dead. Translated by Robert Thurman. 1994.

Vahman, Fereydun. *Ardā Wirāz Namāg: The Iranian 'Divina Commedia.'* 1986.

Vitebsky, Piers. *Dialogues with the Dead: The Discussion of Mortality among the Sora of Eastern India.* 1993.

Wilson, Liz. *Charming Cadavers: Horrific Figurations of the Feminine in Indian Buddhist Hagiographic Literature.* 1996.

See also **Birth and Rebirth; Death; Gender Roles; Salvation.**

KAREN LEE ANDERSON

Agricultural Rituals

The rituals associated with agriculture are underestimated in their significance; yet they developed almost with the discovery of agriculture itself, and thus are a community's most consequential activities. Agriculture began during the rather creative Mesolithic era, between one form of civilization—hunting and gathering—and another—cultivating cereals (Eliade, 1978). There is general agreement among scholars that innovations in agriculture developed in Southwest Asia and Central Africa in the subsequent Neolithic period (9000–7000 B.C.E.).

With the development of language and the turn from hunting and gathering to farming and agriculture, early humans endeavored to control agricultural processes through ritual so as to assure subsistence. Such rituals aimed to increase fertility of the soil, to promote the sprouting of seed, and to encourage the harvesting of crops.

From earliest times it is women who have devised and implemented ritual control over agricultural processes and secured agriculture as their exclusive domain. As in the Paleolithic period, when a mystical relation existed between the hunter and the animal, women cultivated a mystical link between the soil and vegetation. In the dominant ideology and myths of many early societies, the earth and vegetation are feminine, whereas the sky is masculine. A large segment of world communities use simple subsistence farming that produces limited yields and depends mainly on cultivation with the hoe. Evan Zuesse (1979) observed that African societies of the hoe tend to exhibit matrilineal kinship and inheritance systems, especially in places least prone to centralized government, such as "segmentary" societies in Zaire. Among the Ila of Zambia, while their husbands engage in war, herding, and hunting, women cultivate the land (Zuesse, 1979).

Throughout the world agricultural rituals in which women play a central role are intrinsically linked to cultural activities, especially human sacrifice, the rites of rainmaking, possession rituals, menstrual taboo, and what has often been referred to as territorial cults. Among the Aztecs of Mexico, in the eighth month of the year a woman who stood for the corn goddess, Xilonen, was sacrificed. As a part of this ritual, on the eve of the sacrifice a vigil was staged in which participants sang praises to Xilonen throughout the night (Duverger, 1989).

Without rain, planting and agricultural activities cannot flourish; thus, rainmakers are regarded as sacred. Men and women who are spiritually gifted at communicating with the supernatural ancestral world can ensure adequate supplies of rain. Rainmaking rituals are performed whenever there is a drought. In a classic example, the queen of the Luvedu people in South Africa combines the position of a political figurehead with the spiritual leader of the kingdom (Mbiti, 1990). Concerning agriculture and possession rites, Richard Webner (1989) observed that among Kalanga women the performance of possession is correlated with the agricultural

A group of young women perform a harvest dance in a field in Sri Lanka (Hulton-Deutsch Collection/Corbis).

cycle, signifying a relationship to food production. Possession occurs during three significant occasions among the Kalanga: (1) hoeing and ploughing, (2) the first biting of the new fruits, and (3) the first stamping of the new maize (Webner, 1989).

One of the most illuminating explanations of the menstrual taboo lies in its connection with agricultural processes. Among the Beng of Ivory Coast, a menstruating woman avoids the fields and offers sacrifices of chickens or goats to the earth if the taboo is broken. Although menstruation has often been interpreted by scholars as pollution, the anthropologist Alma Gottlieb (1992) argues that, in fact, for the Beng menstrual blood is a symbol of human fertility. By placing a taboo between menstruation and the forests, the Beng separate menstruation from agricultural fertility, which is intricately linked to the field.

Women take actives roles in the African territorial cults (Schoffeleers, 1979). In sacred centers women perform rituals to maintain abundant production in the fields. Women often serve as the custodians of shrines, offering counseling about planting and harvesting and performing divination and other rituals in consultation with the enshrined deity. Terrence Ranger (1985) reported an interesting case of a territorial cult in Zimbabwe in which an elderly woman named Ninakapansi (mother of the ground) in charge of a Nwari shrine reprimanded people for their failure to bring gifts to the shrine and to consult with the spirits before embarking on plantings. Ninakapansi explained the current natural drought as a consequence of her people's disobedience. People responded by bringing gifts to the shrine, and the drought ended.

In places where the ideology of sacred kingship dominates, the king is intimately linked to agricultural productivity. In order to ensure the fertility of the land, the king enters into a sacred marriage (*hieros gamos*) with the goddess (Reiner, 1994), as in Babylonian religions. The symbolic marriage energizes the field and causes abundant harvests.

BIBLIOGRAPHY

Duverger, Christian. "The Meanings of Sacrifice." In *Fragments for a History of the Human Body*. Edited by Michel Feher. 1989.

Eliade, Mircea. *A History of Religious Ideas: From Stone Age to the Eleusian Mysteries*. Vol. 1. 1978.

Gottlieb, Alma. *Under the Kapok Tree: Identity Difference in Beng Thought*. 1992.

Kriger, F. J., and J. D. Kriger. *The Realm of a Rain Queen*. 2d ed. 1960.

Mbiti, John S. *African Religions and Philosophy*. 1969. Reprint, 1990.

Ranger, Terrence. "Religious Studies and Political Economy." In *Theoretical Exploration in African Religions*. Edited by Wim van Binsbergen and Matthew Schoffeleers. 1985.

Reiner, Erica. "Babylonian Religion." In *Religion and the Social Order: What Kind of Lessons Does History Teach?* Edited by Jacob Neusner. 1994.

Schoffeleers, Matthew. *Guardians of the Land: Essays on Central African Territorial Cults*. Gwelo, Zimbabwe, 1979.

Werbner, Richard P. *Ritual Passage, Sacred Journey: The Process and Organization of Religious Moments*. 1989.

Zuesse, Evan M. *Ritual Cosmos: The Sanctification of Life in African Religions*. 1979.

JACOB OLUPONA

'A'ishah

'A'ishah, beloved wife of Muhammad, was the daughter of Abú Bakr (one of Muhammad's earliest and most important companions) and Umm Ruman. The Muslim tradition has generally held that she was born in Mecca around 613–614 C.E. and that she was married to Muhammad at the age of six after the death of his first wife Khadija in 619 C.E., though the marriage was not consummated till three years later at Medina. However, this tradition has been strongly challenged in a book in Urdu entitled *Tehqiq 'umar-e 'Aisha Siddiqa* (Research on the age of 'A'ishah, the Truthful) by Hakim Niaz Ahmad, published in Pakistan. Through painstaking critique of the sources of the traditional view regarding 'A'ishah's age as well as of related historical circumstances, this scholar endeavors to establish that 'A'ishah was not a child-bride but a mature woman when Muhammad married her.

'A'ishah is very important in Muslim history not only because she became Muhammad's favorite wife after the death of Khadija, but also because she is one of the major transmitters of the oral sayings (hadith) ascribed to him. According to one well-known hadith, Muhammad had said, "Learn half of the 'Din' (Principles of Faith) from me and the other half from 'A'ishah." That 'A'ishah was regarded as a learned woman during Muhammad's lifetime supports the contention that she was more than eighteen years old—as is generally believed—at the time of his death in A.H. 10 (632 C.E.).

There were some serious personal and political crises in the life of 'A'ishah, whose role in the politics of the Prophet's household as well as in the early Muslim community is regarded by some as controversial. In the Shiite tradition in particular, 'A'ishah is represented negatively due to the long-standing hostility that existed between her and Fatima, Muhammad's daughter, and Fatima's husband 'Ali, whom 'A'ishah confronted in "the Battle of the Camel" in A.H. 35 (656 C.E.). Defeated, 'A'ishah withdrew from active politics and retired to Medina. She continued, however, to be influential until her death in A.H. 58 (578 C.E.) and is still greatly venerated in Sunni Islam.

A multifaceted, dynamic woman, 'A'ishah is also to be remembered for her strong feminist consciousness, which is reflected in a number of her sayings.

BIBLIOGRAPHY

A'ishah, the Beloved of Mohammed is a full-scale biography of 'A'ishah by Nabia Abbott (1897, repr. 1942). A recent book on aspects of 'A'ishah's life is D. A. Spellberg's *Politics, Gender, and the Islamic Past: The Legacy of 'Aisha Bint Abi Bakr* (1994). Another biographical book on 'A'ishah is *Umm al-Mu'minun 'Aisha Siddiquh: Life and Work* by Mumtaz Moin (1979, repr. 1995).

Useful biographical information is also contained in W. Montgomery Watt, " 'A'ishah Bint Abi Bakr," in *The Encyclopedia of Islam* (new ed., 1960), edited by H. A. R. Gibb, J. H. Kramers, E. Levi-Provencal, and J.

Schacht, vol. 1, pp. 308–309; and Jane Dammen McAuliffe, " 'A'isha Bint Abi Bakr," in *The Encyclopaedia of Religion*, edited by Mircea Eliade (1987), vol. 1, pp. 162–163.

Reference to 'A'ishah is made in all books on Muhammad's life. Brief accounts of 'A'ishah's life are contained in Bint alShati, *The Wives of the Prophet*, translated by Matti Moosa and D. Nicholas Ranson (1971); *The Wives of the Holy Prophet* by Farzana Hasan (1984); and S. M. Madani 'Abbasi, *Family of the Holy* (1982, repr. 1994).

Accounts of 'A'ishah's life are to be found also in books about significant Muslim women including *Middle Eastern Muslim Women Speak*, edited by Elizabeth Warnock Fernea and Basima Qattan Bezirgan (1977, repr. 1980) and Muhammad Saeed Siddiqi, *The Blessed Women of Islam* (1982).

NONENGLISH SOURCES

Ahmad, Hakim Niaz. *Tehqiq 'umar-e 'A'isha Siddiqa.* Karachi, 1972.
Hussain, Syed Asghar. "Hazrat 'A'isha Siddiqi." In *Naik Bibian.* Karachi, 1968.
Jeerajpuri, Aslam. "Umm ul Momineen Hazrat 'A'isha." In *Namwar Musulman Khwateen.* Lahore, 1996.
Khan, Mahmood Ahmad. "Hazrat 'A'isha Siddiqi." In *Umhatul Momineen.* Lahore, 1996.
Nadvi, Syed Sulaiman. *Seerat-e-'A'isha.* Lahore, 1993.

See also Fāṭimàh.

RIFFAT HASSAN

Ala

Ala is a female deity associated with the powers of the land in the religious traditions of the Igbo of southeastern Nigeria. She is also known as Ale and Ani in certain Igbo dialects. Within the broader context of West African religions, Ala bears some resemblances to Onile, the Yoruba earth goddess, and with Asase Ya, the Ashanti earth goddess.

Though not as powerful as the supreme being, Chineke or Chukwu, who embodies both feminine and masculine ideas of spiritual power, Ala is considered to be the most powerful of the lesser deities (*agbara*). In some traditions Ala was said to be married to Igwe, the deity associated with the sky; in others she was married to Amadioha, the god of thunder, but she was regarded as significantly more powerful than her spouse. Above all, Ala is associated with the life-giving powers of the land, of the fertility of women, livestock, and the earth. Before planting and during the yam harvest, major fes-

tivals are held in her honor. Because the growth of life requires a proper moral order to sustain it, Ala is also the primary deity associated with Igbo concepts of ethics and morality. Generally regarded as a loving and generous deity, she can be harsh in dealing with those who violate important Igbo ideas of proper conduct. This has made her the most important deity for the maintenance of an Igbo system of justice.

Ala is seen as the embodiment of feminine power, but her priests are male. Shrines exist at the level of a village cluster, in individual villages, in village quarters, and within particular lineages. Though many of her shrines are quite simple in structure—a pottery bowl near a tree—many of her devotees construct special houses (*mbari*) in which Ala's image, richly adorned with a special type of body painting reserved to Igbo women (*uli*), occupies a central place in the company of other gods and spiritual beings drawn from Igbo and Christian traditions. When women give birth, there are immediate offerings to Ala. Barren women seek Ala's assistance in becoming fertile. She also governs the world of the dead and directs the process of reincarnation, guiding the spirits of ancestors back into the world of the living. Those who died because they offended the land, however, are denied the right to be buried in the earth or are limited to burials in land set aside for wrongdoers.

BIBLIOGRAPHY

Cole, Herbert M. *Mbari: Art and Life among the Owerri Igbo.* 1982.
McCall, Daniel F. "Mother Earth: The Great Goddess of West Africa." In *Mother Worship: Theme and Variations.* Edited by James J. Preston. 1982.
Meek, C. K. *Law and Authority in a Nigerian Tribe: A Study in Indirect Rule.* 1937. Reprint, 1970.

ROBERT M. BAUM

Alchemy

In alchemical "Work," the recombination of male and female elements or essences, both in their mineral and sexual forms, was essential for effecting a return of all contraries or opposites back into their primal source, for a primordial union of matter and spirit, of microcosm and macrocosm, that preceded their "fall" into differentiation. Although transmutation of base metals into gold was a portion of their Work, the alchemists' highest goal was of a soteriological order: the redemption or reintegration of a shattered yet interconnected natural world, and the transformation or transubstanti-

Illustration showing two witches brewing up a bewitching concoction to heal all ills of the soul and body. Woodcut from a book on alchemy published in 1487 (Corbis-Bettmann).

ation of the mortal human body, through the ingestion of an alchemical elixir, into a supernatural, immortal body.

For example, three alchemical sources offer nearly identical instructions for the extraction of fluid mercury, or quicksilver, from the "wells" in which it naturally occurs: A maiden who has bathed following her menstrual period is to walk or ride naked beside the mercurial well. The mercury, sensing her presence, rushes up out of its well to pursue her. She flees ahead of the mercury, which is captured in troughs dug into the ground by alchemists.

This description is found in Syriac recensions of the fourth to fifth centuries of the works of Pseudo-Zosimus, the Indian *Rasaratnasamucchaya* of the thirteenth to fourteenth centuries, and the *Ho han sans ts'ai t'ou hui*, a seventeenth-century Chinese encyclopedia. Although historians of alchemy trace the spread of this tradition in the opposite direction along the Silk Road (i.e., from China westward), this account is exemplary in that it illustrates the most salient feature of all the world's alchemical traditions: the notion that the primary alchemical reagents, mercury and sulfur, are gendered; and that these mineral manifestations of the male and female principles interact with or are identified with human sexual emissions. Thus, in all of these traditions a body of "inner" physiological or eroticomystical practice complements the "outer" laboratory operations of the alchemist.

Sexual union, on a concrete or symbolic level, was central to the alchemical effort; and, because nearly every alchemist of legend and history was male (with the exception of Mary the Jewess of Hellenistic alchemical legend), the alchemical Work could not be realized without a female consort or laboratory assistant. In Taoist inner alchemy, the union of male yang and female yin could be effected through the conjoining of male semen with female uterine blood. In Western Renaissance alchemical imagery, operations involving the "perfect solution" of mercury and sulphur were portrayed as the alchemical wedding and sexual union of a White Queen and her Red King, or Lady Alchimia and her Athanor King.

It was in the Hindu and Tibetan Buddhist alchemical traditions in the eleventh to fourteenth centuries that the role of the female alchemical consort was most fully concretized. Here, the male alchemist was incapable of "fixing" volatile (male) mercury without the menstrual blood of his assistant, menstrual blood that was the mineral homologue of (female) sulfur, which has similar fixative properties. Furthermore, in the final process of his own transformation into an immortal, invulnerable, perfected being, the alchemist had to engage in sexual intercourse with his consort in order for said mercury to be activated within him.

BIBLIOGRAPHY

The best general overview of the world's alchemical traditions remains Mircea Eliade, *The Forge and the Crucible* (1962; repr. 1978), a work that emphasizes the sexual symbolism inherent in these traditions. On sexual symbolism and femininity in Western alchemy, see especially Françoise Bonardel, *Philosophie de l'alchimie, grand oeuvre et modernité* (1993). A fine anthology of illustrations of Western alchemical imagery, much of it sexual, is J. Fabricius, *Alchemy: The Medieval Alchemists and Their Royal Art* (1976). The most comprehensive work on the ninth-century Persian Jābirian alchemical tradition is Paul Kraus, *Contribution à l'histoire des idées scientifiques dans l'Islam: Jābir et la science grecque* (1986). On the Hindu and allied Tibetan Buddhist alchemical traditions, in which sexual symbolism and the role of the feminine are greatly highlighted, see David Gordon White, *The Alchemical Body: Siddha Traditions in Medieval India* (1996). The most comprehensive treatment of the Chinese alchemical tradition is Joseph Needham et al., *Science and Civilisation in Ancient China*, 6 vols. (1954–). In volume 5 of that work, "Chemistry and Chemical Technology: Spagyrical Discovery and Invention," see "Historical Survey, from Cinnabar Elixirs to Synthetic Insulin" (pt. 3, 1976); "Apparatus, Theories and Gifts" (pt. 4, 1980); and "Physiological Alchemy" (pt. 5, 1983). The classic essay is by Sally Allen and Joanna Hubbs, "Outrunning Atalanta: Feminine Destiny in Alchemical Transmutation," *Signs* 6, no. 2 (1980): 210–221.

See also Blood; Esotericism; Magic; Menstruation; Occultism; Tantra.

DAVID WHITE

Alinesitoué

Alinesitoué Diatta (c. 1920–1943), was an important West African prophet who led a major religious movement among the Diola ethnic group in Senegal, Gambia, and Portuguese Guinea from 1941 until 1943. Although she was not the first Diola to claim direct revelation from the Diola supreme being, Emitai, Alinesitoué and some less-known contemporaries transformed an exclusively male tradition of prophetic leadership into a predominantly female one during the period of French colonial rule. Alinesitoué's visions began during a particularly repressive period of French rule in Senegal. An understaffed Vichy regime sought to obtain large quantities of Diola rice to supply the urban areas with food (at a time when drought had shrunk Diola grain reserves) and encouraged vigorous campaigns of Christian and Muslim proselytization in Diola communities. By building on earlier traditions of male prophetic revelation, Alinesitoué was able to introduce a series of new cults and to reform Diola religious practice in such a way as to provide access to religious authority for women and young adults. Furthermore, she challenged French colonial development plans that were based on the introduction of a new cash crop, peanuts, in the region. Among the northern Diola, men had already abandoned the primarily subsistence crop of rice to women so as to concentrate on peanuts. This interfered with a family mode of production and placed the entire burden of rice cultivation on women. She challenged these development schemes, asserting that the new cash crop of peanuts disrupted a covenantal relationship between the Diola and Emitai, in which Emitai provided rain for rice cultivation and Diola women and men provided labor. She taught that peanuts were not spiritually situated within a Diola ecology and that they fostered both a dependence on the French and infertility of the land, while eroding the economic importance of women.

As pilgrims flocked to Alinesitoué's village in 1942, Vichy officials worried about her potential to lead a revolt against an already weakened colonial authority. In 1943 French officials arrested her and many of her followers. She was exiled to Tombouctou, where she died of starvation. Since her exile there have been twenty-eight other prophets, most of them women, all of whom claim to be following in her tradition of revelation from the supreme being and of opening up the tradition to previously marginalized groups. A separatist movement in Senegal's southern region of Casamance has also embraced the legacy of Alinesitoué, claiming her as the Joan of Arc of Casamance.

BIBLIOGRAPHY

Fall, Marouba. *Aliin Sitooye Jaata ou la Dame de Kabrus.* Dakar, 1993.
Girard, Jean. *Genèse du pouvoir charismatique en Basse Casamance (Sénégal).* Dakar, 1969.
Waldman, Marilyn R, with Robert M. Baum. "Innovation as Renovation: The 'Prophet' as an Agent of Change." In *Innovation in Religious Traditions.* Edited by Michael A. Williams et al. Berlin, 1992.

ROBERT M. BAUM

Almsgiving

Almsgiving is the giving of food, other requisites, and money to either the poor and needy or the spiritually worthy. It is usually understood as an ethical or social obligation placed upon the donor bringing not only assistance to the recipient but spiritual benefit to the giver as well. In many traditions, almsgiving came to devolve not only upon individual donors but also upon institutions such as churches, temples, monasteries, and hospitals. In time, the religious setting of almsgiving was augmented by charity as a secular activity championed by philanthropists, social workers, and activists for the disenfranchised. The particular locus of women as almsgivers was often at the household door bestowing gifts, especially food, on petitioners. Additionally, women in many traditions became donors, frequently with their own resources, of substantial largesse such as requisites in bulk, land, and buildings.

In Western traditions, alms are normally given to the poor and needy by pious donors, except in mendicant traditions such as Christianity, where the recipient is a religious who has taken a vow of poverty. In Judaism, charity is an act whereby the individual imitates God's ways, using God-given wealth to rectify a social imbalance. Book seven of Maimonides' (1135–1204) *Mishneh Torah,* for example, is devoted to charity, and tithing (as in Christianity and Islam) is regularly used for benefit to the poor. Apprehensive of the possession of wealth, Christian views focus on the linkage of charity and love to pattern human action after the divine. Contemporary Roman Catholic social teaching further emphasizes the obligation of Christians to effect basic justice and human rights for all. In the Qur'an, no obligation is more noted than that of almsgiving (*zakat*), and this institution, the foundation for social responsibility in Islam, is often used for relief of the poor, as detailed in al-Ghazzali's (1058–1111) *The Mysteries of Almsgiving.*

In Asian traditions, the normal context of almsgiving is the gift of cooked food and other requisites for the religiously worthy. *Dana,* or donation, the main practice of the present age (Kali Yoga) in Hinduism, is obligatory for householders and has parallels in hospitality etiquette for honored guests. The petition for alms is essential to the *brahmacarin*'s (student) and *samnyasin*'s (renunciant) daily rounds, and giving for the donor not only produces merit but eases debts to the religious. In Buddhism, there is particular emphasis on pleasing the donor and on the exchange involved in the relationship: donors have an obligation to give requisites (*danadharma*), while recipients may return with a gift of teaching (*dharmadana*). In countries like China, Buddhist and Taoist institutions themselves have been known for undertaking extensive community charity works. Like Buddhists, Jain mendicants are instructed to receive donations however they come but are also mindful of issues of ahimsa (nonviolence) in the process.

Patronage, or matronage, by women donors is assumed throughout the ages in most traditions. In the New Testament, Jesus uses the example of the poor widow given two copper coins (Luke 21:1–4; Mark 12:41–44) to illustrate the great proportion of holdings a gift should be, and in the Qur'an women are expected to contribute equally in charity with men. In South Asian contexts, women are traditionally styled managers of the household goods and are the representatives of the household in donation to petitioners. In

Women hold up offerings of food to monks in Vientiane, Laos (Nik Wheeler/Corbis).

Buddhism, when women encounter petitioners at the door, they give less out of hospitality obligation and more out of individual agency. The expanded urban context and the rise of mercantile activity helped provide for two new donor groups—courtesans and nuns—amply attested as donors, along with widows, in inscriptional evidence of many periods.

As objects of giving, women receivers fall most naturally into two groups: mendicant women are normally under vows of poverty and propertylessness. Nuns in Christian, Buddhist, and Jain traditions receive gifts of maintenance, though are known at times to engage in support-producing work. Hindu female ascetics who have given up the obligations of housewife (*stridharma*) now must rely, as male renunciants do, on the gifts of others. Injunctions to support women of special needs occur in the cases of widows and of poor maidens needing dowry; both Judaism and Islam, for example, urge the maintenance of widows and the dowering of impoverished brides.

Whether women, by nature, are any more generous with their resources or any more needy than men is not routinely addressed by traditions. The special prominence of women in any area of almsgiving is usually understood as a product of culturally and religiously configured circumstances.

BIBLIOGRAPHY

Acharya, Kala. *Puranic Concept of Dana.* 1993.

Bremner, Robert H. *Giving: Charity and Philanthropy in History.* 1994.

Dundas, Paul. *The Jains.* 1992.

Economic Justice For All: Pastoral Letter on Catholic Social Teaching and the U.S. Economy. 1986.

Findly, Ellison Banks. "The Housemistress at the Door: Vedic and Buddhist Perspectives on the Men-

dicant Encounter." In *Debating Gender.* Edited by
Laurie L. Patton. Forthcoming.

McCash, June Hall, ed. *The Cultural Patronage of Medieval Women.* 1996.

Nath, Vijay. *Dāna: Gift System in Ancient India (c. 600 B.C.–c. A.D. 300): A Socio-Economic Perspective.* 1987.

Tamari, Meir. *"With All your Possessions": Jewish Ethics and Economic Life.* 1987.

ELLISON BANKS FINDLY

Amaterasu

Formally called Amaterasu Omikami (Great Divinity Illuminating Heaven), Amaterasu is the sun goddess in Shinto mythology. Considered the origin of the Japanese imperial line, she is the most important female deity in Shinto. Amaterasu has been enshrined at the Grand Shrine at Ise where pilgrims have come to worship for centuries. Ise has close connections with the imperial family; to preserve ritual purity the numerous shrines there are rebuilt every twenty years.

The story of Amaterasu's birth is recorded in legends found in the earliest Shinto texts, *Kojiki* 712 and *Nihon shoki* 720, where the primal couple is identified as Izanami and Izanagi. According to the *Kojiki,* Amaterasu emerged when Izanagi purified his left eye after visiting the underworld. According to the *Nihon shoki* she was born of the union of Izanami and Izanagi. The most famous legend about Amaterasu tells of when she hid herself in a cave to protest her younger brother Susano's misdeeds. The world immediately went dark until she was tempted out by the dancing and singing of other deities. Amaterasu's absence is considered an explanation of an eclipse, and the other deities' dancing is said to account for the origin of the theatrical arts in Japan. Amaterasu later sent her grandson, Ninigi no Mikoto, to the islands of Japan equipped with a sacred mirror, jewel, and sword (the imperial regalia). The first emperor of Japan, Jimmu, is said to be the great-grandson of Ninigi no Mikoto. Hence, the emperors of Japan are considered to be descendants of the sun goddess, Amaterasu, and until the end of World War II were thought to be divine themselves.

BIBLIOGRAPHY

The Kojiki: Records of Ancient Matters. Translated by Basil Hall Chamberlain. 1981.

Tsunoda, R., and W. T. de Bary, eds. *Sources of Japanese Tradition.* 1959.

MARY EVELYN TUCKER

Amaterasu appears from the cave. Woodblock print, Taiso Yoshitoshi, 1882. (Asian Art & Archaeology, Inc./Corbis)

Amazons

The Amazons, a mythic race of female warriors, appear in Greek literature as early as the epic poems of Homer (c. eighth century B.C.E.). The Amazons were said to dwell beyond the northern edge of the civilized regions of the Greek world at Themiscyra on the Thermodon River (Herodotus 9.27). Devoted to warfare and the hunt, the Amazons are portrayed as the antithesis of Greek women, who stay at home and spin (Homer *Odyssey* 1.356–357; Xenophon *Oeconomicus* 7.30). Diodorus Siculus relates that the Amazons were so called because they made a practice of searing one or both of their breasts to improve agility with the bow (2.45; 3.53), although artistic representations show them with both breasts intact. Traditionally, the name *Amazon* is derived from the Greek alpha privative *a*, which expresses absence of want, and the word for breast, *mazos*. According to Diodorus Siculus, the Amazons were devotees of the Great Mother of the gods, Cybele, and celebrated her in orgiastic rites (3.55).

Among their mythic exploits were various invasions of the Greek world. In book six of Homer's *Iliad*, the Trojan king Priam recalls fighting against attacking Amazons whom he calls "a match for men" (*antianeira*). According to Aeschylus, the Amazons invaded Athens and encamped on the hill known as the Areopagus, where they sacrificed to the god Ares, who is often called the father of the Amazons (*Eumenides* 685ff; Lysias 2.4; Isocrates 4.68). Traditionally, the Amazons were said to have come to the aid of the Trojans at the end of the Trojan War (*Aeneid* 1.490ff.). We are told in Quintus of Smyrna's *Fall of Troy* (1.671 ff) that Achilles fell deeply in love with the Amazon queen Penthesilea upon killing her.

The defeat and subjugation of the Amazons is a motif in the literary tales of Greek heroes and a mark of Athenian glory in art. Conquering the Amazons was among the heroic labors of Bellerophon and Heracles (*Iliad* 6.186; Euripides *Heracles* 408ff). Theseus, the mythic king of Athens, was said to have subdued the Amazons and married their queen, Hippolyta or Antiope, when they attacked Athens. The depiction of Amazonian defeat gained prominence in the decorative programs of many civic buildings during the heyday of the Athenian empire (fifth century B.C.E.). It can be found on the frieze of the Parthenon as well as on the Theseum, a sanctuary to Theseus. At the annual fifth-century Athenian festival of the Thesea, the Athenians offered sacrifice to the Amazons, commemorating their defeat by Theseus.

In recent years many scholars have considered the Amazon myth an expression of the evolution of civilization from matriarchy to patriarchy; it symbolizes the paradoxical repulsion, deep fear, and anxiety coupled with sexual attraction the Greeks had with respect to women.

BIBLIOGRAPHY

Bamberger, Joan. "The Myth of Matriarchy; Why Men Rule in Primitive Society." *Women, Culture, and Society*. Edited by Michelle Zimbalist Rosaldo and Louise Lamphere. 1974.

Bennett, Florence Mary. *Religious Cults Associated with the Amazons*. 1967.

Lefkowitz, Mary. *Women in Greek Myth*. 1986.

Tyrrell, William Blake. *Amazons: A Study in Athenian Mythmaking*. 1984.

See also **Warriors.**

DANIELLA REINHARD

Amulets

Amulets are material substances that women and men use alone or as part of a larger ritual for protection against evil and dangerous forces, healing, safe pregnancy and childbirth, erotic purposes, attacks against other people, or to gain ritual power and favor from a holy person or deity. The primary mark of an amulet is its efficacy in conveying power to the one who wears it, places it in a house or workplace, buries it in a cemetery, or leaves it in a sacred place. Plants have been used as amulets, when, for example, leaves are tied in bundles and hung around the neck of a sick person. Many amulets consist of incantations or holy words (verses from the Qur'an or the Bible), symbols of power (the cross or the footprint of the Buddha), or sacred and powerful images (for example, of a saint) engraved or inscribed on precious gems, stones, metal or ceramic bowls, lamps, rings or coins, parchment, papyrus, or paper.

Both women and men use amulets. In sixty-century C.E. Mesopotamia, Jewish, Christian, and pagan women and men inscribed earthenware bowls with incantations and buried them near or under their houses to protect their families from demons (Joseph Naveh and Shaul Shaked, *Amulets and Magic Bowls*, 1987, pp. 13–21). In early modern England and New England, "cunning" women and men gave out pieces of paper inscribed with words of power to people afflicted with various illnesses (Keith Thomas, *Religion and the Decline of Magic*, 1971, pp. 177–192). In contemporary Thailand, women and men wear amulets on necklaces for protection and prosperity. Urban and forest-dwelling Buddhist monks sacralize the amulets by uttering sacred words over them. Their users feel that they are infused with the power of the Buddha or *arahant* (perfected saint) depicted on the amulet. Both women and men wear these amulets, but it is monks who transmit power to the amulets (Stanley J. Tambiah, *The Buddhist Saints of the Forest and the Cult of Amulets*, 1984, pp. 195–229, 243, 273).

The difference between women's and men's use of amulets shows up most clearly in the needs that they meet. Because of the factors of chance and danger in pregnancy and childbirth, women around the world have used amulets to become pregnant and to ensure safe pregnancy and childbirth and a healthy newborn. In the Greco-Roman world (and in Europe through the sixteenth century), many male philosophical and medical writers (e.g., Plato, *Timaeus*, 91c) believed that the womb was a separate creature in a woman's body that caused illness when it wandered out of its proper place. Ritual practitioners in turn regarded the womb as a god or daimon and believed they could address it directly through prayer or adjuration. They made stone amulets on which they engraved commands to the womb to stay in its proper place. Ancient handbooks on the properties of stones specified those that assisted a woman in pregnancy and birth. Women would wear them, put them in the vagina, or use them in fumigations and potions.

Jewish women made use of similar amulets. A medieval amulet on paper from Cairo requests the zodiacal sign Leo to beseech God to keep evil spirits away from the womb of Habiba the daughter of Zahra, to prevent pain during her menstrual period, and to allow her to give birth without miscarriage. The incantation includes the names of biblical matriarchs: "If you transgress against this adjuration of mine, I shall strike you with iron rods, that are the four holy mothers, Bilhah, Rachel, Zilpah, Leah" (Joseph Naveh and Shaul Shaked, *Magic Spells and Formulae*, 1993, pp. 152–157). Jewish amulets for safe childbirth or to protect the newborn can still be found in religious shops in Israel and other Jewish centers. These amulets are hung by the pregnant woman's bed or on the baby's crib. Both ancient and modern amulets usually direct the incantation against Lilith, the first wife of Adam, who is alleged to kill children.

Women in nineteenth and early twentieth century China wore amulets in order to give birth to a son (Alvin P. Cohen, "Symbolic Amulets and Jewelry in Chinese Popular Culture," in Julian F. Pas, ed., *The Turning of the Tide: Religion in China Today*, 1989, pp. 107–108). In medieval and early modern Japan, pregnant women who wished to have a safe birth would place an amulet made of the text of the "menstruation sutra" into a waistband. This sutra teaches that women who die in childbirth, or even all women, because they menstruate, will fall into hell. Rituals associated with the sutra, including its use as an amulet, were designed to prevent this fate (Takemi Momoko, "'Menstruation Sutra' Belief in Japan," *Japanese Journal of Religious Studies* 10 (1983), pp. 229–246). Women in eighteenth and nineteenth century Ghana would also use amulets in order to have an easy birth. Qur'anic verses would be written on a wide wooden slate, the texts would be

washed off into a vessel, and the woman could drink or wash in the resulting liquid. In this way she could take the holy power of the Qur'an into herself and protect the child in her womb (David Owusu-Ansah, *Islamic Talismanic Tradition in Nineteenth-Century Asante*, 1991, pp. 81–87, 108–111).

Is women's use of amulets evidence for their independent ritual activities, or does it reveal dependence upon male authorities? The evidence presented here is mixed. Contemporary Thai women wear amulets sacralized by male religious figures. English "cunning women" wrote amulets for healing. Jewish women in late antiquity could have received amulets from a male amulet-writer, or could have made and inscribed an earthenware bowl. Like many other religious or ritual activities, the practice of making and using amulets reflects women's complicated relationship to male-dominated cultures. Although many of the most important ritual and symbolic elements are dictated by educated men, women use and remake these rituals and symbols, as well as create rituals of their own.

BIBLIOGRAPHY

Very little has been specifically written about women's, as distinct from men's, creation or use of amulets. Most sources give examples of amulets used by either women or men, and describe both women and men as the practitioners who made the amulets and gave them to their clients. The following three articles, however, specifically consider amulets for women: Jean-Jacques Aubert, "Threatened Wombs: Aspects of Ancient Uterine Magic," *Greek, Roman, and Byzantine Studies* 30 (1989): 421–449; Sarah Iles Johnston, "Defining the Dreadful: Remarks on the Greek Child-Killing Demon," in *Ancient Magic and Ritual Power*, edited by Marvin Meyer and Paul Mirecki, 1995; and J. A. Scurlock, "Baby-snatching Demons, Restless Souls, and the Dangers of Childbirth: Medico-magical Means of Dealing with Some of the Perils of Motherhood in Ancient Mesopotamia," *Incognita* 2 (1991): 137–185. A number of good editions publish examples of amulets from the ancient world: John Gager, ed., *Curse Tablets and Binding Spells from the Ancient World* (1992); Joseph Naveh and Shaul Shaked, eds., *Amulets and Magic Bowls: Aramaic Incantations of Late Antiquity*, 2d ed. (1987); Marvin Meyer and Richard Smith, eds., *Ancient Christian Magic: Coptic Texts of Ritual Power* (1994). A number of studies consider the use of amulets within the ritual systems of particular societies. Stanley Tambiah discusses the relationship between the use of amulets and Thai Buddhist monastic orders in *The Buddhist Saints of the Forest and the Cult of Amulets* (1984). In Keith Thomas's *Religion and the Decline of Magic* (1971), chapters 7–8 describe both folk and elite practices and discuss how amulets were used in healing. Chapter 1 of Richard Godbeer's *The Devil's Dominion: Magic and Religion in Early New England* (1992) describes the use of amulets for both healing and destructive purposes, especially "poppets" or dolls used for malevolent attacks.

See also **Fertility and Barrenness; Magic; Womb.**

REBECCA LESSES

Ānandamayī Mā (Ananda Ma)

Ānandamayī Mā (1896–1982) was a Hindu spiritual teacher and mystic from Bengal (now Bangladesh). Born Nirmalā Sundarī ("Flawlessly Beautiful") Bhattā-chārya to Vaiṣṇava brahmin parents in the village of Kheora, she received very little formal education but is remembered by tradition to have exhibited kindness, obedience, and an affinity for devotional songs (*kīr-tana*) and the chanting of God's name (*nāmajapa*). Just before age thirteen she was joined by arranged marriage to Ramani Mohan Chakravārtī (Bholānāth) and went to live in his brother's household for the first five years of their marriage, while Bholānāth traveled in search of work. Tradition says that their marriage was never physically consummated; when they set up house together in 1914, Nirmalā began the conscious intent (*kheyāla*) to enter into spiritual discipline (*sādhana*) as a mature realization of her childhood spirituality.

After 1918 she began to enter into lengthy meditations and *nāmajapa*s, culminating in her initiation, on 3 August 1922, in which she experienced the identification of the seemingly disparate realities of master (guru), sacred words of initiation (mantra), initiate (*śiṣya*), and Lord (*iṣṭa*). Her realization led to her teaching that everything is One (*advaita*, nonduality), and that all apparent distinctions are due to the *līlā* (divine play) of God. Gradually disciples began to come to her in her new home in Dhaka to attend her frequent entrance into *samādhi*, or state of intensive contemplation, and her regular performances of *kīrtana*. From 1926 until her death, Ānandamayī Mā undertook spontaneous pilgrimages throughout Bengal and across northern India, stopping at ashrams her disciples had established, such as the main ashram at Asi Gha in Banaras. She came to be understood in many ways—as the embodiment of Bliss (*ānandamayī*), as a healer, and as an incarnation of the goddess Kālī; some say she gave Indira Gandhi a *mālā* (sacred beads) in 1977 that helped return her to the prime ministership in 1980. Her disciples are active in India today.

BIBLIOGRAPHY
Authoritative Bengali sources for Śrī Ānandamayī Mā's teachings include *Ānanda Vārta*, the official journal of the Śrī Ānandamayī Charitable Society in Calcutta, and the multivolume study published by the Society: Guru Priya Devi, *Sri Sri Ananda Mayi* (vols. 1 and 2 in English, 1985–1986; vols. 2, 3, and 7–17 in Bengali; vols. 1, 4, 5, and 6 in Bengali [new ed.], 1986). In English, the classic book-length study remains Alexander Lipski, *Life and Teaching of Śrī Ānandamayī Mā* (Delhi, 1977; new ed., Calcutta, 1985). Articles focusing on her, including photographs, are Lisa Lassell Marlin, "Embodied Truth: The Life and Presence of a Hindu Saint," *Harvard Divinity Bulletin* 17, nos. 5–6 (Jan.–May 1987); and Bithika Mukerji, "Śrī Ānandamayī Mā: Divine Play of the Spiritual Journey," in *Hindu Spirituality: Vedas Through Vedanta,* edited by Krishna Sivaraman (1989). Articles offering comparative discussions of Ānandamayī Mā include David Miller, "Karma, Rebirth and the Contemporary Guru," in *Karma and Rebirth: Post Classical Developments,* edited by Ronald W. Neufeldt (1986); and John E. Mitchiner, "Three Contemporary Indian Mystics: Ānandamayī, Krishnabai and Rajneesh," in *The Yogi and the Mystic: Studies in Indian and Comparative Mysticism* (1989).

KAREN PECHILIS PRENTISS

Anat

See **Ishtar and Anat.**

Ancestor Worship

Ancestor worship consist of rituals performed beyond the time designated for primary and secondary funerary rituals, along with beliefs that the dead need ritual care in the afterworld. The primary distinguishing feature of ancestor worship is that the group of people who worships or gives ritual attention to a particular ancestor or group of ancestors is limited to those people considered legitimate members of the family of the deceased.

The significance of ancestor worship for the study of women and religion depends on the domestic and familial character of the phenomenon. Along with rules regulating marriage, the beliefs and practices surrounding ancestor worship help to define the "family," that group of persons linked together by bonds constructed through birth, adoption, and marriage who, as

A family makes offerings to their ancestors at the Wo Hok Shep Cemetery in Hong Kong (Nik Wheeler/ Corbis).

a result, are expected to act together in pursuit of some common purpose. By reinvoking memories of deceased kin and reconfirming one's relatedness to them and through them to others, ancestor worship helps to give affective depth to the matrilineal or patrilineal descent ideologies that govern group membership and inheritance. Moreover, ancestor worship is closely associated with the ethic of filial piety; it tends to consolidate social hierarchies that privilege elders over juniors, and men over women. From a feminist perspective, one sees the tendency in ancestor worship to efface women's crucial role in reproduction. It thus gives religious sanction to beliefs that men and not women in fact have the power to perpetuate the kin group over the generations.

In the societies of China, Japan, and Korea, ancestors are sharply distinguished from their negative counterparts in the world of supernatural beings, the hungry wandering ghosts. Ancestors are the spirits of people who have died after producing sons capable of performing their ancestral rites. According to Confucian practice, after death, tablets representing the individual are installed and worshiped in both the ancestral hall maintained by the lineage and in domestic shrines maintained by individual families. Ghosts, on the other hand, are the spirits of those who die without producing legitimate heirs. Since no one is obliged to perform ancestral rites for them, these pathetic, potentially dangerous beings roam about the settlements of their kin seeking comfort from the living.

In the patrilineal, virilocal communities of East Asia, when a married woman dies, her affinal kin make an ancestral tablet for her and place it among those of her husband's family's ancestral hall. Consequently, on her death-day and at yearly festivals commemorating the dead, her spirit will enjoy the offerings of food made by the living members. In return, she cooperates with the other ancestors to collectively ensure the prosperity and fertility of the lineage. The fate of unmarried women, however, reveals the insecure and ambiguous status of women in Confucian societies, which is concealed by the ideal life history. Unmarried women neither have a husband nor affinal kin to carry out their ancestral rites, nor are they welcome in their natal household's ancestral hall. Their problematic social identity is confirmed when families must either place the ancestral tablets of their socially mature, yet unmarried, daughters in temples specially built for this class of spirits, or marry her spirit posthumously to an appropriate single, deceased male.

In Korea, an alternative to the Confucian discourse on ancestors is available through shamanistic ritual performances called *kuts*. At these rituals, religious specialists, generally lower-class women, go into trance and make direct contact with the spirits of the ancestors, finding out through long, emotionally intense performances the reasons for various kinds of affliction sent by the ancestors. Men of the lineage attend the early segments of the ritual, but leave before the emotionally expressive possession sequences begin. Dawnhee Yim Janelli and Roger Janelli account for the gendered nature of participation in these rituals with the explanation that men and women base their very different conceptions of ancestors on their very different real-world experiences with elders. In the *kuts*, attended largely by women, the ancestors appear as vindictive, easily offended beings, a representation true to the experience of a Korean wife—and a far cry from the mild-mannered spirits who receive their offerings gratefully and return to the spirit world evoked by the rituals of the Confucian ancestral hall.

Ancestor worship in India is supported by the belief that the spirits of the dead exist in an unpleasant state of limbo until they fully expiate their sins. Brahminical practice is centered on the ritual of Śrāddha, in which the eldest son offers balls of rice and ghee on new moon days to his parents, and to maternal and paternal grandparents. Such offerings build up the spiritual body necessary for entering the land of the ancestors; without sons to offer the oblations a dead person may languish perpetually in hellish limbo. Men's wives may help prepare the materials in this rite, but they play no direct role in it. In a different ritual performed exclusively by women, brahmin wives linked by marital ties will gather to celebrate the death anniversaries of the patrilineal family's *sumaṅgali* women, women who died before their husband. They offer saris and food in front of her garlanded portrait and sing devotional songs in homage to this auspicious woman, the moral opposite of a widow in a cultural context in which widows are often suspected of having caused the premature death of their husbands through sinful conduct in this or a previous life.

Even among a matrilineal nonbrahmin caste, the Nayars of Kerala, ancestor worship in India tends to reflect the patriarchal aspects of society. The traditional Nayar kinship structure, now mostly defunct, is based on the *taravād,* an extended family unit owning property in common, which consists of a group of brothers ranked by age, their sisters, and sisters' children. On days commemorating the matrilineage's ancestors, although Nayar women prepare the different varieties of food offered to the ancestors, they do not partake of it during the feasting that follows, and they are forbidden from entering the ancestral shrine. Similarly, when they are menstruating, or are in a state of ritual pollution because they have just given birth, they may not enter the shrine. E. Kathleen Gough, an anthropologist who worked in Kerala in the 1950s, suggests that the taboos surrounding ancestor worship reinforce the sharp distinction made in Nayar culture between the moral authority that devolves on women due to their reproductive capacities and the legal and economic power wielded by men.

Ancestor worship in Africa likewise varies greatly according to tribe and region. Ancestors who are neglected in the central ancestor cult will frequently afflict their descendants with reproductive problems, illness, or persistent failure in hunting. The treatment for such a condition involves a ritual which re-invokes kinship ties that have become weakened or strained in the course of time, sometimes establishing links against the grain of the dominant descent ideology. For example, in Taleland, a region of West Africa where Meyer Fortes did his fieldwork among the patrilineal Tallensi, the only person in a household who can directly approach the ancestors and interpret their will through

sacrifice is the most senior male, who is also the legal head of the family. The senior male is responsible for communicating with his deceased parents, his male ancestors going back several generations, and a special class of ancestor whose role is to protect the lives of his wards—the spirit guardians, ancestors assigned at birth through divination to promote the well-being of an individual child. One of the most significant ties a Tallensi woman maintains throughout her life with her natal home consists of the ritual interactions her male kin perform on her behalf to maintain the relationship with her spirit guardian. On the basis of this connection, a woman has the right to a portion of the grain collected by her parental family at harvest time as well as the freedom to return to her natal home if she is not adequately provided for by her husband. Thus, though the descent ideology enshrined in the ancestor cult is definitely agnatic, it also recognizes the significance of kinship ties through women, and rewards them to a certain extent.

BIBLIOGRAPHY

There is a rich literature on ancestor worship in East Asia. Emily Ahern's *The Cult of the Dead in a Chinese Village* (1973), a study of ancestral lineage halls in northern Taiwan, and Helen Hardacre's study of Japanese new religions, *Lay Buddhism in Contemporary Japan: Reiyukai Kyodan* (1984), are both sensitive to the gendered dynamics of ancestor worship in East Asia. David K. Jordan's *Gods, Ghosts, and Ancestors: The Folk Religion of a Taiwanese Village* (1969) and Diana Martin's "Chinese Ghost Wedding," in *An Old State in New Settings: Studies of the Social Anthropology of China in Memory of Maurice Freedman*, edited by Hugh D. R. Baker and Stephen Feuchtwong (1991), furnish important material on Chinese spirit marriage. Although Dawnee Yim Janelli and Roger Janelli's *Ancestor Worship in Korean Society* (1982) remains the most comprehensive study on the subject, there is a growing body of literature on Korea's female shamans: See Youngsook Kim Harvey, *Six Korean Women: The Socialization of Shamans* (1979); Laurel Kendall, "Caught Between Ancestors and Spirits: Field Report of a Korean Mansin's Healing *Kut,*" *Korea Journal* 17, no. 8 (1977): 8–23; and Kim Kwang-iel, "Shamanistic Healing Ceremonies," *Korea Journal* 13, no. 4 (1973): 41–47. The literature on African ancestor work is voluminous, but not very helpful when it comes to questions of gender. Important in terms of their contributions to anthropological theory are Meyer Fortes's classic studies of the Tallensi, including the most accessible, *Oedipus and Job in West African Religion* (1959), and Igor Kopytoff's "Ancestors as Elders in Africa,"

Africa 41 (April 1971): 129–142. Though basically a cross-cultural analysis of sacrificial ideology, Nancy Jay's *Throughout Your Generations Forever* (1992) provides a fresh feminist perspective on canonical Africanist anthropology. Some excellent scholarship on "muted" forms of African ancestor worship that institutionalize descent lines through women even in patrilineal societies can be found in *The Creative Continuum: African Folk Models of Fertility and the Regeneration of Life* (1990), edited by Anita Jacobson-Widding and Walter van Deek. E. Kathleen Gough's "Cult of the Dead Among the Nayars," in *The Journal of American Folklore* 71 (1958): 446–478, and David Knipe's "*Sapiṇṭakaraṇa:* The Hindu Rite of Entry into Heaven," in *Religious Encounters of Death* (1977), edited by Frank E. Reynolds and Earle Waugh, provide the best descriptions available of ancestor worship in the nonbramin and brahminical Hindu traditions, respectively.

See also Ghosts; Shamans.

ELIZA F. KENT

Ancient Egyptian Religions

The religious activities of women in ancient Egypt are well documented, and some women had active leadership roles though they varied over time. Studies done in the 1980s and 1990s of the goddess Hathor's cult, for instance, have demonstrated the burgeoning and decline of female leadership over a span of some five hundred years.

WOMEN IN THE TEMPLES

The first known priestesses were members of the royal family that built the great pyramids of the Fourth Dynasty (2625–2510 B.C.E.). They served as priestesses for the cults of major goddesses such as Neith and Hathor (a creator and a solar goddess respectively) and some gods, among them Thoth (wisdom and the moon) and Wepwawet (a funerary deity). The wife of King Khafre, Meresankh, was a priestess of the god Thoth, and her mother, Queen Hetepheres, was a prophet of King Khufu, officiating in the mortuary cult of the predecessor of her husband, King Radedef, in what may have been the largest temple of her era. The tombs of principal royal wives and mothers of kings reveal that they shared with the king the exclusive rights to pyramid tombs, solar boats, and funerary literature, which would propel them into the company of the great gods in the sky after death.

Later in the Old Kingdom private individuals are found more widely positioned in government and the temples, and women appear as prophets for the cults of Thoth and the creator god Ptah, but the most popular deity may well have been Hathor, who was regarded as the divine mother of the king of Egypt. Her priesthood was predominantly female until the late Old Kingdom when men suddenly appear, especially in a leadership role as Overseer of Prophets, although this may have been an administrative rather than cultic position. However, queens would remain as chief officiants in the cult and, indeed, living incarnations of this preeminent goddess for centuries to come.

While prophets were full-time clerics, there were also lay women with the rank of a *wabet* or pure one who served in the temple for one month at intervals spaced through the year and who received the same payment for their services as did the men of this category. Other women appear in Old Kingdom temples as *meret* priestesses, singing welcomes to the king in royal celebrations, or served as members of the temple's *hener* or troop of sacred musicians. These originally belonged to goddess cults (Bat, Isis, Nekhbet, Bast, and Hathor) but later appear as celebrants in the cults of gods such as Horus and Onuris as well.

Elite women are still found as priestesses in the important state cult of Hathor in the first half of the Middle Kingdom (c. 2000 B.C.E.). However, by the late Middle Kingdom (c. 1700 B.C.E.) the leading positions in the Hathor cult may have been exclusively held by royal women and, in the provincial cult centers, left to men. From the Middle Kingdom on, certain women impersonated goddesses (like Isis, the widow of Osiris, and her sister Nephthys) in the mystery plays, the most famous of which were held at the temple of Osiris, Lord of the Dead, in his temple at Abydos.

In the second half of the second millennium B.C.E., the Egyptian empire period (New Kingdom) yields still more private monuments on which the title of chantress and musician often follows an elite lady's title of House Mistress. Elite women are often portrayed holding the *menat* necklace of many strands and sistrum rattle associated with Hathoric rituals. Temples were off-limits to the average person in ancient Egypt. The temple personnel, or servants of the resident deity, were the only ones allowed within the sacred house. The laity, who would bring votive offerings and petitions, might be allowed in the front outdoor courtyard, but no farther. Thus anyone with intimate contact with the deity was a specially privileged person. This fact was not lost on earlier Egyptologists, who frequently use the term *priestess* for the chantresses or members of *heners*. Chantresses of Amun actually participated at

A pharaoh receives life—the hieroglyph is an *ankh* from a goddess on a bas-relief sculpture in Buhen, Egypt (Roger Wood/© Corbis).

a number of different temples. The singers of Hathor seem to have impersonated that goddess, as did the *hener* of Amun Re as they participated in the great national festivals, like the Feast of the Valley, held annually in the necropolis, which reunited (through intoxication and revelry) the living with their dead loved ones.

The professionalization of the priesthood in the New Kingdom positioned literate men at the top of the hierarchy, but their wives and daughters are invariably found also playing important supportive roles in the same temple. In this way priestly families became entrenched, intermarried, and controlled much of the wealth of the kingdom that was bestowed generously by the pharaohs upon the gods. Usually the wife of the chief prophet of a temple was the leader of the *hener* of his temple and bore the title Chief of the Hener. These women not only participated in temple services but helped administer the temple as well by receiving and disbursing commodities, particularly those destined for the sacrificial altar.

PERSONAL RELIGION

Within private households, the mother of the family maintained the cult of the household gods (usually those who, like the pregnant hippopotamus, Taweret, and the grotesque dancing dwarf, Bes, were beneficial to her fertility and children) and sacrificed before the image of the family's ancestor or ancestress. Letters left at the tomb of deceased relatives by persons troubled with crises in their lives show that the Egyptians believed the dead could be responsible either for afflicting the living or effectively solving their problems.

The concern for fertility, the protection of women in childbirth, and the health of the newborn are all reflected by wall paintings and furniture decorations depicting the supernatural beings considered as protective and helpful on the domestic scene. Of course, amulets were worn by people of both sexes and all ages to ward off malevolent forces. Oracular decrees issued by temples were worn by women for their "guarantees" of safe delivery and healthy babies. A female purification ritual accompanied by celebrations seems to have followed a period of fourteen days following giving birth.

In a society where oral tradition handed down the complicated myths for which no early manuscripts have been found, women must have helped preserve and pass along to the younger generation religious teachings and lore. Female entertainers are often depicted in the tomb paintings, and villages had "wise women" who may have played the role of a shaman, interpreting phenomena, finding lost articles, explaining and solving problems.

WOMEN AT FUNERALS

Perhaps because of their connection with Hathor—whose responsibilities included the welcoming of the justified dead into the nether world and assisting in their "rebirth" there—the funeral rites in the cemetery were attended by the cult personnel of Hathor and featured acrobatic bare-breasted women in short skirts portrayed in what seem to be highly ecstatic dances. Tomb scenes show more fully clothed women clapping accompaniment and singing. These performers are placed in front of the tomb or in the funeral procession. Throughout most of Egyptian history, both men and women are found together in such sacred troops, but again women originally held leadership positions that they eventually lost to men.

The funerary literature that once was reserved for royalty became, around the end of the third millennium B.C.E., the prerogative of commoners too; now ordinary women as well as men might own, if they could afford them, the necessary offering tables, stelae, and coffins with religious spells that could aid them in attaining eternal life beyond the grave. Usually an eldest son officiated at the funerals of his parents, but if none existed a daughter could do this as well. Both male and female *ka*-servants were hired to look after the mortuary cults of the deceased elite, pouring libations, making offerings, and reciting the proper prayers that would ensure the continuance of sustenance for the deceased in the next world. There are many tomb scenes depicting groups of what may be professional wailing women at elite funerals, but both male and female relatives of the deceased brought floral bouquets and participated in final rites at the cemetery.

NEW CULTIC ROLES FOR ROYAL WOMEN

Already by the Middle Kingdom, at the upper end of the social scale a high female functionary, known as a God's Wife, served the cult of the gods Amun of Thebes and Min of Akhmim. Following the long Second Intermediate Period, New Kingdom records show this God's Wife position held by the queen in the greatest temple of the land, the home of Amun-Re in his new role as King of the Gods at Karnak. The wife of the founder of the Eighteenth Dynasty, Queen Ahmose-Nefertari, who was distinguished later by deification after death and a cult that lasted for centuries, also held the title originally of Second Prophet of Amun at Karnak, but she exchanged this post with her husband in trade for enough lands and personnel to create an endowment to support a "college" of female temple musicians and singers. After Ahmose-Nefertari carried the title of God's Wife of Amun, it was born by her daughter Meritamun and next by Hatshepsut, who was God's Wife until she became King when her daughter assumed the cultic role. The mother of Hatshepsut's successor is also credited with this rank, and it can be traced through royal women until the monotheistic revolution of Akhenaten and Nefertiti, after which it was resurrected for the royal women of the Nineteenth Dynasty. Then the God's Wife title was held by princesses, but queens, such as Ramses II's Nefertari, are shown sacrificing at the high altar, just as Nefertiti had functioned as high priestess for the Aten; Nefertiti is often shown alone on temple walls or with her daughter, who played the sacred musical instrument to accompany whatever was spoken in adoration by her mother.

Like the King of Egypt, the principal queen and mother of the heir to the throne was also considered a divinity, be it Hathor (daughter-wife of the sun-god with whom the king was equated) or, as Isis, the personified throne. Artistic portrayals of queens as the earthly manifestation of the goddess Hathor or the primeval mother-goddess Tefnut are supplemented by frequent portrayals in temples and colossal statuary of the royal wives and daughters of the New Kingdom—in comparison to the royal sons, who almost never appear on existing monuments. This has led some to suggest that divine kingship was really an androgynous or bipolar concept dependent on both the male and female element that kept the cosmos functioning properly. However, the much greater prominence given to the king on the monuments and in the burial place casts some doubt on this theory. Nevertheless, it must be significant that the queen and princesses are usually present (if not prominent) on a large number of pharaonic monuments.

At the end of Egypt's empire period the country split politically between north and south, with the First Prophet of Amun-Re at Karnak controlling the south and maintaining the numerous great temples of the region. His daughters filled the role of God's Wife of Amun, and his wife became the Prophetess of Mut, the goddess who was Amun's consort. Whether this office had always been filled by women is not known owing to scarcity of records. By the Twenty-third Dynasty Egypt was under Libyan rule, and the fourth king of that dynasty, Osorkon III (777–749), consecrated his own daughter as a celibate God's Wife who would live in Thebes and give all her attention to the important cult. This priestess was Shepenwepet I, who received all the estates and property formerly possessed by the High Priest. She ensured her succession by adopting a successor, and this younger woman carried the old title of Divine Votaress, which in the Eighteenth Dynasty, was occasionally held by women of considerable status at court or by the wife of the First or Second Prophet at Karnak Temple. As these women enjoyed long lives that spanned kingly reigns, they were a source of moral and political stability and leadership in the southern half of the country. In religious matters this woman was very like a female pope and would have ruled by the word of Amun, probably by manipulating his oracle.

The Nubian invasion wrested Egypt away from the Libyans. These people also were devoted to Amun and installed a princess as God's Wife of Amun, the first being Amenirdis, the sister of the general who had led the successful invasion. She in turn adopted as her successor his daughter, to be known as Shepenwepet II. The large pyloned funerary chapels of this line of women may be seen today at Medinet Habu on the west bank of Luxor.

The Twenty-sixth Dynasty was a new royal house, and its princess Nitocris became God's Wife. Nitocris outlived her father and the administrators he had appointed for her; during her reign of over fifty years she came to administer through men of her own choosing, without even adopting a successor in order to keep the kings in the north from having influence in the south. Finally in 594 B.C.E., Nitocris in her eighties adopted her great niece Ankhnesneferibre, daughter of Psammetichus II, soon after he came to the throne of Egypt.

This young woman was given the title of First Prophet or High Priest of Amun and is thus the only woman known to have held this high clerical office. It would seem that Nitocris engineered this move so as to preserve the importance of women at Karnak. During the 130 years of these two women's reigns their power definitely rivaled the kings of their time, at least in Upper Egypt, and they were portrayed in art holding the crook and flail scepters of Egypt.

BIBLIOGRAPHY

Blackman, Aylward M. "On the Position of Women in the Ancient Egyptian Hierarchy." *Journal of Egyptian Archaeology* 7 (1921): 8–30.

Borghouts, Joris F. "Magical Practices Among the Villagers." In *Pharaoh's Workers: The Villagers of Deir el Medina.* Edited by L. H. Lesko. 1994.

Fischer, Henry G. "Priesterin." In *Lexikon der Ägyptologie* IV. Edited by W. Helck and E. Otto. 1982. Cols. 1100–1105.

Friedman, Florence D. "Domestic Life and Religion." In *Pharaoh's Workers: The Villagers of Deir el Medina.* Edited by L. H. Lesko. 1994.

Gillam, Robyn. "Priestesses of Hathor: Their Function, Decline and Disappearance." *Journal of the American Research Center in Egypt* 32 (1995): 211–237.

Lesko, Barbara S. *The Remarkable Women of Ancient Egypt.* 3d ed. 1996.

Nord, Del. "The term *hnr* 'harem' or 'musical performers.' " In *Studies in Ancient Egypt, the Aegean, and the Sudan.* Edited by William K. Simpson and W. V. Davies. 1981.

Pinch, Geraldine. *Votive Offerings to Hathor.* 1989.

Sadek, Ashraf I. *Popular Religion in Egypt during the New Kingdom.* (Hildesheimer Ägyptologische Beiträge 27.) 1988.

Troy, L. *Patterns of Queenship in Ancient Egyptian Myth and History.* (Studies in Ancient Mediterranean and Near Eastern Civilizations 14.) 1986.

BARBARA S. LESKO

Androcentrism

The first agenda for the study of women and religion was to challenge the androcentrism that underlies most traditional scholarship. A simple example of androcentrism, in lieu of a definition, follows. Consider the statement: "the Egyptians allow (or don't allow) women to. . . ." For both those who make such statements and for those who hear them without wincing, "Egyptians" are men. Egyptian women are objects acted upon by real Egyptians, but are not themselves "Egyptians." The androcentric model of humanity has three central characteristics that, when stated bluntly, suffice to demonstrate both the nature and the inadequacy of androcentrism.

First, the male norm and the human norm are collapsed and seen as identical. Recognition that maleness is but one kind of human experience is minimal or nonexistent. In androcentric thinking, any awareness of a distinction between maleness and humanity is clouded over, and femaleness is viewed as an exception to the norm.

The second characteristic of androcentrism follows directly from the first. For generations, we were told that the generic masculine included the feminine, making it unnecessary to study women specifically. This is a logical implication of collapsing maleness with humanity, but the result is that research about religion actually deals mainly with the lives and thinking of males, while women's religious lives are treated much more peripherally, as a footnote or a short chapter toward the end of the book.

The third, and most problematic, aspect of androcentrism is its attempt to deal with the fact that, since men and women are taught to be different in all cultures, the generic masculine simply does not cover the feminine. The generic masculine would work only in religions or cultures that had no sex roles, but no such culture exists. At this point, adherents of the androcentric model of humanity reach a logical impasse. Their solution to this impasse is the most devastating component of the androcentric outlook. Because women inevitably deviate from male norms, androcentric thinking deals with them only as objects exterior to "mankind," needing to be explained and fitted in somewhere, having the same epistemological and ontological status as trees, unicorns, deities, and other objects that must be discussed to make experience intelligible. Therefore males are presented as religious subjects and as namers of reality, while females are presented only in relation to the males being studied, only as objects being named by them, only as they appear to them.

Nothing less than a paradigm shift in our model of humanity will remedy these problems. Instead of the current androcentric, "one-sexed" model of humanity, we need an androgynous "two-sexed" or bisexual model of humanity that forbids placing one gender in the center and the other on the periphery. Androgyny as a two-sex model of humanity involves the conviction that despite gender and sexual differences, women and men are equally human, while both traditional androcentrism, which objectifies women, and a sex-neutral model of humanity, which ignores the reality of culture-based gender roles, do not.

BIBLIOGRAPHY

Christ, Carol P., and Judith Plaskow, eds. *Womanspirit Rising: A Feminist Reader in Religion.* 1979.

Daly, Mary. *Gyn/Ecology.* 1978.

Falk, Nancy Auer, and Rita M. Gross. *Unspoken Worlds: Women's Religious Lives.* 1989.

Gross, Rita M. *Beyond Androcentrism: New Essays on Women and Religion.* 1977.

———. *Buddhism After Patriarchy: A Feminist History, Analysis, and Reconstruction of Buddhism.* 1993.

———. *Feminism and Religion: An Introduction.* 1996.

King, Ursula, ed. *Religion and Gender.* 1995.

———. *Women and Spirituality: Voices of Protest and Promise.* 1989.

RITA M. GROSS

Androgyny

The term *androgyne* (from the Greek *andros*, "man," and *gyne*, "woman") often occurs in mythology to denote creatures considered half male and half female. The terms *androgyny* and *androgynous traditions*, however, as opposed to *hermaphrodite*, which refers specifically to the physical body, describe the attempt to incorporate both male and female characteristics into an overall scheme of sacrality. An androgynous religious view expresses the hope for an ultimate reconciliation of the opposing or conflicting qualities of male and female.

Androgynous figures have appeared in both the West and East since ancient times. In the West, for example, the Orphic poets spoke of androgynous beings. There are traces of primordial androgyny in Hesiod's *Theogony*. In *Orphic Hymn* XLII, Dionysos is identified with Misa, both being androgynous. In the fourth century C.E. the Christian Rufinus wrote this summary of the Orphic cosmology: "In the beginning was Chaos eternal, immense, uncreated, from whom all is born; neither darkness nor light, nor damp nor dry, nor hot nor cold, but all things mingled, eternally one and limitless. The time came, when, after infinite ages, in the manner of a gigantic egg, he caused to emanate from himself a double form, androgynous (*masculofeminam*), made by the conjunction of the opposites" (Delcourt, p. 69). Other creatures, the phoenix being a prime example, are deemed androgynous. The Stoics saw the god Zeus as the synthesis of the fertilizing God-Heaven and the fertilized Earth.

Summarizing the sweep of androgynous symbols in Western antiquity, Marie Delcourt (1956) writes: "An image of autogenesis derived from Orphism by way of gnosticism, allusions to Plato's *Ideus,* to the Stoic *pneuma,* to the mathematical harmonies of Pythagoras—all these are associated with the combined and, indeed, synonymous symbols of bisexuality and reversion: the double being fertilises and engenders himself" (p. 71). Plato's *Symposium* posits a similar scenario when it describes how, in the beginning, humanity consisted of spherical double beings with four arms and legs, and two identical faces back to back on a circular neck, that had double sexual organs, too. Drawing from the famed passage in Genesis where it is stated that "male and female created he him" Judaism's Talmudic scholars posited the doctrine of primitive humanity as bisexual—a doctrine that passed into Jewish mysticism as well as into Arabic esoterism, and in which the unity of Adam and Eve represents universal man. (The Midrash quoted Jeremiah as stating that God created Adam androgynous.)

Eastern religious traditions also feature the idea of the unity of opposites as a description of primordial being. The Taoist symbol of the circular union of the yin and yang is well known, for example. Indian mythic traditions present a great number of specifically paired anthropomorphic deities, the best known being the joined pair of Śiva and Pārvāti. In *Women, Androgynes, and Other Mythical Beasts* (1980), Wendy Doniger O'Flaherty presents the most complete typology of such pairs, addressing "physical androgynes" as well as "psychological androgynes." The latter type is defined as either "splitting"—beings originally joined are split so as to create, and thereafter try to get back together; "fusing" after an original separation at creation the two must fuse so as to create; and "two-in-one"—representatives of the hierogamy, or sacred marriage, the joining of complementary opposites. Ultimately, however, as O'Flaherty's analysis suggests, the androgyne is usually male at base, and the male (of the pair) is normative. The male has brought under his control the female, or he has assimilated female qualities and powers.

In fact, regardless of whether one is looking at the analyses of androgyny offered by such scholars as O'Flaherty, Mircea Eliade, Clifford Geertz, or Carl Jung, it would seem to be universally the case that even when a religious tradition presents abundant androgyne symbolism, androcentric perspectives still predominate.

A movement among scholars of Tibetan tantric Buddhism seeks, through a melding of Buddhism and feminism, a revalorization of the feminine principle. This approach, followed by such scholars as Rita Gross, Janice Willis, Anne Klein, and Miranda Shaw, focuses on either single female saints or divinities (such as Yeshe Tsogyel or Vajrayoginī) or tantric Buddhism's penchant for paired male and female deities in sexual union (for

"historical agency of women." Still, those scholars who study the iconographic forms of Tibetan Buddhist deities in sexual union (the so-called father–mother, or *yab-yum* forms) must note the preponderance of male deities as dominant figures.

Theorists examining the social construction of gender identity are coming to see it as nonbinary, encompassing a wide range of genders not reducible to masculine men and feminine women. However, dualistic perspectives—subject–object, white–black, male–female—remain deeply ingrained. For a given tradition to hold androgyny as a religious ideal, it would have to embrace nondualism and the notion of difference without conflict or opposition. Yet, a survey of the history of the world's religious traditions reveals that such an ideal is at best only hinted at, at worse entirely lacking.

BIBLIOGRAPHY

Delcourt, Marie. *Hermaphrodite: Myths and Rites of the Bisexual Figure in Classical Antiquity.* 1956.

Gross, Rita M. *Buddhism After Patriarchy: A Feminist History, Analysis, and Reconstruction of Buddhism.* 1993.

———. "Yeshe Tsogyel: Enlightened Consort, Great Teacher, Female Role Model." In *Feminine Ground: Essays on Women and Tibet.* Edited by Janice D. Willis. 1989.

Klein, Anne C. *Meeting the Great Bliss Queen: Buddhists, Feminists, and the Art of the Self.* 1995.

———. "Nondualism and the Great Bliss Queen: A Study in Tibetan Buddhist Ontology and Symbolism." *Journal of Feminist Studies in Religion* 1 (1985): 73–98.

———. "Primordial Purity and Everyday Life: Exalted Female Symbols and the Women of Tibet." In *Immaculate and Powerful: The Female in Sacred Image and Social Reality.* Edited by Clarissa W. Atkinson, Constance Buchanan, and Margaret Miles. 1985.

O'Flaherty, Wendy Doniger. "Androgynes." In *The Encyclopedia of Religion.* Edited by Mircea Eliade. 1987. Vol. 1. Pp. 276–281.

Paul, Diana. *Women in Buddhism: Images of the Feminine in the Mahayana Tradition.* 1979.

Shaw, Miranda. *Passionate Enlightenment: Women in Tantric Buddhism.* 1994.

Willis, Janice D. "Dakini: Some Comments On Its Nature and Meaning." In *Feminine Ground: Essays on Women and Tibet.* Edited by Janice D. Willis. 1989.

Zolla, Elemire. *The Androgyne: Reconciliation of Male and Female.* 1981.

See also **Pārvatī**; **Vajrayoginī**.

JANICE D. WILLIS

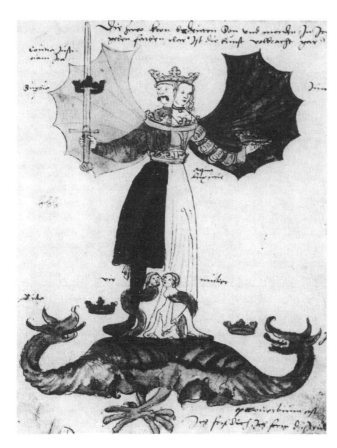

A sixteenth-century alchemy manuscript depicts an androgynous figure, half king, half queen, standing on a two-headed dragon, to illustrate the androgynous nature of human beings (Leiden University Library).

example, Cakrasaṃvara and Vajrayoginī) as a model for the ultimate complementarity (of male blissful energy and female nondual wisdom). Gross (1993) defines androgyny as "lack of patriarchy," "mutuality between women and men," and "a balance between feminine and masculine principles." She criticizes Jung for his failure to give equal standing to the anima and animus and argues that, though Jung acknowledges the feminine principle, he still gives primacy to the masculine (p. 201).

According to Anne Klein, the Tibetan tantric worship and cult of the goddess Vajrayoginī leads the way toward a realization of a type of nondualism that would make possible a true androgyny—the recognition of difference without opposition. Yet, Klein acknowledges that such a nondualism is far from being realized in the lived experience of that tradition's practitioners. Miranda Shaw (1994) has focused on the presentation of female tantric practitioners. Like other feminist historians (she cites Gerda Lerner, Elisabeth Schüssler Fiorenza, and Joan Scott), her aim is to reclaim the

Angela of Foligno

The few facts known about Italian Christian visionary and holy woman Angela of Foligno (c. 1248–1309) derive from scattered clues in the text of her renowned revelations, commonly designated the *Book*. The deaths of her mother, husband, and children sometime during the middle of her life freed her to devote herself fully to the spiritual journey she had begun a few years earlier. Angela was part of a vast, amorphous movement of lay penitents, who sometimes affiliated with one of the mendicant orders, dedicated to poverty, self-sacrifice, and prayer. Angela's promise to follow the "rule of St. Francis" of Assisi prompts some scholars to label her a "tertiary" or member of the "Third Order," but such terms, absent from her revelations, imply a degree of lay institutionalization still inchoate at this time. Her religious life, shared with a female companion, was largely self-styled, unencumbered by rules, and free from ecclesiastical supervision.

The *Book* has two parts, the *Memorial* and the *Instructions*. The thirty-six *Instructions* are discrete texts by anonymous devotees, some alleging to report Angela's own words, whose relationship to her has yet to be established. The *Memorial* recounts her visions, locutions, and spiritual insights as she reported these in Umbrian to her Franciscan relative and confessor, Brother A., who then rendered them into Latin, liberally interpolating his own commentary. Angela's spiritual experience, characterized by attention to human sin, Christ's passion, the Eucharist, and the primacy of experience over worldly learning, oscillates wildly between intense desolation and doubt and joyful consolation and certitude. Angela attracted a large following of devotees, dominated by Franciscan men, both during her lifetime and after her death in 1309.

BIBLIOGRAPHY

The best edition to date of the revelations, with Latin and an early Italian translation on facing pages and extensive bibliography, is *Il libro della Beata Angela da Foligno (Edizione critica)*, edited by Ludger Thier and Abele Calufetti (1985); English translation by Paul Lachance, *Angela of Foligno: Complete Works* (1993). On Angela's life and spirituality, see *Angela da Foligno: Terziaria francescana*, edited by Enrico Menestò (1992); *Vita e spiritualità della Beata Angela da Foligno*, edited by Clément Schmitt (1987); and Paul Lachance, *The Spiritual Journey of the Blessed Angela of Foligno According to the Memorial of Frater A.* (1984). On the collaborative authorship of the *Memorial*, see Catherine M. Mooney, "The Authorial Role of Brother A. in the Composition of Angela of Foligno's Revelations," in *Creative Women in Medieval and Early Modern Italy: A Religious and Artistic Renaissance*, edited by E. Ann Matter and John Coakley (1994), pp. 34–63.

CATHERINE M. MOONEY

Animals

Animal iconography is found on artifacts dating from the Paleolithic era. Whatever the original intention, it is clear that animal imagery entered into the social, symbolic, spiritual, and imaginary life of humans everywhere at an early date.

As the first imaging of the divine was female it is not surprising to find goddess symbolism expressed in animal forms. The most universal and ancient are strongly connected with her life-giving or nurturing aspects and with death and rebirth as the regenerative extension of those creative functions. Preeminent are the snake, the bird, the fish, the deer, and the bear; domesticated animals such as the horse, the cow, the pig, the dog, and the cat; among insects, the bee, the butterfly, and the spider. Each of these symbols is multivalent. Some meanings have experienced the kind of symbol reversal that followed the onset of the patriarchal era. No animal has suffered more from this process than the snake.

From its earliest depiction in the cave art of Southern France, the serpent is both woman and goddess. (Johnson, 1988, p. 123). Because in shedding its skin the snake seems to die and be reborn and because of its poisonous bite, it is strongly associated with both the creator and destroyer aspects of the goddess.

All around the Mediterranean rim, snakes were also associated with wisdom and healing. In Egypt, the hieroglyph for goddess was the cobra, and pharaohs wore the Uraeus or rearing cobra on their foreheads. Elsewhere in Minoan and Greek cultures, snakes were associated with divination, particularly at Delphi where the priestesses were known as pythonesses.

The most compelling inversion is the Biblical creation myth. Traditionally, the serpent is male, but many paintings endow it with a female head, thus conflating snake, woman, and evil. This reversal has been so effective that about the only surviving positive image of serpents in Western culture is the medical symbol, the caduceus. In India, the snake continues to be revered. It appears as part of the iconography of Kali and Manasa, the Bengali serpent goddess, and is the symbol of female energy in Kundalini yoga.

Two characteristics of birds—their ability to fly and their double birth first as egg and then as chick—

stirred the imagination of ancient peoples. Neolithic bird goddesses are heavily ovoid in shape or incised with egg shapes. Later, various birds became associated with particular goddesses, such as the owl of wisdom with Athena. The owl, the crow, and the raven are also aligned with death goddesses, like the Celtic Morrigan. As a creature of the sky, the bird represented the human spirit or soul.

The dove, the temple bird of Astarte and Aphrodite, is a primary symbol of female sexuality as are the swan and the goose. The dove was co-opted by Christianity to represent the third person of the Trinity, the Holy Spirit, who embodied the love between the Father and the Son.

Another animal now primarily identified with Christianity, the fish, started out as a symbol of fecundity and rebirth because of its watery habitat, its womb-like shape, and the prolific number of its progeny. At Lepenski Vir (6000 B.C.E.), ovoid fish sculptures exhibit vulvas, breasts, and watery chevrons or zig zags, all of which specify this symbol as a generative womb (Gimbutas, 1989, p. 260). In Japanese and Chinese mythology carp are particularly important as creators, fertility symbols, and charms against evil.

From Neolithic times, both deer and bear have strong associations with goddesses and mothers, the bear in particular as the nurturing mother (Gimbutas, 1989, p. 113). Celtic legends speak of women who shape-shift into deer as did Artemis, the Greek Mother of all Creatures, who was also known to assume the appearance of a bear. Athenian girls danced clothed in bear skins or masks in her honor. The very word *bear* comes from Germanic and Norse roots and means "to bear children" and "birth" (Gimbutas, 1989, p. 116). The Inuit people and Haida tribes of Canada both worship the bear as a female deity. In fact the Haida consider the whole tribe to be descended from the Bear Mother (Johnson, p. 344).

The horse is a chthonic animal identified with instinctive levels of human consciousness and with sexuality and death. Though parts of its anatomy are phallic symbols, the animal as a whole has long been associated with women. The horseshoe in particular is a yoni symbol. The Amazons were thought to be gifted horsewomen, and remnants of the cult of the Celtic goddess Epona (whose name means horse) can be seen on numerous sculptured plaques from France and Germany. Most notable is the great chalk horse carved out of the turf on a hillside in Uffington, England.

As a death animal, the horse carried souls to paradise. Yet the ride of Lady Godiva, a corruption of the old May-Eve procession by the goddess, was to bring fertility for the new crops (Graves, 1958, p. 451). Mohammed received his spiritual visions during his famous night ride on the alborak, a white horse with a woman's head and a peacock tail (de Givry, 1971, p. 315).

The great traditions of India and Egypt give us the cow as a sacred animal. Hathor, the cow goddess of Egypt, was supreme before the appearance of Isis. As a mother flowing with milk, she gives birth to the sun and to the Milky Way. In the Hindu tradition the world is formed from her curdled milk. Cow and goat horns are associated with goddess incarnations.

Pits were sacred to the exclusively female Thesmaphorian rites in Greece which honored Demeter. The pig and its wild cousin the boar were sacred and sacrificial animals used by such widely separated tribes as the Celts and New Guinea peoples of Oceania. The pig's habit of rooting in the ground evoked a natural link with the life-giving activities of sowing and reaping.

The strongest reference for the cat as a sacred animal comes from the Egyptian worship of the cat goddess Bast, but other feline forms are closely associated with goddesses—leopards with the mother deity at Çatal Hüyück, lions that drew Cybele's chariot through the sky, and the great lion woman of the desert, the Sphinx. As the familiar of witches, cats later shared women's condemnation as devils. Dogs, while associated with women in prehistoric and classical periods, often transmogrify into masculine deities. Considered primarily nocturnal animals, dogs were connected to moon goddesses and underworld goddesses of death. Their dog companions guard the gates of hell to ward off evil.

Butterflies appear as symbols of regeneration because of the transformations involved in their development. The activities of bees and spiders mirror women's work. The spider spinning its web of fate using threads from its own life mirrors the work of the Crone or the Fates who measure out the thread of human life. The queen bee, an obvious symbol for the goddess, lives attended by her "subjects" in the centre of the beehive. Priestesses of Artemis at Ephesus were called *melissae* (bees) (Gimbutas, 1982).

BIBLIOGRAPHY

Campbell, Joseph. *The Mythic Image.* 1974.
———. *The Way of the Animal Powers.* 1983.
Cirlot, J. E. *A Dictionary of Symbols.* 1962.
Givry, Grilot de. *Zoological Mythology or the Legends of Animals.* 2 vols. London, 1972.
Gubernatis, Angelo de. *Witchcraft, Magic and Alchemy.* 1971.
Graves, Robert. *The White Goddess.* 1958.
Johnson, Buffie. *Lady of the Beasts; Ancient Images of the Goddess and Her Sacred Animals.* 1988.
Gimbutas, Marija. *Goddesses and Gods of Old Europe, 6500–3500 B.C.* 1982.

———. *The Language of the Goddess: Images and Symbols of Old Europe.* 1989.

Green, Miranda. *Symbol and Image in Celtic Religious Art.* London, 1989.

Lonsdale, Stephen. *Animals and the Origins of Dance.* London, 1981.

Mundkur, Balaji. *The Cult of the Serpent: An Interdisciplinary Survey of Its Manifestations and Origins.* 1983.

Rowland, Beryl. *Animals with Human Faces: A Guide to Animal Symbolism.* 1973.

Walker, Barbara. *The Women's Dictionary of Symbols and Sacred Objects.* 1988.

———. *The Women's Encyclopedia of Myths and Secrets.* 1983.

See also **Artemis (Diana); Athena (Minerva); Cybele; Fate; Goddess; Greek Religion; Isis; Durga and Kālī; Muses.**

E. ANN PEARSON

Anonymous

Critical examination of Virginia Woolf's "Anonymous Was a Woman," reveals the state of female anonymity to be both a blessing and a curse. For Woolf it served as a stark negative commentary on women's cultural, economic, and spiritual condition in a society dominated by maleness out of control. She recognized women's persistent historical need, as authors of courageous, daring, unconventional, and even heretical literary and artistic works, for the safety provided by personal anonymity (withholding one's name, seeking androgynous rather than female identity, or even using a male pseudonym, for example), and she could see no different future.

In her final, unfinished essay, "Anon.," Woolf at first included all uncited artists, writers, and musicians, female and male; later, she restricted the meaning to women. In *Between the Acts*, which immediately preceded "Anon.," Woolf called her main character, Miss LaTrobe, "Whatsername" and wrote that her disembodied voice coming from among the bushes was "a megaphonic, anonymous, loud-speaking affirmation." Given the opportunity to be recognized, LaTrobe remained anonymous, thus reconnecting her woman's song to nature. Woolf noted that from Anon. all literature, drama, and art originally came forth.

Over time, though losing much of Woolf's cutting-edge anger about conditions dictating women's name-lessness, "Anonymous" has come to signify a mythically prolific female artist, composer, and writer who has authored thousands of articles, books, poems, plays, musical scores, and songs; and has created countless etchings, paintings, quilts, clay pots, and other works. Under the name "Anonymous" or "Anon." women of all times and in all cultures have produced art, spun stories, and given voice to wise sayings.

Some women figuratively or even literally veiled themselves to hide their identities. Some omitted their names deliberately to avoid punishment (social, political, religious, etc.). Other women's names (devalued under patriarchy) were forgotten or lost. Some used pen names to preserve their otherwise "virtuous" reputations, to prevent punishment, or to add to their invisibility; women who sought public identity were thought to be immoral or "loose." Twenty-five pages in the British Museum catalog are headed by the title "Lady" with no given first or surname; a nineteenth-century pamphlet listing works by English authors gives more than a hundred and fifty entries under the same title; and a 1992 world treasury of women's quotations from around the world contains more than fifty entries under "Anon." and collects nearly as many anonymous proverbs. Some women used only their initials or adopted male names in order to have their works accepted as produced by men, H. D., George Eliot, Isak Dinesen, and George Sand, to name only a few. bell hooks chose to write under a pseudonym in order to belong to and participate in a feminist community of thinkers and activists who were seriously committed to intellectual and social development.

Anonymous applies to the composite works of countless universally situated ordinary women who produce domestic handiwork that they would not identify as art work but who regularly decorate and ornament the artifacts of their lives: clothing by knitting, tatting, crocheting, and lace-making; meals by cake decorating, pottery making, and china painting; homes by lintel decorations and quilt making. The power, ingenuity, beauty, and sagacity of anonymous is infinite.

Recognizing this in the late 1970s, Mirra Banks used *Anonymous Was a Woman* as the title of her film and related book on traditional eighteenth and nineteenth century women's folk art in the United States. Banks sought to lay positive claim to the innumerable creative works, especially handicrafts, that have been created but left unsigned by women over centuries. In Banks' examples anonymity reflected the patriarchal devaluing of women's identity and work, by even the women themselves.

By the end of the twentieth century the largely secular feminist movement was using the adage "Anonymous was a woman" somewhat noncritically. This allowed for its detachment from the web of interrelated insights of Woolf and Banks, as well as of other feminist philosophers and religionists who understood the lack of personal identity or namelessness in both its positive and negative aspects. Curiously, at this same time anonymous self-help groups, modeled after male-founded Alcoholics Anonymous, proliferated among women who often vastly outnumbered males in mixed groups and who also established women-only anonymous recovery groups.

At least to outsiders, anonymous also are the millions of women and girls devalued, subordinated, raped, maimed, or eliminated by the patriarchal institutions of their own societies, including and especially their religions. Notable are the abandoned or aborted female children in China; the countless brides and widows burned to death in India; the genitally mutilated girl children of Ethiopia, Sudan, and elsewhere; the women of childbearing age duped and experimented on by reproductive "technologists" in North American and Western Europe; the females raped and impregnated by victors of wars and by slaveholders worldwide throughout the history of "civilization."

Mary Daly has laid claim to the experiences and treasures of unnamed or forgotten women over the centuries. In her courageous outrageous work, *Quintessence ... Realizing the Archaic Future: A Radical Elemental Feminist Manifesto,* (1998) Daly not only exposed the atrocities against unnamed millions of women committed at the end of the twentieth century, but reversing the patriarchal reversals, she also imagined and communicated with a future network of women called "Anonyma," who used this name to honor and signify their bonding with the countless women of the patriarchal era who could not publish under their own names.

Inspired by the work of Woolf, Daly, and other members of the Anonyma Network, radical feminist religionists and thealogians seek to name and claim Anonyma herself. She includes the goddesses; the wives and consorts of the gods; the mothers of male religious founders, such as the Buddha, Muhammed, Jesus; and even Yahweh. Disguised as Athena, Durgā, Kuan-Yin, Gnosis, Sophia, Theotokos, Isis, she is the origin of Life, the Nameless One.

BIBLIOGRAPHY

Useful works by or about anonymous women and Anonyma in addition to Mary Daly's *Quintessence* include Mirra Bank, *Anonymous Was a Woman* (1979); bell hooks, *Outlaw Culture: Resisting Representations* (1994); Cheris Kramarae and Paula A. Treichler, *Amazons, Bluestockings and Crones* (1985); Dale Spender, *Mothers of the Novel* (1986); Carol Travis, *Mismeasure of Woman* (1992); Lise Weil, "Entering a Lesbian Field of Vision," in Eileen Barrett and Patricia Cramer, eds., *Virginia Woolf: Lesbian Readings* (1997); and Virginia Woolf, "Anon," in Brenda R. Silver, ed., *Twentieth Centure Literature* 25, nos. 3 and 4 (1979): 356 ff.

LORINE M. GETZ

Antal

Antal was the sole woman among a group of twelve Vaiṣṇava saints who lived in the Tamil country of South India between the seventh and tenth centuries. Her hymns, composed around the year 800, emphasize utter surrender to god Vishnu whom she addressed as his intended bride. According to legend, the Lord Vishnu accepted her, allowing her body to merge into a stone replica of his form. The Tamil Vaiṣṇava saints were given a unique status as *amsas* or secondary incarnations of Vishnu's attributes; pride of place went to Antal, or "she who rules [the lord]," who was regarded as an *amsa* of Vishnu's second consort Bhudevi, or goddess earth.

Antal's two poetic works reveal her learning and her mastery of metrical structure. In the popular *Tiruppavai,* Antal is one of a group of girls who go to wake up Lord Krishna and ask him to bathe with them in the waters (a euphemism for sexual union). It is sung today by unmarried girls desirous of an early and happy marriage, while brides on their wedding day are frequently bedecked as Antal in the hope that divine favor will descend on them. The *Nacciyar Tirumoli,* by contrast, is a lone journey undertaken by Antal through a set of fourteen hymns. Having once experienced the joy of union with the Lord, Antal expresses the pain of separation and her incessant yearning for the presence of her beloved; the occasional uninhibited use of sexual terminology doubtless resulted in its omission from formal temple chants.

BIBLIOGRAPHY

Dehejia, Vidya. *Antal and Her Path of Love: Poems of a Woman Saint from South India.* 1990.

Hudson, Dennis. "Bathing in Krishna: A Study in Vaishnava Hindu Theology." *Harvard Theological Review* 73 (1980): 539–566.

Sundaram, P. S. *The Poems of Andal* (Tiruppauai *and* Nacciyar Tirumozhi). Madras, 1987.

VIDYA DEHEJIA

Anthropology

Anthropology, the study of culture, was greatly affected in the United States by Franz Boas (1858–1942). Boas's view that the collection of objective data was vital to the study of twentieth century anthropology led to a theoretical approach known as cultural relativism. He stressed the emotional and mental aspects of humans and studied the ways individuals fit into culture. His views weakened evolutionary theories, which assume that universal laws govern all human culture, and prompted many scholars to discard studies to recover absolute origins. He also gave careful consideration to historical contacts in order to understand similarities of religious beliefs in neighboring tribes. Similarities in religious systems, according to Boas, were the result of diffusion and not a matter of a universal history of origins. His theoretical emphasis was responsible for the emergence of diffusionist schools of anthropology. The study of distribution and diffusion was carried on by such scholars as Leslie Spier (1893–1961) and Alexander Goldenweiser (1880–1940), who used historical perspectives to understand culture rather than seek an absolute beginning of religion. Other theorists, such as Paul Radin (1883–1959), continued trying to reconstruct psychologically the origin and evolution of magic and religion by theorizing that religion originated from fear of difficult economic conditions (Malefijt, 1968).

Bronislaw Malinowski (1884–1942) began what is known as the participant-observer approach to anthropological fieldwork by immersing himself in the language and customs of a culture in order to view the world from an insider's perspective. Malinowski's theoretical emphasis, functionalism, assumed that the function of a cultural trait is to satisfy some basic or derived need of the members of the group. Arthur Reginald Radcliffe-Brown (1885–1955), a British social anthropologist, also based his theory of social behavior on the concept of functionalism. But in contrast to Malinowski, Radcliffe-Brown theorized that various aspects of social behavior existed in order to sustain a society's social infrastructure, not the needs of the individual.

In the 1930s a psychological approach to anthropology evolved. Ruth Benedict, a student of Boas, was interested in personality, and the assumption emerged that in each culture there may be several personality types. Benedict introduced the configurational view, according to which the various elements of a culture are interdependent, forming a coherent whole and constituting a unique pattern; each culture, like each individual, is in itself unique.

Margaret Mead (1901–1978), another student of Boas, made groundbreaking contributions to the cross-cultural study of gender roles. In contradiction to the idea that gender roles are innate, she maintained that individuals are born with the potential to develop whatever gender role society dictates. It was during this period of anthropological study up until the 1930s, where cultural studies assumed male dominance as natural and ignored sexual differences, that arguments were raised regarding women's roles in other societies. Such feminist anthropologists as Mead, Elizabeth Fernea, Susan Carol Rogers, and Annette Weiner began to argue that many of the women being studied enjoyed a higher status within their culture than was first recorded, sometimes even higher than that of contemporary Western women.

Claude Lévi-Strauss (b. 1908), known as the leading voice in the approach to cultural analysis called structuralism, concentrated on the origins of systems rather than on their elements within a society. To Lévi-Strauss, a culture is actually a surface representation of the underlying structure of the human mind and is expressed through such things as art, ritual, and the patterns of daily life.

Although women have always been present in ethnographical accounts, they were usually described for their role in subsistence, the importance of their rituals, and the way they were treated by men because of the anthropological concern with kinship and marriage. It was not until the early 1970s that the problem of how women were represented in anthropological study began. By confronting the problem of how women were being represented in ethnographical accounts, scholars made the study of male bias in ethnology the cornerstone of the study of women in the field of anthropology. Henrietta Moore (1988) argues that there are three types of male bias: The first is the anthropologist's assumptions and expectations regarding relationships between women and men and regarding the significance of those relationships to a wider society. The second is inherent in the society being studied, given that women are subordinate to men in many cultures and that these gender differences are usually communicated to the anthropologist. The third bias is based on the inherent prejudice of Western culture. The asymmetrical relationships of men and women in other cultures are often assumed by the anthropologist to be similar to the hierarchical nature of gender relations found in Western society. Taken together, male biases cause the anthropologist to overlook female status as a whole and therefore to perceive it as low.

With the advent of the new anthropology of women, which has come to be known as feminist anthropology, also came new concerns and new fears: Would treating women as a category lead to marginalization and ghettoization? And even as the problem of male bias was being addressed, issues of race and ethnocentrism, growing in response to anthropology's colonial past, were revising the assumptions that underlay much of anthropological theorizing and writing till then.

The study of women in the last three decades has brought the focus of women's representation back into the discipline of anthropology. In the pursuit of understanding women's roles in various societies, anthropologists were constantly drawn into the controversial debate over the origins and universality of women's subordination. This gave rise to new ethnographic studies of women's lives and their perceptions of their lives. Feminist anthropologists argued that in precolonial societies women were not subject to male domination or patriarchal structures, upon which today's male-oriented societies are built. Eleanor Leacock (1978) argues that women's subordination to men, the development of the family as an autonomous economic unit, and monogamous marriage are all related to the development of private ownership of the means of production. She states that in preclass agricultural societies, women and men were autonomous individuals who held positions of equal value and prestige, and functioned publicly in making economic and social decisions. These relationships were transformed under the impact of colonization, Westernization, and international capitalism. Other economic factors, such as the rise of the state and the consequent devaluation of kinship ties, are considered to have lowered the status of women. Hunter-gatherer societies tend not to differentiate between male and female status, and therefore women are not relegated to the domestic sphere; this cultural feature disputes the theory of the universal subordination of women. But when production for consumption becomes production of commodities for exchange, women lose control of their production and become relegated to individual households, where they become private dispensers of services and producers of children. Sexual egalitarianism is displaced by male dominance.

Some theorists argue that greater male levels of aggression are responsible for the phenomenon of universal female subordination, although this argument has been largely discredited as a crude and oversimplified view of the social and ideological nature of gender relations. Other theorists have tended to focus on the importance of childbearing and the "natural" roles women must play as child bearers and mothers, which therefore limits their mobility and restricts them to the domestic sphere. In contrast to this argument is the argument that society imposes the role of primary care giver upon women and that it is not based on a biological distinction.

Other theorists argue that subsistence economies and sex-role behavior in childbearing directly correspond to the role of the sexes in creation stories. Mead argued that the more men were removed from the phenomenon of childbirth, the more the male imagination contributed to the "cultural superstructure of belief and practice regarding child-bearing" (1968, p. 236). John and Beatrice Whiting (1975) contend that religious beliefs are a projection of early human experience and that child-care customs can be found in the psycho-cultural model of the relationship between personality and culture.

Anthropologists who focus on the role of the environment argue that origin myths establish who we are and why we behave in accordance with custom. Myths and stories of origin have been shown to reflect many aspects of social life. Susan Carol Rogers, in explaining the notion of mythical male dominance, argues that a nonhierarchical power relationship between males and females is maintained by "the acting out of a 'myth' of male dominance." The myth of male dominance is expressed "in patterns of public deference toward men, as well as their monopolization of positions of authority and prestige" (1974, p. 729).

Various theorists argue that the universality of male dominance is due to ecological pressures, women's reduced participation in, and therefore contribution to, agricultural societies, and even unbalanced sexual division of labor cross-culturally. Sherry Ortner (1974) argues that the subordination of women is based on cultural ideologies and symbols. In Ortner's formulation, a woman's body dooms her to a mere reproduction of life; she is identified, or symbolically associated, with nature, whereas men are associated with culture. The role of culture in human societies is to control or transcend nature, and therefore women, by virtue of their alliance with nature, are to be controlled and contained.

Social, economic, political, and religious contexts of women's roles are important themes in the debate over gender relations, the sexual division of labor, the organization of kinship and marriage relations, and women's access to power. The study of the anthropology of religion has brought into question the frameworks of domestic versus public and nature verses culture and has broken down the assumed identity between mother and woman; it has caused a rethinking of the individual in relation to society. Moore (1988) claims that feminist anthropology has made an outstanding contribution to anthropology by developing theories relating to gender identity and the cultural construction of gender; it allows for a rethinking of what it is to be a "woman" or a "man." The early period of the study of women was concerned with origins and universalities. The study of gender within anthropology, which was introduced into feminist studies in the 1970s, challenges the view of a universal sociological category of woman, therefore denying any universal attitudes attributed to women, such as universal subordination and oppression. The earlier studies of women considered difference based on gender, asking what difference it makes to be a woman, to see things from a woman's point of view, and to be a woman anthropologist. It reduced the variances in sexual roles to the inevitable natural and universal fact of sex differences. This anthropological study of women is now considered an exclusionary discourse, for women who did not feel that the term *woman* applied to them were left silent. This discourse is seen to have been concerned with the revision of Western cultural assumptions and considered exclusively constructed in dialogue with these same assumptions. The issue of race is not addressed but rather subsumed within the argument of gender difference. The new phase of feminist anthropology has shifted its study of gender relations to analyze class and historical context, while retaining a focus on difference based on race and the intersection of gender, class, and race within specific historical contexts. The anthropological study of gender now challenges the earlier biological essentialisms and transcends it by analyzing the ways cultures construct differences between men and women.

The 1990s has seen the emergence of critiques regarding white middle-class feminism by women of color and lesbians. The publication *This Bridge Called My Back* in the 1980s has made feminist anthropologists rethink the ways in which First World women had unselfconsciously constructed a cultural other in their images of "Third World" or "minority" women. It marked the significance of creating new alliances among women that would acknowledge differences of race, class, sexual orientation, educational privilege, and nationality. It brought up the question of who has the right to write culture for whom. As ethnographic writings have come to acknowledge the words of "othered" women through critical as well as creative writing forms, as seen in the anthology *Women Writing Culture*, it has now brought to the study of anthropology "a rebellious undoing of the classical boundary between observer and observed" (p. 8).

BIBLIOGRAPHY

Anzaldúa, Gloria, and Moraga, Cherríe, eds. *This Bridge Called My Back: Writings by Radical Women of Color.* 1983.

Barrett, Stanley, *The Rebirth of Anthropological Theory.* 1984. Offers a concise critique of various British and American anthropologists and their theoretical orientations in social and cultural anthropology.

Behar, Ruth, and Gordon, Deborah A., eds. *Women Writing Culture.* 1995.

Etienne, Mona, and Leacock, Eleanor, eds. *Women and Colonization: Anthropological Perspectives.* 1980. A good overview of feminist perspectives and arguments on women and the theory of universal subordination.

"Franz Boas: The Shackles of Tradition." Directed by Andre Singer. Films for Humanities and Sciences, Princeton, N. J., 1985. Focuses on Boas's theory challenging the concept of racial inferiority, which was once prevalent in the United States.

Leacock, Eleanor. "Women's States in Egalitarian Society: Implications for Social Evolution." *Current Anthropology* 19 (1978): 247–255.

di Leonardo, Micaela, ed. *Gender at the Crossroads of Knowledge: Feminist Anthropology in the Postmodern Era.* 1991. Comprehensive examination of current thinking in feminist anthropology. One of the few books that deals with issues of racism and gender explicitly and constructively.

Malefijt, Annemarie de Waal. *Religion and Culture: An Introduction to Anthropology of Religion.* 1968.

"Margaret Mead: Coming of Age." Directed by Andre Singer. Films for Humanities and Sciences, Princeton, N. J., 1985. Deals with her fieldwork examining child development, sex, and temperament to see what role society plays in making people what they are. Emphasizes her theory that humans arrange their social world in many different ways.

Mead, Margaret. *Male and Female.* 1968 (originally published in 1949).

Moore, Henrietta L. "The Differences Within and the Differences Between." In *Gendered Anthropology.* Edited by Teresa del Valle, 1993.

———. *Feminism and Anthropology.* 1988.

Ortner, Sherry B. "Is Female to Male as Nature is to Culture?" In *Woman, Culture, and Society.* Edited by Michelle Zimbalist Rosaldo and Louise Lamphere. 1974.

Rogers, Susan Carol. "Female Forms of Power and the Myth of Male Dominance: A Model of Female/Male Interaction in Peasant Society." *American Ethnologist* 2 (1975): 727–756.

Sanday, Peggy Reeves. *Female Power and Male Dominance: On the Origins of Sexual Inequality.* 1981. Comprehensive examination of various patterns of male dominance and female power in different historical and cultural settings.

Visweswaran, Kamala. *Fictions of Feminist Ethnography.* 1994.

Whiting, John W. M., and Whiting, Beatrice B. "Aloofness and Intimacy of Husbands and Wives." *Ethos* 3 (1975): 183–207.

RUBINA RAMJI

Anthropology of Religion

Although the origins of the anthropology of religion are rooted in Émile Durkheim's *Elementary Forms of Religious Life* (1912) and Max Weber's *Sociology of Religion* (1922), the discipline begins with the study of indigenous sacred traditions through sustained fieldwork. U.S. and British anthropologists such as Franz Boas and E. E. Evans-Pritchard rejected the evolutionary theory of religion implicit in Durkheim's work; they eschewed the idea of primitive "survivals" associated with E. B. Tylor (1913) and the conception of "primitive mentalities" developed by Levy-Bruhl (1926), in part for their racist implications, arguing for the systematic study of specific religious systems and the documenting of their rich cultural diversity. Drawing on both Marx and Freud, British functionalism accounted for religious myths and rituals in terms of their social and psychological functions and is perhaps best exemplified by Bronislaw Malinowski's *Magic, Science and Religion, and Other Essays* (1952), which treats religion as a compensatory reaction to mundane deprivation, suffering, or violence.

Anthropological studies of religion conducted from a Durkheimian perspective showed how rites and beliefs given in collective representations or symbol systems reflected and naturalized social divisions and political hierarchies. Such representations, psychologically inscribed through participation in religious activities, shape people's understanding of their experience in terms of socially given constructs. An excellent example of such an approach is Louis Dumont's study of hierarchy and reciprocity as a Hindu value system, *Homo Hierarchicus: An Essay on the Caste System* (1966). However, anthropological studies of religious practice led scholars to revise the Durkheimian model; most notably, Victor Turner, in *The Ritual Process: Structure and Anti-Structure* (1969), observed that some rituals involved the suspension of the normal social order so that hierarchical distinctions were replaced by equality and symbolic poverty, creating an egalitarian ethos of social solidarity. Thus, people also use ritual to contest the legitimacy of political hierarchies—an observation that led anthropologists to pay special attention to the ways that ritual constructs forms of power. In an important comparative study of shamanism and spirit possession cults, *Ecstatic Religion* (1971), I. M. Lewis described how marginalized women use spirit possession to advance their interests and improve their lot. In general, however, the role of women has been neglected in the Durkheimian approach to the study of religion. In *Anthropological Studies of Religion* (1987), Brian Morris provides a list of 102 monographs, only two of which focus on women.

A Weberian approach to the study of religion is best seen in Clifford Geertz's *The Religion of Java* (1960). In his influential essay, "Religion as a Cultural System" (1973), Geertz argued that religion is a system of philosophical ideas represented symbolically, a model *of* the world and *for* the world that gives meaning to human existence. Geertz's cultural hermeneutics opens the door to multiple perspectives that show how religious traditions sustain ambiguity and ambivalence as essential aspects of a moral tradition. This theoretical perspective is more congenial to feminist scholars and scholars who focus on the ways in which a religious tradition is continually reinvented. Many excellent ethnographic monographs focusing on women's role in religious traditions were published in the last decades of the twentieth century, as evidenced by the excellent collection of essays edited by Nancy Falk and Rita Gross, *Unspoken Worlds: Women's Religious Lives* (1989).

BIBLIOGRAPHY

Elizabeth Fernea's *Guests of the Sheik: An Ethnography of an Iraqi Village* (1986) was one of the first ethnographies to explore the lives of Muslim women. It has been followed by several excellent studies, including Erika Friedl's *Women of Deh Koh: Lives in an Iranian Village* (1989), Lila Abu-Lughod's *Veiled Sentiments: Honor and Poetry in a Bedouin Society* (1986), and Abu-Lughod's *Writing Women's Worlds: Bedouin Stories* (1993). One of the first studies on women and Hinduism is *The Powers of Tamil Women* (1980), edited by Susan Wadley. Other ethnographic monographs focusing on women's role in religious traditions include Anne Klein's *Meeting the Great Bliss Queen: Buddhists, Feminists, and the Art of the Self* (1995) and Miranda Shaw's *Passionate Enlightenment: Women in Tantric Buddhism* (1994). Other works, such as *Mama Lola: A Vodou Priestess in Brooklyn* (1991) by Karen McCarthy Brown, and *Wisdom's Daughters: Conversations with Women Elders of Native America* (1993), edited by Steve Wall, allow women to speak in their own words of their religious understanding and how it has shaped their lives.

See also Hermeneutics; Hierarchy; Phenomenology of Religion; Women's Religions; Women's Studies.

ELIZABETH FULLER COLLINS

Antisemitism and Jewish Identity

In 1930, Theodor Lessing formalized a theory about the psychopathological condition of Jewish self-hatred: in effect, he proclaimed it, in *Der jüdische Selbsthass,* a profound—if not the most profound—psychic ramification of a history of antisemitism. Others had described and dramatized it, but he became its official signatory. And most important, Lessing, a convert to Lutheranism from Judaism, was himself, by his own admission, a sufferer. What he describes there is a divided self, the "jew who hates the jew in the jew" (Herring, p. 119), as James Joyce characterized it in his notesheets for the novel *Ulysses,* which constructs a "divided" Jewish character named Leopold Bloom. This pathology results from an internalization of the outside projection of the Jewish self as detestable, unacceptable ("accepting your enemy's estimation of you," as Ludwig Lewisohn put it; cited in Gilman, 1993), a wish to transcend that identification or emulation of the non-Jew–accuser, with the result of extreme self-division (*zerrisenheit*); one is neither able to escape nor accept the self, since such characteristics that are identified as Jewish are defined as intrinsic, characterological, and unmistakable. Sander Gilman (1986) outlines the development and the dimensions of this phenomenon, including the connections within it between antisemitism and sexism. Two significant tangential studies of antisemitism and Jewish identity are Max Horkheimer and Theodor W. Adorno's chapter on "Elements of Anti-Semitism" in *Dialectic of Enlightenment* (1944) and Jean Paul Sartre's *Anti-Semite and Jew* (1948).

Though Lessing may have claimed the position of documentor, he was by no means the only or even the best exemplar of Jewish self-hatred, a condition that Freud would refer to as "exquisitely Jewish." Freud might be counted in that number as would, more notoriously, Otto Weininger. Weininger was a Viennese intellectual whose doctoral thesis became one of the most lauded and most often reprinted antisemitic tracts of the early twentieth century. *Sex and Character* (1906) has become in the second half of the century a casebook study of self-hatred, as much as a prototype of the discourse of antisemitism. Weininger was of Jewish origin and converted to Christianity. On the day his book was published he committed suicide in the house of Beethoven. In his theories about Jews, he contradicto-

rily defines Jewishness as both an essential and constructed type—a state of mind rather than a biological condition. It follows, then, that one's Jewish origin by birth may make no constitutional claim, providing for Weininger the escape hatch he seemed to be seeking and in pursuit of which, perhaps, he wrote his tract. Yet it seems that his theories, though convincing to a generation of intellectuals and practitioners of what was called "psychobiology," could not persuade him finally either that he was free of Jewishness or that he should be.

Another significant aspect of Weininger's theories about Jews is the analogue he creates with sex. In fact, the German word *Geschlecht,* the first word in the German title of Weininger's book (*Geschlecht und Charakter*), is used to mean "race" as well as "sex" and "gender," thereby seemingly conflating these linguistically in a way that history often has. Weininger claims that the lesser, illogical, and corrupt side of every individual is the female side, and that therefore those races that are "lesser"—such as Jews, "negroes and Mongolians," among whom he sees an "anthropological relationship," are womanly (Weininger, pp. 302–303).

CHRISTIAN ANTI-JUDAISM

The roots of antisemitism are most often located in the presumption of Jewish responsibility for the crucifixion of Christ. The charge of "christkiller" has been used to justify a long history of misrepresentation and violence against Jews: pogroms, expulsions, false accusation (e.g., Jews as the source and bearers of disease, such as the Black Plague and syphilis), typological recastings of the Hebrew Bible, and a general vilification of Jewish liturgy and theology by the mainstream Christian establishment. Some might argue that this long history has culminated in this century in the Holocaust.

The charge of Jewish "bloodthirstiness" with respect to Christ has been translated into an accusation of blood libel and the unmanning of Christ: the ritual need for Christian blood to make matsoh (Blood Libel) provides the symbolic interface and divider between Christianity and Judaism, representing the Passover into Christ's body (matzoh into wafer). To unman Christ, that is to kill him, is both to render him into everlasting life—to deify him—and suggestively to castrate him. More contemporary scholars, tracing the history and roots of modern antisemitism, have argued (along with Freud) that the source of antisemitism resides in the metonym of lack presented by the circumcised penis, which is the mark of the Jewish male's covenant with God, and the mark of difference (from Christians). This lack signifies sexually as female, thereby tells or portends of castration, and is arguably the source of a great deal of symbolically related expression of antisemitism. Surely the King of the Jews (the Roman epithet for Christ) was circumcised. Therefore, in order for Jesus to be properly deified, he had to be masculinized—the true Son of God the Father; and for this to occur he had to be dissociated from Jewishness altogether.

FEMINISM AND JUDAISM

Weininger's work has also been revisited by contemporary feminism as a way of examining the historical sources of misogyny. To dissociate from Jewishness or Judaism in Weininger's terms becomes a dissociation from womanness or femininity, making them integral to one another. Some feminists have sought not only to disentangle the two (and in the process to reveal the prejudices therein), but also, in some cases, to show the incompatibility of Orthodox or traditional Judaism with feminist aims. A debate over the feminine or even feminist nature of Jesus has at times claimed Christianity over Judaism as more woman-oriented, with Judaism representing an unyielding patriarchal institution (see, for example, Swindler, 1971). This view reinforces the idea of a feminized Jesus but stands strangely in contradistinction to what has been seen, as cited above, as the source of that idea of Jesus (the womanly Jew). Some, like E. M. Broner (*The Woman's Haggadah*, 1994), have sought to fortify the connection between traditional Judaism and women by rewriting it. One takes a stand on the potential for a connection between Judaism and women or Jewishness and womanness, depending on whether one is addressing the issue from a more religiously identified or gender-identified position. Some Jewishly identified women nevertheless perceive established Judaism to be hostile to woman and seek a means of reclamation (e.g., Cynthia Ozick, Rachel Adler). In her fascinating essay "Notes Toward Finding the Right Question" (1983), Cynthia Ozick demonstrates the way in which the very fabric of Jewish life as determined by the halakhah (Jewish codes of behavior and practice) equates women with a sense of loss, evocative of the metonym of lack. For example, a man may be excused from performing the religious duties that women are legally exempted from by dint of their domestic role only when he is in certain states, such as that of bereavement—suffering from, as Ozick puts it, "an irreversible loss. Ah, Freud!" (Ozick, p. 127).

Whatever the position taken, even when conforming to certain historical stereotypes of Jews, the inside patriarchal view provides a stark, sometimes paradoxical contrast to the predominant outside view that Jewishness as an inferior "race" is necessarily postulated and represented in stereotypes of the feminine. In other words, the discourses and practices of antisemitism and misogyny have been intricately entwined in the history of Western culture.

BIBLIOGRAPHY

Adler, Rachel. "The Jew Who Wasn't There: *Halakhah* and the Jewish Woman." In *On Being a Jewish Feminist: A Reader.* Edited by Susannah Heschel. 1983.

Boyarin, Daniel. "Épater l'embourgeoisement: Freud, Gender and the (De)colonized Psyche." *Diacritics* (Spring 1994): 17–41.

Freud, Sigmund. "Analysis of a Phobia in a Five-Year Old Boy," "The Economic Problem in Masochism," and "The Passing of the Oedipus Complex." In *Collected Papers.* 1950.

Gilman, Sander. *Freud, Race, and Gender.* 1993.

Geller, Jay. *The Jew's Body.* 1991.

———. *Jewish Self-Hatred.* 1986.

———. "A Paleontological View of Freud's Study of Religion: Unearthing the *Leitfossil* Circumcision." *Modern Judaism* 13, no. 1 (1993): 49–70.

Herring, Phillip F., ed. *Joyce's Ulysses Notesheets in the British Museum.* 1972.

Heschel, Susannah. "Jesus as Theological Transvestite." In *Judaism Since Gender.* Edited by Miriam Peskowitz and Laura Levitt. 1996.

Horkheimer, Max, and Theodor W. Adorno. *Dialectic of Enlightenment.* Translated by John Cumming. 1944; 1982.

Lessing, Theodor. *Der jüdischer Selbsthass.* Berlin, 1930.

Ozick, Cynthia. "Notes Toward Finding the Right Question." In *On Being a Jewish Feminist.* Edited by Susannah Heschel. 1983.

Poliakov, Léon. *The History of Anti-Semitism: From the Time of Christ to the Court Jews.* Translated by Richard Howard. 1974.

Sartre, Jean-Paul. *Anti-Semite and Jew.* Translated by George J. Becker. 1948; 1970.

Swindler, Leonard. "Jesus Was a Feminist." *The Catholic World* (January 1971): 177–183.

Weininger, Otto. *Sex and Character.* 1906.

MARILYN REIZBAUM

Aphrodite (Venus)

Aphrodite was a Greek goddess whose most important area of concern was sexuality; indeed, in ancient Greek her name could be used as a common noun to mean sexual intercourse. She developed out of Middle Eastern goddesses who were also connected with sexuality,

Classical Greek sculpture head of Aphrodite (Corbis-Bettmann).

such as Ishtar. When the Romans encountered Aphrodite, they identified her with an obscure goddess of their own named Venus, whose name means beauty. Eventually, this hellenized form of Venus became an important Roman goddess due to Aphrodite's mythic role as the mother of the hero Aeneas, whom the Romans regarded as their founder.

Although myth made the god Hephaestus her husband, Aphrodite had many affairs with other gods and mortals, most notably Ares, the god of war, by whom she bore the child Eros. Usually, she is portrayed as having initiated these affairs herself. Sometimes, as in the case of Adonis, her lovers meet with death or disfigurement after their tryst; the implicit message, which we find in other Greek sources as well, is that uncontrolled female sexuality leads to disaster for men. A famous myth explains that the sea gave birth to Aphro-

dite after the castrated genitals of the sky-god, Ouranos, were tossed into its waves. In another myth, she causes Helen to run away with Paris, an act that leads to the Trojan War and the deaths of hundreds of men.

In cult, Aphrodite was called on by lovers, by young women about to make the transition into married life and productive sexuality, and, occasionally, by those who wished to ensure the fecundity of animals and crops.

BIBLIOGRAPHY

The best overview is provided by Walter Burkert, *Greek Religion* (1985), pp. 152–156. For further analysis, see Deborah Boedeker, *Aphrodite's Entry into Greek Epic* (1974).

See also Ishtar and Anat.

SARAH ILES JOHNSTON

Apsāras

Apsāras (moving in water) is a female celestial who inhabits the Hindu and Buddhist worlds. A beautiful, uniquely gifted woman, she is enchanting to both mortals and gods.

In the Buddhist context, *apsāras*es are portrayed merely as celestial beings without great dramatic or narrative presence. But in the story of Mara's Temptation, in which Mara, the demon king, uses his daughters to try to charm the Buddha away from his goal on the night of his enlightenment, Mara's daughters fulfill many of the functions that *apsāras*es serve in the Hindu context.

In Hindu literature, *apsāras*es are simultaneously dangerous and sexually desirable. When the gods become alarmed at the power of a (male) ascetic, they send an *apsāras* to lure him away from his penances. Later Hindu texts, known as the purānas, recount the *apsāras*es' origin. When the cosmic ocean was churned, various creatures emerged out of its foam, including gods, demons, and *apsāras*es. Because neither the gods nor the demons wished to marry them, *apsāras*es became creatures for the enjoyment of all, or *sumadātmajās* ("daughters of joy"). Whereas this story appears to indicate that *apsāras*es were the instruments of others, some narratives represent them as acting in their own interests, within the space created between their sexual duties to their leader, the god Indra, and the demands made by earthly lovers.

The first reference to an *apsāras* is in the Rig Veda (2000–1500 B.C.E.), a foundational Hindu text. Urvaśī marries the mortal king Purūravas on the condition that they have intercourse three times a day. The hymn re-

Apsārases **in the Hall of Dancers at Prah Khan, Cambodia, 1150–1200** C.E. (Kevin R. Morris/© Corbis)

lates a conversation in which she expresses frustration with their union and her intention to leave him. She complains about Pururavas's neglect of his kingly duties and his lovemaking. She dislikes his boorishness and describes being "pierced with his rod," perhaps because he often fails to obtain her consent. In one of the most quoted passages describing Vedic attitudes toward women, Urvaśī tells the forlorn Purūravas, "Do not die; do not vanish; do not let the vicious wolves eat you. There are no friendships with women; they have the hearts of jackals." This instance of misogyny on the part of a woman can be read either as a sincere appraisal of the whole sex's duplicitous nature or as a duplicitous statement in itself—as, in fact, an attack on *men*, who only purport to love their women. This is perhaps the most enduring feature in literary characterizations of *apsāras*es: as the "other" of the human courtesan and the good wife and mother, they are allowed to say and do things forbidden to mortal women. In the fifth century C.E., the story of Urvaśī was further elaborated into a play by Kālidāsa.

In art, *apsāras*es are found in many Buddhist cave paintings; those at Ajanta, India, and Dunhuang, China, are particularly striking examples. They often share the stage with other celestial beings such as *vidyādharas* and *gandharvas*. *Apsāras*es are also depicted in memorial stones for Hindu warriors, conducting the hero to heaven, perhaps luring and guiding him to his destination.

BIBLIOGRAPHY

Kālidāsa. *Vikramorvaśīya*. Translated by David Gitomer as "Urvaśī Won by Valor." In *Theater of Memory: The Plays of Kālidāsa*. Edited by Barbara Stoler Miller. 1984.

O'Flaherty, Wendy Doniger, trans. "Purūravas and Urvaśī." In *The Rig Veda*. 1981.

Singh, Madanjeet. *India: Paintings from the Ajanta Caves*. 1954.

Srivastava, K. M. "*Apsāras* at Angkor Wat." *Arts of Asia* 14 (1984): 55–67.

Thurman, Robert, trans. *The Holy Teaching of Vimalakirti: A Mahayana Scripture*. 1976. Chap. 4.

Xingru, Fan, copier. *Flying Apsaras in Dunhuang*. Lanchou, China, 1995. A compilation of the copies made by Xingru of the *apsāras* painted in the Dunhuang caves.

ANNAPURNA GARIMELLA

Archaeology

Archaeology is the science of recovering the past through the excavation and analysis of material culture remains. These remains are understood to be the deliberate works or unwitting by-products of human activities, and as such their investigation facilitates our understanding of human behavior in bygone days. Regardless of the location, date, and unique qualities of any individual site, certain archaeological standards and conventions prevail.

Over time the definition of material culture remains has become increasingly broad. In archaeology's early years (mid-nineteenth to mid-twentieth centuries), most excavation focused on the recovery of texts, treasures, and the architecture of society's elite. In consequence, big city life was explored and village life ignored; temples and palaces were favored over domestic quarters; the gleam of gold and silver outshone the dullness of food preparation tools; the tales of texts were repeated endlessly while the voices of the illiterate majority, women included, were rarely heard.

With a more modern sensibility and a new sensitivity to the importance of the everyday and the average, the goals of archaeology have been modified. Now, attention is paid to reconstructing ancient lifeways, to understanding the fabric of daily existence, and to the experience of all people and not only of the male and the privileged. No longer content to conserve the magnificent and discard the mundane, archaeologists look at seed and pollen remains, wear patterns on tools for food and textile preparation, geomorphology and site formation processes. The symbiosis between those in authority and those who made authority possible by acceding to it, between those who were wealthy and those who created the means for their wealth, is increasingly explored. When power is no longer the single important criterion for the excavator, it becomes possible to use archaeology to explore the place of women in ancient religion.

THE QUANDARY OF INTERPRETATION

The process by which things become part of the archaeological record is random rather than deliberative. Sites are often plundered of all valuables in their own time. What is left in its original setting is often only that which is considered useless or too unwieldy to be moved. The materials uncovered through excavation are unedited in the sense that the people who left things behind did so unconsciously, with no effort to create an accurate picture of their lives for later generations. They are mute in the sense that they themselves tell no story. It remains for the excavator and for other professionals to interpret and speak for them. In this way, the voice of the modern social scientist may be heard as clearly as the voice of the ancient inhabitant of an excavated site. Thus, archaeologists and others interested in the past are presented with a professional, and perhaps even an ethical, dilemma. Given our reliance on random remains for reconstructing lives, can accuracy be achieved? Are definitive interpretations possible?

Archaeologists grapple with these questions in various ways. Perhaps the most effective response is that of explicitness. Like other social scientists, archaeologists must design their research with clear objectives, declared suppositions, and well-delineated methods of interpretation. They must describe sites and their multiple finds and develop cogent interpretative stances without skewing information in such a way that it cannot be reanalyzed and reinterpreted by others. By being aware of and sensitive to developments in related fields, including history, anthropology, gender studies, religious studies, art history, and so forth, the archaeologist can work both meticulously and think broadly.

AN EXAMPLE: WOMEN IN ANCIENT ISRAEL

It is not feasible here to attempt a global accounting of the contribution of archaeology to our understanding of the role women played in ancient religions. Context and setting are critical to developing good descriptions of women's many religious roles.

Instead, let us examine a specific geographic and chronological setting, the region of modern Israel (ancient Israel and Judah) during the Iron Age II (1000–587 B.C.E.). Because Israel is well explored archaeologically, the body of excavated data is large. In addition, the Tanakh (Hebrew Bible) provides a superlative literary corpus contemporary to the archaeological remains, one that enriches our understanding of ancient Israelite religion. The religion of ancient Israel has been the focus of tremendous scholarly attention by both archaeologists and Biblical scholars. In the last decades of the twentieth century, a number of talented scholars have worked on reconstructing the roles of women in the religion of ancient Israel. In consequence, the field is rich in information and in critical scholarly studies, making it an excellent example of what can be accomplished—and of pitfalls to avoid.

For the first hundred years and more of archaeological exploration, the role of women in Israelite society was rarely examined. In part, this was due to prevailing assumptions about the unimportance of women in society. Most archaeologists in this region were male clerics, predisposed by their own religious beliefs to disparage women's roles in religion or to discount them entirely.

The androcentric bias of archaeologists and biblicists was matched by that of their fundamental textual resource, the Tanakh. This ancient text is neither neutral description nor accurate history. Rather, it is a complex statement of the relationship between the people of Israel and their God. The Tanakh is composite; its various heavily edited documents describe priests and kings, prophets and scribes, leaders preoccupied with issues of state and temple. Since men dominated both state and temple in ancient Israel and Judah and since literacy was limited to a male elite, the Tanakh emphasized men's place in religion. Archaeologists of previous generations often interpreted excavated materials by exploring the ways in which they could be used to prove the accuracy of Biblical passages. It comes as no surprise, then, that women's religious responsibilities and contributions were rarely examined.

Beginning in the mid-1970s, a new generation of Biblical scholars began looking at gender roles in ancient Israel. Acknowledging that the nature of the Tanakh had long precluded an awareness of women's many critical roles in society, scholars learned to read behind the text, to listen to the whispers of women whose lives, both private and public, had been placed in the Biblical margins. In addition, they began to look for alternate resources that would help them better understand women's roles in ancient Israelite society, including their place in Israelite religion. Archaeology came to be seen as a natural foil to the biased version of Israelite life depicted in the Tanakh, providing a resource unedited by intellectual or theological presumptions.

One example of this effort is the ongoing study of the more than three thousand small ceramic figurines found in Judaean domestic, funerary, and sacred contexts. These figurines depict a nude woman, her head simply formed and her body from waist to feet a flared column or pillar. In all cases the figure's hands support her breasts, giving rise to the name *dea nutrix*, or nursing goddess. In the past the figurine was often dismissed as a token used by women to ensure fertility or to aid in lactation. Efforts to identify her or to understand her place in the religion of Israel were rare.

With increasing interest in the role of women in Israelite religion, a more comprehensive approach to analyzing this pillar-based figurine was developed. Scholars looked to archaeological evidence from pre-Israelite sites to help identify the goddess. Their evidence included well-known Canaanite texts and depictions of goddesses crafted in clay and precious metals or painted on pottery. They examined written references and graffiti art at Judaean shrines and tombs. Attention turned to scant written references to goddesses found in the Tanakh. Understanding the bias in the text, efforts were made to be aware of context and putative authorship. In addition, scholars looked to modern ethnographic studies to better understand the role women fill in the religious life of agrarian societies.

Gradually, an understanding of the place of the originally Canaanite goddess Asherah within the normative Israelite cult of the Iron Age II began to emerge. Scholars continue to disagree on the details, but few will now deny her a place alongside Yahweh, the God of Israel. Her special importance to women is apparent, but no longer is she disparaged as meaningful only to women. Her importance to all Israel is acknowledged, despite the fact that the Tanakh's late editors, who promoted a "Yahweh-only" religion for Israel, had virtually eliminated her from the Biblical text. For more than two thousand years she went unnoticed; now archaeology helps return her to her rightful place in the religion of ancient Israel.

BIBLIOGRAPHY

Conkey, Margaret W., and Spector, J. "Archaeology and the Study of Gender." In *Advances in Archaeological Method and Theory.* Edited by Michael Schiffer. Vol. 7. 1984.

Dever, William G. "Archaeology Reconstructs the Lost Background of the Israelite Cult." In his *Recent Archaeological Discoveries and Biblical Research.* 1990.

Gero, Joan M., and Margaret W. Conkey, eds. *Engendering Archaeology: Women and Prehistory.* Oxford, 1991.

Gilchrist, Roberta. *Gender and Material Culture: The Archaeology of Religious Women.* 1994.

Hestrin, Ruth. "Understanding Asherah: Exploring Semitic Iconography." *Biblical Archaeology Review* 17 (1991): 50–79.

Joukowsky, Martha. *A Complete Manual of Field Archaeology: Tools and Techniques of Field Work for Archaeologists.* 1980.

Meyers, Carol L. *Discovering Eve: Ancient Israelite Religion in Context.* 1988.

Trible, Phyllis. "A Love Story Gone Awry." In her *God and the Rhetoric of Sexuality.* 1978.

BETH ALPERT NAKHAI

Architecture

An Overview

As a term for both a process and product, architecture is the built environment that results from the fusion of thought, action, and matter in the context of social and cultural life. It is too often conceived in terms of permanent, extraordinary buildings and monuments—an

The ruins of a kiva at the Chimney Rock Anasazi ruins at Pagosa Springs, Colorado (Tom Bean/Corbis).

outlook which is even more pronounced in relation to religious structures such as temples, basilicas, stupas, mosques, shrines, and mausolea. But architecture is concomitantly a matter of daily practice and ordinary domestic constructions. It also has a place in collective memory and discourse.

This article surveys religious architecture, both ordinary and extraordinary, built mainly by, for, or about women and female representations. Though some architectural projects clearly express women's spirituality, many buildings for goddesses or female saints have been created by religiopolitical systems where men hold sway. Conversely, constructions for patriarchal religious institutions may be financed, maintained, and designed by powerful and determined women.

RELIGION AND GENDER IN DOMESTIC SPACE

For ordinary buildings, as with extraordinary ones, religious function and significance are above all matters of difference and unity—making spatial and temporal distinctions between culture and nature, sacred and profane, pure and impure, life and death, and organizing them within an architectural system. In some societies, difference is reflected in the creation of segregated places for men and women. This is exemplified in the rectangular layout of the Fang village (western Africa), where the sleeping and cooking huts are female spaces, as opposed to men's council houses. In the female space, metaphorically associated with the womb, birth and death rituals occur. Marriage and other ceremonies go back and forth between the male and female spaces. Some societies establish special rooms and buildings for women during menstruation, childbirth, and puberty rites. When a Bambuti girl (in Zaire) reaches puberty, she lives with a cohort of other girls in a house or domestic extension for an initiation festival period of one or two months, after which she joins the adult women of the tribe and becomes eligible for marriage. This type of spatial segregation is present not only among tribal groups in Africa but also in Southeast Asia and the Americas. The Apache, for example, erect a tipi for girls' puberty rites that emulates the home of the spirit White-Painted Woman, the archetype of Apache femininity.

In many cultures such primary orders of difference are included within elaborated domestic systems. In Timor the roof beams, pillars, and platforms of Atoni houses mirror and symbolically mediate oppositions between male and female, wife-givers and wife-takers, outside and inside, right and left, east and west, sky and earth, host and guest, ruler and ruled, and so forth. The prototypical hogan described in Navajo myth associates women with the left (northern) side of the interior, and with the five chief support poles. According to one blessing song, whatever beauty the Navajo home possesses "extends from the woman." In Batammaliba architecture (of Togo and the Benin Republic), houses are divided symbolically into male and female sections, wherein the latter is the right (northern) half that contains places for storing female crops and game animals killed by women, and for the shrine of the female initiation god. The domestic compound as a whole is identified with the body of the androgynous sky god, Kuiye, whose testicles and mouth are located at the entrance, and whose womb is the woman's circular bedroom in the compound's center, where children are conceived.

Gendered ritual and symbolic formations of domestic space also occur in cultures where translocal religions have taken root. Jewish women manage domestic life and take preeminent roles during Sabbath and Passover observances, when the home is a major focus of ritual activity. In Middle Eastern Islamic societies, the home's interior is considered in patriarchal terms to be a forbidden, sacralized space (ḥaram, ḥurma)—the realm of women par excellence. Thus entrances, windows, terraces, balconies, and accommodations for male visitors are situated and designed so as to uphold the boundaries of sacrality. In Roman Catholic and Orthodox households, niches are set aside within the house for domestic shrines, tended by female inhabitants. Victorian writers in England and the United States promoted a Gothic revival in middle-class domestic architecture to make the Protestant home a church for the family, and a replica of nature where women could properly direct their energies. Given such evidence, it is not surprising to find that historically synagogues, churches, and mosques developed from domestic architecture. However, because these were places of assembly governed by male authorities, women were segregated and peripheralized in adjoining galleries and rooms of the building, especially in communities where purity codes were observed.

ARCHITECTURE DEDICATED TO FEMALE DEITIES AND HOLY WOMEN

Temples and shrines have been conceived and designed as monumental houses for sacred beings, with entryways, courtyards, storage and kitchen areas, meeting areas, and inner chambers. In a number of contexts, such as ancient Mesopotamia and Egypt, Israel, Islamic cultures, Christian cultures, and India, they have been widely known as "houses of god." Moreover, there is ample evidence that such buildings have been constructed for the worship of female deities and saints, as well as for male ones.

Goddess temples are widely attested in ancient Greco-Roman milieus. The Parthenon on the Acropolis at Athens was dedicated to Athena; at nearby Eleusis monumental buildings were dedicated to the mystery religion of the grain mother Demeter and her dying and rising daughter Kore (Persephone). The city of Rome contained temples for Fortuna, Ceres, Venus, Diana, and Juno. The most striking architecturally was the circular shrine of Vesta, goddess of the hearth, where the prestigious vestal virgins conducted sacred fire rituals. Roman rulers also dedicated temples to foreign goddesses, such as Cybele (from Asia Minor) and Isis, who were identified with local deities. Outside the capital, women frequented the lakeside temple of Diana at Aricia with its sacred grove, and the hillside sanctuary of Fortuna at Praeneste, with its famous arcade. Ephesus in Asia Minor was home to the temple of Cybele-Artemis (sixth century B.C.E.–third century C.E.), one of the Seven Wonders of the World; and nearby Aphrodisias, with its grand Venus Aphrodite temple, enjoyed imperial patronage.

Since the fifth century churches dedicated to Mary, the mother of Jesus, have become ubiquitous wherever Christianity, especially Roman Catholicism and Eastern Orthodoxy, has taken root—in some instances replacing the temples of pre-Christian goddesses. Many are based on a cruciform floor plan. Some house her relics, such as the splendid Gothic cathedral at Chartres; others celebrate a Marian vision, such as those at Tinos, Lourdes, and Fatima, which have become significant pilgrimage centers. The shrine complex of the Virgin of Guadalupe in Mexico City, location of Marian visions and relics, comprises a broad plaza with old and new basilicas, a baptistery, a monumental timepiece, subsidiary chapels, a cemetery, and a religious sculpture garden; the new basilica (dedicated in 1975) is built on a modern elliptical plan, representing the cloak and embracing arms of the Virgin. Christians have also dedicated churches to other female saints, such as Elizabeth, Anne, Barbara, and Teresa.

At Mecca, the running course between the hills Safa and Marwa that all Muslim pilgrims must traverse seven times commemorates Hagar's frantic search for water for her son Ishmael. In Mecca and Medina shrines for Muhammad's female relatives, including at least five for his daughter Fatimah, stood until leveled by Wahhabi warriors in the 1920s. Cairo has honored a number of women from the Prophet's household—most notably Nafisa, Zaynab, and Ruqayya—with large domed shrines and mosques dating to the twelfth–thirteenth centuries. Many are still frequented by devotees and pilgrims. In Shia lands, mosque-shrines have been dedicated to female relatives of the imams, the most remarkable of which is Qum's shrine of Fatima (sister of the eighth imam, Ali Reza), the resting place of a number of kings, and birthplace of Ayatollah Khomeini's Islamic revolution.

Hindu temples conjoin male and female symbolisms. As models of the universe, they may be built in a walled compound according to a geometric ground plan containing the cosmic man (*Puruṣa*), and have as their focal point an inner "womb chamber," which houses the image of the chief deity, or the divine couple. Throughout India, since the fourth century B.C.E., innumerable temples and shrines have been dedicated to the goddess Devī and her many manifestations. In Banaras, the city of Siva in north India, the most prominent goddess temples belong to Durgā, a tiger-riding demon slayer; Annapurna Bhavani, the giver of food; and Shitala, goddess of fever diseases. Shrines for other goddesses are situated throughout the city and at the sacred Ganges landings. Nearly everywhere, Sri/Lakṣmī, the goddess of wealth, is worshiped as a mediator between her devotees and her husband Vishnu. In the region of Mathura, pilgrims worship Krishna together with his beautiful lover, Radha, at temples, shrines, and sacred ponds. One of the most modern goddess temples is that of the new goddess Bharat Mata, "Mother India," in the pilgrimage city of Hardwar.

In China one of the deities widely worshiped was Pi-hsia Yuan-chün, Goddess of the Green Clouds, a compassionate earth goddess who could bestow the gifts of fertility and good health. Her first temple (eleventh century C.E.) was part of an ancient imperial shrine complex at a mountain site southeast of Beijing. By the end of the seventeenth century, she had two dozen temples in the vicinity of Beijing alone, the most important being the popular Taoist pilgrimage site located at Miao-Feng Shan. In addition, many temples and pilgrimage sites were devoted to white-robed Kuan Yin, the female bodhisattva. A pilgrimage complex of temples, monasteries, shrines, and caves for this goddess formed on the island of Puto Shan in the East China Sea, starting in the tenth century. She is likewise worshiped at temples in Malaysia, Singapore, and Japan, where she is known as Kannon. In Japan the leading Shinto shrine at Ise is the ancient home of the sun goddess, Amaterasu.

Monasteries are another kind of religious architecture dedicated to women, particularly in the Christian and Buddhist traditions. In medieval Europe they were often established in common houses or manors that had been donated for the purpose. They included living quarters, kitchens, and chapels, as well as agricultural properties to help provide for the daily needs of the order. Sometimes monasteries were shared by male and female religious, but medieval church authorities made concerted efforts to segregate them. In Buddhist communities nuns have lived together with monks and apart from them.

BUILDERS, PATRONS, AND ARCHITECTS

Although women have actively participated in the construction, maintenance, and decoration of domestic architecture, men have predominated in the planning and implementation of large-scale ceremonial, monumental, and public buildings. Nonetheless, history shows that women can play a palpable role in the creation of religious architecture, especially when they acquire enough wealth and power to do so. Some have devoted their attentions to buildings for religious women and female deities, but many have followed the same architectural and endowment conventions as their male counterparts.

In Egypt the pharaoh and queen Hatshepsut (ruled 1503–1482 B.C.E.), improvising on the tradition of her male predecessors, commissioned the building of a distinctive three-tiered mortuary temple against the cliffs of the Theban hills, the site of a Hathor temple. It remains to this day one of the most remarkable constructions in the Nile Valley. Wealthy laywomen in India, such as Visakha of Sravasti (c. fifth century B.C.E.) and queens of northern Buddhist kingdoms (c. third–twelfth centuries C.E.) sponsored the construction of Buddhist monasteries and stupas. In Jewish communities women have contributed to the building and maintenance of synagogues since the Hellenistic era.

Although often excluded from public participation in many key Islamic institutions, considerable numbers of women among the Muslim ruling elites, especially royal families, financed the building and maintenance of mosques, religious colleges, Sufi monasteries, devo-

tional centers, and mausolea. They became patrons and supervised the pious endowments that funded building projects, while their kinsmen were preoccupied with dynastic feuds and battles. Zubayda (d. 831), Harun al-Rashid's queen, commissioned mosques and provided amenities for pilgrims to Mecca and Medina. In medieval Yemen one-third of the religious foundations in the chief cities were built by women affiliated with the Rasulid dynasty (1230–1438). High-ranking women in Mamluk Cairo and Damascus (thirteenth–sixteenth centuries) sponsored the construction of mosques, colleges, and funerary complexes. Royal Ottoman women are said to have been unsurpassed in their architectural patronage, as exemplified by the religious buildings sponsored by Hürrem Sultan (d. 1558), wife of Süleyman the Magnificent, and their daughter Mihrimah Sultan (d. 1578) in Istanbul, Edirne, and Jerusalem.

The modern architectural profession, which has its roots in the Enlightenment and the industrial age, has until recently been regarded as a gentleman's enterprise. Julia Morgan (1872–1957), who helped open the profession to women in the United States, was involved in 800 architectural projects, including churches and Young Women's Christian Association centers, which were designed to help single women adapt to urban life. Professional women architects involved in designing both religious and secular buildings can be found in any countries today. Nonetheless, their numbers remain relatively small.

BIBLIOGRAPHY

Asian Art 6 (Spring 1993). Five articles devoted to the topic "Patronage by Women in Islamic Art."

Bahloul, Joëlle. *The Architecture of Memory: A Jewish-Muslim Household in Colonial Algeria, 1937–1962.* 1992.

Blier, Suzanne Preston. *The Anatomy of Architecture: Ontology and Metaphor in Batammaliba Architectural Expression.* 1987.

Boutelle, Sara Holmes. *Julia Morgan, Architect.* 2d ed. 1995.

Campo, Juan E. *The Other Sides of Paradise: Explorations into the Religious Significance of Domestic Space in Islam.* 1991.

Cunningham, Clarke E. "Order in the Antoni House." In *Right and Left: Essays in Dual Symbolic Classification.* Edited by Rodney Needham. 1973.

Dubisch, Jill. *In a Different Place: Pilgrimage, Gender, and Politics at a Greek Island Shrine.* 1996.

Eck, Diana L. *Banaras: City of Light.* 1982.

Fernandez, James. "Emergence and Convergence in Some African Sacred Places." *Geoscience and Man* 24 (1984): 31–42.

Hawley, John Stratton, and Donna Marie Wulff, eds. *Devi: Goddesses of India.* 1996. See esp. chapters by Hume, Narayanan, and McKean.

Humphreys, R. Stephen. "Women as Patrons of Religious Architecture in Ayyubid Damascus." *Muqarnas* 11 (1994): 35–54.

McCash, June Hall, ed. *The Cultural Patronage of Medieval Women.* 1996.

McDannell, Colleen. *The Christian Home in Victorian America, 1840–1900.* 1986.

Nabokov, Peter, and Robert Easton. *Native American Architecture.* 1989.

Naquin, Susan, and Chün-fang Yü, eds. *Pilgrims and Sacred Sites in China.* 1992.

Nixon, Lucia. "The Cults of Demeter and Kore." In *Women in Antiquity: New Assessments.* Edited by Richard Hawley and Barbara Levick. 1995.

Thompson, Sally. *Women Religious: The Founding of English Nunneries after the Norman Conquest.* 1991.

Valone, Carolyn. "Roman Matrons as Patrons: Various Views of the Cloister Wall." In *The Crannied Wall: Women, Religion, and the Arts in Early Modern Europe.* Edited by Craig A. Monson. 1992.

Warner, Marina. *Alone of All Her Sex: The Myth and the Cult of the Virgin Mary.* 1976.

Weadock, Penelope N. "The *Giparu* at Ur." *Iraq* 37 (1975): 101–198.

Young, William C. "The Ka'ba, Gender, and the Rites of Pilgrimage." *International Journal of Middle East Studies* 25 (1993): 285–300.

See also **Domestic Rites**; **Home**; **Patronage**; **Shrines**; **Space, Sacred.**

JUAN E. CAMPO

Nomadic or Seasonal

In contrast to the architecture associated with rural and urban sedentary lifestyles, nomadic architectures have traditionally been considered temporary and valueless, neglected by those who define the world's architectural heritage in terms of earth, stone, masonry, and marble. This neglect derives in part from a classic definition that continues to rest on monumentality and individual creativity, and from ignorance of the reality of nomadic architecture as women's creation.

In both traditional and contemporary circumstances, women build the domestic domicile. It is they who carry responsibility for creating, pitching, maintaining, striking, and transporting the architecture. All domestic (in contrast to real) property relating to the domicile, including the tent cover, its framework, and its furnishings are in their hands and, for the most part, of their making. The loading and unloading, the construc-

Bedouins in their tent, Iraq, 1974 (Nik Wheeler/Corbis)

tion and reconstruction of the domestic household, is equally their doing.

Nomadic architectures are as permanent as any other architecture using natural resources, since the knowledge, design, technology, and materials that contribute to the finished architectural product are transmitted from one generation to another, reused, reassembled, and inherited by women via ritual behavior and belief systems as peoples move across the landscape. The creative processes remain embedded in the collective memory, and the physical components themselves constitute a poignant cultural heritage that is handed down from mother to daughter.

Indigenous nomadic architectures can be classified according to shape, material, and structural principles: the skin-covered, vertically extended conical structures such as the Lapp *kattaa* or the American Indian tepee, the felt-covered cylindrical, trellis-frame structures such as the Mongol yurt or *kibitka*, the textile or skin-covered rectangular tensile structures such as the North African Tuareg *ehen* or the Near Eastern *beyt*, and the domed, ribbed bentwood arch structures covered with mats, skins or thatch such as the West African Fulani *suudu* or the East African Somali *aqal*. These types are in response to a range of climatic conditions: Conical tents are found across the cold, northern margins of Eurasia and North America; felt-covered trellis-type tents spread out across the plateau lands of central Asia, westward to Iran; tensile structures are dispersed over the Arabian, Turkish, North African, and sub-Saharan savannahs.

The collective creation, reuse, and multiuse of women-owned building components, embedded in marriage and birthing practices, are handed down from mother to daughter through generations. Tent components acquire a symbolic, meaningful existence of their own, translated through use into ritual and metaphor. The communal aspects embodied in both ritual and the generation of metaphors are equally critical to the learning process. Such knowledge is often transmitted orally, by participation, through in-situ observation, and via the collective memory of women.

Both the transportation process and women's work in a nomadic lifestyle establish an interface between striking, transporting, and pitching a domicile. The loading, transporting, and unloading techniques and processes use the same structural elements that the tent itself is composed of. Among the Tekna and Tubu camel herders of the Sahara desert, armatures, poles, and vellums are transformed into litters and camel-loading armatures; the Inuit Eskimos turn their summer tents into winter sleds; the Siberian Koryaks wedge their sleds against building walls to resist the fierce Arctic winds; Qasqai nomads in the Near East convert their tent poles into rafts to ford swollen rivers; North American Plains Indians created travois and platforms out of their tent poles; and the Gabra in northern Kenya convert bed rails and partition screens into litters and palanquins to protect them during travel.

Nomadic architecture is a process of placemaking. It involves not only the enclosure of, but the definition of space. Nomads utilize a tightly prescribed geometric system of spatial organization within the volumetric spaces of the domicile and in the settlement pattern itself. In the seemingly featureless environments of snow or sand, where the harsh climate rapidly bleaches out color, weathers exterior surfaces, and obliterates exterior ornament, the moving architecture serves as a tightly prescribed container setting the scene with intense interior detail, vivid colors, and intricate iconography. The definition of inner-outer space expressed by this contrast provides the altar and sets the stage for the unfolding of womens' rituals. Entrances and key interior architectural elements opposite are counterpoised, equally attributed with aspects of a culture's myths of origin and symbols of cultural value. The tent interior is divided into a geometric grid or quadrants, within which predictable social, ritual, and technical activities unfold. This spatial order also reflects a gender-discrete division: the daily life of each gender unfolds in separate or segregated quarters. In the circle of a conical or domed tent, the hearth or the center pole establishes a line of bisection. In a rectangular space, the division is articulated by a pair or a row of poles. Spaces thus divided into public and private, male and female domains, are often associated with the cardinal directions. Nomadic women often define space by anthropometric measure. The hand and arm span establish the width and breadth of woven textile tent covers that dic-

tate the tent area, and the woman's height establishes the length of the bed rail used to trace the tent perimeter.

Almost always, the creation of the nomadic domicile evolves directly out of behaviors and rituals associated with the marriage ritual. For example, the word for house often derives directly from the verb for marriage itself. Embodied in these synonymous terms are the metaphors for social support in the moral sense as well as in generational continuity. Traditionally, in the course of each daughter's marriage, or the birth of each grandchild, a mother will donate architectural elements from her own tent for her daughter's new tent. The domicile of an old widow can always be recognized by its diminutive size. Continuity becomes a more vivid physical reality when the architecture is inherent in the rituals that usher in a new generation.

Nomadic architectures are frequently composed of materials that engage the same skills which other parts of the material cultural repertoire depend upon. Thus, the weaver who weaves the cloth for clothing also weaves the *flijs* that make up the North African or Near Eastern *beyt;* the felt maker who creates the felt for clothing also manufactures the felt for the *yurt;* the embroiderer who embellishes the tunic or vest also embroiders the reinforcing edges of the tent vellum and the trappings that are used to transport the tent; the basket maker who coils the reeds and grasses into containers also weaves the mats that cover both floor and roof of the domicile; the leather worker who tans the skins provided by her husband also cuts the leather trappings for the tent and often braids the multitude of ropes required to assemble it. Nomadic architectures are thus an amalgam of the arts and skills that permeate the nomadic woman's aesthetic. As a consequence, the designs and motifs used in the creation of the nomadic cultural repertoire are integrated into the built environment through the agency of women. Housing is a feminine noun, and the language of both transport technology and architecture is spoken in a woman's voice.

BIBLIOGRAPHY

Although many of the sources cited below do not explicitly address the interrelationship between women's roles and rituals and the creation of nomadic architecture, they provide the best, albeit implicit, illustrations of the subject matter discussed in this entry.

Cahiers des arts et techniques d'Afrique du Nord 4. 1955.

Casajus, Dominique. *La tente dans la solitude (Kel Ferwan).* 1987.

Creyaufmüller, Wolfgang. *Nomadenkultur in der Westsahara: Die Materielle Kultur des Mauren.* 1983.

Drew, Philip. *Tensile Architecture.* 1979.

Kharuzin, N. *History of the Dwellings of the Turkic and Mongolic Nomads of Russia* (in Russian). 1896.

Musil, Alois. *The Manners and Customs of the Ruwala Bedouins.* 1928.

Nabokov, Peter, and Robert Easton. *Native American Architecture.* 1989.

Prussin, Labelle. *African Nomadic Architecture: Space, Place, and Gender.* 1995.

Szabo, Albert, and Thomas J. Barfield. *Afghanistan: An Atlas of Indigenous Domestic Architecture.* 1991. Pp. 27–110.

LABELLE PRUSSIN

Arctic Religions

In Asia

The native peoples of Arctic Asia encompass many language families, ethnic origins, and local variations. They share a range of ecological settings, from windswept tundra along the Arctic coast to thick forests inland. In a region where crops are almost impossible to grow, all were traditionally dependent on the hunting and herding of animals. The traditional shamanistic religions were heavily repressed by the Soviet regime, and many traditional customs barely survived.

A widespread complementarity between women's and men's space extended from the interior of the tent or hut to the layout of the cosmos. Often, women and men occupied the left and right (inferior and superior) sides respectively of the dwelling, along with all the tools of their occupations such as equipment for sewing and hunting. Similarly, a man's wife or daughter might be buried to his left, his son to his right.

Many peoples understood the sky as male and the earth as female. Female spirits were located especially in streams, rivers, and forests, where they appeared to male hunters in dreams, sometimes in erotic form. Sometimes, they were the daughters of the Master of the Forest, who controls game and success in hunting.

Women's religious activity largely concerned the domestic sphere, such as tending the spirit of the hearth. Much of their activity also combined an acknowledgement of their reproductive functions with taboos associated with the bloodshed of the male activity of killing animals. These taboos often reflect a sense of the pollution and the power of menstrual blood. Among the Nenets of northwestern Russia, for example, a girl who has started menstruating can no longer touch men's implements, spirit dolls, or sacred sledges, while the

A lithograph dating from approximately 1835 depicts Siberian shamen performing a ritual (Christel Gerstenberg/Corbis).

Nenets spirit of childbirth, Yaminya, is given offerings without animal blood.

The men's hunt was everyone's main subsistence activity, and women participated in it in essential ways, such as observing various taboos while their husbands were away hunting in order to ensure the hunters' safety and success. In many parts of eastern Siberia, a woman would hang an amulet or animal skull on a thread and ask it questions, to which it would swing to answer yes or no. Among the Orochon of Sakhalin Island, north of Japan, a woman aided her husband's hunting expedition by suspending a little wooden doll in this way, narrating his route and asking it to confirm or deny various events and dangers that confronted him.

Such dolls and effigies were widely used by women of the Asian north. Among the Nenets, many women keep a doll of the spirit Myadpukuche (The Old Woman of the House). This is handed down from mother to daughter, and men are not allowed to see it or handle it. The doll is kept on the women's side of the tent and during migrations is packed on a women's sledge. In childbirth, a traditional midwife lays the doll on the woman's stomach for easy delivery. After each delivery, the mother sews new clothes for the doll and puts them on top of the old ones, so that a mother of many children will have a very fat doll.

Spirits may also be embodied in living beings. In some regions, the male bear as Lord of the Forest is killed in a rite that is highly charged with implicit sexuality. Among the Khanty of western Siberia, the bear is killed in the forest and women cover their faces when the men carry its body into the village, later kissing its snout only through a handkerchief, while never looking it in the eye. Men may dress and behave as women, and women dance to the bear but with their faces covered so that the bear's spirit cannot see any part of their bodies. Among the native peoples of Sakhalin Island, a male bear was captured as a cub and reared like a human baby, even being breastfed by the women, who would then lament it after it had been sacrificed. Throughout its captivity, the women would talk to the bear, emphasising how tenderly they were fostering it and reminding it to carry a good report about their kindness to its parents in the sky, who would then send abundant game in return.

The main religious specialist was the shaman. There were many terms for male and female shamans in various languages (the English word *shaman* is an Evenk term from the Siberian Pacific coast). Especially among the Chukchi of the far northeast, female shamans were more numerous than male, though individually less powerful. Ethnographic assessments of the power of female shamans are often contradictory. Though they could not perform the major rituals to obtain game or to honor the dead of the patrilineal clan, they were also sometimes considered more accomplished and more dangerous, perhaps because of their own capacities for menstruation and childbirth, though they were unable to practice at these times. Female shamans tended to concentrate on healing and divination, especially on foretelling the future and finding lost objects, animals, and souls. This last action resembles beating vegetation to flush out game in the hunt, a women's activity in daily life. Female shamans often invoked female spirits such as Mother-Elk or Sun-Mother.

Shamans' practice reveals a fluidity of gender identity. The male shaman's costume bears many female emblems. But female costumes generally did not contain symbols of male sexuality, such as antlers on the head. Nor did female shamans "marry" a spirit of the opposite sex to gain their powers, like some male shamans. The implication may be that the female state was regarded as more fundamentally human than the male.

Soviet rule suppressed indigenous religion and culture and promoted Western-style education for women. The role of traditional midwife was almost entirely replaced by the hospital. Women were taken off the land and placed in industrial towns, along with their children. They thus lost contact with the natural environment, and in many communities women became less traditionally oriented than those men who remained on the landscape to continue to work as hunters and reindeer herders. Since the mid-1980s, many women scholars and activists have become involved in attempts to revive traditional religion, though in a modified form since they live in the cities, have Soviet-style careers, and no longer depend on hunting. Generally speaking, their ideological base lies, not in feminism, but in ethnic revivalism and the rediscovery of spirituality.

BIBLIOGRAPHY

The copious anthropological literature in Russian contains much information about women's religion in this region, but it is very time-consuming to seek this out in books that contain no index. Few if any works in English have focused on religion, but much information will be found scattered in the following works, which discuss shamanism, hunting, and gender symbolism among native Siberian peoples: Marie Czaplicka, *Aboriginal Siberia* (London, 1914); Anna-Leena Siikala, *The Rite Technique of the Siberian Shaman* (Helsinki, 1987); Roberte Hamayon, *La chasse a l'âme: Esquisse d'une théorie du chamanisme sibérien* (Nânterre, 1990; in French, comprehensive index); Marjorie Mandelstam Balzer, *Shamanism: Soviet Studies of Traditional Religion in Siberia and Central Asia* (1990); Vilmos Diószegi and Milhály Hoppal, eds., *Shamanism in Siberia* (Budapest, 1978); Anna-Leena Siikala and Mihály Hoppal, eds., *Studies on Shamanism* (Budapest and Helsinki, 1992). A brief description of a rite of one of the last surviving traditional female shamans is given in Nadezhda Bulatova, "The Evenk *Alga* Ritual of Blessing," in Marjorie Mandelstam Balzer, ed., *Shamanic Worlds: Rituals and Lore of Siberia and Central Asia* (1997).

Two important works that focus on an area slightly south of the scope of this article are S. M. Shirokogoroff, *Psychomental Complex of the Tungus* (London, 1935), and Caroline Humphrey with Urgunge Onon, *Shamans and Elders: Experience, Knowledge and Power among the Daur Mongols* (Oxford, 1996).

There is much about the Soviet attack on women's traditional attitudes in Part III of Yuri Slezkine, *Arctic Mirrors: Russia and the Small Peoples of the North* (1994). For its consequences, see Piers Vitebsky, "Landscape and Self-determination among the Eveny: The Political Environment of Siberian Reindeer Herders Today," in Elisabeth Croll and David Parkin, eds., *Bush Base: Forest Farm: Culture, Environment and Development* (1992), and "Women Modernise while Men Go Back to the Spirits of the Land: Reindeer Herders of Siberia," in Soraya Tremanie, ed. *Women as "Sacred Custodians" of the Earth* (forthcoming).

For transvestism and transsexuality, see Waldemar Bogoras, *The Chukchi, Memoirs of the American Museum of Natural History*, vol. 11 (1909) and Marjorie Mandelstam Balzer, "Sacred Genders in Siberia: Shamans, Bear Festivals and Androgyny," in Sabrina Petra Ramet, ed., *Tender Reversals and Gender Cultures* (1996). For the bear cult, see also Irving Hallowell, "Bear Ceremonialism in the Northern Hemisphere," *American Anthropologist* 28, no. 1 (1926).

See also **Cross-dressing; Gender Roles; Shamans.**

PIERS VITEBSKY

In North America

Although the Eskimos and Aleuts fall within a distinct language family and are recognized as belonging to the same major culture area, their social organization and religious traditions show significant regional differences. This disparity reflects their wide-ranging habitat, which stretches over several thousand kilometers along the Arctic coasts of North America, Greenland, and Siberia's northeastern tip, thus making it difficult to summarize women's place in their religion. This problem has become all the more evident given that interest in the study of religion has waned among Arctic researchers since the beginning of the 1970s.

Studies on sex and gender categories and on women's status in Eskimo society are still in their infancy, despite the new theoretical and methodological tools that advancement in feminist thought has made available to researchers. There is also a growing need to consider the viewpoint of the Eskimos themselves, ever since they came together under a common political umbrella, the Inuit Circumpolar Conference (ICC), to defend their interests vis-à-vis the four nations (Russia, the United States, Canada, Denmark) within which they live. Women leaders often dominate ICC politics, to the surprise of observers. *Inuit*, the word Eskimos use to describe themselves, means "humans" in the area from northern Alaska to Greenland, albeit with local variants in Pacific, southwest Alaskan, and Siberian groups.

The Igloolik region of Canada's central Arctic is widely recognized as a focal point for religious activity. It affords great opportunities to define "womanhood" as (a) women's place in myths, rites, and shamanistic practices; and (b) feminine traits observable in the great male figures of mythology and in male shamans through actual or symbolic transvestism. Many of the great female figures are nontraditional women, a fact that led researchers to define a "third gender" as the foremost instrument of religious mediation.

Danish explorer Knud Rasmussen successfully collected accounts from the last of the Igloolik shamans between 1921 and 1924. His fluency in the language has made the quality of his ethnography unequaled, and interpretations of Inuit religion are based on his accounts. However, Rasmussen, and everyone else who has used his work, underestimated women's contribution to Inuit religion. Having mainly worked with men,

Elder Martha Harry sings while she plays the drum during the drum dance, Inuvik, Northwest Territories, Canada, 1994 (Raymond Gehman/Corbis).

he was impressed by the number of male shamans and by their public seances of shamanism in which women participated more discreetly. That women accounted for only 20 percent of all shamans does not mean, however, as is often written, that they could not accede to great shamanistic powers. On the contrary, several cases prove that some of them had powerful helping spirits and could travel to the great beyond in the heavens or under the water and therein act as mediators with the great cosmic spirits.

A dichotomy was said to exist between private, family-oriented female shamanism, geared to individual care for the sick and for women in labor, and public male shamanism, geared to hunting and the group's collective interests. Rasmussen and those citing him, however, failed to understand that the reproduction of life was a model at the core of Inuit social life and representations. Indeed, it is one of the all-encompassing metaphors of Inuit culture: cosmogenesis is conceived as a form of ontogenesis, as a pregnancy giving birth to humanity; the uterus, the igloo, and the firmament differ only in scale, as evoked time and again in myths, rites, precepts, and prohibitions. Nor did scholars see that the sexual boundary was fragile and could be crossed, or that the origin myth of the first woman—a man whose companion turned him into a woman through a magic song—reflected the belief that all infants could change sex at birth. Indeed, one to two percent of the people are presumed to be *Sipiniit* ("transsexuals"), men and women said to have the temperament of the other's sex.

This mythical differentiation of the sexes goes on to pattern all of the other great differentiations along the lines of a man/woman split: night (fox woman) and day (crow man); immortal life (man) and mortal life (woman); sun (woman) and moon (man). At the same time, the universe of myths and rites closely relates the human reproduction process (man/woman/child) to the hunting production process (hunter/Mistress of the Game Animals/game animals), a relationship that constantly stresses the necessary complementarity of the sexes.

Although Rasmussen's male informants told him that trances and shamanism were invented at the initiative of a man during a famine, female informants surveyed between 1970 and 1990 traced the invention of healing back to even older times. They say there once was an orphaned woman with two husbands who was unfit for woman's work, not knowing how to sew or prepare skins, and unable to have children. Through the assistance of her deceased parents, however, she discovered the magic power of air emitted from the body (breath, flatulence). She began to care for and heal the sick, who showed their appreciation by giving her children for adoption and preparing and sewing the skins her husbands brought her.

In actuality there is a sharing of powers between male and female entities. The male moon spirit, an incestuous brother, dispenses shamanistic clairvoyance and protects young boys, orphans, battered or sterile women, and unlucky hunters. In the ocean's depths, however, it is a woman who controls the marine mammals. They are her creatures, having originated from the transformation of her fingers—which her father had lopped off.

In Igloolik 15 to 20 percent of all children were cross-dressed to different degrees from birth to adolescence because of the name or names they had received from deceased forebears of the opposite sex. At adolescence, the cross-dressed boy was supposed to cut his braids, discard female clothing, give up household work, and learn the life of a hunter. At her first menstruation, the cross-dressed girl was similarly supposed to give up the hunting life, put on female clothing, have her face and part of her body tattooed, and learn to do female chores. This transition to adult life was much more painful for the cross-dressed than for other young people their age. Lying astraddle the gender boundary, they showed more often than others the signs of a calling for shamanism and an ability to straddle all boundaries. Fairly visible forms of transvestism and androgynous behaviors would also result from male and female shamans acquiring a helping spirit of the other sex. So, although men may have dominated Inuit social and religious life, some did so in female guise and some women nonetheless enjoyed a high profile in all political, social, and religious spheres.

BIBLIOGRAPHY

Damas, David, ed. *Arctic.* Vol. 5, *Handbook of North American Indians.* Edited by William C. Sturtevant. 1984. The most up-to-date work on Inuit anthropology in the early 1980s. Notable for inclusion of data on religious organization of the twenty-three Eskimo and Aleut regional groups. Unfortunately, the gender issue is developed very little.

Études/Inuit/Studies 10, nos. 1–2 (1986), special issue titled "On the Border of Genders"; and 14, nos. 1–2 (1990), special issue titled "Hunting, Sexes and Symbolism."

Fienup-Riordan, Ann. *Boundaries and Passages: Rule and Ritual in Yup'ik Eskimo Oral Tradition.* 1994. A stimulating contemporary work on the cosmology and ritual cycles of the Yupiit from Alaska's Bering Sea region. Structuralism has influenced the author's approach. She quotes from many accounts by women but says little about gender. See also Fienup-Riordan's *The Nelson Island Eskimo: Social Structure and Ritual Distribution.* 1983.

Giffen, Naomi Musmaker. *The Roles of Men and Women in Eskimo Culture.* 1930. The only exhaustive study on the sexual division of labor among the Inuit. Thoughtfully written, this compilation quickly addresses all aspects of the issue of women's role in religion.

Haase, Evelin. *Der Schamanismus des Eskimos.* 1987. An interesting recent compilation about Eskimo shamanism. The author has incorporated German-language publications largely unknown to the English-speaking public. She discusses the issue of female shamanism and transvestism.

Lantis, Margaret. "Alaskan Eskimo Ceremonialism." *Monographs of the American Ethnological Society* 11. Edited by Marian W. Smith. 1947. An interesting summary of Inuit rituals from Alaska, where they are much more developed than in the eastern Arctic. Discusses the role of women in religion but does not give them any special attention.

Marsh, Gordon H. "A Comparative Survey of Eskimo-Aleut Religion." *Anthropological Papers of the University of Alaska* 3, no. 1 (1954). A brief overview of the main religious concepts and beliefs and the rules of life from the Eskimo-Aleut area. Although the author addresses neither shamanism nor women's place in the myths and rites, this survey may be useful as an initial general view of the subject.

Rasmussen, Knud. *Intellectual Culture of the Iglulik Eskimos. Report of the Fifth Thule Expedition 1921–24.* 7, no. 1. 1929. The first of an exceptionally interesting series of monographs on the different regional Inuit groups. It lists taboos and precepts and describes shamanism, rites, and myths. All data were collected during conversations with shamans.

Saladin d'Anglure, Bernard. "From Foetus to Shaman: The Construction of an Inuit Third Sex." In *Amerindian Rebirth: Reincarnation Belief among North American Indians and Inuit.* Edited by Antonia Mills and Richard Slobodin. 1994. An abridged version of a longer article published in *Études/Inuit/Studies* 10, nos. 1–2 (1986) on the Inuit belief in transsexualism from birth, on the reversed socialization and cross-dressing of children, and on the social construction of a third gender.

———. "Penser le féminin chamanique, ou le 'tiers-sexe' des chamanes inuit." *Recherches Amérindiennes au Québec* 18, nos. 2–3 (1988). Addresses women's place in Inuit myths, rites, and shamanism, and the place of shamanistic mediation along the third gender axis.

Sonne, Birgitte. "The Acculturative Role of Sea Woman, Early Contact Relations Between Inuit and Whites as Revealed in the Origin Myth of Sea Woman." *Meddelelser om Grønland* (Man and Society) 13 (1990). The author raises the issue of the relationship between myth and history in regard to one of the most famous Inuit origin myths, The Mistress of the Sea Mammals. Using a history of religions perspective, she tries to show that the versions of this myth collected by the first ethnographers had already been influenced by missionaries and early voyagers. She addresses neither the gender issue nor the question of women's place in Inuit society.

Weyer, Edward Moffat, Jr. *The Eskimos: Their Environment and Folkways.* 1932. Reprint, 1962. The best systematic compilation on Eskimos at the time of its publication. It is one of the best sources for traditional religion, half the book being devoted to this topic. Its portrayal of women's place in religious rep-resentations and practices is purely descriptive and reflects the dominant ideas of that time.

See also **Dualism; Sex Change.**

BERNARD SALADIN D'ANGLURE

Art

Study of artistic images reveals cultural perceptions of gender, power, and religion. The arts are critical vehicles for both the formation of cultural and religious histories and the analysis of them. Since they evoke authority and reality in a process of sensory analogy, religious and secular images, by being internalized by the viewer and therefore known, have profound effects on individual members of a community—not least on such individuals' notions of male and female. The arts are central to the socialization process by which one enters into the societal and cultural order and signifies oneself as being male or female within that societal construct. In the contemporary world, the relationship among religion, art, and gender has become ever more complex, what with the sheer multitude of religions, cultures, and the increasing power of images through technology and globalization.

Ironically, the fallout of history, with its wars and political conflicts, is that many works of religious art, from paintings to dramas, have been lost. Misogyny and patriarchy, especially as enacted by many world religions, have played a critical role in the loss of images of women in the religious arts. The destruction of works of art—voluntarily in the instances of religious wars and iconoclasm or involuntarily in the cases of disasters such as earthquakes and fires—resulted in an irretrievable and perhaps unaccountable loss of the images of women in religious art. Simultaneously the patriarchal bias of many religious traditions led to a diminution, if not total elimination, of the iconography of women, in particular those motifs of power and authority.

ART AND GENDER

Images in works of art have made visible and tangible the cultural perceptions of appropriate and inappropriate female behavior. The recognition that images are gendered and that the prevalence of gendering through images is formative as well as reflective of cultural attitudes makes it impossible to regard images simply as benign expressions or neutral objects. Traditionally, analysis and implementation of the power of images has

A nun depicts a sacred figure at a Minas monastery. A variety of other religious works hang before her (Hans Georg Roth/Corbis).

been premised upon an overwhelmingly male-oriented framework of knowledge and scholarship. The few critical studies of the images of women in religious traditions that predate the 1970s were characteristically rich in description but lacking in critical analysis of the assumptions about women inherent in different religions and cultures. Feminist scholars of the late twentieth century have examined the symbolism of religious art to gain an understanding of women's roles both within religious traditions and in the wider culture.

RELIGIOUS ART IN A CROSS-CULTURAL CONTEXT

Traditionally, the religious arts are understood to perform certain functions: to teach the faith; to encourage spirituality and contemplation; and to beautify the spiritual environment and heighten the sensory nature of a ritual or act of devotion. The art of various religious tra-

ditions can be classed as iconic, or representative of sacral figures or ideas; aniconic, or symbolic of sacral figures or ideas; and iconoclastic, that is, the denial or destruction of images.

A rapid visual survey of the depictions of female forms of the sacred in the Eastern and Western religious arts yields a recognition of sharp distinctions between Eastern and Western conceptions of the feminine. For example, simply contrast the voluptuous goddesses of Hinduism with the typically asexual female saints of Christian art. Historically, images or descriptions of the divine in female form are found as often as those in male form. Even in male-dominated religions, such as the monotheistic traditions of Judaism, Christianity, and Islam, critical categories of female imagery exist despite women's subordinate position.

Popular practice of religions (and thereby of the religious arts) reveals the religious experience of the "non-elite," including women. Often such practice focuses upon a goddess or female saint whose story or activity is central to women's experience, from domestic activity to the conception or birth of a child.

Gendered images are more than a mode of sexual identification in the religious arts; they are a symbolic communication through gestures, postures, attributes, and signs of the common experiences of being human. A comparative or cross-cultural study of religious images, such as divine warriors or messengers, reveals the engendered interpretations of being male and female in a given religion and culture and serves to sharpen our own religious and cultural perceptions. This is especially significant for a Western viewer, who gains the scholarly realization that the categorizations and structuralisms of Western religions and cultures are not necessarily valid universally or that traditional Western concepts of both gender and the power of images must be reconsidered; the diversity of characteristics and roles in which women are represented in non-Western religious art points to the female power and creativity otherwise "lost" to monotheistic and patriarchal cultures. This is not to say that non-Western cultures are not patriarchal in social and power structures but rather that gender and power may be imaged and experienced differently. The exploration of this "difference" opens new avenues for understanding gender and power, with revised formulations in the iconology of women in religious art.

WOMEN'S PARTICIPATION IN THE ARTS

Any analysis of the images of women in religious art is dependent on an understanding of women's participation in or exclusion from the creation of that art. The use of women's lives, histories, and experiences does not ensure feminist art. Traditionally, women have been considered appropriate subjects for works of art, whether sacred or secular, but their abilities as makers, collectors, or patrons of art were contested if not simply neglected. Although women have vigorously participated in the creation and the implementation of works of art in virtually every discipline, their active roles did not garner sufficient public or scholarly notice until the modern feminist movement.

Throughout history, whenever women were in positions of power they seized the opportunity to patronize or commission works of art. Their commissions can often be distinguished in theme and presentation from those commissioned by men. For example, the iconography of the Virgin Mary in medieval Western Christian art changed significantly as a result of the illuminations created for those Books of Hours commissioned by literate medieval women. The development of the visual motif of the Annunciate Virgin reading bestowed religious legitimation upon this activity for all women. Patronizing and commissioning works of art conferred prestige on women as on men. Art was the vehicle for public signs of female power and authority, whether that of the female pharaoh Hatshepsut in ancient Egypt or of the queen Marie de Médicis (1573–1642) of France.

The long-standing distinction between elite and popular culture was mirrored by the debate about art versus craft, especially in relation to the works created by women artists. For many centuries, especially in the West, artists were often anonymous; it may be that future research will yield evidence that more among these artists were women than we might have originally believed. Nevertheless "women's art" was separated from the high art of men, so women's art flourished amid domesticity, from embroidery to tapestry to "simple" songs and hymns. Although to be sure singular women, such as the French writer Christine de Pisan (1363–c. 1431) and the Italian baroque painter Artemisia Gentileschi (1593–1652 or 1653), stood as exemplars of women's creativity and skill, it was not until the nineteenth and twentieth centuries that women's creative gifts were readily recognized and accepted and women began to be trained formally as artists. From the mid-nineteenth century to the present day, women, whether single or married, with or without children, have taken a dominant position as creators, patrons, and critics of the arts. In so doing, they have moved away from the characterization that women artists were either the daughters or wives of successful men artists, and have even begun a new tradition of women artists who are the daughters or partners of successful "mother"

artists. As creative women have sought to establish a female voice, female imagery, and a female sensibility in the arts, female creativity has become a focus of study. Feminist scholars committed to the study of images of women as sources of (women's) history have noted that this "missing history" demands a reinterpretation of traditional history.

WOMAN AS SUBJECT

Woman as subject matter for art is by definition a passive role. Women have been represented as goddesses, heroines, prophetesses, demonesses, seductresses, daughters, wives, mothers, lovers—all the established proper and fantasized improper roles as envisioned by men. Initially, in the West, female and male figures were rendered in the same manner; the specific gender of an image was clarified by the action of the narrative. As history, and hence the establishment of the monotheistic and patriarchal traditions, evolved, the iconography of women took a series of turns that matched their societal and religious subordination. The female was depicted in relation to the major elements of the life cycle: birth, initiation, marriage, reproduction, death. Having their origin in fertility figures, women's images appeared as fulfillments of societally recognized and sanctioned stages of life: the virgin, the wife, the mother, and the widow.

FEMINISM AND ART

Feminist art is not necessarily that which emphasizes only women's experience or is created only by women artists or depicts only a female image or situation. Rather, feminist art is grounded in the analyses and commitments of contemporary feminism and thereby contributes to a critique of the political, economic, and ideological power relations of contemporary society. Feminist art is subversive insofar as it questions and challenges the power and authority of patriarchy and also critiques the premises of a patriarchal culture.

That women have influenced and shaped religion and religious values in all world cultures, whether officially or privately, is without doubt; precisely how religion has influenced, shaped, oppressed, and liberated women is a new and challenging question. The arts are an integral element in that analysis, for the arts, especially the religious arts, reveal cultural values.

BIBLIOGRAPHY

Resources on the topic of women and the arts are predominantly surveys or monographs on the history of women artists in Western culture; few specialized sources exist from the perspective of world religions or non-Western cultures. Fewer sources are available on the specific themes or motifs related to the images or roles of women in the religious arts, especially with regard to non-Western religions. The relationship of creativity and gender is a relatively new field of study. The sources listed below are a sample of the types of texts and sourcebooks available.

GENERAL

Apostolos-Cappadona, Diane. *Encyclopedia of Women in Religious Art.* 1996.

Apostolos-Cappadona, Diane, and Lucinda Ebersole, eds. *Women, Creativity, and the Arts: Critical and Autobiographical Perspectives.* 1995.

Dotterer, Ronald, and Susan Bowers, eds. *Gender, Culture, and the Arts: Women, the Arts, and Society.* 1993.

ART HISTORY

Anderson, Janet A. *Women in the Fine Arts: A Bibliography and Illustration Guide.* 1991.

Bachmann, Donna G. *Women Artists: An Historical, Contemporary, and Feminist Bibliography.* 1978.

Broude, Norma, and Mary D. Garrard, eds. *The Expanding Discourse: Feminism and Art History.* 1992.

Chadwick, Whitney. *Women, Art, and Society.* 1990. 2d ed., rev. and exp., 1996.

Dunford, Penny. *A Biographical Dictionary of Women Artists in Europe and American Since 1850.* 1989.

Flowering in the Shadows: Women in the History of Chinese and Japanese Painting. 1990.

Gouma-Peterson, Thalia, and Patricia Mathews. "The Feminist Critique of Art History." *The Art Bulletin* 69, no. 3 (1987): 326–357. Specially featured bibliographic essay, "The State of Research."

Greer, Germaine. *The Obstacle Race: The Fortunes of Women Painters and Their Work.* 1979.

Harris, Ann Sutherland, and Linda Nochlin. *Women Artists, 1550–1950.* 1976. Catalogue of the first international exhibition of eighty-four women painters from the Renaissance to 1950.

Langer, Cassandra L. *Feminist Art Criticism: An Annotated Bibliography.* 1993.

Nochlin, Linda. *Women, Art, Power, and Other Essays.* 1989. See especially "Why Have There Been No Great Women Artists?".

Pettys, Chris, with the assistance of Hazel Gustow, Ferris Olin, and Verna Ritchie. *Dictionary of Women Artists: An International Dictionary of Women Artists Born before 1900.* 1985.

Rubenstein, Charlotte Streifer. *American Women Artists: From Early Indian Times to the Present.* 1982.

Turner, Jane Shoaf, ed. *The Dictionary of Art.* 1996. See especially Lisa Tickner, "Feminism and Art."

Watson-Jones, Virginia. *Contemporary Women Sculptors.* 1986.

WOMEN AS ART CRITICS, DEALERS, AND PATRONS

Collischan, Judy. *Women Shaping Art: Profiles of Power.* 1984.

Sherman, Claire Richter, and Adele M. Holcomb, eds. *Women as Interpreters of the Visual Arts, 1820–1979.* 1981.

CINEMA STUDIES

Acker, Ally. *Reel Women: Pioneers of the Cinema, 1896 to the Present.* 1991.

Apostolos-Cappadona, Diane. "From Eve to the Virgin and Back Again: The Image of Woman in Contemporary (Religious) Film." In *New Image of Religious Film.* Edited by John R. May. 1997.

Erens, Patricia, ed. *Issues in Feminist Film Criticism.* 1990.

Foster, Gwendolyn Audrey. *Women Film Directors: An International Bio-Critical Dictionary.* 1995.

Haskell, Molly. *From Reverence to Rape: The Treatment of Women in the Movies.* 1974.

Heck-Rabi, Louise. *Women Filmmakers: A Critical Reception.* 1984.

Kowaiski, Rosemary Ribich. *Women and Film: A Bibliography.* 1976.

DANCE

Adair, Christy. *Woman and Dance: Sylphs and Sirens.* 1992.

Getz, Leslie. *Dancers and Choreographers: A Selected Bibliography.* 1995.

FOLK ART

Bank, Mirra. *Anonymous Was a Woman.* 1979.

Dewhurst, C. Kurt. *Artists in Aprons: Folk Art by American Women.* 1979.

ICONOGRAPHIC STUDIES

Baring, Anne, and Jules Cashford. *The Myth of the Goddess: Evolution of an Image.* 1991.

Kuryluk, Ewa. *Veronica and Her Veil: History, Symbolism, and Structure of a "True" Image.* 1991.

Langener, Lucia. *Isis lactans-Maria lactans: Untersuchungen zur koptischen Ikonographie.* Altenberge, 1996.

Larson, Gerald J., Pratapaditya Pal, and Rebecca Gowens. *In Her Image: The Great Goddess in Indian Asia and The Madonna in Christian Culture.* 1980.

Neumann, Erich. *The Great Mother: An Analysis of an Archetype.* 1974.

Russell, H. Diane, with Bernadine Barnes. *Eva/Ave: Woman in Renaissance and Baroque Prints.* 1990.

LITERATURE

Buck, Claire, ed. *The Bloomsbury Guide to Women's Literature.* 1992.

Eigler, Frederike, and Susanne Korde, eds. *The Feminist Encyclopedia of German Literature.* 1997.

Fister, Barbara. *Third World Women's Literature: A Dictionary and Guide to Materials in English.* 1995.

Ledkovsky, Marina, Charlotte Rosenthal, and Mary Zirin, eds. *Dictionary of Russian Women Writers.* 1994.

Schlueter, Paul, and June Schlueter, eds. *An Encyclopedia of British Women Writers.* 1988.

Todd, Janet, ed. *A Dictionary of British and American Women Writers, 1660–1800.* 1985.

Wilson, Katharina M., Paul Schlueter, and June Schlueter, eds. *Women Writers of Great Britain and Europe: An Encyclopedia.* 1997.

MUSIC HISTORY

Bowers, Jane, and Judith Tick, eds. *Women Making Music: The Western Art Tradition, 1150–1950.* 1986.

Cohen, Aaron I. *International Encyclopedia of Women Composers.* 1987.

Neuls-Bates, Carol, ed. *Women in Music: An Anthology of Source Readings from the Middle Ages to the Present.* Rev. ed., 1996.

O'Brien, Lucy. *She Bop: The Definitive History of Women in Rock, Pop, and Soul.* 1996.

Sadie, Julie Anne, and Rhian Samuel, eds. *The Norton/Grove Dictionary of Women Composers.* 1994. Reprint, 1995.

PHOTOGRAPHY

Fisher, Andrea. *Let Us Now Praise Famous Women: Women Photographers in the U.S. Government, 1935–1944: Esther Bubley, Marjory Collins, Pauline Ehrlich, Dorothea Lange, Martha MacMillan Roberts, Marion Post Wolcott, Ann Rosener, Louise Rosskam.* 1987.

Palmquist, Peter E. *A Bibliography of Writings By and About Women in Photography, 1850–1990.* 1994.

Rosenblum, Naomi. *A History of Women Photographers.* 1994.

RELIGIOUS STUDIES

Adams, Doug, and Diane Apostolos-Cappadona, eds. *Art as Religious Studies.* 1987.

Miles, Margaret R. *Image as Insight: Visual Understanding in Western Christianity and Secular Culture.* 1985.

THEATER HISTORY

Ferris, Lesley. *Acting Women: Images of Women in Theatre.* 1989.

Keyssar, Helene, ed. *Feminist Theatre and Theory.* 1996.

Scolnicov, Hanna. *Woman's Theatrical Space.* 1994.

DIANE APOSTOLOS-CAPPADONA

Artemis (Diana)

Artemis is an early, ancient Greek divinity who seems to have close connections with goddesses of western Asia Minor. From the earliest times Greek sources portray her as an eternally virginal daughter of Zeus, king of the gods, who delights in hunting. This aspect of her personality also appears frequently in art, where she is represented as a "mistress of beasts" who both protects those who should not be killed (the young and the pregnant) and helps the hunter kill those that he may.

Her mythic role as a virgin is linked to her important cultic role as a goddess who helps girls make the transition into marriage and motherhood. At cult sites such as Brauron (near Athens) girls danced in Artemis's honor to ensure her good will, sometimes pretending to be the animals whom she now protected, now killed in her role as mistress of beasts. Myths tell of Artemis's anger at girls who fail to protect their virginity until marriage,

A statue of Artemis (Nik Wheeler/Corbis)

such as Callisto, or her rescue of girls who are threatened by rape or death, such as Iphigenia. Myth also tells of her destruction of men who accidentally violate her chastity, such as Actaeon, who sees the goddess naked. Because Artemis protects women who make the transition from virgin to mother properly, she is also one of the goddesses called upon during childbirth.

Artemis is well known as a moon goddess, but she assumed this role only late in the ancient world (approximately the second century B.C.E.) and perhaps primarily because her twin brother, Apollo, is associated with the sun. When the Romans adopted the Greek gods, they identified Artemis with Diana, a goddess who shared many of her attributes, including involvement with hunting and childbirth.

BIBLIOGRAPHY

An excellent overview of Artemis can be found in Walter Burkert, *Greek Religion* (1985), pp. 149–152. A good discussion of female maturation rites and the myths that express them, including those involving Artemis, is presented in K. Dowden, *Death and the Maiden* (1989); his bibliography will lead readers further.

SARAH ILES JOHNSTON

Asceticism

Asceticism involves the practice of voluntary physical austerities, abstinence from food, sexual intercourse, sleep, and often renunciation of possessions, for a spiritual purpose. Ascetic practice may be limited by time or it may be life-long, as in the case of certain ritual specialists (priests and priestesses) or monastics. In some tribal religions, shamans, inspired persons who have special contacts with the spiritual world, "clear" their bodies, minds, and spirits for the entrance of spirit-beings by fasting and abstinence from sex and sleep. While male shamans predominate in many religious traditions, there are those in which shamans are women or transvestite men, as in Japan and Korea. Often female shamans are chosen by the spirits through an illness that disrupts the expected roles of women. Ascetics may live in communities, may be mendicant or itinerant, or may withdraw totally from society, like hermits and anchorites. Some traditions, such as Hinduism, Buddhism, and Christianity treat asceticism as a valued religious behavior; others, such as the Parsis, reject it as unnatural. While women's ascetic practices have in many instances followed or paralleled those of men, they often appear to be ways of resisting cultural stereotypes of acceptable behavior.

Following the ascetic path, which requires renouncing sex, home, and family life, has been difficult for women in most religions, particularly in societies that value women's reproductive role and its regulation to ensure the survival and stability of the group. Women have undertaken this ascetic life, commonly the domain of men, in the face of many obstacles, and usually only if they have already married, borne, and raised children. Fewer women than men in ancient societies practiced life-long asceticism, and their ascetic practices were confined to austerities like fasting, rather than wandering or begging, that could be undertaken within the confines of the home. In many ancient religious traditions, priestesses and prophetesses were postmenopausal women or life-long virgins, like the Pythia, prophetess of Apollo at Delphi, and the priestesses of Artemis and Athena. Periods of sexual abstinence, fasting, and sleeplessness were required of initiates of some deities like the Egyptian goddess Isis, whose worship was widespread in the first four centuries of the common era.

HINDUISM

In the traditions of the Indian subcontinent known collectively as Hinduism, ascetic behavior (*tapas*) has been recognized since the fifth century B.C.E. as one of the acceptable stages of life for men and in some cases for women. Renunciation (*sannyasa*) prepares one for the perfect unity of the soul (atman) with the Universal Soul (*Brahman-Atman*), the ultimate knowledge that ends the cycle of reincarnation. The discipline (yoga) required for this purpose is rarely possible even for men unless the earlier stages of life—student and householder—are completed. Women, whose primary role is to marry and have children, especially sons, have seldom become *sannyasinis*, although widows can and often do lead lives of severe austerity, while older married women perform temporary ascetic vows to secure the health and long life of their husbands. Despite tales of renunciants in the Hindu literature, the role has been adopted by few Hindu women, an exception being the contemporary Satguru Swami Sri Jnananda Sarasvati, revered as both spiritual guide (guru) and renunciant.

Jainism, an Indian religion that believes taking life (*jiva*) causes one's soul to be weighed down into continuing incarnations, has always promoted a nonitinerant monastic life as most conducive to salvation, although laity also make vows. There are still orders of Jaina monastic women, but the two main sects of Jain monastics are divided over women's ability to achieve full release from reincarnation. For the Svetambaras, the nineteenth Jain saint (*tīrthaṅkara*), Mallinatha, was female, while the Digambaras deny this, believing that women, as temptations to men, are unable to undertake the monastic life.

BUDDHISM

Buddhism was the first major world religion to have an ascetic order, the *saṃgha*, founded by Gautama, the original Buddha (Enlightened One) in the sixth century B.C.E. Theravada, the oldest Buddhist tradition, continues to emphasize mendicant monasticism as the preferred road to enlightenment. The Buddha was reluctantly persuaded by his disciple Ananda, influenced by the ascetic example of Gautama's aunt Mahapajapati and five hundred other women, to allow an order of Buddhist nuns (*bhikṣuṇīs*), adding eight vows that put the women under control of the men. Early Buddhist female monastics of India produced a number of hymns celebrating their enlightenment, the *Therigatha* (*Songs of the Sisters*). Buddhist monastic life for women died out in India but continued to flourish in China, Korea, and Japan, where nuns still follow traditional asceticism. Theravada countries such as Sri Lanka and Thailand do not ordain nuns, but women follow an ascetic life either at home or in the temple as *jis*, ascetic women. Tantric or Vajrayāna Buddhism counts among its many "accomplished" women ascetics (*siddhis*) Yeshe Tsogyel (c. 757–c. 817), who was instrumental in bringing Buddhist teaching to Tibet.

JUDAISM AND CHRISTIANITY

The traditional emphasis in Judaism upon family life makes marriage a mitzvah (commandment) and the choice of an ascetic life rare, even for those scholars, almost entirely male, who are devoted to the study of the Law (Torah). Before receiving the Torah at Sinai, the Israelites are cautioned by Moses not to "go near a woman" (Exod. 19:15), while the prophet Jeremiah is told by God never to marry in order to dedicate himself fully to the divine task of prophecy (Jer. 16:2). Unmarried prophets in Israel were rare, however, and unmarried prophetesses are not recorded. Only the philosopher Philo (first century C.E.) mentions a Jewish ascetic community, the Therapeutes, which included unmarried male and female scholars.

The early Christian apostle Paul prized the unmarried and abstinent state as fitting all Christians who carry on the work of Christ. Paul's followers, however, believing women better suited to marriage and childbearing, cautioned against an ascetic lifestyle for all except elderly widows. Under the influence of teachings like those of the fourth-century monk Anthony of Egypt, male and female Christian renunciants lived a severely ascetic life as solitaries in the desert or in like-

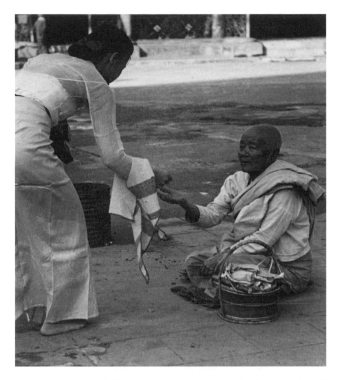

A Burmese Buddhist nun accepts a gift from a local woman. Like their male counterparts, nuns follow an ascetic life. They have no money, very few possessions of their own, and depend on gifts of food for their one meal of the day (Hulton-Deustch Collection/Corbis).

minded communities. Eventually, the wandering or withdrawn ascetics were gathered into communities, with nuns completely enclosed and under the supervision of male clerics. The abbesses or foundresses of certain female monastic orders, however, had great authority over their own domains and influenced male religious leaders. Orders of nuns continue to practice both an active and contemplative ascetic life in the Catholic and Eastern Orthodox churches. Except for radical sects like the Shakers, which flourished in the United States during the nineteenth century, Protestant Christians, since their break with Roman Catholicism in the sixteenth century, have eschewed asceticism for clergy and laity alike.

ISLAM

Islam encourages a stable family in most of its sects. All Muslims are enjoined to practice forms of asceticism, avoiding the display of costly clothing and jewelry, fasting during the month of Ramadan, shunning alcohol, and abstaining from food, sex, and ornament during certain periods of the hajj, the journey to Mecca. Only practitioners of the Sufi tradition, at its height from the eighth to twelfth centuries, among whom the most famous woman is the poet Rabi'ah al-'Adawiyyah (d. 801), believed a stringently ascetic life was needed to achieve spiritual communion with the heavenly Beloved, God.

BIBLIOGRAPHY

Cohen, Shaye. "Asceticism." In *Universal Jewish Encyclopedia.* 1969.

Denton, Lynn Teskey. "Varieties of Hindu Female Asceticism." In *Role and Rituals for Hindu Women.* Edited by J. Leslie. 1991.

Falk, Nancy Auer, and Rita M. Gross, eds. *Unspoken Worlds: Women's Religious Lives.* 1989.

Gross, Rita M. "Yeshe Tsogyel: Enlightened Consort, Great Teacher, Female Role Model." *Tibet Journal* 7, no. 4 (Winter 1987):1–18.

Kendall, Laurel. *Shamans, Housewives, and Other Restless Spirits: Women in Korean Ritual Life.* 1985.

Mernissi, Fatima. *Beyond the Veil: Male-Female Dynamics in Modern Muslim Society.* Rev. ed., 1987.

Miles, Margaret R. *Practicing Christianity: Critical Perspectives for an Embodied Spirituality.* 1988.

Paul, Diana Y. *Women in Buddhism: Images of the Feminine in Mahayana Tradition.* 1979.

Sharma, Arvind, ed. *Today's Woman in World Religions.* 1994.

———. *Women in World Religions.* 1987.

Smith, Margaret. *Rabia the Mystic and Her Fellow Saints in Islam.* 2d ed., 1984.

Wimbush, Vincent L., and Richard Valantasis, eds. *Asceticism.* 1995.

GAIL CORRINGTON STREETE

Asherah

Asherah is a mother goddess of West Semitic origin, known from fourteenth-century B.C.E. Ugaritic texts from the coast of northern Syria, Akkadian and Hittite documents, South Arabian and Judean inscriptions, and the Bible. In the Ba'al cycle from Ugarit, she is the consort of the high god 'El, mother of a variety of deities, and compassionate intercessor. The suggested etymology of her name is complex: shining (S. Arabian), happy, rich (Hebrew), walk, advance, trample (Ugaritic). Her titles may include Athirat of the Tyrians and the Goddess of the Sidonians, Great Lady Who Treads the Sea, Lady of Voluptuousness and Happiness, and Lady of Patient Mercy. She appears as consort of Amurru, another West Semitic high god, and in one Aramaic inscription she is related to the southern region of Tema(n), of interest because in biblical traditions Tema(n) is especially associated with the Israelite god (Hab. 3:3). In the Hurrian-Hittite myth called "El, Ashertu and the Storm-God," she presents a significant variant for the episode of Potiphar's Wife (cf. Gen. 39; Egyptian "Tale of Two Brothers").

Asherah appears forty times within the Hebrew Bible, the word sometimes preceded by the definite article. It is not clear whether these references refer to the goddess herself or to her cult object, a sacred, stylized tree or wooden pole. It may be that only with later reform efforts undertaken in the pre-Exilic period (prior to 587 B.C.E.) by the Judean group called the Deuteronomistic historians (twenty-four references occur within their materials) that the worship of Asherah came to be viewed as foreign and illicit. The Bible associates her with the (censured) activity of two queens: Maacah makes a special item for her cult object in 1 Kings 15:13 (=2 Chron. 15:16); Jezebel houses four hundred prophets of Asherah in her court (1 Kings 18:19). Asherah may have been the particular focus of worship by queen mothers (Hebrew, *Gebîrâ*), since in mythology she is the one who suckles (i.e., creates) kings. The Jerusalem Temple housed a group of women who wove clothing for "the asherah" (the goddess or her cult object?), later abolished by King Josiah's reforms (2 Kings 23:4–7). Significantly, prophets like Hosea, known for their condemnation of foreign or fertility-based worship, seldom mention her (see Isa. 17:8, 27:9; Jer. 17:2; Mic. 5:13), which may mean that she enjoyed widespread popularity in Israel and Judah as the "legal" (official or respected) consort of Yahweh (whose persona is, after all, a composite of elements found in the Ugaritic deities 'El and Ba'al, and who shares a connection both to Teman and Amurru).

Inscriptions from Judean sites Khirbet el-Qom (near Hebron between the mountains and the coast) and Kuntillet 'Ajrud (northern Sinai), both dated to the eighth century B.C.E., make reference to the blessing of so-and-so "by Yahweh and his Asherah" ("Yahweh of Samaria" in the Kuntillet 'Ajrud find). Grammatical difficulties preclude a decision about whether this is the goddess or her cultic tree-pole, but in either case her presence seems to be both normative and intimately connected with Yahweh. Tree of Life imagery for Lady Wisdom in Proverbs 1–9 may be a literary survival of Asherah's former prominence.

BIBLIOGRAPHY

Ackerman, Susan. "The Queen Mother and the Cult in Ancient Israel." *Journal of Biblical Literature* 112 (1993): 385–401.

Hadley, Judith M. "Yahweh and 'His Asherah': Archaeological Evidence for the Cult of the Goddess." In *Ein Gott Allein.* Edited by W. Dietrich and M. A. Klopfenstein. Göttingen, 1994.

Maier, W. A. *Asherah: Extrabiblical Evidence.* Harvard Semitic Monographs 37. 1986.

Margalit, Baruch. "The Meaning and Significance of Asherah." *Vetus Testamentum* 40 (1990): 264–297.

Olyan, Saul M. *Asherah and the Cult of Yahweh in Israel.* Society of Biblical Literature Monograph Series 34. 1988.

CAROLE R. FONTAINE

Asian and Asian-American Traditions

The traditions of Asian (North) American reveal heterogeneity and complexity of a diverse group that do not subscribe to a set of regulating ideals of cultural identity or integration. The adherents of Asian American traditions are for the most part descendants and mixed-race of Asian Pacific Islanders (API); their ancestors were immigrants and refugees who spoke little or no English and were affiliated with Buddhism, Christianity, Confucianism, Islam, Shamanism, Sufism, Taoism, and numerous other "folk" religions and spiritualities. Given the diversity and transnationality of their adherents, Asian American traditions resist formal canonization and abstract doctrine.

Asian American traditions are constantly forming and reforming as their constituency shifts and changes and as they are infused with new voices and perspectives. Both the motif and experience of pilgrimage is central to the spirituality of these traditions. This emphasis on pilgrimage is to be understood as a bridge between people's diverse lived experiences in the context of (North) American social locations and their collective memories of a shared Asian heritage. Pilgrimage also signals the need to reinvent alternative and holistic traditions neither solely Asian nor solely American. Asian American traditions include "practices that are partly inherited, partly modified, as well as partly invented" (Lowe, 1996, p. 65). As part of the development of Asian American culture, these practices have emerged to challenge the dominant representations of Asian and Asian American traditions as "other."

BIBLIOGRAPHY

Amerasia Journal 2, no. 1 (1996). Special issue: "Racial Spirits."

Asian Women United of California. *Making Waves: An Anthology of Writing By and About Asian American Women.* 1989.

Constable, Nicole. *Christian Souls and Chinese Spirits: A Hakka Community in Hong Kong.* 1994.

Journal of Asian and Asian American Theology 2, no. 1 (1997). Special issue edited by Pui-lan Kwok.

Kim, Jung Ha. "Sources Outside of Europe: 'Accidental Tourists' and Spiritual Matchmakers." In *Spirituality and the Secular Quest.* Edited by Peter H. Van Ness. 1996.

Lowe, Lisa. *Immigrant Acts: On Asian American Cultural Politics.* 1996.

Women of South Asian Descent Collective. *Our Feet Walk the Sky: Women of the South Asian Diaspora.* 1993.

JUNG HA KIM

Astrology

Astrology is a symbolic system that postulates a meaningful relationship between earthly and celestial phenomena. It is based on the belief that the universe is an organic whole in which the motions and configurations of the planets and stars, believed to be divine beings, influence human events. The interpretation of and the means for propitiating these movements usually were studied and guarded by priesthoods. As a textual tradition astrology requires literacy and thus historically has been closed to women. (Several exceptions to this rule come from Asia, including the Chinese princess Wen Cheng who, through her marriage to King Srongsten Gampo, influenced Tibetan astrology, and Empress Wu and the Korean queen Sondok, both of whom erected observatories.) As opposed to the natural or spontaneous forms of divination that were open to women, astrology is classified as a "scientific" form, and therefore placed in the hands of men.

Early Christianity attempted to break free of this belief system by stressing that baptism protected one from astrological influences, but astrologers continued to function, albeit under frequent threat of excommunication. In Buddhism and Hinduism astrology often has been in the hands of monks and priests who are consulted by the laity, especially before marriages.

Most astrological systems have been based on a primordial duality described in terms of gender. This duality is sometimes perceived as a necessary complementarity—you need both in order to have anything; just as often, though, such pairings are oppositional. Dualities, whether complementary or oppositional, are cultural constructions and thus tend to be hierarchical, with one side inevitably evaluated as better than the other. The system becomes a subtle, and sometimes not so subtle,

Illustration depicting a view of the heavens with the constellation Virgo (Corbis-Bettmann).

support for the control or oppression of one gender by the other.

The Western system of the individual's horoscope as we know it today began when the ancient Greeks applied their mathematical skills to centuries of Babylonian observational data (c. fourth century B.C.E.). Some of the earliest ideas about gender and astrology were articulated by the great Greek synthesizer, Ptolemy (fl. 127 B.C.E.–48 C.E.), whose *Tetrabiblos* remains the primary classical work on astrology, and which influenced European, Islamic, and Asian systems. Ptolemy, and most other astrologers, used the zodiac, an integrated system of twelve constellations referred to by astrological signs, such as Aries and Taurus, and the planets, including the sun and the moon. Both the astrological signs of the zodiac and the planets are divided by gender: alternating signs are male and female (e.g., Aries is male, Taurus is female), while planets such as the moon and Venus are usually female and the sun and Mars are male. Ptolemy followed Aristotle's theory that the universe, including human beings, is constructed from four elements: dry, cold, hot, and moist. Dry and hot are masculine, moist and cold female. Correspondingly, air and fire signs are masculine, water and earth signs feminine; the sun, being hot and dry, is masculine, the moon, cool and moist, feminine. Going further, the sun is diurnal and therefore active, the moon nocturnal and passive. Though Ptolemy presented astrology as a deductive science, we are left with the familiar duality of female as passive and dark and male as active and light. As this suggests, astrology was vigorously heterosexist, viewing lesbianism and homosexuality as symptomatic of afflicted astral configurations. Significantly, the gendered ideology of astrology had a tremendous influence on medical theory and practice, which understood illness as an imbalance of bodily, and therefore gendered, elements.

Astrological ideas and techniques spread from Greece to India in the early centuries of the common era, during which astrology became an extremely popular form of prognostication. A classical work of Indian astrology is the *Bṛihatjātaka* of Varāha Mihira (c. sixth century), which essentially follows Ptolemy's gender distribution for astrological signs and planets (chapter 4). One of the significant modifications made in the Indian tradition was the addition of *nakṣatras*, or lunar mansions for predictive purposes. This is an integrated system of stars through which the moon (the male deity Soma) travels, with each star thought to be inhabited by one of his twenty-eight wives with whom he spends one night each month. Ancient China had a similar, possibly Indian-influenced, system, though the moon is decidedly feminine in China.

Some of these techniques were passed from India on to the Arab world, possibly as early as the seventh century, where they met with Hellenistic practices and texts that had been preserved in Persia. They then traveled into Europe through the Muslim cultures of Spain and Sicily. Through Buddhism, Indian astrology entered Tibet, China, Japan, and other parts of Southeast and East Asia. In each case, the new astrological ideas were integrated with preexisting indigenous astral and calendrical beliefs and practices.

The ideas of Alan Leo (1860–1917) came to dominate modern astrology in Europe and the United States. Leo played down the predictive side of astrology and instead emphasized its esoteric meaning within the teachings of the Theosophical Society, which, with its many chapters throughout the world, helped spread his name and publications.

Leo elaborates the gendered ideology of astrology in *The Art of Synthesis* (1912; repr. 1949; see esp. pp. 28–51), a guide to interpreting horoscopes. For instance, he says that exoterically the sun represents men, particularly the father, the husband, and authority figures, while the moon represents women, particularly the mother and the wife. From the esoteric point of view, both the sun and the moon represent aspects of the self—though, not surprisingly, it is the male sun which represents the higher self while the female moon represents the lower self.

In the United States Evangeline Adams (1865–1932) became the great popularizer of astrology. Like Alan Leo, she made her living from astrology; she published several popular books on the subject (some of which are still in print, including *Astrology for Everyone* [1931; repr. 1972]) and was arrested in 1914 for fortune telling. The trial gave her an enormous amount of publicity, especially when she was acquitted on account of having shown the astronomical basis of astrology and successfully interpreted the horoscope of the judge's son in court (*New York Criminal Reports*, vol. 32, December 11, 1914, p. 343). Most of Adams's descriptions of the signs are directed toward men, but from time to time she makes some telling remarks about the different effects the signs have on women and men. For instance, she describes the Aries man as having a natural gift for leadership, but the Aries woman is warned that she must guard against being too dictatorial; indeed women should forget their leadership abilities, or at least pretend to, so men will be attracted to them (pp. 31–37).

Today astrology remains a popular means of disseminating both ancient religious and contemporary occult and New Age ideologies about women. Its rich gendered imagery and interpretations of that imagery, though often muddled, tend to hew to the familiar line of the female as passive support or helpmate to the active male. The frequent use of this symbol system for purposes of divination leads to a tacit acceptance of their meanings. Astrological ideas, though they often advance the spiritual superiority of women, do not favor actual women, but instead promote unrealistic and unattainable, to say nothing of possibly undesirable, models of womanhood.

BIBLIOGRAPHY

For the various astral systems of the ancient world, see Robert Brown's *Researches into the Origin of the Primitive Constellations of the Greeks, Phoenicians and Babylonians,* 2 vols. (London, 1899–1900); Ptolemy's *Tetrabiblos,* bilingual ed., translated by F. E. Robbins (1940); *Ancient Astrology Theory and Practice: The Mathesis of Firmicus Maternus,* translated by Jean Rhys Bram (1975); and Franz Cumont, *Astrology and Religion Among the Greeks and Romans,* (1912; repr., 1960). For their scientific background, see Otto Neugebauer's *The Exact Sciences in Antiquity* (1951; repr., 1969). For the *nakṣatras* and general Indian views, see Varāha Mihira, *Brihat Jataka,* bilingual ed., translated by Bangalore Suryanarian Rao (1918; 5th ed., New Delhi, 1986); and Robert De Luce, *Constellational Astrology According to the Hindu System* (1963). Edward H. Schafer's *Pacing the Void: T'ang Approaches to the Stars,* presents a wonderful view of Chinese astrology and is useful for its abundance of information on stories of Star Women and the meaning of female stars and for elucidating the connections between astral beliefs with Taoist practice (1977; see esp pp. 131–148 and 232–233, and the chap. on the moon, pp. 171–210). See also Raoul Birnbaum, "Introduction to the Study of T'ang Buddhist Astrology: Research Notes on Primary Sources and Basic Principles," in *Society for the Study of Chinese Religions Bulletin,* no. 8 (Fall 1980): 5–19. An extremely accessible introduction to various Tibetan astrological systems is *Tibetan Astronomy and Astrology: A Brief Introduction,* no editor, published by the Astrology Department of the Tibetan Medical and Astrological Institute (Dharmasala, 1995). P. V. Kane's monumental *History of the Dharmaśāstra* (vol. 5, part I) contains a rich and wide-ranging history of astronomy, astrology, and calendar systems (Poona, 1974). Marcel Griaule offers an intriguing view of African zodiacal ideology among the astronomically sophisticated Dogon people in *Conversations with Ogotemmêli: An Introduction to Dogon Religious Ideas* (1965), pp. 209–216. Serinity Young, "Stars," in *The Encyclopedia of Religion,* vol. 14 (1987), pp. 42–46 is a typology of religious beliefs about stars, various constellation systems, and zodiacs.

Jim Tester, *A History of Western Astrology* (1987), is an excellent historical study. Ellic Howe, *Urania's Children: The Strange World of the Astrologers* (1967), brings the history of astrology into the twentieth century and is particularly interesting for its descriptions of the uses of astrology in Germany before and during the Nazi period.

Helen Lemay's "The Stars and Human Sexuality: Some Medieval Scientific Views," *Isis* 71, no. 256 (March 1980): 127–137, contains a useful discussion of gender and sexuality issues in medieval Islamic astrology and has references to ancient and medieval European astrology.

Also by Alan Leo is *How to Judge a Nativity* (repr. 1983).

SERINITY YOUNG

Athena (Minerva)

Known in Greece since the second millennium B.C.E. as a citadel goddess, Athena is primarily a protective deity, a guardian of high places such as the Athenian Acropolis or the Capitoline in Rome as well as a protectress of heroes (e.g., Odysseus, Herakles, Theseus, Jason). In texts and imagery she is represented as a martial figure, armed with helmet, shield, spear, and her father's aegis (breastplate) to which the gorgoneion (head of Medusa) is often attached. Born from the head of Zeus after he swallowed his pregnant consort Metis (Wise Counsel), Aeschylus has her state in *Eumenides*: "There is no mother anywhere who gave me birth and, but for marriage, I am always for the male with all my heart, and strongly on my father's side" (Richmond Lat-

Ancient Roman statue of Athena wearing a helmet (Mimmo Jodice/Corbis).

timore trans., 736–740). Her reputation for technical skill (*sophia*) derived not only from warfare but also from handicrafts, as in the contest with the weaver Arachne. At her chief festival in Athens, the Panathenaia, her cult statue was presented with a robe (peplos) specially woven by select women of Athens. As tutelary goddess of the city, she was associated with its small owls and the olive tree, her gift to Athens in a contest with Poseidon. A virgin goddess, Athena nonetheless served a quasi-maternal role in the rearing of the earth-born Athenian king Erichthonios. Given her strong allegiance to males, namely her father and most mythological heroes, Athena was always a popular deity in the patriarchal, male-centered world of ancient Greece.

BIBLIOGRAPHY

Blundell, Sue. *Women in Ancient Greece.* 1995. Pp. 26–29.

Kerenyi, Karl. *Athene: Virgin and Mother in Greek Religion.* 1978.

Lexicon Iconographicum Mythologiae Classicae II. 1984.

Neils, Jenifer. *Goddess and Polis: The Panathenaic Festival in Ancient Athens.* 1992.

Simon, Erika. *Die Götter der Griechen.* 3d ed., 1985. Pp. 179–212.

———. *Die Götter der Römer.* 1990. Pp. 168–181.

JENIFER NEILS

Athletics

Athletics and religion are associated in a number of the world's religious traditions, but most prominently in ancient Greek culture, in which the gods themselves engage in athletic contests and sanction human sporting events. Famous among the mythic traditions is that of Atalanta, associated with the goddess Artemis. Atalanta was a great runner and huntress, who offered to marry any man who could outrun her; those who lost, she speared. She was finally defeated by Hippomenes, with the assistance of the goddess Artemis; Atalanta's and Hippomenes' child was one of the Seven who fought against Thebes after the death of Oedipus.

Homer's *Iliad* offers the earliest extended account of a human sporting event, the funeral games for Patroclus. The famous Olympic Games, honoring the god Zeus, were among four sets of games, the others taking place at Delphi, Corinth, and Nemea. Winners received religious and literary honors (as the commemoration of athletes in Pindar's odes attests), as well as material rewards. Women did not participate, and it seems that the only women spectators were female religious functionaries. The women of Sparta did take part in some athletic competitions, and according to Pausanius (second century C.E.), women's games in honor of Hera took place at Olympia.

The emperor Theodosius suppressed the Olympic games as a "pagan rite," signaling the predominant Christian attitude toward these contests. Beginning with Paul's letters, however, early Christians used athletics as a metaphor for understanding the life of the Christian. The metaphor was particularly apt for describing the early Christian martyrs, whose deaths were understood as their reception of the "palm of victory." This extends to both men and women, sometimes creating tensions when athletic practices conflict with gender expectations. In the third-century *Passion of Saints Perpetua and Felicitas*, for example, the soon-to-be-martyred Perpetua describes a dream in which she strips down and wrestles an Egyptian opponent—but before she can do so she becomes a man. She interprets her victory over the Egyptian as evidence that she will be martyred and thus achieve victory over her pagan oppressors.

Despite negative attitudes toward athletics in the early Christian period, there is evidence that sporting events dedicated to the Virgin Mary or other religious figures occurred in the medieval and early modern periods. The association of athletics and religion reemerges most distinctively, however, in nineteenth-century England and the ideal of "muscular Christianity." The new emphasis on physical, as well as mental and spiritual, vigor manifests itself in the rise of sports clubs for boys and men. The first cricket club for women appeared in 1887, yet women's participation, not surprisingly, lagged far behind that of men. Men's sporting associations played a crucial role in British imperialism, where indigenous games—particularly those viewed as sexual or magical—were replaced with soccer, cricket, and hockey.

As the history of the modern Olympic games demonstrates, women's participation in athletics has increased dramatically over the course of the twentieth century. The modern Olympics were conceived as a movement to replace military and economic rivalry with competition on the playing fields and, like military and economic contests, as taking place between men. From the beginning, however, women pushed for admittance. At Paris in the second Olympic games of 1900, women competed in golf and lawn tennis, and archery was added in the 1904 St. Louis games. By the time the Olympics returned to Paris in 1924, more than 100 women took part, competing in fencing, swimming, and lawn tennis. Women's track and field was introduced in Amsterdam in 1928, with 290 women participating in the games. These numbers continued to increase with each Olympic meeting, as did the number of sports in which women were eligible to compete. By the summer games of 1996, the U.S. press was devoting as much attention to women athletes as to men (in part because of the greater medal prospects among the U.S. women athletes).

The modern Olympic games are not tied to any specific religious beliefs or practices, and yet they arguably constitute a religious spectacle, one that propounds—for its Western observers, at least—the values of liberal democracy. The mythologizing of the modern athlete is perhaps even more apparent in late-twentieth-century advertising, where the malleability of the human body and the ascendance of the human will is celebrated through images of finely toned male and female athletes. Rather than athletics' serving as a metaphor for salvation through asceticism, the athletic body itself becomes the salvific goal to which we can all aspire—with the right pair of shoes.

BIBLIOGRAPHY

Boutilier, Mary A., and Lucinda SanGiovanni, eds. *The Sporting Woman.* 1983.

Guttmann, Allen. *Women's Sports: A History.* 1991.

Huizinga, Johan. *Homo Ludens: A Study of the Play Element in Culture.* 1950.

Lenskyj, Helen. *Out of Bounds: Women, Sport, and Sexuality.* 1986.

Musurillo, H. R., trans. "The Passion of Ss. Perpetua and Felicitas." In *The Acts of the Christian Martyrs.* 1972.

Nelson, Mariah Burton. *Are We Winning Yet? How Women Are Changing Sports and Sports Are Changing Women.* 1991.

See also **Perpetua and Felicity.**

AMY HOLLYWOOD

Auspicious and Inauspicious

Deriving from the concept of good omen or sign, the root word *auspice* connotes kindly or favorable patronage; by extension, *auspicious* refers to signs whereby the favor of Heaven, the gods, or other source of sacred power may be discerned. An examination of major world religious traditions, particularly Judaism, Islam, Hinduism, and Buddhism, along with data from folk traditions, suggests a high degree of similarity in the interpretation, if not application, of the concept. In the context of ritual performance, persons, offerings, and actions deemed pure or purifying are defined as auspicious in that their presence augurs well for the outcome of the ritual; examples include the confession of sins in Catholicism, Shinto ritual washing of the mouth and hands, and the observation of fasting in many traditions. Similarly, objects or actions deemed polluted are inauspicious insofar as their presence taints other participants or even the ritual itself.

Women's bodies and social status weigh heavily in the ascription of auspiciousness or inauspiciousness to religiously significant events. Virginal brides are understood as pure, and weddings are generally considered to be auspicious events; exceptions occur when a bride is menstruating, a polluting event which, in Chinese folk traditions, for example, augurs poorly for the future of the match. As discussed below, menstruation—or the possibility of its onset—often renders a woman's presence inauspicious, in turn barring her from entry into sacred precincts, such as mosques and Hindu temples, or keeping her at a distance from the central shrine, as in Theravadin Buddhist temples. Widows, tainted by their association with the polluted corpse (as well as by the "death" of their controlled social status and confined sexuality), are themselves often deemed polluted; funerals are commonly characterized as inauspicious events.

Linking and defining purity-efficacy over and against impurity-inauspiciousness, however, blurs critical distinctions between the latter two concepts, as well as between auspiciousness and purity. Orthodox Judaism and Hinduism provide the examples of childbirth, being simultaneously highly auspicious and dangerously polluting. Another striking example of the conjunction of auspiciousness and pollution is provided by Frédérique Apfel Marglin's study of *devadāsīs* (female servants of the deity) at a Hindu temple in Puri devoted to Jagannatha, a form of the god Vishnu. The *devadāsīs* are called "auspicious women" (*mangala nari*) in part because they are considered married to god, who is eternal—thus they will never become inauspicious widows. They are the ones who dance and sing "auspicious songs" (*mangala gita*), yet they are never permitted to enter the inner sanctum of the temple—a prohibition stemming from their courtesan status and the impurity of their active sexuality.

Close analysis of particular religious rituals reveals the complexity of relationality between these oppositional poles. James Watson's work on funerary practice in rural Hong Kong demonstrates the management of death pollution as encompassing both the dissipation of its disruptive potential and the transformation of its destructive power into auspicious and creative energy: during a man's funeral, his daughters-in-law will rub their unbound hair (itself a symbol of polluting sexuality) over the coffin to ensure their fertility and the continuity of the family line.

Without any ritual performance, then, the categories of auspiciousness and inauspiciousness and purity and pollution may be simultaneously present; in the East Asian context, ancestor veneration comprises these categories in ever-mutating combinations. Death is polluting, as are the funeral ritual and chief participants, yet the ritual goal is to inaugurate the transformation of all participants, living and dead, into auspicious entities. The life force of the deceased crosses over into the bones of a man's descendants, and as the flesh decays, the inauspicious corpse becomes an ever-more auspicious, that is "pure," ancestor.

A rather different interpretation of the convergence and transformation of pollution and inauspiciousness in traditional Chinese culture adheres to deceased females and is found in the traditional uses of the Buddhist *Blood Bowl Sutra*. The sutra itself, of Chinese origin, describes all women as destined for torment in the Hell of the Bloody Pond—retribution for having polluted the earth god with the blood of childbirth and for having offended all the gods and holy individuals by sullying the earth's waters through washing menstrual cloths. Penances are described in the text, some of which later formed the basis for ceremonies undertaken by filial sons in order to free their deceased mothers from the terrible bonds of their karmic status. Paradoxically, traditions developed around the sutra such that the text came to have talismanic properties: its recitation could save the souls of dead women from the Bloody Pond; belief in the sutra could lead a woman to rebirth in the Western Paradise (i.e., acceptance of the inherent pollution of the female body is auspicious and yields liberation from it); and the physical text could be used as an amulet to guarantee a pregnant woman a safe delivery, and, if kept on her person, could guarantee a woman that her offerings to the Buddha, even if made while in an impure state, would be as pleasing, acceptable, and auspicious as if there were no pollution.

Recent years have brought signs of changing attitudes toward the female body as both polluted and inauspicious. In Taiwan the ceremony of "breaking the blood bowl" is still practiced at many funerals, but in Japan, despite the presence of "bloody ponds" at some temples, belief in the menstruation sutra (*Blood Bowl Sutra*) is virtually nonexistent. Finally, unpublished preliminary research by anthropologist Lingling Weng suggests that young Taiwanese women in the late 1990s, in sharp contrast to women of their mothers' generation, no longer see menstruation as polluting or as an inauspicious obstacle to temple worship—especially when the deity, like themselves, is female.

BIBLIOGRAPHY

Adler, Rachel. "Tumah and Taharah: Ends and Beginnings." In *The Jewish Woman: New Perspectives.* Edited by Elizabeth Koltun. 1976.

Carman, John B., and Frédérique Apfel Marglin, eds. *Purity and Auspiciousness in Indian Society.* 1985.

Marglin, Frédérique Apfel. "Female Sexuality in the Hindu World." In *Immaculate and Powerful: The Female in Sacred Image and Social Reality.* Edited by Clarissa W. Atkinson, Constance H. Buchanan, and Margaret R. Miles. 1987.

———. *Wives of the God-King: The Rituals of the Devādasīs of Puri.* 1985.

Seaman, Gary. "The Sexual Politics of Karmic Retribution." In *The Anthropology of Taiwanese Society.* Edited by Emily Martin Ahern and Hill Gates. 1981.

Takemi, Momoko. " 'Menstruation Sutra' Belief in Japan." *Japanese Journal of Religious Studies* 10, nos. 2–3 (1983): 229–246.

Watson, James L. "Of Flesh and Bones: The Management of Death Pollution in Cantonese Society." In *Death and the Regeneration of Life.* Edited by Maurice Bloch and Jonathan Parry. 1982.

See also Devadāsīs.

VIVIAN-LEE NYITRAY

Authority

Authority denotes the power to privilege opinions or actions selectively. Though religions usually encompass many interpenetrating (and sometimes indissociable) forms of authority (including political authority, the authority generated by reasoned argument, and the implicit authority of custom), specifically religious authority derives its ultimate sanction from a divine or cosmic source. By linking them to such a source, religions often clothe the bearers of other forms of authority with religious authority. The absolute, superhuman character of its source differentiates religious authority and leads some scholars to posit a causal connection between religion and violence.

Events, texts, and persons can wield religious authority. Both uncontrived and induced events can privilege opinions or actions. The interpretation of the behavior of wild birds (ornithomancy), for instance, carried authority in the Greco-Roman world. Many cultures have developed intricate astrologies that interpret the movements of the stars and planets. Medieval Christians, on the other hand, frequently conducted divinatory lotteries (sortilege), and the Azande of Africa poison a fowl and observe the effects to discern the influence of witchcraft.

Texts of various sorts also bear religious authority. Myths often derive their authority from their purported contemporaneity with their subject matter: the origin of the cosmos. Other myths and religious texts, like the Bible and the Qur'an, claim authority on the basis of inspiration or revelation. Some texts, moreover, derive their religious authority from other texts. The Laws of Manu, an ancient Indian ethical treatise, demonstrates how many texts employ multiple strategies to authorize themselves. Manu, the superhuman narrator, explains how Brahmā, the self-existent creator of the cosmos, taught him the contents of the text. The Laws of Manu also, however, authorizes itself and the prescriptions it contains by establishing a connection to the Vedas, the most ancient and sacred Indian texts. The eternal and fathomless Vedas, which mirror and inform the cosmos, contain all knowledge, Manu argues, so the duties it prescribes carry Vedic authority. This strategy, significantly, has a reciprocal effect. Manu, while authorizing itself through the Vedas, also serves to reinforce the authority of the Vedas. Manu concludes by inveighing against non-Vedic teachings.

Finally, persons can possess religious authority. In a distinction first devised by the German sociologist Max Weber, scholars recognize two ideal types of authoritative persons. Authority devolves on a person either because of his or her extraordinary personal qualities (charisma), or because of his or her institutional role or office. The person's relation to the divine or cosmic source differs in these two cases. Although religious authority always depends on those who acknowledge it, charismatic authority depends on the recognition of a direct divine or cosmic commission for the specific person, while institutional religious authority depends on the recognition of a divine or cosmic sanction for the institution, its rules, and roles. To vest authority in a charismatic's hereditary or spiritual lineage following his or her death routinizes the authority and renders it something closer to institutional authority.

Various personal qualities can signal charismatic authority. Spirit possession or ecstatic experience indicate a direct connection to the divine. Extraordinary skill in the interpretation of sacred texts can also betoken divine inspiration. The leader of the Dead Sea Scroll community at Qumran, the Teacher of Righteousness, gained authority from hermeneutic virtuosity. Similarly, many Protestant communities base authority on skillful exegesis because of the "astonishing" authority of Jesus' teaching in the synagogue (Mark 1:22). An unusually virtuous or ascetic life can also indicate a special relation to the divine or the cosmos. In medieval Europe, moreover, stereotyped bodily afflictions like the stigmata (miraculous bleeding marks on the hands and feet like those of Jesus on the cross) could confer authority. Some medieval women, including Margery Kempe, exhibited the sanctifying gift of holy tears. Women in many religions, Afro-Brazilian Umbanda for instance, gain religious authority through illness or great suffering. For women excluded from institutional authority, illness may both act as an unauthorized rite of passage and symbolize the crossing of a social boundary.

The authority of events, texts, and persons interrelate. In many cases, for instance, only authorized persons (of one type or the other) can conduct or interpret events. Sometimes the interpretation of the event depends on an authoritative text. In some settings an institutionally authorized person interprets the behavior or utterances of a charismatic. Similarly, interpretive skill can indicate charisma, while sometimes charismatics compose authoritative texts. Authoritative events, moreover, can confer charismatic or institutional authority. Tibetan Buddhists rely on the time of birth and behavior of a child to determine if he is a *tulku,* a reincarnated religious authority.

In general, the more social and economic power a culture permits women, the more institutional religious authority women possess. Religious groups dissenting against a dominant institution, like the medieval Waldenses and Cathars, often give women more institutional authority. Because women have rarely exercised institutional religious authority, however, women more commonly bear charismatic authority. Charismatic women, though, are generally less likely than charismatic men to produce authoritative texts because women are more frequently illiterate. Unsurprisingly, religions that create a gender-neutral institutional function for charisma also exhibit the most egalitarian distribution of institutional authority. Women Pentecostal preachers are not uncommon, and the Shakers, a group that cultivated inspiration, had dual offices: elder and eldress.

Scholars have offered psychoanalytic, sociological, and psychosexual explanations of the widespread prevalence of one variety of charisma among women: spirit possession. I. M. Lewis's theory that it functions to protest male dominance is perhaps the best known. Caroline Walker Bynum nuances Lewis's theory in a study of thirteenth-century Christian women mystics. She argues that the nuns of Helfta, through mystical union with Christ, devised an authority to countervail the growing institutional authority of the male priesthood. The nuns' mysticism also demonstrates how the structures of religious authority influence religious expression. In their piety the images of food, blood, and fountains express a concern with the clerical control of the Eucharist. Ultimately, however, Bynum sees the world-renouncing authority of the mystics as complementing, rather than simply challenging, world-affirming clerical authority.

BIBLIOGRAPHY

Bynum, Carolyn Walker. *Jesus as Mother: Studies in the Spirituality of the High Middle Ages.* 1982. Bynum considers the problem of authority central to an understanding of the twelfth and thirteenth-century Christian religiosity.

Kienzle, Beverly Mayne, and Pamela J. Walker. *Women Preachers and Prophets through Two Millennia of Christianity.* 1998. A collection of essays that probes the relationship between preaching and authority in different historical contexts.

Lewis, I. M. *Ecstatic Religion: A Study of Shamanism and Spirit Possession.* 1971. 2d ed., 1989. A classic of deprivation theory. Women's deprivation at the hands of a male-dominated social order explains elements of their religious life.

Proctor-Smith, Marjorie. *Women in Shaker Community and Worship: A Feminist Analysis of the Uses of Religious Symbolism.* 1985. Describes the effects of women's leadership on religious imagery.

Russell, L. M. *Household of Freedom: Authority in Feminist Theology.* 1987. An attempt to consider nontraditional models of authority.

Schwartz, Regina M. *The Curse of Cain: The Violent Legacy of Monotheism.* 1997. Recognizes a connection between religion and violence, but implausibly limits it to monotheism.

Sered, Susan Starr. *Priestess, Mother, Sacred Sister: Religions Dominated by Women.* 1994. A search for commonalities between religious groups all of which have mostly women leaders and participants. A good source for data.

Stout, Jeffrey. *The Flight from Authority.* 1981. The use of the concept of authority to analyze and compare religions only arises, as do so many of the concepts central to the modern study of religion, after the Protestant Reformation. Stout describes the conceptual resources that developed in response to the Reformation conflict of religious authorities.

Weber, Max. *From Max Weber: Essays in Sociology.* Translated and edited by H. H. Gerth and C. Wright Mills. 1946. Contains Weber's fullest discussions of charisma and its routinization.

See also **Leadership; Ordination; Suffering.**

MATTHEW BAGGER

Autobiography and Biography

An Overview

As an examination of Serinity Young's *An Anthology of Sacred Texts by and about Women* (1993) shows, women in many cultures have striven to tell and write the stories of their lives; men too have found value in reproducing women's stories. Religious experiences, beliefs, and practices have often been central to these stories; even in the twentieth century, during which fewer people have given credence to official religion, accounts of religious journeys by women have been plentiful. Seven women—a Lakota Sioux, a Bengali Hindu, a Japanese Zen nun, a Jewish Holocaust survivor, a Honduran Catholic, an African-American Protestant, and an Egyptian Muslim—tell their very different stories in Gary L. Comstock's *Religious Autobiographies* (1995).

Whereas women like these have written their lives autobiographically, others have used the novel, short story, or poem as a means to examine their religious identities and histories (e.g., Maxine Hong Kingston, *The Woman Warrior* [1976]; Alifa Rifaat, *Distant View of a Minaret and Other Stories* [1983]; and Jeanette Winterson, *Oranges Are Not the Only Fruit* [1985]).

Anthropologists have made available, through transcription or via the media of their own voices, the stories of women in cultures they have studied. Notable examples include Marjorie Shostak, *Nisa: The Life and Words of a !Kung Woman* (1981); David E. Jones, *Sanapia: Comanche Medicine Woman* (1972); and Karen McCarthy Brown, *Mama Lola: A Vodou Priestess in Brooklyn* (1991).

The value of the term *life-writing* (Kadar) is that it encompasses not only autobiography and biography but other literary forms, such as journals and diaries, letters, transcribed oral or other personal testimonies, even novels and poems that tell stories of lives. Additionally, bringing together fiction and nonfiction and different literary forms allows us to take a fresh look at the place of truth. Whose truth is represented in biography? Is the author of a personal narrative necessarily telling truth? Does a fictional account of a life tell a truth about the author or about the imagined subject and her world?

The issue of truth-telling emerges noticeably where women choose to break with tradition and tell their own truths against the grain of conventional wisdom and expectations, or where their truth-telling may be conditioned by religious and social norms and the means of expression open to them as women. Prose fiction, visionary writing, and poetry may in such cases offer an ambiguous but subversive means for telling truths. It could be argued that the desire and pursuit of self-representation undertaken in life-writing is itself a spiritual process.

Much life-writing by and about women ventures beyond the implicitly spiritual acts of self-representation and self-creation to deal directly with more formal religious matters, such as confession, conversion, discipleship, vocation, discipline and service, and the pursuit of enlightenment or salvation. In fact, the traditional, humanist view of the genre of autobiography sees it originating with the fifth-century C.E. *Confessions of a Sinner* by Augustine of Hippo, in which he writes his life as a prayer to God through the lens of his conversion. According to this view, the genre later acquires its particular modern character through the private confessional journals of the Puritans and the Enlightenment focus on individual selfhood, thus proceeding from an orientation to God as the one to whom truth must be told and the self revealed, to one that favors

the reader as confessor. (Janet Varner Gunn's entry "Autobiography" in *The Encyclopedia of Religion* is representative of this view.)

In accounts of autobiography that adopt the traditional view, women's life-writing has often been ignored or marginalized for failing to demonstrate these characteristics. Feminist critics from Estelle Jelinek onward have challenged this view, identifying innumerable examples of ground-breaking self-accounts by women. These critics reconsider the boundaries of the genre itself, questioning the confessional focus and evaluating the applicability of humanist notions of individualism, selfhood, and linear continuity to women's writing. They offer a new agenda of themes for discussion, such as gender and self-representation, the role of the body in writing, the adequacy of conventional language and narrative, authorization and truth-telling (see Benstock, Gilmore, Heilbrun, Kadar, Lawless, Personal Narratives Group, Stanley).

Once the nature of autobiographical writing is questioned and these new issues taken seriously, many texts by religious women become available for our consideration. The *Therigatha*, for example, attributed to Buddhist nuns living around the time of the Buddha (but collected some thousand years later), contains many poems in the first person exploring the nuns' transition from material suffering to enlightenment through ascetic practice. Common themes are the subordination of nuns to male authority and female bodily disfigurement as a means of enacting the Buddha's teachings on impermanence and the control of desire (L. Wilson). A third-century Christian text, *Passio Sanctarum Perpetuae et Felicitatis*, which contains prison journals by Perpetua, a new convert, also deals with the abuse and mutilation of the female body in conformity with contemporary ideas about the nature of women's ascetic practice. Perpetua, imprisoned for her conversion and then executed, recounts her dream vision of dying for her beliefs, sacrificing everything for eternal life. Thomas Heffernan suggests that this text was paradigmatic for later accounts by and about women that present their visions and their stress on faith above law.

The charting of exemplary lives and their imitation by others were important in the writings of the European medieval church, and certainly among women writers for whom the need both to legitimize their lives and authorize their accounts was urgent. Clarissa Atkinson explains how Margery Kempe and her scribes (for she was illiterate) turned to other lives, such as those of Birgitta of Sweden and Marie d'Oignies, a Beguine, so as to locate Margery's experiences of spiritual tears, visions, and celibacy. Her early-fifteenth-century book offers a first-person testimony of a married laywoman and mother, and her later experiences as a pilgrim and visionary. Margery differed considerably from most of the other Christian women who wrote self-accounts in medieval Europe; these women, such as Hildegard of Bingen, Julian of Norwich, and Teresa of Avila (K. Wilson), lived in Christian orders or as anchorites.

During the same period, in Hindu India, where the monastic life was not open to women, married women were also breaking out of the confines of domestic existence to live in devotion to God. Poets like Mahadeviakka and Mirabai wrote of the intrusion of God into their lives, their feelings of poignant but loving separation from him, and his claims upon them (Ramanujan). Another bhakti poet, the seventeenth-century Bahina Bai, arguably the first true Indian autobiographer, wrote of her mystical experiences of God and guru in a moving account of her childhood, marriage, and domestic life (Abbott). Unlike other mystics, she showed how a life of devotion could be lived without formally transgressing the married state. However, hers was a painful experience, with tension between duty and devotion, husband and God.

Also of importance in this examination of premodern self-accounts by women is a cluster of Japanese Buddhist texts that consider the themes of the wandering life, the problem of the female body for spiritual progress, the ties of the world, and the discipline required for enlightenment. The writings of Lady Nijo (thirteenth century) and Ryonen Genso (seventeenth century), both courtly women who became nuns, and the twentieth-century nun Satomi Myodo are fascinating personal accounts of women in a particular geographical and religious context (Young, Comstock).

These early texts, written in a range of genres and styles but all in the first person, clearly do not present autonomous women, and their purpose is not the exploration of individual selfhood. Rather, they raise questions about women's status as ascetics, the possibility of their liberation or salvation, the identification of signs of spiritual progress, the validation of their personal experiences, and the control of their bodies for orthodox ends.

Arguably, early modern and modern autobiographical writings are more self-focused, many being confessional in style, others experimenting with the model of the life-course or life-journey (Davis). Some, like the seventeenth-century journals of nonconformist Christian women, continued to have a public purpose, recording women's sense of vocation in their acts of resistance and their experience of arrest and imprisonment for reasons of conscience (Graham et al.). Others, like the nineteenth-century spiritual accounts of black women preachers in America, told stories of women's achievement in uncharted religious territory (Foster,

McKay). The social, political, and religious challenges to women under colonialism, negotiating tradition and modernity, were explored in a number of autobiographies by Indian Hindu, Muslim, and Christian women in the early twentieth century (Harish). The spiritual experiences of survival and resistance to oppression were recounted autobiographically by Jewish women, Native American women, women living in dictatorships, and those who suffered domestic and sexual abuse. With greater freedom of expression and expansion of opportunities for women in many countries in the late twentieth century, a broader range of women are able to write their lives—though, as the consideration of premodern self-accounts has shown, determined women from many cultures have succeeded in leaving written testimonies of their own experiences.

The place occupied by women in the history of biography is somewhat different from that of men, for it is men who have often been the writers of such texts. Key questions when considering biographical writing about women are, What was the purpose of writing the life of a particular woman? How was she inscribed in the biography? Was the primary purpose to tell a woman's story, to tell a truth about the author, to reveal a society's ideals of womanhood, or to teach a particular community how to live? A look at what scholars (Williams, LaFleur, Hefferman) have referred to as "sacred biography," the written accounts of lives of holy people, provides some answers.

The earliest accounts of women's religious lives were those that appeared in scripture—for example, the lives of Sarah, Esther, and Jael in the Hebrew Bible, and of Gargi and Maitreyi in the Sanskrit Upanishads—and told of the exploits of powerful women. Though these accounts have been important in women's reclamation of male-oriented history, they do not constitute sacred biography as such, as they are deemed of divine rather than human provenance. Additionally, some legal, prescriptive, and exhortative religious literature contained accounts of the ideal woman, focusing not on particular historical figures but on imagined women shaped by the requirements of the societies that produced them. The Confucian *Book of Rites*, the Hindu *Manusmrti*, selected suras from the Qur'an, and the New Testament writings of Paul provide good examples.

Sacred biographies, by contrast, were those texts, generally by male authors, that told the lives of saintly figures in order to teach the faithful and to encourage the imitation of exemplary behavior. Texts of this kind can be found in many religious traditions, primary examples being the Confucian biographical text, *Lieh Nu*, attributed to an author from the first century B.C.E.; *Liu Hsiang*, in which womanly virtues were identified and exhorted; and the biographies of Yeshe Tsogyel, an eighth-century Tibetan Buddhist practitioner, and the Taoist Sun Bu'er from the twelfth century, both of which expressed the accomplishments of unusual and powerful women. In the thirteenth century Sufi women mystics were hailed in biographical works by Ibn Arabi, who admired their spiritual powers, and Attar, whose *Tadhkirat al-awliya* included accounts of several women, including Rabi'ah, whom Attar maintained became a man in order to make spiritual progress. In a popular Christian text from the same period, *The Golden Legend*, compiled by Jacobus de Voragine, the lives of saintly women, like Agnes, Christina, Lucy, and Agatha, appeared alongside those of men. A life of virgin martyrdom was held up as an ascetic role model to encourage obedience to the church's teachings. These stories were not the products of women saints themselves, but were written by men, often revealing contemporary male attitudes to women's roles and behavior.

As scholars have noted, the interweaving of myth and history in sacred biographies makes the reconstruction of actual lives problematic. Readers may learn more about the beliefs and values of the authors and their social and doctrinal contexts than about the women of whom they write.

BIBLIOGRAPHY

Abbott, Justin, trans. *Bahina Bai: A Translation of Her Autobiography and Verse*. 1929.

Atkinson, Clarissa W. *Mystic and Pilgrim: The Book and the World of Margery Kempe*. 1983.

Benstock, Shari, ed. *The Private Self: Theory and Practice of Women's Autobiographical Writings*. 1988.

Davis, Natalie Zemon. *Women on the Margins: Three Seventeenth-Century Lives*. 1995.

Foster, Francis Smith. "Neither Auction Block nor Pedestal: 'The Life and Religious Experience of Jarena Lee, A Coloured Lady.' " In *The Female Autograph*. Edited by Domna C. Stanton. 1984.

Gilmore, Leigh. *Autobiographics: A Feminist Theory of Women's Self-Representation*. 1994.

Graham, Elspeth, Hilary Hinds, Elaine Hobby, and Helen Wilcox. *Her Own Life: Autobiographical Writings by Seventeenth-Century Englishwomen*. 1989.

Gunn, Janet Varner. "Autobiography." In *The Encyclopedia of Religion*. Edited by Mircea Eliade. 1987.

Hefferman, Thomas J. *Sacred Biography: Saints and Their Biographers in the Middle Ages*. 1988.

Heilbrun, Carolyn G. *Writing a Woman's Life*. 1988.

Jelinek, Estelle, C., ed. *Women's Autobiography: Essays in Criticism*. 1980.

Kadar, Marlene. *Essays on Life Writing: From Genre to Critical Practice*. 1992.

LaFleur, William R. "Biography." In *The Encyclopedia of Religion*. Edited by Mircea Eliade. 1987.

Lawless, Elaine J. "Rescripting their Lives and Narratives: Spiritual Life Stories of Pentecostal Women Preachers." *Journal of Feminist Studies in Religion* 7 (1991): 53–72.

McKay, Nellie Y. "Nineteenth-Century Black Women's Spiritual Autobiographies: Religious Faith and Self-Empowerment." In *Interpreting Women's Lives: Feminist Theory and Personal Narratives*. Edited by the Personal Narratives Group. 1989.

Personal Narratives Group, ed. *Interpreting Women's Lives: Feminist Theory and Personal Narratives*. 1989.

Ramanujan, A. K. "On Women Saints." In *The Divine Consort: Radha and the Goddesses of India*. Edited by John Stratton Hawley and Donna Marie Wulff. 1982.

Ranjana, Harish. *Indian Women's Autobiographies*. 1993.

Reynolds, Frank E., and Donald Capps. *The Biographical Process: Studies in the History and Psychology of Religion*. 1976.

Stanley, Liz. *The Auto/biographical I: The Theory and Practice of Feminist Auto/biography*. 1992.

Williams, Michael A. *Charisma and Sacred Biography*. 1982.

Wilson, Katherina M., ed. *Medieval Women Writers*. 1984.

Wilson, Liz. "Seeing Through the Gendered 'I': The Self-Scrutiny and Self-Disclosure of Nuns in Post-Asokan Buddhist Hagiographical Literature." *Journal of Feminist Studies in Religion* 11 (1995): 41–80.

KIM KNOTT

In Asian Religions

Scholars of religion distinguish among sacred biography, or religiously authoritative accounts of the lives of holy individuals, typically founders of religious traditions or pivotal reformers; hagiography, usually the lives of saints, or those who realize an accepted religious ideal; and secular biographies of religious figures. A similar typology exists for autobiographical accounts, whether sacred or secular, of founders or followers. In all cases, biographical and autobiographical texts exhibit a variety of tensions, including that of the incorporation or avoidance of critical historical detail in the constructed biographical image of the subject. Moving between the realms of myth and chronicle, the life of a religious subject may be significant as much for its universality as for its individuality.

The parameters of biography in Asian religious traditions are elusive. Broad expanses of a life may be compressed into a few lines, the biographer foregoing ency-clopedic coverage of detail in favor of a sharpened focus on signal events and their aftermath. In an extreme but not uncommon form, a "biography" may encompass little more than a demonstration of a particular virtue illustrated through a single incident in the subject's life. Finally, notions of individual identity may be absent, especially for female subjects. Historically, women's lives, perceived as ancillary to men's, were not deemed worthy of full or independent recording, and identification of a female subject might be in terms of her relation to a male ("Mencius' mother"), her location ("the young woman at A-ku"), or her occupation ("the virtuous wetnurse of Wei").

Primary sources for pious women's lives may consist of little more than literary fragments. Although not strictly biographies by any definition, the songs of Mirabai, the sixteenth-century Rajasthani bhakti-poet, have been appropriated by later devotees as autobiographical miniatures or silhouettes. In these poem-songs, many of which were doubtless composed by later hands, "Mira" recounts the obstacles set up by her husband's family, who reject her piety. Against a backdrop of social pressure to submerge her personal identity into that of wife and daughter-in-law, the Mira reconstructed from her poems moves to claim for herself the role of Krishna's bride.

In China, the first compilation of women's lives was that of Liu Xiang (77–6 B.C.E.), whose *Leinu zhuan* (Biographies of exemplary women), offered models of virtuous women who exemplified filiality, loyalty, or other core Confucian virtues; some of these women, "wise" or "able in reasoning," adroitly remonstrate with their husbands, sons, and even their rulers for failure to heed good advice. The text first presents lives of virtuous mothers, thereby underscoring women's primary role as transmitters of cultural norms. Women in this early collection, although sometimes lacking personal identity (referred to as the wife or daughter of a named male), are nonetheless portrayed as the virtuous equals or superiors of male family members. As the biographical genre developed over time, however, the portrayal of Chinese women moved increasingly toward stereotyped cameos of self-effacing filiality and chastity, fueled by the rise and popularity of didactic texts for women. The earliest of these was Pan Ch'ao's (c.48–c.120) *Nüjie* (Instructions for women), wherein women's education was valued chiefly as insurance for correct performance of family rituals. Such texts drew on and reinforced images of female subordination drawn from canonical Confucian works such as the *Shijing* (Book of odes) and the *Liji* (Book of rites). Subject to "Thrice Following," i.e., following the dictates of fa-

ther, husband, and eldest son over the course of life, women were held up as moral custodians of the household. Beyond China, the interwoven traditions of exemplary biography and didactic texts influenced the lives (and the telling of lives) of women in Korea and, to a lesser extent, Japan.

Despite records of small numbers of women at various points in Chinese and Korean history (and in limited geographical areas) who defied, circumvented, or enjoyed freedom from restrictive norms, the majority of premodern biographical accounts preserved in *ni-anpu* (life annals written for the family), official biographies composed for the public record, and surviving correspondence and belles lettres portray women whose lives were circumscribed to greater or lesser extent by restrictions to the domestic realm, lower levels of literacy (e.g., Korean women's use of the hangul alphabet rather than the Chinese characters educated men used in their writing), and a code of male-established propriety, which precluded reportage or reflection on uniquely female events such as denial of education, concubinage, childbirth, or footbinding.

In the Buddhist tradition, accounts of Siddhartha Gautama's life came to be cast in dramatic literary terms as a prophecy of the prince either succeeding his father as ruler or else embarking on a dedicated religious life, the latter path predicated on the dissolution of familial roles and social responsibilities. Parallel to Siddhartha's eventual abandonment of wife and child, indeed the condemnation of his wife to virtual widowhood, his "Great Renunciation" is celebrated and recapitulated in the lives of later Buddhist saints—as with the Japanese poet-monk Saigyo, who kicks his young daughter off the veranda as he leaves the householder's life.

In contrast, lives of Buddhist women depart from the paradigm by requiring justification of their rejection of normative women's roles of wife and mother, e.g., they were orphaned, widowed, or left behind by husbands (or, in the case of courtesans, sons) who had previously renounced the world. Following the monastic Buddhist path was the noblest action for any man but remained questionable for young unmarried women, and closed to married women—the likely result of male monastic anxiety about the temptations occasioned by women, particularly sexually knowledgeable ones, in their midst. Even the hagiography of Gotami, the Buddha's foster mother, vaunted as founder of the nuns' order and winner of full enlightenment, can be read as a life that reinforces the necessary dependence and submission of women: the death of her husband is the catalyst for her entry into the faith, her relationship to the Buddha is of disciple to master rather than of mother to foster child, she wills herself to die in anticipation of the loss of the significant males in her life (the Buddha and his cousin and son, Ananda and Rahula, respectively), and even her name is but a marked form of Siddhartha Gautama's.

Despite variation across traditions and cultures, Buddhist hagiographical literature displays frequent ambivalence to its female subjects. The *Therigatha* (Songs of the nuns), early Indian Buddhist verses attributed to nuns, document the women's adoption of the male monastic gaze in their aversion to their own female form. In China, the *Biqiuni zhuan*, lives of Mahayana nuns compiled in the sixth century, and modelled in part on the Confucian-oriented *lienu zhuan* tradition, focus on the nuns' accomplishments as teachers or pious role models rather than on the inherent loathsomeness of their bodies; however, normative social roles for women as wives and mothers are upheld, and thus entrance into the monastic community typically requires explanation if not justification.

Even Tibetan Buddhism, replete with enlightened female figures such as Yeshe Tsogyel (eighth-century consort of Guru Padmasambhava), and harboring a tradition of female teachers and adepts, presents a hagiographical tradition in which women who attempt to take on roles beyond that of pious laywoman are discouraged and restrained. Inspirational though the autobiographical "full liberation" accounts of independent seekers such as A-yu Khadro (c. 1839–1953) may be, they betray a conservative culture that values female procreative abilities and capacity for physical labor far more than respecting their theoretically equal spiritual endowments and drive.

BIBLIOGRAPHY

Allione, Tsultrim. *Women of Wisdom.* 1984.

Gyatso, Janet. *Apparitions of the Self: The Secret Autobiographies of a Tibetan Visionary.* 1988. Especially helpful discussion on "biography" in a tradition that emphasizes the centrality of "no-self."

Hawley, John Stratton, and Mark Juergensmeyer, eds. "Mirabai." In their *Songs of the Saints of India.* 1988.

Sung, Marina H. "The Chinese Lieh-nü Tradition." In *Women in China: Current Directions in Historical Scholarship.* Edited by Richard W. Guisso and Stanley Johannesen. 1981.

Tsai, Katherine Ann, trans. *Lives of the Nuns: Biographies of Chinese Buddhist Nuns from the Fourth to Sixth Centuries.* A translation of the *Biqiuni zhuan,* compiled by Shi Baochang. 1994.

Wilson, Liz. *Charming Cadavers: Horrific Figurations of the Feminine in Indian Buddhist Hagiographic Literature.* 1996.

See also **Literature**; **Mirabai**; **Monasticism**; **Pan Ch'ao**.

VIVIAN-LEE NYITRAY

In Monotheistic Traditions

The differing cultural contexts of historical Judaism, Christianity, and Islam have resulted in widely different portraits of Jewish, Christian, and Muslim women from within the traditions. This essay considers each tradition separately and then remarks generally on the relationship of biography and autobiography to women's roles in the monotheistic traditions.

JUDAISM

It seems clear that Judaism has preserved many stories about holy male rabbis but few biographies of important women. In fact, outside of the Biblical narratives, it is hard to find lives of holy or exemplary women written by others. Scholars working on the mystical traditions of the city of Safed in the Holy Land are beginning to uncover information from the early modern period about holy women of the Kabbalistic tradition; even though this information has not yet been translated into English, it indicates that some Jewish holy women's lives were retold within the context of some spiritual traditions.

Medieval and early modern Jewish women tended to be literate and had devotional works written for them in Yiddish. Some of the prayers known as *Tkhines* are ascribed to women, such as the elusive Mistress Sarah Rebecca Rachel Leah, and reveal important details of women's religious lives. There are also a number of letters from early modern Jewish women to their children, husbands, sisters, and friends. One of the most celebrated women's autobiographical accounts of early modern Europe is the long letter to her children (widely understood as more of a memoir) written by the seventeenth-century Ashkenazic woman known as Glukl of Hameln (from the city of her husband's birth). This author presents her life as pious, devoted to God, husband, and children, as well as worldly, with business interests—the two are not incompatible.

CHRISTIANITY

Patristic and medieval Christianity, with its enthusiasm for traditions of holy people and literary conventions of self-reflexive soul-searching, offered fertile ground for autobiography and biography of women. Besides the narratives about women in the Gospels, several of the Christian apocryphal writings tell stories of women such as Tecla and Mary Magdalene. The third-century

Passion of Saints Perpetua and Felicitas includes an autobiographical narrative that is thought to be in the voice of one of the martyrs described in the story, Perpetua of Carthage.

By the fourth century the lives of women saints were written down along with the lives of holy men: Gregory of Nyssa wrote a noted life of his sister, Macrina, and anonymous accounts of famous exemplars of female chastity (Catherine of Alexandria, Agnes, Agatha, Barbara, Cecilia) began to circulate in hagiographical collections. The first autobiographical account of a Christian woman pilgrim is Egeria's diary of her fifth-century journey from Spain to Jerusalem; at the end of the Middle Ages, the fifteenth-century Margery Kempe wrote a similar pilgrimage narrative that is counted as the first autobiography in the English language. Women also wrote letters of various types; one of the most famous is the ninth-century Latin letter of Dhuoda to her young son.

The greatest collection of biographical and autobiographical material on Christian women comes from the tradition of visionary accounts and lives of mystical women, a literary genre that flourished especially between the twelfth and the seventeenth centuries. Almost any holy woman of this period (Hildegard of Bingen, Elizabeth of Hungary, Catherine of Siena) had a *Vita* written about her, usually by her confessor; some (Heloise, Teresa of Avila) also left testimony to their own life stories. Many more (Mechtild of Magdeburg, Julian of Norwich) wrote first-person visionary narratives that might be counted as autobiography, although in some cases (Elisabeth of Schönau, Angela of Foligno) this "autobiographical" narrative is filtered through a male scribe, usually the holy woman's father confessor.

ISLAM

In Islam, much information about women is found in the tradition of biographical dictionaries. One impetus for this genre of literature was to collect and pass along as much information as possible about the Companions of the prophet Muhammad; in this way, the biographical dictionaries form a continuum with Islamic hadith. Many women are counted among the Companions; their lives were told especially in the early period of Islam. Ruth Roded's study of women in Islamic biography indicates that the high period of inclusion of women's lives among exemplary Muslims continued until the fifteenth century, when ten percent or more of lives covered in several collections were those of women.

Many Muslim women whose lives were retold were remembered as Sufis. In the biographies of Sufis put together by Ibn al-Jawzi (d. 1200), women's biographies make up almost one quarter of the total, although these are placed in a separate section of the book. The most famous woman Sufi was Rabiʻa al-ʻAdawiyya, who lived in eighth-century Basra; her life is retold in several biographical collections and has been the subject of a modern scholarly biography.

Autobiographical accounts in Islam are found in the fiction and poetry of contemporary Muslim women, particularly Saudi Arabian authors such as Fowziyya Abu-Khalid and Ruqayya Ash-Shabib, but also women writers of Pakistan, Lebanon, and Egypt. The twentieth century is certainly the period of greatest autobiographical expression among Muslim women.

Although the occurrence of biography and autobiography of Jewish, Christian, and Muslim women before the modern period differs greatly, care must be taken not to let external factors lead one to stereotypical conclusions. For example, even though there are more Christian than Jewish women's biographies, this does not mean that Christian women participated more fully in their religious culture. In fact, Jewish women were literate in much higher percentages than Christian women and tended to write their own accounts rather than having lives written about them. Christian women's lives were retold more often because of the Christian emphasis on holy exemplarism, not because women's lives were considered more important than in Islam and Judaism. Likewise, it is striking that, even though we do not have many voices of medieval and early modern Muslim women, we know so much about them because of the role played by biographical dictionaries in Islamic history. It is only in the twentieth century, under the pervasive influence of Western culture, that Jewish, Christian, and Muslim women's autobiographical voices have more similarities than differences.

BIBLIOGRAPHY

The best study of the *Tkhines* is Chava Weissler, *Voices of the Matriarchs: Listening to the Prayers of Early Modern Jewish Women* (1998). For Jewish women's letters, see *Four Centuries of Jewish Women's Spirituality: A Sourcebook*, edited by Ellen M. Umansky and Dianne Ashton (1992), especially Part I, "1560–1800: Traditional Voices." The first English translation of Gluckl's letter, *The Memoirs of Glückel of Hameln*, translated by Martin Lowenthal (1932), was reprinted with a new introduction by Robert S. Rosen (1977). Neither this translation nor a newer one by Beth-Zion Abrahams, *The Life of Glückel of Hameln, 1646–1724, Written by Herself* (1963) is either complete or particularly accurate; a new translation is planned by Schocken. The best English study of Gluckl is Natalie Zemon Davis, "Arguing with God: Glikl Bas Judah

Leib," in her *Women on the Margins: Three Seventeenth-Century Lives* (1995).

For descriptions of and selections from ancient, medieval, and early modern Christian women's biography and autobiography, see Peter Dronke, *Women Writers of the Middle Ages: A Critical Study of Texts from Perpetua (203) to Marguerite Porete (1310)* (1984); Elizabeth Alvilda Petroff, *Medieval Women's Visionary Literature* (1986); and Emilie Zum Brunn and Georgette Epiney-Burgard, *Women Mystics in Medieval Europe,* translated by Sheila Hughes (1989).

For Muslim women's biography, see Ruth Roded, *Women in Islamic Biographical Collections: From Ibn Sa'd to Who's Who* (1994). Margaret Smith, *Rabi'a the Mystic and Her Fellow-Saints in Islam* (1928; repr. with a new introduction by Annemarie Schimmel, 1984) is a classic study that includes attention to the place of Rabi'a in biographical collections. For contemporary Muslim women's autobiography, see Saddeka Arebi, *Women and Words in Saudi Arabia: The Politics of Literary Discourse* (1994).

See also **Angela of Foligno; Catherine of Siena; Elisabeth of Schönau; Elizabeth of Hungary; Gluckl of Hameln; Heloise; Hildegard of Bingen; Julian of Norwich; Kempe, Margery; Literature; Mechtild of Magdeburg; Perpetua and Felicity; Rabi'a; Teresa of Avila.**

E. ANN MATTER

Beauvoir, Simone de

French writer, philosopher, feminist, and social activist Simone de Beauvoir (1908–1986) was perhaps best known for her phenomenological-existential study of the situation of women, *Le deuxième sexe* (1949; tr. *The Second Sex*, 1953). With her famous claim that "one is not born, but rather becomes, a woman," Beauvoir introduces the distinction crucial to much second-wave Western feminist thought between what would be later termed sex and gender. Grounded in a phenomenological differentiation between the body as an object in the world and the body as experienced, the sex-gender distinction allows Beauvoir and later feminists to demonstrate the historical nature of gender conceptions. Although the distinction has recently been critiqued by those who argue for the historically grounded nature of sexual difference itself, renewed analysis of the philosophical complexities of Beauvoir's text suggests the continued relevance of her thought to these issues.

Raised in a conservative, bourgeois, Roman Catholic household, Beauvoir describes herself as discovering early on that religion was the domain of woman. Her father's skepticism and her sense that men were intellectually superior to devout women like her mother led the young Beauvoir to reject the mystical forms of Christian piety she embraced as a child. Her experience of the constraints that religion places on girls and women and her belief that religion serves as an illusory justification for women's oppression play a crucial role in her analysis of women's condition in *The Second Sex*. Mary Daly's *The Church and the Second Sex* (1968) was the first of many attempts to take seriously Beauvoir's critique of Christianity from within Christian traditions.

BIBLIOGRAPHY

Bair, Deirdre. *Simone de Beauvoir: A Biography*. 1990. The standard biography, although recently subject to much feminist critique.

Beauvoir, Simone de. *Mémoires d'une jeune fille rangée*. 1958. (*Memoirs of a Dutiful Daughter*. Translated by James Kirkop. 1963.)

Hollywood, Amy. "Beauvoir, Irigaray, and the Mystical." *Hypatia* 9 (1994): 158–185.

AMY HOLLYWOOD

Beguines

See Porete, Marguerite.

Benedict, Ruth

Ruth Fulton Benedict (1887–1948) was one of the foremost American anthropologists of the twentieth century. She received her Ph.D. in anthropology from Columbia University under the guidance of the founder of American anthropology, Franz Boas. Benedict was also a mentor and close friend of another important American anthropologist, Margaret Mead. She is best known for two books, *Patterns of Culture* (1934) and *The Chrysanthemum and the Sword: Patterns of Japanese Culture* (1946). In the former Benedict analyzes the range of difference in human cultures in terms of the polar concepts of Apollonian and Dionysian, as defined by the nineteenth-century German philosopher Friedrich Nietzsche.

Much of Benedict's work focused on the study of religion, especially the interpretation of Native American religious concepts, myths, and folklore, including her first published paper on the vision quest in Plains Indian culture and her dissertation on the concept of the guardian spirit in North America. For Benedict, the study of religion and mythology was a way to explore a culture's often unconscious values, as well as economic, legal, artistic, and political domains of social life. It was also a personal as well as a professional endeavor. Although she did not focus specifically on the analysis of women's roles in religion, she was intrigued by the irrational dimension of Native American religions—of the ecstatic vision in Plains religion, for example—and its contrast to the rational approach of middle-class American Protestantism. Frustrated by many of the conventions of her own society, especially traditional roles for women, in an unpublished manuscript she celebrated nineteenth-century feminists such as Mary Wollestonecraft as women engaged in spiritual quests for vigorous and unconventional lives.

Fieldwork that Benedict carried out during the 1920s among the Zuni, Cochiti, and Pima Indians in the southwestern United States led to the publication of the two-volumes *Zuni Mythology* (1935) and numerous short articles on animism, myth, magic, religion, and ritual (1930, 1933, 1934, 1938).

BIBLIOGRAPHY

WORKS BY BENEDICT

"Animism." In *Encyclopedia of the Social Sciences*. Edited by E. R. A. Seligman and A. S. Johnson. Vol. 3. 1930. Pp. 395–397.

"The Concept of the Guardian Spirit in North America." Ph.D. diss. Columbia University. Published in *Memoirs of the American Anthropological Association* 29 (1923): 1–97.

"Magic." In *Encyclopedia of the Social Sciences*. Edited by E. R. A. Seligman and A. S. Johnson. Vol. 10. 1933. Pp. 39–44.

"Myth." In *Encyclopedia of the Social Sciences*. Edited by E. R. A. Seligman and A. S. Johnson. Vol. 11. 1933. Pp. 170–173.

"Religion." In *General Anthropology*. Edited by Franz Boas. 1938.

"Ritual." In *Encyclopedia of the Social Sciences*. Edited by E. R. A. Seligman and A. S. Johnson. Vol. 13. 1934. Pp. 396–398.

"Tales of the Cochiti Indians." *Bureau of American Ethnology Bulletin* 98 (1931).

"The Vision in Plains Culture." *American Anthropologist* 24 (1922): 1–23.

Zuni Mythology. 2 vols. 1935.

WORKS ON BENEDICT

Babcock, Barbara. "'Not in the Absolute Singular': Rereading Ruth Benedict." In *Women Writing Culture*. Edited by Ruth Behar and Deborah Gordon. 1995.

Caffrey, Margaret M. *Ruth Benedict: Stranger in This Land.* 1989.

Lutkehaus, Nancy. "Margaret Mead and the 'Rustling-of-the-Wind-in-the-Palm Trees' School of Ethnographic Writing." In *Women Writing Culture*. Edited by Ruth Behar and Deborah Gordon. 1995.

Mead, Margaret. *An Anthropologist at Work: The Writings of Ruth Benedict.* 1959.

Modell, Judith Schachter. *Ruth Benedict: Patterns of a Life.* 1983.

See also **Mead, Margaret.**

NANCY C. LUTKEHAUS

Benten

Benten is the only female of the seven Japanese deities of luck or happiness, the worship of whom dates back to the fifteenth or sixteenth century. Every New Year's Eve, the *takara-bune*—the treasure ship—is said to sail into port carrying the seven deities and various treasures, including a hat of invisibility, a lucky raincoat, a sacred key, an inexhaustible purse, a precious jewel, a weight, and a flat object that represents a coin. Pictures of the *takara-bune* are bought at New Year and placed under people's pillows in the hope that they will bring lucky dreams.

Probably derived from the Hindu goddess Sarasvatī, Benten's worship began in the mid-eighth century because of her role in the then-popular Buddhist text *Konkomyo-saishookyo* (Supreme King of the Golden Radiance). In this scripture, Benten promises increased eloquence and wisdom as well as various material advantages, freedom from calamity, cures for sickness, long life, victory, and repute to those who possess the text. In the fifteenth century, Benten became a popular object of worship for the merchant class and was thus integrated into the pantheon of the seven deities of luck or happiness.

Depicted as a very beautiful woman with a very white complexion and ornate garments, Benten usually holds either a lute or the sword and jewel. She is also sometimes depicted with eight arms, holding various items and generally has a *torii* (Shinto temple gateway) on her forehead. Benten's devotees include, besides merchants, speculators, gamblers and actors, and the geisha. Japanese women sometimes carry charms in the form of Benten to help display beauty, accomplishments, and attractiveness. In a popular Japanese ritual, one seeks wealth by washing money—and then keeping it—in a basin of water dedicated to Benten; such basins of water are common at Shinto shrines.

BIBLIOGRAPHY

Ann, Martha; and Dorothy Meyers Imel. *Goddesses in World Mythology.* 1993.

Durdin-Robertson, Lawrence. *The Goddesses of India, Tibet, China and Japan.* 1976.

Kitagawa, Joseph. *On Understanding Japanese Religion.* 1987.

Piggott, Juliet. *Japanese Mythology.* 1991.

Saunders, E. B., and B. Frank. "Japan: Cults and Ceremonies." In *Larousse World Mythology.* Edited by Pierre Grimal. Translated by Patricia Beardsworth. 1965.

See also **Sarasvatī.**

JENNIFER DUMPERT

Bhakti

The Sanskrit term *bhakti,* usually translated as "devotion," can be applied to a range of devotional attitudes and practices in Indian religions. In its most specific sense, however, bhakti refers to a type of religiosity that developed primarily in Hinduism and denotes personal and emotional devotion directed exclusively to a god of one's choice, conceived of as a path to liberation (*mokṣa*) from the chain of birth-and-death. As suggested by the meaning of the verbal root from which the word is derived, *bhaj* (to share or to participate), bhakti implies a reciprocal, loving relationship between deity and devotee. Although it is mentioned in the Bhagavad Gita (first century) and was gradually incorporated into many levels of Hindu practice, bhakti has its roots and primary contexts in popular religion and in regional languages and cultures.

Arising in the Tamil region of South India around the fifth century C.E., over a period of 1,400 years, bhakti religion spread all over India through popular movements centered on various deities, led by men and women who were venerated as "saints" and as the founders of sects. In spite of regional differences, bhakti movements shared important features. In contrast to the ritualistic traditions from which they had arisen, bhakti sects stressed inclusivity, the equality of all in the eyes of God, and the right of all to achieve sal-

vation through love of God. Unlike the ascetic traditions, they stressed passionate, emotional devotion. Bhakti cult leaders came from low as well as high caste origins and included women and untouchables among their number. Their followers came from equally diverse backgrounds, but bhakti religion has always had the greatest appeal for persons from marginalized groups such as women and the lowest castes. The central texts of bhakti sects are narratives of the lives of the saints and the poems and songs composed by the poetically gifted among them. Valued as expressions of passionate devotion and personal experience as well as vehicles of the saints' teachings, these poems in the regional languages challenge the authority of traditional scriptures, critique social inequalities and mechanical ritual, and extol the primacy of emotional devotion. They are accessible to all and continue to be sung and recited by the sects' followers. Taking their cue from the saint–poets, members of bhakti communities practice devotion through ecstatic and expressive modes, which include singing, dancing, and dramatic performance.

GENDER AND BHAKTI

Until the rise of bhakti devotionalism, the chief path to personal religious quest and expression available to women in ancient India was to enter Jain or Buddhist monastic orders. Bhakti offered ordinary men and women who could not or did not wish to become world-renouncers a spiritual path that could be practiced without abandoning one's duties toward the family and society. Bhakti rituals, too, were largely unstructured and open to both men and women. Today, women continue to head bhakti sects and lead communities in devotional worship. Most important, however, bhakti religion is one of the few contexts within Hinduism in which women have consistently been recognized as leaders, teachers, and exemplars. It is also one of the few Indian traditions that have preserved the histories and writings of individual women.

Most famous among the women saints are Kāraikkāl Ammaiyār (c. fifth century) and Antal (ninth century), who belonged to Śaiva (Siva-worshiping) and Vaiṣṇava (Vishnu-worshiping) cults in the Tamil region; Mahādēviyakka (twelfth century), a Vīraśaiva saint from Karnataka; Bahiṇābāī (seventeenth century), a devotee of the god Viṭhobā in Maharashtra; and Mirabai of Rajasthan (sixteenth century), a devotee of Krishna. Known beyond their own regions and celebrated for their extraordinary careers, these and other women saints are authors of the few works of literature known to have been composed by women in ancient and medieval India, and their poems are acknowledged to be among the most eloquent expressions of bhakti religion.

Bhakti sects have conceived of the relationship between devotee and God along the lines of diverse models of human relationship, including the relationships between servant and master; friends; parent and child; child and parent; a woman and her lover or husband. As exemplified by the male Bengali Śākta (goddess-worshiping) devotee Rāmaprasād Sen's (eighteenth century) poems to Kālī, devotees of goddesses usually adore and address the goddess as a child (usually a son) would a mother figure. The mythology of bhakti, however, accords primacy and great value to feminine sensibilities and attitudes on the part of the devotee. In the bhakti sects focusing on the cowherd-god Krishna, the love between devotee and God is most often visualized as the relationship between a woman and her lover, played out through alternating phases of separation and union. The poems of the Bengali Vaiṣṇava saints allow devotees of Krishna—male and female—to experience devotion by identifying with the cowherdswomen (*gopīs*) or the favored cowherd-girl Rādhā of the Krishna story, women who abandon their husbands and families to give themselves over to an adulterous love relationship with Krishna. A. K. Ramanujan (1982) has suggested that, by identifying with female sensibilities, male devotees are able to access the deep, "natural" emotional aspects of their psyches. In the Indian context, where the faithful wife is held up as the ideal woman and women are constrained by complex codes and institutions of patriarchal control, especially over their sexuality, the married woman in love with an unattainable lover is seen as a paradigmatic devotee, since she takes such great risks. After recounting the dangers she has had to face in her lonely journey along a difficult path in the dark of night to her assignation with Krishna, the female lover in a poem by the Bengali Vaiṣṇava saint Govindadāsa declares: "I no longer count the pain of coming here" (Dimock and Levertov, 1967, p. 21).

WOMEN BHAKTI SAINTS

Although each of the women bhakti saints has a unique history, the many shared motifs and parallels in their hagiographical narratives and poems illuminate the implications of gender identity for the saintly career and persona in the bhakti tradition. One of the four principal saints of the Vīraśaiva tradition, Mahādēviyakka (Mahādevī) is the author of 350 prose-poems called *vacanas* in her mother tongue of Kannada, in which she speaks of her passionate devotion for Siva. According to her biographies, after initiation into the community of Vīraśaiva devotees as a young girl, Mahādevī wan-

dered naked all over the countryside, singing her songs and keeping company with other devotees until she miraculously merged with her god at a famous pilgrimage shrine. Mirabai (also known as Mīrā), the author of 1,400 bhakti songs (*pada*) in Gujerati and Hindi, flourished in Rajasthan in western India in the sixteenth century and spent her last years at Brindavan, the North Indian center of Krishnaite devotion. Born a princess to one Rajput clan and married into another, the widowed Mīrā left her husband's family to devote her life to singing songs about her love for Krishna.

In the traditional biographies of Mīrā, Mahādevī, and other women bhakti saints, a woman's life in the context of marriage and family appears as a metaphor for the oppression and bondage from which the saint breaks away to forge her personal, spiritual freedom through a life dedicated to bhakti. The saints' songs often evoke this theme, as here, in a poem by Mīrā: "And though my mother-in-law fights, / my sister-in-law teases, / [. . .] and a lock is mounted on the door, / How can I abandon the love I have loved / in life after life?" (Hawley and Juergensmeyer, 1988, p. 134). When a woman saint cannot break away from her marriage, a miraculous transformation might effect her freedom, as in the case of Kāraikkāl Ammaiyār, whose husband leaves her, terrified by the occult powers she acquires on account of her devotion to Siva.

In the lives and poems of the women saints, the love for God is often expressed in the language and imagery of sexual and social transgression. Mahādevī speaks of Siva as the lover who "claimed as tribute / my pleasure" and of herself as ". . . the woman of love / for my lord, white as jasmine" (Ramanujan, 1973, p. 125). "Lord white as jasmine" (Chennamallikarjuna), an epithet stressing Siva's beauty, is Mahādevī's favorite name for the god, as well as her signature in her poems. In words that are unthinkable in a society where women are expected to worship their husbands as gods, Mahādevī speaks out against the hypocrisy of men: "take these husbands who die, / [. . .] and feed them to your kitchen fires!" (Ramanujan, 1973, p. 134). In another poem, she celebrates her nakedness, asking those who deride her: "To the shameless girl / wearing the White Jasmine Lord's / light of morning, / you fool, where's the need for cover and jewel?" (Ramanujan, 1973, p. 129). Mīrā's poems are equally bold in their eroticism and defiance of norms. Mīrā speaks of tearing off her veil of many colors, putting on anklets and dancing in front of her lord (only professional courtesans are permitted to dance), dyeing herself in her lover Krishna's color, and lying on his couch.

For bhakti audiences, the voice of the female lover in Mīrā's and Mahādevī's poems is not a poetic persona, but the saint's own voice, bearing testimony in direct, vivid terms to the woman devotee's personal relationship with her god. In the Hindu tradition, the lives and works of the women bhakti saints offer women an imaginative, personal space for religious experience that is not bounded by the dominant and mainly patriarchal norms of Indian society. Anthologies of women's literature (for example, *Women Writing in India,* 1991) and feminist interpretations of the lives and poetry of the women saints (the articles in the journal *Manushi,* 1989, for example) that have been published in India in recent years confirm the continuing significance of this traditional yet alternative model for women's empowerment and self-affirmation in India today, even outside the sphere of religious practice.

BIBLIOGRAPHY

Hindu bhakti religion and literature, and the contributions of women saints to Indian literature and culture, have attracted much scholarly attention. The poems and hymns of the major women saints are available in excellent translations, and there is a wealth of interpretive studies of bhakti religion and of the lives and works of the women saints from feminist and social historical perspectives as well as in the context of religious studies.

In *Speaking of Śiva* (1973) A. K. Ramanujan offers an outstanding introduction to bhakti religion and superb translations of the prose-poems of the saints of the Vīraśaiva tradition, including Mahādēviyakka. Friedhelm Hardy's *Viraha-Bhakti: The Early History of Krishna Devotion in South India* (Delhi, 1983) is a study of the concept of love in separation in Tamil Vaiṣṇava bhakti. The essays in J. S. Hawley and D. Wulff, eds., *The Divine Consort: Rādhā and the Goddesses of India* (1982), offer discussions of gender roles and the love of Rādhā and Krishna in devotional religion.

Among the best studies on women saints in bhakti are: A. K. Ramanujan, "On Women Saints," in *The Divine Consort;* the essays in *Manushi*'s special volume on women saints, *Manushi,* 50–51 (1989); and Uma Chakravarty, "The World of the Bhaktin in South Indian Traditions: The Body and Beyond," *Manushi* (1989): 18–29. On Mirabai, see Madhu Kishwar and Ruth Vanita, "Poison to Nectar: The Life and Work of Mirabai," *Manushi* (1989): 74–93; Kumkum Sangari, "Mirabai and the Spiritual Economy of Bhakti," *Economic and Political Weekly* 25 (1990): 1465; and Lindsey Harlan, "Abandoning Shame: Mīrā and the Margins of Marriage," in L. Harlan and P. B. Courtright, eds., *From the Margins of Hindu Marriage* (1995).

For poetic translations of the Bengali Vaiṣṇava saints' poems on Krishna and Rādhā, see E. C. Dimock and D. Levertov, *In Praise of Krishna: Songs from the Bengali* (1967). *Poems by Indian Women,* the volume on women's poetry edited by Margaret Macnicol (1923), is still useful for its breadth of coverage of women bhakti poets, although the translations are outdated. For more recent translations of selected poets, along with excellent introductions, see Susie Tharu and K. Lalita, eds., *Women Writing in India,* vol. 1 (1991). J. S. Hawley and M. Juergensmeyer include translations of Mirabai's poetry in their anthology, *Songs of the Saints of India* (1988). A. J. Alston offers a broader selection of Mīrā's poems in *The Devotional Poems of Mīrabāī* (Delhi, 1980). J. E. Abbot's translation of Bahiṇābāī, although outdated, gives access to a fascinating bhakti saint and writer: *Bahiṇābāī: A Translation of Her Autobiography and Verses* (Poona, 1929). Vidya Dehejia provides a fine study of Antal's life and translations of her poetry in: *Āṇṭāḷ's and Her Path of Love: Poems of a Woman Saint from South India* (1990), and Norman Cutler offers selections from Kāraikkāl Ammaiyār's poems in *Songs of Experience: The Poetics of Devotion* (1987).

See also Mirabai; Rādhā.

INDIRA VISWANATHAN PETERSON

Bible as Literature, The

The study of the Bible as literature has a long history dating back to the time of the early church and beyond. But it has been in the nineteenth and twentieth centuries that women have had a significant influence on the endeavor. Reading and studying the Bible as literature involves thinking about issues such as the plot of the story (of the whole Bible) and of the individual stories that comprise it; it involves studying the characters and their development or lack of it, the narrative style or the poetic structure and language of a passage of poetry. Those engaged in such study pose such questions as: What is the beginning and ending of this story and how are they related to each other? How does a character develop through a section of the Bible? How do the characters relate to each other? Who has the power or control in this story? Who is telling this story and from what perspective? Women's studies of the Bible as literature have expanded our understanding of the female characters, the effect of structure on our reading and understanding of the text, and the symbolic and representative use of language in the Bible. Since the 1970s critical approaches to the Bible have included reader-response theory, structuralism, cultural criticism, deconstruction, psychoanalysis, and feminism. The devel-

A scene from the play *Esther* by Racine, based on the Biblical story, depicted in a nineteenth-century French print (Gianni Dagli Orti/Corbis)

opment of feminist criticism has been an especially strong influence on literary interpretation of the Bible, encouraging attention to aspects of the Bible that had been previously undervalued, such as minor women characters, gendered language, and patriarchal structure.

One of the most important aspects of women's study of the Bible as literature is the reassessment of female characters. Biblical characters belong to a particular world, whether that of the ancient Hebrews or the Greco-Roman world of the New Testament. Both male and female characters are limited by the world to which they belong, and in the Bible that world is one in which power and control generally belong to males. However, literary feminist criticism draws out the often heroic roles women play in both the Hebrew Bible and the New Testament. Female characters often employ their particular power—deriving from their sexuality and their position as wives (Esth. 5), mothers (Gen. 27), or prostitutes (Gen. 28)—to obtain what they desire. Some of the most heroic actions undertaken by women in the Hebrew Bible happen only because they are women. Their skills at cooking, seduction, hospitality, and mothering enable them to influence the rise and fall of nations as well as families. In the New Testament women are responsible for financing the work of Jesus and providing meeting places for the early church; they risk their lives for the sake of the news of the gospel. The work of feminist scholars has brought to the forefront women from both texts who were previously overlooked either because they had no names or because they played minor parts in the overall Biblical story. For example, studies are available that explicate the place and role of the unnamed women in the book of Judges (Bal, 1987) and of the woman at the well (Moore), who is referred to only as "the Samaritan woman."

Women scholars have also done significant work on the language of the Bible, particularly its use of gender symbolism, language that makes use of male or female characteristics or identity to represent a person (e.g., a ruler) or an object or an idea. Scholarly analysis of gender symbolism provides insight into the divisions Biblical texts make between male and female. God is represented in ways that correspond to both male and female imagery. Though traditionally God has been understood through the metaphor of the father, the metaphorical understanding of God as mother—a one who labors to give birth (Deut. 32:18), suckles her children (Isa. 66:12–13), and shelters and protects (Matt. 23:27)—is an equally important part of the Biblical text. The language of woman, mother, daughter, or sister has been applied to such concepts as wisdom (Prov. 8 and 9) and such places as Jerusalem and other cities (Ezek. 16). For example, the nation of Israel and the city of Jerusalem have been depicted through images of prostitution (Hos. 4), rape and humiliation (Ezek. 23), domestic abuse (Jer. 23), and abandonment (Ezek. 16). For many centuries these images were accepted without question, but new approaches raise issues about how we read and understand symbolic language. Do we accept the image of a raped city because it belongs to a book with a long history? Do we accept the image of a people abandoned like a child because the perpetrator (of what contemporaries would consider a crime) is God? The study of gender symbolism in the Bible acknowledges and examines the feminine images in the Bible, both their positive and negative implications.

The study of the Bible as literature is open to all readers who think seriously about issues of story, plot, character, and language. Women who read the Bible in a literary way may raise questions about how women (and men) are portrayed in the Bible, about the language the Bible employs to describe God and the world of the Biblical text, and about the story or stories the Bible tells. As they reflect on the text and the questions raised, new understandings may lead to the deepening and broadening of women's participation with and in the Biblical text.

BIBLIOGRAPHY

Alter, Robert, and Frank Kermode, eds. *The Literary Guide to the Bible.* 1987.

Bal, Mieke. *Lethal Love: Feminist Literary Readings of Biblical Love Stories.* 1987.

Bellis, Alice Ogden. *Helpmates, Harlots, and Heroes.* 1994.

Berlin, Adele. *Poetics and Interpretation of Biblical Narrative.* 1983.

Büchmann, C., ed. *Out of the Garden.* 1994.

Camp, Claudia. "Metaphor in Feminist Biblical Interpretation: Theoretical Perspectives." *Semeia* 61 (1993): 3–36.

Exum, J. Cheryl. *Fragmented Women: Feminist (Sub)versions of Biblical Narratives.* 1993.

Moore, Stephen. "Are There Impurities in the Living Water that the Johannine Jesus Dispenses? Deconstruction, Feminism, and the Samaritan Woman." *Biblical Interpretation* 1, no. 1 (1993): 207–227.

Schwartz, Regina. *The Book and the Text: The Bible and Literary Theory.* 1990.

Trible, Phyllis. *God and the Rhetoric of Sexuality.* 1978.

———. *Texts of Terror: Literary-Feminist Readings of Biblical Narrative.* 1984.

RUTH ANNE REESE

Birth and Rebirth

The idea and experience of childbirth shape religious belief and practice across a wide range of cultural settings. Birth enters religious life as (1) an event to be celebrated and controlled through ritual; (2) a symbolic process in myth, ritual, and spiritual practice; and (3) a topic of metaphysical speculation.

In many cultures childbirth results in potent ritual pollution. In the villages of central India, a woman is relieved of her household duties, isolated, and fed a restricted diet for as long as forty days after childbirth. At the end of this period, she is bathed and ritually reintegrated into the community at the village well. Well worship celebrates her fertility (water being the source of life) and also gives witness to her regained purity. She is now ritually clean enough to draw water for her family and resume participation in religious festivals and worship.

In China birth is highly polluting, especially when the new baby is a girl. So potent is the blood associated with female offspring that it is said to invisibly soak the mother's hair, flood the birth room, and spill out into the family courtyard. Similarly, Leviticus 12 stipulates that the new mother is unclean for seven days if she bears a son, two weeks for a daughter. Until pure, she is barred from the sanctuary and may not have contact with consecrated objects.

Some birth rituals, by contrast, are dramatizations of significant myths of origin. When a child is born to the Tetum people of Indonesia, family members ritually reenact their ancestors' emergence from the underworld onto the surface of the earth. In this story three siblings climb up through a vagina-like vent in the ground with the help of a creeper, the Tetum word for which also means "descent group" and "umbilical cord." The aboriginal people of Australia believe their birth rituals and songs were mandated and performed by female totemic ancestors at the first aborigine birth. Infant baptism is another childbirth ritual that repeats a myth of origin: the beginnings of Christianity. The baby's submersion in water and subsequent emergence into a new Christian life symbolize the death and resurrection of Christ.

As a concrete event in the lives of men and women, childbirth is the object of ritual activity. In the religious imagination the processes of childbirth represent creation and spiritual rebirth. Cosmic creation myths often contain embryological detail. The *Nihongi*, for instance, a Japanese collection of myths redacted in the eighth century, describes the beginnings of the cosmos as an undifferentiated egglike mass full of life-giving germs. This nebulous substance separates into heaven and earth, which in turn unite to spawn the first divine beings. The *Purāṇas*, classical Hindu collections of religious and dynastic lore, contain the motif of the golden egg, from which was born the world and all of its creatures.

Entry into a religious community represents rebirth into a new mode of life. Appropriately, birth symbolism is typical of initiation rites. Anthropologists Arnold Van Gennep and Victor Turner produced classic works theorizing the ritual separation, liminality, and reintegration undergone by initiates during puberty rituals, initiation into spiritual orders, and other rites of passage. The tripartite ritual process mimics death and rebirth and often employs symbols deriving from local understandings of the physiological life cycle. A swelling-sickness, for example, sometimes afflicts Siberian shaman-initiates, inflating their bodies so they cannot see or move. This illness effectively returns them to an infantile state, from which they are reborn as shamans. The clothing of the initiate in *dīkṣā*, or Vedic consecration, originally practiced by the Aryan people of ancient India, is likened by Vedic commentators to the embryonic sac, and the consecration hut in which he sits to the womb. Inside, the initiate (always a male householder) crouches with his fists clenched, in imitation of a fetus. In the initiation rite of the Kālacakra (a Tibetan Buddhist tantric meditation practice), the student visualizes himself or herself being absorbed into the spiritual teacher's body through the mouth, ejaculated into the womb of the teacher's consort, and reborn as an infant buddha.

The idea of Christian baptism as a rebirth is apparent in the gospel of John (see Chapter 3) and explicitly stated by Paul in Romans 6:4: "we have been buried with him by baptism into death, so that, just as Christ was raised from the dead by the glory of the Father, so we too might walk in newness of life."

Just as physiological birth provides a potent cluster of symbols for spiritual rebirth, embryology and infant development is of symbolic value for describing modes of spiritual practice. In his essay, "Solving Symbolic Language," Liu I-Ming, a nineteenth-century scholar of the Complete Reality School of Taoism, describes the stages of spiritual practice in terms of the natural growth of a child. Like everyone else, the Taoist practitioner begins in the womb and traverses certain stages to maturity. But he or she is able then to reverse that process, spawning and tenderly incubating a "spiritual embryo" within. When spiritual attainment is accomplished, the practitioner suddenly breaks through into the pure body of that embryo, entering the "state before birth." Liu I-Ming likens immortality to regaining the womb, the door between life and death.

In Hindu and Buddhist philosophy, the relationship between human birth and spiritual progress is quite direct. Birth is a matter of religious concern not only because of its social importance or power as a symbol, but also because of its soteriological consequence. Taking rebirth in the realm of cyclic existence (*saṃsāra*) is a mark of ignorance, while breaking the cycle of death and birth is the very definition of salvation. Because women are perceived to be the locus of somatic birth and the source of emotional attachment to this life and this body, they are closely associated with the entrapping nature of *saṃsāra*. In the monastic and ascetic traditions of India, Tibet, and East and Southeast Asia, leaving women and family life behind is largely synonymous with entering the path of spiritual progress.

BIBLIOGRAPHY

CHILDBIRTH RITUALS AND BIRTH POLLUTION IN VARIOUS CULTURES

Ahern, Emily M. "The Power and Pollution of Chinese Women." In *Women in Chinese Society.* Edited by Margery Wolf and Roxane Witke. 1975.

Gross, Rita M. "Menstruation and Childbirth as Ritual and Religious Experience Among Native Australians." In *Unspoken Worlds: Women's Religious Lives in Non-Western Cultures.* Edited by Nancy A. Falk and Rita M. Gross. 1980.

Jacobson, Doranne. "Golden Handprints and Red-Painted Feet: Hindu Childbirth Rituals in Central India." In *Unspoken Worlds: Women's Religious Lives in Non-Western Cultures.* Edited by Nancy A. Falk and Rita M. Gross. 1980.

Weissler, Chava. "*Mizvot* Built into the Body: *Tkhines* for *Niddah,* Pregnancy and Childbirth." In *People of the Body: Jews and Judaism from an Embodied Perspective.* Edited by Howard Eilberg-Schwartz. 1992.

INDIAN AND TIBETAN TRADITIONS

Davis, Richard H. *Ritual in an Oscillating Universe: Worshiping Śiva in Medieval India.* 1991.

Lubin, Timothy Norman. "Consecration and Ascetical Regimen: A History of Hindu *Vrata, Dikṣā, Upanayana, and Brahmacarya.*" Ph.D. diss., Columbia University, 1994.

O'Flaherty, Wendy Doniger, ed. *Karma and Rebirth in Classical Indian Traditions.* 1980. Excellent collection of essays on Indian theories of rebirth.

Tenzin Gyatso, the Dalai Lama, and Jeffrey Hopkins. *Kalachakra Tantra Rite of Initiation.* 1985.

GENERAL

Eliade, Mircea. *Rites and Symbols of Initiation: The Mysteries of Birth and Rebirth.* 1958. Provides a cornucopia of examples.

Liu I-Ming. "Solving Symbolic Language." In *The Inner Teachings of Taoism.* Translated by Thomas Cleary. 1986.

Martos, Joseph. *Doors to the Sacred.* 1981. A solid historical overview of Christian baptism.

Sered, Susan Starr. *Priestess, Mother, Sacred Sister: Religions Dominated by Women.* 1994. Groundbreaking study differentiating between birth rituals and beliefs in male- and female-dominated religions.

Classic works of ritual theory that discuss the structure of initiation rites are Victor Turner, *The Ritual Process: Structure and Anti-Structure* (1969) and Arnold Van Gennep, *The Rites of Passage* (1909; Eng. ed., 1960).

See also **Fertility and Barrenness; Pregnancy; Womb.**

AMY PARIS LANGENBERG

Blackwell, Antoinette Louisa

Antoinette Louisa Brown Blackwell (1825–1921), author, reformer, and Congregational and Unitarian minister, made her first and arguably most important mark on the historical record when she became the first American woman to be ordained by a mainstream Protestant church on 15 September 1853. Her formal education and religious training began several years earlier at Oberlin College, where as a student she published in the *Oberlin Quarterly* her first scholarly analysis, a critique of Paul's prohibitions against women's public speech. Against great odds and over the objections of the faculty Blackwell completed the theological course of study; however, Oberlin refused her degree, belatedly awarding honorary degrees to her in 1878 and 1908. At Oberlin she also formed a lifelong friendship with Lucy Stone, a colleague who would become a leading woman's rights advocate as well as Blackwell's sister-in-law when Antoinette married Samuel Charles Blackwell in 1856.

This marriage into the first family of American reform accelerated both her religious liberalism and political activism; severing her formal ties to Congregationalism, Blackwell found a new spiritual home within Unitarianism. Although she never secured a full-time pulpit as a Unitarian minister, she did have a lengthy career as a guest preacher and served as pastor emeritus at All Soul's Unitarian Church in Elizabeth, New Jersey, from 1908 until her death. Like many female religious leaders of the nineteenth century, Blackwell devoted considerable energies to the woman's rights movement, particularly the American Woman Suffrage Association and the Association for the Advancement of Women. Blackwell was also a prolific author who published eight books. By the end of her life, her intellectual interests turned to philosophical questions as she contemplated the impact of Darwinism and the possibility of immortality. Among her other achievements, Blackwell raised five daughters and voted in the first presidential election open nation-wide to women voters on 2 November 1920.

BIBLIOGRAPHY

Blackwell, Antoinette Louisa Brown. *The Physical Basis of Immortality.* 1876.

Carol, Lasser, and Marlene Deahl Merrill, eds. *Friends and Sisters: Letters between Lucy Stone and Antoinette Brown Blackwell, 1846–93.* 1987.

Cazden, Elizabeth. *Antoinette Brown Blackwell: A Biography.* 1983.

KATHI KERN

Blood

Blood—whether human, animal, or that believed to emanate from dieties—has played many significant roles in the history of religions. Although the ritual uses of blood vary widely, they are usually based on an underlying ambivalence about the nature of blood. As a perceived source and sustainer of life, blood located within a body has generally been regarded in positive, life-affirming ways. On the other hand, blood outside of a body—due to menstruation, accident, illness, sacrifice, or ritual wounding—has usually been treated as a dangerous, polluting, and mysterious substance requiring special handling or avoidance. Many religions, embodying these ambivalent attitudes toward blood as both life essence and death-dealer, have developed distinctive cosmological, soteriological, symbolic, ritual, hygienic, and social structures based on these attitudes. Although blood may at times be perceived as neutral or generic, it is also frequently gendered, depending upon the culture, context, and source of the blood (e.g., a cut finger or vagina).

The general religious contexts involving the ritual uses of blood include menstruation, sacrifice, and ritual wounding. Gender implications are found to varying degrees in each category. Reflecting the widespread androcentrism and misogyny of many world cultures, menstrual blood has frequently been interpreted as a dangerous and polluting substance, with many traditional societies segregating menstruating women from the rest of society. The association of menses with fertility has often been celebrated during puberty rites for young women; among the Apache of North America, a young woman experiencing her first menses would be

Masai women drink blood from the carcass of a goat, Kenya, 1984 (Yann Arthus-Bertrand/Corbis).

ritually identified with the creatrix Changing Woman. In this case, the onset of menstrual blood confers spiritual power as well as the capacity to procreate.

More gruesome interpretations of feminine blood, fertility, and death may be found in the numerous myths of the sacrifice of a female deity in various traditional agricultural societies. For example, in the well-known Southeast Asian and Melanesian island stories of Yam Woman or Coconut Woman, the sudden appearance of a gift-giving goddess is followed by her ritual murder, dismemberment, and burial—from which eventually emerge the basic tuberous food plants cultivated by the society. In these cases, the blood and flesh of the sacrificed goddess are transformed into edible plants. Native American myths tell of the betrayal of Corn Maiden, whose bleeding body is dragged over the soil; from her drops of blood emerge the first corn plants. The meaning of feminine blood is extended here: instead of such blood producing human offspring, it is instead ritually transformed into the necessary food plants that in turn support and nourish the subsequent society. Thus, although the feminine blood is spilled by a culture-defining murder, it ironically leads to the continued life of society, and thus requires ongoing rituals of commemoration and expiation. A male variation of this is found among the Mehinacu of central Brazil, who believe that long ago an alligator being, caught by the men of the tribe as it had sex with two sisters, was murdered and dismembered. From its buried genitals and blood there eventually developed various food sources. This mythic paradigm regarding the conversion of divine blood into human food is also enacted ritually, especially during yearly harvest festivals. The central Christian myths regarding the crucifixion of Jesus and the soteriological powers of his blood (illustrated graphically, for example, in the Cultus of the Sacred Heart and by various styles of crucifixes) appear much later historically, but still reflect this ancient connection between divine sacrifice, blood, and human sustenance and survival.

Profound ritual uses of human blood and sexual fluids have been found throughout the world. For example, in the Pacific region a recently married couple might sprinkle the collected semen, blood, and lubricatory fluids from their love-making upon the nearby fields, thus transferring their human fertility to promising seeds in the fields (a reversal of the Yam Woman model). A controversial early Christian heretical cult called the Phibionites is reported to have collected and then consumed male semen and menstrual blood as offerings of the body and blood of Christ. In the various tantric yogic mystical traditions of Asia, many rituals involving sexual fluids were used to confer spiritual

and magical powers, summon deities, and fashion a body of immortality. The Vaiṣṇava Sahajiyās of seventeenth-century Bengal believed that men and women could use ritual sexual intercourse to draw a woman's uterine blood into the male body through the urethra, creating an androgynous inner being of bliss and light. In more recent times, so-called vampire cults have developed in some American cities, and human blood is drunk in imitation of the literary and legendary fanged beings.

Sacrifices entail another major ritual use of blood. This may range from animal sacrifice to simple ritual wounding to penile bloodletting (Pacific islands, Mesoamerica) and clitoridectomy (Africa, Near East) to actual human sacrifice. The general model seems to be one in which a mediation or boon or protection is sought from a divine being or force, and the shedding of blood or a life provides a vehicle or negotiation for such ends. In northeast India, as in the ancient Near East and in Islam, the sacrifice of a goat is used to appease or honor the sacred, while the Ainu of northern Japan raised and sacrificed a bear cub. Here the flow of animal blood serves as a connection between the human and divine levels and may serve as a substitute for human blood. Ritual wounding, in which scars may be inflicted, small chunks of flesh excised, or blood drawn (as in the Lakota Sun Dances), provides human blood and flesh for similar ends: expiation, commemoration, exhortations, protection, boons, and harmony. Human sacrifices seem to have been practiced in many places on the planet, but evidence suggests that they have been most prominent among certain later agricultural societies, for example among the Mayans, Toltecs, and Aztecs of Mesoamerica.

The many ritual uses of blood provide windows into how human beings have conceived of the human body, gender, fertility, sexuality, death, rebirth, and relationships with the divine. Expressed through language, art, social institutions, and symbols of a culture, blood is likely to remain an essence of religion.

BIBLIOGRAPHY

Douglas, Mary. *Purity and Danger: An Analysis of the Concepts of Pollution and Taboo.* 1992.

Eliade, Mircea. *A History of Religious Ideas.* 3 vols. 1981–1988.

———. "Spirit, Light, and Seed." *History of Religions* 11, no. 4 (1971): 1–30.

Gill, Sam. *Native American Religions: An Introduction.* 1990.

Hayes, Glen Alexander. "The Vaiṣṇava Sahajiyā Traditions of Medieval Bengal." In *Religions of India in Practice.* Edited by Donald S. Lopez Jr. 1995.

O'Flaherty, Wendy Doniger. *Women, Androgynes, and Other Mythical Beasts.* 1980.
Reichel-Domatoff, Gerardo. *The Forest Within: The World View of the Tukano Amazonian Indians.* 1996.
Sproul, Barbara. *Primal Myths: Creation Myths around the World.* 1992.

See also Alchemy; Menstruation; Sacrifice.

GLEN ALEXANDER HAYES

Body

In Microhistorical Societies

All around the world, from the moment of birth to its ultimate treatment after death, the body is shaped to conform to cultural standards of health, beauty, identity. It can be pierced, painted, scarified, tattooed, mutilated, disguised; a corpse can be wrapped, dessicated, buried, burned, or even cannibalized. The body as it is conceived and experienced in the actual lives of human beings is not "natural," that is, a brute fact of nature; it is rather a cultural construction. However, a body is more than a tabula rasa upon which culture inscribes its values. It is the very locus of culture: the focal point of the pain and physical challenges of initiation, the conduit for ecstatic encounter through trance, the arena of combat in ritual healing.

The focus of African religiosity is pragmatic: its rituals are strategies for reinforcing life, fecundity, and power. The body is therefore not only the primary instrument of religious knowledge, the body is itself "religiously experienced and religiously expressed" (Sullivan, 1990, p. 88).

African mythology and ritual commonly depict the cosmos as an anthropomorphic entity. The human body, as a microcosm, incorporates the same primordial elements and essential forces that make up the universe. The human being is where these forces meet in dynamic conjunction. Therefore, neither the body nor the person is conceived as a discrete and independent entity but a nexus of relations and vital energies. Ideas about the body are, in turn, projected onto conceptions about the universe, the structures that control fate, invisible powers. The flow of vital fluids correlates with the course of cosmic substances. Blood, for example, is thought to contain the power of the life force. The shedding of blood in ritual sacrifice releases this vital force and "feeds" the ancestors, divinities, or spirits who are called upon for reciprocal blessing and sustenance. Similarly, body organs are charged with specific kinds of spiritual forces, and the basic impulses of

Igbomina (ibeji) (twin figures), late nineteenth or early twentieth century, southern Nigeria (North Carolina Museum of Art/Corbis)

the body are understood to fulfill cosmic purposes. The womb is the creative sphere of the cosmos and gestation its integrative force.

Cosmogonic myths typically relate that the seamless primordial totality broke apart to give rise to the phenomenal world. The fragmented elements are joined in a dynamic unity; so too is the body. In a sense, then, the human body is the twin of the cosmic body. Twinship is a predominant theme in much West African myth and ritual. According to cosmogony shared by the Dogon, Bambara, and Malinké peoples of Mali, the primordial beings were twins. Twins therefore represent the incarnation of a mythic ideal. Every unique individual shares in the structure of twinship, for the placenta is believed to bear the prenatal destiny chosen by the soul and considered the "twin," or spiritual "double." The placenta is buried in the family compound and watered for the first week of the child's life. Among the Ashanti of Ghana, twins were permanently assigned a special status akin to that of living shrines, for as a sign of abundant fertility they were repositories of sacredness. For the Ndembu of Zaire, twins present a troubling paradox: the "exuberance of fertility" that twinship displays is more characteristic of the animal world than the human (Turner, 1975). Therefore rituals are undertaken to protect the community from this anomalous condition.

The Yoruba of Nigeria describe the person as being comprised of a material body, as well as immaterial soul, spirit, and conscience. Nevertheless, immaterial aspects have a locus within the body—heart, stomach, and entrails or womb. The energy that infuses the person with vitality, *esè*, is often merely referred to as "legs," the physical site of this life force. The head is the seat of *orí*, the "inner head" or guardian spirit that controls personal destiny. Although embodied, these forces are simultaneously dynamic aspects of the supernatural world and can be ritually invoked. This is especially the case with the *orí*. The head is the living altar to which sacrifice is made; fortifying spiritual "medicines" are infused into small cuts in the scalp. Identity is thus embodied, but ritual knowledge of the body is necessary to its fulfillment.

Sexual identity, too, must be implemented through an act of culture upon the "natural" body. The Bemba of Zaire say that the purpose of female ritual initiation, *chisungu*, is to "make a woman." Girls are taught domestic skills, sexual etiquette, and the religious significance of womanhood. In ritual, gender is consciously constructed, modeled, practiced, and imprinted, and the body is inscribed with the indelible mark of this new identity. Circumcision and the excision of the clitoris are widespread initiatory ordeals. Such genital operations rid the body of extraneous flesh that represents the counterpart of the opposite sex. By removing these vestigial signs of androgyny, the sexes are clearly distinguished, and this ensures their fruitful union. Dogon say excision is "opening the mouth of the world" and likened to a generative act of God upon the earth. A more extreme procedure, the removal of the labia as well as the clitoris, is performed in Sudan, where it is thought to make a woman's body resemble the seamless totality of an egg.

The body, bearing the indelible marks of a cultural identity and a religious worldview, is thus the ground of experience through which one achieves an intimate understanding of religious values and grasps abstract principles as "sensible truths." African religions teach and transmit traditions through bodily techniques. The body also supplies the metaphor for the inherent power invoked. The Yoruba Gelede performance in Nigeria is a spectacle in which sacred masks honor the invisible powers of the "Great Mothers." It celebrates the innate power of all women as transmitters of life and pays homage to the forces they master. In Gelede, male masqueraders represent the Great Mothers, but the costumes emphatically exaggerate the features of women's fecund bodies: prominent and pendulous breasts and massive buttocks. The masks present visual statements about the greater significance of femaleness in the cosmos. Women's anatomical features and capacities are metaphors of their spiritual power. Women's power to usher in life or to curse and destroy it is said to make them greater than the gods.

African religions are therapeutic rather than redemptive. Their focus is not the afterlife but wrestling with the pragmatic facts of this life and its afflictions. Given the premium placed on fecundity, it is hardly surprising that much ritual is expressly concerned with women's fertility. For the Yaka of southwest Zaire, female infertility is a tear in the very fabric of life. The *khita* healing cult ritually establishes a vitalizing resonance between a woman's body and the cosmos. It celebrates and arouses the "primal womb" to elicit the body's healing capacities.

The body is not a discrete and bounded entity but is subject to the intervention of other agents, both human and supernatural. Ancestral spirits "remind" their descendants of neglected obligations by afflicting them with misfortune, illness, or even death. Illness may also be due to the malevolence of an evil spirit or witch. Therefore, although banal ailments are treated with medical remedies, chronic illness occasions an examination of the social and spiritual matrix upon which well-being depends. Illness is a moral dilemma as much as a biological crisis. Health depends upon conformity to the ideal model established in the codes and customs of the ancestors. Healing is the secondary effect of the reparation of disturbed relations.

BIBLIOGRAPHY

Blacking, John, ed. *The Anthropology of the Body.* A.S.A. Monograph 15. 1977.

Boddy, Janice. *Wombs and Alien Spirits: Women, Men and the Zar Cult in Northern Sudan.* 1989.

Buckley, Thomas, and Alma Gottlieb, eds. *Blood Magic: The Anthropology of Menstruation.* 1988.

Csordas, Thomas J., ed. *Embodiment and Experience: The Existential Ground of Culture and Self.* 1994.

Devisch, René. *Weaving the Threads of Life: The Khita Gyn-Eco-Logical Healing Cult Among the Yaka.* 1993.

Douglas, Mary. *Natural Symbols: Explorations in Cosmology.* 1970.

Drewal, Henry, and Margaret Thompson Drewal. *Gelede: Art and Female Power among the Yoruba.* 1983.

Jackson, Michael. *Paths Toward a Clearing: Radical Empiricism and Ethnographic Inquiry.* 1989.

Jackson, Michael, and Ivan Karp, eds. *Personhood and Agency: The Experience of Self and Other in African*

Cultures. Uppsala Studies in Cultural Anthropology, 14. 1990.

Jacobson-Widding, Anita, ed. *Body and Space: Symbolic Models of Unity and Division in African Cosmology and Experience.* Uppsala Studies in Cultural Anthropology. 1991.

Janzen, John. "African Cults of Affliction." In *The Encyclopedia of Religion.* Edited by Mircea Eliade. Vol. 1. 1987. Pp. 55–58.

——. *The Quest for Therapy in Lower Zaire.* 1978.

Maw, Joan, and John Picton, eds. *Concepts of the Body/Self in Africa.* Vienna, 1992.

Reynolds Whyte, Susan. "Anthropological Approaches to African Misfortune. From Religion to Medicine." In *Culture, Experience and Pluralism: Essays on African Ideas of Illness and Healing.* Uppsala, 1989.

Richards, Audrey. *Chisungu: A Girls' Initiation Ceremony among the Bemba of Northern Rhodesia.* London, 1956.

Sullivan, Lawrence E. "Body Works: Knowledge of the Body in the Study of Religion." *History of Religions* 30, no. 1 (1990): 86–99.

Turner, Victor. *Revelation and Divination in Ndembu Ritual.* 1975.

See also Blood; Mutilation, Genital.

LAURA GRILLO

In the East

Eastern religious traditions explore a wide range of images relating to the nature and significance of the body, sometimes overlapping with the Western philosophical perspective of the mind-body duality, but often in contrast to it. For example, the *advaita* or "nondualism" philosophy in Hinduism views the sacred as formless, with the concomitant theory that the world of form, and thus the body, is illusory (maya). In contrast, many theistic traditions view the body as a legitimate vehicle for the sacred, including the pervasive sacrality of *kami* in Shinto and the *viśiṣṭādvaita* or "qualified nondualism" philosophy in Hinduism. Both these traditions include goddesses prominently in their pantheons of deities. In nontheistic philosophical traditions, it is the actions and attitudes of the human founder that inform perspectives on the body. The Confucian world of bureaucracy conferred high status on women of prominent political families who refined themselves through the arts. In contrast, both the Buddha and Lao Tzu of Taoism are said to have rejected the materialism of social conventions of their day. Traditions in Buddhism celebrate the Buddha's mother as the first Buddhist nun, communi-

ties of nuns, and female figures of compassion, such as Kuan Yin and Yeshe Tsogyal. Taoism transforms the Confucian image of the submissive female into an image of strength through flexibility.

Generally speaking, the cross-cultural pattern of the male as universal and the female as limited applies to Asian perspectives on the body: whereas male bodies are normative, and thus supply the model for the univeralizing tendencies of philosophy, female bodies are limited, and ritually bound to life-cycle events, especially the ability to produce male children. In Asian countries, being born female can be a liability because of the traditional value placed on men as transmitters of family identity through generations, actualized by the designation of men as heads of household and by the pre-eminent role of men in funerary rituals. Although abortion is uncontroversial as a means of birth control in Asian nations such as Japan, China, and India, the overwhelming tendency to abort female babies has met with protest by feminist groups.

LIFE-CYCLE RITUALS

Examples from South Asian traditions illustrate the ritual binding of women's bodies to mark life-cycle events, especially reproduction. Some of these traditions may not be practiced by the urban upper classes, but they maintain a presence in the lives of most people. In general, a woman's life-cycle is defined through the presence or absence of menstruation. Premenarcheal girls are protected by their families, since their reputations, especially virginal purity, will be a major factor in their marriageability. In Nepal, young girls are chosen to be *kumāris* (virgins) of temples; there they are celebrated and worshiped until the onset of their menstruation, when they return to civilian life. Stories of religious women in India abound with images of virginity; for example, Ānandamayī Mā, a modern woman mystic, was said not to have consummated her marriage.

The onset of menstruation is celebrated in Hindu south India by a family gathering to perform several rituals, including the parents pouring turmeric water over the girl, followed by her first wearing of a sari, which is tied around her body in the traditional manner. In some priestly families, women are secluded during their periods. A young woman may spend the rest of her teenage years performing domestic duties, studying at school, or working outside the home; in all cases, it is expected that she will be married by her mid-twenties. Arranged marriage, with dowry, is the norm. The most important element in the marriage ceremony is the tying of the *tāli*, when the groom fastens a turmeric-stained cord with gold ornaments around the neck of

A Hindu bride and groom wear flowers and jewelry at their wedding, Bombay, India (© Monkmeyer/Kummels).

the bride. The persistent activities that literally bind young women in life-cycle rituals are designed to channel a woman's power into procreation. Traditionally, the best possible result is for a married woman to produce sons. The primary duty of a woman is to raise her children; this role confers social status on her. A woman's status plummets not at the cessation of her menses, for she still has her children and husband to look after, but at the death of her husband. Traditionally, a widow in Hindu south India is forbidden to wear jewelry, have long hair, wear colored garments, or enter into the presence of her son-in-law. Symbolically, the carefully channeled power of womanhood is not liberated in widowhood but simply used up.

BODILY TRANSFORMATIONS

The social expectations encoded in the ritually bound biological transformations of women form a contrasting context for the imagined bodily transformations of religious women preserved in traditional legends and biographies. Significantly, the stories of these bodily changes, with rare exception, do not depict a change in gender; rather, they tend to portray women as freed from a body that male society imprints with primarily sexual meaning. It is a freedom from male projections and male molestation. For example, the Hindu south Indian saint Kāraikkāl Ammaiyār asked the Lord to transform her from a beautiful wife into a skeletal demonlike observer of His Dance. In legends the Chinese and Japanese Buddhist boddhisattva Kuan Yin is created from a princess who gouges her eyes and amputates her arms for the sake of healing her parents. Chinese Buddhist nuns, in biographies that bear the influence of Taoism, had marks of the Buddha on their bodies, went into meditational trances in which their

bodies resembled wood or stone, and immolated themselves to create a lamp (of Buddhism) to others. These women religious adepts achieved pure, spiritlike bodies, free from male sexual attention. The problem is not women per se, because they remain women in their spiritual identities, but the male response to women.

THE SUBTLE BODY

Traditions of the subtle body highlight the spiritual depth of images of the feminine. These traditions, most prominently developed in Indian yoga practices and in Chinese Taoism, envision the corporeal body as having a subtle, spiritual double, of which only the adept will have knowledge. In many yoga traditions the body is mapped by power centers called chakras. The goal of meditation is to awaken the feminine power of *kundalinī śakti* or "the coiled one," and lead it through the chakras to the point of enlightenment just above the head. In Taoism the subtle Tao is associated with feminine qualities such as submission; texts within the Taoist canon describe the visualization of Jade Woman as a technique to achieve immortality. In both traditions men are exhorted to recognize the feminine within as a path to salvation.

BIBLIOGRAPHY

For an interesting comparison of Western and Asian philosophical positions on the body, albeit a male-dominated discussion, see Thomas P. Kasulis with Roger T. Ames and Wimal Dissanayake, eds., *Self as Body in Asian Theory and Practice* (1993). Anthropological studies contain important information on women's rituals across cultures: see the classic study by Margaret Mead, *Male and Female: A Study of the Sexes in a Changing World* (1949, 1975), and *Toward an Anthropology of Women,* edited by Rayna R. Reiter (1975).

For examples of myths on women from many traditions, including those from Hinduism and Buddhism discussed in this article, see Serinity Young, ed., *An Anthology of Sacred Texts By and About Women* (1993). On South Indian customs and rituals pertaining to women, see Susan Snow Wadley, ed., *The Powers of Tamil Women* (1980). On the transformation of the princess into Kuan Yin, see Glen Dudbridge, *The Legend of Miao-shan* (1978). On legends of Chinese Buddhist nuns, see Kathryn Ann Tsai, *Lives of the Nuns: Biographies of Chinese Buddhist Nuns from the Fourth to Sixth Centuries* (1994). On yoga traditions in India, see Jean Varenne, *Yoga and the Hindu Tradition,* translated by Derek Coltman (1976).

See also Ānandamayī Mā (Ananda Ma); Feminine, The; Kāraikkāl Ammaiyār; Kuan Yin (Kannon);

Marriage and Singleness; Maya; Menstruation; Sex Change; Yoga.

KAREN PECHILIS PRENTISS

Female Body as Text in Imperial China

The body occupied a prominent place in Confucian thinking and practice. Not only were the words for the physical body (*shen; ti*) used to denote selfhood in the classics, the body was also the subject of moral cultivation. In other words, the physical body was at once the site of selfhood and the vehicle for its transcendence. A famous passage from *Mencius* highlights this conjoining of bodily discipline and morality: "When Heaven is about to confer a great office on any man, it first exercises his mind with suffering, and his sinews and bones with toil. It exposes his body to hunger, and subjects him to extreme poverty. It confounds his understandings. By all these methods it stimulates his mind, hardens his nature, and supplies his incompetencies" (translation by James Legge).

Although the gender of the human destined for great offices is unmarked, it was presumed to be male. The female body appeared to be nowhere and everywhere: its physicality—often linked to the dangers of desire—was too alluring to be celebrated in Confucian texts, yet its utility to social and familial reproduction had to be recognized and harnessed. The textual absence of the woman's body, in other words, stood in stark contrast with the social reality of its vitality to the perpetuation of a key Confucian institution: the family. The female body was textually invisible but socially indispensable.

This paradoxical existence of women became more pronounced in the Han dynasty (140 B.C.E.–220 C.E.), when, according to historian Patricia Ebrey, the Chinese family codified three characteristic modes of operation: patrilineal descent, patriarchal authority, and ethics of filial piety. The family was thus imagined to be an organic entity constituted by a male-to-male transmission of bodies, surname, property, and ritual obligations. Women's sexuality was acknowledged only after it donned the textual guise of the desexualized mother, as evinced by the portraits of ideal women in didactic texts written in the Han dynasty by Liu Xiang (79–8 B.C.E.) and Ban Zhao (41–115 C.E.).

THE WORD–POWER NEXUS

Besides the sociology of family, the absence of female bodies in the canon has to be assessed in a second context: a tension between the body and the word in the Confucian formulation of culture and civility (*wen*). The conventional translations of *wen*—writings and the civil arts—describe a word–power nexus that was intended to be a male prerogative. This male-centered nature of *wen*

was expressed politically in the barring of women from the imperial civil service examinations, the gateway to bureaucratic appointments from the Sung dynasty (960–1280 C.E.) to 1905. In other words, official power was coextensive with scholarship and the written word; women had no formal place in either realm.

Yet *wen* also encompasses a nonliterary dimension: a culture–power nexus which historian Angela Zito has rendered "cosmic text-pattern." This expanded vision of Confucian textuality sees male and female bodies not as bound entities but as cosmological locations and sites of transformation. Properly attired bodies, well-behaved bodies, and bodies performing in rituals all figured as vehicles of *wen*. This interpretation opens the possibility of viewing women as producers of cultural values—Confucian or otherwise—and recognizes the uses of female bodies other than for the perpetuation of the male line.

From the perspective of the Confucian tradition, the literary and performative aspects of *wen* created a tension between body and word that it was never able to resolve. In the radical period of the late Ming dynasty (1570s–1644), novelists, dramatists, and thinkers openly spoke of a battle between emotions (*qing*) and reason or principle (*li*). From the perspectives of literate and illiterate women, however, the power of "writing" with their bodies was as real as their absence in the canonical texts and their formal exclusion from scholarship and bureaucratic power.

THE FEMALE BODY AS TEXT

The most important message inscribed on female bodies is the virtue of fidelity. From the Sung dynasty on, a large number of women's tales were preserved as part of the imperial state's efforts to canonize women of extraordinary deeds. Be it cutting off her nose to signal her resistance to raging soldiers, hurling herself into a well to avoid rape, or steadfastly passing lonely nights as a widow, a woman achieved virtues in highly *bodily* acts. To say that the body is a vehicle of virtues is to understate the centrality of the body's physicality: there was in fact no way to enact such virtues as chastity and filiality other than through embodiment.

Given the patrilineal structure of the family, filiality imposed exacting demands on a female: upon marriage, the subject of her devotion shifted from her parents to her in-laws. Being filial to the latter required the symbolic abandonment of the former. A female did in fact serve two masters, yet morally she could not: therein lies the singularity of her body. This singularity, however, is a metaphorical construct. In the realm of practice, the filial body is dispersed and often sacrificed; it bows, prostrates, starves, freezes, and is offered up as a substitute for that of the elder. The ambiguity of the virtue of filiality is highlighted in the process of its embodiment.

Nowhere is this ambiguity more evident than in the case of *gegu*, slicing off a piece of one's flesh as an ingredient of medicinal soup to revive ailing elders. The Yuan (1260–1368) and Ming (1368–1644) governments issued prohibitions against the practice, arguing that in harming the body, the progeny of parents, *gegu* was in fact an *anti*filial act. *Gegu* is thus an irony if not an oxymoron, insisting that the ultimate expression of filiality is not embodiment but dismemberment. Although both males and females were known to have sliced off their thighs or buttocks if not their livers, Chün-fang Yü, an expert in Asian religions, has shown how *gegu* became a key element of the cult of the bodhisattva Kuan Yin in Ming–Qing times. Since Kuan Yin was a female deity who held a special appeal to women, *gegu* thus acquired a special significance for its female practitioners.

Chinese virtuous bodies were thus amorphous, cut up, and often disfigured. The medieval Christian church, obsessed with policing the boundaries of an idealized body impervious to evil possessions, construed virginity as a key female virtue. In contrast, chastity in China was predicated on the integrity of the woman's will instead of physical intactness. In the late imperial times, a woman's willingness to destroy her body was increasingly taken as believable evidence of her determination to remain chaste. Indeed, if the body of a female was her tablet and her willpower her stylus, then in the act of "writing" virtues she often ended up immolating the medium, the instrument, and the author. The maiming of the chaste girl's body, like the erasure of the chaste widow's sexuality, are faint echoes of the textual absence of the female body in the Confucian canon.

It is not surprising, then, that female bodily "writing" took extreme and violent forms. Many a Taoist woman saint of the Tang dynasty (618–907), as historian Suzanne Cahill has shown, fasted and ingested drugs until her flaky white skin sloughed off and her body was transformed into that of an immortal. Elite women of the Ming and Qing dynasties practiced footbinding until their toes sloughed off and their feet were remade into an arch shape. Not only did these practices share a semiotic resemblance with the embodiment and dismemberment of virtues, they were in fact produced by the same dynamics of power. If the hegemonic discourse made its power visible through the textual absence of female bodies, the counter-discourse authored by women insisted on being seen in terms of a profusion of bodies in their most concrete physicality.

BIBLIOGRAPHY

The Confucian canon is a rather amorphous body of texts. The Sung thinker Zhu Xi (1130–1200) codified the Four Books (*The Great Learning; Doctrine of the Mean; Analects; Mencius*) with commentaries; henceforth they attained canonical status, comprising the core curriculum of the civil service examination. The absence of female bodies in the Four Books can be gleaned from a cursory reading. Various translations exist; James Legge's *The Four Books* (1861; repr. 1990) is helpful in the copious commentaries he included.

The absence or presence of female bodies in other Confucian classics is more problematic. The Book of Songs (*Shijing*), for example, is full of rhymed ballads unabashed in expressions of longing and desire. Standard translations are Bernhard Karlgren, *The Book of Odes* (1950), and Arthur Waley, *The Book of Songs* (1937; new ed. 1960). The central problem in *Shijing* hermeneutics is that of allegorical reading: is the desire expressed in the songs sexual or is it an allegory for political loyalty? For a recent treatment of this problem informed by theories of comparative literature, see Haun Saussy, *The Problem of a Chinese Aesthetic* (1993).

A summary of the development of the Han family can be found in Patricia Ebrey, "Women, Marriage and the Family in Chinese History," in *Heritage of China,* edited by Paul Ropp (1990). Japanese scholar Takao Shimomi has discerned a concomitant visibility of motherhood in Confucian thinking and society. His arguments are outlined in *Ryû Kyô "Retsujoden" no kenkyû* (A Study of Liu Xiang's *Biographies of Exemplary Women*) (1989) and further developed in "Ryû Kyô *Retsujoden* yori miru jokyô shakai to boseigenri" (The Mother-principle in Confucian Society as Seen from Liu Xiang's *Biographies of Exemplary Women*), *Hiroshima daigaku bungakubu kiyô* 50 (1991): 1–21. The former also includes a copiously annotated Japanese translation of Liu Xiang's didactic text.

The rise of the desexualized mother can also be gleaned from *Nüjie*, instructions for women authored by a female scholar-historian, Ban Zhao. An English translation is furnished by Nancy Lee Swann, *Pan Chao [Zhao]: Foremost Woman Scholar of China* (1932). For a revisionist interpretation that argues that *Nüjie* is a Taoist, not Confucian, text, see Yu-Shih Chen, "The Historical Template of Pan Chao's *Nü Chieh* [*Nüjie*]," *T'oung Pao* LXXXII (1996): 229–257.

Wen is such an important yet ambiguous concept that scholars have illuminated its historical meanings from many perspectives. Lothar von Falkenhausen has examined its use in early ritual texts and argued that it was a stock epithet of ancestors associated with values of civility and merit: "The Concept of *Wen* in the Ancient Chinese Ancestral Cult," *Chinese Literature: Essays, Articles, Reviews* 18 (1996): 1–22. Peter K. Bol, in turn, has analyzed the shifting meanings of *wen* during the Tang–Sung transition, delineating the nexus of writing, family, and governance thus formulated: *"This Culture of Ours": Intellectual Transitions in T'ang and Sung China* (1992).

Angela Zito has explained her rendition of *wen* into "cosmic text-pattern" in "Silk and Skin: Significant Boundaries," in *Body, Subject and Power in China,* edited by Angela Zito and Tani E. Barlow (1994). The conceptual importance of *wen* and its opposite, *wu* (martial), to gender construction is discussed in Kam Louie and Louise Edwards, "Chinese Masculinity: Theorizing Wen and Wu," *East Asian History* 8 (1994): 135–148. For a discussion of the late-Ming rupture in the uneasy balance between *wen, li,* and *qing,* see Wai-Lee Li, *Enchantment and Disenchantment: Love and Illusion in Chinese Literature* (1993).

Feminist theorist Elizabeth Grosz has provided a provocative way to construe female bodies as texts in "Inscriptions and Body Maps: Representations and the Corporeal," in *Feminine/Masculine and Representation,* edited by Terry Threadgold and Anne Cranny-Francis (1990). One form of body-writing in China was the enactment of virtues. An overview of imperial canonization of virtuous women can be found in Mark Elvin, "Female Virtue and the State in China," *Past and Present* 104 (1984): 111–152. Discourses of chaste widowhood in the Qing dynasty have been discussed in Susan Mann, "Widows in the Kinship, Class, and Community Structures of Qing Dynasty China," *Journal of Asian Studies* 46 (1987): 37–56. For the importance of the trope of physical ordeal in multiple genres of good woman tales, see Katherine Carlitz, "Desire, Danger, and the Body: Stories of Women's Virtue in Late Ming China," in *Engendering China: Women, Culture, and the State,* edited by Christina Gilmartin et al. (1994).

The divergent strategies of female bodily "writing" beside the embodiment of virtues have only recently received scholarly attention. The history and contestations over the propriety of *gegu* is discussed in Chün-fang Yü, "The Cult of Kuan-yin [Guanyin] in Ming-Ch'ing [Qing] China: A Case of Confucianization of Buddhism?" in *Meeting of the Minds,* edited by Irene Bloom and Joshua Fogel (1997). Suzanne Cahill has revealed the utility of the physical body to Taoist women saints in her "Discipline and Transformation: Body and Practice in the Lives of Taoist Holy Women of the T'ang [Tang] Dynasty (618–907)," and Dorothy Ko has made a revisionist argument in "Footbinding as Female Inscription," both papers delivered at a 1996 conference at the University of California at San Diego, "Women in Confucian Culture in Premodern China, Korea, and Japan." Ko's views were first articulated in *Teachers of the Inner Chambers: Women and Culture in Seventeenth-Century China* (1994).

Focusing on bodily aspects of writing, this article does not treat the subject of female writing in the literal and literary sense. Readers interested in this related issue may consult Susan Mann's *Precious Records: Women in China's Long Eighteenth Century* (1997) and an anthology, *Writing Women in Late Imperial China,* edited by Ellen Widmer and Kang-i Sun Chang (1997).

DOROTHY KO

In the West

The divergent understandings of the body within and across religious traditions make generalizations and cross-cultural comparisons difficult. These problems are compounded by the multiplicity of methodological approaches to the body, each of which defines differently its object of analysis. The body is an ambiguous entity: it is both limitation and possibility, it is experienced both subjectively and objectively, and subjective bodily experience is marked by absence as well as by presence. Most crucially, bodies—both conceptually and experientially—have a history. There is no "body," for bodies are always culturally inscribed in terms of sex, sexuality, race, ethnicity, and other differences. Bodies are not given but are shaped by practices, material conditions, and beliefs.

Despite recognition of the historicity of the concept and lived experience of the body, most discussions of the body imply a general understanding of it as the physical aspect of human nature. Two issues are immediately raised by this commonsense understanding: 1) To speak of the body as an aspect of human nature implies that there are other aspects of the self with which it coexists. This view contradicts those of a number of religious traditions, including ancient Israel. There *ruah,* often translated as spirit, literally means breath; every aspect of humanity is tied to corporeality. 2) Physicality and materiality can themselves be understood in very different ways, even in the same time, place, and religious tradition. In thirteenth-century Christian Europe, for example, Thomas Aquinas argued that the soul defined the specificity of the person. The resurrection of the body occurs when the soul is rejoined to matter—which bits and pieces of matter is unimportant. Among his contemporaries, however, many believed that the resurrection of the body entailed the reassemblage of the very same bits and pieces of matter that made up the person while alive.

With these complications in mind, it can be said that Judaism, Christianity, and Islam share the conviction that bodies are essential to human personhood. This is most apparent in the Christian and Islamic belief, most prevalent in the premodern period, that resurrection was of both soul and body. Judaism and Islam also emphasize the religiosity of the body through their detailed prescriptions for ritual practice. These include regulations concerning every detail of bodily life, particularly what comes into and goes out of the body. Similar concerns exist in Christianity, yet are downplayed in the West by an Augustinian emphasis on inwardness.

Recognition of the centrality of the body to human personhood comes together, within all three Western religious traditions, with some version of philosophical dualism between body and soul. An inheritance of Platonism, this dualism is perhaps most striking in Christianity and stands in constant tension with Christian emphasis on the Incarnation (the becoming flesh of God) and the resurrection of the body. Much work has been done to trace the configurations that Christian conceptions of human nature and bodiliness take in the early Christian and medieval periods. Scholars often focus on gender and sexuality in an attempt to complicate the predominant modern view of Christianity as ascetic and antibodily, and, antibodily, virulently misogynist. According to this account, Christian asceticism denigrates the body. It is associated with woman, whereas the soul is associated with man. Therefore, with the denigration of the body comes that of women.

Although there is truth here—Christian misogyny is certainly real—Peter Brown, Caroline Bynum, and others offer a more nuanced view. Bynum shows that in the Christian Middle Ages, although women are associated with bodiliness, Christ's salvific humanity is also identified with the body. Women, then, in identification with the humanity of Christ, make their bodies a source of salvation. They are willing to undergo enormous suffering not because they despise their bodies, but rather because the painful limitations of fallen human existence can only be overcome through imitation of Christ's suffering on the cross. Brown uncovers the subtlety of early Christian asceticism, a movement that rejected prevailing social ideals and practices. In rejecting procreative sexuality, early Christian polemicists often associated women with sexuality in misogynist ways, yet also put forth a religious ideal that could empower women.

Although dualism between the body and the soul is known in Islam, the central distinction is between this world and the afterlife. The common Arabic term for soul, *nafs*, refers to the self who desires, reminiscent of Plato's appetitive soul. Aspects of what contemporary scholars associated with the bodily life, then, are understood as soul within Islam. The afterlife, moreover, is described in the Qur'an and other classic sources as corporeal and sensual. Although some within medieval and modern Islamic traditions argue that the Prophet Muhammad uses this method of description in order to accommodate limited intellects, orthodox medieval traditions stress the resurrection of the body.

Given the centrality of lineage within Islam, legal traditions discuss in detail acceptable modes of sexual intercourse and special regulations for women. There are also complex purificatory systems governing men's and women's participation in ritual. Purification is not antibodily; rather it marks off certain activities as religiously salient. Given the centrality of orthopraxy (correct practice) to Islam, the body then is central within it. Although menstruation and childbirth are seen as infirmities (and so will not exist in heaven, though sexual intercourse will), the legal tradition is much less disdainful of women's bodies and less likely to see them as contaminating than Islamic mystical traditions, which associate women with body and men with soul or intellect.

Howard Eilberg-Schwartz demonstrates that Jewish struggles over identity and place in the modern world evince an ambivalence toward the body. On the one hand, Christian European culture, particularly in the eighteenth and nineteenth centuries, described Jewish bodies as lacking, diseased, and weak, yet at the same time accused Judaism of being too carnal because of ritual practices that focused on the regulation and purification of the body. As Eilberg-Schwartz shows, Jews reacted in two ways to this twofold stigmatization: some characterized Judaism as a religion of the book, a spiritualizing move that downplays the centrality of the body to Jewish identity (through biological genealogy—one is a Jew if one's mother is a Jew—and religious practice). Some Zionist thinkers, such as Max Nortan, conversely, accepted Christian European characterizations of the weak Jewish body and argued for the necessity of new bodily regimes (most important the pursuit of agriculture in Israel) to restore the health of Jewish bodies. Accounts of the emasculation of Jewish bodies within Christian culture, by Sander Gilman, Joy Geller, and others, however, seem to erase Jewish women's bodies; if to be a Jewish man in a Christian culture is to be feminized, what are the ramifications for Jewish women and their position within the history of Judaism? Although important to the genealogical continuity of Judaism, women were (and still are within many communities) routinely denied access to the study of Torah, which is seen by the rabbis and many modern Jews as essential to Jewish identity. Associated with embodiment, women's position within Judaism has been as ambivalent as the traditional attitudes toward the body itself.

BIBLIOGRAPHY

Biale, David. *Eros and the Jews.* 1992.
Boyarin, Daniel. *Carnal Israel.* 1993.

Brown, Peter. *The Body and Society: Men, Women, and Renunciation in Early Christianity.* 1988.

Bynum, Caroline Walker. *Fragmentation and Redemption: Essays on Gender and the Human Body in Medieval Religion.* 1991.

———. *Holy Feast and Holy Fast: The Religious Significance of Food to Medieval Women.* 1987.

———. *The Resurrection of the Body in Western Christianity, 200–1336.* 1995.

Coakley, Sarah, ed. *Religion and the Body.* 1997.

Eilberg-Schwartz, Howard, ed. *People of the Body: Jews and Judaism from an Embodied Perspective.* 1992.

Feher, Michel, ed. *Fragments for a History of the Human Body.* 3 vols. 1989.

Foucault, Michel. *The History of Sexuality.* Vol. 1: *An Introduction.* Translated by Robert Hurley. 1980.

Law, Jane Marie, ed. *Religious Reflections on the Human Body.* 1995.

Miles, Margaret. *Carnal Knowing: Female Nakedness and Religious Meaning in the Christian West.* 1989.

Smith, Jane Idleman, and Yvonne Yazbeck Haddad. *The Islamic Understanding of Death and Resurrection.* 1981.

AMY HOLLYWOOD

Body Postures and Trance

Human subjects have been represented in Western and non-Western art for millennia. Remarkably, with very few exceptions, the human effigies are female, beginning with the oldest one discovered to date, a female figure 32,000 years old found in Austria (Neugebauer-Maresch, 1993). Marija Gimbutas (1982) describes numerous other examples of female representation from the sixth to the fifth millennium B.C.E. in southeastern Europe. The archaeological record of the Kyklades Islands during the entire third millennium B.C.E. also shows many female images. Predominantly male representations begin to appear much later in the Western Hemisphere (Bernal, 1969; Gimbutas, 1982; Leyenaar, 1992), Oceania (Wardwell, 1994), and Africa (Wingert, 1970). We do not know why this shift occurred over time. It does, however, indicate that the power of ritual tended to become male centered during this period.

In addition to the male-female dichotomy, many of the early human effigies exhibit nonordinary body postures, which may have been connected to rituals. Some figures show the head tilted back, the mouth open, and the hands clutched in the middle of the body or placed asymmetrically. As was discovered in 1977 (Goodman, 1990), such postures combined with rhythmic stimulation produce visionary experiences. The rhythmic stimulation institutes the ecstatic trance, a dramatic physiological change (Goodman, 1990) that makes possible the entrance into the spirit world. And the specific posture is the ritual that defines the visionary experience, such as magical flight to the lower, middle, or upper world; shape shifting into animals or, more rarely, plants; healing or being healed; and divining. During the course of research, more than fifty different postures were tested that appear repeatedly in many different tribal traditions, often thousands of years ago.

The archaeological sites where these postures were found as well as the societies that still represent ritual postures in their art are predominantly hunting and gathering societies that originated in the very distant past. These postures, which induced trance experiences, were later richly elaborated among horticulturalists (hunters working with small gardens in many parts of the world, both ancient and modern). By contrast, there are no traces of ritual body postures in agricultural societies, only postures of symbolic significance.

A young Balinese girl performs a trance dance for the purpose of exorcism, Indonesia, 1958 (Hulton-Deutsch Collection/Corbis).

CHARACTERISTICS OF THE TRANCE

Trance involves a dissolution of gravity, making the spirit journey possible. The dimension of time is absent, so there is unlimited access to the present, the past, and the future. Most important, the trance state gives access to the abode of a multitude of spirits eager to assume the role of helpers and guides. Foremost among them are the Bear Spirit, the mighty healer, and the Buffalo, who often chooses women to train and protect. The quintessence of the experiences stimulated by body postures agrees with that reported from the vision-quest traditions of the Plains Indians (Irwin, 1994).

These trance and visionary experiences describe a worldview that is free of good and evil; the spirits, although powerful, do not assert any dominance and are not hierarchical. Rather, they reflect an egalitarian system. Expressed in cultural terms, the trance visions of early peoples—hunters, gatherers, and horticulturalists—take us into a moral universe.

A WOMAN'S PLACE

In most hunting tribes the initiation rituals for boys are lengthy and strenuous, while the corresponding rituals among girls are usually brief. The reason given by the tribes for this discrepancy is that it is harder for men to learn how to enter the trance state, which women seem to know innately. Women seem to feel comfortable in the egalitarian world to which the postures afford them entry. Men and women are equal there, and so are humans and spirits: they roam without fear in an alternate reality free of malevolence.

BIBLIOGRAPHY

Alva, Walter. *Royal Tombs of Sipan.* 1993.
Badiches Labdesmuseum Karlsruhe. *Kunst der Kykladeninseln im 3. Jahrtausend v. Chr.* (exhibit). 1976.
Bernal, Ignacio. *The Olmec World.* 1969.
Dockstader, Frederick. *Indian Art in America.* 1973.
Furst, Jill L., and Peter Furst. *North American Indian Art.* 1982.
Gimbutas, Marija. *The Goddesses and Gods of Old Europe.* 1982.
Goodman, Felicitas D. *Ecstasy, Ritual, and Alternate Reality.* 1988.
———. *Where the Spirits Ride the Wind: Trance Journeys and Other Ecstatic Experiences.* 1990.
Irwin, Lee. *The Dream Seekers: Native American Visionary Traditions of the Great Plains.* 1994.
Lehrer, Johann, et al. *Ecuador: Gold and Terrakotten.* 1990.
Leyenaar, Ted, et al. *From Coast to Coast.* 1992.
Neugebauer-Maresch, Christine. *Altsteinzeit im Osten Osterreichs.* 1993.
Wardwell, Allen. *Island Ancestors.* 1994.
Wingert, Paul S. *African Art.* 1970.

See also **Native American Religions; Shamans; Visions.**

FELICITAS GOODMAN

Boundaries

Boundaries separate women from men at many levels of religious practice, from participation in ritual to the expression of religious experience in the myths that communicate meaning within a particular tradition.

In the early histories of the three monotheistic traditions, men and women were separated not only at the time of ritual worship but also in the cultivation of leadership and learning. Jewish women were ritually excluded from the Jerusalem Temple during the time of their menses. Christian women, although they could receive the sacrament of the Holy Eucharist from the hands of male priests, were prohibited from distributing or even touching the consecrated bread themselves. Muslim women, after the death of the Prophet Muhammad, were not only prohibited from entering the place of prayer but were obliged to cover themselves when praying outside. Until the twentieth century, when these customs were relaxed in certain segments of each community, Christian women were required to cover their heads when entering a church to visibly separate themselves from the men, while Muslim and Orthodox Jewish women kept their heads covered in any place outside the home.

But perhaps most significantly, while the sacred language of scripture was open to men as rabbis, priests, and imams, women in these traditions were prohibited from receiving an education in the word of God, except in unusual cases.

Certain exceptional women found ways to cross into this world of men to learn the scriptures for themselves or to assume positions of leadership within the larger religious community. But most of these women were understood (whether in their own time or later) to be saints and prophetesses who could, by virtue of their holiness, communicate directly with God. These women refused to live the designated female roles of their time, following instead the traditional male paths of leadership or saintliness. A few examples of such women are the heroines of the Hebrew Bible, Judith and Esther; female Christian saints such as Catherine of Alexandria and Teresa of Avila; and the famous Sufi Muslim saint Rabi'ah al-'Adawiyyah.

Female devotees dance around the god Krishna in a pasture (The Metropolitan Museum of Art).

In the Asian traditions of Buddhism and Hinduism, the boundaries separating the religious worlds of women and men must be understood within the broad context of the fundamental law of karma and transmigration. In both the Buddhist and Hindu traditions, a present birth (and gender) is limiting only for the duration of this particular lifetime, and stories within both traditions experiment with this fluid boundary separating life, death, and rebirth and the always potential gender changes inherent in this process. In a well-known Hindu story, the god Vishnu gives the male sage Narada the body and identity of a woman in order to teach him the mystery of life. At the end of "her" life, amidst tears of grief mourning the deaths of "her" loved ones, Narada, again a man, reflects on his existence as a woman as having been a "terrible fate." While recognizing the importance of knowledge gained as a woman, the story emphasizes that spiritual knowledge and liberation are won as a man.

Within the Hindu traditions, some of the more interesting gender boundaries are those that are purposely transposed or blurred. In the devotional (bhakti) tradition, devotees of Krishna describe their love for the god in images of human longing and passion. More specifically, all devotees, including the men, identify with the role of the cowherding girls (*gopīs*) who were overwhelmed with feelings of love for Krishna when he appeared among them as a handsome, sensual, and fun-loving cowherding boy, enchanting them with his mischief and flute-playing. Male devotees ritually become the female *gopīs*, a practice that inspired the great male poet-saint, Sur Das, to write of the intense ecstasy he felt when, like a long-separated lover, he was again united with Krishna.

A renowned sixteenth-century male saint, Caitanya, is revered as a unique incarnation of both Krishna and his favorite female lover, Rādhā. According to the tradition, because Krishna wanted to feel Rādhā's passionate longing for him at the same time as feeling his own passion for her, Krishna and Rādhā together incarnated in the person and body of Caitanya. Iconographically, this united image of Krishna-Rādhā depicts the male and female deities so intertwined that they appear as two bodies whose boundaries have become so completely enmeshed that the viewer cannot easily see where Krishna stops and Rādhā begins.

Like Jewish, Christian, and Muslim holy women, female Hindu saints defy the boundaries set for women. Refusing the roles of wife and mother, Hindu holy women who take up religious lives, either as ascetics (*sannyasi*) or as devotees, transgress a number of boundaries. According to the lawbooks (Manavadharmashastra), women are bound by their relationships to men: "In childhood a woman should be protected by her father, in youth by her husband, in old age by her son. Verily, a woman does not deserve freedom" (The Laws of Manu 5.148). However, a woman saint refuses these relationships to dedicate herself entirely to the divine.

In Indian and Tibetan Buddhism, the virtue called the "Perfection of Wisdom" (*prajñā*), the highest of the Mahāyāna Buddhist virtues, is portrayed as a feminine bodhisattva, who stands either alone or as the consort of Manjushri, the male bodhisattva of wisdom. Yet in many early Buddhist texts (e.g., *Sutra of the Perfection of Wisdom in Eight Thousand Verses* and *Lotus Sutra*), the boundary separating women and men also separates those who may attain bodhisattvahood from those who are not ready. In order to achieve enlightenment, women must first become men, either in another birth or in an advanced spiritual state of mind.

Contemporary Buddhist practice allows much greater flexibility for women in terms of attaining the enlightenment of a bodhisattva or a buddha, but few monastic communities allow the ordination of women as nuns. The explanation for this situation is traced to the life of Gautama Buddha in the sixth century B.C.E., when he only grudgingly allowed women to take monastic vows and to join the monastic community. Anticipating special problems for female monastics, the Buddha instituted extra rules for them, and placed all Buddhist nuns under the authority and guidance of the monks.

BIBLIOGRAPHY

Attar, Farid al-Din. *Muslim Saints and Mystics.* Translated by A. J. Arberry. 1966. A translation of the work of a thirteenth-century Persian poet, and hence a thirteenth-century description of the eighth-century Rabi'ah.

Berger, Pamela. *The Goddess Obscured: Transformation of the Grain Protectress from Goddess to Saint.* 1985.

Bynum, Caroline et al., ed. *Gender and Religion: On the Complexity of Symbols.* 1986.

Gross, Rita M. *Buddhism After Patriarchy: A Feminist History, Analysis, and Reconstruction of Buddhism.* 1993.

Hawley, John S., and Donna Marie Wulff, eds. *The Divine Consort: Radha and the Goddesses of India.* 1986.

Hiltebeitel, Alf. *The Cult of Draupadi.* Vol. 1, *Mythologies: From Gingee to Kuruksetra.* 1988.

————. *The Cult of Draupadi.* Vol. 2, *On Hindu Ritual and the Goddess.* 1991.

Marglin, Frederique Apffel. *Wives of the God-King: The Rituals of the Devadasis of Puri.* 1985.

O'Flaherty, Wendy Doniger. *Dreams, Illusion and Other Realities.* 1984.

————. *Women, Androgynes, and Other Mythical Beasts.* 1980.

Paul, Diana Y. *Women in Buddhism: Images of the Feminine in the Mahayana Tradition.* 1985.

Sered, Susan Starr. *Priestess, Mother, Sacred Sister: Religions Dominated by Women.* 1994.

See also Androgyny; Bhakti; Buddhas, Bodhisattvas, and Arhats; Buddhism: An Overview; Gender Roles; Hinduism: An Overview; Ritual; Sex Change; Wisdom: An Overview.

CATHERINE BENTON

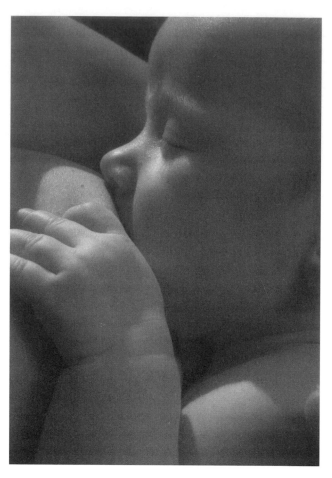

An infant nurses at the breast (Jim Sugar Photography/ Corbis).

Breasts

Breasts figure prominently in the symbolism of many religious traditions. As markers of reproduction and nurturing they often invoke a culture's hope of sustaining itself in fullness and health. Breasts and breast-feeding also can signify more abstract economies of exchange such as between a people and their god(s), or between the soul and its savior. In literate cultures, the symbolism of breasts is often appropriated in male rhetoric to soften demanding disciplines and to draw private emotions into public spaces where they can be redirected toward cultural ideals.

In pre-Aryan India, many of the surviving figurines are of buxom women that likely belonged to fertility cults. Following the arrival of the Aryans in the second millennium B.C.E., Vedic myth (composed and preserved by men) arrogated to itself breast symbolism with the claim that religious literature was milked out of the elements (Manu I.23). Breast-feeding continues to be an important mythic element in the cycle of Krishna myths, and Krishna himself, plump and full of butter and milk, seems breastlike. Significant in later mythology is the noticeable bifurcation of women's bodies into good breasts and bad vaginas (O'Flaherty, 1980).

In Buddhism, the special tie between the Buddha and his mother, Maya, is represented as an enduring milk-bond. According to later tradition, the Buddha's wet nurse, Mahapajapati, is said to have convinced the Buddha to establish the order of nuns based on the logic of milk-debts: she gave to him her milk and now he should reciprocate with the dharma (Sponberg, 1992). In medieval Chinese Buddhism, the logic of milk-debts was developed in a triangle of reciprocation that begins with the mother's breast: every son is to remember the love and sustenance he received as an infant and feel obliged to repay it by ensuring his mother's salvation with donations to the monastery (Cole, 1998). Milk-debts still pervade East Asian thought and are prevalent in modern Japan where icons of breasts appear instrumental in establishing children in exacting capitalist programs (Allison, 1996).

In the West, the Bible has few references to breasts, but early Church Fathers, as well as gnostic writers, drew extensively on the image of Jesus as a mothering figure (Pagels, 1976). Later, in the medieval period many male authors chose breast symbolism to convey the boons of submitting to male authority that, either in the form of Jesus or the abbot, promised the elixir of everlasting life (Bynum, 1982). The cult of the Virgin also draws heavily on images of breast-feeding, and one detects a tension as the strength of this cult pulls at its patriarchal confines. Breast imagery also appears in religio-political discourses such as in the case of Marianne, the bare-breasted heroine carrying the tricolors at the head of the French Revolution (Agulhon, 1979). Similarly in late capitalism, arguably a religion of sorts, breasts function as a primary draw in advertisement.

In sum, breasts seem to promise plenitude in a particularly powerful way because the effect (fullness/health) is already present and visible in the cause (the breast), and because images of a prosperous future simultaneously invoke a nostalgized past.

BIBLIOGRAPHY

Agulhon, Maurice. *Marianne au combat: L'imagerie et la symbolique républicaines de 1789 à 1880.* 1979.

Allison, Anne. *Permitted and Prohibited Desires: Mothers, Comics, and Censorship in Japan.* 1996.

Bynum, Caroline Walker. *Jesus as Mother. Studies in the Spirituality of the High Middle Ages.* 1982.

Cole, Alan. *Mothers and Sons in Chinese Buddhism.* 1998.

O'Flaherty, Wendy Doniger. *Women, Androgynes, and Other Mythical Beasts.* 1980.

Pagels, Elaine. "God the Mother." *Signs* 2 (1976): 293–303.

Sponberg, Alan. "Attitudes Toward Women and the Feminine in Early Buddhism." In *Buddhism, Sexuality, and Gender.* Edited by José Ignacio Cabèzon. 1992.

See also Fertility and Barrenness; Motherhood and Grandmotherhood; Virgin Mary.

ALAN COLE

Buddhas, Bodhisattvas, and Arhats

The scriptures of Buddhism present three ideals of human perfection: the arhat (or, in Pali, *arahant*), one who has completely "destroyed" (from *han,* "to destroy," or "to kill") the three "enemies" (*ari*), namely ignorance, desire, and hatred; the bodhisattva, one who, following in the Mahayana way, is intent on gaining the complete enlightenment of a Buddha and who does so by cultivating both wisdom and compassion; and the Buddha, one who has accomplished this goal, and who thereby embodies these virtues and has as a consequence the ability to teach the way to others. Strictly speaking, none of these three ideals is limited by considerations of sex or gender. However, one finds throughout the orthodox scriptures of Buddhism abundant passages in which there is a clear bias against women's abilities to attain these ideals. In fact, both the early and later scriptures profess the general assumption that the highest goals can only be attained by men and that women who desire these goals must first be reincarnated in male form in order to do so.

Given the cultural context of India in the sixth century B.C.E., as well as the importance of strict celibacy to the earliest community of male renunciants, it is not surprising that women would have been devalued. Women were viewed as having the "three obediences," that is, to their parents when children, to their husbands when adults, and to their sons when aged. Although some women were exempt from the rigid strictures of Aryan society, the great majority were bound by a worldview that deemed them equivalent to children at best and, at worse, to Sudras, the lowest members of society.

Therefore, to the question, "Can a woman attain enlightenment?" one finds, in Buddhist texts, differing answers. Many Hinayana texts assert that, owing to her having the three obediences, a woman is so bound up in domestic life that she cannot devote herself to the religious practice necessary to the attainment of enlightenment. Hence, these texts generally assert that women cannot attain arhatship. According to the more progressive texts of the Mahayana tradition, however, it is declared that all beings can attain Buddhahood. Even so, the authors of Mahayana scriptures have often had to resort to quite clever narrative schemes so as to reconcile the two conflicting ideas that all beings are able to become Buddhas and women are unable to become Buddhas. Texts like the Lotus sutra, for example, have portrayed female figures who, in order to become Buddhas, had first magically to transform their sex, first changing into men and only then into Buddhas. In the Mahayana Śrīmālā sutra, however, a woman character, the princess Śrīmālā, takes center stage, teaching as a Buddha herself (without having first to abandon her female form), and announcing that all beings possess Buddha-nature (here, the theory of *tathāgata-garbha*)

Seated Buddha with bodhisattvas (Luca I. Tettoni/Corbis).

and hence all, regardless of sex or gender, are equally able to attain Buddhahood.

The Buddhist community has always consisted of monks, nuns, laymen, and laywomen—in that order, largely in deference to the social and cultural structures and conditions of the birth of the tradition. However, women's place and standing within Buddhism has remained a problematic and contentious issue. The problem seems perhaps more acute in Buddhism because its doctrines contain such revolutionary and equalizing notions as *anātman*, or "nonself," and *śūnyatā*, or "the emptiness of an independent, inherently existent self." Yet, in spite of such doctrines, Buddhist institutions have continually evidenced discrimination against women. Many modern-day Buddhist scholars have addressed this problem. One text in particular, which purports to describe the founding of the nuns' order *Cullavagga X*, is often cited as evidence of the early community's antifemale gender bias. Nonetheless, other texts, most notably the *Therīgāthā*, show that women, once admitted to the Buddhist order, lost no time in proving their capabilities for attaining arhatship.

In some of the earliest Mahayana texts, such as the Diamond sutra, one finds clear articulation that gender has no bearing on one's attainment of enlightenment.

There, the Buddha himself is said to have stated: "Those who by my form (that is, body, or sex) did see me, and those who followed me by my voice, wrong the actions they engaged in, Me those ones will not see." And in the Vimalakīrtinirdeśa sutra, when the goddess is questioned by Śāriputra (a representative of the highest wisdom of the Hinayana tradition) about why she, being wise, has not yet transformed herself out of her female form, she announces: "Although I have sought my 'female state' for these twelve years, I have not yet found it. . . . Reverend Śāriputra, the Buddha has taught that in all things, there is neither male nor female."

As is the case with other great religious traditions, Buddhism's doctrines espouse egalitarian ideals; yet its institutions, for the most part, have remained quite conservative.

BIBLIOGRAPHY

Conze, Edward. *Buddhist Wisdom Books.* 1958.

Katz, Nathan. *Buddhist Images of Human Perfection.* 1982.

Paul, Diana. *Women in Buddhism: Images of the Feminine in the Mahayana Tradition.* 1979.

Rahula, Walpola. *What the Buddha Taught.* 1959.

Rhys Davids, Caroline A. F., and K. R. Norman. *Poems of Early Buddhist Nuns.* 1909. Reprint, 1989.

Schelling, Andrew, and Anne Waldman. *Songs of the Sons and Daughters of Buddha.* 1996.

Sponberg, Alan. "Attitudes toward Women and the Feminine in Early Buddhism." In *Buddhism, Sexuality, and Gender.* Edited by José Ignacio Cabezón. 1992.

Willis, Janice D. "Nuns and Benefactresses: The Role of Women in the Development of Buddhism." In *Women, Religion, and Social Change.* Edited by Yvonne Haddad and Ellison Findly. 1985.

See also **Buddhism: An Overview; Sex Change.**

JANICE D. WILLIS

Buddhism

An Overview

What (harm) could the woman's state do to us, when the mind is well-concentrated, when knowledge exists for someone rightly having insight into the doctrine? (*Therīgāthā*, p. 7)

This poem, traditionally attributed to the fifth-century B.C.E. Buddhist nun and poet Soma, encapsulates many of the issues, not only of early Buddhism but of the whole tumultuous period of ancient India, referred to as the period of the heterodoxies (sixth to fifth centuries B.C.E.), that culminated in the founding of the new religious sects of the Buddhists, Jains, and Ājīvikas. The religious virtuosi of these sects referred to themselves as *śramaṇas*, in distinction to the *brāhmaṇas* (brahmans) of orthodoxy. The *śramaṇas* emphasized the practice of asceticism, and some rejected not only the ritualism of the brahmans but also their social distinctions, especially those of caste and gender. Essentially, this was a period of conflict about the sources of authority for sacred knowledge. For the *brāhmaṇas* sacred knowledge was divinely revealed to certain *ṛṣis* (seers), who then transmitted it through their holy texts, the Vedas, while in Buddhism a new sacred knowledge came from the Buddha's direct and personal experience of enlightenment. IIis teachings emphasized the necessity of proving spiritual truth for oneself through reason and experience. As Soma's poem shows, women could and did achieve enlightenment, the ultimate goal of Buddhism, and they came from various castes.

Most information about the women of the early Buddhist community comes from canonical sources, for instance the Pali canon, a voluminous collection of sermons, rules, folklore, philosophical discourses, and poems such as the *Therīgāthā*, which contains Soma's poem, among others. The Pali canon was compiled and edited by Theravada monks in Sri Lanka (formerly Ceylon) beginning around the first century B.C.E., primarily from much earlier oral sources, although additional material continued to be added until at least the fifth century C.E. In various forms a significant part of this literature is the shared canon of all Buddhists, although compilers of Mahayana and tantric canons also made their own additions. At least two basic points need to be made about this literature. First, comparisons of the same events described in different canons show gendered disjunctions. For example, in the Pali telling of the Buddha's funeral women are absent, whereas in the *Mūlasarvāstivādin Vinaya* of the Mahayana (completed by about the third century C.E.) women held the processional canopy over the Buddha's bier, which was carried by the men. This leads to the second point: most of the texts of world religion have been compiled and written by men and have a misogynist edge. Oral traditions, too, suffer from a male bias in at least two ways, and all the early documents of Buddhism mostly remained in oral form for several centuries. First, when women tell stories, they tend to have both women and men as main characters, whereas the vast majority of stories told by men have men as their main characters. Second, when men do tell stories that have female main characters, they cast them into masculine roles, thereby revealing the male preoccupation with male social roles as well as their inability to either perceive or value female social roles. In other words, when men tell stories about women they transform them into men (Mills). An example of this in Buddhism is the argument that one had to be male in order to achieve liberation, which led to many stories about sex change. Thus, it is not only quite amazing that we have any information at all on early Buddhist women, but its very existence is strong evidence for the persistence of a powerful female presence and suggests that much more material has been lost.

The serious reader must be prepared to read through a male lens and to accept that even those texts written in a female voice or under female authorship may not be authentic. In ancient India authorship was more a form of anonymity than one of disclosure. For instance, admirable as Soma's poem is, perhaps a more authentic female voice is found in Muttā's poem, also from the *Therīgāthā*:

> I am well-released, properly released . . . by means of the three crooked things, by the mortar, pestle, and my crooked husband. I am released from birth and death; that which leads to renewed existence has been rooted out. (*Therīgāthā*, p. 2)

Soma denies the importance of female existence for liberation; Muttā emphasizes it as a means to that end. Soma's poem is in answer to being challenged as a woman pursuing liberation; Muttā's is its own statement.

Nonetheless, the canons reveal what Buddhists have believed about women for centuries and provide authority both for women seeking to reform sexist tendencies in Buddhism and those who oppose such reforms. The information provided by these texts gets slippery, however, as they move with an easy fluidity between myth and real life, blurring any distinction between the two; and therefore they must be grounded in the archaeological, epigraphic, and iconographic evidence that documents women's participation, especially as donors (on female donors see Findly, forthcoming). For instance, at the most famous Buddhist pilgrimage site, Bodh Gāya, where the Buddha was said to have achieved enlightenment in the first century C.E., Queens Kurangī and Nāgadevī donated funds for a railing to surround the main temple, a walkway, and a throne. These two women alone made a tremendous public and visual impact on a site that was central to the experience of early Buddhism. Additionally, the Buddhist custom of raising stupas (shrines) that contain the relics of saints was extended to female saints, though not as often as to male saints (Schopen, "An Old Inscription," 1991). These are concrete and often datable evidence of women's history in Buddhism.

Buddhism began with the life of its founder Gautama of the Śākya tribe, called the Buddha (a title meaning "the enlightened one"), who lived from 566 to 486 B.C.E. The traditional account of his life is that he was born the son of a king. At the time of his birth a holy man predicted that he would either rule the world or renounce the world. In order to ensure his glorious future as a great king, the Buddha's father brought him up in luxury and prevented him from seeing anything unpleasant. When he was about twenty-nine years old, however, the Buddha traveled outside the palace grounds. Here he encountered four aspects of human experience that his father had prevented him from seeing: a sick man, an old man, a dead man, and a wandering ascetic. This ascetic represents the solution to the problem of the first three visions, namely, enlightenment, which involves the struggle to become free of the wheel of existence that leads to countless rebirths inevitably attended by sickness, aging, and death. Enlightenment is a profound shift of consciousness that frees one from worldly desires, which lead to continual reincarnations.

Because of these four visions, the Buddha was profoundly shaken by the transitoriness and the suffering endemic to all existence and decided to become a wandering ascetic in the hope of finding a way beyond the merely transitory. This story is told in all the major biographies of the Buddha along with the other main events of his life: his miraculous conception and birth, the death of his mother, his marriage, life in his father's palace, his years of ascetic practices, and, after great effort, his enlightenment. A pivotal event is the Buddha's departure from home, when he abandoned not only his wife but the many women of his harem. This popular textual and iconographic scene represents women both as sexual temptresses and as physically disgusting, the Buddha seeing them asleep, lying in awkward positions, drooling and snoring.

Some biographical texts, especially the *Lalitavistara* on which the following is based, also contain positive representations of women. For six years after leaving home the Buddha practiced such severe forms of asceticism that he was near death. His dead mother, Queen Māyā, descended from heaven to remind him of his spiritual destiny, and at her prompting the Buddha decided on a more moderate path, the Middle Path, between the severe asceticism he had been practicing and the worldly life of pleasure he had led as a prince. (This path is why precolonial Buddhists called Buddhism the Middle Way.) To this end, he accepted the food offered

A painting of the birth of the Buddha in the Temple of Yongju, Suwon, South Korea (Leonard de Selva/Corbis)

to him by some young village women led by Sujātā. His five male followers, who later became the first monks, abandoned him to food, females, and the forces of nature, doubting he would achieve enlightenment. Meanwhile, the Buddha continued his drawn-out process of reconciliation with females from all realms of existence: human (living and dead), divine, and animal. At one point, after eating he entered a cemetery where he removed the cloth covering a female corpse to replace his own ragged robe. He then bathed in a nearby pond but was too weak to get out by himself. Seeing his distress, a tree goddess lowered one of her branches to help him, after which a female *nāga* (powerful snake beings) made offerings to him.

The Buddha, refreshed and strengthened by these female encounters, proceeded to reintegrate positive experiences of women and female forces and reverse his pointed earlier rejection of them. Then, and only then, was he ready to move toward the Bodhi tree, under which he battled the demon Māra and his seductive daughters. But the battle turned in favor of the Buddha only when he met Māra's challenge to find a witness for his merit by calling on the Earth herself, which he did by extending his right hand downward. Iconographically, this is one of the most popular Buddha images, called the *bhūmisparśa*, the earth-touching pose. This is the main icon of the Buddha's supreme achievement, enlightenment, and by the gesture of his right hand it signals the necessary female component of that achievement.

After his enlightenment the Buddha established a religious community which practiced his ideas; he continued to preach and shape this community until his death at age eighty, forty-five years later. Its center was composed of the nuns and monks who renounced worldly life: they were celibate, ate only one meal a day, begged for their food from the laity, and spent most of the year wandering from place to place so as not to become attached to one spot. This path is a model for a moderate life, emphasizing meditation as a way to change one's conscious perception of the world in order to reach enlightenment in this life. An enlightened person sees the world differently from one who is still bound by desire and suffering; consequently, that person is released from the wheel of existence and moves beyond death and rebirth. Included in this community were the lay supporters who gained merit by giving to the monastics, which helped them to be reborn in a position deemed more favorable to spiritual progress. The lay supporters adopted five precepts: not to take any life (animal or human), not to steal, not to engage in illicit sex, not to lie, and not to use intoxicating substances. Most of this description of the early Buddhist community remains in place today, with the exceptions that monasteries became established communities that limited wandering, and the goal of enlightenment was eventually seen as less attainable in one lifetime. Thus, lay practitioners especially began to concentrate on achieving a better future life. Nonetheless, for Buddhists salvation is still achieved through the highly individual and personal experience of enlightenment. One consequence of this emphasis on individual experience has been a valuing of the biographical literature of those individuals who have achieved it and thus describe the way for others.

The Buddha's stepmother and aunt (she was Māyā's sister), Mahāprajāpatī, is a pivotal figure in early Buddhism, for she became the first Buddhist nun and maintained a lifelong relationship with the Buddha. The textual record of her ordination (*Cullavagga*.X of the Vinaya, II.254–283) is highly problematic, though many scholars accept the story of the Buddha's reluctance to ordain women and the stipulation of eight additional rules for nuns as if it were historical fact. Actually, it is quite possibly a later interpolation or merely a dramatic device (see Findly, 1993; Sponberg; Walters; Young, 1994). What we have is a passage that is descriptive of existing conditions, the subordination of the nuns to the monks, rather than a prescription by the Buddha that this is the way it should be. Of note, however, is the propagation of this story as fact throughout the Buddhist world and the eventual decline of the nuns' ordination lineage. This entire scenario is perhaps best viewed in light of the routinization of charisma whereby followers eventually retract the innovations of charismatic leaders. Additionally, it needs

to be understood within the context of contemporaneous views about the activities of other ascetic women such as the Jain order of nuns and their rather different history (Young, 1994). Significantly, the tradition also states in connection to this first ordination that the Buddha affirmed women's ability to achieve enlightenment, and Mahāprajāpatī's own biography is a testament to that ability (Walters), as are the nuns' poems in the *Therīgāthā*. The main goal, the sine qua non, is enlightenment, and here women are equal to men.

The Buddha's wife, or wives (depending on the tradition), also deserves careful attention, not necessarily for what may have been her actual relationship to the Buddha but for what various traditions have done with her as a symbol of womanhood (see Bareau; Shaw; Strong; Young, forthcoming; and Zelliot). She is also a particularly intriguing figure in the *Jātakas*, the past life stories of the Buddha, most of which he shared with her.

The early tradition emphasized the human qualities of the Buddha, making the point that enlightenment is open to all sentient beings who strive for it. In time, however, the Buddha is increasingly described in more divine terms, which suggests that achieving a direct, personal enlightenment experience is less of a human possibility. Instead, emphasis is placed on acquiring merit in order to win a rebirth that will lead to enlightenment, or to be reborn in a particular Buddhist heaven.

These and other changes and innovations in doctrine occurred slowly over the centuries, with various schools distinguishing themselves, most of which eventually disappeared. This early period of Buddhism is best described as Nīkāya or Sectarian Buddhism. By around the first century B.C.E., two distinct schools of Buddhism are established. The first is Theravada, the only surviving school of the early period, which spread south from northern India into Sri Lanka and eventually east to Burma, Thailand, Cambodia, and Laos. Its ideal type is the arhat, a nun or monk who has achieved enlightenment; many monastic women achieved positions of prominence and prestige, but over time this opportunity declined, as did the order of nuns. The other school is Mahayana, which grew out of various sectarian groups to take shape as a separate school of Buddhism in northern India around the first century B.C.E.; it is the form of Buddhism that spread north to Tibet and east to China, Korea, and Japan. This school understands itself to contain the esoteric doctrine of the Buddha, the teachings he did not preach publicly; its religious ideal is the bodhisattva, an enlightened being of infinite compassion who postpones final personal enlightenment in order to continue to reincarnate and help all other beings to achieve enlightenment. The bodhisattva can be female or male, thus leaving the path of spiritual accomplishment open to women, though they often met with the usual difficulties of sexist societies and religious hierarchies.

A third school of Buddhism, variously called esoteric Buddhism, Vajrayana, or tantra, began sometime around the fifth century C.E. This movement had its roots in the popular religions of northern India, which contained many magical and shamanistic features as well as the worship of goddesses. All these elements are incorporated into tantric practices, which spread throughout the Buddhist world. The movement stresses enlightenment in one lifetime in contradistinction to the idea of gradual enlightenment over several lifetimes, which had developed in some sects of Mahayana and Theravada; it emphasizes individual visionary experiences. Its ideal type is the *siddha*, and there were and are women *siddha*s; but most often the tradition is described from the male point of view.

Women, both lay and monastic, were instrumental in spreading all three schools of Buddhism as missionaries (Bode), teachers, practitioners, and donors. Royal support for the spread and maintenance of Buddhism was historically important and contributions by royal women tremendously so. Most of this support, however, was directed toward monks, not nuns. This hinges on the concept of merit (Sanskrit, *puṇya;* Pali, *puñña*), the idea that donations, whether monetary or through actions and prayers, create merit that will lead to better future lives in Buddhist heavens or in circumstances that will be conducive to achieving enlightenment. In practice, merit is usually dedicated to the good of all sentient beings or to the donor's parents. At issue is the belief that monks make a better, that is, more productive, field of merit than nuns, from which inevitably followed, and continues to follow, the wealth of monks' establishments and the poverty of nuns'. Despite such views about the qualities of actual women, important Buddhist values were often conceived in feminine terms such as compassion and wisdom.

In keeping with the cyclical worldview of Buddhism, and to capture its paradoxical nature, it seems appropriate to end at the beginning, with the Buddhist creation story. Buddhists and Hindus alike share the Indian belief that the life of the universe is cyclical: it comes into being, destroys itself, and comes into being again, in the endless turning of the wheel of existence. In one Buddhist version of creation from the *Visuddhi-Magga* (c. fifth century C.E.), the earth was formed gradually. Beings of light were attracted to it and began to eat pieces of it. As a consequence of this primordial meal distinctions arise: handsome and ugly, female and male, possessions (mine and yours). This story does not emphasize one sex over the other; both participate in the creation of the world as we know it. The division into sexes is seen as part of the process, even though this division has the negative consequence of leading to dualistic thinking, such as a sense of self as distinct from others, that blocks the path to enlightenment. In the tantric tradition highly trained adepts attempt to reverse this process of creation in their meditational practices in order to arrive at a purer, nonearthly, and androgynous form.

In Buddhism gender is considered an illusion, and to take it seriously is to fall into the trap of limited dualistic thinking. Consequently, many Buddhists will argue for the irrelevance of gender studies in Buddhism, dismissing the whole enterprise as missing the point. Unfortunately, frail human nature all too easily does fall into the trap of dualism. There are Theravada monks who, as they argue for the illusory nature of sexual difference, will not accept an offering from a woman's hand: she must put it down before the monks will take it, whereas men can hand anything directly to them. Mahayana and Vajrayana monks will accept offerings directly from women, but women are often prohibited from entering their monasteries, or certain sections of them. Of course, many Buddhist women have also internalized these views. Perhaps the greatest harm of dualistic thinking is the tremendous, almost unbridgeable, gap it creates between theory and practice.

BIBLIOGRAPHY

CANONICAL SOURCES ON BUDDHIST WOMEN

See *The Elders' Verses*, vol. 2, *Therīgāthā*, translated by A. K. Norman (1971), Pali edition by Richard Pischel (1983); I. B. Horner's translation of the *Vinaya* entitled *The Book of the Discipline*, 6 vols. (1938–1966; repr. 1992); as well as the biographies of the Buddha: Aśvaghoṣa, *Buddhacarita*, edited and translated by E. H. Johnston (1936; Delhi, 1984); Sanskrit edition of the *Lalitavistara*, edited by P. L. Vaidya (Darbhanga, 1985); and an English edition, Gwendolyn Bays's translation of Edouard Foucaux's French translation from the Sanskrit, *The Voice of the Buddha: The Beauty of Compassion* (1983); the *Nidāna-Kathā*, in *The Jātaka Together with Its Commentary*, edited by V. Fausboll (1877), translated by T. W. Rhys Davids as *Buddhist Birth Stories* (1880; repr. 1925). The *Buddhacarita* and *Lalitavistara* were composed in India between the first century B.C.E. and the first century C.E., a period that saw the rise of the Mahayana school of Buddhism; the *Nidāna-Kathā* is a Theravada text composed in Sri Lanka in the fifth century C.E. A fourth biography is contained in *The Gilgit Manuscript of the Saṅghabhedvastu, Being the 17th and Last Section of the Vinaya of the*

Mūlasarvāstivādin, edited by Raniero Gnoli (Rome, 1977), no English translation available. This was compiled around the third century C.E. and became an important source in Mahayana traditions. Despite some differences, all four texts were based on much earlier, shared oral material. The *Jātakas* themselves are an additional biographical source on the Buddha as they are folktales about his past lives; English translation, *The Jātaka,* edited by E. B. Cowell (1895; London, 1973).

Some general sources for background on the early period of Buddhism are: Richard Gombrich, *Theravāda Buddhism: A Social History from Ancient Benares to Modern Colombo* (1988); Luis O. Gomez, "Buddhism: Buddhism in India," in *The Encyclopedia of Religion,* vol. 2, edited by Mircea Eliade (1987); Akira Hirakawa, *A History of Indian Buddhism: From Śākyamuni to Early Mahāyāna,* translated and edited by Paul Groner (1990; Delhi, 1993); Padmanabh S. Jaini, "Śramaṇas: Their Conflict with Brahmanical Society," in *Chapters in Indian Civilization,* vol. 1, edited by Joseph W. Elder (1970); Étienne Lamotte, *History of Indian Buddhism: From the Origins to the Śaka Era,* translated by Sara Webb-Boin (1958; Louvain-la-Neuve, 1988). John C. Huntington's two series of articles on the eight major Buddhist pilgrimage sites in *Orientations* are extremely helpful for material evidence. See first "Sowing the Seeds of the Lotus: A Journey to the Great Pilgrimage Sites of Buddhism," part I, 16, no. 11 (November 1985): 46–61; part II, 17, no. 2 (February 1986): 28–43; part III, 17, no. 3 (March 1986): 32–46; part IV, 17, no. 7 (July 1986): 28–40; and part V, 17, no 9 (September 1986): 46–58. See second "Pilgrimage as Image: The Cult of the Astamahapratiharya," part I, 18, no. 4 (April 1987): 55–63 and part II, 18, no. 8 (August 1987): 56–68. These sites commemorate the Buddha's birth, enlightenment, first sermon, death, ascent, and descent from the Trāyastriṁśa heaven (two separate places), the taming of the mad elephant, and the gift of honey from a monkey. Gregory Schopen, "Archaeology and Protestant Presuppositions in the Study of Indian Buddhism," *History of Religions* 31 (August 1991–May 1992): 1–23, raises important issues about conflicting textual and archaeological evidence in early Buddhism as well as Western presuppositions about early Buddhism. His "An Old Inscription from Amarāvatī and the Cult of the Local Monastic Dead in Indian Buddhist Monasteries," *Journal of the International Association of Buddhist Studies* 14, no. 2 (1991): 281–329, discusses some stupas dedicated to nuns.

SOURCES ON OR RELATED TO WOMEN AND BUDDHISM

I. B. Horner, *Women Under Primitive Buddhism* (1930; Delhi, 1975) is the first serious book-length study of women in Buddhism; the mantle is then assumed by, among others, Diana Paul, *Women in Buddhism: Images of the Feminine in the Mahāyāna Tradition* (1979; repr. 1985), for which I. B. Horner wrote the introduction. It also contains Francis Wilson's groundbreaking essay "The Nun." Yuichi Kajiyama's review of Paul's book, although critical, actually points to the complexity of the materials to be studied and the issue of periodization: "Women in Buddhism," *The Eastern Buddhist* 15, no. 2 (Autumn 1982): 53–70. See also:

Bareau, André. "Un Personage Bien Mysterieux: L'espouse du Buddha." In *Indological and Buddhist Studies: Volume in Honour of Professor J. W. de Jong on His Sixtieth Birthday.* Canberra, 1982.

Bartholomeusz, Tessa. *Women Under the Bō Tree: Buddhist Nuns in Sri Lanka.* 1994.

Bode, Mable. "Women Leaders of the Buddhist Reformation." *The Journal of the Royal Asiatic Society.* 1893.

Falk, Nancy. "The Case of the Vanishing Nuns: The Fruits of Ambivalence in Ancient Indian Buddhism." In *Unspoken Worlds: Women's Religious Lives in Non-Western Cultures.* Edited by Nancy Auer Falk and Rita M. Gross. 1980.

Findly, Ellison Banks. "Ananda's Case for Women." *International Journal for Indian Studies* (July–December 1993).

———. Study of women donors of Buddhism. Forthcoming

Mills, Margaret. "Sex Role Reversals, Sex Changes, and Transvestite Disguise in the Oral Tradition of a Conservative Muslim Community in Afghanistan." In *Women's Folklore Women's Culture.* Edited by Rosan A. Jordan and Susan J. Kallčik. 1985. Though not about Buddhism, this is a particularly provocative and therefore quite helpful essay for understanding gender and oral traditions.

Richman, Paula. "The Portrayal of a Female Renouncer in a Tamil Buddhist Text." In *Gender and Religion: On the Complexity of Symbols.* Edited by Caroline Walker Bynum et al. 1986.

Shaw, Miranda. *Passionate Enlightenment: Women in Tantric Buddhism.* 1994.

Sponberg, Alan. "Attitudes toward Women and the Feminine in Early Buddhism." In *Buddhism, Sexuality, and Gender.* Edited by José Ignacio Cabezón. 1992. Thoughtful essay on the first ordination of Buddhist nuns; contains citations to its many textual versions.

Strong, John S. "A Family Quest: The Buddha, Yaśodharā, and Rāhula in the *Mūlasarvāstivāda Vinaya*." In *Sacred Biography in the Buddhist Traditions of*

South and Southeast Asia. Edited by Juliane Schober. 1997.

Walters, Jonathan S. "A Voice from the Silence: The Buddha's Mother's Story." *History of Religions* 33, no. 4 (May 1994): 358–379. Though actually about his stepmother and aunt Mahāpajāpatī, this article is also useful for Walters' thoughtful overview of scholarly sources on women in early Buddhism.

Willis, Janice D. "Nuns and Benefactresses: The Role of Women in the Development of Buddhism." In *Women, Religions, and Social Change.* Edited by Yvonne Yazbeck Haddad and Ellison Banks Findly. 1985.

Young, Serinity. *Dreaming in the Lotus: Buddhist Dream Practices and Imagery.* Forth coming. Includes a discussion of the Buddha's relationship to his wife or wives, both in his historical life and in his past lives. Also discusses Māyā's conception dream and has a chapter on the meaning of gender in Buddhist dreams and dream practices.

———. "Gendered Politics in Ancient Indian Asceticism." *Union Seminary Quarterly Review* 48, nos 3–4 (1994): 73–92. Discusses the relationship of Buddhist, Brahmanical, and Jain ideologies about ascetic women. Also available on the Internet at <http://www.uts.columbia.edu/~usqr/

Zelliot, Eleanor. "Buddhist Women of the Contemporary Maharastrian Conversion Movement." In *Buddhism, Sexuality, and Gender.* Edited by José Ignacio Cabezón. 1992.

See also Androgyny; Buddhas, Bodhisattvas, and Arhats; Compassion; Ḍākinīs; Desire; Durgā and Kālī; Jainism; Kuṇḍalinī; Machig Labdron; Mahāprajāpatī; Oral Tradition; Ordination: In Buddhism; Periodization; Saṅghamittā; Shaktism; Tantra; Tārā; Vajrayoginī; Wisdom: Prajñā and Prajñāpāramitā.

SERINITY YOUNG

Religious Rites and Practices

Women's roles in Buddhism have largely been configured by the exigencies of Buddhist monasticism, which survived by encouraging ritualized exchanges between private (domestic) and public (monastic) spheres. Though Buddhism is regularly depicted as a world-renouncing tradition that severs all ties to the family, research suggests that Buddhist ideologies often extended into the family to construct ideals for women that encouraged specific attitudes and practices. However, given the structural requirements of monastic–family relations, most Buddhist rites for women draw them and their resources out into the public space of

Elderly Buddhist woman praying, Bodhanath Stupa, Kathmandu, Nepal (Craig Lovell/ Corbis)

the monastery, and thus there are few strictly domestic Buddhist rites for women. This tendency is compounded by the fact that Buddhism, as a mobile and transcultural tradition, usually piggybacked on local non-Buddhist customs that were relied on to define domestic procedures relating to marriage, birthing, cooking, and menstruation.

In Indian Buddhism three main roles were available for women. The first, and most evident, was that of donor. Buddhism courted women's patronage with many sutras specifically addressing both female and male listeners. There is ample evidence of wealthy female donors making significant contributions to Buddhist causes and participating in the teachings that this support generated. Given that Buddhism asked for contributions that overstepped traditional patriarchal lines of expenditure, it makes sense that women, who likely were less invested in their husband's patriline, were relied on to redirect resources. Today, in many Asian cultures, women continue to play the role of "donor for the family," making offerings whose merit is thought to accrue to the entire family. Second, Buddhism sanctioned female monasticism, albeit reluctantly. Women were permitted to leave their domestic situations to organize their lives around ritual practices that largely mirrored those of their male counterparts, though they were never given equal status (Sponberg). Last, women were praised for producing Buddhists (Keyes). The Buddha's mother, Maya, and his aunt, Mahapajapati, figure prominently in Buddhist literature as ideal women who served Buddhism by giving bodily form to men as they progressed through Buddhist careers that stretched across lifetimes (*Mahavastu*).

However, in Buddhism the value of feminine fertility is undercut in two ways. First, many narratives explicitly or implicitly elide women's somatic contributions by attributing fecundity to the force of Buddhist asceticism (*Mahavastu; Buddhacarita*). Second, there are numerous passages in Mahayana Buddhist literature that offer women personal rites that they can perform so as to ensure that they will not be reborn as women in the future (Paul). Variations on these rites are also said to be effective in turning women into men after death so that they may ascend to the Pure Land. With Buddhist authors asserting control over gender production and fertility in general, it is not surprising that one also finds sutras that promise pregnancy and easy childbirth to any woman who will follow said text and worship the Buddhist divinities described therein.

In China, Buddhism produced an elaborate mythology involving mothers and sons that, once inaugurated in the fifth century, became a mainstay of East Asian Buddhism up to the present (Cole). Based on the trials of the monk Mu Lian saving his sinful mother, Buddhist authors sculpted roles for mother and son that seem to have encouraged a fusion of family and Buddhistic disciplines. Sons were taught to venerate Buddhism for its ability to save their mothers, and women were taught that producing sons was their most viable avenue for ascendance within the Buddhist cosmology. Reading these prescriptions carefully also suggests that mothers were implicitly asked to school their sons in Buddhist beliefs. Though there is no evidence of formalized Buddhist instruction from mothers, nonetheless there is much that implies that mothers became important purveyors of Buddhist myths. Similarly, obedience to one's mother became a prominent Buddhist virtue in several medieval discussions of ethics, suggesting that Buddhist authors recognized the vital role women played in producing obedient Buddhist children.

More concretely, it seems that women were full participants in many kinds of public Buddhist services. In particular, in the seventh century the Pure Land advocate Shan Dao wrote manuals for organizing week-long retreats for lay women and men (Stevenson). During these retreats women and men would adopt monastic codes of conduct and devote themselves to chanting the name of the Buddha of the Western Paradise, Amitabha. Public Buddhist groups such as these seemed to have been popular, and evidence drawn from the Tun Huang caves suggests that in the following centuries women were active in a variety of Buddhist or Buddhist-inspired groups, centered on financing religious works (Gernet).

In line with Buddhist tendencies in India, Chinese women were also told that they were second-class human beings who should propitiate Buddhist powers for a change of sex in the future. These doctrines were expanded in Chinese texts such as the *Bloody Bowl Sutra*, which explained that all women are sent to hell for menstruation and the blood that they spill in childbirth (Cole). Besides dramatically bringing women's bodies within the purview of Buddhist "ethics," the sutra concludes with the promise that women can save their own mothers by spreading this doctrine of hell. Here again Buddhist ideologues seem to be asking women to participate in informal proselytization. In another fusion of Buddhist ideology and women's practice, we find that beginning in the Ming period (1368–1644), the female bodhisattva Kuan Yin was prayed to as patron saint of footbinding, along with her more traditional role of "son-giver" (*Song Zi Guan Yin*) (Yü).

Many of these traditions were exported to Japan, where in the twentieth century a new form of Buddhist practice for women appeared. Beginning in the 1970s, Buddhist temples offered women the chance to redeem aborted fetuses by buying two-foot-high statues of the bodhisattva Jizo (Kṣitigarbha), placing them in Buddhist cemeteries, and then coming to offer them worship. This practice is similar to other Buddhist rites by urging women to find closure to personal problems in the public space of the monastery but has the onerous function of focusing the pain of abortion on the woman and not on the widely criticized failure of Japanese family planning policies (LaFleur).

BIBLIOGRAPHY

Though there is a growing body of literature dealing with feminist issues in the history of Buddhism, it seems that thus far too many discussions labor to prove that Buddhism is an egalitarian tradition; evidence to the contrary is then dismissed as symptomatic of a fall from an earlier, more consummate form of egalitarianism. Future research will likely overturn this presumption of equality and present a less contrived view of gender roles in Buddhism.

Bartholomeusz, Tessa. *Women Under the Bo Tree.* 1994.

Buddhacarita: Aśvaghoṣa's Buddhacarita, or Acts of the Buddha. Translated by E. H. Johnston. Reprint, 1978. This text is replete with images of women, most of whom are notable for their sexual allure and their libidinal urges.

Cole, Alan. *Mothers and Sons in Chinese Buddhism.* 1998.

Gernet, Jacques. *Buddhism in Chinese Society.* 1995.

Keyes, Charles. "Mother, Mistress, but Never a Monk: Buddhist Notions of Female Gender in Rural Thailand." *American Ethnologist* 11, no. 2 (May 1984): 223–241.

LaFleur, William. *Liquid Life: Abortion and Buddhism in Japan.* 1993. This work seems uninterested in investigating the more dubious side of Buddhist ideology and practice. Clearly there is much more to say about Buddhism and patriarchy in Japan than this book covers.

Mahavastu. Translated by J. J. Jones. London, 1949. This early Mahayana text, dated roughly to the beginning of the common era, provides rich images of women in Buddhism; relations between mothers and sons are detailed in a particularly dense and thought-provoking way.

Paul, Diane. *Women in Buddhism.* 1979. This is a good collection of Buddhist narratives about women.

Sponberg, Alan. "Attitudes toward Women and the Feminine in Early Buddhism." In *Buddhism, Sexuality, and Gender.* Edited by José Ignacio Cabezón. 1992. This is a fine article but works too hard to preserve an original Buddhist egalitarianism.

Stevenson, Daniel B. "Pure Land Buddhist Worship and Meditation in China." In *Religions of China in Practice.* Edited by Donald Lopez. 1996.

Walters, Jonathan S. "Gotami's Story." In *Religions of China in Practice.* Edited by Donald Lopez. 1996. The author is right to see in this story a good example of the tradition acclaiming women's spirituality, but he underplays the simultaneous submission of women to male authority that forms a major part of the narrative.

Yü, Chun-fang. "Sutra Promoting the White-robed Guanyin [Kuan Yin] as Giver of Sons." In *Religions of China in Practice.* Edited by Donald Lopez. 1996.

ALAN COLE

Himalayan Buddhism

One should always honor women.
Women are heaven, women are truth,
Women are the supreme fire of transformation.
Women are Buddha, women are the religious
  community,
Women are the perfection of wisdom.

Caṇḍam ahārosanatantra
(George, 1974, p. 33; by permission)

The Buddhism of the Himalayan countries of Tibet, Bhutan, Sikkim, and Ladakh, as well as large parts of northern India and Nepal, predominantly belongs to the Vajrayana or tantric branch of the Mahayana, especially as articulated in Tibet. Before the advent of Buddhism, the Tibetan landscape was dominated by local deities, many of them female, such as the Five Long Life Sisters who dwell on the Himalayan peaks. One sister, Lady Leviathan, lends her name to Mount Everest—Chomolangma. Other deities include the Medicine Women (*menma*) and the Twelve Steadfast Women (*tenma*), who guard the passes that lead into Tibet from the south. Serpent Goddesses (*lumo*), who are milk-white and worshiped with offerings of milk, inhabit streams, springs, lakes, and roots of trees.

FEMALE DEITIES

If Buddhism was to flourish in Tibet, it had to deal with the indigenous female deities, including those perceived as malefic. For instance, a supine demoness was pinned down by building Buddhist temples on her limbs. When Padmasaṁbhava arrived in the eighth century to found the nation's first monastery, the Steadfast Women tried to stop him. After an epic battle, he empowered them as Guardians of the Buddhist Teaching. In this role they remain, guarding the passes into Tibet from other religions just as they once guarded them against Buddhism itself. Yet the struggle was not a simple clash of genders: Padmasaṁbhava also fought male divinities, while women of power such as the Realization Yoginīs converted the Long Life Sisters and other indigenous deities.

The Buddhism that came from India already had its own pantheon of goddesses. Many of these, such as Tārā, were fully enlightened Buddhas or bodhisattvas dedicated to the enlightenment of all living beings. Others included Prajñāpāramitā, who embodies the Perfection of Wisdom Scriptures and the wisdom of all Buddhas, and Nairātmyā, who personifies selflessness, the philosophical truth that wisdom apprehends. Fearsome protector goddesses such as Śridevī (in Tibet, Palden Lhamo) and Ekajaṭī guard Buddhism from its enemies, protect the land, and punish those who break their vows.

The *ḍākinīs*, Women Who Travel the Sky, are a vast class of goddesses. Artists show them garlanded with

A Tibetan Buddhist nun wears ceremonial clothing for a midspring festival in the Rumtek Monastery in Sikkim, India (Nazima Kowall/Corbis).

skulls, naked and dancing ecstatically. Complex figures, they embody wisdom and the power of inspiration, among other elements. A special class of *ḍākinīs* guard the doors of mandalas. Embodying immeasurable compassion, love, joy, and equanimity, these Door Women aid in the spiritual transformation of those who enter the sacred space. The highest *ḍākinīs* rank as Buddhas and can serve as personal deities for men and women alike. The best known of these are Vajravārāhī, who symbolizes the transformation of ignorance into wisdom, and Vajrayoginī, who was the personal deity of the Indian saint Nāropa.

Such personal deities (*yidam*) are not considered as merely external supernatural entities to be worshiped. They represent a practitioner's inner capacity for enlightenment and serve as a role model, an image of the Buddha the meditator vows to become by grace of her meditations. Other *yidam* are male, but the practice cuts across gender lines. Women may visualize themselves as male deities; men may visualize themselves as female deities. A large number of personal deities are seen in a dual-gender form (*yab yum*), a male deity who represents compassion embraced by a female deity who represents wisdom. Their embrace encodes the Mahayana Buddhist principle that enlightenment is the blissful union of wisdom and compassion.

Individual goddesses like Tārā and pairs like Cakrasaṁvara and Vajravārāhī figure in the other great Buddhist tradition of the Himalayas, that of the Newars, the indigenous people of Nepal's Kathmandu Valley. Tantric theorists posit that men and women must practice together to attain enlightenment. The key Newar tantric rite, initiation (*dikṣa*), is performed by a husband-and-wife team; the recipients too should be couples. The tradition of paired meditators is also found in India and Tibet (Niguma and Nāropa are a famous example from eleventh-century Bengal). The attitudes to celibacy among the four sects of Tibetan Buddhism vary. The Nyingma give the greatest place to married practitioners, whereas the Geluk emphasize monastic celibacy. The Sakya and Kagyu fall in between.

WOMEN IN BUDDHIST HISTORY

Women have played an impressive role in the history of Himalayan Buddhism from its beginnings. In the seventh century, Princess Wen Chen of China and Princess Bhṛkuti of Nepal brought the first Buddhist images to Tibet, the Jowo and Jowo Mingyur Dorje, which are still visited by thousands of pilgrims each year. The eighth-century saint Yeshe Tsogyal, consort of Padmasambhava, was a great teacher in her own right as well as the major force in preserving Padmasambhava's spiritual legacy. Her biography is a unique and moving document of a woman's spiritual quest. Machig Labdron (1055–1145) founded the Pacification School of meditation around a practice called *chö*, Cutting Off [the Ego]. The practice of *chö* became widespread in Tibet. Like Yeshe Tsogyal, Machig Labdron is widely worshiped and emulated. Jomo Menmo (b. 1248), a *terton* (revealer of spiritual treasures), is believed to have received an important text still in use, *The Gathering of All the Secrets of the Ḍākinīs*, from the goddess Vajravārāhī. In the eighteenth century, the renowned teacher and author Mingyur Paldron rebuilt the great monastery of Mindroling after it was sacked by the Dzungar Mongols.

Biographies are an important genre of Buddhist literature. Some of their subjects are women, especially famous saints. Others celebrate lesser-known practitioners, such as the twelfth-century *terton* Machig Ongjo or Ayu Khandro, teacher of contemporary lama Namkai Norbu. One genre recounts the spiritual journeys of women who have returned from the dead (*delog*), such as the twelfth-century Nangsa Obum or twentieth-century Delog Dawa Drolma.

The reincarnating lama, or *tulku*, is a unique feature of Tibetan Buddhism. Although the vast majority of *tulkus* were men, women *tulkus* were also known. The most famous are the Abbesses of Samding Monastery, a mixed-gender institution. Considered earthly incarnations of the *ḍākinī* Vajravārāhī, they are venerated on a par with Tibet's highest lamas.

NUNS AND LAYWOMEN

The Himalayan Buddhist world encompasses many nunneries. In Tibet proper, most were free-standing institutions. Others, as is typical in the Everest region of Nepal, are paired with male monastic institutions. Although in general there are fewer nuns than monks, at Thubten Chöling, Nepal's largest monastery, nuns outnumber monks by roughly three hundred to two hundred. The world's largest nunnery, Gechak Tekchenling in East Tibet, was home to one thousand nuns. Still, it was considerably smaller than Tibet's largest monastery, which housed ten thousand monks. The religious practice of monks and nuns is similar, and in paired institutions they may worship together. Nuns are often known for their beautiful chanting of *ḍākinī* rituals.

Educational opportunities for nuns have rarely equaled those for monks. Tibet's famed monastic universities were all-male institutions. Recently, nunneries in the exile communities of India have begun to redress this by establishing philosophy classes of their own, often with the help of Western nuns. And in Central Tibet, nuns are in the forefront of the struggle for freedom from China. Many nuns, some of them only teenagers, serve long sentences in Chinese prisons for their political activities.

Most Himalayan Buddhist women are householders. Their religious practice, by-and-large, is not gender specific. Women recite prayers and mantras, perform prostrations and fasts, circumambulate holy places, go on pilgrimages, and donate to monks and nuns. Certain practices are favored by women, such as household purification rituals, and, among accomplished practitioners, *chö* and meditation on Tārā and Vajrayoginī.

In Tibetan Buddhist societies, there is an inequality of the sexes in terms of sociopolitical power. Compared to other traditional Asian societies, however, the status of women is high. Women can inherit property, enter into contracts, obtain divorce, and retain their property after divorce.

Tibet inherited the entire history of Buddhism from India and, with it, the history of Buddhism's evolving attitude toward women. Although early Buddhist opinion of women was mixed, by the time of the tantric tradition, which Tibetans consider the pinnacle of Buddhist practice, women are exalted. Despising women is counted among the Root Tantric Downfalls, the greatest faults that can befall a practitioner. Women played a vital role in the tantric milieu of ancient India and Nepal, reached high spiritual attainment, celebrated their achievement in ecstatic song, and pioneered important meditative practices. The fasting practice (*nyungne*) introduced in the tenth to eleventh centuries by the Kashmiri nun Bhikṣuṇī Lakṣmī (in Tibet, Gelongma Pamo), is repeated annually in villages and convents across the Himalayas. The long-life empowerment formulated by the twelfth-century yoginī Siddharājñī is also widespread. In the words of Padmasaṁbhava, the founder of the Tibetan tantric tradition: "The basis for realizing enlightenment is a human body. Male or female—there is no difference. But if she develops the mind bent on wisdom, the woman's body is better" (Tarthang Tulku, 1983, p. 102).

BIBLIOGRAPHY

Allione, Tsultrim. *Women of Wisdom.* (1984). An invaluable collection of biographies of six great women practitioners of Tibet: Nangsa Obum, Machig Labdron, Jomo Menmo, Machig Ongjo, Drenchen Rema, and Ayu Khandro.

Aziz, Barbara Nimri. *Tibetan Frontier Families: Reflections of Three Generations from D'ing-ri.* 1978. An ethnography of southern Tibet with valuable information on women and their religious lives.

Beyer, Stephan. *The Cult of Tārā: Magic and Ritual in Tibet.* 1973. The classic study of this important goddess.

Bruno, Ellen. *Sayta: Prayer for the Enemy.* Transit Media/Film Library. Ho-ho-kus, N.J., 1993. Moving documentary film on Tibetan nuns as political activists.

Bskal bzang rgya mtsho, Dalai Lama VII [1708–1755]. *Nyung Nö: The Means of Achievement of the Eleven-Faced Great Compassionate One, Avalokiteśvara of the (Bhiksunī) Laksmī with the Fasting Ceremony and the Requests to the Lineage Gurus.* 1995. An English translation of a Gelug version of the popular religious practice founded by the eleventh century nun, Bhikṣuṇī Lakṣmī.

Chodron, Pema. *Start Where You Are: A Guide to Compassionate Living.* 1994. Two books by an influential American teacher trained in the Tibetan Buddhist lineage.

———. *The Wisdom of No Escape and the Path of Loving-Kindness.* 1991.

David-Neel, Alexandra. "Women of Tibet." *Asia* 34, no. 3 (1934): 176–181. An article by the courageous Frenchwoman who traveled throughout Tibet in disguise during the earlier part of this century.

Dawa Drolma, Delog. *Delog: Journey to Realms Beyond Death.* 1995. Chronicle of a twentieth-century Tibetan woman's after-death experience.

Devine, Carol. *Determination: Tibetan Women and the Struggle for an Independent Tibet.* 1993.

von Fürer-Haimendorf, Christoph. *The Sherpas of Nepal: Buddhist Highlanders.* 1964. The classic ethnography of the Sherpas. Contains much information on women's social role and religious practice.

Gellner, David N. *Monk, Householder, and Tantric Priest: Newar Buddhism and Its Hierarchy of Ritual.* 1992. A thorough ethnography of Newar Buddhism in the Kathmandu Valley. Contains much useful information on Newar women as well as a fascinatingly detailed account of the tantric initiation ceremony.

George, Christopher S., trans. *The Caṇḍam ahāroṣaṇatantra, Chapters I–VIII: A Critical Edition and English Translation.* American Oriental Series, no. 56. 1974. A translation of a key tantric text that emphasizes the role of women and the worship of them.

Gyatso, Janet. "The Development of the Good Tradition." In *Soundings in Tibetan Civilization.* Edited by Barbara N. Aziz and Matthew Kapstein. 1985. An incisive summary of the early history of the meditative tradition codified by Machig Labdron.

Havenik, Hanna. *Tibetan Buddhist Nuns.* 1990.

Hermanns, Matthias. "The Status of Women in Tibet." *Anthropological Quarterly* 26, no. 3 (1953): 67–78.

Karma Lekshe Tsomo, Bhiksuni. *Sisters in Solitude: Two Traditions of Buddhist Monastic Ethics for Women. A Comparative Analysis of the Chinese Dharmagupta and the Tibetan Mulasarvastivada Bhiksuni Patrimoksa Sutras.* 1996. A scholarly study of the monastic rules that govern Buddhist nuns.

Klein, Anne Carolyn. "Primordial Purity and Everyday Life: Exalted Female Symbols and the Women of Tibet." In *Immaculate and Powerful: The Female in Sacred Image and Social Reality.* Edited by Clarissa W. Atkinson, Constance H. Buchanan, and Margaret R. Miles. 1985. A valuable discussion of the difference between symbolic and social status of Tibetan women.

Kohn, Richard. "*Mani Rimdu:* Text and Tradition in a Tibetan Ritual." Ph.D. diss., University of Wisconsin–Madison. 1988. A lengthy work on Tibetan Buddhist ritual that contains full translations of the liturgies of several major and minor protector goddesses.

Miller, Beatrice D. "Views on Women's Roles in Buddhist Tibet." In *Studies in the History of Buddhism.* Edited by A. K. Narain. 1980.

Ortner, Sherry B. "The Founding of the First Sherpa Nunnery, and the Problem of 'Women' as an Analytic Category." In *Feminist Re-Visions: What Has Been and What Might Be.* Edited by Vivian Patrika and Louise A. Tilly. 1980. A balanced study of the founding of a Sherpa nunnery and its implications for the study of women in religion.

Paul, Diana. *Women in Buddhism. Images of the Feminine from the Mahāyāna Tradition.* 1979. Classic study of the evolution of attitudes toward women in Buddhism.

Rhie, Marylin M., and Robert A. F. Thurman. *Wisdom and Compassion: The Sacred Art of Tibet.* 1991. A large catalog of Tibetan art that includes numerous color plates of goddesses as well as scholarly contributions by a number of authors.

Sakya, Jamyang. *Princess in the Land of Snows: The Life of Jamyang Sakya in Tibet.* 1990. Autobiography of a woman of the ruling class of the Sakya Order of Tibetan Buddhism.

Samuel, Geoffrey. *Civilized Shamans: Buddhism in Tibetan Societies.* 1993. An encyclopedic work on Tibetan Buddhism with valuable information on the role of women.

Shaw, Miranda. *Passionate Enlightenment: Women in Tantric Buddhism.* 1994. A controversial but valuable work on the role of women in the early centuries of tantric Buddhism in India.

Taring, Rinchen Dolma. *Daughter of Tibet.* 1970. A Tibetan noblewoman's account of her life.

Willis, Janice Dean. "Nuns and Benefactresses: The Role of Women in the Development of Buddhism." In *Women, Religion and Social Change.* Edited by Yvonne Haddad and Ellison Findlay. 1985.

Willis, Janice Dean, ed. *Feminine Ground: Essays on Women and Tibet.* 1989. An essential collection of essays by many of the leading woman scholars of Tibetan Buddhism.

Ye shes mtsho rgyal. *The Lotus-Born: The Life Story of Padmasaṁbhava.* 1993. Translated by Erik Pema Kunsang [Schmidt]. (Nyang ral nyi ma'i 'od zer, 1124–1192.) A shorter biography of Padmasaṁbhava by Yeshe Tsogyal in English translation.

RICHARD KOHN

East Asian Buddhism

Buddhism reached China via Central Asian trade routes by the first century C.E., became quite popular by the fourth century, and from there spread to Korea,

Japan, and northern Vietnam. Strongly influenced by Chinese culture, this region has created some distinctly East Asian forms of Buddhism, notably including the intuitive wisdom, love of nature, and world-affirming esthetic of Zen. East Asian Buddhism continued the Indian Buddhist renunciant cenobitic monasticism as its institutional backbone and preeminent form of practice, though in Japan a noncelibate priesthood and large, lay-led Buddhist religious groups have challenged the universality of that model. But East Asian Buddhism's greatest role in society has often been providing ways for lay people to care for their ancestors and the recently deceased. In East Asia a strong link between native traditions of filial piety and imported Buddhism has enabled monks and nuns to perform important priestly functions for lay women and men seeking to transfer merit to ensure the health and well-being of living and dead family members.

Women in East Asia have maintained the *bhikshuni sangha* of renunciant monastic women for sixteen centuries up to the present. Women have been important as donors to the *sangha* and as exemplars of purity (popularly understood as a renunciation of marriage and sexuality) and piety. In China and the rest of East Asia the most revered and beloved object of Buddhist piety since the eleventh century C.E. is the bodhisattva Kuan Yin (Kannon), who rescues those who call upon her from every sort of danger, and in China responds to women's prayers to give birth to sons. The change in representation of Kuan Yin—from masculine in India to feminine in China and the rest of East Asia—was an important contribution to worldwide Buddhism, which as a whole has lacked popular feminine representations of religious realities.

Within East Asian Buddhism nuns have attained a certain degree of equality with monks. Nuns in East Asia have been able to perform the same practices and priestly functions as do their male counterparts, and have in a number of times and places been able to conduct their personal and institutional life without strong assertions of male control. In Japan, where new noncelibate forms of Buddhism have largely replaced the older monastic institutions, temple wives have become an important though underrecognized part of priestly families, nuns have continued the traditional celibate practice, and laywomen have energized and in some cases founded syncretic Buddhist lay "new religions" like Risshō Kōsei-kai and Reiyu-kai that have attracted millions of members since World War II.

At the same time Buddhism in East Asia has reflected and supported misogynist constructions of gender and sexist social practices. Buddhism has taught that birth

A woman stands below a statue of Buddha in a temple near Seoul, Korea (Horace Bristol/Corbis).

as a woman shows heavier negative karmic fruits from past lives, and that one's hope as a woman is that great faith will enable one to be born a man and in that form become a Buddha. Buddhism has taught that giving birth is sinful and menstruation polluting—a menstruating woman should not attend ceremonies or enter into the presence of Buddha images in the temple's worship hall. Buddhism has strongly supported the notion that women's virtue lies in fulfilling their destiny to be wives and mothers.

CHINA

The Buddhist nuns' order was established in China in the fourth century C.E., and it has survived as an unbroken tradition to the present. Nuns and monks in China, northern Vietnam, and Korea take the precepts of the Dharmagupta school (*Ssu-fen lu*), a set of rules designed to serve as a guide for living the Buddhist life of few possessions, simple dress in the secular style of the Tang dynasty in China, not taking life (in East Asia this included a vegetarian diet), not taking anything that is not given, avoiding all greed in relationships with lay donors, and avoiding any actions that might be construed as encouraging or leading to sexual contact. Differences in culture and climate have occasioned acceptance of some differences between actual behavior and the precepts; Chinese nuns handle money, have bank accounts, and eat after noon, for example.

The first Buddhist convent of which we have clear records was founded in 312 C.E. A lack of adequate Vinaya texts in the early history of Buddhism in China delayed the first full ordination of Buddhist nuns by monks until 357 (a procedure not sanctioned by the Vinaya). The first full ordination of nuns by both nuns and monks who were members of an unbroken *bhikshuni* lineage as prescribed by the Vinaya occurred in 434, thanks to Sri Lankan nuns who traveled to China.

About 516 C.E. a scholar monk named Baochang recorded the biographies of sixty-five exemplary nuns, mostly from the social elite, in a text called *Biqiunizhuan* (Lives of nuns). A majority of these nuns excelled in erudition and sophisticated literary skills, as well as in faith, ascetic practices, meditation, learning, and teaching. Unfortunately, Baochang's work of recording the lives of eminent nuns was not continued in later periods. Later women were not entirely forgotten, though. In the eighteenth century Peng Jiging (Peng Shaosheng) complied the *Shan nuren zhuan* (Lives of good women) in which he brought together biographies and stories of exemplary nuns and laywomen preserved in the earlier records of the Ch'an, T'ien-t'ai, and Pure Land schools.

Chinese Buddhist schools such as T'ien-t'ai, Huayen, and Ch'an, which spread throughout East Asia, did stress that all beings have the same potential to reach Buddhahood, and that distinctions of gender are not essential but rather empty of any permanent, substantial, independent nature and thus of any ultimate reality. However, these same East Asian schools did not completely discard the notion found in early Mahayana scriptures that the fact of birth in a woman's body entails more obstacles than does birth as a man in attaining full awakening or nirvana. Nonetheless, in Ch'an beginning in the twelfth century women were fully recognized as teachers and spiritual guides in no way inferior to men.

The assembly of nuns provided an alternate family in China and East Asia for many women who lacked male protection. The *sangha* in China eventually developed a family system parallel to the sanctified secular blood lineages, with an elaborate hierarchy of relationships based on tonsure, the first act required of one leaving the household life. The newly tonsured nun moved from her secular to her Buddhist family, becoming the dharma son of the nun who was her tonsure master, and the dharma brother of all the nuns given tonsure by the same master.

Buddhism ran directly counter to Confucian norms in many aspects of life, one of the most important being that Buddhist monastic life required celibacy. Buddhists had to try to convince the Chinese that a child's monastic practice not only was not unfilial but also was the highest form of filial piety. Particularly on the popular level, chastity was equated with purity, which dedication to Buddhist monastic vows and practice allowed one to preserve. Buddhist monasticism as well as semimonastic lay Buddhist vegetarian societies allowed women to avoid marriage or remarriage; there is evidence that the popularity of the monastic path for women correlated with the degree to which in a given historical era women were required by their in-laws and natal families to seek financial support by remarrying after widowhood.

After the triumph of Confucianism among the elite beginning in the eleventh century, some officials, such as the famous Sung dynasty philosopher Chu Hsi, refused to approve of ordination for women within their districts, believing that the Heaven-ordained purpose of life for women was motherhood.

One of the severest eras of repression of Buddhism in China occurred in the twentieth century. Except for brief respites, the period from 1949 to 1980 was extremely painful for Buddhists and other religious groups in the People's Republic of China. Since 1980 policy has changed; the government has supported the reopening of monasteries and nunneries, and seminaries have opened to give novices a good Buddhist and secular education. Both women and men have been ordained in considerable numbers. Ordination and seminary training have attracted more women than men, in fact more than the government-regulated nunneries can accommodate. In China since 1985 women have been actively taking part in lay Buddhist activities at every point on the social scale. Women participate in dharma assemblies (*fa-hui*) in temples, in which they chant sutras for several days at a time, and sponsor and attend elaborate tantric "release of the burning mouths" (*fang yankou*) ceremonies performed by nuns and monks for the liberation of those suffering in their next rebirth.

In Taiwan, a society in which marriage, food, wealth, and children are highly valued as life's chief joys, nuns have generally been pitied more than admired. Nonetheless, in Taiwan there are many laywomen actively supporting Buddhism, and sixty to seventy percent of those ordained as monastics since 1952 have been nuns. Some have entered convent life because they lacked a dowry to marry or did not want to marry the man chosen for them. Others have found attractive the possibility of higher education offered by Buddhist seminaries for nuns, or are glad not to enter a life of service to husband and parents-in-law. In Taiwan a nun, Shig Hiu-wan, has founded an academic Buddhist studies program and a university; another (Shih Heng-ching) is a professor of Buddhist studies at the nation's premier university. The donations and active service of lay women are what make Buddhism possible in Taiwan. A large charitable organization focused on health care for the poor called the Buddhist Compassion Relief Love and Mercy Foundation was founded in 1966 by a Taiwanese nun, Dharma master Cheng Yen (b. 1937).

KOREA

Buddhism was officially recognized by the state in Korea in the fourth century, at a time when Korea's clans had been consolidated into three separate kingdoms, Koguryŏ, Paekche, and Silla. As in China, the royalty of each kingdom welcomed Buddhism as a religion offering supernatural protection for the nation as well as a way of unifying and pacifying powerful clans. Members of the royal families entered the *sangha* as monks and nuns. One prominent Paekche nun, Pŏpmyŏng, traveled to Japan in 655 C.E., where she cured illness by chanting the *Vimalakīrti-nirdesa* sutra. Her regional Korean accent is said to be responsible for the way the Japanese pronounce the words of sutra passages as they chant them to this day.

From the late seventh century to the early tenth century Korea was unified under the Silla dynasty. During this period various doctrinal and practice schools were brought to Korea from China. Koreans formed five doctrinal schools, of which Hwaŏm was the most important. Ch'an lineages arrived, becoming organized by the early tenth century into the Sŏn school, with its Nine Mountains system. Though its contributions remain largely invisible to historians, the order of nuns continued to maintain itself during this period.

In the succeeding Yi/Choson dynasty (1392–1910) the state was hostile to Buddhism and promoted Confucianism. Beginning in the late nineteenth century traditional Sŏn school began to revive. A teacher named Mang Gong (1872–1946) was notable for teaching Sŏn not only to monks but also to nuns and laypeople. Of his twenty-five *dharma* heirs, four were nuns. One of them, Manseŏng (1897–1975), founded a Sŏn monastery for women, T'aesong-am, outside Pusan.

The Japanese ruled Korea from 1910 to 1945 and adopted a policy of encouraging Buddhism while using it to mold public opinion in Japan's favor. The Japanese required Buddhist abbots to remove all rules against marriage by monks and granted ecclesiastical positions only to married monks, though they allowed nuns to remain celibate. After independence the celibate monks, with state support, reclaimed the major monasteries of the Chogye Order, which now unites the Sŏn and Doctrinal schools. The married priests formed their own T'aego Order, now in decline.

In South Korea today there are more than 6,000 *bhikshunis* and *sramanerikas*, and nuns play a more prominent role in *sangha* affairs than ever before. Korean nuns now have two independent orders, affiliated with the Chogye and T'aego orders. In 1982 the practice of ordination for nuns with representatives of both male and female *sanghas* present as the Vinaya requires was revived by the Chogye Order after a one-hundred-year lapse. There are more than two hundred nuns receiving *bhikshuni* ordination each year, which is usually preceded by at least five years' training. There are a number of schools, and one Buddhist university for women, that offer higher education for nuns; a number of nuns who teach at those schools have doctorates from Buddhist universities in Japan. There are currently several hundred nuns practicing intensive meditation in Korea at more than a dozen meditation halls. Nuns and lay women have found new ways to serve society: counseling prisoners, running homes for the aged and Buddhist Sunday schools for children, hosting radio shows, starting a Buddhist magazine for children, offering healing through meditation, and providing instruction in traditional arts as forms of spiritual training.

In Korea today there are four large "forest" monasteries that specialize in intensive Sŏn meditation training under a master. A compound is set aside in each for nuns who wish to study there. In this fashion the highest levels of religious training available to monks are also made available to nuns.

VIETNAM

Vietnam as a political and cultural entity is largely a product of the modern era. For centuries the country now known by that name was divided politically and culturally into two parts, north and south. Beginning in the fifteenth century the sinicized culture of the north came to dominate the Indianized culture of the south, and Vietnamese Buddhism came almost entirely under Chinese influence. As in the case of China, Confucianism came to dominate the court during the Later Le Dynasty (1428–1788), and Buddhism became the religion of the masses.

The French colonial period produced a political environment hostile to Buddhism, and higher education for Buddhists virtually disappeared within the country. After the end of French colonial rule some monks were sent abroad to India and Japan to study, but the same opportunities were not made available to nuns. They returned, though, to found an excellent Buddhist university in Saigon at which nuns, monks and Buddhist lay people were encouraged to study for university degrees. Still, Vietnamese Buddhism tended to take a paternalistic attitude toward monastic and lay women, and to replicate a patriarchal hierarchy associated with a Confucian social order, so that while women and men in theory played the same roles in the order and in society, in fact men were given more authority. During the period of American involvement there were a large number of nuns in Vietnam. There were a somewhat smaller number of monks in Vietnam, since young men were inducted into the military.

Since the end of the war, Buddhism has entered another period of repression within Vietnam. Monks and nuns have been returned to lay life, sent to remote villages, and held under house arrest. For Buddhist women as for Buddhist men, there are few opportunities for education, training, and leadership. Buddhist nuns offer leadership in exile communities in France, the U.S., and elsewhere, but in these communities there are more monks than nuns being ordained and trained.

JAPAN

The first ordained Buddhist in Japan was a woman whose dharma name was Zenshin-ni. In 588 she and two other Japanese nuns traveled to Korea to study the Vinaya. On their return the first Buddhist temple in Japan was built, a nunnery (*amadera*) called Sakurai-ji. During the Nara (710–784 C.E.), Heian (794–1185 C.E.), and Kamakura (1185–1333 C.E.) periods many Japanese women from elite families became nuns, often upon being widowed. Cutting their hair was the principal sign of their retreat from the world. During the Heian period women were banned from entering the major Buddhist study and practice centers such as Mt. Hiei and Mt. Kōya so as to prevent sexual liaisons. This succeeded in stigmatizing women and creating the impression that they were spiritually defiling and inferior. In the Zen school in the Kamakura period, nuns studied with the most prominent male masters; in the Muromachi period and thereafter, some received recognition as *dharma* heirs and organized their major convents into a "Five Mountains" system paralleling that of the Zen monks. Some talented women, including the author of *Confessions of Lady Nijo*, became nuns so that they could move freely in all levels of society.

Beginning in the twelfth century Pure Land Buddhism, a movement that was neither monastic nor lay, gained great popularity under the leadership of Hōnen, Shinran, and Shinran's wife Eshin-ni. Nichiren in the thirteenth century likewise taught that faith in the truth of the Lotus sutra and recitation of its name would save women and men alike. Some convents, such as Tokeiji, later became important as places where abused wives could flee for refuge. There are nuns today in Japan in Pure Land schools as well as in Rinzai and Sōtō Zen schools. In general, nuns in Japan have not been as numerous as nuns in Chinese cultural areas, and have not in recent centuries received much social recognition or support from the larger Buddhist schools to which they belong. Through a determined campaign, nuns in the Sōtō school in the twentieth century were able to attain recognition by the school as a whole as formally equal with monks.

BIBLIOGRAPHY

HISTORICAL STUDIES

Barnes, Nancy J. "Striking a Balance: Women and Images of Women in Early Chinese Buddhism." In *Women, Religion, and Social Change.* Edited by Yvonne Haddad and Ellison Findly. 1985.

Grant, Beata. "Female Holder of the Lineage: Linji Chan Master Zhiyuan Xinggang (1597–1654)." *Late Imperial China* 17, no. 2 (1996): 51–76.

Levering, Miriam L. "Lin-chi (Rinzai) Ch'an and Gender: The Rhetoric of Equality and the Rhetoric of Heroism." In *Buddhism, Sexuality and Gender.* Edited by José Ignacio Cabezón. 1992.

Robinson, Richard H., and Willard L. Johnson, assisted by Sandra Wawrytko. *The Buddhist Religion: A Historical Introduction.* 4th ed. 1997.

Shih Pao-ch'ang, and Kathryn Ann Tsai, trans. *Lives of the Nuns: Biographies of Chinese Buddhism Nuns from the Fourth to the Sixth Centuries.* 1994.

Uchino, Kumiko. "The Status Elevation Process of Sōtō Sect Nuns in Modern Japan." In *Speaking of Faith.* Edited by Diana L. Eck and Devaki Jain. 1987.

Yü, Chun-fang. "Guanyin: the Chinese Transformation of Avalokiteshvara." In *Latter Days of the Law: Images of Chinese Buddhism 850–1850.* Edited by Marsha Weidner. 1994.

CONTEMPORARY AND FIELD STUDIES

Arai, Paula. *Women Living Zen: Sōtō Buddhist Nuns in Japan.* Forthcoming.

Barnes, Nancy J. "Buddhist Women and the Nuns' Order in Asia." In *Engaged Buddhism: Buddhist Liberation Movements in Asia.* Edited by Christopher S. Queen and Sallie B. King. 1996.

Levering, Miriam. "Women, Religion and the State in the People's Republic of China." In *Today's Woman in World Religions.* Edited by Arvind Sharma. 1994.

Li Yu-chen. *T'ang-tai ti Pi-ch'iu-ni.* 1989.

WRITINGS BY AND ABOUT INDIVIDUAL BUDDHIST WOMEN

Chân Không (Cao Ngoc Phuong). *Learning True Love: How I Learned and Practiced Social Change in Vietnam.* 1993.

Ching, Yu-ing. *Master of Love and Mercy: Cheng Yen.* 1995.

Levering, Miriam. "Ting-kuang Miao-tao and Her Teacher Ta-hui Tsung-kao." In *Buddhism in Sung China*. Edited by Peter N. Gregory and Dan Getz. 1998.

Tae-heng Se Nim. *Teachings of the Heart: Zen Teachings of Korean Woman Zen Master Tae-Heng Se Nim*. 1990.

FILMS

Choice for a Chinese Woman. Films for the Humanities and Sciences, Princeton, N.J., 1993.

Guanyin Pilgrimage. Directed and distributed by Yii Chun-fang. Rutgers University, New Brunswick, N.J., 1988.

See also **Kuan Yin (Kannon)**; **Ordination: In Buddhism**.

MIRIAM LEVERING

A Buddhist nun at Wat Tham Mongkorn Thong Kanchanaburi in Thailand, 1994 (Robert Holmes/Corbis)

Southeast Asian Buddhism

South and Southeast Asian Theravada Buddhist ideology about the female aims at producing good wives and mothers who maintain the home where they socialize the next generation of Buddhists. In other words, in the worldview of Theravada Buddhism (lit., "the doctrine of elders"; the Buddhism of South and Southeast Asia), a woman need not renounce her home life in order to be religious; rather, by fulfilling her social duties as wife and mother, a woman performs her religious duties. As wife, she supports her husband in his endeavors, ensuring a peaceful home life for all. As mother, it is her duty to instill in her children a sense of religious and moral awareness. The model for her behavior, and of female religiosity in general, is Visakha, the most well-known woman of the Pali canon, the authoritative corpus of texts of Theravada Buddhism. Visakha, wife and mother, provides alms to the monastic community, and sons for its continuance. In fact, she, rather than a Buddhist nun, is the religious female par excellence of the Pali canon. In short, as the canonical stories about Visakha assert, the Theravada Buddhist woman fulfills her religious duties by marrying, having children, ensuring the prosperity of her family, and supporting the monastic community.

Despite the Pali canon's portrayal of Visakha rather than a nun as the exemplary religious woman, it records that women could, and did, become nuns. The Chronicles of Sri Lanka claim that nuns acted as Buddhist missionaries. Indeed, according to the Chronicles, the Mahāvaṃsa and the Dīpavaṃsa, both monks and nuns were responsible for spreading Buddhism throughout the island of Sri Lanka. Chinese tradition asserts that Sri Lankan nuns as Buddhist missionaries established an order of nuns in China. While at present there are no officially recognized Buddhist nuns (*bhikkhunīs*) in

any Theravada community of South Asia (Nepal, India, Sri Lanka) or Southeast Asia (Thailand, Burma, Laos, Cambodia, Vietnam), some women nevertheless renounce their roles as wives and mothers and lead celibate, monastic lives. Such lives are antithetical to the life of the valorized lay woman, Visakha. Due to a variety of historical exigencies, and to strict interpretation of the canonical rules regulating ordination, the Theravada woman desiring to lead a monastic life cannot receive ordination from Theravada Buddhist clerics. She may, however, choose to receive ordination from full-fledged Mahayana nuns in Korea or Taiwan, but her ordination is not sanctioned by most persons in her own community. Thus, if a woman desires to leave lay life, one of her only options is to become a "lay nun" (Sinhala: *dasa sil mata;* Thai: *mai ji;* Burmese: *thila shin;* Nepali: *anagarika*). The category of lay nun is a paradox in that it recognizes that a female can live as a nun without changing formal status, without entering the *sangha,* the monastic community. Their ambiguous status notwithstanding, some lay Theravada nuns aspire to attain nirvana, or enlightenment, Buddhism's soteriological goal, which the Theravada tradition claims is the purview of monks. Though some Pali canonical and postcanonical texts recognize that lay people can attain nirvana, traditional ideology is that one must enter the *sangha* to be liberated. Thus, from the point of view of conservative Buddhists, the lay nun's aspiration for enlightenment and her attempt to attain it amounts to a heterodoxy. For them, as women cannot enter the *sangha,* women should not aspire to attain nirvana. In this line of thinking, women should support the *sangha* by providing alms and sons for its well-being, that is, emulate Visakha. While conservative males embody this ideology, it is shared by many women throughout Theravada Buddhist strongholds. Moreover, some conservatives, both male and female, argue that not only must one enter the *sangha* to attain enlightenment, but one must also be male to seek nirvana. Women who subscribe to this line of thinking, arguing that women are morally weaker than men, hope to be reborn as men so that they may have a chance at salvation. These claims are made by conservatives—both male and female—despite the canon's allegation that the Buddha pronounced that gender is no impediment to salvation. Indeed, the internal evidence of the canonical *Poems of the Elder Nuns* and *Poems of the Elder Monks* suggests that more nuns than monks attained enlightenment; when we compare the incidence of the attainment of nirvana in the ancient poetry, we find that among world-renouncers, nuns were the most successful. In short, the canon vaunts that females could and did attain enlightenment as nuns.

While there is an abundance of material concerning the (ideal) lives of women as nuns and lay women in ancient Buddhism, there is a dearth of information on Buddhist women and their practices in contemporary Vietnam, Laos, and Cambodia, doubtless due to the volatile situation in those countries, which has inhibited research, and to scholars' disinterest in women's religious lives. Some scholars, however, have conducted studies in Theravada communities to which they have access, namely, Nepal, Thailand, Sri Lanka, and Burma. Those studies suggest that while negative attitudes concerning the female's ability to attain nirvana are pervasive throughout South and Southeast Asia, so are countervailing, egalitarian ideas. Indeed, some Buddhists, both men and women, hold that females can attain enlightenment. Much of the ideology that places nirvana in the reach of the female also construes nirvana as a goal for all lay people, male and female alike. Underpinning this ideology is the notion that one can attain enlightenment while in lay life, bringing to the fore one claim of canonical and post-canonical works, namely, that lay people can be enlightened. In the present, some lay Theravada practitioners in Sri Lanka, Nepal, Thailand, and Burma practice insight meditation and hope to be enlightened; these men and women claim, contrary to their more conservative counterparts, that one need not enter the monastic community to seek and find salvation. In Theravada Buddhist communities, this has meant that women, despite being excluded from the *sangha,* have been able to engage in religious practices, particularly insight meditation (*vipassanā*), traditionally associated with the *sangha,* that is, with male Buddhist monastics. Indeed, in Sri Lanka, Thailand, and Burma women are in the majority at insight meditation centers, which suggests that meditation appeals to more women than men. Moreover, most of the women who patronize the centers are in their childbearing years.

Gender ideology can account for the marked participation of women in meditation centers: given the pervasive belief that one's gender is a result of one's karma, and that female gender is a consequence of bad karma, women are said to suffer more than men. Thus, it is not surprising that more women than men find relief from suffering through meditation. In addition, it is also widely held that women, because they give birth and are responsible for child rearing, are more connected to the world around them and thus understand the suffering of others better than men. Due to their gender, women thus not only symbolize suffering but the empathy associated with the suffering of others as well. As meditation is traditionally viewed as the vehicle of liberation, or the absence of suffering, it therefore is to be expected that women's religious practice should center on meditation.

Views about women and suffering, in conjunction with ideas about the spiritual capacities of the laity in Nepal, Sri Lanka, Thailand, and Burma, have helped some Buddhists in the modern period to contest views concerning the proper role for women in Theravada Buddhism. The contestation has allowed women to embrace their new found religiosity by moving from the private sphere of the home, to the public sphere of monasteries (lay nunneries) where they live as lay nuns. Others choose meditation centers, where they practice as lay women. Yet, while women are persuaded to practice insight meditation, sometimes even by their governments (this is particularly the case in Thailand), it is as lay women; women are not usually encouraged to renounce their lay lives.

If a woman chooses to live the monastic life, however, her decision to do so can often be costly. There are two reasons for this. First, according to traditional ideology about the female, she is to be under the guidance of a male, whether father, husband, or son. Thus, if a woman renounces her lay identity, she renounces a male, which is tantamount to autonomy, a condition that is not socially acceptable for a female in traditional Theravada Buddhist communities. In short, one strand of contemporary ideology concerning women, as we have seen, maintains that women need not (and should not) renounce lay life in order to be religious. Thus, if she does so renounce it, she is very rarely patronized by society in the same way as a monk because she has acted in defiance of traditional norms. She therefore must rely for sustenance on her family, which, paradoxically, she has renounced (and which, in many cases, has renounced her). Second, because she is not officially recognized as a member of the *sangha,* giving to her does not draw to the giver the type of merit associated with monks, so she is not patronized in the same way as a monk. In most cases the lay nun's life, indeed, underscores suffering in a way that the monk's life does not. Moreover, her life suggests that Hindu ideas about women, namely, that they should be under the guidance and protection of the men with whom they are affiliated, have permeated Theravada Buddhist cultures, making difficult her life of renunciation.

Because the traditional ideology concerning women's proper religious roles is pervasive throughout South and Southeast Asia, in all Theravada communities, with the exception of Nepal, women encounter much resistance from their families when they decide to leave lay life. Nepal, which since the late nineteenth century has been experiencing a Theravada Buddhist revival, provides a different picture of Theravada women. In Nepal, Theravada women, in addition to men, are exemplars of monastic living, notwithstanding their inability to enter the *sangha*. The Nepalese lay nun, the *anagarika*, receives financial support from lay supporters that equals, if not surpasses, alms given to monks. Lay nunneries in Nepal are highly organized, far exceeding the organization of monastic dwellings for women in Theravada communities elsewhere. In fact, one such lay nunnery in Kathmandu, Dharmakirti Vihara, is the center of life for the Theravada Buddhists in its area. While in most Theravada communities the monks' monastery functions as the spiritual and social center, in Kathmandu the lay nunnery serves this function. In Nepal lay nuns rather than monks are believed by many, including monks, to be more instrumental in reviving Buddhism, bringing into prominence the idea that women, rather than men, are more connected to the world around them. In Nepal monks interpret the rules incumbent upon *sangha* members to mean that the *sangha* should stay aloof from the laity and the concerns of the world. *Anagarikas*, on the other hand, not bound by the conventions of the rules because they are not ordained, remain immersed in the lives of their lay supporters while pursuing their own enlightenment. They thus have closer contact with lay Buddhists than monks and often are responsible for organizing activities to enliven Theravada Buddhism in Nepal. Moreover, traditional ideology that suggests that women should be religious by being mothers is reinterpreted in Nepal. Lay nuns are encouraged to be mothers by engaging in social work, in which they can nurture Buddhism and see to its well-being in the present-day Buddhist revival.

Indeed, there are more Theravada *anagarikas* in Nepal today than there are monks, although the most recent statistics suggest that there are fewer than one hundred lay nuns and roughly eighty Theravadin monks. The practical consequence of the numbers is that lay nuns wield at least the same degree of authority over the laity as monks, precisely because there are more of them. In the Nepalese Theravada Buddhist revival, all efforts to resuscitate Theravada practice are encouraged, including the help of females as lay women or as world renouncers. In many ways, the situation at present in Nepal is much like the situation in Sri Lanka at the turn of the twentieth century. At that time, Buddhists encouraged all people—male and female—to preach and teach, and rally for, Buddhism, despite traditional notions concerning the proper role of the Buddhist female. Thus, women were encouraged to become mothers of Buddhism, that is, to nurture the religion by playing public roles. Some women even left lay life, acted as religious exemplars, and were encouraged to do so. In short, their contribution—as lay women and as world renouncers—was valued. Once Buddhism was considered revived, however, positive ideology about women and the monastic life began to wane. Today, lay nuns in Sri Lanka are for the most part impoverished, whereas at the turn of the twentieth century they enjoyed a comfortable existence. Whether this will be the fate of Theravada women in Nepal, once Theravada Buddhism is considered revived there, remains an open question. One cannot help but notice, however, that in Theravada Buddhism the laity respects the monastic robe, rather than the person who wears it. Reverence of the robe suggests that, despite historical exigencies that marginalize her, the woman who dons it will always be supported to some degree, yet rarely to the same degree as the monk.

Though women have been drawn to monasticism, and though they have made contributions to the health of Buddhism as lay nuns, most Theravada women live out their religious lives as lay women. In fact, in most Theravada communities, lay women, rather than lay men, predominate at almsgiving ceremonies and in temple life. In other words, a very marked characteristic of Theravada Buddhist women is that they are far more involved in overt religious activities and practices than men. Indeed, in South and Southeast Asia, lay women contribute to the life of monasteries and lay nunneries in a variety of maintenance roles, far exceeding the contribution of lay men. This is a significant dimension of the social reproduction of Buddhism, along with the inculcation of morality, both of which are considered a woman's religious duty. Women tend to the upkeep of monastic dwellings and the organization of the daily almsgiving. However, lay nuns, too, fulfill part of their religious obligation by supporting monasteries, either as groundskeepers (which is particularly true in

Thailand) and as preparers of food and distributors of alms (Burma, Sri Lanka, and Thailand). In other words, in many cases the lay nun's role is a continuation of the lay woman's, affirming the subordinate status of women in contemporary Theravada Buddhism. Nonetheless, these support roles are considered indispensable, and thus of the utmost importance, for without them the *sangha* could not survive.

While the Buddhism of Buddhist temple life is the mainstream religion of Sri Lanka, Thailand, Burma, Cambodia, Laos, and Vietnam, there are other dimensions of Buddhism in those countries that afford women different religious roles than mainstream Buddhism. In the Burmese Nat (spirit) religion, for instance, which mixes with, and exists alongside, Buddhism, women are considered authoritative in a contradistinction to Buddhism. In fact, the religious officiant in the Nat religion is usually a female medium, who becomes possessed by one of a variety of spirits and serves as its mouthpiece. In return, clients compensate her, either in cash or in kind, reversing the traditional idea of exchange that operates in monasteries, which sanctions that women give (alms; services; sons) while men receive. Yet, female mediums are never patronized to the same degree as monks, underscoring the traditional ideology that giving to men yields higher rewards than giving to women. Moreover, whereas a monk is respected (and, to a certain degree, a lay nun, because she wears the robe), a Nat medium is not; rather, because she often drinks alcohol and dances to facilitate her communications with spirits, behavior that is unacceptable for women in traditional Buddhist societies, her vocation is not regarded as a suitable one for women. In sum, nonetheless, a conclusion one can draw from contemporary religious life in Burma, especially if one takes into account whose voice is authoritative, is that the Nat religion is aligned with women, while Buddhism is aligned with men, despite ambiguity associated with the roles of mediums and lay nuns. Yet, at the same time, from the vantage of lay Buddhism—essential to the prosperity of the *sangha*—another conclusion one can draw is that women play as important a role as the *sangha* in keeping Buddhism alive: women (more so than lay men) provide the necessary requisites to monks, who are then able to see to the spiritual well-being of the laity, both men and women. Though (negative) stereotyping deems support roles to be the woman's ambit, the way they are regarded as absolutely essential for the social reproduction of Buddhism suggests that we should rethink whose voice in Buddhism is subaltern.

Like Burma, Sri Lanka provides Buddhist women the opportunity to speak with authority as mediums. Indeed, according to traditional beliefs, deities possess more women than men. Undergirding this ideology is the belief that women are weak, both morally and physically, and thus are more vulnerable to possession than men. In this instance, negative stereotyping paradoxically empowers women: once possessed, the female can make demands on others for things otherwise out of her grasp as an ordinary housewife and lay woman, including the respect that comes with religious authority. Moreover, once possessed, in addition to insisting on certain tangibles and intangibles, the medium also can use her possession to help others. In this way, she carves spaces for women in public life that, like religious roles for men, including monkhood, require the support of others.

Thus, in the Theravada Buddhist societies of South and Southeast Asia, there is no consensus on the spiritual equality of men and women even though the Pali canon considers men and women to be spiritually equal. Perhaps due to the lack of clarity on this issue, some women's religious lives revolve around the physical and social reproduction of Buddhism, both of which involve nurturing. Other women enact their religious lives in opposition to the family, as world renouncers, or outside the mainstream, as mediums. One thing is clear, however: the richness of female religiosity in South and Southeast Asia forces us to attend to the importance of women in keeping Buddhism alive. It also invites us to shift the focus of our studies from monastic to lay Buddhism, in which the maintenance and continuance of the religious traditions, upon which Theravada Buddhist identity depends in South and Southeast Asia, hinges on the regular involvement of women.

BIBLIOGRAPHY

Dewaraja, Lorna. "The Position of Women in Buddhism with Special Reference to Pre-Colonial Sri Lanka." Paper presented to the Third Sri Lanka Conference, Amsterdam. April, 1991.

Horner, I. B. *Women Under Primitive Buddhism.* 1930. Reprint, 1975.

Kabilsingh, Chatsumarn. *Thai Women in Buddhism.* 1991.

Keyes, Charles. "Mother or Mistress but Never a Monk: Buddhist Notions of Female Gender in Rural Thailand." *American Ethnologist* 11, no. 2 (1984): 223–241.

Khaing, Mi Mi. *Burmese Family.* 1962.

———. *The World of Burmese Women.* 1984.

King, Winston. *A Thousand Lives Away: Buddhism in Contemporary Burma.* 1964.

Kirsch, A. Thomas. "Text and Context: Buddhist Sex Roles/Culture of Gender Revisited." *American Ethnologist* 12, no. 2 (1985): 302–320.

Law, Bimala Churn. *Women in Buddhist Literature.* 1981.

Murcott, Susan. *The First Buddhist Women.* 1991.

Obeyesekere, Gananath. *Medusa's Hair: An Essay on Personal Symbols and Religious Experience.* 1981.

Rhys Davids, C. A. F. *Sacred Writings of the Buddhists: Psalms of the Sisters.* 1986.

Thamel, Sr. Cleophas. "The Religious Woman in a Buddhist Society: The Case of the Dasa Sil Maniyo in Sri Lanka." *Dialogue* 11, nos. 1–3 (1984): 53–68.

TESSA BARTHOLOMEUSZ

Modern Movements

Buddhist activities among women that have become important religious, social, and educational movements fall into three categories: those aimed at greater recognition, unity, or the enlightenment of other Buddhists; those in the Triloka Bauddh Mahasangha Sahayaka Gana (TBMSG) in India; and those of the conversion movement begun in 1956 by Dr. B. R. Ambedkar.

Thailand offers an interesting example of what women can do even when barred from religious orders. As Leedom Lefferts has shown, women's participation is essential for providing cloth to monks and temples (Gittinger, 1992). A new effort by educated women is under way to claim both recognition and the right to Buddhist education. Voramai Kabilsingh, the only Thai *bhikshuni* (a female member of a Buddhist order), was ordained in Taiwan and has established the Dharmajinaree Wittya nunnery in Ratchiburi province, west of Bangkok. She has gathered a sizeable following and is able to offer schooling to poor women. Her daughter, Chatsumarn Kabilsingh, a professor of religion at Bangkok's Thammasat University and a prolific writer on Buddhism and women in Thailand, says that there is some mild encouragement for change in attitudes toward women as religious participants within the Buddhist order.

John Van Esterik (1982) studied two educated laywomen in Bangkok who lead major Buddhist meditation societies. Achan Naeb Mahaniranonda is the head of large lay and monastic groups of meditators found throughout central Thailand. Monks have appeared with her on the dais in public lectures, even though normally women would not presume to teach monks. Achan Naeb's work began in 1950 with a meditation center in a major monastery. Twenty years later, some twenty centers taught meditation under her auspices. Another meditation teacher, Achan Naeb's former student, Achan Suchin, has given radio broadcasts and has monastic, military, and bureaucratic supporters. The women have built their teaching on the *Abhidhamma*, which is a text not normally studied by Thai monks.

They also bring a more intellectual and sophisticated approach to Buddhist thought and meditation than do the many monks who rely strictly on ritual and use of the Therigatha, the songs of the early Buddhist *bhikshunis*.

Sri Lanka is also seeing something of the same effort by women to organize and to teach. Ranjiini de Silva, president of Sakyadhita (daughters of the Buddha), a society dedicated to the revival of ordination for nuns, has asked that Chinese *bhikshunis* be invited to Sri Lanka for ordination ceremonies and claims that the difference between the Mahayana Buddhism of the Chinese and the Theravada Buddhism of Sri Lanka regarding *bhikshunis* is insignificant. In another illustration of unity, almost the entire body of Sri Lankan nuns (the term is used even though the women are not officially ordained) gathered in 1986 in the sacred city of Anuradhapura to celebrate the anniversary of the arrival of the daughter of the emperor Ashoka in the third century B.C.E. to form the order. Abhaya Weerakoon reports in *Sakyadhita* that monthly programs for nuns in each district have proved popular and successful. A few dharma classes for nuns have been organized with *bhikshus* (monks) serving as teachers. Kusuma Devendra, also in *Sakyadhita*, notes that the Commissioners of Buddhist Affairs have arranged for the *dasa sil mata* (women who have taken the ten precepts) to take *vipassana* medication courses. Another group concerned for the unity and education of the *dasa sil matas* in the Sarvodaya movement, the "social gospel" wing of Buddhism in Sri Lanka founded in 1958. Efforts are made to help the women with schooling and the gaining of respect and to organize them in service to community development. Sarvodaya's work is even more important to laywomen, and more women than men partake in the many activities of Sarvodaya, especially at the grassroots level.

Anagarika Dhammavati reports in *Sakyadhita* that she has been able to establish a nunnery in Katmandu, Nepal, and that a youth group reaches out to rural areas, invites foreign scholars to Nepal, and puts out literature. The nunnery, Dharmakirti Vihar, also publishes in Newari and Nepali languages and is involved in social service, including health and sanitation, all of which are new activities for Buddhist nuns.

The autobiography of Chan Khong (Cao Ngoc Phuong) (1993) tells not only of her becoming a nun in a new Buddhist order in Vietnam but also of the work of many Buddhist women in political protest and social work, such as the highly organized School of Youth for Social Service during the war period. After leaving Vietnam in 1968, she worked with Europeans to support projects in Vietnam such as day-care centers run

A Nepalese Buddhist nun, Solo Khumbu, Nepal (Christine Kolisch/Corbis).

by Buddhist nuns; the work was stopped with the unification of Vietnam in 1975.

The movement toward social service and the education of all Buddhists is perhaps most evident in Taiwan. A forest monastery, Fo Kuaang Shan, largely run by nuns, promotes "humanistic Buddhism" and sponsors the training of dharma teachers and medical programs; it publishes books and tapes on dharma talks and Buddhist chanting, a biweekly newsletter that circulates to 25,000 people, and a monthly magazine. The abbess of Fo Shan Ssu directs the re-editing of the Chinese Tripitaka and compiling of a Chinese Buddhist dictionary. Purifying the minds of Buddhists through pilgrimage is promoted through twenty branches, most of them directed by nuns (Shih Yung Kai in *Sakyadhita*).

The most important event in this new movement among religious Buddhist women was the 1989 gathering of *bhikshuni*s at Bodh Gaya, attended by some seventy monks and nuns and eighty lay people with the Dalai Lama as the keynote speaker. Burmese, Cambo-

dian, Chinese, Japanese, Korean, Nepalese, Thai, Tibetan, and Vietnamese traditions were represented. The International Association of Buddhist Women called Sakyadhita (note the use of the word *women* rather than *bhikshuni*) was formed on the final day of the conference. The word *sakyadhita* means "daughters of the Buddha." Eight years later, the International Sakyadhita Conference was held in Ladakh. Seventy delegates from the United States, Europe, and Australia and two hundred from Asia attended. In a seven-day event, Tibetan practices, the problem of prostitution in Thailand, and the loss of the *bhikshuni* order in Theravada Buddhism were discussed.

Women are ordained as *dhammacharinī* in the Triloka Bauddh Mahasangha Sahayaka Gana or TBMSG movement, which was founded by the English convert Sangharakshita and now has large centers in Pune, Ahmedabad, and Nagpur in India. Meditation courses and retreats on the dharma are held specifically for women, and women may lead these. Buddhist women are in charge of the TBMSG hostels for women and serve as doctors and workers in the health clinics of the organization. From the beginning, the TBMSG has been concerned with the health, welfare, and religious life of women, and increasingly women are participating in its work.

In 1956 in India, B. R. Ambedkar founded a conversion movement, chiefly among ex-Untouchables, which now numbers in the millions. While Buddhist women do hold conferences and one edits a Marathi publication (Meenakshi Moon's *Maitrani*), most of their participation in this Buddhist movement is individual. Many women express their beliefs in poetry or other writing, and this work is both in print and read or recited at literary conferences held in Maharashtra. Their work is an ever more important part of *dalit* literature, "the literature of the oppressed." One woman has translated Paul Carus's important work on Buddhism into Marathi. Others attend either the TBMSG meditation classes or go to Igatpuri for *vipassana* meditation. Many women participate in the social, educational, and political phases of the Ambedkar movement as committed Buddhists, working to better the condition of Dalits, to push for equality and justice, and to further Buddhism. Buddhist women in the Ambedkar movement participate in great numbers in the campaign to restore the Mahabodhi temple in Bodh Gaya to Buddhist control.

BIBLIOGRAPHY

Chân Không (Cao Ngoc Phuong). *Learning True Love; How I Learned and Practiced Social Change in Vietnam.* 1993.

Gittinger, Mattibelle, and H. Leedom Lefferts. *Textiles and the Tai Experience in Southeast Asia.* 1992.

Handley, Paul. "Unequal Struggle." *Far Eastern Economic Review* 153, no. 27 (1991): 24–25.

Kabilsingh, Chatsumarn, *Thai Women in Buddhism.* 1991.

Lynch, Owen. Unpublished untitled manuscript on the Mahabodhi Temple Liberation Movement.

Macy, Joanna. *Dharma and Development: Religion as Resource in the Sarvodaya Self-Help Movement.* 1983.

Padmasuri. *But Little Dust: Life amongst the 'Ex-untouchable' Buddhists of India.* 1990, 1997.

Tsomo, Karma Lekshe, ed. *Sakyadhita: Daughters of the Buddha.* 1988. See entries by Tsomo, Anagarika Dhammavati, Kusuma Devendra, Abhaya Weerakoon, and Shih Yung Kai.

Van Esterik, John. "Women Meditation Teachers in Thailand." In *Women of Southeast Asia.* Edited by Penny Van Esterik. 1982.

Zelliot, Eleanor. "Buddhist Women of the Contemporary Maharashtrian Conversion Movement." In *Buddhism, Sexuality, and Gender.* Edited by José Ignacio Cabezón. 1992.

See also Ordination: In Buddhism.

ELEANOR ZELLIOT

Buddhism in the West

Buddhism was introduced to eighteenth- and nineteenth-century Europe and North America primarily through the intellectual activities of men who collected, translated, and analyzed Asian religious texts. These scholarly Orientalists were not interested in the practice of Buddhism or in living Buddhists, male or female. Their research was philological and philosophical; most had no personal religious interest in Buddhism. But starting in the late nineteenth century the religious tradition the Orientalists made known in the West did elicit personal interest from some Occidentals.

In 1880 the Theosophists H. P. Blavatsky and H. S. Olcott formally undertook the five traditional precepts (*pansil*) of lay Buddhists in a public ceremony in Ceylon (present-day Sri Lanka), thereby becoming the first modern Westerners to become Buddhists and fueling the Buddhist revival movement in Ceylon. Western interest in Buddhism was deepened by the participation of several Asian Buddhist teachers in the World's Parliament of Religions held in Chicago in 1893. By 1902 a British man had become the first Occidental to join a Buddhist monastic order.

Asian immigration also influenced the establishment of Buddhism in North America. From the Chinese who came to California during the Gold Rush, to the Japanese who arrived in the United States at the beginning of the twentieth century, to the post–Vietnam era immigrants from Cambodia, Thailand, Vietnam, and Korea, Asians brought Buddhism to the West, not for Western consumption but as part of the culture of their own ethnic communities. For the most part, these two streams of Buddhism in America have remained separate, serving very different needs. Whereas Buddhism served Asian-Americans as a link with their traditional past, it appealed to Westerners who were seeking a kind of spiritual fulfillment they considered lacking in their own religious traditions.

The Asians who figured prominently in the initial establishment of Buddhist practice among Occidentals were men. At first Western Buddhism perpetuated the male dominance that had characterized both Asian and Western religious communities for centuries, where virtually all leadership and institutional power was reserved for men. Despite the prominence of such exceptional women as Blavatsky in the spread of Buddhism westward, traditional gender-role expectations were seldom challenged in religious circles East or West prior to the second half of the twentieth century. Yet during the latter half of the twentieth century—as Buddhism was increasingly established among Occidentals in Europe and North America, where women were striving to gain some social power—the traditional forms of Buddhism encountered significant challenges. The ensuing changes rendered such different patterns of institutional and spiritual practice that Western Buddhists often speak of the process as producing a new "turning of the wheel of dharma"—an expression that traditionally explains the generation of the three "vehicles" or branches of Buddhism (Theravada, Mahayana, Vajrayana).

Many Occidental followers of Buddhism in the later half of the twentieth century have challenged traditional gender-role expectations. Asian teachers have been joined by Occidentals (male and female) at the highest ranks, and female Buddhist practitioners have rivaled and sometimes surpassed their male counterparts in numbers and in spiritual accomplishments. In some cases the transition of these religious communities toward gender balance has been relatively smooth. Where it has not, there is evidence of deeply entrenched gender role expectations that, at their worst, have led to sexual and other power abuses on the part of male leaders. Even in less extreme cases, the inclusion of women at all levels of Buddhist communities has required reexamination of traditional expectations concerning monastic rules, institutional hierarchies, lay practice, and even child care.

By the 1980s enough women had joined Buddhist communities and begun to take leadership roles that Sandy Boucher, in researching her book *Turning the Wheel: American Women Creating the New Buddhism* (1988), spoke to more than one hundred influential Buddhist women. Boucher's book shows the wide range of women's influence in Buddhism in the West: there are women who have developed strong arguments for gender equality, both in scholarly publications (e.g., Janice Willis, Rita Gross, Diana Paul) and within Buddhist communities (e.g., Jacqueline Mandell, Judith Simmer-Brown). Other women have taken on, and sometimes transformed, Buddhist monastic vows (e.g., Pema Chodron, Ayya Khema). A number of the more well-known female Buddhist leaders are best known as teachers (e.g., Ruth Denison, Maureen Stuart Roshi). Other Buddhist women are active at the intersection of Buddhist practice and political-social activism, applying their understanding of Buddhism to such issues as environmental degradation, the threat of nuclear war, sexual abuse, inhumane treatment of animals, and racism (e.g., Joanna Macy, Charlene Spretnak). Of course the names of the vast majority of Buddhist women are not well known. Boucher includes some of them in her discussion of integrating Buddhist practice with the realities of everyday life, work, and community.

At the twentieth century's end women are active in every form of Buddhism that has taken root in the West. In Zen, the Mahayana school that has had the widest occidental following in North America, a number of women have become Zen *roshi*s (masters); several have established Zen centers of their own (e.g., Toni Packer, Charlotte Joko Beck). Some of these women preserve the traditional forms of Zen practice, wearing the robes of the Japanese *roshi* and requiring strict adherence to meditation postures and procedures. Others have questioned traditional symbols and institutional hierarchies and are exploring new teaching methods.

Western women have also been drawn to Vajrayana Buddhism, mainly through the teaching activities of influential Tibetan men (the Dalai Lama, the Karmapa, Chogyam Trungpa). A number of the leading women associated with Vajrayana in the West combine personal practice with research and publication and academic teaching (e.g., Anne C. Klein, Judith Simmer-Brown, Jan Willis, Rita Gross, Miranda Shaw). Others have dedicated themselves to practicing and teaching Vajrayana in monasteries and study centers in North America and Europe (e.g., Pema Chodron, Tsultrim Allione).

The impact of women's participation is evident, to a lesser degree, in the conservative Theravada school of Buddhism. In Theravada a central issue has been the unavailability of full monastic ordination for women. Although some Western women have sought to have the full ordination reinstated in the interest of equal opportunity for men and women, others have questioned the appropriateness of the traditionally celibate monasticism as an institution in the modern Buddhist world.

All of the branches of Buddhism in the West are undergoing significant transformation in response to the needs and worldviews of their Western adherents. The participation of women in this process continues to steer Buddhism's development in the West in creative directions, both institutionally and doctrinally.

BIBLIOGRAPHY

Batchelor, Stephen. *The Awakening of the West.* 1994.

Boucher, Sandy. *Turning the Wheel: American Women Creating the New Buddhism.* 1988. Rev. ed., 1993.

Butler, Katy. "Encountering the Shadow in Buddhist America." *Common Boundary* (1990): 14–22.

Fields, Rick. *How the Swans Came to the Lake.* 3d ed. 1992.

Friedman, Lenore. *Meetings With Remarkable Women: Buddhist Teachers in America.* 1987.

Humphreys, Christmas. *Sixty Years of Buddhism in England (1907–1967).* 1968.

Hunter, Louise. *Buddhism in Hawaii.* 1971.

Kashima, Tetsuden. *Buddhism in America.* 1977.

Kosho, Yamamoto. *Buddhism in Europe.* 1967.

Layman, Emma. *Buddhism in America.* 1976.

Lopez, Donald S., Jr., ed. *Curators of the Buddha.* 1995.

Prebish, Charles. *American Buddhism.* 1979.

Sidor, Ellen S., ed. *A Gathering of Spirit: Women Teaching in American Buddhism.* 1987.

Tsomo, Karma Lekshe, ed. *Buddhism Through American Women's Eyes.* 1995.

Tworkov, Helen. *Zen in America.* 1994.

See also **Asian and Asian-American Traditions; Ordination: In Buddhism.**

GRACE G. BURFORD

History of Study

Buddhists have been actively engaged in the study of their religion since the third century B.C.E. Although historically Buddhists have written accounts of the spread and establishment of their religion (from the *Mahāvaṃsa* in Sri Lanka and similar chronicles throughout Southeast Asia, to the histories of Tibetan Buddhism by Bu-ston and Taranatha), the majority of traditional Buddhist writers have tended to focus their efforts on interpretation of doctrine, via analysis of scriptural texts. Buddhist scholastic writings have recorded little social history and seldom discuss actual Buddhists, women or men. Early Buddhist tradition records the participation of both men and women in both lay and monastic Buddhist practice, yet from its beginning Buddhist scholastic analysis and systematization of doctrine appear to have been the exclusive domain of male monastics. The focus on text-based doctrinal interpretation and the exclusion of women from this analytical process characterize the scholastic aspect of the Buddhist tradition throughout Asia.

Nineteenth- and twentieth-century Western scholars of Buddhism, like their Asian Buddhist counterparts, have focused on analysis of doctrines preserved in Buddhist texts, and—also like their counterparts—almost all of these scholars have been men. The study of Buddhism in the West began in earnest during the nineteenth century, when European academic scholars, called Orientalists, began to analyze Buddhist texts sent to them from Asia by adventurous Occidental travelers. Interpretation of Buddhism came to be seen as the task of professional scholars, who could base their analyses on the growing collections of Pali, Sanskrit, and Tibetan texts in European libraries. The scholar's authority to describe Buddhism superseded that of the traveler to Buddhist countries, as well as that of any living Buddhist. For—in keeping with the colonial attitude of superiority to the native—the Orientalist claimed access, via the texts, to a transhistorical form of Buddhism that the Europeans projected as original, and thus pure, Buddhism, in contrast to what was perceived as the degenerate manifestations of this religion in contemporary Buddhist societies. By the middle of the twentieth century, Japanese scholars trained in European scholastic methods had expanded the range of Buddhist texts being analyzed to include the vast Chinese canon, but both in Japan and in the West the focus continued to be on doctrinal interpretation of texts.

Given that the Buddhism that interested Buddhist and non-Buddhist scholars alike was abstract, doctrinal, philosophical, and rational, it is not surprising that the topic of women in Buddhism seldom arose in their discussions; in fact, issues of actual human beings seldom arose, regardless of gender. This pattern appears to have been broken in 1893 by Mabel Bode, who drew attention to "Women Leaders of the Buddhist Reformation" in the *Journal of the Royal Asiatic Society*. The first person to give the role of women in Buddhism systematic treatment was I. B. Horner (1896–1981), a British scholar of the Pali texts of Theravada Buddhism. Horner had begun her study of Pali texts in the 1920s under the guidance of C. A. F. Rhys-Davids (1857–

1942), a Theosophist and scholar of Pali texts who had succeeded her husband T. W. Rhys-Davids (1843–1922) as president of the Pali Text Society, which he had founded in 1881. On the suggestion of C. A. F. Rhys-Davids, Horner undertook a study of women in Buddhism, in which she analyzed a wide range of Pali texts. She published her work in *Women Under Primitive Buddhism: Laywomen and Almswomen* (1930). Horner's analysis conformed to the norm of Buddhist scholarship in its method: Horner interpreted texts in search of original Buddhism. It differed, however, from that of her fellow scholars in its content, since, prior to Horner's work, Buddhist studies had essentially ignored women. It is also interesting to note that both Isaline Horner and Caroline Rhys-Davids chose to publish using their initials, as I. B. Horner and C. A. F. Rhys-Davids. This could have been a strategy aimed to disguise, or at least to downplay, their gender.

While Horner was undertaking her career in Buddhist studies, the French adventurer Alexandra David-Neel's writings on Buddhism began to appear. David-Neel (1868–1969) is best known for her fourteen-year journey through Asia, which culminated in an accomplishment that ensured her fame: she was the first Western woman to reach the Tibetan city of Lhasa. When David-Neel returned to France in 1925, she began to write and lecture about her Asian adventures and her study of Buddhism. Her account of her most famous trip, *My Journey to Lhasa* (1927), was widely read. Her subsequent works on Buddhism combined her firsthand information about Buddhism in Asia with her personal practice of this religion. In the context of twentieth-century Buddhist studies, however, neither David-Neel's experience in Asia nor her personal commitment to Buddhism won her scholarly work a great deal of respect among professional academics. In Buddhist studies the ideal remained one of academic distance from one's subject; texts contained the true religion, and the scholar did not get personally involved.

For the remainder of her long and distinguished career, I. B. Horner concentrated her efforts primarily on furthering the work of the Pali Text Society by collecting, editing, and translating the literature of Theravada Buddhism. The topic of Horner's first book was not taken up again until Diana Y. Paul published *Women in Buddhism: Images of the Feminine in the Mahayana Tradition* (1979). Just as Horner had analyzed the Theravada texts, in this work Paul mined the Mahayana texts for information about women in that branch of Buddhism. Although her research subject was not considered serious enough to win her university tenure, Paul's work stimulated further research on women in Buddhism at a time when study of women and religion in general—and women's roles in specific religions in particular—was taking off in Western scholarship.

In the 1980s and 1990s the growing presence of women among Buddhist scholars contributed to increased attention to the topic of women in Buddhism, and to gender issues. Methodologically, Buddhist studies shifted under the influence of both women and men in the next generation of Buddhism scholars, who supplemented their textual study with travel to Asian countries and who exhibited the kind of personal religious interest in Buddhism that David-Neel modeled. The ideal of studying Buddhism from a distance, via texts alone, has come under significant scrutiny. The boldest explicit revision of this method appears in Rita Gross's *Buddhism After Patriarchy: A Feminist History, Analysis, and Reconstruction of Buddhism* (1993), in which Gross argues for a feminist merging of an "insider" approach (typified by theological methods) and an "outsider" approach (as in the methods of the history of religions).

Many women are contributing new work in Buddhist studies—too many, happily, to mention here. Selected works of some of these scholars are listed below.

BIBLIOGRAPHY

Allione, Tsultrim. *Women of Wisdom.* 1984.

Bartholomeusz, Tessa. "The Female Mendicant in Buddhist Sri Lanka." In *Buddhism, Sexuality, and Gender.* Edited by José Ignacio Cabezón. 1992.

———. *Women Under the Bo Tree: Buddhist Nuns in Sri Lanka.* 1994.

Bode, Mabel. *The Pali Literature of Burma.* Rangoon, 1909. Reprint, 1965.

———. "Women Leaders of the Buddhist Reformation." *Journal of the Royal Asiatic Society* (1893): 517–566, 763–798.

Cabezón, José Ignacio, ed. *Buddhism, Sexuality, and Gender.* 1992.

David-Neel, Alexandra. *Buddhism: Its Doctrines and Its Methods.* 1939. Reprint, 1979.

———. *Magic and Mystery in Tibet.* 1931. Reprint, 1971.

———. "Women of Tibet." *Asia* 34 (March 1934): 176–181.

Gross, Rita M. *Buddhism After Patriarchy: A Feminist History, Analysis, and Reconstruction of Buddhism.* 1993.

Horner, I. B. *Women Under Primitive Buddhism: Laywomen and Almswomen.* Delhi, 1930. Reprint, 1975.

Kabilsingh, Chatsumarn. *A Comparative Study of the Bhikkhuni Patimokkha.* Varanasi, 1984.

King, Sallie B., trans. *Journey in Search of the Way: The Spiritual Autobiography of Satomi Myodo.* 1993.

Klein, Anne C. *Meeting the Great Bliss Queen: Buddhists, Feminists, and the Art of the Self.* 1995.

Paul, Diana Y. *Women in Buddhism: Images of the Feminine in the Mahayana Tradition.* 1979.

Rhys Davids, C. A. F., trans. *Psalms of the Sisters.* Vol. 1 *Psalms of the Early Buddhists.* London, 1948.

Shaw, Miranda. *Passionate Enlightenment: Women in Tantric Buddhism.* 1993.

Willis, Janice, ed. *Feminine Ground: Essays on Women and Tibet.* 1989.

GRACE G. BURFORD

Cabrini, Frances Xavier

Frances Xavier Cabrini (1850–1917), the first American citizen canonized a Roman Catholic saint, founded the Institute of the Missionary Sisters of the Sacred Heart of Jesus. The tenth of eleven brothers and sisters, of whom only four survived to adulthood, Maria Francesca Cabrini was born in Lombardy, Italy. Her consistently poor health never stopped her from working strenuously to fulfill her desire to be a missionary. After initial difficulties she was allowed in 1880 to organize her religious institute. Her interests were channeled by Pope Leo XIII in 1889 to missionary work not in Cabrini's intended destination, China, but to the United States, where she would assist the growing community of Italian immigrants in New York. In the wake of the great Italian immigrations in the late nineteenth and early twentieth centuries, Mother Cabrini expanded her ministries to both North and South America and the activities of the Missionary Sisters to Spain, France, England, and Italy. She exhibited tireless perseverance and independence as she personally established a network of convents, schools, parishes, orphanages, and hospitals among the Italian immigrant communities. In the United States, she worked in New York, New Orleans, Chicago, Philadelphia, Denver, Seattle, and Los Angeles among other locations. Though not fluent in English herself, she stressed ability in the language as a necessity for living in the United States. She also favored maintaining Italian language and culture within the immigrant community. Despite her fear of travel over water, she sailed to Central and South America, leaving sisters and new institutions in Nicaragua, Panama, Argentina, and Brazil to assist Italian immigrants, especially women and children. Her letters to her sisters, in the form of travel diaries, which she began in 1890, and her personal spiritual notes written when on retreat are especially helpful in understanding her spirituality. She was canonized on 7 July 1946. In 1950, Pope Pius XII declared her "Patroness of Immigrants."

Mother Frances Xavier Cabrini in 1880 at the time of the founding of her order (Cabriniana Room, Cabrini College, Radnor, PA).

BIBLIOGRAPHY

Maynard, Theodore. *Too Small A World: The Life of Mother Cabrini.* 1945. Prepared in anticipation of Cabrini's canonization, this book was for years the standard work on her in English.

Serpentelli, Giovanni, trans. *The Travels of Mother Frances Xavier Cabrini.* 1944. Selections from Cabrini's travel diaries and personal notes.

Sullivan, Mary Louise, MSC. *Mother Cabrini, Italian Immigrant of the Century.* 1992. The major documented study of Mother Cabrini. Brings together many scattered primary sources about her life and activities and includes photographs.

LEONARD NORMAN PRIMIANO

Canaan-Phoenicia, Religions of

In the Hebrew account of the creation of humankind, it is told that Adam ("Earthling") could not find a mate to suit him from among the animals paraded before him, so God built one of Adam's ribs into a helpmate. She was labeled "woman," but Adam did not fully appreciate her true function until after she brought him knowledge and vigor. He then named her Eve, meaning mother of the human species.

This parable may have been current among Israel's close neighbors, the Canaanites and the Phoenicians, with whom they had much in common. Inhabiting today's Lebanon, Israel, and (western) Syria, these people have left hardly any tales of creation. But what they do say suggests that their faith and cult resembled what the Hebrews believed in all but two crucial aspects: they venerated many gods, and women actively participated in this veneration. What the Bible says about their orgiastic worship can be dismissed as slander; its claim that they practiced sacral infanticide is likely to be false.

Canaan and *Phoenicia* refer to the same geographic region, the eastern Mediterranean littoral; but *Canaan* (a term derived from the Bible), commonly refers to the region in the period before the first millennium B.C.E., whereas *Phoenicia* (originating in classical sources) is used for subsequent periods. The distinction is largely artificial and is not followed here.

THE THIRD MILLENNIUM B.C.E.

Almost all the documentation for Canaan and Phoenicia (hereafter C/P) is artifactual. Because it includes a significant amount of female statuary, there has been endless speculation about the religion and society of these regions but little certainty on their manifestation. Whether this artifact suggests a goddess-dominated pantheon or a matriarchal society is often discussed.

The earliest written record hints at a number of regional city-states, a pattern that was to remain characteristic of C/P even when brought under the control of foreign powers. The archives found at Ebla (Tell Mardikh, south of Aleppo) record about fifty years (three rulers) in the life of an active metropolis around 2500 B.C.E. and mention a number of places that have been inconclusively equated with towns later known in C/P.

Although the titular gods of Ebla, Kura, and his consort Barama will not be known from C/P of later periods, the city's pantheon includes many male and female deities that survive into subsequent centuries: the male Dagan, Hadda ([H]Adad or H[A]ddu, storm god), and Rashap (Reshep, pestilence god), and the female Ishkhara, Ishtar, and (believed to be female) Sipish (sun goddess). What distinguishes Eblaite society is the major role played by the queen (*maliktum*) in all phases of the city's culture. In a series of rituals that lasted twenty-one days and in which a priestess occasionally took part, the future queen was at the center of activities that led to her marriage and to the enthronement of the royal couple. The celebrations included her making sacrifices to diverse deities and ancestors, anointing her head with oil, journeying to a series of shrines for purification and incubation, and banqueting. Ebla princesses often married rulers of neighboring principalities or became high priestesses (*dam.dingir*, literally "wife of the god").

THE SECOND MILLENNIUM B.C.E.

A significant shift in population took place around 2000 B.C.E., bringing Amorites to the fore in C/P. The Amorite were Semites whose language was close to the Canaanite and Phoenician of subsequent centuries. The sources for the second millennium are the archives found in Mari, Emar, Ugarit, and Tell el-Amarna.

Mari (c. 1775 B.C.E.)

The archives from Mari (Tell Hariri, on the Euphrates, north of the Syria-Iraq frontier) are only tangentially informative about religious life in C/P. Names of Amorites have elements that refer to regional gods, among the (H)Addu, El, Ishtar, and Dagan. The Mari texts include many letters exchanged between individuals, and they permit fuller portraits for palace women who originated in northwest Syria. The kings of Mari readily sought wives from the C/P region, and when these women move east they did not sever their connections with their past. When Beltum of Qatna (modern Mishrife) married Yasmakh-Addu of Mari, a sheepish Mari official tried to shift responsibility for the following misfortune that struck the new queen:

> When Beltum was leaving Qatna, [her nanny] was singled out and was sent to us with Beltum to Mari. But she knows nothing about the palace's operation. Because of this unreliable woman who now mentors my lady, during the siesta, when the palace's gate-bolts were drawn, [Beltum] had [the nanny] bring women-singers out to Ishtar's temple for the *shurarum* ceremony. While in the "multicolor" court, Beltum got a sunstroke and has been ill ever since (*Archives royales de Mari* 26, no. 298 [1988]).

Beltum, who had not yet adapted to the hotter clime of Mari, was evidently resuming cultic practices she had learned in Qatna. She recovered from her illness, and her father requested that she come home "to conciliate the gods of her city." Evidently, women from C/P did not forsake their native gods. Other texts tell us that women offered blood sacrifices themselves, a right denied them in Israel.

More informative are the letters regarding Shiptu, a princess from Aleppo who married another Mari king, Zimri-Lim. Because a delegation sent to fetch her arrived just as her grandmother died, the letters describe funerary rituals for royalty in C/P that stretched for a full month. The nuptial terms indicate that menstrual taboos forbade sexual activities, just as in later Israel. A series of letters written when Shiptu took control of her husband's palace tells of her involvement in affairs of state. Not content merely to forward messages the gods communicated through male and female prophets, Shiptu drugged soothsayers of both genders and, by skillfully quizzing them, forced the gods to give unequivocal answers to the issues of the day.

Emar, Ugarit, Tell el-Amarna (1400–1200 B.C.E.)

A number of archives tell about religious life in C/P in the Late Bronze Age. Although those from Emar (modern Meskene, on the Euphrates) illuminate a largely nonsemitic culture that lies beyond the fringes of C/P, nevertheless one of its rituals, dealing with the selection and installation of a high priestess (*nin.dingir*), is of interest. A daughter of any Emar citizen could be chosen for the honor by lot. Her head shaved and scented with oil, she was seated on a temple throne. She then presided over a seven-day banquet at the end of which she was said to "ascend her bed and lie down." The priestess was treated as a "bride of Baal"; but it is unclear whether a "sacred marriage" took place and whether the priestess held sacerdotal functions.

The richest information on the religion of C/P comes from Late Bronze Age Ugarit (Ras Shamra, on the Mediterranean coast, facing the "finger" of Cyprus).

This statuette of Astarte, the consort of Yam, dates back to the Late Bronze Age (Gianni Dagli Orti/Corbis).

Ugarit had a number of temples to such major deities as Dagan, Baal ("Lord," epithet for Haddu) and his sister-consort Anat, El and his spouse Ashera, Yam ("Sea") and his consort Astarte, Mot, ("Death"), Athtar and Athtart, and Reshep ("Plague"). "Rephaim," dead ancestors (apparently only males), were also venerated, probably for their power to heal the sick and reverse sterility.

Mythological tablets "copied" (possibly from oral dictation) by an Elimilku, part of the "private" archives of a priest, for the first and only time in C/P literary history give direct access to beliefs in the C/P region. The most frequently adopted sequence of events has Baal defeating his nemesis Yam before building a palace. With Anat's help, Baal eventually triumphs. The whole aims at reassuring believers of the constancy of nature and the gods.

The cultic vocabulary at Ugarit is highly reminiscent of the biblical idiom. Terms for temple personnel (*khnm* [Hebrew *kohanim*]; *qdšm* [Hebrew *qedošim*, used pejoratively]) often have female equivalents, whereas in Israel the only term associated with women (*ṣōbeʾōt,* Exod. 38:8) is for a menial occupation, possibly courtyard sweepers. Whether C/P women participated in cultic activity during menstruation is not yet known.

As in Israel, worship centered on caring for and feeding the gods. Sacrifice included animal, vegetal, and libation, commonly twice a day, but more frequently during seasonal and agrarian festivals. During crises, first-born (animal rather than human) were vowed.

THE FIRST MILLENNIUM B.C.E.

Shortly after the turn of the millennium, the geographical horizons of C/P expanded when such port cities as Sidon and Tyre established colonies extensively in North Africa (most famously Carthage, near Tunis), Spain, Sardinia, Corsica, southern France, and beyond Gibraltar. Moreover, the nonsemitic Sea Peoples that entered southern C/P early in the twelfth century B.C.E. eventually were assimilated to the population, becoming known as the Philistines. Paradoxically, except for information derived from burial grounds, less is known about cultic matters after 1000 B.C.E. than before because around that time documents ceased to be written on clay tablets in C/P. Papyrus, always favored in an area influenced by Egypt, became the dominant writing medium throughout the Mediterranean littoral; it does not withstand humidity and fire.

Although the gods of previous millennia continued to be worshiped throughout C/P, each city gravitated toward a deity, with or without a (female) consort: Baal Shamem ("Sky Baal") and Baalat ("The Lady") in Byblos, "Poseidon" (Yam?) in Beirut, Eshmun and Astarte in Sidon, Melqart ("City King") and Astarte in Tyre, but Melqart and Tanit in Carthage. Among the Philistines of Gaza, Askelon, Ashdod, Gath, and Eqron, there was worship of Dagan (Dagon), Baal-Zebul (Beelzebub), and Astarte (Hebrew *aštōret*).

The participation of women in cultic activities is best known from funerary inscriptions, mostly of the elite. According to one such inscription, Addu-guppi, mother of King Nabonidus of Babylon, probably was a Syrian from Haran (sixth century), at the edge of C/P. When the moon god abandoned her city, she vowed herself to an ascetic life until, touched by her piety, the god dampened his anger. Ama'Ashtart, married to her (half-?) brother Tabnit of Sidon, was mother of the child Eshmunazar when her husband died. A priestess of Astarte and regent in Sidon, she soon also lost her young son. The pathetic tone struck in her son's sarcophagus inscription ("I died prematurely, very young, an orphan, son of a widow"—repeated twice) may well have been her own. Her body was likely the one found in an inscribed and undecorated sarcophagus, possibly confirming her feeling of doom.

A major controversy, with credible scholarship on both sides, concerns whether the discovery of hundreds of urns (mostly from the "Tophet" shrine in Carthage) containing charred remains of infants is evidence of child sacrifice or of the "purification" of dead infants. The debate is almost hopelessly complicated by reference to the hostile (and largely unfounded) biblical polemic attributing child sacrifice (*mōlek,* see 2 Kings 23:10, Jer. 7:31–32) to the Phoenicians. While the gender of these infants cannot be determined (their bodies are too small and too badly charred), 10 percent of the four thousand inscribed dedications that accompanied burials in the tophet were done by women. Many identified themselves through their fathers or ancestors rather than through their husbands, confirming that, as Alexander's armies were conquering the C/P region, women were independent enough to make their own promises to the gods.

BIBLIOGRAPHY

OVERVIEW

Sabatino Moscati, ed., *The Phoenicians* (Milan, 1988), is encyclopedic about Phoenician civilizations and contains many excellent illustrations, especially of terracotta figurines, sarcophagi, jewelry, and scarabs associated with women. Useful to consult is E. Lipinski, ed. *Dictionnaire de la civilisation phénicienne et punique* (Bruxelles, 1992), and V. Krings, ed., *La civilisation phénicienne et punique: Manuel de recerces* (Leiden, 1995). Diverse aspects of Canaanite myth and religion are presented in J. M. Sasson et al., eds., *Civilizations of the Ancient Near East,* vol. 3, pp. 2031–2094 (1995). See also Jonas C. Greenfield, "The Hebrew Bible and Canaanite Literature," in *The Literary Guide to the Bible,* edited by Robert Alter and Frank Kermode (1987).

A fine compendium on the gods of C/P is Edward Lipiński, *Dieux et déesses de l'univers phénicien et punique* (Leuven, 1995). A focused study of a major Phoenician goddess is Corinne Bonnet's *Astarté: Dossier documentaire et perspectives historiques* (Rome, 1996).

THIRD MILLENNIUM B.C.E.

On the gods of Ebla, see P. Mander, "Los Dioses y el Culto de Ebla," in *Mitología y Religión del Oriente Antiguo, II/1: Semitas Occidentales (Ebla, Mari),* edited by P. Mander and J.-M. Durand (Sabadell, 1995). On the cult, see P. Fronzaroli, "The Ritual Texts of Ebla," *Quaderni di Semitistica* 18 (1992): 163–185. On the role of royal women, see Maria Giovanna Biga, "Prosopographie et datation relative des textes d'Ébla," *Amurru* 1 (1996): 29–72.

SECOND MILLENNIUM B.C.E.

On the religion and cult of Mari, which includes inspection of material from Aleppo and Qatna, see J.-M. Durand, "La religión en Siria durante la época de los reinos amorreos según la documentación de Mari," *Mitología y Religión del Oriente Antiguo, II/1: Semitas Ocidentales (Ebla, Mari)*, edited by P. Mander and J.-M. Durand (Sabadell, 1995). For the roles of palace women in cult and prophecy, see J. M. Sasson, "The Posting of Letters with Divine Messages," *Florilegium marianum, 2: Recueil d'études à la mémoire de Maurice Birot*, edited by D. Charpin and J.-M. Durand (Paris, 1984).

The rituals from Emar are most conveniently assembled in D. Fleming, "Rituals," in *The Context of Scripture* I, edited by W. W. Hallo and K. J. Lawson, Jr. (Leiden, 1997). D. Pardee translates and annotates the Ugaritic "Baal and Anat" in the same volume.

FIRST MILLENNIUM B.C.E.

For expansion to the West, see M. E. Auber, *The Phoenicians and the West* (1993). Addu-guppi's life is (partially) recounted by T. Longman, also in *Context of Scripture*. On the issue of infant sacrifice at Carthage, see M. Gras, P. Rouillard, and J. Teixidor, "The Phoenicians and Death," *Berytus* 39 (1991): 127–176 ("Les Phéniciens et la mort," chap. 6 of *L'univers phénicien* [Paris, 1989]). On the gender of vow-makers at the tophet, see M. G. Amadasi Guzzo, "Dédicaces de femmes á Carthage," *Studia Phoenicia* 6 (1987), 143–149.

See also **Sacred Marriage**.

JACK M. SASSON

Caribbean Religions

The Caribbean islands and the Orinoco basin on the South American coast provided a cohesive habitat to several cultural groups in the pre-Hispanic period. The most numerous were the Arahuacan-speaking communities that came to be called Taínos. As population increased, threatening the availability of fish and animals for food, kinship groups split apart, sending bands of mostly younger males into migration to search for new regions to settle. Migration created problems for the endogamous patterns of marriage exchange and occasioned conflicts over land and water. The seventeenth-century French missionary friar Raymond Breton compiled a dictionary that proves two languages were used among the inhabitants of St. Vincent: the women spoke a variant of Arahuacan, whereas the men employed an idiom dependent on a vocabulary derived from the Karina (Carib) linguistic family. This bilingual pattern along gender lines probably reflects a migration pattern dating from before the European invasions, in which male Caribs had invaded and replaced Arahuacan-speaking male rivals, settling with the females already there.

The Taíno division of labor often coincided with gender. As in many societies, hunting and fishing were male occupations, while agricultural tasks and especially food preparation were left to females. We can classify the Taíno society as matrilineal, with residence required in the village of the woman's grandfather. According to some chronicles, women ruled over their peoples after the death of their husbands. But virtually all the texts that make Taínos into queens come from Castilian sources. Castile's feudal law, in contrast with that of Aragon, permitted female ascension to the throne. Were the Castilians reading into Taíno society a European institution when they reported women rulers? With hindsight, we can assert that caciques, Taíno kinship leaders, likely were chosen on account of leadership abilities and not in accord with the rights of primogeniture. Any male—even a Spaniard—acquired an opportunity to inherit a cacique's responsibilities if he married a Taína daughter of a cacique. Thus, in its gender relationships Taíno society did not follow European legal notions of power. Indeed, rule may have been a power jointly shared by man and woman and not entirely resident in a single individual.

Taíno cultural and religious experience is characterized by fissure—that is, the separation of the kinship group into sedentary and migratory segments. In passages similar to the Mesoamerican Popul Vuh, Taíno mythology describes the first humans as two sets of twins, born from a woman without the aid of a male parent. Other religious explanations legitimate union with women from other tribal and linguistic groups. Thus, Matininó was an island where women had "No Fathers" and any man could find a mate there. The island was a mythical place, of course, but the Spaniards identified it with the Amazon society of classical Greek legend. The notion that the islands (Canary and Caribbean) did not form a "new" world, but were instead a rediscovered part of the lost Greco-Roman empires, colored Spanish colonization until the seventeenth century.

Taíno mythology describes women personages who instruct male characters in the skills of sedentary social life. Interestingly, what the West considers feminine characteristics—patience, forbearance, sexual continence—were required of the masculine hero Guayahona before he could become a cacique. These traits were taught to him by a woman, Guabonito, who arises from the bottom of the sea and has mastered a magic calibrated with the *maraca*.

The Taínos' religion reflects a dualism in which the numinous is found only in the combination of opposing forces. Resembling the yin and yang of Chinese experience, this perception of the spiritual relies on the coalescence of femininity and masculinity, of emotion and reason, of action and passivity. Taíno healing and the balance of the cosmos are built upon what philosophy has called *coincidentia oppositorum.*

There are two important feminine spirits in Taíno religion. The fertile Atabeira is spirit of the earth and provider of potable water in the mountains and lakes. Represented as pregnant, with breasts filled with milk, one of her stone reproductions has been compared to the Venus of Willendorf. The other feminine spirit is Guabancex, depicted as a floating woman's face with sinuous arms whirling about her head. She is identified with salt water and the driving storms of the hurricane. The Taínos drew her arms in the exact pattern of the hurricane's winds, so that the Guabancex pictogram can be superimposed on a contemporary satellite photograph of a hurricane: her head is the eye of the storm, her arms its winds.

These feminine spirits integrated telluric and cosmic forces of fertility with the social order and psychological maturity. Atabeira is the fertile Venus, sexual object and mother to all; Guabancex is the menstruating woman, companion and Amazon competitor to men. Both figures together represent the fullness of Taína femininity. This rich and complex reading of Taíno symbolism has spurred a reimaging of the pre-European roots of Caribbean societies. Today, Taíno themes are frequently found in art, cultural expression, and literature both on the islands and among the Caribbean diaspora in the United States A few organizations, such as The Taíno Intertribal Council, Inc., profess to have restored practice of the Taíno religion.

BIBLIOGRAPHY

In religion, the best text remains *Cave of the Jagua: The Mythological World of the Taínos,* by Anthony M. Stevens-Arroyo (1988). See also two articles by the same author, "The Inter-Atlantic Paradigm: The Failure of Spanish Medieval Colonization of the Canary and Caribbean Islands" (*Comparative Studies in Society and History* 35, no. 3 [1993]: 515–543) and "Juan Mateo Guaticabanú, September 21, 1496: Evangelization and Martyrdom in the Time of Columbus" (*Catholic Historical Review* 82, no. 4 [1996]: 614–636). In archaeology, see Irving Rouse, *The Tainos: Rise and Decline of the People Who Greeted Columbus* (1992) and William F. Keegan, *The People Who Discovered Columbus* (1992). For a more historical slant, see Troy S. Floyd, *The Columbus Dynasty in the Caribbean, 1492–1526* (1973); Samuel M. Wilson, *Hispaniola: Caribbean Chiefdoms in the Age of Columbus* (1990); and Wilson's edited volume, *The Indigenous People of the Caribbean* (1997).

For a deconstruction of European depiction of the Taína women, see *Iconografía política del nuevo mundo,* edited by Mercedes López-Baralt (1990), and in English, Peter Hulme's *Colonial Encounters: Europe and the Native Caribbean, 1492–1797* (1986).

ANTHONY M. STEVENS-ARROYO

Castration

Castration is mentioned in a religious context in the oldest written texts, the Hittite and Hurrite cosmogonic myths of the middle of the second millennium B.C.E. In these tales the god Kumarbi bites off his father's penis and swallows it, an act that results in his becoming pregnant with a generation of gods who will defeat him. Whereas this myth focuses on the procreative power of the male organ, ritual castration often aims at feminizing males. The feminizing aspect of castration applies particularly to Christianity and to the religions of Anatolia and India.

Through Greek and Roman accounts we learn of the Galli, the priests of the mother goddess, the Magna Mater, or Cybele of Pessinus in the middle of modern Turkey. Pessinus was their center, but the castrated priests also are widely attested in ancient Anatolia and Syria. They wore female clothing and make-up, displayed feminine hairstyles, and practiced ecstatic rites. Greek and Roman males considered them "half-men" or "half-women." The use of flint for their castration seems to point to a tradition dating to the Stone Age, but its origin is lost in obscurity. The Galli have not left their own explanation for this practice, but from a functionalist point of view we may observe that castration rendered them unthreatening to other males. This may have been the reason the institution could survive over such a long period of time in Anatolia.

Early Christianity did not practice castration as a rule, but it is mentioned as an option for the sake of sexual purity in the middle of the second century in Justin's *Apology I* (chap. 29). The practice was condemned at the Council of Nicaea (325) and by Pope Leo I (c. 395). Unfortunately, the most cited examples of castration are known only from the writings of opponents of the practice. Origen (c. 185–c. 253), a Greek writer and early Church Father, supposedly castrated himself, but this is known from unreliable sources and only after his death. The same is true about the mysterious sect of the Valesians, who are mentioned by the fourth-century bishop Epiphanius in his *Panarion*, which is an enumeration of heresies. Much better attested are the Russian Skopcy ("the castrated"), an ecstatic sect that emerged in the last quarter of the eighteenth century. The Skopcy believed that male castration and the removal of female breasts opened the road to salvation. Their founder, Kondratij Selivanov (d. 1832), was politically active and was therefore confined by authorities to a monastery. Due to many arrests by the Russian authorities, the sect started to decline at the beginning of the twentieth century and now seems to have disappeared altogether.

The best known modern practitioners of castration are the Indian *hijras*, an Urdu word meaning eunuch, transvestite, or hermaphrodite. They are not enumerated in census reports, and estimations vary between fifty thousand and half a million adherents; the great majority of them live in the big cities of northern India. *Hijras* may be Hindus, Muslims, or Christians, but are outcast by traditional society on account of their emasculation, which violates the male norm of begetting children. They often organize in small groups under the leadership of a guru who is responsible for the wellbeing of his pupils (*chelas*). The hierarchical relationship is supplemented by fictive kinship relations, such as "mother" and "daughter," which are reinforced during religious and secular annual gatherings.

Hijras are often connected with Bahucharamata, a Hindu goddess associated with birth and fertility. Childless couples visit her shrine during the full moon and new moon, when they dance in the temple compound. Traditionally, *hijras* earn their living by singing and dancing during birth ceremonies, Islamic weddings, and at some festivals during which they have the right to beg for alms. They are not supposed to engage in sexual activities but are required to store their energy as ascetics. This unspilt sexual power enables them to bless or to curse in the above mentioned situations (birth, marriage) in which this power is of vital importance.

BIBLIOGRAPHY

Bianchi, Ugo, ed. *La tradizione dell' enkrateia: Motivazioni ontologiche e protologiche.* 1985.

Bradford, N. J. "Transgenderism and the Cult of Yellama: Heat, Sex, and Sickness in South Indian Ritual." *Journal of Anthropological Research* 39 (1983): 307–322.

Burkert, Walter. *Structure and History in Greek Mythology and Ritual.* 1979.

Grass, K. K. *Die geheime heilige Schrift der Skopzen.* 1904.

———. *Die russischen Sekten.* 2 vols. 1907–1914.

Nanda, S. "The Hijras of India: Cultural and Individual Dimension of an Institutionalized Third Gender Role." *Journal of Homosexuality* 11 (1986): 35–54.

———. *Neither Man nor Woman: The Hijras of India.* 1990.

Schmolitsch, I. *Geschichte der russischen Kirche.* Vol. 2. 1990.

Sharma, S. K. *Hijras: The Labelled Deviants.* 1989. Flawed from a scholarly point of view.

Vermaseren, Maarten J. *Cybele and Attis.* 1977.

See also Celibacy; Cross-dressing; Gender Roles; Men's Spirituality Movement; Mutilation.

LOURENS P. VAN DEN BOSCH

JAN N. BREMMER

Catherine of Genoa

Catholic holy woman Catherine of Genoa (1447–1510), was born to the aristocratic Fieschi family in Genoa, Italy. In 1463, three years after being refused entrance into a convent, Catherine was forced into an unhappy marriage to a spendthrift and philandering nobleman. A profound religious experience in 1473 prompted her to begin severe penitential practices as well as charitable works. In 1479, her by then converted husband joined her at the Pammatone Hospital where, residing celibately, they ministered to the poor and sick. Catherine was director of the hospital from 1490 to 1496, distinguishing herself especially during a devastating plague.

Central to Catherine's spirituality are the notions of suffering, purgation, and the soul's struggle against the body and self-love. Her virulent penances included lengthy fasts, sleep deprivation, and eating pus and lice to conquer her aversions. In contrast to most holy women, Catherine pursued her spiritual life independently for over twenty-five years, accepting a confessor only in 1499. Renowned for her benevolent activities, as well as her eucharistic devotion, visions, and ecstasies, Catherine attracted numerous disciples, including priests, sisters, and laity, and inspired the foundation of eminent charitable and religious institutions.

Catherine's life and teaching are recounted in three texts composed shortly after her death: a widely read *Life*; *The Treatise on Purgatory*, which relates her teachings regarding spiritual purgation; and *The Spiritual Dialogue*, a three-part text including a dialogue between the soul and body, arbitrated by self-love; a dialogue recounting the struggles of human frailty against the spirit; and a graphic narrative of her excruciating final illness and death. The precise authorship of these texts, compiled variously by her confessor and spiritual disciples, has been much disputed.

BIBLIOGRAPHY

The best edition in the original Italian of the texts associated with Catherine appears in the second volume of Umile Bonzi da Genova's *S. Caterina Fieschi Adorno:* vol. 1, *Teologia mistica de S. Caterina da Genova;* vol. 2, *Edizione critica dei manoscritti cateriniani* (1960–1962). For English translations of the *Life,* see *Life of Madame Catharine Adorna,* translated by Thomas Cogswell Upham (1845); for *The Treatise on Purgatory* and *The Spiritual Dialogue,* see *Catherine of Genoa: Purgation and Purgatory, The Spiritual Dialogue,* translated by Serge Hughes (1979).

Friedrich von Hügel's *The Mystical Element of Religion as Studied in Saint Catherine of Genoa and Her Friends* (2 vols., 1908) remains the foundational work about her. On her life and the disputed authorship of texts associated with her, see Pierre Debongnie, "Sainte Catherine de Gênes, vie et doctrine, d'après des travaux récents," *Revue d'ascétique et de mystique* 38 (1962): 409–446; and Hughes' note in *Catherine of Genoa,* pp. 47–67. For further bibliography, see S. Pezzella, "Caterina Fieschi Adorno (Caterina da Genova), santa," *Dizionario Biografico degli Italiani,* vol. 22 (1979), pp. 343–345.

CATHERINE M. MOONEY

Catherine of Siena

Catherine of Siena is known equally for her mystic visions, devoted religious life, and political influence. Catherine was born in Siena, Italy, in 1347, one of twenty-five children, to the Christian family of Jacopo Benincasa and Lapa di Puccio di Piacenti. From a very early age she reported visions of Christ, and by age seven had dedicated her virginity to him. She became a member of the Dominican third order (tertiary) in 1365 and lived an austere life of prayer and dedicated service to the poor and the sick. Catherine adopted a leadership role within the order and became a spiritual guide and teacher to many important religious and political rulers of the time. She founded her own ascetic women's order in Belcaro, Italy (1377). Catherine's theological reflections were dictated in her *Dialogue,* which speaks of a path to God through self-knowledge, love, and penance. The "bridge" of Christ, the central metaphor of the *Dialogue,* is the earthly connection be-

tween humankind and God, who "draws everything to himself through love" (chaps. 26–87). Catherine's ecstatic visions and theology of love are also contained in her prayers. The correspondence (382 letters) between Catherine and various monarchs, popes, cardinals, and other European dignitaries demonstrates her competence and acumen in the political arena. Catherine is credited with having influenced Pope Gregory XI to return the Curia from Avignon to Rome (1376). After Gregory's death a dispute arose over the election of the subsequent pope, and for a time there were three popes (the Great Western Schism): Urban VI in Rome, Clement VII in Avignon, and Alexander V in Pisa causing a division among the church hierarchy and European political alliances that lasted until 1418. Catherine was instrumental in encouraging many European rulers to recognize Urban VI in Rome as the true pope. She died of a stroke in 1380 at the age of thirty-three and was canonized by the Roman Catholic Church in 1461. Catherine was declared the patron saint of Siena in 1461 and in 1866 declared copatron of Rome. She was made Doctor of the Church in 1970, along with the first woman so honored, Teresa of Avila. Catherine is depicted in many paintings, often holding a lily. Her feast day is April 29 (formerly April 30). Her monumental achievements, as a political mediator, a mystic visionary, mentor, and writer, affected the course of European history and Catholic theology and constitute a remarkable contribution from a single life.

BIBLIOGRAPHY

There are innumerable studies of Catherine that could be divided into the following categories: commentaries, hagiography, literary analyses, and artistic representations. The primary source material from which these studies draw includes the vast body of work translated by Suzanne Noffke: *The Letters of St. Catherine of Siena* (1988; vol. 1 of what proposes to be the first complete English translation of the letters); *Catherine of Siena: The Dialogue* (1980) (replacing the original fifteenth-century English translation, known as *The Orcherd of Syon,* and the subsequent 1896 translation by Algar Thorold); and *The Prayers of St. Catherine of Siena* (1983). The anthology edited by Mary O'Driscoll, *Catherine of Siena: Passion for the Truth, Compassion for Humanity* (1993) contains a critical selection of these primary sources. *Catherine of Siena: Vision Through a Distant Eye* by Suzanne Noffke (1996), in addition to providing an excellent examination of Catherine's theological and spiritual writings, contains an annotated bibliography of the primary sources and an extensive listing of secondary sources organized by category.

KATHLEEN O'GRADY

Celibacy

Celibacy is the voluntary renunciation of sexual activity, usually practiced within an ascetic lifestyle, that includes other physical disciplines such as fasting and periods of solitude. The fact that celibacy is a voluntary commitment not based on previous sexual abstinence distinguishes it from virginity, which refers to the biological state of never having engaged in sexual intercourse. The historical Buddha and St. Augustine, for example, became celibates after having fathered children and therefore were not virgins. Celibacy also differs from chastity, which refers to refraining from inappropriate or unlawful sexual activity. For example, a married person is chaste if she or he is monogamous and modest in social relationships. Thus, one can be chaste while not being celibate, and one can be celibate while not being a virgin.

Throughout history celibacy has been embraced by both men and women but often for different reasons, in different forms, and with different effects. Male celibacy developed predominantly in those religions whose goal is a transcendent spiritual reality directly opposed to this world's mutable earthly existence. Hence, achieving salvation in these religions requires renouncing the material world and its pleasures, including sexuality and, consequently, women. Moreover, males in these religions chose celibacy to isolate themselves from women, whose sexuality was viewed as possessing a dangerous power that seduces, an impurity that pollutes, or a physical quality that weakens the will and spirit. Over time, however, women themselves became ascetics, practicing celibacy for different purposes—to be free of men's beliefs about them, which subjected their spirits and bodies to male domination.

In Hinduism, woman's sexuality is considered potentially dangerous. As mother, a woman is revered as the center of domestic life, but as wife she is often feared because her sexuality could impede her husband's spiritual progress. According to the early Upanishads written prior to the sixth century B.C.E., a man could attain *mokṣa*, or liberation from the cycle of death and rebirth, by leaving all worldly ties behind and becoming celibate after he had raised a family and had performed the necessary rituals.

For the most part, a woman's asceticism in India is associated with her chastity and obedience within marriage. However, there were women renouncers, devotees of Siva or Krishna, who proclaimed their god to be their lover. By doing so these women freed themselves of society's expectations and the oppression of in-laws. There are several stories about women such as Ma-

A female Hindu swami crosses her legs in Haridwar. Like many women swamis, she renounced the material world and its pleasures (Earl Kowall/Corbis).

hadeviyakka and Mirabai who leave their husbands and in-laws to pursue a life of a celibate renouncer.

Buddhism, too, from its inception in sixth century B.C.E. India, included celibacy as a necessary step to liberation. Buddha himself achieved enlightenment only after abandoning family life and sexuality, thereby becoming the model for his followers. He taught that one needs to be free of all attachments in order to pursue liberation. Sexuality, though not necessarily evil in itself, was one of the greatest of these attachments. The history of Buddhism indicates that both women and men could join monasteries and that their robes and shaved heads eliminated sexual distinctions; yet there is also a tradition that states that women will be reborn as men before attaining enlightenment. The social resistance to women taking up the religious life is reflected in the Buddha's reluctance to admit women to the monastic order. He did so only after imposing on them eight additional rules that stipulate obedience to their male counterparts. Such difficulties account for the fact that the Theravada women's order died out more than a thousand years ago and even in this day the Theravada sect does not ordain women.

Although Buddhist women joined monastic orders to achieve the same spiritual goal as held by men, they also sought freedom from their restrictive domestic roles. The words of the first nuns found in the *Therigatha* reveal their quest for freedom, both spiritual and social.

Christianity is the only Western tradition that holds celibacy as a value for both men and women. The dualism of matter versus spirit and earth versus heaven entered Christian thought through Greek philosophy and mystery religions, such as Gnosticism, that were popular at the beginning of the common era. This dualism also separated genders and associated men with the spiritual realm or the good and women with the material or the bad. It is not surprising, then, that in these philosophies abstinence from sex and from the contaminating influence of women is essential for the attainment of the eternal good or salvation. Christian Scriptures, however, are ambiguous on the issue of celibacy. This is especially true of the epistles of Paul, which, while advising Christians that celibacy is a preferred state (1 Cor. 7:1 and 7:38), also uphold marriage as the paradigmatic relationship of Christ and his Church (Eph. 5:22–33). In the early Church writings there were arguments for both the sanctity of marriage and the value of celibacy, and, as a result, women were free to practice either. Based on the evidence of these writings, some scholars claimed that early Christianity stood out as a religion that was more egalitarian than others at the time. Indeed, Christianity's first women celibates were widows who held special positions in the community, often as collaborators with the clergy.

In the fourth century, when persecution of Christians ceased, the celibate ascetic life became institutionalized because many, wanting to commit themselves totally, fled to the desert and renounced all earthly pleasures. The first monks were men, but women soon formed their own communities that took their place alongside their male counterparts.

Largely because of St. Augustine, the fourth-century theologian, the role of sexuality was reduced to that of procreation and was divorced from any pleasure that might accompany the act. He saw sensual pleasure as the result of original sin, serving only to pull the person away from the life of the spirit and union with God. Although one could be good in the married state, one had to embrace celibacy to achieve perfection; and although both married and celibate were eligible for salvation, the former would have to meet many more obstacles along the way. The purpose of leading a celibate life was to keep the temptation of carnal pleasures at bay and also to reap rewards of abstinence in this life, that is, union with God and the freedom to serve others.

The purpose of women's monastic life was also union with God, but it offered another dimension: for many, the convent provided an alternative to marriage and an escape from the prevailing misogynistic attitudes throughout the Middle Ages, an opportunity for an education, and expression of artistic, literary, and philosophical talent. It also provided Christian women an opportunity to live together in an association that would be impossible in society because of the traditional dependence of women on men. This community gave women the support and creative energy to be independent and to develop a spirituality and ideology that was particularly female. Women who exemplify such lives are Hildegard of Bingen, Julian of Norwich, Catherine of Siena, Teresa of Avila, and Mechthild of Magdeburg.

In the mid-sixteenth century, the Protestant Reformers abolished the monastic life from new-found sects of Christianity. The monastic traditions survived in Roman Catholicism and Eastern Orthodoxy and retured in the nineteenth century to the Anglican church. In these branches, celibate religious communities provided alternatives for women who wished to remain single and pursue careers. They also provided a social support system for a woman to be creative, self-assured, and fulfilled independent of male influence and the imposition of male views of women. In fact, such socialization achieved many of the goals of the modern women's movement long before it began. Only toward the end of the twentieth century, with single life becoming more acceptable, more career opportunities opening to women, and greater choices for missionary work, are Catholic religious orders declining in numbers.

Whether in the East or West, celibacy provided religious and educational opportunities for women. Celibate communities also provided support systems for a uniquely feminine spirituality and ideology in the face of the androcentrism both within male celibate communities and in society as a whole.

BIBLIOGRAPHY

Brown, Peter. *The Body and Society: Men, Women and Sexual Renunciation in Early Christianity.* 1988.

Clark, Elizabeth A., and Herbert Richardson, eds. *Women and Religion.* 1977.

Gies, Frances, and Joseph Gies. *Women in the Middle Ages.* 1978.

Gross, Rita M. *Buddhism after Patriarchy: A Feminist History, Analysis, and Reconstruction of Buddhism.* 1993.

Hopkins, Thomas. *The Hindu Religious Tradition.* 1971.

Jaini, Padmanabh S. *Gender and Salvation.* 1991.

Kinsley, David R. *Hinduism: A Cultural Perspective.* 1993.

Lannoy, Richard. *The Speaking Tree: A Study of Indian Culture and Society.* 1971.

Murcott, Susan. *The First Buddhist Woman: Translations and Commentary on the* Therigatha. 1991.

Young, Serinity. "Gendered Politics in Ancient Indian Asceticism." Website <http://www.uts.columbia. edu/~usqr/young.htm>. April 5, 1997.

See also **Catherine of Siena; Chastity; Hildegard of Bingen; Julian of Norwich; Mahādēviyakka; Mechthild of Magdeburg; Mirabai; Teresa of Avila; Virginity.**

MAURA O'NEILL

Celtic Religions

At its height, pagan Celtic Europe stretched from Ireland to Romania and part of Turkey and its religion spanned a period from 700 B.C.E. to the middle of the first millennium C.E. Due to the virtual nonliteracy of pre-Roman Celtic Europe, we possess no contemporary indigenous accounts of religion and ritual. Consequently, there are three main sources of evidence: the comments of writers from the Graeco-Roman world about their "barbarian" Celtic neighbors; the vernacular myths of Ireland and Wales, compiled by Christian monks in medieval times; and archaeological evidence.

We cannot tell whether women played an active role in all religious ceremonies; whether some cults were exclusively for female participants or whether certain rites excluded women. Classical literature and the testimony of archaeology combine to describe a Celtic society in which women could and did achieve social and political parity with men. Thus, in describing the great rebellion of the British queen Boudica in 60 C.E., the Roman historian Tacitus mentions that the British Celts were accustomed to female battle commanders. Early Celtic graves likewise indicate the aspiration of women to a high and independent status, as reflected in rich grave-goods (frequently wealthier than neighboring male tombs). The graves of the women buried at Vix in Burgundy (late sixth century B.C.E.), at Reinheim and Waldalgesheim in Germany (early fourth century B.C.E.), and at Wetwang in northeast Britain (second century B.C.E.) are indications of the senior rank attainable by women.

Goddesses were important in the Celtic pantheon. Archaeological findings, in the form of images of female deities and dedicatory inscriptions (from the Roman period), provide testimony as to the wide-ranging functions of Celtic goddesses. They had responsibilities for warfare, hunting, healing, death, and animals, as well as fertility; some female divinities were unifunctional, others were multifaceted. Prominent divine females include the horse-goddess Epona; the triple Mother-Goddess; and goddesses associated with sacred healing springs, such as Sulis in western Britain and Sequana in Burgundy.

The Celtic myths provide abundant evidence for supernatural females who clearly possessed divine status. "Goddesses" are described, for instance, in the Irish *Táin Bo Cuailnge* and in the Welsh *Four Branches of the Mabinogi.* The legendary Queen Medb of Connacht, the sinister Battle Fury known as the Morrigán, and Macha are all associated with myths of sovereignty, in which the divine female personification of the land of Ireland conferred kingship on men by means of ritual marriage. In Welsh mythic tradition, it is possible to recognize divinity in Rhiannon (a horse-goddess), in Arianrhod, whose name means "silver wheel" and who may therefore have been a moon-deity, and in many others.

Archaeology and classical literature show that women were fully involved in some religious practices. The Greek Strabo (first century B.C.E.) and the Roman Pomponius Mela (first century C.E.), both geographers, record priestesses of island cults off the coasts of Gaul (France) and Britain. Strabo speaks of an island inhabited by priestesses who, every year, dismantled and re-roofed their temple in one day, accompanying this ritual by the sacrifice of one of their number. Mela's holy island (probably located in the Scilly Islands, off the coast of Cornwall, England) was inhabited by nine virgin priestesses who guarded a sacred oracle. These women had the power to cure disease, control the elements, and predict the future. Strabo alludes to female religious officials who belonged to the tribe of the Cimbri, who were involved in the sacrifice of prisoners. Tacitus mentions an influential Cimbrian prophetess named Veleda, who had quasi-divine status. The *Augustan Histories,* compiled in the fourth century C.E., make reference to encounters between Roman emperors and druidesses, who told their fortunes. The Irish myths similarly record the presence of prophetesses: in the *Táin,* Queen Medb is confronted by Fedelma, a female oracle from the Otherworld.

Celtic iconography endorses the ancient literature: images of priestesses, like the small bronze figurines of the Roman period from South Shields and Crewelthorpe (both in northern England), are indicative of the presence of female clergy. The role of women in ritual is demonstrated by imagery associated with the Rhenish Mother-Goddesses at Bonn: on a stone altar dated to the second century C.E., a female sacrificial procession is depicted. A fascinating piece of evidence for magical practice consists of an inscribed lead sheet from Larzac in southern Gaul, which mentions the presence of two rival guilds of female magicians.

Inscribed dedications from the Roman period refer to the worship of Celtic divinities by female devotees: some of the lead curse-tablets from the shrine of the healer-goddess Sulis at Bath in western Britain are inscribed with messages from women. Some of the jewelry and the specifically feminine votive objects given to goddesses were offerings from women: gifts of objects associated with spinning, or personal items like tweezers, were surely female gifts. Likewise, the anatomical models of breasts and female genitalia offered at healing shrines are best interpreted as feminine gifts.

The Celtic myths are full of references to powerful women. But despite these rich allusions to prominent females, we lack information that tells us how far women were responsible for myth making. Many Irish scholars who wrote down the stories were monks in early Christian monasteries. We do not know whether abbesses and prioresses were involved in story writing, though there is no inherent reason to discount such activities. The medieval Welsh storytellers, traveling between royal courts, were responsible for disseminating many of the Welsh tales: some of them may have been women.

BIBLIOGRAPHY

Allason-Jones, Lindsay. *Women in Roman Britain.* 1989. An archaeological survey of evidence for all aspects of women in the Celtic province of Britain during the Roman period, with one section devoted to religion.

Billington, Sandra, and Miranda Green, eds. *The Concept of the Goddess.* Contains several papers from a conference held at the University of Glasgow (1993) relating to the female aspects of Celtic religion.

Ehrenberg, Margaret. *Women in Prehistory.* 1989. Looks at archaeological evidence for women in prehistoric Europe, from Palaeolithic times to the Iron Age. Written by an archaeologist, specifically from a feminist perspective, this work includes material pertaining to the role of females in religious activity.

Gilchrist, Roberta, *Gender and Material Culture: The Archaeology of Religious Women.* 1994. Examining the role of women in medieval Christian religious houses, this work presents a useful and innovative framework for the more general study of women and religion.

Green, Miranda J. *Celtic Goddesses.* 1995. Examines the archaeological and mythological evidence for goddess worship in Celtic Europe, from about 600 B.C.E. to the early medieval period. One chapter deals with priestesses and other female religious functionaries.

———. *Exploring the World of the Druids.* 1997. One chapter explores the evidence from the classical writers, archaeology, and the Celtic myths for druidesses and other priestesses in Celtic Britain, Ireland, and Europe.

James, Simon. *Exploring the World of the Celts.* 1993. Presents a broad overview of ancient Celtic society, including the role of women. Useful for providing a context for understanding women in Celtic religion and ritual.

Markale, Jean. *Women of the Celts.* 1975. A useful general overview of women in Celtic society, including their participation in religious activity.

Wood, Juliette. "Celtic Goddess: Myth and Mythology." In *The Feminist Companion to Mythology.* Edited by Caroline Larrington. 1992.

MIRANDA J. ALDHOUSE GREEN

Charisma

Charisma is direct experience of the sacred that imparts knowledge and revelation and is often associated with the power of healing. The earliest forms of charisma are found among shamans who function within animistic religions. Charisma is seen in the Christian Pentecostal belief in contact with the Holy Spirit, and in any person who claims divine revelation or enlightened wisdom. Charisma can empower persons of lower social status to significant leadership, and it is the first type of religious leadership exercised by women.

Shamanism or charisma is especially important for women living in patriarchal cultures. Possession rituals involving dancing and singing permit women to articulate issues in their lives that they are usually forbidden to mention; a possessed woman can address taboo topics such as conflict with her husband and his relatives because the spirit, not the woman, is speaking. In the nineteenth-century United States, it was not socially acceptable for women to speak in public before audiences that included men. The first significant number of American women to make public addresses were trance mediums in the 1850s.

Charisma has the effect of breaking through the restrictions of patriarchal society for an individual woman. The charismatic woman often becomes the head of her family. She gains the economic means to support her family through her role as shaman. Nevertheless, the advice and teachings of charismatic women often enforce the patriarchy experienced by other women while simultaneously healing and providing them with spiritual solace to cope with their restricted gender roles. Charismatic women who succeed in founding new religions typically facilitate the leadership of men—not women—who will take over after their deaths: charisma does not necessarily make a woman a feminist.

For a charismatic woman to found a religion that continues to empower women to leadership even after the death of the founder (examples are the Theosophical Society and Unity), other factors must be present. These include a broad social expectation of equality, a view of the divine that is not strictly masculine, a view of human nature that does not blame women for the limitations of the human condition, and gender roles within the religion that do not restrict women to the roles of wife and mother. Of these, the most important is the broad social expectation of equality. If there is the social expectation of equality, the other factors will be created if they are not already present.

The German sociologist Max Weber noted that a person's charisma is established by social consensus. If people reject a person's claim to charisma, she or he will have no impact on society. A woman becomes a shaman, prophet, messiah, or guru because people around her acknowledge her special access to the sacred. Women are noteworthy as significant early followers, financial benefactors, administrators, and missionaries in new religious movements focused on charismatic individuals. Some examples of charismatic individuals, both male and female, include Jesus of Nazareth; Muhammad; Gautama Buddha; Mother Ann Lee, founder of Shakerism; Helena P. Blavatsky, cofounder of the Theosophical Society; Mary Baker Eddy, founder of the Church of Christ, Scientist; Myrtle Fillmore, cofounder of Unity; David Koresh, the messiah of the Branch Davidians; and Elizabeth Clare, prophet of the Church Universal and Triumphant. Note that religions led by charismatic women are more likely to be regarded by people with mainstream patriarchal values as marginal and problematic. Not all religions founded by charismatic men become culturally dominant, but the great world traditions of Buddhism, Christianity, and Islam look back to revered male founders.

By increasing access to ordination, contemporary women are moving beyond charisma as a means to religious leadership. However, charisma remains important because it expresses belief in the immanence of the divine. Feminist theologies affirm the immanence of the sacred. Religious feminists often cultivate ways of discovering the sacred within. For Christian women, charisma remains an important legitimation due to the idea that a person is "called" by God to the ministry.

BIBLIOGRAPHY

Blacker, Carmen. *The Catalpa Bow: A Study of Shamanistic Practices in Japan.* 1975.

Boddy, Janice. *Wombs and Alien Spirits: Women, Men, and the Zar Cult in Northern Sudan.* 1989.

Braude, Ann. *Radical Spirits: Spiritualism and Women's Rights in Nineteenth-Century America.* 1989.

Falk, Nancy Auer, and Rita M. Gross, eds. *Unspoken Worlds: Women's Religious Lives.* 1989.

Hackett, Rosalind I. J. "Sacred Paradoxes: Women and Religious Plurality in Nigeria." In *Women, Religion, and Social Change.* Edited by Yvonne Yazbeck Haddad and Ellison Banks Findly. 1985.

Hardacre, Helen. *Kurozumikyo and the New Religions of Japan.* 1986.

Harvey, Youngsook Kim. "Possession Sickness and Women Shamans in Korea." In *Unspoken Worlds: Women's Religious Lives.* Edited by Nancy Auer Falk and Rita M. Gross. 1989.

Jacobs, Claude F., and Andrew J. Kaslow. *The Spiritual Churches of New Orleans: Origins, Beliefs, and Rituals of an African-American Religion.* 1991.

Nakamura, Kyoko Motomochi. "No Women's Liberation: The Heritage of a Woman Prophet in Modern Japan." In *Unspoken Worlds: Women's Religious Lives.* Edited by Nancy Auer Falk and Rita M. Gross. 1989.

Sered, Susan Starr. *Priestess, Mother, Sacred Sister: Religions Dominated by Women.* 1994.

Weber, Max. "The Sociology of Charismatic Authority." In *Max Weber on Charisma and Institution Building: Selected Papers.* Edited by S. N. Eisenstadt. 1968.

Wessinger, Catherine, ed. *Religious Institutions and Women's Leadership: New Roles Inside the Mainstream.* 1996.

———, ed. *Women's Leadership in Marginal Religions: Explorations Outside the Mainstream.* 1993.

See also Authority; Possession; Possession Cults; Shamans.

CATHERINE WESSINGER

Chastity

Chastity most often refers to marital fidelity and modesty in appearance and behavior, though it can include premarital virginity and celibacy. Religious authorities usually idealize the chaste woman as a paragon of virtue and devotion and promise her spiritual fulfillment, religious merit, or divine salvation. Although theoretically chastity indicates culturally appropriate sexual discretion regardless of gender, religious texts overwhelmingly focus on female chastity, claiming it a paramount religious duty, describing how to ensure its preservation, and recommending harsh punishments for its loss. For reasons that vary throughout history and culture, women's sexuality is usually perceived as a threat to religious and social order, and thus its regulation has been a matter of public rather than private concern. Views on chastity substantially influence the style and structure of women's lives: dress, demeanor, mobility, and behavior are restricted and monitored in various ways, and transgressions often are punished severely. By declaring the maintenance of chastity as a primary duty of women, religious texts often buttress systems that render women inferior to men in economic power, social standing, legal prerogative, and religious role and importance.

Patriarchal traditions such as Hinduism, Judaism, and Islam are vigorously concerned with ensuring female chastity, for paternity must be legitimate and determinable in order to fulfill a number of religious rites and ensure purity of lineage, class, or caste. Thus, a woman's procreative function must be limited to the proper partner, that is, a husband, and she must marry in order to carry out religious duties and achieve her spiritual aspirations. Her sexual fidelity and loyal service to her husband are seen as measures of her faith, and her adultery and neglect are likened to heresy, apostasy, or idolatry. In the Hindu case, scriptures literally enjoin a woman to worship her husband as god.

These religions encourage sexual activity within marriage but traditionally have appeared not to trust women to restrict their sexual encounters to their husbands. In one text or another, each tradition expounds on the evils of women, portraying them as insatiably lustful, morally lax, adulterous, and seductive by nature. In addition, a woman's chastity is often directly linked to her male relatives' honor. Any act of impropriety on her part defiles not only herself but also her entire lineage. Insisting that women cannot be trusted to maintain chastity on their own, religious authorities license fathers, husbands, brothers, sons, and sometimes kings to monitor women and mete out punishments for immodesty. In cases of adultery, women frequently are killed. Under the guise of implementing a religious order, some contemporary governments in countries such as Iran, Pakistan, and Saudi Arabia have dispatched "moral" police forces to monitor women's movements and enforce laws that prohibit them from "unchaste" behavior such as driving cars, wearing short sleeves, or appearing bareheaded or unveiled in public. Within classical Judaism, adultery is defined as relations between a married woman and a man other than her husband; in contrast, a married man who has relations with an unmarried woman is not considered to have committed adultery.

Handprints on a gate at Jodhpur Fort serve as memorial for widows who immolated themselves in order to accompany their husbands to heaven (Brian Vikander/ Corbis).

Gender segregation is perhaps the most common means of ensuring chastity. Many societies have traditionally relegated women's social and religious duties to the domestic sphere, whereas men's duties have been located in the more prestigious public arena. The practice of purdah in South Asia renders this segregation explicit as both a religious observance and a male right. Purdah refers to a range of practices concerned with the seclusion of women from public (i.e., male) observation. Although associated primarily with Islam, purdah varies more by culture and class than religious boundaries, and its more elaborate forms are generally privileges of the rich. Women don the veil (customs vary from covering the hair to the entire body), avoid contact with men who are not relatives, and spend most of their time inside the precincts of the home or the women's quarters of the house. When forced to travel, women have been carried through the streets in closed palanquins and deposited in windowless women's-only train carriages. Husbands have even forbidden physicians from looking at their wives and have demanded that examinations be conducted through a small opening in a sheet.

More extreme practices for ensuring women's chastity include genital mutilation performed in parts of Africa, which ranges from the removal of the clitoris to sewing closed the labia of the vagina. The controversial and sporadic incidence of sati in India can be read as the ultimate expression of female chastity. The ideal Hindu wife should fully worship her husband as god. After his death, she proves her ultimate virtue by becoming a sati and immolating herself on his funeral pyre. By ending her life she precludes any possible sexual interaction with other men; she also brings merit and auspiciousness to his lineage for generations.

Celibacy is highly regarded in Buddhist and Christian religions but has been met with hostility in traditions such as Islam and Judaism that locate women's religious duty and fulfillment within marriage. Although severe in its abstinence from all sexual activity, celibacy ironically frees women from marriage and the most direct forms of male control.

Although there are valid reasons for choosing a chaste life-style, it should be recognized that religious and cultural systems impose heavy penalties on women who choose to do otherwise. It is extremely difficult, if not impossible, for women deemed unchaste to remain respected members of society. Persuaded by religious ideals, social customs, economic dependence on men, and the threat of physical violence, women usually cooperate in monitoring their sexuality.

BIBLIOGRAPHY

Abu-Lughod, Lila. *Veiled Sentiments.* 1988.

Ahmed, Leila. *Women and Gender in Islam: Historical Roots of a Modern Debate.* 1992.

Biale, Rachel. *Women and Jewish Law: An Exploration of Women's Issues in Halakhic Sources.* 1984.

Chakravarti, Uma. "Conceptualizing Brahmanical Patriarchy in Early India: Gender, Caste, Class and State." *Economic and Political Weekly* (April 3, 1993): 579–585.

El Sadaawi, Nawal. *A Woman at Point Zero.* Translated by Sherif Hetata. London, 1983.

Kumari, Ranjana. *Female Sexuality in Hinduism.* Delhi, 1988.

Narayanan, Vasudha. "Hindu Perceptions of Auspiciousness and Sexuality." In *Women, Religion, and Sexuality: Studies on the Impact of Religious Teachings on Women.* Edited by Jeanne Becher. 1990.

Wegner, Judith Romney. *Chattel or Person? The Status of Women in the Mishnah.* 1988.

See also Celibacy; Mutilation, Genital; Sexuality; Virtue.

TREVOR M. WADE

Christianity

Historical Overview from 300 to 1800

The study of women in the history of Christianity has advanced from critiques of exclusionary ideologies and practices as represented in classical (male) theological texts and ecclesiastical sources to recovery and reconstruction of women's lives and accomplishments as revealed in their own works and in the evidence of material culture. Detailed investigations of particular contexts have begun to yield analyses of privilege and differences among women. Yet despite these gains, exceptional women with access to cultural resources and power continue to dominate the historiography of women and Christianity.

LATE ANTIQUITY (300–600)

During the last Roman persecutions of Christians (303–311 C.E.), women figured prominently among the martyrs (Agape, Irene, and Chione; Crispina). Once Christianity was tolerated (313) and established (391) as the religion of the empire, Christian imperial women influenced the religious policies and preferences of emperors (Helena [c. 255–c. 330], mother of Constantine, discovered the True Cross, 326), brought about the banishment of bishops (Eudoxia exiled John Chrysostom, 403), and guided the outcome of doctrinal controversies (Pulcheria called the Council of Chalcedon, 451).

Aristocratic women converts brought Christianity to the Roman elite in the late fourth century. Notable wealthy women practiced asceticism and philanthropy (e.g., Paula [347–404] endowed monasteries in Bethlehem for Jerome and herself, supporting his biblical scholarship while pursuing her own studies); others built churches and saints' shrines and subsidized episcopal sees. But women's power as patrons did not translate into public leadership in the churches. By about 400, misogynist theologies of women's nature combined with understandings of ordained male priesthood to exclude women from most formal ministries other than deaconess.

Sexual asceticism offered early Christian woman some freedom from conventional social roles, but teth-

Fresco depicting Constantine with his mother, Saint Helena, who found the True Cross (Chris Hellier/Corbis).

ered them to male norms of sexuality and sanctity. Some upper-class women (e.g., Macrina [327–379] sister of powerful bishop-theologians) formed ascetic communities on their family estates; others practiced asceticism in their city homes. Women of varying social status lived in monastic communities or as solitaries in the deserts of Egypt, Palestine, and Syria. The teachings of several desert mothers (Sarah, Syncletica, Theodora) are preserved in collections of sayings of the desert fathers.

EARLY MIDDLE AGES (600–1000)

Christian women married to pagan kings played a pivotal but private role in evangelizing the Germanic kingdoms that replaced the Roman empire in the West after the late fourth century. They urged their husbands' conversions (Clothild and Clovis, king of the Franks, 496) and predisposed them to receive Christian missionaries (Bertha, Christian Frankish wife of Ethelbert

of Kent, aided Augustine of Canterbury, 596). Often ruled by powerful abbesses, Anglo-Saxon and Carolingian women's monasteries were centers of local Christianity in recently converted areas. As monasticism became a dominant institution in the West, some women entered monasteries by choice to pursue a vocation or seek personal advancement; others did so of necessity, having been dedicated as child oblates or deemed unmarriageable.

In the Byzantine (eastern Roman) empire, imperial women were instrumental in overturning the iconoclastic policies of their predecessors: the empress Irene championed the icons and promoted their vindication at the Second Council of Nicaea in 787; the empress Theodora again restored their use in 843, in the so-called Triumph of Orthodoxy. In the West privileged women began to produce Christian literature. The Frankish noblewoman Dhouda (803–c. 843) wrote a manual of instruction in Christian faith and virtue for her son; the tenth-century Saxon canoness Hrotsvitha wrote plays, legends, and epics.

THE MEDIEVAL WEST (1000—1500)

Religious communities under the Rule of Benedict offered both elite and common women some measure of security and educational opportunity. Hildegard of Bingen (1098–1179) is an exceptional example of monastic achievement. From the twelfth century onward, both women and men founded new, or reformed older, monastic orders (e.g., Cistercians, 1098, and Premonstratensians, 1120), but male communities often refused to acknowledge their female counterparts or undertake their pastoral care.

Urban growth and cultural expansion fostered nonmonastic forms of religious life (e.g., canonesses, first known in the Carolingian era) and popular movements that emphasized poverty, penitence, and charitable works. Women pursued evangelical ideals in newly approved mendicant orders such as the Dominicans, and Clare of Assisi (1194–1253) for example, in the Franciscans; informal associations such as the Beguines (who had no Rule or permanent vows); third (lay) orders; and individually fashioned ways of life. By 1400 many popular religious movements had been suppressed, and most Beguines forced to enter established orders with a recognized Rule and strict cloister.

Women mystics and visionaries found receptive audiences but were regarded with suspicion by the clerical hierarchy. Mysticism flourished at the Cistercian monastery of Helfta (Gertrude the Great, d. 1301 or 1302) and among the Beguines, who were often harried by church authorities, as was Mechthild of Magdeburg, and sometimes executed for heresy, as was Marguerite

Porete. Some women mystics, such as Julian of Norwich, Catherine of Siena, and Bridget of Sweden, wrote and spoke unharmed, but others, such as Joan of Arc (c. 1312—1431), were burned at the stake for heresy and witchcraft. From the fourteenth to seventeenth centuries, churchmen pursued witches and condemned as many as one to three hundred thousand to death.

EARLY MODERN PERIOD (1500–1800)

During the Protestant Reformation, women voluntarily left convents and monasteries or were turned out by local reformers. Many former nuns married, some, like Katherine von Bora, who married Martin Luther, to reform leaders. Luther considered marriage a religious vocation but restricted women to the confines of the patriarchal family. Nevertheless, pastors' wives, such as Katherine Zell, and other married women furthered the aims of the Reformation through the family, even while their economic opportunities outside it declined.

In England and Scotland female monarchs both advanced and hindered the reforming cause: Mary Stuart (Queen of Scots, r. 1561–1567) remained Roman Catholic; Mary Tudor (called "Bloody Mary," r. 1553–1558) executed English Protestant leaders in an effort to reimpose Roman Catholicism; Elizabeth I (r. 1558–1603) was so politically astute that she secured the establishment of the Church of England through policies known as the Elizabethan Settlement.

Among radical Protestants, Anabaptist women were martyrs, visionaries, and prophets. Puritan and Quaker women, such as Anne Hutchinson (1591–1643) and Margaret Fell (1614–1702), claimed the egalitarian authority of the Spirit for their ministries of Bible studies, women's meetings, public preaching, and missionary work and defended women's right to speak on religious matters. Pietist emphasis on affective religious experience created openings for women's influence in Moravianism, early Methodism, and revivalism (the Great Awakening).

Women advanced the Catholic Reformation through the cultivation of prayer, as did the *beatas*, holy women in urban Spain, and the renewal of existing religious orders (witness Teresa of Avila's reform of the Carmelites). They founded new congregations of women for "apostolic" service of the poor, (e.g., the Ursulines and the Daughters of Charity), most of which eventually were compelled to accept cloister but maintained their educational and charitable works within its constraints. Particularly in France and England, upper-class women nurtured Roman Catholicism in their families.

Following Spanish and French conquests in the Americas, women religious undertook missions to establish convents, schools, and hospitals to serve the colonists and, to a lesser extent, to evangelize the indigenous peoples. In Mexico the learned poet Sor Juana Inés de la Cruz (1648–1695) flourished and was silenced. In Canada, Marie of the Incarnation (1599–1672), a French Ursuline, opened the first school for girls in Quebec (1639) and compiled dictionaries of several Native American languages. French Ursulines established a convent in New Orleans in 1727, but it was not until the nineteenth century that religious orders of women took root in the United States.

BIBLIOGRAPHY

The scholarship on women in the history of Christianity is continually expanding, both in regard to the life and works of particular women and to movements, institutions, periods, geographical areas, theology, and spirituality. Works noted here are gateways to primary sources and current scholarship.

BIBLIOGRAPHIES

Blevins, Carolyn DeArmond, ed. *Women in Christian History: A Bibliography.* 1995. Occasionally misses important works, but still useful.

Irwin, Joyce. "Society and the Sexes." In *Reformation Europe: A Guide to Research.* Edited by Steven Ozment. 1982. Essay on approaches to the topic.

Norberg, Kathryn. "The Counter Reformation and Women: Religious and Lay." In *Catholicism in Early Modern Europe: A Guide to Research.* Edited by John O'Malley. 1988. Essay on approaches to the topic.

Wiesner, Merry E. "Studies of Women, the Family, and Gender." In *Reformation Europe: A Guide to Research, II.* Edited by William Maltby. 1992. Essay on approaches to the topic.

SOURCES IN TRANSLATION

Irwin, Joyce. *Womanhood in Radical Protestantism 1525–1675.* 1979. Translations of primary sources, mostly by men about women.

Kors, Alan C., and Edward Peters, eds. *Witchcraft in Europe, 1100–1700: A Documentary History.* 1995. Reprint of a classic sourcebook, with short postscript.

Oden, Amy, ed. *In Her Words: Women's Writing in the History of Christian Thought.* 1994. Selections from the second through twentieth centuries, with some short works in their entirety. Brief introductions and bibliography of primary sources in translation (most, but not all, current).

Wilson, Katharina M., ed. *Medieval Women Writers.* 1984. Selections in translation, with helpful introductory essays, notes, and bibliographies.

——. *Women Writers of the Renaissance and Reformation.* 1987. Selections in translation, with helpful introductory essays, notes and bibliographies.

COLLECTIONS OF ESSAYS

Marshall, Sherrin, ed. *Women in Reformation and Counter-Reformation Europe: Public and Private Worlds.* 1989. Essays organized around country or area.

Nichols, John A., and Lillian Thomas Shanks, OCSO, eds. *Medieval Religious Women.* 3 vols. Vol. 1: *Distant Echoes.* 1984. Vol. 2: *Peaceweavers.* 1987. Vol. 3: *Hidden Springs: Cistercian Monastic Women.* Books 1 and 2. 1995. Rich collections of essays on aspects of medieval religious women's history, including individual women, movements, monasteries.

Ruether, Rosemary and Eleanor McLaughlin, eds. *Women of Spirit: Female Leadership in Jewish and Christian Traditions.* 1979. Now-classic collection of essays surveying the achievements of Christian women from early Christianity through the twentieth century (with one essay on contemporary Jewish women).

MONOGRAPHS

Lerner, Gerda. *The Creation of Feminist Consciousness: From the Middle Ages to Eighteen-Seventy.* 1993. Survey of Western European proto-feminist accomplishments; outside her area of expertise (American women's history), Lerner relies on the work of other historians. Extensive bibliography.

McNamara, Jo Ann Kay. *Sisters in Arms: Catholic Nuns through Two Millennia.* 1996. This massive study of the history of women's religious communities in Western Christianity is best in the medieval period, the author's specialty. Extensive bibliography

Wemple, Suzanne Foney. *Women in Frankish Society: Marriage and the Cloister, 500 to 900.* 1985. Thorough study of a formative period in Western European history. Extensive bibliography and notes.

See also Catherine of Siena; Christianity: Apostolic Religious Orders and Communities; Clare of Assisi; Hildegard of Bingen; Joan of Arc; Juana Inés de la Cruz; Julian of Norwich; Mechthild of Magdeburg; Porete, Marguerite; Teresa of Avila.

FRANCINE CARDMAN

Religious Rites and Practices

In Western cultures, Christian women's ritual and religious domains tend to be more informal than men's, often flourishing in the domestic environment, outside of institutionalized rites and practices. Women's religious expression may be interpreted as reactive, the direct result of male domination and the exclusion of women from institutional roles. Such a viewpoint assumes a powerlessness to act within a patriarchal framework. Scholars such as Kay Turner argue for the relative autonomy of women's traditions from institutional structures and suggest within Christianity women find pathways to exercise religious power and creativity. This theoretical perspective grants women active agency in their religious lives and asserts that women can and do create or reinterpret symbolic modes of expression to articulate a religiosity that differs from the dominant (male) culture.

Within Roman Catholicism and Eastern Orthodoxy women interact with the sacred through a tradition of sacramental praxis expressed through ritual activities that parallel a priest-mediated formal tradition. This culture of women's religion is expressed in such activities as the recitation of the rosary, home prayer, novenas, votive making and offering, laments, the making of traditional foods associated with special religious holidays, devotion to particular saints, construction of altars in the home, feminist liturgies, and other creative endeavors.

Praying the rosary, for example, is found across many Catholic cultures and occurs in the church or in the Roman Catholic home. The rosary encompasses a ritualized formulaic prayer form accompanied by the use of prayer beads and is recited privately or communally. In the United States, from the nineteenth into the twentieth century, the rosary was the most important prayer form used in the home by Catholic families.

While both men and women pray the rosary, women predominate in its use and incorporate the rosary in contexts not shared by men. Women across several Catholic cultures enact the rosary as part of a complex of informal rituals surrounding death. Among some indigenous Mexicans in Oaxaca, for example, women prepare the area in the home where the body lies with candles and flowers and chant the rosary throughout the entire night. The women are solely responsible for leading the prayers and expressing the grief of the family. On the ninth and fortieth day following the funeral, the women re-enact the wake, gathering around a stimulated corpse, and again pray the rosary for the deceased. As in everyday life, the women nurture deceased family members as they make their gradual transition into the next world.

Many traditional practices centered in the home articulate concerns with family and community. The creation and ritual use of altars by women in the Roman Catholic home represents such an activity. Altars are placed in a special area of the house and utilized for intercessory prayer. The altars are created out of an assemblage of religious paraphernalia such as statues of particular saints, Mary, or Jesus; holy cards and other images, or rosaries; votive candles; photographs of family members; and flowers. While certain elements are common to home altars, such as the use of images, flowers, and candles, each altar is tailored to express the spiritual needs as well as the aesthetic inclinations of the altar maker.

Prayer to a particular saint has long been incorporated within the Catholic doctrine. However, the choice of particular saints and the ways in which women actually interact with them are uniquely personal and independent of clerical authority. Recent studies of home altar traditions among women of Mexican and Italian descent document the ways in which the creation and use of altars sacramentalize women's activities of care, symbolically expressing women's power within the home and connections to sacred passages, family, and community.

Women dominate activities of traditional healing across many Christian cultures. Greek Orthodox women healers are found both in Greece and in immigrant communities in the United States. Healers utilize verbal incantations drawn from traditional prayers combined with religious objects to effect cures for illness. Particular sacred images known as icons, considered efficacious against various illnesses, are physically placed near the sick person by the women of the family. Women also pin amulets and charms onto family members, particularly children, to cure illness or protect one's family from the evil eye.

The influence of white Protestant women on their families from the mid-nineteenth century was profound. Because of the scriptural orientation of Protestantism, reading from the Bible was the center of home worship, accompanied by prayer and hymn singing. Men presided over the daily family worship service, but women were perceived as the moral center and example of Christian living in the home. As a reflection of women's roles as the moral force within the domicile, middle-class Protestant women created and displayed religious objects in the home. These included family Bibles, embroidery with mottos and scriptural verses, wax and wooden crosses, pin cushions shaped in the form of churches, and woven hair art used to commemorate deceased relatives and friends. In contrast to the Roman Catholic and Eastern Orthodox traditions, with the exception of the Bible religious artifacts were not used for prayer or ritual purposes. However, their presence imbued the home with a sense of the sacred, relating the supernatural realm with everyday life.

A stand sells religious figurines to be used in homes outside of the Church of San Francisco in Quito, Ecuador (Pablo Corral V/© Corbis).

Protestant women of the nineteenth century were denied ordination, leadership on church boards, and participation in established structures of the denominations. However, in the late nineteenth century church women developed a plethora of all-female organizations. The most common were missionary societies ministering both at home and abroad, and the establishment of deaconess orders in a number of denominations. These organizations broadened women's public and ministerial roles within Protestant Christianity. While denied official status as ministers, a number of women were well-known evangelists and preached on a regular basis within the context of public worship and revivals.

The nineteenth century was punctuated by the first ordination of a woman into the Congregational church in 1853. Following World War II, a number of denominations began to ordain women, a movement that continued into the 1970's. The decision to ordain women among Lutherans, Episcopalians, Methodists, Disciples of Christ, and other churches opened the doors to full participation and leadership in all rites and practices found within their respective traditions.

A number of American congregations still ban or are extremely ambiguous about women ministers. Despite these limitations, women within certain congregations, such as Holiness, Pentecostals, Church of God in Christ, and independent Baptists, dominate areas within the public arena of the worship service. Worship services in these traditions are marked by charismatic experiences among participants as well as distinct styles of preaching and testimony. In both African-American and white churches women dominate the genre of oral testimony. Testimony is a distinct, spontaneous verbal art form, which employs highly stylistic and traditional speech patterns. Women often utilize testimony to engage in a style of informal preaching. As a result, women restricted from formally recognized acts of preaching still forcefully voice interpretations of experiences of God's action in the context of public worship.

Since the 1970's, many women within Catholic and Protestant churches critique male dominance found in their own theological traditions and structures. Today within Catholicism, for example, women explore and reinterpret institutionalized rituals, particularly the central sacrament and liturgy of the Eucharist. Progressive parishes and communities of women religious struggle with a ritual that clearly restricts women from mediation of institutionally defined sacraments and interpretation of scripture. Such explorations attempt to eliminate the inequalities in the ritual, often stretching and even breaking institutional rules. Alternative Eucharists, which are celebrated without the participation of a priest, are also part of the ritual landscape of many Catholic women. Such emerging practices are yet another example of the process of creation and reinterpretation in which Christian women engage.

BIBLIOGRAPHY

Badone, Ellen, ed. *Religious Orthodoxy and Popular Faith in European Society.* 1990. Series of ethnographic articles focusing on the tensions between institutional religion and "folk" or "popular" religion in Europe and the ways in which people actively create their religious domains. Includes an article on women's participation in pilgrimage at a Greek Orthodox shrine.

Bynum, Caroline Walker, Stevan Harrell, and Paula Richman, eds. *Gender and Religion: On the Complexity of Symbols.* 1986. Excellent volume of articles focusing on gender as culturally constructed meaning, the multivocality of gender symbols, and the ways in which men and women interact and interpret symbols differently. Covers many religious traditions such as Christianity, Islam, Buddhism, and others.

Caraveli-Chaves, Anna. "Bridge between Worlds: The Greek Women's Lament as Communicative Event." *Journal of American Folklore* 93, no. 368 (1980): 129–157. Ethnographic study of the lament tradition among Greek Orthodox women of Crete. Argues that the lament tradition creates a domain of cultural power where women articulate their own view of the world.

Carroll, Jackson W., Barbara Hargrove, and Adair T. Lummis. *Women of the Cloth: A New Opportunity for Churches.* 1983. Cross-denominational study and survey of ordained women in the mainline Protestant churches.

Collins, Mary, O.S.B. "Women and Eucharist—Women and Ecclesial Power: A Clash of Eucharistic Horizons." *Benedictines* 46 (1992): 32–43. A Benedictine sister documents the rise of tensions over the Eucharist among communities of Roman Catholic women religious (sisters) because of articulations of clerical power found within the ritual.

Dubisch, Jill. *In a Different Place: Pilgrimage, Gender, and Politics at a Greek Island Shrine.* 1995. Ethnographic study of a Greek shrine. Author analyzes how Greek Orthodox women create religious and social constructions of themselves in public, ritualized performances at the shrine, which are often at odds with institutional understandings of what the shrine is all about.

Juster, Susan, and Lisa McFarlane, eds. *A Mighty Baptism: Race, Gender and the Creation of American Protestantism.* 1996. Excellent collection of articles examining the lived religion of women in the nineteenth century across a variety of denominational and sectarian churches. Of special interest are articles documenting the tradition of magic and healing practices among African-American women since slavery.

Lawless, Elaine J. *God's Peculiar People: Women's Voices and Folk Tradition in a Pentecostal Church.* 1988. An ethnographic study of Pentecostal worship services. Author focuses on how women utilize opportunities to testify as a way to gain control of the service and make their voices heard.

———. *Handmaidens of the Lord: Pentecostal Women Preachers and Traditional Religion.* 1988. A study of preaching styles of white Pentecostal women pastors in mid-Missouri. The author claims that women pastors subvert the usual cultural claims of Pentecostalism, which states that women's roles should be restricted to home and family. At the same time they subvert male dominance and utilize traditional maternal imagery in their sermons in order to maintain their position as women pastors in the community.

———. *Holy Women, Wholly Women: Sharing Ministries Through Life Stories and Reciprocal Ethnography.* 1993. Ethnographic study of the life stories of Protestant women ministers across several denominations.

McDannell, Colleen. *The Christian Home in Victorian America, 1840–1900.* 1986. Author documents the rise of a domestic centered religiosity both among Protestants and Irish Catholics in the United States. Examines domestic architecture, religious objects found in the home, religious rituals performed within the home, and conceptions of the appropriate religious role of women in the domestic setting.

Orsi, Robert Anthony. *The Madonna of 115th Street: Faith and Community in Italian Harlem, 1880–1950.* 1985. A fine historical study that documents the popular religiosity of Italian immigrants in Harlem. Includes a thorough study of women's roles as the keeper of the faith within the domicile, women's devotional life, and the meaning of the festival devoted to the Madonna among women of that community.

Quaggiotto, Pamela. "Altars of Food to St. Joseph: Women's Ritual in Sicily." Ph.D. diss., Columbia University, 1988. Ethnographic study of women's participation and creation of altars offered to St. Joseph on his feast day.

Radnor, Joan Newlon. *Feminist Messages: Coding in Women's Folk Culture.* 1993. A series of articles that document the ways in which women code creative activity such as oral performances and material creations to articulate subversive messages. Includes an article on the subversive content of Irish women's lament rituals.

Teske, Robert Thomas. *Votive Offerings among Greek-Philadelphians.* 1980. Ethnographic study of the votive offering tradition still actively practiced by Greek Philadelphians. This study is not intentionally a study of women. However, the author discovered that votive offerings are made and used much more frequently by women than men.

Titon, Jeff Todd. *Powerhouse for God: Speech, Chant and Song in an Appalachian Baptist Church.* 1988. An ethnographic study of the use of language in the practice of religion. In-depth analysis of song, testimony, chant, prayer, and preaching in the context of worship services. Shows how the testimony genre affords an opportunity for women's solo performance.

Turner, Kay Frances. "Mexican American Women's Home Altars: The Art of Relationship." Ph.D. diss., University of Texas, 1990. A fine dissertation documenting the vitality of home altar traditions among Mexican women in Texas despite clerical pressure to dismantle the altars. Analyzes how popular religious practices centered in the home are a source of empowerment for these women.

Turner, Kay, and Suzanne, Serrif, " 'Giving an Altar to St. Joseph': A Feminist Perspective on a Patronal Feast." In *Feminist Theory and the Study of Folklore.* Edited by Susan Tower Hollis, Linda Pershing, and M. Jane Young. 1993. Ethnographic and feminist analysis of how altars express the power of women's activities within the home and relationships with family and sacred figures.

Wessinger, Catherine, ed. *Religious Institutions and Women's Leadership: New Roles Inside the Mainstream.* 1996. Series of articles focus on the ministerial roles of women within a number of Christian denominations and Judaism. Includes histories of the ordination of women within these denominations.

DEBORAH ANN BAILEY

New Testament Canon

The New Testament, the second part of the Christian canon, offers a partial sourcebook of Christian origins consisting of narratives (four Gospels and the Acts of the Apostles) and letters; even the visionary prophecy Revelation manifests letter form. All the narratives are anonymous and many of the letters pseudonymous. Retrieving historical information about women from this material is a complex process whose results are subject to constant revision.

The earliest written sources, Paul's undisputed letters (c. 52–62 C.E.), reflect some memories of the participation of women in Christian beginnings. Paul refers to at least one woman, Junia (Rom. 16:7), as an apostle (i.e., an evangelizing missionary and witness to the resurrection [1 Cor. 9:1, 1:17]). A substantial proportion of other missionary "laborers" and "co-workers" in Paul's context were women: Prisca (Rom. 16:3; 1 Cor. 16:19), Mary (Rom. 16:6), Tryphaena and Tryphosa, Persis (Rom. 16:12), Julia and the "sister" of Nereus (Rom. 16:15); Evodia and Syntyche (Phil. 4:2) Women also exercised prophecy (1 Cor. 11:4–5, cf. Acts 21:8–9), the function most highly regarded by Paul after apostleship (1 Cor. 12:28, 14:1), and were accorded the vague but authoritative title *diakonos* (Phoebe, Rom. 16:1), used by Paul of himself (2 Cor. 3:6). The leadership may have been partially enabled by the early communities' practice of meeting in the houses of its members, where women exercised the authority of the materfamilias; churches in the house of Prisca and Aquila (Rom. 16:5) and of Nympha (Col. 4:15) receive greetings.

The evidence of women's leadership attests at least some communal implementation of the baptismal tradition that "there is no 'male and female' " (quoted in Gal. 3:28, revising Gen. 1:27b). But other dicta from these letters conflict with this picture. Headcovering (in 1 Cor. 11:2–16) enforces the gender distinctions of Genesis. Thessalonians (1 Thess. 4:4) reflects a highly androcentric view of marriage. The stipulations of 1 Corinthians 7, even when formally egalitarian, endorse both marriage and celibacy in ways that reflect identification of women with sex and ultimately contribute to misogyny. In Romans 1:18–31, Paul makes

Christ is mourned by the women who witnessed his death—his mother, Mary Magdalene, Mary mother of James and Salome (National Gallery, London/Corbis).

female "unnatural" sexuality, primarily female homo-eroticism, the foremost example of idolatrous perversity; 1 Corinthians 14:34–35, which requires that women be silent in the assembly, is often seen as a product of the later Pauline tradition.

The interpreters of Paul who wrote Colossians, Ephesians, 1 Timothy, Titus, and 1 Peter insist upon the submission of women, children, and slaves to husband, father, or master in the "household codes," partly to accommodate Christianity to Roman imperial "family values." Timothy (1 Tim. 2:9–15) prohibits women from teaching and makes women's salvation dependent on childbearing and child rearing. Although these restrictions may have had little effect on contemporaries, their canonization restricted the roles of women in later Christianity.

The Gospels and the Acts of the Apostles present a different set of problems: whereas these narratives reflect some memories of women (and men) who were active in the early Christian mission and during the career of Jesus, their real interest is in explaining the death and resurrection of Jesus and directing the lives of the survivors by his living voice. Other figures appear only to illuminate the person and message of Jesus as the authors sought to make him present to the needs and experience of later communities. Tensions between early Christianity and the Judaism from which it arose are also reflected in the Gospels, further obscuring the original context of Jesus and his companions. Attempts to reconstruct the attitude of Jesus toward women or the interest of women in Jesus have largely depended on contrasting the Gospels with highly negative reconstructions of the roles of women in Judaism.

Even so, the Gospels and Acts reflect the participation of women. Mark 15:40–41 (thought to be the earliest of the four canonical gospels) names Mary Magdalene, Mary the mother of James and Joses, and Salome to provide consistent witnesses to the death of Jesus, his burial (15:47), and the empty tomb (16:1–8). They "followed" and "ministered to" (*diekonei*) Jesus in Galilee; that is, they were disciples and ministers in the movement, among numerous other women. The Gospel of John, which may be independent of Mark, places Mary Magdalene at the cross and tomb in the company of Jesus' mother, his mother's sister (and?) Mary of Clophas (John 19:25). Other women treated as disciples are the mother of the Zebedees (Matt. 27:56, cf. 20:20), Joanna the wife of Chuza, Susanna, Mary (wife or mother) of James (Luke 8:3, 24:10), and Martha and Mary (John 11:1–12:8, Luke 10:38–42). Luke alone limits women's ministry to the patronage subsidizing the movement. Matthew and Luke follow Mark in representing women as on the road with Jesus in Galilee. Because recent scholarship on the historical Jesus has largely depicted his context as an itinerant, mendicant, and antipatriarchal movement of preachers of the reign (kingdom) of God, locating women on the road attests women's central participation in the movement. The association of women with the resurrection stories argues that women were among the first visionaries to encounter Jesus alive from the dead.

In addition to women members of the movement, the authors of the Gospels and Acts proffer stories about women who were healed by Jesus, or who provide him with the occasion of a wise saying, as well as parables in which women provide the analogy. Women rarely appear as interlocutors of Jesus who question and evoke teaching on discipleship and God's reign as they do in extra-canonical works, such as the Gospel of Thomas, Gospel of Mary, and Dialogue of the Savior. The exception is the Gospel of John, which includes lengthy dialogues between Jesus and a woman of Samaria (4:6–42) and Martha (11:17–44), and brief exchanges with Mary, Martha's sister (11:32–35), his own mother (2:3–5), and Mary Magdalene (20:14–18). Even in texts that explicitly raise issues of gender, women (like male interlocutors, and indeed Jesus himself) express the theology or articulate the problems of the writer or community, rather than those of the "historical" Mary Magdalene or Salome.

Thus, inquiring into women's motives for participating in the movement requires adopting a reconstruction of the movement itself. The recognition that Jesus died as an enemy of the Roman order and that "God's reign" preached an alternative to the imperial order is crucial to eliminating anti-Judaism in feminist New Testament scholarship. For scholars who reject future expectation and view its preaching of God's reign as radical Jewish moral wisdom, women in the movement might be seen as wandering sages whose activity challenged the paterfamilias' control of women within the household. Most feminist scholars continued to see the movement as prophetic, announcing God's imminent just reign, and the women of the movement as prophets as well as sages.

BIBLIOGRAPHY

The earliest feminist treatment of women in the whole of the canonical New Testament was Elisabeth Schüssler Fiorenza's *In Memory of Her: A Feminist Theological Reconstruction of Christian Origins* (1983); of methodological importance was her modification of sociological approaches to the New Testament by focusing on the evidence for participation of women in both the Jesus movement and the early Christian mission (Pauline and pre-Pauline churches). Ross Shepard Kraemer's *Her Share of the Blessings: Women's Religions Among Pagans, Jews and Christians in the Greco-Roman World* (1992) approaches the canonical New Testament in the context of other evidence from early Christianity to construct an anthropological description of early Christianity among other women's religions of antiquity. Luise Schotroff's *Lydia's Impatient Sisters: A Feminist Social History of Early Christianity* (1995) attempts a feminist reading of Christianity that presents it as a Jewish movement of the poor. She stresses the necessity of placing Jesus' death at the hands of the Romans in the center of reconstruction, as do both Mary R. D'Angelo, in "Re-membering Jesus: Women, Prophecy and Resistance in the Memories of the Early Churches," *Horizons* 19 (1992): 199–218, and Elisabeth Schüssler Fiorenza, in *Jesus: Miriam's Child, Sophia's Prophet: Critical Issues in Feminist Christology* (1994).

There are two complete feminist commentaries on the New Testament: *The Women's Bible Commentary,* edited by Carol Newsom and Sharon Ringe (1992), and *Searching the Scriptures,* edited by Elisabeth Schüssler Fiorenza. The latter is a more extensive treatment: volume 1, *A Feminist Ecumenical Introduction* (1993), provides a hermeneutical and methodological introduction; volume 2, *A Feminist Commentary* (1994), covers both the canonical New Testament and some important works from its context. *Women in Christian Origins: A Reader,* edited by Ross Kraemer and Mary R. D'Angelo (forthcoming), is a collection of essays forming an introduction to the topic.

Specialized studies of particular importance on the Gospels include Amy-Jill Levine, "Who's Catering the Q Affair? Feminist Observations on Q Paranesis," *Semeia* 50 (1990): 145–161; Elisabeth Schüssler Fiorenza, *But She Said: Feminist Practices of Biblical Interpretation* (1992); Kathleen Corley, *Private Women, Public Meals: Social Conflict in the Synoptic Tradition* (1993); Turid Karlsen Seim, *Double Message: Patterns of Gender in Luke–Acts* (1994). Ivoni Richter Reimer offers the only book-length study of women in Acts: *Women in the Acts of the Apostles: A Feminist Liberation Perspective* (1995). Among significant contributions to the study of women through the letters of Paul are Antoinette Clark Wire, *Women Corinthian Prophets: A Reconstruction through Paul's Rhetoric* (1990), and Bernadette J. Brooten's *Love between Women: Early Christian Responses to Female Homoeroticism* (1996).

See also Liberation Theologies; Mary and Martha; Ministry.

MARY ROSE D'ANGELO

Paul and the Pauline Tradition

Thirteen letters in the New Testament bear Paul's name, yet there is no consensus on which letters he actually composed. Most scholars agree that Romans, 1 and 2 Corinthians, Galatians, Philippians, 1 Thessalonians, and Philemon were written by Paul. The authorship of Ephesians, Colossians, and 2 Thessalonians continues to be debated. 1 and 2 Timothy and Titus are almost unanimously assigned to the early second century C.E. and thus to a later follower of Paul. In the seven uncontested letters women hold leadership roles and are included among Paul's inner circles. In the contested (deutero-Pauline) letters women's roles are restricted. Paul, it seems, had less difficulty with a more egalitarian community of believers than did his later, pseudonymous interpreters.

WOMEN IN PAUL

Although Paul wrote infrequently about women in his letters he sometimes described them with special titles. In Romans 16:1–2 Phoebe is called a deacon (*diakonos*) of the church in Cenchreae (a port city near Corinth) and patron or protector (*prostatis*) of Paul and others. As a result, Paul highly commends her to the community. In Romans 16:7 Paul sends greetings to Junia, who is called an apostle (*apostolos*). What is striking about this verse is that a woman is not only included among the group Paul identifies as apostles but she is also prominent among them. Prisca is called a coworker (*synergos*) of Paul in Romans 16:3 and head of a house church (along with Aquila) in 1 Corinthians 16:19 (see Acts 18:24–26). Euodia and Syntyche are also called co-workers of Paul in Philippians 4:2–3. Paul asks the Philippian community to help these women reach agreement on an undisclosed conflict, one important enough to merit Paul's epistolary attention.

Other women's names also appear. Romans 16 acknowledges the hard work of Mary (16:6) and Tryphaena, Tryphosa, and Persis (16:12) and greets Julia and Nereus's sister (16:15). 1 Corinthians 1:11 mentions the report of Chloe's people, which suggests she was the leader of a pro-Paul faction in the Corinthian community. Philemon 2 includes Apphia as one of three people to whom the letter is addressed. This is the only example of a woman addressee in all thirteen letters.

Paul comments on the nature of woman in 1 Corinthians 11:2–16, although his primary concern is the necessity of headcoverings for women in public worship. He explains that man is the image (*eikōn*) and glory (*doxa*) of God, whereas woman is the glory of man; that woman was created from man and for man (Genesis 2:21–22). Hence, as a derivative person, the woman must cover her head because to leave her hair uncovered is as shameful as a shaven head (the alternative to uncovered hair). Nowhere in the passage does Paul prohibit the verbal participation of women in worship, whether through prayer or prophecy. In contrast to this passage, 1 Corinthians 14:33b–36 demands that women should keep silent in church since woman's voice is shameful in public worship settings. Because the latter directly contradicts 1 Corinthians 11 and sounds suspiciously similar to 1 Timothy 2:11–12, some scholars have concluded that 1 Corinthians 14:33b–36 is an interpolation, a later non-Pauline addition to the text.

Two final texts that neither mention real women nor discourse on women's nature should be addressed. Galatians 3:28 ostensibly breaks down social distinctions between people—Jew and Greek, slave and free, and male and female. Paul appears to be quoting a pre-Pauline baptismal prayer to demonstrate that in baptism such categories are rendered meaningless. Yet he clearly did not mean that individuals somehow became sexless. In the practice of the early Christian communities, as in Greco-Roman society generally, such distinctions did in fact remain.

Romans 1:26–27 is the only explicit biblical reference to female homosexuality yet this topic is not the focus of the larger text (Romans 1.18–32). Paul condemns those who worship images (human, animal, and reptile) rather than the true, imageless God. This passage is especially troubling because the image worshipers are consigned by God to all kinds of depravity, including

"unnatural" intercourse of women with women (and men with men). Homosexuality in this passage is understood as an imposed outcome of a more egregious sin, and along with the vice list in 1:29–31 should be seen as a rhetorical device, one which nevertheless suggests that Paul would also condemn individual same sex relations.

WOMEN IN THE DEUTERO-PAULINE LETTERS

Colossians 4:15 names Nympha as head of the house church in Laodicea, yet this letter also depicts woman's role as subordinate. Both Colossians 3:18–4.1 and Ephesians (written with Colossians as its source) 5:21–6.9 share similar household codes, hierarchical models of social relations based on the ancient household. In these codes wives (*gunai*) are to be submissive to their husbands (see also Titus 2:4–5). Ephesians 5:23–24 intensifies Colossians 3:18 by adding that the submission of the wife to the husband is analogous to the church's submission to Christ; women's subordination is theologically necessary and mandated. Ephesians 5:25–27 further develops the Christ–husband analogy by stating that husbands have similar obligations to sanctify their wives as Christ sacrificed himself to make the church holy. Wives are depicted as submissive and in need of a sanctification that can only be obtained through their husbands. Woman in and of herself in this model is essentially impure.

In 1 Timothy 2:8–12 women are required to dress modestly for worship, they are to be silent, and they are not allowed to teach or have authority over men. 2 Timothy 3:6–7 further describes women as overwhelmed by their "sins and desires," and though they are constantly instructed they cannot learn. The justification for these restrictions is given in 1 Timothy 2:13–15: woman was created after man (as Paul claims in 1 Corinthians 11:8); the woman, not the man, was deceived by the serpent (Genesis 3); and woman will be saved through childbearing. Thus woman's salvation seems to rest on her submission to her husband together with the bearing of his children.

CHRISTIAN ATTITUDES ABOUT WOMEN'S TODAY

The desire to find Biblical precedents for women's ordination today, as well as religiously conservative interests in deconstructing such texts, has fueled much recent interest in Paul and women. Given that ordination, Jewish or Christian, was not part of Paul's historical context, methodological caution is needed with this trajectory. Nonetheless, women were active participants, leaders, teachers, and patrons of the early Christian communities. The trend in later interpreters of Paul to constrain and silence women in the church suggests women were too successful in these roles.

BIBLIOGRAPHY

Brooten, Bernadette J. " 'Junia . . . Outstanding among the Apostles' (Romans 16:7)." In *Women Priests: A Catholic Commentary on the Vatican Declaration.* Edited by Leonard S. Swidler and Arlene Swidler. 1977.

———. *Love between Women: Early Christian Responses to Female Homoeroticism.* 1996.

———. *Women Leaders in the Ancient Synagogue: Inscriptional Evidence and Background Issues.* Brown Judaic Studies 36. 1982.

D'Angelo, Mary Rose. "Women Partners in the New Testament." *Journal of Feminist Studies in Religion* 6 (1990): 65–86.

Kraemer, Ross Shepard. *Her Share of the Blessings: Women's Religions among Pagans, Jews and Christians in the Greco-Roman World.* 1992.

MacDonald, Dennis R. *The Legend and the Apostle: The Battle for Paul in Story and Canon.* 1983.

Newsom, Carol A., and Sharon H. Ringe, eds. *The Women's Bible Commentary.* 1992.

Schüssler Fiorenza, Elisabeth, ed. *In Memory of Her: A Feminist Theological Reconstruction of Christian Origins.* 1984.

———. *Searching the Scriptures: A Feminist Commentary.* 1994.

Wire, Antoinette Clark. *The Corinthian Women Prophets: A Reconstruction through Paul's Rhetoric.* 1990.

JACQUELINE PASTIS

Apocrypha

The word *apocrypha,* literally "hidden things," when coupled with the words *new testament,* designates numerous Christian writings from late antiquity that are not part of the canon (generally defined as the twenty-seven books comprising the New Testament). Among them are gospels (narrative proclamations centering on Jesus) including Christian gnostic post-resurrection dialogues from Nag Hammadi, acts (travelogues of apostles), letters, and apocalypses (revelations). Women feature prominently in the first two collections.

The *Gospel of Mary* is an account of a revelation of the resurrected Christ to the woman Mary (or Miriam; Mariamme). It conveys the source of her spiritual authority. In the *Sophia of Jesus Christ* the figure of the female Sophia identifies a gendered Christ—elsewhere Sophia is a female revealer.

Among *The Acts of the Christian Martyrs* is the third-century *Martyrdom of Perpetua and Felicitas,* a narrative that includes Perpetua's diary of her last days. It is the earliest Christian text written by a woman. During her imprisonment Perpetua slowly divested herself of cultural expectations for women (motherhood and familial ties) and chose instead a martyr's death. This process was symbolized by her visions and culminated in her "becoming a man" during an athletic struggle in a public arena. This transformation signifies her sanctification because in the lives of ascetic holy women, the mark of true holiness is to become men.

The second- and third-century *Apocryphal Acts of the Apostles* recount the conversions of several upper-class women to a form of ascetic Christianity. Whether the subjects are real is not important since they represent idealized and popular forms of piety. Shorn heads and men's clothing together with sexual renunciation and virginity signify the new lifestyle of Thecla, Mygdonia, and Charitine. Thecla renounces her engagement after hearing the apostle Paul, and dressed as a man follows him on his travels. She baptizes herself in a pool of water. The connection between status and gender ambiguity continues into the fourth century. Jerome says of the abbess Olympias, "don't say 'woman' but 'what a man!' " because this is a man despite her physical appearance." However, in the same period, John Chrysostom counterbalances Jerome's praise by warning that such changes upset the natural order, and Tertullian expresses anxiety about women modeling themselves on Thecla.

A new Christian movement called Montanism emerged in the second century and continued into the eighth, in which women prophets played an important role. This public, ministerial, and sometimes priestly activity of Montanist women, such as Priscilla, Maximilla, and Quintilla, was the product of the Montanist belief in a Spirit-guided breaking in of a new order. As the Hebrew prophet Joel (2:28) had promised, women and men were recipients and proclaimers of the spirit. These were celibate women leaders whose oracles were preserved along with those of the founder, Montanus. Maximilla's oracle "I am driven away like a wolf from the sheep. I am not a wolf; I am word and spirit and power" is the voice of a persecuted woman's ecstatic and inspired speech evoking the apostle Paul (I Cor. 2:4). Nothing is known of their lives.

BIBLIOGRAPHY

Castelli, E. " 'I will make Mary male': Pieties of the Body and Gender Transformation of Christian

Women in Late Antiquity." In *Body Guards: The Cultural Politics of Gender Ambiguity.* Edited by J. Epstein and R. Straub. 1991.

Cloke, G. *This Female Man of God: Women and Spiritual Power in the Patristic Age,* A.D. *350–450.* 1995.

Schneemelcher, W. *New Testament Apocrypha.* 2 vols. 1992 and 1994.

Trevett, C. *Montanism: Gender, Authority and the New Prophecy.* 1996.

See also **Christianity: Gnostic Writings; Sophia.**

DEIRDRE GOOD

Gnostic Writings

The gnostic writings from Nag Hammadi are an invaluable source of information about Christian and non-Christian (pagan) gnosticism. They enhance the reconstruction of Christian origins as first-hand accounts of revelation texts and resurrection dialogues.

Texts written by Gnostics containing female imagery and describing women disciples (the *Books of Jeu,* the *Codex Brucianus,* the Berlin Gnostic Codex, *Pistis Sophia,* and much of the Nag Hammadi Library) are part of a larger world of gendered language pervading gnostic texts. Some texts (*Thunder, Perfect Mind*) describe the character of divinity as female revealer while others describe androgynous inhabitants of the light-world (aeons) including Sophia, the principle associated with material creation (*The Apocryphon of John*). Among this group are the female savior figures of Norea (in *the Hypostasis of the Archons*) and Ennoia (in *Trimorphic Protennoia*). Additional texts portray male and female disciples of Jesus (*The Sophia of Jesus Christ; The Gospel of Mary*). Some of these texts correlate men and women to male and female aeons (*Pistis Sophia; The Treatise on Resurrection*); others do not. *The Gospel of Philip,* for example, understands the sacraments in gendered imagery: bridal chamber, baptism, eucharist, and redemption unite male and female originally separated in creation. In these texts the gender of the presider over acts of worship is not important. However, readers must be cautious in deducing social practice from religious theory.

Among the female disciples of Jesus, Mary (Mariamme) plays an important role. She is the recipient of divine revelation (John 20) and the revealer of it to other disciples in *The Gospel of Mary, Pistis Sophia,* and Manichaean hymns. That Jesus and Mary protest and affirm the validity of her revelation in response to the incredulity and scorn of some male disciples in these texts not only affirms the authority of female discipleship and the validity of revelation as a medium of spiritual truth but also the particular and even higher insight of Mary herself.

The sheer number of references to female figures and imagery in accounts of gnostic communities by early Christian hereseologists suggested to ancient readers that women were prominent in gnostic communities. Around 180 C.E., for example, Irenaeus writes that Marcus, a Valentinian gnostic leader in the south of France, deliberately cultivates women followers. These women are easily seduced, he says, by assurances of their own spiritual gifts. The fourth century writer Jerome lists heretics and their female companions from earliest times to the present. In contrast, the gnostic teacher Ptolemy writes a letter perhaps from Rome in the second century to a woman named Flora clarifying tenets of gnostic teaching about the law. Clearly there were women interested in gnostic Christianity, but to extract information about them is problematic, since male catologers of heresies such as Jerome utilize the figure of the heretical female as a vehicle for the negative expression of their own orthodox male self-identity.

BIBLIOGRAPHY

Buckley, Jorunn J. "An Interpretation of Logion 114 in the Gospel of Thomas." *Novum Testamentum* 27 (1985): 245–272.

Burrus, Virginia. "The Heretical Woman as Symbol in Alexander, Athanasius, Epiphanius, and Jerome." *Harvard Theological Review* 84 (1991): 229–248.

King, Karen L., ed. *Images of the Feminine in Gnosticism.* 1988.

Marjanen, Antti. *The Woman Jesus Loved: Mary Magdalene in the Nag Hammadi Library and Related Documents.* Nag Hammadi and Manichaean Studies 40. 1996.

McGuire, Anne. "Women, Gender, and 'Gnostic' Traditions." In *Women and Christian Origins.* Edited by Ross Kraemer and Mary Rose d'Angelo. 1998.

Williams, Michael. "Uses of Gender Imagery in Ancient Gnostic Texts." In *Gender and Religion: On the Complexity of Symbols.* Edited by Caroline W. Bynum, Steven Harrell, and Paula Richman. 1986.

See also **Christianity: Apocrypha.**

DEIRDRE GOOD

In Africa

Although Africa encountered Christianity in Biblical times, with countries such as Ethiopia and Egypt developing indigenous forms of Christianity, it was only in the nineteenth century through European missions that Christianity reached more of the African interior.

The Berlin Conference (1884–1885, which provided a procedure for annexing African territories), European exploration and commerce, the British slavery abolitionist movement, the slave trade, and Christian efforts at evangelism and missionizing all contributed to European intervention in Africa, often seen by the Europeans as bringing the benefits of Christianity and Western civilization to an allegedly "dark continent."

The nineteenth century missionary project was a predominantly male enterprise. Initially Protestants did not admit women for mission work, though wives were allowed as part of the domestic support that male missionaries needed to succeed in their work. Despite this, a significant number of single women became missionaries in their own right. By 1915, out of a total of 1,354 Church Missionary Society missionaries in Africa, 444 were single women missionaries while 374 were missionary wives. The documentation of the contributions of such women to the success of the missionary enterprise is largely absent from missionary historiographies.

The nineteenth century Catholic missionary project was male centered and clergy centered. It was, however, supported from the start by numerous orders of nuns, who were largely subordinate to the male clerical hierarchy. Such orders of nuns, however, constituted viable spheres of female autonomy and initiative. They pioneered in introducing formal education to African women and became role models for African women, some of whom aspired to be nuns themselves, seeing this as a plausible alternative to the near inevitability of marriage as the only vocation hitherto open to them. As early as 1858 African orders of nuns were formed—initially under the mentorship of European nuns and clergy but quite frequently through the initiative of African women themselves.

Because of a variety of interlocking factors, including missionaries' prior loyalty to their respective countries of origin as well as the sense of racial superiority which characterized European attitudes to Africa at the turn of the century, the Christian missionary project became implicated in colonialism. Consequently, it had an ambiguous impact on Africans and elicited a similarly ambiguous response from them.

On the one hand, missionaries, both men and women, endured many hardships and worked diligently to bring what they considered gifts of Western civilization, namely Western education and medicine. This dedication inspired many Africans to join mission churches in search of these benefits. Some became such fervent followers that they became priests, nuns, and evangelists themselves. Others, such as the young pages in Kabaka Mwanga's Court in the 1890s, preferred martyrdom than to betray their new-found faith.

On the other hand, much of missionary praxis contradicted Christianity's central message of the universality of God's love for humanity and the equality of all before God. Missionaries failed to treat adequately even Christianized Africans as equals. This failure manifested itself in the aggressive methods of conversion and disciplining converts when they seemed not to comply with prescribed Western ways. Missionaries also actively destroyed many aspects of African culture, which they considered incompatible with Christianity.

Africans throughout the continent actively resisted this "bull in a China shop" approach to African cultures. Some rejected Christianity outright. The most spectacular resistance to what was in effect a forced acculturation came in the formation of over six thousand so-called Independent Churches, including the numerous Zionist and Ethiopian Churches in South Africa, the ubiquitous Roho (Spirit) Churches in Kenya, and the Aldura Churches in West Africa. Such churches eloquently testify to Africans' determination to maintain their cultural integrity and autonomy.

A significant number of these churches were founded by women, such as Alice Lenshina of the Lumpa Church (Zambia), Gaudencia Aoko of the Legio Maria Church (Kenya), Mai Chaza of the Guta ra Jehovah (Zimbabwe), Christina Nku of St. John's Apostolic Church (South Africa), and Christiana Akinssowon of the Cherubim and Seraphim Church (Nigeria). Though women do not exclusively lead in these churches their conspicuous presence in such churches constitutes a critique of missionary Christianity and its alliance with colonialism, as well as a critique of patriarchal missionary ecclesiology, which in many cases eroded the religious leadership roles of women recognized in African traditional religions and is also perceived as a betrayal of Biblical teaching.

In the case of South Africa, entanglement of missionary Christianity with apartheid in South Africa led not only to the emergence of hundreds of Independent Churches to which over 25 percent of the Christians in South Africa belong today but also to the emergence of Black Theology of Liberation, which named and challenged the alliance between the theology upheld by the state (so-called State Theology) and racism. In 1985, a number of black theologians drafted the Kairos Document, in which they rejected State Theology as heretical. They adopted what they called Prophetic Theology, the task of which was to challenge apartheid and to mobilize people to take action against it. For many black theologians like Desmond Tutu, Tsakatso Mofokeng, Simon Maimela, and Alan Boesak, Black Theology signified a prophetic rejection of a theology in the service of oppression and a reclamation of the liberative aspects of Christianity in their struggle against apartheid.

Another alternative theology that has emerged to challenge the apparent alliance between colonialism and mission Christianity is Inculturation Theology, which is a response to forced inculturation and aims to rearticulate and reclaim the Christian message in a language that resonates with the African world view, thus meeting African spiritual needs more adequately. Such efforts at inculturation include the vernacularisation and indigenization of the liturgy as well as the translation of Christian doctrine into African categories. To what extent Inculturation Theology meets the African need for cultural liberation remains to be seen. Much will depend on the extent to which such theologians perceive African religions and spirituality as viable alternatives, or at least mutually enriching, to Christianity. Christianity in Africa as elsewhere has yet to come to adequate grip with the religious and cultural pluralism that faces the world today.

While such formal challenges to western Christian theology have for a long time been a male enterprise with women involved more informally and obliquely, more recently African women have also organized themselves and embarked on a sustained and formal analysis of the impact of religion (including Christianity) and culture in their lives. The impetus and the will to take initiative crystallized in 1989 in the formation of the Circle of Concerned African Women Theologians. Under the leadership of Mecy Amba Oduyoye, the Circle has a growing membership comprising both academically trained women, church leaders, and women in Christian and other communities of faith, particularly Islam and African traditional religions.

African responses to Christianity have claimed its positive and emancipatory dimensions and appropriated these in their search for justice. Many African women have appropriated the central message of liberation implicit in Christianity in their struggle against sexism and other forms of injustice that they face. More recently, the search for healing and reconciliation, given the trauma and damage caused by colonialism and neocolonialism, has led to a new phase of African Christian theology, suitably called Reconstruction Theology. In the process of this reconstruction, women are claiming their rightful place as moral agents rather than as mere victims of the interlocking webs of oppression in Africa. For many Africans, the challenge is how to re-envision the Christian project in Africa so that it moves beyond a preoccupation with the conversion of non-Christians, to a project that claims the insights of Christianity along with those of other religions also embraced by Africans, and to press these into the service of healing the battered continent and its inhabitants.

BIBLIOGRAPHY

Chidester, David. *Religions of South Africa.* London, 1992.

Comaroff, Jean. *Body of Power, Spirit of Resistance.* 1985.

———. *The Culture and History of a South African People.* 1985.

De Gruchy, John, and Charles Villa-Vicencio. *Apartheid Is a Heresy.* 1983.

Ela, Jean Marc. *African Cry.* 1986.

Gifford, Paul, ed. *New Dimensions in African Christianity.* Nairobi, 1992.

Hastings, Adrian. *African Catholicism: Essays in Discovery.* 1989.

———. *The Church in Africa, 1450–1950.* 1994.

———. *A History of African Christianity, 1950–1975.* 1979.

Hinga, Teresia M. "Women, Power and Liberation in an African Church: Theological Assessment of The Legio Maria Church in Kenya." Ph.D. diss., Lancaster University, 1990.

Isichei, Elizabeth. *A History of Christianity: From Antiquity to the Present.* 1995.

Mudimbe, V. Y. *The Invention of Africa.* 1988.

Mugambi, J. *From Liberation to Reconstruction: African Christian Theology after the Cold War.* Nairobi, 1995.

Musimbi, Kanyoro, and Nyambura Njoroge. *Groaning in Faith: African Women in the Household of God.* Nairobi, 1996.

Oduyoye, Mercy, and Musimbi Kanyoro, eds. *The Will to Arise: Women, Tradition and the Church in Africa.* Nairobi, 1996.

Sanneh, Lamin. *Translating the Message: The Missionary Impact of Culture.* 1990.

Shorter, Aylward. *Towards a Theology of Inculturation.* 1988.

TERESIA MBARI HINGA

In Asia

Asia is a multiracial, multireligious, and multicultural continent, the birthplace of major historical religions of humankind. Christianity has very ancient roots in Asia. In India, Thomas Christians trace their roots back to Thomas the Apostle. After Nestorian Christianity was condemned as a heresy in the fifth century, Nestorian missionaries spread the gospel in Persia, Afghanistan, Central Asia, and India and reached China in the seventh century.

Although Catholic missionaries had visited Asia in earlier periods, mission work did not gain a foothold until the discovery of sea routes, which increased trade prospects and military expansion. Portuguese missionaries began work in west India after Goa was occupied (1510) and in Southeast Asia as Melaka in Malaysia was defeated (1511). The Spanish colonized the Philippines in 1565 and imposed Catholicism on the population. French missionaries were active in Southeast Asia and China.

Protestant missions arrived simultaneously with colonial expansion. In the so-called great century of mission (nineteenth century), missionaries from Europe and North America were sent to preach the gospel at the same time that lands were taken from the people. Believing in the superiority of Western culture, missionaries also established mission schools, mission presses, health clinics, and introduced social reforms.

Since Christianity came to Asia as a foreign religion, often backed by colonial interests, Christian missionaries often met with strong suspicion and resistance. In Japan, for example, missionaries and Christians were persecuted by the Tokugawa government in the seventeenth century, and many were forced to become "hidden Christians." In China, the gentry and local populace spread antimissionary propaganda, culminating in the Boxer Uprising in 1900. Not until Asian countries became more open to the West did Christian missionaries enjoy a more favorable reception.

In the long struggle for independence from colonial rule, Christians in some Asian countries played a significant role. For example, Philippine Christians were instrumental in overthrowing Spanish rule, and Korean Christians participated in the independence movement against the Japanese. In order to gain autonomy from Western control, independent churches or movements were initiated, such as the Philippine Independent Church, the "no-church" movement in Japan, and various independent churches in China. The Church of South India was formed in 1947 and the Church of North India in 1965. When the Chinese churches were reopened in the late 1970s after religious persecution, the church in China became post-denominational.

Many Christian leaders in Asia are aware that Christianity must be indigenized into Asian soil, using the idioms and languages of the people. Radical Asian theologians insist that religious processes of humankind are all syncretistic, with constant adaptation and borrowing from other cultures. Asian Christians, therefore, should have the freedom to use their indigenous resources in theological reflection. As a result of dialogue with people of other faiths and participation in political struggles, various theological currents have emerged in Asia. These include *minjung* theology (theology of the

Chinese Catholics worship at Easter mass in Beijing, China, 1983 (Owen Franken/Corbis).

masses) in Korea, homeland theology in Taiwan, and grassroots theology in the Philippines.

Much of the history of Christianity in Asia has been written from the missionary perspective. When church history is written from the Asian side, the writers focus on the lives and thought of male Christians. Recently, Asian female scholars have begun to study the very complex relationships between Christianity and women's lives in Asia, in which Christianity sometimes advanced and sometimes impeded women's situation. In the Philippines, Catholicism superimposed a more patriarchal structure onto the indigenous traditions, which were more egalitarian. In other parts of Asia, Christianity introduced an alternative worldview, enabling women to challenge indigenous patriarchal cultures.

The Christian church and mission schools in Asia provided education for poor girls and women, nurtured women's leadership, and enabled women to organize reform activities. Women missionaries provided role models and alternative understandings of womanhood. Female religious orders enabled the formation of women's communities dedicated to education and ministry. Protestant women were employed as Bible women and evangelists, who were instrumental in literacy campaigns and local reforms. The Young Women's Christian Association (YWCA) and the Women's Christian Temperance Union (WCTU) provided opportunities for women to participate in wider society. Christian women in Asia also participated in revolutionary movements and political struggles for democracy.

Asian Christian women in earlier periods have written testimonies, articles in religious newspapers and magazines, and autobiographies reflecting on their faith. A more conscious attempt to develop Asian feminist theology began in the 1970s through various ecumenical networks of Asian women. Today Asian feminist theologians have made significant contributions to feminist theological discourse.

BIBLIOGRAPHY

Chung, Hyun Kyung. *Struggle to Be the Sun Again: Introducing Asian Women's Theology.* 1990. An introduction to the historical contexts and major themes of Asian women's theology.

David, M. D., ed. *Asia and Christianity.* 1985.

————. *Western Colonialism in Asia and Christianity.* 1988.

Fabella, Virginia, and Sun Ai Lee Park, eds. *We Dare to Dream: Doing Theology as Asian Women.* 1989. A collection of essays by Asian feminist theologians.

Gnanadason, Aruna. *No Longer a Secret: The Church and Violence against Women.* 1993. An insightful study of violence against women and the church's responsibility.

Kinukawa, Hisako. *Women and Jesus in Mark: A Japanese Feminist Perspective.* 1994. A study of Mark combining Western scholarship with feminist insights from Japan.

Kwok Pui-lan. *Chinese Women and Christianity, 1860–1927.* 1992. An analysis of Chinese women's interactions with the missionary movement and their religious and social activities, and theological construction.

————. *Discovering the Bible in the Non-Biblical World.* 1995. A critical study of issues of Asian feminist hermeneutics: orality and textuality, multifaith hermeneutics, postcolonial criticism, and ethnocentrism in feminist biblical interpretation.

Mananzan, Mary John. "The Filipino Woman: Before and After the Spanish Conquest of the Philippines." In *Essays on Women.* Edited by Mary John Mananzan. 1991. Compares the social status of women before and after colonization in the Philippines.

See also Christianity: In North America: American Protestant Women's Foreign Missionary Activity.

KWOK PUI-LAN

In Europe

Most European women in the nineteenth and twentieth centuries were or are Christian. Regretably, patriarchal interpretations distorted the Christian message to legitimate women's subordination as divinely ordained. With no record of foremothers' experience, women struggled toward full humanity, despite church conspiracy with misogynistic political regimes. Following isolation at home, women discovered common stories shared in jobs, college, wartime mobilization, and concentration camps. They bonded, survived, and together demanded their rights.

English writer and early feminist Mary Wollstonecraft (1759–1797) debunked women's innate inferiority, advocating their inclusion in political and legal life, since education could remedy the apparent inequality with men. During the next century, women achieved universal access to primary education, notably through women's religious communities. New congregations emerged, such as the Sisters of Mercy's noncloistered, walking nuns, bringing education to neglected women and girls in the 1831 Dublin slums.

English novelist Virginia Woolf (1882–1941) wrote metaphorically of Shakespeare's sister—all women deprived of educational opportunities to make creative contributions to society apart from motherhood. Unlike men, women had to choose between marriage and professional life. They needed economic independence for higher education, politics, law, medicine, and so on. Women sacrificed their interests to nationalist causes but failed to obtain voting rights and were forced to struggle well into the twentieth century. The daring Catholic Women's Suffrage Society emerged in 1910. It became Saint Joan's Social and Political Alliance, once suffrage was achieved in England and Ireland in 1928.

The nineteenth and twentieth centuries encompassed feminist ebb and flow. Two Catholic dogmas, Immaculate Conception (1854) and Assumption (1950), emphasized Mary's uniqueness, which did not further women's emancipation. Marie Curie (1867–1934), first woman science professor at the Sorbonne, won Nobel Prizes in physics and chemistry. German theologian Charlotte von Kirschbaum (1899–1975), lived the divinely ordained subordination she internalized as helper to Protestant theologian Karl Barth. French Simone de Beauvoir (1908–1986) wrote her landmark women's liberation manifesto, *The Second Sex* (1949). Margaret Thatcher became England's prime minister (1979) and Mary Robinson Ireland's president (1990).

Neither Protestant nor Catholic churches supported women's liberation initially. The World Council of Churches (WCC), an aggregate of Protestant churches since 1948, actively promotes equality through its women's department, studies on Women and Men in the Church, and Ecumenical Decade of Churches in Solidarity with Women (1988–1998). WCC European leaders Marga Bührig and Madeleine Barot each held the ceremonial office of president. No woman has held the highest position of General Secretary.

The Roman Catholic Church backed the 1804 Napoleonic Code, classifying women with children, criminals, and the insane as politically incompetent, and married women as subject to their husbands. Despite manifested job competence during World War I and World War II, a postwar backlash relegated women to the domestic sphere. Contraception and abortion were outlawed in Catholic countries and where an increased birth rate was desirable. Women were coerced and encouraged to have more children. Mother's Day was invented in France and Germany, and women were honored with bronze, silver, or vermeil medals for five to ten children. Italian mothers bearing fourteen to nineteen children received a medal from Fascist premier Mussolini with Pope Pius XI's encyclical, condemning married women's employment, contraception, abortion, and marital sex without procreative intent. Paul VI's 1968 encyclical on human life prohibited contraception.

Paul VI invited twenty-three women auditors to the Second Vatican Council (1962–1965) for the first time, but not Swiss lawyer Gertrud Heinzelmann, who advocated women's ordination. The pope promoted Rosemary Goldie from executive secretary of COPECIAL (Permanent Committee for International Congresses of the Lay Apostolate) to under-secretary of the Pontifical Council of the Laity. He supported the first women's ecumenical meeting in 1965. He challenged women to active church membership but responded negatively to the ordination question in 1976. John Paul II reiterated his arguments in a definitive 1994 statement, forbidding all discussion. The Vatican backlash legislated sexist language in the *Catechism* and liturgical texts. In some Protestant churches, as elsewhere in society during World War I and World War II, women did jobs previously viewed as male domains. Those with theological education were ordained and became pastors in the absence of men. The Orthodox tradition, however, like the Roman Catholic Church, has consistently refused to ordain women.

Qualified Catholic women today do voluntary or low-paid work as pastoral associates in priestless parishes, as hospital chaplains, or as religion teachers. A few are university professors on theological faculties in universities but not in seminaries. Organizations for women's rights span the continent. Women's Ordination Worldwide was launched in Austria in 1996. Referenda solicit supportive signatures for inclusive church reform.

Paradoxically, women's communities, regulated by patriarchally approved rules, imaged the autonomous woman others could emulate, although women religious, long conditioned to docility and hierarchical loyalty, do not lead in feminist theology. Lacking feminist mentors and sources, pioneers produced traditional doctoral dissertations.

Mary Wollstonecraft was an English writer and early feminist. She is known for her *Vindication of the Rights of Women* (Library of Congress/Corbis).

Feminist consciousness took a giant leap since women perceived their common oppression and united ecumenically for liberation. The third millennium could generate a feminist culture, structured by inclusive language that shapes, transforms, and redeems society.

BIBLIOGRAPHY

Anderson, Bonnie S., and Judith P. Zinsser. *A History of Their Own: Women in Europe from Prehistory to the Present*, vol. 2. 1988. A most valuable, carefully researched work. Excellent extensive bibliography, notes, and index. Four main sections in volume 2 deal with women of the courts as rulers, patrons, and attendants; women of the salons and parlors as ladies, housewives, and professionals; women of the cities as mothers, workers, and revolutionaries; and a history of feminism in Europe.

Aubert, Jean-Marie. *L'exil féminin: Antiféminisme et Christianisme*. 1988. A revised edition of an earlier work by this renowned male historian. Critiques biblical and historical data and their interpretations concerning women. Deals with contemporary questions in the light of feminist scholarship and the gospel message. Shows how Christianity has contributed to antifeminism, thus distorting the creative, liberative force of the gospel. Useful bibliography.

Brotherton, Anne, ed. *The Voice of the Turtle Dove: New Catholic Women in Europe.* 1992. An interesting, substantial collection of essays by women in eight European countries, plus an introductory and concluding chapter by the editor, putting the research project in context. The essayists follow uniform guidelines in speaking of women in ministry, theology, religious communities, and their attitudes toward the institutional church.

Jackson, Eleanor, ed. *The Question of Woman: The Collected Writings of Charlotte von Kirschbaum.* Translated by John Shepherd. 1996. Excellent extended introduction by the volume editor, followed by von Kirschbaum's own writings. Important as the first English translation of an unknown theologian whose brilliance was eclipsed by her partnership with Karl Barth, though he admitted his dependence on her for his *Church Dogmatics.*

Lerner, Gerda. *The Creation of Feminist Consciousness from the Middle Ages to Eighteen-Seventy.* 1993. A sequel to Lerner's earlier work, *The Creation of Patriarchy.* (Regrettably, this work does not include a study of the twentieth century.) Valuable in how it defines feminist consciousness and its emergence through twelve hundred years of women's struggle for liberation. With the skill of a historian and the insight of her own feminism, Lerner highlights key individuals and turning points. With the experience of a scholar and teacher, she presents priceless bibliography carefully categorized and user-friendly.

McEnroy, Carmel E. *Guests in Their Own House: The Women of Vatican II.* 1996. A contribution to ecclesiology, especially of Vatican II. Tells the story of women's presence at a church council for the first time in history, a story not included by male ecclesiologists. Based mainly on the primary research of oral sources derived from personal interviews with several conciliar women, personal letters, and the testimonies of others who knew them.

McNamara, Jo Ann Kay. *Sisters in Arms: Catholic Nuns through Two Millennia.* 1996. A mammoth historical work, beautifully written, and likely to evoke a wide range of emotions as one reads the incredible story of convent life, hitherto untold. Deserves high praise for providing this overdue testimony to those whose lives and work were mostly misunderstood and unappreciated. Extensive bibliography.

Owings, Alison. *Frauen: German Women Recall the Third Reich.* 1994. Oral history at its best as presented by a professional journalist whose fluency in German and English enabled her to carry out this task with honesty and sensitivity to the nuances of a foreign language and culture. Based on interviews with twenty-nine German women who survived the Third Reich. An exhortation to withhold judgment and enter a difficult mindset at a tragic time in history. German women were caught between loyalty to the mother country, instilling in the young obedience, respect, and trust for authority—virtues that contributed to their undoing under the Nazi regime.

Schüssler Fiorenza, Elisabeth, and Mary Collins, eds. *Women Invisible in Church and Theology. Concilium* 182. 1985. A collection of enlightening essays by ten women, five from the United States and five from Europe.

Uglow, Jennifer S., comp. and ed. *The International Dictionary of Women's Biography.* 1982. An important reference work featuring over 1,500 fascinating biographies of leading women, mostly in the United States and Europe. Covers a broad range of interests, professions, and achievements. Helpful subject index and biographical references.

Ward, Margaret. *Unmanageable Revolutionaries: Women and Irish Nationalism.* 1983. Documents Irish women's struggle for independence since 1881. Deals with divisions between nationalists and feminists—a common phenomenon in Europe. As elsewhere, Irish women were mobilized only in time of crisis but never consistently given positions of influence.

See also **Monasticism: In the West; Orthodox Christianity.**

CARMEL ELIZABETH MCENROY

In Latin America and the Caribbean

Since the 1980s, the name *Abya-Yala* (ripe earth) has been used by indigenous communities to replace *Latin America,* the name imposed on this continent by Europeans. From its beginning in 1492, the history of Christianity in Abya-Yala has been marked by conflict over socioreligious relations of power. This history includes the search for alternative models that accept the cultural plurality of Christianity, social justice, and the contribution and self-determination of women.

This conflict is expressed in four interconnected dimensions: first, the massive expansion of European Christianity toward Abya-Yala as an integral factor of the processes of conquest and colonization of the new territories; second, the imposition of Western Christianity as the absolute and universal expression of the gospel, which demonized Indo-American and Afro-American religious traditions; third, the religious justification of cultural norms of patriarchy, which sustain social and spiritual privileges of men over women; and fourth, the construction of a sociocultural model articulated by the international, racial, and sexual division of work in society to the advantage of powerful social groups, most commonly, white men.

This combination contributed to the establishment of a social model that has been and continues to be profoundly unequal and unjust because it is based on hierarchical conceptions and practices of the relationships between social groups, races, sexes, cultures, and religions. Western Christianity developed many religious principles to legitimize this hierarchy, but it has also been interpreted and lived critically by the victims of injustice, who have appropriated liberating principles from both the gospel and their own religious traditions to support practices of opposition and resistance to injustice. From the nascent capitalism of the sixteenth century through the period of national independence movements of the eighteenth and nineteenth centuries to the current model of global capitalism, these practices in Abya-Yala continue to challenge the capacity of Christianity to overcome its colonizing, patriarchal-androcentric, and solely European-based cultural expressions.

The emergence and development of liberation theology in the second half of the twentieth century made it possible to think and live Christian faith as a transformation of social reality. This theology also opened doors for the contribution of Catholic and Protestant women who developed central Christian principles to analyze critically the contribution of Christianity to either the preservation or the transformation of unequal models of power based on social origin, race, or sexual condition. Women's initiatives are compatible with the social justice agenda of the Catholic Church, as is evident in the conclusions of the conferences of Bishops in Medellín, Colombia (1968), Puebla, Mexico (1979), and especially Santo Domingo, Dominican Republic (1992). The Santo Domingo Conference shows that the Catholic Church is adopting, even in mild terms, a stand on the side of women victims of violence. The growth of Protestantism in modern Abya-Yala has made possible a distinct ecumenical experience among women, which can rightly be called "ecumenism from the base community," and which has the shared goal of the eradication of violence against women. Catholic and Protestant women have joined in the effort to counter a politically conservative and sexist Christianity. Especially in the 1990s, a number of Pentecostal and right-wing fundamentalist Christian groups based in North America have attempted to co-opt the feminist organizations, diminish the justice-based understanding of the church, and distort the liberation social movements. This type

Aztec youth march in a Candlemas procession, San Juan de los Lagos, Jalisco, Mexico, 1996 (Denny Lehman/© Corbis).

of Christianity reinforces patriarchal church institutions and has served the expansion and domination of a neoliberal market economy.

At the dawn of the third millennium, Christianity faces a challenge to the relationship between faith and culture that comes from feminist theologies and is rooted in experiences that seek a culturally pluralistic Christianity. This challenge is met in an understanding of the gospel as a gift of God announced by Jesus Christ and experienced as the salvation or liberation from all evil and sin that oppress human beings. Christianity's contribution is in the establishment of new cultural models free of hierarchical social relations to overcome existing patriarchal models.

The growth of diverse critical feminist theologies, both in Abya-Yala and in Latina communities of North America, requires a critical comprehension of Christianity beyond its monocultural and androcentric historical expression. As a force in the recreation of cultures, Christianity has the capacity to accept the feminist vision of justice and liberation as a dynamic expression of the incarnation of the gospel in present reality. Feminist theologies, in dialogue with native cultural traditions, offer new keys to understanding the Christianity of the third millennium in new cultural climates that, although diverse and plural, share common objectives to uphold the human integrity of men and women and the well-being of creation.

BIBLIOGRAPHY

Aquino, María Pilar. *Our Cry for Life: Feminist Theology from Latin America.* 1993.

———. "Santo Domingo Through the Eyes of Women." In *Santo Domingo and Beyond: Documents and Commentaries from the Historic Meeting of the Latin American Bishops' Conference.* Edited by Alfred T. Hennelly. 1993.

————. *La teología: La iglesia y la mujer en América Latina.* 1994. This book includes a detailed examination of the approach to women's issues by the Bishops' Conferences of Medellín and Puebla.

Aquino, María Pilar, ed. *Aportes para una teología desde la mujer.* 1988.

Espín O., Orlando. *The Faith of the People: Theological Reflections on Popular Catholicism.* 1977.

Gebara, Ivone. *Teología a ritmo de mujer.* 1995.

Gracio das Neves, Rui M., and Ana María Bidegáin. *América Latina al descubierto.* 1992.

Mananzan, Mary John, et al. *Women Resisting Violence: Spirituality for Life.* 1996.

Lima Silva, Silvia Regina. *Mulher negra e jubileu: Desafíos à teología Latino Americana.* 1994. Guided by Elsa Tamez, the author provides the most recent scholarly articulation of the black feminist Latin American theology.

See also Liberation Theologies; Theology: Feminist Theology.

MARÍA PILAR AQUINO

In North America

CANADA

Christianity in Canada has been formed by patriarchal European colonialism, immigration, and geographical proximity to the United States. A history of antagonism between Roman Catholics and Protestants and cultural biases favoring Anglo-Saxon peoples add to the uniqueness of Canadian Christianity. While women have often been overlooked within Canadian Christian history, they have always been present.

Land stretching along the St. Lawrence waterway into the interior of the continent were explored and then claimed by France in the early sixteenth century. The original women of this area—the aboriginal women of the Indian First Nations—had little formal interaction with French Roman Catholicism; they became sexual partners to, and traders with, male colonists. European women came to New France in the seventeenth century. Many of these women were religious sisters who developed hospitals, schools, and basic social services. Marie de l'Incarnation organized the Ursuline mission in Quebec and was a mystic and writer.

The British absorbed New France in 1763. The Church of England became the established religion, but the Roman Catholic Church was allowed to continue in Quebec. Before and after the United States Declaration of Independence in 1776, significant numbers of loyalists migrated to the northern British colonies. They brought with them their identity as Angelicans, Presbyterians, Baptists, Congregationalists, and Methodists. Immigrants from Ireland and Great Britain also arrived, bringing Irish Roman Catholicism and Scottish Presbyterianism. The various Protestant sects (as they were then called) were granted "liberty of conscience" under British law. Roman Catholicism continued to thrive, despite Protestant attempts to discredit it.

In the eighteenth and early nineteenth centuries (indeed, through the early twentieth century), Roman Catholic women exerted influence primarily through their religious orders, while most Protestant women were relegated to household duties and pioneer survival tasks. Some women, however, were itinerant preachers and missionaries. In fact, revivalist and evangelical Protestantism empowered some women to speak, pray, and even preach in public. Women active in such traditions tended to be of lower social class than Anglican or Congregational women and were sometimes former Americans, who were less strict about gender roles than British North American colonists.

Immigration and migration westward were the immediate results of national confederation in 1867. Hundreds of thousands of immigrants came to Canada; most arrived as members of ethnic groups who shared strong cultural and religious traditions. Although invited by the Canadian government—which wanted to settle the interior prairies to allay their fears of American expansion—much concern was expressed by public leaders over immigrants' lack of English language skills and often differing or "radical" brands of Christianity. Ukrainian Catholics and Ukrainian Orthodox, Russian Mennonites, and even German Lutherans were viewed by already planted Christian denominations as needing cultural assimilation, if not Christian conversion. Political and religious leaders upheld a narrowly defined Christianity and blurred it with a British-style Canadianism.

Social and religious movements in the nineteenth and early twentieth centuries, in which many white women were involved, were directly related to the fear that the influx of ethnic peoples would make the Dominion of Canada less Christian. Sunday schools were established in the Atlantic provinces and spread westward. Teaching children reading, writing, arithmetic, and Bible was a way to Canadianize and Christianize new immigrants. Temperance and prohibition became central to the cultural and nation-building campaign. Letitia Youmans, a Methodist Sunday School teacher in Ontario, founded the first local Woman's Christian Temperance Union in 1874. Independent missionary societies were formed by Baptist, Presbyterian, Methodist, and Anglican women in the 1870s and 1880s. Such organizations focused on raising funds and personnel for home and foreign missions. They created opportunities for social interaction and, in some ways, provided parallel church structures for women who were otherwise prohibited from ordination and elected church leadership positions.

After industrialization occurred in the first decades of the twentieth century, urban missions became more numerous. Anglicans, Methodists, and Presbyterians formed deaconess orders—open only to single women—and founded women's vocational training schools between 1893 and 1908. Deaconesses provided cheap and dedicated labor to peoples' missions (as they were often called) and local congregations. Women within more sectarian groups, such as the Salvation Army, also emphasized city missions. Residential schools for native children were founded and were often staffed by white women who desired to teach the English language and impart Euro-Canadian values. While theological beliefs differed among Christian women, ideals of self-sacrificing service were often espoused. Organizations such as Canadian Girls in Training (f. 1917) shaped thousands of girls to this mindset and simultaneously provided significant opportunities for leadership and skill development.

Two world wars, economic depression, and prairie drought radically changed Canadian society in the twentieth century. Women's suffrage, under the leadership of Nellie McClung and others, was first legalized in the western provinces and became national in 1919. Quebec women received the ballot only in 1940, however, due to an opposing alliance of Catholic and political leaders. The Persons Act of 1929 declared that women were legally persons and therefore eligible for all political appointments.

The advancement of women within Christian churches lagged behind that of political and social institutions. The first white woman, Lydia Gruchy, was ordained in 1936 by the United Church of Canada, a union formed in 1925 by Methodist, Presbyterian, and Congregationalist denominations. The first black woman, Addie Aylestock, was ordained in 1951 by the British Methodist Episcopal Church. Ordination did not result in ecclesiastical equality but was a crucial step in that direction.

Canadians continue to struggle with issues of diversity, unity, and identity. In 1969, Canada became officially bilingual (French and English), and in 1972, it adopted a national policy supporting multiculturalism. While Christianity in Canada is predominantly tri-denominational (Roman Catholic, Anglican, and United Church), it exists in a variety of forms, from ultraconservative to ultraliberal. Women reflect this mosaic. Their beliefs differ on feminism, inclusive language, sexual orientation, and understandings of racism and classism. Some women have been empowered by Christianity and others have been oppressed by it. Privileged women have also used Christianity—even unknowingly so—to perpetuate imperialism and injustice against the less powerful, be they new immigrants or aboriginal peoples. At the end of the twentieth century, Christianity in Canada remains a mixed legacy.

BIBLIOGRAPHY

Bristow, Peggy, coordinator. *'We're Rooted Here and They Can't Pull Us Up': Essays in African Canadian Women's History*. 1994. One of the few sources available on this topic.

Butcher, Dennis L., et al., eds. *Prairie Spirit: Perspectives on the Heritage of the United Church of Canada in the West*. 1985. Essays on women's missionary societies and Nellie McClung.

Danylewycz, Marta. *Taking the Veil: An Alternative to Marriage, Motherhood, and Spinsterhood in Quebec, 1840–1902*. 1987. An important analysis.

Muir, Elizabeth Gillan, and Marilyn Fardig Whiteley, eds. *Changing Roles of Women within the Christian Church in Canada*. 1995. A variety of traditions and movements are highlighted in this volume.

Prentice, Alison, et al. *Canadian Women: A History*. 1988. The only historical survey on Canadian women yet published.

Simon, Sarah, et al. (as told to Joyce Carlson and Alf Dumont). *Bridges in Spirituality: First Nations Christian Women Tell Their Stories*. 1997. Biographical accounts of the spirituality and life experiences of five aboriginal women in Anglican and United Church traditions.

Warne, Randi R. *Literature As Pulpit: The Christian Social Activism of Nellie L. McClung*. 1993. Explores the feminism and social activism of one of Canada's significant leaders.

Numerous videos are available from The National Film Board of Canada, including documentaries on Roman Catholic, black, aboriginal, and contemporary Christian women. Contact The NFB, 3155, rue Cote de Liesse, St-Laurent, PQ H4N 2N4. http://www.nfb.ca

ELEANOR STEBNER

UNITED STATES

The two themes of cultural pluralism and the activity of women have been interwoven throughout the history of Christianity in the United States, beginning with European colonization in the seventeenth and eighteenth centuries.

COLONIAL SOCIETY

Convent life, brought to the Mississippi valley and the Southwest by French and Spanish nuns, offered some Native American converts a sphere of social respect, comfort, education, and some autonomy. However, most Native American women who were reached by European missionaries remained in their villages and grafted selective aspects of Christianity onto their own religious traditions, exhibiting more willingness to penetrate the mysteries of European Christianity than was true in reverse.

In Puritan society in New England, most white women accommodated to their socially prescribed subordination as helpmates to their husbands and co-authorities over children and servants, essential to maintenance of the Puritan order. However, Ann Hutchinson and circles of seventeenth-century women challenged religious and sexual subordination by applying the gift of God's grace and unity in Christ to themselves, often leading to their banishment from the colonies or trials for heresy and witchcraft. Domestic piety characterized the world and vision of most southern white women of Anglican and Catholic descent, while Quaker women developed a theology and Biblical exegesis of women's spiritual equality with men.

When full and equal participation was not extended to African Americans by the Church of England or dissenting Methodist and Baptist churches, they began to found their own denominations. However, preaching authority was not granted officially to black women by the African Methodist Episcopal Church and subsequent black denominations. This led black women to develop their own ministerial roles as revivalists, missionaries, charity workers, and educators, highly acceptable functions for them within these denominations during the eighteenth and nineteenth centuries.

THE REVOLUTIONARY WAR AND THE NINETEENTH CENTURY

Republican womanhood, the belief that women were meant to be guardians of the home and responsible to inculcate virtue in their sons, daughters, and husbands, increasingly defined white women's roles from the era of the American Revolution, during the 1770s and 1780s, through the nineteenth century. With the disestablishment of mainline Protestant denominations after the war, religion increasingly became a private concern located within the home—plural, personal, and voluntary. "The cult of true womanhood," defined by piety, domesticity, and submissiveness, characterized women's

role within Protestantism and Catholicism and is maintained today by the right wing of Christianity.

On the other hand, the Biblical mandate of equality before God and the revolutionary ideology of religious freedom and human rights provided the justification for human liberation employed by nineteenth-century feminists. Christianity became an infinitely variable instrument for enlarging women's sphere for white and black women, through utopian movements, revivals, evangelism, ordination, missionary work, and social reform.

Two female-founded sects, the utopian and millennialist Shakers, started by Mother Ann Lee, and the harmonial and metaphysical Christian Scientists, begun by Mary Baker Eddy, linked the perfection of humanity with the feminine as the higher element representing divine wisdom and love. The Shakers, however, were the only utopian community to develop a consistent theory of equal empowerment of women.

Nuns in immigrant Catholicism, founders and builders of schools, hospitals, and social service institutions, possessed a mobility, autonomy, and control over their own organizations possible for few other American women during the nineteenth century. However, in a predominantly Protestant society, the celibate woman was an object of superstitious fear, and nuns received the brunt of anti-Catholic bigotry.

Black and white women were often well-received as evangelists for revival meetings, as long as they did not seek actual ordination, because they were effective in bringing converts to Christ. Antoinette Brown became in 1853 the first fully ordained woman in a recognized American denomination, the Congregational Church.

Though usually denied ordination and leadership in mainline Protestantism, women created parallel church societies and sent deaconesses and female missionaries throughout the world. The development of separate spheres of service for women in church structures became the primary expression of women's work in Christian churches during the late nineteenth to mid-twentieth centuries. Separatist women's societies had the dual potential to contain and isolate women's work from the major service of clergy, and to enable women to develop autonomous power and self-conscious sisterhood.

Social reform became a religious calling to a large and active segment of women in nineteenth-century United States. Female reformers worked for the rights of women and entered all other areas of social action, including abolitionism, education, temperance, peace and arbitration, antilynching, prison reform, and professional social work. Among those religiously motivated female leaders were Jane Addams, Catherine

Jane Addams was an American social reformer and pacifist. She is best known as the founder of Hull House, one of the first social settlements in North America (National Archives).

Beecher, Dorothea Dix, Sarah and Angelina Grimke, Frances Willard, and Ida B. Wells-Barnett.

There was little participation by Catholic women in the nineteenth-century feminist movement. As an embattled cultural group, Catholic women put their energy into affirming their Catholic identity and proving to the Protestant majority the compatibility of Catholicism with American values. Only when the battle of Americanization was won by the mid-twentieth century, as exemplified in the election of John F. Kennedy to the presidency, did they turn to confrontation with the male hierarchy for enlarged roles in religious leadership.

THE TWENTIETH CENTURY

When a religious and ethnic subculture is oppressed by the dominant culture, as has been the case with American Indians, blacks, and Catholics, as well as with Jews, women put their ethnic identity first and concede leadership in the distinctive institutions of the subculture to men. Only when a certain cultural and social parity is established between the minority and majority communities do women turn their attention to feminist questions within their own communities. Accordingly, it is not surprising that the women's rights movement was dominated by middle-class Anglo-Saxon Protestant women in the nineteenth and early twentieth centuries. Only in the late 1960s, as Catholics emerged into cultural parity and middle-class status, have distinctive Catholic feminist movements begun to arise that challenge the patriarchalism of Catholic communal institutions. This process has also begun for a smaller group of middle-class black women. It has scarcely started at all for Indian women, whose primary battle is still the survival of their people as a distinct cultural community.

Like Catholic antimodernists, fundamentalists saw reaffirming women's "place" in a patriarchal social order as the key to reestablishing "true" Christianity. The Evangelical, Holiness, and Pentecostal traditions, however, diverge from fundamentalism in that they derive from experiential and charismatic movements which included women precisely because their presence validated the existence of the Holy Spirit. These movements found signs of the spirit outside rather than within institutions. In the 1930s this charismatic tradition became more institutionalized, and women were shut out of many roles in religious leadership that they had held in earlier days. Yet in the late 1960s, a new evangelical feminism was reborn which revived the earlier struggle between a liberatory and patriarchal charismatic tradition.

From the late nineteenth century, Protestant churches have followed a pattern in which women win laity-governing authority first at the local level and then at the level of conferences and synods. Only when women have gained full lay rights do these churches turn to granting ordained status to women. The process of winning full lay rights and finally ordained ministry for women began for Protestant churches at the end of the nineteenth century and did not progress to the granting of full ordination until the period from the mid-1950s to the 1970s. The winning of ordained status for many women by the mid-1970s has created a new era in the churches. Now fundamentalist, Roman Catholic, and Orthodox churches, which do not ordain women, feel mounting pressure from within and without to reconsider their historic position.

Women have increasingly enrolled in theological schools since the 1970s and now comprise more than 50 percent of the students at many liberal Protestant seminaries. Their presence has created a new base for feminist criticism within Biblical, theological, historical, and practical fields of Christian theological studies.

The last quarter of the twentieth century marked a major turning point in the relationship between women and religion in the United States. Only since the 1970s has the history of women and religion begun to be recovered on a broad scale and has an authentic female voice, individuated from men's, emerged through feminist theology. In the latter part of the twentieth century, women also were being integrated into mainline structures of religious institutions on a basis of more legitimate parity than had ever happened before. In the process, religious justifications constricting women to subordinate roles within the family and workplace were overthrown by large numbers of women and men. Ethnic minority women also discovered their own identity and interests, distinguished from that of men within their subcultures. Recovery of the history of women and the voice of feminist theology growing out of it, coupled with advances in the status and role of females, promise new issues arising from liberation in the twenty-first century.

BIBLIOGRAPHY

Axtell, James, ed. *The Indian Peoples of Eastern America: A Documentary History of the Sexes.* 1981.

Baum, Charlotte, Paula Hyman, and Sonya Michel. *The Jewish Woman in America.* 1976.

Braude, Anne. *Radical Spirits: Spiritualism and Women's Rights in Nineteenth Century America.* 1989.

Cott, Nancy. *The Bonds of Womanhood: "Woman's Sphere" in New England: 1780–1835.* 1977.

———. *The Grounding of Modern Feminism.* 1987.

———. *Root of Bitterness: Documents of the Social History of American Women.* 1972.

Creel, Margaret Washington. *"A Peculiar People": Slave Religion and Community-Culture Among the Gullahs.* 1988.

Douglas, Ann. *The "Feminization" of American Culture.* 1977.

Fox-Genovese, Elizabeth. *Within the Plantation Household: Black and White Women of the Old South.* 1988.

Hardesty, Nancy. *Women Called to Witness: Evangelical Feminism in the Nineteenth Century.* 1984.

Hill, Patricia R. *The World Their Household: The American Woman's Foreign Mission Movement and Cultural Transformation, 1870–1920.* 1985.

James, Edward T., Janet W. James, and Paul Boyer, eds. *Notable American Women, 1607–1950: A Biographical Dictionary.* 3 vols. 1971.

Karlsen, Carol F. *The Devil in the Shape of a Woman: Witchcraft in Colonial New England.* 1987.

Lindley, Susan Hill. *"You Have Stept Out of Your Place": A History of Women and Religion in America.* 1996.

Loewenberg, Bert James, and Ruth Bogin, eds. *Black Women in Nineteenth-Century American Life.* 1976.

Morgan, Edmund. *The Puritan Family: Essays on Religion and Domestic Relations in Seventeenth-Century New England.* 1944. Rev. ed., 1966.

Muncy, Raymond Lee. *Sex and Marriage in Utopian Communities.* 1973.

Painter, Nell Irvin. *Sojourner Truth: A Life, A Symbol.* 1996.

Premo, Terri L. *Winter Friends: Women Growing Old in the New Republic.* 1990.

Ruether, Rosemary R., and Rosemary S. Keller, eds. *In Our Own Voices: Four Centuries of American Women's Religious Writing.* 1996.

———. *Women and Religion in America: A Documentary History.* 3 vols. 1981.

Scott, Anne Firor. *Natural Allies: Women's Associations in American History.* 1991.

Sicherman, Barbara, and Carol H. Green, eds. *Notable American Women*, Vol. 1, *The Modern Period.* 1980.

Sweet, Leonard. *The Minister's Wife: Her Role in Nineteenth-Century American Evangelicalism.* 1983.

Ulrich, Laurel. *Good Wives: Images and Reality in the Lives of Women in Northern New England, 1650–1750.* 1982.

Weaver, Mary Jo. *New Catholic Women: A Contemporary Challenge to Religious Authority.* 1985.

Weisenfeld, Judith, and Richard Newman, eds. *This Far by Faith: Readings in African-American Women's Religious Biography.* 1996.

Welter, Barbara. *Dimity Convictions: The American Woman in the Nineteenth Century.* 1976.

Wessinger, Catherine, ed. *Religious Institutions and Women's Leadership: New Roles Inside the Mainstream.* 1996.

See also **Blackwell, Antoinette Louisa; Evangelical, Holiness, Pentecostal, and Fundamentalist Christianity; Feminisms; Fundamentalism; Ordination.**

ROSEMARY KELLER

AMERICAN PROTESTANT WOMEN'S
FOREIGN MISSIONARY ACTIVITY
The involvement of American women in world missions changed dramatically over the nineteenth and twentieth centuries. Before 1800, American Protestant women had little or no involvement in world mission, except for a few who accompanied their missionary

husbands in foreign mission work. These women generally were limited to the role of housewife and mother.

Active evangelization and reform involvement on the home front among poor southern blacks and whites, Native Americans, Hispanics, and European and Asian immigrants was a powerful stimulant for women to expand into foreign mission work. Denied participation by denominational general mission boards, American women began in the early 1800s organizing themselves to support foreign missions. During the first half of the nineteenth century women's support of foreign missions grew but was mostly limited to fund-raising, education, correspondence, and prayer. At the same time, the roles of single and married domestic missionary women began to expand to include evangelistic work among women and children, medical and educational instruction, and numerous other kinds of training. Some individual women initiated frontier mission work, and their reports home greatly inspired their female supporters at home.

By 1860 American women started to form their own denominational training schools and missionary societies as sending agencies. However, the movement did not gain momentum until after the Civil War. White women, many of them former abolitionists and experienced activists, who had assumed new roles and responsibilities while their men were fighting the war, found a new focus for their energies. The formation of women's missionary societies ballooned until by 1910 there were forty-four such groups in the United States with three million members from every denomination. By this time there were two thousand missionaries abroad, mostly single women doing work that focused on women and children.

Support and administrative personnel in these missionary societies were all female and mostly volunteers. The organizations were highly successful and fully supported and staffed by women. Not only did women missionaries significantly outnumber men during these years, but they also were given a certain amount of administrative latitude. These women's mission groups started teacher training institutions, hospitals, and medical training programs for women abroad. They also ran diverse ministries among women and children.

By the end of the nineteenth century, there was an extensive network among women missionary leaders who developed programs to more effectively carry out work in the field. Two notable women mission leaders were Helen Barrett Montgomery and Lucy Peabody who encouraged ecumenical unity among mission societies. Their most lasting accomplishment was the establishment of the interdenominational Central Committee for the United Study of Foreign Missions, the first interdenominational project of the women's boards. The committee published and distributed books, and participated in education programs across the country that featured short-term summer schools in missions. By 1917 there were twenty-five such schools, which enrolled almost twelve thousand women and girls. After thirty-eight years the committee had distributed more than four million copies of books on Christian missions around the world.

Agencies governed by men began to pressure women's societies to consolidate with the denominational mission boards. They argued that women's missionary societies drained off limited church funds. Eventually, women gave in and merged but stipulated that they retain leadership in their societies. Within twenty years, forty-eight women's societies closed. At first, women retained some administrative positions, but slowly they were replaced by men. By the 1950s very few women held leadership positions in missionary societies. Women's missionary societies shrank in size and effectiveness and often were absorbed into denominations' general women's organizations.

American mission thinking in the late nineteenth and early twentieth centuries emphasized direct evangelism and "civilizing" activities to convert peoples in Asia, the Middle East, and Africa to the "American" version of Christianity. Women missionaries hoped to transfer Western gender-linked roles and functions to these women and girls. Women missionaries could teach female converts the Bible and, in so doing, would prepare these women to be proper wives for new male convert pastors.

The motivation for mission work did not vary much for black, white, or other women. Some were influenced through experiences at churches, camps, or colleges with missionaries who had returned home from overseas or were home on furloughs. Others went because they had married someone who had been appointed a missionary or who had returned home on a furlough. In addition, it was popular and acceptable for a woman to serve as a missionary.

Some women felt the advantage of being a woman missionary in working with women and girls. Others felt that there was a lack of opportunity for women to advance into the church hierarchy. They also complained that indigenous men would not take directions or suggestions from women. Local government officials would not accept women as equals. Women were not allowed to preach and, to a large extent, single or married women missionaries remained in the shadow of men who were doing "real" mission work. The salary of a single woman missionary was ten to fifty percent less than a single male missionary. Until the 1960s married women missionaries did not receive an actual salary, although a male missionary's salary was increased by about thirty percent when he married.

Administrative opportunities in the mission field came to men and women fairly equally. When they first went to the field women were given more freedom for church leadership than was possible in the United States. Opportunities for leadership and participation in decision making came earlier and to a greater extent for women in the mission field than in the church at home. But because women could not be ordained ministers, they also could not receive full missionary status and were limited to serve as "assistant missionaries."

Frustrations that women faced in their early years of foreign mission service included the lack of language instruction or preparation for the new culture. Nurses struggled with the problems of not enough drugs or staff, or being put in charge of a whole hospital without being given adequate training or support. Women missionaries also suffered because their children frequently were far away in boarding schools.

Disappointment in church work was also felt by many women missionaries. American church leaders refused to use the nationals' music in the church. There never seemed to be enough resources for all of the programs, particularly those geared to women and girls.

However, there were plenty of times of fulfillment and joy for women's missionary work. It was especially rewarding to these missionaries when indigenous women teachers went back into their communities or nurses returned to mission hospitals after certification. Women missionaries also were fulfilled by seeing growth in women's work and district women's meetings, or having women lead a worship service for the first time.

Although the American Protestant women's mission movement was predominantly white, African American, Chinese American, Native American, and Latina women also were involved. American women missionaries worked overseas in Africa, China, India, Japan, Korea, Latin America and the Caribbean, and the Middle East. Most of their work was in converting women to a Protestant faith, but they also reached out to women of other religions, including Islam and Buddhism. Their efforts among women of these religions did not result in large numbers of conversions. Yet relationships did often develop between American women and the indigenous women of diverse foreign cultures and religions.

The most important and lasting contribution of these women missionaries was in the transformation of societies. They founded schools and colleges, opened medical clinics and hospitals, and supported orphanages. These women missionaries underwent a cultural transformation themselves, which allowed them to identify with a foreign culture and empathize with the condition of foreign women.

BIBLIOGRAPHY

Beaver, R. Pierce. *All Loves Excelling: American Women in World Missions.* 1968.

———. *American Protestant Women in World Mission: A History of the First Feminist Movement in North America.* 1968.

Beck, Lois, and Nekki Keddie, eds. *Women in the Muslim World.* 1978.

Bode, Mable. "Women Leaders of the Buddhist Reformation." *Journal of the Royal Asiatic Society* (1893).

Borthwick, Meredith. *The Changing Role of Women in Bengal, 1849–1905.* 1984.

Bowie, Fiona, Deborah Kirkwood, and Shirley Ardener, eds. *Women and Missions, Past and Present: Anthropological and Historical Perceptions.* 1993.

Flemming, Leslie A., ed. *Women's Work for Women: Missionaries and Social Change in Asia.* 1989.

Graham, Gael. *Gender, Culture and Christianity: American Protestant Mission Schools in China, 1880–1930.* 1995.

Hill, Patricia R. *The World Their Household: The American Woman's Foreign Mission Movement and Cultural Transformation, 1870–1920.* 1985.

Hunter, Jane. *The Gospel of Gentility: American Women Missionaries in Turn-of-the-Century China.* 1984.

Hutchison, William. *Errand to the World.* 1987.

Jacobs, Sylvia M., ed. *Black American Missionaries in Africa.* 1982.

Robert, Dana Lee. *American Women in Mission: A Social History of Their Thought and Practice.* 1997.

See also **Christianity: In Africa; Christianity: In Latin America and the Caribbean; Christianity: In Asia.**

SYLVIA JACOBS

Apostolic Religious Orders and Communities

Any survey of Christian women's religious orders, congregations, and institutes has an implicitly conservative dimension since they are by definition communities that have been authorized by the male ecclesiastical hierarchy. This entry therefore surveys Christian women, regardless of their labels, who self-identify as religious communities; live celibately, poorly, and in obedience to a religious discipline or superior; and dedicate themselves not only to prayer but also to active service of their neighbors.

Christian women have gathered together in celibate communities devoted to prayer and contemplation since early Christian times. Although little is known regarding early Christian communities of women described, for example, as virgins, widows, and *kanonikai,* sporadic references indicate that many showed generosity toward the needy. Thereafter and prior to 1100 C.E., women's communities were overwhelmingly monastic and dedicated primarily to prayer. The occasional services they provided, such as schooling for children, hospitality to travelers, and provision of food, shelter, and nursing to the poor and sick, tended to be offered within their monasteries, although nuns and canonesses sometimes left their residences to perform charitable deeds.

The first abundant evidence of women's communities dedicated specifically to "apostolic" service of neighbor dates from about the twelfth century, the very period when many Christians sought to imitate Christ and his apostles specifically through good works. Through the fourteenth century growing numbers of women in the newly formed cities of Western Europe dedicated themselves to a life of piety involving prayer, celibacy, and, often, charitable works, especially toward the poor and sick in urban streets, homes, hospices, and hospitals. These women lived both individually and in communities and were variously identified by a host of names still poorly understood by historians—for example, Sisters of Penance, *mulieres sanctae, mantellate, pinzochere, beatas,* Beguines, and tertiaries. Many of these women were inspired by the same impulses toward poverty and service then giving rise to the male Franciscans, Dominicans, and other mendicant orders; however, because church legislation consistently encouraged and often forced these women to curtail such active engagement through the imposition of cloister, they never received recognition equivalent to that accorded to the mendicant males (who, it should also be noted, often wished to have little to do with them).

As this diverse movement of pious women increased, so did the church's interest in regularizing it by placing these women under the authority of an approved religious rule, such as the rule of St. Benedict, and subjecting them to direct clerical control, trends often supported by civil authorities. The papal bull *Periculoso,* issued in 1298 and mandating the enclosure of all nuns, not only typified the reaction of many male authorities to women's new visibility, but also provides evidence that women identified specifically as nuns also desired to serve outside the cloister. While some communities accepted or even welcomed regularization and cloister, others submitted only reluctantly. Those who refused to submit opened themselves to a variety of charges, including heresy, and rarely survived.

Women in and out of cloister, however, continued to serve their neighbor. While most cloistered women and quasi-religious, especially those in northern Europe, led withdrawn lives dedicated to contemplation, others, particularly Italian women, engaged in charitable

activities as well. Some cloistered nuns, for example, educated young girls attending schools attached to their monasteries. Religious women in military orders, such as the Order of the Hospital of St. John of Jerusalem and the Teutonic Knights, tended the sick and indigent, as did many women following the Rule of St. Augustine, who lived in or alongside the numerous hospitals appearing in towns across Europe, such as the Hôtel-Dieu in Paris. Although the many late medieval nonmonastic and unregulated communities, including Dominican and Franciscan tertiaries, indicate that *Periculoso* was by no means universally observed, the fate of others, such as Bernardina Sedazzari's community of Corpus Domini in Ferrara (1406), indicate a pattern of forced monastic enclosure. Nonetheless, women's ministries continued to multiple and, by the early sixteenth century, included initiatives in the areas of health care, religious education, care of orphans, and assistance to "fallen women."

The Protestant Reformation and subsequent Catholic legislation mark a new stage in attempts to corral women's communities into cloister and limit their activities, and in women's resistance. The apostolate of Louise Torelli's Sisters of St. Paul, working alongside the male Barnabites, aiding orphans, the sick, and providing religious instruction, abruptly ceased when a papal visitor enforced enclosure in 1552. Significantly, Torelli herself refused cloister and founded instead a new community dedicated to the education of girls. Groups such as Angela Merici's Company of St. Ursula (1535), dedicated to the education of young girls, escaped cloister by wearing secular dress and living individually in their homes. Shortly after Merici's death in 1540, however, in response to conservative social and religious pressures both within and outside of the Company, the women were urged to adopt a standard form of dress, live in communities, and submit to strict clerical control. Legislation by the Council of Trent (1545–1563), extended by the papal edict *Circa pastoralis* in 1566 and supported by civil authorities, aimed to impose cloister on all nuns and female religious. Nevertheless, some uncloistered communities of Ursulines succeeded in continuing their work "in the world" until the early seventeenth century in France and even beyond that in Italy.

Through the nineteenth century, women in female institutes that did not accept solemn vows and cloister were no longer considered "true religious." This ecclesiastical pressure eventually led communities such as the Visitation of Holy Mary, founded in France in 1610 by Francis de Sales and Jane Frances de Chantal, reluctantly to accept cloister and forgo their visits to the sick. Many others, encouraged by bishops and lay people who had come to rely on the women's work, found ways around the new legislation using legal and semantic niceties. The Daughters of Charity, for example, founded by Vincent de Paul and Louise de Marillac (1633), proudly claimed the lesser designation "secular daughters" rather than "religious," which freed them to run soup kitchens and care for needy constituencies.

Papal legislation adapted only slowly to women's persistent efforts to offer social services. In England in 1609, Mary Ward tried to found the Institute of the Blessed Virgin Mary as an order of uncloistered nuns styled after the Jesuits. Although her "Jesuitesses" were suppressed in 1631 and she herself briefly imprisoned as a heretic, schismatic, and rebel, in 1703 the papacy finally recognized the Institute and its educational work, albeit identifying the women as "ecclesiastical persons" rather than true religious. Numerous post-Reformation women's communities, in contrast to the more contemplatively oriented medieval women's communities, now considered their good works a primary and essential expression of religious vocation.

Women's communities fared better than their male counterparts as revolutionary movements in the late eighteenth and early nineteenth centuries spread throughout Europe, in part because the women were more courageous and in part because their charitable and educational works were viewed more positively by revolutionary authorities than the activities of male clerics and religious. Many religious women in France temporarily abandoned their convents but remained faithful to their vows and continued their good works discreetly by wearing secular dress and living singly, in pairs, or in very small groups in private homes.

In the nineteenth century women's apostolic communities, still overwhelmingly institutionalized within the church, achieved what is known as a "golden age," in which their numbers grew dramatically, especially in France, but also elsewhere in Western Europe. Religious women came for the first time to outnumber religious men. Many of these new communities arose in reaction to revolutionary violence and ideology and promoted a spirituality focused on making reparation to God and reestablishing societal order. While explicitly rejecting Enlightenment thinking, many communities actually reflected it through their interest in education, especially for the young. Orders such as the cloistered Society of the Sacred Heart of Jesus, founded in France by Madeleine Sophie Barat (1800), educated both well-to-do and poor girls, albeit in separate schools. The social and economic problems consequent upon nineteenth-century industrialization also contributed to the astonishing growth of women's communities, many of them semicloistered, and intensified their activities in various kinds of medical and social work—without diminishing their emphasis on interiorized spirituality.

In the nineteenth century many women's communities intensified their work in various kinds of medical and social work (National Institutes of Health/Corbis).

Missionary growth also mushroomed in the nineteenth century, especially in regions colonized by Europeans. Many communities retained their European cast for some time, whereas others were quicker to attract indigenous young women and hand over authority to them. Communities of religious women completely indigenous to Latin America, Africa, and Asia, were slow to flourish.

Although apostolic religious communities of women belong overwhelmingly to the Roman Catholic faith, there are a few Protestant communities engaged in active works of charity, teaching, and social work, including Anglican-Episcopalian groups in Ireland, Great Britain, and the United States, the Evangelical Marian Sisterhood founded in Germany, and the Swiss-founded ecumenical communities of Grandchamp.

The Second Vatican Council (1962–1965) proved to be a watershed for Catholics around the world, but most especially for female religious. They generally responded more enthusiastically than did the clergy, male religious, and many sectors of the laity to its new vision of Christian life: the Council affirmed and extended recent theological formulations emphasizing a more open and horizontal ecclesiastical community, participatory decision making, and the Christian obligation to eliminate rather than simply alleviate poverty and suffering. Inspired as well by the burgeoning women's movement, nuns and sisters began to challenge and indeed dismantle what they saw as outdated and unjust structures of authority not only "in the world," but also within their communities and in an overwhelmingly male-dominated church. A desire "to be in the world for the world" led to a radical decline in distinctive religious dress, regimented and institutional life-styles, and cloister and semicloister and the spiritual elitism they fostered. Work in schools, hospitals, and other social services continues to occupy the majority of nonretired religious women; a very visible minority engages in political activism, professions such as law, and movements of liberation of all sorts around the world.

Many women have left religious life, some disillusioned by the changes, many more dissatisfied with their pace, or no longer feeling a need for a separate, celibate religious life-style. The decline in membership, most notable in the United States, Canada, and Europe, reflects also a lack of new members and losses through the deaths of an aging population. Within the United States, for example, numbers of women religious rose 23 percent from 1950 to 1966, and then sharply plummeted after Vatican II by 50 percent from 1965 to 1995. Communities of religious women are growing elsewhere: in East Africa the number of sisters has increased from about 2,800 in 1961 to almost 11,000 in 1992, paralleling the increase among Catholic laity there.

Although women's religious communities have radically diminished in number, they have increased in strength in terms of their education, social awareness, and courage in the face of an uncertain future.

BIBLIOGRAPHY

Although there is much scholarship devoted to the history of individual female religious leaders and founders, particular women's communities, and women religious within specific chronological and geographical boundaries, there are very few general historical overviews of Christian women's communities. On female and male religious, see "Vie consacrée," *Dictionnaire de spiritualité*, vol. 16 (1994), coll. 663–705. For monographs on women religious in particular see Jo Ann Kay McNamara, *Sisters in Arms: Catholic Nuns Through Two Millennia* (1996), and Patricia Ranft, *Women and the Religious Life in Premodern Europe* (1996). Helpful introductory essays include, despite its lack of notes, Jeanne de Charry, "Vita religiosa femminile: Evoluzione e sviluppi fino al Vaticano," translated from unpublished French into Italian by G. G. Sarzi Sartori, *Qua-derni di diritto ecclesiale* 4 (1991): 355–369; Philip Sheldrake, *Spirituality and History: Questions of Interpretation and Method* (1992), pt. 2, chap. 5 on religious life and chap. 6 on the beguines; and, despite a debatable correlation of historical periods with issues regarding the vows, Marie Augusta Neal, "From Nuns to Sisters: Three Significant Changes," in her *From Nuns to Sisters: An Expanding Vocation* (1990).

A sampling of works on women religious who engaged in serving others includes: Herbert Grundmann, *Religious Movements in the Middle Ages: The Historical Links Between Heresy, the Mendicant Orders, and the Women's Religious Movement in the Twelfth and Thirteenth Century*, translated by Steven Rowen (1995; orig. German ed., 1935), helpful despite its lack of comment on women's ministries; Ruth P. Liebowitz, "Virgins in the Service of Christ: The Dispute over an Active Apostolate for Women During the Counter-Reformation," in *Women of Spirit: Female Leadership in the Jewish and Christian Traditions*, edited by Rosemary Radford Ruether and Eleanor McLaughlin (1979), pp. 131–152; Charmarie J. Blaisdell, "Angela Merici and the Ursulines," in *Religious Orders of the Catholic Reformation*, edited by Richard L. DeMolen (1994); Patricia Burns, "Aux origines de la Visitation: La vraie pensée de St. François de Sales," in *Les religieuses dans le cloître et dans le monde* (1994); Elizabeth Rapley, *The Dévotes: Women and Church in Seventeenth-Century France* (1990); Marguerite Jean, *Évolution des communautés religieuses de femmes au Canada de 1639 à nos jours* (1977); M. Ursula Stepsis and Dolores Liptak, *Pioneer Healers: The History of Women Religious in American Health Care* (1989).

Helpful introductions regarding contemporary women's religious life in the United States include Patricia Wittberg, *The Rise and Fall of Catholic Religious Orders* (1994), and Sandra M. Schneiders's influential work, *New Wineskins: Re-imagining Religious Life Today* (1986).

Unless otherwise indicated, further bibliography is provided in all of the above works.

CATHERINE M. MOONEY

History of Study

The history of Christianity has been told in many different ways over two millennia. The New Testament Book of Acts, which immediately follows, in the Bible, the story of the life of Jesus as told in the four Gospels, has traditionally been understood as the first self-consciously Christian church history. By the fourth century C.E., the time of the consolidation of Christianity into an official religion of the Roman Empire, there were a number of additions to this history, notably those written by Eusebius of Caesaria, a confidant of Emperor Constantine. Eusebius sought to demonstrate that Christianity supersedes all other earthly traditions. Women are mentioned in these early works only when they stand out as the mothers or wives of the great male protagonists of the official story, although some are depicted as the ones who brought the male members of their family to Christianity.

The modern idea of Christian history arose during the Enlightenment as a reconsideration of the relationship between political, religious, and intellectual movements in Western history. Edward Gibbon's *Decline and Fall of the Roman Empire* (2 vols., 1776–1788) is a classic example, claiming a connection between the rise of Christianity and the fall of Roman civilization. Much of modern study of Christianity has been in dialogue with Gibbon, often attempting a sympathetic view of Christianity as world culture.

Three modern projects of Christian history deserve mention in this context. At the end of the nineteenth century, Adolph von Harnack's seven-volume work concentrated on Christian dogma, the officially proclaimed beliefs of the Christian community as mediated by the ecclesiastical hierarchy, from the first to the sixteenth century. A century later, Jaroslav Pelikan published a five-volume history of Christian doctrine, exploring what the church has believed, confessed, and taught in every age, as a guide to what a historian might consider "the church" in each historical context. Bernard McGinn's still unfinished four-volume history of Christian mysticism has by far the widest and most comprehensive view of Christianity, including its liturgical theology and affective spirituality.

Of all of these sweeping studies of Christianity, only McGinn's makes room for the experience of women at any significant level. Yet, even McGinn sets up a definition of "mysticism" that favors a systematic, and to some degree philosophical, quest. Because McGinn focuses exclusively on the "high" theological traditions from which women were systematically excluded, his study excludes many of the most influential Christian female mystics and spiritual leaders, notably the twelfth-century German Benedictine Elisabeth of Schönau.

Women have been excluded from Christian history for various reasons: because women were not the main players of the story; because so little evidence of their lives is available; and because their religious activities fall outside the defined parameters of study. Certainly, women's voices have been muted: until very recently, the original sources were badly edited (if at all), and English translations were woefully inadequate, both technically and conceptually. The difficulty of finding good critical editions and translations of works by important literate medieval Christian women, such as Hildegard of Bingen, has been an ongoing problem. This shortcoming has been partially addressed by large publishing projects, for example the Paulist Press *Classics of Western Spirituality,* which have made the writings of Christian women widely available in English for the first time.

These limitations are largely due to the assumption that Christian women's voices and experiences were not as important as men's. This is an inevitable conclusion as long as the study of Christianity is limited to the works that shaped the official world of the medieval hierarchy, a male construction. Under the influence of feminist historiography, a reconstruction of women's roles in the Christian tradition has led to a new understanding of women's special role in the Christian ascetic tradition. These new primary and secondary resources have changed the discourse of the study of Christianity with regard to women. A number of scholars, notably Penelope Johnson and Jo Ann McNamara, have contributed to this revised history, but the work of Caroline Walker Bynum has had the widest and deepest influence.

Bynum's conception of major trends and ideas in Christian history paints a new picture that is not fixated on the official acts of the hierarchical elite but considers the religious experience of the wider Christian community. She has portrayed the language surrounding Jesus as mother, the intricate connections between women, food, and eucharistic piety, and the theological implications of ancient and medieval theories of bodily fragmentation. This new perspective on Christian history helps us to see some traditional elements of piety, for example, mimesis of the passion of Christ, in relation to centrally important concepts. The inclusion of women's piety has led to a dramatic shift in the foreground and background of the study of Christianity. Teachers, scholars, and students of Christianity find themselves in a new landscape, defined by a wider discourse of their historical roles.

This new landscape also reveals an insufficient accounting for a number of medieval men, who, as deviants from the Christian consensus, have been excluded from the larger history. There has been a revival of intellectual interest in Christian spiritual traditions, orthodox and heterodox, elite and popular. Because so much of our evidence for women in Christian culture fits into this broad definition of *spirituality,* the two movements of historical rediscovery, of women's history and the history of Christian spiritual traditions, have strengthened and complemented one another. Mystics, prophets, and spiritual leaders, male and female, are now a part of the portrait of "official" Christianity. We now have the resources, both primary and secondary, for a whole new study of Christianity.

BIBLIOGRAPHY

The works of Caroline Walker Bynum are the best place to see the impact of feminist thought on the contours of the historiography of Christianity. Three of Bynum's books are especially important in this regard:

Bynum, Caroline Walker. *Fragmentation and Redemption: Essays on Gender and the Human Body in Medieval Religion.* 1991.

———. *Holy Feast and Holy Fast: The Religious Significance of Food to Medieval Women.* 1987.

———. *Jesus as Mother: Studies in the Spirituality of the High Middle Ages.* 1982.

The first history of Christianity dates from the fourth century:

Eusebius of Caesaria. *Ecclesiastical History.* Translated by Roy J. Deferrari. 2 vols. 1953–1955.

For classical multivolume histories of Christianity, each with its own particular point of view, see the works of Edward Gibbon and Adolph von Harnack:

Gibbon, Edward. *The Decline and Fall of the Roman Empire.* 2 vols. 1776–1788.

von Harnack, Adolph. *History of Dogma.* 7 vols. 1885. Translated by Neil Buchanan. Reprint 1961.

Many contemporary women scholars are exploring problems and questions having to do with women's participation in Christian society. Two of the most important scholars in this area are Penelope D. Johnson and Jo Ann McNamara:

Johnson, Penelope D. *Equal in Monastic Profession: Religious Women in Medieval France.* 1991.

McNamara, Jo Ann. *A New Song: Celibate Women in the First Three Christian Centuries.* 1983.

McNamara, Jo Ann, ed. and trans., with John E. Halborg and E. Gordon Whatley. *Sainted Women of the Dark Ages.* 1992.

Recent multivolume histories of the Christian tradition, each from a particular standpoint of inquiry, are by Bernard McGinn and Jaroslav Pelikan:

McGinn, Bernard. *The Presence of God: A History of Western Christian Mysticism.* 4 vols. 1991–.

Pelikan, Jaroslav J. *The Christian Tradition.* 5 vols. 1971–1989.

E. ANN MATTER

Circle

The circle, as a potent symbol of perfection and plenitude, figures prominently in religious imagination and history. It often represents the primordial womb or cosmic egg, the source of creation itself. The solar and lunar disks are the most obvious natural inspirations for circle symbolism. Their circular movement and celestial cycles, perfect and immutable, symbolize the endless flow of time, the turning wheel of life. The Sanskrit word *cakra*, meaning "wheel," refers to the sun's chariot, a potter's wheel, and the circle of the zodiac.

The Babylonians used the circle, divided into 360 degrees, as a measure of time, transmitted in the image of a serpent swallowing its own tail, *uroboros* ("tail eater"). In classical antiquity this icon designated the fullness of time and the endless universe. Indian iconography shows the god Siva dancing inside a cosmic ring, depicted as a serpent with a head at each end. In Benin the divinity, Dan, is represented as a snake wrapped in a coil that binds heaven and earth. Here the encircling snake represents the spatial as well as the temporal cosmos.

In Christian medieval imagery the terrestrial paradise is circular; the twelve disciples of Christ circle the vault of heaven as zodiacal constellations. Muslim mystics, the Sufis, are known for their circular dancing that imitates the rotation of the planets orbiting the sun. In Eastern religions, the circle represents the realm of human action and the labor of perfection; mandalas (a Sanskrit word meaning circle) are depictions of a divine cosmos drawn in ritual and used to aid contemplation. The circular design of cities such as Varanasi (Benares) and Jerusalem and ritual constructions such as the Sun Dance lodges of the North American Plains Indians replicate the cosmic model. At the center of the microcosm is the palace or temple, an *axis mundi* that provides access to power and orientation within the universe.

The circle may symbolize the hidden perfection and diffused goodness of the creator. Alchemical philosopher Hermes Trismegistus stated "God is a circle whose centre is everywhere and the circumference nowhere." In Taoism, a circle with a point marking the center represents the supreme power, the Tao. The circle as sign of both cosmos and creator is also common in the iconographic traditions of Africa. Among the Baluba of Zaire, God is called "the circle of the beginning," and is represented on ritual objects by a simple circle (Faïk-Nzuji, p. 77). In ancient Benin, circular patterns representing cosmological dynamics were inscribed on royal brass plaques. Even today, these signs are associated with Olokun, god of the waters, and are drawn in chalk at the center of Olokun shrines.

Associated with mystical insight, concentric circles symbolize stages of interior, spiritual perfection. In Christian tradition, three concentric circles depict the Trinity. Throughout sub-Saharan Africa, three concentric circles represent abundance and cosmic harmony. In Nigeria, they are the triple sign of the Yoruba Earth

In a painting by Haitian artist Nicolas Jallot, a Vodou priest draws on the ground within a circle of worshipers clothed in white, while observers in brightly colored clothes stand outside the circle (Gamma-Liaison, Inc.).

goddess; for the Baluba, this sign, *mànyìngu,* indicates the plenitude of the supreme being. A ubiquitous variant is the concentric circle twisted at its center. Having neither beginning nor end, this motif represents the supreme being, eternity, and permanence.

Making a ritual circuit around a holy person, place, or object, one correlates everything within the circumference with the center and circumscribes a sphere of protection and sanctification. As a rite of orientation, circumambulation also bears a cosmic value. The traditional Muslim pilgrimage to Mecca, the hajj, literally means "to describe a circle." It includes circling the Kaaba monument (regarded as the navel of the universe) seven times, the presumed number of the celestial spheres. Encircling movements are often ascribed to primordial beings. The Yoruba divinity, Eshu, is said to have circumambulated the world and so is considered the original iconographer of the cosmos.

The circle and its center, cycles, and encircling motions are the marks of sacred and generative powers. They are to an extent analogous to women's physiological attributes and processes: the creative sphere of the womb, the menstrual cycle, and gestation. These are indeed valued in religion as embodied sacrality. Yet the signification of the circle surpasses gender and reproductive powers, however compelling and determinative they are in the human career.

BIBLIOGRAPHY

Aniela Jaffé. "Symbolism in the Visual Arts." In *Man and His Symbols.* Edited by Carl G. Jung. 1964.

Chevalier, Jean, and Alain Gheerbrant, eds. *Dictionnaire des symboles: Mythes, rêves, coutumes, gestes, formes, figures, couleurs, nombres.* 1969. Reprint, 1982.

Cooper, J. C. *An Illustrated Encyclopedia of Traditional Symbols.* 1978.

Faïk-Nzuji, Clémentine M. *Symboles graphiques en Afrique noire.* 1992.

Jung, C. G. *Collected Works.* Translated by R. F. C. Hull. 1959.

McClain, Ernest G. "Circle." In *The Encyclopedia of Religion.* Edited by Mircea Eliade. 1987.

LAURA GRILLO

Clare of Assisi

Clare of Assisi (c. 1194–1253), Christian saint and foundress, was born to a well-to-do family in Assisi, Italy. Extensive hagiographic documents, including a Legend and the Acts of the process for her canonization, in addition to her own writings, provide the main sources for her life. Inspired by the charismatic Francis of Assisi, Clare escaped from her family home in 1211 or 1212, promised obedience to Francis, and withdrew to a church he had repaired, San Damiano, where she resided enclosed the remainder of her life. With other women joining her there and entire monasteries following her lead, Clare became founder of the female branch of the Franciscan order, later designated the Poor Clares. Exalted for her prayer, humility, virginity, and silence, Clare is best known for her commitment to radical material poverty, notably when many male Franciscans were modifying this ideal. She struggled successfully to obtain a papal "privilege of poverty" permitting the "poor ladies," as they were then known, to live without property, a significant departure from previous monastic practice.

The authenticity of her writings has been disputed. Virtually all scholars accept as hers four letters to Agnes of Prague. The "form of life" attributed to Clare, often acclaimed as the first religious rule for women written by a woman, includes signs of her influence and even her words but borrows from earlier rules and likely involved another compiler. Debate continues regarding a testament and a blessing, notwithstanding their acceptance by many scholars. A letter to Ermentrude of Bruges appears to be a seventeenth-century summary of two now lost letters.

After many years of illness, Clare died on 11 August 1253. She was canonized just two years later.

BIBLIOGRAPHY

The best edition of Clare's corpus in the original Latin, with concordances and indices, is *Concordantiae ver-*

bales opusculorum S. Francisci et S. Clarae Assissiensium, edited by Giovanni M. Boccali (1976; rev. and enl., 1995). An earlier edition with Italian on facing pages but without concordance is *Opuscula sancti Francisci et scripta sanctae Clarae Assissiensium,* translated by Luciano Canonici (1978). A more accessible and somewhat inferior edition, with Latin and French on facing pages, is *Claire d'Assise: Écrits* (1985), edited and translated by Marie-France Becker, Jean-François Godet, and Thaddée Matura. In addition to her corpus, pivotal medieval documents about Clare including the Legend, letters, and legislative texts, may be consulted in their original Latin with Spanish translation in *Escritos de Santa Clara y Documentos Contemporáneos,* edited by Ignacio Omaechevarría et al. (1970; rev. and enl., 1982). For the Acts of the Process of Canonization, no longer extant in Latin, see the fifteenth-century Italian version edited by Zeffirino Lazzeri in "Il processo di canonizzazione di s. Chiara d'Assisi," *Archivum Franciscanum Historicum* 13 (1920): 439–493. An English translation of texts attributed to Clare and medieval texts about her is *Clare of Assisi: Early Documents,* edited by Regis J. Armstrong (1988; rev. and enl., 1993).

Scholarship regarding Clare has recently burgeoned, although much of it uncritically repeats earlier views regarding Clare and the texts associated with her or is otherwise of mediocre quality. A useful biography is Marco Bartoli's *Chiara d'Assisi* (1989); English translation by Sister Frances Teresa, *Clare of Assisi* (1993). For further bibliography see the above works; *Bibliografia di Santa Chiara di Assisi: 1930–1993* (1994), edited by Isidoro de Villapadierna and Pietro Maranesi; and *St. Clare of Assisi and Her Order: A Bibliographic Guide,* edited by Mary Francis Hone (1995).

CATHERINE M. MOONEY

Classism

Classism refers to groupings within societies along major hierarchical lines, particularly those based on the capitalist mode of political economy, which originated with the Enlightenment of the seventeenth and eighteenth centuries. In classist societies, human dignity is denied to individuals, families, and groups according to authoritative interpretations of subtle as well as highly theoretical concepts and consequences of social origins, patterns of cultural dispositions, and stratifications of political power. The injustice of class oppression has three dimensions: social capital (ancestry, education, language, social distance), cultural capital (style of life, interpersonal relations, etiquette), and political capital (economic income, ideology and politics,

religious affiliation, motivation, expectation). Class elitism demands that persons validate their humanness by conspicuously possessing these social, cultural, and political properties in accordance with the orientation and inscriptions of the small, but wealthy, ruling class.

Oliver C. Cox has presented the thesis that the capitalist political economy generates a political order that is ostensibly democratic but leaves economic power unchecked. Cox insists that race and gender dynamics must be understood basically as aspects of labor relations. The more that employers depress women's wages, restrict women to poor working conditions, and limit job opportunities, the greater is the opportunity to seize surplus and maximize profits. Women of color, occupying the lowest rungs of the labor hierarchy, are subjected to the full force of ruthless entrepreneurial exploitation. Neither racism nor sexism can be eliminated unless these divisions of labor are broken.

In Cox's view, a capitalist political economy also generates a suitable religion to loosen those social restraints that are rooted in mysticism and cultural rituals. In other words, Cox argues that capitalism is a form of social organization in which the distinctive economic order slowly shapes government and religious structures into a neutralized network of national and territorial units, so that commercial and exploitative economic relationships can flourish.

BIBLIOGRAPHY

Cannon, Katie G. *Katie's Canon: Womanism and the Soul of the Black Community.* 1995.
Cox, Oliver C. *Capitalism and American Leadership.* 1962.
———. *Caste, Class and Race.* 1948.
———. *The Foundations of Capitalism.* 1959.
Marable, Manning. *How Capitalism Underdeveloped Black America.* 1983.

KATIE CANNON

Clothing

In its presentation of social, religious, or psychological information, clothing is a cogent form of communication. Individuals have used apparel to express self-awareness, particularly within the context of a public affiliation such as a religious group, whereas authority figures have used dicta about attire and dress as the means to telegraph attitudes and policies about tradition, hierarchy, and ethics. Clothing has been protection and refuge for the wearer, but it has acted also as a protection and a refuge for society against the nudity of the wearer. Over the course of history, it has been quite

A young Algerian woman is heavily veiled and covered. The women of Islam have been charged with the necessity of being modest to the point of being invisible in public (Michael Maslan Historic Photographs/ Corbis).

usual for invading or colonizing powers to regard the nudity of tribal and native peoples with not only cultural discomfort but moral indignation. Nudity calls into question the messages of clothing, which is rarely arbitrary but rather a set of clues to the identity of the wearer.

The majority of Neolithic figurines that wear clothing are female: the female form is presented in a kind of wrap-around skirt, of varying lengths, that in some cases especially hugs the hips. Some others also indicate stoles or covers for the shoulders. In ancient Crete and early Vedic India, among other cultures, representations of goddesses and other women usually depicted them clothed below the waist but with the upper torsos, including the breasts, uncovered. Some scholars have speculated that the prevalence of such a skirt in the early representations of goddesses and in the dress of common women suggests that such clothing was both a protective device (for that most critical area, the area of conception and birth) and possibly a sign of fertility and procreative availability, notably in ritual performance. In ancient Mesopotamia, Sumerian women

were more likely to wear linen tunics from shoulder to ankle that were wrapped to expose the right arm and shoulder (men generally wore "skirts" of sheepskin until the third millennium). In the divine pantheon of the ancient Sumerians, the deities were patrons of culture; both gods and goddesses were responsible for the emergence of human civilization, which itself was gender-patterned according to the knowledge bestowed upon it by the divinities. The goddesses were especially responsible for three activities deemed intrinsic to a civilized life: eating grain (*nisba*), drinking beer (*ninkasi*), and wearing clothes (*uttu*). The Mesopotamian epic *Gilgamesh* demonstrates the cultural significance of eating, drinking, and wearing clothes: it is through the intervention of a courtesan who teaches him how to wear clothing and how to eat and drink that Enkidu is able to learn the essentials of civilization and, thus "humanized," confront the powerful Gilgamesh.

Clothing is therefore transformational by its own creation and in its ability to alter the social pedigree, spiritual status, gender value, or cultural role of the wearer. Male authorities have used the transformational process of clothing to control what they insist is the female tendency toward lustful sexuality and seduction of men, envy, jealousy, pride, and narcissism—vices that the female penchant for finery abets and celebrates. Because the vitality as well as the viability of internal virtue depends, in this view, on the suppression of external extravagance, religious and secular authorities of many cultures and traditions have emphasized self-effacing, plain, and unpretentious dress for women. For example, women members of the ancient Greek Pythagorean community in southern Italy (third century B.C.E.) were urged by the male leaders toward purity, even austerity, in their attire, in an effort to nullify what was worst in the female personality: they were expected to dress all in white, without adornment, of humble (i.e., not silken) natural material; avoid the wearing of gold or emeralds especially, since such jewels were expensive and proud; and refrain from applying makeup or anything artificial to their persons since such adornment would excite jealousy among the women of the community.

The Augustan poet Ovid became well known for his poems *Amores, Ars Amatoria,* and *Medicamina faciei feminae,* satirical verses about the lives of Roman women and their predilection for fine (read foreign, un-Roman) clothing, makeup, and adornment. Roman women, particularly *matronae,* were required to assume somber and staid attire befitting their roles as wives and mothers; their *stolae* and *pallae* were made of woven material, in appropriately sober colors. Only the (semidivine) emperor could wear a robe entirely of "royal purple"; high-ranking priests could wear a similarly designed but lighter-colored robe with a stripe of purple, but Roman women of any class were forbidden for centuries to wear such purple at all. The toga, the garment symbolizing citizenship in ancient Rome, could be worn only by men and women who were prostitutes or who had been found guilty of adultery. The holiest women of Rome, the vestal virgins, were, like all holy women, constrained to wear simple yet particular clothing. When first initiated into the vestal priestesshood, the candidates wore the red headdress (*flammeum*) and the six braids (*sex crines*) of a bride, after which, for the next thirty years, though avowed virgins, vestals wore the long gown (*stola*) and the hairbands (*vittae*) of married women: their clothing coincided with the public perception of marital status.

Biblical Judaism gave a married woman the freedom to enjoy cloth and material finery; however, she was expected to reserve her most attractive apparel for private enjoyment in the home (Ps. 45:14). The prophets depict harlotry as the excessive adornment with jewels, silken robes, and other expensive raiment (Hos. 2:2–13; Ezek. 23:5–31). The Sabbath, however, must be honored by sumptuous and fine dress. The Mishnah obliged married women to keep their hair covered, and Orthodox Jewish women still may wear head covering.

Christianity, beginning with the New Testament (in passages such as Corinthians 11:2–16 or 1 Timothy 2:8–15) preserves the admonition for women to assume modest attire and to cover their heads. The early Christian Fathers, such as Clement of Alexandria (*Stromata* and *The Teacher*, passim) and Tertullian (*On the Apparel of Women* and *On the Veiling of Virgins*), formalized concern over female dress, with varying defenses: decorous clothing was associated with non-Christian, especially pagan, women, and thus Christian women were to distance themselves externally as well as internally from any suggestion of a heathen connection; the preference for ornate dress was perceived as an attachment to things of the corporeal world from which Christianity urged its followers to detach themselves; and a preoccupation with clothing and physical attractiveness was regarded by Christian leaders as an act of seduction and as proof of pride, that original sin which caused Eve to disobey God and lead humankind out of Eden. The Christian tendency to look with fierce misgiving upon external embellishment and regard it as a form of sinful pretension, defiance of divinely ordered nature, and an offense to spiritual health, finds echoes in the sartorial injunctions of such Christian sects as the Puritans, the Shakers, and the Old Amish, who required of their followers, male and especially female, to clothe themselves with "plain" and simple attire.

The women of Islam have also been charged with the necessity of being modest to the point of being invisible in public, dissociated from and unavailable to the secular world. Muslim women are enjoined to clothe themselves apart from the rest of the world. Depending on the specific Islamic society, all women must wear special clothing at all times outside the confines of the home and at prayer, in the presence of Allah, such as *jilbab* (cloak or mantle), chador (square of dark fabric that falls from the head to the ankles and is pinned under the chin), *dir'* (chemise), *izar* (wrap for the body), *khimar* (veil, kerchief), *niqab* (head veil that completely covers the face), *burqu'* (face mask of leather or stiffened fabric covering the entire face except the eyes and worn primarily by Islamic women of the Gulf nations), or *magneh* (head covering for Iranian women). Proscriptions against the adoption, especially in public, of "secular" (and therefore immodest) dress by Islamic women attest to the evolution of an acculturated norm that was broadly derived from the divine legislation in the Qur'an of the *hijab* (curtain, screen) as revealed in sura 33:53. This revelation to the Prophet by Allah is considered to have been initially little more than a provision to secure for the Prophet's wives a degree of privacy and security from visitors to his domicile. The *hijab* was originally just that, then: an actual screen or curtain that separated the women's quarters from the more public areas of the dwelling and so protected the women from the unwanted attentions of unfamiliar men. Soon, the revelation of female cloistering was extended to all upper- and upper-middle-class women of Islam. In the hadith the text indicates that the meaning of the term had evolved to include not only its literal meaning, but also its more analogous connotation: *hijab* is not just the object that causes separation and seclusion, but the very seclusion itself.

Seclusion away from the public became seclusion *in* public (sura 33:59 and sura 24:31). Although the initial revelation was probably directed toward the family of the Prophet, its injunction was gradually extended to all Muslim women, who were expected to model themselves after the women of the Prophet's family. As Islam expanded into foreign territories and alien mores, the interpretation of the degree of seclusion and the extent of veiling was colored by cultural influences. However, the Islamic imprint of female veiling became so pronounced, especially in countries with an Islamic majority or strong presence, that other faiths, like the Baha'i in the Middle East and the Hindus in India, enjoined their women to be veiled (a full chador in the case of the Baha'i faith; head veiling, especially for married Hindu women) in public. It should go without saying, however, that for the devout Muslim woman (especially the educated of the middle class), conservative dress (e.g., *hijab*) is not only an emblem of religious piety and cultural authenticity, it is also an instrument of liberation that provides her with a form of "seclusion" in public so that she may engage in tasks and businesses outside the domestic boundary.

Women throughout history have been intimately connected to the making of clothing, especially the weaving of cloth. Across cultures, representations of the good wife in art and literature usually depict the woman engaged in three essential tasks: tending to children, cooking, or weaving and spinning. In the mythic constructs of most civilizations, however, the making of clothing was considered more than a functional task. In fact, weaving and the creation of cloth (and thereby clothing) came to represent another act of transformation associated with the feminine, in this case, a magical craft that generated mythologies and mythic symbols. Woman was charged not only with guardianship of the human body, in her creation of its cloth coverings, but also, by analogy, with the spiritual protection of the fabric of its existence.

BIBLIOGRAPHY

Ahmed, Leila. *Women and Gender in Islam.* 1992.

Alexandre, Monique. "Early Christian Women." In *A History of Women: From Ancient Goddesses to Christian Saints.* Edited by Pauline Schmitt Pantel. 1992.

Balsdon, J. P. V. D. *Roman Women: Their History and Habits.* 1962.

Barber, Elizabeth Wayland. *Women's Work, The First 20,000 Years: Women, Cloth, and Society in Early Times.* 1994.

Beard, Mary. "The Sexual Status of Vestal Virgins." *Journal of Religious Studies* 70 (1980): 12–27.

Carmody, Denise Lardner. *Women and World Religions.* 2d ed. 1989.

Casagrande, Carla. "The Protected Woman." In *A History of Women: Silences of the Middle Ages.* Edited by Christiane Klapisch-Zuber. 1992.

Hughes, Diane Owen. "Regulating Women's Fashions." In *A History of Women: Silences of the Middle Ages.* Edited by Christiane Klapisch-Zuber. 1992.

Kraemer, Ross Shepard. *Her Share of the Blessings.* 1992.

Lannoy, Richard. *The Speaking Tree: A Study of Indian Culture and Society.* 1974.

Lefkowitz, Mary R., and Maureen B. Fant. *Women's Life in Greece and Rome: A Source Book in Translation.* 1982.

Neumann, Erich. *The Great Mother.* 2d ed. Translated by Ralph Manheim. 1991.

Pickthall, Mohammad Marmaduke, trans. *The Meaning of the Glorious Koran.* 1963.

Scheid, John. "The Religious Role of Roman Women." In *A History of Women: From Ancient Goddesses to Christian Saints.* Edited by Pauline Schmitt Pantel. 1992.

Stowasser, Barbara Freyer. *Women in the Qur'an: Traditions and Interpretations.* 1994.

See also **Body**; **Craft**; **Hair**; **Weaving**.

JUNE-ANN GREELEY

Colonialism and Postcolonialism

Until the last quarter of the twentieth century, studies of women and religion were largely institutional (convents or sisterhoods) or hagiographic (saints). With the devolution of European empires after World War II, scholars have developed a postcolonial analysis of the relations between colonizers and colonized that has important implications for such studies. This postcolonial approach asks new kinds of questions about the colonizers and the colonized, takes gender, race, and class as critical analytical tools, and seeks a better understanding of the complexities of women's experiences in relation to religion and religious practices. Addressing southern Africa and the Indian subcontinent, to take two examples only, this new scholarship has sought to examine the impact of the social structures of power on women and religion in both colonial and precolonial eras and has been acutely conscious of the specificities of historical context. New historical and ethnographic questions have probed socially and culturally imposed constraints on women's behavior as well as women's resistance and agency. Postcolonial scholarship explores the ways ideologies and cultural prescriptions have been critical to establishing self-identities and the identification of "others." Both colonial and precolonial periods have come under scrutiny, which has meant the reassessment of women's interactions with religion, indigenous and imposed.

Postcolonial scholarship has redefined the study of colonialism by stressing how the structures of power and authority were exercised by strong states over weak ones, by colonial administrators and missionaries over colonized peoples, and men—in kinship and institutional structures—over women. Past histories of colonization were written primarily by the colonizers themselves, and primarily from their point of view. Postcolonialist studies recognize the need to question all old assumptions and to seek to understand the interplay of the ideologies and structures of gender, race, and class that underpinned both the imperial centers themselves and their empires. The process includes the deconstructing of notions of tradition as used throughout the colonial period and a new appreciation of the dynamics of change always at work. This process reveals the complementary and conflicting stances taken by missionaries, travelers, settlers, and government officials and the vested interests and adaptations characterizing colonized societies.

Christian missionaries have been a particular focus of postcolonial studies. Whether the attempt to convert involved black Jamaican slaves, the Tswana or Xhosa of southern Africa, or the young women and men of India, the scrutiny of missionary efforts has examined the links between deeply embedded cultural beliefs of gender, race, and class and their religious messages. The complex relationships between European Christianity and local converts, a majority of them low-caste or marginal women, as well as the way European and colonized women interacted have called into play new questions and new methodologies made possible by feminist analyses and cultural studies. This exploration has redrawn the boundaries between precolonial, colonial, and postcolonial periods, emphasizing continuities in the midst of change.

BIBLIOGRAPHY

Berger, Iris. *Religion and Resistance: East African Kingdoms in the Precolonial Period.* Gwelo, 1979.

Blunt, Allison, and Gillian Rose, eds. *Women and Space: Colonial and Postcolonial Geographies.* 1994.

Chakravarti, Uma. "Whatever Happened to the Vedic *Dasi*? Orientalism, Nationalism, and a Script for the Past." In *Recasting Women: Essays in Indian Colonial History.* Edited by Kumkum Sangari and Sudesh Vaid. 1992.

Chanock, Martin. *Law, Custom, and Social Order: The Colonial Experience in Malawi and Zambia.* 1985.

Cock, Jacklyn. "Domestic Service and Education for Domesticity: The Incorporation of Xhosa Women into Colonial Society." In *Women and Gender in Southern Africa to 1945.* Edited by Cheryl Walker. 1990.

Comaroff, John, and Jean Comaroff. "The Colonization of Consciousness." In their *Ethnography and the Historical Imagination.* 1992.

Guy, Jeff. "Gender Oppression in Southern Africa's Precapitalist Societies." In *Women and Gender in Southern Africa to 1945.* Edited by Cheryl Walker. 1990.

Hall, Catherine. "Missionary Stories: Gender and Ethnicity in England in the 1830s and 1840s." In *White, Male and Middle Class: Explorations in Feminism and History.* 1992.

Hobsbawm, Eric, and Terence Ranger, eds. *The Invention of Tradition.* 1983.

Jeater, Diana. *Marriage, Perversion, and Power: The Construction of Moral Discourse in Southern Rhodesia.* 1993.

Mani, Lata, "Contentious Traditions: The Debate on *Sati* in Colonial India." In *Recasting Women: Essays in Indian Colonial History.* Edited by Kumkum Sangari and Sudesh Vaid. 1992.

Parker, Kenneth. "Fertile Land, Romantic Spaces, Uncivilized Peoples: English Travel Writing about the Cape of Good Hope, 1800–1850." In *Expansion of England: Race, Ethnicity and Cultural History.* Edited by Bill Schwartz. 1996.

Pratt, Mary Louise. *The Imperial Eye: Travel Writing and Trans-culturation.* 1992.

Tharu, Susi. "Tracing Savriti's Pedigree: Victorian Racism and the Image of Women in Indo-Anglican Literature." In *Recasting Women: Essays in Indian Colonial History.* Edited by Kumkum Sangari and Sudesh Vaid. 1992.

Viswanathan, Gauri. "Coping with (Civil) Death: The Christian Convert's Rights of Passage in Colonial India." In *After Colonialism: Imperial Histories and Postcolonial Displacements.* Edited by Gyan Prakash. 1995.

Wright, Marcia. "Bwanikwa: Consciousness and Protest among Slave Women in Central Africa." In *Women and Slavery in Africa.* Edited by Claire Robertson and Martin Klein. 1983.

DOROTHY HELLY

Community

While there are some religious practitioners, such as hermits and *sunnyasins*, who require a solitary existence, the more common religious experiences occur within communities, which may be more or less cohesively organized. These religious communities are social groups that interpret, nourish, and sustain a particular tradition's experiences of the sacred. Although there is a modern trend to see religion as an individualistic experience, many people find a communal setting supports and nourishes their spirituality. This spiritual dimension of religious communities derives from a visible structure that provides identities, roles, and privileges for members, both female and male.

On one level, both women and men participate in the life of a religious community. Hindu women bathe in the Ganges river along with Hindu men; Muslim women accompany Muslim men on the hajj to Mecca; Jewish women observe the Sabbath along with Jewish men, and Christian women receive the same blessed bread that Christian men receive.

But in the more specific structures of these communities gender makes a difference. Woman's identity in religious communities is largely determined by the fact that she bears and nurtures children, which, in the monotheistic faiths, are viewed as functions belonging to God's natural law. Because of her roles as wife and mother, her primary community is that of home and family, and here is where she fulfills her religious obligations. Muslim women, for example, contribute to Islam by keeping the family united and strong (Stowasswer, 1994, p. 127). In Judaism, the mother is exempt from reading Torah so that she may have more time for her family role (Plaskow, 1991, p. 84), which becomes ritualized when she lights the candles at the beginning of the Sabbath meal (p. 48). Men, on the other hand, are assigned the more public functions of maintaining the larger community found at the synagogue, mosque, or church. While in most religions women are full members of the larger community and recipients of all spiritual benefits, it is only recently that they have been able to perform more public roles such as rabbi, elder, or minister, and then only in the more modernized branches of traditional religious communities such as Reform Judaism and some Protestant sects of Christianity.

In some religious communities there are opportunities for women to assume roles outside the traditional ones of wife and mother. While there are histories of solitary women ascetics in Hinduism and Islam, these women have diverted from the normative roles. For the most part, when a woman chooses to remain single and follow a spiritual path she usually does so within a single-sex community such as a Catholic convent or a Buddhist *sangha*. These communities are entered into freely and for the purpose of achieving the spiritual goal of contemplation or liberation. Catholic nuns live together, taking vows of poverty, celibacy, and obedience. They hold all things in common and perform the work that they believe is God's will as expressed through their sisters. They believe that their good works and their personal and communal prayer life will achieve for them union with God, which is a preview of the life to come. Catholic religious communities of brothers also take such vows and dedicate their lives in a similar manner. Male communities of priests, however, support their members not only in their goal of union with God but also in a ministry that more fully participates in Christ's work by representing him in the sacramental rituals (McBrien, 1981, p. 811).

Buddhist nuns also hold all things in common but do so in obedience to the precepts of the historical Buddha. Because in his era the Buddha feared the negative impact of having a female following, he set up eight special rules as well as a book of additional rules for women's communities (Murcott, 1991, p. 196). These rules serve mainly to assure that nuns would always remain under the guidance and protection of the monks. However, even though she is politically subordinate to monks, a nun who follows these rules is considered a spiritual equal to her male counterpart, possessing the same opportunity to achieve enlightenment and to help others along the path (Murcott, p. 10).

In more recent times some women have criticized traditional institutions as being male dominated and therefore have attempted to form communities that would enable them to practice a more female-centered spiritual life. Some of these communities are loosely organized and come together mainly for the purpose of worshiping in a context of feminine symbols and feminist theology. For example, some Christian women have formed WomanChurch (Ruether, p. 1985, p xii) for the purpose of transforming Christian rituals to deepen and nourish their spirituality. Jewish women are attempting to create communities where they are called to read Torah and fully participate in a minyan, the quorum of ten required for worship. These structural elements of religious communities are becoming as egalitarian as the spiritual elements have been in the past. In short, the structure of religious communities is gradually evolving alongside the more modern view of the equality among women and men.

BIBLIOGRAPHY

McBrien, Richard P. *Catholicism.* 1981.
Murcott, Susan. *The First Buddhist Women: Translations and Commentary on the Terigatha.* 1991.
Plaskow, Judith. *Standing Again at Sinai: Judaism from a Feminist Perspective.* 1991.
Ruether, Rosemary Radford. *Womanguides: Readings Toward a Feminist Theology.* 1985.
Stowasser, Barbara Freyer. *Women in the Qur'an: Traditions and Interpretation.* 1994.

MAURA O'NEILL

Comparative Religion

"Comparative religion" is one of many terms used to designate ways of studying religion that take seriously the diversity of religions. The term has gone into and out of fashion over time, and it is not always clear how comparative religion should be differentiated from the history of religions or the phenomenology of religion, if at all. Studying religion non-confessionally, cross-culturally, and comparatively is an academic discipline that first emerged in Europe in the latter quarter of the nineteenth century but did not become common in North America until the 1960s. By whatever name it is called, however, the cross-cultural comparative study of religion used methods that are radically different from all previous ways of studying religion and reaches conclusions that have revolutionized previous understandings of religion.

The most basic and distinctive trait of comparative religion is the insistence that religion cannot be adequately understood unless the scholar is familiar with several different religions, preferably religions quite dissimilar from one another and often widely divergent in time and place. Max Müller (1823–1900), the German Indologist often credited as "the father of comparative religion," stated, "To know one religion is to know none." Thus, without the "comparative mirror," to use the felicitous phrase of historian of religions William E. Paden, one is ill-advised to assume that one understands even familiar religions. Certainly one would be extremely ill-advised to assume that familiar religions are the gauge and measure of religion everywhere. As with foreign travel or the study of another language, one often learns as much about what is familiar as about what is "other" when one engages in comparative study.

The emergence of the comparative method depended on several other factors. Foremost was increasing knowledge of the non-European world. As European colonialism penetrated into every corner of the globe, it became increasingly evident that Christianity was not the only religion with highly developed intellectual, spiritual, and aesthetic resources and a widespread, loyal following. Also crucial was an explosion of archaeological discovery that pushed back knowledge of religious history into pre-Biblical times. When this new information about religions of pre-Biblical antiquity was combined with newly available information about the religions of small-scale societies around the world, interest in questions about the origin and development of religion soared. This interest was also fueled by evolutionary theory, new to the European intellectual world.

Partly derived from the intellectual currents listed above and partly derived from the humanism common to the European Enlightenment, the most far-reaching conclusion of the comparative study of religion is that religion is a human phenomenon subject to historical and cultural causes and conditions. However else they may differ, all modern understandings of religion based on the comparative method agree that human creativity in response to the mysteries of life and death and the awesomeness of the phenomenal world, rather than extra-human intervention into human activities, is sufficient to explain the presence of religion in all human cultures. Since they are human phenomena, religions reflect the economies, political structures, and social worlds of the cultures in which they are located and change with the changing concerns and conditions of the societies in which they are practiced. Studying religion as a human activity best illumined by use of the comparative mirror is radically different from previous Western understandings of religion that had stressed a nonhuman source for one uniquely relevant religion. According to this school of thought, religion is better explained by comparative than by theological methods, and the comparative method, according to its contemporary practitioners, though not its nineteenth-century practitioners, does not include criteria for judging that one religion is unequivocally superior to all others.

Also important to the study of comparative religion are attempts to investigate and analyze whether common structures and functions can be found beneath the widely varying beliefs and practices of religion viewed cross-culturally. Is there something so essential to religion that without it religion ceases to exist? Are there discernible outlines or common building blocks constitutive of most or all religions? Do the vastly different religions of humankind serve similar purposes through time and across space? Different schools of thought have grown up in answer to these questions. But the cross-cultural comparative study of religion could accurately be credited with discoveries essential to a modern understanding of religion: that symbols, not doctrines, function as the primary building blocks of religious universes, that myth or sacred story is more basic than empirical history in religious narrative, and that ritual is the most basic type of religious behavior.

Despite its many virtues, however, comparative religion until recently shared the major defect of religion and religious studies in general. Comparative religion was unrelievedly androcentric until a significant number of women entered the field and feminist scholars began their critique of the discipline in the early 1970s. None of the major early theoreticians of the discipline that are mentioned in most histories of comparative religion were women. However, a few prominent women scholars did make important contributions to the study of non-Western religions. Mrs. C. A. F. Rhys Davids (1857–1942) and I. B. Horner (1896–1981) made significant contributions to Buddhist studies, and Jane Ellen Harrison (1850–1928) was one of the more important scholars of ancient Greek religion of her generation.

Early theoreticians in comparative religions assumed that universal principles could be applied to all cultures everywhere and paid little attention to the specifics of race, class, gender, or culture. They wrote and thought in the generic masculine, in common with all scholars of their day. As a result, few considerations of women and religion are found in the early classical literature of the field. The sole exception is early matriarchal theory associated primarily with J. J. Bachofen (1815–1887). According to him, male-dominated religions and cultures were universally preceded by a stage of "mother-right" in which women's interests and the "feminine" pole of cosmic duality—the moon, night, earth, darkness, and death—were favored over men and the masculine elements, and goddesses were universally worshiped. But this peaceful society was destined to be overcome by its opposite and, according to Bachofen, superior stage of cultural evolution. Matriarchal theory was debated seriously for some decades at the end of the nineteenth century, but it was forgotten soon thereafter and is rarely mentioned today in histories of comparative religion.

When the first women's movement ceased to be important in public consciousness, between the 1920s and the 1950s, women's participation in the field of comparative religion and scholarly interest in women's religious roles declined, as happened in all other professions. That situation changed only slowly with the second wave of feminism. The percentage of women engaged in comparative religion is not nearly so high as in theological fields and problems of androcentrism are not as widely acknowledged. Several important recent accounts of comparative religion, by W. E. Paden and W. H. Capps, mention the impact of feminist methods on the discipline only in passing.

Nevertheless, important feminist scholarship in comparative religion has been written since the middle 1970s. Three trends stand out: first, a new, more sophisticated version of a prepatriarchal hypothesis; second, interest in views about women found in the world's religions; and third, attention to the lived reality of women's religious lives.

Though interest in the origin of religion has waned considerably, feminist scholars such as Marija Gimbutas and Peggy Reeves Sanday have renewed the question of the origin of male dominance, and the suggestion that male dominance is a late development in human history has become controversial. Some popular versions of this hypothesis merit little scholarly attention, since they are based more on fantasy than on research, but the more carefully researched and cautiously phrased versions of the prepatriarchal hypothesis deserve serious consideration. The prepatriarchal hypothesis is based on archaeological reconstructions from Çatal Hüyük in Antolia, prehistoric Old Europe, and Crete, which indicate widespread worship of god-

desses and appreciation of the sacredness of females. The conclusion that women were relatively self-determining and important in society as a whole is not unreasonable, given that none of these societies was aggressive or warlike and none featured great economic inequities. Cross-cultural inferences from anthropological studies of recent foraging and horticultural societies strengthen this interpretation. Though gender roles are virtually universal, male dominance is not; interdependence between women and men is much more common, even though men and women are rarely, if ever, equal in the modern meaning of the term, which implies a complete absence of gender roles. However, though the case has not been made for all lines of cultural evolution, the situation does seem to change with the emergence of complex stratified societies; significant gradations of wealth and power, urban culture, state systems, and the invention of complex agriculture (as opposed to horticultural gardening) are more conducive to male dominance than the conditions found in simpler societies. Many scholars have traced the religious and mythological consequences of these social changes as male deities eclipse female deities and women are relegated to an increasingly passive role, at least in public rituals.

The world's major religions all emerged relatively recently, so it is no surprise that they are publicly male dominated, and often misogynist (fearing or hating women) as well. Androcentric scholarship took public male dominance at face value and concluded that studying women would be irrelevant or uninteresting. But feminist scholars have insisted on revisiting the topic of what the world's religions have to say about women, with often surprising results. Everywhere, overt male dominance hides many important female religious leaders, and teachings about the inferiority of women are often contradicted in less well known layers of the tradition. Women often react with frustration, anger, and reforming zeal when they discover that their religion may not be as male dominated as they had been led to believe by their male religious teachers. Feminist scholars are also attempting to compare the world's religions on the basis of how women fare in these traditions, rather than on the more usual bases for comparison, such as views about deity or human nature. To date, no definitive or satisfying comparisons have emerged.

The most significant topic to emerge in feminist comparative religion is the rich variety of women's religious lives. Rather than studying only traditional prescriptions about women, usually male-authored, early feminist theoreticians in comparative religion suggested that the focus be shifted to women's religious lives. The first book to do this, N. A. Falk and R. M. Gross's *Unspoken Worlds: Women's Religious Lives*, demonstrated how fruitful such scholarship could be. Later, S. S. Sered demonstrated that in many parts of the world, everyday domestic cults, which parallel the male-dominated major world religions, are almost entirely in the hands of women. Studies such as these make clear several generalizations. The most important is that whatever a religion may say about women's limitations and however restricted their public religious lives may be, in every culture women do have religious lives. Because of sexual segregation, their religious lives are often totally inaccessible to male researchers, which helps explain why they were so little known and so misunderstood by androcentric scholarship. Women's opinions, shared with other women, about their tradition's attitudes toward women, the extent to which they conform to male demands, the ways in which they cope with institutionalized inferiority, and women's covert avenues to power and self-determination all are interesting and important topics for the feminist scholar who does not assume that public male dominance is the whole story for any religion. A second significant generalization is that in many religious contexts, women have highly developed rituals and traditions that are not shared with men and do not depend upon the presence or approval of male religious authorities. Often these religious practices are little known to men of the culture and only rarely are they discussed in the tradition's sacred texts. A third generalization follows from the tendency for textual religions to be male dominated; insofar as religion is defined as a textual tradition largely in the hands of institutionalized authority figures, women are usually at the margins of religion. But religion usually cannot be limited to texts and formal authorities; in most cases ecstatic emotional practices more dependent on the appropriate psychological temperament are also important. Women are rarely successfully barred from such dimensions of religion; as a result famous mystics and founders of new religious movements are frequently female.

BIBLIOGRAPHY

Bianchi, Ugo. "History of Religions." In *The Encyclopedia of Religion*. Vol. 6. Edited by Mircea Eliade. Pp. 399–408.

Bynum, Caroline Walker, Steven Harrell, and Paula Richman. *Gender and Religion: On the Complexity of Symbols*. 1986.

Capps, Walter H. *Religious Studies: The Making of a Discipline*. 1995.

Eck, Diana. *Encountering God: A Spiritual Journey from Bozeman to Benares*. 1993.

Eliade, Mircea. *Patterns in Comparative Religion*. 1958, 1963.

Falk, Nancy A., and Rita M. Gross, eds. *Unspoken Worlds: Women's Religious Lives*. 1989.

Gross, Rita M. *Feminism and Religion: An Introduction*. 1996.

King, Ursala, ed. *Religion and Gender*. 1995.

Paden, William E. *Religious Worlds: The Comparative Study of Religion*. 1988.

Sered, Susan Starr. *Priestess, Mother, Sacred Sister: Religions Dominated by Women*. 1994.

Sharma, Arvind. *Today's Women in World Religions*. 1994.

———. *Women in World Religions*. 1987.

Sharpe, Eric J. *Comparative Religion: A History*. 1975.

———. "Comparative Religion." In *The Encyclopedia of Religion*. Vol. 3. Edited by Mircea Eliade. 1987. Pp. 578–580.

Smart, Ninian. "Comparative-Historical Method." In *The Encyclopedia of Religion*. Vol. 3. Edited by Mircea Eliade. 1987. Pp. 571–574.

———. *The Science of Religion and the Sociology of Knowledge: Some Methodological Issues*. 1973.

Young, Serinity. *An Anthology of Sacred Texts by and About Women*. 1993.

See also **Gimbutas, Marija; Harrison, Jane Ellen.**

RITA M. GROSS

Compassion

A sympathetic concern for others' well-being, a good heart, is the foundation for all Buddhist practices of ethics, meditation, and wisdom, for a beginner as well as an enlightened being. To act for the welfare of all beings was Gautama Buddha's chief motivation for seeking enlightenment and, after attaining it, for teaching others the path to enlightenment. This altruistic attitude is comprised of compassion (Sanskrit *karunā*) and loving kindness (Sanskrit *maitri*) for all beings. A vast compassion is to be developed together with deep wisdom (*prajñā*), insight into emptiness or no-self; these are the two chief causes and qualities of an enlightened being.

Compassion and love need to be enhanced by meditative practices in order not to be limited to just one's friends and to ultimately include all living beings as one's objects. Thus one needs to cultivate immeasurable compassion—the fervent wish that immeasurable numbers of beings be free from suffering—and immeasurable loving-kindness—the wholehearted wish that they all have happiness.

A mural painting depicts White Tārā, goddess of compassion, in the Potala Palace, Lhasa, Tibet (Christine Kolisch/Corbis).

Great compassion (Sanskrit *mahākarunā*) in Mahāyāna Buddhism is an even more active form of compassion—the attitude of universal responsibility, one's own wholehearted determination to help all beings become free from suffering. This evolves into a Buddha's compassion, conjoined with profound wisdom, which is expressed in superknowledges and powers that enable her or him to manifest in infinite universes to help infinite numbers of beings be free from the misery of countless rebirths. The bodhisattva path to buddhahood, which is comprised of the six transcendent perfections—generosity, patience, ethics, enthusiastic effort, meditation, and wisdom, is based on the motivation of great compassion.

An important model for compassion prevalent in many texts from the Theravada and Mahayana traditions is feminine—the kindness of one's mother (and all one's mothers in previous lives). The goal is to attain the level of great compassion for all beings like that of a mother's intense loving concern for her sick child. This example is the key image in one of the two main meditation lineages for becoming a bodhisattva in the Indo-Tibetan Mahāyāna tradition: the sevenfold method that begins by contemplating one by one the infinite number of beings who have been one's kind mothers in countless previous lives. This will generate in the meditator a sense of closeness and gratitude and the heartfelt need to reciprocate their kindness with love and compassion. A preliminary step begins with cultivating an even-mindedness to all beings, which removes the prejudices evoked by attachment, neglect, and hostility toward friends, strangers, and enemies respectively. A prerequisite is an awareness and understanding of one's own sufferings and its causes in order to be able to understand the depth and scope of all beings' misery and dissatisfaction. When an affectionate, loving, and compassionate attitude is expanded into great compassion and love for all, it can finally be transformed into *bodhicitta*—the heartfelt spontaneous aspiration to attain enlightenment for the sake of helping all beings. The second meditation method—the equalizing and exchanging of self and other, eloquently described in Shantideva's eighth-century guide to the bodhisattva path—is developed through combining compassion generation with analytical insight into the lack of an inherent difference between oneself and others.

Compassion is also symbolized by masculine models in the form of a male Buddha or bodhisattva in some sutras, tantras, and iconography, though this has its feminine counterpart in wisdom, personified as a female Buddha or bodhisattva. According to the great fifteenth-century Tibetan scholar Je Tsong-kha-pa in his classical comprehensive text the *Great Stages of the Path to Enlightenment*, wisdom is like the mother of all Buddhas because it nurtures and gives birth to all the three types of enlightened beings: the *śrāvaka* and *pratyekabuddha* (Hinayāna followers), and the bodhisattva (the Mahayana follower).

The valorization of the masculine symbol of compassion must be seen in balance with the value given to the motherly compassionate model that Mahayana practitioners use in other meditative practices such as that outlined above. Moreover, even in the practice of deity yoga in Tantra, the female or male meditator can identify with a feminine or masculine Buddha or bodhisattva. Since all Buddhas and bodhisattvas embody both compassion, power, and wisdom, though their attributes often emphasize one or the other quality, all practitioners must generate the good qualities of both masculine and feminine symbols. In the tantric or Vajrayana traditions, the use of this duality in female-male symbolism does not theoretically imply hierarchy in which maleness is superior nor does it imply consistent gendered stereotypes such as male activity or female passivity. Both compassion and wisdom can be passive and active; for example, wisdom may be vast open awareness or active analytical wisdom, and compassion can be an open acceptance or a motivating active force for one's good deeds.

The fluidity of gender in relation to compassion can be seen in the figure of Avalokiteśvara, the epitome of compassion, and one of the most popular of all Mahayana bodhisattvas. In Indo-Tibetan Buddhism he always appears in male form. However, devotion to Tārā, a female Buddha who is a manifestation of compassion and is said to be born from Avalokiteśvara's tears, is also widespread in Tibet. She has promised to always take female form while working for the sake of all beings until all attain enlightenment.

In Chinese and East Asian Buddhism, Avalokiteśvara was transformed into Kuan Yin (later Kannon in Japan) by the time of the Sung dynasty, and she most often appears in female form. In Chinese texts and iconography she is depicted as a beautiful, white-robed woman associated with yin (female) symbols, and she is an important object of devotion for Chinese women even today.

Seen as a savior from suffering, Kuan Yin was invoked especially in relation to female suffering, but not only did she serve as a role model of unselfish giving and piety, she also appeared as a model of independence from family restrictions, such as in her manifestation as Miao-shan, who rejected marriage, dedicating her life to meditation. Thus Kuan Yin, though not a symbol for equality, could encourage a more independent social role.

Anne Klein, José Cabezón, Rita Gross, Karma Lekshe Tsomo, Tsultirm Allione, and others have analyzed the symbolism of female Buddhas, bodhisattvas, and *ḍākinīs*, and written on the lives of extraordinary women in the Indo-Tibetan tradition who were nuns, yoginis, and teachers. Although in Tibet ordinary women often had some economic freedom and independence, and some female meditators became renowned teachers and even abbots of monasteries as well as nunneries, these women often had to overcome many social and cultural obstacles to pursue their goals. In general, the exhalted female symbols of wisdom and compassion and the special religious achievements of some women were not mirrored in high religious, political, social, or economic roles for women in patriarchal Buddhist countries. Yet perhaps those heroic women practitioners were encouraged by these female symbols of Buddhas and bodhisattvas which embodied compassion and wisdom, and inspired also to engage in meditative practices that emphasized equal development of these qualities symbolized in both feminine and masculine forms.

Modern Western scholars are continuing to examine the psychological, cultural, and gender assumptions behind traditional Indo-Tibetan Buddhist meditations on compassion, to explore their impact in their cultures, and to suggest ways of understanding and adapting these meditations for use in modern societies. Buddhist texts and conferences as well as ecumenical seminars analyze Buddhist psychology and meditations for insight into and practical techniques for handling anger and hatred and developing patience, love, and compassion.

Meditating on compassion for all including one's enemies and actively working for peace are practices of modern Buddhist leaders such as the Dalai Lama, the Burmese Nobel Prize winner Aung San Suu Kyi, and the Vietnamese peace activists and meditation teachers Thich Nhat Hanh and Sister Cao Ngoc Phuong. Western Buddhist peace and environmental groups call for both meditation and action in finding peaceful compassionate solutions to problems.

BIBLIOGRAPHY

Allione, Tsultrim. *Women of Wisdom.* 1984.

Aronson, Harvey. *Love and Sympathy in Theravada Buddhism.* 1980.

Cabezón, José Ignacio, ed. *Buddhism, Sexuality and Gender.* 1992. See Cabezón, "Mother Wisdom, Father Love: Gender-based Imagery in Mahayana Buddhist Thought" and Barbara Reed, "The Gender Symbolism of Kuan-Yin Bodhisattva."

Dalai Lama. *Healing Anger: The Power of Patience from a Buddhist Perspective.* Translated by Thupten Jinpa. 1997.

Dresser, Marianne, ed. *Buddhist Women on the Edge: Contemporary Perspectives from the Western Frontier.* 1996.

Gross, Rita M. *Buddhism After Patriarchy.* 1993.

Hopkins, Jeffrey. *Compassion in Tibetan Buddhism.* 1980.

Klein, Anne C. *Meeting the Great Bliss Queen.* 1995.

Lemle, Mickey, director. *Compassion in Exile: The Story of the 124th Dalai Lama.* 1992. Distributed by Direct Cinema, Los Angeles.

Macy, Joanna. *World as Lover, World as Self.* 1991.

Maxwell, Natalie (Hauptman). "Great Compassion: The Chief Cause of Bodhisattvas." Ph.D. diss., 1975.

Newland, Guy. *Compassion: A Tibetan Analysis: A Buddhist Monastic Textbook.* 1984.

Pabongka Rinpoche. *Liberation in the Palm of Your Hand.* Translated by Michael Richards. 1991. Comprehensive instructions on Tsong-kha-pa's stages of the path to enlightenment, including compassion, by a renowned Tibetan scholar-yogi in the 1920s.

Paul, Diana Y. "Kuan-Yin: Saviour and Saviouress in Chinese Pure Land Buddhism." In *The Book of the Goddess.* Edited by Carl Olsen. 1983.

Paul, Diana. *Women in Buddhism: Images of the Feminine in the Mahayana Tradition.* 1979.

Saddhatissa, Hammalawa. *Buddhist Ethics: The Path to Nirvana.* 1987.

Salzberg, Sharon. *Lovingkindness: The Revolutionary Art of Happiness.* 1995.

Śāntideva (seventh century C.E.). *A Guide to the Bodhisattva's Way of Life (Bodhisattvacaryāvatāra).* Translated by Steven Batchelor. 1987. See also *A Guide to the Bodhisattva's Way of Life.* Translated by Vesna A. Wallace and B. Alan Wallace. 1997.

Tsomo, Karma Lekshe, ed. *Buddhism Through American Women's Eyes.* 1995.

———. *Sakyadhītā: Daughters of the Buddha.* 1988.

Tsong-kha-pa (d. 1419). *The Great Treatise on the Stages of the Path to Enlightenment (Lam Rim Chen Mo).* Translation team. Tibetan Buddhist Learning Center and the Library of Tibet. Edited by Joshua Cutler. Forthcoming.

Willis, Janice D. "Ḍākinī: Some Comments on Its Nature and Meaning." In *Feminine Ground: Essays on Women and Tibet.* Edited by Janice D. Willis. 1987.

NATALIE MAXWELL HAUPTMAN

Confession and Penitence

The basic issues of confession and of penitence are related to soteriological concerns in which the goals, symbols of power, authority, and organization of religion insist on transcendence of the mundane sphere in order to attain a higher dimension of freedom. The basis for this position is a sense that the ways of this visible world are not ultimately satisfactory; whether identified as ignorance, defilement, sin, passion, or illusion, the fundamental defect requires healing, cleansing, atonement. The way to freedom thus passes through the forest of penitential practice, conceived as atonement for past transgressions and purification of the root causes of alienation, thus providing the basis for the transformation of human beings into saints.

SURVEY OF RELIGIONS

Ancient Indian tapas

Tapas, which originally meant "heat" and was an essential element in the process of creation, came to be seen as the power derived from asceticism. The goddess Pārvatī performs *tapas* to obtain Siva for her husband (*Skanda Purana* 1.2.25.24–84), and thereby rejuvenates the world. Similarly, the renewal of health and vigor in the Hindu family brought about by the wife's practice of *vrat* (penitential vows, usually emphasizing rituals, prayer, and fasting) corresponds to a reenactment of Pārvatī's *tapas,* and brings faithful women inner peace.

Buddhism

In the early Buddhist scriptures there are two principal sources for penance or confession related to women. The short poems of liberation in the *Therigatha* (Hymns of Women Elders) celebrate the ascetic life while the *Vinaya* (*Cullavagga* and *Parivara*), the monastic rule, gives the rather disturbing account of the origins of the monastic order for women, and outlines the rules (*Prātimokṣa*) for confession and reparation of faults in this the world's earliest extant monastic legislation.

The rigorous attitude against women in the *Vinaya* seems to arise from the way the law of karma is interpreted with regard to the moral capacity of the body that arises from the concatenation of prior causes and conditions. A being born as a woman is considered to have serious karmic limitations that make it highly unlikely that she will be able to persevere in the practices necessary to attain nirvana in that lifetime. In Jainism, the same attitude prevails with the denial that a woman can be born with an adamantine body capable of sustaining prolonged penitential practices required for liberation from evil karma.

In contrast, the women of the *Therigatha* sing of their attainment: "Bhadda Kapilani, . . . bears her last body, having conquered Mara . . . with impure actions annihilated, tamed, has become cool, quenched" (Bhadda Kapilani, 65–66). Practicing the most rigorous penance, these women were among the earliest Buddhist saints and were recognized as having attained perfect liberation; their "last body" was female. It is thus quite possible that the *Vinaya* account is not the original teaching of Śākyamuni, but a later intensification of the usual norms governing the separation of male and female monastics, which also occurred in Jainism.

Over the centuries, penitential practices of male and female Buddhist monastics have tended to center on the collective formal recitation of the *Prātimokṣa* on the nights of the full moon and new moon, the lighting of butter lamps, fasting, and prostrations. Individual "confession" of sins to another monk or nun is not unknown; one may confess to a visualized image of Buddha or other enlightened beings. In the Vajrayana context, purification of faults and downfalls is accomplished by the recitation of the long mantra of Vajrasattva and by fasting practices related to the cult of Avalokiteśvara. Penitential observances typical of early Buddhism (*dhutagunas*) are found in the Vajrayana biography of Machig Labdron as a manifestation of her realization, free from dualism and conceptualization. The penances (*vrats*) typical of Hindu women's spirituality are explicitly repudiated in Buddhism. In Śvetāmbara Jain practice, lay or monastic practitioners confess infractions of their vows to a monastic of the same sex.

Christian monasticism and lay female piety

In early Christianity small groups of Christian women withdrew from urban centers to create small communities that nourished the roots of later Christian monasticism. However, one of the primary models of women's penitential practices in early Christian through medieval times was devotion to Mary Magdalene and the hagiographical accounts of converted prostitutes.

The sacrament of penance/confession in Catholicism

The early thirteenth-century rule for hermitesses, the *Ancrene Wisse*, gives a summary of the changes in penitential practice that were already animating the religious life of twelfth-century Western Europe. The task of the penitent solitary anchoress, according to Linda Georgianna, is to "come to understand herself, her desires and memories, her motives and habits of mind, as a unique individual whose relationship with God is defined . . . in terms of the every day, which is always in flux." The same themes remain central to the subsequent tradition of Catholic women's spirituality.

The two principal streams of medieval penitential movements in Western Europe were the Beguines and the Third Orders. Both movements inspired women to undertake a life of renunciation, either in solitude or in community, embodying in new institutions the spiritual ideals of evangelical poverty, penitential austerity, and poetically affective mystical prayer. Highly educated and outspoken lay men and women spearheaded these complex penitential movements: the Beguines in northern Europe and the more widespread Third Orders associated with the various groups of friars (Franciscan, Dominican, Carmelite, and Trinitarian). In spite of their links with established religious orders, the penitents emphasized lay autonomy and were often in communication and sympathy with the heretical movements of the era. The new groups reflect a growing interest in mystical experience, apostolic life, and autonomy from clerical control. As a women's movement, they preferred the relative freedom and flexibility of life in very small groups to the more rigorously enclosed life of the older women's monastic communities. Their penitential observances included wearing simple clothing of austere colors, recitation of the Liturgy of the Hours or a rudimentary form of the rosary, regular confession and communion, fasting, peacemaking, detachment from worldly diversions, and charitable works to the marginalized members of society and chastity (either perpetual for the unmarried or according to the penitential seasons of the church calendar for the married). Margaret of Cortona (d. 1297) and Angela of Foligno (d. 1309) were typical examples of Third Order sanctity; Marguerite Porete (executed 1310), author of a doctrine of the annihilation of the will in the state of perfection, represents a notorious example of Beguine spirituality.

Within the cloister, the case of Teresa of Avila illustrates common problems over the centuries in the spiritual direction and confession of women. Contemplative prayer and mystical graces, the fruits of extensive penances and long periods of meditation, were evaluated negatively by suspicious confessors (influenced by several notorious cases of pseudo-saints) who were inclined to interpret these experiences as diabolical. Teresa was subjected to extreme psychological abuse by several confessors, but was fortunate to find among the others understanding and help from a number of notable kindred spirits. Here as elsewhere, violence was inspired by a fear of a woman's use of the symbolic language of ineffability, severe penances, and claims of extraordinary graces to acquire prestige and power.

The problem of sexual abuse and canonical censure against confessors (only male priests were authorized to hear sacramental confession) who used the confessional for seduction is illustrated in the life of Miguel de Molinos, a Spanish priest of the seventeenth century whose ministry of spiritual direction electrified Rome and Naples in the period 1663–1687. Accused of sexual abuse of his women penitents and of formal heresy, he was arrested by the Inquisition and narrowly escaped the stake, dying in prison in 1696. Molinos' teachings are known as Quietism and entailed a once-and-for-all act of perfect abandonment and love for God in which the contemplative presumes to be in perfect union with God without further need for effort either in prayer or in one's way of life. Thus neither the ordinary acts of piety, nor resistance to negative thoughts, nor confession of sins had any value for the true contemplative. Molinos explained the sins of contemplatives as "diabolic violence" directed against the bodies of those who had made this perfect act of abandonment; such sins were not to be confessed, but simply endured as a kind of humiliation that serves to perfect the contemplative's love of God. On the basis of this and similar cases, Roman Catholic canon law imposed severe penalties on confessors guilty of sexual abuse.

The most popular discussion of penance and confession of women is the classic *Introduction to the Devout Life* of Francis de Sales, first published in 1609, and ever since a handbook for parish clergy and laity. The emphasis here is on psychological rather than bodily penances, with everything ordered to a progressive distancing from sinful tendencies and a corresponding increase in devotional intensity and growth in the virtues. In total contrast to Quietism, the Salesian emphasis is on day-by-day renewal of the struggle against temptation and commitment to the path toward holiness. Although the sanity and gentleness of this work are only to be admired, it has always been considered a book of spiritual guidance for the laity, and it tended to confirm the general view that the heights of sanctity were only for the cloistered religious.

In recent times the guidance of women away from the cloister toward engagement with the world has been typical of Catholic penitential practice. For example, Padre Pio of Pietralcina, in a long correspondence with the young teacher Maria Gargani, helps her overcome her negative self-image by encouraging her to be a witness to Christian values in the secularized, anticlerical world of the Italian school system. In a few years Gargani was transformed from a woman filled with self-doubts and a desire to withdraw to a contemplative monastery into the foundress of an apostolic community of women who work in precisely those situations that so traumatized her in the first years of her teaching career.

Judaism

Under Jewish law, sins against God are forgiven through penitent prayer, fasting, and the annual Day of Atonement. Pietistic movements of the medieval and modern period included such means as flogging and abstention from meat to evoke a spirit of penitence. Sins against human beings are forgiven only after restitution is provided and forgiveness requested in a penitent spirit. Confession of sins is a regular part of Jewish liturgy. Confessions are written in the first-person plural, indicating that all Jews are responsible for the entire community's sins. Confession and penitence have historically been open to women as well as men, though public flogging seems to have been restricted to men.

Contemporary Sri Lankan women penitents

Gananath Obeyesekere's study of the psychology of religious symbolism in Sri Lanka, *Medusa's Hair*, shows the relationship between guilt, madness, and penitential practice among contemporary women in a syncretic Asian culture. These women experience guilt based on family relations gone awry; tormented by the spirits of the dead, they manifest radical alienation by wandering in cemeteries, screaming, and extreme anorexia. In seeking to resolve their anguish, the outward manifestation of private feelings of guilt come to be seen as expiatory penances. Transformed by the traumatic but convincing public idiom of magical asceticism, matted hair, and spirit-possession, they become oracles of the gods, both dangerous and powerful in their own right. Such experiences correspond to patterns observable in other "traditional" societies undergoing the crisis of modernization.

BIBLIOGRAPHY

Babinsky, Ellen L., trans. *Marguerite Porete: The Mirror of Simple Souls*. 1993.

Edou, Jérôme. *Machig Labdrön and the Foundations of Chöd*. 1996.

Heinze, Ruth-Inge. *Trance and Healing in Southeast Asia Today*. 1988.

Georgianna, Linda. *The Solitary Self: Individuality in the* Anorene wisse. 1981.

Jaini, Padmanabh S. *The Jaina Path of Purification*. 1979.

Lachance, Paul, trans. *Angela of Foligno: Complete Works*. 1993.

Lea, Henry C. *A History of Auricular Confession and Indulgences in the Latin Church* [1896]. 1968.

Pearson, Anne Mackenzie. *"Because It Gives Me Peace of Mind": Ritual Fasts in the Religious Lives of Hindu Women*. 1996.

Petroff, Elizabeth. *Consolation of the Blessed*. 1979.

Obeyesekere, Gananath. *Medusa's Hair: An Essay on Personal Symbols and Religious Experience*. 1981.

O'Flaherty, Wendy Doniger. *Siva: The Erotic Ascetic*. 1973.

Ryan, John K. *St. Francis de Sales: Introduction to the Devout Life*. 1955.

Savage, Ann, and Nicholas Watson, trans. *Anchoritic Spirituality: Ancrene Wisse and Associated Works*. 1991.

Ward, Benedicta. *Harlots of the Desert: A Study of Repentance in Early Monastic Sources*. 1987.

See also **Angela of Foligno; Jainism; Ordination: In Buddhism; Porete, Marguerite; Teresa of Avila.**

FRANCIS V. TISO

Confucianism

An Overview

After four centuries of Western scholarship on Confucianism, presenting its basic features to an English-reading audience would seem to be a straightforward task. However, because it is now clear that Confucianism is as much a modern construction as a past historical actuality, one must ask anew: What is *Confucianism?* Like the word *Hinduism*, the term itself betrays its foreign origin and is similarly used to cover a wide range of moral, social, political, religious, and philosophical elements that were not always joined under one banner. Also, since it is a derivation of "Confucius," the Jesuits' Latinized name for Kong Zi (Master Kong, 551–479 B.C.E.), it is a term that, like the now discredited term *Mohammedanism*, betrays the Christian tendency to name each so-called world religion after its putative "founder."

The word *Confucianism* thus bears little semantic relationship to its Chinese counterparts, *rujiao* and *rujia*, which, respectively, mean "teaching of the Ru" and "thought-lineage of the Ru." *Ru* refers to the Literati, an East Asian social elite characterized by their general commitment to literary arts and their specific faith in a set of classical Chinese texts with distinctive views on ritual, social morality, government, and self-cultivation. "Literati Tradition" perhaps best captures the sense of the original Chinese terms, while also placing this pan–East Asian movement in the wider history of religious traditions.

We must never forget that the nature of the tradition was deeply shaped by the Han dynasty circumstances under which it emerged as a major social force, perhaps even more than it was shaped by the moral and spiritual teachings of Master Kong and other founding figures of the late Zhou dynasty (c. 1050–256 B.C.E.), such as Master Meng (Mencius, c. 372–289) and Master Xun (third century B.C.E.). For this reason, I will trace its history from the time that it became an influential movement during the Han dynasty (206 B.C.E.–220 C.E.), the first of many times that East Asian Literati would seek to define the texts, rituals, ideas, and so forth that constitute their tradition. The tradition is treated here as a social, political, and religious movement that has had tremendous impact on the lives of East Asian peoples, especially women.

HAN DYNASTY DEVELOPMENTS

Han Literati had a wealth of resources on which to draw, including the remembered words of their Zhou predecessors as well as a large repository of texts that purported to tell of the history of ancient China, the transmission of the Literati Way (*tao*), and the nature of the Zhou ritual and political institutions established to embody that Way. Nonetheless, at the start of the Han period, neither the tradition's content nor its imminent acceptance was self-evident to proponents. The preceding Qin dynasty (256–206 B.C.E.) had burned the Literati's favored texts because of their implicit support for the institutions of the Zhou dynasty. Han Literati debated about which texts to accept as well as about what the texts meant. Of course, they agreed that Master Kong and the ancient culture heroes that he had idolized (e.g., legendary Emperors Yao and Shun as well as Zhou dynasty founders Kings Wen and Wu) were great sages. They considered him not only the source of the famous *Analects* (*Lunyu*), but also the author or editor of a set of texts that would come to be known as the Five Scriptures or Five Classics (*wujing*): *Book of Odes, Classic of Changes, Book of Historical Documents, Ch'un Ts'ew [Chunqin]with the Tso Chuen*

Portrait of Chinese philosopher Confucius (Corbis-Bettmann)

[Zuozhuan] (Spring and Autumn Annals with commentary of Zuo), and *Li Chi [Liji]: Book of Rites.* A sixth scripture, said to concern music, was also mentioned, but it is no longer extant. They grew in stature to the point that an emperor of the Later Han (25–220 C.E.) was moved to have the Five Scriptures carved in stone. In 175 C.E. Han Xiaoling issued an edict to have stone stelae with the texts of the scriptures erected outside the gate of the national university.

One thing the Literati had in their favor as they eclipsed representatives of other traditions, including Taoists, was that they were custodians of ancient rituals. Chinese rulers early learned that magnificent ceremonies conferred an air of majesty and that the ceremonial dimension of statecraft was as important as practical affairs. It not only kept a ruler in good graces with the royal ancestors and the forces of nature (such as through the sacrifices to Heaven, Earth, Sun, and Moon), but it also brought order and civility to a ruler's relations with his officials and foreign quests (such as through audience rituals).

Perhaps the first Literatus to gain imperial favor was Dong Zhongshu (176–104 B.C.E.) under Han Wudi. On his advice, the emperor established doctoral chairs for the study of Literati scriptures as well as the aforementioned national university. Moreover, in setting up an imperial examination (*mingjing shi*, examination on understanding of the scriptures), he established the basis for the system of state examinations that most East Asian governments later used to recruit qualified officials.

Dong was himself an expert on the Spring and Autumn Annals, and his famous commentarial work, Luxuriant Dew of the Spring and Autumn Annals (*Chunqiu Fanlu*), indicates key trends of Han Literati thought. It assumes that the Annals' reputed author, Master Kong, was a great sage and uncrowned king. This fit well with ongoing efforts to deify the Master and develop the practice of performing sacrificial rites at his tomb and, later, at Master Kong Temples and government-supported schools. Dong's work also sought to establish numerological and cosmological correspondence between Heaven (*tian*) and humanity. This macrocosm–microcosm model linking Heaven to humans helped reinforce the view that Heaven would respond to acts in the human world and vice versa. It also supported the principle of the Mandate of Heaven (*tianming*), according to which Heaven granted the right to rule to a dynastic line and could through natural phenomena or omens express its approval or disapproval thereof.

This principle exemplified perhaps the most fundamental of all Literati beliefs—that the human order must replicate the cosmic order in the harmonious relations between its parts and in the hierarchical structuring of high and low parts (Heaven and Earth, yang and yin, and so forth). To keep the Mandate of Heaven, a ruler must observe moral and ritual propriety; and to maintain harmony with Heaven, his subjects must observe the doctrine of the Three Bonds: subject to ruler, son to father, and wife to husband. This doctrine is often viewed as a hierarchical and oppressive reinterpretation of the Five Relationships (father-son, older brother–younger brother, ruler-subject, husband-wife, and friend-friend) discussed in the *Mencius* (Book of Master Meng), which represents the teachings of the Second Sage of Literati tradition. Master Meng was probably no less androcentric in his outlook than were Han Literati, but politically he was much more of a populist. The *Mencius* calls for benevolence and justice (*ren* and *yi*) in government and advocates the overthrow of rulers who fail to implement these virtues.

For the most part, Han Literati either followed Dong's cosmological ideas, with their implicit support of autocratic rule, or they favored textual exegesis over politi-

cal thought. Han emperors, for their part, supported Literati thought but ruled in the autocratic fashion of the First Emperor of Qin (Qin Shihuangdi), who had burned Literati texts. From this time forward, Literati would face a dilemma in their dual role of obsequiously supporting the emperor as Son of Heaven and of forthrightly reminding him that Heaven desired its Son to practice benevolence and justice.

Moreover, from this time forward, general trends in the wider society favored the spread of authoritarian tendencies in Literati teachings. In the name of Masters Kong and Meng, social leaders stressed interpretations of the virtues of harmony and filiality according to which individuals must subordinate themselves to prevailing social units, and certain persons must be subservient to others who rank higher in terms of generation, age, or gender. With specific reference to gender, Han Literati defined women's roles in various ways. Stories of self-sacrificing women were collected by the scholar Liu Xiang (77–6 B.C.E.) in his famous work, Biographies of Exemplary Women (*Lienu Zhuan*). There were also works summarizing the virtues of ideal womanhood and ideal male-female relations, such as Instructions for Women (*Nujie*), a work by Ban Zhao (Pan Chao, d. 116 C.E.), a female scholar from a leading Han Literati family. Each of these texts was important not only in its own right but also as a model for most of the later texts produced by Literati for the education of women.

Representing a central feature of Literati doctrine, Biographies of Exemplary Women presented women in their role as upholders of social morality, although Liu also included (in one of seven chapters) negative examples of women whose selfish, sensual demands destroyed social morality, their husbands, and even dynasties. The emphasis was on mothers who reared their sons well and gave their husbands moral guidance. While these were not independent women, they were certainly neither weak nor feeble-minded. Ideal mothers included Tairen, whose skill in prenatal education brought sagacity to a Zhou dynasty founder (King Wen) and the widow Meng, whose son's future as a great Literati philosopher was attributed to her perseverance in finding a suitable neighborhood (next to a school) for her young son. Ideal wives are a more mixed group, including both women who had the strength to criticize their husbands for failing to be ideal rulers and women who had the "courage" to sacrifice their own welfare, even their lives, in order to prove their chastity.

In Instructions for Women, we find strong statements against spousal abuse and other indications of the need for male care of and respect for women. Alongside these we see a picture of the ideal (marriageable) girl, who is a model of subservience because she possesses the "four virtues." The first virtue is "womanly virtue" itself, which involves being chaste and demure. Second comes "womanly words," which should be always polite, never clever or quarrelsome. Third, there is "womanly bearing," which should be ever erect and clean, never slovenly or dirty. Finally, we have "womanly work," which should be domestic in content and industrious in spirit. Later, the term for "four virtues" (*si-de*) would join one meaning "three followings" (*san-cong*) in a simple four-character phrase that has, more than any other, shaped Chinese attitudes toward rearing daughters. A girl who understands the principle of the "three followings" knows she should obey her father in youth, her husband after marriage, and her sons in old age.

Ultimately, for a woman the Literati Way meant seeking personal fulfillment in preparing for and living a life of virtuous service to the men in her life. Excluded from the path of formal study and state exams that led to a life of public service to Literati men, this private and domestic "vocation" was her only path. A woman who desired a more individualized or public moral-spiritual life would need to seek it elsewhere, for example, as a Buddhist nun or Taoist priestess.

POST-HAN DEVELOPMENTS

The centuries following the Han period also saw ritual traditions based on Literati scriptures spread among social elites and then to lower levels of society. Having a proper marriage for one's daughter, coming of age ("capping") ceremony for one's son, or funeral for one's deceased parent became markers of upward social mobility. Yet this was a long, slow process, which, moreover, came under the influence of trends in the development of Taoism and the continued influx of Buddhism in post-Han China. By the middle of the Tang dynasty (618–907), many important new commentaries on Literati texts had been written, and a rudimentary state examination system had begun to operate.

Tang Literati were for the most part content to share the stage with Buddhism and Taoism as two among China's "three teachings" (*san jiao*). However, there were Literati loyalists, such as Han Yu (768–824), who felt the true Way of the Literati had been lost and was being denigrated. By the time of the Sung dynasty (989–1279), this view became more widely held, and a major Literati renaissance movement began. This movement was so impressive and contained so many new elements that most contemporary Western scholars term it neo-Confucianism.

New elements can be traced mainly to Taoism and Buddhism. The most significant of these was from Bud-dhism, which had imported the originally Indian notion that ascetic self-denial was central to the religious life. This had special repercussions for women, as it undermined the somewhat salutary elements of early Literati thought, which was rooted in a rather positive evaluation of human emotions, the human body, and the natural world. Of course, neither Buddhism nor Sung Literati bears direct responsibility for such misogynist practices as footbinding and female seclusion. Nonetheless, the ascetic turn in Literati thinking helped usher in such practices during Sung and later dynasties.

Moreover, because Sung and later Literati developments, in particular, determined the nature of the tradition in Vietnam, Korea, and Japan, this ascetic turn in Literati values has had a momentous effort on the lives of women throughout East Asia. It was surely Buddhist influence that (though unacknowledged) led Zhu Xi (1130–1200), the leading Sung Literati thinker, to stress the tension between Heavenly Principle (*tianli*) and human desires (*renyu*) as the fundamental problematic for those seeking moral certainty and cognitive clarity.

However, the Literati debt to Buddhism was not limited to the realm of ascetic attitudes. After exposure to Buddhism, reflection on traditional Chinese cosmological texts, including the *Classic of Changes,* produced more sophisticated metaphysical ideas, such as the notion of interdependence between the Heavenly Principle (*tianli*) in things and the vital force (*qi*) which gave them physical actuality. It also produced a cosmological grounding for ethics, such as we see in the reinterpretation of benevolence (*ren*) as, first, a cosmic entity interconnecting all life forms and, second, a particular human virtue. The man of benevolence in later Literati thought shares some qualities of the Indian bodhisattva. This provided the possibility, at least, for the Literati tradition to develop a universal ethic rather than one limited to fulfilling the responsibilities of given social roles. The moral intuitionism of Wang Yangming (1472–1529), which became the basis for a Literati school that challenged Zhu Xi orthodoxy, took the tradition in that direction. Although the Literati Tradition as such never evolved popular, universalistic belief systems, it contributed, along with Buddhism and Taoism, a range of moral and spiritual ideas to the universalistic beliefs of numerous popular sects in late imperial China. These syncretic lay sects allowed many women to fill nondomestic spiritual roles and even to hold leadership positions.

TRANSMISSION TO VIETNAM, KOREA, AND JAPAN

When the Literati teachings were transmitted from the Sung, Yuan (1279–1368), and Ming (1368–1644) dynasties to Vietnam, Korea, and Japan, their acceptance was related to many of their new features, not to mention the new level of sophistication they had reached in developing systems of recruitment and administration (which ideally were intended to be the basis for benevolent and honest governance). In other words, the tradition was accepted for its value as 1) a challenging way of thinking about ethics and metaphysics, 2), a system of governmental ideas and practices, and, perhaps most important, 3) a set of social norms and rituals that "civilized" peoples should adopt. Throughout East Asia, Zhu Xi (Chu Hsi) was known as much for *Chu Hsi's Family Rituals* (*Zhuzi Jiali*) as he was for his philosophical writings.

The Literati tradition first arrived in Vietnam long before China's Sung era, as it was an area frequently under Chinese control. As early as the Han period, Chinese writing and literature were introduced. Later, scholars from the area competed in state examinations and became officials of the Chinese government. Nonetheless, as in Korea and Japan, the extensive Literati penetration, or so-called Confucianization, of Vietnam occurred under native dynasties of later periods: the dynasties called Ly (1010–1225), Tran (1226–1428), "Second" Le (1428–1789), and Nguyen (1802–1883). Against the background of an originally less patriarchal society, Vietnamese social elites encouraged adoption of the rituals and values in Literati scriptures as interpreted by Zhu Xi and other Sung, Yuan, and Ming Literati. State ceremonial, including attendance at Chinese imperial audiences for vassal states and sacrifices at Master Kong Temples in Vietnam, followed Chinese models, as did state administrative practice. Vietnamese society sought to model itself according to hierarchical dyads of father-son, husband-wife, ruler-subject, and, in addition, teacher-student relationships.

In Korea we see a similar situation. It early was exposed to isolated elements of Literati tradition, such as the *Analects* of Master Kong, who, after all, was active in the Shandong area that borders on the Korean peninsula. Yet it was after the Sung Literati renaissance that Korean elites became the kind of Literati converts that would attempt a full-fledged transformation of the Korean state and society in the name of the Literati Tradition. To statecraft, they introduced examinations to recruit officials, rules to establish honesty in government, ceremonial to add civility to public life, and the ideal of benevolent rule. At the same time, perhaps to an even greater extent than in Vietnam, Literati loyalists sought conformity at all levels of society to social norms that deprived women of previously enjoyed social privileges in the areas of inheritance, mobility outside the home, relations with their natal families, and status

within their marriages. This process began during the Koryo dynasty (918–1392) and continued with a vengeance during the Yi dynasty (1392–1910). Indeed, the latter dynasty became so strongly aligned with the Literati Tradition—in fact, with a narrow orthodoxy based on Zhu Xi's school—that it ended up suppressing Korean Buddhism.

In Japan the first wave of Confucian influence also preceded the Sung period, but was not quite as early as the waves that first rolled into Vietnam and Korea. During the seventh and eighth centuries Japan adopted a wide range of social norms, administrative practices, and intellectual trends from the Tang dynasty. Both the Literati and Buddhist traditions began to have influence in Japan from this time. Literati governmental traditions were particularly important in Japan's first efforts at centralized rule, which borrowed much directly from the Tang dynasty state codes. Nonetheless, it was the second wave of Literati influence, in the post-Song era, that created lasting schools of interpretation of Literati scriptures and widespread social effects in Japan.

During the Kamakura (1185–1333) and Muromachi (1392–1568) periods, Zen Buddhists were instrumental in the spread of new Literati ideas and practices. For example, the practice of both Buddhist *zazen* and Literati *seiza* (Chinese, *jingzuo*, quiet sitting) became popular, even at Buddhist monasteries, along with the synthesis of Buddhist and Literati views on moral self-discipline. Against this background, Bushido (way of the warrior) later developed as the Samurai way.

Samurai ascendancy under Tokagawa rule (1600–1868) was accompanied by Tokagawa support for Literati scholars, especially those who followed Zhu Xi. For example, Yamaga Soku (1622–1685), admired posthumously for formulating the Bushido code, was banished from the capitol (Edo) for ten years (1666–1675) for advocating that the Literati bypass Zhu Xi and adopt the *kogaku* (ancient learning) of early Literati sages. Generally, political conservatives preferred the scholasticism of Zhu Xi orthodoxy, while progressives adopted the activist and intuitionist alternative associated with Wang Yangming. Indeed, progressive Literati were among those who brought about the Meiji Restoration of 1868, beginning Japan's modernization.

While thus contributing to the male world of warriors and statecraft, the Literati tradition also had an impact on women in Tokagawa Japan that mirrored its effects under pro-Literati regimes in Korea and Vietnam. One difference was that the Japanese emphasis on the emotional and sensual dimensions of life kept the puritanical features of the later Literati value system from penetrating Japanese society as deeply as it had other East

Asian societies. Nonetheless, since Japanese society was the most explicitly feudal of the four societies just prior to modernization, Literati views on loyalty and filiality, including assumptions about female subservience, reinforced the Tokagawa social structure.

BIBLIOGRAPHY

Anh, Dao Duy. "Influence of Confucianism in Vietnam." *Vietnamese Studies,* no. 111 (1994): 23–35.

Bellah, Robert. *Tokagawa Religion: The Cultural Roots of Modern Japan.* 1957.

Blake, Fred. "Foot-binding in Neo-Confucian China and the Appropriation of Female Labor." *Signs: Journal of Women and Culture in Society* 19, no. 3 (1994): 676–712.

Brandauer, Frederick P. "Women in the *Ching-hua yuan:* Emancipation Toward a Confucian Ideal." *Journal of Asian Studies* 36, no. 4 (1977): 647–660.

Carlitz, Katherine. "The Social Uses of Female Virtue in Late Ming Editions of Lienu Zhuan." *Late Imperial China* 12, no. 2 (1991): 117–148.

Chan, Wing-tsit, trans. *Reflections on Things at Hand: The Neo-Confucian Anthology Compiled by Chu Hsi and Lü Tsu-ch'ien.* 1967.

Dardess, John. *Confucianism and Autocracy.* 1983.

deBary, William Theodore, ed. *The Unfolding of Neo-Confucianism.* 1975.

deBary, William Theodore, and Jahyun Kim Haboush, eds. *The Rise of Neo-Confucianism in Korea.* 1985.

Deuchler, Marina. *The Confucian Transformation of Korea.* 1992.

Ebrey, Patricia Buckley. *Confucianism and Family Rituals in Imperial China: A Social History of Writing about Rites.* 1991.

Ebrey, Patricia Buckley, trans. *Chu Hsi's Family Rituals.* 1991.

Jensen, Lionel M. *Manufacturing Confucianism: Chinese Traditions and Universal Civilizations.* 1997.

Karlgren, Bernard, trans. *The Book of Odes.* 1950.

Kelleher, Theresa. "Confucianism." In *Women in World Religions.* Edited by Arvind Sharma. 1987.

Lau, D. C., trans. *Confucius: The Analects.* 1970.

———. *Mencius.* 1975.

Legge, James, trans. *Book of Historical Documents.* 1865. Reprint, 1960.

———. *Ch'un Ts'ew with the Tso Chuen.* 1872. Reprint, 1960.

———. *Li Chi: Book of Rites.* 1885. Edited with an introduction by Ch'u Chai and Winberg Chai. 1967.

Lim, Chin-chown. "Reading 'The Golden Cangue': Iron Boudoirs and Symbols of Oppressed Confucian Women." *Renditions,* no. 45 (Spring 1996): 141–149.

Lynn, Richard John, trans. *The Classic of Changes.* 1994.

Maruyama, Masao. *Studies in the Intellectual History of Tokagawa Japan.* Translated by Mikiso Hane. 1975.

Nivison, David S., and Arthur F. Wright, eds. *Confucianism in Action.* 1959.

Nosco, Peter, ed. *Confucianism and Tokagawa Culture.* 1984.

Shryock, John. *The Origin and Development of the State Cult of Confucius.* 1966.

Smith, R. B. "The Cycle of Confucianism in Vietnam." In *Aspects of Vietnamese History.* Edited by Walter F. Vella. 1973.

Swann, Nancy Lee. *Pan Chao: Foremost Woman Scholar of China.* 1932.

Taylor, Rodney L. *The Religious Dimensions of Confucianism.* 1990.

Tu, Wei-ming. "Confucianism." In *Our Religions.* Edited by Arvind Sharma. 1993.

Woodside, Alexander Barton. *Vietnam and the Chinese Model.* 1971.

See also **Philosophy: In the East.**

CHRIS JOCHIM

Modern Movements

Historically, Confucianism has not relied on distinct institutional forms—churches, movements, sects—as much as on existing social institutions, such as family and state, to preserve and transmit its teachings. As these institutions have changed or disappeared, it has had to make major readjustments in each of the East Asian societies where it has traditionally held sway: China, Japan, Korea, and Vietnam.

The fall of China's Qing dynasty (1644–1911), Japan's Tokugawa shogunate (1600–1868), Korea's Yi dynasty (1392–1910), and Vietnam's Nguyen dynasty (1802–1945) marked the disappearance of the institutional vehicles that had carried Confucianism. Moreover, in each country it came under severe attack from modernizing intellectuals. As a result, the Confucian tradition, its very survival threatened, entered an identity crisis.

Confucianism was born in China and, according to many, produced a good number of Chinese society's existing ills. In 1915, during the first decade of the new Chinese republic, a group of intellectuals led by Chen Duxiu (1879–1942) of Beijing University founded the journal *New Youth* and initiated a movement that would culminate in mass student demonstrations on 4 May 1919. Known as the May Fourth Movement, it made Confucianism a key target of its critique of traditional

Offerings are burnt as a way of sending them to the dead at a Confucian temple in Taiwan (Michael S. Yamashita/Corbis).

culture. The movement, using *New Youth* as its voice, saw Confucianism as the main obstacle to achieving China's key goals: male–female equality, scientific thinking, economic development, and democracy. The journal came to symbolize the spirit of the era and inspired many others, including at least two dedicated specifically to women's rights, *The New Woman* and *The Woman's Bell.*

Chen, who later founded the Chinese Communist Party, was joined by literary figures such as Lu Xun, the period's greatest short-story writer, and political essayists such as Hu Shi. Although Hu and other proponents of the Western liberal tradition disagreed with Chen and his colleagues' Communist views, both groups of social reformers agreed on the need to criticize Confucianism.

To defend Confucianism in this milieu required a great deal of courage. Yet there were those who not only defended the tradition but insisted that a Confucian revival was just what would lead China out of its doldrums and into a bright future. Building on the work of turn-of-the-century thinkers such as Kang Youwei and Liang Qichao, Liang Shuming (1893–1988) was the first of Confucianism's post–May Fourth defenders. In 1921 he published *Eastern and Western Cultures and Their Philosophies,* a work in comparative thought and culture which concluded that Chinese culture was supreme and that true Confucianism could save China. For Liang, as for other modern Confucians, "true" Confucianism transcended the imperial system with which it was once identified; it was even compatible with science and democracy. Xiong Shili (1885–1968), another scholar of Liang's generation, was not famous for his own work but trained many students who continued to revive and redefine the Confucian tradition into the

twentieth century. These students included a famous group of four self-styled New Confucians: Mou Zongsan, Tang Junyi, Xu Fuguan, and Zhang Junmai.

Owing to its apologetic tone, the new Confucians' attempt at Confucian revival has been termed Fundamentalism. Yet these scholars and their living students, notably Liu Shu-hsien and Tu Wei-ming, see themselves as modernizers of their tradition, seeking to find a place for it in twentieth-century world theology and philosophy. Following Mou, Tu has referred to a Third Epoch of Confucianism emerging in response to Western thought and comparable to its earlier responses to other native movements—to Taoism and Legalism during the Han period (206 B.C.E.–220 C.E.) and to Indian Buddhism during the Sung period (960 C.E.–1279 C.E.).

Until recently these Confucian apologists have been alone in their defense of the tradition. But since the economic success of Japan and the so-called Four Little Dragons (Hong Kong, Singapore, South Korea, and Taiwan), a new breed of apologists—more social-scientific than philosophical—has emerged. Armed with data on rapid economic development as well as surveys demonstrating the perseverance of so-called Confucian values like diligence, thrift, loyalty to authority, and conformity to social norms, they have reversed the judgment of their predecessors. Now, they say, Confucianism facilitates rather than obstructs economic modernization.

Even if this new judgment of Confucianism's economic role is correct, many are less sanguine about its role in social and political modernization. Confucianism's key representatives, all of whom are men, have yet to deal seriously with its patriarchal norms and sexist historical record. Socially, while other traditions (Buddhist, Christian, Islamic, etc.) strive to deal with feminist movements, it has yet to see one emerge within its ranks. Politically, its champions, such as Chiang Kaishek and Lee Kuan-yu, have been authoritarian rulers rather than democratizers. This has hurt Confucianism's chances for developing what W. T. deBary, doyen of Confucian studies in the United States, for example, has called its "liberal tradition." Although it is still possible that the Confucianism of the future, freed of its imperial past, will develop its latent potential to be socially progressive and politically liberal, the early signs are not good.

BIBLIOGRAPHY

Chow, Tse-tsung. *The May Fourth Movement: Intellectual Revolution in Modern China.* 1960. Standard work on the central movement in modern China attacking conservatives, including Confucians, and furthering the rights of women and others believed to have been victims of oppression in the traditional Chinese social order.

deBary, William Theodore. *The Liberal Tradition in China.* 1983. An effort to trace certain open, reformist trends in the Confucian tradition.

Deuchler, Martina. *The Confucian Transformation of Korea.* 1992. An excellent study, coming down to the twentieth century, explaining how Confucianism was consistently and explicitly used to create a thoroughgoing patriarchal social system in Korea.

Furth, Charlotte, ed. *The Limits of Change: Conservative Alternatives in Republican China.* 1976. Modern Confucians are among the conservatives treated here by leading scholars, such as Guy Allito, Hao Chang, and Wei-ming Tu.

Kelleher, Theresa. "Confucianism." In *Women in World Religions.* Edited by Arvind Sharma. 1987. Brief but good coverage of the views of women in traditional Confucianism and of the social and religious effects of these views.

Levenson, Joseph R. *Confucian China and Its Modern Fate: A Trilogy.* 1968. Excellent treatment of Chinese intellectual history from the Qing Dynasty (1644–1911) through the 1960s, now controversial for prematurely announcing the death of Confucianism.

Liu, Shu-hsien. "Postwar Neo-Confucian Philosophy: Its Development and Issues." In *Religious Issues and Interreligious Dialogues: An Analysis and Sourcebook of Developments since 1945.* Edited by C. W. Fu and G. Spiegler. 1989. Concise summary of the contributions of the Contemporary Neo-Confucian school of thought by a leading proponent.

Reed, Barbara. "Women and Chinese Religion in Contemporary Taiwan." In *Today's Woman in World Religions.* Edited by Arvind Sharma. 1994. Assesses the effects on women of recent changes in religion and society in Taiwan, with coverage of efforts to de-Confucianize society as well as to make Confucianism itself more woman-friendly.

Tu, Wei-ming. "The Search for Roots in Industrial East Asia." In *Fundamentalisms Observed.* Edited by M. Marty and R. S. Appleby. 1991. A good brief overview of what the author considers a kind of Confucian revival.

Tu, Wei-ming, ed. *Confucian Traditions in East Asian Modernity.* 1996. The advantage of this volume is that it covers a wide range of societies from various perspectives; the disadvantage is that many articles cover the contribution of Confucian values to economic development.

CHRIS JOCHIM

Politics and Authority in the Confucian System

The nature of authority in the Confucian system is difficult to separate into public and private spheres. *The Great Learning,* an essential Confucian text, proclaims that cultivation of the self leads to the cultivation of the family, which leads to the cultivation of the state, and eventually to the creation of peace for all in the human and natural realms. Historically, this teaching has been put into practice by constituting the family and the state as corresponding structures. The correspondence is expressed in the idea that the ruler is a father to the people and that the loyal minister is like a virtuous wife. More than just metaphor or analogy, these correspondences convey the belief that the relations within familial and state structures are essentially homologous. In terms of actual practices, the extended clan structure of aristocratic Chinese and Korean families resembled the network of royal power relations, which were themselves composed of familial and lineage claims. The structural and psychological similarities between formal and informal contexts of power in the Confucian system stand in striking contrast to the contractual, voluntary association that is the hallmark of modern Western political, economic, and social organizations.

In turning to the familial roles of women in Confucian societies, the porousness between private and public authority encourages a reexamination of the view that women's roles are limiting or lacking in authority. It has been commonplace for Western theorists to divide Confucian ritual functions along gender lines. Women, as wives and mothers, are concerned with immediate household affairs and fortunes, whereas men maintain the formal ancestral rites that assure the overall ceremonial integrity and perpetuation of the clan. This neat distinction, which has the effect of confining women's actions, is belied by the actual range of women's ritual roles, which often contribute directly to the maintenance of the broad social structure. The predominantly female participation in shamanism in Korea is an example. Women use the services of shamanistic mediums in order to confront and bargain with the ancestral spirits and household gods held responsible for current misfortunes. In this practice, the dead are accounted as participants and powerful family members who can be cajoled into cooperation and supernatural aid. Often the requests involve resolution of illness and successful childbirth, but the overall concern with the economic and psychological well-being of the family extends to the larger community, which also has its pantheon of local spirits. The dominant role of women in negotiating relations between the living and the dead is integral to broader social purposes.

A woman's role as wife and mother is not only the basis for religious and ritual authority, but for political power as well. In a weaker sense, women have functioned as the vehicles of male bids for authority, given that such bids were based primarily on familial ties of birth or marriage. Confucianism officially frowns on women rulers, although it has engendered the poetic habit of fallen statesmen likening themselves to rejected wives pining for their sovereigns. The familial locus from which rulers and ministers emerge, however, has made the female exercise of royal power a regular historical occurence. In Chinese dynastic history, Empress Lu Zhi of the Han, Empress Wu Zetian of the Tang, and the Empress Dowager Ci Xi of the Qing are the most notable examples. This list is augmented by the numerous regencies of empress dowagers who momentarily stepped into the position of power as a prerogative of their role as the wife or mother of an incapacitated ruler. Empress Wu Zetian is perhaps the most exceptional of this list because of her efforts to establish her rule as permanent and even to found a new dynastic lineage in her name. This unorthodox bid for rulership was initially and typically based on the favor she held with the emperor as a consort and wife. Although official Confucian historiography has judged Wu Zetian harshly, as recently as the twentieth century Jiang Qing prepared her bid to replace her husband Mao Zedong as chair of the Communist Party by expressly associating herself with Chinese empresses of the past.

At first glance, it appears that Confucianism limits the latitude of woman by confining her exercise of ritual and political authority as extensions of her functions as a wife and mother. On the other hand, any assessment must first take into account the overarching model of authority that makes binding claims upon men and women alike, irrespective of their differentiated roles. This model is distinguished by the degree to which it makes family structure and relations the paradigm for all realms of authority. The "family" here conveys little of our current connotations of affective warmth and nurturing, focusing instead on the importance of structural roles and ritual interactions. Thus even in contemporary and industrialized Asian nations such as Singapore and Taiwan, the rhetoric and practice of familial obligation eclipse the legalistic relations that we normally expect of state institutions. The cultural divergence between Eastern and Western paths of modernization can be traced to this basic difference in how authority and social interactions are patterned.

BIBLIOGRAPHY

Chan, Wing-tsit, trans. *The Great Learning.* In *A Source Book in Chinese Philosophy.* Translated and compiled by Wing-tsit Chan. 1963.

Chung, Priscilla Ching. "Power and Prestige: Palace Women in the Northern Sung (960–1126)." In *Women in China: Current Directions in Historical Scholarship.* Edited by Richard W. Guisso and Stanley Johannesen. 1981.

Day, Tony. "Ties that (Un)Bind: Families and States in Premodern Southeast Asia." *Journal of Asian Studies* 55, no. 2 (1996): 384–409.

Elvin, Mark. "Female Virtue and the State in China." *Past and Present* 104 (1984): 111–152.

Hsieh Chen-ping. "The Rise and Fall of Comrade Chiang Ch'ing." *Asian Affairs* 5 (January–February 1978): 148–164.

Kendall, Laurel. *Shamans, Housewives, and Other Restless Spirits: Women in Korean Ritual Life.* 1985.

Keyes, Charles, ed. *Asian Visions of Authority: Religion and the Modern States of East and Southeast Asia.* 1994.

O'Hara, Albert Richard. *The Position of Women in Early China.* 1971.

Yang, Lien-sheng. "Female Rulers in Imperial China." *Harvard Journal of Asiatic Studies* 23 (1960–1961): 47–61.

Zakaria, Fareed. "Culture is Destiny: A Conversation with Lee Kuan Yew." *Foreign Affairs* 73, no. 2 (1994): 109–126.

See also **Leadership; Motherhood and Grandmotherhood; Shamans; Wives.**

FRANCISCA CHO

Contraception

Contraception has been known to humankind from the earliest times. Ancient Jewish sources, early Islamic medical texts, and Hindu sacred scriptures all indicate that herbal contraceptives could induce temporary sterility. Today, however, there exists no uniform position on contraception within each of the major religious traditions; rather, the issue is marked by a plurality of views from followers, religious leaders, and scholars. All of the traditions discussed below are founded on notions of fertility and procreation within the family; while the views on contraception vary widely, no religion advocates the goal of a childless marriage or the use of contraception outside of the marriage contract.

The Hebrew Bible promotes prolific childbirth; "be fruitful and multiply" (Gen. 1:28), has been taken by both Jews and Christians as God's "first commandment." Yet there is only one explicit reference to birth control: Genesis 38:9–10 states that during intercourse Onan "spilled his seed on the ground" (*coitus interruptus*). This was "evil in the sight of the Lord" and was punished by Onan's death. Jewish Talmudic literature builds on this passage and prohibits the use of any contraceptive device for use by men that would waste the "male seed"; female contraceptive may be permitted for health reasons (danger to the mother or to the potential child). The Orthodox position on contraception accepts abstinence as the only permissible birth control method except where health reasons apply. Conservative and Reform views, which note that sexual pleasure between married partners is permissible and sanctioned by the rabbinical literature, authorize social, environmental, and economic reasons for the use of birth control in addition to health factors, and leave the decision to individual choice (declared formally at the Central Conference of American Rabbis, 1930, and the Rabinical Assembly of America, 1935).

Prior to the 1930s all Christian denominations were united in their firm rejection of contraceptives. The Lambeth Conference of the Church of England (1930) marks the first departure from this unanimous prohibition by advocating the use of artificial contraception where abstinence was deemed impracticable. The Federal Council of Churches (1931) also adopted a policy of conservative advocation of artificial birth control methods. Most major Protestant traditions followed suit, and by 1961 the National Council of Churches declared a liberal policy on contraceptive use, subject to mutual consent between couples.

The total prohibition of artificial birth control methods by the Roman Catholic Church, declared by Pope Pius XI in his 1930 encyclical, *Casi Connubii*, was maintained by the 1968 *Humanae vitae* (the encyclical of Pope Paul VI), and constitutes the present-day policy of the church. The Catholic position on contraception is highly influenced by the natural law theory of Aristotle, Augustine, and Aquinas, which deems that sexuality has as its end purpose procreation; to interfere in this end would be a violation of the natural law and thus a sin. This view is maintained by some Anglicans, Evangelicals, and Christian fundamentalist denominations as well. The Catholic Church sanctions only abstinence and the rhythm method as suitable techniques for birth control.

Unlike the Catholic tradition, the Eastern Orthodox Church does not discern a moral difference between artificial or natural birth control methods. They note that many Church Fathers, as well as the Pauline texts in the New Testament, do not strictly limit sexual intercourse to procreation; the Orthodox position is that sexual intercourse also constitutes an expression of love within the marriage contract. No official statement has been made on prohibitions for artificial contraceptives, whereas abortion, infanticide, and permanent sterilization have been condemned. The Orthodox Church allows a married couple to make their own decisions on contraceptive use.

There is a widespread variation on attitudes to contraception in the Islamic faith. The Qur'an states: "You should not kill your children for fear of want" (17:31, 6:151). Critics of birth control argue that this can be extended to include a ban on all family planning methods; advocates of birth control indicate that this passage explicitly refers to infanticide and note that there is no prohibition against birth control in the Qur'an. Further, the hadith and *sunnah* literature clearly permit the practice of *coitus interruptus* (*'azl*), and sources indicate that *'azl* was practiced by the Prophet Muhammad himself (*sunnah* related by Habir). Those in favor of contraception argue that artificial birth control is morally the same as *'azl* and therefore to be accepted. Most Muslim traditions permit the use of birth control where health reasons are an issue or where the well-being of the family is concerned; this flexibility affords latitude in interpretation and is reflected by the vast differences in policies on family planning by distinct Muslim groups and countries. Despite varying viewpoints, the emphasis remains on procreation within the family as a religious duty. There is unanimous rejection of sterilization and abortion.

Hinduism actively encourages prolific procreation within marriage, but there is no prohibition against birth control in the Hindu religion. The Upanishads describe a birth control method (Brihadaranyaka Upanishad), and temporary abstinence is advocated in the Shastras, while abortion is condemned. Still, Hindu scholars' views on contraception vary widely: Gandhi advocated birth control based on abstinence and not through artificial means, while philosopher and statesman Sarvepalli Radhakrishnan and the poet Rabindranath Tagore, on the other hand, promoted the use of artificial methods. India was the first nation to establish a governmental population strategy based on birth control measures.

The critics of family planning in all major religious traditions fear that contraceptive use will encourage immorality and illicit sex. Furthermore, critics in many non-Western faiths fear that liberal contraceptive policies encourage a Western model of living that would destroy the family and family values. Among supporters of family planning, feminist commentators have viewed prohibitions on birth control as a means to control female sexuality and independence.

BIBLIOGRAPHY

Most of the literature in contraception and religion is contained on sociological, health, or environmental studies on population control. Very little work has been completed specifically on the relation between birth control and religious institutions, but references to contraception (particularly with a feminist analysis) can be found in more general texts on women and religion or in articles dealing with religious views of abortion.

Catholic and Islamic opinions of birth control are the most comprehensively covered in the secondary literature. Janet E. Smith's *Humanae Vitae: A Generation Later* (1991) offers a systematic examination of the moral and theological implications of the arguments against the present Catholic prohibition on artificial birth control methods, and argues that the church ruling on birth control is a logical extension of its traditional teachings on morality and the family; although this is a conservative text that supports the ban on contraception, it nevertheless offers the most detailed historical information on the arguments against birth control in the Catholic Church to date. Similarly, *Abortion, Birth Control and Surrogate Parenting: An Islamic Perspective,* by Abul Fadl Mohsin Ebrahim, supports a conservative Muslim position on contraception, yet offers a clear and concise listing of the primary text references and religious commentaries on the subject. Feminist analyses of contraception in the Islamic tradition include *Islam, Gender and Social Change,* edited by Yvonne Yazbeck Haddad and John L. Esposito (1998), and Theodora Foster Carroll, "Islam and Population," in her *Women, Religion, and Development in the Third World* (1983). Information on religious views of contraception can be found in the proceedings of the September 1994 United Nations Conference on Population and Development held in Cairo (Document A/Conf. 171/13). See specifically Chapter 7, "Reproductive Rights and Reproductive Health," and the reservations about this chapter held by various Islamic countries and the Holy See. Proceedings of the International Islamic Conference in Rabat, 1971, are also available in printed form as *Islam and Family Planning,* edited by Isam R. Nazer et al., from the International Parenthood Federation (1974).

S. Cromwell Crawford, "Hindu Ethics for Modern Life," in his edited volume, *World Religions and Global Ethics* (1989), includes an extensive section on birth control in a Hindu context. Bardwell Smith, "Buddhism and Abortion in Contemporary Japan," in *Buddhism, Sexuality, and Gender,* edited by José Ignacio Cabezón (1992), offers an account of Japanese Buddhist views on contraception. Susan Power Bratton, *Six Billion and More: Human Population Regulation and Christian Ethics* (1992), links a Christian moral theology with issues of contraception and population control. Chrysostom Zaphiris (an Orthodox theologian), "The Morality of Contraception: An Eastern Orthodox Opinion" (*Journal of Ecumenical Studies* 11, no. 4 (1974): 677–690), contrasts the views of the Roman Catholic Church with those of the Eastern Orthodoxy on the concept of family planning generally. Similarly, Harmon L. Smith, "Contraception and Natural Law: A Half-Century of Anglican Moral Reflection," in *The Anglican Moral Choice,* edited by Paul Elmen (1983), contrasts Anglican views of contraception with Catholic natural law theory.

See also **Abortion.**

KATHLEEN O'GRADY

Conversion

The term *conversion* evokes for many modern persons the sense of a radical reorganization of identity, meaning, and life—a fundamental transformation of self. Historically, conversion more often represented a communal action and resultant affiliation to a new group rather than a choice of individual conscience.

In each case, there are dimensions of the conversion experience in which gender is significant. In societies and historical periods dominated by patriarchal constraints, it is likely that a woman's experience of conversion would be mediated by the males who had power over her. For example, many cases of mass conversion in the premodern period involved whole tribes or communities following their male leaders into new political alliances.

The integration of new belief systems and altered identities and life-styles would only take place gradually, as in historical processes such as the Christianization of Europe and the New World, or Islamization in Asia and Africa. Here women's experience was often reflected in the composition of popular religious poetry, songs, and ritual which enabled the absorption and assimilation of elements of the new tradition, for example the threshing songs of women converted to Islam in the Indian Deccan (Eaton, 1978) or Buddhist poems of converted Hindu untouchables in modern-day Maharastra. Studies of conversion across Asian religions are rare and specifically female experiences remain to be explored.

CHRISTIANITY

In Western Christian history women have been portrayed as taking leadership roles in the conversion process. For example, the conversion of Augustine, the model of transformation, not only to Christianity but to a new Western consciousness, was preceded by that of his saintly mother, Monica. Rodney Stark argues that this conversion wave on the part of women arose from Christianity's giving a relatively higher status to women than Greek and Roman practices of the period.

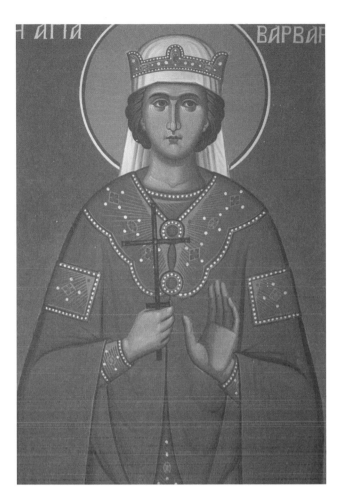

In Christian history women have been portrayed as taking leadership roles in the conversion process. Augustine's conversion was preceded and encouraged by that of his saintly mother, Monica (Dave G. Houser/ Corbis).

Female martyrdom is a particularly striking element in early Christian conversion accounts. The staunchness and bravery of the female in the face of torture and death became a symbol of heroic faith-based resistance. Even in nineteenth-century America, Protestant conversion narratives of women indicate that it was they who more often converted to revivalist or Evangelical Christianity and consequently faced the opposition of less religious husbands and fathers.

While nineteenth-century female conversion narratives in America often featured a critique of the subject's sinful and rebellious tendencies, many twentieth-century female subjects focus on interior states of feeling unloved and unlovable, of isolation, abandonment, and hatred turned inward.

In the twentieth-century West, the traditional language of conversion as transformation and renewal, enhanced by discourses of liberation and reorientation, influenced secular movements that incorporated women's conversion experiences such as recovery literature from addictions to food, drugs, and alcohol, as well as women's narratives of lesbian coming out or feminist awakening (Brereton, 1991).

Female conversion literature in the West can expose tensions between the theme of surrender to a higher power versus a woman's taking control of her life and daring to speak out. Thus, female conversion to a religious vocation or commitment can in some cases represent her creation of a space that transcends traditional reinforcement of the patriarchy, or it can be co-opted into serving and reinforcing norms of humility and submission. In both modern and premodern contexts conversion might represent a woman's breaking with prevailing cultural norms. For example, the conversion of some women to ascetic Christianity constituted a break with traditional expectations of women as wives and mothers.

FACTORS IN FEMALE CONVERSIONS

Theological aspects

Real differences occur across religious traditions, historical settings, and the class and power positions of female converts. Theologies of conversion may vary. For example, converts to Islam may claim to "revert" to what they have always been, since, according to the Qur'an (7:131) all souls have already recognized God at the time of a "primordial convenant." In Judaism and Islam, there is a process occurring in which women or men become more observant of legal and ritual norms, a conversion in the sense of altered behaviors and meaning, without a change in formal religious affiliation.

Social status and assimilation

Conversion, deconversion, or apostasy of females can also be related to issues of status and assimilation. For example, in Germany as lower-middle-class Jewish women entered paid employment in increasing numbers in the late nineteenth and twentieth centuries, their rates of conversion to Christianity rose. Similarly, wealthy German Jewish families of the same period would marry their daughters to impecunious German Christian noblemen in order to gain access to broader and more prestigious social networks (Endelman, 1987). There can be issues of acceptance involved in whether a female enters into a new religious community through marriage or by her own individual choice.

Studies of twentieth century conversions to Islam in America and Europe indicate that there are variations in styles of religiosity adopted by female converts that may be associated with generational cohort profiles within their original cultural environment.

psychology and gendered styles of conversion

Questions of whether there are distinct, gender-based styles of moral reasoning, and the extent to which these are innate or imparted by society, are relevant to the understanding of female conversions. Literature on the individual psychology of religion as well as Carol Gilligan's argument that females have distinctive styles of moral reasoning suggest that female styles of conversion may entail greater influence from responsible committed relationships as opposed to the evaluation of abstract ethical principles associated with males. This distinction likely reflects cultural and historical factors as well as gender differences.

In her article, "Women's Ministry in the United Methodist Tradition," Rosemary Skinner Keller contrasts a male model of conversion entailing an individualistic understanding of sin with a female one that additionally critiques sinful social structures. This is resonant with feminist reevaluations of "conversion," notably Rosemary Ruether who in *Sexism and God-Talk* (1983) posits a conversion from group egoism and passivity to a free and individuated self grounded in community.

Since convert narratives are one of the principal sources for determining motives for conversion, it should be noted that conventions and cultural patterns may have tended to make females write in noncanonical genres such as letters, diaries, and memoirs, although in Europe and the United States a body of edifying female conversion narratives has circulated along with male ones from the seventeenth century. A study of nineteenth-century Protestant conversion narratives found female accounts to reflect "more struggle, more painful self-examination, more intensity, more agonizing about 'sins' " than contemporary male narratives (Brereton, 1991).

The gendered elements of "deconversion," or the processes by which one abandons previously held views and associations, have been considered by Janet Jacobs, who suggests an object relations model to explain the distinctive challenges to females leaving new religious movements and by John D. Barbour, who considers twentieth-century women, including Mary Daly, who write about their loss of traditional faith.

Many works on conversion note the lack of information and analysis regarding gender-based elements of the phenomenon and view it as a desideratum for future investigation.

BIBLIOGRAPHY

Barbour, John D. *Versions of Deconversion: Autobiography and the Loss of Faith.* 1994.

Brereton, Virginia. *From Sin to Salvation: Stories of Women's Conversions, 1800 to the Present.* 1991. A groundbreaking historical and literary study focusing on American Protestantism.

Davidman, Lynn. *Tradition in a Rootless World: Women Turn to Orthodox Judaism.* 1991.

Eaton, Richard M. *Sufis of Bijapur, 1300–1700.* 1978.

Endelman, Todd M., ed. *Jewish Apostasy in the Modern World.* 1987. Several chapters consider cases of European Jewish conversions to Christianity.

Gilligan, Carol. *In a Different Voice: Psychological Theory and Women's Development.* 1983.

Hermansen, Marcia. "Two-Way Acculturation: Muslim Women in America." In *Muslims of America.* Edited by Yvonne Haddad. 1991.

Jacobs, Janet Liebman. *Divine Disenchantment: Deconverting from New Religions.* 1989.

Keller, Rosemary Skinner. "Conversions and their Consequences: Women's Ministry and Leadership in the United Methodist Tradition." In *Religious Institutions and Women's Leadership: New Roles Inside the Mainstream.* Edited by Catherine Wessinger. 1996.

Kraemer, Ross S. "The Conversion of Women to Ascetic Forms of Christianity." In *Sisters and Workers in the Middle Ages.* Edited by Judith M. Bennett. 1989.

Ruether, Rosemary Radford. *Sexism and God-Talk.* 1983.

Shatzmiller, Maya. "Marriage, Family, and the Faith: Women's Conversion to Islam." *Journal of Family History* 21, no. 3 (1996): 235–266. On social and legal aspects in premodern contexts.

Stark, Rodney. *The Rise of Christianity: A Sociologist Reconsiders History.* 1996.

Viswanathan, Gauri. "Coping with (Civil) Death: The Christian Convert's Rights of Passage in Colonial India." In *After Colonialism: Colonial Histories and Post Colonial Displacements.* Edited by Gyan Prakash. 1994. Considers the deeper issues involved in defining the legal status of Hindu females converted to Christianity.

Zelliot, Eleanor. "Buddhist Women of the Contemporary Maharashtrian Conversion Movement." In *Buddhism, Sexuality, and Gender.* Edited by José Ignacio Cabezón. 1992.

FILMS

"The Return of Sarah's Daughters." Edited by Lise Braden and Ken Schneider. Patchworks. 1997. On American Jewish women including Jewish returnees to Orthodoxy

"A Veiled Revolution." Directed by Elizabeth W. Fernea. Icarus Films. 1982. Studies Muslim women in

Cairo who are returning to traditional forms of Islamic dress.

MARCIA K. HERMANSEN

Couples

Typically an affective union of two, the couple is a cardinal theme running through the creeds, codes, ceremonies, and communities of religious traditions throughout the world. From worship seating arrangements at a Hindu temple or a Muslim mosque to the distribution of aesthetic elements in a Tibetan Buddhist mandala, the couple or a dynamic of coupling informs practices and beliefs of the world's religions in countless ways. Among world religions, the couple generally occurs in one of three categories: divine couples, in whose form religious traditions depict the transcendent or divine; ideal or heroic human couples, wherein the relationship of a particular human couple is elevated as a model for the religion's adherents; and paired principles, which function as a couple in the brief structure of a religion and tend to be personified as such in symbol or myth.

DIVINE COUPLES

Divine couples figured prominently in ancient religions, including those associated with archaic Egypt, Greece, Rome, and South Asia; yet whether the couple is the earliest form in which divinity was imagined by humanity remains uncertain. Feminist archaeologist Marija Gimbutas, along with feminist historian Gerda Lerner, interprets the female statues discovered in Paleolithic and Neolithic archaeological remains as evidence that a Great Goddess who represented "life, death [and] regeneration" was the earliest form in which divinity was conceived (Lerner, 1986). While this interpretation remains controversial, results from this research indicate that in many cases initially independent goddesses or female principles gradually became eroticized and then, in the case of the former, coupled with a male deity (Gimbutas, 1989) or, in the case of the latter, suppressed and absorbed by incorporation of her or their attributes into a male principle or monotheistic deity (Pintchman, 1994; Schüssler Fiorenza, 1983).

While divine couples primarily are presented as voluntary (or involuntary) heterosexual pair bonds, they are not limited to them. Divine couples come in the form of mother–daughter pairs such as Demeter and Persephone and twins such as Castor and Pollux. In early Mormon tradition the divine couple was described as the divine parents and addressed as "our mother and father in heaven" (Hanks, 1992). Contemporary religious traditions that embrace a depiction of the divine as a couple or a series of couples include Hinduism, most Native American traditions, and the neopagan movement (Eller, 1993).

IDEAL AND HEROIC HUMAN COUPLES

In many of the world's religious traditions, a human couple serves as the ideal or norm for followers of the religion to emulate. In Christianity, Eve and Adam slowly were embraced as the founding parents of humanity and the story of their early life presented as a teleology for the world's ills. When the Protestant Reformation resulted in the second major schism of Christian tradition, the marriage of Martin Luther and Katherine Von Bora provided an early norm for marital relationships—a novelty for a religious tradition that

Painting depicting the divine couple of the Rāmā-yaṇa, Rāma and Sītā (David Cumming; Eye Ubiquitous/Corbis)

had eschewed sexuality for much of its history (Clark and Richardson, 1977). In Islam, stories found in the hadith of the treatment by Muhammad of his first wife, Khadija, and his subsequent wives after her death, most notably 'Ā'ishah, serve as a guideline for determining appropriate behavior among Muslims in marriage (Mernissi, 1975).

PERSONIFIED PAIRED PRINCIPLES

While stories of divine or human couples percolate through religious history, the couple also appears in many world religions in the form of paired principles. The yin–yang principle of Confucianism and religious Taoism is perhaps the best known of these. Other religious traditions present individuals as personifying paired principles. Among these are Mother Ann Lee, founder of the Shakers and female Messiah, who was believed to function as a parallel and balance to Christ, thereby fully incarnating the nature of God as both male and female (Humez, 1993), and the mythic twins or dual creators of Native American Zuni tradition (Tedlock, 1992). Feminist criticism of personified paired principles in world religions focuses on a historic tendency to arrange such paired principles in oppositional hierarchies and to associate the female with the least valued members of the pairings—that is, heaven, civilization, and intellect are associated with the male and valued over and in opposition to earth, nature, and emotion, which are associated with the female (Ruether, 1983).

BIBLIOGRAPHY

Clark, Elizabeth, and Herbert Richardson. *Women and Religion: A Feminist Sourcebook of Christian Thought.* 1977. Reprint, 1996.

Eller, Cynthia. *Living in the Lap of the Goddess: The Feminist Spirituality Movement in America.* 1993. Reprint, 1995.

Gimbutas, Marija. *The Language of the Goddess.* 1989. Reprint, 1991.

Hanks, Maxine, ed. *Women and Authority: Re-emerging Mormon Feminism.* 1992.

Humez, Jean, ed. *Mother's First-born Daughters: Early Shaker Writings on Women and Religion.* 1993.

Lerner, Gerda. *The Creation of Patriarchy.* 1986.

Mernissi, Fatima. *Beyond the Veil: Male-Female Dynamics in Modern Muslim Society.* 1987.

Pinchtman, Tracy. *The Rise of the Goddess in the Hindu Tradition.* 1994.

Ruether, Rosemary Radford. *Sexism and God-Talk: Toward a Feminist Theology.* 1983.

Schüssler Fiorenza, Elisabeth. *In Memory of Her: A Feminist Theological Reconstruction of Christian Origins.* 1983.

Tedlock, Barbara. *The Beautiful and the Dangerous: Encounters with the Zuni Indians.* 1992.

See also Dualism; Family; Yin/Yang Polarity.

BRENDA E. BRASHER

Couvade

Derived from the French, *couver,* meaning "to hatch," or "to brood," the term *couvade* has come to refer to widespread ideas and practices that intimately relate a father to the birth of his child. The term was first used by Edward Tylor in *Researches into the Early History of Mankind and the Development of Civilization* (1865). Described as a "strange custom" by many early ethnographers, couvade generally takes two forms: an individualized male psychosomatic complaint accompanying his wife's pregnancy, often called couvade syndrome, and ritual couvade, in which seclusion and dietary restrictions and other practices are formally established within particular societies for the husband of a pregnant woman. These restraining behaviors have the effect of prohibiting productive activity by the male participant often during and immediately after the period in which his wife has given birth to the child.

Ritual couvade practices, though not universal, are found among divergent hunting-gathering peoples and agricultural societies that have retained some features of hunting and gathering.

Couvade is described in a Basque legend, the epic of Aitor. In one episode, attributed to the bard Larsa at the time of the Punic Wars, Aitor and his wife take refuge in a cave on a high mountain from the raging flood waters of the great deluge. There in the darkness of clashing elements a son is born. Having delivered her son, Aitor's wife returns to the search for food with her husband. Upon hearing her infant's cries from the cave, she fears that wild beasts will carry the child away. Thus, she asks Aitor to lay on the bed of skins and hold the infant in his strong arms. Aitor takes the infant and lays down upon his wife's bed, keeping the infant warm with his breath and body heat while she gathers food. Aitor's acts continue to be handed down in rural Basque country so that "when a young mother leaves her bed of confinement, her husband at once takes her place with the newborn child, so that, by its inhaling the manly and paternal breath, the strength of the small and puny being is endowed with sympathetic influence" (Hall and Dawson, 1989, p. 140). Couvade here suggests strong protective relationships established by sympathetic magic between a father and his child as well as legitimization of paternity.

Among the Carib-speaking Waiwai of northwestern Brazil, couvade entails both the wife and husband's leaving the main communal house for a smaller hut at a little distance. This seclusion during the period of the delivery ensures that the communal house is not contaminated by the blood of birth. The husband may come and go, but he is prohibited from undertaking normal hunting activities and submits himself to dietary restrictions. Ideally, these latter prohibitions and restrictions are in place for three years. During this time, according to Waiwai anthropological and cosmological beliefs, the child acquires his or her spiritual integrity from the spiritual reservoir at the end of the world. Not only does the couvade here suggest the religious ties, vulnerabilities, and responsibilities of the parents and child to each other but also provides an arena for the father to assert his paternity and femininity in a male-affirming context.

Couvade is documented for Black Caribs in Belize where particular men experience pregnancy symptoms. This type of couvade syndrome has been documented in urban settings in Mexico (Nutini, 1968), the United States (Munroe, 1980), and Europe (Hall and Dawson, 1989). No longer accepted as evidence of an evolutionary shift in cultural patterns from matriarchy to patriarchy, couvade is still understood as expressive of deep empathic forces within the male that surface in childbirth, "making fathers" as well as children.

BIBLIOGRAPHY

Hall, Nor, and Warren Dawson. *Broodmales.* 1989. Includes "A Psychological Essay on Men in Childbirth" and "The Custom of Couvade."

Munroe, Robert L. "Male Transvestism and the Couvade." *Ethos* 8 (1980): 49–59.

Nutini, Hugo. *San Bernardino Contla: Marriage and Family Structure in a Tlaxcalan Municipio.* 1968.

Paige, Karen, and Jeffrey Paige. *The Politics of Reproductive Ritual.* 1981.

Reed, Evelyn. *Woman's Evolution: From Matriarchal Clan to Patriarchal Family.* 1975.

Riviere, P. G. "The Couvade: A Problem Reborn." *Man* 9, no. 3 (1974): 423–435.

Wilson, H. Clyde, and Aram A. Yengoyan. "Couvade: An Example of Adaptation by the Formation of Ritual Groups." *Michigan Discussions in Anthropology* (Winter 1976): 111–133.

JOHN GRIM

Craft

An Overview

It is generally acknowledged that basketry and pottery are the inventions of women (Lucie-Smith, 1981). The caveat must be added that, although the making of crafts may divide along strict gender lines within a given culture, cross-cultural studies show that who makes what differs over time and place, embroidery perhaps being the exception to the rule.

The construction of community depends on all healthy members contributing economic labor to ensure the survival of the group; a useful model for determining whether an ancient society relied upon women to be the principal supplier of a particular labor is one that examines "'the compatibility of the pursuit with the demands of child care'" (Judith Brown as quoted in Barber, 1994, p. 29). This model suggests that if women were able to perform a task that posed no threat to children, whose care was entirely in their hands, then women were most likely to be the principal providers of that labor. The fabrication of textiles (i.e., the crafts of spinning, weaving, and sewing) meets the criteria of high compatibility between task and child care. Thus reliance to complete a task on behalf of the community, and not necessarily ability, became the key factor in the development of textiles as the female-gendered craft par excellence (Barber).

When considering the question of women, craft and religion, one must be careful not to overlook those perishable arts such as the making of bread or flower arranging. Bread has been so little recognized as a craft, especially in relation to religious practices, that it deserves special belated attention.

Bread baked in the form of cakes is known to have been used by women in antiquity as a sacrificial offering to gods and goddesses during cult celebrations, in sacred ceremonies such as weddings and funerals, and in worship activities. Cakes would be placed upon the goddess's or god's altar as a way of honoring and pleasing the divinity. The devotee, by consuming bread made from a grain identified with the goddess or god, was thought to be thereby united with that deity. An individual could also be healed by eating divine bread— that is, bread that had been sacrificed on the altar of a god or goddess (Benko, 1993). A cake mold (c. fifteenth century B.C.E.) in the form of Ishtar, Babylonian goddess of love and fertility, was found in the palace of Mari near the Euphrates River, thus confirming the religious use of breads more than 3,500 years ago in the ancient Near East (Benko).

EMBROIDERY AS RELIGIOUS EXPRESSION

If one had to name the craft that most clearly demonstrates the religious expression and experience of women across cultures, the most likely choice would be the textile technique of embroidery. Working with a needle to embellish an already existing fabric, usually woven cloth, the embroiderer adds carefully constructed designs to bring protection, fertility, or prosperity to the wearer of the garment. The earliest known samples are from Egyptian tombs dating back to the fourteenth century B.C.E. (Harris, 1993), but the practice of embroidery is undoubtedly much older. Elizabeth Barber (1994) writes that needles became common between 26,000 and 20,000 B.C.E., as did a knowledge of sewing. Primitive embroidery consisted of sewing beads of shell, tooth, and bone onto hide (Barber). Even today for many women around the world, embroidery is a way of practicing their religion. From the peyote-induced designs stitched by the Huichol Mesoamerican women, who learn how to embroider religious knowledge from the time they are seven, to the young Jewish bride who embroiders a blessing onto a tallith (prayer shawl) for her new husband, there are many paths to religious experience. Some contemporary women who embroider, even those who claim not to be religious, find the act of making to be calming and meditative. In some cases it may even put the maker in a trancelike state, in which the sense of self recedes and the work itself becomes a kind of spirit-directed practice.

HISTORY OF THE STUDY OF CRAFT

Scholarship on craft is dispersed across various disciplines, including anthropology, the new art history, women's studies, sociology, design studies, archaeology, museology, cultural theory, classics, and religion. The efforts of anthropologists of the nineteenth and early twentieth centuries (setting aside the ethical problems with the practice of collecting objects from non-Western cultures) ensured that commentaries and catalogues on irreplaceable craft objects from indigenous cultures exist alongside preserved artifacts. The same is true for objects of ancient societies found by archaeologists. Craft as an object of study suitable for art historians and historians of religion has suffered, however, from a particular mode of academic thinking that judges 1) art by the culturally limiting standards of a philosophy of aesthetics; 2) texts as a more reliable indicator of ideas than visual representations; 3) males as inherently more capable of rendering masterpieces than females; and 4) painting and sculpture as media more worthy of academic study than embroidery or beadwork.

It is now recognized that craft, as a product of civilization, is of critical importance in the study of humans in relation to their object environment. With regard to the history of women, it is fair to say that in some cases our only knowledge of the female in non-Western or ancient cultures has been through the objects that have been left behind.

ART VERSUS CRAFT

The concept of fine art is a relatively recent notion that comes down to us from Renaissance Europe, an era in which artistic genius was judged to be superior to physical skill. Prior to this time, the word *artisan* could just as easily identify a weaver as a painter. Unlike the term *fine art*, *craft* connotes both science and technology (although of course the practices of painting and sculpture, as much as weaving or metallurgy, rely on scientific knowledge). Where fine art commands attention with respect to culture, craft may be seen as embodying the enduring traditions of a given culture.

The division between fine art and craft is a socially constructed one, used to reinforce the ideologies of gender. This construction may best be illustrated by the example of embroidery in post-Renaissance Britain, a time when this craft was becoming increasingly associated with women and amateurism—hence a lack of remuneration (Parker, 1989). Rozasika Parker, the feminist art historian, states: "The art–craft hierarchy suggests that art made with thread and art made with paint are intrinsically unequal. . . . But the real differences between the two are in terms of where they are made and who makes them" (Parker). Dissociated from gender—being simply what women do—the practice of embroidery is difficult to classify. As it is not really utilitarian, it does not fall under a strict definition of craft. Though a pictorial form, it cannot be considered as painting. Yet it does employ color, style, and iconography and express cultural meaning (Parker). There is a strong association between embroidery, femininity, and pastime, just as there is one between painting, masculinity, and professionalism. It is not surprising then to find voluminous scholarship dedicated to the history of art but only scanty scholarship on the history of craft. Those histories that do exist tend to emphasize the so-called "manly" crafts, such as woodworking, metallurgy, and glass blowing.

ROLE OF CRAFT IN RELIGION

Within the context of religious expression, *craft* may refer either to a practice or an object. As a practice, craft falls within the realm of cult ritual, in which the precise correct performance of a rite is of paramount importance. As an object, craft denotes cult articles, their

Women of the Hichol Indians learn how to embroider religious knowledge from the time they are seven. Here is an example of their embroidered artwork (Morton Beebe-S.F./Corbis).

uniqueness and function. In both senses it registers skill, expertise, or special knowledge and cunning. These two aspects of craft come together in the performance of ritual. Rarely does a rite take place, for example, in which a cult object is not involved.

Craft and Identity

Craft more than the fine arts has been traditionally associated with the expression of cultural and religious identity. Cultural identities have been and continue to be asserted and constructed through crafted objects that express a shared system of meanings. The clans of the Northwest Coast Amerindians identify themselves through boldly colored geometric designs known as clan crests; these designs appear on cedar totem poles, painted house fronts, and woolen button blankets to proclaim the hereditary rights, duties, and ancestral histories of the individual native clans.

Craft and Power

Craft acts as a type of protocol between the worshiper and the divinity, calling attention to the devotee and routing power between her and the divinity. Still practiced by contemporary Christians, among others, the ritual of the votive offering to goddess or god in thanks for or in expectation of a blessing is ancient and widespread. In the past votive objects were most commonly made of wood or terra-cotta and featured a wide variety of images. Common among archaeologists' finds are models of body parts, such as hands and feet, which were either in need of being healed or had been healed. Left by worshipers at shrines, sacred trees, or consecrated fountains, the votive object effected an immediate and direct relationship to salvation (Freedberg, 1989).

Some crafted objects, like the talisman or amulet, are meant to protect the wearer from harm. Made from terra-cotta, wood, stone, metal, thread, and other materials, and possibly containing a substance associated with or having direct contact with the source of supernatural power, a talisman, often worn as jewelry, or embroidered as a protective design into garments, is thought to ward off hostility directed at the wearer. The exact nature of their efficacy however is subject to debate among scholars (Freedberg).

Among some peoples, a craft can serve as an instrument to give temporary cosmological power or strength to humans. The seamstresses of the Koniag Eskimo of the North Pacific Coast expressed magical beliefs and the ideology of spiritual transformation between people, animals (sea otters), and spirits in the clothes they made for the male hunters of their group. Such clothing had to be beautifully made so as to coax the spirit of the animal to give up its life to the men and women who respected and depended upon it for survival (Chaussonnet, 1988).

Craft and Sacred Space

One of the most common uses of craft across different religions is in decorating a sacred space in which a religion's deity or deities may be worshiped. Culture-specific ideas of purity, perfection, enlightenment, protection, sacred geography, and religious history must all be taken into consideration as part of the architect's and craftperson's task. The Byzantine church expressed its adoration of Christ by using kingship symbolism and materials, such as ornate stained-glass windows, gold and silver chalices, marble altars, silk vestments and altar cloths, gem-covered reliquaries, and intricately designed wall mosaics.

Craft and Rites of Passage

The safe deliverance of the body through the unstable passages of life when humans are considered to be most vulnerable—conception, birth, puberty, marriage, parenthood, and death—has been the motivation for various cultures to paint coming-of-age motifs on the bodies of young girls, to sew unique and beautiful garments for newlyweds, and to carve protective amulets for the deceased. This role of craft in life's pivotal changes becomes most salient in ceremonies that honor an individual's passing from life into death. Around the world, in the crypts, tombs, and catacombs of the dead, elaborately embroidered burial shrouds, gold-printed and -painted silk robes, tunics decorated with beads and shells, linen- and wool-wrapped burial couches, and ceramic plates and cups attest to the centrality of craft in humanity's attempt to find and give meaning.

BIBLIOGRAPHY

Amir, Ziva. *Arabesque: Decorative Needlework from the Holy Land.* 1977.

Anscombe, Isabelle. *A Woman's Touch: Women in Design from 1860 to the Present Day.* 1984.

Barber, Elizabeth W. *Women's Work: The First 20,000 Years.* 1994.

Benko, Stephen. *The Virgin Goddess: Studies in the Pagan and Christian Roots of Mariology.* 1993.

Brown, Judith. "Note on the Division of Labor by Sex." *American Anthropologist* 72 (1970): 1075–1076.

Chaussonnet, Valerie. "Needles and Animals: Women's Magic." In *Crossroads of Continents.* Edited by William W. Fitzhugh and Aron Crowell. 1988.

Dean, Beryl. *Ecclesiastical Embroidery.* 1968.

Eger, Susan. "Huichol Women's Art." In *The Art of the Huichol Indians.* Edited by Kathleen Berrin. 1978.

Flanders, John. *The Craftsman's Way: Canadian Expressions.* 1981.

Freedberg, David. *The Power of Images: Studies in the History and Theory of Response.* 1989.

Harris, Jennifer, ed. *Textiles 5000 Years: An International Survey.* 1993.

Hendrickson, Carol. *Weaving Identities: Construction of Dress and Self in a Highland Guatemala Town.* 1995.

Hickey, Gloria A., ed. *Making and Metaphor: A Discussion of Meaning in Contemporary Craft.* 1994.

Johnstone, Pauline. *Byzantine Tradition in Church Embroidery.* 1967.

Kelly, Mary B. "Goddess Embroideries of Eastern Europe." In *Gender, Culture and the Arts: Women, the Arts, and Society.* Edited by R. and S. Bowers. 1993.

Lucie-Smith, Edward. *The Story of Craft: The Craftsman's Role in Society.* 1981.

Parker, Rozsika. *The Subversive Stitch: Embroidery and the Making of the Feminine.* 1989.

Salomon, Kathryn. *Jewish Ceremonial Embroidery.* London, 1988.

Smith, Susan L. "The Power of Women Topos on a Fourteenth-Century Embroidery." In *Viator: Medieval and Renaissance Studies,* no. 21 (1990): 203–228.

See also **Amulets**; **Visual Arts**.

JANET HELEN TULLOCH

In Microhistorical Traditions

The microhistorical traditions are those of the indigenous peoples that anthropologists usually describe as living today in small-scale societies. (Some indigenous peoples today live in small-scale societies; many others do not.) Small-scale indigenous populations are small; they share the same culture, beliefs, and traditions; and they are predominately, if not exclusively, homogenous or homogenetic. Their economies emphasize a local self-sufficiency. They are usually capable, at least in provident times, of supporting their populations with resources near at hand.

Not long ago, the populations of small-scale societies were typically categorized by scholars as "primitive cultures," their beliefs and traditions labeled "primitive religions," and their crafts gathered together under the heading "primitive art." Nothing could be further from the truth. The beliefs and traditions of surviving small-scale societies are complex and sophisticated. The objects embodying these beliefs and traditions are similarly complex and sophisticated in form, construction, and configuration. Research, however, is spotty and insufficient overall. For starters, such words as *art, craft,* and *religion* are generally unknown in most of the world's spoken languages and the languages of today's indigenous peoples.

The reader would be further misled if he or she thinks the peoples of the microhistorical traditions have always lived in small-scale societies. Some small-scale societies today are all that remain of ancient civilizations once part of vast trading and political alliances of considerable population densities. Their numbers were reduced for a variety of reasons, singly or in combination, including the ecological collapse of food resources, introduced diseases, conquest and colonialization, loss of homelands, outward migration, and genocide.

These factors all contribute to the poverty and insufficiency of scholarship in this field with regard to sacred myths and practices centered on women's crafts. At this point in cross-cultural scholarship it is not possible to say with certainty that any particular material or technique is usually restricted to women's domain worldwide. The techniques of spinning and weaving, for example, are not "women's work" everywhere nor is sculpting and carving "men's work" only.

Microhistorical traditions survive because they are adaptable and accommodating to change, a fact too often overlooked by scholars. For example, Canadian artist Freda Diesing (b. 1925), a Haida elder, is internationally renowned for her traditional cedar sculpture. How is this possible when cedar is believed to be a wood only men may carve because cedar is seen as a grandmother? Diesing, however, claims descent from the mythical ancestress Djilagons of the Eagle clan. The artist received specific permission to carve cedar from her own powerful dream and the approval of her mother's uncle, a chief. As a result, it is not unusual today to find Haida masks or bentwood boxes carved by women. Diesing's vision validated not only her own work but that of other women, too. What is missing from the ethnographic research are the particular stories of who does the work, when is the work performed, and why is it done this way.

Although embroidery—the elaboration of cloth or leather with stitched thread—is very often women's work, exceptions abound. According to the American artist Lucy Arai, the practice of *sashiko,* a form of Zen art, developed from a practical and inexpensive simple embroidery technique that Japanese peasants of both sexes once employed to create warmer, less expensive work garments. Arai herself learned the stitching technique from her Japanese uncle.

It is important for researchers to keep several questions foremost in their research: when is a particular activity done by one sex (and not the other), what are the reasons given for this differentiation, under what circumstances are roles reversed or borrowed (if ever), and, most importantly, are particular roles delimited to both sexes or to only one? Some research in this complex area has been exemplary and the stories collected paradigmatic.

OCEANIA

Throughout central New Guinea, one finds women and men whose traditional culture is centered on the manufacture and use of the bilum, an astonishingly versatile string bag. *Bilum* is a pidgin term meaning string bag, pockets, marsupial pouch, and human placenta. The importance of the bilum is only suggested by its name. A bilum can carry babies, food, fuel, fibre, the sick and injured, or whatever else that needs to be carried. For example, a mother working her field will suspend the baby in a bilum from a stick stuck in the field. This keeps the baby near at hand and close to breast. However, as Maureen Anne MacKenzie discovered in her extraordinary and exhaustive study of the bilum culture (1991), the practice also is believed to transmit power from the earth via the stick into the bilum and ultimately into the baby. Thus, the baby learns ritual lessons awake and asleep. Perhaps no other human-made object in the world today is as multifunctional as the bilum nor as important.

Bilums can be made in any size. Small ones are worn as amulet covers. A man with much ritual knowledge can be identified by the number of bilums he wears. Large bilums carry home the brush for making more bilums. Bilums may be worn in layers as capelike clothing, too. In some settlements, the age of a woman is known by the number of bilums she wears. Among the Eipo, when a man dies it is believed that he is carried away by a female power whose name, *Ninye Tomolim Alenq,* means "the net bag collecting men." Women make all of these bags, employing a not-easy-to-learn looping technique, from bark fibers that are handspun

into a two-ply string. Men, women, and children all collect the fibers that are spun into string. Each of the bags is looped from a single string. The bags are almost unbreakable and can be looped in any size, limited only by the string available and the particular women's skill. Women learn to make bilums as young girls. Much of the looping is done away from public view. When a woman dies, she is buried with her personal bilum so that she may continue her good works after her death.

Women do not ornament their bags. The contents of their bilums are always on display. Men, however, do cover the outer surfaces of their bags with bird feathers and plumes so that no one can see inside. Only the side of the bag worn next to the skin is left unadorned.

The existence of the entire community centers on its status as children of Afek, the female creator who gave birth to the people and all aspects of human life. Afek's complete name, Paatakanib or Fitipkanib, translates variously as "marsupial pouch mother" or cassowary. Before Afek left this world, she organized and divided all of her mothering tasks into two equal groups—the tasks men should perform and the tasks women should perform—just as a good mother would assign her children each their particular chores in the home. Men must care for the ancestral relics Afek left behind when she built the men's houses in the various villages, and women must loop together the life of the community by means of their continuous manufacture of bilum. MacKenzie was not able to uncover even a suggestion of acknowledged male or female dominance in the division of labour.

Nevertheless, women and men lead almost completely separate lives. According to MacKenzie, women are identified with Afek as natural mothers. That is why women always wear their bilum suspended from their heads with the handle of the bilum serving as a tumpline. Worn in this manner, with a bilum spread across their backs, the women actually take on the form of a cassowary as they bend over to work in their vegetable gardens. Men do not have this possibility of a worldly, mundane identification with Afek. Their identification with the geneatrix must be more esoteric. It can only be completed within the men's house, which is thought of as a womb. Inside these houses, men become ritual mothers, caring for the ancestor's relics and initiating boys into their social responsibilities. In public, men wear their bilum simply as shoulder bags. Men ornament their bilums in private while inside the men's house.

THE AMERICAS

Early in the 1930s noted anthropologist Ruth Landes set out to chronicle the lives of Ojibwa women in a western Ontario hunting band in hard times. One of her most striking findings was the discovery that men and boys led disciplined lives delimited by what they must do to be men and, therefore, to be successful hunters and warriors. Women's education as such was ignored. They were not given any particular standard for being a woman. Indeed, they (and their menstrual cycle) were viewed as dangerous, potentially "bad medicine" for everyone. Landes concluded that the contemporary Ojibwa woman's life had become chaotic because there was little incentive to learn or practice any of the traditional women's skills now that "white" clothing and household items had replaced the traditional material culture. Interestingly, Landes also noted, no social barrier now stood in the way of any Ojibwa woman who wanted to hunt or do any of the things men did.

The Huichol women of the Sierra Madres of Mexico have obtained a very different situation. According to researcher Susan Eger, Huichol women are encouraged to become "good women" by learning the skills of traditional weaving, beadwork, and embroidery. Their artwork brings sacred power into their personal lives and that of the community because the Huichol woman's talent and skills are believed to be on loan from a divine source. Her visible esoteric knowledge is respected as much as that of the male shaman. The designs the Huichol woman works into her products are exclusively hers. They have been received in visions. Huichol men, too, also learn to do fine traditional embroidery, weaving, and beadwork, but sacred knowledge is not thought to be encoded in their work. Importantly, too, Huichol work has become an important source of income for the community because it is also prized by non-Huichol collectors.

SIBERIA AND ALASKA

In the Bering Sea region researchers find yet another understanding of women's work. All of the traditional material culture is focused on the hunt and the sacred interrelationship of women and men to the animals hunted. The relationships are complex ones, crisscrossed between sexual identity and animal and human identity. The female seamstress's transformation of the skins of slain animals into second skins for humans to wear is a delicate balance of opposing and complementary powers. For example, when the male hunters are away from the camp, women may not sew. Such work would offend the animals being hunted. In some situations women in the camps are so closely identified with the animals that the hunter seeks, that the success or failure of the hunt is believed to depend on what the women are doing back at the camp.

The boundary between animal and human is a porous one because many animals are persons who share the quality of *inua* with humans. Each may—and at times

does—wear the skin of the other. The human clothing women construct, consequently, is made to reveal the sexual characteristics of the one wearing it. In this manner all animals hunted are construed to be female, and all hunters male—even if, in fact, the hunter is female and the animal slain is male.

AFRICA

Among the Mafa and Bulabay people of northern Cameroon in Africa women of a particular caste, the Nqwazla, are responsible for all the ceramic production used throughout the community. These women are also the community midwives and healers. Their life-sustaining roles are intertwined with the pots they make. According to researchers Nicholas David, Judy Sterner, and Kodzo Gavua (1988), the pots have personhood and that personhood is decidedly human, a fact reflected in the manner in which the pots are decorated. The ornamentation is anthropomorphic. Pots representing men, for example, might have an abstracted moustache or a stylized penis; pots representing women could be emblazoned with a stylized breast or vulva. Decorated pots are part of the living human community. The pots, just like human bodies, are oiled for special occasions. Some pots are so powerful that a sacrifice must be made to the powers held in the pots—for example, the deceased mother's soul pot or the deceased father's soul pot. The only pots Nqwazla women do not decorate are pots that are not part of human social life. Thus, an old woman who lives by herself would eat her food from an undecorated pot because there is no danger of any man accidentally coming in contact with her food pot.

Although women throughout Africa are widely credited with responsibility for domestic ceramic production and all other domestic crafts, historian Marla Berns notes there are many poorly understood exceptions to this supposed pattern. Further, Berns argues, unsubstantiated androcentric assumptions in past and present African studies unnecessarily complicate the researcher's role. The same could be said of other studies in any of the microhistorical traditions.

BIBLIOGRAPHY

Berns, Marla. "Art, History, and Gender: Women and Clay in West Africa." *The African Archaeological Review* 11 (1993): 129–148. Critical bibliographic and methodological discussion of scholarly incongruities in studies of West African materials.

Berrin, Kathleen, ed. *Art of the Huichol Indians.* 1978. Illustrated catalogue for museum exhibition with scholarly essays from a variety of art historical and anthropological viewpoints.

David, Nicholas, Judy Sterner, and Kodzo Gavua. "Why Pots are Decorated." *Current Anthropology* 29, no. 3 (1988): 365–389. Description of the sacred nature of ceramic production by women of a particular caste among the Mafa and Bulahay peoples of northern Cameroon, Africa. See related video: "Vessels of the Spirit: Pots and People in North Cameroon." Directed by Nicholas David. University of Calgary, 1989.

Fitzhugh, William W., and Aron Crowell. *Crossroads of Continents: Cultures of Siberia and Alaska.* 1988. Illustrated, comprehensive scholarly catalogue that accompanied a blockbuster exhibition tracing the joint history of the circumpolar peoples who had been separated by fifty years of the Cold War. Contains authoritative essays by North American, European, and Russian scholars.

Hackett, Rosalind I. J. *Art and Religion in Africa.* 1996. Unlike other descriptive studies of African art that focus on an often decontextualized artwork, in this comprehensive survey of sub-Saharan art and religion Hackett describes the social and religious nature of becoming an artist and the traditional and contemporary roles artists play in their communities.

Hauser-Schäublin, Brigitta. "The Thrill of the Line, the String, and the Frond, or Why the Abelam Are a Non-Cloth Culture." *Oceania* 67, no. 2 (1996): 81–106. The Abelam people of Papua-New Guinea have created a sex-specific culture that contrasts the female softness of the string bag (looped by women) with the masculine hardness of the shell ring (cut by men). All relationships are transactional and oppositional and possible only when individual elements are temporarily conjoined.

Landers, Ruth. *The Ojibwa Woman.* 1938. Ethnological field study of the roles women play and the options open to them in a hunting culture at a time of great social transition. The author provides forceful and cautionary descriptors of women's lives at the time of this writing.

MacKenzie, Maureen Anne. *Androgynous Objects: String Bags and Gender in Central New Guinea.* 1991. A richly textured study that loops together myth, technique, social custom, tradition, and variance all centered on the bilum. The bilum keeps the universe knotted together for the peoples of central New Guinea, a complex of nations all claiming descent from a female geneatrix. The author's photographs and diagrams are persuasive evidence of the diligence with which she set out to learn all that might be known about the bilum. She also includes discussion of the impact of contemporary land use and Christian missionizing on the once-isolated societies.

Oakes, Jill, and Rick Riewe. *Our Boots: An Inuit Women's Art.* 1995. Although both women and men know how to sew and repair sealskin and caribou boots (*kamik*), the most beautiful and valued work is that done by women of the central Arctic. The boots are symbolic of personal and group identity.

Tepper, Leslie H. *Earth Line and Morning Star: Nlaka'-pamux Clothing Traditions.* 1994. The Nlaka'pamux people (formerly known as the Knife or Couteau Indians or Thompson River Indians of British Columbia, Canada) traditionally believed that the center of the world is where the Thompson and Fraser rivers meet. Their clothing, both woven fibers and hides, reflected this belief. Much of the clothing was made by women; today these skills are taught to both girls and boys to ensure that these beliefs survive.

Weiner, Annette B. *Inalienable Possessions: The Paradox of Keeping-While-Giving.* 1992. Comprehensive discussion of the ritual role of women focused on their cloth production in the traditional societies of New Zealand, Australia, Samoa, and the Trobriand Islands. Common themes explored include the role of cloth as a secondary "skin" and the religious and social role of women as life-giver and societal legitimator.

Weiner, Annette B., and Jane Schneider, eds. *Cloth and HUman Experience.* 1989. Selected essays loosely organized under three headings. Five essays discuss cloth production among the peoples of the Trobriand Islands and Samoa in Oceania; the Kuba people of Zaire; and the Kodi people of eastern Indonesia. Three essays consider shifts of metaphorical meaning in cloth production created by the introduction of capitalist economics, specifically in the economics of early modern Europe, seventeenth-century Holland, and contemporary Oaxaca, Mexico. The last section of the anthology consists of four essays dealing with cloth production in periods of political change, specifically ancient Peru, nineteenth-century and early-twentieth-century India, and late-medieval Okinawa.

MAUREEN KORP

In Asian Traditions

The term *craft* is usually taken to mean the making by hand of items that are used, especially those used in daily life. This article focuses specifically on items that are made for use in religious ceremonies or otherwise have religious significance. A given religious tradition will generally support both arts, which are held to a broadly conceived cultural aesthetic standard, and crafts, which are locally specific. However, some traditions do not support both; for example, Confucianism, with its emphasis on refinement and precise skills of execution, tended not to find expression in the making of crafts. Thus, this article presents both arts and crafts in the interest of providing an overview of religiously significant items made by women in a variety of religious traditions.

The study of women's participation, both historically and in contemporary times, in the making of any type of craft is an emerging field. Many dictionaries and gallery produced coffee-table books provide information and illustrations of arts and crafts in Asian traditions; however, there are few gender-specific discussions among them. To understand women's participation in making arts and crafts, one must assess, first, the traditional involvement in particular arts and crafts of women, whose names, historical periods, and works are known through scholarly studies of historical records; second, the present involvement of women in arts and crafts traditionally associated with women, but about whose predecessors historical evidence is lacking, either because there are no records or the records have not yet been a subject of study; and third, the present involvement of women in arts and crafts not traditionally associated with women.

PAINTING

Confucianism

Painting was one of the arts suitable to Confucian philosophical and social principles; the "three perfections" were painting, poetry, and calligraphy. The earliest known woman artist in China was a calligrapher, Wei Furen or Wei Shuo (272–349). Although her works have been lost, she was celebrated as the teacher of Wang Xizhi, the most famous and influential of all Chinese calligraphers. A celebrated woman painter, Guan Daosheng (1262–1319) was also admired for her calligraphy; the emperor at the time collected samples of her writing, along with those of her husband and son. She is said to have innovated a new style in monochrome ink bamboo painting, which featured new-growth bamboo after rain.

Women were also taught Confucian values through scroll paintings that illustrated the *Ladies' Filial Piety*, a work traditionally attributed to a woman with the surname Cheng who lived during the Tang dynasty (618–906). Some of the extant scrolls were painted by male artists, but scholars suspect that this could have been an art by and for women as well. Through the paintings women were taught virtues especially appropriate to them, such as the decorum of a noblewoman, appreciation of classical texts, spinning and weaving as arts that demonstrate filial behavior, and reverence for one's husband.

The Ming dynasty (1368–1644) is known as a time when the participation of women in the arts increased, owing to economic prosperity and growing literacy;

during this period, skills in painting became identified as a social asset for women, enhancing their ability to attract a husband. A major woman painter around this time was Ch'en Shu (1660–1736), idealized as an exemplar of Confucian virtue in a biography written by her scholar-official son. Her figural paintings focused on religious themes, such as the bodhisattva Kuan Yin and the Taoist immortal Lü Tung-pin, as well as classical images, such as the return of the Han Dynasty noblewoman Ts'ai Yen (Lady Wen-chi) to China. She is most famous for her landscape studies of mountains.

Hinduism

The celebrated art of Tanjore painting on glass and canvas was traditionally performed exclusively by a class of male artisans, since it involved status (royal patronage), religious significance (the paintings are images of God), and expense (the paintings use gold paint or gold leaf). In the changing political times of the nineteenth and early twentieth centuries, the art became less prominent. Today, Tanjore painting has been revived and is practiced by women in the city of Madras.

Popular sentiment attributes the recent revival of Tanjore painting in Madras to Meena Mutiah, a princess of the Chettinad royal family, whose father had patronized Tanjore painting. Drawing upon this tradition, Mutiah runs a school of Tanjore painting at her family's Chettinad Palace in the city. Some one hundred young men receive training in Tanjore painting at this school, which includes a workshop where contemporary masterpieces are created and sold at high prices to domestic and foreign customers.

Although Mutiah's school carries on the tradition of male production of Tanjore painting, many urban women artisans are drawn to the art. For many of these women artists, who were trained in classical Western painting styles, their making of Tanjore paintings represents their participation in a distinctively Indian classical tradition.

Tanjore paintings are devotional works of art, depicting Hindu gods—in classical versions, Vishnu, but Sarasvatī, the goddess of learning and the arts, is increasingly popular. In canvas paintings the god's clothing and ornaments are represented in raised portions, encrusted with pieces of glass and then covered with gold leaf. The image is painted around these areas in an intentionally flat style with minimal shading and completely outlined in red. The classical palette includes rich reds, browns, blues, and greens.

Other devotional painting traditions of India have been the province of women. The wall and paper-canvas paintings of village women of Kumaon in Uttar Pradesh and Mithila of Bihar render images of Hindu gods and goddesses in brightly colored designs. Throughout India women decorate their doorways with rice or chalk-powder line designs. These impermanent white or colorful patterns, known as *kolam, alpona,* or *rangoli,* depending on the region, signify a flourishing household.

WEAVING

Buddhism in Thailand

Women are traditionally responsible for the production of cloth, work they perform on looms in their homes in Thai villages. They produce clothing for men and women, textiles for the home, and clothing and materials for Buddhist monks, which is a merit-making activity. Traditionally, cotton is woven to a specified length, then presented to monks for their daily wear. Other donations, often from female relatives, include a square of white cloth surrounded by decorative designs, which initiates wear as a head covering at the ordination ceremony. Gifts to the monastery include patterned covered pillows and banners that are raised on ceremonial occasions.

Traditional Beliefs in Thailand

Among the Yao hill peoples of northern Thailand, traditional beliefs are embroidered into clothing and ornaments. For example, the classic Star Design, executed by a weave or running stitch, symbolizes ancestor spirits that have reached the heavens and protect their kin on earth. In northeast Thailand, white cloth is used in traditional practices that predate Buddhism. For example, at traditional funerals white cloth is used as dress for the deceased's children and as a flag of commemoration; it also symbolizes the power of a system of natural medicine derived from Indian teachings.

Buddhism and Shinto in Japan

A tradition in Japanese Pure Land Buddhism attributes the sacred depiction of Amida Buddha in woven cloth (an image known as the Taima Mandala) to a woman. According to this depiction, in 763 a young noblewoman, Chūjōhime, prayed to the Buddha Amida. In response to her prayers, Amida Buddha and his disciple Kannon descended; Kannon wove the mandala, while Amida explained its meaning. Throughout the centuries, the legend of Chūjōhime has been depicted in text, painting, and drama; there are temples at her birth and grave sites; and an annual ritual reenacts her involvement in the original creation of this salvific woven image of the Buddha in Paradise.

In Shinto tradition ancient texts portray the sun goddess Amaterasu as responsible for planting the rice fields, performing the harvest ritual, and weaving the clothes for all of the gods. The texts relate these duties to senior women of the household, who weave clothes for their families and offer mulberry-fiber thread and

Ikat weaving of ancestors, Indonesia (© Werner Forman/ Corbis)

cloth as first fruits for worship in a special household harvest ritual. The legend also informed classical rituals at the famous Ise temple. The scriptural *Engi-shiki* text, dating from the tenth century but containing much older material, refers to two groups of women weavers, the Hatori Uji (*hata,* "to weave on a loom" and *oru,* "to weave") and Omi Uji (*o,* "hemp, flax" and *umu,* "to tear into thin strips"). These women would weave both coarse and soft cloth for presentation at the annual Festival of the First Fruits ceremony and then participate in the ritual procession to offer the cloth.

POTTERY

Zen Buddhism

In contemporary Japan women perform the tea ceremony (*chanoyu*), which has been traditionally practiced by Zen masters and noblemen. The first woman to serve as senior instructor in the influential Urasenke school of tea was Hamamoto Sōshun (d. 1986), who was appointed by the fourteenth-generation grand master Tantansai (1893–1964) during World War II. The tea ceremony embodies simplicity, refined poverty, purity, meditation, and the sacredness of everyday items. The popularity of the tea ceremony underlies the interest in and development of ceramics in Japanese tradition; even today, manufacture of tea ceremony ware is the cornerstone of a potter's business. Because it is unusual for women to be accorded the status of master craftsperson of a traditional art, women contribute to the making of tea ceremony items in a supporting, though still an important, capacity, such as as carver of decorative designs on the clay forms. More commonly, young women are encouraged to study ceramics as a course in their refinement, to enhance their marriageability.

Hinduism

Women play a supporting role in the creation of earthenware pots for temple food offerings (*mahāprasād*) at the famed Jagannāth Temple in Purī, on the coast of Orissa in eastern India. This community of potters has traditionally enjoyed high status even though potters are low-caste as a group, since they create vessels in which the food blessed by God is placed and then distributed to worshipers. The creation of large pots, finished with a paddle and anvil to have a faceted appearance that evokes the sacred lotus design, is the most prestigious work, since these pots can be used in the temple kitchen. Women in the community can make some of these pots, but in general it is male-defined labor. Women make many varieties of small unfaceted pots and lamps, all of them fashioned by hand without the wheel, which are used in the temple but not in the temple kitchen.

BIBLIOGRAPHY

The Dictionary of Art, 33 vols., edited by Jane Turner (1996), has a brief entry on handicraft and a longer one on folk art, which discusses the theoretical distinctions between fine art and folk art but provides no examples of the latter.

Marsha Weidner, ed., *Flowering in the Shadows: Women in the History of Chinese and Japanese Painting* (1990) is a rare and exemplary single volume devoted to the study of women's historical participation in making Asian art. In Weidner, see especially Julia K. Murray, "Didactic Art for Women: The *Ladies' Classic of Filial Piety*," Ellen Johnston Laing, "Women Painters in Traditional China," and Marsha Weidner, "The Conventional Success of Ch'en Shu." Gallery catalogues featuring women artists are Marsha Weidner et al., *Views from Jade Terrace: Chinese Women Artists, 1300–1912* (Indianapolis Museum of Art, 1988) and Patricia Fisher, *Japanese Women Artists 1600–1900* (Lawrence, Kansas: Spencer Museum of Art, 1988).

On Indian craft traditions, *Arts and Crafts of India*, by Nicholas Barnard with photographs by Robyn Beeche (1993), contains informative text and outstanding photographs, including a brief section on Tanjore painting. For more information on Tanjore painting in Madras, see Karen Pechilis Prentiss, "From Modern Madras to Enterprising Chennai," in *Baboos, Bohras and Banyas to Bureaucrats and Businessmen: The Mid-*

dle-Classes and the Building of Modern Religion(s) in South Asia, edited by Joanne Punzo Waghorne (forthcoming). *Mathila Painters: Five Village Artists from Madhubani, India* (40 min., 1994) a color video produced and directed by Ray Owens and Joseph Elder, explores the lives and artistic styles of four women and one man to show how the change from the traditional technique of painting on village walls to the painting on heavy handmade paper for commercial sale has affected village life.

An overview of Southeast Asian craft traditions is provided in Thelma R. Newman, *Contemporary Southeast Asian Arts and Crafts* (1977). An overview of Thai craft traditions is provided in William Warren and Luca Invernizzi Tettoni, with consultant Chaiwut Tulayadhan, *Arts and Crafts of Thailand* (1994). On Thai weaving traditions, see Mattiebelle Gittinger and H. Leedom Lefferts, Jr., *Textiles and the Tai Experience in Southeast Asia* (Washington, D.C.: The Textile Museum, 1992). On Thai weaving, women, and Buddhism, see H. Leedom Lefferts, Jr., "The Power of Women's Decisions: Textiles in Tai Dam and Thai-Lao Theravada Buddhist Funerals," *Southeast Asia Journal of Science* 21, no. 2 (1993): 111–129, and the same author's "The Ritual Importance of the Mundane: White Cloth Among the Tai of Southeast Asia," *Expedition* 38, no. 1 (1996): 37–50.

On Japanese weaving traditions, see Elizabeth Ten Grotenhuis, "Chūjōhime: The Weaving of Her Legend," in *Flowing Traces: Buddhism in the Literary and Visual Arts of Japan*, edited by James H. Sanford, William R. LaFleur, and Masatoshi Nagatomi (1992); Alan L. Miller, "Ame no miso-ori me (the heavenly weaving maiden): The Cosmic Weaver in Early Shinto Myth and Ritual," *History of Religions* 24 (August 1984): 27–48; and Louise Allison Cort, "The Changing Fortunes of Three Archaic Japanese Textiles," in *Cloth and Human Experience*, edited by Annette B. Weiner and Jane Schneider (1989).

An excellent, anthropological introduction to the tea ceremony is Jennifer L. Anderson, *An Introduction to Japanese Tea Ritual* (1991). An excellent, experiential discussion of contemporary potters and their craft in Japan (similar in style to the paradigm of writing on craft, Michael Owen Jones, *The Hand Made Object and Its Maker* [1975]) is Leila Philip, *The Road Through Miyama* (1989).

On the Jagannāth Temple community of potters, see Louise Allison Cort, "Temple Potters of Purī," *Res 7*, no. 8 (Spring/Autumn 1984): 33–43. An important theoretical discussion of pottery and possession is Stephen Inglis, "Possession and Pottery: Serving the Divine in a South Indian Community," in *Gods of Flesh Gods of Stone: The Embodiment of Divinity in India*, edited by Joanne Punzo Waghorne and Norman Cutler, with Vasudha Narayanan (1985); as Inglis notes, the potters in the community he studies are male, yet possession is a prominent female strategy of relating to the divine.

KAREN PECHILIS PRENTISS

In Monotheistic Traditions

Women's religious activities, including practices and production of artifacts of religious meaning and use, are not always specific to or dictated by their religious affiliation. Such activities are often more connected to women's rituals in the domestic sphere, where ethnic identification is often perceived as synonymous with religious identification. Emphasizing the timely, the specific, the personal, the ephemeral and the nondoctrinal, women's crafts foster the cohesion of families in time and space as they mark both the cyclical passage of time and the individual rites of passage of the family members, even when these are not officially religiously marked.

An individual woman's skill, experience, or knowledge in producing and reproducing religious crafts can distinguish her from other women and constitute sources of personal pride and prestige. Even if particular items or services are purchased, women choose which these will be and what form they must take.

In the home women keep the calendar of ethnically and religiously meaningful holidays and holydays. They decide seasonal food menus and recipes, decorations, celebratory clothing, hairstyles and makeup, and the choice and arrangement of family mementos. If the home contains a shrine, even if it is only a crucifix on the wall, women install and maintain it. In the public sphere, women coordinate group events, set protocol and dress codes, decorate and clean the site. If they have access to public areas of worship, women worshippers clean and decorate; make, embellish, and maintain vestments and ritual textiles; prepare food (both social and ritual); arrange flowers; constitute the choir; produce items for fund-raising events; organize pageants, theatrical events, and parish activities; and produce the visual aids to provide religious instruction to the young. A last common responsibility for women is the public display of emotion. They openly grieve, rejoice, or curse. Depending on the ethnic and religious context, these displays take specific forms such as the ululation of North African women.

JUDAISM

Leviticus 19:19 and Deuteronomy 22:11 specifically proscribe the combination of materials in clothing, in particular of linen and wool. To safeguard, against this, Jews have had a long tradition in the garment trade. Women have also been skilled lace makers and thread,

Here are examples of embellished vestments hanging in the backroom of the Cataldo Mission, in Coeur D'Alene, Idaho (Kevin R. Morris/© Corbis).

gold-thread, and bead embroiderers. As such, they have produced ritual textiles for Christian, Muslim, and Jewish communities in Europe and the Middle East until recent times. Work studios were often made up of the women of a family headed by the father and husband who worked as a tailor (Salomon, 1988).

It is not always possible to identify the gender of the maker, but enough synagogue textiles are signed by their maker (or their purchaser) that we know that women are active in their production. These textiles included curtains (*parokhet*) for the Ark, Torah scroll covers and binders, and men's prayer shawls (tallith) and skullcaps (*kippah*). Used both at home and in the synagogue would be the marriage canopy (*chuppah*), which is sometimes made by the bride-to-be as a gift for her husband to wear as a prayer shawl after the wedding (Salomon, 1988). Skullcaps were also produced by the bride as wedding gifts for the men of her bridegroom's family. If childless, she might later embroider a Torah binder as a special gift to the synagogue in hopes of having her wish for a child granted.

In the home, site of many Jewish religious ceremonies, the wife is responsible for maintaining the ritual purity of food and serving dishes (kosher). She cooks the ritual meals and leads the weekly kiddush prayers before the Shabbat (sabbath). Fine white tablecloths, challah cloths for the braided bread, and matzo cloths for the unleavened bread, passover pillows, the *mizrach* panel to mark the east—all these have been traditionally made by women for their families.

CHRISTIANITY

Byzantine church textiles were often the gift of rich patronesses (Johnstone, 1967) who paid to have them made by embroidery guilds or female monasteries.

Both nuns and commercial factories, mainly employing women, continue to produce Catholic ritual textiles and vestments to this day. Since the reforms of Vatican II, many Canadian Catholic parishes have forgone commercial products and encouraged parish women to produce the vestments instead. This continues a long tradition in Canada of women, mainly in religious communities, producing textiles, embroideries, lace, vestments and altar cloths, parade banners, religious paintings, guilding, candles, silk and dried flower arrangements, wax statues for Christmas crèches, rosary beads and holy images, and finally both leavened and unleavened bread for Mass. The teaching of these skills by nuns to other women, both native and white, has also been an important missionizing strategy (Marchand, 1984; Simard, 1989).

Anglican women have produced important quantities of lace and embroideries for ritual vestments, while the making of canvas wool-work prayer kneelers has been a popular group endeavour (Dean, 1968). Protestant women in Europe and America often embroidered religious sayings on samplers, which then became cherished home decorations. Certain denominations, such as the Shakers, made the production of any item a religious exercise for both women and men. American Protestant congregations have tended to use few ritual textiles other than choir and ministerial robes. What has remained are rites-of-passage garments for individuals, from christening robe to wedding gown and funeral suit.

In both the religious and secular home, Easter, Thanksgiving, Christmas, and even Independence Day are marked by the production of embroidered, quilted, or appliqued textiles and seasonal foods. Even the buying and sending of greeting cards can be seen as a ritual activity.

ISLAM

Little has been written about Islamic women's ritual productions and practices, but much can be inferred from their textile production. In North Africa and the Middle East, embroidery is an integral part of a young woman's education. As a child, she may have worn unadorned clothing but at about age 12, she begins to embroider her *kissweh* (trousseau). Blankets, cushions, veils, headgear, jackets, and dresses for both everyday and special occasions must be made and decorated, as adornment will proclaim married status. The clothing covering her head, neck, and chest are most heavily embroidered as these are the main life centers of the body. Such vulnerable areas are protected with traditional talismanic patterns. This wedding clothing will also serve on later festive occasions in her life. Embroidered cushions made by the mothers of the bride and groom are exchanged between families, and the bride also produces embroidered items for the groom's family as wedding presents.

Even though men and women often celebrate in areas separated from each other, women prepare the appropriate foods for the festive occasions. In many parts of North Africa, a celebration also is not complete without the presence of professional women dancers and singers. For example, in Egypt in the late twentieth century, a traditional wedding is marked by the *shamadan* procession of the bride and groom preceded by a dancer holding a candelabra on her head and dancing to a rhythm reserved for this one occasion.

Finally, it is Muslim women who most often maintain the shrines of saints found outside the mosque. These are periodically cleaned, covered in flowers, and given food offerings appropriate to the saint.

BIBLIOGRAPHY

Amir, Ziva. *Arabesque: Decorative Needlework from the Holy Land.* 1977.
Barbeau, Marius. "From Gold Treads to Porcupine Quills." *Antiques* 5, no. 45 (1944): 24–26.
———. *Saintes artisanes.* Vol. 1, *Les brodeuses.* Montreal, 1944.
Dagneault, Sr. Gabrielle. "La broderie d'art chez les Ursulines." *Musées* (September 1981): 15–20.
Dean, Beryl. *Ecclesiastical Embroidery.* London, 1989.
Gray, Elizabeth Dodson, ed. *Sacred Dimensions of Women's Experience.* 1988.
Johnston, Pauline. *The Byzantine Tradition in Church Embroidery.* London, 1967.
Kelly, Mary B. "Goddess Embroideries of Eastern Europe." In *Gender, Culture and the Arts: Women, the Arts and Society.* Edited by R. Dotterer and S. Bowers. 1993.
Luciow, Johanna, et al. *Eggs Beautiful: How to Make Ukrainian Easter Eggs.* 1975.
Marchand, Thérèse. "La collection des broderies historiées des Ursulines de Québec." M.A. diss., University of Laval, Canada. 1984.
Porter, John R. *L'art de la dorurer au Québec.* Québec, 1975.
Rabuzzi, Kathryn Allen. *The Sacred and the Feminine: Toward A Theology of Housework.* 1982.
Redekop, Gloria Neufeld. *The Work of Their Hands: Mennonite Women's Societies in Canada.* 1996.
Routtenberg, Lilly S., and Ruth R. Seldin. *The Jewish Wedding Book: A Practical Guide to the Traditions and Social Customs of the Jewish Wedding.* 1967.
Salomon, Kathryn. *Jewish Ceremonial Embroidery.* London, 1988.
Simard, Jean. *Les arts sacrés au Québec.* Ottawa, 1989.

Stone, Caroline. *The Embroideries of North Africa.* Essex, 1985.

Weibel, Adèle Coulin. "Ursuline Embroideries of French Canada." *Art Quarterly* 10, no. 1 (1947): 31–39.

LUCIE DUFRESNE

Creation and Recreation

Creation myths are concerned with the fundamental problems of human life: those of the origin of our own existence and the existence of the world. The multiplicity of creation stories testifies to the diversity of their cultural, social, and political contexts. Some scholars point to the positive role of creation stories as the sources of moral values that encourage cohesiveness of the society (Bronislaw Malinowski, *Sex, Culture and Myth,* 1962). Recently, however, feminist thinkers have argued that many of the creation myths have had a negative influence on the life of women. Since most creation stories mirror the patriarchal structures of their culture, they often encourage women's subordination and passivity.

TAOISM

Taoism relates a creation myth rich in feminine metaphors and symbols. The account of creation comes from the *Tao te ching* (sixth century B.C.E.) and *Chuang tzu* (fourth century B.C.E.). In Taoism all reality springs from Tao, the "Mysterious Female," "Mother of All-under-heaven." Creation comes from the womb of the Mother and is continually dependent on her for its existence. Tao is not only the source of all existence but also a model for the human creative power. All people fulfill their creativity when they follow the nonaggressive, flexible attitude of the Mother and reject strength, hardness, or superiority of stereotypically male behavior.

According to Taoism, the whole universe is sustained by the proper balance between yin and yang, or female and male principles that belong to Tao. Yin stands for negative forces and yang stands for positive forces, complementary principles that depend on each other. The cooperation between those two principles sustains the world and brings balance to each human existence.

While Taoism still has some elements of patriarchal structures (highest religious leadership is carried by men), perhaps due to the strong presence of the feminine images coming from the presence of yin, women have participated in spiritual and moral leadership.

HINDUISM

A study of Hinduism reveals various creation accounts that are more patriarchal than Taoism in tone. Ultimately all reality comes from *brahman,* or the absolute principle that is everything and nothing, is everywhere and nowhere. The oldest Hindu account of creation (2000 B.C.E. speaks of the cosmic primal man out of whose body emerges the rest of the universe. According to another set of stories (1000 B.C.E.) the world arises from the primeval sea, which produces a golden egg. Out of the egg is born the primal man who creates the rest of the world by his word. In later accounts (200 B.C.E.) creation comes from Brahma, the masculine expression of *brahman,* who creates through his thought (out of nothing).

While in principle *brahman* is beyond gender, the expressions of the divine are often portrayed in masculine images. Later Hindu tradition (500–1800 C.E.) refers to feminine creative energy (*śakti*) from which come other forms of life. In Tantrism, the male principle (Śiva) is subordinated to the female principle, Kālī, who is presented as the cherishing mother and creative power, as well as a destroyer. Some interpreters see Kālī as a stereotype of female chaotic sexuality, which is blamed for bringing destruction, while others believe that Kālī provides a needed counterbalance to the too soft concepts of femininity. Furthermore, contemporary Hindu women find in Kālī a hope for liberation from all sorts of oppressions (Sharada Sugirtharajah, "Hinduism," in *Women in Religion,* 1994)

JUDAISM AND CHRISTIANITY

In Judaism and Christianity, God is described as creating the universe out of nothing by the power of divine words. There are two creation stories describing the creation of the first human couple, Adam and Eve, in Genesis 1:1–2:3 and Genesis 2:4–3:24. The first account (about 400 B.C.E.) stresses the equality of the sexes as it speaks of both as being created in the image of God. In the second narrative (about 900 B.C.E.), Eve is created out of Adam's rib and is the one who leads Adam to disobey divine commandment. Traditionally this second story was understood as a sign of women's subordination to men since Eve was created after Adam, from Adam, and for Adam. Furthermore, her disobedience was taken as an evidence of her vicious nature that brings evil into the world. (Other females viewed as sources of chaos include Pandora in Greek mythology; the whore demoness in Zoroastrianism; and Tiamat in Mesopotamian myth.) Contemporary feminist scholars either reject completely the second story as intrinsically patriarchal or reinterpret the myth. New interpretations point to the fact that creation from Adam symbolizes the mutual need for companionship while eating of the fruit symbolizes the joint disobedience of the first couple.

Both Judaism and Christianity affirm that God, the creator, is beyond gender and provide feminine images of the divine. In the later sections of the Hebrew Bible, Sophia mediates the work of creation and continues to sustain the universe together with God. Moreover, Jewish tradition has a rich creation symbology based on the Kabbalah that speaks of a primordial, andrygynous unity (*ayn soph*), which splits itself into two principles of divinity. The products of splitting are YHVH, which stands for the male, transcendent aspect of God, and Shekhinah, the immanent, female part of God indwelling all creation. Such images from the Hebrew Bible and the Kabbalah provide inspiration for creating new egalitarian metaphors for the relationships between the sexes.

AFRICAN AND NATIVE AMERICAN RELIGIONS

While the majority of creator gods in African religions are male, there are a number of female creators: Temearu (the Uzo, Nigeria), Mawu and Nana Buku (Republic of Benin), and Obudua (the Yoruba, Nigeria). If male gods are often portrayed as "above the sky," female creators are identified with creation (earth, river, and moon) and are symbols of fertility. Some African creation myths blame women for creating the distance between the supreme being and the creation (Efik tribe, Nigeria).

Native American religions also speak of female creator gods in terms of their motherhood and immanence in creation. Earth the Mother often performs the role of the creator. The Changing Woman (Navajo) cooperates with the First Man in the acts of creation, and the Spider Woman (Hopi) breaths life into the first human beings. Still, patriarchal elements are present in the Native American traditions: male creators are prevalent and women are sometimes blamed for the misfortunes brought on the tribes, as in the Blackfoot creation story.

BIBLIOGRAPHY

Carmody, Denise Lardner. *Mythological Woman: Contemporary Reflections on Ancient Religious Stories.* 1992.

Hoch-Smith, Judith, and Anita Spring, eds. *Women in Ritual and Symbolic Roles.* 1978.

Holm, Jean, and John Bowker, eds. *Women in Religion.* 1994.

King, Ursula, ed. *Women in the World's Religions, Past and Present.* 1987.

Kumari, Ranjana. "Femaleness: The Hindu Perspective." *Religion and Society* 32 (1985): 3–19.

Larrington, Carolyne, ed. *The Feminist Companion to Mythology.* 1992.

Leeming, David Adams, and Margaret Adams Leeming. *Encyclopedia of Creation Myths.* 1994.

O'Brien, Joan, and Wilfred Major. *In the Beginning: Creation Myths from Ancient Mesopotamia, Israel and Greece.* 1982.

Sharma, Arvind, ed. *Religion and Women.* 1994.

———. *Women In World Religions.* 1987.

Sirwardena, R., ed. *Equality and the Religious Traditions of Asia.* 1987.

Walker, Barbara G. *The Woman's Encyclopedia of Myths and Secrets.* 1983.

WIOLETA POLINSKA

Critical Theory

Sometimes known as the Frankfurt school, critical theory is the intellectual heir to the tradition of G. W. F. Hegel (1770–1831) and Karl Marx, bringing together as well themes in sociology and psychoanalysis. The most important representatives of the Frankfurt school are Max Horkheimer (1895–1973), Theodor W. Adorno (1903–1969), and Herbert Marcuse (1898–1979). Horkheimer's essay "Traditional and Critical Theory" (1937) outlined the basic features of critical theory and gave it its name. Although never a systematic, unitary body of thought, the early critical theorists were primarily interested in what they understood to be the "self-betrayal" of the Enlightenment, inquiring into the ways in which reason itself becomes a mode of domination in patriarchal, performance-driven capitalist societies. Adorno in particular analyzed the conceptualizing practices of identity thinking in which the relations between subject and object are structured by domination, violence, and coercion. Nonidentity thinking or "negative dialectics" holds rich theoretical potential for feminist thinkers, some of whom are influenced by Adorno, such as Drucilla Cornell. Although Horkheimer, Adorno, and Marcuse were well aware of the long history of the male domination of women, their work does not address this in a sustained fashion. Patricia Jagentowicz Mills (1987) and Marsha Aileen Hewitt (1995) represent feminist critical appropriations of critical theory in the fields of philosophy and religious studies respectively. Critical theory analyzes the triumph of instrumental reason in modernity and its disastrous consequences for the dehumanization of the world; it scrutinizes the complexity of domination, including the recognition of the centrality of the domination of women within the fabric of civilization, as outlined in Horkheimer and Adorno's diagnosis of modernity in *Dialectic of Enlightenment*. These practices and insights together with the theory of negative dialectics provide a rich methodological and critical resource that contemporary feminist theory can use to expand and deepen its own critical focus on the myriad structures of sexism that reside in social institutions, social relationships, and within the human psyche, both male and female.

BIBLIOGRAPHY

Hewitt, Marsha Aileen. *Critical Theory of Religion: A Feminist Analysis.* 1995.

Horkheimer, Max. *Critical Theory: Selected Essays.* Translated by Matthew J. O'Connell. 1970.

Horkheimer, Max, and Theodor W. Adorno. *Dialectic of Enlightenment.* Translated by John Cumming. 1944, 1972.

Mills, Patricia Jagentowicz. *Woman, Nature, and Psyche.* 1987.

See also Deconstruction.

MARSHA AILEEN HEWITT

Cross-dressing

Cross-dressing, assuming the style of dress or actions culturally associated with the opposite sex, is one of the many forms of disguise that appear internationally in folk tale, legend, myth, and ballad; it is common as well in vernacular, dramatic performances (primarily farcical in nature) associated with festivals or carnivals. In narrative, the broader category of disguise includes male or female characters dressing not only as members of the opposite sex but also as members of a socioeconomic class not their own (for example, "Cinderella" [tale type AT510A; tale type references from Aarne and Thompson, 1961]). By extension, the category also includes the marking or branding of a member of one sex with the genitalia of the opposite sex as well as the physical transformation of a character (usually male) into the gender of the opposite sex (for example, the classical Greek tale of "Tiresias" and tales involving the prophet Muhammad's conversion of a male skeptic to Islam [motif D12; motif references from Thompson, 1966]). Finally, disguise may involve assuming the shape of animals or objects (for example, a goose in "The Black and White Bride" [tale type AT403]). Cross-dressing is thus related to various forms of disguise that involve symbol inversion and transformation; female-to-male and male-to-female cross-dressing must be "read" together in order to understand gender construction within particular cultures and their attendant ideologies.

Cross-dressing, whether as female or male, almost always enables a character's freedom of movement that is not traditionally available within a particular cultural setting. Generally, male characters cross-dress as a female so as to gain access to private female spaces, usually for the purpose of seduction, or to escape from life-threatening situations. Generally, female characters cross-dress as a male so as to enter and gain broader mobility in the "outside" public world or to escape socially threatening as well as life-threatening situations (usually an unsuccessful seduction by a predatory male that nonetheless results in questions concerning the woman's chastity). Whereas cross-dressing of male characters as a female, except for the purpose of seducing a woman, almost always leads to sexual or another form of abuse or humiliation for the male, interestingly, just the opposite is usually true of female characters who cross-dress as a male.

The most extensively documented story-telling tradition of female characters dressing as males is that of the female warrior. The female warrior is a young woman who cuts her hair and dons male or martial attire and enters the public realm to save or revenge family, tribe, or nation or to look for a lost lover: Joan of Arc (Western European), Mary Ambree (English and American), Fa Mu Lan (Chinese), Subanbali and Phulan Devi (India). Historical and legendary, the female warrior's disguise not only conceals identity, thus giving her broader freedom of movement and action, but "reveals the social constraints under which [women] normally live" (Flueckiger, 1996, p. 69).

Other tales involving female cross-dressing fall within the category of folk legends about transvestite saints, who, as Marjorie Garber (1992) explains, cross-dressed as men to obtain entry into all-male religious communities. Occasionally these women are forced to reveal their sex when they become pregnant by a member of their order. Garber notes the examples of saints Eugenia, Perpetua, Anthanasia, Apollinaris or Dorotheus, Euphroysne, Anastasia, Patricia, and Wilgefortis, who is said to have additionally grown a beard in order to stay virginal and devotional when her father tried to marry her off to the king of Sicily. Such legends also include stories of women becoming bishops or popes, as in the case of Pope Joan (motif K1961.2.1).

In a genre that has been called the "Innocent Persecuted Heroine," two internationally widespread tale types, "The Wager on the Wife's Chastity" (AT882) and "The Innocent Slandered Maiden" (AT883A), involve the ruining of a young woman's reputation by an attempted seduction, sexual assault, or accusation of infidelity or uselessness. The woman is forced to flee dressed as a man, and in this disguise she both makes her way in the world and ultimately forces a revelation of the villain's true character, which in turn enables her

Tomoe Gozen was a twelfth-century noblewoman famous both for her beauty and her courage. She saved her husband at the Battle of Uji in 1184. Here she is depicted in her armor (Asian Art & Archaeology, Inc./Corbis).

to disclose her "true" sex and participate in normative conjugal relations. Male and female narrators of the tales tend to foreground and downplay different parts of the tales, suggesting that women's and men's everyday life experiences create gendered understandings of what is or is not important. James Taggart (1990) has noted that, among storytellers of Cáceres, Spain, both women and men seem to concur that only when dressed as a male can the female character "make 'other' men hear her and . . . extract confessions from the men who did her harm," suggesting that "in terms of morality the male voice is the ultimate arbiter" (p. 57). In an Afghani narrative, by contrast, a female character's masculine behavior limits her public mobility; the story, part of a women's ritual, sanctions women's more normative appropriation and use of the institutionalized practice of veiling (Mills, 1985).

Finally, cross-dressing narratives suggest the possibility of same-sex erotic desire, even as the tales' het-

erosexual framings seek to erase such possibilities or at least cast them as cultural taboos. A male character dressed as a woman may be subject to amorous male advances, including rape; a female character dressed as a man may similarly evoke other women's romantic attentions, as well as actively perform such male acts as winning a bride.

Cross-dressing in folk narrative is about gender confusion. Traditional gender categories are disclosed as social constructions, and the authority of those constructions is, at least momentarily, challenged. When performed in the midst of local festivals, such narratives serve to reveal and question the existing social order—even when, as is often the case, that order is restored in the narrative's concluding scene.

BIBLIOGRAPHY

Aarne, Antti, and Stith Thompson. *The Types of the Folktale: A Classification and Bibliography.* Helsinki, 1961. For European tale types involving female characters cross-dressing as males, see types AT514, AT880, AT881, AT882, AT883A, AT884, AT890.

Dugaw, Dianne. *Warrior Women and Popular Balladry, 1650–1850.* 1989.

Flueckiger, Joyce Burkhalter. *Gender and Genre in the Folklore of Middle India.* 1996.

Garber, Marjorie. *Vested Interests: Cross-Dressing and Cultural Anxiety.* 1992.

Greenhill, Pauline. " 'Neither a Man nor a Maid': Sexualities and Gendered Meanings in Cross-Dressing Ballads." *Journal of American Folklore* 108 (1995): 156–177.

Mills, Margaret. "Sex Role Reversals, Sex Changes, and Transvestite Disguise in the Oral Tradition of a Conservative Muslim Community in Afghanistan." In *Women's Folklore, Women's Culture.* Edited by Rosan A. Jordan and Susan J. Kalcik. 1985.

Taggart, James H. *Enchanted Maidens: Gender Relations in Spanish Folktales of Courtship and Marriage.* 1990.

Thompson, Stith. *Motif-Index of Folk-Literature.* 1966. See motifs K1836, "Disguise of Man in Woman's Dress," and K1837, "Disguise of Woman in Man's Clothes."

CATHY PRESTON

Crossroads

Intersections of roads have been recognized as significant sites of liminal, sacred, and supernatural activities in many cultures; the horizontal convergence of crossroads is understood religiously to signal vertical passageways between realms.

Deities associated with crossroads exhibit strongly gendered characteristics. Many male crossroads deities, such as the Greek Hermes and the Japanese Shinto categories of *sae-no-kami* (gods-who-prevent-misfortune) and *chimata-no-kami* (road-fork gods), are represented phallically, establishing boundaries and protecting travelers.

Many female crossroads deities emphasize permeable boundaries between realms of existence. Nirrti, a Vedic goddess of death, witchcraft, decay, and old age, demands various sacrifices at desolate crossroads. In Japan, when deceased mortals reach the underworld crossroads at Sanzugawa—The River of Three Ways—they are met by Sanzu-no-baba, an old woman who strips them prior to judgment.

The Greek goddess Hecate is strongly connected with liminality and transitions: magic, doorways, fire, the underworld, and zoomorphic shape-shifting. Statues of her were placed at crossroads, in her form as Hecate Trioditis (Goddess of the Three Ways), with three faces, each gazing down a road. In Roman religion and throughout Celtic Europe there were related goddesses known as Bivia, Trivia, and Quadrivia. The word "trivia" is derived from this: everyone passed the crossroads and so worshiped its goddess every day.

In later Roman esoteric paganism Hecate functioned positively as a cosmic and theurgic mediator at the crossroads of existence. The ancient rite of leaving food-offerings—known as "Hecate's suppers"—at intersections, continued in a host of northern European crossroads practices, including divination rites, votive candles, midsummer fire festivals, and offerings. These magical customs were discouraged and sometimes explicitly suppressed by Christian authorities.

This combination of vertical passage between realms and pagan female deities led to the association of crossroads with witches in Europe. The crossroads were notorious for attracting a diversity of beings, including demons, ghosts, and criminals. A Portuguese account mentions how witches gather for "the Devil's assembly at the crossroads" where "they immediately join a motley throng of Portuguese, Moorish, Jewish, French and other witches" (Puhvel, 1989, p. 30). Suicides and executed criminals were often buried at crossroads, reinforcing affinities with ghosts.

The gendered apotheosis for crossroads deities comes from the Shinto cosmogonic myth. The male creator, Izanagi, fleeing the underworld after having stared at the decaying Izanami against her wishes, is chased by eight Shikome (female furies). Izanagi flings his staff at them, "erecting" a boundary that they cannot pass. The name of the staff—*tsuki-tatsu-funado-no-kami*—means "thrust-erect-come-not-place kami." This phallic border definitively splits the world of the living from the underworld of death and pollution, cementing the male-female split in spheres of sovereignty between Izanagi and Izanami. The staff is worshiped as a crossroads deity named Funado.

The crossroads in Native American traditions are cognate with spatial orientation around the four cardinal directions. The center functions as an *axis mundi* but also induces dynamic outflow, as in an Inca ritual for dispelling evil spirits. Four lines of male warriors with lances run in relays from the ceremonial center to the outskirts of the city, planting the lances at compass point boundaries.

Haitian Vodou incorporates crossroads as a paragon of syncretism, representing the convergence of African and Christian symbols; this is actualized in numerous crossroads rites and personified by male spirits (*lua*) associated with death and liminality: Legba, Gede, and Baron Samedi.

Contemporary North American feminists have reclaimed the spiritual significance of the crossroads. Mary Daly embraces the pervasive encounter with the everyday sacred represented by Trivia. Chicana lesbian-feminist Gloria Anzaldúa suggests that the mestiza is "becoming the officiating priestess at the crossroads" (1987, p. 80), and Judy Grahn develops a metaphor of "Gay as Crossroads" to describe the perpetual spiritual liminality of lesbians and gay men.

BIBLIOGRAPHY

Specific studies on the crossroads are rare, whether cross-cultural or more narrowly topical. The only full-length study, Martin Puhvel's *The Crossroads in Folklore and Myth* (1989), provides myriad examples but is marred by dated source materials, a Eurocentric bias, and the lack of any discernible gender analysis. The two articles "Crossroads" and "Hecate's Suppers" in James Hastings' *Encyclopedia of Religion and Ethics* (1951) are rich in detail and can be effectively supplemented by the more recent extended entry in *A Dictionary of Symbols* (1994) by Jean Chevalier and Alain Gheerbrant (translated by John Buchanan; see pp. 257–261). The bibliography of Hecate is extensive. Two recent feminist studies complement each other on the subject of this goddess' many functions. Deborah Boedecker's "Hecate: A Transfunctional Goddess in the *Theogony*?," *Transactions of the American Philological Association* 113 (1983): 79–93, maintains that Hecate's ability to combine the functions of sovereignty, physical force, production, and fertility provides a paradigm for Zeus's acquisitive accumulation of sacred powers while not directly threatening him. Sarah Iles Johnston, in her book *Hekate Soteira: A Study of Hekate's Roles in the Chaldean Oracles and Related Literature* (1990), argues that Hecate's role in late classical thought, as a cosmic and theurgic mediator, was an extension of her role as a goddess associated with liminality. Carl Jung's discussion of Hecate, in which he interprets the crossroads as both the union of opposites and the inevitable division from the mother, can be found in *Symbols of Transformation: An Analysis of the Prelude to a Case of Schizophrenia* (1956; vol. 5, *Collected Works,* translated by R. F. C. Hull). On Shinto, Genchi Kato's monograph, *A Study of the Development of Religious Ideas among the Japanese People as Illustrated by Japanese Phallicism* (1924; *Transactions of the Asiatic Society of Japan,* supp. to 2d ser., vol. 1), is a brief seminal study, rather enthusiastically illustrated, containing numerous examples connecting crossroads, agriculture, boundaries, and sexuality. The feminist references mentioned come from Mary Daly (with Jane Caputi), *Websters' First New Intergalactic Wickedary of the English Language* (1987); Gloria Anzaldúa, *Borderlands/La frontera* (1987); and Judy Grahn, *Another Mother Tongue* (1984).

JENNIFER RYCENGA

Cults

Since the late 1970s most discussions of "cults" have taken place in a highly contentious and emotionally charged atmosphere. A loose network of amateur and professional opponents, including troubled parents and relatives, freelance "deprogrammers" and "exit counselors," and organizations such as the now defunct Cult Awareness Network, has successfully popularized the notion that all cults are alike. In their opponents' view cults are led by dangerously unstable charismatic leaders who deceptively recruit followers and unscrupulously manipulate them for their own, often violent, purposes. But despite the cultbusters' claim that a proliferation of cults is unique to the late twentieth century, emergent forms of religion can be identified throughout history and across cultures.

Sects, as offshoots from established religious bodies, and cults, as either imports from another culture or as innovations within a host culture, display similar characteristics. Features supposedly characteristic only of contemporary cults, however, including heavy reliance on a charismatic leader, dramatic conversions, and adoption of unconventional patterns of family, sexual, and economic life, are actually characteristic of most religions in their formative stages. The cult controversy that has periodically flared into public consciousness in North America and Western Europe simply transposes into a different key the perennial antagonism between new religions and the status quo. In common usage, therefore, the term *cult* primarily expresses a polemical desire to locate a group beyond the pale of normalcy; and since what is normal varies from one observer to another, it is impossible to develop a substantive definition of the term. The scholarly preference for the terms "new religious movements" or "alternative religions" puts the study of contemporary cults on a much more sound historical and comparative footing.

Since every new religion has a distinctive history, context, and logic, no single generalization can account for the manifold relations between women and new religions. Conceptions of divinity, opportunities for leadership, and gender roles within the religious community vary significantly in alternative religions. In some cases, such as contemporary paganism and witchcraft and the related revival of goddess-worship, new religious movements explicitly portray the divine as feminine. Many practitioners of Wicca, both male and female, cite the focus on a female deity as a part of their attraction to neopaganism. Other alternative religions have emphasized the dual gender of the supreme God. For example, in a striking reinterpretation, Christian Scientists proclaim the addressee of the Lord's prayer (Matt. 6:9–15) to be "Our Father-Mother God." The God of the Unification Church, however, is the more androgynous "One True Parent of Mankind." On the other hand, women will also be found among the adherents of alternative religions, such as Rastafari, the Children of God (now the Family), where the divinity is unequivocally depicted as male.

Although male leadership is predominant, there have been numerous opportunities for female leadership in new religions. In the second century C.E., for example, the female prophets Priscilla and Maximilla led the Montanist movement within Christianity. Female *manbos* have long served as ritual specialists in Vodou communities in Haiti and particularly in the Haitian diaspora. In the nineteenth-century United States, the Fox sisters made crucial contributions to the rise of Spiritualism; Mary Baker Eddy founded the Church of Christ, Scientist; and Helena Petrovna Blavatsky organized the Theosophical Society. In the twentieth century Elizabeth Clare Prophet has guided the Church Universal and Triumphant, and many female teachers, including J. Z. Knight and Jane Roberts, have been influential in the amorphous New Age movement. Women also frequently serve as ritual specialists in neopagan groups and some, perhaps most prominently Zsuzsanna Budapest, have led all-female covens.

Gender roles within alternative religions can conform to traditional patriarchal models, as is largely the case in the Unification Church of Sun Myung Moon and the International Society for Krishna Consciousness and was the case in the Branch Davidian community led by David Koresh. But even in those situations women can wield extensive influence through their relationships with male leaders. Susan Palmer's typology of gender roles in new religions identifies three typical forms. Some groups see each sex as having different but complementary spiritual qualities and consequently may focus on marriage as a process of spiritual unification, as in the Blessing ceremony of the Unification Church. Other groups emphasize the differences between the sexes and often privilege males over females. The comment of a female Krishna devotee that "a man's body is a finer instrument of developing Krishna Consciousness" (Palmer, 1994, p. 16) vividly portrays that perspective. Palmer's third type sees gender characteristics as superficial phenomena that obscure a completely sexless spirit. The desire of the Heaven's Gate community to progress to the "evolutionary level above human" and leave all traces of sexuality behind reflects such an outlook.

In new or alternative religious groups, specific attention is often directed to the regulation of sexuality. The early Mormons were enjoined to practice "plural marriage" in the form of polygyny. John Humphrey Noyes's Oneida community implemented among members of the group a form of "complex marriage," in which they abandoned special attachments to particular individuals in favor of "the honor and faithfulness that constitutes an ideal marriage, [which] may exist for two hundred as well as two" (Foster, 1984, p. 72). David Koresh simultaneously imposed a rule of celibacy on all Branch Davidians while claiming the right to take any woman in the community as his bride. Both the International Society for Krishna Consciousness and the Unification Church advocate a traditional patriarchal model in which sexual relations are solely for the purposes of procreation. Other groups, such as Mother Ann Lee's Shakers and Bonnie Lu Nettles and Marshal Applewhite's Heaven's Gate community have imposed a rigorous rule of celibacy.

Clearly, women's experience in new and alternative religions is neither inherently liberating nor repressive, but must be carefully investigated in its diverse particularities. The manifest diversity of new religious movements completely undermines the caricature promulgated by the anticult movement that all cults are alike. It also signals the need for continuing efforts at ethnographic, historical, and comparative understanding of new and alternative religions.

BIBLIOGRAPHY

Adler, Margot. *Drawing Down the Moon: Witches, Druids, Goddess-Worshippers and other Neo-Pagans Today.* Rev. ed. 1986.

Beckford, James. *Cult Controversies: The Societal Response to New Religious Movements.* 1985.
Bromley, David G., and Anson D. Shupe, Jr. *The New Vigilantes: Deprogrammers, Anti-Cultists, and the New Religions.* 1980.
Foster, Lawrence. *Religion and Sexuality: The Shakers, the Mormons, and the Oneida Community.* 1984.
Miller, Timothy, ed. *America's Alternative Religions.* 1995.
Palmer, Susan Jean. *Moon Sisters, Krishna Mothers, Rajneesh Lovers: Women's Roles in New Religions.* 1994.
Puttick, Elizabeth. *Women in New Religions: Gender, Power and Sexuality.* 1997.
Stark, Rodney, and William Sims Bainbridge. *The Future of Religion: Secularization, Revival, and Cult Formation.* 1985.
Wessinger, Catherine, ed. *Women's Leadership in Marginal Religions: Explorations Outside the Mainstream.* 1993.

EUGENE V. GALLAGHER

Cultural Studies

In the 1950s a postwar desire for an intellectual project that could avoid the traps of a rigid and deterministic Marxism while remaining open to possibilities of connection between the theoretical activity of the academy and the practice of progressive social movements gave rise to the academic field known as cultural studies. This moment of desire—the "culture and society" moment (after Raymond Williams's 1958 study)—represented an attempt to connect the social (structural) analysis of Marxism with the cultural activities and movements of working-class peoples. The endeavor became important to feminist movements; thus, the feminist journal *Signs*, begun in 1975, is subtitled *A Journal of Women in Culture and Society*.

Cultural studies does not just analyze aims to intervene in the historical processes and relations of domination shaping modern (and, now, postmodern) society. It was, therefore, conducive to those new social movements, like feminism, that did not want to privilege class analysis or struggle to the exclusion of other axes of social differentiation and domination: gender, race, sexuality, nation, the environment, and militarism.

Cultural Studies also draws on those theories loosely aligned under the name poststructuralism, originating mainly in France, which argue that social structure is not itself fully determinative of "culture," but that culture or "discourses" form the parameters of possibility for social life and its "structures."

Interdisciplinary to the point of being post- or even antidisciplinary, cultural studies privileges no one methodology or theoretical paradigm. If, as Stuart Hall has said, "Cultural Studies is not one thing . . . has never been one thing," it yet seems to have resisted one thing in particular: getting religion. This resistance is not surprising. Both progressive political movements and the academy are heirs of the Enlightenment progress narrative. Accordingly, they often define themselves over and against religion, construed as irrationality and regressive dogmatism. However, prompted by worldwide social movements that challenge the assumption that religion will or has become progressively privatized and socially irrelevant, many scholars are now turning to the cultural study of religion.

It is too soon to predict what this critical meeting might produce, but it is not too soon to ask: What is the relationship between something called "religion" and the narratives of modernization, rationalization, and secularization, which are the legacy of the European Enlightenment? What might it mean to study "religion" given that academic "study" is implicated in these narratives and in the relations of (post) colonialism that these narratives legitimate(d)? Is the cultural study of religion thus an incoherent project, or might religion's resistance to the status of "proper object" of study also become a site for reworking the meaning of cultural studies itself? Moreover, how do feminist scholars and activists negotiate their place and their objects of concern in this shifting landscape? Will, for example, the specificity of the various studies associated with women's movements in religion—feminist, womanist, *mujerista*—be lost under the "general" rubric of the cultural? What might it mean to combine the study of "women" and "religion" in relation to "culture"? Can "women" be an object of cultural study any more than "religion"?

Although these questions name both rifts and inadequacies within cultural studies, they also warrant excitement over the work that needs to be done and indicate possibilities for reworking the bases of "study" itself. Indeed, to pose these questions is already to intervene in the way practitioners of cultural studies get religion.

BIBLIOGRAPHY

Aronowitz, Stanley. *The Politics of Identity: Class, Culture, Social Movements.* 1992.

Grossberg, Lawrence, Cary Nelson, and Paula Treichler, eds. *Cultural Studies.* 1992.

Hall, Stuart. "The Emergence of Cultural Studies and the Crisis of the Humanities." *October* 53 (1990): 11–90.

Jakobsen, Janet R., and Ann Pellegrini. "Getting Religion." *One Nation Under God? Religion and American Culture.* Edited by Marjorie Garber and Rebecca Walkowitz. Forthcoming.

Rooney, Ellen. "Discipline and Vanish: Feminism, the Resistance to Theory, and the Politics of Cultural Studies." *differences: A Journal of Feminist Cultural Studies* 2, no. 3 (1990): 14–28.

Thompson, E. P. *The Making of the English Working Class.* 1963.

Williams, Raymond. *Culture and Society, 1780–1950.* 1958. Reprint, 1983.

See also **Feminisms; Mujerista Tradition; Structuralism; Womanist Traditions.**

JANET R. JAKOBSEN
ANN PELLEGRINI

Cybele

Cybele was originally an Anatolian goddess of fertility, worshiped as a symbolic black stone. She was also a mistress of animals, often pictured in a chariot pulled by lions. Her myth told of the tragic death of her beloved, Attis, a vegetation spirit, and of his miraculous resurrection. Both of these events were celebrated in

The goddess Cybele driving a lion-drawn chariot in a fountain amid Plaza de Cibeles in Madrid (Richard T. Nowitz/Corbis)

ritual, but it was the mourning carried out by her priests, the Galli, that most impressed the onlookers. To the sound of flutes and drums, priests and worshipers would stab themselves and sprinkle their blood on the goddess's altar. Those who entered fully into ecstatic union with her divinity would castrate themselves and thus become priests.

By the fifth century B.C.E. the worship of Cybele had arrived in Greece, where she was identified with Rhea, mother of the gods. Cybele was brought to Rome in 204 B.C.E. because of an oracle that only her presence could save the city from the Carthaginians. Roman women played an important role in the official installation of Cybele's black stone in her temple on the Palatine.

The cult of Cybele was very appealing to women. Cybele's role in myth as mother, bereaved lover, and mistress of fertility and of untamed nature projected a powerful image for women to identify with or supplicate. The ecstatic nature of her cult, with its wild Phrygian music and bloodshed, reminiscent of the early cult of Dionysius, offered the cloistered wives of Athens, as well as the upright matrons of Rome, an opportunity for expressive religious behavior that was not available to them in their everyday lives.

BIBLIOGRAPHY

Cumont, Franz. *Oriental Religions in Roman Paganism.* 1911.

Farnell, Lewis R. *The Cults of the Greek States.* 5 vols. London, 1896–1909. See vol. 3 for Cybele.

Vermaseren, Martin J. *Cybele and Attis: The Myth and the Cult.* 1977.

For classical reference to the Anatolian deity Kybele (Cybele), see Herodotus (v. 102); to the arrival of Cybele at Rome, see Livy (29. 14. 10–14); to the ritual of Cybele at Rome, see Lucretius (De *rerum natura* 2. 594–632).

ALLAIRE BRUMFIELD

Dākinīs

A *ḍākinī* (the Sanskrit word for "ogress") is a feminine spiritual guide whose appearance has been documented primarily by Indo-Tibetan Vajrayāna adepts of northern Buddhism. Tantric yoga flourished in northeast India during the Pāla era (eighth to twelfth centuries) and simultaneously in Uḍḍiyāna or the "Land of *Ḍākinīs*" (Tibetan *khandroling*)—which is both the Swat Valley in Pakistan and a domain of inner geography. Consistent with the mystic continuity of outer and inner worlds at Uḍḍiyāna is the ontologically ambiguous sense that *ḍākinīs* can be human or imaginal. Highly realized *yoginīs* are counted as human *ḍākinīs*, while imaginal *ḍākinīs* materialize in connection with the rushing of subtle wind through four lotuses situated along the central channel of a tantric adept's inner landscape. The geographical character of *ḍākinīs* (Tibetan *khandroma*, "sky walker") was enhanced in Tibet where pre-Buddhist cultural influences strengthened their association with impressive natural phenomena such as stars, rocks, lakes, and mountains.

Indo-Tibetan Buddhists composed numerous "tales of liberation" (Tibetan *namthar*) in which *ḍākinīs* appear glamorously decked in jewels as florescent fairies, or mount a terrific aspect as crones and ogresses. Some are enlightened wisdom *ḍākinīs* who bestow empowerment and instruction; others are worldly *ḍākinīs* who assist adepts in exchange for religious teachings.

In spite of their diverse natures and tempers, all *ḍākinīs* promote spiritual development by shocking, testing, advising, initiating, or feeding fortunate adepts. When Milarepa (1040–1123) had trouble controlling his subtle wind, *ḍākinīs* demonstrated remedial yoga postures; during a fast, they rode the sun's rays and of-fered him yogurt from a ladle of blue jewels. Nāropa (1016–1100) met a swift lady messenger (Tibetan *pho-nyamo*) manifesting as a hag (none other than *ḍākinī* Vajrayoginī) who cracked his rationality, freed his intuition, and sent him on a wild-goose chase to find her "brother" for tantric instruction. A naked, red *ḍākinī* gave Yeshe Tsogyel (757–817) a drink from her copious flow of menstrual blood; and she was inspired to give her kneecaps to a cripple after being transported by radiant meditation to a gruesome "*ḍākinī* land" where *ḍākinīs* offered their body parts to Vajrayoginī. Yeshe Tsogyel herself was a human *ḍākinī* who remains central to ritual of the Nyingma lineage founded in Tibet by her consort, Padmasaṃbhava (d. 802). Cutting across boundaries of time, space, and substance, Yeshe Tsogyel still appears to tantric adepts through ritual invocation. Moreover, a human *ḍākinī* abides presently at Terdrom, Tibet, near Yeshe Tsogyel's footprint and Padmasaṃbhava's cave.

Ḍākinīs facilitate extraordinary modes of communication. In the verbal sphere they inspire the composition of songs and tales of liberation permeated with multivalent "twilight language" (Sanskrit *sandhyābhāṣa*). In the preverbal sphere, wisdom *ḍākinīs* reveal "hidden treasure" texts (Tibetan *terma*) whose contents may be written on leaves, water, or tiny scrolls of paper. *Ḍākinīs* also function as curious figures of speech homologous to the Indian *mātṛkā* (Tibetan *mamo*) the smallest literal unit of a *dhāraṇī*, mnemonic formula. For example, Nāropa read the crone's thirty-seven hideous features to denote several lists of thirty-seven items in Buddhist philosophy. In the nonverbal sphere *ḍākinīs* present secret gestures where words fail between consorts. They also draw people with strong spiritual connections together through dream messages and events of meaningful coincidence or synchronicity (Tibetan *tendrel*).

Ḍākinīs initiate adepts into the lineages of the Indian mother tantras. The *Cakrasaṃvaratantra* features Vajrayoginī (diamond *yoginī*) and Vajravārāhī (diamond sow) as *ḍākinī* consorts of Cakrasaṃvara, while the *Hevajratantra* includes Ḍākinī Vetali (ghoul lady) among fifteen *yoginīs* dancing in Hevajra's mystic circle (Sanskrit *maṇḍala*). In tantric practice the predominance of male adepts in the literature is belied by evidence that groups of tantric women, sometimes accompanied by men, gathered to dance in liminal environments such as cremation grounds for ritual feasts (Sanskrit *gaṇacakra*)—a fact that may account for the tendency of *ḍākinīs* to favor bone ornaments. *Ḍākinīs* show themselves to both male and female adepts apparently without discrimination. However, because tantric women were regarded as *ḍākinīs* (especially in the role of consort) they were at risk of being coopted by male social and psychological interests. On the other hand, the *ḍākinīs*' empowerment of women through their identification cannot be ignored; and there was a movement in the late 1990s to explore the positive relationship between *ḍākinīs* and women practitioners based upon traditional Vajrayāna teachings.

BIBLIOGRAPHY

Articles treating the nature and function of *ḍākinīs* include Nathan Katz, "Anima and mKha'-'gro-ma: A Critical Comparative Study of Jung and Tibetan Buddhism," *Tibet Journal* 2 (1977): 13–43; Victoria Kennick Urubshurow, "Tibetan Fairy Glimmerings: *Ḍākinīs* in Buddhist Spiritual Biography" in *Women in the Indic Religious Traditions*, edited by Arvind Sharma (forthcoming); Janice D. Willis, "Ḍākinī: Some Comments on Its Nature and Meaning" in *Feminine Ground: Essays on Women and Tibet*, edited by Janice D. Willis (1989). On *ḍākinīs* from a feminist perspective as idealized mothers or sexual consorts, see June Campbell, *Traveller in Space: In Search of Female Identity in Tibetan Buddhism* (1996). On tantric women as unencumbered by patriarchy, see Miranda Shaw, *Passionate Enlightenment: Women in Tantric Buddhism* (1994). On the *ḍākinī* Yeshe Tsogyel from a Tibetan ritual perspective, see Anne Carolyn Klein, *Meeting the Great Bliss Queen: Buddhists, Feminists, and the Art of the Self* (1995). On the lives of Vajrayāna women, see Tsultrim Allione's *Women of Wisdom* (1984) and Reginald A. Ray, "Accomplished Women in Tantric Buddhism of Medieval India and Tibet" in *Unspoken Worlds*, edited by Nancy Auer Falk and Rita M. Gross (1989). English translations of Vajrayāna biographies most relevant to a study of *ḍākinīs* include Garma C. C. Chang's *The Hundred Thousand Songs of Milarepa*, 2 vols. (1962); Keith Dowman's *Masters of Mahāmudrā: Songs and Histories of the Eighty-four Buddhist Siddhas* (1985), and *Sky Dancer: The Secret Life and Songs of the Lady Yeshe Tsogyel* (1984); Herbert V. Guenther's *The Life and Teaching of Nāropa* (1963); and Lobsang P. Lhalungpa's *The Life of Milarepa* (1977).

See also **Buddhism: Himalayan Buddhism; Tantra; Vajrayoginī; Yoginīs.**

VICTORIA KENNICK URUBSHUROW

Dance and Drama

An Overview

Anthropologists and theater scholars have long supposed that dance and theatrical forms throughout the world originated in ancient religious rituals and ceremonies. The progressivist view that theater and dance emerged out of ritual has recently lost favor to the less linear notion that ritual and theater have typically coexisted as modes of expression using the same or similar elements for different functions.

Religious practice often has much in common with theater and dance performance, including a departure from ordinary representations of time, the designation of special performance sites, the participation of specially qualified people, the use of costumes, masks, or other symbolic objects, and the enacting of a role and scenarios accompanied by music and movement. The difference between religious and theatrical events may depend on whether they serve as entertainment or as effective, transformative acts. However, it is often difficult to draw a clear distinction between theater and ritual, especially for traditions in which performance itself is an act of devotion. Moreover, many ritual events are celebratory and include communal feasting, dancing, singing, and other forms of entertainment.

Women have played a part in religious performance since ancient times. The Hebrew Bible tells of the prophet Ezekiel denouncing women for "weeping for Tammuz." According to the *Universal Jewish Encyclopedia* the reference is to a dramatic play, possibly a source of Greek drama, performed by Israelite women in honor of the Phoenician god Adonis-Tammuz. For the Greeks the divine patroness of astronomy, Urania, was also the Muse of dance. In Japan the *Kojiki* records the legend of an erotic dance performed by the female deity Ame-no-uzume to entice the sun goddess Amaterasu from her cave.

Dances and theatrical performances of seasonal renewal are found throughout the world, from the Abydos passion play of ancient Egypt to the sacred circle dances of Native American Indians. In many religious and performance traditions, dances involving masks and costumes serve to attract the good spirits and fend off the bad. Bad spirits may be exorcised as a way of combating disease, war, or famine, while good spirits may ensure peace, a good harvest, the replenishment of game and livestock, and human fertility.

Masquerades figure in religious practices throughout Africa. Masqueraders, usually from a special cult group, don masks made of wood, grass, leaves, or textiles, sometimes covering the entire body. Harmful or benevolent spirits are not merely represented by the mask, rather they are said to possess the performer wearing it. In many cases there are sanctions against women wearing the masks, or even touching or seeing them, or knowing who is wearing them. In practice, however, women often have knowledge of the rites but will publicly pretend ignorance.

Many masquerade traditions tell of women as the original maskers whose rites were taken over by men who had been made privy to the secrets. Anthropologist Margaret Drewal interprets such stories in the Yoruba culture of Nigeria as effecting a symbolic identification of women with containers and men with things contained. Woman as childbearer is therefore the original mask, harboring the new spirit within her, while the child is the original masker. Drewal's interpretation also accounts for women's prominent role as mediums within Yoruba culture, containing the spirit that comes to them without the need of a mask. Nonetheless, in the Sande cult, a women's secret society found in Liberia, Sierra Leone, Ivory Coast, and Guinea, initiation rites involve women dancers wearing masks and embodying the spirits of their female ancestors.

Possession is one of the most common religious performative practices for women throughout the world. Possession may serve to convey a special message from the spirit world to the community or to effect a communion with the gods. In many cultures women dance in order to become possessed by spirits. The manifestation of the gestures and speech of distinct, identifiable spirits warrants comparison with the theatrical enactment of dramatic characters.

In the *zar* cult of North Africa and the Middle East women convene to dance, feast, and incarnate the spirits that have called them to join the cult. The spirits the women act out are often men or foreigners (for example Chinese, Ethiopian, British). In the Vodou practices of Haiti, women are also the primary mediums who, through dancing, become possessed by spirits. In Ko-

A group of women in ceremonial costume perform a Rejang dance in Tengannan, Bali, Indonesia (Reinhard Eisele/Corbis).

rea women shamans perform family ceremonies, known as *kut mudang*, in which they may incarnate a number of different spirits in succession who advise the family. In the *san hyang dedari* ritual of Bali, two young, untrained female dancers between the ages of nine and twelve go into trance by inhaling incense and then improvise a dance performed through them by visiting goddesses.

Whereas in possession spirits act through human agents, performance practices are often occasions for human beings to entertain visiting gods, ancestors, or spirits. An example is the *rejang*, a processional group dance involving some forty to sixty women, which is part of the *wali*, or most sacred category of Balinese dance. This ritual demonstrates respect for the spirits, who descend into doll-like wooden effigies and are given offerings of food and flowers during their visit.

Throughout the world song and dance have played a role in worship as a way of expressing devotion, giving thanks, and celebrating important moments of transition such as marriage, birth, and death. The Hebrew Bible tells of Miriam leading other women in a dance of celebration after the crossing of the Red Sea. In the egalitarian Shaker communities, both men and women engage in ecstatic dancing as a form of worship. Funeral rites in the Yoruba culture of Nigeria involve family members playing and dancing throughout the village in the deceased's honor.

Religious stories have been passed down through dramatic enactment as a means of conveying religious teachings, proselytizing, or explaining religious practices. In India and Indonesia the Hindu epics, the *Rāmāyaṇa* and the *Mahābhārata*, are the primary sources for theatrical dramatizations. Since the Middle Ages the Catholic Church has used performance as a means of spreading Christian belief and church doctrine. Women rarely performed in the large Corpus Christi Cycle plays cosponsored by the church and craft guilds throughout Europe from 1350 to 1550. In Chester, England, however, production of *The Assumption of the Virgin* was allotted to "the wives of the town," and there are records in France of a woman in Metz performing the role of Saint Catherine in 1468 and of women performing all the female roles in *Le Mystère des Trois Doms* in Romans in 1509.

In convents, where they had access to learning and time to write, some women became notable playwrights. Hrosvitha of Gandersheim (c. 935–973), a canoness from northern Germany, is credited not only as the first known woman playwright but also as the first Western dramatist of the postclassical period. Hrosvitha wrote six plays on Christian themes (*Paphnutius, Dulcitius, Gallicanus, Abraham and Maria, Callimachus,* and *Sapientia*), using the Roman playwright Terence as a model. *Sapientia* features as its main characters an early Christian mother and her three brave daughters, who are tortured at the hands of Roman soldiers rather than renounce their belief in Christ. The Benedictine abbess Hildegard of Bingen (c. 1098–1179) wrote *Ordo Virtutum*, a Latin morality play. Sor Juana Inés de la Cruz (c. 1648–1695) of Mexico became a nun in order to avoid marriage and to pursue her passion for writing. She wrote plays, poems, and theological pieces. Marcela de San Félix (1605–1687), daughter of the Spanish Golden Age playwright Lope de Vega, joined a convent to escape her father's profligate life-style. There she wrote six one-act religious plays and numerous poems.

Other religious performative practices include ritual clowning, story-telling, cross-dressing, the use of puppets as mediums or objects of worship, and the performance of magical feats for displaying power or manifesting spirits.

BIBLIOGRAPHY

Arenal, Electa, and Stacey Schlau, eds. *Untold Sisters: Hispanic Nuns in Their Own Works.* Translated by Amanda Powell. 1989.

Bandem, I Made, and Fredrik Eugene de Boer. *Balinese Dance in Transition: Kaja and Kelod.* 2d ed. 1995.

Boddy, Janice Patricia. *Wombs and Alien Spirits: Women, Men, and the Zār Cult in Northern Sudan.* 1989.

Bonfante, Larissa, trans., with the collaboration of Alexandra Bonfante-Warren. *The Plays of Hrotswitha of Gandersheim.* 1986.

Brandon, James R., ed. *The Cambridge Guide to Asian Theatre.* 1993.

"Divine Horsemen: The Living Gods of Haiti." Mystic Fire Video. 1985.

Drewal, Margaret Thompson. *Yoruba Ritual: Performers, Play, Agency.* 1992.

Garrett, Clarke. *Spirit Possession and Popular Religion: From the Camisards to the Shakers.* 1987.

"The JVC Video Anthology of World Music and Dance." Fujii Tomoaki, series editor. Rounder Records. 1990.

Lawler, Lillian B. *The Dance in Ancient Greece.* 1964.

"Lord of the Dance" and "Dancing in One World." From the PBS Television series *Dancing.* Produced by Rhoda Grauer. Home Vision. 1993.

Merrim, Stephanie, ed. *Feminist Perspectives on Sor Juana Inés de la Cruz.* 1991.

Schechner, Richard. *Performance Theory: Revised and Expanded Edition.* 1988.

Sered, Susan Starr. *Priestess, Mother, Sacred Sister: Religions Dominated by Women.* 1994.

Tonkin, Elizabeth. "Women Excluded? Masking and Masquerading in West Africa." In *Women's Religious Experience.* Edited by Pat Holden. 1983.

Turner, Victor. *From Ritual to Theatre: The Human Seriousness of Play.* 1982.

See also **Hildegard of Bingen; Juana Inés de la Cruz.**

CLAUDIA ORENSTEIN

In Microhistorical Traditions

Dance as a form of human communication and experience is a universal art in which people move their bodies in a way that reflects a known, conscious cultural existence in time and space, in thought and matter. Even before history there was dance and the ability to achieve trance or ecstasy. In what has been called "tribal dance" it is often believed that it is not the person who dances, but the spirits that enter and move the body. The dancer's body is only the means by which the spirit's work is accomplished. The dancer, if successful, is capable of being inspired because of the belief in supernatural power imbued into the enlightened mind and receptive body of the dancer. Receiving and communicating with the sacred carries the dancer into another reality. This ability to communicate, inspired by supernatural entities, influences the dancer as well as those in the presence of the dancer(s).

Precise movement by the dancer is considered extremely important because it is charged with supernatural power—the dancer after extensive training is prepared to submit to the ritual transformation that changes the person into a spirit or deity. This process usually requires body adornment, special regalia, masks, purification, bathing, and sweating. In Apache culture, the use of special language (chanting) and cultural restrictions, such as forbidding women and others to identify the male dancers once they are ritually prepared, still prevails. Those responsible for providing accompaniment either by vocal singing, chanting, esoteric language, or playing musical instruments such as rattles and drums are seen to give support or sometimes protection and guidance to the dancers.

Dance, often called the mother of the arts, and language—whether spoken, chanted, or sung—are considered by many of the indigenous peoples in the Americas as the two qualities that distinguish people from the animal world. In Yaqui culture, for example, the two are linked. While the Yaqui deer dancer is exquisite in replicating the movement of the deer, he can only dance the deer when he hears the music of the deer singers, which is the language of the deer. Oral traditions in the American Southwest tell of the times when humans and animals could understand each other and were able to learn from one another. One can imagine that by following the prevailing rules and through careful observation of animals and their activities that people learned how to develop the enduring art form we call dance even as they learned to cope with the difficulties of survival.

Today tribal dances are often ritual manifestations of history and events from the mythological past that are recreated or reimagined in the present. The intention of making animal movements in dance and contemplation about how to convey the spirit of the animal and its behavior to those present, so that the details are revealed, is the inspiration for many of the dances that have survived. According to Yupik cultural traditions, animals were capable of transforming into humans and interacting with them; both humans and animals are considered incomplete without each other. Attitudes about the animal and the dancers' ability to arouse emotions in the people are made visible through dance. Even though over time people have learned to distinguish themselves from animals, they realize that the dance about the bear is a way to reconnect over and over again with the bear's power and to communicate feelings of both respect and fear of a powerful animal. Through this use of metaphor and ritual transformation it is understood that one thing can stand for another. This weaving of thought and body, idea and motion—this visible representation of a cultural ideal—is the result of reflection by the dancer as well as a powerful source of human motivation for human self-understanding and sense of place.

One of the most important elements in indigenous dance is the demarcation of an area that is acknowledged and set aside for the ceremonial dance. Usually the creation myths make reference to paradigms that are ritualized for the purpose of preparing ceremonial or sacred space. Crossing one biological boundary into another, then, often refers to a people's cosmology. This area is blessed and prepared for dancing as carefully as the dancers are prepared. Once this space is ready, special regalia, body adornment, facial paints, and ceremonial masks are employed to reaffirm that the dancer has been ritually marked and has become a spirit. Under the scrutiny of the head dancer, dancers are carefully observed since there are many restrictions they are obliged to observe. The highly ritualized form of dance and its accompaniment by repetitive sound as well as strict adherence to religious traditions creates a sense of awe still experienced today.

Every important event with the cycle of nature and the human life cycle is considered an opportunity for communicating with the spirit world. It follows, then, that there are many rituals and many dances.

THE AMERICAS

Religious dance in the American Southwest is highly stylized and carefully executed, as for example in the Baile de Matachines, a reenactment of the Spanish expulsion of the Moors from Spain and the later conquest of Mexico. Every year in masked dance and celebration, the people of the Rio Grande Pueblo ritually and symbolically recreate the Matachines dances on Christmas day and on December 12 to honor the Virgin of Guadalupe. The dancing, like many of the regional dances of Mexico, evokes ordinarily invisible power, bringing spiritual forces into the real world where they are experienced by the dancers and audience. Power is made concrete through dance masks and costumes and complemented by music and song. Just as the dance evokes power, so also do the songs and music. All of the dancers are male except for the young girl who dances the role of La Malinche.

Aztec history informs us that in these early tribal societies dance functioned as an integral component of the religious life of the people. All aspects of their lives had a religious significance, which was often symbolized by the gestures and movements of the body with reference to nature or the human life cycle. Today in Chicana/o culture, contemporary dance, or *danza,* is performed mostly by women who study and follow Mexico's folk traditions. Danza Azteca is a reminder of the cultural connection between Mexican and Chicana/o culture. In general in Mexico there are a variety of categories of dances that are different from dances that have specific implications for rites of passage, healing, or when a person dies. Some Mexican dances are performed to mark historical occasions, such as the just-mentioned Baile de Matachines. These dancers reflect the native point of view, representing the conquest of Mexico as an evil force that destroyed Indian cultures. The arrival of infused native dances and performances with Christian implications—the dances began to characterize native deities as evil and turned their masks into devil masks. Today such devil dances provide the release of tension; the usually male dancers wear horned masks and are trickster-like in that they amuse the people by behaving inappropriately. The Dances of Mexico are the artistic expression of the imagination of the Mexican people, who reveal their ability to remember their past cultural and religious beliefs and to connect them to their present experience.

ASIA

In India, the Vedas, the most ancient literature of the Indian culture, mentions that dancing is practiced as a form of Hindu religious reverence rendering divine honors to a deity, showing respect and devotion. Śiva, the Hindu god of dance often referred to as the Lord of Dancers, is also capable of destroying and renewing, and it is he who is responsible for the movement pattern or rhythm of the earth. As in tribal dance in the Americas, Hindu religious traditions include dance as a rich heritage handed down over the generations. Female dancers, *devadāsīs*, dedicated their lives to serving in temples where they performed daily duties, but most importantly they propitiated the divinities and performed before their symbolic representations. Nryta, the dance centered on the movements made with the arms and feet of the dancers as well as stylized facial expressions, is intended to communicate ideas and opinions of the dancer. But by performing like the deity they also become personalities responsible for keeping the world in balance as they dance the divinity inherent in their own being. Dance in India is endowed with an extensive variety of folk dance, and like Mexico's ritual dances reflect the cyclical nature of life. The context of Indian dances seeks to create a heightened awareness of the interconnectedness between nature and the supernatural and to encourage visionary experience for the dancer and those present.

As in the Americas, dance was forbidden by missionaries and by the British government in India. In both cases, as dance was suppressed, it later surfaced again sometimes in altered forms. In Java dancers influenced by mythology and the ancient tradition of ancestor worship developed a highly ritualized artistic form influenced in part by India yet set in a format that utilizes masked dancers and shadow puppets. The performance is exemplified by slow movement with erect back and accompanied by flutes, gongs, and the chanting of the narrative of the origin of the dance.

In Bali, dance is a significant cultural manifestation. Everyone is thought to possess the attributes of a dancer. Balinese dance is elaborate in its head dresses, facial paint, and the textures of fabrics adorning the body as well as in the vigorous angular movement of the hands and arms, which celebrates the various aspects of the life cycle. Religious festivals were danced not only by trained dancers but by the people as well.

By contrast, dance in China developed into a highly stylized form of gesture and movement. It was characterized by ingenious refinement of thought, insights, and perception reflected in delicate distinctions of movement and subtle gestures, face painting, and colors that reflected the attributes of the dancers.

OCEANIA

In Hawaii the ancient myths that tell of Pele, female deity of volcanoes (specifically of the Kilauea volcano) are closely associated with the daily lives of the people. Pele's personal characteristics reflect those of her volcano: unpredictable, fiery, glowing, ardent, passionate, irritable, sensuous, and luminous. The practice of Pele religion today and the religious debates on the impact of Christianity taking place at annual hula competitions indicate that the native peoples of Hawaii are deeply concerned with the continuation of their religious and cultural traditions. Dancing is a form of religious worship, in the Hawaiian case the hand gestures create a highly stylized religious aesthetic and, more importantly, a language of the dance.

In Oceania where missionization and the colonial agenda forced indigenous cultures to speak foreign languages, practice foreign religious traditions, and create foreign arts the devastation is still felt. There is today a resurgence of dance traditions that were dominant for centuries in Hawaii, Samoa, Tahiti, and the Philippines. Some of these traditions have been maintained such as the dances associated with Pele. Others have undergone transformation due to new forms introduced during the colonial period. In the Philippine Islands, indigenous forms took on new characteristics but had elements that could be traced back to dances of the mountain tribes as well as dances of the peoples of the lowlands, thanks to the efforts of Francisca Reyes Acquino, who documented the traditional indigenous dances as well as the dance forms that were changed because of the colonial encounter. The Spanish colonization in the Philippines for more than three centuries left its imprint in the form of the Fandango, which later becomes the Pandanggo. The Spanish music is retained and many regional adaptations are developed through which the people manifest their graceful virtuosity. Both men and women dance, and movement and feeling are interwoven.

AFRICA

The significance of dance in Africa is closely associated with patterns of adaptation to the land and the environment. Africans have danced their religions with complicated footwork and body movement as a form of nonverbal communication with the spirit world. As elsewhere, Christian missionizing had a devastating impact. African dance is a religious and ritual expression that allows the human body to elaborate on what David Abram calls the "spell of the sensuous." Both women and men spontaneously dance to movements that come to them from within the body. This improvisation and freedom allows dancers to express themselves both religiously and creatively in performance. Through the movement of the dancer's body, both the dancers and the observers can achieve altered states of consciousness. In Africa there are also highly ritualized dances used to mark all aspects of life from birth through other rites of passage to hunting, gathering, marriage, political and social conflicts, and death. A dance involves selecting a sacred dance arena, special dancing regalia, face painting or masks, and tattoos and scarification. All of these ritual acts emphasize the fact that the dancer undergoes ritual transformation. In the !Kung tradition of the Kalahari Desert of southern Africa, Richard Katz has observed that for these people the ritual of the healing dance integrates all aspects of the culture. Both women and men participate. Singing, clapping, and dancing are engaged in summoning *num*, or spiritual energy, which is manifested as the dance intensifies; male dancers then sense an altered consciousness known as *kia*. At this time they are able to heal those present. This ritual continues throughout the night. The dance has great significance in the daily lives of the !Kung people, as it is uniquely the key to healing in their society. There is evidence here that the combination of the body's neuromuscular movement with the thoughts and emotions of the dancer as she moves toward altered states of consciousness accomplishes the healing that is the purpose of this dance. In present day !Kung society the Giraffe Dance is the main form of the healing dance. In the Dobe area there are two other dances where the use of *kia* is a part of healing: the Trees Dance and the Drum Dance. In the Drum Dance, women dance and sing to receive *kia*, though here there is less emphasis on healing. The same is true for the boys' initiation dance, called *Chimera*, and the Eland dance, which marks a girl's menarche. Dances performed solely for the purposes of entertainment are also common throughout Africa.

BIBLIOGRAPHY

Abram, David. *The Spell of the Sensuous: Perception and Language in a More-Than-Human World.* 1996.

Acquino, Francisca Reyes. *Philippine National Dances.* 1946.

Andersen, Johannes C. *Myths and Legends of the Polynesians.* 1969.

Basso, Keith H. *Wisdom Sits in Places: Landscape and Language among the Western Apache.* 1996.

Briggs, Charles L. *Competence in Performance: The Creativity of Tradition in Mexicano Verbal Art.* 1988.

Cordry, Donald. *Mexican Masks.* 1980.

Devi, Regina. *Dance Dialects* of India. 1972.

Erickson, Robert A. *The Language of the Heart, 1600–1750.* 1997.

Evers, Larry, and Felipe S. Molina. *Yaqui Deer Songs.* 1987.

Fienup-Riordan, Ann. *Boundaries and Passages: Rule and Ritual in Yup'ik Eskimo Oral Tradition.* 1994.

Gunji, Masakatsu. *Buyo: The Classical Dance.* 1970.

Hanna, Judith Lynne. *The Performer Audience Connection: Emotion to Metaphor in Dance and Society.* 1983.

Huet, Michel. *The Dance, Art and Ritual of Africa.* 1978.

Katz, Richard. *Boiling Energy: Community Healing among the Kalahari Kung.* 1982.

King, Noel Q. *African Cosmos: An Introduction to Religion in Africa.* 1986.

Marglin, Frédérique Apffel. *The Wives of the God-King: The Rituals of the Devadāsīs of Puri.* 1985.

Prokosch Kurath, Gertrude. *Half a Century of Dance Research.* 1986.

Ray, Benjamin C. *African Religions: Symbol, Ritual and Community.* 1976.

Sullivan, Laurence E. *Icanchu's Drum: An Orientation to Meaning in South American Religions.* 1988.

Talamantez, Ines M. Review of Champe, Flavia Waters, *The Matachines Dance of the Upper Rio Grande: History, Music and Choreography. New Scholar* 10 (1986): 378.

Tinker, George E. *Missionary Conquest: The Gospel and Native American Cultural Genocide.* 1993.

INES M. TALAMANTEZ

In Asian Traditions

Despite historically having been barred from holding key leadership positions in the various Asian religions, Asian women have often played pivotal roles in worship practices by means of creative abilities. Music, dance, and dramatic enactment are performance media that have been employed for centuries by Asian women in the context of religious worship. The number and diversity of sacred performance traditions featuring female artists is perhaps greater in Asia than in any other part of the world.

The function and form of women's sacred performance in Asia has varied among cultural and religious groups and through time. Sacred female performance traditions can roughly be divided into shaman performance, trance performance, sacrificial offering, entertainment for the spirits, and educational performance. Because of the complexity of many of the sacred traditions in Asia, it is not unusual to find that a single performance tradition may serve multiple functions.

Throughout Asia animistic religions predate the development of the more highly codified belief systems such as Buddhism and Islam. Animism holds that spirits inhabit inanimate objects, such as mountains and trees, and that these spirits can, and frequently do, operate within the human realm. Spirits are thought to possess the power to alter the balance between positive and negative forces, which in turn can affect a community's health, climate, and economic condition. Theatrical performance is one means employed by believers to appease or influence the spirit world. In many cultures the person who serves as the mediator between human and deity is the shaman. In Korea female shamans conduct sacred performances known as *kut* (or *gut*). During a *kut* the shaman will attract the spirits through the singing of epic poems or mythological tales. Gifts of food, music, and dance are offered to the spirits to secure their aid in solving the problem.

In Burma (Myanmar) female and male transvestite mediums known as spirit-wives (*nat kadaw*) conduct sacred performances for private seances as well as during public festivals. Through the singing of sacred songs the spirit-wives become possessed by one of the thirty-seven guardian deities (*nat*) worshiped in Burmese animistic practice. While possessed the spirit-wives perform ecstatic dances characterized by a highly percussive movement style. Unlike shamans, who attempt to influence the spirits while possessed, the spirit-wives are trance performers who serve as empty vessels through which the spirits can communicate directly with the human realm—both through the dancer's body and through her voice. In *sanghyang dedari* (divine nymph), practiced on the island of Bali in Indonesia, prepubescent girls serve as spirit mediums. Their performances, generally held on temple grounds, are well-attended public events; intended to solicit protection from the gods and heal sickness, they also serve as popular entertainment for the community. *Sanghyang dedari* performance is characterized by rapid eye movement, the holding of the elbows at shoulder level, and quick changes of body posture and position.

The *Natyasastra*, an Indian treatise on theater written by Bharata Muni sometime between 200 B.C.E. and 200 C.E., carefully details the Hindu god Brahmā's role in establishing the art of dramatic performance. According to Brahmā, theater was to be a tool for educating and entertaining, and all classes of people and spir-

its (even demons) could attend performances. The first theater artists were said to be Hindu priests and heavenly nymphs created by the god specifically for this purpose. Later a professional class of theater artists—both male and female—took over this tradition, which is now referred to as Sanskrit drama. Performances took place in sacred spaces and were always initiated by ritual offerings to the gods. Although plays are known to have contained sacred material, they were not overly didactic and often dealt with themes of love and heroism. The *Natyasastra* calls performances visual sacrifices (*yajña*) and states that all who view them or take part in them shall receive protection from evil and enjoy success in life. Performances of Sanskrit drama coincided with important religious and temple celebrations. During India's Mogul period, when Islam became the state religion, theater performance (sacred as well as secular) was not condoned and Sanskrit drama disappeared.

The vast majority of sacred theater forms in India are performed by men. The one exception is the South Indian theatrical tradition known as *kutiyattam*, a descendant of Sanskrit drama. The female roles in *kutiyattam* dramas have for centuries been played by women of the Nangyar community, who also perform sacred dances at temples. These dances are not only considered to be offerings to the deities from the dancers themselves, but also from the audience in attendance. Until the 1920s another class of sacred performers, known as *devadāsīs*, could be found in India. Like the Nangyar, the *devadāsīs* also performed sacrificial dances to the deities. Although the *devadāsīs* were ritualistically married to male deities, they often served as courtesans to Hindu priests and kings. British morality and declining

The royal dancers of Cambodia perform an ancient traditional dance at the Angkor Wat Temple (Hulton-Deutsch Collection/Corbis).

economic support helped bring an end to this tradition. Today the dances of the *devadāsīs*, which often depicted the stories found in the sacred epics Rāmāyaṇa and Mahābhārata, form the basis of India's *bharatanāṭyam* dance tradition. Although sacrificial offerings are made at the beginning of *bharatanāṭyam* performances, the tradition is now regarded as a secular form.

Cambodian (Kampuchean) legend has it that through sexual intercourse with heavenly dancing nymphs the former kings of Kambuja made their land fertile. Until the 1970s the descendants of these dancing deities were the women who performed *lakon lueng* (king's dances) at the royal palace. Known to many outside the culture as the Royal Cambodian Ballet, these dancers were living symbols of the land over which their king ruled. The repertoire included both secular and sacred works such as dance dramas based on Rāmāyaṇa tales and offertory dances soliciting rain. In some sacred dances the women were thought actually to embody divine spirits.

Japan's earliest historical document, *Records of Ancient Matters* (*Kojiki*, 712 C.E.), recounts the culture's creation myth. It is within this account that the first reference to sacred female performance can be found. According to the legend, the sun goddess Amaterasu becomes angry with her brother and shuts herself up in a cave. Her disappearance plunges the world into darkness. At the urging of several lesser gods, the goddess Ame no Uzumi steps up onto an overturned wooden tub, bares her chest, drops her skirt, and performs an erotic dance. The cheers and applause that erupt from her audience pique the curiosity of the sun goddess and draw her from hiding. Not only is light returned to the world, but theater performance is established as an integral part of Japan's spiritual life. Out of this event the sacred dance style known as *kagura* ("entertainment of the gods") developed. For centuries in Shinto temples, young women (called *miko*) have performed the religious rites and slow-moving dance style of the *kagura* tradition as an offering to Shinto deities. In the sixteenth century a *kagura* dancer named Okuni from the shrine of Izumo is said to have performed a program of dance on a riverbed stage near Kyoto. Dressed in kimono yet wearing a Christian crucifix around her neck, Okuni performed Shinto dances, a genre of Buddhist offertory dances known as *nembutsu odori*, and enacted dramas of contemporary urban life. It was from this eclectic performance that the all-male theatrical tradition kabuki is thought to have developed.

Most female sacred performance traditions in Asia emphasize movement and song. Although the major dramatic script-based theater forms of Asia such as Japanese *noh*, Indian *kathakali*, or Chinese opera (*xiqu*) have roots in sacred traditions, they have now evolved into either all-male forms or forms performed primarily in a secular context. The dramatic repertoires of these theater forms contain female characters. In the Chinese Kun opera (*kunqu*) play *Longing for Laity* (*Si fan*), for example, a young Buddhist nun character is depicted debating the value of monastic life over love and marriage. Japanese *noh* plays are laden with Buddhist and Shinto symbolism and ideology. Many focus on the stories of tormented individuals who after death cannot relinquish attachment to the human realm. In the play *Sotoba Komachi* the spirit of a courtesan possessed by the spirit of a young man who died while trying to win her love encounters two Buddhist monks on a religious pilgrimage. Before the spirit's soul is freed from its possession and laid to eternal rest, the courtesan and monks debate the virtues of Zen versus Shignon Buddhism. The *Jakata* stories, which relate the previous lives of the Buddha, are widely performed throughout Southeast Asia.

BIBLIOGRAPHY

Brandon, James R. *The Cambridge Guide to Asian Theater.* 1993.

Blumenthal, Eileen. "Cambodia's Royal Dance." *1990 Los Angeles Festival Program Book.* 1990.

Daughtery, Diane. "The Nangyar: Female Ritual Specialist of Kerala." *Asian Theater Journal* 13, no. 1 (1996): 54–67.

Kang, Joon hyuk. "Korean Shamanism." *1990 Los Angeles Festival Program Book.* 1990.

Malm, William P. "Music in Kabuki Theater." *Studies in Kabuki: Its Acting, Music, and Historical Context.* 1978.

Meduri, Avanthi. "Bharata Natyam—Where Are You?" *Asian Theater Journal* 5, no. 1 (1988): 1–22.

Muni, Bharata. *Natyasastra.* Edited and translated by M. Ghosh. Calcutta, 1967.

Ortolani, Benito. "Shamanism in the Origins of the No Theater." *Asian Theater Journal* 1, no. 2 (1984): 166–190.

See also **Devadāsīs, Shamans.**

SUSAN PERTEL JAIN

In Monotheistic Traditions

The monotheistic traditions have been ambivalent toward dance and drama, with attitudes ranging from hostility to toleration under restrictive conditions. Restrictions usually affected women more than men: in dance, the public display of the female body was considered offensive under a patriarchal, male gaze; in drama, the contentious issue was the female voice and women's subjectivity in general. Hence, women claiming dance and drama as sources of female spirituality had to overcome a triple prejudice: first, the historical marginalization of dance and drama within the dominant traditions of Judaism, Christianity, and Islam; second, the marginalization of women within the performing arts, notably in drama; and third, the suspicion of the monotheistic traditions toward women as cultural agents and public figures.

DRAMA

Historically, drama has been perceived as a threat to monotheistic truth claims. Since Judaism, Christianity, and Islam are built upon sacred stories, rites, and liturgies that are highly dramatic themselves, a clear distinction had to be drawn between celebrations of faith in the One God and other performative genres so as to avert any kind of idol worship. Dramatized and ritualized worshiping of God was not to be confused with the make-believe world of theater and its potentially subversive, polymorphic alternatives to the sacred representation of ultimate reality. Theatrical performances have been variously condemned as pagan rites, profane entertainment, or licentious spectacles. Women were particularly absent in the history of theater: excluded from the performance of sacred rites, they were also barred from assuming key roles in popular religious dramatizations as well as from appearing on the secular stage.

In Judaism and Islam, drama as an art form developed only under the influences of the Enlightenment and modernity. Rabbinic and Qur'anic literature is mostly silent with respect to drama. In Islam, theater's mimetic threat was discussed as the dangers of *shirk* (idolatry) and *tashbīh* (anthropomorphizing of God), though Muslim scholars of religious law frequently ruled in favor of religious dramatizations. Popular and religiously inspired drama existed (e.g., the passion play *ta'ziyah* in Shiism commemorating the martyrdom of Imam Hosein, or the Jewish Purim *shpels* commemorating Esther's success in foiling the persecution of Jews), but female characters were often played by cross-dressing or transgendered men and boys (as in the *ta'ziyah*, or the Iranian comic theater of *ru-hozi*).

In Christianity, religious dramatizations were tolerated when they served moral and didactic purposes (e.g., medieval miracle, passion, and morality plays). The guilds staging these plays were, as in England, exclusively male, but mixed-gender casting was known in Spain and France. Even more exuberant, transgressive, and carnivalesque forms, which remained a constant source of anxiety for religious authorities, excluded women (e.g., male clergy played in the Feast of Fools, in the twelfth to the seventeenth centuries, and the choir

boys in the related Festival of the Choristers). Women attended those festivals as audience, participated in local processions (e.g., in honor of Christian saints), and sometimes accompanied vagrant renewal movements. But in the convents and as mystics, women enjoyed creative and spiritual freedom. A few religious women wrote plays (among them the Latin plays by Hrosvita von Gandersheim [c. 932–983]; the musical drama *Ordo Virtutum* by Hildegard of Bingen [1098–1179]; or the allegorical plays by Juana Inés de la Cruz [1651–1691]), but women playwrights did not become a visible force in Europe until the seventeenth century.

As theater moved slowly from the churchyard to the marketplace, the dominance of Christian plays was eventually broken by the classical Renaissance; and when theater companies became more professionalized, some women gained prominence, such as Isabella Andreini (1562–1604) in the *Commedia dell' Arte*. But women as cultural producers and ritualizing agents remained under attack: in Shakespeare's Elizabethan theater, male performers played women's roles; the Reformation relegated women to the private realm and further restricted theatrical elements within the church. On the North American continent, the Puritan spirit initially condemned theater as idleness, but under the influence of secularism numerous performative genres developed that included women.

The fact that women have mostly performed in the interstices of religious acceptability of the monotheistic traditions and at the margins of professional theater has led to what drama historian and feminist critic Sue-Ellen Case (1988) describes as the absence "of the female subject, whose voice, sexuality and image have yet to be dramatised within the dominant culture." As a response, feminist theories have called for a redefinition of drama that would render visible the spaces in which women have been active as dramatizing agents (covens; gnostic and mystical circles; local folk traditions, processions, and carnivals; or homes and religious institutions where women prepare feasts, plan celebrations, or rewrite liturgical traditions, such as a Jewish feminist seder).

DANCE

Gender-specific restrictions imposed on dance usually affected women more than men because the female body—according to patriarchal modes of thinking the site for sexuality—threatened to bring disorder and chaos to the social body. The public display of the "shameless" female body in dancing was of great concern to the monotheistic religions. Nevertheless, women always remained present in liturgical and popular dances.

The biblical tradition itself is a rich resource for images of dancing. As many as ten different verbs have been identified in the Hebrew Scriptures referring to some type of dance or dance-related movement, and a number of stories have sparked the Western imagination. Whereas the dance around the golden calf (Ex. 32) and Salome's dance (Mk. 6:22; Mt. 14:6) traditionally exemplify the dangers of dance (disloyalty to God; the evil of erotic seduction), the dances of Miriam (Ex. 15) and David (2 Sam. 2:14), among others, are cited as positive examples. In the New Testament, Luke provides a few references to dance (7:32; 14:25), and the apocryphal *Acts of John* (c. 160) contains a gnostic hymn that portrays a dancing Jesus. Some rabbis in the Midrashic and Talmudic literature envision a heavenly communal dance and consider dancing in honor of the bride a religious act. In Islam, dance-derived expressions include the *dhikr*, ritualized phrases accompanied by physical movements and breathing patterns.

In Christianity, a repressive body politic often coincided with a bias against both women and dance (e.g., the Council of Elvira [306], with its disciplinary, antisexual rulings, also refused to baptize mimes and circus performers), but dancing was not entirely proscribed. Church fathers like Ambrose (340–397) admonished Christians not to "abandon [themselves] to the actorlike movements of indecent dances and to the romance of the stage" (*On Repentance*), yet praised spiritual dances of women in the church; Chrysostom (349–407) commented on Salome's dance: "For where is dance, there is also the Devil. For God has not given us our feet to use in a shameful way . . . but to dance ringdances with the angels" (*Homiliae in Mattheum*). Attempts at curbing the dancing (and singing) of women in general and nuns in particular (as well as male clergy) continued until the fifteenth century. But as the various European dance epidemics beginning in the fourteenth century reveal, dancing could never be fully repressed. At best, it could be channeled into morally acceptable standards, either by separating men and women (as in Orthodox Jewish wedding dances or American Shaker formation dances), or by excluding women (as in Hasidic dance on the holiday Simhat Torah, or the rejoicing in the Torah, or by creating fraternal orders, like some of the Islamic dervishes, or the Christian flagellants in fourteenth century Europe). Renewal movements frequently made the gendered body the site of expressing religious discontent, with differing results for women and dancing: some incorporated ecstatic dancing and included women (especially mysticism, like Sufism), others exhibited strong iconoclastic and antisexual views, which led to the prohibition of dancing but allowed greater gender-equality

A mid-twentieth-century performance of the medieval play Noah at the Mermaid Theater, London, England, one of thirty-two biblical plays in the Wakefield cycle, composed between the mid-fourteenth and fifteenth centuries (Hulton-Deutsch Collection/Corbis)

(e.g., the Brothers and Sisters of the Free Spirit, twelfth–fifteenth centuries). Women also danced in their own spaces—in Sephardic homes to welcome the Sabbath, or in European covens—and took part in creating new dances in the New World (witness Afro-Brazilian rituals, like the Candomble, with its Yoruba and Catholic roots; or the African-American ring-shouts and polyrhythmic clapping that developed against Puritan proscriptions of drumming and dancing).

TWENTIETH CENTURY

In the twentieth century the search for female subjectivity has been at the center of performing women in Europe and North America, challenging the definition of traditional theatrical spaces and the role of the gendered body. Frequently, concerns for gender and ethnic identity have superseded religious issues (e.g., in lesbian or Chicana theater and among feminist performance artists or womanist playwrights), but women have also turned to dance and drama to rejuvenate their spirituality. On stage, women in modern dance and ballet revitalized biblical themes (e.g., Isadora Duncan, Ruth St. Denis, Rina Nikova, Martha Graham, Mary Wigman, Doris Humphrey, Judith Jamison, Ze'eva Cohen, Anna Sokolow, Sara Levi-Tanai), created choreographies influenced by New Age philosophies (e.g., Anna Halprin), and in their scripts emphasized women's rites of passage and other religious themes (e.g., Karen Malpede, Caryl Churchill, Adrienne Kennedy). Others created new performative genres that no longer distinguished among art, religion, and healing, including Jewish and Christian liturgical dances (by such artists as Judith Rock, Carla de Sola, and Fanchon Shur); Sufi-inspired explorations (Laura Dean's choreographic spinning techniques, or Ivy O. Duce's syncretistic performances); ritual performances incorporating African traditions (Katherine Dunham, Glenda Dickerson, Barbara Ann Teer); revival of goddess rituals and covens (Z. Budapest and Starhawk); and movement therapies emphasizing the artistic, therapeutic, and spiritual unity of dance (Franziska Boas). In these and similar performative genres, women have found creative ways to express and celebrate their spiritual freedom—sometimes within, sometimes at the margins of, and sometimes against their respective faith traditions.

BIBLIOGRAPHY

For historical information, consult Judith Lynne Hanna's *Dance, Sex and Gender* (1988), Sue-Ellen Case's *Feminism and Theatre* (1988), and Helen Krich Chinoy and Linda Walsh Jenkins's (eds.) *Women in American Theatre* (1981). Important information, though not written from a gender-conscious perspective, can be found in Louise E. Backman, *Religious Dances in the Christian Church and in Popular Medicine* (1952); Richard Kraus, *History of Dance in Art and Education* (1969); Edwin G. Brockett, *History of the Theatre* (1995; 7th ed.); Lynne Fauley Emery, *Black Dance: From 1619 to Today* (1972; 2d rev. ed., 1988); Genevieve Fabre, *Drumbeats, Masks, and Metaphor* (1983); and Peter J. Chelkowski's (ed.) *Ta'ziyeh: Ritual and Drama in Iran* (1979). William O. Beeman provides a gender-conscious treatment of *ta'ziyah*, "Mimesis and Travesty in Iranian Traditional Theatre," in Laurence Senelick's (ed.) *Gender in Performance* (1992).

For works on dance and drama that contain information on spirituality and gender, consult the following: for the revitalization of biblical and spiritual themes in twentieth-century dance, two excellent books are Doug Adam and Diana Apostolos-Cappadona's edited volume *Dance as Religious Studies* (1990; it includes a good list of references for liturgical dance), and Giora Manor's *The Gospel According to Dance* (1980), containing hundreds of photographs put together by the editors of *Dance Magazine*. Among the many biographical and autobiographical works, a well-known text is Isadora Duncan's *Isadora: My Life* (1928). For liturgical dance, see Carolyn Deitering's *The Liturgy as Dance and the Liturgical Dancer* (1984) and Judith Rock and Norman Mealy's *Performer as Priest and Prophet* (1988). A Jewish perspective is offered by Fanchon Shur's "My Dance Work as a Reflection of a Jewish Woman's Spirituality" (in *Four Centuries of Jewish Women's Spiritual-*

ity, edited by Ellen M. Umansky and Dianne Ashton, 1992). In Lesley A. Northup's (ed.) *Women and Religious Ritual* (1993), Melva Wilson Costen's "African-American Women and Religious Ritual" and Amitiyah Elayne Hyman's "Womanist Ritual" provide a womanist perspective. For goddess spirituality, two pioneering works are Starhawk's *The Spiral Dance* (1979) and Margot Adler's *Drawing Down the Moon* (1979; rev. and enl., 1986). Fran J. Levy's *Dance/Movement Therapy: A Healing Art* (1988; rev. ed., 1992) is a comprehensive introduction to the therapeutic use of dance.

For general information on women and performance, many excellent publications exist, including Jill Dolan's *The Feminist Spectator as Critic* (1991) and Sue-Ellen Case's edited volume *Performing Feminisms: Feminist Critical Theory and Theatre* (1990), the latter with contributions by Glenda Dickerson on womanist theater, Yvonne Yarbro-Bejarano on Chicana theater, and Vivian Patraka on Jewish women playwrights. The volume *Acting Out: Feminist Performances* (1993), edited by Lynda Hart and Peggy Phelan, provides a good overview of various feminist plays and theater productions. Christy Adair's *Women and Dance* (1992) addresses many of the problems women face in dance.

BJÖRN KRONDORFER

Day, Dorothy

A dynamic and influential figure in twentieth-century American Catholicism, Dorothy Day (1897–1980) was a passionate advocate for the improvement of the lives of the poor and marginalized. She was born in Brooklyn, the daughter of a journalist, and spent her youth absorbing books. In the 1920s she was a part of the Greenwich Village avant-garde of writers and radicals, and she wrote for various leftist publications. In 1926 the birth of her daughter, Tamara, restored her to a belief in the love of God after years of doubt and depression. She converted to Catholicism and was baptized in December 1927. Day was troubled by what she perceived to be the complacency of Christianity and the lack of direct involvement of lay Catholics and the institutional hierarchy in the social concerns of the world. Together with Peter Maurin, the French Catholic émigré whose ideas inspired and focused her, in 1933 she founded the Catholic Worker Movement in New York City. This movement and its newspaper, *The Catholic Worker*, challenged individuals to commit themselves to social and economic justice and peace but had no institutional ties to the Roman Catholic Church.

Day believed that responsibility to the poor, the workers, and the racially disenfranchised was the lived religion called for by Jesus in his Sermon on the Mount and was relevant to all the laity, not simply the Catholic Left. Day exemplified her movement's call to action by leading a life of voluntary poverty, personalist or individual nonviolent social activism, communitarian Christian living, and pacifism. She established and lived in Catholic Worker Houses of Hospitality and farms where she worked to feed and house the poor. She went to jail for her pacifism and was at the forefront of a U.S. Catholic movement against the Vietnam War in the 1960s and 1970s. Her personal Catholicism, though, blended her social radicalism with staunch theological conservatism.

A prolific writer, Day wrote six books and more than fifty articles, not including her innumerable columns in *The Catholic Worker.* Her activist social Catholicism marked a maturation of the U.S. Catholic community from the period of late-nineteenth-century European mass immigration to a more distinctive and reflective national Catholicism of the late twentieth century. Her death in New York City at the age of eighty-three was followed by calls for her canonization—an idea she disdained during her lifetime.

BIBLIOGRAPHY

Coles, Robert. *Dorothy Day: A Radical Devotion.* 1987. A rich biography formed from Coles's personal conversations, correspondence, and taped interviews with Dorothy Day.

Day, Dorothy. *The Long Loneliness.* 1952. One of Day's richest spiritual autobiographies.

Ellsberg, Robert, ed. *By Little and By Little: The Selected Writings of Dorothy Day.* 1983.

Merriman, Brigid O. *Searching for Christ: The Spirituality of Dorothy Day.* 1994.

Miller, William D. *Dorothy Day: A Biography.* 1982.

LEONARD NORMAN PRIMIANO

Death

Death marks the cessation of understandable human existence. Consideration of what lies beyond that threshold has been the impetus for much of the world's religious speculation, thought, and ritual. The fear of death and the need to control the mystery of that inevitable passage has resulted in the creation of a rich and complex set of symbols and rituals.

In many societies women played special roles in death rituals. The Egyptian goddess Isis became the very embodiment of lamentation in her search for her beloved husband Osiris. Her tireless search brought about his resurrection from the dead. Jeremiah 6:26

and Ezekiel 32:16 indicate that women performed the mourning lamentations in ancient Judaism. Ancient Greece and Rome also gave women the sacred duty of ritual lamentation and preparation of the dead body. Antigone, the daughter of Oedipus, believed it was a sacred duty to prepare the dead. She herself was condemned to death for defying King Creon by scattering a ritual handful of dust over the body of her brother, the traitor Polynices. In Roman Judea it was evident that women prepared the dead for burial. The Gospels report that women carrying embalming unguents were the first to visit the sepulcher of Jesus (Mark 16:1).

Many cultures associate death with the female, especially in that aspect of the chthonic absorbing earth matrix. The chthonic Mother gives birth, but her womb also demands nourishment. Eric Neumann called these destructive manifestations the Terrible Mother: she is the hungry earth fattened on the corpses of her children. Some cultures have suppressed this aspect of the Mother, while others have celebrated it.

This duality of the divine female as both life giver and destroyer is represented in many traditions. In Egyptian mythology the cow-headed goddess Hathor is both the nurturing mother of all and the Goddess of the West (the realm of the dead). In the Abrahamic religions (Judaism, Christianity, Islam) it was Eve, the first woman, who brought death and sorrow into the world. With Eve's disobedience God cast Adam and Eve out of Eden, lest they also partake of the Tree of Life and live forever and cheat death. In Islam Adam and Eve were equally disobedient, so that Eve is not solely burdened with the introduction of death and suffering. In hero cycles such as the *Odyssey,* it is a woman, Circe, who knows how to traverse the land of the dead and yet survive. In Norse mythology it was the Valkyries, terrible but seductive maidens who chose the honored dead and welcomed them into Valhalla, the paradise of worthy warriors.

India is particularly rich in goddesses who both give and destroy life. In traditional Indian thought, death was not perceived as an end; it was a transformative event that led to a new birth and consciousness. Death was the final achievement of life, the necessary step before renewal through the next birth. For this reason death was not perceived to be an evil that must be avoided or postponed, or a frightening event that must be hidden. Male and female images of transformative death are ubiquitous in Indian art, but it is as the dark side of the Great Goddess, the Mahādevī, that the most powerful expression of death emerges. She has many forms, which embody the symbols of destruction, death, and renewal.

The *Vedas* mention few goddesses, but the goddess Nirṛti is singled out as the deity of death and sorrow. In

An engraving by the French printmaker Gustave Doré of "Furies Before Gates of Dis," a scene from Dante's *Inferno* (Chris Hellier/Corbis)

Hinduism Kālī is the destructive aspect of time (*kāla*). She is often portrayed with dark skin and disheveled hair, her bloody tongue lolls from her mouth. She is dressed in a skirt of severed arms, a necklace of severed heads circles her neck, and she grasps a knife while holding another freshly severed head. Delightedly she dances on the inert body of her corpse-like consort, Śiva. She haunts the cremation grounds. Although Kālī sums up the horrors of decay she is also acknowledged as the *shakti* or enabling power of her consort. Like Isis she is the catalyst to jolt her male partner from passivity, a point made in the well-known phrase "Śiva without Shakti is Śava (corpse)."

Kālī has other yet more fearsome manifestations, such as Cāmuṇḍa, the goddess of the battlefield, who has a skeletal body and withered breasts. Her ornaments are snakes and scorpions. She carries a noose, a chopper, and a staff topped with a skull—emblems of her ruinous powers. She is described as howling with delight on the battlefield, drunk on the blood of the slain, her gaping maw ready to devour the vanquished.

Old age and its decay are personified by the goddess Jyeṣṭhā (The Eldest). She sums up the miseries of poverty and misfortune, yet she was worshipped in south India as a force that must be acknowledged. Diseases are often personified as female deities. The goddess Śītalā (The Cool One) is the Hindu goddess of smallpox; her Buddhist counterpart Hāritī (She who Steals) is also paradoxically the protectress of childbirth and children. The goddess Jarā also steals the lives of children. Manasā, the goddess of serpents, both embodies and protects from the deadly bite of the cobra. The Saptamātṛkās (The Seven Mothers) are a group of *ugra* (violent) goddesses whose identities change but whose intentions are usually associated with the sorrows of life, such as disease and death.

The tantric Hindu and Buddhist goddess Chinnamastā is a symbol of death and renewal. Despite her violent and destructive aspects, Chinnamastā is portrayed as a beautiful youthful woman, not the withered hag usually associated with Kālī iconography. Images of the self-decapitated Chinnamastā show the goddess in a cycle of destruction and creation fed by blood and sexuality. Typically, Chinnamastā is shown standing on the embracing lovers Rati and Kāma. They lie on a lotus, the symbol of renewal and an emblem of the Mahādevī. With one hand the goddess holds a knife with which she has cut off her own head; she holds her head aloft in her other hand. Despite the horror of the scene her face is serene: this is her *dharma*. She feeds herself and her two female attendants with the blood spurting from her severed neck. Chinnamastā is an example of the goddess as the Jaganmātā, the world mother, infinitely giving of blood, the fluid of creation, yet also needful of blood for the reinvigoration of life.

Some goddesses are associated with death because they demand blood sacrifice. Kālī, Cāmuṇḍa, Durgā, and Chinnamastā all continue to receive animal sacrifice, and at one time took human sacrifice. Other regional forms of these goddesses also needed blood, and sometimes accepted human oblations. It was believed that the goddess must be renewed and refreshed with blood to maintain her fertility and nurturing qualities.

All of these female manifestations of death from around the world are reminders that the Goddess is a complex deity who both takes and gives life. She represents the cyclical pattern of birth, degeneration, death, decay, and renewal. Her devotees worship the Goddess in these dark aspects as an acknowledgment that life emerges from the detritus of death and that meditation on the face of death will liberate the worshiper from the bonds of ego tied to the concerns of a mortal body.

BIBLIOGRAPHY

Banerjea, J. N. "Some Folk Goddesses of Ancient and Medieval India." *Indian History Quarterly* 14 (1938): 101–109.

Benard, Elizabeth Anne. *Chinnamastā.* New Delhi, 1994.

Bleeker, C. Jouco. "Isis and Hathor: Two Ancient Egyptian Goddesses." In *The Book of the Goddess Past and Present: An Introduction to Her Religion.* Edited by Carl Olson. 1983.

Holst-Warhaft, Gail. *Dangerous Voices: Women's Laments and Greek Literature.* London, 1992.

Kinsley, David. "Freedom from Death in the Worship of Kālī." *Numen,* 22, no. 3 (1975): 183–207.

Kramrisch, Stella. "The Indian Great Goddess." *History of Religions.* 14, no. 4 (1975): 235–265.

Neog, Maheswar. *Religions of the North-East: Studies in the Formal Religions of North-Eastern India.* New Delhi, 1984.

Neumann, Erich. *The Great Mother: An Analysis of the Archetype.* 1955.

Storm, Mary N. "Chinnamastā." *Journal of Asian Culture* 16 (1993): 75–93.

MARY STORM

Deborah is well understood as a Biblical reflex of Anat, although she has been rendered as human rather than divine by an Israelite tradition that recognized the existence of only one God.

BIBLIOGRAPHY

Craigie, Peter C. "Deborah and Anat: A Study of Poetic Imagery." *Zeitschrift für die alttestamentliche Wissenschaft* 90 (1978): 374–381.

Dempster, Stephen G. "Mythology and History in the Song of Deborah." *Westminster Theological Journal* 41 (1978): 33–53.

Rasmussen, Rachel C. "Deborah the Woman Warrior." In *Anti-Covenant: Counter-Reading Women's Lives in the Hebrew Bible.* Edited by M. Bal. *Journal for the Study of the Old Testament* Supplement Series 8. Bible and Literature Series 22. 1989: 79–93.

See also Ishtar and Anat.

SUSAN ACKERMAN

de Beauvoir, Simone

See Beauvoir, Simone de.

Deborah

According to the Bible, Deborah was a prophet and judge during the period of Israelite history that immediately preceded the establishment of kingship. This so-called League Period, which dated from c. 1200–1050 B.C.E., was characterized by a tribal form of government; each tribe was generally autonomous, with some occasions of intertribal assembly. Although called in the Bible "judges," those who led in these times of tribal interaction were really undifferentiated judicial, religious, and military authorities. Thus the judge and prophet Deborah assumes both a judicial and a religious role; she also seems to assume a military role in Judges 4:6–16 by commissioning a man named Barak to lead a coalition of Israelite tribes into battle against the Canaanite general Sisera. Judges 5:1–23, a second account of the battle against Sisera, demonstrates even more vividly Deborah's military role, as it describes her arising to lead the people (v. 7), sounding the reveille that calls the tribes into battle (v. 12), and singing the Israelite victory hymn (v. 1). She can also be understood as a participant in the battle itself (v. 15). Deborah's depiction here as a woman warrior is highly reminiscent of descriptions of the warrior goddess Anat found in the mythology of Israel's west Semitic neighbors. Indeed,

Deborah (Chris Hellier/Corbis)

Deconstruction

Deconstruction is a term associated with the work of the philosopher Jacques Derrida, particularly with his use of the neologism *différance* (*Positions*, pp. 8–9). The term is adapted from Derrida's reading of the linguistic scholar Ferdinand de Saussure, whereby language is described as a system of differential signs whose semiotic meanings derive from synchronic (dis-)placements within the system. There is no point of reference that would provide meaning outside this system. Thus, ideas of stable definitions, such as those of identity, truth, and representation itself, which depend on ahistoric ideals, are challenged. For Derrida the word *différance* has two connotations: 1) a radical difference that cannot be contained by antithetical formulas and that permits a playful interrogation of alternate possibilities of meaning; 2) a deferral of closure, which introduces a chain of endless postponements of definitive meaning. Their concomitant strategies can be employed either separately or together to question the finality of universalizations or absolutes, which often function by excluding an oppositional term. From a more general perspective—and here Derrida has been influenced by Nietzsche and Heidegger—deconstruction puts into question the ideals of reference and presence which have been the mainstay of Western metaphysics. The aim of the exercise is not nihilism or relativism, but the destabilization of conventional, limited categories so as to promote new insights and meanings.

Initially, Derrida focused on a style of reading texts that revealed the exclusionary presuppositions at work by introducing alternate meanings. Such a tactic was assumed to illustrate the inherent instability and incapacity of language (and texts) to sustain a uniform position. For example, in "Plato's Pharmacy," Derrida plays on the dual meaning of *pharmakon* as remedy or poison to explore alternate readings to the univocal meaning that Plato intended. In later work Derrida has exploited logico-formal paradoxes, as in his examination of the aporia of the gift. Here Derrida illustrates that the very conditions of gift giving within an economy of exchange cancel the gratuity of the gift and undermine both the definition and practice of gift giving itself.

Many feminists have been wary of adopting a deconstructionist approach, regarding it as one more tool of patriarchy. Such feminists regard Derrida's proclamation, "There is no such thing as the essence of woman" (*Spurs*, p. 51), as just one more example of the list of male philosophers who have presumed to impose their views on women. Other feminists, such as Susan Hekman, advocate its use to displace the prevailing dualistic structures that have relegated women to an inferior status. Diane Elam would employ it within an ethical framework to investigate the presumed hierarchy of values that become entrenched in any institution, even that of feminism itself. In the field of religious studies, feminists have tended to restrict their use of deconstruction to Derrida's early approach of a suspicious way of reading texts. However, Elizabeth A. Johnson and Anne Carolyn Klein introduce it in ways that critique accepted definitions of women and disclose the vested interests of mores in religion, which are symptomatic of the rigid rejection of both women and traditional "feminine" attributes.

BIBLIOGRAPHY

Derrida, Jacques. "Given Time: The Time of the King." Translated by Peggy Kamuf. *Critical Inquiry* 18, no. 2 (1992): 161–187.

———. *Margins of Philosophy.* Translated by Alan Bass. 1982.

———. "Plato's Pharmacy." In *Dissemination.* Translated by Barbara Johnson. 1981.

———. *Positions.* Translated and annotated by Alan Bass. 1981.

———. *Spurs: Nietzsche's Styles.* Translated by B. Harlow. 1979.

de Saussure, Ferdinand. *A Course in General Linguistics.* Edited by C. Bally and A. Schehaye. Translated by W. Baskin. 1959.

Elam, Diane. *Feminism and Deconstruction: Ms. en Abyme.* 1994.

Hekman, Susan J. *Gender and Knowledge: Elements of a Postmodern Feminism.* 1990.

Johnson, Elizabeth A. *She Who Is: The Mystery of God in Feminist Theological Discourse.* 1992.

Klein, Anne Carolyn. *Meeting the Great Bliss Queen: Buddhists, Feminists, and the Art of the Self.* 1995.

See also **Semiotics**; **Structuralism**.

MORNY JOY

Delphi

Delphi is a rural sanctuary on the slopes of Mount Parnassus in central Greece and home of the foremost oracle in classical antiquity. From the eighth century B.C.E., the focus of the sanctuary was a temple to Apollo that housed the *omphalos*, a stone considered by the Greeks to be the center of the world. A priestess called the Pythia mediated for the god; sitting on a tripod next to the *omphalos* she spoke words inspired by Apollo to

Ruins of Sanctuary of Athena at Delphi (Kevin Schafer/ Corbis)

priests who then transferred her prophecy into verse. Delphi provided both political and personal advice to those who consulted it and is associated with some of ancient Greece's most renowned wisdom: "Know thyself" and "Nothing in excess." Delphi reached its peak of political influence in the classical period, and after Alexander it continued to be a source of moral guidance until it was destroyed by Christians in the fourth century C.E.

Delphi was known principally as a sanctuary to Apollo since it was there that Apollo traditionally slew a she-dragon associated with Gaia and thereafter assumed his oracular powers. Delphi also contained older Bronze Age shrines to Athena and Gaia, neither of which can be associated with prophecy. A myth of Gaia's "previous ownership" of the oracle does not necessarily reflect actual cultic history; rather it expresses the cultural tensions between the civilizing functions of Apollo and his priests, and the perceived disorder of Gaia and the Pythia. Female deities continued to be venerated even after Apollo's arrival: within Apollo's classical temple stood an altar to Hestia, and a nearby archaic temple to Artemis and Athena was later rebuilt as a round *tholos* temple sacred to the two virgin goddesses. Although literary sources (e.g., Euripides' *Ion*) depict women traveling there, we cannot be sure how many Greek women actually went to Delphi to consult the oracle.

BIBLIOGRAPHY

Fontenrose, Joseph. *The Delphic Oracle: Its Responses and Operations.* 1978.

The Homeric Hymn to Apollo. The Homeric Hymns. Translated by A. Athanassakis. 1976.

Parke, H. W., and D. E. W. Wormell. *The Delphic Oracle.* 1956.

Price, Simon. "Delphi and Divination." In *Greek Religion and Society.* Edited by P. E. Easterling and J. V. Muir. 1985.

Sourvinou-Inwood, Christiane. "Myth as History: The Previous Owners of the Delphic Oracle." In *Interpretations of Greek Mythology.* Edited by Jan Bremmer. 1986.

NANCY EVANS

Demeter and Persephone

Demeter was the Greek goddess of grain and patron of agriculture, considered to preside over all gifts the earth provides. She was often worshiped together with her daughter, Persephone, or Kore (Maiden), and the two goddesses were closely identified with female experience and a female clientele. Their sanctuaries were modest, usually located in the countryside rather than in the city. Their most popular festival, the Thesmophoria, celebrated by women throughout the Greek cities of the Mediterranean, guaranteed both the food supply and the successful reproduction of the community. Men were not allowed to see these rites, celebrated at night and considered so sacred that they could not be described. Ancient writers, however, indicate that the Thesmophoria included fasting, ritual obscenity, and abnormal sacrifice (including the throwing of newborn piglets into underground pits and the retrieval of the rotted flesh). At some of Demeter's festivals the menu for women's banquets included meat from pregnant sows. The Thesmophoria concluded with a day called Kalligeneia (bearer of beautiful offspring), a description that could refer to the earth, the day, or the goddess herself.

The Thesmophoria were part of an annual cycle of female rituals that marked critical periods in the cycle of the agricultural year. In Attica the Proerosia was celebrated in early autumn, to prepare for the plowing of the winter grain crop. Sowing followed, but not before the Stenia and Thesmophoria anticipated the month of intense work and hazards of planting, followed in midwinter by the Haloa and the Chloia, timed to coincide with the first stages of plant growth. In early summer women celebrated the Kalamaia for protection of the grain stalks, and just before harvest in mid-June, the Skira, anticipating the threshing that ended the harvest in late June and July.

Female rituals for Demeter punctuated the cycle of male agricultural labor, but, as Plato's Aspasia says, "In conception and birth it is not the land that imitates the

Demeter. Archaic Greek sculpture, 500–400 B.C.E.
(Mimmo Jodice/Corbis)

woman, but the woman the land" (*Menexenus* 238a). Myths about Demeter emphasize her role as mother. The *Homeric Hymn to Demeter* tells how her anger compelled Zeus and the other male gods to meet her terms after her daughter, Kore, was abducted by Hades, king of the underworld. As Persephone, Demeter's daughter is bride of Hades and queen of the dead, but the story also tells how she returns to spend time with her mother each year. In this way Demeter and Persephone are connected to the annual cycle of birth, death, and rebirth. The hymn explains famine and food shortage by the anger of Demeter, who requires the fulfillment of motherhood in order to maintain the successful agricultural cycle. Many cities celebrated this story, even claiming to have locally the very place where Korea disappeared or returned.

The hymn also describes the building of Demeter's famous temple at Eleusis, site of the Eleusinian mysteries. By the sixth century B.C.E. the Eleusinian mysteries were open to all, male and female, Athenian and foreigner, both Greek and non-Greek. Emphasizing personal ritual experience, the mysteries focused on individual rather than community benefits. Concerned

with experience after death as well as before, the mysteries seem to have promised divine protection extending to the land of the dead. Ritual was carefully structured, and administration centralized under control of the city of Athens.

Demeter and Kore were identified so strongly with a female clientele that it was considered improper for a man to use the woman's exclamation, "By the two Goddesses!" Nevertheless, even the women's rites for these two were performed for the sake of the community, and all their public rituals, whether exclusive to women or open to all, were administered by public (always male) officials.

BIBLIOGRAPHY

Clinton, Kevin. *Myth and Cult. The Iconography of the Eleusinian Mysteries.* 1992.

Cole, Susan Guettel. "Demeter in the Ancient Greek City and Its Countryside." In *Placing the Gods: Sanctuaries and Sacred Space in Ancient Greece.* Edited by Susan E. Alcock and Robin Osborne. 1994.

Foley, Helene. *The Homeric Hymn to Demeter: Translation, Commentary, and Interpretive Essays.* 1994.

Foxhall, Lin. "Women's Ritual and Men's Work in Ancient Athens." In *Women in Antiquity: New Assessments.* Edited by Richard Hawley and Barbara Levick. 1995.

Kron, Uta. "Frauenfeste in Demeterheiligtümern: Das Thesmophorion von Bitalmi." *Archäologischer Anzeiger* 44 (1992): 607–650.

Lang, M. *Demeter and Persephone in Ancient Corinth.* 1987.

Nixon, Lucia. "The Cults of Demeter and Kore." In *Women in Antiquity: New Assessments.* Edited by Richard Hawley and Barbara Levick. 1995.

Zeitlin, Froma. "Cultic Models of the Female: Rites of Dionysos and Demeter." *Arethusa* 15 (1982): 129–157.

See also Festivals.

SUSAN GUETTEL COLE

Desire

Desire plays a pivotal role in religion. Human desire generates both a dissatisfaction with the way things are and the will to improve the current situation. Thus desire can be seen as an important motivating factor in the pursuit of spiritual progress. Yet desire is also seen in many religious contexts as a hindrance to spiritual advancement. Some religious traditions consider all desire to be counterproductive. Humanity's spiritual progress lies not in changing the way things can fulfill our desires, but either in lowering our expectations to allay disappointment (as in Stoicism) or in eliminating desire altogether (as in philosophical Taoism and some forms of Buddhism). In Taoism, the tao (way) is completely desireless and one can only achieve the ideal by simply letting go of all desires. Only the action that is no action (*wu-wei*) flows with the tao, and desires always disturb that natural harmony.

Religions that regard desire as potentially helpful usually distinguish between higher and lower forms of desire. The Christian theologian Augustine distinguishes between good desire (love of God) and evil desire (worldly lust). Similarly, according to the Theravada School, the Buddha describes both desire for conditioned (caused, mundane) things, which leads only to more conditioned things, and desire for the unconditioned (nirvana), which leads to nirvana. In such dichotomies, the lower, or worldly, desire is often associated with a loss of control. The emotional aspect of profane desire overwhelms humanity's higher aspirations, dragging it down into carnality. Descriptions of this level of desire often include misogynist depictions of women as hopelessly desirous. Women who are susceptible to their own worldly desires cannot control themselves, and women out of control are dangerous, both to themselves and to otherwise righteous men. Thus men must control women at every stage of their lives, a principle clearly described by the Hindu philosopher-lawgiver Manu, who stipulates that a woman must be controlled first by her father, then by her husband, and finally by her sons. Even women dedicated to a spiritual life, such as the nuns in medieval Christianity, it was thought must be carefully controlled by their male superiors, to ensure they do not succumb to their worldly desires for men, or for each other. Women whose desires are out of men's control are likely to be labeled witches or lesbians, both accusations that have led to the deaths of untold numbers of autonomous women.

Women are also castigated for planting the desire in men that leads them to lose control over themselves. This type of depiction occurs most often in male-dominated religions that uphold an ideal of celibacy. Whereas women's lust results from women's lack of self-control, men's worldly desire is blamed on women. The world's religions are full of images of temptresses who obstruct the religious progress of virtuous men. In Judaism and Christianity the first woman, Eve, typifies this dangerous behavior when she tempts Adam with the forbidden fruit from the tree of knowledge. In Hinduism, the goddess Pārvatī recruits Kāma, the god of love, to shoot Siva (Kāma, like Cupid, uses arrows) while he is medi-

tating, in order to win his love for her. In the story of the Buddha, the evil Mara (whose name means death and desire) sends his three beautiful daughters to prevent (unsuccessfully) the Buddha's enlightenment experience.

While a woman's desire, uncontrolled by men, is dangerous, and a man risks his own well-being by desiring a woman, many religions celebrate a woman's male-controlled desire for a man. In the world of the Egyptian pharaohs, Isis's desire for her husband Osiris leads her to give him both proper treatment after his death and a legitimate heir. In Hindu bhakti (devotion), the cowgirl Rādhā, who submits to the sexual desires of the cowboy Krishna and subsequently falls in love with him, provides the model of ideal human behavior toward God. The positive imagery of desire in Western religious mysticism is frequently associated with women, such as the sixteenth-century Christian Teresa of Avila and the eighth-century Muslim Rabi'ah, who is said to have been the first Sufi to practice love as a path to God.

In the major religious traditions, desire is usually seen as inherently dangerous. It must be controlled, eliminated, or redirected to a spiritual object. These androcentric traditions often identify women's desire as particularly intractable and dangerous. Thus images of temptresses abound, alongside the ideal of the pure virgin dedicated to the sacred. The fact that such condemnation of desire is a product of otherworldly patriarchies implies that new developments in women's religion and spirituality could lead to a reformulation of desire in a more positive light, as a tool of spiritual growth.

BIBLIOGRAPHY

Brown, Peter. *The Body and Society: Men, Women, and Sexual Renunciation in Early Christianity.* 1988.

Burford, Grace G. *Desire, Death, and Goodness: The Conflict of Ultimate Values in Theravada Buddhism.* 1991.

Flinders, Carol Lee. *Enduring Grace: Living Portraits of Seven Women Mystics.* 1993.

Matte, E. Ann. "My Sister, My Spouse." In *Weaving the Visions: New Patterns in Feminist Spirituality.* Edited by Judith Plaskow and Carol P. Christ. 1989.

O'Flaherty, Wendy Doniger. *Asceticism and Eroticism in the Mythology of Siva.* 1964.

Rousselle, Aline. *Porneia: On Desire and the Body in Antiquity.* Translated by Felicia Pheasant. 1988.

Young, Serinity, ed. *An Anthology of Sacred Texts By and About Women.* 1993.

See also **Body; Friendship; Love; Sexuality.**

GRACE G. BURFORD

Devadāsīs

In traditional India women who were formally dedicated to the Hindu temple as ritual servants to the gods were known as *devadāsīs*. This Sanskrit term literally means "servants of the gods," and the duties of such servants covered a variety of specific ritual areas. Because one of the major ritual activities of these women was sacred dance, the term has also come to mean, albeit somewhat inappropriately, "ritual dancer."

The *devadāsīs* played an integral part in the ritual life of Indian kingdoms, for in their specialized status these women served to embody the presence of the goddess Lakṣmī in the kingdom. The goddess of auspiciousness and prosperity, Lakṣmī was propitiated by the king so that she, along with her properties, might dwell in the court beside him and thereby bring prosperity to the entire kingdom. The *devadāsīs* performed rituals to invoke the ruling deity of the temple, but they maintained a special relationship with Lakṣmī in that they transmitted her power and blessings by becoming her representative on earth. The rituals entailed specific dances, songs, waving the sacred lamps before the deity, and, under certain circumstances, sexual intercourse with the king. All of these activities were performed with the intent to ward off evil and degenerative psychic influences and to usher auspicious, life-enhancing energies into the kingdom.

Devadāsīs did not constitute a separate caste as such, but entrance into their ranks was restricted. Ritual purity of the young woman, as well as that of her family, was required. This is but one example in traditional Indian culture in which ritual purity and ritual sexuality are necessarily linked. The strict ritual prohibitions surrounding the behavior of the *devadāsīs* insured that their sexuality—and thus their cosmic playing out of the female's sacred role in creativity and sustenance of the community—was an integral part of one holistic ritual configuration. The *devadāsīs* were sacred courtesans and never performed as prostitutes in a "secular," or common, sense. They remained within the sacred precincts and had little contact with outsiders.

A *devadāsī* surpassed the highly auspicious state of an ordinary married woman, for a *devadāsī* was married to God, specifically in the form of the deity of the temple in which she served. Her husband, being divine, was therefore immortal and could never abandon her to a state of inauspicious widowhood. Such a woman was therefore lauded with the epithet *maṅgala nārī*, "auspicious woman," or *nityasumaṅgalī*, "forever highly auspicious."

A major part of the ritual duties of the *devadāsīs* was to perform sacred dance, called *nāṭya* in Sanskrit. In vernacular Indian languages the term transformed into *nāc*, and during the British colonial period in India, the vernacular Indic term was anglicized to "nautch." By this time the ritual duties of the *devadāsīs* had been construed, by outsiders at least, simply as those of prostitutes who also performed dances as part of their work, and the term "nautch girl" came to carry the connotation of something like "exotic dancer." With the cultural changes that took place throughout the centuries of British rule, culminating in the Indian social reform movements of the early twentieth century, *devadāsīs*, far from being revered, were actually scorned. The traditionally ambivalent Hindu view toward sexuality—in the sense that its expression was both highly sacred yet highly profane—was losing out to the increasingly reformed interpretations of Hindu customs, which found sexuality within religiosity to be something of an embarrassment. Outside the context of ritual temple life, the "eternally auspicious" women came to be regarded simply as "nautch girls." Such fragmentation and thus misunder-

Two Indian classical dancers perform a traditional Bharat Natyam dance outside a temple at Bhubane in the Orissa region of India (Barnabas Bosshart/Corbis).

standing of the role of the *devadāsīs* within Hindu religious practice, compounded with a growing reform movement from within Hinduism to rid itself of archaic practices, especially as they concerned women, led in 1947—the year of India's independence from British rule—to the Devadasi Act, which made it illegal for women to be dedicated to temples or to religious images.

With the decline and eventual outlawing of the institution of the *devadāsīs*, a major feature of their role—that of sacred dancer—was salvaged in what is known generally as Indian classical dance. Although the dance is distinguished in various regional styles, the dominant style, which originated in South India, is known as *bhāratanāṭyam*. Work toward reviving and reinventing the sacred dance of the *devadāsīs* began in the early twentieth century, eventually entailing a reversal in what was emphasized in its study and performance: where once the focus was on ritual meaning, now aesthetics was the primary consideration.

Today's performers of Indian classical dance are artists and entertainers without the ritual status and significance of the former *devadāsīs*. Working within a necessarily secular mode, they can circumvent the inherent ambiguity of the sexuality of the dancer and thus avoid any of the past stigma. But by working outside of the traditional context of ritual, today's performers of *bhāratanāṭyam* do not gain admittance into the other side of the dance's ambiguity, for the perfect execution of artistic form alone would not have been enough to earn the traditional dancer the title of *nityasumangalī*, the sacred and powerful designation for the "ever-auspicious" woman.

BIBLIOGRAPHY

Gaston, Anne-Marie. "Dance and the Hindu Woman: Bharatanatyam Re-ritualized." In *Roles and Rituals for Hindu Women*. Edited by Julia Leslie. 1991.

Kersenboom, Saskia C. "The Traditional Repertoire of the Tiruttani Temple Dancers." In *Roles and Rituals for Hindu Women*. Edited by Julia Leslie. 1991.

Kersenboom-Story, Saskia C. *Nityasumangalī: Devadasi Tradition in South India*. Delhi, 1987.

Khokar, Mohan. "A Momentous Transition." *Sangeet Natak: Journal of the Sangeet Natak Akademi* (Delhi) 84 (April–June 1987): 41–47.

Marglin, Frédérique Apffel. "Types of Oppositions in Hindu Culture." In *Purity and Auspiciousness in Indian Society*. Edited by John B. Carman and Frédérique Apffel Marglin. Leiden, 1985.

———. *Wives of the God-King: The Rituals of the Devadasis of Puri*. Delhi, 1985.

Ramanatham, Leela, ed. *Bharata Natyam: Yesterday, Today, Tomorrow*. Delhi, 1985.

Srinivasan, Amrit. "The Hindu Temple-Dancer: Prostitute or Nun." *Cambridge Anthropology, Art and Society* 8, no. 1: 73–99.

Starza, O. M. *The Jagannatha Temple at Puri: Its Architecture, Art, and Cult*. Leiden, 1993.

CONSTANTINA RHODES BAILLY

Dharma

People in the West distinguish between private morality and state legislation, between religious rules and the scientific laws of nature. In India, the notion of dharma unites all these different aspects. Derived from the Sanskrit root *dhr* (to sustain, uphold, support), dharma is a designation for religion in general. But it also denotes specific injunctions to specific castes at a specific stage of life (*varnashramadharma*). Integrating right with rite, and description of the way things are with inscription for the way they ought to be, dharma integrates religion, virtue, duty, propriety, morality, cosmic order, and civil and criminal law.

DHARMA IN HINDUISM

While many texts elaborate dharma for men in great detail and precision, women's dharma is mentioned only tangentially. For instance, the Dharmasastras vividly describe the four stages of life of men with very little about women's dharma.

Most of the Vedic hymns extol powerful male figures, requesting in return longevity, prosperity, and heroic sons. The husband is the head of the household, and he is in charge of hosting guests both human and divine. Yet, woman as wife and mother is regarded as auspicious in this life-affirming weltanschauung. Her role in the family and the rituals is related to a harmonious social and cosmic order. The wife-mother in the home who gets up early in the morning is connected with the female cosmic phenomenon of dawn. Throughout the Rig Veda, the first recorded literary work in India, woman is essential to the well-being of her family and necessary for the presence of gods. We also encounter women fulfilling esteemed religious functions. There are examples of women reciters of Vedic chants, singers of the sacred hymns, and seers (*rsika*) into the divine reality, while in the Upanishads (Vedic treatises) women like Maitreyi and Gargi affirm and valorize female voices questioning, arguing, and searching for the nature of the ultimate.

As the polarity of pure (*sauca*) and impure (*asauca*) became central to religious activities, especially in the Dharmasastras, women came to be viewed as increas-

A golden Dharma-chakra, a wheel symbolizing the teachings of the Buddha, stands between statues of deer, representing the first sermons of the Buddha at Deer Park, Sarnath Jokhang Temple, Lhasa, Tibet (Christine Kolisch/Corbis).

ingly impure at times of menstruation and childbirth. For men, Vedic learning became the highest virtue; for women, chastity and purity. While a man's duties and obligations extended to the economic, social, political, and even to the transcendent realm of the Infinite Brahman, a woman's world came to be confined within the narrow walls of her home.

The *ashrama* (stages of life) requisites are different for men and women as well. Whereas the ideal life cycle of the Hindu man is demarcated into four stages—that of the student, householder, forest dweller, and renunciate—the life of woman came to be divided into three main phases: maidenhood (*kaumarya*), marriage (*vivaha*), and self-immolation on the funeral pyre of the husband (sati) or widowhood (*vaidhavya*). Through sati (literally "good wife") a woman performed her dharma by consummating her life of devotion to her husband. Widowhood was an expression of *adharma* (evil), a wife's failure in her supreme sacrifice to her husband.

Upanayana sacrament or the initiation into Vedic learning for the young boy was substituted by the nup-

tial ceremony for the girl (Laws of Manu, 2.67). Instead of residing and studying at the house of the guru, she was to serve her husband. In place of the male student's daily worship of the sacred fire, she was to perform her household chores.

The Laws of Manu propose that women be honored and adorned by all the males in the family, especially on holidays and festivals with gifts of ornaments, clothes, and dainty food (3:55–59). In the Laws of Manu, women's dharma is the opposite of men's, for what ought to be shunned by men is an honor for women. Material gifts to be showered on women fall in the category of *preyas* (pleasing), which are to be rejected by venerable males. The distinction between *preyas* and *sreyas* is emphasized in the Katha Upanishad, one of the oldest verse Upanishads, composed in the last few centuries B.C.E., where the young Brahmin boy who opts for knowledge (*sreyas*) over material delights (*preyas*) is lauded for his virtue.

The Laws of Manu repeatedly define the dependence of women on men: fathers, husbands, sons, brothers-in-law. This legal code lists a wife's duties to her husband both while he is alive and after he is dead. He is the constant subject of her devotion, obedience, and worship.

The Laws of Manu permit a husband to remarry after performing the funeral rituals for his wife (5.168), but they absolutely forbid the remarriage of a wife after the death of her husband (9.65). On the positive side, the sale of women into marriage is forbidden, and their right to own separate property is protected (3.51). Close female relatives, including mothers-in-law, are to be revered as is a teacher's wife (2:131).

Hindu scriptures apotheosize both men and women. "A husband must be constantly worshipped as a god by a faithful wife" (5:154). The wife, too, is the goddess, and in fact *striyah* (woman) is identified with *shriya* (goddess of prosperity). But again there is a major difference between male dharma and female dharma. While the husband is unconditionally a god who owes no obedience to his wife and could never be her subordinate, the wife must always be obedient to her husband in word, deed, and thought. Her exaltation depends upon her devotion and surrender to her lord-master "even if he behaves badly, freely indulges his lust, and is devoid of any good quality" (5:154). In an often quoted passage from the Ramayan, Lord Rama says, "By obedience to her husband, a woman attains the highest heaven. . . . To be subject of her consort and seek to please him is the strict duty of a woman, laid down by the Veda and acknowledged by the world." While the man holds the divine status as a birthright, the woman's divine status is contingent upon her bearing offspring, and her being physically and psychologically bright and cheerful.

Women were excluded from hearing and reading sacred texts. The Laws of Manu advocate that women's rituals are to follow the timing and sequence of the men's, "but without the recitation of sacred texts" (2.66). A later text, Devi Bhagavata Purāna, exalts the triumphs of the goddess Durga. But in its final chapter, women (along with Sudras, Hindus of the lowest caste) are forbidden outright from reciting the very text that lovingly and lavishly celebrates female power.

The three yogas that are put forth in the Bhagavad Gita by Lord Krishna, *karma* (action), *jnana* (knowledge), and *bhakti* (love), converge for women in yet a fourth: *patiyoga* (literally, husband yoga). The yogic discipline of restraint, purification, concentration on a single point, equanimity, and desirelessness is exercised by the woman—for her *pati* and his family. Dharma for the wife prescribes an understanding of herself in relation and connection with her husband and in-laws. In various ways women try to build positive energy so that they can transfer it to their husbands and families. For example, in the north of India, Karva Chauth is an important festival during which women have to fast for the entire day for their husband's long life and prosperity.

There are many figures in Hindu mythology that are paradigms of feminine beauty, sexual fertility, serenity, radiance, ardent devotion, self-control, self-sacrifice, and goodness in relation to others. This ideal behavior of the Hindu woman, popularly known as *stridharma*, is embodied in heroines such as Sītā and Savitri, and goddesses such as Laksmi. The virtues of goddesses such as Durga and Kali are not appropriated by women in the real world.

DHARMA IN OTHER INDIAN RELIGIOUS TRADITIONS

Later religious developments in India, such as Jainism, Buddhism, and Sikhism, rejected the *varnashramadharma* and instead promoted a more egalitarian form of morality, ethics, and propriety. Dharma in Jainism, Buddhism, and Sikhism is doctrinally the same for both men and women, and for all people, irrespective of their birth.

JAINISM

Ahimsa, nonviolence, is the dharma of all Jains, be they monks, nuns, laymen or laywomen, and it is geared toward all beings, animate or inanimate. Both Jain monks and nuns take the same five great vows (*mahavrata*) against injuring life, false speech, stealing, unchastity, and attachment to material wealth. In spite of these vows, the nuns are always subservient to the monks. Male and female lay believers share the ethical injunctions of the monks and nuns but to a lesser degree, so their vows are *anuvrata* (small vows). Husbands and wives, mothers and fathers practice charity, meditation, fasting, and other obligatory duties. Many young Jain children also observe the fasts rigorously.

BUDDHISM

The *Dharmasangiti* says: "The Law [Dharma] is equal, equal for all beings: For low or middle or high the Law cares nothing." Every Buddhist, male or female, young or old, rich or poor, takes refuge in the Buddha, dharma, and the *samgha* (the Three Jewels of Buddhism). The Buddhist goal of enlightenment or nirvana is a recognition of the utter vacuity of the self and the universe; such recognition ends all desire and craving, and frees the individual from the cycle of birth and death. The Buddha opened nirvana to both men and women disciples equally: both have the same aspiration, both are given the same teachings and the same spiritual path to follow. Yet, the status of the nun is always inferior to that of the monk.

SIKHISM

Guru Nanak (1469–1539) and his successors repeatedly claimed that dharma was the same for men and women of all races, classes, and ages. Contemplation of the Transcendent One (*Ikk Oan*) is the supreme and immutable dharma in Sikhism. Rules of conduct and religious duties are the same for both men and women; there is no specification of *stridharma*. Both have identical status, and as early as Guru Amar Das (1552–1574), women were appointed as religious leaders along with men.

The intimate link between dharma and *dharti* (earth) is underscored in Sikh literature. Both share the etymological root (*dhr*). Earth is called dharma, and even *dharmasala*, the House of Dharma. Earth gives humans their very existence and the opportunity to engage in moral and ethical action. Rather than reach another and distant realm, the Sikh spiritual goal for men and women devotees is to draw the Transcendent into the everyday routine.

Sikh scripture also celebrates the body as dharma. Celibacy and the notion of female pollution are denounced, while the wife is regarded as an essential partner for moral and spiritual development. In fact, female tone, imagery, sentiments, actions, modes of dressing up, all receive a transcendent value. In spite of the high status of women accorded in Sikh sacred and secular literature, Sītā and Savitri still remain the unconscious models for Sikh society.

BIBLIOGRAPHY

The Griha-Sutras: Rules of Vedic Domestic Ceremonies. Translated by Hermann Oldenberg. 1986.

Jamison, Stephanie W. *Sacrificial Wife, Sacrificer's Wife: Women, Ritual, and Hospitality in Ancient India.* 1996.

Laws of Manu. Translated by Wendy Doniger. 1991. See also G. Buhler's 1886 translation.

Paul, Diana. *Women in Buddhism: Images of the Feminine in Mahayana Tradition.* 1985.

Singh, Nikky-Guninder Kaur. *The Feminine Principle in the Sikh Vision of the Transcendent.* 1993.

Young, Katherine K. "Hinduism." In *Women in World Religions.* Edited by Arvind Sharma. 1987.

TEXTUAL SOURCES—HINDUISM

Sruti (literally, that which is heard) is the primary source for normative guidance. Considered as divine revelations, *Sruti* texts are comprised of the liturgical hymns of the Rig, Yajur, Sama, and Atharva Vedas, the ceremonial instructions of the Brahmanas, and the philosophical treatises—the Aranyakas and Upanishads. *Smriti* (literally, that which is remembered) are later texts; they are the interpretations, philosophies, legal systems, and traditions passed down through the generations. *Smriti* literature consists of the six Vedangas (including Srautrasutras that explain public rituals; the Grihasutras, which teach ways of performing domestic ceremonies; and Dharmasutras, which interpret the duties of the community), the epics Mahābhārata and Rāmāyaṇa, and the Puranas. *Sruti* also includes Dharmasastras, which were developed around 100 C.E. with a focus on the injunctions in Vedic dharma. Manava Dharmasastra, popularly known as the Laws of Manu, has been the most authoritative code on Hindu ethics and law for centuries.

See also **Buddhism: An Overview; Hinduism: An Overview; Jainism; Sikhism.**

NIKKY-GUNINDER KAUR SINGH

Diana

See Artemis (Diana).

Diatta, Aline Sitové

See Alinesitoué.

Diotima

Diotima, a prophetess of the ancient Arcadian city of Mantinea, is portrayed by Socrates as discoursing to him on the nature of eros (love, desire) in the *Symposium* of Plato. Her name is synonymous with female intellectual and religious authority. Diotima has become the locus of feminist reclamation of women's history and theorization of sexual difference.

In the *Symposium*, Socrates describes Diotima as his teacher in "erotic matters" and recounts her pronouncements on the nature of eros, at once psychological and cosmic force, and on its personification as mythic individual (Plato, *Symposium* 201D–212C). Diotima argues that desire desires the beautiful and the good. But since desire is always desire for what it lacks, Eros cannot be a god, perfectly possessed of beauty and good. Rather Eros is a daimon, one of those spirits mediating between mortal and divine. She recounts the myth of his birth to Resource, his father, and Poverty, his mother. Eros, at once needy and resourceful, pursues what is beautiful, hence wisdom, and so must be conceived as philosopher, a lover of wisdom. All desire is the desire for happiness as eternal possession of the beautiful and good.

Eros aims, however, not at mere possession of the beautiful, but at "giving birth in beauty." Beauty is the goddess of birth in whose presence alone all creativity comes to fruition. Diotima claims the urgency of eros in all breeding and bearing in the animal and human world as impulse to immortality, likewise positing every body, every mind, as a sort of fountain of being that must continually renew itself to continue to exist.

Creativity may be of the body or of the soul. Men "pregnant" in body seek to produce children. Men "pregnant" in mind produce virtue, and with it poetry and those laws that order human communities, which provide their begetters with "immortal fame." Diotima explicitly associates this latter eros with male homoerotic love and describes in the language of religious initiation a ladder of love, whereby a man who loves boys correctly can ascend from love of one beautiful body, to love of all beautiful bodies, to love of the soul, to love of laws and institutions, to love of kinds of knowledge, so begetting beautiful ideas and theories. Finally, at the summit of eros, he apprehends beauty itself, "absolute," "pure," and "unpolluted" by mortality. Quickened by the absolute reality of beauty, he gives birth to real virtue, and "could any human being become immortal, it would be he."

Two interlocking questions trouble any account of Diotima: her historicity and the relation of her teaching to Plato's philosophy. She is described by Socrates as responsible for a purification of Athens that postponed the great plague (430 B.C.E.) by ten years, yet no extant contemporaneous source makes any reference to Diotima or to the purification. Thus certain commentators consider Diotima an invention of Plato (or possibly of the historical Socrates). Some theorists link her with Aspasia, the brilliant mistress of Pericles. Failing strong historical evidence, interpreters argue for her historicity on the basis of claimed contrast between Diotima's speech and Plato's philosophy.

Has Plato preserved, falsified, or created Diotima? Only in submitting ourselves to reflection on the doctrine of this founding philosopher of the Western metaphysical tradition can we call up Diotima's voice, to hear her and yet not know in whose voice she speaks.

BIBLIOGRAPHY

The best single treatment of Diotima is Mary Ellen Waithe's "Diotima of Mantinea" in vol. 1 of *A History of Women Philosophers* (1987), a collection of essays on ancient women philosophers edited by Waithe. Waithe makes the strongest possible case for a historical Diotima, reviewing the historical evidence, archaeological and textual, and positing differences between the doctrines of Diotima and those of Plato.

Luce Irigaray's "Sorcerer Love: A Reading of Plato's *Symposium,* Diotima's Speech" (in French, 1984) is a key text for feminist analyses of Plato. This essay appears in English together with a critique by Andrea Nye, "Irigaray and Diotima at Plato's Symposium" and other essays directly relevant to Diotima in *Feminist Interpretations of Plato,* edited by Nancy Tuana (1994).

The most prominent circle of feminist philosophers in Italy today has taken as a collective name the "Diotima Group." Adriana Cavarero, a leading member, offers an important reading of Diotima's speech in her *In Spite of Plato* (in Italian, 1990; English translation, 1995).

A language of conception and birth characterizes Diotima's discourse, which some read as woman-oriented, while others criticize as an instance of male appropriation of the feminine that characterizes much androcentric theory. David Halperin utilizes this dimension of feminist criticism in "Why Is Diotima a Woman?" which appears in fullest form in his *One Hundred Years of Homosexuality* (1990). Halperin's work is a particularly rich source for bibliography on the relevant classical scholarship. He sharply criticizes the claims of Gustave Fougères and Roger Godel, who posit a Mantinean tradition of philosopher-priestesses.

LUCIA LERMOND

Disciples

As with many terms that Western-trained historians of religion have come to apply in their treatments of religions cross-culturally, the word *disciple*—based on the Latin *discipulus,* meaning "learner" or "pupil"—originally had a Christian connotation. Employed frequently throughout the Gospels and Acts, the word appears to be applied in three ways: 1) to distinguish the most fervent followers of the teacher Jesus Christ; 2) to designate anyone who follows a great movement or leader; and 3) to describe all people who believe in Christ. Considering how the term has been expanded upon and used in the transreligional sense, one can see that while the third meaning is too broad, in that when we speak of disciples we are rarely referring to all members of a particular religion, the first two meanings can be easily and instructively applied. In almost every religion, the normative tradition established first by its founder or founders, and later promulgated by its leaders, is largely preserved and transmitted by the immediate followers of those founders and leaders, who are known as disciples. Those who are defined as disciples are also typically regarded as those who most completely accept a religion's philosophical or theological doctrines, apply its system of moral values, and engage in its program of spiritual practice.

In Christianity, the New Testament term *disciple* (Greek, *mathētēs*) first applies to the inner circle who shared the mission of Jesus and walked in his company.

In the broader sense of the term, as including all believers in Christ, the early Christian vision of a discipleship of equals practiced in the house and church attracted many women to the religion. Before and after Easter, the community of Christ granted women equal rights with men to participate in worship, and gave traditional female roles new significance in the context of discipleship. Over the course of the subsequent centuries, however, forces that promoted patriarchal and hierarchical structures, supported in part by certain late New Testament writings that subjugated women, increased in prevalence to the point where most Christian assemblies counted women as second-class citizens, generally not admitting them to the ranks of ministers and powerholders. Still, given the more restricted Pauline and post-biblical definition of disciple as one who not only follows, but also endeavors to imitate the poverty, humility, and charity of the earthly Jesus as closely as possible, opportunities continued for women to serve as Christian disciples, especially with the institution of the nun's vocation, which provided an environment for living according to this "imitation of Christ" ideal. The Catholic saints Catherine of Siena and Teresa of Avila perhaps stand out as models of this mode of discipleship, both because of their moving mystical experiences of God and their hard-won positions of authoritative leadership in the church.

Of all the major religions, Judaism has tended to place the least amount of distinction on the most dedicated followers and bearers of its traditions, choosing instead to focus on the God whose word the prophets have spoken and whose law all Jews are to obey. The leaders who have been distinguished in its scriptures, such as Moses, Elijah, and Jeremiah, and their divinely appointed successors, such as Joshua and Elisha, have almost always been men. There are notable exceptions, such as the Israelite judge and prophet Deborah and the heroines Judith and Esther, whose courageous actions helped liberate their people, as well as the figures Ruth and Naomi, whose exemplary lives have provided Jews with models of strong and loyal friendship.

Despite a continuing focus in later eras of Jewish history on the revealed law of God over and above the human person of the religious master, in traditions such as rabbinic and Hasidic Judaism one does find a greater

Christ Appearing to the Magdalen (National Gallery, London/Corbis)

emphasis on master-disciple relations, in which teachers provided guidance by example and personal contact, as well as by lecturing on sacred texts, and pupils reciprocated by revering and serving their teachers. Again, the environment was largely patriarchal, with women's roles often being limited to the more passive ones of follower and wife. Nevertheless, some women, as followers of great Jewish leaders, have emerged as renowned disciples, as is the case with individuals such as Beruiah, the learned wife of Rabbi Meir, and Oudil, the charismatic and pious daughter of the Hasidic founder Baal Shem Tov.

In Islam, disciples of the founder are known as "companions" (Arabic sing., *ṣāḥib* or *ṣaḥābī;* pl., *aṣḥāb* or *ṣaḥābah*) of the Prophet Muhammad. While general opinion holds that a companion is anyone who saw Muhammad and embraced Islam, the more strict view maintains that the only true companions were those who were chosen by the Prophet, who kept frequent and close company with him, and who became the memorizers and transmitters of the traditional accounts of his deeds and utterances (hadith) and of the Qur'an, before they were written down and compiled.

While sources tell us that there were many women who lived in close proximity with Muhammad, emigrating with their families to Abyssinia in the early years of Islam and accompanying him into battle where they cared for the wounded and even sometimes engaged in the fighting, there are really three women who stand out as great Muslim disciples, both in terms of their fulfilling traditional female roles and serving as models of piety, regardless of gender. The first is Muhammad's first wife, Khadija. Besides being the mother of most of his children and providing a haven of security and serenity for him, Khadija was in many ways Muhammad's greatest disciple, for she was the first believer, consoling him after his initial visions and auditions, and convincing him that the revelations he received were of divine, not demonic, origin. She also supported his mission both materially and spiritually. In all these capacities, Khadija played a crucial part in defining the role of women as followers of Islam. The second is 'A'ishah, regarded not only as Muhammad's most beloved wife, but also as a most important authority on hadith and God's law (sunna) after his death. She is said to have been so knowledgeable about the religious duties (fara'id) of Islam that even men who had been the most senior companions of Muhammad came to her for counsel and instruction. The third great female disciple is Fāṭimah, Muhammad's daughter and the wife of his cousin 'Alī, who was the Prophet's first male believer and the eventual fourth Caliph. Fāṭimah is regarded by Muslims everywhere as the religion's fountainhead of female spirituality, because she continually occupied herself with maintaining the purity that stems from belief in the unity of God.

Sufi sources tell of a considerable amount of women disciples (faqīrāṇi) who have been celebrated for their piety, spiritual achievement, and teaching and leadership ability. Perhaps the most famous faqīrāṇi is Rabi'a of Basra, a key figure credited with introducing the element of absolute love into the strict ascetic Sufism of her time.

Although the Sufi orders have been considered "families" that were not to be separated by gender, or to exclude women from full participation in their life of practice, over the course of history most orders have come to accept women only as lay members, who may observe but not take part in ritual activities. As a corrective response to this, Sufi orders were established that have been open only to women, especially to those of particularly ascetic and celibate inclinations. Noting the tremendous love and enthusiasm of female adherents, the Bektashi order of Turkey have placed women on an equal plane with men, having them undergo the same initiations rites and partake in all community ceremonies. This custom has led to frequent accusations of immorality against them.

The misogyny inherent in a cultural tradition that succumbs to the seemingly perennial negative image of women as seductresses who evince lust, temptation, and other worldly weaknesses has been a familiar aspect of almost all religious movements, especially those marked by an ascetic strain. For instance, this tendency is manifest in many Indian-based traditions, which also place a high premium on the master-disciple (Sanskrit, *guru-śiṣya*) relationship and the continuation of a lineage (*paramparā*) that bears a system of teachings. In the case of Buddhism, it seems that there was great reluctance on the part of the Buddha and the early monastics to include lay women in their community (sangha). Eventually a nuns' order was established, but only after it was agreed that the nuns would have to abide by an extra set of disciplinary rules, most of which were based on assumptions of women's inherent sexual licentiousness. It was also prophesied by the Buddha that the Buddhist tradition would be short-lived because of the presence of nuns in the community, and indeed, the nuns' orders at least, due largely to entrenched prejudices, have typically not endured or flowered in most Buddhist cultural settings, with lineages dying out in many cases. On the other hand, there is evidence—perhaps found most impressively in a collection of poems composed by members of the early nuns' order, known as the *Therīgāthā*—that Buddhist (like Christian) nuns have often enjoyed greater social and religious freedom than women in their cultures who live outside the monastic community.

Hinduism, in which the social status of women has been largely one of dependence upon their families, which they serve, has greatly limited women's opportunities to live lives of religious discipline. However, there have also been major popular religious movements of pan-Indian religiosity, namely those of theistic devotionalism (bhakti) and esoteric yoga (tantra), which have provided avenues for women to go beyond normative controls and pursue alternative religious roles. The Bhagavadgītā has famously declared that the discipline of devotion is open "even to women," and indeed subsequent history shows that many bhakti and tantra groups, honoring expressions of love of the divine above social conventions, have welcomed women as fully participating members. For example, many women, such as Mirabai in the north and Mahādēviyakka in the south, have been leading exponents of bhakti and its values. In modern times, neo-Hindu movements that blend classical forms of spiritual teaching with more egalitarian community structure have provided the world (for many of them have spread to Europe and North America) with powerful women leaders, such as Ma Jñānānanda and Guru Chidvilasānanda, who count many women as their devoted disciples.

BIBLIOGRAPHY

Bartholomeusz, Tessa. *Women Under the Bo Tree.* 1994.

Baskin, Judith. "The Separation of Women in Rabbinic Judaism." In *Women, Religion, and Social Change.* Edited by Yvonne Y. Haddad and Ellison B. Findly. 1985.

Chishti, S. K. K. "Female Spirituality in Islam." In *Islamic Spirituality.* Edited by S. H. Nasr. 1987.

Falk, Nancy A. "The Case of the Vanishing Nuns: The Fruits of Ambivalence in Ancient Indian Buddhism." In *Unspoken Worlds: Women's Lives in Non-Western Cultures.* Edited by Nancy A. Falk and Rita M. Gross. 1980.

Findly, Ellison B. "Gargi at the King's Court: Women and Philosophic Innovation in Ancient India." In *Women, Religion, and Social Change.* Edited by Yvonne Y. Haddad and Ellison B. Findly. 1985.

Fiorenza, Elizabeth Schüssler. *In Memory of Her.* 1983. Reprint, 1994.

Freyer, Barbara. *Women in the Qur'an: Traditions, and Interpretation.* 1994.

Horner, I. B. *Women under Primitive Buddhism.* 1930.

Murcott, Susan, trans. *The First Buddhist Women.* 1991.

Ramanujan, A. K. "On Women Saints." In *The Divine Consort: Radha and the Goddesses of India.* Edited by J. S. Hawley and Donna M. Wulff. 1982.

Schimmel, Annemarie. *My Soul Is a Woman: The Feminine in Islam.* 1997.

Smith, Jane I. "Women, Religion, and Social Change in Early Islam." In *Women, Religion, and Social Change.* Edited by Yvonne Y. Haddad and Ellison B. Findly. 1985.

Smith, Margaret. *The Life and Works of Rabi'a and Other Women Mystics in Islam.* 1994.

Sponberg, Alan. "Attitudes Towards Women and the Feminine in Early Buddhism." In *Buddhism, Sexuality, and Gender.* Edited by José I. Cabezón. 1992.

Thera, Nyanaponika, and Hellmuth Hecker. *Great Disciples of the Buddha.* 1997.

Tsomo, Karma Lekshe. *Sakyadhita: Daughters of the Buddha.* 1988.

Willis, Janice D. "Nuns and Benefactresses: The Role of Women in the Development of Buddhism." In *Women, Religion, and Social Change.* Edited by Yvonne Y. Haddad and Ellison B. Findly. 1985.

Witherington, Ben. *Women in the Ministry of Jesus.* 1984.

See also 'A'ishah; Deborah; Esther; Fāṭimah; Khadija; Mahādēviyakka; Mirabai; Monasticism; Ordination; Rabi'a.

BRADLEY S. CLOUGH

Divination

Divination is not simply the business of telling one's fortune or predicting the future. Rather, it is a highly specialized discourse based on an equally specialized practice. In general, the diviner may be understood as one who knows how to read and interpret a subtle, obscure text that is enormously revealing, but inaccessible or illegible to others. Sometimes this text is a written record of esoteric import, like the *Sibylline Oracles,* books of Nostradamus, or *I Ching.* More often, diviners use randomizing operations—such as casting sticks, stones, chains, coins, or bones; spreading oil on water; or heating tortoise shells until they fracture—to produce visible patterns to which they can then apply a traditional, if arcane, system of interpretation. Within other systems, the text in question is written in, on, and by nature itself, as when flights of birds, the organs of sacrificial victims, the procession of celestial bodies, or the lines that traverse human palms are construed as signifying objects amenable to interpretation.

In general, divinatory hermeneutics follow rational schemata that practitioners master as part of their training, and on which they base their conclusions (Sabbatucci, 1989; Vernant, 1974). Maya diviners, for instance, work with complex calendrical data, augmented by philological associations to the names of the days (Colby, 1981; Tedlock, 1992). Etruscan haruspices, for their part, identified different portions of the liver with specific deities, and examined the liver of sacrificial victims for abnormalities in one area or another, from which they could draw appropriate conclusions based on the nature of the associated deity (van der Meer, 1987).

Whatever the details of their system, diviners claim they can apprehend the way things really are at a given moment within a family, lineage, tribe, nation, or other group: the problems that face them, the forces that affect their well-being, and the nature of the sentiments that bind them together or threaten to tear them apart. Further, they may tell how their clients' situation reflects the current disposition of ancestors, deities, or other supernatural beings, and how it results from events of the past. This past may be either recent or remote, but since any events causally related to the present state of affairs were themselves caused by others still further in the past, any exercise in divination has the potential to produce an account of cosmic history in its entirety.

Consulting a diviner is rarely an exercise born of idle curiosity. Typically, those contemplating any enterprise that entails serious risk—founding a city or home, contracting a marriage, giving birth to a child, taking a voyage, waging a battle, or launching a business venture, to cite some obvious examples—may seek a diviner's counsel, hoping to learn how they might avert danger and maximize opportunity. Others, motivated more by suffering than ambition, seek not just an etiological explanation of their woes but practical advice about how to rectify whatever is responsible, be it angry kin, envious neighbors, neglected ancestors, ritual faults, and so on.

Within such contexts, diviners regularly play a therapeutic role, allaying the anxieties of the afflicted, ascertaining the critical points where their lives have gone astray, and reweaving the frayed fabric of social relations. In the process, however, they regularly identify their clients' plight as the consequence of their infractions against conventional norms, which the diviners misrepresent as if they were the demands of a cosmic or divine order. People in pain are thus counseled to heed the commands of their parents and elder siblings, pay their debts to in-laws, apologize to authorities, submit to husbands, offer sacrifice to ancestors, and so forth. More generally, they are told that the norms are eternal, inviolable, and self-enforcing. Trouble comes when one transgresses them, and relief can be gained by confessing guilt, making restitution, pledging to do better, and reconciling one's self to the way things are and must be.

In this way, divination can become not just a therapeutic practice, but also a powerful instrument of social control. Through divination, experts—people authorized to speak with profound knowledge on behalf of the social cum cosmic order—respond to their clients' life crises by identifying and sanctioning their deviance, impressing on them the demands of tradition, all at a time when they are neediest and most vulnerable. Although most studies have focused on the ideology of divination rather than its concrete practice, two studies of the latter sort have produced important results. Thus, Eugene Mendonsa (1982) found that Sisala diviners most often defend the interests of elders against impatient or rebellious youths, who chafe against their subordinate position, while Rosalind Shaw (1985; forthcoming) found that among the Temne, divination affected women and men in markedly different ways. Thus, the two genders were likely to consult different sorts of diviners (men going to men of high renown, women seeking female practitioners to whom they had some connection and whom they expected to be sympathetic), for different reasons (men contemplating risks or when seriously afflicted, women for reproductive disorders, the illness of a child, or when domestic harmony was threatened), and under different sorts of circumstances (men in public, women more often in private).

Other studies suggest that among certain peoples, specialized forms of divinatory practice were categorized according to gender. Among the earliest and most

The ruins of the Temple of Apollo, ancient site of the Delphic oracle, Delphi, Greece (Wolfgang Kaehler/ Corbis)

important examples is Cicero's division of Roman divination into two broad types, which he called "artificial" and "natural" (*De Divinatione* 2.26–27; cf. 1.4, 12, 34, 109–1120, 113, 127–130, and 2.42). The former of these was a science and the latter a gift. The artificial forms—astrology, extispicy, ornithomancy, and so on—involved disciplinary knowledge transmitted and jealously preserved in priestly colleges like that of the augurs, all of whose members were male (Cicero himself included). In contrast, the natural forms involved experiences of inspiration and ecstasy given to people who had lost rational control of their souls.

A weak form of such experiences was available to everyone in the form of dreams. Statistical analysis of the examples Cicero cited, however, shows that women were much more inclined to have premonitory dreams than were men, whom Roman misogyny credited with a much higher degree of reason and fuller control over their soul. The gendered character of dreams is also indicated by the ease with which Cicero and others dismissed them as little more than "old wives' tales" (*De Divinatione* 2.125, 129, 141).

The strongest forms of inspiration—oracular utterances like those of the Pythia at Delphi and the Sibyl at Cumae—were exclusively female. Yet this situation was so fraught with destabilizing potential that the speech of these women was subjected to several sorts of containment and control. At the ideological level, it was denied that they spoke with their own voice; rather, it was the god Apollo, whose spirit filled the bodies their souls had abandoned in ecstasy. More practically, their words were treated as extremely difficult to understand, both for their obscurity and for the bizarre intonation that marked them as divine. As a result, specialists like the Roman Quindecemviri (a priestly college of fifteen men) had to write them down and interpret them, censoring any inappropriate portions in the process.

BIBLIOGRAPHY

Bascom, William. *Ifa Divination: Communication between Gods and Men in West Africa.* 1969.

Bloch, Raymond. *La divination: Essais sur l'avenir et son imaginaire.* 1991.

Colby, Benjamin, and Lore Colby. *Daykeeper: The Life and Discourse of an Ixil Diviner.* 1981.

Guillaumont, François. *Philosophe et augure: Recherches sur le théorie cicéroniene de la divination.* 1984.

Lincoln, Bruce. *Authority: Construction and Corrosion.* 1994.

Loewe, Michael. *Divination, Mythology and Monarchy in Han China.* 1994.

Mendonsa, Eugene. *The Politics of Divination.* 1982.

Peek, Philip M. *African Divination Systems: Ways of Knowing.* 1991.

Pfeffer, Friedrich. *Studien zum Mantik in der Philosophie der Antike.* 1976.

Sabbatucci, Dario. *Divinazione e cosmologia.* 1989.

Shaw, Rosalind. *The Dangers of Temne Divination.* Forthcoming.

———. "Gender and the Structuring of Reality in Temne Divination: An Interactive Study." *Africa* 55 (1985): 286–303.

Smith, Richard. *Fortune Tellers and Philosophers: Divination in Traditional Chinese Society.* 1991.

Starr, Ivan, ed. *Queries to the Sun-God: Divination and Politics in Sargonid Assyria.* 1990.

Tedlock, Barbara. *Time and the Highland Maya.* 1992.

Turner, Victor. *Revelation and Divination in Ndembu Ritual.* 1975.

van der Meer, L. B. *The Etruscan Bronze Liver of Piacenza: Analysis of a Polytheistic Structure.* 1987.

Vernant, Jean-Pierre, ed. *Divination et rationalité.* 1974.

See also **Dreams**; **Possession**; **Shamans**.

BRUCE LINCOLN

Divine Child

When the divinity is imaged as a child, it awakens feelings that are usually kept secret and protected. This interior aspect of devotion to the divine child seems particularly important in the religious lives of women at certain times and in certain places; it is often connected to social conflict, and is fraught with theological paradox.

HISTORICAL EXAMPLES

The Child Jesus

The cult of the infant Jesus is traceable to the canonical and apocryphal Gospels in which the newborn Messiah is presented as fulfilling the prophecies of the Hebrew scriptures, manifesting his deity in humility, and anticipating in part the sufferings that he will endure on the cross.

In the Byzantine icon of the virgin of the Passion (immensely popular in Roman Catholicism as Our Lady of Perpetual Help), angels show the Child the symbols of the Passion; seized by fear, he grasps Mary's hand while a sandal falls from his foot. Here, paradoxically, the human emotion of fear is divinized. Devotion to this image responds to the search for meaning and hope of assistance in perplexity, especially in family life.

Late medieval and Renaissance iconography is noteworthy in the context of the construction of gender in its insistence on the maleness of the Child (Mary points to the genitals as proof that the Christ is truly human) and on the presence of a navel (although Adam had no mother, this Child does have one).

The Child Jesus as an expression of religious conflict is particularly evident in the well-known statue of the Infant of Prague, brought from Habsburg Spain to Prague in 1655, shortly after the end of armed conflict between Catholics and Protestants during the Thirty Years War. The message is clear: Christ, however sweet, is King and his reign on earth is coextensive with the Catholic Reformation. Other child-images of power include El Santo Niño de Atocha, in which the Infant Jesus is clothed in the garb of Santiago (the Moor-slayer), and the recent apparitions of the Bambino Gesù of Gallinaro (province of Frosinone, central Italy), who works miracles, exorcises demons, and predicts a universal cataclysm, in total contrast to standard parish Catholicism.

Similarly, Christmas carols dwell on the Child as a sign of contradiction. St. Alphonsus Liguori's "Tu scendi dalle stelle" plays on the humiliation of the

Word-made-flesh, showing how it attracts wonder, admiration, and desire. The hymn evokes the feeling function of the popular psyche in an era in which the skepticism of the Enlightenment was distancing both the commoner and the philosopher from traditional piety. The more mystical and theological traditions might question whether this appeal to the feeling function achieves an integration of faith and life, or if it represents a retreat into sentimentalism.

Krishna the Butter Thief

The popular stories of Krishna as a butter thief relate a whole complex of beliefs about motherhood and divinity in India. When Krishna steals the butter (mischievous adventures not found in the usual Purānic and other scriptural accounts of his life), he is stealing love (*Prema*), stealing hearts, and above all he is stealing the essence of femaleness. Butter is the product of the cow and the labor of milkmaids; the cow itself is identified in India as Mother par excellence. Cow's milk is a basic and universal symbol of the bond of love between mother and child (*vātsalya*). It is no wonder that today in popular Hinduism "someone is always ready to tell, sing, dance, act out, or even worship" the stories of the Butter Thief. According to J. S. Hawley, beneath the playful surface of these tales lies an insistent tension that also defines for many people their relationship with God: the tension between love and fear. In addition, the butter stories are a metaphor for the vulnerability of people in love: "Nothing is so open to being stolen as love, the most private possession of all, for love can never truly be possessed" (Hawley, p. 10). That love, in the context of devotion to Krishna, is *prem*, "the sort of fully devoted love that is motivated solely by the desire to serve or satisfy the beloved" (Hawley, p. 263). The essence of *prem* is self-forgetfulness, not in the sense of mystical annihilation, but rather in giving oneself through the emotions to a divine attraction that undermines that world of structure, propriety, and hierarchy. In its Vaiṣṇava social context, the fascination with the Divine Butter Thief sums up perfectly the conviction of devotees that emotion, and not intellect, is the supreme human faculty, for it is emotion that attracts us to God and that convinces us immediately without any need for appeals to the intellect.

Various Figures

It is of note that child divinities are inevitably male, though they often provide an important form of piety for women. Asia offers several examples, such as: Mahavira, the founder of Jainism, as a fetus in his mother's womb, is said to have practiced *ahimsa* (nonviolence) by not kicking until he perceived that she had become concerned that her child had died, at which point he

A divine child, Santo Nino de Atocha

kicked gently. In tantric Buddhism, the red form of Avalokiteśvara (Chen re zig Khor wa drung truk) is visualized as eight years old; the child bodhisattva is said to "stir up the depths of cyclic existence" by his power to liberate beings from the six realms of rebirth. And, in the rNyingma pa school of Tibetan Buddhism, Guru Rinpoche (Padmasambhava) is represented at his spontaneous birth in the heart of a lotus as an eight-year-old child. Another type is found in ancient Egypt in a figure of Horus, the posthumously conceived child of Isis and Osiris.

CONCLUSIONS AND OBSERVATIONS

The divine child represents more than a mere cult of sweetness that presumably appeals to feminine or childish emotions. On the contrary, the appearance of divine children almost always reflects an awareness of socioreligious conflict on the level of collective expressions of the feeling function of the psyche. The cult of Krishna not only bespeaks the value of love in the Vraj feminine idiom, it also mirrors the strong attachment of the Hindu masses to the images of divinity that are constantly called into question by Islam, Christian missionaries, and the modern secular world. The cult of the Child Jesus often expresses lay and women's insistence on nonclericalized forms of piety. Moreover, in feminine monasticism, it joins the high theology of the magisterium to the cloistered quest for mystical intimacy.

BIBLIOGRAPHY

Clark, John, trans. *St. Thérèse of Lisieux: Story of a Soul.* 1976. This classic autobiography presents Thérèse's teachings on the "way of spiritual childhood," which is the basis for a practical application of devotion to the divine child.

Deberre, É. *Histoire de la vénérable Marguerite du Saint-Sacrement.* Paris, 1907. A biography of one of the most extravagant examples of devotion to the child Jesus in Christian hagiography.

Hawley, John Stratton. *Krishna, The Butter Thief.* 1983.

Hawley, John Stratton, with Shrivatsa Goswami. *At Play with Krishna: Pilgrimage Dramas from Brindavan.* 1981.

Norcia, Giuseppina. *Una Culla per Gesù Bambino nella Terra di Gallinaro.* n.d. (1990s)

FRANCIS V. TISO

Divinity

Divinity and Humanity

The word *divinity,* derived from the Latin *divinus,* has the same Indo-European root, *div,* meaning to shine, as *deva,* the gods or deities who represented supernatural energies or natural forces, worshiped by the Aryan peoples of ancient India, Greece, and Rome. As a concept, *divinity* developed from the animism of the sacred traditions of tribal peoples to monotheism in the Abrahamic religions, Judaism, Christianity, and Islam, and to a transcendental principle that orders reality in the Asian religions of Hinduism, Buddhism, and Taoism.

Tribal peoples outside of the world's major textual religions generally conceptualize the divine as a sacred power manifest in nature, which can be worshiped as a spirit present in natural objects or a sacred place. This power is often associated with ancestor spirits who represent the power of tradition. In these traditions, humans may be considered vessels for sacred power, and ritual specialists may contact the divine through a shamanic journey to the realm of the spirits or through bodily possession. Because tribal peoples are primarily agriculturists or hunters and gatherers, they are concerned with the fertility of the land, of animals, and of human beings. The sacred power that produces new

life is generally understood to be bipolar, that is, like human sexuality, it has both a male and female aspect. When female fertility is considered to be a manifestation of sacred power, goddess worship is often present in religious life in which women may have a prominent role. However, women may also be considered dangerous or polluting because of menstruation and excluded from ritual practices central to the tribe.

The concept of *shakti,* or sacred energy that pervades the universe, is also found in Hinduism. The Brāhmaṇas are priestly manuals prescribing ritual ways of controlling this power. Texts on yoga outline techniques that human beings may use to transform this power, manifest as human sexual energy, into spiritual power. This sacred power may be worshiped in the form of natural phenomena, such as ant hills or an unusual stone, or in aniconic images, such as the lingam that represents the phallus of Siva. In theistic Hinduism, divine power is conceived to be manifest in gods, goddesses, and demons. The myths associated with these deities make evident the creative and destructive aspects of divine power and its sexual polarity. For example, the lingam of Siva represents his creative energies, while the destructive aspect of his power is represented in his dance of destruction. Similarly, the goddess Devī, in her benevolent form as consort, brings prosperity, but as Kālī, the devouring mother with her necklace of skulls, she brings destruction. Theistic Hinduism also provides the most well-developed theory of a hierarchy of the divine. The highest form of divinity is unembodied essence, the atman. Next are the high gods who maintain the world order: Brahmā, Siva, and Vishnu, followed by deities who are more accessible to their worshipers, but have more limited powers, such as Skanda and Gaṇeśa. Below these benevolent deities are the unmarried forms of the Goddess, who must be propitiated lest they bring destruction. Below the Goddess are guardian deities, fierce demonic spirits that she has brought under her control. Finally come the dangerous spirits of people who died an unnatural death; these attack and possess unwary humans. This hierarchy of the gods is based on a logic of purity and pollution: the latter must be contained so as to preserve the moral order of the universe and maintain the rule of the high pure gods. The principle of a moral hierarchy based on purity also legitimates caste distinction and a hierarchical social structure and naturalizes the rule of men over women, who are less pure. The Śāstras explain that a woman is unfit to enjoy independence and should be ruled by her father, husband, or son.

Philosophical texts known as the Upanishads, written in India between 800 and 300 B.C.E., develop a metaphysical understanding of sacred power as the reality

Painted sculpture of Devis at Ekambaresvara Temple (Macduff Everton/Corbis)

or principle that is the substrate of the cosmic order. This principle was called atman, meaning self or soul, understood as the manifestation of divine energy in an individual being. The cosmic self was called brahman. The practice of meditation or yoga is taught as a way to understanding of the nature of the divine and a super-conscious state of union with the Absolute.

The core texts of Theravada Buddhism reject this concept of divinity as an eternal, unchanging order, while retaining the idea that meditation leads to an awareness of eternal truths. The Four Noble Truths of Buddhism rest on the teachings of impermanence and no-self, or *anātman*. The no-self teaching denies the reality of an individual self or soul. In the *Majjhimanikaya*, the Buddha also teaches the futility of metaphysical speculation about the nature of reality, by way of the parable of the man wounded with an arrow, who wants to know by whom the arrow was shot, by whom it was made, from what materials, and so on, before hav-

ing the arrow removed. However, in later Buddhism, particularly schools of Mahāyāna Buddhism, divinity is conceived as Buddha-mind, immanent in all beings, or as Buddha-nature, manifest in a bodhisattva who accepts reincarnation (in Tibetan Buddhism) or postpones nirvana until all sentient beings have achieved enlightenment. Although texts insist on the principle of emptiness (*śūnyatā*) and deny the permanent reality or essence of things and beings, in popular Buddhism a concept of the universe as divine and an understanding of nirvana as a blissful dissolution of the self into at-oneness with the universe reemerges. Furthermore, in the Vajrayana School of Tibetan Buddhism, the divine is represented as having both a female and male aspect, and the highest form of the divine is symbolically represented as the union of male and female deities or *yab-yum*.

As compared with Hinduism, Buddhism, and Taoism, where divinity is understood as the nature of reality and good and evil are illusions to be overcome, a radically different concept of an ethical divinity is developed in the monotheistic religions. In Judaism, Christianity, and Islam, God stands above nature, which he has created. He cannot be worshiped in idols or in nature; rather, he reveals himself to those he has chosen.

The anthropomorphic God of Abraham is said to have created human beings in his own image. Grammatically and in popular imagination, this God is gendered male; he created woman as a companion for the first man. A loving and merciful patriarch, he guides his people, with whom he makes a covenant and to whom he has given free will. He is an ethical God who requires of his people that they obey his law. He is just and righteous; he humbles the proud and raises up the lowly. His will is realized through history, understood as the fulfillment of his covenant. This understanding of human history as the realization of a divine plan acknowledges human beings as agents and makes people responsible for the world they live in, encouraging social and political activism as exemplified by the prophets of the Hebrew Bible.

In Christianity the emphasis on the incarnation of God in his son Jesus Christ creates a new relationship based on love between God and humanity. In Islam, however, the separation between God and humanity reemerges, and the divine is given to humanity in the Qur'an as the word of God spoken to the Prophet Muhammad. Religious figures associated with mystical traditions (such as Meister Eckhart and in Sufi Islam, al-Hallaj) and Ibn Arabi and some modern Christian theologians (following the philosopher Ludwig Feuerbach) have taken humanity's participation in a divine plan to mean that divinity is immanent in humanity. In this way a concept central to Asian religious traditions can be found in Christianity and Islam. Similarly, the concept of an ethical God in monotheistic theology has in turn influenced figures like Gandhi and new movements in Asian religious traditions such as Engaged Buddhism to encourage social activism to create a more ethical society.

Neopaganism, goddess worship, and new religious movements of the twentieth century have tended to turn to indigenous sacred traditions for a concept of the divine that does not reinforce patriarchal structures of power. Generally, these new religious movements, like Asian religions and mystical traditions, see divinity as immanent in humanity, but they also draw from monotheistic theology a concept of divinity as ethical.

BIBLIOGRAPHY

Armstrong, Karen. *A History of God.* 1993.

Atkinson, Clarissa, Constance Buchanan, and Margaret Miles, eds. *Immaculate and Powerful: The Female in Sacred Image and Social Reality.* 1985.

Carmody, Denise. *Women and World Religions.* 1989.

Daly, Mary. *Beyond God the Father: Toward a Philosophy of Women's Liberation.* 1973.

Gross, Rita. *Beyond Androcentrism: New Essays on Women and Religion.* 1977.

———. *Feminism and Religion.* 1996.

Lienhardt, Godfrey. *Divinity and Experience: The Religion of the Dinka.* 1961.

Miles, Jack. *A Biography of God.* 1995.

O'Flaherty, Wendy Doniger. *Women, Androgynes and Other Mythical Beasts.* 1980.

Paul, Diana. *Women in Buddhism: Images of the Feminine in Mahayana Tradition.* 1979.

Pinchtman, Tracy. *The Rise of the Goddess in the Hindu Tradition.* 1994.

Ruether, Rosemary Radford, ed. *Religion and Sexism.* 1974.

Sharma, Arvind, ed. *Women in World Religions.* 1987.

ELIZABETH FULLER COLLINS

In Judaism

In any given culture, divinity wears many masks. The nature of the mask is to reveal and conceal simultaneously, indeed to reveal in the mode of concealment and to conceal in the mode of revelation. In the religious history of Judaism, those masks are signified above all else by the names of God. If holiness is understood as the manifestation of divine power, then nothing is holier than God's names, and of those names none more so than the four-letter name YHWH. The traditional account of the ineffability of this name attests to its ultimate power as the iconic representation of the deity in visible and audible form.

The linkage of divine embodiment to the notion of the name should not mislead one into thinking that the idea expressed in Scripture is predicated on the denial of a body to the divine. On the contrary, the unqualified rejection of an anthropomorphic conception of divinity is the distinctive legacy of the rationalist theology cultivated by Jewish thinkers in the Middle Ages under the influence of Greco-Roman philosophy mediated through Islamic sources. The approach to anthropomorphism in the biblical and rabbinic corpora is more complex. According to a growing consensus in biblical scholarship, the textual evidence indicates that for the ancient Israelites the burning issue was not God's corporeality per se, but the problem of materially representing the divine in corporeal images. Even archaeological evidence that has recently emerged attests that in ancient Israel Yahweh was represented iconographically, in spite of the fact that the official cult, already in the early monarchic period, was aniconic. The phenomenon of the empty throne in the Temple of Jerusalem confirms the paradoxical idea that the God of Israel is enthroned in unseen majesty.

This aniconism, however, did not imply the incorporeality of God, an inference made repeatedly by rationalist interpreters of Judaism. One must distinguish between the prohibition of depicting God in images and the claim that God cannot be manifest in a body. There is no reason to suppose that the anthropomorphic characterizations of the divine in Scripture are to be treated figuratively or allegorically. The epiphanies of God in human form have the texture of a tangibility that one would normally associate with a body of flesh and bones. The issue, then, is not how one speaks of God, but how God is experienced in the phenomenal plane.

Of late a variety of scholars have also reexamined the centrality of anthropomorphic representation in the mythic imagination of the rabbis. Although it is premature to speak of a scholarly consensus, it would not be incorrect to refer to a new paradigm that affirms the mythopoeic nature of rabbinic theological pronouncements predicated on the belief that God takes shape within the margins of human experience. To posit as theologically viable an incarnate God is not merely to portray God in figurative terms; it is to say that God is configured phenomenally in an embodied state. Within the aniconic framework of classical Judaism, only an imaginal body could be attributed to God—that is, the somatic form ascribed to God inheres in the human imagination as a symbolic configuration.

The imaginal body, as the nature of embodiment more generally, involves the attribution of gender to the divine as well. Biblical and rabbinic sources reflect a thoroughly androcentric theology. Even if we acknowledge vestiges of a belief in a feminine deity in some of the biblical narratives, the overriding picture is surely of a masculine God. Similarly, in the vast corpus of rabbinic writings, the masks worn by God are of a decisively male persona. To be sure, the Shekhinah, the rabbinic term for the presence of God, is a feminine grammatical form, but there is little evidence in the earlier sources that this word refers to a feminine hypostasis that complements the masculine potency. In midrashic sources from the Middle Ages, one can detect a change in this direction, an orientation that was fully exploited in medieval kabbalistic symbology.

One of the cardinal principles of kabbalistic ontology is the belief that the divine anthropos is configured as male and female. But just as the engendering myth of human creation is based on the claim that the female is taken from and constructed out of the male (the account of the creation of Adam in the first chapter of Genesis is read in light of the account in the second chapter), so in the case of the divine anthropos the female is characterized as deriving from the male. Redemption, therefore, is understood as the restoration of the female to the male, the heterosexual union that results in the reconstitution of the androgynous state wherein the gender dimorphism is overcome.

Heterosexuality is valorized as a positive act to the degree that it is the means by which the ontic fission is overcome by the unification of male and female. The ultimate ideal, however, is one wherein the female is restored to the male, an ontological condition that is reflected socially in the adoption on the part of kabbalists of an ascetic renunciation. The sacralization of human sexuality, which lies at the heart of kabbalistic myth and ritual, is dialectically related to the ascetic impulse. Ascetical sublimation, however, did not result in the effacing of gender differences in either a sociological or theological sense. On the contrary, the contemplation of the imaginal body of God ensues from the erotic attachment of the mystic to the divine, which is predicated in turn on the subjugation of physical eros. The subjugation, which is sometimes portrayed as a symbolic castration (based on Isa. 56:4–5), did not imply sexual impotence, which would be equivalent to effeminization, but the transformation of the phallic energy from carnal intercourse with one's earthly wife to spiritual intercourse with the Shekhinah. However, insofar as the union of the sexes results in the integration of the feminine to the masculine in the form of the corona of the phallus, one can speak of the phallicization of the feminine, which implies that heterosexual eros (desire for the other as self) gives way to homoeroticism (love of self as other). In the symbolic worldview of the kabbalists, homoeroticism is the carnality of celibate renunciation. An anticipation of the eschatological metamorphosis of erotic energy from the bisexual to the monosexual is found in the fraternity of mystics whose study of Torah takes the place of sexual mating with their female partners.

BIBLIOGRAPHY

Adler, Rachel. *Engendering Judaism: A New Ethics and Theology.* 1997.

Boyarin, Daniel. *Carnal Israel: Reading Sex in Talmudic Culture.* 1993.

Eilberg-Schwartz, Howard. *God's Phallus and Other Problems for Men and Monotheism.* 1994.

Green, Arthur. "Bride, Spouse, Daughter: Images of the Feminine in Classical Jewish Sources." In *On Being a Jewish Feminist.* Edited by Susannah Heschel. 1983.

Hauptam, Judith. *Rereading the Rabbis: A Woman's Voice.* 1998.

Idel, Moshe. "Sexual Metaphors and Praxis in the Kabbalah." In *The Jewish Family: Metaphor and Memory.* Edited by David Kraemer. 1989.

Neusner, Jacob. *The Incarnation of God: The Character of Divinity in Formative Judaism.* 1988.

Patai, Raphael. *The Hebrew Goddess.* 1967.

Persowitz, Miriam B. *Spining Fantasies: Rabbis, Gender, and History.* 1997.

Plaskow, Judith. *Standing Again at Sinai: Judaism From a Feminist Perspective.* 1990.

Satlow, Michael. *Tasting the Dish: Rabbinic Rhetorics of Sexuality.* 1995.

Scholem, Gershom. "Shekhinah: The Feminine Element in Divinity." In *On the Mystical Shape of the Godhead: Basic Concepts in the Kabbalah.* 1991.

———. "Shi'ur Komah: The Mystical Shape of the Godhead." In *On the Mystical Shape of the Godhead: Basic Concepts in the Kabbalah.* 1991.

Wolfson, Elliot R. *Circle in the Square: Studies in the Use of Gender in Kabbalistic Symbolism.* 1995.

———. "Eunuchs Who Keep the Sabbath: Becoming Male and the Ascetic Ideal in Thirteenth-Century Jewish Mysticism." In *Becoming Male in the Middle Ages.* Edited by Jeffrey Jerome Cohen and Bonnie Wheeler. 1997.

———. "Iconic Visualization and the Imaginal Body of God: The Role of Intention in the Rabbinic Conception of Prayer." *Modern Theology* 12 (1996): 137–162.

Wyschogrod, Michael. *The Body of Faith: Judaism as Corporeal Election.* 1983.

ELLIOT R. WOLFSON

Divorce

The term *divorce*, meaning sundering, is applied to the severing of matrimonial relations between husband and wife. In a religious context, a marriage, the union of two individuals of opposite genders who establish a household and may start a family, is generally celebrated with sacred rites. The severing of this union usually transpires when one or both partners decide they are not compatible. The requirements for the dissolution or negation of marriage vary among religious traditions but in most cases address two associated issues—division of material property and custody or living arrangements for the offspring of the couple. In many contemporary societies, secular regulations replace religious injunctions on divorce.

In Judaism, the rules for divorce and marriage have evolved over centuries with different groups following a variety of norms. Though accepted as an established custom in ancient Israel, divorce was considered a "calamitous necessity." A bill of divorcement, termed *sepher keritut* in the Pentateuch or *get* in the Talmud, is formally presented by the husband to his wife in the presence of witnesses. Only the husband may initiate and procure the divorce bill, which may not require a detailed explanation of his action. In certain situations, such as when the husband has a contagious disease or abuses or neglects his wife, the wife may seek a divorce from the rabbinical courts, but unless the courts convince the husband to grant the divorce bill, the wife is not free. In modern Israel rabbinical sanction is necessary for divorce.

Christians follow a range of practices and beliefs with regard to divorce. In the Roman Catholic Church marriage is considered a sacrament and thus divorce is not permitted. If a couple want to end their marriage, they may apply to the church for an annulment. (This, however, poses a problem as to the status of the couple's children.) In the case of couples who obtain a civil divorce, the church proscribes them from participation in the sacrament of Holy Communion. In the Eastern Orthodox Church, divorce and remarriage are permitted under certain situations, such as the disappearance, insanity, criminal conviction, or unfaithfulness of a partner (usually the husband). While the first marriage is called "the Crowning," the second marriage includes an element of penitence for the unsatisfactory outcome of the first union. Protestant churches allow for divorce and remarriage when certain criteria are met.

In Islam, while both men and women may seek divorce, it is usually initiated by the husband. In a relatively easy repudiation, *talaq,* the husband utters the intent of divorce three times. Though infrequent, the tradition allows for the wife to initiate the divorce in cases of mistreatment or desertion or other extenuating circumstances. The marriage may be rescinded, *khul* or annulled, *faskh,* with the acceptance of the petition from the wife by the Shari'a courts. Traditionally, custody of children is awarded to the father after the male children reach the age of nine and the females the age of eleven. However, modern courts in some Muslim

countries, such as Egypt, favor the child's remaining with the mother until the child is no longer a minor.

In the Hindu tradition, marriage is considered a sacrament that may not be voided. The couple circumambulates the sacred fire to solemnize the union that is popularly believed to continue in the afterlife if the partners are faithful. A husband may marry more than once, especially in the case of a wife who bears no children. With the institution of the Hindu Code by the Indian Government, contemporary law courts in India can grant a civil divorce, but technically that does not constitute a religious rupture of the union. Classical Hindu texts present wifely obedience and service as a moral obligation. In ancient lore there are instances of a wife leaving her husband that may seem tantamount to a divorce. For example, in the Hindu legend of King Yayati, Queen Devayani, daughter of Shukra the priest of the Daityas, leaves her husband and returns to her father's house when she discovers that her husband has taken as his consort Sarmistha, her maidservant. Her action of leaving her husband also entails leaving behind her two sons, Yadu and Turvasu, with their father.

Traditionally in China women could achieve a worthy social status only through marriage. Divorce was not an available option even when the bride was ill-treated by the groom's mother; the pitiful condition of the new daughter-in-law is a common portrayal in Chinese literature. These practices where the daughter-in-law had to be deferential and submissive stem from the Confucian ideal by which various members of the family must live. Frequently, women married young, and in the early period of marriage a wife could be sent back in shame to her parents as being unsuitable if the husband's mother did not like her. Children remained with the husband's family. In communist China much effort was made to protect the "moral environment" of the family. Thus the authorities could deny permission to work to divorcing couples, especially if they had children. Extramarital affairs and illegitimate offspring could lead to public rebuke, forced abortion, and even criminal proceedings. By the fifteenth century, when Confucian norms were adopted in Korea, divorce and remarriage (including for widows), became very difficult. Since the 1950s and the revised civil codes, the position of women has improved with regard to divorce and inheritance.

In most African communities polygyny is a domestic norm, and divorce is governed by a variety of native customs. Among the Ashanti, where matrilineal descent dominates, either party may initiate a divorce. Traditionally a wife could opt to return to her parents if she felt neglected by her husband. Generally, the mother's brother had more rights over the children than did the father. Among various Native North American tribes, traditional marriage and divorce processes were relatively simple. A woman could initiate a separation of the marriage by going back to her parents or by placing her husband's moccasins outside the dwelling, indicating that he was no longer welcome. A man could simply walk away and not return. Children usually stayed with their mother.

In contemporary Western society, in the United States as in other countries, for many couples religious norms are replaced with secular civic regulations on marriage and divorce. Issues of property division and child custody are increasingly decreed by civil courts and not by religious laws.

BIBLIOGRAPHY

Cowan, Philip A., ed. *Family, Self and Society: Toward a New Agenda for Family Research.* 1993.

Esposito, John L. *Women in Muslim Family Law.* 1982.

Freid, Jacob, ed. *Jews and Divorce.* 1968.

Ingoldsby, Bron B., and Suzanna Smith. *Families in Multicultural Perspective.* 1995.

Mehta, Rama. *Divorced Hindu Women.* 1975.

O'Mahony, Patrick J. *Catholics and Divorce.* 1959.

Platte, Erika. "Divorce Trends and Patterns in China: Past and Present." *Pacific Affairs* 61 (1988): 428–445.

Radcliff-Brown, A. R., and Daryll Forde, eds. *African Systems of Kinship and Marriage.* 1987.

Rozman, Gilbert, ed. *The East Asian Region: Confucian Heritage and Its Modern Adaptation.* 1991.

Sharma, Arvind, ed. *Women in World Religions.* 1987

Sonbol, Amira El Azhary. *Women, the Family, and Divorce Laws in Islamic History.* 1996.

Stephens, William N. *The Family in Cross-Cultural Perspective.* 1963.

Young, Serinity, ed. *An Anthology of Sacred Texts by and About Women.* 1993.

HABIBEH RAHIM

Doctrine

The term *doctrine* has its roots in the development of Christianity, where the word is derived from the Latin *doctrina* (basic teaching), which is, in turn, a translation of the Greek *didaskalia* (the activity of teaching) and *didachē* (that which is taught). Doctrine has two meanings in studies of religion: the first denotes the theoretical dimension of a religion, where doctrine is usually understood in the sense of intellectual context, an intellectual guide for behavior or action. Joachim Wach and other sociologists of religion often employ the term in this way. The second meaning focuses on the interplay between the content of certain doctrines and the acts of teaching doctrines; Jaroslav Pelikan's five volumes on *The Christian Tradition: A History of the Development of Doctrine* (1971–1989) is perhaps the best example of this definition of doctrine.

In a pejorative sense, doctrine stands for something that is abstruse and abstract, with little relation to lived experience. Some studies of religious doctrine focus on it as a matter of the intellect; others have tried to cast it in the realms of both thinking and acting.

Scholars have increasingly sought to clarify the function of doctrine in religious traditions. These examinations of the category of doctrine *qua* doctrine have emerged largely from two circles: theology and comparative philosophy. Contemporary theologians have raised useful questions about the study of doctrine using anthropological approaches such as those of Clifford Geertz. George Lindbeck explores the place of doctrine within the content of intra-Christian religious dialogue and suggests that scholars turn their attention to the regulative function of doctrines. That is, instead of treating doctrines as propositions about the nature of what is ultimately true, or as symbols, Lindbeck explores how doctrines function as authoritative rules that govern discourse, shape religious attitudes, and determine behavior. Paul J. Griffiths, in *On Being Buddha* (1994), on the other hand, has shifted the discussion of doctrines within the context of contemporary Christian practice into that of comparative philosophy, particularly into the study of Buddhism. Taking Lindbeck, William Christian, and studies of legal doctrine as starting points for his methodology, Griffiths engages in what he calls a doctrinal study of doctrine. By this he means a study of religious doctrines that focuses on doctrines as expressive of certain claims about truth within a specific religious community (rather than doctrines functioning as symbols or rules). The attention that Lindbeck pays to the role of action and the clarity Griffiths brings to the definition of primary doctrine provide useful starting points for studies of doctrine that seek to understand it as something more than a matter of the intellect.

It is hardly surprising that these studies make no direct contribution to the study of women and doctrine. For the most part, doctrines are the means by which women are subordinated within religions, as was argued by Matilda Joslyn Gage (1893). Mary Daly (1978) deconstructs such Christian doctrines as the Immaculate Conception and the Trinity as forms of Christian mythology that deceive and mystify women about the true nature of patriarchy; in her view, particular doctrines serve as manifestations of the patriarchal mind whose principles are implemented in ritual actions. Like Gage and Daly, Susan Starr Sered (1994) suggests that doctrine is a category that belongs to patriarchal religions, explicitly arguing that female-dominated religions, with the exception of Christian Science, are marked by an absence of doctrine and dogma.

The question of doctrine and women becomes more intricate when the analysis moves beyond a definition of doctrine as an intellectual proposition to which women must assent. For example, feminist theologians such as Anne Carr and Carter Heyward have provided arguments and evidence to reform certain doctrines of Christianity, or at least to change the interpretations of those doctrines. Work done toward inclusive-language lectionaries are one example of such reinterpretations. The subject of women and doctrine would be enriched by studies of nineteenth-century religious movements in Britain and the United States that produced traditions in which the words of the founders may be understood as forms of doctrine—such as the writings of Mary Baker Eddy and H. P. Blavatsky of the Theosophical Society—as well as traditions as discussed by Ann Braude that categorically reject any form of doctrine.

BIBLIOGRAPHY

Almond, Philip C. *Mystical Experience and Religious Doctrine: An Investigation of the Study of Mysticism in World Religions.* 1982.

Braude, Ann. *Radical Spirits: Spiritualism and Women's Rights in Nineteenth Century America.* 1989.

Christian, William A. *Doctrines of Religious Communities: A Philosophical Study.* 1987.

———. *Oppositions of Religious Doctrines: A Study in the Logic of Dialogue among Religions.* 1972.

Cooey, Paula M., ed. *After Patriarchy: Feminist Transformations of World Religions.* 1991.

Daly, Mary. *Gyn/Ecology: The Metaethics of Radical Feminism.* 1978.

Gage, Matilda Joslyn. *Woman, Church, and State.* 1893. Reprint, 1992.

Griffiths, Paul J. "Doctrines and the Virtues of Doctrine: The Problematic of Religious Plurality." *Proceedings of the American Catholic Philosophical Association* (1992): 29–44.

———. "Religious Diversity." *The Thomist* 52 (1988): 319–327.

Lindbeck, George A. *The Nature of Doctrine: Religion and Theology in a Postliberal Age.* 1984.

McGrath, Alister E. *The Genesis of Doctrine: A Study in the Foundations of Doctrinal Criticism.* 1990.

Neuner, Josef. *Christian Revelation and World Religions.* 1967.

Sered, Susan Starr. *Priestess, Mother, Sacred Sister: Religions Dominated by Women.* 1994.

CAROL S. ANDERSON

Domestic Rites

Domestic rites are ceremonies, religious practices, or gatherings conducted in the home, at shrines, or other informal arenas rather than in public buildings specifically designated for use in orthodox religious rituals. Since the historical development of religious specialists and the compartmentalizing of religious life from the rest of human life, males generally became the religious specialists, and public, orthodox religious rites fell under male control. Women's religious lives and spiritual connections with the holy in orthodox, formal, public rituals were often minimized, leaving their religious proclivities little outlet other than home-based or private rituals and domestic rites. Through home-based, informal, female-generated and conducted religious rites, women found the means to express their own spiritual concerns and develop religious practices more appropriate to their own lives.

Women's domestic rites are usually devoted to maintaining family and home welfare, obtaining the benevolence of holy forces, and keeping the home and family safe from disruptive malevolent forces. Women's goals focus on the health, welfare, and success of family members and on the self-presentation of the family to the outside world. Further, women attend to the emotional, social, psychological, spiritual, and cultural well-being of family members as well as maintaining family cohesion, mutual respect, affection, and bonds with kin and community.

More closely tied than men to family members in day-to-day interaction and caring, women are more attentive to and interested in human relations and development. They are involved in life-cycle events, such as engagements, pregnancies, childbirth, birthdays, anniversaries, illness and mourning, and honoring ancestors. Enacting cultural or religious traditions, women prepare and manage family holiday celebrations. Usually women are able to influence the form and content of home rites, acting out their concerns and views in ceremony. However, not all domestic rituals are self-initiated or express a woman's views unambiguously. Domestic rites may be determined by a new mother-in-law, for example, and performed by the new bride for the benefit of her husband's family. Some domestic rites, such as harrowing wedding preparations while arousing respect for a woman and her family, can seriously harm or injure her.

A woman may engage in home rites by herself or with others. For example, among Christians, Jews, and Muslim of Europe and the Middle East, women could take measures to protect against the evil eye or rectify damage already done. Where religious traditions consider menstruation, sexual activity, elimination, or childbirth polluting for women, an individual woman may go through purification motions while saying the necessary phrases. A woman may pray, read from holy texts, meditate, or worship by herself at a home shrine in Buddhist, Hindu, Christian, and South Asian Muslim societies, as may the newly emerging devotees of individualized home altars in the United States. Hindu women have elaborate rites to purify and protect home and family.

Alternatively, a group of women may gather for a home ritual. In comparison to public, orthodox rites, women's home rites tend to be informal, less hierarchical, and more personalized. Participants in home religious gatherings are family, relatives, and neighbors, and notification of gatherings tends to be through informal word of mouth and networking. Home rites may focus on family, health, protective, reproductive, child or relative-centered issues.

In women's domestic rituals, spirituality is often personal, involving women's emotional connections with spiritual or holy figures. Mexican American women can talk woman-to-woman to Our Lady of Guadalupe, and Muslim women interact like intimate relatives with female saintly figures. Home rites may take the form of narratives, spilling out to other women personal stories of grief and loss. Home gatherings likely include a social element, with time to interact before, during, or afterward with others in the community, reflective of women's merging of their social and spiritual worlds. The gathering frequently includes exchange of news and information and demonstrations of emotional support and empathy. Home rites usually include partaking in some refreshments. In their domestic rituals, women can express and recognize their personal concerns, emotions, and unique perspectives to a greater degree than can participants in public rites.

Although men and orthodox religious leaders generally dismiss women's home rites as unorthodox, even superstitious, and cite the "gossiping," socializing, and refreshments to demonstrate women's lack of spiritual motivation, women's rites and rituals are a stronghold of religiosity. When men's or male-dominated public rituals are precluded by political force, displacement, secularization, or economic responsibilities, women's ongoing religious practices can keep devotion and spirituality alive. When males wish to promote religious identity and cohesion for political reasons or sectarian interests, they encourage women's home devotions and networking through ritual. Home rites may contain religious beliefs when specialized religious practitioners and formal rituals are not available, for example, among white settlers on the early American frontier. Women in the United States may construct home rites to mark events and changes not recognized by formalized rituals, such as girls' first menstruation, bridal and baby showers, or menopause.

BIBLIOGRAPHY

Betteridge, Anne H. "Gift Exchange in Iran: The Locus of Self-Identity in Social Interaction." *Anthropological Quarterly* 58, no. 4 (1985): 190–202.

Brink, Judy. "Lost Rituals: Sunni Muslim Women in Rural Egypt." In *Mixed Blessings: Gender and Religious Fundamentalism Cross Culturally.* Edited by Judy Brink and Joan Mencher. 1997.

Burman, Rickie. " 'She Looketh Well to the Ways of Her Household': The Changing Role of Jewish Women in Religious Life, c. 1988–1930." In *Religion in the Lives of English Women, 1760–1930.* Edited by Gail Malmgreen. 1986.

di Leonardo, Micaela. "The Female World of Cards and Holidays: Women, Families, and the Work of Kinship." *Signs: Journal of Women in Culture and Society* 12, no. 3 (1987): 440–453.

Eglar, Zekiye. *A Punjabi Village in Pakistan.* 1960.

El-Or, Tamar. *Educated and Ignorant: Ultraorthodox Jewish Women and Their World.* 1994.

Fernea, Robert A., and Elizabeth W. Fernea. "Variation in Religious Observance among Islamic Women." In *Scholars, Saints, and Sufis. Muslim Religious Institutions since 1500.* Edited by Nikki R. Keddie. 1978.

Freeman, James. "The Ladies of Lord Krishna: Rituals of Middle-Aged Women in Eastern India." In *Unspoken Worlds: Women's Religious Lives in Non-Western Cultures.* Edited by Nancy A. Falk and Rita M. Gross. 1989.

Friedl, Erika. "Islam and Tribal Women in a Village in Iran." In *Unspoken Worlds: Women's Religious Lives.* Edited by Nancy A. Falk and Rita M. Gross. 1989.

Grima, Benedicte. *The Performance of Emotion among Paxtun Women.* 1992.

Gross, Rita M. "Menstruation and Childbirth as Ritual and Religious Experience among Native Australians." In *Unspoken Worlds: Women's Religious Lives in Non-Western Cultures.* Edited by Nancy A. Falk and Rita M. Gross. 1989.

Hegland, Mary Elaine. "The Power Paradox in Muslim Women's *Majales:* North-West Pakistani Mourning Rituals as Sites of Contestation over Religious Politics, Ethnicity, and Gender." *Signs: Journal of Women in Culture and Society* 23, no. 2 (1998): 391–428.

Jacobson, Doranne. "Golden Handprints and Red-Painted Feet: Hindu Childbirth Rituals in Central India." In *Unspoken Worlds: Women's Religious Lives in Non-Western Cultures.* Edited by Nancy A. Falk and Rita M. Gross. 1989.

Kerns, Virginia. "Black Carib Women and Rites of Death." In *Unspoken Worlds: Women's Religious Lives in Non-Western Cultures.* Edited by Nancy A. Falk and Rita M. Gross. 1989.

Lincoln, Bruce. *Emerging from the Chrysalis: Rituals of Women's Initiation.* 1991.

Myerhoff, Barbara. *Number Our Days.* 1980.

Powers, Marla N. *Oglala Women: Myth, Ritual, and Reality.* 1986.

Rice, C. *Persian Women and Their Ways.* 1923.

Sered, Susan. "Rachel's Tomb and the Milk Grotto of the Virgin Mary: Two Women's Shrines in Bethlehem." *Journal of Feminist Studies in Religion* 2, no. 2 (1986): 7–22.

Tapper, Nancy. "Changing Wedding Rituals in A Turkish Town." *Journal of Turkish Studies* 9 (1985): 305–313.

———. "*Ziyaret:* Gender, Movement, and Exchange in a Turkish Community." In *Muslim Travellers: Pilgrimage, Migration, and the Religious Imagination.* Edited by Dale F. Eickelman and James Piscatori. 1990.

Tapper(Lindisfarne), Nancy. "Changing Marriage Ceremonial and Gender Roles in the Arab World: An Anthropological Perspective." *Arab Affairs* 8, no. 1 (1988–89): 117–135.

Wadley, Susan S. "Hindu Women's Family and Household Rites in a North Indian Village." In *Unspoken Worlds: Women's Religious Lives in Non-Western Cultures.* Edited by Nancy A. Falk and Rita M. Gross. 1989.

Westermarck, Edward. *Ritual and Belief in Morocco.* 1926.

MARY ELAINE HEGLAND

Dona Beatriz

Dona Beatriz (c. 1686–1706), Christian healer, was born Beatriz Kimpa Vita to aristocratic parents in the Mbidizi Valley, in the eastern part of the kingdom of Kongo, a Christian kingdom in modern Angola. In youth she acquired a reputation for mystical powers and was initiated into various healing and priestly cults, which she left when she concluded they were contrary to Christianity. In August 1704 she believed she died and Saint Anthony took over her body. In this guise she began a movement to stop the civil wars then raging between factions of Kongo's ruling family and to resettle the abandoned capital. Rebuffed by factional leaders, she led her own followers to the ruined city and established herself near the cathedral. Her following

grew and soon some factional leaders joined her, bringing her into the civil war. In 1706 she became pregnant and, returning to her home, was captured by officers of faction leader king Pedro IV. She was tried in a civil court on charges of witchcraft (the ecclesiastical authorities, primarily Italian Capuchin missionaries, did not wish to try her), found guilty and burned at the stake in July 1706. Her remaining followers were crushed by Pedro IV's troops in 1709, and there is no evidence that her movement survived this defeat.

Beatriz's teaching included the ideas that she, as Saint Anthony, was the primary intermediary between the people and God, and that proper intentions were more important than the sacraments. She made prophetic pronouncements concerning Kongo's future and performed miracles of healing and occult knowledge.

BIBLIOGRAPHY

French translations of the original sources and a long essay placing Beatriz's life in Kongo's history are found in Louis Jadin's "Le Congo et la secte des Antoniens: Restauration du royaume sous Pedro IV et la 'Sainte Antonie' congolaise (1694–1718)," *Bulletin, Institut historique belge de Rome* 33 (1961): 411–615. John Thornton's *Dona Beatriz: The Kongolese Saint Anthony* (Cambridge, forthcoming, provisional title) is a full-length biography of Beatriz and her times.

See also **Sex Change**; **Witchcraft: In Africa**.

JOHN THORNTON

Draupadī

Draupadī, common wife of the five Pāṇḍava brothers whose name is a patronymic of Drupada (her royal father), has been a significant figure in Indian story and cult since the composition of the Sanskrit Mahābhārata began (c. fifth century B.C.E.). Often called Kṛṣṇā (dark), she has not traditionally been regarded as a role model for Hindu women, presumably in part because polyandrous marriage is an anomalous practice in most of South Asia.

In the Sanskrit Mahābhārata , the public humiliation of Draupadī by her husbands' cousins (the Kauravas) is a proximate cause of the internecine war between the cousin groups. Draupadī's desire for revenge of this offense helps fuel the epic's narrative development and culminates in a gruesome scene in which she washes her hair in the blood of Duḥśāsana, who insulted her.

A cult of Draupadī as the Hindu supreme goddess remains an important feature of religious life in the South

Indian regions of Tamil Nadu and Kerala but is also known in Mahābhārata cults in Uttar Pradesh and Nepal. Documented in print and on film by Indologist Alf Hiltebeitel, who has also examined Draupadī's complex mythic and religious associations in the Sanskrit Mahābhārata, the cult includes an (ideally) eighteen-day festival in which the epic story is narrated and enacted. Hiltebeitel argues that the cult was probably consolidated in the early fourteenth century.

In modern-day popular culture, Draupadī has at times been considered a heroine, particularly by some women who admire her assertive behavior toward men, including her husbands.

BIBLIOGRAPHY

Hiltebeitel, Alf. *The Cult of Draupadī*. Vols. 1 and 2. 1988, 1991.

"Lady of Gingee: South Indian Draupadī Festivals." Pts. 1 and 2. Directed by Alf Hiltebeitel. University of Wisconsin South Asia Center. 1988.

van Buitenen, H. A. B. *The Mahābhārata*. Vol. 1, *The Book of Beginnings;* vol. 2, *The Book of the Assembly Hall* and *The Book of the Forest;* vol. 3, *The Book of Virāṭa* and *The Book of the Effort*. 1973, 1975, 1978.

See also **Hinduism: Modern Movements.**

BARBARA GOMBACH

Dreams

Almost all ancient and modern dream narrations include their interpretations and fulfillments in later events. And, even though most of the preserved dreams are those of men, some of the earliest dream interpreters are women. For example, in the ancient Sumerian story "Dumuzi's Dream," it is Dumuzi's sister Geshtinanna who correctly interprets his dream (Wolkstein and Kramer, 1983). Similarly, Gilgamesh's mother, Ninsun, interprets his dreams (Sandars, 1960). Other second millennium texts from Mesopotamia and Asia Minor confirm that dream interpreters were often women, though dream interpreters usually had low standing (Oppenheim, 1996). By contrast, the Bible emphasizes male dream interpreters such as Joseph and Daniel. This gendered disjunction suggests there is something of value at stake in dream interpretation—most obviously the ability to interpret otherworldly or divine discourse, an awesome power indeed—with ramifications in both the human and divine worlds. Indeed, Richard L. Kagan (1990) has uncovered an analogous situation in sixteenth-century Spain where male Catholic priests competed with low-status women for expertise in dream interpretation. Shifting the perspective to the dreamers rather than the interpreters, Bruce Lincoln (1994) has presented some relevant and pervasive examples of dream discourse as one of the few authoritative voices available to women in the Roman world, albeit an easily challenged one, a point echoed by Kagan.

Patricia Cox Miller (1994) argues that in late antiquity, dreams helped people to find solutions for everything from the practical problems of daily life to the highest spiritual aspirations. For instance, the Christian martyr Perpetua, while awaiting execution in the Roman arena in 203 C.E., was reconciled to her fate by dreaming she was transformed into a man. Conversely, Jerome said that while living in the desert he was often surrounded by dancing girls. Miller takes these to be dreams rather than visions and argues that in much the same way that Perpetua transformed her body into a male body (i.e., a heroic body), Jerome used his "dreams" to transform or remake his body into an ascetic body, a body unmoved by sexual desire.

Intriguing inversions of erotic women invading male dreams are described in Greek magical papyri (second century B.C.E. to fifth century C.E.), in which spells are cast and amulets made in order to invade someone's dream life. The vast majority of these concern male manipulation of female dreams with the aim of arousing sexual desire in the women. In imagery reeking of bondage and humiliation the man projects all his erotic symptoms onto the passive (sleeping) object of his desire (e.g., Betz, ed., [1993] spells nos. IV.2441–2621, VII.862–928, and XIV.1070–1077). These spells, which are a record of actual men who actively decided to infiltrate women's dreams, stand in sharp contrast to frequent representations of men as passive or resisting recipients of dream invasions by erotic women or *succubi*, such as Lilith. In the religious literature of the world when men have erotic dreams they feel invaded by demonesses, but the evidence of these spells shows that erotic dream invasion was a conscious male pastime, not a female one.

In the literature of world religion one of the most commonly preserved dreams of women are conception dreams, the dreams women have just before their children are conceived. This is a form of passive conception that represented women as incubators for predominantly male heroes. Such dreams are fairly common in the stories of heroes and religious figures from all around the world, such as Alexander and Zoroaster (Rank, 1990), while medieval Christianity and Islam are also quite rich in such dreams (Bitel, 1991; Bulkeley, 1994). They emphasize a divine involvement in the life of the children and in some cases actual divine father-ing. One famous example is the conception dream of the Buddha's mother, Queen Māyā, in which she sees a magnificent white elephant. With its trunk, the ele-phant strikes her right side, through which it enters her womb (Young). This dream is pervasive in Buddhist iconography and texts, so it is not surprising that con-ception dreams figure in the biographical literature of highly revered Buddhists, both women and men. Such a dream both predicts and confers spiritual authority on the child.

In one of the best known biographies of Tibetan Bud-dhism, that of Milarepa (1040–1123), the text both be-gins and ends with dreams involving five divine women (Sanskrit: *ḍākinī*s; Tibetan: *mkha' 'gro ma*, meaning "sky-goer" and indicating their role as crossers of the celestial and terrestrial realms). These women encour-age the dreamer, Milarepa's disciple Rechungpa, to ask Milarepa to recite his life story. In another dream at the end of the biography Rechungpa sees the same woman carry away the relics from Milarepa's cremation cell (Lhalungpa, 1984).

These five *ḍākinī*s become the protectors of Mi-larepa's lineage, which includes teachings about Dream Yoga. This is a practice that in its simplest form encourages initiates to examine their dreams before an initiation to see if they will be accepted by the deity. However, *ḍākinī*s most often show up in dreams to tell adepts what teachings they need and sometimes pre-dict who they will receive them from; or often just see-ing a *ḍākinī* in a dream is evidence of spiritual accom-plishment, though they sometimes grant spiritual powers that immediately manifest in waking life. Per-haps the greatest *ḍākinī* of them all is Niguma, a renown teacher of Dream Yoga, who may or may not have existed in waking reality, but who remains avail-able through dreams and visions (Mullin, 1985).

A fertile climate for such dreams is created by the Ti-betan emphasis on the iconography and visualization of *ḍākinī*s and on other female deities. Such imagery rep-resents the internalization of the feminine, the coopta-tion of female power and insight, which is the often stated goal of Tantric Buddhism. However, there is no complimentary male imagery for women dreamers or practitioners and could only function in symbolic roles, whether as dream-women, or as the subject of (mostly male) visionary experience, or as passive, mostly sym-bolic, participants in marginal tantric rituals. Similarly, Jewish Kabbalists relied on the Shekinah, the feminine presence of God in the world, to understand their prophetic dreams, while some Shiite Sufis rely on Fa-tima, the daughter of the Prophet Muhammad (Blood, 1996). One finds an echo of this female role in C. G.

Jung's concept of the Psychopomp, the female guide to the unconscious. But the most ancient source for this idea is in the myths and stories from around the world in which male heroes always require a female guide to complete their quest.

This brings us back to Perpetua's dream of transform-ing into a man. Indeed, in the spiritual life of most world religions that is exactly what women need to do. The contrast between Christian male celibates who perceived the beautiful and erotic women of their dreams as demons and Tibetan monks who viewed such dreams as the blessings of auspicious, divine women does not mean that women had a higher status in Bud-dhism; in neither case are they actual living women.

BIBLIOGRAPHY

Betz, Hans Dieter, ed. *The Greek Magical Papyri*, vol. 1. 1986; 2d ed., 1992.

Bitel, Lisa M. "*In Visu Noctis:* Dreams in European Hagiography and Histories, 450–900." *History of Re-ligion* 31 (August 1991): 39–59.

Bloom, Harold. *Omen of the Millenium: The Gnosis of Angels, Dreams, and Resurrection.* 1996.

Bulkeley, Kelly. *Wilderness of Dreams.* 1994.

Kagan, Richard L. *Lucrecia's Dreams: Politics and Prophecy in Sixteenth-Century Spain.* 1990.

Lhalungpa, Losang P. *The Life of Milarepa.* 1984.

Lincoln, Bruce. *Authority: Construction and Corrosion.* 1994.

Miller, Patricia Cox. *Dreams in Late Antiquity: Studies in the Imagination of a Culture.* 1994.

Mullin, Glenn H., ed. and trans. *Selected Works of the Dalai Lama II: The Tantric Yogas of Sister Niguma.* 1985. Pp. 92–151 discuss Niguma and Dream Yoga.

Oppenheim, A. Leo. "Mantic Dreams in the Ancient Near East." In *The Dream and Human Societies.* Edited by G. E. von Grunebaum and Robert Caillois. 1966.

Rank, Otto. "Myth of the Birth of the Hero." Repr. in *In Quest of the Hero.* Edited by Robert A. Segal. 1990.

Sandars, N. K., trans. *The Epic of Gilgamesh.* 1960, 1964.

Wolkstein, Diane, and Kramer, Samuel Noah. *Inanna, Queen of Heaven and Earth: Her Stories and Hymns from Sumer.* 1983.

Carol Schreier Rupprecht's "Women's Dreams: Mind and Body," in *Feminist Archetypal Theory: Interdisci-plinary Re-Visions of Jungian Thought,* edited by Es-tella Lauter and Carol Schreier Rupprecht (1985), of-fers a useful presentation and integration of dream theory, dream data, feminist thought, and the differ-ences between women's and men's dreams. See also her "Sex, Gender and Dreams: From Polarity to Plurality" in *Among All These Dreamers: Essays on Dreaming and Modern Society*, edited by Kelly Bulkeley (1996).

John J. Winkler, *The Constraints of Desire: The Anthropology of Sex and Gender in Ancient Greece* (1990), discusses erotic spells in the Greek magical papyri, erotic dreams in the context of Artemidoros' *Dream Analysis*, and lists women's dreams reported by Artemidoros. As a professional dream interpreter, Artemidoros collected dreams from thousands of clients. See also Winkler's brief discussion of one of Penelope's dreams.

Serinity Young, *Dreaming in the Lotus* (1998) has chapters on conception dreams and the symbolic role of women in Buddhist dreams.

Anthropological studies of dreams provide a much needed balance to these textual traditions, which are almost completely dominated by male dream experience. Laurel Kendall's *The Life and Hard Times of a Korean Shaman: Of Tales and the Telling of Tales* (1988) records several dreams of Yonsu's mother and those of her female family members, as well as their interpretations. Kendall brings us into a rich world, where spirits advise and empower women through dreams, thereby changing their lives. Similarly, Karen McCarthy Brown, *Mama Lola: A Vodou Priestess in Brooklyn* (1991), records many of Mama Lola's dreams as well as those of her mother and her daughter, all of which are believed to be advice or warning from the spirits. These women share a powerful community of dreaming and dream interpretation. The aboriginal women of Australia, through their access to the *jukurrpa* (the Dreamtime), establish and maintain their relationships and rights to land, their connections to the past and the present (Diane Bell, *Daughters of the Dreaming* [1983; 2d ed., 1993]) and their ritual roles as nurturers. Lee Irwin's *The Dream Seekers: Native American Visionary Traditions of the Great Plains* (1996) is a good typology of dream experience that attempts to compensate for the preponderance of male dreams collected by ethnologists, arguing that they tended to favor the sought after dreams of males over the spontaneous dreams of females. It contains dreams that changed the dreamer's gender identity as well as the dreams of a few women; further, it discusses the role of women in male dreams as well as the general belief that women are more receptive to such experiences. T. M. Luhrmann, *Persuasions of the Witch's Craft: Ritual Magic in Contemporary England* (1989), briefly discusses neopagan dream groups. A more detailed guide to such practices is Diane Mariechild, *Mother Wit: A Feminist Guide to Psychic Development* (1981). This contains a chapter on dreams, including exercises to enhance dream and visionary experiences.

See also Ḍākinīs; Jung, Carl; Perpetua and Felicity.

SERINITY YOUNG

Dualism

Dualism is the single most common feature of the foundational myths of virtually all world religions from the beginning of recorded history. Its functions are multiple, including: cosmogonic (explanation of the origin of the universe); cosmological (explanation of the order and structure of the universe); and anthropological (explanation of the origin, nature, and destiny of humankind). Whether explicitly or implicitly, dualism represents the male-female bipolarity present in many myths of origin. Insofar as such myths mirror a culture's political and social economy, they reflect the gendered nature of the grammar of power that is established in and through them. Furthermore, they also reflect culturally constructed attitudes toward the sexes and about sexuality.

Creation myths are fundamental to a culture's self-understanding and provide the necessary paradigms for religious and political rituals. Dualism is an aspect of myths that involve a supreme creator; gradual emergence; primordial parents whose offspring is the world; a cosmic egg; and primordial battles between a good "god" and an evil force or entity. In all cases, at issue is differentiation or separation of human reality from the originary or primordial matter.

Despite cultural differences among the descriptions of the divine creator, some common elements emerge. First and foremost, the creator is often described as an omniscient, omnipresent, and all-powerful father through whose generative act creation happens. Assumptions about gender inform these myths and also determine their interpretation. Genesis 1–3, the myth of origin for Judaism, and subsequently for Christianity and Islam, describes creation as generated by the word of God, the essential patriarch. Similar representations of the divine creator are found in the mythologies of Egypt (Ptah and Kheper), Polynesia (Io), and the Winnebago (Earthmaker).

Dualism and gender are central in Genesis, both in the fundamental act that announces the separation of creator from creation and in Adam's dominion over nature and Eve. In the folkloric rendering of the creation narrative found in the Talmud, the first woman, Lilith, refuses to submit to Adam and is turned into a primordial monster who kills children. In the canonical myth, Eve disobeys God and is made to suffer the pain of childbearing; Adam is made to till the soil. In each case,

Six panels illustrating the six days of the creation of the World (Corbis-Bettmann)

and evil; spirit and matter; body and soul; sacred and profane; life and death. In the case of Hinduism, for example, dualism is seen in the oppositions between the one and the many, and between reality and appearance. It is also present in the description of two eternal but conflicted cosmic principles: original matter and spirit believed to be the substance of the universe. By contrast, in China the dualism of yin and yang is of a complementary rather than oppositional nature. Yin is associated with the feminine, earth, darkness, passivity, receptivity, yang with the masculine, heaven, light, activity, and penetration. Emerging from the ultimate power, the T'ai Chi, the interplay of the yin and yang, creates harmony in the universe.

The female-male dualism of yin and yang represents a cultural predisposition to harmony and balance; nevertheless, the cultural power dynamic ascribes a subservient role to women and privileges attributes related to masculinity. As in the case with Western religions, in Asian religions women are, in general, of lesser status than the normative male.

Classic dualisms have saturated the worldviews of many traditions: woman is to nature as man is to culture; woman is to body as man is to spirit and reason; woman is passive and receptive, man active and penetrating. History offers myriad examples of the infelicitous effects on women's lives of religious belief systems that glorify masculinist values and practices. Religious dualism, rather than affirm each side's power to effect its own place in the universe, tends to legitimate the right of one side to have power over the other.

BIBLIOGRAPHY

Campbell, Joseph, and Mircea Eliade. *The Universal Myths*. 1976.
Highwater, Jamake. *Myth and Sexuality*. 1991.

IRENA S. M. MAKARUSHKA

women and men who appear to subvert the natural order of things must pay the price.

Dualism and gender play a role in creation accounts that tell of a cosmic battle between opposing forces or the sacrifice of a god. In the Mesopotamian myth *Enuma Elish,* for instance, the primordial mother, Tiamat, is killed in her battle with the warrior sun god, Marduk. With a final blow he splits her into two parts, from which are formed heaven and earth. From her blood and bone, he creates earth's human inhabitants, destined to be slaves to the gods. Similarly, for the aboriginal people of Borneo, the creation myth recounts that the first couple sprang from a rock in the ocean. After they create the earth from a handful of dust and pieces of rock, they have a human son and daughter. The daughter becomes the first human sacrifice from whose buried body grow fruit trees and animals.

Creation narratives assume a fundamental distinction between creator and creation; female and male; good

Durgā and Kālī

Durgā and Kālī are two Hindu goddesses often portrayed—mythically and philosophically—as different forms of the same goddess, the divine female energy, *śakti*. Though both have independent histories dating from the Vedic and Upanishadic periods, respectively, they are linked textually for the first time in the sixth-century "Devī Māhātmya" section of the *Mākaṇḍeya Purāṇa*, where wrathful Kālī springs from Durgā's forehead to slay demons. Thereafter they maintain philosophical ties, since both are martial goddesses, powerful

Clay statues of Durga for her annual festival are offered for sale at a sculpture shop, Calcutta, West Bengal, India, 1996 (Jeremy Horner/© Corbis).

and independent of male deities, but they also develop distinct iconographic, ritual, and textual traditions. Recognized today as goddesses of pan-Indian popularity and importance, Durgā's major annual festival is Navarātrī, Festival of the Nine Nights, in September–October, whereas Kālī's occurs in October–November.

Iconographically, Durgā is more benign; in her most famous exploit, she slays the buffalo demon, Mahiṣa, but with a serene and beautiful countenance. In Kālī's most celebrated depiction, by contrast, she stands atop a corpse in the cremation grounds, her tongue lolling and her naked body ornamented with instruments of death. Both goddesses, however, are understood as divine mothers who offer grace and salvation; their demon enemies are sins or obstructions, not their own devotees.

Many women in positions of spiritual and political leadership—including the former prime minister, Indira Gandhi—have derived inspiration from the models of independence and power that Durgā and Kālī provide. On the other hand, these deities are also anti-models, as ordinary women are not generally allowed to express aggression or autonomy.

BIBLIOGRAPHY

Coburn, Thomas B. *Devī Māhātmya: Crystallization of the Goddess Tradition.* Delhi, 1985.

Hawley, John Stratton, and Donna Marie Wulff, eds. *Devī: Goddesses of India.* 1996.

Kinsley, David R. *Hindu Goddesses: Visions of the Divine Feminine in the Hindu Religious Tradition.* 1986.

RACHEL FELL MCDERMOTT

Earth

Earth figures prominently in numerous creation stories of different religions. Earth is mother, source of life, partner of sky, and the womb to which human beings return in death.

Great mother

In Hesiod's *Theogony*, earth is Gaia, the mother who existed before time. She creates her son-lover, Ouranus, the sky, and then bears many children. Ouranus quickly imprisons their children in the earth—both underground and in the womb of their mother, Gaia. This angers Gaia, who asks her children to take revenge against their father. One of the children, Kronos, ambushes Ouranus and the children are released from their confinement. Gaia as earth mother is generative and nurturing.

To the Thompson Indians of the North Pacific coast, earth was the primal woman, who was transformed into solid land and became the mother of people. Earth is presented like a human being, with her flesh as clay, her hair the trees and grass, her bones the rocks, and her blood the springs of water. People live in her bosom, derive nourishment from her, and use all parts of her body. This idea of earth as mother is shared by many Philippine tribes who believe that deep bowels of the earth are the original habitat of humans. In many of these creation stories, earth gives birth through parthenogenesis (without male assistance), thus emphasizing the fullness of the creative powers of mother earth.

Earth and sky as partners

Another image presented in creation stories is that of the earth and sky as divine partners responsible for populating the earth. In Chinese mythology, the combined essences of earth and heaven became the *yin* (earth, female) and *yang* (sky, male), which brought about the four seasons, which in turn brought about the creatures of the world. A creation myth of the Luiseno Indians of California tells of the creation of a primal pair, Tamayowut (earth, female) and Tukomit (sky, male) who gave birth to mountains, rocks, trees, and birds, then to Towish, the human spirit that survives the body, and to Wiyot, from whom sprung all human generations. To the Toradjas of Celebes and the Minahassa of Borneo, this primal pair of earth and sky produced offspring who people the earth. Japanese cosmogony speaks of heaven and earth taking the form of humans, Izanagi and Izanami, and giving birth to the gods.

Earth's role in creation

Earth brings forth life, and at the same time it is an element in the creation of life. Jews, Christians, and Muslims share a common story of God's creation of humanity. God shaped a man from clay, breathed life into his nostrils, and together with a woman whom God created later, this primordial pair became the progenitors of humans. The Shilluks of the Nile attribute the origin of human races to the different colored clays that the creator, Juok, used. Juok wandered the earth, and from pure white sand, he created a white progenitor; from Egypt and out of the mud of the Nile, he made red or brown, from the land of the Shilluks, he created black. He shaped humans from lumps of earth, gave them arms, ears, mouth, tongue, eyes and sent out to the world a perfect person from each kind of clay.

Earth as the womb

The process of creation involving earth serves as a metaphor for birth and involves motifs of primal egg, primal water, and the womb. Life emerges out of the

The female earth spirit Yakshi from Indian mythology depicted as a voluptuous woman, second century B.C.E. (Angelo Hornak/Corbis)

womb and as earth is the giver of life, humans return to it in death until, as many traditions claim, they are transformed into another existence.

BIBLIOGRAPHY

Demetrio, Francisco R. *Myths and Symbols, Philippines.* Manila, 1981.

Eliade, Mircea. *From Primitives to Zen: A Thematic Sourcebook of the History of Religions.* 1977.

———. *Patterns in Comparative Religion.* 1958.

Gantz, Timothy. *Early Greek Myth: A Guide to Literary and Artistic Sources.* 1993.

Gill, Sam D. *Mother Earth: An American Story.* 1987.

Gimbutas, Marija. *The Civilization of the Goddess.* 1991.

Hultkrantz, Ake. *The Religions of the American Indians.* 1967.

Leeming, David Adams. *The World of Myth.* 1990.

Leeming, David Adams, and Jake Page. *Myths of the Female Divine Goddess.* 1994.

Versluis, Arthur. *Sacred Earth: The Spiritual Landscape of Native America.* 1992.

VIVIENNE SM. ANGELES

East Asian Religions

An Overview

For three millennia masculine voices have largely dominated elite discourse on feminine sanctity in East Asia. Despite such dominance, however, the figure of the female religious leader and the attendant configuration of feminine sanctity have had longevity and viability, occurring at the earliest mentions of religion in East Asia, and important still today in China, Korea, and Japan. The female religious leader is, in essence, a divine "intermediary," the potent link between the mundane and the extra mundane; her functions are to communicate with the gods and ancestors, to heal, to serve as psychopomp (escort of the soul to the afterlife), and, in some incarnations, to serve as ascetic, visionary, and religious teacher. Within this overarching sacred persona, however, the authority of the female intermediary varies considerably according to the four major religious traditions of East Asia: (1) In the so-called popular or folk religions she dominates; (2) in Chinese Taoism she has a highly significant role, equal to that of the male religious leader; (3) in Confucianism her influence is much filtered through the cults of motherhood and marriage; and (4) in Chinese, Korean, and Japanese Buddhism her significance is muted; hegemonic discourse tends to demonize her, although in popular contexts she figures importantly.

FOLK RELIGIONS

The female divine intermediary has pride of place in the "folk religions" of East Asia. Folk religion consists of a loose aggregation of practices that orders, sanctifies, purifies, and protects the individual and the community, practiced typically at the local level and preserved by oral tradition or in noncanonical, alternative sources such as popular literature. In the folk religions of East Asia the female intermediary is referred to as a shamaness: Chinese *wu*, Korean *mudang*, Japanese *miko*. (All three expressions utilize the same character.)

At the earliest strata of religious history in East Asia the shamaness—*wu*—appears. In ancient China during the Shang Dynasty (c. 1766–1027 B.C.E.) she served as the chief adept for rites of propitiation directed at gods of the natural world; she summoned the rain, performed rituals governing seasonal purification, and was in charge of healing rituals. In the rituals of the Shang and Zhou (c. 1027–221 B.C.E.) her rituals were exorcistic; to bring rain the shamaness was burned in a fire, or exposed naked to the heat of the sun, thus driving out the drought and compelling the rain. Deities allied with shamanistic rituals were fertility gods, usually female; chief among these goddesses was the dragon. She was the overarching symbol of the rain: curved, watery, snakelike, magical, and, in this ancient period, female. No sacred texts are preserved from the Shang, but the song cycle of the state of Chu (*The Songs of the South*) is thought to be heavily filtered libretti for shamanistic ritual performance. The shamaness diminished in status in periods after the Shang and Zhou. In the Han Dynasty (202 B.C.E.–220 C.E.) the performance of women in the role of rainmaker was labeled "licentious"; by the Late Imperial period in China—the Ming (1368–1644) and Qing periods (1644–1911)—shamanism became a feature of popular life, disdained by elites. The folklore of feminine fertility, however, with its imagery of snakes, water, swampy settings, and springtime growth continued to find expression in alternative sources, surviving in medieval poetry, as well as in popular narratives of the Ming and Qing.

In Korea shamanistic practices have served as the religious foundation for Korea and have demonstrated a powerful presence up through the modern era. The *mudang* of Korea performs for communities and households, engaging the gods and ancestors to obtain divine benefits and to ward off malign influences. The role of the female shaman reached its apogee in Korea in the fourteenth century; but with the advent of neo-Confucianism from China in the Chosŏn period (1392–1910), with its configuration of the family as a lineage of males, the status of the shamaness diminished. Female religious leaders did not disappear, however, but found expression rather in nonhegemonic, alternative sources. Vernacular narrative and popular theater from the seventeenth century through today have articulated an influential mythology of the feminine. The legend of Sim Ch'ŏng, the filial daughter, has been retold in *p'ansori* novels of the early modern period. These popular narratives on filiality derive from an amalgamation of religious tenets and texts, with elements from shamanism, Buddhism, and Confucianism. Despite the intellectual diffuseness, however, of the *matière de* Sim Ch'ŏng, her legend and texts reflect a widespread and deeply felt sense of the cultural authority of feminine sanctity.

Shintoism of Japan is also an "indigenous" folk religion and is defined as "the way of the *kami*" or the "way of the gods." It is a diffuse set of practices honoring gods of the natural world, of the state, and of the home. Shinto originated in Japan at the earliest period of prehistoric Japan and was articulated as a mythology in the time of Emperor Temmu (672–687) when the *Kojiki* and *Nihonshoki* were likely compiled. Shinto evolved differently than did shamanism in China and Korea, however, for Shinto was never sanitized out of hegemonic religious discourse, nor limited to local communities of worship; rather it was established as a feature of national religious life. As Shinto grew in importance so did many of the female divinities of Shinto. The goddess Amaterasu originated as a local clan deity. During the sixth and seventh centuries, however, she gradually evolved into the protective deity of the state; her thirteen-hundred-year-old shrine at Ise is one of the most important religious sites in Japan. So-called folk Shinto has continuously preserved shamanic rituals and the importance of the shamaness. In 1981 the shamaness Fujita Himiko of a folk Shinto sect was awarded the title *kami-miko*, Divine Shamaness.

TAOISM

Taoism was founded in ancient China and has had largely indirect influence in Korea and Japan, but its canon and practices contain some of the most elaborate and forceful articulations of feminine sanctity in East Asia. In the Warring States period of China (403–221 B.C.E.), Taoism emerges from archaic religious practices. Early texts of Taoism articulate the role of the Goddess, the Queen Mother of the West, and her importance in the mythology of rulership. In the Six Dynasties period (222–589 C.E.) we begin to see a clearly defined class of Taoist religious leader, as during this period of growth the Taoist monastic movement provided a forum for Taoist women of all classes. Women found vocations as cleric, nun, novice, adept, recluse, healer, warrior, and lay heroine. Nor were Taoist women limited to minor roles in Taoist communities—they served as visionaries, priestesses, and adepts, conduits for divine communication, the focus of national religious movements and "living auspicious omens" allied with dynastic legitimacy. The Taoist discourse on the feminine thus greatly enhanced East Asian notions of the idealized feminine. Solitary, ascetic women in monastic settings who practiced the intense disciplines associated with transcendence became female icons; and the roles of religious teacher and dynastic talisman configured women as charismatic community leaders. In the Late Imperial period vernacular narratives of the woman warrior and millenarian rebel further advanced this construct of the feminine.

Scholars have theorized that Taoist emphasis on the role of the feminine religious teacher derives from Taoism's historical and ongoing reliance on shamanic religion. Brigitte Berthier (1988) has traced the cult of the shamanic deity, the Woman of the Water's Edge (Linshui Furen), establishing the ways the powers of the shamaness, especially in her role as psychopomp, rain-maker, and healer, have been co-opted into Taoism. Taoism is seen to have preserved the lore of the female divine intermediary but transformed it: recasting folk practice as liturgy and recording oral tradition as canon. Thus, the shamaness, though banished from elite articulations of religion, is transformed into the Taoist adept and cleric.

CONFUCIANISM

Confucianism of China, Korea, and Japan represents the greatest contrast with "folk religions," and the female intermediary appears to be the most diminished in her significance. Yet despite the emphasis on the masculine, Confucianism still articulates important aspects of feminine sanctity that are established firmly within both elite and popular discourse. Ancient Confucianism evolved during the Zhou period in China as an elaboration and codification of the cult of family and ancestor worship. Confucians emphasized filial piety (*xiao*), placing human conduct on a continuum of filial obligations due to elders, parents, and ancestors; essential to this continuum of piety was domestic life. The family was configured as a cult space, and a spirit of self-sacrifice for the consecrated family characterized family membership. Men and women were considered, in their domestic roles, icons of piety. For women, the extreme realization of this ethos was known as the "cult of the martyred (or chaste) woman." The "chaste woman" was idealized as a type of domestic ascetic who sacrificed herself under the conditions of familial crisis. In the case of the illness of a parent or parent-in-law, the devout Confucian woman performed rites of mutilation, sacrificing her own flesh to produce healing concoctions. With the death of a spouse or of a betrothed she either withdrew completely from the community for a life of mourning, or she suicided. These acts of fanaticism were not, however, purely moral acts, but were cultic and magical as Confucian women achieved apotheosis through them. The community also reinforced the cultic by deifying the martyrs as local divinities capable of protecting the community from natural disasters. Nor was this mystifying of domestic asceticism and characterization of feminine sanctity limited to Confucianists. Widespread throughout the culture, the pious daughter represented an authoritative and compelling ideal, resurfacing in Buddhist, Taoist, and folk religions, in popular literature and in theater. The belief in the magical efficacy of self-sacrificing, self-mutilating acts was at the core of the idealized feminine in both elite and popular contexts.

A shrine attendant dressed in gold, red, and white sells a branch offering at the Ebisu shrine to the god of business, Osaka, Japan (Nik Wheeler/Corbis).

Confucianism entered Korea and Japan in approximately the third century C.E., and by the seventh to eighth centuries Confucianism's emphasis on hierarchical relationships and the correlation between a moral, harmonious home and a virtuous state were well established in Korea and Japan. It was not until the late seventeenth century, however, that Confucianism and the *Confucian Classics* achieved wide circulation. It is Confucianism of the Song Dynasty (960–1279)—as recast by Zhu Xi (1130–1200) and referred to as "neo-Confucianism"—that has had the greatest influence in Japan and Korea. In Korea, neo-Confucianism greatly influenced notions of feminine sanctity. During the Chosŏn dynasty (1392–1910) the explicit goal of the educated class was the transformation of Korea into a Confucian state. An aspect of this transformation was a change in the treatment of women and a change in perceptions of the feminine. Since the Koryŏ period (918–392) (and probably earlier), until the beginning of the Chosŏn, daughters performed family ritual, inherited property equally with sons, and could succeed to the family line; widows were not forbidden to remarry, and the shamaness had exalted status. As neo-Confucianism became increasingly important and Zhu Xi's *The Family Ritual of Master Zhu* became widely accepted for ordering domestic relations, Korean domestic life became configured as a lineage of males, with accompanying changes in Korean law and society that eclipsed indigenous practices. Despite the importance of neo-Confucianism, however, scholars have noted an undercurrent of resistance to the male-centered homogenization, which articulated a valorized feminine sanctity. Martina Deuchler (1977) has maintained that native Korean practices remained important, as the wedding ceremony, for example, adhered to folk rituals; likewise did popular literature continue to express a counter tradition that was opposed to the male-based discourse on sanctity.

BUDDHISM

Buddhism first entered East Asia from India in the second century C.E. During the Six Dynasties period the successes of Turkic and Mongolian peoples in establishing through conquest cultural and political centers helped convert Northern China into a center for Buddhist activity in East Asia. By the sixth century Buddhism had spread to Korea and Japan. From the perspective of doctrine, East Asian Buddhism relied on the configuration of the feminine as defined originally in Indic texts that articulated a harsh perspective on feminine physiology and feminine sanctity. Despite, however, the demonizing of the feminine, which occurred in doctrine, the Buddhism that evolved in practice in East Asia was far more accessible to women and, in fact, both enhanced local notions of feminine sanctity and, in turn, relied on women for its spread and survival. Buddhist monasticism and ascetic disciplines contributed especially to the roles of women in religion. Buddhist monasteries served as centers of worship for women, offering an explicit alternative to marriage, where practitioners might become local religious leaders famous for learning, discipline, and wisdom. In Japan during the pre-Nara period, by 623, there were over 569 nuns in monastic life, as compared to 816 men. In China during the Six Dynasties period nuns served as religious teachers to aristocratic families, and in the Late Imperial period in China popular movements often formed around women in monastic settings (Buddhist or Taoist), who became centers of cults, millenarian rebels, or warriors. East Asian hagiography and literature articulated, likewise, a tolerant notion of Buddhist feminine sanctity. The Priest Keisei (1189–1268), in his *The Companion in Solitude* (*Kankyo no Tomo*), a compilation of hagiographies of women and men who attained enlightenment, depicted women who, though declared impure by canonical text, achieved salvation through acts of asceticism and sacrifice. Women also provided important support for the Buddhist religion. During the Chosŏn period in Korea women of the upper classes continued to support Buddhism despite official proscription. Yoshikawa Buntaro (as cited in Lancaster [1984]) attributes the survival of Buddhism in Korea to their patronage.

Strict doctrinal notions of Buddhist feminine sanctity were also changed, in turn, by local belief systems as cults centered around the feminine influenced Buddhism; the most notable of these changes occurred in the cult of the bodhisattva Avalokiteśvara. A male in the Indic tradition, she becomes a goddess in the Chinese tradition, Kuan Yin (Guan Yin); her sect becomes one of the most widespread sects in East Asia. The spread of her sect was aided by the absorbtion of two female deities from the local religions of China. The cult of Mazu centered originally around a filial daughter who rescued her brother and father at sea; by the Sung she was an important goddess of the sea with thousands of shrines along the coast. Miaoshan was another filial daughter; she sacrificed her eyes and arms to make a sacred healing concoction for her ailing father. Both "popular" cults were absorbed into the Kuan Yin sect and partially accounted for the spread of Buddhism.

In East Asia the female divine intermediary and her mythology have had the greatest elaborations in religions linked to life at the local level and in religious discourse that articulates the magical connections between community and the divine. Conversely, the female intermediary becomes increasingly alien in the traditions that are more state-centered, more typically preserved in written, canonical, hegemonic texts. It is important, however, to acknowledge the significance of local practices, for the sects of "folk religions"—with their reliance on the female intermediary—are not tangential to the religious panorama of East Asia. Rather the two traditions of elite and popular relate to one another as concentric circles of practices and beliefs, imitating each other as they repeat larger mythic patterns. Thus do sects centered around local female cult figures constantly replenish the organized, codified religions, and, likewise, do female intermediaries for the divine constantly reappear—as shamaness, adept, nun, cleric, or pious daughter.

BIBLIOGRAPHY

Ahern, Emily. "The Power and Pollution of Chinese Women." In *Women in Chinese Society*. Edited by Margery Wolf and Roxanne Witke. 1975.

Berthier, Brigitte. *La Dame-du-Bord-de-l'Eau*. Nanterre, 1988.

Blofeld, John. *Bodhisattva of Compassion: The Mystical Tradition of Kuan Yin*. 1978.

De Groot, J. J. M. *The Religious System of China*. Leiden, 1892–1910.

De Vos, George A., and Takao Sofue, eds. *Religion and the Family in East Asia*. 1984.

Deuchler, Martina. "The Traditions: Women During the Yi Dynasty." In *Virtues in Conflict, Tradition and the Korean Woman Today*. Edited by Sandra Mattielli. Seoul, 1977.

Dudbridge, Glen. *The Legend of Miaoshan.* London, 1978.

Haboush, JaHyun Kim. "Filial Emotions and Filial Values: Changing Patterns in the Discourse of Filiality in Late Choson Korea." *Harvard Journal of Asiatic Studies* 55 (1995): 129–177.

Kendall, Laurel, and Mark Peterson, eds. *Korean Women: A View from the Inner Room.* 1983.

Lancaster, Lewis. "Buddhism and Family in East Asia." In *Religion and Family in East Asia.* Edited by George A. De Vos and Takao Sofue. 1984.

Nosco, Peter, ed. *Confucianism and Tokugawa Culture.* 1984.

Ono, Sokyo. *Shintō: The Kami Way.* 1962.

Pandy, Rajyashree. "Women, Sexuality, and Enlightenment, *Kankyo no Tomo.*" *Monumenta Nipponica* 50 (Autumn 1995): 325–356.

Qu Yuan et al. *The Songs of the South: An Anthology of Ancient Chinese Poems by Qu Yuan and Other Poets.* Translated by David Hawkes. 1985.

Rozman, Gilbert, ed. *East Asian Religion.* 1991.

Schafer, E. H. *The Divine Woman.* 1973.

———. "Ritual Exposure in Ancient China." *Harvard Journal of Asiatic Studies* 14 (1951): 130–184.

T'ien, Ju-k'ang. *Male Anxiety and Female Chastity: A Comparative Study of Chinese Ethical Values in Ming-Ch'ing Times.* Leiden, 1988.

Tsai, Kathryn Ann. *Lives of the Nuns: Biographies of Chinese Buddhist Nuns from the Fourth to Sixth Centuries: A Translation of the Pi-ch'iu-ni chuan.* Compiled by Shih Pao-ch'ang. 1994.

Walraven, B. C. A. *Muga: The Songs of Korean Shamanism.* Leiden, 1985.

See also Amaterasu; Body: Female Body as Text in Imperial China; Kuan Yin (Kannon); Miaoshan; Monasticism: In the East; Ordination: In Buddhism.

VICTORIA CASS

Religious Rites and Practices

Throughout East Asia, pantheons of household gods coexist with ancestor cults. Ethnographers describe gods who are dispersed throughout the family dwelling: reigning household tutelary gods sometimes associated with the stove or hearth, fertility and childbirth goddesses in inner sanctums, and site guardians outside the house but somewhere within the compound. The location of deities within the physical house and the subsequent sanctification of the household as a ritual unit reflects the traditional importance of the small family farm as the fundamental unit of economic life for most of the population of this region until recent decades. Birth spirits and ancestor cults reflect both the family's immediate need to replicate its work force and its desire to perpetuate kinship, wealth, and reputation across generations through ritual acts and inheritance.

Despite common themes, the ways men and women divide ritual tasks in China, Korea, and Japan convey variations upon the themes of "family"—a unit of biological kinship that extends through time—and "household"—a temporally bounded unit of common residence. Different notions of male and female and of the interactions between men and women within domestic groups are implicit in these distinctions.

CHINA

In China individual households and the broader family present a clash of interests and strategies, a conflict between sons who would keep the father's family intact, and brothers who are greedy and impatient to stake independent households. Although brothers may be the actual initiators of family division, the Chinese themselves blame brothers' wives (Cohen, 1976). According to Maurice Freedman, the Chinese consider women "by nature quarrelsome, jealous, petty-minded, and preoccupied with the interests of their own husbands and children at the expense of the wider family" (1979). Margery Wolf (1972) suggests that this perception is natural where women are sent to live as aliens among the husband's kin. Women build their own "uterine families," deriving emotional sustenance and the promise of future support from their own children.

We might logically expect ritual life to reflect gendered experiences with women worshiping the Kitchen God, the household tutelary, and men honoring the ancestors of their extended family, but in fact, we find just the opposite. Women tend the ancestors, at least in their daily and routine care, and men worship the Kitchen God in the New Year, smearing his lips with honey so that he will carry a good report of the family to the Jade Emperor of Heaven. Freedman suggests that this arrangement adds a supernatural counterweight to women's divisive proclivities. Women fall under the family ancestors' authority; men represent the household before a supernatural authority associated with "domestic discipline."

Menstruation and birth pollution render Chinese women ritually unclean, and unclean women deal most directly with unclean spirits, with the dead, and with "little low goddesses" who are tainted by association with childbirth. Emily [Martin] Ahern notes that "The common relegation of women to the worship of the low,

A woman at the Edo-mura Village, a reconstruction of life in Edo times, writes an *ema*, a prayer plaque, for the village's Shinto temple. Prayer papers flutter behind her, Nikko, Japan, 1995 (Richard T. Nowitz/Corbis).

unclean end of the hierarchy is appropriate because women are so frequently unclean themselves. Conversely, the near-monopoly by men of the clean, high end of the hierarchy is appropriate because they are much less often unclean" (1975, pp. 206–207). Ahern interprets pollution beliefs as simultaneously rationalizing women's ritual subordination and commenting upon the structural danger that women pose to Chinese families. Death, birth, and menstruation pollute because they rupture the integrity of bodies and families. Women's greater perceived uncleanliness is a function of women's borderline position as strangers who break into collectivities that are based on male lines of descent. Women must give birth for the sake of the family, but at the same time, children provide the nucleus of particularistic interests—one's own children versus a sibling's children—that will eventually tear the family into separate households.

"Unclean" and "dangerous" are specific to Chinese notions of "wife" and "daughter-in-law" rather than to the full symbolic potential of "woman." Steven Sangren (1983) reminds us that nominally "Buddhist" goddesses whose veneration is also a part of Chinese domestic practice—particularly by elderly women—appear as "mothers" who promise universalistic love and acceptance transcendent of the narrow strictures of family and gender.

KOREA

Korea shares China's strong androcentric traditions. Sons are the family's social and ritual heirs while daughters are sent away to husbands' families. We would expect to find gendered tensions akin to those

described for China and a consequent similar gendering of domestic religion. We find instead the "logical" arrangement that Chinese ethnography confounds. In Korea, men perform the formal rites of ancestor worship as sons and grandsons who make offerings to parents and grandparents on death anniversaries and on holidays. These rituals map the immediate extensions of family as nephews and cousins gather to venerate their common grandparents (Janelli and Janelli, 1982). The rites also tacitly affirm the exclusion of daughters who leave the family and who prepare ancestral offerings in other families' kitchens.

Wives and daughters-in-law prepare elaborate food for the ancestral offerings and for the feast that follows, but only sonless widows officiate at ancestor rites. Women deal with the family dead in other contexts, however. During the mourning period, women make twice-daily offerings to the recently deceased, feeding the dead along with everyone else as a sign that the soul has not yet completely departed from the household (Janelli and Janelli). Women also deal with the restless dead whose baleful presence brings illness or misfortune. Housewives perform simple exorcisms and sponsor elaborate rituals where shamans send unquiet souls to Paradise (Kendall, 1985).

If Korean women are marginal to the formal rites of ancestor veneration, they play a central role in honoring the household gods. The senior housewife makes rice cake offerings after the harvest and minor offerings when prompted by particular circumstances such as a bad dream or a sudden windfall from the sale of a cow. In some households, women offer secret prayers for their families at the village shrine or make silent pilgrimages to sacred mountains or to Buddhist temples. These traditions are passed from a mother-in-law to her daughters-in-law. A woman assumes responsibility for a household pantheon when her mother-in-law retires from active management of the household, or when a couple establishes an independent household (Kendall).

Although menstruation and childbirth pollute Korean women, menstruating and postpartum women are only temporarily unfit to honor the household gods or to visit temples and sacred mountains. Following the logic of Ahern's structural argument, Korean women are simply not perceived to be as threatening as Chinese women. Where Chinese households are torn apart in a single acrimonious act of dissolution by brothers who have equal claims on the family property, Korean households segment sequentially as a matter of course. The eldest brother and his wife, as primary heirs, remain in the "main house." Other brothers are expected to establish independent households, one by one, once their brides have learned the family's customs (Kendall).

Birth order among brothers fuels family division, not the perceived acrimony of brothers' wives.

JAPAN

Japan provides another contrast. Women prepare and serve both the gods' and the ancestors' offerings along with the family food, but men might occasionally make these offerings when they have the time and inclination to do so. Men are expected to officiate at major offerings, but venerable widows often claim dominant roles in the household ancestors' cult (Morioka, 1968; Smith, 1974).

The Japanese do not seize upon a ready gender dichotomy to distinguish the household cult from family ritual for they have no need to make this distinction. The ancestors and gods belong to the *ie*, a collectivity of those who reside in the house, who have lived there in the past, and who may do so in the future. *Ie* members are likely to share ties of biological kinship, but this is not essential (Nakane, 1967). Known ancestors (*hotoke*) are eventually absorbed into the *ie*'s anonymous collectivity of tutelary gods (*kami*) (Smith, 1974). Although pollution beliefs barred women from certain ritual sites, sacred mountains, and monasteries (Befu, 1971), these beliefs seem not to inhibit women's active participation in domestic ritual practices.

These three societies have been described in general terms and in an ethnographic present that should be qualified. In the last decades of the twentieth century, all of East Asia has seen massive industrialization and urbanization. Urbanites sometimes simplify or even abandon practices that were attuned to the agricultural calendar and were less burdensome when relatives lived close at hand in rural villages. Housewives who live in isolation from their mothers-in-law sometimes turn to ritual specialists for skills that most housewives once possessed. Governments throughout the region have denounced many of these activities as "wasteful" and "superstitious." Protestant Christianity in Korea and indigenous new religions in Japan have redefined domestic religion for significant segments of these societies, but still grant important roles for women.

BIBLIOGRAPHY

Ahern, Emily [Martin]. "The Power and Pollution of Chinese Women." In *Women in Chinese Society.* Edited by Margery Wolf and Roxanne Witke. 1975.

Befu, Harumi. *Japan: An Anthropological Introduction.* 1971.

Cohen, Myron L. *House United House Divided: The Chinese Family in Taiwan.* 1976.

Freedman, Maurice. *The Study of Chinese Society.* Edited by G. W. Skinner. 1979.

Janelli, Roger L., and Dawnhee Yim Janelli. *Ancestor Worship and Korean Society.* 1982.

Kendall, Laurel. *Shamans, Housewives, and Other Restless Spirits: Women in Korean Ritual Life.* 1985.

Morioka, Kiyomi. "Religion, Behavior, and the Actor's Position in His Household." *Journal of Asian and African Studies* 3, nos. 1–2 (1968): 25–43.

Nakane, Chie. *Kinship and Economic Organization in Rural Japan.* 1967.

Sangren, Steven. "Female Gender in Chinese Religious Symbols: Kuan Yin, Ma Tsu, and the 'Eternal Mother.'" *Signs: Journal of Women in Culture and Society* 9, no. 1 (1983): 4–25.

Smith, Robert J. *Ancestor Worship in Japan.* 1974.

Wolf, Margery. *Women and the Family in Rural Taiwan.* 1972.

See also **Ancestor Worship; New Religions: In East Asia; Purity and Pollution.**

LAUREL KENDALL

New Buddhist Movements

The place of women in East Asian Buddhism since the end of World War II is intimately related both to the legacy regarding women that has been handed down within the Buddhist tradition and to the situation that the Buddhist establishment as a whole has encountered in each of the East Asian countries (here understood to encompass China, Taiwan, Korea, and Japan). Within Buddhist history, although certain Buddhist texts argue for the equality of men and women as regards their capacities to attain religious insight and liberation, the dominant tradition has been to regard women as suffering from certain obstacles related to their sex that has made it difficult for them to achieve true equality within the *sangha* (Buddhist community). This view of women originally arose in India but was reinforced in the male-dominated cultures of East Asia. However, this tradition has by no means prevented women from participating in Buddhist religious life over the centuries, both as nuns and as laywomen. Today, the extent and forms of their participation are related to the specific histories of Buddhism in each country as well as to larger political, economic, and social trends.

CHINA

After the Communist party took over the mainland in 1949, Buddhism was placed on the defensive. Buddhist teachings were classified as superstition, monks and nuns were often forced back into the laity, and the *sangha* rapidly dwindled in size and vitality. Many Buddhist properties were taken over and maintained by the state. The situation worsened dramatically during the

Cultural Revolution (1966–1976), when Buddhist temples and art treasures were destroyed by the Red Guard and monks and nuns were ridiculed as parasites and remnants of the old feudal order.

Buddhism's fortunes began to improve in the late 1970s when the government adopted a more liberal attitude toward the religion, in part so that the government might benefit from the tourist dollars that the Buddhist sites might attract. The government has supported the rebuilding of many Buddhist temples destroyed during the Cultural Revolution. Although still regulated by the government, monks and nuns are being permitted to enter the religious life in increasing, though still small, numbers, and lay Buddhists, especially women, are commonly seen visiting Buddhist temples and sacred sites.

Although monks far outnumber nuns, where nuns' communities exist they operate along traditional lines. Their regular activities include study, the recitation of texts, meditation, participation in the ritual celebrations of their institutions and in local Buddhist festivals, along with the usual chores associated with monastic life. Entrance into such a community provides women with a variety of benefits, among them freedom from what some view as the burdens of married life in a society run by men. It also offers them the chance to pursue their religious interests in supportive and close-knit communities of like-minded women.

Among lay Buddhists in China, women are clearly the most active. It is women far more than men who visit the temples and who undertake religious pilgrimages. As has been the case in the past in many cultural settings, participation in a pilgrimage gives women freedoms otherwise largely beyond their reach—the chance to get away from home, to see new sites, and to enjoy the company of fellow, largely women, travelers. Today, groups ranging from several tens to more than two or three hundred may undertake pilgrimages to famous Buddhist temples or sacred sites, such as those dedicated to Avalokiteśvara (Kuan Yin) in Hangchow. The prayers made by women on such occasions reflect perennial concerns; requests are made for the birth of sons, for health, for happiness in the family, or thanks are offered for blessings received. Although the current political climate in China is still repressive, in an era of economic liberalization it appears that the opportunity for Buddhist women to participate in their religion as nuns and laity will continue to grow.

TAIWAN

Because Taiwan did not become Communist at the end of the war, Buddhist traditions on the island were not as dramatically disrupted by postwar developments. The Nationalist party that set up government on Taiwan favored Christianity and Confucianism, but Buddhism was allowed to follow its own course. Particularly in the 1980s and 1990s, there has been a rebirth of interest in Buddhism on the island; rapid economic growth and a less authoritarian style of government have led to the creation of an environment more conducive to religious activity.

Men have held the leadership positions in most temples and monastic institutions, but the rapid growth in the participation of women, as nuns and laypersons, has been one of the most remarkable features of recent Buddhist history on the island. The institution of the nunnery, as always, has given women an independence difficult for most to attain in the larger society, and while laywomen continue to live in the secular world, their visits to and service at Buddhist temples and religious sites afford them some small taste of independence. Further, Buddhist women in Taiwan have also distinguished themselves in the field of charity work. Today, perhaps the best example of the latter is the Buddhist Compassion, Relief, Love and Mercy Foundation, established in 1966 by the nun, Dharma Master Cheng Yen. After a troubled youth and years of religious searching, Cheng Yen decided to devote herself to the bodhisattva path presented in Mahayana Buddhism and became a nun. In the mid-1960s, aware of the suffering experienced by the poor among native Taiwanese, she formed a small group that dedicated itself, in the tradition of the bodhisattva of compassion, Kuan Yin, to care first for their medical needs. With the passage of time, her group also worked to feed and house the poor. Today, Cheng Yen's foundation has attracted more than three million followers and, with support from overseas Chinese, has built hospitals and schools for the training of doctors and nurses.

KOREA

The institutional structure of the present-day Korean Buddhist establishment has its roots in the period of Japanese colonial rule. From 1910 to 1945 the Japanese forced the Korean clergy to break with Buddhist monastic practice and permit their clergy to marry, as the clergy already did in Japan. Although the Japanese succeeded in pressuring the Korean clergy into accepting this practice, with the end of World War II a small minority that had continued to follow the rule of celibacy called for a return to that ideal and eventually won the day. Hence, the so-called Chogye Order, which is based on Zen (Ch'an) teachings along with certain philosophical traditions and which accepts celibacy as the norm, has become the dominant group. The so-called T'aego Order, which includes the married clergy, is only a small minority. The nuns' community is also split along the same lines.

Although Christianity has been the fastest-growing religion in postwar Korea, Buddhism too is popular among many Koreans and appears to be growing. The monastic life in Korea, for nuns as well as monks, is demanding and involves serious study of Chinese and the sutras and adherence to a disciplined life within the monasteries. As is the case in Taiwan, the nuns in particular have become leaders in social welfare activities, caring for the elderly and looking after the poor, as well as working as teachers. Laywomen are also active at temples as *posals* (or bodhisattvas), who clean, assist in cooking and the like, and help in the instruction of other lay folk.

Buddhism and women are also brought together in the native Korean religious figure of the female shaman. Whereas the monks and nuns of the mainstream monasteries distance themselves from the practices of the shamans, the shamans in contrast have actively appropriated elements of the Buddhist tradition. In certain rituals the shaman invokes such celestial bodhisattvas as Avalokiteśvara and Bhaisajyaguru as well as other Buddhist saints. In her celestial travels she gains information about the state of the dead as they are believed to exist in various Buddhist purgatories, and she often leads them out of those hellish existences into a Buddhist Lotus Land. Just as the nunnery has provided women with a rare degree of autonomy in Korean society, so has the long-standing tradition of the female shaman, which, though independent of Buddhism in its origins, has drawn as it has seen fit from the Buddhist repertoire of saints, rituals, and teachings. At the local level the shaman is also most commonly concerned with the needs of women, serving both as counselor and healer.

JAPAN

Although rapid economic development and the increase in opportunities to enjoy the amenities of contemporary living have made the monastic life less appealing for the younger generation in all East Asian countries, this phenomenon is perhaps most apparent in Japan. The traditional monastic standard had already begun to disappear in the nineteenth century, when monks openly began to marry, but the trend toward the secularization of Japanese society proceeded with still greater speed in the twentieth century as Japan turned first to military expansion and then, in the postwar years, to economic growth. The possibility of entering the monastic life still exists in certain segments of the Buddhist community, but individuals choosing to take up that way of life are few. The number of young women

so inclined is especially small. Further, although the local Buddhist temple continues to function as the focus of religious and social activities for some laywomen, for most, contact with Buddhism comes chiefly at the time of some relative's or friend's funeral.

More than the traditional Buddhist sects, it has been the so-called new religions in Japan that have attracted the support of religiously active women. The earliest of the new religions first appeared in the mid-nineteenth century, but groups have continued to arise down to the present. The new religions tend to exhibit a shared cluster of traits, including charismatic leadership, syncretic teachings, the promise of concrete benefits (cures, the solution of family problems, wealth), and a critical stance toward the older, established forms of Japan's native religion, Shinto, and of Buddhism. Estimates of the number of people involved in the new religions varies widely; perhaps a quarter of Japan's population is associated with them in one way or another. Regardless of the actual number, however, it is clear that women have had prominent roles in the new religions. Reflecting the special access that women had to religious authority in premodern Japan as shamans, several of the new groups have been founded by women who exhibited shamanic qualities and, in virtually all of the new religions, women have constituted the majority membership.

The Reiyūkai (Society of Friends of the Spirits) and Risshō Kōseikai (Society for the Establishment of Righteousness and Fellowship) are examples of Buddhist-based movements that have been led by women. Kotani Kimi (1901–1971), cofounder with her brother-in-law of Reiyūkai, was born into a family of farmers, lost her father when she was a child, and helped her mother raise seven children and care for a sick father-in-law. After her marriage, her husband became ill and her brother-in-law urged her to embrace the teachings of the Lotus sutra, a central Mahayana Buddhist text, and to take up the practice of austerities. Kotani followed his advice and as a result was able to cure her husband. She then became an advocate for the power of the Lotus sutra. Naganuma Myōkō (1889–1957), cofounder of the Risshō Kōseikai with Niwano Nikkyō, also experienced hardships as a young person. Her mother died when she was six and she was raised by her mother's family. Her marriage ended in divorce, and while attempting to support herself as a single parent she lost a three-year-old daughter. She married again, but herself soon became ill. Devoting herself to Buddhism, and especially to the teachings based on the Lotus sutra and to the care of the poor and the sick, she came to be regarded by her followers as a "living Buddha."

Within such religious movements, women are also chiefly responsible for the day-to-day operations of the group and take on important roles as counselors and healers. In a society in which a woman's place has been, first and foremost, associated with the family, religious movements such as these have provided women with one of the relatively few accepted avenues to positions of public leadership and prestige. They have also provided structures through which women could join together to address issues of common concern.

BIBLIOGRAPHY

"Choice for a Chinese Woman: Enlightenment in a Buddhist Convent." Films for the Humanities, Inc., 1993.

Hardacre, Helen. *Lay Buddhism in Contemporary Japan.* 1984.

Ko, Hesung Chun. "Religion and Socialization of Women in Korea." In *Religion and the Family in East Asia.* Edited by George A. DeVos and Takao Sofue. 1984.

Lancaster, Lewis R. "Elite and Folk: Comments on the Two-Tiered Theory." In *Religion and the Family in East Asia.* Edited by George A. DeVos and Takao Sofue. Discusses the theme of elite and folk religious traditions with special attention to the Korean case.

"Pilgrimage, 1987: Pilgrimages to Tianzhu and Putuo." Videocassette directed by Chun-fang Yu. 1988. Covers pilgrimages to two Chinese sites associated with Kuan Yin.

Robinson, Richard H., and Willard L. Johnson. *The Buddhist Religion: A Historical Introduction.* 4th ed. 1997. Contains useful overviews of the contemporary Buddhist situation in several South, Southeast, and East Asian countries.

See also **Kuan Yin (Kannon).**

PAUL WATT

History of Study

The history of study of East Asian religions is complex and varied. Korea, Japan, and China each have a unique cultural and political history and relationship with the West. As a result of these separate histories, the religions chosen for study and the attitudes that formed toward these traditions have varied through the centuries, often illuminating the concerns of those investigating religious phenomena as much as the subjects they studied. Sustained contact between Europeans and East Asians began in the sixteenth century; due largely to China's geographical, political, and cultural domination of the region, the first centuries of study were almost exclusively focused on China.

The study of Chinese religious traditions from the sixteenth through the nineteenth centuries focused primarily on Confucianism, as religious Taoism and Buddhism were considered idolatrous and superstitious and therefore not worthy of scholarly attention. In the sixteenth through the eighteenth centuries Jesuit missionaries described Confucianism as the enlightened, rational ethic of imperial China, a notion eagerly embraced by Enlightenment thinkers in Europe, who saw China as an exemplar of a monarchy dissociated from religious bodies. Consideration of women in the study of Chinese religions was restricted mainly to their role within the paternalistic Confucian hierarchy. In the nineteenth century, after humiliating defeats at the hands of Western powers, Chinese civilization came to be viewed by Westerners as degenerate and weak. During this time the role of women in Confucianism was seen as proof of Chinese degeneracy because Confucian values legitimized practices considered debased, such as concubinage.

The study of the religions of Korea and Japan has flourished only since the mid-twentieth century. Early studies in the West on Korean religions reflected Korea's historical status as a tributary state of the Chinese Empire; it was only in the later part of the twentieth century that Korean studies emerged as a field in its own right. The first Western commentators on Japanese religions were Jesuit missionaries in the 1500s. However, the Seclusion Edict in 1639 almost entirely closed Japan to Western contact until 1853. The foundations of the modern study of Japanese religions were laid at the end of the nineteenth and early twentieth centuries by Westerners and by Japanese scholars inspired by Western methods of study; even so, critical study of Shinto was prohibited by the Japanese government from 1882 to 1945.

The twentieth century has seen a sea change in the study of East Asian religions. In the early part of the century, Paris-based scholars, notably Henri Maspero, began the study of religious Taoism. The Paris school has continued to be tremendously influential, and scholars such as Anna Seidel and Isabel Robinet have helped define the field of Taoist studies with their path-breaking work. Seidel's involvement with the monumental work on Buddhism, the *Hobogirin,* has also advanced the field of Buddhology. The study of Japanese religions has grown rapidly since World War II, with formative works exploring Japanese religious traditions as well as issues in the study of religion. Helen Hardacre and Carol Gluck, for example, have provided insights into important methodological issues as well as analysis of State Shinto.

In the late 1960s and early 1970s the focus of study began to include not only formal traditions but also popular and sectarian religions. This shift in subject matter necessitated a reevaluation of the role of women, who characteristically dominate the practices of these traditions. A number of prominent women scholars have been instrumental in opening new topics and pioneering fresh approaches of study. Hardacre's work on Japanese new religions elucidates the importance of these religious phenomena for women and the centrality of women in these groups. The emergence of the field of Korean studies has in large part coincided with the shift to a focus on folk traditions, in which women figure prominently. Anthropologist Laurel Kendall has researched the folk practices of female shamans and their place in Korean society. In Chinese religions the historians Susan Naquin and Patricia Ebrey have provided insight into sectarian groups and religion in daily life in imperial China.

As there has been a shift in topics of study, some methodological questions and debates have come to the forefront. There is debate as to whether the traditions of a culture should be viewed separately, as is customary in the West—with, for example, Shinto, Confucianism, Buddhism, and new religions designated as "Japanese religions"—or holistically, as the traditions are experienced by practitioners—that is, "Japanese religion." Another issue concerns Western models, which tend to favor doctrinal orientations, not a primary characteristic of most East Asian religions. Scholars have worked to develop ways to approach the liturgical and ritual focus of East Asian religions. Finally, as open discussion of women's concerns continues to grow in academia and the wider culture, the study of East Asian religious practices produces scholarship in previously unexamined areas, such as religious rites concerning abortion.

BIBLIOGRAPHY

A number of books examine important aspects of East Asian religious traditions. Carol Gluck's *Japan's Modern Myths* (1985) and Helen Hardacre's *Shinto and the State* (1989) are major contributions to the topic of State Shinto. Many works specifically address women and religion in East Asia. Patricia Ebrey's *Inner Quarters: Marriage and the Lives of Chinese Women in the Sung Period* (1993) pays particular attention to the role of women in Chinese society, including religion. Helen Hardacre's *Kurozumikyo and the New Religions of Japan* (1986) pays detailed attention to women in Japanese religion and the motivation and appeal of such religions for women. Hardacre's *Marketing the Menacing Fetus* (1997) addresses rites performed for aborted fetuses. Laurel Kendall's *Shamans, Housewives and Other Restless Spirits* (1985) examines the dichotomy between Korean women's roles in public com-

pared to that in the home, and the way in which their roles in religious practices bring status and power. Joseph Kitagawa includes a rich historical overview of the study of Japanese religions in his book *On Understanding Japanese Religion* (1987). Norman Girardot's article "Chinese Religion: History of Study" in *The Encyclopedia of Religion*, edited by Mircea Eliade (1987) is a superb, detailed overview of the subject.

JENNIFER OLDSTONE-MOORE

Ecofeminism

See Environmentalism

Economics

As Aristotle argued in his *Politics,* the well-being of androcentric society rested on the male citizen's control over his household, or *oikonomia.* This vision of political economy, which served as the fountainhead for ancient Hellenic and Roman societies, was predicated on the exploitation of women's labor. Physically women proved to be the means by which society produced and reproduced itself. Although the power of woman as mother and midwife was metaphorically appropriated by Hellenic philosophers in the "birth of ideas" (e.g., Plato, *Theaetetus*), women themselves were deemed inferior beings, deformed males who lacked souls and were good for only menial tasks (Aristotle, *On the Generation of Animals*). In ancient Hebrew society, women fared little better, being regarded in some respects as persons but in many more as chattel. A woman could, in limited circumstances, make religious vows, have a right to inheritance, or be entitled to maintenance by her husband and to the return of her marriage portion if divorced. But a woman's sexuality was regarded as the property interest of, first, her father who received a bride-price from the prospective groom, and, later, her husband (*ba'al,* master). A woman's barrenness or infidelity jeopardized the lineage and well-being of the paternal house.

Class distinctions during the Middle Ages in Western Europe divided women between those who fulfilled their feudal role by advancing the interests of the noble or gentried house through marriage, and those who labored as serfs. The doctrine of eucharistic transubstantiation—eating Christ's body and drinking his blood—echoed the role of women who, as the bearers and sustainers of new life, symbolized nourishment and re-

The socialist economist and political philosopher Karl Marx (1818–1883) with his wife (Hulton-Deutsch Collection/Corbis)

generation, that is, food itself. This imitation of Christ provided the means by which women could overcome the medieval teaching that stigmatized women as flesh and valorized men as spirit. If women regarded themselves as the food on which the patriarchal order thrived, then control over food was a means of asserting authority over their own lives and ascending to the spiritual realm. Hence, fasting was far more common among women mystics than among their male counterparts.

Founded on the normative claim of equality before the law, modern Western secular societies allegedly endorse the revolutionary promise of shattering the patriarchal order and liberating women from the domestic economy of the household. Yet, despite the first and second waves of feminism in the nineteenth and twentieth centuries, women have not reached economic parity with men, particularly in the United States, where

occupations are still largely gender-specific, "glass ceilings" still exist, and the movement for comparable worth has failed. In households where both women and their male partners work, studies show that fathers may be spending 20–30 percent more time with the children than they did twenty years ago, but women still contribute 200–300 percent more time than men in domestic tasks, particularly in preparing meals and attending to children's physical needs. The "feminization of poverty" within the United States, especially in minority communities, poses a difficult challenge to Western religious traditions—some of which call for the return of women to supposedly "traditional Biblical roles" and others who lobby the government to defend affirmative action and expand opportunities for women in a male-dominated society.

Whereas Western Christian societies, influenced by the Pauline "household code" (e.g., in Titus and 1 Timothy) traditionally limited a woman's activities to the immediate family, Islamic societies of the Middle East and indigenous societies of sub-Saharan Africa shaped women's roles in terms of the broader extended family or clan. A woman's sexuality was the property of the non-nuclear family rather than the husband alone; she was subordinate not only to her husband and male relatives but also to older women; and her productive and reproductive capacities served the clan as a whole. Polygyny entailed the segregation of women from the male world, but also gave women the opportunity to form a separate women's society which, in the transition from indigenous agrarian or herding societies to capitalism, provided a forum for resistance to European culture and religion. Likewise, among Central American indigenous peoples, such as the Maya, women's society insulated these groups from European-identified elites, such as the Ladino, and preserved traditional beliefs and customs.

Nonetheless, women's reproductive capacity serves a taxonomic function in both Western and non-Western societies as a repository for blood regimes and hence the distribution of wealth and property. Whether in India, China, or numerous other developing countries, a woman (as is said in Guyana) is "born with an acre of land between her legs." In traditional brahminic society, young brides are expected to produce ten children, resulting in their assignment to the domestic sphere and their exclusion from education. Yet, as the ground of the patriarchial order, the power to reproduce must be kept in check; hence, the wife is to treat her husband as a god and her marriage as a Vedically-sanctioned form of self-sacrifice, asceticism, and devotion. Likewise, in China where marriage is a union of two clans rather than of individuals, and the birth of a daughter is shameful, the feminine yin of Confucianism is identified with the inferior or weak and enforced through a discipline of obedience to father, husband, and son. In Hinduism, the image of the mother is marked by ambivalence: on the one hand, she is essential to the patriarchal scheme of the male householder; on the other, her very physicality symbolizes the material world (maya) repudiated by the Hindu ascetic. Although, unlike Hinduism, Buddhist doctrine permits women to follow the path of nonattachment, the scriptures portray women's bodies themselves as an impediment to enlightenment, which women could achieve only through transfiguration into male buddhas or bodhisattvas. As in the writings of such early church fathers as Jerome, a woman transcends her role as mother and domestic laborer by becoming "male"—a religious metaphor that has its secular analogue in contemporary economic developments.

BIBLIOGRAPHY

Alperin, Mimi. "The Feminization of Poverty." In *Women of Faith in Dialogue.* Edited by Virginia Ramey Mollenkott. 1987.

Bell, Rudolph M. *Holy Anorexia.* 1985.

Bynum, Caroline Walker. *Holy Feast and Holy Fast: The Religious Significance of Food to Medieval Women.* 1987.

Clark, Elizabeth. *Ascetic Piety and Women's Faith: Essays on Late Ancient Christianity.* 1986.

duBois, Page. *Sowing the Body: Psychoanalysis and Ancient Representations of Women.* 1991.

Haj, Samira. "Palestinian Women and Patriarchal Relations." *Signs* 17, no. 4 (Summer 1992): 761–778.

Hollinger, Dennis and Joseph Modica. "The Feminization of Poverty: Challenge for the Church." In *Envisioning the New City.* Edited by E. Myers. 1992.

Moore, Dwight, and Fred Leafgren, ed. *Men in Conflict.* 1990.

"Presbyterian Women Address the Feminization of Poverty [selected proceedings, Conference, Women and Economic Justice, Washington, DC, 1984]." Edited by Mildred McKee Brown and Sydney Thomson Brown. *Church and Society* 76, no. 3 (1986): 3–54.

Ruether, Rosemary Radford, ed. *Religion and Sexism: Images of Women in the Jewish and Christian Traditions.* 1974.

Schmidt, Elizabeth. "Patriarchy, Capitalism, and the Colonial State in Zimbabwe." *Signs* 16, no. 4 (Summer 1991): 732–756.

Sharma, Arvind, ed. *Women in World Religions.* 1987.

Smith, Carol A. "Race/Class/Gender Ideology in Guatemala." In *Women Out of Place.* Edited by Brackette F. Williams. 1996.

Starrels, Marjorie, Sally Bould, and Leon J. Nicholas. "The Feminization of Poverty in the United States: Gender, Race, Ethnicity and Family Factors." *Journal of Family Issues* 15, no. 4 (1994): 590–607.

Wagner, Judith Romney. *Chattel or Person? The Status of Women in the Mishnah.* 1988.

Williams, Brackette F. "A Race of Men, A Class of Women: Nation, Ethnicity, Gender, and Domesticity Among Afro-Guyanese." In *Women Out of Place.* Edited by Brackette F. Williams. 1996.

See also **Couples; Divorce; Fertility and Barrenness; Liberation Theologies; Marriage and Singleness: An Overview; Marxism.**

JAMES MCBRIDE

Eddy, Mary Baker

Mary Baker Eddy (1821–1910), is a rare phenomenon in American religious history: a woman who founded a new religion. She constructed the worldview, healing method, and form of governance of Christian Science, and ensured that her authority would persist after her death.

Eddy's limited education, chronic emotional and physical illnesses, early widowhood, poverty, dependence on relatives, and unhappy second marriage gave little evidence of her eventual prominence. Her illnesses began to diminish in 1866, when she experienced a spontaneous healing while reading the Bible after a serious fall. The central claim of Christian Science—that spirit is real and matter is ultimately illusion—evolved from her interpretation of this healing. Eddy spent the next nine years laying out the theological implications of her radical ontology and published them in 1875 as *Science and Health,* which she revised up to fifty times until the final version in 1910.

Eddy published several interpretations and defenses of Christian Science, among them *Christian Healing* (1880), *Christian Science: No and Yes* (1887), *Unity of Good and Unreality of Evil* (1888), and *Retrospection and Introspection* (1892). In 1895 she published the *Manual of the Mother Church,* by which the Church of Christ, Scientist is still governed, although, like *Science and Health,* it was revised again and again until her death. In 1908 she established the *Christian Science Monitor,* a highly regarded general newspaper, designed as a Christian Science response to public issues.

Eddy's personal eccentricities and authoritarianism, her controversies with former students, and the radical claims of her theology and healing method have made her easy to dismiss and ridicule. But she remains the most prominent woman in a long lineage of female metaphysical healers, many of whom were at one time her students. Her responses to major religious questions—What is God like? Why do we suffer?—offer insights into indigenous American alternative religions, and, in particular, one founded by a woman.

BIBLIOGRAPHY

Mary Baker Eddy's *Science and Health with Key to the Scriptures* (1910) and *Prose Works other than Science and Health* (1925) contain Eddy's major works. For a sympathetic but not uncritical biography (written by a Christian Scientist with access to Mother Church archives), see Robert Peel, *The Years of Discovery* (1966); *The Years of Trial* (1971); and *The Years of Authority* (1977). A classic criticism is Mark Twain's *Christian Science* (1907). Feminist interpretations of Eddy include:

Bednarowski, Mary Farrell. "Mary Baker Eddy and Theological Reform." In *American Reform and Reformers*. Edited by Randall M. Miller and Paul A. Cimbala. 1996.

Lindley, Susan Hill. "The Ambiguous Feminism of Mary Baker Eddy." *Journal of Religion* 64 (1984): 318–331.

McDonald, Jean A. "Mary Baker Eddy and the Nineteenth-Century 'Public' Woman: A Feminist Appraisal." *Journal of Feminist Studies in Religion* 2 (1986). 89–111.

MARY FARRELL BEDNAROWSKI

Education

Education and Literacy

The global history of education is characterized by large gender differences. While we know much about the education of women in modern times, it is more difficult to obtain concrete data on their education in earlier ages, especially in relation to religion. What did particular world religions contribute to the literacy and education of women? Traditional histories of religion, as well as histories of education, rarely provide much gender-specific information. No significant systematic study on the education of women in world religions exists, and this large topic remains such a thoroughly underresearched area that information has to be gleaned from widely scattered sources.

Literacy, the ability to read and write, presupposes not only the historical development of writing systems but also the existence of educational structures for the transmission from one generation to another of systematically gathered knowledge codified through writing.

Secular knowledge had its earliest origin in religion and was initially much influenced by religious world views. In stark contrast to the archaic, primal, and tribal religions of nonliterate societies, which transmitted their cumulative knowledge orally and produced no writings, the great historical religions all possess large bodies of sacred writings created by a male social and religious elite. Strongly institutionalized, these religions are mostly dualistic, hierarchical, and patriarchal, qualities that have worked to the general detriment of women and contributed to their relative deprivation from education.

In patriarchal, functionally differentiated religions with strong distinctions among members, women have generally not been part of official authority structures, and thus have usually not enjoyed the privileged access to education possessed by certain classes of men. Women's own religious experiences and practices, often distinct from those of men, have played little part in the creation of canonical sacred texts and their commentarial traditions, so important for all subsequent religious and theological thought. As women were almost universally excluded from access to the sacred scriptures, it followed that they were also mostly excluded from literacy and higher learning. The question then is whether women were excluded from access to sacred scriptures because they were thought to be inferior, or they were inferior because the scriptures said so, and therefore they could not gain access to knowledge deemed superior.

While this question remains ultimately unanswerable, it is generally true that women's access to education is directly related to whether they were allowed to learn to read and write. As Albertine Gaur (1984, p. 162) has stated: "Whenever the ability to write was associated with power and influence, women were, as a rule, excluded. There were no professional female scribes in Egypt or Mesopotamia. In Judaism and Islam the position of women was generally too low to allow them to tamper with the writing of the name of God, though this did not necessarily condemn them wholesale to illiteracy. Hinduism did. . . . Indeed until very recently the belief prevailed . . . that disaster would befall the family if a woman so much as held a book or pen in her hand."

In view of the vastness of the field, only a few selected comments on female education as it relates to several religions can be made here. In Indian religions, women had more access to religious knowledge and education in ancient times than during the medieval and early modern period (Altekar, 1987; Chaudhuri, 1982). Vedic texts mention that some learned women seers and poets, as women of higher castes, could study the Vedas under the guidance of a teacher or become teachers themselves. But it is doubtful whether their number were ever as great as men's. Some women learned to recite the Vedas, knew about Vedic rites, grammar, and other branches of study, and participated in various cultural activities, especially music and dancing (as is evident from classical Indian sculpture). But the Dharmashastras, especially the Laws of Manu (200 B.C.E.– 100 C.E.), later prohibited women from undertaking Vedic study and ritual, so that officially women could not perform any sacrifice, vow, or fast independently from their husbands.

During the nineteenth century Indian female education was first developed by Christian missionaries, especially the wives of Protestant missionaries. Hindu reformers, well aware that social reforms would not be effective without changing the status of women, soon championed women's access to education, supported by all the reform movements. The modern history of women's education in India is closely intertwined with the development of religious reform groups, such as the Brahmo and Arya Samaj, and with the history of the Indian women's movement.

The Pali canon of Buddhist scriptures also mentions several learned women who taught the Vinaya (rules on religious discipline). Buddhism acknowledges some distinguished women preachers and influential laywomen who were important patrons. Early Buddhist writings contain no reference to unmarried girls going to school or being educated at home, although educated women are known to have existed. This paradoxical situation highlights the relatively low status of women, for even when women acquired knowledge and learning, men did not consider it worth recording how they did so. Buddhist nuns have always held a lower status than monks and thus were largely confined to learning the rules of the order. Yet there are records of women engaged in learned debates with the Buddha himself, and the Pali canon contains the early Song of the Sisters, or Therigatha, which indicates a high level of learning among at least some women in early Buddhism.

In East Asia the most widely shared intellectual, ethical, and spiritual heritage has been that of Confucianism, which still prevails, at least in Korea and Japan, and to some extent also in modern China. Traditional Confucianism puts women in the same class as inferior men and slaves, and women's subordinate position within the patrilineal Confucian family has meant that girls' education prepared them largely for being good wives and mothers, with higher learning the prerogative of men. Although Confucianism always placed great value on learning, it had little to offer women, contributing to their oppression and victimization by restricting them to the private sphere of family life.

A woman teaches children to read from the Qur'an, Kabul, Afghanistan, 1995 (Baci/Corbis).

Confucianism did give women an esteem for learning, and some women from the upper strata of society were able to gain access to education. Best known is the famous Chinese woman scholar Pan Ch'ao (first century C.E.), the only woman ever appointed as a historian at the imperial court and author of several writings, including *Instructions for Women.* This treatise on education exerted a tremendous influence on Chinese women and later provided a model for other women writers. Yet Pan Ch'ao's plea to give girls the same education as boys received no support until the late twentieth century, when East Asian women finally entered into political and social activities effectively and in large numbers.

In ancient times Jewish women were know for their gifts of poetic expression, prophecy, and seership, as is evident from the Hebrew Bible. During most of Jewish history the education of girls was undertaken at home, and, in addition to domestic skills such as weaving, cooking, and midwifery, they were taught prayers,

Bible and Jewish law, which they would then follow for observance of holidays, dietary laws, mourning rituals, and so on. Women were exempted from the general religious duty of studying and teaching the Torah, excluded from reading the Torah aloud in synagogues, and could not become rabbis. Yet women knew the Hebrew prayerbook and often psalms and prophetic sections of the Bible better than did men. Reform Judaism has stressed the equality of women since the nineteenth century, and ordination of women is a development of the twentieth century. The secular education given to Jewish women—begun long before it was given to men—was, in fact, a gateway from traditional Judaism to the secular world and modernity.

In Islam, women were allowed to read the Qur'an but not to preach it. Although there is no prohibition on women's education, women were largely excluded from Muslim ritual and scholarship. There is relatively little known about the education of girls before the nineteenth century. Considerable variations among Muslim countries notwithstanding, whatever girls learned, they learned at home; they did not attend *madrasah*, the Qur'an school, as did their brothers. Muslim women enjoyed a higher position in Sufism than in orthodox Islam, and a number of Sufi *shaykhas*, or female spiritual leaders, were renowned for their preaching, spiritual guidance, and contribution to Islamic mysticism. Women also worked as calligraphers and excelled in copying the Qur'an all over the Islamic world.

In Christianity, too, although there has been no official prohibition of female literacy, women were largely barred from advanced education, and the leading positions of authority in church and state were closed to them. Yet women have made substantial contributions to Christian religious literature, especially during the Middle Ages, where we know of many European women writers, both religious and lay, such as Hildegard of Bingen, Margery Kempe or the Beguines. At a time when the church virtually held a monopoly over education, girls from aristocratic families were mostly educated in convents, but some laywomen also ran schools in cities, with mixed education for girls and boys.

We know of Christian women poets and mystics, of women troubadors, and of nun-scribes who pursued the art of copying and illustrating religious manuscripts. The education of women religious in convents was generally better than that received by men and women outside, but the higher grades of education were closed to women, apart from a few exceptions, until the late nineteenth century. Women's access to higher education, especially to religious learning and theology, has been a decisive factor in shaping the mod-ern women's movement. Women's access to theological education led to the struggle over women's access to the ordained ministry in Protestant churches, and also to the development of feminist theology, which could not have occurred without women becoming theologically literate and academically trained to the highest level.

Education and literacy are essential for gaining access to official positions of power and authority in the religions of the world. Scholarly writing and teaching on religion has been the prerogative almost solely of men, and to this day women have difficulty in gaining full recognition in this field. It was in mystical and devotional literature that women could freely express their own religious experience, although such expressions did not remain uncontested by male religious leaders, and sometimes cost women their lives, as was the case with Marguerite Porete. Today, with formal education open to women as well as men around the world, the traditional teachings of world religions may eventually become radically transformed.

BIBLIOGRAPHY

Altekar, Anant Sadashiv. *The Position of Women in Hindu Civilisation: From Prehistoric Times to the Present Day.* 1956. Reprint, 1987. A classic, often-cited study of the status and roles of Indian women from Vedic to modern times, with details on women's participation in sacrifices, the early access to sacred knowledge, and the later prohibition of such study. Also discusses women in Buddhism and Jainism.

Bosworth, C. E., E. van Donzel, B. Lewis, and C. Pellat, eds. *The Encyclopedia of Islam.* New ed. 1986. "Madrasa," vol. 5, pp. 1123–1134. A comprehensive discussion on Qur'anic instruction and Islamic studies in mosques that excludes women from its consideration.

Bowie, Fiona, Deborah Kirkwood, and Shirley Ardener, eds. *Women and Missions: Past and Present—Anthropological and Historical Perceptions.* 1993. Contains some interesting chapters on female Christian missionaries' contribution to the education of women in various countries.

Carmody, Denise L. *Women and World Religions.* Reprint, 1989. Widely used textbook surveying women in world religions, with some attention to their educational opportunities and attainments.

Chauduri, Nupur, and Margaret Strobel. *Western Women and Imperialism: Complicity and Resistance.* 1992. Contains several significant essays on the influence of colonialism on the education of indigenous women in India and Africa.

Chauduri, Roma. "Women's Education in Ancient India." In *Great Women of India.* Edited by Swami

Madhavananda and R. C. Majumdar. 1953. Reprint, 1982. Shows that women's education in ancient India was superior to what later became the norm in Indian society. Describes ancient Jains as especially progressive in opening religious education to women, which may be related to the fact that Jainism in its early days, before the arrival of Buddhism, had more women than men followers.

Chung, Edward Y. J. "Confucianism and Women in Modern Korea." In *The Annual Review of Women in World Religions,* vol. 3, 1994. Although mainly concerned with modern Korea, this well-annotated article contains much general information on women in Confucianism.

Falk, Nancy Auer. *Women and Religion in India: An Annotated Bibliography of Sources in English, 1975–92.* 1994. Contains many bibliographical references to women, religion, and education in various Indian religions, dealing with traditional teachings regarding the nature and duties of women, the opposition to women's education, and the impact of modern education on orthodox practices and social and political developments.

Ferrante, Joan M. "The Education of Women in the Middle Ages in Theory, Fact and Fantasy." In *Beyond Their Sex: Learned Women of the European Past.* Edited by Patricia H. Labalme. 1980. Discusses the complex developments of medieval education at a time when the Christian church held a monopoly over education and women in religious orders attained high levels of learning.

Gaur, Albertine. *The History of Writing.* 1984. A small but informative cross-cultural study with manuscript illustrations in color on the development of the art of writing, including information on women's participation in writing.

Kelleher, Theresa. "Confucianism." In *Women in World Religions.* Edited by Arvind Sharma. 1987. A helpful survey article on women in Confucianism.

King, Ursula. "World Religions, Women and Education." In *Comparative Education* 23, no. 1 (1987): 35–49. Raises general questions about the education of women and world religions and looks in particular at female education in Indian religions, Judaism and Islam, and Christianity.

Sakala, Carol. *Women of South Asia: A Guide to Resources.* 1980. Lists numerous works on all aspects of women's education in ancient and modern India.

Sharma, Arvind, ed. *Women in World Religions.* 1987. *Religion and Women.* 1994. Both works contain seven phenomenological studies on the position of women in world religions with occasional attention to literacy and education. They include material not easily found elsewhere on, among others, women in the Baha'i faith, Confucianism, Taoism, Jainism, Zoroastrianism, and Sikhism.

Willard, Charity C. *Christine de Pizan: Her Life and Works.* 1984. Considered a definitive biography of the first woman writer of the West who earned her living by her pen. Among her many writings are several treatises on education, which express Christine's progressive view on women's education, and literacy.

Wilson, Katharina M., ed. *Medieval Women Writers.* 1984. One of the first anthologies devoted to the writing of women in the Middle Ages dealing with diverse religious and secular topics. Contains the first Western treatise on education written by the ninth-century Carolingian laywoman Dhuoda.

Young, Serinity, ed. *An Anthology of Sacred Texts by and About Women.* 1994. This wide-ranging selection of historical and contemporary texts from world religions includes fascinating material from quite a few women authors. Their works provide powerful evidence of the rich religious worlds and experiences of women across time and from many places, indicating a high level of literacy and educational sophistication reached by at least some women in the past.

URSULA KING

Teaching Women and World Religions

Scholarly interest in the world's religions was awakened during the eighteenth century as the Enlightenment gave rise to a critical examination of both religion and theology. It was not until the 1870s, however, that the academic study of religion was recognized as an autonomous discipline and introduced into universities. Taught under the headings of history of religions and the comparative study of religion, this discipline was seen as providing an objective, nonconfessional approach to the study of humans as religious beings.

The purported neutrality of this approach was seriously challenged a century later when, in the early 1970s, women theologians and scholars of religion not only generated research that documented the androcentric bias of existing scholarship, but succeeded in persuading members of the American Academy of Religion to redress the imbalance by providing a venue for networking in the area of women and religion. The groundbreaking work of this network of scholars was soon complemented and supplemented by developments in the parallel field of women's, or feminist, studies, which likewise emerged in the early 1970s.

The encounter between these two fields in interdisciplinary, cross-cultural, woman-centered scholarship proved to be mutually enriching. On the one hand, those engaged in women's studies and the secular feminist movement who had been largely indifferent or hostile toward religion gradually came to recognize that they could not responsibly ignore the significant impact religion has on women's lives. Similarly, the study of women and religion was influenced by academic feminism to use gender, together with race and class, as primary categories of analysis.

To appreciate the scope and implications of this methodological shift, it is helpful to examine Peggy McIntosh's often-cited work, *Interactive Phases of Curricular Revision: A Feminist Perspective* (1983). Using gender as a category of analysis to determine how (or whether) women are presented in the curriculum, McIntosh uncovers five phases in the approach to historical studies that also apply to the teaching of world religions.

In the first phase, designated "womanless history," disciplines are defined solely in terms of what men think and achieve; although women are virtually excluded as historical subjects, their absence is not missed. For example, the Hindu life-cycle is routinely described solely in terms of what Hindu men do, despite the fact that the religious life-cycle of Hindu women is significantly different. Phase two attempts to correct this neglect of women's accomplishments by including references to heroines and other exceptional women, like Joan of Arc, Deborah, and Mahaprajapati, who qualify as historical subjects by virtue of playing roles similar to that of the great men of history. At this point, the contributions of ordinary women are overlooked and often hard to recover. As Bernadette Brooten, a scholar of early Christianity, has said, "The lack of sources on women is part of the history of women" (1985, p. 85). In the third phase, so-called "women's issues" come to the fore with studies focusing on women as a disadvantaged group seeking access to a man's world, church, mosque, temple, and so on. Although race, class, and gender are recognized as interlocking political phenomena, the analysis of the issues is still made from the perspective of those in power. For example, the question is asked whether women can be ordained instead of why were women excluded from ordination. The fourth phase marks a major paradigm shift away from an androcentric to a more inclusive model of scholarship, which the feminist scholar of religion Rita Gross (1996) terms the androgynous or bisexual approach. In this approach, female and male scholars work to transform rather than reform the study of religion as well as the disciplines of history, psychology, anthropology, sociology, and philosophy, on which the study of religion relies. This is accomplished by exploring the actual lives and thoughts of women, since these

are often richer and more diverse than standard texts, myths, and notions of what is female or feminine. Included in the study of women's experiences would be personal and historical accounts of what it means to live in a female body. When applied to the study of women in the world's religions, this approach reveals that, in actual practice, the range of options for women is linked to their education and social location and often differs from the ideals set down for them in traditional religious texts. Finally, the anticipated fifth phase envisages a gender-balanced portrait of the world's religions that includes the stories and perspectives of us all, women and men.

Complementing these curricular developments, feminist pedagogy can be distinguished by its commitment to empower all students by helping them see and describe the impact that androcentric and patriarchal traditions have had on the lives of women and men, past and present; by inspiring students to reflect on how their own social positioning influences their views on women and religion; by fostering communities of learners who become involved with such pressing issues as spirituality, social justice, ecology, and interreligious dialogue, as well as the problems of sexism, heterosexism, racism, classism, and ethnocentrism; and by preparing them to participate in shaping the symbol systems and social structures that promote equality among human beings and respect for the ecosystems that sustain us.

Like the growing network of religious feminists who are transforming the societies and religious traditions to which they belong, the number of feminist scholars of religion has reached a critical mass that is not only changing the way women are studied in the world's religions, but transforming the way religions themselves are being conceived. By providing comprehensive feminist deconstructions and reconstructions of Christian, Jewish, and Buddhist religions, pioneers like Rosemary Radford Ruether (1983), Judith Plaskow (1990), and Rita Gross (1993), respectively, are laying the foundations for the study of postpatriarchal forms of the world's religions and theologies.

BIBLIOGRAPHY

BOOKS

Brooten, Bernadette. "Early Christians and Their Cultural Context: Issues of Method in Historical Reconstruction." In *Feminist Perspectives on Biblical Scholarship.* Edited by Adela Yarbro Collins. 1985.
Carmody, Denise Lardner. *Women and World Religions.* 1979; rev. ed., 1989.
Christ, Carol P., and Judith Plaskow, eds. *Womanspirit Rising: A Feminist Reader.* 1979; rev. ed., 1992.

Clark, Elizabeth A., and Herbert Richardson, eds. *Women and Religion: The Original Sourcebook of Women in Christian Thought.* 1977; expanded 1996.

Cooey, Paula M., William R. Eakin, and Jay B. McDaniel, eds. *After Patriarchy: Feminist Transformations of World Religions.* 1991.

Falk, Nancy A., and Rita M. Gross. *Unspoken Worlds: Women's Religious Lives.* 1980; 2d ed., 1989.

Gross, Rita M. *Buddhism After Patriarchy.* 1993.

———. *Feminism and Religion: An Introduction.* 1996.

Hohm, Jean, with John Bowker, eds. *Women in Religion.* 1994.

King, Ursula, ed. *Women in the World's Religions: Past and Present.* 1987.

Kyung, Chung Hyun. *Struggle to Be Sun Again.* 1990.

Plaskow, Judith. *Standing Again at Sinai: Judaism from a Feminist Perspective.* 1990.

Ruether, Rosemary Radford. *Sexism and God-Talk: Toward a Feminist Theology.* 1983.

Sharma, Arvind, ed. *Religion and Women.* 1994.

———. *Today's Woman in World Religions.* 1994.

———. *Women in World Religions.* 1987.

Young, Serinity, ed. *An Anthology of Sacred Texts By and About Women.* 1993.

VIDEOS AND CD-ROMS

"The Burning Times." Directed by Donna Read. Direct Cinema Ltd.; Studio D, National Film Board of Canada, 1990. Discusses legends and misconceptions regarding the term *witch;* also church- and state-sanctioned torture and killing of women during witch-burning times. Explores the history, repression, and resurgence of the women's spirituality movement.

"Discovering the Feminine." Directed by John Swindells. More than Illusion Films, Sydney, Australia, 1993. After a stroke, Father Bede Griffiths experienced a remarkable transformation. He discusses with humility and humor his understanding of love, nonduality, and the feminine aspects of life.

"Fighting Back." Directed by Bill Jersey. PBS Video, Alexandria, VA, 1992. Part of a series on fundamentalist movements in various religions. This episode focuses on fundamentalism in Christianity, with good excerpts on the role of women.

"Full Circle." Directed by Donna Read. A coproduction of the Great Atlantic and Pacific Film Company and the National Film Board of Canada, Ontario Centre, 1993. Explores the history and present practices of goddess religions. Authors, social activists, and teachers describe spirituality and the rituals that give them strength to transform their personal belief into political and social action, advocating a reverence for the earth.

"Half the Kingdom." Directed by Francine E. Zuckerman and Roushell N. Goldstein. Kol Ishah Productions, Inc. in coproduction with the National Film Board of Canada, 1990. American, Canadian, and Israeli women talk about their struggle to redefine their roles in Jewish life and attempt to incorporate feminist values into their religion.

"Mother Wove the Morning." Written and performed by Carol Lynn Pearson. Walnut Creek, CA, 1992. A powerful look at sixteen women throughout history, including a paleolithic woman, an Egyptian priestess, a Biblical woman, a Gnostic woman, a medieval witch, a Shaker deaconess, and others whose lives dramatize the search for God the Mother.

"On Common Ground: World Religions in America." Diana L. Eck and the Pluralism Project at Harvard University. New York, NY: Columbia University Press, 1997. A CD-Rom that explores the history, beliefs, and current practices of fifteen religious traditions in the United States.

"Remaking the World." Directed by Steve York. PBS Video, Alexandria, VA, 1992. Part of a series on fundamentalist movements in various religions. This episode focuses on fundamentalism in Islam, with a useful section on preaching about women.

"Woman and Islam." Directed by Mahmood Jamal. Films for the Humanities, Inc., Princeton, NJ, 1994. Leila Ahmed, professor of women's studies at Amherst, argues the case for revision of the Islamic world's widely held views about the role of women. She explains the origin of the veil and discusses the issue of marriage and women's rights within marriage.

JUDITH G. MARTIN

Egg

Cultures from the Middle East to Asia tell creation myths that describe a cosmic egg which hatches to form the universe.

In an ancient Indian text, the Rig Veda (1200–900 B.C.E.), the creator of the world is said to be the Golden Embryo Hiranyagarbha, which arose in the beginning. Later commentators on this Sanskrit passage suggest that the creator god "possessed" the golden seed or egg, or that the golden egg existed within his belly like an embryo. The Chandogya Upanishad (700–500 B.C.E.), a later Indian text, describes the beginning of creation as an egg that developed out of nonexistence. This egg split, forming from the silver half the earth, and from the gold half the heavens.

Christian communities celebrate Christ's resurrection by exchanging decorated Easter eggs like the ones pictured above painted by Ukrainian-American women and girls (Jim Sugar Photography/Corbis).

An early Egyptian manuscript (1569–1085 B.C.E.) refers to a world egg emerging from primeval waters. Several Egyptian gods were then associated with this cosmic egg, but as in the texts of other cultures, no female deities were connected with it. Although creation myths of different cultures use the image of a cosmic egg, the production and nurturance of this egg rarely involves a female presence. In most cultures, the texts stress the role of either a male deity or specifically asexual elements of nature.

In religious rituals and mythology, eggs are used as symbols of life and fertility. The Jewish feast of Passover, commemorating the Exodus from Egypt, customarily begins with a hard-boiled egg as a symbol of fertility and survival. After returning from a family member's funeral, Jewish mourners are commonly given an egg to eat, as a symbol of renewed life.

Christian communities celebrate the resurrection of Christ on Easter Sunday and during the subsequent Easter Week by exchanging decorated Easter eggs among friends and relatives. In anticipation of the regeneration promised by the Feast of Easter, on the fourth Sunday in Lent (Laetare Sunday), Christian households in some parts of Germany decorate an "egg tree" in their garden. In some European countries, eggs are also exchanged between betrothed couples and their families at Easter, in order to promote fertility for the soon-to-be-married couple. Women are responsible for the cooking and decorating of these Easter eggs, in keeping with their role of providing nurturance through food. However, women do not play a significant role in the ritual celebration of these religious festivals.

In some cultures, eggs are used in funeral and burial rituals. The Maoris of New Zealand place an egg in the hand of the corpse, and certain hill tribes in northeast India place an egg in the navel of a corpse. Such customs reflect the concern of the mourners to effect an auspicious rebirth for the person being buried or cremated.

Because of the association in nature of eggs with the fertility and brooding of the hen, one might expect a strong ritual association of eggs with women. But only rarely is such an association indicated. As in the creation myths of the cosmic egg, most religious rituals involving the egg, such as those performed at Easter and Passover, as well as those funeral rites performed among some communities in India and New Zealand, involve no particular explicit association with women. The egg repeatedly represents the resurgence of new life, both physically and spiritually, but without any special reference to women in either the performance of the ritual or in the symbology of the tradition. Even rituals that expressly use eggs to ensure many children for a newly married couple, or to ease childbirth, emphasize the powerful and auspicious quality of the egg rather than any association with the female of the species, either fowl or human.

BIBLIOGRAPHY

Basham, A. L. *The Wonder That Was India.* 1959.
Monkey. Translated by Arthur Waley. 1943.
Newall, Venetia. *An Egg at Easter: A Folklore Study.* 1971.
The Rig Veda: An Anthology. Translated and annotated by Wendy Doniger O'Flaherty. 1981.
Upanisads. Translated by Patrick Olivelle. 1996.

See also **Birth and Rebirth; Fertility and Barrenness; Mourning and Death Rites.**

CATHERINE BENTON

Eliade, Mircea

Romanian-born Mircea Eliade (1907–1986), one of the most influential figures in the academic study of religion in the latter half of the twentieth century, spent several impressionable years in India (1928–1931) and the most important years of his scholarly career in Paris (1945–1955) and in Chicago (1955–1986). More than any other figure, he could be credited with shifting the focus in the study of religion from Christian theology to the phenomenology of religion. His discussions of symbol, myth, and ritual were especially important to this shift.

Nevertheless, his published works contributed greatly to the pervasive androcentrism of religious studies before the rise of feminist scholarship in the late 1960s and early 1970s. Like so many others, his theoretical and linguistic styles fostered the impression that humanity consists of only one relevant sex—men—and their objects of interest and curiosity—women, not two sexes, women and men. His books are filled with the construct *homo religiosus* or "religious man." The construct *homo religiosus* has now received a great deal of criticism for its essentialism and universalism, but since it is a model or a type, rather than an empirically existing individual, *homo religiosus* would have to be a universal, a platonic form of the type so out of favor today. Much more serious is the fact that *homo religiosus* is clearly a universal of the male gender, with all of the limitations and ambiguity attendant on any generic masculine terminology. Most of the time, Eliade writes about women as symbols to *homo religiosus*, rather than as real people. For example, in his famous and influential phenomenology of religion, *Patterns in Comparative Religion* (1963), "woman" is discussed as a symbol after discussions of the symbolism of the sun, the moon, the waters, sacred stones, and the earth but before vegetation, sacred places, and sacred time. When Eliade does, infrequently, write about women as real people, it is because their behavior represents a special case that does not fit his general descriptions or theories. In a notable early work, *Rites and Symbols of Initiation: The Mysteries of Birth and Rebirth* (1958), women's initiations, which deviate from the model of male initiations that he has constructed throughout the book, are dealt with in seven pages. In this book, Eliade claims that female initiations are determined by "natural" events, such as menstruation and childbirth, in contrast to male initiations, which belong, "not to the natural world, but to culture" (p. 47). The cultural choice to interpret female biology as a sacred symbol is overlooked in this common androcentric claim that "male is to female as culture is to nature."

Although Eliade never overcame the androcentrism of his own methodology, in some later works he did devote more attention to women's rituals and female symbolism, as in his study of Australian aboriginal religion, published in book form in 1973 as *Australian Religions: An Introduction*. His most noteworthy contribution to women's studies in religion involved his supportive mentoring of some of the early pioneers studying women and religion and his public endorsement of some important early discussions of women's religious lives.

BIBLIOGRAPHY

Cave, David. *Mircea Eliade's Vision for a New Humanism.* 1993.

Eliade, Mircea. *Cosmos and History: The Myth of the Eternal Return.* 1954, 1959.

———. *A History of Religious Ideas.* Vols. 1–3. 1978, 1982, and 1985.

———. *Patterns in Comparative Religion.* 1958, 1963.

———. *The Sacred and the Profane: The Nature of Religion.* 1957, 1959.

See also **Phenomenology of Religion.**

RITA M. GROSS

Elisabeth of Schönau

Christian nun and visionary Elisabeth of Schönau (1128 or 1129–1164 or 1165) entered at the age of twelve the monastery at Schönau, a community of Benedictine monks and nuns in the Rhineland, and eleven years later began to have visionary experiences. Elisabeth confided these visions to other nuns of Schönau, and then to her brother Ekbert who, in 1155, entered the monastery and became her secretary. Ekbert transcribed Elisabeth's words, discussed with her the contents of her visions, sought revelations from her about topics of interest to himself, suppressed what he feared would not be edifying to her audience, and wrote introductions to her various works. Thus the texts that record her visions are the product of a complex collaborative relationship shaped by Elisabeth's power as female visionary and Ekbert's power as learned male secretary who believed in her visions.

Elisabeth's experiences are described in three visionary diaries as well as texts on the various paths of the Christian life, the martyrdom of Saint Ursula and her companions, and the bodily resurrection of the Virgin Mary. In these works, Elisabeth proclaimed her condemnation of a corrupt church, reshaped images of female holiness (that of Mary, of the Ursuline martyrs, and of herself as visionary devotee), and offered a vision of salvation and the means to gain it. These works were widely copied in the later Middle Ages, attesting to the interest in Elisabeth's attempt to articulate her experience of divine intervention in her life and her understanding of herself as messenger of divine revelation.

BIBLIOGRAPHY

Clark, Anne L. *Elisabeth of Schönau: A Twelfth-Century Visionary.* 1992.

Roth, F. W. E., ed. *Die Visionen der hl. Elisabeth und die Schriften der Aebte Ekbert und Emecho von Schönau.* 1884.

ANNE L. CLARK

Elizabeth of Hungary

Elizabeth of Hungary (1207–1231) was a canonized bene-factor of the poor and exponent of the poverty move-ment. The daughter of Count Berthold IV of Andechs-Merania, she arrived at age four at the Wartburg, the court of Hermann I of Thuringia, to whose son Ludwig she had been betrothed as a child for dynastic reasons. As an adult she criticized the mundane life at court and, following the spiritual counsel of her confessor, Conrad of Marburg, adopted a life of poverty and humbleness which she led with utmost severity. Ludwig trusted and supported her. After his death in the crusade of 1227, Elizabeth left the Wartburg together with her three children. In Marburg she founded a hospital dedicated to Francis of Assisi in which she lived as a *soror in saeculo* (lay sister), serving the needy as a poor woman in Christ with no regard to her noble descent. She died in November 1231 of physical exhaustion.

Elizabeth of Hungary in a fourteenth-century Italian painting by Ambrogio Lorenzetti (Corbis-Bettmann)

At the instigation of her brother-in-law Conrad, the master of the Teutonic Order, she was canonized on 27 May 1235 by Pope Gregory IX, who compared her to Francis of Assisi. On 1 May 1236, in the presence of Holy Roman emperor Frederick II, her body was trans-ferred to the not yet completed church of St. Elizabeth at Marburg. Elizabeth is venerated by the faithful as a benefactor of the poor and characterized by historians as one of the foremost female exponents of the poverty movement of the thirteenth century.

BIBLIOGRAPHY

Werner, M. *Mater Hassiae; Flos Ungariae; Gloria Teu-toniae.* In *Politik und Heiligenverehrung im Hochmit-telalter* (*Vorträge und Forschungen* 42). Edited by J. Jetersohn. Sigmaringen, 1994

KASPAR ELM

Emotion

Emotion affects us both physically and mentally. The Latin root of the word *emotion* connotes action and movement. It is juxtaposed to cognitive and volitional consciousness and thereby represents a mental feeling or affection. Reason and emotion are construed as op-posites. It is then but a small step to cast emotion as a weak and negative surrender to feelings and passions.

Religion is frequently associated with emotion by both supporters and detractors. Supporters find the uniqueness of religious expression in profound emo-tional attachment and demonstration. Detractors make the claim that understanding religion is difficult be-cause religion is emotional, not cognitive and reason-able. Both women and minorities are seen by many to favor emotional religious practices.

Religious ritual can be seen as emotive change. The emotional transformation of consciousness in ritual profoundly affects the practitioner. In modern witch-craft, emotion is seen as the vehicle of magical change. Europe in the Middle Ages represented women as weak in their will and ruled by emotion (Fausto-Ster-ling, 1992). This, combined with bodily weakness and sexual desire, makes them easy prey for the Devil. The Furies, ancient female fertility figures of Greek reli-gion, represent irrational and emotional elements. In Aeschylus's *Eumenides,* they are subdued by the virgin goddess Athena who uses her "masculine" logic to con-vince the Furies to calm their passions and renounce their behavior.

In *Generation of Animals* Aristotle stated that men and women have different understandings of temper-

Two members of the family of Pai de Santo (High Priest) Antonio Pereira, in a Candomblé trance ceremony, evoke several deities, or Orixas, and allow them to take over their bodies, Salvador, Brazil, 1985 (Stephanie Maze/Corbis).

ance, courage, and justice, and that courage in a woman is expressed by obedience, making her what he calls a natural slave. For him, women are inferior because they can apprehend rationality but not possess it. Women are material, of the body as animals are, and ruled by emotion. For Aristotle, therefore, as the soul rules the body and the mind rules the passions, so too men, because of their superior natures, rule women.

In contradistinction to the German philosopher Immanuel Kant (1724–1804), who saw reason as the source of morality, the ethics of the Scottish philosopher David Hume (1711–1776) derived from the capacity for sympathy or fellow-feeling and was based ultimately on sentiment and the overcoming of conflicting emotions. In a reaction against the Enlightenment's overdependence on the power of reason, Friedrich Schleiermacher's German Romanticism of the early 1800s tended to identify woman as possessing more ap-

titude for emotion; she therefore becomes a more complete religious being than man, who was seen as imbalanced by rationality. Schleiermacher's belief that the true person is whole, encompassing both female and male aspects, was echoed in Carl Jung's later works.

Psychology is divided as to the role of emotion in gender. Love, fear, and compassion are traditionally assigned to the female, but the pejorative charge of emotionalism is common. Freudian theory supports this charge; Jungian theory, on the other hand, complicates the view of both male and female. Jung states that a male experiences his deep unconscious, or soul, in a feminine archetypal form, the anima, and that the female experiences her unconscious in a masculine archetypal form, the animus. Ann Ulanov and others dispute this association of the animus with the female, arguing that the woman experiences her own deep unconscious soul in a feminine archetypal form as well.

Polarities of male and female are common in both Eastern and Western conceptions. In Chinese theory the cosmos is divided into the feminine, yin, energy and the masculine, yang, energy; these energies are present everywhere. Yin is described as weak, dark, passive, and yielding, and is predominant in the female. Yang is strong, light, aggressive, and firm, and is predominant in the male. That the yin is equal with the yang is crucial. Jung based much of his theory in this notion of distinct but equal energies.

Emotion is identified in Western thought particularly with women, and reason with men. Carol Gilligan and several other feminist theorists have argued that rationality and objectivity are indeed male qualities, whereas Mary Field Belenky and others have argued for a specifically feminist rationality distinct from male reason. The compellingly familiar opposition of emotion to reason appears to be a Western dichotomy, but in fact this bifurcation of consciousness takes place cross-culturally (Harre, 1986). The Japanese Neo-Confucians, who also link the female with the yin energy and thus cast women as sensitive and petty, propose the cultivation of yang energy in the mind as a remedy.

In Chinese medicine excessive emotion is thought to be dangerous not only to a woman but to the fetus she carries. To be moved by emotions like passion and anger is to risk a pathological "fire" that endangers the fetus. This "fetal poison" is transferred to the mother's milk and thus continues to affect the newborn child (Harre, 1986).

Indian aesthetic theory focuses not on plot or character but on emotion. Through the concept of *rasa*—flavor, mood, or emotion—the sentiments of all humans are united and transcend the particulars. According to the treatise on dramaturgy by the first-century C.E. aesthetician Bharata, the universalization and abstraction of emotion are achieved through its expression in art, and it is this universal emotion that the person responds to. Human emotions are divided into nine *rasas* (flavors): love, humor, pathos, violence, heroism, fear, loathsomeness, wonder, and quietude. Thirty-three transitory feelings accompany them.

Generally Buddhists follow Hindus in their conclusion that women cannot control their passions. In order to become a Buddha, a woman must first be reborn as a man. To accomplish this she must control her excess emotions, which are her hallmark, in this life, and then "she will not be bound to the limitations of a woman's state of mind" (Gross, 1993). By contrast, Vajrayana Buddhism of Tibet states that emotions are energy that is in itself neutral and becomes negative or positive depending on the degree of insight with which they are experienced. The emotions themselves always contain wisdom, and one must work through the negativity or positivity of the emotions to find this wisdom.

A traditionally feminine emotion, compassion, is raised in Buddhism to the status of the ideal and embodied in the bodhisattva or savior figure. Through this emotion all lives are linked; Buddhists cultivate caring as a religious act. In Confucian religious conduct a traditionally feminine emotion, benevolence, is seen as the seat of virtuous action (Klein, 1986). The Confucian *Classic of Filial Piety* states that the feelings of love and affection for one's parents begin in childhood. By cultivating this loving emotion the person can extend this benevolence to become the foundation of the other Confucian virtues. David Hume also saw familial love as the basis for morality and developed his ethics from the central bond of family love.

Many contemporary feminist ethicists who criticize the conventional dichotomy of intellect and emotions and the inferior status of emotions are examining the positive role of emotions in being and knowing (Kittay and Meyers, 1987). They are developing a morality that is based on caring and functioning with emotion. Emotion flows through the channels of the mind, enlivening, making connections and distinctions. The rigid dichotomy of intellect and emotion is based on the distrust of the motion of the mind. Unfeeling intellect blocks the flow, and undirected emotion floods the mind. As the river flows, emotion simply is.

BIBLIOGRAPHY

Aristotle. *Generation of Animals.* Translated by A. L. Peck. 1943. This translation gives Aristotle's views of conception as well as the nature of women in general and serves as the basis for much of his later thought.

Belenky, Mary Field. *Women's Ways of Knowing: The Development of Self, Voice, and Mind.* 1986. Studies the use of emotion in development.

Clark, Elizabeth, and Herbert Richardson. *Women and Religion: A Feminist Sourcebook of Christian Thought.* 1977. Traces the development of perceptions about women; many selections describe changing attitudes toward women's emotions.

Fausto-Sterling, Anne. *Myths of Gender: Biological Theories About Women and Men.* 1992. Shows how biological variation led to theories of gender differences.

Gilligan, Carol. *In a Different Voice: Psychological Theory and Women's Development.* 1982. Presents a discussion of ethics, emotion, and relational thinking.

Gross, Rita M. *Buddhism After Patriarchy: A Feminist History, Analysis, and Reconstruction of Buddhism.* 1993. A detailed source for the discussion of emotions in Buddhist thinking.

Harre, Rom, ed. *The Social Construction of Emotions.* 1986. Cross-cultural analysis of the construction of emotions and the effects on women.

Kittay, Eva Feder, and Diana T. Meyers, eds. *Women and Moral Theory.* 1987. Essays based on a care perspective morality.

Klein, Ann. "Gain or Drain?: Buddhist and Feminist Views on Compassion." *Women and Buddhism: A Special Issue of the Spring Wind Buddhist Cultural Forum* 6 (1986): 105–116. A discussion of the cultivation of emotion for Buddhist religious advancement.

Lerner, Harriet G. *The Dance of Anger.* 1985. Focuses on the positive and negative effects of one turbulent emotion.

Schleiermacher, Friedrich. *Speeches on Religion and Christmas Eve.* Translated by T. Rice. 1967. Early work said by theologian Karl Barth to show his preoccupation with the nature of women and their religious propensity.

Ulanov, Ann Belford. *The Feminine in Jungian Psychology and in Christian Theology.* 1971. A discussion of the female, in both theological and psychological contexts, that poses a challenge to Jungian views.

See also **Furies**; **Jung, Carl**; **Romanticism**; **Yin/Yang Polarity**.

LINDA L. LAM-EASTON

Emptiness

Emptiness refers to the nature of reality as defined in Mahayana Buddhism and the Buddhist understanding that all things lack or are "empty" of inherent existence and an intrinsic, enduring self. Throughout Buddhist history, the term *emptiness* or *śūnya* has been the subject of numerous philosophical, doctrinal, and polemical debates. Emptiness accrued significance as a key doctrinal concept with the rise of early Mahayana Buddhist schools in India around the first century B.C.E. Emptiness, an innovation and expansion of the earlier Buddhist concept of *anātman* (no-self), implies all dharmas (phenomena) are subject to change and devoid of enduring characteristics. Understanding the significance of emptiness enabled nuns, monks, and lay practitioners to free themselves from attachment to the self (the cause of suffering) and strive for enlightenment. Since Buddhists throughout history have understood emptiness as a lack of self-substantial reality and as a lack of distinction between all phenomena, emptiness can potentially serve as an egalitarian doctrine and Buddhist critique of gender.

In the collection of Buddhist texts known as the *Perfection of Wisdom Sutras*, emptiness is associated with the bodhisattva path to enlightenment, which involves the direct perception of the emptiness of all phenomena. This cognition enables the bodhisattva to cultivate and practice compassion for all sentient beings without regard for distinctions. Through meritorious actions, the bodhisattva generates "seeds of virtue" that mature into the mind of enlightenment (*bodhicitta*). In the *Perfection of Wisdom in Eight Thousand Lines*, wisdom is symbolized as the Mother of the Buddhas. As the Mother of the Buddhas, perfection lays the foundation for the subsequent enlightenment (or birth) of the Buddhas. Buddhas, like good children, are said to protect and worship her, for, as their mother, she reveals wisdom and shows them reality as it truly is—empty.

The association of female symbols with emptiness can also be found in other Mahayana texts such as the *Lotus Sutra* and the *Holy Teaching of Vimalakirti*. Both sutras employ the image of gender and sex-changes from female to male and male to female to teach the significance of emptiness. While these sources lend themselves to the potential to view emptiness as an egalitarian symbol and concept, there are two important factors for consideration. First, like all symbols and concepts, emptiness is subject to a variety of interpretations; therefore, one cannot assume that positive or negative symbols of emptiness valorizing the feminine apply to all Buddhists. Furthermore, while the concept of emptiness has been equated with female roles such as motherhood in sutras like the Perfection of Wisdom, the texts use of symbols or ideals of femininity are problematic when automatically assumed to imply equality for all. While the *Perfection of Wisdom* urges its readers to treat the sutra as their mother and generative matrix of the Buddhas, the fact remains that throughout Buddhist history, many women have considered motherhood and the pressures of childrearing as a hindrance to their own enlightenment. Such texts can be seen to uphold and even reinforce motherhood at the expense of other possible avenues for women. What appears are idealized conceptualizations of motherhood that do not necessarily refer to real women. Rather, the texts envision a male subjectivity and urge their readers to treat the texts reverentially as they would treat their own mother. This abstraction creates an idealized image of motherhood which may, paradoxically, not even be available to women, for women were still depicted in much Mahayana Buddhist literature as weak, inferior, or polluted. The above examples serve to caution against positing an overall egalitarian principle onto the concept of emptiness, for texts dedicated to elucidating emptiness equate the feminine only with motherhood, and motherhood is then equated with an "ethics of care" to be taken up primarily by men. The use of female-based imagery or gender ambiguity to clarify the concept of emptiness should not be automatically equated with a Buddhist critique of gender, for interpretations of emptiness have varied in quite complex manners throughout the Buddhist world and should, therefore, be approached according to time and place.

BIBLIOGRAPHY

Allione, Tsultrim. *Women of Wisdom.* 1984.

Cabezón, José. "Mother Wisdom, Father Love." In *Buddhism, Sexuality and Gender.* 1992.

Cooey, Paula M. "Emptiness, Otherness and Identity: A Feminist Perspective." *Journal of Feminist Studies in Religion* 6 (1990): 7–23.

Gross, Rita. *Buddhism After Patriarchy.* 1992.

Huntington, C.W., Jr. *The Emptiness of Emptiness: An Introduction to Early Indian Madhyamaka.* 1989.

Keyes, Charles. "Ambiguous Gender: Male Initiation in a Northern Thai Buddhist Society." In *Gender and Religion: On the Complexity of Symbols.* Edited by Caroline Walker Bynum. 1986.

Klein, Anne Carolyn. *Meeting the Great Bliss Queen: Buddhists, Feminists, and the Art of the Self.* 1995.

———. "Primordial Purity and Everyday Life: Exalted Female Symbols and the Women of Tibet." In *Immaculate and Powerful: The Female in Sacred Image and Social Reality.* Edited by Clarissa Atkinson, Constance Buchanan, and Margaret Miles. 1985.

Levering, Miriam L. "The Dragon Girl and the Abbess of Mo-Shan: Gender and Status in the Ch'an Buddhist Tradition." *Journal of the International Association of Buddhist Studies* 5, no. 1 (1982): 19–35.

———. "Lin-chi (Rinzai) Ch'an and Gender: The Rhetoric of Equality and the Rhetoric of Heroism." In *Buddhism, Sexuality and Gender.* 1992.

Napper, Elizabeth. *Dependent Arising and Emptiness.* 1989.

Paul, Diana. *Women in Buddhism.* 1985.

Sangren, P. Steven. "Female Gender in Chinese Religious Symbols: Kuan-yin, Ma Tsu and the 'Eternal Mother'." *Signs* (Autumn 1993).

Streng, Frederick. *Emptiness: A Study in Religious Meaning.* 1967.

Willis, Janice D. *Feminine Ground: Essays on Women and Tibet.* 1987.

See also Buddhas, Bodhisattvas, and Arhats; Compassion.

SHARON A. SUH

Environmentalism

Environmentalism involves defense of the value of nature. Environmentalists identify ecological degradation as a serious problem and seek in diverse ways to remedy it. The roots of this stance are ancient, stretching back, for example, to Plato's concerns in the Critias about soil erosion and deforestation in fourth-century b.c.e. Greece. Its present form dates from the 1960s, when humans began to realize they could cause permanent and worldwide ecological damage. An important catalyst to the contemporary environmental movement was the 1962 publication of Silent Spring by marine biological Rachel Carson. Carson spoke out against the dangers of insecticides in one of the first books to predict and document the pending ecological crisis.

Within traditions of faith, religious thinkers have a long-standing interest in the relation of nature to humanity and the divine. Debates on the significance of religion for environmentalism took off with Lynn White, Jr.'s highly influential and oft-cited article, "The Historical Roots of Our Ecological Crisis" (*Science* 155 [March 1967]: 1203–1207). White argued that the Western Christian worldview was responsible for much of the ecological crisis; he criticized the idea that nature is separate from us and that God intended for us to dominate it (from Genesis 1:28, in what became known as the dominion thesis). Scholars of religion responded with lively discussion on whether his assessment of Christianity was fair and whether other traditions (Asian, tribal) might have concepts of nature from which Westerners could learn.

Before the widespread advent of feminist scholarship in the 1970s and 1980s, environmentalism paid little attention to issues of gender. With the development of ecofeminism, however, such work blossomed into a vibrant and fast-growing field. Ecofeminism—the term was coined in 1974 by Françoise d'Eaubonne in *Le féminisme ou la mort* (Feminism or Death)—melds environmentalism with feminism. Ecofeminists identify gender as a central metaphor in Western constructions of nature-culture relations and see gender analysis as a key to understanding and healing these relations. The ways we think about and treat women, they argue, are related to the ways we think about and treat nature. Common roots in patriarchy relate misogyny to the domination of nature. Both are forms of hierarchical dualism and oppression whereby patriarchy claims the male as superior to the female and humans as superior to nature. Along with their focus on theoretical analysis, ecofeminists are also praxis-oriented activists interested in antinuclear protests, vegetarianism, animal rights, women's and children's health, birth control, and development issues. Ecofeminism intersects with the study of religion in at least two ways, which themselves overlap. Because environmentalism is an interdisciplinary endeavor, it draws widely on ethics, philosophy, theology, comparative religion, ecology, history, feminism, gender theory, and more.

First, ecofeminists critique religion on the criteria of whether it supports practices and beliefs that are environmentally sound and liberating for women. They identify aspects of religious tradition that devalue nature and the female, often in ways that conflate the two. Leading ecofeminist theologian Rosemary Radford Ruether, for example, critiques tendencies within the history of Christianity to place both woman and nature in the category of the other, the inferior, the dangerous, the sensual realm of temptation to sin (*Gaia and God: An Ecofeminist Theology of Earth Healing*, 1992). Anthropologist Sherry Ortner framed this problem in a ground-breaking 1974 article, "Is Female to Male as Nature Is to Culture?" (in *Woman, Culture, and Society*, edited by Michelle Zimbalist Rosaldo and Louise Lamphere. Ortner argued that women are cross-culturally seen as closer to nature than men and that this view accounts for women's universal subordination, since nature is itself universally devalued. Ecofeminists further developed the argument: in patriarchy, women are perceived to merge with nature as servile resource, lacking in full subjectivity. Similarly, nature is perceived as female, as virgin resource or bountiful mother, sharing in woman's semihuman quality. Ecofeminists here reject the cultural association of nature and the female. They see it as objectifying women, reinforcing their traditional exclusion from public realms of culture, and burdening them with a presumption of natural fitness to a housekeeping role of cleaning up the planetary mess men make and cannot be expected to clean up themselves. Religious roots of environmental degradation are traced also to cosmological shifts from animistic to mechanical models of nature during the Scientific Revolution and to a theological agenda behind the quest for control of nature as part of a "return to Eden"; these themes are developed in the influential historical analyses of Carolyn Merchant (*The Death of Nature: Women, Ecology, and the Scientific Revolution*, 1980; *Earthcare: Women and the Environment*, 1996).

Second, ecofeminists transform religion in ways both reformist and revolutionary. Some remain within traditional frameworks and draw on religious resources to formulate an environmental ethic and practice environmentally sound spirituality. The main anthology in environmentalism and the feminist study of religion (*Ecofeminism and the Sacred*, edited by Carol J. Adams, 1993) develops such Jewish, Christian, Buddhist, and Hindu "ecotheologies" to guide the religious lives of women and men. Other ecofeminists find traditional religion irredeemably patriarchal and move outside it to create new religious movements. They revive past traditions of viewing the earth as sacred and revering goddesses associated with nature, such as Gaia, Demeter, or the Great Mother. They develop syncretistic nature-based spiritualities of neopaganism and feminist witchcraft (see, e.g., Carol P. Christ, *Laughter of Aphrodite: Reflections on a Journey to the Goddess*, 1987, and Starhawk, *The Spiral Dance: A Rebirth of the Ancient Religion of the Great Goddess*, 1979). Some draw on archaeology and paleoanthropology to construct inspirational visions of prehistoric Old European religion and society as peaceful, in harmony with nature, Goddess-worshiping, and matrifocal. These ecofeminists view positively the association of nature and the female. Within a postpatriarchal value system in which nature, women, and mothers are accorded high value, they reclaim the association and embrace it as empowering. Mother Nature imagery expresses for them the deep connection women share with nature and celebrates the oneness of women's fertility with that of the earth.

Within the field of women and religion, environmentalism is thus a political stance guiding ethics and activism, an interpretive tool for feminist analysis of religion, and a powerful factor in the spirituality of many women.

BIBLIOGRAPHY

Much ecofeminist writing is contained in anthologies:

Caldecott, Leonie, and Stephanie Leland, eds. *Reclaim the Earth: Women Speak Out for Life on Earth*. 1983.

Diamond, Irene, and Gloria Orenstein, eds. *Reweaving the World: The Emergence of Ecofeminism*. 1990.

Gaard, Greta, ed. *Ecofeminism: Women, Animals, Nature*. 1993.

Plant, Judith, ed. *Healing the Wounds: The Promise of Ecofeminism*. 1989.

Ruether, Rosemary Radford, ed. *Women Healing Earth: Third World Women on Ecology, Feminism, and Religion*. 1996.

Warren, Karen, ed. *Ecological Feminist Philosophies*. 1996.

Some other important works include:

Christ, Carol P. *Rebirth of the Goddess: Lending Meaning in Feminist Spirituality*. 1997.

Dinnerstein, Dorothy. *The Mermaid and the Minotaur: Sexual Arrangements and Human Malaise*. 1976.

Gimbutas, Marija. *The Goddesses and Gods of Old Europe*. 2d ed. 1982.

Gray, Elizabeth Dodson. *Green Paradise Lost*. 1979. Reprint, 1981.

Griffin, Susan. *Woman and Nature: The Roaring Inside Her*. 1978.

Sjöö, Monica, and Barbara Mor. *The Great Cosmic Mother: Rediscovering the Religion of the Earth*. 1987.

CATHERINE M. ROACH

Epistemology

Epistemology is the study of the method and ground of knowledge, a near synonym of the theory of knowledge. In this traditional perspective, opinion, belief, imagination, and faith are kept separate from knowledge; the need to determine principles or criteria of justification leads to a foregrounding of the cultural determination of knowledge, as perceptual, inferential, and linguistic understanding modify both its definition and justification. In the study of religion, perceptual understanding relates to ontology, inference structures theology, and language grounds textual hermeneutics and epistemology itself.

Michel Foucault's work is central to a contemporary understanding of the historicocultural characters of epistemology. He defined *episteme* as the condition of possibility of the recognition of knowledge (*The Order of Things*, X), indicating that understanding and valorization are relative to cultural settings, and that the "sciences of man" are part of the modern episteme. Foucault's work, in spite of his patriarchal language and concerns, is valuable to feminists because he displaces the very questions defining traditional epistemology ("what is knowing and the known?") by the notion of episteme. Inasmuch as the episteme accommodates human sciences, empowering them to "construct man as their object," women's ways of knowing also belong to the contemporary episteme, empowering the inscription of "women" as the constructed object of culturally acknowledged "human/woman sciences."

By the beginning of the seventeenth century, religion had become the object of a human science, since the connection of metaphysics, ethics, and science no longer articulated an episteme of absolute monolithic truth.

Therefore, any modern definition of religion necessarily reflects the worldview of those who articulate it. The difficulty of defining categories to interpret religious facts is visible in the patriarchal acknowledgement of the disruption of realities, resisted also by feminist scholars of religion: for feminists, categorical "weakness" becomes an epistemological strength. The Kantian ideal of "ethical community," the Bergsonian critique of the linguistic articulation of morality and religion, the romantic inheritance of the analysis of symbol creation are reinterpreted within a feminist constructionist epistemology that stresses "the 'time- boundedness' and 'linguisticity' of historical knowledge" (Schüssler Fiorenza, 1984, p 142). This awareness results in the feminist recognition of the "epistemological privilege of the oppressed," who have an unfettered view of cultural hegemonies, and in the valorization of the category of difference in race/ethnicity/ sexuality.

The universalizability of epistemology is called into question by a feminist critique of dichotomies, in which patriarchal terms eclipse feminist ones not only in ethics but also in theology, placing a god over a goddess (Ruether's critique of the dualistic hierarchical mentality that informs Western thought, Daly, Goldenberg). Feminist epistemology cannot acknowledge the positivistic textual scholarship of academic theology because it would forfeit the object of its concern: women's religious past and heritage and the experiences of women as knowledge producers.

Feminist religious epistemology implies the centrality of experience as both object and category, but without turning it into a universal: "There is probably no universal 'women's experience,' but only the experience of women in particular societies and particular social groups" (Plaskow, 1979, p. 47). Epistemologically crucial is the distinction between meaning and reference, not only in reinterpreting religious tradition— "the Torah is not just history, . . . but also living memory" (Plaskow, 1989, p. 39)—but also in revising the theology of creation, based on the epistemological results of different ontological specifications (Daly, Schüssler Fiorenza). Feminist conceptions of a general order of existence can be expressed by retheorizing body, mind, and emotion, often through literary language, while resisting women's invisibility and showing the powerful connection of language and reality.

BIBLIOGRAPHY

Bergson, Henry. *The Two Sources of Morality and Religion.* Translated by R. Ashley Audra and Cloudesley Brereton, with W. Horsfall Carter. 1935.
Christ, Carol P., and Judith Plaskow, eds. *Weaving the Visions: Patterns in Feminist Spirituality.* 1989.
———. *Womanspirit Rising.* 1979.
Daly, Mary. *Beyond God the Father.* 1973.
Foucault, Michel. *Les mots et les choses.* Paris, 1966. (Translated by the author as *The Order of Things: An Archaeology of the Human Sciences.* 1970.)
Goldenberg, Naomi. *The Changing of the Gods.* 1979.
Heschel, Susannah, ed. *How Feminism Is Transforming Judaism.* 1982.
Kant, Immanuel. *Religion Within the Limits of Reason Alone* [1793]. Translated with introduction and notes by Theodore M. Greene and Hoyt H. Hudson. 1960.
Olson, Carl, ed. *The Book of the Goddess: Past and Present.* 1985.
Plaskow, Judith E. "Sex, Sin and Grace: Women's Experience and the Theologies of Reinhold Niebuhr and Paul Tillich." Ph.D. diss., Yale University, 1975.
Ruether, Rosemary Radford. *Sexism and God-Talk.* 1983.
Schüssler Fiorenza, Elisabeth. *Bread Not Stone.* 1984.

CARLA LOCATELLI

Esotericism

Modern scholarship has attempted—notably in the writings of René Guénon, Jacob Needleman, and Antoine Faivre—to define esoteric spirituality and to distinguish esoteric movements, teachings, and traditions from general trends in mysticism. In many respects esoteric spirituality can be regarded as a more specialized case and subset of the trends and phenomena of mysticism. The term *esoteric* is derived from the Greek *eso:* "within," "inside," or "inner." Esoteric teachings and traditions are often seen by adherents as the inner aspect of exoteric traditions: thus, Sufism in Islam; the alchemical, hermetic, and kabbalistic teachings in Jewish and Christian traditions of Renaissance Europe; and the tantric lineages of Buddhism and Hinduism. Additionally, these inner traditions are initiatory in nature, emphasize the oral transmission of knowledge, assume some form of prayer, contemplative, or ascetic practice, and recognize the necessity of a teacher or spiritual guide in some form for this transmission. Because of these features, esoteric movements are often viewed as "secret" or hidden within the life of greater traditions. Finally, in defining the nature of esoteric spirituality, the inner aspect must also refer to the inner life or inner experience of its followers.

All esoteric teachings seem to hold the principle in common that the differences that appear in the world are only apparent, the result of a limited dualistic consciousness that constructs our view of the world along subject-object dichotomies, while the ultimate reality of the world is nondual. Esotericism seeks to acquire an all-encompassing vision or consciousness that discovers the harmony and unity in diversity, a view that transcends duality and eliminates the basis for difference and hierarchy. In this light, the differences between male and female are only aspects of conventional reality and the construction of hierarchies, and perceived limitations based on gender are merely conventional and without basis, even though conventional and ultimate reality pervade each other in nondualistic thought. Esoteric teachings thus resist the objectification of difference based on gender and the gender biases that arise from the architecture of the dualistic view. Evidence of this resistance is sometimes awkwardly expressed in ancient sources: "every woman who will make herself male will enter the kingdom of heaven" (*The Gospel of Thomas*); the hagiographer of Rabi'a, the great Sufi saint, said that she was "clearly superior to men, and that is why she was also named 'the Crown of Men' "; and in the proto-tantric Buddhist text, the *Vimalakīrtinirdeśa*, a long discussion of nondualism culminates in a debate between a goddess and a monk of patriarchal persuasion—the goddess demonstrates the ultimate emptiness of gender by magically transforming the monk into a female form and herself into a male form, reminding "him" that the Buddha proclaimed that in all things "there is neither male nor female." The tendency to relativize conventional views of gender is also embraced by male adepts of esotericism as indicated in the poetry of Vīraśaiva yogins like Basavaṇṇa ("sometimes I am man/sometimes I am woman") and Devāra Dāsimayya ("the self that hovers/in between/is neither man/nor woman"). It would appear that understanding and acceptance that followed from nondualistic views contributed to the equality and greater opportunity enjoyed by women in esoteric teachings.

Evidence of esoteric traditions can be found in several ancient sources. In the West the communities that formed around the figure of Pythagoras included both men and women in equality and attributed some texts to women. Although little is known of the Platonic Academy, and scholars continue to debate whether or not Plato possessed an "unwritten teaching" (that is, an oral tradition outside of his writings, as indicated by Aristotle in *Physics*, 209b15), the general equality of women and men in the pursuit of wisdom and the philosophical life is recognized in Plato's *Republic*, in which the utopian community would recognize and acknowledge the transformation and being of its most elite members, both men and women. In Plato's dialogue on love, the *Symposium*, Socrates identifies a woman, Diotima, as his teacher. The status of women in the mysterious Jewish sect of the Essenes remains unresolved, while the discovery of gnostic texts has reopened the question of women in early Christianity. In a fragment titled "The Gospel of Mary," for example, Mary is asked to recall the words of the Savior since he loved her "more than the rest of women." The gospel also indicates certain gender hostilities as Peter and Andrew doubt the truth of her recitation, although Mary and her account are defended by other men.

The seemingly unrelenting patriarchy of brahminical society in Indian antiquity could be questioned in light of certain Upanishadic passages, notably in the *Brihadāranyaka Upanishad,* in which the great Vedic sage Yājñavalya is portrayed as providing the hidden teachings and entering into spirited exchange with two women, Maitreyī, one of Yājñavalkya's two wives, and Gārgī. In the esoteric schools of Indo-Tibetan Buddhism, there is clear evidence that women (often wives of great gurus or teachers) were respected as extraordinary adepts, *yoginīs* and gurus in their own right. Many of the great tantric sages, as in the case of Maitrīpa, were said to have been taught by women. But as Miranda Shaw (1994) has suggested, even though the participation of women in tantric lineages was full and unrestricted, and despite abundant spiritual biographies and numerous hymns, poems, and songs attributed to women, it remains a difficult if not impossible task to uncover the precise nature of their contribution, linking specific practices and teachings with specific women.

In modern times the influence of women on esoteric spirituality remains profound. Annemarie Schimmel (1997) has noted that some of the most genuine modern representatives of the Sufi tradition in Istanbul and Delhi are women who exert a strong influence upon smaller and larger groups, both in the great city-centers and beyond. In modern thought a new, more complete and sympathetic view has begun to emerge of the central importance of women in the life and ongoing transmission of esoteric teachings. This is due in part to the convergence of feminist thought and scholarship (including critiques of patriarchal orders), the changing status of women in Western culture, and the appearance in the West in the nineteenth and twentieth centuries of esoteric forms of thought and practice with Eastern roots. Although the modes of expression and interest have varied, Western women have been central to the dissemination of Eastern esoteric ideas and practice and to the revitalization of esotericism in the modern world. Extraordinary examples abound: H. P. Blavatsky, founder of the modern theosophical movement; Alexandra David-Neel, whose books chronicle the fourteen years in which she lived and studied with Buddhist teachers in Tibet; and Lizelle Reymond, who worked closely with Śrī Anirvan in the foothills of the Himalayas until he sent her back to the West in search of others who had embraced new forms of esoteric teachings.

BIBLIOGRAPHY

Faivre, Antoine, and Jacob Needleman. *Modern Esoteric Spirituality.* 1992.

Klein, Anne Carolyn. *Meeting the Great Bliss Queen: Buddhists, Feminists, and the Art of the Self.* 1995.

Ramanujan, A. K. *Speaking of Śiva.* 1973.

Shaw, Miranda. *Passionate Enlightenment: Women in Tantric Buddhism.* 1994.

Smith, Margaret. *Rabi'a the Mystic, and Her Fellow Saints in Islam.* 1928; reprint, 1984.

Schimmel, Annemarie. *My Soul Is a Woman: The Feminine in Islam.* 1997.

See also Diotima; Dualism; Mysticism; Occultism; Rabi'a; Theosophy.

STUART SMITHERS

Essentialism

The concept of essence has been an important and contested notion in many Western philosophical systems. While its meaning has varied from thinker to thinker, it has generally been the term that has expressed what is taken to be the identifying element in some object or concept. The essence of something lies in its distinguishing characteristics, nature, or invariant elements that identify something as what it uniquely is.

When the quest for essences or intrinsic natures has been applied to women, it has attempted to identify what is the same in all women across time and space. Essentialist assumptions have characterized both conservative perspectives and feminist orientations. The former have often located essential female nature in biology and have used these claims to argue for differences in nature, roles, and societal position between men and women. Feminist theorists, including theologians, often offered their own version of essentialism in the appeal to women's experience, positing that women's experience had a universal or widely shared character that could be identified. That commonality was located in a variety of places including a distinctive female biology, similar experiences of oppression, and a common form of critical consciousness. Feminist thinkers utilized these notions of common experience not to restrict women's role and place but to argue for a normative perspective from which to challenge the traditional situation of women and transform it.

Since the 1980s there has been a widespread negative reaction to essentialist renderings of women's nature and experience. Increasingly women have raised the issue of what and who are left out when women are identified by virtue of assumed commonalities. Women of color have been especially strong in their criticism of white women's appeal to a common experience that they believe masks the differences among women and often hides the role some women have played in the oppression of other women and men of less power. There is now an intense effort to rethink women's identity in a manner that respects differences, identifies conflicts, and still provides the ground for broad-based action on behalf of women. This exploration of female identity and subjectivity may well be the most central issue confronting feminist thought at the close of the twentieth century.

BIBLIOGRAPHY

Davaney, Sheila Greeve. "The Limits of the Appeal to Women's Experience." In *Shaping New Vision: Gender and Values in American Culture.* Edited by Clarissa W. Atkinson, Constance H. Buchanan, and Margaret Miles. 1987.

Ferguson, Kathy E. *The Man Question: Visions of Subjectivity in Feminist Theology.* 1993.

Fulkerson, Mary McClintock. *Changing the Subject: Women's Discourses and Feminist Theology.* 1994.

Grant, Jacquelyn. *White Women's Christ and Black Women's Jesus: Feminist Christology and Womanist Responses.* 1989.

Guha, Ranajit, and Gayatri Chakravorty Spivak, eds. *Selected Subaltern Studies.* 1988.

Hogan, Linda. *From Women's Experience to Feminist Theology.* 1995.

Mohanty, Chandra Talpade, Ann Russo, and Lourdes Torres, eds. *Third World Women and the Politics of Feminism.* 1991.

Moraga, Cherríe, and Gloria Anzaldúa, eds. *This Bridge Called My Back: Writings by Radical Women of Color.* 1983.

Spelman, Elizabeth. *Inessential Woman: Problems of Exclusion in Feminist Thought.* 1988.

See also Deconstruction; Femininity; Genre and Gender; Theology: Feminist Theology; Women's Studies.

SHEILA DAVANEY

Esther

According to the Biblical book named for her, Esther is a Jewish woman who becomes the queen of the Persian king Ahasuerus (Xerxes I) and then, along with her cousin Mordecai, works to undermine the plot of the

Esther. Print, Philip de Bay, c. 1802 (Historical Picture Archive/Corbis)

king's vizier Haman to kill all the Jews. The Jewish festival of Purim commemorates these events.

Esther is not an unambiguous heroine. She first comes to Ahasuerus's court with other beautiful virgins, all gathered by the king to audition as the replacement for the banished Queen Vashti. Esther wins the favor of the eunuch who oversees these virgins and, following his advice, eventually secures the favor of Ahasuerus as well. Esther also during this time remains in contact with Mordecai and, the text stresses, obedient to him (Esther 2:20). At this point in the narrative, Esther seems to rely on men to guide her actions.

Esther continues to rely on men, and especially Mordecai, as Haman issues his decree condemning the Jews. For example, it is Mordecai who instructs her to make supplication to the king to save the Jewish people. Yet as the supplication proper begins, Esther appears more independent. Without specific advice from Mordecai, she persuades the king to execute Haman and elevate Mordecai in his place. Moreover, despite Mordecai's new role as vizier, it is really Esther who

becomes the power behind the throne. Indeed, by the end of the book, it is the command of Queen Esther alone that establishes the practices of Purim (Esther 9:32).

BIBLIOGRAPHY

Niditch, Susan. "Short Stories: The Book of Esther and the Theme of Woman as a Civilizing Force." In *Old Testament Interpretation: Past, Present, and Future: Essays in Honor of Gene M. Tucker.* Edited by J. L. Mays, D. L. Petersen, and K. H. Richards. 1995.

White, Sidnie A. "Esther." In *The Women's Bible Commentary.* Edited by C. A. Newsom and S. H. Ringe. 1992.

———. "Esther: A Feminine Model for the Jewish Diaspora." In *Gender and Difference in Ancient Israel.* Edited by P. L. Day. 1989.

SUSAN ACKERMAN

Ethics

An Overview

Ethics asks the questions: What is the right act, the good human moral gesture, and what makes it so? What is the meaning and the making of a good life? How is justice best achieved among competing moral appeals? Who ought I to be, and how ought I to treat others, and what are the criteria for knowing such things? In so doing, the discipline of ethics spans two distinctive academic fields of inquiry: philosophy (analytic and moral philosophy) and religious studies (social ethics). As a discipline it engages the insights and observations of sociology, anthropology, linguistics, psychology, and political theory in its description of the phenomena of society; in its normative capacity ethics is an applied theory for the practice of medicine (bioethics) and the conduct of research, business, and political action. Ethics is a discipline that seeks logically to justify choices for right behavior, rules, and activities, particularly in situations that challenge established norms of behavior or require new paradigms for judging behavior. Metaethics evaluates how it is that we can know and speak of such abstract theories.

Ethics, in evaluating the moral gestures that make up human activity, traditionally assumed that humans are rational actors, capable of pre- and post-reflective accounts of their action, and that they can give coherent linguistic justifications for their actions. Ethics as a discipline relies on sociability, accountability, conscience, and rationality. The capacity for speech, for rational justification, and for community are thus prerequisites of ethics. But such a set of assumptions has been under increasing scrutiny. Can a single standard for goodness, rightness of action, or even of evaluative criteria be constructed in a world understood as profoundly diverse? If cultures are constituted and constructed in large part by their complex and differing understandings of what goodness can be, and if we understand the depth of cultural relativism, how can we share a common understanding of ethics? Can there be agreement, if not on the principles or the definitions of good action, then agreement on the rules of engagement of the question, a "common language of ethics"? It is this understanding of ethics as essentially methodological that distinguishes it from morality, rules of proper conduct, or descriptions of cultural norms (Robb, 1985).

TRADITIONAL METHODS OF ETHICS

Ethical inquiry, in looking at any gesture and in constructing a "moral sentence" that can interpret and reflect upon it ("that is a good action," "this is a fair trade"), traditionally has evaluated and centralized one of three elements of action: the moral agent and its character, the motive for the gesture itself, or the effect of the action on others. The varieties of methods emerge at specific historical periods and are shaped by culture, class, and gender of the theorists who defend the methods but are nonetheless useful as starting places in defining the academic field.

Methodology in ethics varies as the culture shifts its emphasis and telos. Specific historical periods privilege different understandings of the nature of the self and the construction of power and its justification. Methods in ethics, of course, are shaped by the social location of the agents who use the method, by class, ethnicity, and by gender, but beginning with an understanding of method allows us to turn to the central arguments for good and right action as they are reflected in the traditional source texts.

Virtue theory, the study of what "excellences" of character are necessary prerequisites for the achievement of a good life, was first developed by the Greek philosophic tradition, notably the Socratic and Aristotelian schools. As such, the virtues described as good and the metaphors used include those that would tend to make a successful, heroicized aristocrat: courage (as in battle), loyalty, and civic friendship. Aristotle argued that the achievement of a good life included the selection of a role model and asking oneself how such a model would act in the situation before one. Also central to Greek ethics, and to all virtue theory, is the idea that habitual actions themselves shape character. Later

Christian theorists, notably Aquinas, expand the virtue theory to include the necessity for compassion, merging the Greek ideal philosophic type with the aspirational goal of acting as Jesus would act.

Deontological ethics is the study of rules, arguments, and motives for behavior. This method makes the claim that certain invariable qualities of the human person and hence of the social contracts that person constructs require rules, obligation, and duties to act well. Fulfilling these duties defines and decides ethical dilemmas. Jewish tradition, with its textual emphasis on a life commanded and obligated to commandment, is one variant of this method. At stake in this method are the duties that lie behind the moral gesture itself. Such duties can be based in God's law ("the yoke of the Kingdom of Heaven," in rabbinic text) or in later understandings of essential categorical imperatives that emerge in any interaction (for example, Immanuel Kant's categorical imperative never to lie, or in an obligation never to use a fellow person as a mere means to an end). Deontological thinking draws heavily on the premise that human persons have rights that cannot be abrogated despite necessity.

Consequentialism is the method of ethics based most classically in the nineteenth-century utilitarian philosophic tradition. The argument for this method is the account of the effect of moral action on the outcome of the act itself. Consequentialists can be act-accountable, or seek more general rules of utility, but what will matter most in the reflection and evaluation of the moral gesture is the future. In contrast to deontological theories—which are rooted in the past, in commitments, essential obligations, or promises—consequentialist thinkers argue for assessment of right action to spring from the emerging and shifting possibilities that the action will create. In this theory the concept of rights is more tenuous, and freedoms depend on the outcome for the general good, or the good for the greatest number (John Stuart Mill), or the avoidance of harm to most (Toulmin, 1981).

CHALLENGES TO THE TRADITION

Such classical historical categories have been significantly challenged. Both the expanding understandings of religion and culture and an inclusivity and attention to feminist insights have been central to the development of the field. Modernity, scientific inquiry, and cultural acuity have focused the attention in ethics toward the particular Other and to the relationship between the self, a particular context, and a particular Other. Religious theorists, such as Emmanuel Levinas (1985) and Stanley Hauerwas (1981), have questioned whether there can be any absolute pole of moral worth apart from a faith in a divine order, command, or Being. Feminists and others have questioned the freighting of theoretical rationality in the tradition, noting the term implies relationships of alliances, power, and expertise that have traditionally marginalized women, emotive or intuitive reflection, and practical wisdom rooted in lived experience.

Ethicists who work in the fields of bioethics and legal or business ethics have attempted to create consensus in broad policy documents, often supported by public civic bodies, or to create principles that could guide future decisions. Still others, such as Selya Benhabib (1990), have focused on how to create ideal speech situations, processes, and methods in which the significant differences that shape our constructs of goodness and rightness could be fully explored, focusing on our ability to speak together rather than to seek a priori principles of conduct.

BIBLIOGRAPHY

Of the many classic sources, readers should consider: Aristotle, *Nicomachean Ethics;* Plato's *Republic;* Thomas Aquinas, *On Politics and Ethics;* Maimonides, *A Guide to the Perplexed;* David Hume, *An Inquiry Concerning the Principles of Morals* (1777; 1978); Immanuel Kant, *Groundwork of the Metaphysics of Morals* (1785; 1990); and John Stuart Mill, *On Liberty,* (1859; 1971). For an understanding of ethical arguments, see Carol Gilligan, *In a Different Voice* (1982); John Rawls, *A Theory of Justice* (1971); and Michael Walzer, *Spheres of Justice* (1983). Alasdair MacIntyre, *A Short History of Ethics* (1966) is a good summary of major arguments, as is Karen LeBacqz, *Six Theories of Justice* (1986). For current debate, see *Hypatia: A Journal of Feminist Philosophy.*

WORK BY WOMEN INCLUDES:

Benhabib, Selya. "Communicative Ethics and Current Controversies in Practical Philosophy." In *The Communicative Ethics Controversy.* Edited by Seyla Benhabib and Fred Dallmayr. 1990.
Code, Lorraine. *What Can She Know?* 1991.
Farley, Margaret. *Personal Commitments.* 1986.
Frazer, Elizabeth, Jennifer Hornsby, and Sabina Lovibond. *Ethics: A Feminist Reader.* 1992.
Gatens, Moira. *Imaginary Bodies: Ethics, Power, and Corporeality.* 1996.
Hirshmann, Nancy. *Rethinking Obligation.* 1992.
Kittay, Eva Feder, and Diana T. Meyers, eds. *Women and Moral Theory.* 1987.
Okin, Susan. *Justice, Gender and the Family.* 1989.
Robb, Carol, ed. "A Framework for Feminist Ethics." In *Women's Consciousness: Women's Conscience: A Reader in Feminist Ethics.* Edited by Barbara Hilkert Andolsen, Christine E. Gudorf, and Mary D. Pellauer. 1985.
———. *Making the Connections.* 1985.
Zoloth-Dorfman, Laurie. *The Ethics of Encounter: A Jewish Conversation on Health Care Justice.* 1997.

OTHER WORKS CITED IN ARTICLE:

Hauerwas, Stanley. *A Community of Character: Toward a Constructive Christian Social Ethic.* 1981.
Levinas, Emmanuel. *Ethics and Infinity.* Translated by Richard A. Cohen. 1985.
Toulmin, Stephen. "The Tyranny of Principles." *The Hastings Center Report* 11 (December 1981): 31–39.

LAURIE ZOLOTH-DORFMAN

Feminist Ethics

The work of feminist ethics is multidimensional. Feminist ethics begins with fundamental assumptions about the immorality of sexism and misogyny and about the intrinsic value of women's experience as an essential lens to be used in the process of moral decision making. Feminist ethics calls into question the morality of ethics as it has traditionally been approached—an approach that, with few exceptions, has contributed to the oppression of women. Feminist ethics, then, is in part a critique of traditional systems of ethics.

Feminist ethicists must then determine what sources will be used in addition to or in lieu of the sources provided by traditional ethics. Those who do their work in feminist theological ethics have the added challenge of finding new sources in which to ground their ethics other than religious texts such as the Bible, Talmud, writings of the Church Fathers, and so on. Feminist ethicists often attempt to uncover and reclaim women's stories from the past and/or to elicit women's stories from the present as a source of guidance in moral decision making. Many feminist ethicists look specifically to the stories of women outside of the academy as a source for doing ethics. Moreover, feminist ethics as it is practiced in the United States is highly interdisciplinary, looking beyond theology and philosophy to sociology, history, psychology, and especially literature for inspiration and moral insight.

Insisting that gender is intrinsic to all issues and using women's experience as an analytical tool, feminist ethics revisits such topics as racism, heterosexism, militarism, colonialism, autonomy, and rationality. Feminist ethics also introduces new, previously neglected issues into the sphere of moral consideration such as domestic violence, motherhood, pornography, friendship, and relationality. In these ways feminist ethics broadens and deepens ethical discourse as it challenges the myopia of masculinist ethics.

WHY FEMINIST ETHICS IS NECESSARY

Ethics, as it has traditionally been approached, is in reality masculinist ethics, focusing as it does on male experience, understanding, and insight. By not naming its masculinist bias, traditional ethics feigns objectivity. This is unethical both because it is misleading and because it unfairly eclipses women. In addition, as philosopher Elizabeth Kamarck Minnich suggests, the false universalization of male perspective means that we are limited to only partial knowledge. Feminist ethics reminds us of the intellectual mediocrity that results from the exclusion of women's experience, understanding, and insight. This is a crucial and ironic point, since women's ways of knowing, communicating, and doing ethics have been the target of ridicule and insult in so many "ethical" writings that deny the moral agency of women.

In fact, masculinist ethics often has manipulated categories of right and wrong to perpetuate and reinforce the subjugation of women. Feminism, lesbianism, and almost any behavior that suggests women's autonomy and empowerment are deemed sinful. Therefore, there is an obvious need for new understandings of morality that take into account the full personhood of women, providing women with a moral compass untouched by patriarchy (if, in fact, that is possible) and by which to determine and pursue what is good.

Perhaps what makes the work of feminist ethics most urgent is the fact that so often in systems of masculinist ethics women have been defined as the incarnation of evil. As Marilyn Frye writes, "Naming women 'evil' makes it open season on women to be 'punished,' used, scapegoated, ignored, abused" (Card, 1991, p. 56). Feminist ethics, then, is not merely an academic discipline. It seeks to have a very real and positive impact on the lives of women as it challenges misogynist assumptions. Feminist ethics, like all feminist endeavors, is about saving women's emotional, spiritual, and physical lives.

In addition, feminist ethics seeks to repair the damage done by an imposed bifurcation of public and private life. This bifurcation places private life, the sphere to which women have traditionally been relegated, beyond the pale of moral scrutiny, thus making domestic violence, for example, immune to critique. Feminist ethics takes seriously the adage that the personal is political and refuses to bracket off the private domain from moral evaluation.

Finally, much of ethical theorizing before the advent of feminist ethics was based on assumptions about the autonomy of the agents involved. Feminist ethics challenges these constructs as androcentric and elitist, ignoring as they do the historical reality of those who have been robbed of their autonomy.

A BRIEF HISTORY OF U.S. FEMINIST ETHICS

During the feminist resurgence of the 1960s, debates in the United States about feminist ethics began taking place in the public arena and eventually spread to the academy. Feminist perspectives on issues of what in philosophic circles is referred to as applied ethics were developed, including discourse about pornography, abortion, sexuality, and so on. In the 1970s such issues as reproductive technology, surrogate motherhood, and militarism began to be explored.

The term *feminist ethics* came into use during the late 1970s and early 1980s and refers to both the work of addressing contemporary moral issues and the work of revealing and challenging the androcentrism of traditional ethical theory.

A watershed in the development of feminist ethics was the publication of *In a Different Voice* by Carol Gilligan in 1982. In this work, Gilligan suggested that women's moral development differs from men's. This raised the question of whether there is a distinctively "feminine" approach to ethics and began a debate about what became known as an "ethics of care" versus an "ethics of justice."

During the late 1980s and throughout the 1990s there has been a proliferation of work in feminist ethics including discussions of the extent to which feminist ethics should rely on abstract principles; whether the notion of a system of ethics is in itself patriarchal; and the extent to which the particularity of a situation should be considered in the course of moral evaluation. Debate still continues around the issue of whether there is a distinctively feminine way of doing ethics and whether an ethics of care is necessarily diametrically opposed to an ethics of justice.

Issues of difference, too, have been a topic of vigorous debate. How do we appreciate and celebrate the differences among and between us without undermining the possibility for a unity that will enable us to work for common goals? Moreover, since there is no one feminist ethical position, there continues to be much debate surrounding specific issues of reproductive rights, pornography, affirmative action, the environment, and power.

Among those who did, and continue to do, significant work in applied ethics are Carter Heyward, who has explored issues of compulsory heterosexuality, racism, sexism, exploitation, "right relationship," and what she calls "the moral deficit of liberal Christianity"; Beverly Wildung Harrison, who has done extensive work on reproductive rights, using natural law tradition creatively to expand the discourse on abortion beyond the act itself to include its social, historical, and political context; Margaret Farley, who has explored issues of relationship; Christine Gudorf, who has looked at sexuality and pleasure; and Karen Lebacqz, who maintains that an understanding of justice necessarily begins with an understanding of the realities of injustice.

WHO DOES FEMINIST ETHICS?

While Christian women have been the most visible in the field of feminist ethics, women of all faiths have made significant contributions to this work. Judith Plaskow, in her book *Standing Again at Sinai*, challenges Judaism's androcentrism and offers, among other things, a vision of a new Jewish sexual ethic. Laurie Zoloth-Dorfman has done work in the field of Jewish medical ethics. Melanie Kaye/Kantrowitz has looked at issues of power in black–Jewish relations and Arab–Jewish relations. Rachel Adler, Ellen Umansky, Naomi Goldenberg, and Susannah Heschel have each made unique contributions to the challenging project of developing a Jewish feminist ethics within the context of a religion that is rooted deeply in patriarchal texts. Jewish feminists have also been vigilant in their critique of Christian antisemitism found both in some masculinist as well as some feminist approaches to ethics.

Muslim feminists, such as Fatima Mernissi, Fatna Sabbah, and Durriyah Shafiq have looked at such issues as war and peace, the phenomenon of Muslim fundamentalism, and the meaning of community in the context of Islamic theocracy. True to the intent of feminist ethics, women of different faiths and races use their unique experience as a lens for doing ethics.

A powerful critique of feminist ethics has been brought by women of color. Just as men have universalized their experience to speak for all people, many African-American and Hispanic women claim that white women have universalized their experience to speak for all women. Womanist theologian Katie Cannon reminds us that what is necessary for survival in the midst of racism's dire oppression may be radically different from the mainstream notion of what is moral. *Mujerista* theologian Ada María Isasi-Díaz looks to the lived experience of grass-roots Hispanic women as the basis for her ethics. Feminist ethics, a term that more and more refers only to the work being done by Euro-American white feminists, is beginning to listen and appropriately respond to critiques by women of varying races and ethnicities in both developed and developing countries.

In conclusion, feminist ethics is more than the introduction of women's voices into what has been a masculinist ethical discourse. Feminist ethics, like feminism generally, is never merely a matter of adding women and stirring. Because gender differentiation and inequality undergird so much of the way we as a culture have constructed and perceived reality, to challenge these notions is to cause a major disruption of our social order. In the words of Elizabeth Minnich, "You don't simply add the idea that the world is round to the idea that the world is flat. You go back and rethink the whole enterprise" (1990, p. 180). Feminist ethics ultimately goads us to redraw our maps of the world.

BIBLIOGRAPHY

Cannon, Katie Geneva. *Black Womanist Ethics.* 1988.
———. *Katie's Canon.* 1995.
Card, Claudia, ed. *Feminist Ethics.* 1991.
Daly, Lois K., ed. *Feminist Theological Ethics: A Reader.* 1994.
Farley, Margaret. *Personal Commitments: Beginning, Keeping, Changing.* 1986.
Framer, Elizabeth, Jennifer Hornsby, and Sabina Lovibond, eds. *Ethics: A Feminist Reader.* 1992.
Gudorf, Christine. *Body, Sex, and Pleasure: Reconstructing Christian Sexual Ethics.* 1994.
Harrison, Beverly Wildung. *Making the Connections: Essays in Feminist Social Ethics.* 1985.
Heyward, Carter. *Our Passion for Justice.* 1984.
———. *Staying Power.* 1995.
Hoagland, Sarah Lucia. *Lesbian Ethics: Toward New Value.* 1992.
Isasi-Díaz, Ada María. *En La Lucha: Elaborating a Mujerista Theology.* 1993.
Kaye/Kantrowitz, Melanie. *The Issue Is Power: Essays on Women, Jews, Violence and Resistance.* 1992.
Lebacqz, Karen. *Justice in an Unjust World: Foundations for a Christian Approach to Justice.* 1987.
Mernissi, Fatima. *Women's Rebellion and Islamic Memory.* 1996.
———. *The Veil and the Male Elite: A Feminist Interpretation of Women's Rights in Islam.* 1987.
Minnich, Elizabeth Kamarck. *Transforming Knowledge.* 1990.
Okin, Susan Moller. *Justice, Gender, and the Family.* 1989.
Plaskow, Judith. *Standing Again at Sinai: Judaism from a Feminist Perspective.* 1990.
Young, Iris Marion. *Justice and the Politics of Difference.* 1990.

See also Morality; Mujerista Tradition; Shafiq, Durriyah (Doria); Womanist Traditions.

DONNA BERMAN

Ethnicity

Broadly defined, ethnicity refers to the condition of belonging to a particular social group whose distinctiveness is based on the sharing of certain characteristics such as religion, language, ancestry, culture, or national origin. In contrast to the common ties of identity that members of dominant social groups also enjoy, the particulars of ethnic group identities historically have been played out against the backdrop of that dominant group culture and thus have typically resulted in the latter's social, economic, and political power over the former. Also designated as "minorities" within a larger society, ethnic groups have often had to struggle to define and maintain their identities in the face of both voluntary and forced calls to assimilation, as well as defend themselves from outright assaults against their humanity, which form a key aspect of the relationship between dominant and ethnic groups. Historical examples of such struggles can be seen in the relationship between persecuted Jewish minorities and ethnic subgroups and the traditionally white majority culture in the United States, and, globally, between so-called Third and First World sociopolitical groups.

Within the study of religion, ethnicity as a theoretical or methodological concept refers to how the social grouping or the characterization of a particular ethnic population has affected the evolution of that group's understanding of divine or ultimate reality. Ethnicity, as a social and discursive category, occupies a pivotal conceptual place in the construction of multiple religious realities—whether one looks at the influence of ethnic identity on the construction of ancient Israel's understanding of God's covenantal relationship with humanity, the role indigenous cultural practices have played in the syncretistic development of major religious bodies, or at the connection between the organized nationalism of historically oppressed peoples and the emergence of various liberation theologies.

As this pertains to the study of women's religious lives, feminist scholars, through their critical engagement of the concept, have been able to represent the diversity of female ethnic identities while simultaneously challenging the very notion of identity as a fixed category. Relying on the positive power of storytelling, feminists—in particular, feminists of color—have managed to broaden the concept of ethnicity by bringing women's previously marginalized voices to the fore within traditions previously configured in monolithically male ways. Most notably, womanist, *mujerista*, Asian, and African women scholars such as Delores Williams, Ada María Isasi-Díaz, Chung Hyun Kyung, and Mercy Oduyoye have helped mine a vast store of resources within their respective ethnic enclaves and thereby shown that the fullness of any peoples' humanity cannot be adequately represented without reference to women's ways of knowing and being. These feminist theologies have had a profound effect on the development of new liturgies and languages about divine love and earthly justice within a variety of faiths.

Feminists are challenging the notion of identity itself as a fixed category by showing that identities, even ethnic ones, might be socially constructed. They encourage women to discuss the extent to which their own experiences of ethnicity often contradict what they have been told it means to be an "authentic" member of a particular group. Scholars such as Renee Hill, Gloria Anzaldua, Maria Lugones, and Audre Lorde have written at length about what it means to live in so-called inauthentic ethnic space. Each of their stories challenges the set of dominant assumptions about what it means to be human; a universalized sense of oneness can crush what these women define, from the crucible of their own experiences, as their ability to attain wholeness through the uncertain and contradictory cultural spaces their unstable identities afford them. Conceptualizing identity broadly and ethnicity more specifically allows for a variety of factors—cultural, geographic, and so forth—to typify what it means to be human, in a way that pleas for ethnic authenticity alone cannot do satisfactorily.

Such ideas can have a positive influence on a religious understanding of the concept of ethnicity. For insofar as human beings are able to put aside their narrow definitions of ethnic self in favor of a more diverse understanding, so too can they begin to imagine and indeed strive to realize a greater sacred and profane realm where a multiplicity of human identities are celebrated.

BIBLIOGRAPHY

Anzaldua, Gloria. "Haciendo caras una entrada." In *Making Faces, Making Soul.* Edited by Gloria Anzaludua. 1990.

Chung Hyun Kyung. *Struggle to Be the Sun Again.* 1991.

Hill, Renee Leslie. "Which Me Will Survive All These Liberations: U.S. Third World Feminist Theories of

Identities and Difference as Resources for U. S. Liberation Theologies." Ph.D. diss., Union Theological Seminary, New York, 1996.

Isasi-Díaz, Ada María. *Mujerista Theology.* 1996.

Lorde, Audre. *Sister Outsider: Essays and Speeches.* 1984.

Lugones, Maria C. "Playfulness, World Traveling, and Loving Perception." *Hypatia: A Journal of Feminist Philosophy* 2 (Summer 1987): 3–19.

Oduyoye, Mercy Amba. *Daughters of Anowa: African Women and Patriarchy.* 1995.

Schwartz, Regina M. *The Curse of Cain: The Violent Legacy of Monotheism.* 1997.

Williams, Delores. *Sisters in the Wilderness.* 1993.

See also **Mujerista Tradition**; **Womanist Traditions**.

LISA ANDERSON

Etruscan and Roman Religion

The main evidence for Etruscan and Roman religion comes from ancient historical and literary texts, including inscriptions, and from representations in art, dating from the sixth century B.C. to the end of the Roman Empire in the fifth century C.E. Based on a limited interpretation of these ancient sources, most scholars have often stated that women had little or no independent involvement in official religious issues in Rome (Scheid, 1992). As suggested in the following text, however, the roles of women in Etruscan and Roman religious practices were strong, albeit different from those of men.

GODS AND GODDESSES

Latin religious nomenclature reveals a major difference between Greek and Etrusco-Roman religious beliefs. Whereas the Greek deities were heavily anthropomorphized, the Latin *numen* indicates an almost abstract divine power, whether male or female. The interaction between the divine power and worshipers is referred to as *religio*, or bond; the deities provide *beneficia* (good deeds), in exchange for which the worshipers show *gratia* (gratitude) and provide *officia* (duties). Although the word *numen* is grammatically neuter, prayers are directed to individually named deities, or to a gender-specific *sive deus sive dea* ("whether god or goddess," Cato the Elder, *On Agriculture*, 139–140).

Both Etruscan and Roman religion emphasize the importance of the deities' names over their mythology or iconography. Lists of names of male and female Etruscan deities are preserved in inscriptions (primarily the inscribed bronze model of a sheep's liver, dated to the second century B.C.E. and found at Piacenza in northern Italy; van der Meer, 1987), and individual names occur in dedicatory inscriptions. Some of these names have Greek and Latin cognates, such as Etruscan Hercle, Greek Herakles, and Latin Hercules; others are specifically Etruscan. The gender of the deity is identified by special endings (masculine names end in -e or in a consonant; feminine names in -i or -a; Bonfante, 1990).

Latin texts provide equations of Greek and Latin names for the foremost deities, such as Greek Zeus and Latin Jupiter, Greek Hera and Latin Juno. Although such equations seem to have been acknowledged by the Romans, the activities of the Greek and Roman deities do not necessarily overlap. Thus Roman deities such as Diana, Juno, or Minerva correspond superficially with their Greek counterparts Artemis, Hera, and Athena but display characteristics that connect them with local Etruscan or Italic deities.

The gender of a Roman deity is usually clear from the ending of the word (masc., *liber*; femin., *libera*), even when there is little evidence that the female deity had any function other than that of being the female component of a pair. Occasionally, the gender of the deity is not clear: Voltumna, the deity of the sanctuary (*fanum Voltumnae*; Livy, 4.23.5), used by a confederation of twelve Etruscan cities, may represent the Latinized form of a masculine Etruscan name, rather than the female counterpart of the male deity Vertumnus. The main Roman deities, including Juno, Vesta, Minerva, Ceres, Diana, and Venus (Ennius, *Annals*, 60–61, in *Remains of Old Latin*, vol. 1), were clearly identifiable and had their distinct roles in the pantheon, whereas others, such as Cluacina, the goddess of sewers, or Tutilina, the goddess of safekeeping, represented the Roman belief that every aspect of life was under the protection of divine powers (*numina*). The Roman belief in these divine powers was scorned by later authors such as the church father Augustine (*City of God*, IV.8) and the fourth century C.E. grammarian Servius (Shelton, 1988, 365–366).

The feast days recorded in the Etruscan and Roman calendars indicate the importance of the deities worshiped throughout the year. Some correspond with the cycle of the agricultural year (for example, Cerialia, in honor of Ceres, the grain goddess, in April); others commemorate some important event in history (for example, Regifugium, commemorating the expulsion of the last king of Rome on 24 February 509 B.C.E.). Evidence for the Etruscan religious calendar is fragmentary but suggests some correspondence between the Etruscan and Roman traditions (Edlund-Berry, 1992). Although the actual calendars record only the name of a feast day, the Roman poet Ovid's poetic calendar, *Fasti*, describes the celebrations of each for the first six months of the year. Roman festivals celebrated exclusively or primarily by women included those honoring Venus (Veneralia, 1 April), Magna Mater (4 April), Mater Matuta (11 June), Fortuna Muliebris (6 July), and Bona Dea (3 December) (Scheid, 1992). Two of the Roman months were named after female deities, (May for Maia and June for Juno).

PRIESTS AND PRIESTESSES

Ancient sources indicate the importance of women in Etruscan religion, primarily for their skill in interpreting the signs of the gods. Most famous is Tanaquil, married to Tarquin, who became the first Etruscan king in Rome in the early sixth century B.C.E. (Livy I.34). Etruscan priestesses may be recognized in inscriptions by the title *hatrencu*, through their clothing on statuettes, or in funerary monuments (Nielsen, 1990). An Etruscan prophetess, Vegoia, is credited with works on natural phenomena such as lightning, and a cosmogony.

State priests were in charge of public forms of religious worship in Rome. The chief priest, the *pontifex maximus*, supervised the group of six young women, the Vestal Virgins (*vestales*), in charge of the sacred hearth, Vesta. Little is known of the Salian Virgins (Saliae Virginies) other than that they performed sacrifices with the *pontifex maximus*.

Other women involved in public worship were the wives of certain priests, primarily the *flaminica*, wife of the high priest of Jupiter (*flamen Dialis*), and *regina sacrorum*, wife of the King of Sacrifices (*rex sacrorum*). In other cults women, in particular freeborn married women (*matronae*), served as priestesses (*sacerdotes*), either by themselves or in conjunction with a priest. A prophetess, the Sibyl from Cumae in southern Italy, is said to have brought her sacred writings, the Sibylline books, to Rome for consultation by the Romans during the reign of the Tarquins.

The importance of Etruscan and Roman deities in the daily life of their worshipers is difficult to establish. The poets and other literary texts describe processions, sacrifices, and prayers, usually involving the matrons (*matrons*) of Rome. The matrons were also present at particularly important events, such as the introduction of the goddess Cybele to Rome at the end of the Second Punic War in 204 B.C.E. Although the ceremonies were performed by state officials and priests, the presence of matrons and certain priestesses, such as the *flaminica* or the Vestal Virgins, was required. Less well documented in the texts is the involvement of women in the rituals of daily life, involving offerings of miniature clay vases or clay models of anatomical body parts or of swaddled infants. Archaeological discoveries of such offerings deposited at sanctuaries throughout the cities and the countryside suggest that women were in charge of the cults that involved birth and healing. It is this more personal aspect of Etrusco-Roman religion, combined with the worship of deities such as the Egyptian goddess Isis, which facilitated the acceptance of Jewish and Christian beliefs in Italy during the Roman Empire. These rituals of daily life seem to have existed parallel with the state ceremonies regarding the deities in charge of the political life of the city. Only in cases where rituals not sanctioned by the state gained popularity to the point of becoming a threat to the established political system do we find evidence of religious persecution, such as the decree of the Roman senate in 186 B.C.E. to outlaw the cult of Bacchus (*Corpus Inscriptionum Latinarum* I² 581; *Remains of Old Latin*, vol. 4, 254–259). The women worshipers, Bacchantes, were in charge of this cult, and the office of priesthood (*sacerdos*) was reserved for women, although a Roman city official, the *praetor urbanus*, had to grant approval for participation in the cult.

MYTHOLOGY

Whereas Roman religion centers on a legalistic interaction between deities and worshipers, Roman mythology is based on stories from Roman history in which deities take part or where supernatural events explain the outcome. Many of these stories appear as a mixture of Greek, Etruscan, and Roman traditions, especially in Ovid's *Metamorphoses* or in Virgil's *Aeneid*. It is often difficult to draw the line between history and story in the accounts of early Roman history where the god Hercules interacts with the monster Cacus (Livy I.7) or where heroes and heroines take on superhuman roles (Gardner, 1993). Although some authors express an interest in the philosophy of religion (for example, the Roman orator and philosopher Cicero [106–43 B.C.E.], *De Natura Deorum*), there is less concern with creation myths other than those translated or adapted from the Greek (for example, Ennius' [239–169 B.C.E.] translation of the Greek fourth century B.C.E. mythographer Euhemerus (*Remains of Old Latin*, vol. 1, 414–430). Etruscan mythological stories are best known from representations on funerary urns (Small, 1981) or mirrors (de Grummond, 1982), which, in addition to Greek deities and heroes, display typically Etruscan figures such as the winged Lasa and the death demon Vanth (Sowder, 1982).

BIBLIOGRAPHY

ANCIENT SOURCES

Beard, Mary, John North, and S. R. F. Price. *Religions of Rome.* Vol. 1, *A History.* Vol. 2, *A Sourcebook.* Forthcoming.

Shelton, Jo-Ann. *As the Romans Did: A Sourcebook in Roman Social History.* 1988. See esp. chapter on religion and philosophy, pp. 360–437.

Warmington, E. H., ed. *Remains of Old Latin.* Vol. 1 (Ennius) and Vol. 4 (Archaic Inscriptions). 1967.

There are few studies dedicated specifically to issues of women's roles in Roman and Etruscan religion. This is a selection of general works.

Adkins, Lesley, and Roy A. Adkins. *Dictionary of Roman Religion.* 1996.

Beard, Mary, and John North, eds. *Pagan Priests.* 1990. Contains scattered references to women in the priesthood and Vestal Virgins.

Bonfante, Larissa. "Etruscan Women." In *Women in the Roman World.* Edited by Elaine Fantham, Helene Peet Foley, Natalie Boymel Kampen, Sarah B. Pomeroy, and H. Alan Shapiro. 1994.

———. *Reading the Past: Etruscan.* 1990.

de Grummond, Nancy T., ed. *A Guide to Etruscan Mirrors.* 1982.

Edlund-Berry, Ingrid E. M. "Etruscans at Work and Play: Evidence for an Etruscan Calendar." In *Kotinos: Festschrift für Erika Simon.* Mainz, 1992.

———. "Whether Goddess, Priestess or Worshipper: Considerations of Female Deities and Cults in Roman Religion." In *Opus Mixtum: Essays in Ancient Art and Society.* Edited by Eva Rystedt, Charlotte Scheffer, and Charlotte Wikander. Stockholm, 1994.

Gardner, Jane F. *Roman Myths.* See esp. chapter on "Legendary Ladies," including Claudia and the cult of the Great Mother. 1993.

Grant, Michael. *Roman Myths.* 1971.

Harmon, Daniel P. "The Family Festivals of Rome." In *Aufstieg und Niedergang der römischen Welt.* Vol. 16:2. Edited by Hildegard Temporini and Wolfgang Hase. 1978.

———. "The Public Festivals of Rome." In *Aufstieg und Niedergang der römischen Welt.* Vol. 16:2. Edited by Hildegard Temporini and Wolfgang Hase. 1978.

Nielsen, Marjatta. "Sacerdotesse e associazioni cultuali femminili in Etruria: Testimonianze epigrafiche ed iconografiche." *Analecta Romana Instituti Danici* 19 (1990): 45–67.

Radke, Gerhard. *Die Götter Altitaliens.* Münster, 1979.

Rallo, Antonia, ed. *Le donne in Etruria.* Roman, 1989.

Scheid, John. "The Religious Roles of Roman Women." In *A History of Women.* Edited by Pauline Schmitt Pantel. 1992.

Scullard, H. H. *Festivals and Ceremonies of the Roman Republic.* 1981. Detailed analysis of the Roman calendar.

Simon, Erika. *Die Götter der Römer.* Darmstadt, 1990.

Small, Jocelyn Penny. *Studies Related to the Theban Cycle on Late Etruscan Urns.* Rome, 1981.

Sowder, Cheryl L. "Etruscan Mythological Figures." In *A Guide to Etruscan Mirrors.* Edited by Nancy T. de Grummond. 1982.

van der Meer, L. Bouke. *The Bronze Liver of Piacenza.* Amsterdam, 1987.

INGRID EDLUND-BERRY

Eucharist

The Eucharist (Greek, "to offer willingly"), also known as communion, is a central Christian sacrament. It derives from the symbolic association Jesus made between the bread and wine of the Last Supper and the giving of his body and blood in sacrifice on the cross. The moment is described in the synoptic Gospels (Matt. 26:26–29, Mark 14:22–25, Luke 22:14–20), while the "farewell discourse" of the Gospel of John (John 14–17) elaborates many of the same themes. In 1 Cor. 10:16, the apostle Paul stresses that the cup of blessings and the breaking of the bread constitute "participation" in the blood and the body of Christ; at 1 Cor. 11:23–26, echoing the Gospel of Luke, he invites the believer to eat the bread and drink the cup "in remembrance" of Christ.

Many texts from the first and second centuries show that the early Christian community celebrated a blessing of bread and wine in ritual commemoration of Christ's body and blood. As Christian theology developed, eucharistic theology slowly became more complex, culminating in the doctrine of transubstantiation defined in 1215 as the process by which the bread and wine of the ritual actually become (in interior truth if not in external manifestation) the body and blood of Christ. Although this formulation is only accepted by the Roman Catholic and Orthodox churches, a vaguer notion that Christ is really present in the bread and wine of the Eucharist is held by Episcopal, Anglican, and Lutheran Christians. Other Protestant Christians understand the presence of Christ in the communion as wholly symbolic. It is noteworthy that this participation in the body of Christ is extended to the believer regard-

A Catholic nun carries consecrated hosts and a chalice to patients in a maternity clinic in Cite Soleil, Port au Prince, Haiti, 1986 (Owen Franken/Corbis).

less of gender; by participating in the Eucharist, women also, in some way, become Christ.

The Western Middle Ages was the period of the greatest eucharistic devotion, and the apex of women's eucharistic piety in particular. Here, the connection between embodiment, suffering, and salvation was articulated with increasing complexity. By the twelfth century, identification with the suffering Jesus was central to a popular spiritual revival. As Caroline Walker Bynum has shown, women were in the forefront of this spiritual movement, particularly because of the awareness of the functional likeness (giving life, giving food) of their bodies to the body of Christ. In this theological climate, devotion to the Eucharist flourished in new ways, such as vigils before the consecrated host and visions of divine union inspired by contemplation of the Eucharist. Women were beyond doubt the leaders of this new piety.

It was, in fact, the fervent eucharistic piety of a Belgian nun, Juliana of Mont-Cornillon, which provided the direct catalyst for the first liturgical feast dedicated to the Eucharist. Shortly after her profession in 1207, Juliana began having a vision of the full moon with a small breach in its body. Christ revealed to her the meaning of this vision: the moon was the Church, and the breach was the absence of a feast in honor of the body and blood of Christ. Juliana's plea to fill this gap was endorsed by powerful clerics who promoted the new feast of Corpus Christi (the body of Christ). In 1264, six years after Juliana's death, Pope Urban IV declared Corpus Christi an official feast for the universal church. A new liturgy for the feast was composed by the famous theologian Thomas Aquinas. Corpus Christi remains a part of the Roman calendar, celebrated the

Thursday after Trinity Sunday, at the very end of the Easter season.

Juliana was one of many holy women of medieval Europe whose extraordinary feats of eucharistic piety brought them some measure of power in their society. Rudolph Bell has studied 261 Italian women who were famous for what he calls "holy anorexia," the ability to survive on only the nutrition found in daily reception of the Eucharist. These include such famous medieval women as Clare of Assisi, Angela of Foligno, Catherine of Siena, and Catherine of Genoa, but Bell also includes thirteen twentieth-century Italian women in his study. A more renowned contemporary "holy anorexic" was Theresa Neumann, a Bavarian woman who bore the stigmata (the marks of the crucifixion) on her body and lived for long periods of time on the eucharist alone.

The Roman Catholic and Orthodox hierarchies continue to insist that women cannot be ordained to the priesthood nor preside at the Eucharist because, as women, they are not fully in the image of Christ. This is an ironic denial of women's importance in the development of eucharistic theology and devotion.

BIBLIOGRAPHY

The classic argument that medieval women's eucharistic piety constituted a pathology which can be identified in modern psychological terms is Rudolph M. Bell, *Holy Anorexia* (1985). The counter-argument, based on an analysis of embodiment in medieval culture, is Caroline Walker Bynum, *Holy Feast and Holy Fast: The Religious Significance of Food to Medieval Women* (1987). For the origins of the feast of Corpus Christi and its founder, see *The Life of Juliana of Mount Cornillon*, translated by Barbara Newman (1990). For Theresa Neumann, the modern German "holy anorexic," see Paul Siwek, *The Riddle of Konnersreuth: A Psychological and Religious Study* (1953). For an anthropological study of the Eucharist, see Gillian Feeley-Harnik, *The Lord's Table: The Meaning of Food in Early Judaism and Christianity* (1994).

See also Christianity: Religious Rites and Practices; Mysticism.

E. ANN MATTER

Evangelical, Holiness, Pentecostal, and Fundamentalist Christianity

Although the term *evangelical* is often applied to Pentecostal and Fundamentalist groups as well, each of these is a distinct group, with varying views on women's roles in home and society and attitudes regarding women's leadership.

Evangelical has a variety of historical meanings. In its widest sense, it often means Protestant. In Latin America all Protestants are referred to as Evangelicos. The term also refers to groups that practice revivalism, meetings that encourage people to experience conversion, to make a personal commitment to Jesus Christ as savior and lord. These groups, including Baptists, Methodists, and Presbyterians, represent a particularly American phenomenon. The evangelical form of Protestantism dominated the nineteenth-century United States and is still the cultural religion of the South.

In the late nineteenth century, more intense forms began to develop. The first was called Holiness. Based on John Wesley's *Plain Account of Christian Perfection* (1766), it was taught by Phoebe Palmer (1807–1874) in *The Way of Holiness* and her magazine *The Guide to Holiness*. She encouraged people to seek an additional experience called "holiness" or "entire sanctification." To receive it, one must consecrate oneself entirely to God. A transatlantic form called "Keswick holiness," named after an English meeting site, was based on the book *The Christian's Secret of a Happy Life* by Philadelphia Quaker Hannah Whitall Smith (1832–1911).

Eventually Holiness people formed different denominations such as the Wesleyan Methodist Church, Church of God (Anderson, Indiana), Christian and Missionary Alliance, the Church of the Nazarene, and the Salvation Army. The latter was founded in England by Catherine and William Booth; their daughter Evangeline succeeded her father as General. Women continue to serve as pastor-officers within the Army. Women served as evangelists and pastors in many of these denominations at their beginnings, but as the denominations became more middle class at midcentury gender roles became more patriarchal.

In the 1870s and 1880s some Holiness groups adopted two more distinctive beliefs. First, they embraced faith healing. Faith healers included African-American Sarah Mix (1832–1884), Carrie Judd Montgomery (1858–1946), and Maria Woodworth-Etter (1844–1924). Second, they adopted John Nelson Darby's (1800–1882) "dispensationalism": he taught that Jesus would come in the clouds (the "rapture") to rescue faithful Christians from a "great tribulation" under the rule of a cruel "Anti-Christ."

The experience of holiness was sometimes called "baptism of the Holy Spirit." As Charles Parham (1873–1929) traced this concept in Scripture, he decided it should be evidenced by speaking in tongues. This was initially conceived as the ability to spontaneously speak another language (as in Acts 2:1–12); later it was understood as a private prayer or praise language used to commune with God. The first person to do so was Parham student Agnes Ozman (1870–1937) on January 1, 1901. This isolated experience was not repeated until 1906, when another Parham student, African-American William Seymour, began preaching in Los Angeles. His work spawned a worldwide movement termed Pentecostalism.

Denominations such as the Assemblies of God, the Church of God (Cleveland, Tennessee), the Church of God in Christ, and the Pentecostal-Holiness Church are all characterized by exuberant worship styles, tongues speaking, prophecy, healing, and other manifestations of the Spirit. Again, in the early years women held prominent places as preachers, teachers, founders, and healers. For example, healer Aimee Semple McPherson (1890–1944) founded the International Church of the Foursquare Gospel. In the 1960s tongues speaking broke out in Roman Catholic and many mainline Protestant churches. This was called the "charismatic renewal." Although many participants and leaders were women, their views on gender roles were often more conservative than those of their denominational peers.

Meanwhile, in the late nineteenth century, other conservative Protestants were becoming alarmed by science, particularly Darwin's theory of evolution, and by German higher criticism of the Bible. Scholars at Princeton Seminary declared that the Bible was "verbally inspired" and "inerrant in the original authographs." This movement came to be called Fundamentalism after publication of *The Fundamentals*, a series of twelve volumes of essays published between 1910 and 1915 and sent to every Christian leader in the world, courtesy of a wealthy oilman. Theologically, the fundamentals were defined as the plenary inspiration and verbal inerrancy of the Bible, the virgin birth of Jesus, his miracles, his death as a substitutionary atonement for sin, and his bodily resurrection. Debates over these issues racked the Presbyterian Church, U.S.A., and the Northern or American Baptist Convention. This movement was almost entirely male and it continues to deny women any leadership roles in the church and to insist on subordinate roles of wives to husbands.

Fundamentalists are often independent and separatist but they include such denominations as the Orthodox Presbyterian Church and the Independent Association of Bible Churches. Independent Baptists such as Jerry Falwell share their beliefs.

Some Fundamentalists in the 1940s became more open to other Christians while retaining their distinctive theology. They appropriated for themselves the name Evangelicals. Most representative of this group is evangelist Billy Graham, who helped to found Fuller Seminary in Pasadena, California, and the magazine *Christianity Today.*

In 1974 some Evangelicals founded the Evangelical Women's Caucus (now the Evangelical and Ecumenical Women's Caucus) to promote women's equality in home, church, and society. When they adopted a more systemic feminist critique, including support for gay rights in 1986, Christians for Biblical Equality was formed, limiting its focus to women's equality in marriage and church. In the early 1990s a more conservative group founded the Council on Biblical Manhood and Womanhood to support male headship in the home and women's subordination in church ministries.

BIBLIOGRAPHY

Bendroth, Margaret. *Fundamentalism and Gender, 1875 to the Present.* 1993.

Dayton, Donald. *The Theological Roots of Pentecostalism.* 1987.

Dieter, Melvin. *The Holiness Revival of the Nineteenth Century.* 1980.

Hardesty, Nancy A. *Women Called to Witness: Evangelical Feminism in the Nineteenth Century.* 1984. Rev. ed., 1998.

Harrell, David, Jr. *All Things Are Possible: The Healing and Charismatic Revivals in Modern America.* 1975.

McLoughlin, William. *Revivals, Awakenings and Reform.* 1978.

Marsden, George. *Fundamentalism and American Culture: The Shaping of Twentieth-Century Fundamentalism, 1870–1925.* 1980.

Sandeen, Ernest. *The Roots of Fundamentalism.* 1970.

See also **Christianity: In North America: United States.**

NANCY A. HARDESTY

Eve

Three religious traditions trace their ancestry to Adam and Eve—Judaism, Christianity, and Islam. In Genesis 1, human beings are created simultaneously, male and female together. However, in the account of human creation in Genesis 2, Eve is created by God from one of Adam's ribs to be his helpmate. Historically, this second account has been used in each of the three traditions to justify the subjugation of women. In Genesis 3, a serpent persuades Eve to eat fruit from the forbidden tree of knowledge of good and ill, and she offers some to Adam to eat. God's punishment for their transgression involves hard labor for both—Eve's in childbirth, Adam's in cultivating food. With the new terms for their life together spelled out, Adam names the woman Eve (from the Hebrew root for "life") because she will be the mother of all the living. After making clothing for Adam and Eve out of skins, God expels the pair from Eden to prevent their eating from the tree of life. In Genesis 4, Eve gives birth to Cain and Abel, and later to Seth, whose birth appears to comfort her after Abel's murder. Eve appears no more in the biblical text.

The history of interpretation of these biblical events in Judaism and Christianity elaborates and interprets the biblical text, as does Islam in the Qur'anic text. In Judaism, rabbinic exegesis connects the Hebrew name for Eve with the Aramaic word for serpent (*ḥewyā*), suggesting that the serpent was Eve's undoing as Eve was Adam's. Rabbinic sources and Greek and Latin Apocrypha continue the stories of Eve and Adam beyond Genesis 4. Jewish sources focus on the nature of their sin, strongly suggesting that God would have for-

The creation of Eve, marriage, temptation, and expulsion from the Garden of Eden (© The Barnes Foundation/Corbis)

given the primeval pair had they confessed their transgression and repented instead of protesting their innocence and attempting to shift blame. For this sin, sources of the first century C.E. suggest, God punishes Eve and Adam with expulsion from paradise and with the twin banes of illness and mortality that are passed on to all their human descendants. The Apocryphal books and rabbinic exegesis emphasize Eve's and Adam's belated, and inadequate, attempts at repentance and contrition throughout their lives subsequent to expulsion from Eden, and the finality of their punishment until the anticipated ultimate messianic redemption.

In Christianity, the expulsion from Eden is interpreted as a fall from grace experienced by all human beings descended from Adam and Eve. This fall is attributed specifically to Eve. For the early Church Fathers, like Justin and Irenaeus, Mary is a "new Eve," whose obedience and faith are contrasted with the disobedience of the first woman. Based on Paul's writing in Romans 5 in the New Testament, and also on the writings of the early Church Fathers, St. Augustine articulated the Catholic doctrine of Original Sin, holding that the deliberate sin of the first man is its cause, and that Eve was Adam's pitfall, seducing him to sin. The Catholic Church defines Original Sin beyond mere physical mortality (which it acknowledges as the punishment for sin) but as sin itself, which the Council of Orange (529 C.E.) defined as the death of the soul, depriving the soul of the sanctifying grace, union with God, that belongs to the soul according to God's initial plan for humanity. Original Sin is passed on to every descendant of Eve and Adam and is removable only by waters of baptism. Many Protestant groups reject the Catholic view of Original Sin, and articulate a view closer to the Jewish equation of the primeval punishment with human mortality.

As in the Genesis account, Islamic scripture assigns no specific blame for the transgression of Adam and his mate to the woman alone. The Qur'an treats the primordial couple as equally receiving the prohibition of God, equally succumbing to temptation, and together being expelled from the garden (2:35–36; 7:19, 24). In the Qur'an, Eve is not named, although Islamic tradition gives the Arabic name Hawwa' to Adam's wife. Eve is not created from Adam's rib in the Qur'an. Rather, man and woman are created from a single soul, finding respite in one another (7:189). Later Islamic interpretations are probably influenced by Christian attitudes toward Eve, ascribing her origin to Adam's rib (sometimes to the most crooked part of that bone) and blaming her for the expulsion from the garden.

BIBLIOGRAPHY

Ahmed, Leila. *Women and Gender in Islam: Historical Roots of a Modern Debate.* 1992.

Alexandre, Monique. "Early Christian Women." In *A History of Women in the West: I. From Ancient Goddesses to Christian Saints.* Edited by Pauline Schmitt Pantel. Translated by Arthur Goldhammer. 1992.

Bellis, Alice Ogden. *Helpmates, Harlots, Heroes: Women's Stories in the Hebrew Bible.* 1994.

Bronner, Leila Leah. *From Eve to Esther: Rabbinic Reconstructions of Biblical Women.* 1994.

Ginzberg, Louis. *The Legends of the Jews.* Translated by Henrietta Szold. 1909; 1937. Reprint, 1968.

Milne, Pamela J. "Eve and Adam: Is a Feminist Reading Possible?" *Bible Review* 4 (June 1988): 12–21.

Shanks, Hershel, ed. *Feminist Approaches to the Bible.* 1995.

Stowasser, Barbara Freyer. *Women in the Qur'an: Traditions, and Interpretation.* 1994.

Wilfong, Marsha M. "Genesis 2:18–24." *Interpretation* 42, no. 1 (1988): 58–63.

See also **Hawwa' (Eve)**; **Sin**.

DIANE M. SHARON

Evil

Life manifestly includes evil. Human beings suffer from natural disasters, such as earthquakes, floods, famines, but they also inflict pain on themselves and others. In Western monotheistic religions human actions that defy divine law are called sins. For those traditions the problem of evil involves concepts of the nature of God: how can God, who is both all-powerful and all-good, allow evil to exist? Eastern religions speak of individuals' suffering, which is caused by self-centered desire and can be ended by destroying desire; moral evil or suffering is a matter of human action and human responsibility.

Given that most religions were founded and organized by men, the visions of individual and social life described in their sacred texts reflect male points of view. In the religious literature of most traditions, women's basic function is defined as reproduction, and that is what determines her place in the social and religious hierarchy. Her sphere is home and family. Women are subordinated to men, either because this is understood to be the natural way of the universe (as in the Confucian Book of Rites); or because this has been divinely ordained (as in the Torah, the Christian Bible, and the

Qu'ran); or because women are not thought capable of public life (as in the Buddhist sutras).

The male norm is right and good, and women do not fit it; women are "other." That does not necessarily mean that women are regarded as evil, however. In fact, in those religions where evil is thought of as a power opposed to divine goodness, and personified, the Evil One is most often male: Satan in the Hebrew and Christian Bibles, Iblis in the Qu'ran, Mara in the Buddhist sutras, Ahra Mainyu in the Zoroastrian Gata (Songs). Just as supreme good is personified as male in these religions, so is supreme evil: the head of every hierarchy is always male.

Yet women, as other, pose a special problem. Religious texts of many traditions, as well as common beliefs, identify women with physical matter, nature, the body, and worldly concerns, especially with sex, and men with soul, intellect, and spirituality. Christian and Buddhist religious texts agree that women can reach the ultimate spiritual goal just as surely as men can; but when men reach the goal they remain in harmony with their own essential nature, including their male bodies, whereas when women reach it they must transcend their essential nature, including their female bodies. Some early Christian authors, such as Augustine, following classical philosophical assertions, held that only the male is the true image of God. Several Buddhist scriptures describe the visionary transformation of a woman's body into that of a male ascetic at the moment she attains supreme enlightenment.

Women are primarily sexual beings, in the eyes of many religious teachers, and their bodies and behavior are a constant temptation to all men, whether ascetics or laymen. Sex is what female otherness is all about. Most misogynist outbursts in religious texts are about women as temptresses. The Hindu Mahābhārata (Epic of Great India, book 13) proclaims that women are sexually insatiable: they are ready to have sex with any man at any time and are incapable of self-control or fidelity. Buddhist scriptures sometimes voice the same sentiments, saying that even as a woman lies dying, she will try to ensnare the heart of a man, and therefore it is safer to sit down beside a deadly snake than to sit alone with a woman (*Aṅguttara Nikāya*, Book of the Gradual Sayings, 3).

In many cultures sexual activity and the blood of menstruation and childbirth are considered dangerous and polluting. Leviticus 12 in the Hebrew Bible says that a woman is unclean after childbirth and must be purified by priestly sacrifice of a lamb or a pigeon. Before God announced his presence to the Hebrew people at the foot of Sinai, he had commanded that the men abstain from sexual intercourse with their wives

A picture of demons and devils from *The History and Doctrine of Buddhism* (1829) by Edward Upham (Historical Picture Archive/Corbis)

and cleanse themselves (Exod. 19:15). In ancient Israel and India, as in modern Africa and Taiwan, blood and sex are thought to be dangerous not because they are evil, but because they are powerful. Giving birth is a woman's unique power; blood is the fluid that contains that awesome, life-giving force. The power to give life, and the power to attract men sexually, mark women as dangerous. The strict rules constructed by male religious teachers and social leaders to govern marriage and reproduction are intended to keep female power under male control.

If women are dangerous, does that mean they are evil, or that they are the cause of evil in the world? In many Hindu myths, it was the gods who created evil: Indra or Brahma or another god committed the first sin, and in order to be free of it transferred it to women. Women's recompense was the boon of childbearing and the pleasure of sex. Other Hindu and Buddhist myths describe an originally perfect world that gradually became corrupted over time; no one caused evil to begin, it is simply part of the natural order of the universe. By contrast, generations of Christian teachers have taught that it was Eve, the first woman, who brought sin and death into the world, and all women share her guilt.

The story of the creation and fall in Genesis 2 and 3 does not itself assert that Eve was the cause of sin and evil in the world and was cursed for it. Rather that is how Christian teachers have interpreted it. The second-century writer Tertullian said every woman is Eve, who is the Devil's gateway and destroyer of God's image, man (*De Cultu Feminarum*, 1). Jews and Muslims tell the same story of Adam and Eve, but without putting so great a burden of blame on the woman alone. To Muslims it is the story of human sin, repentance, and Allah's forgiveness, the paradigm for Muslims' relationship with God.

In Christian thought, man alone is the true image of the good and powerful God, and woman's relationship to evil has been ambiguous. Modern Christian feminist writers reject the definition of divinity that leaves women alienated from both goodness and power and recognize moral evil as what humans choose to do to each other. In this respect, and in their emphasis on the necessity of personal action to alter evil conduct, Western religious feminists find rapport with Eastern attitudes toward evil and the human condition.

BIBLIOGRAPHY

Most of the critical studies of religious judgments on the good or evil character of women have been written by specialists in the Christian tradition, partly because of the large number of scholars working in that field, and partly because the connection between women, sin, and guilt is especially close in Christian doctrine. Elaine Pagels, *Adam, Eve, and the Serpent* (1988), explores the historical roots of the Christian position with superb clarity and erudition. Kim Powers, *Augustine on Women* (1996), reexamines Augustine's role in the development of theological arguments concerning evil and women, against the background of Greek and Roman philosophy. Nell Noddings, *Women and Evil* (1989); Wendy Farley, *Tragic Vision and Divine Compassion: A Contemporary Theodicy* (1990); Kathleen M. Sands, *Escape from Paradise* (1994); and the contributors to *A Troubling in My Soul: Womanist Perspectives on Evil and Suffering*, edited by Emilie M. Townes (1993), develop new approaches for Christian feminists to the problem of evil. Paul Ricoeur's classic study on evil in Western religious traditions, *The Symbolism of Evil* (1967), is still richly informative. *Early Modern European Witchcraft, Centres and Peripheries*, edited by Bengt Ankarloo and Gustav Henningsen (1990), is a collection of up-to-date and wide-ranging critical studies of Christian complicity in a special instance of persecution of women and men. Few studies of Judaism and Islam focus on the connection between women and evil, but Judith Plaskow, *Standing Again at Sinai: Judaism from a Feminist Perspective* (1990), and Fatima Mernissi, *The Veil and the Male Elite* (1991), provide relevant information as they view their traditions from new directions. Wendy Doniger O'Flaherty has published two books packed with myths from the Hindu tradition, and her own analyses of their meaning: *The Origins of Evil in Hindu Mythology* (1976), and *Women, Androgynes, and Other Mythical Beasts* (1980). A helpful, though narrowly focused, study of Buddhist misogynist literature is W. B. Bollee, *Kunalajataka* (1970). A more general overview of women in Buddhist literature and life can be found in Nancy Barnes's essay, "Buddhism," in *Women in World Religions*, edited by Arvind Sharma (1987). *Women in China*, edited by Richard W. Guisso and Stanley Johannesen (1981), is a collection of very scholarly and very readable essays on women in the Confucian, Taoist, and other religious traditions. Finally, Mary Douglas's admirable work, *Purity and Danger: An Analysis of Concepts of Pollution and Taboo* (1966), is still indispensable for understanding the relationship between religious ideas, social structures, and gender conflict in tribal cultures and major religious traditions all over the world.

NANCY J. BARNES

Family

As social structure and as metaphor, family shapes women's religious experience. Both nuclear and extended families are systems of order that are typically arranged hierarchically. With some exceptions, both social and religious power and authority have historically been vested in a male head of the family. For example, in the traditional Chinese family organized according to Confucian principles, a woman was required to defer first to her father, then later to her husband, and eventually to her son. Similarly, alongside statements that theoretically support gender equality, the early Christian missionary Paul asserts that "the head of every man is Christ, the head of a woman is her husband, and the head of Christ is God" (1 Cor. 11:3; but see Gal. 3:28).

Family members' religious roles and statuses vary according to their positions. Children are frequently the subjects of rites of passage, especially marking entry into adulthood. They often experience these rites with a specific gender and age cohort. The Bemba of Zambia, for example, describe the process as "growing" a girl into a woman. Successful completion of a rite of passage invests the initiate with new social and religious responsibilities. The Sioux remind a girl newly transformed into a woman that she has become similar to Mother Earth because she too will be able to bear children. Adults have distinct religious responsibilities, often allocated by gender. Muslim women, for example, are responsible for maintaining the religious atmosphere and ritual purity of the home, while Muslim men play much more significant roles in religious activities in the mosque and other arenas outside the home. Like men, however, Muslim women are encouraged to make the pilgrimage to Mecca, though they are not permitted to pray aloud and are subject to other restrictions. Ancestors exert continuing influence over the lives of their descendants and may be worshiped at family shrines within the home, as they are in Japan in both Buddhist and Shinto ritual forms as well as in the "new religions."

In many instances the divine world is imagined as a family, as it is in the ancient Egyptian pyramid texts from the Temple of Re at Heliopolis. Divine families, however, frequently mirror the patriarchal social organization of the religious community. In his *Theogony*, for example, Hesiod vividly chronicles the chaotic family history of the classical Greek pantheon in which successive generations of male deities violently strive to control fertile goddesses. The Babylonian creation epic *Enuma Elish* recounts a similar multigenerational family saga in which the supreme male god, Marduk, establishes cosmic order through the brutal sacrifice of the female Tiamat. Other myths of divine beings give primacy to females, such as the Spider Grandmother who weaves the web of creation in several Native American mythologies of the Southwest. In still other instances, depictions of the divine realm may present an ideal model of gender equity toward which devotees may aspire, as with the Goddess and her male consort among some contemporary pagans.

Family can also serve as a powerful image for the unity and cohesiveness of an entire religious tradition, but the metaphor can be developed in various ways. For example, Jews think of themselves as a people descended from a single ancestor, Jacob or "Israel," and throughout history the predominant definition of a Jew is one who has been born of a Jewish mother. Similarly, until the concept was weakened in the modern era, all Japanese thought of themselves as united in a single *uji*

According to the Babylonian creation myth, Marduk established cosmic order through the brutal sacrifice of the female Tiamat (The British Museum).

or household under the authority of a divine emperor. Likewise, practitioners of Santeria consider themselves *omo-orishas,* children of the spirits, and connect the living community with the ancestors through spirit-possession and other ritual means.

The image of the family, however, can also be used to contrast conscious affiliation to the accident of birth. For example, the synoptic gospels report that Jesus of Nazareth, when informed that his mother and siblings were waiting outside for him while he was teaching, replied, "whoever does the will of God is my brother, and sister, and mother" (Mark 3:35). Some of that imagery recurs when biologically unrelated Christians refer to themselves as brother and sister and when Roman Catholics address their priests as "father" and nuns address their superior as "mother." Many contemporary new religious movements also see themselves as constituting new families based on conversion rather than biology. For example members of the Unification Church understand themselves as forming a single family under the guidance of their "True Parents," the Reverend and Mrs. Sun Myung Moon. The conception of the religious community as a family may also give rise to distinctive living arrangements, as in contemporary groups such as the Family (formerly the Children of God), which is now a loose federation of multifamily communes, and the Branch Davidians, where several of David Koresh's multiple "brides" at the Mount Carmel Center adopted the surname of Koresh.

The rejection of family, and the pleasures, comforts, and routines that it stands for, is often a key ingredient in the formation of ascetics. The thirteenth-century *Confessions of Lady Nijo,* a work by a former concubine of a Japanese emperor who later became a wandering Buddhist nun, movingly recounts the difficulty of renunciation. Others apparently experienced no such troubles. In the Christian apocryphal text The Acts of Paul the young woman Thecla is on the verge of marriage when she first hears Paul preach the gospel. Much to the dismay of her family, she immediately abandons her plans, cuts her hair, and eagerly dons ascetic garb to become an itinerant missionary herself. In many ascetic traditions family, and especially sexual relations, are considered impediments to a life of religious dedication. Nonetheless, communities of ascetics, such as convents and monasteries, may take on many of the characteristics of a family as the common Christian nomenclature of "mothers," "sisters," and "brothers" suggests.

Since some sort of family is such a ubiquitous and fundamental social unit, it is not surprising that family is an important social context and imaginative resource for women's religious experience. But as the specific nature and structure of a family varies significantly through time and across cultures, so also will its contributions to ritual, mythology, and other aspects of religious life.

BIBLIOGRAPHY

Cooey, Paula. *Family, Freedom, and Faith: Building Community Today.* 1996.

Daedalus 106, no. 2 (Spring 1977). Special issue on the family.

Foster, Lawrence. *Women, Family, and Utopia: Communal Experiments of the Shakers, the Oneida Community, and the Mormons.* 1991.

Palmer, Susan J. *Moon Sisters, Krishna Mothers, Rajneesh Lovers: Women's Roles in New Religions.* 1994.

Wessinger, Catherine, ed. *Women's Leadership in Marginal Religions: Explorations Outside the Mainstream.* 1993.

EUGENE V. GALLAGHER

Fasting

Fasting in religious terms may be described as an act of volition whereby a person refrains from nourishment to procure and enhance the spiritual discernment of transcendence. Fasting may be motivated as a means to appease or beseech the Divine in times of difficulties or as an offering of the self in devotion and gratitude or penitence. The institution of a religious fast is frequently accompanied by prayers, designated intentions, and specific rites or rituals. In religious lore, women together with men have fasted to enhance their veneration toward the Supreme Being. Most prescribed religious fasts appear to be gender free, mandated for both men and women. Some fasts may be obligated as part of the grace reserved for the priestly office, which generally is held by men. However, frequently there are fasts specified for the community by feminine religious personalities or by concerns or vows that distinctively encompass women.

In the Judaic tradition, by Mosaic Law the Day of Atonement was to be adhered to by the entire Israelite nation. Subsequently, several other fasts were sanctioned. In the Biblical narrative of Esther, fasting for three days is presented as an important spiritual means to worship God and to seek divine succor for an important task. Prior to the presentation of her petition to her husband, King Xerxes, to protect the Jewish inhabitants from the ruin planned by Haman, Esther fasts for three days and urges Mordecai and the other Jews of Susa to simultaneously fast (Esther 4:16). After the completion of the fast, Esther sets in motion her successful petition to the king and so assists in the deliverance of her community. The Fast of Esther (Ta'anit Ester) is honored on the 13th of Adar (the day before Purim). There are other instances of fasting in the Bible, both at the individual and the community level. According to the halakah, with exceptions for the sick and infirm, fasting is obligatory for boys over thirteen and girls over twelve.

In the Christian tradition, fasting is a vital component of the faith, especially in connection with monasticism. Sometimes fasts and austerities may be taken to drastic extents: Catherine of Siena is reported to have subsisted for several years by consuming only her daily Eucharist wafer. The fasts associated with Lent and Pentecost are, with variations, adhered to by everyone. In the Biblical narrative of Luke, Anna, the prophetess, who joyfully proclaimed the birth of Jesus, is reported as never leaving the temple but worshiping night and day, praying and fasting (Lk. 2:36–38). In the Coptic tradition a fifteen-day fast is kept in commemoration of Mary, which ends with the feast of the Assumption of the Virgin Mary. For the duration of the fast, fish is abstained from, as is fat and oil. Many people may practice full abstention, eating only one meal at the end of the day subsequent to the liturgy.

In the Islamic tradition, fasting for the entire community is mandated during the month of Ramadan from dawn to dusk, when no food or drink may be ingested. Fasts may also be kept during the year for various purposes such as repentance for a wrong action. Celebrat-

ing the sanctity of Fāṭimah, in some Indian Muslim communities, women occasionally keep a fast and feed young girls from a *thali* (large food tray) as part of a vow taken for an aspiration or need. In many Sufi orders, praying and fasting for a day or consecutively for several days, while common for men, are frequently practiced by women as well. For instance, Rabi'ah al-'Adawiyah, a ninth century Sufi, is celebrated for her devoted prayers, austerities, and fasting.

In Hindu lore, ascetic practices inclusive of fasting provide immense merit. The deity Pārvatī is celebrated for her ascetic exercises that entailed not eating. As a result of her austerities she gained great spiritual merit (*tapas*) and eventually exterminated the mighty demon chief, with the collective energy of the deities encapsulated within her. Though special fasts are instituted for Brahmin priests, several fasts are reserved for women only. In popular Hindu convention, women frequently fast and perform special devotional veneration (*pūjā*) for procuring a boon, such as a child or a good husband, or for the welfare of their families. To obtain a kind husband, the *molakata* fast is observed by both Jain and Hindu women, when all food containing salt is not eaten for a day. To ensue married felicity, Jain women keep the fast of Oli or Ambela in honor of the princess Mayana Sundari, whereby they give up tasty foods for a few days.

Only women participated in the ancient Greek three-day Thesmophoria fertility festival held in Pyanopsion (October 24–26). Restriction from certain foods and behavioral regulation, including abstention from cohabitation, were part of the ceremonies.

In Chinese Buddhism, the *Qinggui* (Regulations of the priesthood) and *Jingvang Mingjing* (The bright sutra of golden light) give instructions on the days for festivals and fasts; among other occasions, fasts are kept to commemorate the birthdays or anniversaries of diverse male and female Buddhas and bodhisattvas.

In many tribal customs, fasting appears as an integral part of the religiosocial realm. In many cases young boys are required to fast at the start of puberty as part of the initiation ceremonies, but young girls too may be required to undergo certain austerities. Traditionally, among the maidens of the indigenous inhabitants of British Columbia, a girl would fast for four days at the time of the first menses. In ancient China, the *Liji* (Book of Rites) had ordained a similar practice accompanied by austerities.

Childbirth and pregnancy become the occasion for fasts and abstinence among Melanesian women. It was customary among pregnant Koita women of New Guinea and the Andaman Islanders to refrain from certain foods; following childbirth the women of southern

Hindu women flock to the Pashupatinath Temple and waters of the Bagmati River in Kahma, Nepal during the Tij Brata festival, a fasting festival for women only (Alison Wright/Corbis).

Massim could only ingest boiled taro and the okioki fruit for a month. Special complete fasts were also adhered to following the birth of a child, especially the first birth. Often the father joined the mother for these fasts and austerities, as among the Bororo of South America where both parents refrained from food for two days after childbirth.

Fasting has also been observed as an important expression of grief in many parts of the world. While many tribes enjoin fasting for the entire community, frequently women are expected to participate more completely. Among the Copts all near relatives generally fasted between death and burial. Yoruba widows and daughters were secluded for twenty-four hours and refrained from nourishment during this period.

A negative fast referred to as Black Fast has been banned by the church since the sixteenth century. Practiced in England, it was used as a potent spell. For in-

stance, Mabel Brigge hired a woman to fast on her behalf to cause the death of a man, who actually did fall, break his neck, and die before the fasting period was completed. Mabel was subsequently executed in 1538 for causing his death.

BIBLIOGRAPHY

'Attar, Farid al-din. *Muslim Saints and Mystics.* Translated by A. J. Arberry. 1990.

Baird, John E. *What the Bible Says about Fasting.* 1984.

Brown, George. *Melanesians and Polynesians: Their Life-histories Described and Compared.* 1910. Reprint, 1972.

Burmester, Oswald Hugh Ewart. *The Egyptian or Coptic Church: A Detailed Description of Her Liturgical Services and the Rites and Ceremonies Observed in the Administration of Her Sacraments.* 1967.

Butcher, Edith Louisa. *The Story of the Church of Egypt: Being an Outline of the History of the Egyptians under Their Successive Masters of the Roman Conquest Until Now.* 2 vols. 1897.

Bynum, Carolyn Walker. *Holy Feast and Holy Fast: The Religious Significance of Food to Medieval Women.* 1987.

Chatham, Romara Dean. *Fasting: A Biblical-Historical Study.* 1987.

Ellis, Alfred Burdon. *The Yoruba-speaking Peoples of the Slave Coast of West Africa: Their Religion, Manners, Customs, Laws, Language etc., with an Appendix Containing a Comparison of the Tshi, Gaa, Ewe, and Yoruba Languages.* 1970.

Groot, Jan Jakob Maria de. *Religion of the Chinese.* 1910.

Hastings, James, ed. *Encyclopaedia of Religion and Ethics.* 13 vols. 1908–1926. See especially "Calendar," "Fasting," "Festivals and Fasts."

Hopkins, Edward Washburn. *The Religions of India.* 2d ed., 1970.

Kitov, Eliyahu. *The Book of Our Heritage: The Jewish Year and Its Days of Significance.* 1978.

Leach, Maria, ed. *Funk and Wagnalls Standard Dictionary of Folklore Mythology and Legend.* 1984. See especially "Fasting."

Lopez, Donald, ed. *Religions of China in Practice.* 1996.

———. *Religions of India in Practice.* 1995.

O'Flaherty, Wendy Doniger. *Hindu Myths.* 1975.

Oman, John Campbell. *The Brahmins, Theists, and Muslims of India.* 1907.

Sastri, Natesa. *Hindu Feasts, Fasts and Ceremonies.* Introduction by Henry K. Beauchamp. 1903.

Thompson, Laurence G. *The Chinese Way in Religion.* 1973.

See also **Catherine of Siena; Fāṭimah; Menarche; Mourning and Death Rites; Pārvatī; Rabiʿa.**

HABIBEH RAHIM

Fate

Fate (derived from the Latin *fatum,* "something spoken" or "oracle"), the preordained, unalterable pattern of cosmic and human events, is a concept associated with the feminine in some religions, notably the Indo-European traditions. In Greek mythology, fate takes the form of a goddess or group of divine beings. They are known as the Moirai (singular, Moira), which comes from the Greek word meaning "lot" or "share." The three Moirai of ancient Greece (Clotho, Lechesis, and Atropos) spin, measure, and snip the thread of life, determining the life span and fortune of each baby at birth. The Moirai may have originated as chthonic deities whose special area of jurisdiction was human death. Eventually, however, they came to govern the whole of one's lot in life from cradle to grave.

Atropos, the third of the Moirai in Greek mythology, is depicted in this mosaic (Gianni Dagli Orti/Corbis).

In pre-Christian German and Nordic mythology, several classes of female supernatural beings specialized in knowing and controlling the fates of people. The Valkyries, divine female warriors, were said to flock to battlefields where they meted out victory or death to the warriors. Most powerful of all were the three Norns, representing past, present, and future, who watered the ash tree that is the *axis mundi* or structural center of the Nordic cosmos. In addition, both gods and human beings lacked foreknowledge and relied on sibyls or *vǫlur* to prophesize future events.

The image of a wise and powerful woman weaving or spinning presents an important key to understanding the relationship between fate and the feminine in classical Greek and prehistoric Old European traditions. Like the making of cloth, the work of fate is a painstaking process in which fragile human lives are spun out, snipped off, and woven together to create a well-planned human social textile. Women are the instrument of fate's work because they repeatedly spin new life from their bodies. Raising children and weaving cloth, an activity that symbolizes fertility, were both women's work in Greek and northern European culture. Like fate, women were weavers, creating a useful material out of raw matter.

In India, women are also associated with fate, that is, the dispensation of human birth and death. The Sanskrit term samsara, the cycle of birth and death, derives from a verb meaning "to flow together" and connotes the never-ending gush of ignorant life that makes up the ordinary world. The inevitable and cyclical nature of samsara, which dooms unseeing, grasping humans to multiple lives of suffering, is something that most Indian spiritual traditions, including Jain, Buddhist, and Hindu asceticism, seek to escape through the cultivation of detachment. Many actions that fuel the engine of samsara, such as sex, eating, and accumulating wealth, pertain to women's bodies and social roles. Women are sexual partners, makers of food, and birth-givers. Thus, in Indian spiritual traditions, outwitting samsara is usually predicated on circumventing domestic life with women.

BIBLIOGRAPHY

Dietrich, B. C. *Death, Fate, and the Gods.* 1965.
Greene, William C. *Moira: Fate, Good, and Evil in Greek Thought.* 1944.
Jochens, Jenny. *Old Norse Images of Women.* 1996.
Knott, Kim. "Hindu Women, Destiny, and *Stridharma." Religion* 26 (1996): 15–35.
O'Flaherty, Wendy Doniger. *Karma and Rebirth in Classical Indian Traditions.* 1980.

AMY PARIS LANGENBERG

Fāṭimah

Fāṭimah, the youngest daughter of Muhammad and his first wife Khadija, is known in the Muslim tradition as Zahra (the Radiant One) and is greatly venerated by all Muslims. She was born at Mecca but there is divergence regarding her date of birth in the early Arabic sources. It is generally believed that she was born between 605 and 609 C.E.

Among the few incidents reported about Fāṭimah's early life is her profound grief at her mother's death and consolation by her father, and her removal of refuse thrown from the Quraysh tribe at her father when he was at prayer.

Fāṭimah was married to ʿAli, the son of Abu Talib, Muhammad's uncle and protector, when she was between fifteen and twenty-one and he was twenty-five. Their union had many difficulties, ranging from poverty in the early years to marital discord. Muhammad, who loved Fāṭimah dearly, offered financial help to the couple and arbitrated in their disputes. He is also believed to have blocked ʿAli's intention to take another wife.

There are some references to Fāṭimah in historical accounts of events during and after Muhammad's lifetime, but they do not give a clear, comprehensive, or consistent picture of Fāṭimah, who died a few months after her father in 633 C.E.

The importance of Fāṭimah in the Muslim tradition is due primarily to the fact that, as the only surviving child of Muhammad, she continued his bloodline through her marriage to his cousin ʿAli, with whom she had two sons, Hasan and Husayn. The concept of *ahl al-bayt*, or the people of the Prophet's house, became confined to Muhammad, Fāṭimah, and her husband and sons.

As the result of the development particularly of Shiite piety, Fāṭimah became the center of a cult that regarded everything about her as sacred or miraculous, extending to her the attributes of impeccability and infallibility applied to the Prophet and the imams. In his book *Fāṭimah Fāṭimah ast* (Fāṭimah Is Fāṭimah), the modern Iranian scholar ʿAli Shariʿati, making use of both historical and hagiographical sources, represents Fāṭimah as the model to be emulated by all women seeking self-actualization.

BIBLIOGRAPHY

Useful sources of biographical information are Laura Veccia Vaglieri, "Fatima," in *The Encyclopaedia of Islam*, vol. 2, edited by B. Lewis, Ch. Pellat, and J. Schacht (1965); and Jane Dammen McAuliffe, "Fatimah Bint Muhammad," in *The Encyclopedia of Religion*, vol. 5, edited by Mircea Eliade (1987).

Considered an Islamic good luck symbol, the Hand of Fāṭimah is made on this wall by a painted handprint (Bernard and Catherine Desjeu/Corbis).

References to Fāṭimah may be found in historical accounts about events in the life of Muhammad and the early Muslim community. There is also a great deal of hagiographical literature that focuses on Fāṭimah as she became preeminent in Shiite piety.

A popular book in English on Fāṭimah is Mohammad ʿAli Al-Haj Salmin, *Fatima, The Lady of the Light* (1934). Brief accounts of Fāṭimah's life may be found in books about noteworthy Muslim women, such as Muhammad Saeed Siddiqi, *The Blessed Women of Islam* (1982).

Non-English sources include Muhammed Nafiʿ, "Sawaneh Hayat Hazrat Saiyyada Fatimatuz Zahra," in *Binat-e-Arbaʿ*, Lahore, 1997, and Syeda Ashraf Zafar, *Al-Fatima*, Lahore, 1982.

RIFFAT HASSAN

Female Personifications

Personification is the practice of imputing human form to an abstract idea, a natural force or phenomenon, or an aggregate of people such as a city, state, nation, tribe, or clan. Its function in language or visual culture is to give boundaries to a capacious notion or phenomenon. Personifications are prevalent in most ancient religions, including those of the Egyptians, Greeks, Romans, and Semitic peoples, and in historical and contemporary Christianity, Amerindian, Mesoamerican, and Asian belief systems. As applied to natural phenomena such as storms, rivers, or mountains, personifications are a way of personalizing one's relationship to such phenomena, and in some cases may be understood as a way of controlling their unpredictable characters. This article discusses only those female personifications that show evidence of worship or cult activity. Such activity implies the presence of a belief system related to the personified force or idea.

ABSTRACT IDEAS

The Furies

A group of female personifications of vengeance in Roman and Greek religions, they punish guilty humans on earth and in the underworld and especially focus their wrath on murderers who kill their own kinfolk.

Honor

In Chinese cosmology, Honor is associated with selflessness and is known as Yu Nu (Honorable Lady). Connected with the constellation Leo, she is also known as a Taoist stellar deity.

Lady Wisdom or Wisdom

In Christianity, Mary, the mother of Jesus, has been associated with divine Wisdom since about the seventh century C.E. In the Ancient Near East, wisdom or Sophia-achamoth was considered to be the female aspect or mother-face of the God of the Hebrew scriptures. Described collectively as sensuous, maternal, erotic, moral, and a beautiful bride in an array of Hebrew and Christian texts, Wisdom symbolizes both empirical and mystical knowledge.

Prayers

In Hellenistic religion the Prayers were sometimes personified as the daughters of Zeus, the Olympian supreme being. Their role was to intervene with their father on behalf of mortals.

NATURAL FORCES OR PHENOMENA

Corn Mother or Corn Woman

The Corn Mother is known in many of the corn-growing cultures of the traditional peoples of North America but is particularly associated with those Amerindians who dwell on the plains and in the southeast corner of the continent. For the plains Indians she is associated with education and knowledge, for the Huron, Abnaki, and Cherokee, with goodness, hunting, and agriculture.

Death

Personified as the dark aspect of the Great Mother in many belief systems, or as the death aspect of a goddess identified as the creator of life and death, Death may be portrayed as a devouring gorge of the underworld, who nourishes herself by consuming the cadavers buried in her, as in Mesoamerican representations, or as a female figure adorned with skull necklaces. In Hinduism the goddess Kali is known as the "bone-wreathed Lady of the place of skulls."

Fire

Known as Kadlu to the Central Inuit of the Arctic, Fire is one of three goddesses of weather who, when they interact, bring thunder, lightning, and rain to the earth. Fire is the sister who makes lightning by rubbing pieces of flint together.

Lady of the Beasts

An aspect of the Great Goddess and worshiped around the Mediterranean, the Ancient Near East, India, and Africa, Lady of the Beasts, a principle in female form, has all beasts, including phantasms such as the sphinx, as her subjects. In visual form she is often depicted as a winged creature, holding an animal by the neck or foot in either hand. In human beings she is thought to govern instincts and drives by tempering them, thus guiding humans away from the primitive toward civilization.

Lady of the Lake

As the Celtic goddess of Sovereignty, the Lady of the Lake gave Arthur of Britain his kingship and accompanied him on his death barge at the end of his life. Her domain is water, and her Welsh name is Nimue.

Lady of the Plants

Associated with the tree goddess, and an aspect of the Great Goddess, the Lady of the Plants gives nourishment to souls. Often represented as the sycamore or date palm, especially in ancient Egyptian art, the Lady of the Plants is responsible for the birth and death of all living things. The equation of tree worship with a feminine principle has semblances in the cults of Isis and

Tarot card of Justice depicted as a woman, by Bonifacio Bembo, c. 1400–1500 (Gianni Dagli Orti/Corbis)

Dionysus and in the belief systems of Buddhism, Hinduism, and Christianity.

AGGREGATES OF PEOPLE

Haida

Known as the creator deity of the northwest coast of Canada, Haida, or "Foam Woman," whose attribute is water, is represented as a fecund mother with twenty breasts. Each breast suckled one of the grandmothers

of the Raven Clan families who became organized into matrilineal clans or households. The histories of the clan ancestors are visually depicted in potlatch houses, living personifications of the clans' ancestors.

Amaterasu

The great ancestral goddess of the Japanese is known as Amaterasu-no-oho-kami, or "Heavenly Shining Great Deity." To live by the qualities of virtue and uprightness is her mandate for the emperor and his family and all Japanese.

Chinese dynasties

In early Chinese history, in the time of the Three Dynasties before the imperial age of Ch'in and Han, three "ladies" were considered the clan ancestors of these ancient families. Lady Yu, Lady Xie, and Lady Yuan are the female personifications of the Xia (Hsia) dynasty (2205–1766 B.C.E.), the Shang dynasty (1766–1122 B.C.E.), and the Zhou (Chou) dynasty (1115–221 B.C.E.), respectively. Like all Chinese female ancestors, they are identified as being the mothers and guardians of their people.

Roma

Often depicted as a warlike figure wearing a short tunic and helmet and sitting on armor, Roma's first temple was erected not in Rome but in the eastern provinces of the Roman Empire. The emperor Hadrian (117–138 C.E.) brought her cult to Rome, where she was regarded as a personification of the city itself.

Given the great number of female personifications, one may ask how they relate to the place of actual women in a given culture. When female deities or principles are seen to rule intuitively over the affairs of men, as in the case of Roman religion, real women are obliged to do the same: both real and mythical women lack direct political power and must achieve their ends indirectly through manipulation of their men. In a study of the representations of women in Sinhalese myth and Buddhist doctrine, Lorna Rhodes Amara-Singham (1978) concluded that "women represented uncontrolled desire in both doctrinal Buddhism and folk mythology." Yet attitudes toward women in folk mythology and toward real Sinhalese women could not be directly correlated. In cultures that uphold a male-gendered vision of reality, even when the female principle has power mythologically, flesh-and-blood women are still dominated by men socially and politically. David Kinsley, in his comparative study of female goddesses, found that female divinities were either extremely important or in fact central in cultures that were nonetheless still male dominant.

In any study of Western personifications, it is important to remember that over time, worshiped female entities lost their divine attributes and developed into forms of rhetoric (written and visual), forfeiting earlier multiple meanings for ease of communicating a single idea. Thus, their continued presence in Western culture reveals as much about the evolution of ideologies as the devolution of belief systems.

BIBLIOGRAPHY

Adkins, Lesley, and Roy A. Adkins. *Dictionary of Roman Religion.* 1996.

AmaraSingham, Lorna Rhodes. "The Misery of the Embodied." In *Women in Ritual and Symbolic Roles.* Edited by Judith Hoch-Smith and Anita Spring. 1978.

Ann, Martha, and Dorothy Myers Imel. *Goddesses in World Mythology.* 1993.

Apostolos-Cappadona, Diane. *Encyclopedia of Women in Religious Art.* 1996..

Bonnefoy, Yves. *Mythologies: A Restructured Translation of* Dictionnaire des mythologies et des religions des sociétés traditionnelles et du monde antique. Translated by Gerald Honigsblum et al. 1991.

Fitzhugh, William W., and Aron Crowell. *Crossroads of Continents: Cultures of Siberia and Alaska.* 1988.

Kinsley, David. *The Goddesses' Mirror: Visions of the Divine from East and West.* 1989.

Larrington, Carolyne, ed. *The Feminist Companion to Mythology.* 1992.

Neumann, Erich. *The Great Mother: An Analysis of the Archetype.* Translated by Ralph Manheim. 1963.

Ramage, Nancy H., and Andrew Ramage. *Roman Art. Romulus to Constantine.* 1991.

Soskice, Janet Martin. *Metaphor and Religious Language.* 1985.

Warner, Marina. *Monuments and Maidens: The Allegory of the Female Form.* 1985.

See also **Amaterasu; Animals; Death; Furies; Nature; Sophia.**

JANET HELEN TULLOCH

Feminine, The

Many religious traditions postulate the existence of a primordial force or essence characterized as "the feminine." It is imagined in a variety of ways: the yin aspect of the Tao in Taoism; the nurturing or destructive goddesses of Hinduism; the bodhisattva of compassion in Buddhism; the Shekhinah of Jewish Kabbalah, the motherly tenderness of the Virgin in Roman Catholicism. Most religious symbol systems have contributed to the notion that there is such a force or essence, a feminine side of reality or of the divine that is uniquely related to whatever qualities are seen as properly female in that culture.

Some feminist critics have argued that any notion of the feminine is an inherently essentialist concept: to assert the existence of the feminine is to claim that there is an essence of femaleness or of women, an intrinsic, universal, unchangeable nature in which all women either do or properly should participate. To postulate the existence of the feminine would thus be to deny the diversity, variability, and even freedom of actual living women themselves.

The charge of essentialism takes many forms, depending on the concept of the feminine that is proposed. Especially important in the history of the term in contemporary feminist debate are the psychological theories of Sigmund Freud, Carl Jung, and Jacques Lacan.

Freud believed that the feminine is characterized most centrally by penis envy. Women's character, constructed around this envy, is essentially envious, jealous, and narcissistic. Freud was critiqued by Simone de Beauvoir, who revealed how patriarchal restrictions created this supposedly feminine character. But she fell into her own form of essentialism, claiming that the biology of motherhood itself inevitably makes women dependent.

Jung proposed the existence of the anima, a contra sexual aspect of the male psyche that needed to be integrated for true maturity to emerge. Some female Jungian analysts have suggested that women whose egos have followed a "masculine" path of development also need to work to integrate their own feminine soul dimension. Others have argued that women are more naturally in touch with the feminine on the conscious level. Both groups remain vulnerable to the essentialist charge.

Lacan characterized the feminine as lack or otherness, and said that it is unrepresented within Western discourse, functioning either as absence or excess. Luce Irigaray differs with Lacan, asserting that there is indeed a feminine, but that it is *nonrepresentable* rather than just missing, and therefore constitutive of a potentially disruptive locus or strategy outside patriarchal thought patterns. Although critics of Irigaray call her an essentialist she seems to advocate a "practice" of the feminine as a strategic feminist move rather than assert its existence as a natural, biological, or psychic essence.

French deconstructionist philosopher Jacques Derrida frequently invokes the feminine or woman. He ar-

An aboriginal bark painting depicts a feminine Mimi spirit, Arnhem Land, Australia (Charles and Josette Lenars/Corbis).

gues that Nietzsche associates woman with metaphor and writing, which beneficially subvert and transcend metaphysical philosophies of certainty and truth. Derrida says that what escapes capture by "phallogocentric" philosophical discourse is feminine.

Judith Butler questions the substantial existence of any identity such as women or the feminine, and argues for the performative nature of gender itself. If gender arises in the doing or performing of gender, as she suggests, any notion of the feminine preexisting the performance of culturally constructed "femininities" is unthinkable.

BIBLIOGRAPHY

Freud's classic essay is "Femininity" in *New Introductory Lectures on Psycho-Analysis* (1932). Simone de Beauvoir's *The Second Sex* (1949) both analyzes cultural sources of the feminine as "other" and sees it as a result of reproductive biology. *Aspects of the Feminine* collects Jung's writings on the subject from 1921 to 1951, including "The Shadow and the Syzygy: Anima and Animus" (1951). *Feminine Sexuality* includes articles by Lacan from 1966 to 1975. Derrida's most accessible statement on the feminine appears in *Spurs: Nietzsche's Styles* (1978). Luce Irigaray's *This Sex Which Is Not One* (1977) revalorizes "the feminine" as an alternative discourse outside of patriarchal language, while Judith Butler's *Gender Trouble* (1990) proposes a performative theory of gender.

See also **Beauvoir, Simone de.**

JEAN GRAYBEAL

Femininity

Derived from *femina,* Latin for woman, *femininity* refers to the quality or nature of the female gender. Within religious contexts, certain frequently visited themes display cultural and religious judgments of what constitutes femininity. One such recurrent theme involves the chaste woman or the virgin who is moral, regal, and untouchable. She approaches divinity, for through sexual abstinence she achieves a kind of religious purity, a great power that is sometimes dangerous and often surpasses that of males.

In ancient Greece we see her as Athena, the virgin goddess of war, both guardian of civilization and fierce warrior, and Artemis, maiden goddess of the hunt, the "protectress of dewy youth" who nonetheless kept the Greek fleet from sailing to Troy until they sacrificed a maiden to her, and who also caused the death of the youth Actaeon when he happened upon her bathing nude.

In Hindu tradition Sītā, the wife of Rāma (the hero of the epic Rāmāyaṇa) clearly exemplifies the Hindu ideal of femininity—*pativrata,* the faithful, devoted, chaste wife. After having refused the advances of the demon Ravana, who held her captive for years, Sītā called upon the earth to swallow her and thus abandoned Rāma, who wrongly doubted her faithfulness. The greatest Christian symbol of purity is the Virgin Mary, through whom the Savior entered the world. Catholic doctrine affirms she was assumed bodily into heaven where she now lives and intercedes for the faithful.

In contrast to the virgin is the image of the temptress. Enticing and dangerous, she is sexy, self-possessed, and bold. Men desire her, but she will bring about their destruction. In Greek myth sirens swam in the sea and sang their irresistible song to passing sailors, seducing them to jump to their watery deaths. In Western monotheistic traditions, all of humanity suffers downfall owing to Eve's temptation of Adam. In Milton's *Paradise Lost,* when Adam and Eve make love after the Fall, Adam rises afterward, like Samson at the hands of Delilah, "shorn of his strength." This image is seen today in the femme fatale, portrayed perfectly by Marlene Dietrich in the classic German film *The Blue Angel.*

Temptresses, prostitutes, and wayward women, however, can also be vehicles of their own and others' transformations. Herodotus's *Histories* tells of sacred rites of the goddess Mylitta (Aphrodite) involving sexual encounters between men and temple prostitutes, the priestesses of the goddess. In Christianity the reformed prostitute Mary Magdalene becomes a faithful disciple of Jesus and is among the first witnesses of the Resurrection. The popular U.S. film *Pretty Woman* exemplifies the secularized version of this theme, the prostitute with the heart of gold who brings out the best in the male protagonist.

In the image of the mother, the feminine is chthonic, full, giving, and protective but also authoritative and dominating. She is both giver and taker of life. As nature she is fecund, ripe, and generous, providing life and nourishment in the rhythm of the seasons—the grain goddess of ancient myth, the Great Goddess of neopagans, the lush, earthy mother portrayed by Sophia Loren in various Italian films. A mother's power, however, also makes her capable of wreaking disaster, as when the Greek earth goddess Demeter plunges the world into darkness while mourning for her kidnapped daughter Persephone. Another image of the mother is the "queen of heaven," the mistress of the gods. She is the Virgin Mary, the Canaanite Astarte, the Babylonian Ishtar. Hsi Wang Mu (XiwangMu), the Queen Mother of the West from Chinese mythology, is the official giver of the plagues sent from heaven but who can also grant immortality.

The ferocity of the mother's devotion rivals the hero's strength. To protect or avenge her child, she will sacrifice even herself. In the old English epic *Beowulf,* the beast Grendel's mother, "savage in her grief," attacks the troops of Beowulf's company, seeking revenge for the death of her son at Beowulf's hands. Anna Magnani portrays this image in Roberto Rossellini's film *Open City.* Motherly devotion can also, however, be sexually predatory. Sexual relationship with the mother, as between the Sumerian hero Dumuzi and his mother, the goddess Innana, or King Oedipus and his mother Jocasta, brings danger or death to the son. Mothers are also dominating forces. To grow to power within the world, the hero must sometimes reject or even defeat his mother: as Orestes, who kills his mother, Clytaemestra, to avenge her murder of his father, Agamemnon, and who is forgiven for matricide by Apollo, Athena, and Zeus; and Jesus, who by some Gospel accounts asks who is his mother by claiming his followers as his true family.

Other aspects of femininity are underscored by the Taoist idea of yin. Passive and receptive, as opposed to the active, creative yang, yin is water, night, the depths, the dark, the cold, the mysterious. We see her in the common film trope of the mysterious woman, as played by Simone Simon in the classic U.S. film of the 1940s, *Cat People.* According to the I Ching, the Taoist Book of Changes, yin activated and led by yang produces good; yin which tries to stand equally with yang produces evil. As water, yin—the force that slowly and gently

Tokiwa Gozen, a twelfth-century Japanese woman who saved her children and remained loyal to their father's memory, represents feminine obedience in Yoshitoshi Taiso's "Eight Honorable Ways of Conduct," series of woodblock prints, 1878 (Asian Art & Archaeology/Corbis).

wears away the great yang force of rock—is also the deep, mysterious, dangerous abyss.

Various aspects of femininity can be seen in the three-faced goddess, such as Hecate, the ancient moon goddess who is maiden, mother, and crone. The Fates of ancient Greece take the form of these three women; they are portrayed again in Satyajit Ray's film *Pather Panchali.* Crones, or old women, the final phase of these three aspects of femininity, are particularly powerful, for they stand outside the realm of male desire. No longer virgin, maiden, temptress, or mother, the crone has moved beyond the male world. The wise old tea women of Zen koans and the grizzled witch hag who flies by the full moon of Halloween are two images of the crone.

Concepts of femininity become evident in the common religious trope of cross-dressing. Men who take on the dress and appearance of women attempt to emulate some feminine attributes. Some Hindu sadhus—ascetic holy men—such as the rasik sect, called Sakhis, practice a kind of devotional worship in which they dress and make themselves up as women and develop an erotic attachment to Rama or Krishna. Transvestism is also a common trope in shamanism, which sometimes, according to Mircea Eliade, provides a means of accessing the strength and magic of feminine power (perhaps left over from matriarchal times). In the U.S. film *Tootsie*, Dustin Hoffman plays a man who through cross-dressing achieves the New Age goal of getting in touch with his feeling, intuitive, feminine side.

BIBLIOGRAPHY

Birrell, Anne. *Chinese Mythology*. 1993.

Butler, Judith. *Feminist Contentions: A Philosophical Exchange (Thinking Gender)*. 1995.

Eliade, Mircea. *Shamanism: Archaic Techniques of Ecstasy*. 1964.

Hamilton, Edith. *Mythology: Timeless Tales of Gods and Heroes*. 1967.

Kuryluk, Ewa. *Salome and Judas in the Cave of Sex*. 1987.

Mookerjee, Ajit. *Kali: The Feminine Force*. 1988.

Neumann, Erich. *Great Mother: An Analysis of the Archetype*. 1991.

O'Flaherty, Wendy Doniger. *Women, Androgynes, and Other Mythical Beasts*. 1982.

Scott, Joan Wallach. *Gender and the Politics of History*. 1989.

Sproul, Barbara. *Primal Myths: Creating the World*. 1979.

See also Essentialism; Gender Roles.

JENNIFER DUMPERT

Feminisms

Women's movements have traveled under a variety of names since at least the middle of the nineteenth century (King, 1994; Lugones, 1997). As will become clear in what follows, sometimes feminist movements are initiated by and are open to women from various social locations, and sometimes feminist movements are more limited in their appeal.

The history of the women's movement and its variations crosses the field of religion or "the religious" in some interesting and surprising places. In addition to being active shapers of reform movements or schismatic movements, women have often been involved in and created new religious movements (e.g., Quakers, Shakers, Anabaptists, Christian Science, Spiritualism).

What is conventionally referred to as first wave feminism dates to nineteenth-century movements for women's rights in the United States, England, and Germany. Undertaken in part as efforts at both mission and moral reform, these feminist movements have been both distinct from and intertwined with their not specifically religious or "secular" counterparts. One fascinating example here is Bertha Pappenheim, an early twentieth-century feminist who founded the German Jüdischer Frauenbund, or League of Jewish Women. (This is the same Bertha Pappenheim whose case study—Anna O.—launched psychoanalysis and the talking cure.) Though Pappenheim was highly critical of the second-class status of Jewish women within Orthodox Judaism and Jewish society more broadly, her proposed solution was not "secularization" but the radical return of traditional Judaism (Boyarin, 1997; Kaplan, 1979). Pappenheim's example denaturalizes any simple pairing of feminism with "the secular" and against "the religious."

The relations between feminism and religion and between feminism and secularism must be evaluated on a case-by-case basis and with careful attention to historical and cultural content. What each of these terms means will not be everywhere or at all times the same. Kwok Pui Lan (1992) offers the suggestive case of late nineteenth- and early twentieth-century China, where a specifically Christian women's movement was both influenced by and sometimes lagged behind a secular Chinese feminist movement.

Secular Jewish socialist movements in the United States were also among the early conditions of feminism's nineteenth-century emergence. Additionally, feminism or movements for women's rights emerged out of various—and often religiously based—social movements, including the movement for the abolition of slavery, which produced leaders such as Sojourner Truth and the Grimke sisters. While religion, broadly conceived, may have formed the basis of these movements, it also became the object of movements for change, as the pillars of religious institutions were called to account (e.g., sacred texts justifying women's second-class status and denying women equal access to learning and public interpretation of sacred texts). In response, women produced *The Woman's Bible* (Stanton), took up the role of preacher, and founded religious movements of their own.

Moreover, as would be the case in the second wave of a specifically feminist movement, these various "feminisms" took place under different auspices, with different theoretical understandings, and different practical and political effects. Though the founding text of second wave feminism is probably de Beauvoir's *The Second Sex*, which was first published in France in 1949, the advent of second wave feminism is conventionally dated to the second half of the twentieth century, particularly the 1960s and 1970s. These broad rubrics for distinguishing among the political orientations of feminisms have been identified by Alison M. Jaggar (1983) in relation to second wave feminism, but they are in some ways applicable to the first wave as well: socialist, liberal, and radical feminism. Socialist feminist movements have worked to maintain the class-based analysis of Marxism in conjunction with a feminist focus on the specifics of gender oppression. So, for example, socialist feminist movements strive to bring women's (frequently unpaid) labor into the realm of political relevance. Cases in point are movements agitating for wages for housework, perhaps most vocally in Italy; or movements for women's benefits in democratic socialist countries like Sweden; or movements for women's rights as part of Marxist nationalist movements in South Africa or Nicaragua or in avowedly Marxist countries like Cuba.

Liberal feminisms argue that the foundations of liberal or Enlightenment-based democracy are the basis for universal human rights, and thus for women's rights. Making the deceptively simple argument that "feminism is the radical claim that women are human beings," liberal feminisms protest that women's social, legal, and economic inequalities undermine the fulfillment of Enlightenment humanism and its discourse of rights. Thus, liberal feminist movements have been more common in those countries espousing liberal democracy (e.g., Great Britain or the United States). Because liberal feminisms do not contest the underlying assumptions of liberal humanism, the projects of liberal feminism are sometimes identified with or as reform feminism.

Radical feminists place women, rather than Marxism or liberal political ideology, at the center of their analysis and activism, arguing that only by starting from women's lives can feminism produce a theoretical and political framework that is not ultimately intertwined with or collusive with patriarchy. Radical feminisms refuse an accommodation with the liberal state, seeking instead the radical reorganization of social and political life.

None of these distinctions goes all the way through, however. For example, the radical implications of liberal claims for the full humanity of women led Zillah Eisenstein to produce the aptly titled political theory *The Radical Future of Liberal Feminism* (1981). Moreover, a different genealogy of second wave feminism might distinguish between radical feminism and cultural feminism. According to Alice Echols' retelling (1989), whereas radical feminists contested the naturalization of binary gender (a naturalization that is taken

to legitimate or justify women's inequality by referring it to "nature"), attempted to eliminate gender as a meaningful social category, and emphasized the material bases for women's inequality (Firestone, 1970), cultural feminists stressed fundamental differences between women and men, valorizing female nature and seeking to elaborate a distinctively female counterculture in opposition to patriarchal dominance (Alpert, 1993; Daly, 1978).

The point here is not to establish which label is proper to which set of claims, but to suggest how widely disparate claims about what women "are" may yet travel under the same name, whether "radical feminist" or simply "feminist." Moreover, this set of distinctions among feminisms is intertwined with another set based on the variety of women's movements that do not travel under the name of feminism. The forms of study based on these diverse women's movements are perhaps more fully developed in religious studies than in any other field, a reflection of the global and practice-oriented implications of the study of religion.

Throughout the world, various liberation movements and theologies have taken up women's rights as a cause or have been taken up by women in other social movements. The relation between and among women's movements, feminisms, and other radical social movements is articulated differently in different national and politico-cultural scenes. For example, Lou Ratté (1985) reports that the development of Indian feminism in the twentieth century took place in relation to counter-imperialist and nationalist movements that both advanced the cause of women's rights and used "woman" as a symbol of nation in ways that could recuperate feminism into a traditionally patriarchal nationalism. In Latin America, liberation theologies and movements of indigenous peoples have also become women's movements, iconographically embodied most recently by Nobel Peace Prize winner Rigoberta Menchú.

In the United States, a number of distinctive women's movements have formed—womanist, *mujerista*, lesbian, for example—to struggle against the various forms of domination faced in a society stratified along lines of class, race, and sexuality, as well as gender. Moreover, the term "third wave" has been proposed to characterize new forms of feminist organizing, such as riot grrrls, undertaken through new media (zines, Internet, punk rock). These movements point to both the limits and possibilities of any project that might call itself feminist; if women are not one, then there can be no one feminism "proper" to women either. The name *feminism* carries with it the imperative both to move to end the domination of all women and simultaneously to recognize the limits of any single name or movement for women. Only the recognition of these limit(s) can leave feminism(s) open to the various possibilities that might make up a future not marked by domination.

BIBLIOGRAPHY

Alpert, Jane. "Mother Right: A New Feminist Theory." *Ms.* (August 1993): 52–55, 88–94.

Beauvoir, Simone de. *The Second Sex.* Translated and edited by H. M. Parshley. 1953.

Boyarin, Daniel. *Unheroic Conduct: The Rise of Heterosexuality and the Invention of the Jewish Man.* 1997.

Daly, Mary. *Gyn/Ecology: The Metaethics of Radical Feminism.* 1978.

Echols, Alice. *Daring to Be Bad: Radical Feminism in America, 1967–1975.* 1989.

Eisenstein, Zillah R. *The Radical Future of Liberal Feminism.* 1981.

Firestone, Shulamith. *The Dialectic of Sex: The Case for Feminist Revolution.* 1970.

Jaggar, Alison M. *Feminist Politics and Human Nature.* 1983.

Kaplan, Marion A. *The Jewish Feminist Movement in Germany: The Campaigns of the Judischer Frauenbund, 1904–1938.* 1979.

King, Katie. *Theory in Its Feminist Travels: Conversations in U.S. Women's Movements.* 1994.

Kwok Pui Lan. *Chinese Women and Christianity, 1869–1927.* 1992.

Lugones, Maria. "Playfulness, 'World'-Travelling, and Loving Perception." In *Feminist Social Thought: A Reader.* Edited by Diana Tietkjens Meyers. 1997.

Ratté, Lou. "Goddesses, Mothers, and Heroines: Hindu Women and the Feminine in the Early Nationalist Movement." In *Women, Religion, and Social Change.* Edited by Yvonne Yazbeck Haddad and Ellison Banks Findly. 1985.

Stanton, Elizabeth Cady. *The Woman's Bible.* 1895–1898. Reprint, 1972.

See also **Lesbianism; Menchú, Rigoberta; Mujerista Tradition; Pappenheim, Bertha; Womanist Traditions; Woman's Bible, The.**

JANET R. JAKOBSEN

ANN PELLEGRINI

Fertility and Barrenness

Women's fertility is a subject of great seriousness in all of the world's religious traditions. Most religions consider childbearing one of women's most important societal functions. It is very common for women, and in some cases men, to seek religious means to attempt to secure fertility for themselves, or to alleviate problems involving a woman's fertility. Fertility is often conceptualized, in some traditions through cosmogonic myths telling of divine fertility, as instigating the very creation of the physical world and its sentient populations. Ritual practices concerned with women's fertility are often explained as attempts to emulate the mythic forces that incited human procreation.

There are many different perspectives from which to analyze a given religion's approach to fertility. This article focuses on the religious strategies of myth and ritual as they relate to fertility. Myths that address women's fertility help illuminate how certain foundational beliefs arose, and ritual practices illustrate how these beliefs are often concretized through repetitive experience. In this way, fertility rites are passed on from generation to generation often linking the fertility of the field with that of a woman's womb.

It is not uncommon that a religious tradition mythologizes its matriarchs as barren and in need of some kind of divine intervention to instigate conception. For example, in the Hebrew Bible, the wives of the three patriarchs in the Book of Genesis, Sarah, Rebekah, and Rachel, are all barren until God blesses their wombs with a male child. The New Testament also casts Mary's cousin Elizabeth as barren until she is blessed by God with her male child, John. In these instances, fertility is seen as a kind of divine gift, a reward after much suffering and hardship. Such a gift ensures the longevity of the lineage, which has been endowed with God's promise to continue and be fruitful.

The rhetoric common throughout the Bible is that the male carries the seed that will propagate the species while the female is likened to the soil in which the lineage is nurtured. According to this imagery, the seed carries the honor of a patriarchal society while the soil sustains this honor by continuing the male line of succession. In the Islamic tradition, the conception of women as soil implies that women are inherently shameful because they lack the seeds of honor, that is, the power to create and project themselves onto future generations. This shamefulness is a kind of indiscriminate fecundity that requires limits. A woman's value as alleged in Turkish Islamic village society, for example, depends on her ability to guarantee the legitimacy of her husband's seed. The emphasis here, as in many traditional societies, is on producing a male child as an heir to the patriline. A Muslim wife is expected to continue to bear children until a male is born.

Fertility is relevant to both men and women; rarely, however, do the same pressures exist for men within a given tradition to prove the purity and certitude of their fertility as those that exist for women. Some traditions have developed male cults that engage in ritual practice ostensibly to request a deity to bless both the earth and the women with fertile soil (or wombs). The goddess cult of the pagan people in the highlands of Papua New Guinea is one example. Here, it is the male cult that is fully responsible for conducting rituals that will honor and court the goddess who bestows fertility on the women of the tribe. The cult acts as a blueprint for male control over women in all arenas of life. The goddess negates the idea that males themselves create fertility and simultaneously affirms that women are entirely responsible for it.

Many traditions believe that fertility is a reward for propitiation of certain deities or goddesses. In China and Japan, Kuan Yin is the female Buddha believed to be the giver of children. Known as Hariti in Indian Buddhism, she is thought to be both devourer and restorer of children and fertility. Among the Shakta tradition of Hindu worshipers, there is a secret ritual that invokes the goddess to make the womb fertile. A young virgin's menstrual blood is used along with other bodily fluids as food offerings to the insatiable goddess who is invoked by the temple prostitutes, or *devadāsīs*. This secret fertility ritual is performed at night under highly guarded conditions. The purpose of this ritual is to maintain the male line of descendants because the failure of a woman to produce a male heir is considered the ultimate calamity. Thus, the withholding of fertility is alleged to bring finality, death, and terror to the whole group of believers.

One of the most interesting fertility cults exists among North African women, especially in the Sudan and Egypt. The Zar cult incorporates aspects of both Christianity and Islam; it involves spirit possession, which in this particular context may be associated with the loss of virginity. The *zayran* spirits are held responsible for numerous fertility disorders: they are believed to hold or seize the womb to prevent conception, or to loosen a fetus resulting in a miscarriage. Since the production of healthy male children is an imperative among North African women, those women who have successfully negotiated these spirit possessions have the greatest social status within their village. In this society, children are the highest form of capital a woman can hope to accumulate, and any impediments to fertility are believed to have grave consequences for a woman.

Barren women in most religious traditions are met with varying degrees of disrespect, ranging from pity to ostracism to banishment from the social group. In some cultures, such as Japan, there are extensive rituals available for aborted fetuses and miscarriages that are meant to alleviate the pain of a failed birth. In many so-

A colorful fertility tree of baskets and lights, Philippines (Paul Almasy/© Corbis)

cieties, however, the state of being barren is considered a divine punishment that often has no religious remedy and which results in the pronounced lack of status for a woman and often the lack of any opportunity to alter her standing within society. Therefore, where there are rituals available for women that attempt to court divine favor for their wombs, to hope and pray for the blessing usually of a male child, most women have no choice but to participate.

BIBLIOGRAPHY

Boddy, Janice. *Wombs and Alien Spirits: Women, Men, and the Zar Cult in Northern Sudan.* 1989.

Delaney, Carol. *The Seed and the Soil: Gender and Cosmology in Turkish Village Society.* 1991.

Greenhalgh, Susan, ed. *Situating Fertility: Anthropology and Demographic Inquiry.* 1995.

Jamison, Stephanie W. *Sacrifed Wife/Sacrificer's Wife: Women, Ritual, and Hospitality in Ancient India.* 1996.

Marglin, Frederique Apfell. "The Ambiguity of the Fertile Womb." In *The Realm of the Sacred: Verbal Symbolism and Ritual Structures.* Edited by Sitakant Mahapatra. 1992.

McCormack, Carol P., ed. *Ethnology of Fertility and Birth.* 1982.

O'Flaherty, Wendy Doniger. *Women, Androgynes, and Other Mythical Beasts.* 1980.

Sered, Susan Starr. *Priestess, Mother, Sacred Sister: Religions Dominated by Women.* 1994.

Srathern, Andrew. "Fertility and Salvation: The Conflict Between Spirit Cult and Christian Sect in Mount Hagan." *Journal of Ritual Studies* (Winter 1991): 51–65.

See also Devadāsīs; Kuan Yin (Kannon); Shaktism.

AMY LAVINE

Festivals

Festivals, as communal celebrations, are organized according to a set calendar in many religious traditions to mark central moments in the cosmic pattern (e.g., the new year), the subsistence cycle (e.g., harvest), or the life of a religious figure (e.g., Christ's resurrection, Buddha's birth). In some societies noncalendrical festivals are the norm, scheduled by religious and social authorities according to perceived communal need. Family festivals, especially initiatory or funeral rituals, sometimes take a central place in the public ritual life of a people (e.g., girls' initiation rites among the Tukuna of the Amazon basin; funeral rituals among the Garífuna of Belize).

Because of their communal nature, festivals are important to the social lives of women. Where women's daily life is restricted largely to the home, festivals offer a rare opportunity to go out in public and socialize outside the immediate circle of family and friends. Families separated through distance, especially women relocated through marriage, may reestablish ties during festivals, as when Garífuna families travel long distances for death rituals, or when, for various festivals of northern India, women return to their birth families.

Many community-wide festivals have ritual elements that must be performed in gender-specific groups, but it is rare to find civic or public festivals in which females exclusively participate. Our best examples come from ancient Greece, in festivals such as Thesmophoria (a three-day festival to Demeter in which married women camped out and performed fasts and rituals oriented toward communal fertility) and Adonesia (a day of mourning for Aphrodite's consort Adonis). Women may have particular issues that restrict or alter their festival participation (e.g., menstrual or postpartum taboos) and may have gender-specific readings of or activities during festivals that are not a part of "official" protocol (e.g., fasting one day during the celebration of Krishna's birthday in order to conceive a child).

Through formal and symbolic structures and through the duties and behaviors expected of participants, festivals play a significant part in representing to women their role within both community and spiritual world. Because women's roles vary widely from society to society, so, too, do their roles within festivals. Women may serve as priestesses, prominent in the festival's sacred action. For example, in ancient Greece priestesses (usually aristocratic married women) presided over most festivals in honor of goddesses; in India professional temple priestesses (*devadāsīs*) provided dance-drama reenactments of myths at many public and familial festivals. Priestesses provide a model of women's roles as representatives of cosmic order and mediators of relationships between gods and humans.

Similarly, in some festivals issues of prime importance to the entire society, such as maintenance of fertility and renewal of cosmic order, are mediated through a central female figure. For the hunter-gatherer Tukuna, girls' initiation rituals require participation by the entire community. The rituals surrounding the girl's journey through the upper and lower cosmic realms and into adulthood provide the framework for the community's ritual engagement with the crucial issues of balancing human fertility and finite resources. In Emar in ancient Syria, Baal's priestess was installed in a nine-day festival that provided the framework for balancing civic, kingly, divine, and familial order through the metaphor of sacred marriage.

Women's perceived connection with certain sources of power may cast them as festival organizers. Women play a large part in organizing Yoruba Gelede festivals, which honor "the mothers," and Garífuna women organize large-scale funeral festivals because of their expertise in and responsibility for mourning rituals.

In many religions, including Islam, Judaism, and Hinduism, women are generally excluded from public religious leadership while simultaneously acting as the primary practitioners of domestic ritual. Though less likely to play a prominent role in the public ritual aspect of festivals, women symbolically extend the importance of the festival from the public into the familial realm by means of their domestic activity. Among Turkish villagers the *mevlûd* (festival for Muhammad's birth) is celebrated publicly in mosques by men, while women celebrate in smaller groups of fifty or sixty, which provide a close, intense religious experience shared across class boundaries and illustrate the importance of this occasion in women's domestic lives. In many Jewish festivals women's expertise in the rituals of food preparation and service provides a domestic experience central to the festival's communal meaning. In India during Divali (the festival of light), women draw the goddess Lakṣmī's footsteps going into their homes for luck, an extension of the publicly celebrated goddess's importance into domestic space.

Women with arrangements of prepared food, fruit, and flowers piled in huge pyramids on their heads perform at the Odalan festival in the Kehen Temple in Bali (Arne Hodalic/Corbis).

Women's participation in public festivals often echoes their domestic duties: cleaning and decorating sacred spaces or preparing food, as in Indonesian festival offering trays or church dinners in the United States. While these activities may go unspoken, they may also be actively valued; the Lozi of Zambia, for instance, consider women's preparation of special beer necessary to the efficacy of all festivals.

Some festivals encourage transgressive behavior (activities that violate ordinary standards of behavior, such as riotous drinking at spring festivals). This temporary overthrow of order and status allows festival participants both a brief freedom from day-to-day restrictions and an experience of communal identity outside the normal boundaries of gender and status. Women's transgressive behavior may involve a rejection of typical female roles, as in Zulu spring festivals, where young girls dress in men's clothing and, under the guidance of older women, sing derogatory songs about men, or Thesmophoria, where the women's camps intruded into masculine public space. Transgressive behavior that involves obscenity is usually in service of fertility, as in a Tibetan May festival where both sexual joking and riotous water fights ensure plentiful rains, or in the ancient Greek women's festival of Haloa, where women's drinking and obscene talk encouraged an abundant harvest.

Other transgressive behaviors may illuminate aspects of cosmic order. During the early nights of the *molimo* festival of the Mbuti Pygmies, women are largely confined to their homes while men sing songs and perform dances forbidden for women. But in the last nights of the festival, women intrude into masculine space, disrupt the ceremony, and begin to take part in singing

and dancing those very songs. The women's transgressive actions are necessary to reestablish communal and cosmic order. Through the transgressive behaviors prescribed by festivals, women are able to explore conflicts implicit in their sacred systems and in their daily lives.

Festivals contribute to the construction of women's gender identity in several ways. They may illustrate ideas about women's perceived essential nature through symbolic action, as in Gelede, where women's measured style of dance reflects the feminine attributes of control, patience, and balanced power, or the Adoneia, where women's mourning shows their power over the barriers between life and death. Some, like the Turkish *mevlûd,* foster communal identity for women, distinct from men and free from status boundaries. Festivals often provide consciousness of age-specific as well as gender-specific roles. Girls often have a more active, performative role in civic rituals (e.g., maiden choruses in ancient Greece). Married women are frequently cast in a stabilizing background role that parallels their role as maintainers of family. Old women may play transgressive roles or ignore restraints that apply to fertile women. Through the complex symbolism of ritual action, women recognize the ways in which they are perceived as valuable to or dangerous to society and form a context for a wiser comprehension of the spiritual identities open to them, as well as the honors, duties, and restrictions integral to their daily lives.

BIBLIOGRAPHY

Blundell, Sue. *Women in Ancient Greece.* 1995.

Drewal, Henry John, and Margaret Thompson Drewal. *Gelede: Art and Female Power among the Yoruba.* 1983.

Hoch-Smith, Judith, and Anita Springs, eds. *Women in Ritual and Symbolic Roles.* 1978.

Kerns, Virginia. *Women and the Ancestors: Black Carib Kinship and Ritual.* 2d ed. 1997.

Kersenboom, Saskia C. "The Traditional Repertoire of the Tiruttani Temple Dancers." In *Roles and Rituals for Hindu Women.* Edited by Julia Leslie. 1991.

Lincoln, Bruce. *Emerging from the Chrysalis: Studies in Rituals of Women's Initiation.* 1981.

Pearson, Anne Mackenzie. *"Because It Gives Me Peace of Mind": Ritual Fasts in the Religious Lives of Hindu Women.* 1996.

Sax, William S. *Mountain Goddess: Gender and Politics in a Himalayan Pilgrimage.* 1991.

Sered, Susan Starr. *Women as Ritual Experts: The Religious Lives of Elderly Jewish Women in Jerusalem.* 1992.

Tapper, Nancy. "Gender and Religion in a Turkish Town: A Comparison of Two Types of Formal

Women's Gatherings." In *Women's Religious Experience.* Edited by Pat Holden. 1983.

Watkins, Joanne C. *Spirited Women: Gender, Religion, and Cultural Identity in the Nepal Himalaya.* 1996.

Zuesse, Evan M. *Ritual Cosmos: The Sanctification of Life in African Religions.* 1979.

See also Devadāsīs; Lakṣmī; Priestess.

ANDREA DEAGON

Film and Video

Documentary Films and Videos

Since the 1970s there has been an increasing array of media productions taking a wide range of thematic and stylistic approaches that explore the subject of women in religion. Some are ethnographic documentaries distinguished by their intimate and complex portrayals of women within a religious community. Others emphasize a political agenda, illustrating the ways in which women from different religious traditions engage in larger social, economic, and cultural arenas to improve conditions in the secular world. Another type of film offers critical and theoretical reinterpretations of religious traditions.

ETHNOGRAPHIC FILMS

Ethnographic film is a subgenre of documentary film often distinguished by a collaboration between the filmmaker and a social scientist, usually an anthropologist or sociologist. Several such films explore the theme of women as religious initiates and practitioners. The practice of long-term study conducted by social scientists helps to foster more intimate relationships between the filmmaker and the initiate. The development of small-format cameras has liberated filmmakers from cumbersome, obtrusive technology and permitted greater ease of access to sacred spaces where rituals, ceremonies, and worship are performed.

The film "In Her Own Time" (1985) emphasizes the quiet but transformative process by which a woman becomes a member of the Orthodox Jewish faith. In this film the initiate, Barbara Myerhoff, is an anthropologist who looks to religion at a moment of crisis. A diagnosis of cancer at age forty-nine propels her to confront issues of death. Beginning as the consummate social scientist, she consults with a range of people, from rabbis to scholars to Orthodox Jewish women, some of whom have practiced their faith for a lifetime and others who are recent converts. With each of these interviews she

tries to understand what is gained from faith. Myerhoff moves beyond observation to participate in women's Orthodox rituals, but is driven by her intellect rather than emotion. Slowly, her spirituality is awakened, and she begins to be touched by the community of the faithful.

Another collaborative effort between anthropologist and filmmaker, the video "An Initiation *Kut* for a Korean Shaman" (1991), follows the two-day initiation ceremony of a young Korean woman as she is guided by her spirit mother into her new status as shaman. The spirit mother barrages the hesitant, awkward initiate with insults and challenges—"Do you think spirits will appear if you just stand there waiting for them?" This video, by revealing the often mundane, tedious, and exhausting aspects of the ritual, demystifies the process of acquiring religious knowledge.

A series of four works produced by anthropologist Linda Connor and ethnographic filmmakers Timothy and Patsy Asch explores in all its complexity the life and healing practice of Jero Tapakan, a shamanic medium from Bali, Indonesia. The series is distinguished for its minimal voice-over narration; only contextual information is provided. A follow-up film entitled "Jero on Jero" (1981) applies an innovative film technique of self-reflexivity: Jero, rather than the anthropologist or filmmaker, reviews the film and provides her own interpretation, emphasizing what is meaningful about her practices and behavior.

POLITICAL FILMS

Many documentary film and video productions represent women, from Christianity to Islam to Buddhism, as active participants and agents of change in economic, political, and social arenas. One of the more aestheticized productions that illustrates this trend is "Satya: A Prayer for the Enemy" (1994), which addresses the suppression of Buddhism in Tibet by the Chinese. It shows the emergence of Buddhist nuns from forced seclusion to lead public demonstrations on behalf of human rights, religious freedom, and independence. The nuns articulate their choice in forsaking family life in order to defend, to their death, the beliefs of their community. Another video production, entitled "A Lesbian in the Pulpit" (1991), documents the life of an ordained minister in the United Church of Canada and how she and her partner have fought for gay rights and redefinition of the concept of family.

RELIGIOUS TRADITIONS REASSESSED

Feminist theory has propelled a reexamination of female icons and religious traditions. A provocative experimental documentary, "A Biography of Lilith" (1997), examines a curious figure from Jewish tradition. Lilith, Adam's first partner, was expelled from the Garden of Eden for her sexually assertive behavior. References to her have been found in Babylonian, Aramaic, and Jewish folklore dating back to before the birth of Christ. In this film, scholars and elderly Jewish women tell stories about the ambiguous representations of this maligned figure, who traditionally was said to be a threat to pregnant women. The film shows a stunning array of images of Lilith, from pre-Christian ceramics to nineteenth-century Eastern European amulets, which were meant to ward off her demonic spirit.

In a Brazilian video, "Feminino Sagrado" ("Feminine Holiness") (1996), done in the talking-head interview style, women from four religious traditions, Catholic, Protestant, Jewish, and the Afro-Brazilian Condomble, discuss the formation of an interreligious discussion group. They argue that because of inequities created by religious paternalism, such a discussion group is needed as a way to reclaim an affirming relationship to their religious traditions.

With the ever-growing Islamic faith and revival of fundamentalism, many films examine the practice of veiling demanded of Muslim women. "Covered: The Hejab in Cairo, Egypt" (1995), "Hidden Faces" (1990), and "A Veiled Revolution" (1992) explore the issues surrounding the wearing of the veil and its impact on women living in contemporary society.

Perhaps the most critical area undergoing reassessment is that of religious appropriation. In this multicultural, global community, religion is constantly being reshaped and reformed. A video entitled "Sweating Indian Style" (1995) looks at the impassioned and tense debate around non-native women who have appropriated Native American religious practices through the building of a Lakota women's sweat lodge. Who has the right, who has the privilege to practice religious traditions? Religion is deeply rooted in culture, as culture changes, so do religious traditions. Films and videos help to illustrate issues of religious tradition and change that face women around the world.

FILMOGRAPHY

"A Balinese Trance Seance." Directed by Linda Connor, Timothy Asch, and Patsy Asch. Documentary Educational Resources, Watertown, MA. 1980.

"A Biography of Lilith." Directed by Lynne Sachs. Women Make Movies, New York. 1997.

"Covered: The Hejab in Cairo, Egypt." Directed by Tania Kamal-Eldin. New York. 1995.

"Feminino Sagrado." Directed by Eunice Gutman. Rio de Janeiro, Brazil. 1996.

"Hidden Faces." Directed by Claire Hunt and Kim Longinotto. Women Make Movies, New York. 1990.

"In Her Own Time." Directed by Lynne Littman. Direct Cinema, Limited, Santa Monica, California. 1985.

"An Initiation *Kut* for a Korean Shaman." Directed by Diana S. Lee and Laurel Kendall. University of Hawaii Press, Honolulu. 1991.

"Jero on Jero." Directed by Linda Connor, Timothy Asch, and Patsy Asch. Documentary Educational Resources, Watertown, MA. 1981.

"A Lesbian in the Pulpit." Directed by Robin Taylor. Filmakers Library, New York. 1991.

"Satya: A Prayer for the Enemy." Directed by Ellen Bruno. Film Library, Ho-Ho-Kus, New Jersey. 1994.

"Sweating Indian Style." Directed by Susan Smith. Women Make Movies, New York. 1995.

"A Veiled Revolution." Directed by Marilyn Gaunt. First Run/Icarus Films, New York. 1992.

See also Lilith; Myerhoff, Barbara.

ELAINE CHARNOV

Feature Films and Videos

Fictional films portraying women as central figures interacting with religion are numerous and greatly vary in style and intent. Unlike documentaries, these films are free to explore and develop the complex links uniting women and religion. These relations reinforce the etymology of the word: religion is above all, a bond.

A distinction can be made between movies featuring historical characters and those that focus on entirely fictional women.

REVISITING HISTORICAL FIGURES

Among historical characters, the different interpretations of Joan of Arc are particularly striking. In *La Passion de Jeanne d'Arc* (1928), a French production and acclaimed classical version of Danish filmmaker Carl Dreyer, Joan is a martyr, a female Christ. Her suffering and humiliation are clearly shown as redeeming values of Catholicism. That the movie is silent enhances the passion of Joan's martyrdom, as does its black and white format. By contrast, Robert Bresson's *Le Procès de Jeanne d'Arc* (1962) presents Joan as an intellectual resisting her judges and, by extension, the official church. In the debates with the judges, she assumes full responsibility for her destiny and her mission. She strives to convert her persecutors to her vision of Catholicism as well as national unity. Although the voice of God guides her conduct, Bresson makes Joan a free agent. In her 1987 essay on film theory and gender, entitled *Technologies of Gender*, Teresa de Lauretis argues that even in the case of female characters, like Joan, who do not seem to comply with male rule, it is the nature of narrative cinema itself to perform an "inscription of gender" in its visual figuration of the masculine and the feminine positions. The woman becomes an image to be looked at, made to attract the look of both spectator and the male characters. It is the latter, in this case the judges, who at once command the action and the landscape, which they relay to the viewer.

The Egyptian film *Rabi'ah Al Adawiya* (1963) illustrates the life of the famous Sufi mystic Rabi'a, who lived during the eighth century in what is now Iraq. "She was no ordinary woman but rather the equivalent of one hundred men fighting for Islam," says one character in the movie. The film shows Rabi'a abandoning the lures of secular life for an ascetic existence. Through prayer and preaching, she reaches the desired state of charismatic ecstasy. The voice of famous Egyptian singer Om Kalthoum underlines the Sufi tradition of trance-like chanting as a means to reach Allah.

The character of Antigone in Greek mythology inspired various portraits. The Greek movie entitled *Antigoni* (1961) is faithful to the myth: respecting the gods' law, Antigone feels compelled to give her brother Polynice a burial following the rituals prescribed by ancient Greek religion, despite the interdiction of her uncle, King Creon. She winds up burying Polynice with her own hands and being punished by death. Italian filmmaker Liliana Cavani sets her Antigone (*I Cannibali*, 1969) in a modern totalitarian country in which burials of the regime's opponents have been forbidden. Antigone mysteriously comes out at night and buries the bodies; the viewer understands that this gesture is what links Antigone to her own spirituality. In this particular instance, the character is also using religious ritual as a political weapon, where the "personal becomes political."

The French director Jean-Luc Godard proposes an unconventional and controversial look at Mary, the mother of Christ. In *Je vous salue Marie* (1983) the focus is on Mary, not Jesus. A young basketball player, Mary is platonically involved with a taxidriver. She mysteriously becomes pregnant. While surprised, she accepts this pregnancy, although it is sometimes difficult to bear. Despite overtones of what was perceived as irreverence, this film depicts Mary pondering the mystery of birth and creation. She is a complex character inspired by an unshakable faith: opting for chastity, yet, accepting her pregnancy, intuitively sensing her divine selection.

REEXPLORING THE ORDINARY
Devi (1960), directed by Indian filmmaker Satyajit Ray, recounts the story of a beautiful young bride whose father-in-law delusionally believes her to be the goddess Kālī. She, in turn, accepts the role and becomes a living icon, soon acquiring a reputation for miraculous acts. A fascinating example of how history and culture can create an oppressive milieu, Devi is both sanctified and sacrificed, as her personal life disintegrates in parallel with her deification. De Lauretis points out in *Alice doesn't* that woman characters serve as the very ground of representation. They are both "object and support of a desire," which, intimately associated with power and creativity, is the moving force of culture and society.

Another exploration of women's roles in a traditional religious setting is the American film *Hester Street* (1974). Gitl, an immigrant Orthodox Jew, resists her husband's pressure to relax her strict ritual observances and become more "American," preferring Jewish Orthodox tradition in which she finds meaning and solace.

In Lars von Trier's *Breaking the Waves* (1996), Bess McNeill, the central character, lives in an isolated Scottish village ruled by austere Presbyterian men. Bess, though, has direct access to God to whom she speaks aloud: He always answers. Faced with a choice between committing a mortal sin and "saving" her husband, she chooses the former, even though it means becoming an outcast: her husband claims that she can only give him the will to stay alive after his paralysis by having sex with other men and telling him about it. She interprets it as God's command. In this twisted plot, the paradox lies in the fact that Bess finds the real meaning of Christian sacrifice in this strange act of devotion and pure faith in God, an act that ordinarily would appear to be one of betrayal. The movie portrays her as a modern saint, who, according to de Lauretis, curiously reaches sainthood by being "the looking-glass held up to man," a woman whose sexuality is either reduced or assimilated to the man's.

Noce en Galilée (1987), a movie produced in Belgium by Palestinian director Michel Khleifi, also places personal religious practice in opposition to well-established traditions. The movie recounts a Muslim wedding ceremony set in Israeli-occupied Galilee. Three generations of women are involved in the preparations for the ceremony: they carefully make traditional dishes and sing old Arabic songs in which secular and religious references are intricately mingled. During the purifying bath of the young bride, Aicha, the women punctuate their songs with the traditional ululating cry of joy reserved exclusively to women. Aicha joyfully takes part in this ritual. On her wedding night, however, the bridegroom cannot perform his "manly duty," and she defies religious traditions and "deflowers" herself, presenting the family with the much-awaited bloody sheet.

A few films explore religious customs through heroines who find themselves in conflict with these customs, despite wanting to remain faithful to their particular group, opposing what feminist film critic Constance Penley refers to as "patriarchal discourse," which attempts to repress the feminine voice and to eradicate all expression of difference that is not defined in relation to this superior discourse.

The Turkish film *Hazal* (1980) by Ali Ozgentürk tells the story of Hazal, a young widow who has to obey the local custom of her Anatolian village and marry her deceased husband's twelve-year-old brother. She abides by the law but finds herself more and more confined in a religious practice that has lost its meaning. The opposite of Hazal is Rosa in the Israeli movie *Ani ohev otakh, Rosa* (1972). Rosa lives in Old Jerusalem at the turn of the century, scrupulously following Orthodox traditions. When her young brother-in-law must become her husband to honor the very old Jewish practice according to which a widow must marry her husband's brother, she tries and succeeds to integrate this marriage into a network of meaningful gestures belonging to Jewish tradition. In these two movies, women are, according to Teresa de Lauretis, not only goods or objects exchanged by and among men but also signs or messages which circulate among individuals and groups ensuring social communication.

The custom of wearing the veil is still controversial in Muslim countries and many films explore it. *Bez Straha* (1971), a movie from Uzbekistan, sets the story during 1927 in Tashkent. This film documents the campaign of Communist representatives against women wearing the veil (*parandja*), which meets with resistance on the part of women. In this movie, the veil, which had been formerly imposed by religious men, becomes a symbol of resistance for Uzbek women against a new male-dominated Communist order.

In *Le Pari de Bintou* (1994), the director documents the question of female circumcision (excision) still practiced in some Muslim countries. When a family from Mali moves to Paris, the father of Aissatou, the little girl, demands that his daughter undergo this operation. The mother, Bintou, refuses to submit her daughter to this practice, insisting that nowhere in the Koran is it prescribed. Rather, she sees it as a tradition that should be abandoned, particularly as female circumcision is absolutely illegal in their adopted country. In a very moving scene, Bintou reaffirms her respect for Islamic traditions while at the same time, by her firm stand, she fights for her daughter and generations of women to come, for what de Lauretis calls "the politics of self-representation," in which women have to fight not only to make visible the invisible but also to produce the conditions of visibility for a different social subject.

BIBLIOGRAPHY

BOOKS

de Lauretis, Teresa. *Alice doesn't.* 1984.
———. *Technologies of Gender.* 1987.
Penley, Constance. *Feminism and Film Theory.* 1988.

FILMS

Ani ohev otakh, Rosa. Directed by Moshe Mizrahi. Noah Films. 1972.
Antigoni. Directed by Yorgos Tsavellas. Norma Film Productions. 1961.
Bez Straha. Directed by Ali Khamraev. Uzbekfilm. 1971.
Breaking the Waves. Directed by Lars von Trier. Zentropa Entertainments APS. 1996.
Devi. Directed by Satyajit Ray. Satyajit Ray Productions. 1960.
Hazal. Directed by Ali Ozgentürk. Umut Films. 1980.
Hester Street. Directed by Joan Micklin Silver. Midwest Film. 1974.
I Cannibali. Directed by Liliana Cavani. San Marco Produzione. 1969.
Je vous salue Marie. Directed by Jean-Luc Godard. Pegase/JLG Films/Sara Films. 1983.
La Passion de Jeanne d'Arc. Directed by Carl Theodor Dreyer. Société Générale de Films. 1928.
Le Pari de Bintou. Directed by Kirsten Johnson. Production Cams. Julia Pimsleur. 1994.
Le Procès de Jeanne d'Arc. Directed by Robert Bresson. Agnès Delahaie Productions. 1962.
Noce en Galilée. Directed by Michel Khleifi. Marisa Films. 1987.
Rabi'ah Al Adawiya. Directed by Niazi Mustapha. Helmi Rafla Productions. 1963.

IDA KUMMER

Folklore

The concept of folk religion, or folk components of religion, has toward the end of the twentieth century received critical attention. In everyday speech, *folk* carries connotations ranging from "local" and "popular" to "noncanonical" (often "oral tradition") and "erroneous." Folklorists and religious scholars such as William Graham point out, however, that in spiritual practice and everyday interpretation, canonized articles of faith must reenter the oral domain. Religious canon, in all religions that have one, is constantly met with local, vernacular elaboration or reaction. It is perhaps only the existence of a written canon and the prevalence in a literate environment of concepts of authenticity and systematic consistency that give rise to a concept such as folk religion as a residual category of belief and practice. Yet popular piety continues not only to ratify but to feed canon—for example, by recognizing in local contexts saints and miracles that ultimately may be incorporated into canon. If formal religious authority is assigned to men, informal ("folk") spirituality may devolve upon women; beliefs and practices of those not in authority may be deemed "folk," noncanonical, even heretical, not as a result of formal or content differences but of the practitioners' marginal social position.

Thus, the term *folk religion* invites close analysis of the mechanisms of distribution of spiritual authority whereby items of belief or practice are deemed noncanonical, infracanonical, or anticanonical in any tradition. Folklorist Marta Weigle (1989) provided a model for such analysis in her critique of European comparative mythographers' gender-exclusionary definitions of myth in Native American and other traditions. In other contexts, as in Australian aboriginal religion as discussed by Diane Bell (1993), women's sacred narrative may be recognized as just as fundamental and powerful a cosmological discourse as men's, but may be sequestered in separate ritual contexts and made invisible to men and outsiders so as to protect and sustain its power.

When a social category (e.g., women) is excluded from formal authority, the group may elaborate vernacular practices and beliefs to answer the felt need for spiritual agency. Votive activities that emphasize personal or small-group concerns, the well-being of the family or the local community, often are elaborated by women. Vows often entail narratives that may report a problem to the spiritual power whose help is sought or provide evidence for a ritual's efficacy in an origin story. Whether narratives are connected with vows and deemed sacred by tellers, or deemed folktales for entertainment, may depend on the performance context or on the interpreter's position in the formal authority structure of the faith.

Hindu *vrat katha* (vow narratives) generally tell of a woman or someone she cares for in jeopardy and her rescue by a religious offering, which itself might involve the telling of a witness narrative. These tales carry explicit morals, promoting religious faith, the honoring of a pledge, or filial or marital obedience. Kirin Narayan (1997) presented Hindu women's worship-related and nonworship-related stories side by side, showing how women readily identify the moral or spiritual messages of ritual stories but withhold such explicit interpretation of nonvow-related stories. Narayan and other writers on *vrat katha* show women in control of sophisticated interpretive use of narratives. The Brahmin male priests Narayan contacted show only partial knowledge of stories and rituals conducted by women, although they also perform *vrat katha* in certain male-conducted rituals directed to other deities.

The high-caste North Indian male ritual specialists Narayan interviewed do not seem intentionally to marginalize women's religious practices. In Muslim communities, by contrast, women's vow-related narratives are performed on more contested ground. Iranian Shia Muslim women may incorporate certain stories into the offering of a *sofreh,* a dedicated meal to which women invite others, usually women, as an act of charity in connection with a vow. Islam enjoins charity as a basic religious duty, but orthodoxy tends to reject charity offered in hopes of solving a particular problem: God's wisdom and mercy are unconditional, to be taken on their own terms without bargaining for blessings. Yet women sustain these devotional practices on behalf of family members or the wider community (e.g., when a drought affects a village, or for the protection of the soldiers during the Iran-Iraq war in the 1980s).

Stories told in the vow context may report previous interventions of sacred personages (deities in Hinduism, members of the Prophet's family, or other saints in Islam), or may raise to spiritual significance tales told elsewhere in the community for entertainment, such as a version of the Cinderella story used in a women's ritual in eastern Iran. Laments, which routinely include narrative, are a predominantly female form of discourse worldwide. American folklorists Elaine Lawless and Jody Davie have studied and recorded contemporary women's personal experience narratives. It is the importance of reported personal experience, both to establish the legitimate power of faith and to demonstrate women's responsibility and power to protect family and community, both spiritually and physically, that unites all these forms of women's spiritual narrative.

BIBLIOGRAPHY

Alexiou, Margaret. *The Ritual Lament in Greek Tradition.* 1974.

Bell, Diane. *Daughters of the Dreaming.* 1993.

Betteridge, Anne. "The Controversial Vows of Urban Muslim Women in Iran." In *Unspoken Worlds: Women's Religious Lives in Non-Western Cultures.* Edited by Nancy Auer Falk and Rita M. Gross. 1980.

Caraveli, Anna. "The Bitter Wounding: The Lament as Social Protest in Rural Greece." In *Gender and Power in Rural Greece.* Edited by Jill Dubisch. 1986.

———. "Bridge between Worlds: The Greek Women's Lament as Communicative Event." *Journal of American Folklore* 93 (1980): 129–157.

Davie, Jody Shapiro. *Women in the Presence: Constructing Community and Seeking Spirituality in Mainline Protestantism.* 1995.

Jamzadeh, Laal, and Margaret Mills. "Iranian *Sofreh:* From Collective to Female Ritual." In *Gender and Religion: The Complexity of Symbols.* Edited by Caroline Walker Bynum, Steven Harrell, and Paula Richman. 1986.

Lawless, Elaine. *Handmaidens of the Lord: Pentecostal Women Preachers and Traditional Religion.* 1988.

———. *Holy Women, Wholly Women: Sharing Ministries through Life Stories and Reciprocal Ethnography.* 1993.

———. "Rescripting Their Lives and Narratives: Spiritual Life Stories of Pentecostal Women Preachers." *Journal of Feminist Studies in Religion* 7, no. 1 (1991): 53–71.

Mills, Margaret. "A *Cinderella* Variant in the Context of a Muslim Women's Ritual." In *Cinderella: A Folklore Casebook.* Edited by Alan Dundes. 1982.

———. "Oral Tradition." In *The Encyclopedia of Religion.* Edited by Mircea Eliade. 1987.

Narayan, Kirin. *Storytellers, Saints and Scoundrels.* 1990.

Narayan, Kirin, in collaboration with Urmila Devi Sood. *Mondays on the Dark Night of the Moon: Himalayan Foothill Folktales.* 1997.

Raheja, Gloria G., and A. G. Gold. *Listen to the Heron's Words: Reimagining Gender and Kinship in North India.* 1994.

Seremetakis, Constantina-Nadia. *The Last Word: Women, Death and Divination in Inner Mani.* 1991.

Wadley, Susan. "Vrat Katha." In *South Asian Folklore: An Encyclopedia.* Edited by P. Claus, S. Diamond, and Margaret Mills. Forthcoming.

Weigle, Marta. *Creation and Procreation: Feminist Reflections on Mythologies of Cosmogony and Parturition.* 1989.

Yoder, Don. "Toward a Definition of Folk Religion." *Western Folklore* 33, no. 1 (1974): 1–15.

MARGARET MILLS

Folklore Studies

The field of folklore studies has roots in the late-eighteenth-century movement of romantic nationalism and the development of the academic study of "popular antiquities." It originally sought to record traditions believed to be dying out among the rural, native populations—the "folk"—and simultaneously provided a means to address societal changes ushered in by the advent of modernity and the rationalism of the Enlightenment. For this reason, concepts of rurality, tradition, and orality were paramount to early definitions and understandings of both the methods and topics of study. In 1846 the term *folklore*, a composite term designed to reflect this understanding, was coined by the English antiquarian William Thoms.

Over time, approaches borrowed from the many companion fields of folklore—sociology, anthropology, history, literature, music, art, linguistics, and religion—have shaped ongoing theoretical understandings and methodologies of the field. Areas of study have ranged from genre analysis, festivals, proverbs and tales, gesture, foodways, and folk arts and crafts, to means and modes of cultural transmission, narrative formation and performance, folklife and material culture, and the functions of folklore. In modern understandings folklore is defined as a culturally unique mode of communication, distinctive in its formal, thematic, and performative aspects (Ben-Amos, 1971). This definition incorporates both the centrality of the concept of tradition as seen in past definitions and the influence of performance-centered approaches that emphasize individuality, creativity, and the interaction between tradition and innovation.

In the late nineteenth century the new approaches of the young field of folklore were applied to the Biblical text and the comparative study of traditions of the Ancient Near East. Regarding folklore as the oral heritage and antecedent of the Hebrew Bible, scholars sought to locate survivals, or remnants, of folklore in the literary form through the comparison of narrative elements and styles, and through isolation of evidence of the gradual verbalization of religious rites and rituals of the period, based on notions of cultural evolution where more "primitive," traditional elements were thought to be gradually lost as society advanced. Such theories were best personified by the nineteenth-century anthropologist E. B. Tylor. Resting on the concept of the universality of principles that governed the transition from oral to written literature, this comparative approach used the manner and mode of oral tradition in any nomadic, rural, and oral society as models, suggesting, by analogy, that the Hebrew Bible possessed comparable narratives found all over the world, that is, narratives of the flood, the creation of humankind, and so on. Hence, such an approach to the study of religion ought to compare themes, actions, and motifs of the Hebrew Bible and, indeed, other traditional religions to one another and to similar narratives and practices found among contemporary "folk." J. G. Frazer's work, especially *The Golden Bough* (1907–1915), is an excellent example of this approach.

A later approach of folklore studies and religion focused on an ethnographic method of analysis. Here the Hebrew Bible, as a text composed in a society of restricted literacy, reflected the culture in which it was first formulated and was full of allusions to and representations of ideas and performances of folklore in the social life of the group. It was, therefore, a means by which to reconstruct the dynamics of the folklore of the land, the people, and the time. Neither the Hebrew Bible, nor indeed folklore, was regarded as a collection of verbal forms, patterns, and motifs alone, but as a reflection of an artistic process of communication that was performed in face-to-face situations, in a society that shared languages, symbols, and cultural meanings that were expressed in thematic variation, patterned accounts, and repetitive sequences. As a field of study, the ethnographic approach to folklore expands beyond studying the "folk" to the traditions and beliefs of groups and of groups within groups. It incorporates elements of social history, cultural history, and the study of the performative and traditional aspects of society. In such a way, folklore complements and contributes significantly to the study of women in general and to women's history, culture, and belief systems in particular.

Such comparative and ethnographic methods and approaches have also been reflected in folk religion. Defined by folklorist Don Yoder as "views and practices of religion that exist among the people apart from and alongside the strictly theological and liturgical forms of the official religion" (1974, p. 14), it originally focused on the tension between "folk" and official or orthodox forms of belief and the anthropological study of the syncretism between different forms of religion and the acculturation of religious beliefs. Concerned with the religious dimension of culture or the cultural dimension of religion, folk religion has grown to incorporate the analysis of religious celebration, including ritual, drama, and festival, the study of cultural and social approaches, practices, and perceptions of belief, the performative aspects of religious practice, sociopolitical aspects of belief, and the study and analysis of alternative belief systems. Topics of study, therefore, range from Marian worship, Easter egg decoration, holy well veneration, and La Fiesta del Dia de los Muertos, to sermon oration and religious testimony, religious narrative, including myth and legend, the interaction and history of religious communities, and alternative belief systems such as worship of popular figures like Elvis Presley and UFO cults, among many others.

BIBLIOGRAPHY

Ben-Amos, Dan. "Toward a Definition of Folklore in Context." *Journal of American Folklore* 84 (1971): 3–15.

Coats, George W. *Saga, Legend, Tale, Novella, Fable.* 1985.

Davis, Gerald L. *I Got the Word in Me and I Can Use It, You Know: A Study of the African-American Sermon.* 1985.

Gunkel, Hermann. *Folktales in the Old Testament.* Translated by Michael D. Ritter. 1987.

Kirkpatrick, Patricia G. *The Old Testament and Folklore Study.* 1988.

Lawless, Elaine J. *Handmaidens of the Lord: Pentecostal Women Preachers and Traditional Religion.* 1988.

Niditch, Susan. *Folklore and the Hebrew Bible.* 1993.

Turner, Victor. *Dramas, Fields, and Metaphors: Symbolic Action in Human Society.* 1974.

Yoder, Don. "Toward a Definition of Folk Religion." *Western Folklore* 33 (1974): 2–15.

AMANDA CARSON BANKS

Food

The relationship between gender, prescribed foods, and religious practices and beliefs is played out in a multitude of ways in societies around the world.

Sacred ritual foods and related ritual practices can highlight appropriate social roles for each gender. In Indian Hinduism, Kanya-Kubja brahmins risk the loss of their patrilineal honor and prestige in every marriage, especially in its food transactions. Ravindra Khare (1976) notes that upon the marriage of a couple, special ritual foods are given as gifts to the groom's patrilineal relatives by the bride's patrilineage. The bride's first ritual act in her new husband's home is the preparation of special foods; this links the bride to gods and goddesses, her husband's ancestors, and living relatives.

The Inupiat of the Arctic regard the internal organs of the captured whale (the staple food) as the part that should be cut up and processed by women. The important part is the heart, for in Inupiat thinking "the woman catches the whale." This is because men's success in hunting depends on the goodness and spiritual power of their wives (Turner, 1966).

Gwen Kennedy Neville (1987) argues that it is the woman's role to define and perpetuate the family through her contributions of food for American Protestant culture's sacred pilgrimage, the family reunion. In addition to the woman's role in preparing this food, the

Sabbath table with traditional challah bread and candles (Richard T. Nowitz/Corbis)

recipes for prescribed foods shared at the family reunion are valuable heirlooms that pass down through generations of women to become symbols of family heritage and religion.

Ritual exchanges of gendered foods ensure social reproduction and concern women because of the sacred beliefs that validate the exchanges. Miriam Kahn (1986) relates how the Wamirans of Papua New Guinea raise pigs to exchange for brides from other groups. In one version of a Wamiran myth of creation, a boy killed his mother, who then turned into a pig. The Wamirans say that the mother gave her life so that her son could share the pig with others—validating existing exchange networks—and thus teach his people that they should no longer eat humans.

A Ndembu African girl initiate, in her seclusion hut, was not allowed to do any cooking, for she was a creature of the bush, a fisher and honey gatherer for that time of separation. She would dab some of the cassava mush she was given on the *mudyi* ("milk" tree) post of her hut, for her matrilineal ancestors. As each boy was circumcised, he was fed a mush of cassava and beans, both traditional foods, from the point of the circumciser's knife. The white cassava in both cases represents the goodness of living. The symbolic meaning of the cassava and red beans—both cultivated by women—celebrates women's fertility in the reproduction of her matriline and her production of food.

Particular kinds of food reflect the gendered qualities of the ancestors and sacred deities. The Tewa of the

U.S. Southwest (Ortiz, 1969) believe that the first mothers of all the Tewa were the supernaturals known as Blue Corn Woman and White Corn Maiden. Each child acquires his or her soul at birth from these sacred mothers who are symbolically represented during the child's naming ritual by two similarly colored ears of corn. These mothers are also present in other rituals that unify the Tewa with their ancestors, their community, and their deities.

Emiko Ohnuki-Tierney (1993) describes how, for the Japanese, the souls of rice grains reflect the positive power of divine purity. The soul of each kind of grain, including rice, is a female deity. The Japanese harness this positive female power of the deities by performing a ritual using rice or by consuming rice so that the divine becomes part of the human body and its growth.

Christianity and Judaism also feature gendered sacred food in important rituals. In the Bible examples of women's relationship to food include Eve tempting Adam with the fruit (Gen. 3:6); Rebecca cooking the savory goat's meat for her favorite son Jacob so that he could impersonate his hunter brother Esau and win his father Isaac's blessing (Gen. 27:14); the widow's unfailing meal and cruse of oil for Elijah (I Kgs. 17:11–16); the famous praise of the housewife for feeding her family (Prov. 31:14, 15); and Martha, rebuked by Jesus for complaining that Mary did not help with the food (Luke 10:40–42).

Medieval Christian women used food to control and renounce the world and their flawed physicality. By fasting, women moved closer to God. Women's bodies became associated with the food of the Eucharist (see Bynum, 1987).

In preparation for Judaism's weekly Sabbath, Jewish women traditionally bake challah, braided loaves of bread, as well as other special foods. Shortly before sunset on Friday evening she kindles two lights, prays over them, and greets the Shekhinah, the female presence of God.

Ritual food and its preparation can reflect social roles, embody sacred deities, and transform the gender of ritual participants. Ritual food reflects religious beliefs and gender domains while it nurtures the body and the spirit of people around the world.

BIBLIOGRAPHY

Bynum, Caroline Walker. *Holy Feast and Holy Fast: The Religious Significance of Food to Medieval Women.* 1987.

Kahn, Miriam. *Always Hungry, Never Greedy: Food and the Expression of Gender in a Melanesian Society.* 1986.

Khare, Ravindra. *The Hindu Hearth and Home.* 1976.

Neville, Gwen Kennedy. *Kinship and Pilgrimage: Rituals of Reunion in American Protestant Culture.* 1987.

Ohnuki-Tierney, Emiko. *Rice as Self: Japanese Identities through Time.* 1993.

Ortiz, Alphonso. *The Tewa World: Space, Time, Being and Becoming in a Pueblo Society.* 1969.

Turner, Edith. *The Hands Feel It: Healing and Spirit Presence among a Northern Alaskan People.* 1966.

Turner, Victor. *The Forest of Symbols.* 1967.

EDITH TURNER
PAMELA FRESE

Founders

Throughout history and in most world religions, women have founded a variety of religious expressions: religious orders sanctioned by mainstream religions, cults that exist in opposition to or within major religions, and syncretistic religions that blend elements from several traditions. Despite the different forms they take, they all rely on personal charisma, begin locally, and include nurturing functions such as tending the sick, feeding the hungry, and addressing family and personal problems.

RELIGIOUS ORDERS WITHIN DOMINANT TRADITIONS

It is difficult to determine the level of founding activities in the ancient world because the androcentric veneer of history obscures women's activity. In the East, for example, there are two accounts of the origins of Buddhist nuns. One (Nancy Auer Falk, "The Case of the Vanishing Nuns," in *Unspoken Worlds,* edited by Falk and Gross, 1989) depicts Mahapajapati and her five hundred followers demanding ordination from the reluctant Buddha; the other shows the Buddha himself establishing the order. Similarly, in Christianity, the second-century author of the Apocalypse refers to a female founder of a prophetic school with a derogatory term, Jezebel, in place of her name.

Later histories provide better records. Ching Chien (c. 292–361) was the first of many Chinese Buddhist women to found monastic orders. In Christianity, Macrina instituted what was later called the "Basilian Plan" for ascetic life. Women continued to found monastic orders well into the Middle Ages. St. Frideswide (680–727), for example, founded the order at Oxford, England, the site of the present Christ Church (Nancy Bauer, "St. Frideswide: Monastic Founder of Oxford," in *Medieval Women Monastics,* edited by Miriam Schmitt, 1996).

Because Christians do not need a lineage, or direct line to a spiritual master, as Buddhists do, Christian women have continued to inaugurate new orders. The first attempts to establish noncloistered communities occurred during the Counter Reformation. Seventeenth-century women—Angelica Merici, Mary Ward, and Louise de Marillac—wanted to carry their vocations into the world but were vigorously opposed by the patriarchal Roman Catholic Church. Rome pressured Merici's Ursulines into cloistered life. Papal order suppressed Ward's Institute of the Blessed Virgin Mary and imprisoned her as a heretic. Finally in 1633 the church approved De Maurillac's order, The Daughters of Charity.

As opposition to noncloistered orders waned, Christian women established many communities devoted to caring for the sick and the poor, such as Elizabeth Seton's (1774–1821) Sisters of Charity, headquartered in Emmitsburg, and Frances Cabrini's (1850–1917) Missionary Sisters of the Sacred Heart. In 1916, Mother Mary Theodore cofounded the Handmaids of the Most Pure Heart of Mary, which she called "A Community of Colored Sisters for Colored People" (Cyprian Davis, "Handmaids of the Most Pure Heart," in *Black Women in America,* edited by Elsa Brown and Darlene Clark Hine, 1993).

Although the number of female Christian orders continued to grow into the twentieth century, Theravada Buddhist orders disappeared by the eleventh century. Oddly, it was an American woman, Countess Miranda de Souza Canavarro, a Theosophist and convert to Buddhism from Catholicism, who established Sanghamitta Upāsikārāmaya, the first Ceylonese lay nunnery in 1898.

OUTSIDE THE MAINSTREAM: POSSESSION CULTS

When the major traditions completely exclude females from authority of office, women develop cults that exist alongside and sometimes in opposition to them. In both Eastern and Western religions, these cults typically begin with spirit possession. Each *zar* cult, for example, has a female founder who is possessed by an ancestress. *Zar,* which originated in Ethiopia in the eighteenth century, accompanies Islam and Coptic Christianity as they spread into new locations. Similar female-founded groups arise in response to mainstream Buddhism in both the Nat cults of Burma and the nameless religion of the Ryūkyūan Islands. In Korea and China, Shamanism coexists with the dominant traditions, which can be Buddhist, Christian, neo-Confucian, or Taoist. The possession cults give women spiritual authority over both men and women, center on this world by healing the

In Burmese pre-Buddhist folk religion a *nat* represents a group of spirits capable of harming or protecting the believer (Michael Freeman/Corbis).

sick and solving personal and family problems, and are confined to small regions.

SYNCRETISTIC RELIGIONS IN JAPAN

Women founded many of the Japanese New Religions that emerged in relation to Shinto, Buddhism, and Christianity. Personal charisma originating from spirit possession creates the authority to establish a New Religion. All New Religions contain some element of healing; most remain local; a few have become international.

The peasant woman Nakayama Miki (1797–1887) founded Tenrikyo after being possessed by God the Parent. Showing her followers the path to healing and bliss, Nakayama Miki continued her work despite persecution. Today, Tenrikyo has more than 1.5 million members worldwide.

Born in 1900, Sayo Kitamara believed God descended into her body on 11 August 1945 and instructed her to break with Buddhism and Shinto. The miracles that have accompanied her religion, Tensho-kotai-jingu-kyo, brought her movement international fame; followers believe that a dormant Hawaiian volcano became active in preparation for her visit (Harry Thomsen, *The New Religions of Japan,* 1963).

SPIRITUAL AUTHORITY IN AMERICA

Women founders have been at the center of sectarian development in North America since the late eighteenth century. By seizing the authority of the spirit championed by Protestant Christianity, several women formulated new religions despite serious opposition and persecution from mainstream Protestantism.

Ann Lee, founder of the United Society of Believers, called Shakers, ventured from England to the American colonies in 1774. Early Shakers believed Lee to be the second incarnation of Christ and formulated a theology and social structure based on the idea that men and women had become equal through Christ's second coming.

Mary Baker Eddy (1821–1910), founder of the First Church of Christ Scientist, and Ellen Harmon White (1827–1915), founder of Seventh-Day Adventism, both deemed American religion deficient and placed healing at the core of their religions. Christian Scientists and Seventh-Day Adventists invest their founders' revealed words with scriptural authority.

Women played a major role in the Pentecostal and Holiness movements that appeared on the American scene in the late nineteenth century by appropriating their authority from Pentecostal and Holiness emphasis on spiritual gifts. Alma White (1862–1946) severed her ties with the Methodists and established the staunchly feminist Pillar of Fire Church. Canadian-born Aimee Semple McPherson (1890–1944) began her ministerial career as the young wife of a missionary to China only to be widowed and become ill. She was simultaneously healed and called to ministry, a pattern repeated in other charismatic female leaders throughout the world. McPherson founded the Four Square Gospel Church on the principle that all the gifts available to the early Christians, including healing, were available in the present.

Both Holiness and Pentecostal groups originally ordained women. When this practice changed, some women founded their own churches and ordained themselves. The United Holiness Church in America ordained Ida Robinson (1891–1946) but later restricted female ordination. In response, Robinson founded Mt. Sinai Holy Church in America. Robinson is one of only a few Black Pentecostal women to found a separate church.

At the turn of the century, American Jewish women began creating service organizations, charities, and schools. Like their historical counterparts all over the world, Jewish women neither broke with Judaism nor founded religions that coexisted with it but instead supported Judaism from within.

In the last quarter of the twentieth century, American women sought ordination in record numbers. Because female clergy have official voice within mainstream Protestantism, founding activity has slowed but has not stopped. Elizabeth Clare Wulf Prophet (b. 1939) blends spirit possession, healing, and Oriental and Christian theologies in her Church Universal and Triumphant, founded in 1974. Prophet stands with the many female founders who opposed the dominant tradition, seized spiritual authority, and launched their own brands of religion.

BIBLIOGRAPHY

For a thorough discussion of spirit cults and female charismatic leaders, see Susan Starr Sered, *Priestess, Mother, Sacred Sister: Religions Dominated by Women* (1994). The anthology edited by Nancy Auer Falk and Rita Gross, *Unspoken Worlds: Women's Religious Lives* (1989), contains useful articles on several women founders in Eastern and Western religions. For information on Hindu Goddess Cults, see Linda Johnsen, *Daughters of the Goddess: The Women Saints of India* (1994). A video, "Sri Ānandamāyī Ma: Her Life, Her Message," is available from the Matri Satsang in Encinitas, California. Articles and general information about Anandamāyī Ma are also available at http\\www.moksha.org.

For information on Buddhist nuns, see Tessa J. Bartholomeusz, *Women under the Bō Tree* (1994); Kathryn Ann Tsai, *Lives of the Nuns: Biographies of Chinese Buddhist Nuns from the Fourth to Sixth Centuries—A Translation of the Pi-ch'iu-ni chuan* (1994); and Rita M. Gross, *Buddhism After Patriarchy: A Feminist History, Analysis and Reconstruction of Buddhism* (1993). Rosemary Ruether and Eleanor McLaughlin, eds., *Women of Spirit: Female Leadership in the Jewish and Christian Traditions* (1979), contains several important articles on women in early and medieval Christianity. Information on Japanese New Religions is available on the Internet by searching the name of the religious group. For an exhaustive account of women in American religion that contains biographies of many women founders, see Susan Hill Lindley, *"You Have Stept Out of Your Place": A History of Women and Religion in America* (1996).

See also Eddy, Mary Baker; Lee, Ann; McPherson, Aimee Semple; Monasticism; Saints; Women's Religions.

SUSAN M. SETTA

Freud, Sigmund

The founder of psychoanalysis, Sigmund Freud (1856–1939), was born to Amalia Nathansohn and Jacob Freud in a humble house in Freiberg, Moravia. In 1860 the family moved to Vienna. It was there that Freud received all his education, including his medical degree, and did research in physiology and neurology. He was to live in Vienna, the place where he created and developed psychoanalysis, for seventy-eight years.

The number, complexity, and significance of Freud's discoveries is without parallel in the field of psychology. The following is only a glimpse at the vast intellectual terrain explored by Freud: he theorized the unconscious, the existence of repression, and other psychological defenses; he unmasked the meaning of dreams, defined the mechanisms of dream formation, and devised the means by which they could be analyzed; he explored childhood sexuality, the sexual roots of hysteria, and the Oedipus complex; and he wrote seminal works on narcissism, depression, paranoia, obsessive compulsive illness, sexual aberrations, perversion, love, and guilt. He also articulated the psychodynamics of religion.

Having recognized that the study of religion revealed some of the deepest truths about human conflicts and needs, Freud saw religion as a legitimate subject for scientific inquiry. But this did not mean that science would in any way legitimize religious belief. For Freud, there was an irreparable schism between science and religion: the basic procedure of science is to suspend belief and insist on proof; religion insists on the irrelevance of proof and importance of belief. Thus, the claims of science are based on reality; those of religion, on emotion and fantasy. Freud's conclusion, which he details in *The Question of a Weltanschauung* (1933), was that any attempt to reconcile religion and science was doomed to fail. But he valued the use of science to reveal similarities between religious practices and neurotic symptoms. The best example of this is his paper *Obsessive Actions and Religious Practices* (1907b), in which he demonstrates the striking accord between the rituals of obsessive neurotics and those of religious believers. He analyzed the religious ruminations of his patients and diagnosed them as symptoms, one example being the case of Dr. Schreber, known formally as

A portrait of Sigmund Freud (1856–1939) taken around 1930 (Corbis-Bettman)

Psycho-Analytic Notes on an Autobiographical Account of a Case of Paranoia.

In his best known and most comprehensive work on religion, *The Future of an Illusion* (1927), Freud analyzed the motives behind the pervasive influence and emotional power of religious belief. He boldly asserted that the essence of religion is a disguised but universal wish for an omnipotent, omniscient, and protective parent. These wishes, intensified by the fear of death and nothingness, represented the unconscious motive for the emergence of an illusion of God's existence, just as the fantasy of an afterlife of bliss was a thinly veiled compensation for human suffering. Freud saw the religious impulse as a cry for help and a refusal to accept disappointment of the hope for aid to humanity in its struggle against the callousness and indifference of nature and of reality.

Not surprisingly, Freud was an enthusiastic atheist. The description of Freud as a misogynist by some feminists, however, is unfounded. He had numerous female followers before his death, and today the majority of psychoanalysts are women. Although Freud had sons, he entrusted the guardianship of the psychoanalytic movement to his daughter Anna Freud, who became an eminent psychoanalyst in her own right and made major contributions to the field. In 1938 Freud was rescued from the Nazis with the help of Princess Marie Bonaparte, a former patient and loyal follower. He died in London on September 23, 1939.

BIBLIOGRAPHY

Brierly, Marjorie. *Trends in Psychoanalysis.* 1951. Contains the arguments of this British Christian psychoanalyst who opposed Freud's rejection of religion and who, like William James, argued in favor of a Christianity enlightened by reason.

Gay, Peter. *Freud: A Life for Our Time.* 1988. The most comprehensive and detailed biography of Freud since the publication of Ernest Jones's *The Life and Work of Sigmund Freud* (1953).

———. *A Godless Jew.* 1987. A rich discussion of the development of Freud's thought on religion. His point of view is compared to those of the psychologist William James, numerous Enlightenment thinkers, and several female critics, most notably Marjorie Brierly.

Freud, Sigmund, and Oskar Pfister. *On Psychoanalysis and Faith.* Edited by H. Meng and E. L. Freud. 1963. This correspondence between Freud and Pfister, a minister and psychoanalyst, exemplifies the arguments of many in the clergy who saw the truths of psychoanalysis and wanted to reconcile it to the Christian religion.

Freud, Sigmund. *The Standard Edition of the Complete Psychological Works of Sigmund Freud.* 24 vols. 1953–1974. This is the standard reference for Freud's work; it includes indexes, bibliographies, and explanatory notes in addition to all of his published writings.

ARACELIA PEARSON-BROK

Freyja

Freyja, daughter of Njorðr, sister-wife of Freyr, Norse god of fertility, and originally herself among the Vanir (the Norse fertility pantheon), is the most complex goddess in the court of the Æsir, Norse gods of war. Her function as love- and battle-goddess and her eroticism are consistent with her representation in both the Prose Edda (*Gylfaginning; Skáldskaparmál*) and the Poetic Edda. She appears as a discordant and erotic court figure, where she is defamed as licentious, incestuous, adulterous, and otherwise sexually corrupt (*Lokasenna; þrymskviða; Hyndluljóð*) and is associated with battle and the realm of the dead, dividing the spoils of battle with Oðínn. Her realm is Fólkvangr (*Grímnismál*), her hall Sessrúmnir; she moves about in a carriage drawn by cats (*Gylfaginning*) and on occasion rides a boar (*Hyndluljóð*), possibly *Hildisvíni*, an animal emblem she shares with Freyr. Particularly helpful and responsive to humans in matters of love (*Oddrúnargrátr*), she possesses a necklace, the *Brísingamen*. She owns a *hamr* (feather-coat) made of bird skin (*þrymskviða*). Personified meanings of her name appear in the Prose Edda, and there is some fusion of function and identity with Frigg and Gefjon. As an Æsir she is the wife of the wandering Oðr, for whom she sheds red-golden tears (a kenning for gold [*Skáldskaparmál*]) and hence is known as *grátfagra goð*, "the goddess fair in tears" (*Skáldskaparmál*). She is referred to by a number of epithets (Vanadís, Mardoll, Horn, Gefn, Sýr [*Gylfaginning*]) in Skaldic poetry, and is loosely associated with magic (*Ynglinga Saga*). Along with Freyr, Freyja was part of a brother-sister fertility cult that flourished in heathen Uppsala; Swedish kings were priests of Freyr and their queens priestesses of Freyja. The importance of her cult is reflected in the story of Hjalti Skeggjason, a tenth-century skald (highly skilled Norse poet) who denigrated the goddess and was outlawed for the offense (*Islendingabók; Njálssaga*).

BIBLIOGRAPHY

Damico, Helen. *Beowulf's Wealhtheow and the Valkyrie Tradition.* 1984.

Davidson, Hilda Ellis. *Gods and Myths of Northern Europe.* 1964.

———. *Pagan Scandinavia.* 1967.

Dumézil, George. *Gods of the Ancient Northmen.* 1973.

Lindow, John. *Scandinavian Mythology.* 1988.

Turville-Petre, E. O. G. *Myth and Religion of the North.* 1964.

Vries, Jan de. *Altgermanische Religionsgeschichte.* 1956.

See also Goddess: Historical Goddesses; Scandinavian Religions.

HELEN DAMICO

Friendship

Friendship is a common human experience valued and understood quite differently in the many religious traditions. Friends of God is a term used variously to describe holy people. Meanings of both terms have been predicated largely on male experiences of friendship and spirituality, but feminist work in religion is beginning to change that.

Women's friendships have been understood in a contradictory way in patriarchal societies. On the one hand, they are trivialized as girl friends, seen as less important than men's friendships with men or even men's with women. On the other hand, they are suspect, as in the case of so-called "particular friendships" so often found in women's religious congregations. Nuns were counseled to avoid such pairings as sources of temptation, implying that they would have a sexual as well as emotional dimension.

The term *friends* is used by a number of religious groups. For example, the Roman Catholic Sisters of Loretto have as their official name Friends of Mary at the Foot of the Cross. A Buddhist group by the name of Friends of the Western Buddhist Order is dedicated to teaching that faith to women.

In Judaism, Martin Buber's classic formulation of "I-Thou," a relationship for the sake of the other, includes no specific mention of women, but neither are women left out. Jewish feminist theologian Judith Plaskow claims that the normative use of God as lord and king in Judaism needs to be complemented with God as friend with whom human beings, including women, are cocreators. Anthropomorphic language such as *friend* reinforces the relational quality of the divine, the potential for divine-human connection, the bringing together of ever more parts of creation.

Christianity's view of friendship has long been predicated on Aristotle's model of mutual recognition of the well-being of the other. In Aristotle's view, only males could be friends, so that when Thomas Aquinas wrote of friendship with God in the thirteenth century, a term with roots in The Book of Wisdom (7:14, 27) and the Gospel of John (15:14–15), it was not clear whether women were included. However, in medieval Christianity trade guilds developed with some fourteenth-century German mystics calling their fellowships Friends of God (German, *Gottesfruende*). These included some Dominican nuns such as Margaret and Christine Ebner. In the late seventeenth century George Fox and followers who formed the Society of Friends of Truth (popularly known as Quakers) included women members.

Later feminist work in philosophy and theology with roots in the Christian tradition focuses on friendship as a central spiritual issue. Mary Daly calls women's "Be-friending" a radical ethical act. Janice Raymond details women's passionate friendships. Mary E. Hunt uses women's friendships as an overlooked source of revelation and the basis for theo-political justice seeking. Sallie McFague describes God as Friend in an effort to transform root metaphors for the divine.

In Islam the notion of friendship has a number of dimensions. The Qur'an cautions against believers making friends with unbelievers. Women have provided great support to each other as friends in the context of male-dominated societies. Visitation to the tomb of a deceased saint, *wali,* often provides a means of culturally sanctified religious activity for women. Women go in family and friendship groupings to receive blessing from the *wali* who is himself or herself a "friend of God."

The healing power of friendship, depicted in a painting, Healing a Sick Woman, by Violet Oakley, c. 1905 (Photo Disc, Inc.)

Hindu concepts of friendship take on a brotherly quality (*bhratr*). Friendship is a social relationship more than a personal one, including the extended family, the friends of friends. Whether such relationships can also be "sisterly" remains to be seen.

Confucianism includes encouragement to be upright, trustworthy, and learned friends. It discourages friendship with obsequious, flattering, and glib-tongued people. But the emphasis on men who are fit for friendship leaves little evidence of women's role.

In Buddhism, friendship is seen as an intimate relationship of reciprocity, especially among monks. Friendship with wicked or foolish people is against the teaching, but comrades who fulfill the multiple qualities of listening and faithfulness are to be prized for a lifetime. As women increasingly become part of Buddhist communities there is every indication that their friendship will be taken equally seriously.

Lesbian relationships are often seen as a special case of friendship. However, many feminist writers have recognized that such relationships are simply friendships with sexual expression as opposed to friendships without sexual expression. Many religions, for example Christianity, find this view problematic, especially because it implies that lesbianism, like friendship, can be natural, good, and holy.

Women's friendship rituals tend to be informal and private rather than part of the ritual or sacramental system of most traditions. Among followers of Goddess and Wicca spirituality (a revival of religious belief and practice believed to be of pre-Christian origin and focused on nature, magic, and goddess worship) friendship is a common theme, though set rituals are not common. Covenant, commitment, and even marriage ceremonies are now emerging as some women formalize their coupled relationships into what some hope will eventually be legally recognized partnerships.

BIBLIOGRAPHY

Hunt, Mary E. *Fierce Tenderness: A Feminist Theology of Friendship.* 1991.

McFague, Sallie. *Models of God: Theology for an Ecological, Nuclear Age.* 1987.

Plaskow, Judith. *Standing Again at Sinai: Judaism from a Feminist Perspective.* 1990.

Raymond, Janice. *A Passion for Friends: Toward a Philosophy of Female Affection.* 1986.

Rouner, Leroy S., ed. *The Changing Face of Friendship.* 1994.

See also **Lesbianism.**

MARY E. HUNT

Fundamentalism

Fundamentalism is an embattled term. It arose in the United States in about 1920 as a term of self-reference adopted by a group of Protestant Christians who rallied behind a series of pamphlets called *The Fundamentals* (1910–1915). These writings deplored the evils of modernism—especially scientific naturalism, the use of higher criticism of the Bible, and perceived lapses in moral values. They favored returning to "the fundamentals" of Christian belief and practice, eternal pillars of an idealized past inhabited by, as one writer of the period put it, "moral progenitors." In time, liberal Christians and modernists of a more secular hue began to use the term *fundamentalist* in a rather broader sense to designate groups they saw as naive enough to believe they could reverse the course of history in favor of a mythic, dogmatically and socially homogeneous, Christian past.

In the 1980s this pejorative usage became a staple in journalistic analyses of political debates about the Equal Rights Amendment (ERA), abortion, and prayer in public schools, indicating positions articulated by conservative Christian groups, especially evangelical Protestants. It was also employed by extension to designate the stances of religious groups around the world, especially Muslims, who took political action to reject Western secular modernism in its various forms. The Islamic revolution in Iran in 1979 put the term into wide use for the first time. Before long it also came to designate Hindus, Sikhs, Buddhists, and others. Many people so designated understandably came to resent the term's derogatory overtones—its suggestion of atavism and a narrow, rigid mentality. Not without justice, Muslims in particular have often seen it as cultural imperialism of a specifically Jewish and Christian variety.

In the 1990s scholars sensitive to this problem have suggested a series of alternate terms to designate conservative, neotraditionalist, and often militant religious groups whose ideas and actions they continue to see as parallel, and which have on occasion made common cause across religious boundaries. One such term, favored by writers such as Peter van der Veer and Mark Juergensmeyer, is "religious nationalism." Nikki Keddie, implicitly questioning whether nationalism is always the main focus of such efforts, proposed "the new religious politics." The large "Fundamentalism Project," organized by Martin Marty and J. Scott Appleby and funded by the MacArthur Foundation through the American Academy of Arts and Sciences, rejected the idea that there was a single global enemy of an enlightened, pluralist approach to religion-state relations, in-stead recognizing a plurality of "fundamentalisms." Yet the organizers retained as proper the sense that the groups being so described would insist on seeing themselves as standing for a cohesive religious worldview that focused on "the fundamentals."

Until recently, the crucial role played by issues of gender in the language of fundamentalism has been insufficiently appreciated—even on the part of the wide-ranging Fundamentalism Project. While some thinkers (e.g., Bruce Lawrence) continue to emphasize the appeal to inerrant scripture as a principal defining feature of fundamentalist groups, others (Betty DeBerg, Nikki Keddie, Judy Brink, and Joan Menscher, and John Hawley) have focused on the centrality of an appeal not to scriptural fundamentalism but to a certain "social fundamentalism." These authors have noted that shared fears about enlarged domains of relative autonomy for women are a major focus of attention, even in groups that represent themselves as being concerned first and foremost with submission to inerrant scriptural revelation (the Torah, the Bible, the Qur'an, the Guru Granth Sahib) or about the wounded dignity of a particular national culture (*hindutva*, Sinhala Buddhism). In this, American fundamentalist struggles to defeat the Equal Rights Amendment (ERA) and reverse court rulings about a woman's right to choose abortion are hardly exceptional. What is being championed is a divinely sanctioned vision of natural differences between the sexes that make it appropriate for women to live within boundaries that would be restrictive for men—and to live under men's protection and even surveillance.

The abortion debate is particularly instructive in this regard. Opponents of abortion clearly regard a woman's proper space as delineated within the reproductive sphere of family. Antiabortion rhetoric seems to project this space onto the womb and provides for it a threatening opponent: the woman who seeks to destroy the safe space within which a child should dwell. The debate is about whose space that is: hers ("right to choose") or its ("right to life"). If "its," the uterine space stands for the prelapsarian purity of God's creation, which it echoes. The fetus's space is literally the woman herself; but by the same token the woman's space is firmly circumscribed by the infant, who represents and guarantees the mother's embeddedness in patriarchal family structures.

Controversies about women's legal rights and women's visibility in public space have been notable in the sorts of discourse we might call fundamentalist. For example, two interrelated disputes captured wide attention in India in the late 1980s. One had to do with whether Shah Bano, a Muslim woman unwillingly divorced by her husband, should be restricted to the legal

It is important to recognize that women are often vocal and active in organizations that can be characterized as fundamentalist—here Phyllis Schlafly lobbied against the ERA in the rotunda of the Illinois State Capitol (UPI/Corbis-Bettmann).

rights defined by Muslim personal law, as the Indian Constitution allows, or should have access to India's universal civil code. The other dispute concerned whether a young Hindu woman, Roop Kanwar, had the religious right to immolate herself on the pyre of her recently deceased husband, according to the little-practiced and long-outlawed custom of sati. (Whether she acted by her own volition was a separate dispute, extremely dubious from the evidence available, but never entirely resolved.) Both cases became occasions for conservative communities captained principally by men to dispute the right of the secular state to intervene in matters they considered religious, and both became instances in which one religious community portrayed another as the covert enemy. Muslims arguing for their autonomy in the Shah Bano case depicted their opponents as intolerant Hindus. Pro-sati activists in the Roop Kanwar affair suggested there was a bias in granting Muslims a degree of religious freedom denied to Hindus, as in the Shah Bano affair.

It is tempting to argue that in both cases the aggrieved conservatives saw a woman—and perhaps womanhood in general—as the primary sign of the dignity, integrity, and autonomy of their religious community. Such symbology is also present in the desire to place restrictions on a woman's dress and freedom of movement, a theme that emerges with great frequency in fundamentalist rhetoric. Press reports about the self-proclaimedly Islamic actions of Taliban militants in Afghanistan have repeatedly stressed this dimension. It also figures, for example, in dress codes for women that were stipulated by Sikh militants agitating for an independent Khalistan in the late 1980s and in statements of the Vishva Hindu Parishad (World Hindu Council), a group closely associated with the Hindu-nationalist Bharatiya Janata Party (BJP).

Of late, some feminists have launched efforts (e.g., Women Against Fundamentalism, based in London) to stop what they see as the victimization of women by groups such as these. Yet it is important to recognize that women themselves are often vocal and active in organizations one might characterize as fundamentalist. Phyllis Schlafly's efforts to block the ERA and Uma Bharati's anti-Muslim tirades on behalf of the BJP come instantly to mind. Feminist scholars in particular (e.g., Nikki Keddie, Amrita Basu, Tanika Sarkar, Urvashi Butalia) have been eager to account for this apparent anomaly, and have observed that in certain situations some of the most effective avenues open to women desirous of escaping the confinements of domestic space may be precisely those offered by religious or religiopolitical organizations that can make special use of "the woman's voice." And in the upheavals occasioned by rapid social change, "traditional" domestic roles sanctioned by religion do sometimes promise women power and protection more effectively than the available "secular" or "modernist" alternatives.

Hence the debate about women and fundamentalism is not a single controversy easily framed as women versus fundamentalism, but a complicated series of overlapping debates that involve often very different local cultures, histories, and constituencies. On the boundaries between women's lives and politically active neo-traditionalist religious groups, no doubt certain patterns recur. Women regularly serve as the "other" body upon which struggles with the cosmopolitan, modernist "other" are enacted—even when women themselves are speaking. Women easily represent nostalgia for an authoritatively organized childhood now felt to have been lost. And women justify a certain religious machismo on the part of the men who would protect them. Such continuities would seem to support the continued use of a single term for comparative analysis.

But should that term be *fundamentalism?* There are two significant objections. First, it is regarded as pejorative by many whose profile it seeks to describe. Even in the world of conservative Christianity, only a limited group would today choose to identify themselves as fundamentalists. Second, the word carries inescapable historical, cultural, and sectarian baggage by virtue of having arisen in the specific context of American Protestantism: members of other religious communities therefore feel easily misunderstood. We must be aware of these difficulties if we continue to use the term, yet there is good reason for doing so. In contrast to the alternatives that have been proposed, *fundamentalism* foregrounds the sense shared by many militantly conservative religious groups that their cause is a principled one focused on a restoration of divinely sanctioned core values—fundamentals—that have been attacked, obscured, or overridden by the forces of modernity, often in colonial or imperial guise. The proper behavior of women is often key to the articulation of such views.

BIBLIOGRAPHY

Basu, Amritra, ed. "Women and Religious Nationalism in India." *Journal of Concerned Asian Scholars* 25, no. 4 (1993) 3–52.

Brink, Judy, and Joan Menscher, eds. *Mixed Blessings: Gender and Religious Fundamentalism Cross-culturally.* 1997.

Caplan, Lionel, ed. *Studies in Religious Fundamentalism.* 1987.

DeBerg, Betty A. *Ungodly Women: Gender and the First Wave of American Fundamentalism.* 1990.

Hawley, John Stratton, ed. *Fundamentalism and Gender.* 1994.

Juergensmeyer, Mark. *The New Cold War? Religious Nationalism Confronts the Secular State.* 1993.

Keddie, Nikki R., ed. "Comparative Fundamentalisms." *Contention* 4, no. 2 (1995): 19–174, and 4, no. 3 (1995): 79–221.

———. "Women, Gender, and Fundamentalism." *Comparative Studies in Society and History.* Forthcoming.

Keddie, Nikki R., and Jasamin Rostam-Koyali, eds. "Women and Fundamentalism: Perspectives on the New Religious Politics." *Journal of Women's History* 10, no. 1 (1999).

Lawrence, Bruce B. *Defenders of God: The Fundamentalist Revolt Against the Modern Age.* 1989.

Marsden, George. *Fundamentalism and American Culture: The Shaping of Twentieth-Century Evangelicalism, 1870–1925.* 1980.

Marty, Martin E., and R. Scott Appleby. *Fundamentalisms Observed.* 1991.

Marty, Martin E., and R. Scott Appleby, eds. *Fundamentalisms Comprehended.* 1995.

———. *Fundamentalisms and Society: Reclaiming the Sciences, the Family, and Education.* 1993.

Sarkar, Tanika, and Urvashi Butalia. *Women and the Hindu Right: A Collection of Essays.* 1995.

van der Veer, Peter. *Religious Nationalism: Hindus and Muslims in India.* 1994.

JOHN STRATTON HAWLEY

Furies

The Furies, or Erinyes, as they are called in Greek, are archaic female demigoddesses associated with curses, vengeance, and divine justice. In the epic poetry of Homer's *Iliad* and *Odyssey,* Erinyes are often invoked to protect and avenge the rights of parents and elders; they also function as punishers of certain crimes, including murder and oath breaking.

In his cosmogonic poem *Theogony,* the eighth-century B.C.E. poet Hesiod provides a genealogy for the Erinyes. He represents their birth from the blood of the sky god Ouranos, mutilated by his own son, as the birth of vengeance (*Theogony,* 176–185). It is this Hesiodic conception of Erinyes that the tragedian Aeschylus adopts for his trilogy, *Oresteia,* performed on the Attic stage in 458 B.C.E. There they pursue Orestes after he murders his mother Clytemnestra to avenge her slaughter of his father, Agamemnon. Orestes must stand trial for murder in Athens, where his case marks the founding of the Athenian law court. He is defended by the god Apollo, while the Erinyes prosecute, and the goddess Athena presides. Upon Orestes' acquittal, the Erinyes threaten to destroy Athens. It is only by the persuasion of Athena that they agree to put aside their anger in exchange for cult honors.

Semnai Theai (or Awesome Goddesses), the cult title given to the Erinyes in the *Oresteia,* and *Eumenides* (or Kindly Ones), the title of the last play of the trilogy, associated the primarily literary Erinyes with two preexisting cults of goddesses in Athens. Henceforth, the Erinyes, transformed from hostile to kindly, protect the city of Athens and her citizens, ensuring agricultural and human fecundity, wealth, and happiness and forbidding the premature deaths of citizens from sickness and civil war.

BIBLIOGRAPHY

Aeschylus. *Oresteia.* Translated by Richmond Lattimore. 1953.

Gantz, Timothy. *Early Greek Myth: A Guide to Literary and Artistic Sources.* 1993.

Hesiod. *Theogony.* Translated by Richmond Lattimore. 1959.

Homer. *Iliad.* Translated by Richmond Lattimore. 1962.

———. *Odyssey.* Translated by Robert Fitzgerald. 1990.

Lardinois, Andre. "Greek Myths for Athenian Rituals." *Greek, Roman and Byzantine Studies* 33 (1994): 313–327.

Lloyd-Jones, Hugh, "Les Erinyes dans la Tragédie Grecque." *Revue des Études Grecques* 102 (1989): 1–9.

Prins, Yopie. "The Power of the Speech Act: Aeschylus' Furies and Their Binding Song." *Arethusa* 24 (1991): 177–195.

NAOMI FINKELSTEIN

Gage, Matilda Joslyn

"These three names, Stanton, Anthony and Gage . . . will ever hold a grateful place in the hearts of posterity," declared *The Woman's Tribune* in 1888. History proved otherwise. The most radical of the suffrage "triumvirate," antichurch activist Matilda Joslyn Gage (1826–1898) was virtually written out of history for her radical religious beliefs. Although her leadership positions in the National Woman Suffrage Association (NWSA) were roughly equivalent to those of Susan B. Anthony and she penned the important documents of the NWSA with Elizabeth Cady Stanton, her name is all but forgotten today.

Trained early to think for herself in her parents' abolitionist household, Gage entered the free-thought movement in the 1870s, joined the American Theosophical Society the following decade, and became a student of the occult in the 1890s.

The woman's rights movement claimed her primary allegiance; she was an activist at the local, state, and national level. Newspaper correspondent and later, editor, Gage wrote admiringly of the superior position held by women of the Six Nations of the Iroquois Confederacy, while chiding the U. S. government to uphold its treaties.

Unable to stop the conservative Christian direction of the suffrage organization, Gage turned to her "grandest, most courageous work": to free woman "from the bondage of the church," which was the "chief means of enslaving woman's conscience and reason." She formed the antichurch Woman's National Liberal Union (1890), contributed to Stanton's *Woman's Bible* (1898), and published her acclaimed magnum opus, *Woman, Church and State* (1893).

Gage placed the blame for women's oppression squarely at the feet of the Christian church, which "hurled woman from the plane of 'natural rights' " (where indigenous women resided) and crushed "her personal, intellectual and spiritual freedom." Christianity rested on "the theory that woman brought sin and death in the world," she maintained, and, in the most important revolution the world had yet seen, women were rising up "against the tyranny of Church and State." It "will shake the foundations of religious belief, tear into fragments and scatter to the winds the old dogmas upon which all forms of Christianity are based," she predicted. The result "will be a regenerated world."

BIBLIOGRAPHY

Works by Matilda Joslyn Gage include "The Church, Science, and Women," *The Index* (29 April 1886); "The Dangers of the Hour," speech delivered at the Woman's National Liberal Union Convention (24 February 1890); "The Foundation of Sovereignty," *The Woman's Tribune* (April 1887); "What the Church Has Not Done for Women," *The Truth Seeker Annual and Freethinkers' Almanac* (January 1895); and *Woman, Church and State: The Original Expose of Male Collaboration Against the Female Sex* (1880). Her works can be consulted at the Gage Collection, Schlesinger Library, Radcliffe College, in Cambridge, Mass. See also Dale Spender's *Women of Ideas* (1982).

SALLY ROESCH WAGNER

Gender Conflict

The term *gender conflict* implies a situation in which male and female struggle against each other. For such a struggle to be significant, each side must possess some degree of power. Since the rise of patriarchy, women's power in societies and in the religious systems constructed to support the status quo of patriarchy has been severely limited. As a result, most existing religions, particularly monotheistic religions, give more evidence of misogyny, gynophobia, and the oppression of women than of gender conflict. For example, in the Hebrew Bible (Genesis 1–3; Proverbs 1–9), in works of the Apocrypha (Judith, Sirach), and in the writings of early Christians (Tertullian), women are portrayed as profoundly dangerous to men's physical and spiritual well-being. Women's sexuality is often identified as their principal weapon in any conflict with men. As projections of male insecurity and irresponsibility, such portrayals fog the reality that men and male sexuality pose a much greater threat to the safety of women than do women and female sexuality to the safety of men. The conflict such traditions portray is more imaginary than real. What they do suggest, however, is that in conditions of oppression and subjugation, such as characterize the status of women in patriarchy, women must find survival strategies that avoid direct conflict with men.

Gender conflict in religion, as in other human cultural institutions, is spawned by male efforts to control and subordinate women. It is typically strongest during times of transition into and out of male dominance. The transition into male dominance may have been symbolized by the struggle between goddesses-centered religions and god-centered ones. Anthropologist Marija Gimbutas argued that such a transition began to occur in Europe around 4000 B.C.E. Although goddesses did not disappear from religions at this time, their power diminished over the next several millennia. Written traditions from the first and second millennia B.C.E. have preserved traces of this struggle. The Babylonian Enuma Elish myth graphically depicts a divine gender conflict. In it, Marduk becomes king of the gods by defeating the goddess Tiamat in one-on-one physical combat. He bisects her body and uses it to create the world. Marduk's conquest of the primordial mother goddess is seen as bringing order out of chaos.

In the monotheistic religions of the West, Judaism, Christianity, and Islam, the divine female has been obliterated, while dualistic theologies subordinate the human female to the male in oppositional and hierarchical relationships. Eastern religions, though not eliminating the goddess, have similarly negative outcomes of gender conflict for women. In Hinduism, for example, there is a corpus of myths ranging from the Sanskrit story of Renuka in the Mahābhārata to the eighteenth-century Tamil tale of Mariatale, in which a female character is beheaded by a male character. Typically, this act is the male response to conflict over the female character's sexual loyalty or interests. Though this decapitation seldom has a fatal outcome in Hindu myth, it represents, nonetheless, a male response to gender conflict that employs physical violence similar to that found in Western religions.

BIBLIOGRAPHY

Eilberg-Schwartz, Howard, and Wendy Doniger. *Off With Her Head! The Denial of Women's Identity in Myth, Religion, and Culture.* 1995. See esp. chap. 1 by Doniger, " 'Put a Bag Over Her Head': Beheading Mythological Women."

Frymer-Kensky, Tikva. *In the Wake of the Goddesses: Women, Culture and the Biblical Transformation of Pagan Myth.* 1992. See esp. chap. 2, " 'Godwoman': Goddesses, Women, and Gender," and chap. 7, "The Marginalization of the Goddesses."

Gimbutas, Marija. "Women and Culture in Goddess-Oriented Old Europe." In *The Politics of Women's Spirituality: Essays on the Rise of Spiritual Power Within the Feminist Movement.* Edited by Charlene Spretnak. 1982.

Knapp, Bettina. *Women in Myth.* 1996.

Larrington, Carolyne, ed. *The Feminist Companion to Mythology.* 1992.

Ortner, Sherry B. *The Politics and Erotics of Culture.* 1996.

Sered, Susan Starr. *Priestess, Mother, Sacred Sister: Religions Dominated by Women.* 1994. See esp. chap. 10, "Gender Ideology."

See also **Heterosexism**; **Hierarchy**; **Women's Studies**.

PAMELA J. MILNE

Gender Roles

Gender roles are the actualization in community life of assumptions held within a given culture on the distinctively appropriate social contributions that should be made by women and men. Traditionally, cultural ideas on gender and gender roles were nearly universally grounded in observations on anatomy and biology, as well as images and moral lessons provided in mythology, religious doctrine, and religious law. Generally, reflections on these principles resulted in the cross-cultural pattern of supposedly complementary gender roles, in which women were the primary creators and guardians of domestic space (even though they also performed work, such as agriculture, outside of domestic space), while men were responsible for all aspects of leadership, including the family unit, means and modes of production, community organization, and relationships among communities.

Western feminists, who have identified this traditional pattern and its implications, including the binary oppositions of private-public, nurture-war, submission-dominance, as well as its tenacity in postindustrialist societies, have criticized this model of gender roles as not being complementary at all, but rather based on the unequal distribution of power and access to power. Feminists in non-Western cultures are engaged in assessing and challenging the applicability of this insight to their own cultures. Western feminists have observed in their own societies that, although a woman has social status as a wife and mother, her power within the domestic sphere is completely circumscribed by her husband's access to financial resources in the public sphere, which gives him dominance. For women, marriage has served as the primary access to positive status; access to power—including the right to vote, the chances of being voted into elective office, the likelihood of being hired into and promoted within male-dominated professions, and achieving high religious office—has traditionally been denied to women and only slowly accepted in the latter part of the twentieth century. In contrast, groups that do not necessarily accept, or that even directly challenge, biological and traditional religious definitions of gender and gender roles, including homosexuals, transsexuals, and eunuchs, have been marginalized in terms of power and denied the status of marriage.

With the exception of the Hebrew Bible, which explicitly provides rules for marriage and procreation (e.g., Deuteronomy 22:13–29; Numbers 5:11–31; Proverbs 31; Leviticus 12, 15:16–32), scriptural texts such as the Gospels of the New Testament, the Vedas, the Dhammapada, the Qur'an, and the Lun Yu (Analects of Confucius) do not explicitly explore gender roles as a dominant theme; although gender identities are there, the texts often present their teachings as prayers or sayings that apply to both women and men. In contrast, texts by male authors who drew upon scripture did have the nature and place of women as a major concern and generally sought to limit women's access to sacred power: for example, the writings of Philo of Alexandria, the letters of Paul, the Laws of Manu, Ashvaghosha's bi-

ography of the Buddha, and Hadith. In the case of Confucianism, a woman scholar, Pan Ch'ao (first century C.E.), wrote the Instructions for Women, in which she advocates both education and marriage for women.

However, when one examines the stories of religious women and images of the feminine in religious mythology, one finds as many stories that challenge the traditional model of gender roles as those that appear to support it. By taking a new look at traditional and contemporary images of women in religion, contemporary scholars are aiming for a more accurate understanding of the complicated ways in which the access of women to spiritual power has been and is defined and of the implications such paths of access have for gender roles. The following comparative discussion identifies some patterns in traditional representations of women in religion.

AUTHORITATIVE RELIGIOUS WOMEN

Women authors

In some cultures women are the authors of authoritative religious works. Kāraikkāl Ammaiyār and Antal wrote canonical works in Tamil on South Indian Hinduism, Mirabai in Hindi on North Indian Hinduism, and Rābi'a on Sufism. Each of these women wrote influential devotional religious poetry based on her experiences of mystical intimacy with God. In all cases, their biographies represent them as independent women, either unmarried or actively resisting marriage; none of them had children.

Models of Religious Women

Traditionally, religious behavior has been encouraged in women because they are viewed as the preservers of culture, but religious behavior comes in a varied palette. Paradigms of religious women include mothers of religious leaders—for example, the Virgin Mary as the mother of Christ, and Queen Māyā as the mother of Buddha. In both cases, though, the biological details of motherhood have been mythologically eclipsed: the Virgin Mary experienced conception by the Holy Spirit, and Queen Māyā gave birth through her side, without pain. Typically, women have become religious leaders for groups of women, albeit ultimately under the supervision of the male religious hierarchy; for example, the Buddha's stepmother became a leader of the order of nuns in Theravada Buddhist tradition. In Christian tradition, Hildegard of Bingen and Clare of Assisi were medieval mystics who founded convents and authored important confessional texts on doctrine. In Islamic traditions, women trained in the Qur'an lead other women in prayer recitation. In Hinduism, groups of women perform self-described "secret" rituals for fertility. In

Jewish tradition, domestic rituals, including observance of dietary laws and the Sabbath, have traditionally been the province of women.

A few religions have honored women with ritual leadership of the larger community; in general, these religions tend to emphasize mystical vision and possession. Examples include women shamans in Korea, women priestesses in Japanese Shinto and ancient Egyptian religion, and women ritualists in the African religions of Santeria and Vodou. Many individual women visionaries are remembered for their important contributions to religion, including those who founded new religions—for example, Ann Lee of the Shakers in the United States, Mary Baker Eddy of Christian Science, H. P. Blavatsky of Theosophy, Yeshe Tsogyal of Tibetan Tantrism, Ānandamāyī Mā of Hinduism, and Sun Bu-er of Taoism.

GODDESSES

Independent Goddesses

Images of feminine religious power include representations of female deities. Throughout the world, sculptures depicting pregnant women have been found and are considered to be images of the mother goddess, perhaps signifying early religious ideas about women's power. Indeed, myths of sacred ancestors from Australia and the Amazon describe how women originally exclusively possessed sacred power, which was subsequently stolen by men. The maternal qualities of mercy and compassion are represented in female deities such as the Chinese and Japanese Buddhist image of Kuan Yin, a goddess who hears and responds to all human cries for help. Images of independent goddesses can also explore the forceful dimensions of power; in Hinduism, the goddess Kālī conquered demons that threatened heaven and earth when male gods were unable to do so.

Goddesses and Marriage

In many mythologies of creation, there is both a female and a male creative power; often, as in the Hopi Indian story of the Spider Woman, the Hindu story of Puruṣa and Shakti, and the biblical story of Adam and Eve, the male principle is a static figure whereas the female principle provides the activity that results in conditions as we know them. In Hinduism, gods and goddesses are married, with the goddesses symbolic of the wealth that wifely virtue brings to a home and a community. The hero Rāma and the heroine Sītā of the famous Indian epic, the Rāmayaṇa, are held by peoples throughout South and Southeast Asia to represent the ideal husband and wife—he in his moral leadership, she in her devotion to him.

The patterns in traditional accounts of human women's religious careers indicate that women religious adepts had to renounce the social customs of marriage and motherhood. This is similar to stories of some male religious adepts, who renounced wealth (sometimes represented as their renunciation of women). The difference is that men also had access to institutional opportunities for religious leadership, which might offer stability, financial remuneration, and the possibility of marriage. Leadership opportunities for women tended to cluster on the visionary or mystic side of religion, in a kind of entrepreneurial capacity where a consistent audience and patronage were not guaranteed, unless their services were defined for women. In contrast to these realities, images of goddesses were and are a locus for the imagination of a broad range of contributions women could make to religion and society.

BIBLIOGRAPHY

Helpful comparative studies of gender include Peggy Reeves Sanday, *Female Power and Male Dominance: On the Origins of Sexual Inequality* (1981); Caroline Walker Bynum, Steven Harrell, and Paula Richman, eds., *Gender and Religion* (1986); and Nancy Auer Falk and Rita M. Gross, eds., *Unspoken Worlds: Women's Religious Lives* (1989). On gender roles, see Priscilla Rachun Linn, "Gender Roles," in *The Encyclopedia of Religion,* edited by Mircea Eliade (1987), pp. 495–502.

The story of Kāraikkāl Ammaiyār and a translation of selected poems can be found in Norman J. Cutler, *Songs of Experience: The Poetics of Tamil Devotion* (1987). On Antal , with translations from her poetry, see Vidya Dehejia, *Āṇṭal and Her Path of Love: Poems of a Woman Saint from South India* (1990). On Mirabai, with translations from her poetry, see John Stratton Hawley and Mark Juergensmeyer, *Songs of the Saints of India* (1988). On Rabiʻa, with translations from her poetry, see Charles Upton, *Doorkeeper of the Heart: Versions of Rabiʻa* (1988). An excellent, comparative collection of religious writings by women is Jane Hirschfield, ed., *Women in Praise of the Sacred: 43 Centuries of Spiritual Poetry by Women* (1994).

Many of the examples presented in this article were drawn from Serinity Young, ed., *An Anthology of Sacred Texts By and About Women* (1993). See also, on the mother goddess, Elinor Gadon, *The Once and Future Goddess: A Symbol for Our Time* (1989); on Indian Hindu goddesses, John Stratton Hawley and Donna Marie Wulff, *The Divine Consort: Rādhā and the Goddesses of India* (1982); on Kuan Yin, Martin Palmer and Jay Ramsay with Man-Ho Kwok, *Kuan Yin: Myths and Prophecies of the Chinese Goddess of Compassion* (1995); on traditions of Rāma and Sītā, Paula Richman, ed., *Many Rāmāyaṇas: The Diversity of a Narrative Tradition in South Asia* (1991).

For reflections on the meaning of feminine religious symbolism in modern times, see Clarissa Pinkola Estés, *Women Who Run with the Wolves: Myths and Stories of the Wild Woman Archetype* (1992); Clarissa W. Atkinson, Constance H. Buchanan, and Margaret R. Miles, *Immaculate and Powerful: The Female in Sacred Image and Social Reality* (1987); Carol P. Christ, "Why Women Need the Goddess: Phenomenological, Psychological, and Political Reflections," in *Womanspirit Rising*, edited by Carol P. Christ and Judith Plaskow (1979); and Rita M. Gross, "Hindu Female Deities as a Resource for the Contemporary Rediscovery of the Goddess," *Journal of the American Academy of Religion* XLVI, no. 3 (1978): 269–291. A very interesting comparative discussion of the theory and practice of women's ritual roles in Judaism, shamanism in Korea, and Iraquois tradition is Ellen Koskoff, "Both In and Between: Women's Musical Roles in Ritual Life," in *Music and the Experience of God*, edited by Mary Collins, David Power, and Mellonee Burnim (1989).

See also Afterlife; Couples; Femininity; Gender Conflict; Goddess: History of Study; Images of Women.

KAREN PECHILIS PRENTISS

Gender Studies

Gender studies can name a general, interdisciplinary academic field, an approach or methodology within a particular field, or a literally institutionalized program of study. The meaning of *gender studies* in a given instance is dependent on the context in which it is invoked as well as its relation to other possible ways of naming the terrain. Thus, university programs can be named either "women's studies" or "gender studies" and sometimes are named by the conjunction "women's and gender studies."

Women's studies programs are generally taken to imply a focus on studying women as a corrective to the androcentric bias of most academic curricula. Women's studies is a necessary undertaking because the rest of the modern university curriculum is focused on men, which contributes to the maintenance and reproduction of male dominance in society. Yet its political possibilities are not set in advance, but emerge in context. Moreover, the varying meanings of *equality*, and the varying understandings of what woman is and whether she is an "is"—an identity—at all, make the study of

"women" as a means to achieving equality a complicated and even vexed project.

Some feminist thinkers have argued that a focus on "women" does not challenge gender roles and the inequality these roles support but rather may actually reinscribe them. Monique Wittig (1992), for example, argues powerfully that for "women" to be free they must refuse to be "women." Gender is, she suggests, the very mark of inequality, and no amount of recuperating the history of women as women can undo that inequality. According to this line of thinking, gender studies bespeaks a reexamination of the identity category in whose name women's studies has gone forward.

The choice between women's studies and gender studies is thus more than a cosmetic or semantic difference. To see the space between them requires critical consideration of the relations between and among the terms *sex, gender, sexual difference,* and *sexuality*.

The distinction between biological *sex* and the social roles of *gender* is the result of a hard-won battle in the second wave of the feminist movement and theory to resist interpellation into the ideology "biology is destiny" (Beauvoir, de). For example, just because some women are biologically capable of bearing children does not mean that (1) everybody marked as female is so capable, (2) it is the duty of every female body capable of natal reproduction to bear a child, or (3) child care is women's necessary task. Rather, the division of labor such that women are the primary caretakers of children is a socially arbitrary assignment. The conflation of social role with a biological capability makes this cultural assignment appear both natural and necessary. Feminists such as Adrienne Rich (1993) and Gayle Rubin (1975) have also exposed and criticized the "compulsory heterosexuality" of the "sex/gender system," working to disengage the social roles of gender from sexual practice.

Although these theoretical distinctions have proven to be politically useful and powerful, there are limits to their effectiveness. One of the reasons for distinguishing gender from sex is because gender was held to be socially constructed and thus more open to change than the "given" of biological sex. Yet, gender roles have not simply or easily shifted in the face of feminist critique. Not only has the "social" often proven quite resistant to change (Fuss), but the "biological" has not proven to be a mute and passive substrate available to social inscription—a realization leading later theorists to argue that "biology" is not simply "natural" and unchangeable (Haraway).

Further, some feminist theorists, often using psychoanalysis and poststructuralist theories of language, have argued that a focus on gender is too tied to the sociological idea of roles and fails to recognize the underlying structures of psyche and language that make investments by both men and women difficult to dislodge. Theorists who focus on the sexual difference structured into language provide one means of explaining the continuation of phallogocentrism despite movements for social change (Braidotti, Butler, Rose). Some feminists have even suggested that the distinction between sex and gender is no distinction at all. Thus, Judith Butler (1990) argues that gender, far from being the social interpretation of a pregiven sex, is the set of normative arrangements whereby "sex" or "sexed nature" gets produced and naturalized in the first place.

It is by no means a settled question whether destabilizing those analytic categories (e.g., gender and sexuality) and identities (e.g., woman and man) that have been so central to feminist theory and politics can help to destabilize and subvert lived inequalities of gender and sexuality. Though there is no one answer to this question, attacks on gender studies—from both right and left—suggest that this is not simply an academic matter. Advocates on what may loosely be described as the political and religious (Christian) right have attacked gender studies precisely because it has unmoored gender roles and sexual identity from biology; such critics correctly perceive that destabilizing gender effects also the denaturalization of heterosexuality.

Yet gender studies can also be appropriated to conservative ends. For example, the shift from "women" to "gender" can be used to extend androcentric bias, restoring masculinity to the center of analysis without taking on any of the feminist insights about the production and enforcement of sexual difference. Thus, gender studies can sometimes name a conservative refusal to make women central at any academic site, a refusal to allow any space in which women are not primarily named and defined in relation to men. The potential conservation of masculine privilege has made some feminists wary of gender studies.

Wittig's claim that "lesbians are not women" is an attempt to undo the restrictive binary distinction—woman or man—that makes both gender studies and women's studies subject to patriarchal appropriation. The possibility of nonbinary gender positions, which might be named by terms like *lesbian, queer,* or various *transgenders,* has yet to be fully explored either theoretically or politically.

The designation "gender studies" is also limiting for feminist analyses because gender is not the only vector of power or axis of difference that organizes bodies and subjects. The relations of domination that women face and resist are not captured only by the terms of gender: man, woman. Much feminist theoretical work has been devoted to delineating interstructured social and psy-

chical relations along the axes of gender, race, class, sexuality, nation, ability, and age, among others (Anzaldúa, Crenshaw, Fuss, Lorde, Spillers). One of the chief challenges for feminist theory and politics remains how to negotiate the double demands of identity and difference, without seeking to prioritize one at the expense of the other.

In religious studies, in particular, the project of women's empowerment and agency has been crucially linked to an expanding catalogue of identity and difference: womanist, *mujerista*, lesbian, Asian, Asian-American, Native American, and so on (this list can never be completed). The American Academy of Religion now recognizes the importance of such scholarship and concerns with groups and sections like "womanist theology" and "lesbian feminist issues in religion." The first formally institutionalized feminist section of the Academy, the Women and Religion section, has been the staging ground for the development of many of these groups.

In short, *gender studies* names part of a field that is itself a complex matrix of variously articulated, overlapping, but also contradictory parts. In the end, that no one term or name will do may be not a shortcoming but a strength.

BIBLIOGRAPHY

Anzaldúa, Gloria. *Borderlands/La Frontera: The New Mestiza.* 1987.

Beauvoir, Simone de. *The Second Sex.* 1952, 1989.

Braidotti, Rosi. "Feminism By Any Other Name." Interview with Judith Butler. *differences: A Journal of Feminist Cultural Studies* 6, nos. 2–3 (Summer-Fall 1994): 27–61.

Butler, Judith. *Gender Trouble: Feminism and the Subversion of Identity.* 1990.

Crenshaw, Kimberle. "Demarginalizing the Intersection of Race and Sex: A Black Feminist Critique of Antidiscrimination Doctrine, Feminist Theory and Antiracist Politics." *University of Chicago Legal Forum* (1989): 139–167.

Fuss, Diana. *Essentially Speaking: Feminism, Nature and Difference.* 1989.

———. *Identification Papers.* 1995.

Lorde, Audre. *Sister Outsider.* 1984.

Haraway, Donna. *Primate Visions: Gender, Race, and Nature in the World of Modern Science.* 1989.

Rich, Adrienne. "Compulsory Heterosexuality and Lesbian Existence." In *The Lesbian and Gay Studies Reader.* Edited by Henry Abelove, Michèle Aina Barale, and David M. Halperin. 1993.

Rose, Jacqueline. *Sexuality in the Field of Vision.* 1986.

Rubin, Gayle. "The Traffic in Women: Notes on the 'Political Economy' of Sex." In *Towards an Anthropology of Women.* Edited by Rayna R. Reiter. 1975.

Spillers, Hortense. "Mama's Baby, Papa's Maybe: An American Grammar Book." *Diacritics* 17, no. 2 (1987): 65–81.

Wittig, Monique. *The Straight Mind and Other Essays.* 1992.

JANET R. JAKOBSEN
ANN PELLEGRINI

Genre and Gender

Genre is a hypothesis regarding the relation of a single text to one or more other texts with similar structures, styles, topics, and effects. Gender is a hypothesis that relates a person to others with similar biological appearance, predominant societal roles, styles, and interests. With respect to writing, performing, reading, and viewing, gender differences are noticed in the choices made by women and men and the questions they ask about texts of specific genres.

Societies in which gender is the major category for differentiating among human beings show primary correlation between genre and gender. Societies in which gender is only one of several major features or in which more than two genders are recognized show correlations among groups distinguished by features such as class, race, or education, as well as gender.

Gender studies show that similar correlations between genre and gender can be made with respect to folklore and oral traditions. Here the margins of genre and gender are more immediately dependent on the degree to which women and men have opportunities to participate in public rituals.

Sometimes a particular genre changes when it crosses gender boundaries. Ria Lemaire, for example, shows that the earliest medieval Galician-Portuguese love songs (*cantigas de amigo*), sung by two dialoguing women soloists, described women with several positive adjectives and as initiating relationships. Later (male) court poets imitating these love songs reduced women to passive stereotypes.

In androcentric societies, genres will seldom be distributed evenly. Because of the considerable power residing in writing and producing, genres of the dominant gender are likely to be more numerous, more popular, and to be valued more highly. Because both genre and gender are public and culturally bound, they are imitated and parodied successfully by authors regardless of gender. It is better therefore to study the phenome-

Novelist and abolitionist Harriet Beecher Stowe (1811–1896), author of *Uncle Tom's Cabin* (The National Archives/Corbis)

non of "writing as a woman" and "writing as a man" than to study "writing by women" and "writing by men."

Interpreters exhibit three levels of competence with respect to genre and gender: (1) those who naively assume a correlation. These readers are either unaware that gender is an issue in interpreting texts, or they believe that biological or stereotypical factoring of human beings into male and female is sufficient; (2) those who recognize that genre is historically and culturally defined. When these interpreters evaluate genres, they substitute other kinds of certainty about gender categories—such as the degree to which the narrator speaks normatively, degree of success in rendering or understanding male or female characters, or ability to distance the writer's persona from the writer's experience; (3) those who recognize that genres change with the emergence of new texts and new interpretations. These interpreters discriminate among and resist gender stereotypes even as they use them to push back the margins of discourse.

BIBLIOGRAPHY

Gerhart, Mary. *Genre Choices, Gender Questions.* 1992.

Gilbert, Sandra M., and Susan Gubar. "Tradition and the Female Talent." In *Poetics of Gender.* Edited by Nancy K. Miller. 1986.

Heilbrun, Carolyn G. *Writing a Woman's Life.* 1988.

Kamuf, Peggy. "Writing Like a Woman." In *Women and Language in Literature and Society.* Edited by Sally McConnell-Ginet, Ruth Borker, and Nelly Furman. 1980.

Kauffman, Linda S. *Discourses of Desire: Gender, Genre, and Epistolary Fiction.* 1986.

Kristeva, Julia. "Women's Time." Translated by Alice Jardine and Harry Blake. In *Feminist Theory: A Critique of Ideology.* Edited by Nannerl O. Keohanc, Michelle Z. Rosaldo, and Barbara C. Gelpi. 1981.

Lemaire, Ria. "Explaining Away the Female Subject." *Poetics Today* 7 (1986): 729–743.

Modleski, Tania. *Loving with a Vengeance: Mass-Produced Fantasies for Women.* 1982.

Todd, Janet. *Feminist Literary History.* 1988.

Weedon, Chris. *Feminist Practice and Poststructuralist Theory.* 1987.

See also **Deconstruction; Gender Studies; Literary Theory and Criticism; Literature.**

MARY GERHART

Geography, Sacred

Human beings have long held the idea that certain features of the landscape (natural or humanmade) provide special access to or reveal sacred and powerful realities or alternate realities. Evidence from at least as far back as the Paleolithic period suggests that humans have regarded certain caves, mountains, rivers, forests, and other geographical locations as being especially significant. The physical world, in its topographical, mineralogical, floral, faunal, and hydrological dimensions, and the world as shaped by human societies, with its temples, gardens, and cities, thus serve as a type of grid upon which human values are imposed, manipulated, and experienced. Such impositions of human imagination and values upon the landscape have led to important and long-lasting constructions of gender and power.

Any consideration of sacred geography must take into account the importance of cosmogonies (creation stories), since the models of creation that people believe in have had a profound influence on how the physical and social worlds are envisioned. Thus, the different types of creation processes, creative beings, and created realities as presented in myths and rituals have helped to determine how the world, space, and time are imagined and engaged—providing basic models of reality. These models of reality have served as guidelines and arguments for constructions of gender, power, culture, and the sacred. Creation stories are typically expressed using a range of metaphors, allowing for the description and understanding of an often remote and abstract cosmic process using familiar imagery from the natural and human worlds.

Many of the most ancient and widespread types of cosmogonies express creation in terms of procreative and biological metaphors, quite often as the result of either the primordial coupling of a sky "father god" and an earth "mother goddess" or of the actions of a productive goddess herself. As a result, the entire world becomes a sacred geocosm, sometimes regarded as being the "body" of the mother goddess, with all creatures considered her "children." The sacred is thus within nature, not beyond it, as in many Western religious traditions. In most traditional and premodern societies, particular geographic features and landmarks acquired additional importance as being especially significant parts of the goddess's body (e.g., caves as her womb), abodes of her special protection (e.g., groves, springs, valleys), and places of ritual devotion (e.g., grottoes, volcanoes, fields). In many agricultural societies, the correspondence of the seed cycle to the fertilizing power of rain (associated with the sky god) and the fecundity of the earth (associated with the mother goddess) led to the worship of sacred rivers, fields, and valleys, as well as the recognition of women as manifestations of the divinity and productivity of the goddess in the visible world. Later developments of this early perception of sacred geography and personalities included establishment of ritual centers (culminating in the growth of cities), ritual specialists, and extensive expressions of sacred art, literature, and other cultural forms. Although historians continue to argue over the precise nature of gender roles and power in the prehistoric and ancient worlds, it is certain that many societies gave women special religious significance by virtue of their connections to the creatrix and to the sacred world and its features.

Sacred geography and cosmogony have also been expressed through metaphors of divine administration and shaping, of ordering chaos, and of defeating chthonic beings. Many of these suggest underlying attitudes of misogyny and androcentrism, or at least tensions between men and women. For example, in the Babylonian cosmogony known as *Enuma Elish* (c. 2000 B.C.E.), the known world was created when the hero god Marduk slew the unruly mother goddess Tiamat, dismembering her body and using the severed portions to create the mountains, rivers, and other parts of the current world. The Ngaju Dayak people of southern Borneo believe the world was created by a series of clashes between primordial male and female deities, one result of which was the destruction of the Tree of Life and the creation of the compromised world we live in today.

Because of the protective roles more typically attributed to goddesses (outside of the androcentric traditions), it is not surprising that natural geographical features such as coves, seashores, forests, valleys, islands, and springs—as well as constructed areas like gardens and fields—would be given special meanings. As places that provide shelter, water, sustenance, and a sense of wonder, these locales have long served as sacred spaces. In some cases, as in ancient Crete, palaces were built near sheltered valleys and conical hills, which represented respectively the womb and breasts of the goddess. In South Asia rivers have long been regarded as manifestations of the goddess, and many important pilgrimage sites are located along rivers. Some pilgrimage sites in India have the additional significance of marking spots where portions of the goddess Satī's body fell off as her grieving husband Siva carried it on his shoulder; her vagina, for example, is believed to have fallen in Assam and is worshiped at the Kamakhya temple. In general, many premodern and contemporary societies have tended to view the vertical and mountainous dimensions of sacred geography in terms of the masculine sky or sun god (e.g., building temples to the Greek god Zeus atop mountains), while the horizontal, chthonic, and terrestrial dimensions have often been connected to the feminine earth goddess. Such constructions of gender, based upon metaphorical understandings of sacred geography and human bodies, have proven to be widespread and powerful.

In more recent times, attitudes regarding gender and sacred geography have been influenced by events as diverse as the numerous visions of the Virgin Mary (e.g., Lourdes, Medjugorje); reappraisals of the roles of women and the feminine in Western religions; renewals of pre-Christian goddess-centered religions and the growth of "new" religions; postcolonial revivals of the traditional religions of the Americas, Africa, Australia, and Oceania; explorations of space and the planets; heightened ecological consciousness; and the embracing of digital-age notions such as cyberspace and virtual reality. For some, the modern disenchantment with the physical and natural world has led to a diminished appreciation of the mysterious dimensions of geography. Notions of sacred geography and gender will likely change in response to such forces.

BIBLIOGRAPHY

Blacker, Carmen, and Michael Loewe, eds. *Ancient Cosmologies.* 1975.

Eliade, Mircea. *A History of Religious Ideas.* 3 vols. 1981–1988.

Gimbutas, Marija. *The Language of the Goddess.* 1989.

Kinsley, David. "Goddesses and Sacred Geography." In his *Hindu Goddesses: Visions of the Divine Feminine in the Hindu Religious Tradition.* 1986.

O'Flaherty, Wendy Doniger. *Women, Androgynes, and Other Mythical Beasts.* 1980.

Sproul, Barbara. *Primal Myths: Creation Myths around the World.* 1992.

Tuan, Yi-Fu. *Topophilia: A Study of Environmental Perception, Attitudes, and Values.* 1974.

See also **Creation and Recreation; Gender Conflict; Goddess.**

GLEN ALEXANDER HAYES

Ghazali, Zaynab al-

Zaynab al-Ghazali (b. 1917) was the founder of the Association of Muslim Ladies in Egypt and writer and teacher for the Muslim Brotherhood, an organization founded in 1928 to Islamize Egyptian politics and society. Her father, a religious scholar and cotton merchant, had her privately tutored in Islamic studies and encouraged her to assume an Islamic form of leadership, following the example of Nusayba bint Ka'b al-Maziniyya, who fought alongside the Prophet Muhammad in the battle of Uhud (625 C.E.). Initially joining the Egyptian Feminist Union, she came to believe that Islam guaranteed women's rights. At the age of eighteen she founded the Association of Muslim Ladies, which offered weekly lectures on religion and assistance to orphans and the poor and published a magazine. It also demanded that Egypt be ruled by the Qur'an. Hasan al-Banna, founder of the Muslim Brotherhood, requested a merger of her organization with the Muslim Sisters, the women's branch of their organization, but she refused. She nonetheless pledged allegiance to Banna shortly before his assassination in 1949 and played a major role in the organization's attempted revival in 1964 after it was forcibly dissolved by President Gamal Abdel Nasser in 1954. In 1965 she was imprisoned, along with many other members of the Brotherhood, for allegedly plotting to assassinate Nasser, a charge she vigorously denies. She describes her excruciating torture in prison in her book, *Ayyām min ḥayātī* (Days of My Life). The Association of Muslim Ladies was taken over by the government, but after President Anwar Sadat released her and most of the imprisoned Brothers in 1971, and allowed the organization unofficially to function, she resumed teaching and writing for the Muslim Brotherhood. She espouses domesticity and obedience for wives but suggests that women follow the example of women warriors from early Islam who refused to bow to tyrannical male rulers. She divorced her first husband for interfering in her activities and threatened to do the same with her second. She attributes her public activism to her father's encouragement; her husband's wealth, which exempted her from housework; the fact that he had other wives to visit; and her own childlessness, which she sees as a blessing. Although many women have joined Islamist movements in recent decades, she is the only one to become a major Islamist leader.

BIBLIOGRAPHY

Ghazali, Zaynab-al. *Ayyām min ḥayātī* [Days of My Life]. 1977.

Hoffman, Valerie J. "An Islamic Activist: Zaynab al-Ghazali." In *Women and the Family in the Middle East: New Voices of Change.* Edited by Elizabeth W. Fernea. 1985.

Zuhur, Sherifa. *Revealing Reveiling: Islamist Gender Ideology in Contemporary Egypt.* 1992. See esp. chap. 5.

VALERIE J. HOFFMAN

Ghosts

Ghosts are souls of deceased persons (and sometimes animals) who inhabit the unseen world, may appear as visible but not necessarily material forms (apparitions, specters), may or may not speak, and may use means such as noises or invisible forces (poltergeists) to make their presence known to living beings. Although all cultures are known to have this concept and to have experiences with such beings, the word *ghost* has its roots in the West Germanic languages; it appears to be cognate with Old Norse *geisa*, to rage, and Gothic *usgaisjan*, to terrify. Rich narrative traditions about ghosts are found in Celtic, Scandinavian, Icelandic, and German folklore. In Irish tradition the *banshee*, a death omen, cries out and is sometimes seen in the form of a woman. In both Ireland and Scotland a *wraith* may be a spiritual manifestation of a person who is still living, on the point of dying, or dead within the immediate past. A *fetch* (doppelgänger) is one's double. Ghosts traverse the boundary between life and death. Ghosts may be help-ful (on the Internet one can meet Quick Silver, a friendly female teenage ghost), neutral (ghosts that don't bother anyone), evil, or just restless (sometimes because of the inordinate grief of the living); but above all they are presences, experienced as real.

Ghosts tend to inhabit places associated with their lives, thus the use of the word *haunt* meaning ghost, molestation by a ghost, or a place where a ghost may be found. *Haunt* is of uncertain origin, referring to habit (custom) and habitation, and has been used in English to refer to ghosts since the sixteenth century.

In most cultures particular names for ghosts manifest gender-related issues in society. For example, in Great Britain grey ladies are ghosts of women who have died violently for love or have pined away. In India a *churel* is the evil ghost of a woman who dies in childbirth or ceremonial impurity; in Russia a *rusalka* is the ghost of a maiden who drowns by accident or force. In Jamaican folklore, *duppies*, ghosts of the recently deceased, may return desiring sexual intercourse with their spouses. Narratives of experiences with ghosts have long been collected and anthologized, but they are rarely analyzed concerning the gender of the ghosts (some ghosts are reported as having no recognizable gender) or the gender of the person visited by ghosts.

An important difficulty lies in distinguishing between demons, many of whom are characterized as female, some with attributes of insatiable sexuality, and ghosts. The dybbuk in Jewish folklore, an evil spirit that possesses the living, has been seen as a demon or a lost soul. A ghoul (often female) feeds on flesh of the dead and may be associated with a house where tragedy has occurred or with graveyards; its etymological source is the Arabic *ghūl* (to seize), and in Islamic folklore the female *ghŭla* is feared because she can appear as a fully normal woman. (Thus, in this case, a ghoul is a demon rather than a ghost in the sense used above.) The zombie (from Vodou) is a reanimated corpse, summoned through magic or sorcery. In African-American belief systems from the Georgia coastal islands, at night water or food must be made available to ghosts, who are most readily seen at dusk and just after midnight.

Cultures with elaborate systems of ancestor veneration (China, Japan, Southeast Asia, Africa) show correspondingly complex relationships with ghosts. One feature common to these cultures is that frequently the socially marginalized (often women) who die without proper ritual are the cause of trouble and misfortune as ghosts after death. Stevan Harrell, in one of the few studies to consider the gender of ghosts (Harrell, 1986), compared reports of female and male ghosts in Taiwanese folk religion and showed that ghosts are an explanation for misfortune; when men see ghosts, the

Buddhist worshipers make offerings during the Hungry Ghosts festival, Melaka, Malaysia (Eye Ubiquitous/Corbis).

ghosts are usually female, perceived as a threat to men in the society. Shamanic practices in these cultures often entail possession by ancestor spirits (male and female) to solicit their advice and assistance.

The Hebrew scriptures contain surprisingly few descriptions of what we think of as ghosts. On the other hand, spirits—angels—are clearly depicted in the Hebrew Bible. Among the many other supernatural beings in cultures around the world, spirits form a broader category than ghosts and include God or the gods, angels, and demons (in Western cultures).

In Christianity the word *ghost* refers to the third person of the Trinity as Holy Ghost and has been seen by some mystics and contemporary charismatics as a feminine manifestation of God. Holy Ghost is the equivalent of Holy Spirit; the German and Old English *geist* translates the meaning of *spiritus* (Latin). In the English Roman Catholic liturgy the older term Holy Ghost was formally replaced by Holy Spirit during the Second Vatican Council (1962–1965), perhaps to distance the term from negative connotations of ghost. Appearances of holy persons or saints who are deceased (referred to as apparitions in Catholicism) are a common feature of the cults of the saints in historical as well as contemporary Catholicism. *Ghost* is also used to describe the principle of life or spirit—at death one "gives up the ghost."

There has been a strong tendency in secular thought to reduce all belief about or experiences of ghosts to an explanatory paradigm of illusion, delusion, deception, or unreal manifestation of thoughts or dreams; *phantom*, a synonym for *ghost,* suggests a mental illusion or hallucination. A survey conducted by the Princeton Religious Research Center asked members of major Christian religious denominations in the United States about paranormal experiences and found that 16 to 19 percent (unfortunately not categorized by gender) reported experiences of contacting the dead and 6 percent to 14 percent reported having seen a ghost (*Religion in America*, Robert Bezilla, ed., 1993). More productive scholarship accepts the validity of such first-hand experiences.

BIBLIOGRAPHY

Unlike witches, which are the subject of much excellent scholarship by and about women, ghosts, with some exceptions, have received comparatively little attention. Notable, however, is the growing body of work on women's roles in nineteenth-century Spiritualism, with its dramatic contacts with the dead. See, for instance, Diana Basham, *The Trial of Woman: Feminism and the Occult Sciences in Victorian Literature and Society* (1992) and Bret E. Carroll, *Spiritualism in Antebellum America* (1997). For theory on ghosts and other spirits see David J. Hufford, "Beings Without Bodies: An Experience-Centered Theory of the Belief in Spirits," in *Out of the Ordinary: Folklore and the Supernatural,* edited by Barbara Walker (1995). Hufford's earlier work, *The Terror That Comes in the Night: An Experience-Centered Study of Supernatural Assault Traditions* (1982) examines what Newfoundlers and others call "the old hag," an evil presence that presses down on the chests of its victims; Hufford proves that the experience occurs cross-culturally, presents women's and men's experiences in case studies, and discusses the gender of the "old hag." Gillian Bennett, *Traditions of Belief: Women and the Supernatural* (1987), is based on interviews and case studies of women's experiences with ghosts and other supernatural phenomena in contemporary England. For Irish beliefs see Linda May Ballard, "Before Death and Beyond: A Preliminary Survey of Death and Ghost Traditions with Particular Reference to Ulster," in *The Folklore of Ghosts,* edited by Hilda R. Ellis Davidson (1981); Patricia Lysaght, *The Banshee: The Irish Supernatural Death Messenger* (1986); and John Messenger, "A Critical Reexamination of the Concept of Spirits: With Special Reference to Traditional Irish Folklore and Contemporary Irish Folk Culture," *American Anthropologist* 64, no. 2 (1962). West Indian, in particular, Jamaican beliefs are discussed by Venetia Newell, "West Indian Ghosts," in Davidson, ed., cited above. Michiko Iwasaka and Barre Toelken, *Ghosts and the Japanese Cultural Experience in Japanese Death Legends* (1994), is based on translations from the Japanese, with illustrations featuring Japanese artwork of ghosts and a chapter on ghosts of mothers and children; it does not index women as a subject. Stevan Harrell, "Men, Women, and Ghosts in Taiwanese Folk Religion," in *Gender and Religion: On the Complexity of Symbols,* edited by Caroline Walker Bynum, et al. (1986), discusses the gender of ghosts and the contexts for placating or exorcizing them. Robert P. Weller, *Unities and Diversitites in Chinese Religion* (1987), has significant chapters on the complex hierarchies of the social life of ghosts in the religions of Taiwan. See also Mary Beth Mills, "Attack of the Widow Ghosts: Gender, Death, and Modernity in Northeast Thailand," in *Bewitching Women, Pious Men: Gender and Body Politics in Southeast Asia,* edited by Aihwa Ord et al. (1995), and Ruth S. Freed and Stanley Freed, *Ghosts: Life and Death in North India* (1993). Aniela Jaffe, *Death Dreams and Ghosts: An Archetypal Approach to Apparitions* (1997), presents a Jungian viewpoint on ghosts. A general reference source showing the wide cultural diversity of beliefs about ghosts is Rosemary Ellen Guiley, ed., *The Encyclopedia of Ghosts and Spirits* (1992).

MAGGIE KRUESI

Gimbutas, Marija

Marija Gimbutas (1921–1994), anthropologist and leading figure in the study of the goddess, was born in Vilnius, Lithuania. Gimbutas was educated in Lithuania, Austria, and Germany. In 1964 she became a professor of European archaeology at the University of California, Los Angeles. Gimbutas was a member of the American Institute of Archaeology, the Association of Field Archaeology, and the Association of Baltic Studies. She received a number of awards and honors, including grants from the National Endowment for the Humanities and the Smithsonian Institution, and in 1968 was proclaimed the Los Angeles Times Woman of the Year. Of her several books and scholarly articles, three, *The Gods and Goddesses of Old Europe: 7000–3500 B.C.* (1974), *The Language of the Goddess* (1989), and *The Civilization of the Goddess* (1991), have had an especially important influence on contemporary feminist goddess spirituality.

The main conclusion of her later work was that the religion of the Neolithic period in Europe involved the primary worship of the Goddess, indicating the existence of prehistoric societies that were sexually egalitarian, peaceful, agrarian, and aesthetically highly developed. The central and persistent theme of her interpretation of prehistoric European culture is that it was destroyed by aggressive invaders who established patriarchal hierarchies of control, dethroning the Goddess as the central deity and instituting the subjugation of women. The influence of J. J. Bachofen and Riane Eisler is especially evident here. Gimbutas' assertions concerning the overthrow of the matrifocal, goddess-worshiping, harmonious cultures of prehistoric Europe have been described as "archaeomythology," since her method is to combine archaeological research with mythology and folklore. Nonetheless, this dimension of her thought has had a powerful influence on feminist theologians such as Carol Christ, and Gimbutas was a contributor, along with a number of leading feminist religious writers, to *The Politics of Women's Spirituality,* edited by Charlene Spretnak (1982).

BIBLIOGRAPHY

Two works critical of the goddess theories inspired by Gimbutas are Marsha Aileen Hewitt, *Critical Theory of Religion: A Feminist Analysis* (1995), especially pp. 184 ff., and Rosemary Radford Ruether, *Gaia and God: An Ecofeminist Theology of Earth Healing* (1992), especially chapter 6.

See also Goddess: Contemporary Goddess Movement; Goddess: History of Study; Patriarchy; Theology: Feminist Theology.

MARSHA HEWITT

Gluckl of Hameln

Memoirist Gluckl of Hameln (1646–1724), also known as Glueckel von Hameln or Glikl, was born to a prominent Jewish family in Hamburg, Germany. She married Haim of Hameln at fourteen and bore twelve children. She was her husband's business partner and advisor; after his death in 1689, she carried on the family's extensive financial affairs, including trading and manufacturing, attending mercantile fairs, and lending money. Gluckl remarried in 1699 and moved to Metz, France; shortly afterward, her new husband went bankrupt, losing his own and Gluckl's savings. After his death in 1712, Gluckl moved in with her daughter's family, where she died in 1724.

Gluckl's fame rests on her seven "small books," which have been variously described as a memoir and as an "ethical will," a traditional genre of Jewish writing addressed to one's children, typically including moral counsel as well as family history. Gluckl's memoir is the first known autobiography of a Jewish woman and a valuable cultural resource for Jewish life in Germany in the seventeenth century. The original Yiddish manuscript has been lost, but copies circulated among

Gluckl's many descendants until the memoirs were finally published in 1896. Gluckl's descendant, the well-known feminist Bertha Pappenheim, translated the memoirs into German in 1910.

Gluckl began writing the memoirs after her first husband's death "to help against the melancholy thoughts which came . . . during many sleepless nights," completing them in 1719. The memoirs reveal the influence of Yiddish ethical-didactic literature, folktales, the *Tsenerene* (the Yiddish "women's Bible"), and *tkhines*, women's supplicatory prayers.

BIBLIOGRAPHY

Bilik, Dorothy. "The Memoirs of Glikl of Hameln: The Archaeology of the Text." *Yiddish* 8 (Spring 1992): 1–18. An analysis of questions of textual integrity, style, and genre in five translations of Gluckl's memoirs.

Davis, Natalie Zemon. *Women on the Margins: Three Seventeenth-Century Lives*. 1995. A comparative analysis of the autobiographical writings of three women—one Jewish, one Protestant, and one Catholic—who lived "on the margins" of seventeenth-century European, North American, and South American life. The section on Gluckl provides information on her environment and close readings of passages in the memoirs.

Glueckel of Hameln. *The Memoirs of Glueckel of Hameln*. Translated by Marvin Lowenthal. Edited by Robert Rosen. 1977. A somewhat abridged and dated translation of the memoirs, first published in 1932, with a new introduction by Robert Rosen.

NAOMI SEIDMAN

Gnosticism

Gnosticism, a term coined in the eighteenth century, refers particularly to second- and third-century sects whose dualistic teachings claimed to disclose divine mysteries. Contemporary Christian authors such as Irenaeus, Tertullian, Hippolytus, and Epiphanius apply the word *gnostic* to the teachings of Valentinus, Carpocrates, Mani, the Naassenes, and the Ophites, among others. Certain gnostic teachings predate Christianity and are found in philosophical circles within the Greco-Roman world, as well as occurring in Jewish texts, notably those coming from the Alexandrine community. The medieval teachings of the ninth-century Bogomils and twelfth-century Cathari resemble earlier gnostic systems, while the Ismā'īlīyah sect of Islam, founded in the ninth century, and the sixteenth-century Jewish kabbalist Isaac Luria share similar ideas. The teachings of the seventeenth-century German Jakob Boehme inspire gnosticism in the modern period.

Scholars distinguish between the Greek word *gnosis*, meaning knowledge or understanding, and *gnostic* and *gnosticism*. *Gnosis* is narrowly defined as knowledge of divine secrets reserved for an elite; whereas *gnostic*, a rare technical term dating from Plato (fifth-century B.C.E.) and used by patristic writers as a negative label for specific sects, became the designation for the second- and third-century systems. The distinction has not been universally accepted by academics. However, *gnosticism* itself, a word not found in ancient literature, is now recognized as designating a religion.

A large corpus of gnostic writings was discovered in 1945 near Nag Hammadi in Upper Egypt. Much of the literature consists of writings attributed to figures such as Adam and Eve and to Christian disciples such as Thomas, John, and Mary Magdalene.

Gnosticism's complex myth of origins is repeatedly told in the surviving documents. Knowledge of the gnostic cosmogony offers the possibility of deliverance to those who possess it, male or female. Non-gnostics or agnostics are ignorant of this knowledge and cannot benefit from redemption.

Although the creation story is difficult to systematize, all gnostic writings concur that the cosmos is divided into three parts: the kingdom of light or God; an intermediate realm; and the earthly world. The cosmos is created by an Unknown God, also called the Pleroma, or fullness, and his spouse, who is God's mirror. Sophia, or Wisdom, is the last spiritual creature. She wishes to reproduce creation but instead produces the Demiurge, or Ialdabaoth, who subsequently organizes the planets and the stars. The Demiurge thinks he alone exists and proceeds to create the earthly world; he then boasts of his greatness, only to be humbled by the disclosure of a world that is preexistent in space and time. It is the female being Wisdom (Sophia) or Faith (Pistis) who makes this revelation. Next, humanity is manifested through the fashioning of the lower angels. For some time this creature, Adam, or *anthropos*, does not stir. Sophia then causes the Demiurge to breathe the *pneuma* (spirit or breath) he has inherited from her into humanity. Following the animation of Adam, Sophia and the Demiurge struggle, she to awaken the human to spiritual consciousness, he to prevent the awakening.

The *Apocryphon of John*, a text dating from the second century, provides another version of the gnostic myth in which the Pleroma produces a thought (*ennoia*) who is the image of the fullness. She is Barbēlo, and she becomes the "first man, which is the virgin spirit [*pneuma*]." Barbēlo represents the female aspect of the Unknown God, yet she retains bisexual features, her bisexuality being one expression of perfection. Barbēlo brings forth a "blessed spark of light," which is identified with the heavenly Christ. The story of Sophia follows. In this version Sophia repents of her hubris resulting in the Demiurge. She is then restored to the Pleroma.

For the gnostics it is the earthly creation that leads to a separation of the original divine unity. Sophia's desire to reproduce violates that divine unity and results in serious consequences for her and the cosmos. In the *Gospel of Philip* the division of the sexes is blamed on a woman (Eve) and connected with the origin of mortality. The writer is apparently drawing a parallel between Eve's situation and Sophia's fall from the unity of the Pleroma. Probably Barbēlo and Sophia were originally a single being in gnostic mythology. Certainly they occupy a prominent position in the cosmogony; but both female aspects are ultimately subordinated to a male ideal.

Another second-century writing, the *Gospel of Mary,* was known to scholars prior to the discovery of the Egyptian manuscripts. In it Mary Magdalene is portrayed as a spokeswoman, exhorting the male disciples to prepare for the work of preaching that they have been called to perform. Her address to them arouses Peter's opposition and irritation. He disparages her authority, asking "Did he [Jesus] really speak with a woman without our knowledge and not openly? Are we to turn about and all listen to her? Did he prefer her to us?"

Further evidence of the prominence of Magdalene and the tension with Peter (or the Petrine tradition) is recorded in Logion 114 of the *Gospel of Thomas.* Simon Peter declares that women are not worthy of the gift of life. Jesus replies that Mary can be led into becoming male so that she can participate in life like men: "for every woman who will make herself male will enter the Kingdom of Heaven." Once again, the redemption of a woman is possible only on condition of her metamorphosis into a man.

Despite this, both gnostic and orthodox Christian sources indicate that many women found that the gnostic style of Christianity addressed their interests, beliefs, and concerns. The third-century Latin author Tertullian complains about the heretical (gnostic) women who teach, dispute, perform exorcisms and cures, and even baptize. He accuses these women further by declaring their ordinations to be "carelessly administered, capricious and inconsistent" (*Praescr.* 41).

Gnostic sects did not possess a developed hierarchical administration. Women occupied prominent positions as teachers, prophets, and missionaries. Women also took a leading role in cultic ceremonies such as baptism and the celebration of the Eucharist. As long as gnosticism proclaimed salvation solely through knowledge, the salvific potential it offered was accessible to women as well as men. Certainly gnostic writings suggest a more powerful and public status for women than was available to them in patristic (orthodox) Christian communities.

BIBLIOGRAPHY

The corpus of literature on gnostic teachings and communities is vast. The following titles focus on descriptions of the female and the feminine in gnosticism.

Buckley, Jorunn J. *Female Fault and Fulfillment in Gnosticism.* 1986.

Castelli, Elizabeth. " 'I Will Make Mary Male': Pieties of the Body and Gender Transformation of Christian Women in Late Antiquity." In *Body Guards: The Cultural Politics of Gender Ambiguity.* Edited by Julia Epstein and Kristina Staub. 1991.

Fischer-Mueller, E. A. "Yaldabaoth: The Gnostic Female Principle in Its Fallenness." *Novum Testamentum* 32, no. 1 (1990): 79–95.

Hoffman, Daniel L. *The Status of Women and Gnosticism in Irenaeus and Tertullian.* 1995.

King, Karen L. "The Gospel of Mary." In *The Complete Gospels: Annotated Scholars Version.* Edited by Robert J. Miller. 1992.

———, ed. *Images of the Feminine in Gnosticism.* 1988.

McGuire, Anne. "Women, Gender, and 'Gnostic' Traditions." In *Women and Christian Origins.* Edited by Ross Kraemer and Mary Rose d'Angelo. 1997.

Mortley, Raoul. *Womanhood: The Feminine in Ancient Hellenism, Gnosticism, Christianity, and Islam.* 1981.

Perkins, Pheme. *The Gnostic Dialogue: The Early Church and the Crisis of Gnosticism.* 1980.

Williams, Michael A. "Uses of Gender Imagery in Ancient Gnostic Texts." In *Gender and Religion: On the Complexity of Symbols.* Edited by Caroline W. Bynum, Stevan Harrell, and Paul Richman. 1986.

The following books contain translations of gnostic writings.

Pagels, Elaine. *The Gnostic Gospels.* 1979.

Robinson, James M., ed. *The Nag Hammadi Library in English.* 3rd ed. 1988.

A thorough technical discussion of gnosticism in antiquity may be found in Kurt Rudolph's *Gnosis: The Nature and History of an Ancient Religion,* translated by Robert McLachlan Wilson (1983).

See also **Creation and Recreation; Wisdom.**

DIANE TREACY-COLE

Goddess

Prehistoric Goddesses

The only evidence for prehistoric goddesses lies in nontextual evidence such as iconography. Icons, leaving no explanation, must be interpreted, and interpretation is theoretical. The meaning of female statuettes and statues has been debated vigorously. Do these figures represent goddesses, human women, or dolls? Many figures have been found in the general cultural milieu of an excavated settlement: in what may have been houses, often clustered in groups in one locality, such as a bench or altar. They have also been discovered in association with hearths, storage pits, refuse pits, and graves. Figurines found in graves probably represent forms of goddesses who protected the body in death or helped bring it into a new life.

The presence of prehistoric goddess-figures does not give evidence of early matriarchal societies. Worship of goddesses cannot be equated with the position of the woman in society. This point is well-illustrated by goddess-worshiping peoples of India; tantric texts to the goddess Devī beg the goddess for sons, not daughters. However, scholarship indicates that many prehistoric tribes were matrilineal (Battaglia, 1993).

FUNCTIONS OF THE GODDESSES

In order to determine the characteristics of prehistoric goddesses, it is useful to look at the pantheons of the earliest historical cultures of the Near East: the Sumerian, Akkadian, Syrian, and Egyptian. None of these pantheons is dominated by a single monotheistic deity—female or male—but there exist in each culture multifunctional "great"-goddesses: Inanna, Ishtar, Anat, and Hathor, among others, are goddesses of love, war, and in some cases handicrafts. This differs greatly from the functionality of historic European goddesses such as Greek Athena, who remains the patroness of both war and crafts, but who has lost her sexuality. If the goddesses of the earliest historical cultures were multifunctional, it is likely that the goddesses of at least late prehistory shared these characteristics.

The primary function of the prehistoric European and Asian goddesses was not just sexual; nor were they merely mother goddesses. These figures represent the female in many different life epochs, from pubescent girl to elderly woman (Rice, 1981). The prehistoric goddesses must have been responsible for the life continuum: birth, death, and rebirth; human and nonhuman animal fertility and vegetal fertility; wisdom; and crafts. When, in later prehistory, these societies needed defensive protection, the goddesses probably became city protectresses (as did the later Greek Athena) and warrior goddesses.

A multifunctional goddess may have represented both death and rebirth. The early historic Akkadian and Babylonian goddess Ereshkigal, "great lady earth," was goddess of earth and underworld. In the poem "The Descent of Inanna," Inanna, goddess of the heavens and earth, descended to the underworld to visit her sister Ereshkigal. On the way to the underworld, she was compelled to divest herself of all her worldly attributes. Upon her arrival, Ereshkigal fixed upon her the eye of death, and she turned into a slab of rotting meat. Eventually, her attendant Ninshubur was able to compel the freshwater and wisdom-god Enki to save her. Enki created asexual creatures, who sympathized with Ereshkigal as she was going through birth pangs, and Ereshkigal granted life to Inanna. Thus the goddess of the underworld also gave birth to new life. Prehistoric iconography leads one to the same conclusion, that the goddess of death was a cyclic goddess of the life continuum.

EVIDENCE

Geographically, Upper Paleolithic goddess figures range from central Europe (France, Austria) to Mal'ta near Lake Baikal in Siberia. They are generally amply proportioned and characterized by an emphasis upon breasts, buttocks, and pubic triangle. An example is the most famous of the carvings found at Laussel, in the Dordogne region of France: a seventeen-inch-high figure, covered with red ochre, carved onto a limestone block at an overhanging rock shelter, and holding a bison horn carved with thirteen lines. The four-inch-tall figurine from Willendorf, on the north bank of the Danube River, is also amply proportioned. Upper Paleolithic faces lack clear definition. Some, like the figure from Lespugue, France, made of mammoth ivory, seem to represent multiple eggs and may represent the potentiality of birth. Many, such as the Willendorf figure, were covered with red ochre; red, the color of blood, perhaps represents childbirth and life. These goddesses reflect many different life phases of woman, including but not limited to pregnancy. In addition to carvings and figurines, cave paintings give examples of possible female symbolism: cup marks, hands, and vulvae.

Abstract double-breast figures show a continuum from the Upper Paleolithic through the Neolithic, from Palestine, France, Italy, Switzerland, The Czech Republic, and the Cycladic Islands. Vulvar images have a geographic span from The Czech Republic, Germany, France, and eastern Europe; many of them were covered with ochre, implying a ritual usage. Figures of abstracted buttocks are similarly represented geographi-

A Mother Goddess sculpture from the third century B.C.E., found in Mathura, Uttar Pradesh, India (Angelo Hornak/Corbis)

frog, among others. The bird-goddess is often represented with a beaky nose and breasts; the mouth is rarely depicted. Bird and snake figures occur throughout Europe and the Middle East, from Iberia and Ireland in the west to the Balkans and the Baltic cultures of the east, and they continue through the historic era in both iconography and myth. Beaked female figures painted with stripes, dating from the fifth millennium in Israel to the late second millennium in the Greek Cycladic islands, may also be representations of the bird-goddess; the stripes may portray feathers.

From Çatal Hüyük and Hacilar in Anatolia come many female figurines. As early as the seventh millennium B.C.E. these appear in multiples, often in shrines. Many are depicted in association with felines and birds such as vultures; some are represented in the process of giving birth. Female figures also appear in the earliest Neolithic in Israel. Many of these are seated, representing, perhaps, the moment of giving birth or a goddess enthroned. Goddess figures from Neolithic Israel rarely have mouths (Noy, 1985).

The Indus Valley civilization flourished between 2500 and 1500 B.C.E. and produced figurines as anatomically refined as those which the classical Greeks produced over a millennium later.

Neolithic European goddesses were the product of sedentary agricultural populations. Until the later Neolithic, the peoples of southeastern and central Europe were characterized by lack of defensive fortifications, few cutting and thrusting weapons, and often matrilineal descent patterns (Battaglia, 1993). Many small and some large female statues have been found throughout this area.

The goddesses of the prehistoric European culture differ considerably from the goddesses worshiped by the tribes called the "Proto-Indo-Europeans," who venerated a warrior sky-god as king, and who had few female figures. According to etymological and comparative mythological evidence, the Proto-Indo-Europeans worshiped a sun-maiden, a dawn-goddess; an earth-goddess; and a river-goddess (Dexter, 1978). When the Proto-Indo-Europeans assimilated with the Neolithic Europeans, they assimilated the multifunctional Neolithic European goddesses into their own sky-god–oriented pantheon. Multifunctional classical-age goddesses such as the Germanic Freyja, Indic Devī, Lithuanian-Latvian Laima, Iranian Anahita, and Greek Athena were assimilated from the indigenous peoples.

cally. These figures are found inscribed or painted on cave walls, as plaques, and as burial objects. Phallic images show complementary distribution.

Many Mesolithic figures—for example, those depicted with necklaces or pendants with double breast images—show continuity with the Upper Paleolithic. Cave art depicts some female and male figures as well as abstract vulvar signs.

Figurines are found in the earliest Neolithic, in the Middle East, as early as the ninth millennium. They become prolific from 6,000 on in both the Middle East and in southeast and central Europe. As in the Upper Paleolithic, figures probably represent a full spectrum of women's life-phases, from early puberty through old age.

Iconography of the goddess takes many animal shapes: bird, snake, and bird-snake hybrids; hedgehog, and

BIBLIOGRAPHY

On Upper Paleolithic female figures, see André Leroi-Gourhan, *The Dawn of European Art*, translated by Sara Champion (1982); and Alexander Marshack, *The*

Roots of Civilization (1972; rev. and exp., 1991), chap. 13. T. G. E. Powell, *Prehistoric Art* (1966), discusses goddess figures from central Europe. See also Peg Streep, *Sanctuaries of the Goddess: The Sacred Landscapes and Objects* (1994), on cave paintings and clay and stone female figures.

On the contexts for goddess-figures (shrines, graves, and household contexts) in the Neolithic of southeastern and central Europe, see excavation reports such as Marija Gimbutas, ed., *Neolithic Macedonia as Reflected by Excavation at Anza, Southeast Yugoslavia* (*Monumenta Archaeologica*, vol. 1, 1976), particularly chap. 8 on figurines. See also Colin Renfrew, Marija Gimbutas, and Ernestine S. Elster, eds., *Excavations at Sitagroi: A Prehistoric Village in Northeast Greece*, vol. 1 (*Monumenta Archaeologica*, vol. 13, 1986). Miloje Vasić, the excavator, illustrates several female figures in *Preistoriska Vinča* II-III (1936, in Russian). Marija Gimbutas, *The Goddess Civilization: The World of Old Europe* (1991), also gives contexts for female figures.

On the meanings of female figures, see Emmanuel Anati, "The Question of Fertility Cults," in *Archaeology and Fertility Cult in the Ancient Mediterranean*, edited by Anthony Bonanno (1985). Anati does not believe that female figures with exaggerated pubic triangles give enough evidence to posit prehistoric fertility cults. Tamar Noy, "Seated Clay Figurines from the Neolithic Period, Israel," in the same volume, believes that these figures do have connection with fertility cults. See also the arguments in Erich Neumann, *The Great Mother* (1955); Johann Jacob Bachofen, *Myth, Religion, and Mother Right*, [*Das Mutterrecht*, 1861] translated by Ralph Manheim (1926, 1967); see also Robert Briffault, *The Mothers* (1969).

Following Marija Gimbutas' death, several critical articles appeared, discussing her work. See Lynn Meskell, "Goddesses, Gimbutas, and 'New Age' Archaeology," *Antiquity* 69, no. 262 (1995), and Margaret W. Conkey and Ruth E. Tringham, "Archaeology and the Goddess: Exploring the Contours of Feminist Archaeology," in *Feminisms in the Academy: Rethinking the Disciplines*, edited by Abigail Stewart and Donna Stanton (1994).

With regard to the "fertility" function of the female figures, Patricia C. Rice writes on the possibility that the prehistoric female figures represent not only fertility but multiple phases of a woman's life, in "Prehistoric Venuses: Symbols of Motherhood or Womanhood?," *Journal of Anthropological Research* 37, no. 4 (1981): 402–414.

On the animal symbolism of European Neolithic goddesses, see Marija Gimbutas, *The Gods and Goddesses of Old Europe* (1974); *The Language of the Goddess*

(1989); "Old Europe in the Fifth Millennium B.C.," in *The Indo-Europeans in the Fourth and Third Millennia*, edited by Edgar C. Polomé (1982). See Marija Gimbutas, Daniel Shimabuka, and Sean Winn, *Achilleion: A Neolithic Site in Thessaly, Northern Greece, 6400–5600 B.C.* (*Monumenta Archaeologica*, vol. 14, 1989), particularly the plates for chap. 7. For other Greek female figures, see Chrestou Tsounta, in *Proistorikai Akropoleis Dimēniou kai Sesklou* (1908); he includes plates of striped figures, which may represent both birds and snakes, and other female figures found in the Thessalian Greek sites of Dimini and Sesklo. See also Miriam Robbins Dexter, "The Frightful Goddess: Birds, Snakes and Witches," in *Varia on the Indo-European Past: Papers in Memory of Marija Gimbutas*, edited by Miriam Robbins Dexter and Edgar Polomé (1997). On Neolithic snakes and modern folk belief in Spain, see Margarita Bru Romo and Ana Vazquez-Hoys, "The Representation of the Serpent in Ancient Iberia," in *Archaeology and Fertility Cult in the Ancient Mediterranean*, edited by Anthony Bonanno (1985). On the two-faced goddesses from the Gumelnitza site of southern Romania and Bulgaria, see Vladimir Dumitrescu, "New Discoveries at Gumelnitza," *Archaeology* 19, no. 3 (1966): 162–172. These female figures may precede the Janus-figure, which becomes identified as male in the classical era.

Åke Hultkrantz, "The Application of the Method of Religion in Prehistory: The Case of the Goddess," *Saeculum* 42, no. 1 (1991): 71–81, applies ecological evidence to an interpretation of Upper Palaeolithic "Venus" figures, concluding, from a comparison with Eskimo and North Siberian tribes, that the Upper Paleolithic deity was indeed an earth mother, a mistress of animals, and protector of the house and tribe.

For a perspective of female figurines throughout the Middle East, and throughout the Neolithic, see John Nandris, "Early Neothermal Sites in the Near East and Anatolia: A review of material, including figurines, as a background to the Neolithic of temperate south east Europe," *Memoria Antiquitatis* (1969). James Mellaart excavated the Anatolian sites of Çatal Hüyük and Hacilar. See James Mellaart, Udo Hirsch, and Belkis Balpinar, *The Goddess from Anatolia* (1989); James Mellaart, *Ancient Civilizations of the Near East* (1965), and *Çatal Hüyük: A Neolithic Town in Anatolia* (1967).

In chap. 4 of *Digging up Jericho* (1957), Kathleen Kenyon discusses female figures found at this site. Another western Mediterranean site was Gilat, in the Negev desert, discussed by Nili Sacher Fox, in "The Striped Goddess from Gilat: Implications for the Chalcolithic Cult," *Israel Exploration Journal* 45, no. 4 (1995).

On the pre-Greek Minoan culture, see Nannó Marinatos, *Minoan Religion: Ritual, Image and Symbol* (1993).

For Indus Valley goddesses, see John Marshall, "Mohanjo-Daro," in *The World of the Past*, edited by Jacquetta Hawkes (1963); and Mortimer Wheeler, "The Beginning and End of the Indus Civilization," in the Hawkes volume. R. A. Jairazbhoy, *The First Goddess of the Indo-Pakistan Subcontinent* (1990), discusses the meaning of the Indus Valley ring-stones, concluding that they are icons of a prehistoric fertility goddess, similar to the yoni and lingam of the goddess and god depicted in historic Hindu iconography.

On northern European Neolithic female figures, see P. V. Glob, in *The Mound People* (1974). Gro Mandt, in "Female Symbolism in Rock Art," *AmS-Varia* 17: 35–52, discusses Scandinavian female symbols connected with motifs of fertility, sexuality, and rebirth.

The northwestern European Bronze Age is characterized by megalithic monuments that probably provided the architecture of goddess-worship. See Audrey Burl, *Prehistoric Avebury* (1979); Christopher Chippindale, *Stonehenge Complete* (1983); George Eogan, *Knowth and the Passage-Tombs of Ireland* (1986); and Michael J. O'Kelly, *Newgrange: Archaeology, Art, and Legend* (1982). Megalithic monuments in southwestern Europe are discussed in Sir T. Zammit, *The Western Group of Megalithic Remains in Malta* (1931). See also Cristina Biaggi, *Habitations of the Great Goddess* (1994). On the English mound of Silbury Hill, see Michael Dames, *The Silbury Treasure* (1976). Neolithic goddesses have similar iconography throughout western Europe. O. G. S. Crawford, *The Eye Goddess*, describes "eye goddess" figures from the Orkney Islands in the north to the Iberian Peninsula, Malta, and Africa in the south.

Michael Everson, "Tenacity in Religion, Myth and Folklore: The Neolithic Goddess of Old Europe Preserved in a Non-Indo-European Setting," *Journal of Indo-European Studies* 17, nos. 3 and 4 (1989): 277–295, discusses why he believes that the Basque goddess Mari gives clues to the functionality of the prehistoric European "great"-goddess.

Many female figurines were found in southeastern, central, and eastern Europe. See Ruth Tringham, *Hunters, Fishers and Farmers of Eastern Europe, 6000–3000 B.C.* (1971); and Marija Gimbutas, *The Prehistory of Eastern Europe. Pt. I: Mesolithic, Neolithic, and Copper Age Cultures in Russia and the Baltic Area* (1965). On the identity of Proto-Indo-European goddesses, who may have originated in eastern Europe, see Miriam Robbins Dexter, *Whence the Goddesses: A Source Book* (1990), chap. 3; "Proto-Indo-European Sun-Maidens and Gods of the Moon," *Mankind Quarterly* XXV, nos. 1 and 2 (1984): 137–144; "Reflections on the Goddess *Donu," *Mankind Quarterly* 31, nos. 1 and 2 (1990): 45–58; "Dawn-Maid and Sun-Maid: Celestial Goddesses Among the Proto-Indo-Europeans," in *The Indo-Europeanization of Northern Europe*, edited by Karlene Jones-Bley and Martin E. Huld (1996); "Dawn and Sun in Indo-European Myth: Gender and Geography," in *Collectanea Philologia IV Ignatio Richardo Danka sexagenario oblata*, edited by Krzysztof Witczak and Piotr Stalmaszczyk (1997); and "Indo-European Female Figures" (Ph.D. diss., University of California, Los Angeles, 1978).

The above article focuses upon European and Middle Eastern prehistoric goddesses. For sources on the New World, see Betty J. Meggers, Clifford Evans, and Emilio Estrada, *Early Formative Period of Coastal Ecuador: the Valdivia and Machalilla Phases* (1965), and Gordon R. Willey, *An Introduction to American Archaeology* (1966).

See also Athena (Minerva); Freyja; Inanna; Indo-European Religions; Ishtar and Anat; Warriors.

MIRIAM ROBBINS DEXTER

Historical Goddesses

Feminist theology burst on the scene in the 1970s with important works by Mary Daly and Rosemary Radford Ruether among many others. Its mode was a vigorous critique of Jewish and Christian practices and, more generally, of patriarchal religious traditions. Equally vigorous was the beginning of a search for a historical goddess who could provide the basis for a constructive alternative—a feminist thealogy, or spiritual feminism, using archaeological and textual evidence from Asia, Old Europe, Mesopotamia, and the Middle East.

The arguments for the historical goddess were made initially by a combination of theology and history in a critique of what was already written about such goddesses. In her opening volley, *When God Was a Woman* (1976), Merlin Stone showed that scholars who treated the religion of the goddess, if they treated it at all, judged it to be an inferior form of religion—of magic and mystery cult. And yet the persistence of goddess-like finds prompted Stone to posit a forgotten religion that in fact linked many parts of the Neolithic Era (7000–3500 B.C.E.) in the worship of the divine feminine. Scholars also assumed that in many cases the worship of an ancient goddess was accompanied by a matriarchal civilization, existing before the onslaught of patriarchal values and norms.

The evidence for this original matriarchy was built on a number of emerging discoveries. First, Marija Gimbutas argued that figurines found in many areas in and around central and eastern Europe were clearly fertility goddesses used in rites that emphasized maternal values. Found near small household altars, these figurines were frequently large-breasted women and were occasionally depicted in positions of giving birth. Their prevalence, combined with the relative absence of weapons of any kind at the same sites during the Neolithic period, led Gimbutas to argue for a pre–Indo-European culture based on the matriarchal values of giving birth, nurturance, and peace-loving agricultural existence. She also pointed to the work of James Mellaart (*Catal Huyuk*, 1967) in Anatolia for similar figurines suggesting woman-centered practices.

Though Gimbutas's book was not the first of its kind (see Robert Graves, *The White Goddess*, 1972; Raphael Patai, *The Hebrew Goddess*, 1978), it spawned a very important intellectual trend among feminist historians: the gathering of evidence for such woman-centered societies besides that of Neolithic Europe. Minoan Crete, discussed by Gimbutas and studied in depth by Jacquette Hawkes (*Dawn of the Gods*, 1968), pre-Celtic and Celtic Ireland (Mary Condren, *The Serpent and the Goddess*, 1989), and the Indus Valley civilization of the Hindu Kush, among many others, offered up both female figurines and seals featuring trees, animals, and other forces of nature. The Mesopotamian world also offered plentiful evidence of both goddesses and snakelike figures, which suggested a similar alliance between the world of women and that of nature. Together with a relative absence of remains of warfare or violent sacrifice, these artifacts evidently convinced feminist historians of a global pattern involving a prepatriarchal emphasis on the feminine.

Other societies, while not necessarily possessing archaeological remains, did possess "narrative" remains—mythological remnants—that seemed to suggest the same kind of social and religious structure as the archaeological data. Many Native American cultures, particularly the Hopi, the Navaho, and the Lakota, told of a mythological grandmother or mother figures who featured prominently in the creation, sustenance, and healing of the world. In Hindu India, the goddess tradition was full-blown, with its own textual and iconographic tradition in place by the fifth century C.E. In Buddhist India, China, and Tibet, female figures such as Tārā and Kuan Yin served as powerful bodhisattvas of compassion, and even in earlier India the perfection of wisdom, *prajñāpāramitā*, was personified as a goddess. Africa, particularly West African mythological tradition, also became a focus for black spiritual feminists, such as Luisah Teish, looking for black goddess figures. Feminist historians initially hypothesized that many of

these female deities personified compassion and gentleness; if angry, they embodied a righteous anger that served to subdue evil and bring about good.

This historical hypothesis about the existence of goddess traditions took a number of different forms: matriarchy, where rulership by women was the main form of political organization; matriliny, where lines of descent and property rights were passed through the mother; matrifocal societies, where the qualities of motherhood were revered; and "gylany," where political and religious leadership focused on the power and values of women in mutual cooperation with men. In each case, the presence of a divine feminine was seen to inspire these more liberating, gender-equal social structures on earth.

Feminist theology of existing religious traditions was deeply affected by these ideas. The Hebrew patriarchal tradition appeared to be preceded by the fluorescence of Mesopotamian fertility, the Hindu tradition by nature goddesses who guarded steppe-wells, rivers, and forests; the warlike and honor-bound world of Homer held traces of a preexistent gylanic heritage. Each of these patriarchal traditions could have been a kind of fall from an original state of a more gender-sensitive humanity. These early forms of society possessed a wiser understanding of nonviolence and mutuality between the sexes. Moreover, there might be traces of these values in the remnants of the feminine in patriarchal traditions—hints of a goddess figure in Marian worship in Roman Catholic traditions, Lilith in the Hebrew tradition, and so on.

Thus a historical goddess, in a number of religious traditions, provided an actual alternative social organization to which theologians based in Judaism and Christianity could point. The historical goddess proved that patriarchy was not a necessary form of religious organization, and—as some theologians argued even more boldly—a return to such a historical state might even be possible. For many theologians, this meant that Eden might have existed in history; for others, goddess traditions provided social and ethical critique of patriarchy; for still others, it offered the proof that was needed all along as a basis for the already existent goddess-worshiping traditions, such as Wicca. (For a review of these movements, see Eller, 1993.)

Critique of the historical goddess has come in three particular strands: archaeological, mythological, and theological. Archaeologists and literary historians such as Lynn Meskell and Helene Foley have questioned the assumptions of the feminist interpreters of Old European, Greek, and Anatolian data. First, it is not clear that the figurines are in fact goddesses, or represent fertility, but may have been other forms of votive offer-

The temple of the goddess Durgā at Aihole, India, is a freestanding stone building from the seventh century (University of Michigan Library).

ings. Moreover, they are not always found near altar or temple sites, but possibly at domestic sites. Moreover, the similarity among all of the figurines has been challenged, as has their status as representing a single tradition spreading from Anatolia to Denmark.

This questioning of a single, Old European goddess has led to scholarly queries from other traditions such as India and Israel. The local goddesses of many areas of India or the Middle East do not necessarily represent a unified cultural area with a single, unified goddess tradition. To speak of "the goddess tradition" is a historical inaccuracy for almost any religious tradition and amounts to a scholarly fiction. One should, rather, speak of "historical goddesses," which emphasizes the plurality of religious traditions (see Larry Hurtado, *Goddesses in Religions and Modern Debate*, 1990).

Moreover, scholars have questioned the assumption that there is an automatic link between the ways of life suggested by archaeological and historical data and the lives of ordinary women. In societies that reify the female in a goddess figure, there is no evidence that such figures provide positive role models for women; they can, rather, fulfill the opposite role of providing imaginative ground for patriarchal projections of what constitutes the "ideal female." In addition, many of the narrative traditions mentioned above also contain stories depicting the goddess as bloodthirsty and violent, hungry for animal sacrifice and frenzied festivals in her honor. Thus, with closer textual and ethnographic analysis, goddesses emerge in as varied and diverse forms of peacefulness, violence, and abuse of power as do their male, patriarchal counterparts.

The debates in historical, archaeological, and mythological judgment remain lively and engaged. Goddess-

worshiping traditions, such as Wicca and others, tend to stand by the scholarly claims of their thealogical writers and canon-formers. Those within the mainstream academy tend to demur, citing an increasing complexity to the evidence and a clear plurality of traditions, making a single historical goddess, even within a single religious tradition, impossible. The value of the writing on the goddess produced in the last three decades of the twentieth century lies perhaps not in proving the historical existence of a single, mother-centered era of history, presided over by a loving female figure. Rather, thealogical and historical writing about the historical goddess has provided something infinitely more valuable: it has sparked a larger debate that can focus at last on the careful examination of data about women—both in the sky and on the ground.

BIBLIOGRAPHY

Andrews, Lynn. *Medicine Woman.* 1981.

Benko, Stephen. *The Virgin Goddess: Studies in the Pagan and Christian Roots of Mariology.* 1993.

Beyer, Stephan V. *The Cult of Tara: Magic and Ritual in Tibet.* 1978.

Blofield, Richard. *In Search of the Goddess of Compassion: The Mystical Cult of Kuan Yin.* 1990.

Christ, Carol. *The Laughter of Aphrodite: Reflections on a Journey to the Goddess.* 1986.

Condren, Mary. *The Serpent and the Goddess.* 1989.

Daly, Mary. *Beyond God the Father.* 1973.

———. *The Church and the Second Sex.* 1975.

Eisler, Riane. *The Chalice and the Blade: Our History, Our Future.* 1987.

Eller, Cynthia. *Living in the Lap of the Goddess: The Feminist Spirituality Movement in America.* 1993.

Emerson, May. *Edge of the Wave: Great Goddess: Fact, Working Hypothesis, or Feminist Myth?* 1993.

Foley, Helene. "A Question of Origins: Goddess Cults Greek and Modern." In *Women's Studies* 23, no. 3 (1994): 193–215.

Frymer-Kensky, Tikva Simone. *In the Wake of the Goddess: Women, Culture, and the Biblical Transformation of Pagan Myth.* 1992.

Gallagher, Eugene V. "A Religion Without Converts? Becoming a Neo-Pagan." *Journal of the American Academy of Religion* 62 (1994): 851–867.

Gimbutas, Marija. *The Goddesses and Gods of Old Europe: 6500–3500 B.C.: Myths and Cult Images.* 1982.

Gleason, Judith Illsey. *Oya: In Praise of the Goddess.* 1987.

Grigg, Richard. *When God Becomes Goddess: The Transformation of American Religion.* 1995.

Hawley, John S., and Donna Wulff, eds. *Devi: Goddesses of India.* 1996.

Lerner, Gerda. *The Creation of Patriarchy.* 1986.

Luhrmann, T. M. *Persuasions of the Witch's Craft: Ritual Magic in Contemporary England.* 1989.

Meskell, Lynn. "Goddesses, Gimbutas, and 'New Age' Archaeology." *Antiquity* 69, no. 262 (1995): 74–86.

Olson, Carl, ed. *The Book of the Goddess, Past and Present.* 1983.

Orenstein, Gloria Feman. *The Reflowering of the Goddess.* 1990.

Patai, Raphael. *The Hebrew Goddess.* 1978.

Plaskow, Judith, and Carol Christ, eds. *Reweaving the Visions: New Patterns in Feminist Spirituality.* 1989.

Ruether, Rosemary. *Gaia and God: An Ecofeminist Theology of Earth Healing.* 1992.

———. *Religion and Sexism.* 1974.

———. *Sexism and God Talk.* 1983.

Sjoo, Monica. *The Great Cosmic Mother: Rediscovering the Religion of the Earth.* 1991.

Starhawk. *The Spiral Dance: A Rebirth of the Ancient Religion of the Great Goddess.* 1979.

Stone, Merlin. *When God Was a Woman.* 1978.

Teish, Luisah. *Jambalaya.* 1985.

See also **Gimbutas, Marija; Kuan Yin (Kannon); Wicca.**

LAURIE LOUISE PATTON

Contemporary Goddess Movement

The Goddess movement is an international phenomenon emerging in the wake of feminism in North America, Europe, Australia, and New Zealand. In all the places where biblical monotheism succeeded in prohibiting the worship of the feminine divine, hundreds of thousands of women and increasing numbers of men are turning to the Goddess. In her they have found an image of female power and of the human connection to the natural world denied in patriarchal religion. It is increasingly being recognized that they are creating a new religion.

"I found god in myself and I loved her fiercely"—words first spoken in Ntozake Shange's play *for colored girls who have considered suicide/when the rainbow is enuf* (1975)—is the cry of every woman touched by this movement. Whereas Christianity portrayed the naked Eve as the source of sin, evil, and death, Goddess religion honors the female body, its powers and its cycles. Rituals celebrating the onset of menstruation, female sexuality, pregnancy and birth, abortion, and menopause are important in contemporary Goddess religion.

"At the very dawn of religion . . . God was a woman. Do you remember?" So wrote Merlin Stone in *When God Was a Woman* (1976), calling others to claim their connection to a past far more ancient than Judaism and Christianity. Goddess religion draws inspiration from images of the Goddess from Paleolithic, Neolithic, and later patriarchal religions. The reproduction of photographs of ancient images, such as the goddess of Willendorf (c. 25,000 B.C.E.), the goddess of Laussel (c. 25,000 B.C.E.), the Cretan snake goddesses (c. 1600 B.C.E.), and others, helped to bring the Goddess into contemporary consciousness.

Women began writing of the appearance of the Goddess in their lives in the *WomanSpirit* magazine, published from 1974 to 1984. About that time Goddess imagery became a major theme in women's art. Simultaneously, women in churches and synagogues began to feel the need for a feminine divine. Soon *The Feminist Book of Light and Shadows* (1974) by Zsuzsanna E. Budapest and *The Spiral Dance* (1979) by Starhawk provided guidelines for celebrating rituals to the Goddess. These books were used as "cookbooks" in ritual groups that sprung up around the world. More slowly, but just as surely, the Goddess began to make her presence felt within traditional religions. Since the 1970s hundreds of books have been published on the Goddess. Reading has been a primary source of initiation into the movement.

The image of the Goddess as Earth or Mother Earth turns religious consciousness away from heaven, inviting participation in the cycles of the earth body. The Goddess is worshiped on the new and full moons and the seasonal holidays: spring equinox, May 1, summer solstice, August 2 (Lammas), fall equinox, All Hallow's Eve, winter solstice, February 2 (Candlemas). These rituals affirm the human connection to the natural world and its powers of birth, death, and regeneration. The Goddess brings awareness of the deep connection and interdependence of all beings and all people in the web of life. This insight can lead to ecological and social action. The Goddess is an important image in ecofeminism, a movement stressing that the domination, and healing, of women and the earth are interconnected.

As Carol P. Christ argues in *Rebirth of the Goddess* (1997), the Goddess is not considered the female equivalent of the God of monotheistic traditions, and thus cannot be understood using the traditional dualisms that separate spirit and nature, mind and body, rational and irrational, male and female. Whereas God is commonly perceived as transcendent of the body and nature, Goddess is said to be within the world body. Rejecting the God "out there" of traditional theism, some have described the Goddess as immanent, using the language of pantheism (Goddess is all); Carol Christ finds process theology's language of panentheism (Goddess is in all) more appropriate.

The work of archaeologist Marija Gimbutas on the Neolithic religion and culture of prehistoric Europe (c. 6500–3500 B.C.E.) offers scholarly corroboration of many of the movement's claims. According to Gimbutas, the civilization of prehistoric Europe was matrifocal, sedentary, peaceful, artistic, and oriented to earth and sea. Over several thousand years this culture was overthrown by patriarchal Indo-European warrior groups who rode horses, worshiped sky gods, and were indifferent to art. The classical Greeks were the heirs of these invaders. Basing their civilization on that of the Greeks, Westerners have mistakenly come to think of hierarchy, domination, warfare, and male superiority as inevitable. Gimbutas argues that the West's true heritage is a civilization that lived without great differences in rank or wealth among its members, that lived in harmony with nature, and at peace for thousands of years. Gimbutas's view is controversial.

Images of the Goddess from African and African-American, Latin American, native North American, Aboriginal, Chinese, Japanese, Hindu, and other traditions are also emerging in the movement. Some worry that non-European images may be appropriated (especially by white women) without a proper understanding of their historical contexts.

One strand within the contemporary Goddess movement is called witchcraft or Wicca (from Old English). Feminist witchcraft claims solidarity with those who were burned as witches in early modern Europe, asserting that all or many of them were following the "Old Religion" of the Goddess. Feminist witchcraft has roots that can be traced to neopagan witchcraft, a movement created by Englishman Gerald Gardner (who claimed he learned it through secret traditions preserved since the burning times). But it differs from Gardner's version of "the craft" in being feminist and woman-centered and in emphasizing or elevating female power and the Goddess. Both Zsuzsanna E. Budapest and Starhawk refer to their traditions as witchcraft. Magic, which Starhawk describes as the art of changing consciousness at will, is an important part of feminist witchcraft; some covens (worship groups) have specific rituals of initiation, and some are led by a (high) priestess. Although many in the contemporary Goddess movement identify with feminist witchcraft, others find its emphasis on spellcasting and magic unnecessary or unappealing. They prefer versions of Goddess worship that are rooted in nature, intuition, and the wider history of the Goddess.

The contemporary Goddess movement owes a debt to the nineteenth-century scholar J. J. Bachofen, who proposed the theory of primitive matriarchy. Inspired by a great love for his mother, Bachofen argued that civilization was originally ruled by mothers or matriarchies. He also argued that patriarchy (rule by fathers)

was necessary for "man" and "civilization" to "evolve." The Goddess movement draws on the work of scholars inspired by Bachofen, including Jane Ellen Harrison and Robert Graves, but generally it does not uncritically accept the matriarchal hypothesis.

The psychologist Carl Jung defined the Goddess as an archetype of the unconscious and claimed that the reintegration of the "feminine" was necessary for cultural transformation. Jungians such as M. Esther Harding (*Women's Mysteries*, 1935), Erich Neumann (*The Great Mother*, 1955), and others have influenced the Goddess movement. Some find Jungianism attractive, whereas others argue that Jungian theory subordinates the feminine and defines the Goddess using familiar stereotypes.

The contemporary Goddess movement is one of a handful of religions discussed by anthropologist Susan Starr Sered (*Priestess, Mother, Sacred Sister*, 1994) as created and led by women, an attribute making it relatively unusual among contemporary religions. Though some women have emerged as leaders, the Goddess movement is antihierarchal and encourages the leadership potential of every woman. Many covens and ritual circles are exclusively for women because habits of dominance and submission make it difficult for women and men to participate equally in any group. But other circles include men and boys, or open their rituals to them for the major holidays.

In Christian and Jewish circles, God the Mother, God She, Sophia (feminine Wisdom), and Shekinah (the feminine presence of God) are being invoked in language and rituals that show the clear influence of the contemporary Goddess movement. A Unitarian Universalist curriculum called "Cakes for the Queen of Heaven" has introduced many to the Goddess. The Unitarians have accepted the Goddess-oriented "Covenant of Unitarian Universalist Pagans" (CUUPS) as a legitimate interest group within their fellowship. Do these developments herald a new religious syncretism that will result in transformed monotheisms? Or will those attracted to the Goddess eventually leave (or be forced to leave) traditional religions? The suppression of the image of the female divine is foundational to Biblical monotheisms. It remains to be seen whether monotheistic traditions can reincorporate the Goddess excluded "in the beginning."

BIBLIOGRAPHY

Budapest, Zsuzsanna E. *The Holy Book of Women's Mysteries.* 1989. Based on the first manifesto of contemporary Goddess worship, *The Feminist Book of Lights and Shadows*, 1975.

Christ, Carol P. *Rebirth of the Goddess: Finding Meaning in Feminist Spirituality.* 1997. A Goddess thealogy explaining the challenge the Goddess presents to Western philosophy and religion.

Diamond, Irene, and Gloria Feman Orenstein, eds. *Reweaving the World: The Emergence of Ecofeminism.* 1990. The first collection of ecofeminist essays.

Downing, Christine. *The Goddess.* 1981. An archetypal and autobiographical approach to the Greek goddesses.

Eisler, Riane. *The Chalice and the Blade: Our History, Our Future.* 1987. Combines Goddess history, futurism, and a theory of cultural transformation.

Eller, Cynthia. *Living in the Lap of the Goddess: The Feminist Spirituality Movement in America.* 1994. A sympathetic outsider's view of the movement and its history.

Gadon, Elinor. *The Once and Future Goddess.* 1989. A beautifully illustrated synthesis of Goddess history and feminist art.

Gimbutas, Marija. *The Civilization of the Goddess.* Edited by Joan Marler. 1991.

———. *The Language of the Goddess.* 1989. Both works represent the culmination of a distinguished archaeologist's career.

"The Goddess Remembered." Directed by Donna Read. A film from the Canadian National Film Board about the Goddess movement featuring many of its leaders. 1989.

Goldenberg, Naomi R. *The Changing of the Gods: Feminism and the End of Traditional Religions.* 1979. An early recognition of the iconoclastic potential of Goddess religion.

Griffin, Susan. *Woman and Nature: The Roaring Inside Her.* 1978. A moving testimony to the domination, survival, and reemergence of woman and nature.

Starhawk [Miriam Simos]. *The Spiral Dance: The Rebirth of the Ancient Religion of the Great Goddess.* 1979. 2d ed., 1989. A pathbreaking explanation of Goddess religion and its rituals.

Stone, Merlin. *When God Was a Woman.* 1976. The book that brought the history of the Goddess to a wide feminist audience.

Teish, Luisah. *Jambalaya.* 1985. An interpretation of Goddess religion rooted in African and African-American traditions.

WomanSpirit. 1974–1984. Magazine that chronicled the emerging feminist spirituality and Goddess movements.

CAROL P. CHRIST

History of Study

Within the Western religious traditions, the tendency has been to worship a single (or tripartite) god who is either technically genderless but implicitly male or unapologetically male. Therefore, goddesses have been studied only as relics of ancient history or Asian or tribal religions—that is, as they appear in the religions of "others." Until late in the twentieth century "the goddess" was not seen as playing a role in mainstream Western religions themselves; even with the advent of goddess studies, goddess-worship within Judaism, Christianity, and Islam has typically been regarded as metaphorical at best, and heretical at worst.

Nevertheless, since the mid-nineteenth century, the goddess has exerted a strong fascination for scholars, psychologists, and poets in the West. Though the fascination is now predominantly feminist, much of the interest in the goddess originated with men. Some of these late-nineteenth-century male "goddess-watchers" were well disposed toward feminist claims and women's political equality, but just as many were adamantly antifeminist and sometimes misogynist as well.

Scholars in the West had long shown an interest in the goddesses of classical myth and religion, and depictions of these goddesses in Western art were not uncommon. But this benign, aesthetic use of goddesses from the past took a new turn in 1861 with the publication of Johann Jakob Bachofen's *Das Mutterrecht* (Mother-right). Bachofen was the first to make a sustained argument suggesting that our earliest ancestors universally practiced goddess-worship to the exclusion of the worship of gods, and that, indeed, this goddess-worship involved the social dominance of women. Like many others who followed him, Bachofen suggested that ancient goddess-worship stemmed from an awed (male) reaction to women's ability to bear and nurse children, and to bleed—menstruate—without risk of death. By analogy, all life, all nature, was seen to be female, and vice versa. It was only common sense, then, that early humans should appeal to female deities who mirrored and amplified these powers of women.

Following Bachofen's trailblazing work, most theorists who discussed the goddess did so only incidentally; these theorists were more interested in Bachofen's theories on marriage, the status of women, and the development of various human technologies (e.g., agriculture). They regarded the worship of ancestresses or goddesses as only a minor by-product of a culture built on women's kinship relations and/or their social prominence. Indeed, Bachofen was criticized by a number of his contemporaries—men such as John Ferguson McLennan, Edward B. Tylor, and Friedrich Engels—for relying too heavily on religion as a primary agent of social change. An exception to this disinterest in the religious role of the goddess was Jane E. Harrison's pioneering work, *Prolegomena to the Study of*

Greek Religion (1903), which returned, as Bachofen did, to the classics, and found there evidence of a strong and central role for goddesses in the prehistoric Mediterranean.

But with the exception of Harrison, it was not until the goddess was adopted by a more poetic community that she again became what she had been for Bachofen: the symbol of an ancient (golden) age, of nature, of the marvel of reproductive capacity—in short, of a harmony with the universe unattainable through male deities, or through male deities alone. Robert Graves, in his reverential *The White Goddess* (1948), both recovered and created the goddess as a true deity, a deity of nature, and one who encompassed both good and evil. Perhaps more influential were authors in the Jungian tradition, who exalted attention to the goddess as a recapturing of the feminine (which was in danger of being lost through excessive emphasis on the masculine in Western patriarchal culture). Of these, Erich Neumann's *The Great Mother* (1955, 1963) provides the best synthesis and reveals in an especially clear manner the tremendous ambivalence toward the feminine that dogged all early Jungian writing on the goddess: she was awesome, she was universal, she was the all; and yet it was only by escaping her—via masculine consciousness—that human society (not to mention contemporary human individuals) could progress psychologically.

Apart from some scholarly religious interest in tracking goddess worship historically and phenomenologically (for example, E. O. James's *The Cult of the Mother-Goddess* [1959]), the goddess did not again take center stage until she was placed there by feminists of the second wave, and particularly by feminists sharing an interest in constructing female- or feminist-oriented spiritualities. This feminist literature on the goddess dwarfs what came before, both in quantity and in variety: there are now multiple reference works on goddesses, thealogies of the goddess, guides to her worship, and histories of her travels from the earliest hominid social groupings to her reemergence in the late twentieth century as a symbol for feminist regeneration.

BIBLIOGRAPHY

Bachofen, Johann Jakob. *Myth, Religion, and Mother Right: Selected Writings of J. J. Bachofen.* 1861. Translated by Ralph Manheim. 1967.

Engels, Friedrich. *The Origin of the Family, Private Property and the State.* 1884. Reprint, 1972.

Graves, Robert. *The White Goddess: A Historical Grammar of Poetic Myth.* 1948. Amended and enl. ed., 1966.

Harding, M. Esther. *Woman's Mysteries: A Psychological Interpretation of the Feminine Principle as Portrayed in Myth, Story, and Dreams.* 1955. Reprint, 1991.

Neumann, Erich. *The Origins and History of Consciousness.* (1949). Reprint, 1970.

Patai, Raphael. *The Hebrew Goddess.* 1978.

Contemporary feminist studies of the goddess, beginning in the 1970s, are numerous. Key works include: Merlin Stone, *When God Was a Woman* (1976); Starhawk, *The Spiral Dance* (1979); and Marija Gimbutas, *Goddesses and Gods of Old Europe* (1982 [1974]). Two excellent bibliographies by Anne Carson are available: *Feminist Spirituality and the Feminine Divine* (1986), and *Goddesses and Wise Women: The Literature of Feminist Spirituality, 1980–1992* (1992).

See also Graves, Robert Ranke; Harrison, Jane Ellen; Matriarchy.

CYNTHIA ELLER

Goretti, Maria

A well-known child saint in the twentieth-century Roman Catholic Church, and a model of chastity and devotion to the church's moral codes, Maria Goretti (1890–1902) was born in the town of Corinaldo in the province of Ancona, Italy. Her father was a tenant farmer who died in 1900, leaving his wife with several small children. Maria's mother needed to work outside the home, and the young girl took care of the household. Physically mature for her age, Maria attracted the unwanted advances of a neighbor, Alessandro Serenelli. After repeated attempts to seduce the young woman and threats against her safety if she revealed his advances, on 5 July 1902 he attempted to rape her when she was alone in her home. When she resisted, he stabbed her repeatedly. On her deathbed the next day, she forgave her murderer. Serenelli was reportedly an uncooperative, unrepentant prisoner, whose demeanor was transformed after he had a visionary dream of Maria dressed in white in which she gathered and gave him lilies. After this experience, he repented of his sins and upon his release worked to advance the case for her sainthood. Both Maria Goretti's mother and her murderer were among the 250,000 people who attended her canonization on 24 June 1950. On this occasion, Pope Pius XII noted that Maria was the twentieth-century equivalent to Agatha, an early church model of sexual purity and personal modesty. She was used as an exemplar of the chaste life—especially to Catholic schoolchildren in the pre–Second Vatican Council Church—becoming as popular in that role as the Virgin Mary herself. Many schools and parishes were named after her. The feast day of Maria Goretti is 6 July.

BIBLIOGRAPHY

Buehrle, M. C. *Saint Maria Goretti.* 1950. Prepared in the wake of Goretti's canonization, this book is the standard devotional work on her in English.

Guerri, Giordano Bruno. *Povera santa, pover assassino: La vera storia di Maria Goretti.* (*Poor Assassin, Poor Saint: The True Story of Maria Goretti.*) Rome, 1985. This book provoked controversy. The author, a left-wing journalist, accused the Vatican of having manufactured the narrative of Maria Goretti's martyrdom and youthful chastity in cooperation with the Fascist government of Benito Mussolini. Pope Pius XII was said to be especially interested in creating a saint who would stand as a model of sexual morality in the face of the actions of the mainly American Protestant occupying forces in Italy during and after the war. The Vatican criticized the author and his book, citing its factual and interpretive errors.

LEONARD NORMAN PRIMIANO

Robert Ranke Graves (Hulton-Deutsch Collection/Corbis)

Graves, Robert Ranke

Robert Ranke Graves (1895–1985), prolific English poet, novelist, and critic, is best known for his book of World War I memoirs, *Good-bye to All That* (1929), and his fictionalized accounts of history, *I, Claudius* (1934), *Claudius the God* (1934), and *King Jesus* (1946). Scholars of women and religion are more interested in *The White Goddess* (1948), a study of the mythological origins of poetry; his works *The Greek Myths* (1955) and *Hebrew Myths* (1963, written with Raphael Patai); and his translation of *The Golden Ass* by Apuleius, which includes a stunning account of an apparition of the Goddess.

Graves's compilations of sources, variants, and ritual origins of familiar Greek, Hebrew, and North European myths were encyclopedic and should be consulted by anyone who wonders about the story behind the story as conventionally told. Graves's interest in the Goddess has drawn those in search of Goddess history to him. It should, however, be noted that Graves based his study of the Goddess in his conviction, stated in the foreword to *The White Goddess*, that the language of poetic myth is rooted in religious rituals dedicated to the moon goddess. For Graves, the Goddess was the muse of poetry, which he assumed to be created primarily by men. This should alert feminist scholars to ask to what extent Graves depicts the Goddess as the loving mother of a talented son—in other words, as a servant of male creativity.

In addition, Graves was particularly drawn to the myth that the Goddess must sacrifice her beloved son: his work is strewn with references to the sacrifice of the son or the king to the Mother, even though there is little evidence that such sacrifices occurred frequently or cross-culturally. This is puzzling until it is recognized that the poet fancies himself as sacrificed on the altar of his muse. Revelations of Graves's obsession with masochistic sexual behavior with women sheds more light on this issue. His work on the Goddess is thus a resource to be consulted with caution. Sources of his claims, especially those about the relation of the Goddess to her son, should be carefully checked. Unfortunately, Graves has been uncritically quoted in some of the literature of the contemporary Goddess movement.

BIBLIOGRAPHY

WORKS BY GRAVES

Graves, Robert. *The Greek Myths.* 2 vols. 1955.

———. *Hebrew Myths.* With Raphael Patai. 1963.

―――. *The Transformations of Lucius Otherwise Known as the Golden Ass.* Translated from the Greek of Apuleius. 1951.

―――. *The White Goddess.* 1948. Rev. and enl. ed., 1966.

WORKS ON GRAVES

Graves, Richard Percival. *Robert Graves: The Assault Heroic, 1895–1926.* 1986.

―――. *Robert Graves and the White Goddess.* 1995.

―――. *Robert Graves: The Years with Laura.* 1990.

Seymour, Miranda. *Robert Graves: A Life on the Edge.* 1995.

Seymour-Smith, Martin. *Robert Graves: His Life and Work.* 1982.

CAROL P. CHRIST

Greek Religion

It is difficult to determine to what extent the complex literary use of myth by the Greeks reflects their religious beliefs and the evolution of those beliefs. Although archaeological evidence points to religious beliefs in Greece at the beginning of the third millennium B.C.E., the earliest literary remains date to the eighth century B.C.E.; it is impossible to describe with any certainty Greek religious practices before that time.

Hesiod's *Theogony* (seventh century B.C.E.) contains the myth of the birth of the gods, beginning with the original principles of Gaia (female Earth) and Ouranos (masculine Sky) and ending with the overthrow of their children, the Titans, by the third generation of gods (the Olympians); Homer presents a portrait of the anthropomorphized Olympians, ruled over by Zeus, whose realm is the sky and the upper air. He shares his power with his brothers, Poseidon, ruler of the sea, and Hades, ruler of the underworld. His official consort is his sister Hera, who bore him Ares, the god of war; but his affairs with other goddesses have produced Apollo, Artemis, Hermes, and Athena. His sister Demeter, the corn goddess, bore him Persephone. Hera is said to have produced the crippled Hephaistos, the divine blacksmith, by parthenogenesis. Also included among the Olympians are Aphrodite, the goddess of sexuality, and Hestia, the guardian of the hearth.

Nevertheless, although Homer, Hesiod, and their literary successors (especially the tragic playwrights) create a complex portrait of public religious attitudes, they provide little concrete information about private practices and beliefs. Thus, we know relatively little about women's private religion, for there is a paucity of documentary sources for family religion, in which women played a large role. In addition, although ancient Greek religion publicly recognizes the power of the feminine, and although female deities assert themselves within the polis (city) (e.g., Athena as the patron goddess of Athens), Greek religion in the classical period presents the anomaly of a society in which women had few rights and yet, at the same time, in which there were powerful female deities. The world of the fifth-century B.C.E. polis was almost wholly male: priesthoods were civil offices, performance of civic religious obligations was dominated by men (although there were priestesses for various female deities), and festivals were regulated by the state. Although women could participate in many of the festivals (such as the Panathenaia, in honor of Athena as patron of the city), there was a sharp division between the world of men and the world of women, and there is evidence that certain female deities played gender-specific roles in the private lives of women.

Hera, for instance, the patron and guardian of marriage, watched over the lives of women. Although she may have originally been a deity of female fertility or an earth goddess, in the historical period her functions seem to have been confined to the social and sexual relationship of wife, and she is worshiped as the protector of women in childbirth and of young children.

Although in myth Artemis is the virginal goddess who demands chastity from her followers, the mistress of the hunt who prefers nature to civilization, she is often identified with Eileithyia, the goddess of childbirth. Like her brother Apollo, she carries the bow and arrow but aims primarily at women: Zeus made her as a lion among women and let her kill them whenever she chose. The pangs of childbirth are caused by her arrows; as Eileithyia she can protect women but can also cause childbed fever and death.

Like Hera, Artemis is associated with the young; protector of the unborn, she is called *kourotrophos,* the nurturer of children. Every five years at Brauron (in eastern Attica), an initiation festival was held for Athenian girls between the ages of five and ten, who performed a dance to commemorate the killing of a bear, which had led to a plague. Artemis had demanded the sacrifice of a young girl but was offered a goat instead. The goddess, angered, demanded that every girl was to dance the bear dance before marriage.

The worship of Demeter is grounded in the tale of her search for her daughter, Persephone, who had been kidnapped by Hades with the connivance of Zeus. Bereft, Demeter wandered the earth and neglected her domain. Without her help, nothing grew, so Zeus compelled Hades to return Persephone. Although reunited with her mother at Eleusis, Persephone was contaminated by death, for she had unwittingly eaten the pomegranate seeds offered to her by Hades. For each seed she had consumed, she was forced to spend one month in the underworld. Thus, the earth is by turns bounteous, when the maiden is with her mother, and barren, when they are separated.

Two cults had this myth at their center: the Thesmophoria and the Eleusinian mysteries. The festival of the Thesmophoria (the bringing of treasure) was celebrated in autumn at the planting of the new corn by married women throughout Greece and was said to have been initiated by Demeter as she searched for Persephone. In Athens the women spent three days in the hilltop sanctuary of Demeter, fasting, mourning the disappearance of Persephone, and then celebrating a feast in honor of birth. According to Athenian law, it was the obligation of every husband to send his wife and bear the costs. Because men were barred from the rites, however, almost all information about the actual rituals is the product of male fantasy (see *Women at the Thesmophoria* by the fifth-century B.C.E. comic playwright Aristophanes).

The biennial celebration of the cult of Demeter at Eleusis was open to both men and women. The ritual began with a procession from Athens to Eleusis, where Demeter was reunited with her daughter; in gratitude for their warm reception, she gave the Eleusinians the gift of agriculture and taught them her mysteries. Part of the ritual was open to everyone, but the substance of the rites were revealed only to those who had been initiated through the performance of a secret ceremony. Before that ceremony, all worshipers walked in torchlit parades, seeking Persephone in order to make Demeter, the divine mother, happy once more, for the return of the maiden would guarantee the renewed fertility of the earth and themselves. Through human participation in the earth goddess's suffering and happiness, the world of nature and the world of human experience are joined together. And just as the virginal Persephone descended into the underworld and yet returned to the land of the living, participation in the mysteries offered the participant the eternal renewal of life.

BIBLIOGRAPHY

Cameron, Averil, and Amelie Kuhrt, eds. *Images of Women in Antiquity.* 1983.

Cantarella, Eve. *Pandora's Daughters: The Role and Status of Women in Greek and Roman Antiquity.* 1987.

Fantham, Elaine, et al. *Women in the Classical World.* 1994.

Farnell, Lewis. *The Cults of the Greek States.* 1896–1909. Reprint, 1977–.

Halperin, David, et al., eds. *Before Sexuality: The Construction of Erotic Experience in the Ancient Greek World.* 1990.

Kraemer, R.S. *Her Share of the Blessings.* 1992.

———. "Women in the Religions of the Greco-Roman World." *Religious Studies Review* 9 (1983): 127–139.

Lefkowitz, Mary. *Women in Greek Myth.* 1986.

Lefkowitz, Mary, and M. B. Fant. *Women's Life in Greece and Rome.* 1982.

Pomeroy, Sarah. *Goddesses, Whores, Wives and Slaves in Classical Antiquity.* 1975.

Slater, Philip. *The Glory of Hera: Greek Mythology and the Family.* 1968.

See also **Artemis (Diana); Demeter and Persephone; Hera.**

TAMARA M. GREEN

Guyon, Jeanne Marie Bouvier de la Motte

The religious thought of French Christian mystic Jeanne Marie Bouvier de la Motte Guyon (1648–1717) is anchored in negative theology, a doctrine characterized by a form of mental practice that aims at the abandonment of cognition, representation, conceptualization, the memory of God and of oneself. According to this trend of mysticism, the workings of the divine can occur only with the quieting of reason and discursive thought. A powerful spiritual teacher and writer, Guyon courageously challenged the authority of the church in matters of spirituality. Her originality resides in the fact that she radicalized negative mysticism by democratizing its teaching while the church had wanted to keep it esoteric. A true healer of minds, she minimized the suffering brought about by her century's increasing insistence on guilt, and she taught her disciples a benevolent relationship with the divine.

Because mysticism under the name of "quietism" had come under increasing suspicion at the end of the seventeenth century, and because of her independence, Guyon was persecuted for many years. In 1694 her work was formally examined by a commission of theologians. Defended by Archbishop Fénelon, and accused and defamed by Bishop Bossuet, Madame Guyon was never found heretical nor was she excommunicated. Nevertheless, the outcome of the Quietist Affair was Guyon's imprisonment for more than seven years, five of which were spent at the Bastille, a political prison. She was released in 1703, and for the remainder of her life she was surrounded by an international avant-garde of intellectuals attracted by her teaching. Like Guyon, her new disciples drew their inspiration from medieval mysticism while participating in the shaping of a new philosophy with new claims for the individual.

BIBLIOGRAPHY

WORKS BY GUYON

Small works and treatises:

Moyen Court, Les Torrents; Traité de la purification de l'âme; Courte apologie du Moien Court; Petit abrégé de la voie; Règles des associés à l'Enfance de Jésus; Instruction chrétienne d'une mère à sa fille; Discours chrétiens et spirituels; l'Ame amante de son Dieu; Ecrits sur les Michelins. In *Les Opuscules spirituels de Madame J. M. B. de la Mothe Guion.* Edited by Pierre Poiret. Cologne, 1720.

Les Justifications de Madame J. M. B. de la Mothe Guion, écrites par elle-même, suivant l'ordre de Messieurs les Evêques ses examinateurs, où l'on éclaircit plusieurs difficultés qui regardent la vie intérieure [. . .]. 3 vols. Cologne, 1720.

Poetry:

Poésies et cantiques spirituels sur divers sujets qui regardent la vie intérieure, ou l'esprit du vrai Christianisme. 4 vols. Cologne, 1722.

Autobiography:

La Vie de Mme J. M. B. de la Mothe Guion écrite par elle-même. 3 vols. Edited by Jean-Philippe Dutoit. Paris, 1790.

Récits de captivité: Inédit. Edited by Marie-Louise Gondal. Grenoble, 1992.

Correspondence:

Lettres chrétiennes et spirituelles sur divers sujets qui regardent la vie intérieure, ou l'esprit du vrai christianisme. 5 vols. Edited by Jean-Philippe Dutoit. London. 1767–68.

Mme Guyon et Fénelon. Introduction by Etienne Pérot. Paris, 1982.

Letters to the Marquis de Fénelon and to the Duc de Chevreuse. *Revue Fénelon*: nos. 2 and 3 (1910); nos. 3 and 4 (1911); nos. 1 and 2 (1912).

Letters to the Scottish disciples. G. Henderson. *Mystics of the North East.* Aberdeen, 1934.

Anthology with some unpublished texts:

La passion de croire. Edited by Marie-Louise Gondal. Paris, 1990.

WORKS ON GUYON

Brémond, Henri. *Histoire du sentiment religieux en France depuis la fin des guerres de religion jusqu'à nos jours.* Vol. 11. Paris, 1921–33.

Bruneau, Marie-Florine. *Marie de l'Incarnation (1599–1672); Madame Guyon (1648–1717): Female Mystics and the Modern World.* 1997.

———. "Mysticisme et Psychose: L'autobiographie de Jeanne Guyon." Ph.D. diss., University of California, Berkeley, 1981.

Gondal, Marie-Louise. "L'autobiographie de Mme Guyon: La découverte et l'apport de deux nouveaux manuscrits." *XVIIe Siècle* 164 (1989): 307–323.

———. *Madame Guyon, 1648–1717: Un nouveau visage.* Paris, 1989. Contains a list of unpublished manuscripts by Guyon.

Laude, Patrick D. *Approches du quiétisme: Deux études.* Paris, 1991.

Ward, Patricia. "Madame Guyon in America: An Annotated Bibliography." *Bulletin of Bibliography* 52, no. 2 (1995): 107–111.

MARIE-FLORINE BRUNEAU

Hadewijch of Brabant

Hadewijch of Brabant was a Dutch mystic writer of the first half of the thirteenth century. Hadewijch's work is known to us through fourteen visions, thirty-one letters in prose, sixteen letters in rhyming couplets (the *Mengeldichten*), and forty-five stanzaic poems. Very little is known of her life. More than likely Hadewijch belonged to the early Beguine movement, composed of religious women who lived a monastic lifestyle without strict supervision by the church hierarchy. The Brabant writer was highly educated and taught mysticism to a select elite of women and men. Her oeuvre enjoyed great popularity among monastic and lay spiritual circles such as the Carthusians and the Devotio Moderna movement and mystics such as Ruusbroec (1293–1381), but lost currency in subsequent centuries. Her manuscripts were rediscovered in 1838 by the German philologist F. J. Mone. Hadewijch is regarded as one of the most important writers in the history of literature in the Netherlands and, like many other women mystics of the Middle Ages, must be credited with advancing vernacular literature to new levels of sophistication.

Hadewijch, an exponent of bridal mysticism, a movement based on the Song of Songs, used already existing genres such as courtly love poetry, epistolary writing, and visionary literature to express a daring and intellectually complex theological and spiritual model of human nature and ethical responsibility, *Minne* (divine love), and spiritual growth. Trust in divine goodness, an emphasis on Christ's suffering, and an analysis of the nature of human feeling and consciousness are framed by the soul's ardent relationship with the allegory of *Minne*. Both soul and *Minne* are envisioned as feminine, and most of the recipients of Hadewijch's letters appear to be women; Hadewijch's work thus represents an important contribution to the study of gynocentric aspects of Christian spirituality and mystical theology.

BIBLIOGRAPHY

Hadewijch. *Brieven; Mengeldichten; Strophische Gedichten; Visioenen*. 6 vols. Antwerp, 1924–1952.

———. *The Complete Works*. Translated by Columba Hart. 1980.

Mommaers, Paul, and Frank Willaert. "Mystisches Erleben und sprachliche Vermittlung in den Briefen Hadewijchs." In *Religiöse Frauenbewegung und mystische Frömmigkeit im Mittelalter*. Cologne, 1988.

ULRIKE WIETHAUS

Hagar

Hagar, the bearer of Abraham's son Ishmael and the ancestor of Muhammad, could be called "The Mother of Islam." She is the model for the rites of Hajj (Meccan pilgrimage).

In Genesis an old and childless Abraham is promised more sons than the stars, who will inhabit the land given to them, "from the river of Egypt to the river Euphrates" (15:7). Abraham's wife Sarah offers him Hagar, her Egyptian slavegirl, so that the barren Sarah might be "sonned" through her. The proud, pregnant Hagar, a surrogate mother like Bilhah and Zilpah (16:1–16, cf. 30:3–4; 9–10), is abused by Sarah. Hagar flees into the wilds, shedding the first tears of the Bible. The spring where Hagar is given the annunciation of Ishmael (for "God has heard" her suffering) is called Beer-lahai-roi (Well of the-Living-On-Who-Sees-Me) because she

Abraham exiles Hagar and Ishmael to the wilderness (Historical Picture Archive/Corbis).

gives God the name El-roi (The-One-Who-Sees). Though belittled throughout the Abrahamic saga, Hagar is the only female of Genesis addressed directly by God (twice). When Sarah finds the teenage Ishmael laughing at her son Isaac's weaning feast, she commands Abraham to drive out "this slavegirl and her son" (21:9–21). Abraham obeys because God makes clear the covenant is Isaac's alone. The next morning he reluctantly sends Hagar and Ishmael away with bread and water. Hagar and Ishmael wander the wilderness of Beer-sheba; again God hears her suffering, this time opening her eyes to a spring that saves them, though their lives will be harsh in the lands of Paran. This ends Hagar's biblical story. Both Midrashic and Jewish-feminist writings focus on "Sarah's sin" in mistreating Hagar; both see the drama as causal in the tense relations between the Abrahamic cousins' progeny in later history.

In service to Christianity, Paul continues the theme of Hagar's exclusion. To the old covenant of law and flesh (especially male circumcision), she represents slavery in contrast to the heavenly Jerusalem, the new covenant of spirit and faith represented by Sarah (Gal. 4:21–31). Hagar represents the earthly Jerusalem the Galatians are to reject. Womanist theologians read Hagar as the African slave-woman, who, like her sisters in antebellum America, breaks out from the white master and mistress' (Abraham and Sarah) exploitation to win freedom.

In Islamic tradition Abraham accompanies Hagar (Hajar) and the nursing infant Ishmael to the desolate valley of Mecca (or Bakkah) and returns to Sarah in Syria (Qur'an 14:37). Hagar accepts abandonment as God's will. When the waterskin empties and her milk dries up, according to hadith of Muhammad and Qur'an commentaries (on 2:158), Hagar runs in distress between the hills of Safa and Marwah seven times. The nomadic Jurhum tribe asks Hagar's permission to settle near her spring, and through Ishmael's marriage to one of their women the Arab people arise. Abraham returns after her death, and he and Ishmael build the Kaabah next to Hagar's grave, which was visible until Saudi reconstruction. On her account the Prophet ordered leniency during the Egyptian conquest. Thus, Sarah's mistreatment of Hagar (which in legend includes Sarah's punishing her with the first female circumcision) is foreordained to bring Abrahamic monotheism to Arabia by way of Hagar, a wellspring of faith and strength for Muslim women.

BIBLIOGRAPHY

Firestone, Reuven. *Journeys in Holy Lands: The Evolution of the Abraham-Ishmael Legends in Islamic Exegesis.* 1990. Brings Hagar to Mecca from numerous Arabic sources but emphasizes the controversy over the sacrifice (Isaac or Ishmael).

Gordon, Cynthia. "Hagar: A Throw-Away Character among the Matriarchs?" *SBL Seminar Papers* (1985): 271–277. Includes reference to rabbinic commentaries.

Greenblatt, Matis. "Did Sarah Sin against Hagar?" See website <www.torah.org/genesis>.

Stowasser, Barbara Freyer. *Women in the Qur'an, Traditions, and Interpretation.* 1994. See esp. "The Women of Noah, Lot, and Abraham." Ibn 'Arabi's *Futuhat,* al-Tha'labi's *Ara'is,* al-Tabari's *Tarikh,* al-Azraqi's *Akhbar Makkah,* and 'Ali Shari'ati's *Hajj* could be added as further Islamic Hagar sources.

Teubal, Savina J. *The Lost Tradition of the Matriarchs: Hagar the Egyptian.* 1990. Proposes two separate matriarch identities for the Hagar stories of Genesis.

Trible, Phyllis. *Texts of Terror: Literary Feminist Readings of Biblical Narratives.* 1984. Hagar chapter concludes with statement: "All we who are heirs of Sarah and Abraham, by flesh and spirit, must answer for the terror in Hagar's story," p. 29. For further discussion of Trible's points, see Robert Alter, *Genesis: Translation and Commentary,* 1996; Bill Moyers, *Genesis: A Living Conversation,* 1996; *Genesis: As It Is Written,* 1996; Burton L. Visotzky, *The Genesis of Ethics,* 1996; and Gail T. Reimer and Judith A. Kates, eds., *Beginning Anew: A Woman's Companion to the High Holy Days,* 1997.

Williams, Delores. *Sisters in the Wilderness: The Challenge of Womanist God-Talk.* 1993. See esp. "Hagar's Story: A Route to Black Women's Issues."

BARBARA R. VON SCHLEGELL

Hagiography

Hagiography, or writing about the lives of saints, is a common form of religious literature. First used for the lives of Christian saints, the term *hagiography* is now widely applied to accounts of the lives of saints in other religions, although neither *hagiography* nor *saint* are always exact translations of terms used in other religions. Hagiographies may either chronicle the life of one saint or provide brief accounts of many saints. In most religious traditions saints are understood to embody or communicate attributes considered sacred or beyond this world, and therefore sainthood in its very essence is difficult to convey. In contrast to historically oriented biography, hagiography generally relates the historical details of a saint's life only insofar as it contributes to the overall depiction of sainthood. Scholars have often looked to hagiography for historical information about saints' lives but have found that legends and miracle tales predominate; because such accounts serve to communicate the saint's power, they play a crucial role in the hagiographer's endeavor.

Hagiography is nonetheless not ahistorical. A person becomes a saint when she is recognized as such by her followers. When a saint is no longer living, her followers create and perpetuate her memory. It is the power of the saint that inspires the hagiographer, but it is the hagiographer who helps to define and perpetuate the memory of the saint's power. Both male and female hagiographers have used the power of the saint to lend authority to their own positions.

When hagiographers write about a saint from past decades or even centuries, they must relate the saint's life in ways relevant to the concerns of their intended audience. Hagiographies thus often reveal more about the historical situation of their authors than that of the saints they address. This becomes especially evident if we trace the portrayals of one saint over time.

Women's saintly vocations have often been seen as opposing traditional gender roles. Hagiographical traditions concerning women saints reflect prevailing attitudes toward female religious experience. Thus, although female saints have challenged traditional ideas about female religious roles in their own lives (as is well-attested in Christian hagiography), their hagiographers will often present them as fulfilling and endorsing traditional gender roles.

Hagiographers often express the wish that their readers try to pattern their own lives after the life of the saint. Hagiographies of female saints in particular become a means of promoting images of ideal female behavior. One hagiographer's depiction of a saint's life as an endorsement of the status quo may be contested by another hagiographer wishing to use the same saint's life to challenge the status quo. Early hagiographical accounts of Mirabai, a sixteenth-century Hindu saint, describe her contentious relationship with her husband and his family; more recent hagiographies depict her as a dutiful, obedient wife. Because hagiographers both describe and appropriate the power understood to inhere in sainthood, hagiography has served as a useful tool for promoting various social and religious agendas.

BIBLIOGRAPHY

The literature on saints' lives is vast. Listed here are studies that use hagiographies as source material as well as theoretical studies of hagiography as a genre.

Blumenfeld-Kosinski, Renate, and Timea Szell, eds. *Images of Sainthood in Medieval Europe.* 1991. Useful articles on hagiographical images and the development of hagiographical traditions, with particular focus on gender issues.

Delany, Sheila. *A Legend of Holy Women: A Translation of Osbern Bokenham's Legends of Holy Women.* 1992. A fifteenth-century all-female hagiography, with critical introduction. Good example of portrayal of female saints in Christian tradition.

Olsen, Alexandra Hennesey. "'De Historiis Sanctorum': A Generic Study of Hagiography." *Genre* XIII (1980): 407–429. A critique of scholarly approaches to hagiography; suggests new ways of approaching the genre.

Ramanujan, A. K. "On Woman Saints." In *The Divine Consort.* Edited by J. S. Hawley and D. M. Wulff. 1982. Describes the common features of women saints' lives found in Hindu hagiographies.

Smith, Margaret. *Rābi'a the Mystic and Her Fellow-Saints in Islam.* 1928. Reprint, 1984. Dated in its approach, but still a good introduction to the life of an important Muslim female saint, with discussion of her portrayals in hagiographical tradition.

Tsai, Kathryn. *Lives of the Nuns.* 1995. A study of Chinese Buddhist nuns.

ROBIN C. RINEHART

Hair

Hair is a powerful cultural signifier that is often gendered. Women's hair, in particular, has preoccupied many of the world's religions, where it is entangled in codes of ritual purity and impurity, in cosmic creation and dissolution, life-giving and murder, chastity and promiscuity, celebration and mourning, authority and submission. Infinitely pliable as medium and metaphor, hair is significant in marking transformations of many kinds, as well as negotiating social status and group identity.

Unbound hair is an aspect of such powerful goddesses as the Hindu Kālī, destroyer, transformer, inspirer; and the Egyptian Isis, whose hair revived her murdered lover Osiris. The Mahābhārata's Draupadī wears her hair unkempt while menstruating, and again to mark her sexual violation and her vow to "wash her hair in her attacker's blood." *Ḍākinīs*, semidivine partners of male tantric masters, appear with radiant, flowing locks, as did the human Medusa before she was raped by the Greek god Poseidon and transformed by Athena into a snake-haired monster whose gaze turned men to stone. Other women whose unbound or uncovered hair is related to spiritual powers or cultic devotion include the Maenads, whose frenzied ecstasies were tribute to the Greek Dionysus; some Hindu holy women whose matted locks flow from asceticism; tantric adepts, sisters to the supernatural *ḍākinīs*; European witches, whose hair unleashes forces celestial and terrestrial; and the Corinthian Christian female prophets of the New Testament, whose unveiling appears linked to their prophetic powers and perhaps to angelic possession. Possession by a *loa*, or spirit, is sought by Vodou initiates, who undergo the rite of *lave tèt* wherein one's head is "cleansed" and anointed with ingredients particularly inviting to one's personal *mèt tèt*, or "master of the head." Similarly, elaborate hairdos may have served female shamans as "spirit-lures" in prehistoric Japan. Unbound, uncovered hair advertises a bride's virginity, according to earliest rabbinic Jewish accounts, while wives accused of adultery suffer the dishevelment of their hair during the ordeal required by biblical law to determine guilt or innocence.

Conversely, covered hair is generally tied to order and discipline, gender hierarchy, and submission to authority. Rabbinic law requires wives to cover their heads and stipulates divorce as the penalty for refusal; heavy fines are levied against one who assaults a woman by uncovering her hair. Draupadī's sexual assault takes the form of hair-pulling. Paul insisted that women veil themselves while praying or prophesying, as a sign of submission to male authority. Prior to Vatican II, most Catholic nuns, "brides of Christ," wore veils as part of their habits. Veiling of brides appears widely, including in ancient Greek and Roman, Jewish, Christian, Muslim, and Chinese cultures. The *hijab*, or "curtain" of separation spoken of in the Qur'an, has, for many Muslim women, taken forms ranging from simple head scarves to full-body shrouds. *Hijab* is understood by some to protect women from sexual objectification;

The head of Medusa, second to third century C.E. (Wolfgang Kaehler/Corbis)

others suggest it reinforces the identification of women's hair and bodies with sex. Veiling may also advertise sexual availability, as when the biblical Tamar "put off her widows' garb and put on a veil" to pass as a prostitute.

In some cultures, women express mourning through dishevelment and tearing of hair, in some they don veils. Mourning, shame, and penitence for Eve's transgressive search for knowledge appears in Christian and Jewish texts as one explanation for the requirement of women's head-covering. Among other peoples, women cut their hair in mourning.

Shorn hair is part of women's discipline in numerous religious communities. Buddhist nuns, like monks, shave their heads, and the hair of Catholic nuns was traditionally cropped upon entry into an order. Paul found short-haired women and long-haired men equally reprehensible, while other Christian saints, like Thecla and Joan of Arc, wore short hair and men's garb in fulfillment of their holy vocations. Among some Orthodox Jews a bride's head is shaved at marriage, and kept shorn thereafter under a scarf or wig. Biblical law stipulated that Israelites shave the heads of captives they intended to marry. Among some peoples, girls' first haircuts are ritual celebrations. Apache girls' hair is cut in spring, each lock snipped along with a handful of grass, then prayerfully placed in flowering trees.

Finally, many myths tell of women disempowering men through cutting men's hair or displaying their own. The biblical Delilah brings down Samson, and the Greek Scylla her father, Nisus, by cutting off their locks. Even the sight of the dead Medusa's hair petrifies men, while Jewish, Christian, and Muslim traditions insist the sight of women's hair dissolves men's sexual restraint.

BIBLIOGRAPHY

Carson, Ann. "Putting Her in Her Place: Women, Dirt, and Desire." In *Before Sexuality: The Construction of Erotic Experience in the Ancient Greek World.* Edited by David M. Halperin et al. 1990. A provocative article with a subsection on bridal veiling in classical Greek art and literature.

Eilberg-Schwartz, Howard, and Wendy Doniger, eds. *Off with Her Head! The Denial of Women's Identity in Myth, Religion, and Culture.* 1995. An excellent resource comprising several articles that treat a variety of ancient and contemporary traditions concerning women's hair and heads. Extensive notes and bibliography.

Hiltebeitel, Alf. "Draupadi's Hair," *Purusartha* 5 (1981): 179–214. An in-depth treatment of the subject.

Martin, Dale. "Prophylactic Veils." In his *The Corinthian Body.* 1995. A critical rehearsal of most of the available theories about the veiling controversy among Christians at Corinth, followed by Martin's own insightful assessment of the evidence.

Obeyesekere, Gananath. *Medusa's Hair.* 1981. A controversial classic exploring ethnographic and psychoanalytic dimensions of hair in South Asian religions.

Walker, Barbara G. "Hair." In her *The Woman's Encyclopedia of Myths and Secrets.* 1983. More manifesto than sound information, but worth a look.

See also Ḍākinīs; Draupadī; Durgā and Kālī; Isis; Maenads; Mourning and Death Rites; Possession.

CYNTHIA M. BAKER

Hallucinogens

See Intoxicants and Hallucinogens.

Hannah

In the Bible, Hannah is a barren woman who eventually gives birth to the prophet Samuel. The birth narrative, in 1 Samuel 1:1–28, recounts how one year, at the annual vintage festival held at Shiloh, Hannah, grieved over her barrenness, prays that God will give her a son. She vows, moreover, that if her prayer is granted, she will consecrate the child to God's service. In due time this comes to pass, and in 1 Samuel 2:1–10 Hannah sings a song of exultation celebrating God's goodness in reversing her misfortune.

The story of Hannah has many similarities to the stories of the Bible's other barren women (Sarah, Rebekah, Rachel, Manoah's wife, and the Shunammite woman), including the notions that the barren woman has a fertile rival (in Hannah's case, Peninnah) and that the announcement that the barrenness is to be ended should be delivered by a divine messenger (in Hannah's case, the priest Eli). The story of Hannah also shows affinities with Judges 21:15–24, as the song Hannah sings in 1 Samuel 2 is paralleled in the Judges text by a description of women dancing in conjunction with the Shiloh feast. Female musicianship seems further to be associated with the vineyard festival in Jeremiah 31:10–14 and Isaiah 5:1–7 and 32:9–14. Indeed, although generally in Israelite religion ritual duties are solely the province of men, the making of music at the time of the vintage feast seems specifically to be the responsibility of women.

BIBLIOGRAPHY

Ackerman, Susan. "Isaiah." In *The Women's Bible Commentary.* Edited by C. A. Newsom and S. H. Ringe. 1992.

Alter, Robert. "How Convention Helps Us Read: The Case of the Bible's Annunciation Type-Scene." *Prooftexts* 3 (1983): 115–130.

Goiten, S. D. "Women as Creators of Biblical Genres." *Prooftexts* 8 (1988): 3–33.

SUSAN ACKERMAN

Hāritī

Hāritī is the Buddhist goddess of smallpox and other pustular fevers. She is also, paradoxically, the goddess of prosperity and fertility and protectress of children. Hāritī is thus a representation of the Indian Great Goddess as creator, nurturer, and destroyer. A contradictory figure, she gives children to the barren yet causes the fevers of childhood; she bestows wealth yet must rely on charitable offerings.

The *Samyuktavastu,* chapter 31, relates that Hāritī was a human woman who lost her child in a miscarriage. This anguish caused her to be reborn as a demoness with five hundred children. She destroyed human children to feed her own demon offspring. The Buddha taught her compassion by hiding her favorite child, and in her sorrow at the loss of her son, she learned that she had caused misery to the parents of those children she had killed. Although she repented, and became guardian of children, she still belongs to the group of malevolent deities who represent the disturbing power of women deprived of their children.

Though she was honored in monastic Buddhism, Hāritī's most dedicated worshipers were among the laity. Her shrines, often in or near a monastery refectory, gave lay pilgrims a focus for the ordinary concerns of children, disease, and wealth. The shrines were a reminder to visitors that just as the goddess needed daily offerings of food, the monastic community was dependent on the laity for charitable donations. Her cult is indicative of the integration of local goddess worship into mainstream Buddhism and a reminder that most members of the Buddhist assembly were not concerned with the abstract issues of Buddhist philosophy, but lived with all the daily worries of domestic life. Some shrines continue to be important pilgrimage sites for barren women.

Hāritī's cult developed in northwest India in the cultural pluralism of the Kuṣāṇa period (first century C.E.–fourth century C.E.). Kuṣāṇa sculptures reflect her syncretic nature, combining aspects of pre-Buddhist *yakṣas* (nature spirits) and foreign goddesses. She is crowned, wears Roman dress, holds a baby, and sometimes a cornucopia, wine cup, grapes, or a sheaf of grain. Her attributes are usually benign, but in keeping with her violent or *ugra* character, she sometimes has fangs or carries a *triśūla* (a weapon of the Hindu goddess Durgā). She is often seated with her consort, Pāñcika (also known as Kubera), the *yakṣa* general and god of wealth.

BIBLIOGRAPHY

Bivar, A. D. "Hāritī and the Chronology of the Kuṣāṇas." *Bulletin of the School of Oriental and African Studies* 33 (1970): 10–21.

Getty, Alice. *Gods of Northern Buddhism.* 1928. Reprint, New Delhi, 1978.

Coomaraswamy, Ananda. *Yakṣas.* Part I and II. New Delhi, 2d ed., 1980.

Foucher, A. "The Buddhist Madonna." *The Beginnings of Buddhist Art.* 1917.

Hallade, Madeleine. *Gandharan Art of North India.* 1968.

Harle, J. C. *The Art and Architecture of the Indian Subcontinent.* 1990.

Huntington, John C. "Cave Six at Aurangabad: A Tantrayāna Monument?" In *Kalādarśana.* Edited by Joanna Williams. New Delhi, 1981.

Huntington, Susan L., with contributions by John C. Huntington. *The Art of Ancient India.* 1985.

Peri, N. "Hāritī, La Mère de Démons." *Bulletin de L'Ecole Française d' Extrême-Orient* 17, no. 3 (1917): 1–102.

MARY N. STORM

Harrison, Jane Ellen

Jane Ellen Harrison (1850–1928) was a classicist and historian of Greek religion whose work on the goddesses has proved inspiring to feminist scholars. Harrison was one of the first women students at Cambridge University in England, and she later taught at its Newnham College. Her most important works, *Prolegomena to the Study of Greek Religion* (1903) and *Themis* (1912), reflect her lifelong interest in uncovering the religious experience and passion that inspired Greek religion.

In *Prolegomena* Harrison writes that Hesiod (c. 700 B.C.E.), who is usually cited as the most important source on Greek religion, was motivated by "the ugly malice of theological animus." His goal was to dethrone the Earth Goddess and to establish the rule of the fathers and their god Zeus. Through painstaking analysis of the literary and artistic record, Harrison shows that Hesiod's views were not necessarily accepted in his own or later times. For example, Hesiod portrays Pandora as the woman who was responsible for first unleashing evil into the world by opening her infamous jar (sometimes incorrectly translated as box). Yet "Pandora" means "Giver of All" and is an appellation of the Earth Goddess; Harrison finds an amphora that shows Pandora rising from the earth, a classic depiction of the Rising of the goddess. Harrison also discovers prepatriarchal understandings of other goddesses such as Athena, Artemis, and Aphrodite.

Harrison's work anticipates contemporary feminist scholarship in questioning the reliability of patriarchal primary and secondary texts and in developing a methodology for uncovering what those texts, informed by a particular point of view, attempt to suppress. Just as significant is Harrison's challenge to the image of the Greeks as the first rational men on whose shoulders Western civilization and its educational system stands. Harrison argued that men were motivated by the urge to subordinate women and therefore rewrote history in the process. As she continued to uncover the roots of Greek religion in religious practice, Harrison became increasingly convinced that the ideal of rationality attributed to the Greeks was a dangerous and misleading restriction of human experience. Human life is ruled by passions rooted in the body and its needs. To deny this is to deny the life force that gives rise to all the creations of civilization. Here too Harrison anticipated many feminist scholars who reject the oppositions of rational and irrational, mind and body, and spirit and nature enshrined in the classical dualisms. Perhaps because she was a woman and she challenged some of patriarchy's most deeply held beliefs, Harrison's work is often ignored by traditional scholars in classics and religion.

Harrison worked without a community of other women to help her name the feminist impulses that inspired her research and to confirm her insights. Those reading Harrison's work today will find that she often holds back from clearly asserting the radical implications of her work—sometimes retracting what she has just asserted. They might also find it irritating that she says "primitive" religion where we would say "traditional" or "folk" religion and that she uses the word "matriarchal" where we would use "matrifocal" or "matrilineal." But they will be rewarded by discovering the enormously powerful work of a woman who had the courage to challenge both the obvious and more subtle patriarchal assumptions of her field, her colleagues, and her culture.

BIBLIOGRAPHY

Carpentier, Martha C. "Jane Ellen Harrison and the Ritual Theory." *Journal of Ritual Studies* 8, no. 1 (1994): 11–26.

Harrison, Jane Ellen. *Ancient Art and Ritual.* 1913.

———. *Epilegomena to the Study of Greek Religions.* 1921.

———. *Mythology and Monuments of Ancient Athens.* 1890.

———. *Prolegomena to the Study of Greek Religion.* 1903. Reprint, 1991.

———. *Themis: A Study of the Social Origins of Greek Religion.* 1912.

Murray, Gilbert. "Jane Ellen Harrison 1850–1928." Memorial Lecture in *Epilegomena . . . and Themis.* 1962.

Peacock, Sandra J. *Jane Ellen Harrison: The Mask and the Self.* 1988.

Stewart, Jessie G. *Jane Ellen Harrison: A Portrait from the Letters.* 1959.

CAROL P. CHRIST

Hawwa' (Eve)

In Islamic tradition the female partner of the first man created is called Hawwa', although she is not specifically named in the Qur'an. Whereas Adam alone is taught the names of things and given the covenant by God, he and his wife are asked to dwell in the Garden and both are warned not to eat of the tree (of immortality) (2:35, 7:19). The Qur'an makes it clear that both are tempted by Satan, both eat what is forbidden, and both are expelled from the Garden (2:36, 20:123, 7:24). In the scripture, therefore, no special culpability is as-

Nineteenth-century Islamic depiction of Hawwa' and Adam in the Garden (Leonard de Selva/Corbis)

signed to Eve for the fall of humanity. Neither is she described as having been fashioned from a rib of Adam. Rather man and woman are said to have been created from a single soul (4:1, 7:189), and mates given that each might find rest in the other (7:189, 30:21).

In the centuries following the Prophet Muhammad's death, however, a number of narratives came to be circulated concerning Eve's creation and culpability that may have been influenced by biblical stories. She is said to have been brought forth from Adam's rib, sometimes described as coming from the most crooked part of that bone. Some traditions place the blame for the fall from the Garden directly on Eve's duplicity. Contemporary Qur'an interpreters reject these traditions and affirm the Qur'anic picture of Hawwa' as co-created with Adam and sharing equally with him in the events that led to the fall from the Garden.

BIBLIOGRAPHY

Smith, Jane I., and Yvonne Y. Haddad. "Eve: Islamic Image of Woman." In *Woman and Islam.* Edited by Azizah al-Hibri. 1982.

Stowasser, Barbara F. *Women in the Qur'an: Traditions and Interpretations.* 1994.

Wadud-Muhsin, Amina. *Qur'an and Woman.* Kuala Lumpur, 1992.

See also Eve.

JANE I. SMITH

Hebrew Bible

God in the Hebrew Bible

Biblical religion developed out of the polytheistic traditions of Israel's ancient Near Eastern neighbors and especially out of the polytheistic traditions of the Canaanite culture that preceded Israel's emergence in the "promised land" c. 1200 B.C.E. Thus, despite the Bible's claims that its God is utterly different from the gods of the nations, there were in fact manifold similarities between the ways in which the ancient Israelites described the God of the Hebrew Bible and how their Canaanite predecessors described their deities. Even the names of Canaanite deities and the name of the Israelite God could be the same: for example, the head of the Canaanite pantheon is called El, a word that simply means "god" and that is used in the Bible, both in the form El and in a longer form, Elohim, as an appellation for the God of Israel. Scholars have also suggested that another name of Israel's God, Yahweh, which is best analyzed as a verbal form meaning "the one who creates" (literally: "the one who causes to be"), originally applied to El, who is frequently called "creator" in Canaanite religion.

Several other epithets are shared by Canaanite El and the biblical God. In Canaanite tradition, El is "the ancient one," "father," "Bull," and "the god of the covenant," terms all used at points in biblical tradition to describe the Israelite God (e.g., "the ancient one": Gen. 21:33, Isa. 40:28; "father": Deut. 32:6, Isa. 63:16, 64:8 [Hebrew 64:7], Jer. 3:4, 19, 31:9, Mal. 1:6, 2:10; "Bull": Gen. 49:24, Ps. 132:2, 5, Isa. 49:26, 60:16; "the God of the covenant": Judg. 9:46 [Judg. 8:33 and 9:4 suggest that the "God of the covenant," whose temple was in Shechem, was different from the Israelite God, but this is surely wrong: see Gen. 33:20 for evidence that the deity worshiped in Shechem was Israel's]). Also, El and the biblical God share many of the same attributes: both are renowned for their kindness and compassion (according to Canaanite myth, El is the "Kindly One" and the "Compassionate One"; the biblical God is "merciful" and "gracious" [Exod. 34:6; Deut. 4:31; Ps.

86:15; Jon. 4:2]); both appear to humans in dreams and visions (Gen. 20:3, 28:10–17, 31:24); both are tent-dwellers (2 Sam. 7:6; Ps. 15:1, 27:6, 91:10, 132:3); both are lawgivers and judges who preside over assemblies filled with other divine beings (1 Kgs. 22:19; Ps. 82:1, 89:7 [Hebrew 89:8]; Isa. 6:1–8). Even the narratives told about their exploits can be quite similar: the Canaanite Epic of Kirta, for example, describes how El grants a son to the childless King Kirta so that Kirta might have an heir, which parallels in many respects the biblical story of God giving Isaac to Abraham as a son and heir, even though both Abraham and his wife Sarah are old and Sarah is postmenopausal (Gen. 17:15–22, 18:9–15).

Yet El's epithets and attributes are not the only images from Canaanite polytheism adopted by the Israelites in their depictions of Yahweh; Israelite tradition also borrows heavily from Canaanite conceptions of the god Baal. According to Canaanite tradition, Baal is a young warrior whose primary weapon is the storm: his voice, when he speaks, is the roar of thunder; he carries a lightning bolt as his weapon; he rides on a chariot of clouds. Israelite tradition can similarly depict Yahweh as a warrior who uses the storm as a weapon: in Exodus 15, for example, Yahweh defeats the forces of Pharaoh at the Reed (Red) Sea by stirring up a mighty tempest that throws the Egyptian soldiers from the boats on which they presumably travel and tosses them into the tumultuous depths. Judges 5 describes how, in a battle against the Canaanites after Israel has come into possession of the promised land, the enemy's forces are swept away by the storm water Yahweh sends raging through the normally dry riverbed of the Wadi Kishon. In Habakkuk 3, although there is no specific identification of the enemy against whom Yahweh fights, the imagery of Yahweh's using raging waters and mighty rivers in battling against Israel's foes is also present.

Israel's assimilation of Baal imagery into its descriptions of its God, however, is not only found in military contexts. The giving of the commandments at Sinai, where God's presence atop the mountain is marked by thunder, lightning, and thick clouds, draws heavily on the storm language associated in Canaanite tradition with Baal. Sinai's depiction of Yahweh as a lawgiver, however, is more likely derived from traditions of El. Scholars have also located this same juxtaposition of El and Baal imagery in texts such as Genesis 49: 25–26, Deuteronomy 33:26–27, Psalms 18:14–16, and Job 38: 1–42:6. In the latter, Yahweh speaks both as creator (El) and as the one who can call a flood of waters from the clouds, send forth lightning, and roar with a voice of thunder (Baal). Also in the Job text, Yahweh speaks as the one from whose womb ice came forth and the one

The god Baal with a lance, early second millenium B.C.E. (Paul Almasy/© Corbis)

tions of Yahweh, the authors of (at least) these Numbers, Deuteronomy, and Isaiah texts assimilated imagery of the Canaanite mother goddess, Asherah, as well. These authors' understanding seems to be that, if Israel is to have only one God, that God must absorb all the characteristics of the many gods—both male and female— of the older Canaanite pantheon.

Other ancient Israelites, however, described the appropriation of Asherah imagery into Biblical religion differently. Because, according to Canaanite mythology, the mother goddess Asherah was the consort of the patriarch El, some ancient Israelites reasoned that in their own tradition, Asherah should also serve as the consort of El, which is to say, as the consort of El's Israelite counterpart, Yahweh. This belief in turn suggested the erecting of icons to Asherah at cult sites dedicated to Yahweh. Such an icon—which was in the form of a stylized pole or tree—stood at Yahweh's temple in Bethel (2 Kgs. 23:15). Also, throughout much of Israelite history, Asherah's stylized pole or tree stood in Yahweh's temple in Jerusalem. In the ninth century B.C.E., for example, Maacah, the queen mother of King Asa, is said to have dedicated a cult icon to Asherah; and given that Yahweh's temple in Jerusalem stood next door to the royal palace and that the temple essentially functioned as a private chapel for the king's family, it is almost undoubtedly within its walls that Maacah's icon was erected. Second Kings 18:4, from the eighth century B.C.E., also describes an Asherah icon that most probably stood in the Jerusalem temple. Two seventh-century texts, 2 Kings 21:7 and 2 Kings 23:6, are emphatic that there was an image dedicated to Asherah in Yahweh's temple. According to 2 Kings 23:4, moreover, sacrifices were offered to the goddess in the temple, and 2 Kings 23:7 reports that there was a cadre of women temple servants who wove garments to be draped over Asherah's cult image.

Recent archaeological discoveries from the sites of Kuntillet Ajrud, a ninth- or eighth-century site in the eastern Sinai, and from Khirbet el-Qom, an eighth-century site some 10 kilometers east-southeast of the city of Lachish, have further confirmed that at least some in ancient Israel worshiped Asherah and Yahweh side by side. At both these sites, inscriptions (one at Khirbet el-Qom, several at Kuntillet Ajrud) mention Yahweh and Asherah as a pair. Drawings at Kuntillet Ajrud, which have been argued to represent an image of Yahweh in association with an image of Asherah, may also suggest the worship of Asherah in conjunction with Yahweh. A tenth-century B.C.E. cult stand from the site of Taanach, located near the city of Megiddo, has similarly been held to represent images of Asherah together with images of Yahweh.

who gave birth to the hoarfrost of heaven (38:29). This imagery of Yahweh giving birth is found again in Isaiah 42:14, where God, in the context of a hymn of creation, speaks of crying out like a woman in labor. In Deuteronomy 32:18 and Isaiah 66:9, too, birth imagery is associated with the deity. In these latter two passages, the child whom Yahweh bears is either the nation Israel (Deut. 32) or the capital city of Jerusalem (Isa. 66).

This motif of Yahweh as the mother of Israel or Jerusalem manifests itself also in Numbers 11:12–13 and in Isaiah 45:9–10, 49:15, and 66:13. Thus it appears that, in the same way that Israelite tradition assimilated the imagery of Canaanite El and Baal into its descrip-

In general, the books of the Pentateuch (Genesis, Exodus, Leviticus, Numbers, and Deuteronomy), along with the Bible's so-called historical books (Joshua, Judges, 1–2 Samuel, 1–2 Kings, 1–2 Chronicles), are disdainful of this sort of Asherah worship and condemn it as apostasy in Israelite tradition. The prophetic tradition, however, is less sure. According to 2 Kings 13:6, for example, the icon to Asherah that King Ahab erected in Samaria, the capital city of Israel's northern kingdom, was allowed to remain standing by one of Ahab's successors, King Jehu, even though Jehu, inspired by the religious zeal of the prophet Elisha, had otherwise purged from Samaria and from the northern kingdom all the religious imagery that he considered to be apostate within Yahwism. This suggests that Elisha and, by implication, the prophetic tradition more generally did not object to the worship of Asherah in association with the worship of Yahweh. Note in this regard that the prophets Amos and Hosea make no negative comment about the presence of an Asherah icon at Yahweh's temple in Bethel, although both otherwise unleash virulent attacks on the religious practices associated with that sanctuary (Amos 3:14, 4:4–5, 5:4–7, 7:1– 17; Hos. 8:5–6, 10:5–6, 13:2). Also, there is virtually no anti-Asherah polemic in prophetic texts concerning Yahweh's temple in Jerusalem.

All of this data raises the question of how we should understand the concept of monotheism in biblical tradition. Obviously, for some, the supposedly sole God Yahweh could, at a minimum, be associated with a female counterpart. Yet even those ancient Israelites who rejected an Asherah cult in conjunction with that of Yahweh's cannot really be called monotheists, at least not in the word's pure, philosophical, or theoretical sense. Their stance is rather one of monolatry or henotheism: the confession that though many gods exist, there is only one God (Yahweh) who is to be worshiped. Implicit in the first of the ten commandments, for example ("I am Yahweh, your God. You shall have no other gods before me"), is an understanding that other gods do exist: they are just not to be privileged in Israel. Lines of hymnic praise such as "Who is like you among the gods, O Yahweh?" (Exod. 15:11) similarly indicate a belief that there is a plurality of deities in the cosmos while at the same time singling out Yahweh for Israel's special devotions.

It is only in the middle of the sixth century B.C.E., some 650 years after Israel's emergence in the land of Canaan, that the Bible begins to describe a belief in Yahweh as the only deity in the heavens. The second half of the book of Isaiah (Isa. 40–66), penned by an anonymous prophet who wrote during the exile of the Israelite people in Babylon, is the first to give witness to unambiguously monotheistic confessions: "I am the first and the last," Yahweh proclaims in Isaiah 44:6, "besides me there is no God" (see also 41:4; 43:10; 44:8; 45:5–6, 14, 18, 22; 48:12). Yahweh is celebrated as the sole creator of the earth (40:12–31); the idols of the nations are dismissed as worthless (41:21–24, 44:9–20, 46:1–13). The prophet can even imagine the day when all the nations will convert to the worship of the one God, no longer a God who is just the God of Israel but now the God of all peoples.

BIBLIOGRAPHY

Ackerman, Susan. *Under Every Green Tree: Popular Religion in Sixth-Century Judah.* 1992.

Ahlström, Gösta W. *Aspects of Syncretism in Israelite Religion.* 1963.

Albertz, Rainer. *A History of Israelite Religion in the Old Testament Period.* 1994.

Albright, William F. *Yahweh and the Gods of Canaan: A Historical Analysis of Two Contrasting Faiths.* 1968.

Armstrong, Karen. *A History of God: The 4000-Year Quest of Judaism, Christianity, and Islam.* 1993.

Cross, Frank M. *Canaanite Myth and Hebrew Epic: Essays in the History of the Religion of Israel.* 1973.

Dever, William G. "Archaeology Reconstructs the Lost Background of the Israelite Cult." In his *Recent Archaeological Discoveries and Biblical Research.* 1990.

Fohrer, Georg. *History of Israelite Religion.* 1972.

Halpern, Baruch. " 'Brisker Pipes than Poetry': The Development of Israelite Monotheism." In *Judaic Perspectives on Ancient Israel.* Edited by J. Neusner, B. A. Levine, and E. S. Frerichs. 1987.

Lang, Bernhard. "No God but Yahweh! The Origin and Character of Biblical Monotheism." *Concilium* 177 (1985): 41–49.

Mettinger, Tryggve N. D. "Fighting the Powers of Chaos and Hell—Towards a Biblical Portrait of God." *Studia Theologica* 39 (1985): 21–36.

———. *No Graven Image: Israelite Aniconism in Its Ancient Near Eastern Context.* Stockholm, 1995.

Miles, Jack. *God: A Biography.* 1995.

Olyan, Saul M. *Asherah and the Cult of Yahweh in Israel.* 1988.

Petersen, David L. "Israel and Monotheism: The Unfinished Agenda." In *Canon, Theology, and Old Testament Interpretation: Essays in Honor of Brevard S. Childs.* Edited by G. M. Tucker, D. L. Petersen, and R. R. Wilson. 1988.

Ringgren, Helmer. *Israelite Religion.* 1966.

Schmidt, Werner H. *Alttestamentlicher Glaub und seine Umwelt: Zur Geschichte des alttestamentlichen Gottesverständnis.* Neukirchen-Vluyn, 1968.

Smith, Mark S. *The Early History of God: Yahweh and the Other Deities in Israel.* 1990.

Tigay, Jeffery H. *You Shall Have No Other Gods: Israelite Religion in the Light of Hebrew Inscriptions.* 1986.

Trible, Phyllis. *God and the Rhetoric of Sexuality.* 1978.

See also **Israelite Religion**.

SUSAN ACKERMAN

Prophets and Judges

The fundamental public roles in ancient Israel, a patriarchal society like the rest of the ancient Near East, were carried out by males. In the pre-Davidic period of Israel, however, before 1000 B.C.E., several women are cited as having important roles, especially Miriam and Deborah. With the monarchy, public positions became more formalized and the government and priestly roles basically excluded women. All of the governmental heads were male—apart from Athaliah, who had the important but little-understood role of queen mother (and daughter of King Ahab and Queen Jezebel of Israel) and who gained the throne of Judah upon her son's death, only to be overthrown in her seventh year—and all of the recognized priestly roles were filled by males. (Among Israel's neighbors women could serve as priests, especially in the cult of goddesses, but Israel's official cult was limited to male priests.) In Israel, women's chief public roles of a more religious character were as musicians and as specialists in mourning (e.g., 1 Sam. 18:6, Jer. 9:16–20). There were other roles, however, that did not rely either on patriarchal tradition and heredity, on bureaucratic attainment, or on acquired skills. Women could have the charismatically based and socially approved role of "deliverer" or "rescuer"—traditionally translated as "judge"—or prophet, in which they seem to be accepted without surprise, and the achieved role of the unnamed "wise women" (Judg. 5:29; 2 Sam. 14:2; 20:16). Women also filled marginalized roles, officially discouraged, including acting as a "medium" (e.g., the "possessor of a ghostly spirit," a woman from Endor, 1 Sam. 28). Also, women played prominent roles within the more private arena of the family, though these roles are generally ignored in the biblical texts. The limited and androcentric character of the biblical tradition provides little direct information and encourages speculation as to what women actually did. For example, rabbinic tradition (Megillah 14a–b), though not acknowledging Noadiah's identification as a prophet, goes beyond the biblical texts and extends the title prophet to four other important women associated with the well-being of Israel but not with oracles: Sarah, Hannah (a singer, like Miriam and Deborah), Abigail, and Esther.

Women as prophets, that is, as inspired messengers, are well known in the Amorite areas of Mesopotamia and Syria, figuring in many ways with the prehistory of Israel, in the first part of the second millennium B.C.E.; they appear also in Assyria, especially during the seventh century just before the time of Huldah. In connection with Canaanite deities, the 450 prophets of Baal and the 400 prophets of Asherah cited in 1 Kings 18:19 may well have included some women. The women prophets known from Israel's neighbors, like their male counterparts, are especially protective of the well-being of the king. The nature of the prophetic role, including revelatory dreams and ecstatically received messages, encouraged the transcending of traditional gender barriers. Technical forms of divination, such as the examination of animal livers, were almost exclusively in the hands of men. Dreams and ecstasy cannot be denied to women, however, so those who welcomed communications from the divine world by means of dream or ecstatic utterance commonly ignored gender issues.

Both in Mesopotamia and Israel, prophets were individual persons entrusted by a divine power with a special message; they were also individuals and groups who were part of the cultic personnel and expected to respond to direct or indirect requests for a divine message.

MIRIAM

Miriam is the first woman identified in the Bible as a prophet (Exod. 15:20–21). She is so described in connection with being a musician and song leader, a role connected with prophesying in the later tradition (1 Chron. 25:1; see also Ps. 68:26). Miriam invokes the opening line of Moses' Song at the Sea (Exod. 15:1). Together with her brothers, Moses and Aaron, she is among the key leaders in the Exodus-Wilderness period and is so celebrated even in later prophetic tradition (Mic. 6:4). The account in Numbers 12, from the epic tradition, which tells of Miriam and Aaron challenging the exclusive authority of Moses—"Has the Lord spoken only through Moses? Has he not spoken through us also?"—points to a claim as a revealer of God, not only as a singer. (Note also how Aaron, her co-conspirator, is described in Exod. 7:1, from the Priestly source, as Moses' prophet, i.e., as able to speak as Moses' intermediary with Pharaoh, to whom Moses is as god; the same role is assigned to him in Exod. 4:16, by the Elohistic or northern source, without the specific title.) In being identified as a prophet, Miriam is comparable to Abraham, so titled in Gen. 20:7 (Elohistic source; see also Ps. 105:15), to whom God appears and who intercedes with God, though he too is not associated with giving oracles.

In Numbers 12, Miriam is also named first of the conspirators against Moses, and the initial verbal form in Numbers 12:1 is feminine singular. This preferential order (though not maintained in Numbers 12:4–5) together with the subsequent punishment as directed only to Miriam, has suggested to some interpreters that, not only was Miriam the leader in this protest, but also that the claim to separate divine revelation is but a remnant of what was at one time a much more decisive role for Miriam than the present sources indicate. Note also that in Numbers 12:6–7, Moses is described as having "mouth to mouth" encounters with God, unlike prophets who have visions or dreams. This could be taken as a tacit admission that Miriam (and Aaron) also had divine revelations. There is no substantial basis in the biblical texts for constructing a more fundamental role for Miriam. Nonetheless, in the Dead Sea Scroll (Qumran) text 4QRP [4Q365 Frg. 6 ii 7], an expanded text of Exodus 15:21 provides the words of a song, somewhat different from the Song of Moses, in which Miriam tells the women singers to extol God who rescued them from the enemy. Thus this Qumran text exhibits a new song by Miriam, not the suggested repetition of the preceding Song of Moses, and thereby provides a more important role for Miriam.

DEBORAH

Deborah is the only Israelite woman identified with the traditional role of the "judge" in early Israel, a person inspired by God to rescue (some of the people of) Israel from the dominance of outside forces. These judges (*shofetim*) were not judicial figures but temporary military leaders who rescued Israel from attackers and then retired into the background; the term is better translated as "chieftain" or "deliverer," as indicated by alternative titles used, such as "savior" (Ehud; Judg. 3:15). Deborah is also presented as giving judicial decisions; she thus has the dual role of deliverer and judge.

The Song of Deborah in Judges 5, the poetic account, identifies Deborah as joining with Barak, who is then sublimated by feminine singular forms and first-person references to Deborah, in describing the desperate situation of Israel and its subsequent defeat of the Canaanite kings. Deborah is described in a role similar to that of the deliverers, although her only specific title in Judges 5 is "a mother in Israel." In the later prose account in Judges 4, Deborah has many titles. She is identified as "a prophet-woman (literally, a woman [and] a prophet), the wife of Lappidoth, who was judg-

Deborah depicted in an engraving by Gustave Doré in 1866 (Chris Hellier/Corbis).

ing Israel." Unlike the other rescuing judges, she is described as sitting under the palm of Deborah in the Ephraimite hill-country, with the Israelite people coming to her for a decision in some dispute—thus as having a judicial role as well. Deborah is also the one who conveys to Barak God's command to lead the Israelite forces against he Canaanite general, Sisera. As such, by summoning Barak as the "deliverer," Deborah is acting in the traditional role of God, who otherwise is the one who summons the "deliverer." Barak acknowledges Deborah's special role by insisting that she accompany him in the forthcoming battle, which she does. Ultimately, in both Judges 4 and Judges 5 Sisera is dispatched not by Barak but by Jael, the wife of a Kenite, a non-Israelite. Both accounts celebrate the empowerment and initiative of women—Deborah as not only giving judicial guidance but also herself summoning the "deliverer," and Jael as a dangerous opponent who is seriously underrated by Sisera.

Like Miriam, Deborah is portrayed as an inspired singer (Judg. 5:1, 12) and identified as a prophet. Though she does not deliver a formal oracle, in Judges 4 she does convey God's command to Barak. This quality of being inspired might also relate to her judicial role, in which she could have used oracular techniques.

Like other leaders in early Israel, Deborah is described in the tradition as having several roles. She is uniquely identified as "a mother in Israel," reminiscent of Elisha's reference to Elijah as "my father, my father, the chariotry of Israel and its horses" (2 Kings 2:12), and King Joash's similar reference to Elisha (2 Kings 13:14; see also 2 Kings 6:21).

Interestingly, the name Deborah means "bee"; a similar Greek title (and name), Melissa, also meaning "bee," is used of priestesses of the goddesses Demeter and Artemis, among others. Honey, of course, was a primary source of sweet nourishment, suggesting yet another element of Deborah's role.

HULDAH

In the report in 2 Kings 22 and 2 Chronicles 34 of the discovery of the "scroll of the law" during temple repairs in the eighteenth year of King Josiah (c. 622 B.C.E.), the scroll passes from the high priest to the royal scribe to the king. Upon hearing the scroll read out, King Josiah engages in a mourning ritual and commands his close advisors: "Go, inquire of God concerning the words of this scroll." The king's advisors choose to consult a resident of Jerusalem, "Huldah, the prophet, the wife of Shallum, who was the son of Tikvah [or Tokhath], son of Harhas [or Hasrah], the keeper of the wardrobe." Huldah responds with an oracle, like a traditional prophet—"Thus says the Lord"—and authenticates the scroll and its dire consequences, without reference to ameliorating repentance, while assuring the king in another oracle that because of his piety he himself would die in peace. (This latter assurance, which implies the benefits of repentance, did not prove to be true for the king in 609.) Huldah, following this critical moment, is heard from no more, though later redactors have surely pondered—and revised—her words. Huldah parallels prophets such as Nathan, Micaiah, Elisha, and Jeremiah, from whom guidance was sought. That she is apparently closely identified with the Jerusalem aristocracy through her husband (Shallum, in charge of the palace or temple clothing, should not be confused with Jeremiah's uncle) suggests that she may have been viewed by the royal officials as a safe source for authentication. Yet Huldah most clearly exemplifies traditional prophecy and is the only identifiable woman prophet during the monarchical period. The reference in Isaiah 8:3 is to Isaiah's wife, who, even though she may actually have been a court prophet or, as some suggest, a temple singer, is not described as playing a prophetic role.

NOADIAH

The least well-known of the women prophets, presumably omitted in the rabbinic list as a false prophet, Noadiah (Neh. 6:14) even has her gender questioned in the Septuagint text, 2 Esdras 16:14, which uses the masculine form of "prophet" for Noadiah. (Ezra 8:33 mentions a Levite named Noadiah, showing the name's masculine potential.) At a time when Nehemiah's work on the rebuilding of the Jerusalem city walls was nearing completion, Nehemiah 6 reports various efforts to discourage or discredit Nehemiah. These efforts are attributed to Sanballat, governor of Samaria, and his allies Tobiah (of Tarnsjordan) and Geshem, the Arab. Nehemiah even went to the house of Shemaiah, who offered him prophetic advice, but Nehemiah took it as bad advice and concluded that "God had not sent him" but rather than Sanballat and Tobiah had hired him. Nehemiah condemns them and adds condemnation for "Noadiah, the (woman) prophet and the rest of the prophets who were seeking to scare me." Yet the text also indicates that Nehemiah's foes had considerable support from within Judah.

Given the internal difficulties, and the strain still present between those who had returned and those who had remained in Judah during the Babylonian exile, it may well be that Noadiah regarded herself as an authentic Judaean prophet opposing the political authority of the Persian Empire as represented in the person of Nehemiah. She cannot merely be dismissed as a "false" prophet or as a hireling of others. The complexities of that period allow many reconstructions, none of which can be conclusively demonstrated.

OTHER REFERENCES

Ezekiel 13:17–23 refers to Israelite women "who keep on prophesying from their (own) heart," with God instructing Ezekiel to prophesy against them. The practices condemned by Ezekiel do not relate to traditional prophecy, and the specific title prophet is not used of these women. The verbal form employed, though used on occasion for traditional prophets, also has the sense of describing behavior typical of prophets, specifically suggesting some kind of ecstasy. The practices cited make use of various magical techniques, and the women are castigated by Ezekiel as "hunting souls" for hire. Such marginal roles accessible to women do not make them prophets in the traditional sense. However, Joel 2:28 (3:1) "And it will happen that I will pour out my spirit on all persons, and your sons and your daughters shall prophesy, your elders shall dream dreams, and your young men shall see visions" suggests that women may assume prophetic roles and that God's charismatic spirit will come and level all distinctions of gender and age.

BIBLIOGRAPHY

Bellis, Alice Ogden. *Helpmates, Harlots, and Heroes: Women's Stories in the Hebrew Bible.* 1994.

Bird, Phylis A. *Missing Persons and Mistaken Identities: Women and Gender in Ancient Israel.* 1997.

Brenner, Athalya. *The Israelite Woman: Social Role and Literary Type in Biblical Narrative.* 1985.

Burns, Rita J. *Has the Lord Indeed Spoken Only Through Moses? A Study of the Biblical Portrait of Miriam.* 1987.

Carroll, Robert P. "Co-opting the Prophets: Nehemiah and Noadiah." In *Priests, Prophets and Scribes: Essays on the Formation and Heritage of Second Temple Judaism in Honour of Joseph Blenkinsopp.* Edited by Eugene Ulrich, John W. Wright, Robert P. Carroll, and Philip R. Davies. 1992.

Day, Peggy L., ed. *Gender and Difference in Ancient Israel.* 1989.

Pardes, Ilana. *Countertraditions in the Bible: A Feminist Approach.* 1992.

Rasmussen, Rachel C. "Deborah the Woman Warrior." In *Anti-Covenant: Counter-Reading Women's Lives in the Hebrew Bible.* Edited by Mieke Bal. 1989.

Terrien, Samuel. *Till the Heart Sings: A Biblical Theology of Manhood and Womanhood.* 1985.

Trible, Phyllis. "Bringing Miriam Out of the Shadows." *Bible Review* (February 1989):14–25, 34.

Winter, Urs. *Frau und Göttin. Exegetische und ikonographische Studien zum weiblichen Gottesbild im Alten Israel und in dessen Umwelt.* 1983.

HERBERT BARDWELL HUFFMON

Hecate

Hecate was a Greek goddess with a wide range of interests. The poet Hesiod (eighth or seventh century B.C.E.) provides our earliest description, crediting her with the ability to help many different types of people in many ways; he particularly emphasizes her role as a goddess concerned with the care of children (*Theogony,* lines 411–452). This role and the related duty of helping at the time of childbirth are amply attested for Hecate in other ancient sources as well; it is likely that Hecate was identified with such attributes in her homeland of Caria (on the west coast of modern Turkey) before she entered Greece. These qualities closely associated or even identified her with Artemis, who also served as a birth goddess and caretaker of children.

One of Hecate's other important roles was protecting people at dangerous liminal places, such as the doorway or places where three roads met (the latter gave rise to her Roman name, Trivia, which literally means "Three-Roads"). Primarily, she protected them against the demons believed to lurk at these places, a duty that led eventually to the belief that Hecate controlled the demons and thus could also send them against unfortunate mortals when angry. This belief, in turn, led to her function as a goddess expected to help witches and magicians, who needed the help of the demons to perform their spells. This attribute lingered beyond classical antiquity, leading to Hecate's portrayal as a horrific witches' goddess in, for example, Shakespeare's *Macbeth* (act 3, scene 5).

BIBLIOGRAPHY

No recent work thoroughly discusses Hecate's role as a birth goddess and caretaker of children, but the ancient sources are well collected in L. R. Farnell, *The Cults of the Greek City States,* vol. 2 (1896), pp. 501–519. (Farnell's interpretations, however, are outdated.) On Hecate as a protector at liminal places and as goddess of demons, see S. I. Johnston, "Crossroads," *Zeitschrift für Papyrologie und Epigraphik* 88 (1991): 217–244. Generally, see also H. Sarian, "Hekate," in *Lexicon Iconographicum Mythologiae Classicae,* vol. 7.1 (1992), pp. 985–1018, with plates in vol. 6.2, pp. 654–673.

SARAH ILES JOHNSTON

Heloise

Heloise (c. 1100–1163 or 1164), was the wife of Abelard and foundress of the Paraclete. Precise historical data on Heloise are limited and details of her birth are unknown. She was the niece of Fulbert, a canon at the Cathedral of Notre Dame in Paris. As a young girl Heloise studied at St. Marie of Argenteuil, a Benedictine convent near Paris, where she excelled in the arts of grammar and rhetoric.

Until recently, Heloise's significance was understood primarily in terms of her personal relationship to Peter Abelard, the century's foremost though controversial logician and theologian. Heloise met Abelard in 1114 or 1115 when Fulbert hired him as her tutor. The events of the next few years definitively shaped her life: a passionate affair with Abelard, the birth of their son, Astralabe, a secret marriage, and Abelard's punitive castration ordered by Fulbert. Finally, in 1117 or 1118, Abelard entered religious life at the royal Abbey of St. Denis after insisting that Heloise profess religious vows at Argenteuil. She was not yet twenty.

monastic houses and remained an active community until its demise during the French Revolution.

Interest in Heloise and Abelard quickly concentrated on Abelard's *Story of My Misfortunes,* a letter to a friend in which he narrates the events related to their love affair and the foundation of the Paraclete. Heloise's reaction to the letter and their subsequent correspondence provided the perfect paradigm of star-crossed lovers.

Prompted perhaps by modern, critical editions of the literature, contemporary writers continue to challenge the authenticity of the letters and have begun to focus on Heloise in her own right. Many new questions have been brought to bear upon the texts: feminist and psycho-historical perspectives, analysis of her literary skills, and reflections upon her unique position regarding an ethics of pure love. Heloise can now be seen as a woman of distinction because of her contribution to the intellectual and spiritual life of the twelfth-century monastic world.

BIBLIOGRAPHY

With the exception of the *Problems of Heloise,* Heloise's writings have been translated into English by Betty Radice in *The Letters of Abelard and Heloise* (1974). Radice includes the poignant letter to Heloise from Peter the Venerable, the abbot of Cluny, who had befriended Abelard in the last months of his life and arranged for his burial at the Paraclete.

A classic study of the correspondence that highlights Heloise's significance is Etienne Gilson's *Heloise and Abelard* (1960).

Other literature reflecting contemporary research includes three collected essays by Peter Dronke: "Abelard and Heloise in Medieval Testimonies," "Heloise's *Problema* and *Letters:* Some Questions of Form and Content," and "Heloise, Abelard, and Some Recent Discussions," in *Intellectuals and Poets in Medieval Europe,* (1992); Eileen Kearney, "Heloise: Inquiry and the *Sacra pagina,*" in *Ambiguous Realities: Women in the Middle Ages and Renaissance,* edited by Carole Levin and Jeanie Watson (1987); David Luscombe, "Monasticism in the Lives and Writings of Heloise and Abelard," in *Monastic Studies: The Continuity of Tradition, II,* edited by Judith Loades (1991); and Glenda McLeod, "'Wholly Guilty, Wholly Innocent': Self-Definition in Héloïse's Letters to Abélard," in *Dear Sister: Medieval Women and the Epistolary Genre,* edited by Karen Cherewatuk and Ulricke Wiethaus (1993).

Critical editions of the correspondence include Abelard's *Story of My Misfortunes* and Heloise's first two letters in *Historia calamitatum: texte critique avec introduction,* edited by Jacques Monfrin (1959).

Heloise Portrait by Louis-Marie Lante (Leonard de Selva/ Corbis)

In 1129, Suger, Abbot of Saint Denis, repossessed Argenteuil. Along with several companions, Heloise accepted Abelard's offer of his lands located near Troyes. When Innocent II approved the new community of the Paraclete in 1131, Heloise became its first prioress.

Heloise came into her own as foundress of the Paraclete. She took great pains to ensure that Abelard serve as founding father and had a singular influence on the formation of early Paraclete literature. In her letter-commentary on the Benedictine Rule, Heloise asked Abelard to accommodate the rule to the needs of women. Abelard not only provided a Rule of Life but also a treatise on the origin of nuns, a hymnal, sermons, prayers, and a breviary. At her request Abelard commented on the *Hexaemeron* and provided directives for spiritual reading (*lectio divina*) and an exhortation to studies. They collaborated on the *Problems of Heloise,* a series of exegetical questions raised by Heloise with Abelard's solutions.

Heloise's leadership at the Paraclete continued after Abelard's death in 1142. She founded several daughter houses and even allowed the Paraclete to come under Cistercian influence. At her death in 1163 or 1164, the Paraclete had distinguished itself from among other

J. P. Muckle also edited much of the correspondence including the *Historia calamitatum,* "Abelard's Letter of Consolation to a Friend," *Mediaeval Studies* 12 (1950): 163–213; "The Personal Letters between Abelard and Heloise," *Mediaeval Studies* 15 (1953): 47–94; and "The Letter of Heloise on Religious Life and Abelard's First Reply," *Mediaeval Studies* 17 (1955): 240–281.

T. P. McLaughlin edited the Paraclete Rule, "Abelard's Rule for Religious Women," *Mediaeval Studies* 18 (1956): 241–292.

Heloise's letter to Peter the Venerable has been edited by Giles Constable in *The Letters of Peter the Venerable,* 2 vols. (1967), and Peter's "Letter to Heloise" after the death of Abelard can be found in *Peter the Venerable: Selected Letters,* edited by Janet Martin in collaboration with Giles Constable (1974).

Two articles that treat Heloise in a medieval period context are Barbara Newman, "Authority, Authenticity, and the Repression of Heloise," in her collection of essays *From Virile Woman to WomanChrist: Studies in Medieval Religion and Literature* (1995), and Christopher N. L. Brooke, "The Correspondence of Heloise and Abelard" and "The Marriage of Heloise and Abelard" in his major study, *The Medieval Idea of Marriage* (1989).

EILEEN F. KEARNEY

Hera

The ancient Greek goddess Hera is shrouded in mystery. According to Pausanias, Hera was worshiped under various names. The name Pais, meaning "child," emphasized her maidenhood. The name Teleia, meaning "fulfilled," referred to Hera as wife of Zeus, whereas Chera, meaning "widow," evoked an angry Hera separated from her husband, Zeus (Pausanius VIII.22.2; 31.9; IX.2.7). The Argive legend that Hera regained her maidenhood yearly (II.38.2), and Hera's frequent depiction with the *Horai,* or Seasons (II.13.2–4; V.16.6), point to Hera as a fertility goddess embodying seasonal renewal and marriage. Consequently, in Sparta mothers were said to sacrifice to the goddess under the name Aphrodite Hera at the time of their daughters' marriages (III.13.19), and in Olympia the maiden footraces celebrated in honor of Hera were said to be Hippodameia's offering of thanks for her marriage to Pelops (V.16.1–4). Her most important rite was the *hieros gamos,* or sacred marriage, in which participants reenacted the goddess's marriage to Zeus. Argos and Samos were most sacred to Hera, thus she is often called Samian or Argive Hera.

Hera, 470 b.c.e.   (Mimmo Jodice/Corbis)

In literary tradition Hera remains a goddess of marriage (Aeschylus, *Eumenides* 214ff.; Aristophanes, *Thesmophoriazousai* 973ff., *Birds* 1731ff.; Theocritus 17.131ff.). But she is also the angry, vengeful, and scheming wife and sister of Zeus, with whom she forever quarrels (Pausanius IV, etc.). Angry at Zeus for his production of Athena without her, according to the *Homeric Hymn to Apollo,* Hera parthenogenetically produces Typhaon to be a scourge to mortals (305ff.); according to Hesiod, however, she parthenogenetically produces Hephaestus (*Theogony* 927). Hera's anger also flares up at Zeus' philandering with mortal women, and she takes out her wrath on the offspring of these couplings. One object of her anger is Heracles, son of Zeus and the mortal Alcmene. In Hesiod, Hera nurtures the Lernean Hydra and the Nemean Lion to plague Heracles (*Theogony* 313ff.). Although Zeus often finds his pleasures elsewhere, the tale of Ixion's failed seduction of Hera is a testimony to the goddess's steadfast monogamy (Pindar, *Pythian II.*26ff.). Despite her husband's philandering, Hera, the goddess of marriage, never takes a lover other than Zeus.

In Homer's *Iliad* Hera steadfastly stands by the Achaeans and wreaks havoc upon their enemies, the Trojans (I.517ff; II.14,40ff.), who have broken the marriage bond by kidnapping Helen, the wife of the

Achaean Menelaus. In Virgil's *Aeneid*, Hera, as the Roman goddess Juno, brings misfortune upon Aeneas in revenge for her beauty spurned in the Judgment of Paris (I.4,25ff; IV.166; etc.).

BIBLIOGRAPHY

Arafat, K. W. "Pausanias and the Temple of Hera at Olympia." *The Annual of the British School at Athens* 90 (1995): 461–473.

Burkert, Walter. *Greek Religion.* 1985.

Cowan, Louise. "Hera: Goddess and Wife." In *The Olympians: Ancient Dieties as Archetypes.* Edited by Joanne H. Stroud. 1995.

O'Brien, Joan V. *The Transformation of Hera: A Study of Ritual, Hero, and the Goddess in the* Iliad. 1993.

Serwint, Nancy. "The Female Athletic Costume at the Heraia and Prenuptial Initiation Rites." *American Journal of Archeology* 97 (1993): 403–422.

DANIELLA REINHARD

Hermaphrodite

The word *hermaphrodite* combines the names of the Greek fertility deities Hermes and Aphrodite (or possibly her male analogue, Aphroditus). The word is also used of human beings having indeterminate sexual organs or both male and female primary sexual characteristics; real human beings with these characteristics were regarded as ominous by Roman writers and as impaired in Jewish legal contexts. Hermaphrodites appear in older Greek art as lesser divinities, perhaps with apotropaic functions (like the statues called Herms). In Hellenistic and Roman art they inspire an erotic frisson; in literature and moral philosophy of the period, they are associated with eunuchs, passive homosexuals, and cross-dressers, as emasculated males. In Ovid's *Metamorphoses* (4.285–4.388) Hermaphroditus's bisexuality constitutes a loss of virility resulting from melding with a nymph who desired him. Gnostic texts also see these figures as imperfect or evil, representations of unbridled sexuality.

Antiquity knew two other forms of double being: the double-bodied human creature or creation apparently deriving from Plato's *Symposium*, presented most explicitly in early Jewish texts and in the syzygies or divine twins of gnostic and hermetic mythology. Gnostic and early Christian texts also offer the union of opposites as a spiritual ambition, sometimes including the union of male and female. The revision of Genesis 1:27 in Galatians 3:28 may imagine the original and ultimate humanity as androgynous. Hermaphrodites occur in

An Indian hermaphrodite, depicted in a late eighteenth-century engraving (Christel Gerstenberg/Corbis)

the myth and ritual of many, but by no means all, cultures. Wendy Doniger O'Flaherty's study of Indian androgynes divided such figures into male and female types; male androgynes are positive figures, females negative.

BIBLIOGRAPHY

Much of the interest in hermaphrodites and androgyny in antique religion was inspired by Marie Delcourt's studies of art and ritual in Greek antiquity: *Hermaphrodite: Myths and Rites of the Bisexual Figure in Classical Antiquity*, translated from the French by Jennifer Nicholson (1961), pp. 43–46, 60; *Hermaphroditea: Recherches sur l'être double promoteur de la fertilité dans le monde classique* (1966); and *"Utrumque-Neutrum,"* *Mélanges d'histoire des religions offerts à Henri-Charles Puech* (1974), pp. 117–123. Interest in the figure in Judaism, Christianity, and gnosticism was sparked by Wayne A. Meeks, "The Image of the Androgyne: Some Uses of a Symbol in Earliest Christianity," *History of Religions* 13 (1974): 165–208. Dennis Ronald MacDonald developed some aspects of Meeks's essay in *There Is No Male and Female: The Fate of a Dominical Saying in Paul and Gnosticism* (1983); for a critical approach to the imagery, see M. R. D'Angelo, "Transcribing Sexual Politics: Images of the Androgyne in Discourses of Antique Religion," in *Description and Inscription/Descrizione e Inscrizione: Politiche del Discourso,* edited by Carla Locatelli and Giovanna Covi (forthcoming). For a cross-cultural anthropological study, see Hermann Baumann, *Das Doppelte Geschlecht* (1955). Wendy Doniger O'Flaherty, *Women, Androgynes and Other Mythical Beasts* (1980), treats the figure in the perspective of psychology and the history of (primarily Indian) religions.

See also Androgyny; Sexuality.

MARY ROSE D'ANGELO

Hermeneutics

An Overview

Hermeneutics has had several meanings over the centuries. Used in a general sense, it denotes "the study of interpretation" or "the art of interpretation." The Greek roots *hermeneutikos* (for interpreting) and *hermeneuein* (to interpret) convey this broad meaning. In a more specific sense, the word has been used to signify the practice of interpreting sacred texts; this meaning is connoted by its etymological link to the Greek god Hermes, who acted as intermediary between the gods and humankind. Thus, the most ancient usage of the term denotes the art of reading divine messages, such as oracular signs, and only later came to be used to indicate the interpretation of sacred texts generally.

During the patristic and medieval ages of Biblical criticism, *hermeneutics* began to apply to the various methods available for the interpretation of the Jewish and Christian scriptures, characterized by a fourfold model: literal, tropological or moral, allegorical, and anagogical readings of the Bible. It was not until the eighteenth and nineteenth centuries that "modern hermeneutics" emerged with the writing of Freidrich Schleiermacher and Wilhelm Dilthey, which shifted the debate from methods of interpretation to the philosophical study of interpretation itself. Schleiermacher first raised the problem of the "hermeneutic circle" to delineate his theory that interpretation rests on the relation between "the whole" (the text) and its "parts" (such as the language, culture, and life of the author, which contribute to the production of any text): One cannot understand the whole without first comprehending the elements of which it consists, and vice versa; the parts cannot be understood without grasping the whole, resulting in a perpetual and reciprocal rela-

tion of interpretation (diagrammed as a circle). Further, Dilthey adjoined the social sciences to the study of interpretation and explored the possibility of a psychological transposition between a reader and the writer of a historically informed text. The subsequent study of hermeneutics evolved to include the anthropological, psychological, social, and historical contexts of both the writer and reader in a complex relationship of meaning and interpretation.

It was not until the twentieth century that hermeneutics took on its particularized meaning to designate the specific philosophical school of interpretation informed by the existential writings of Martin Heidegger and Hans-Georg Gadamer. In this distinct sense, hermeneutics constitutes an investigation of Being (and later for post-Heideggerians, "the self" or "subject" who interprets), particularly in relation to language production. Heidegger asks: "how is understanding possible at all?" and insists that any theory of interpretation must first be based on an investigation of the meaning of "Being" (Dasein) itself, which, in turn, is founded and expressed in the revelatory medium of language. Gadamer further contributed a complex model of interpretation as a product of embedded knowledge, a reflection of the cultural, historical, and linguistic "horizons" of the reader. A "fusion of horizons" can occur between the reader and the equally embedded text as a result of the dynamic nature of linguistic production, thus affording a further shift in the reader's "horizons." Philosophical writings of the late twentieth century that fall within the realm of a Gademerian or Heideggerian-informed (though often "critical") hermeneutics include those of such disparate figures as Paul Ricoeur, Jacques Derrida, Jürgen Habermas, and Julia Kristeva, who all, through highly diverse methodologies, connect linguistic performance and the subjective process with interpretation.

Today the word hermeneutics can be used to describe a number of interpretive processes not limited to those delineated above. One of the most significant interpretive models to emerge and develop in the twentieth century is feminist criticism. For the study of women and world religion, feminist hermeneutics has included within its realm: a) the demonstration of a patriarchal order or agenda implicit in the structure of sacred texts and their exegesis; b) the examination of women's substantial contribution to religion; and c) uncovering women's history (lost stories, lives, and texts that challenge the view that all cultural productions are "man"-made. Feminist hermeneutics thus reveals new information about women and their religious lives that had previously been concealed by inadequate and prejudicial interpretive models; it further questions the "objective" and "impartial" standpoint on which so much patriarchal scholarship claims to rest.

BIBLIOGRAPHY

The primary texts for hermeneutics can be located in a small number of dense and difficult works. Schleiermacher did not write a localized account of his hermeneutical theory, but his study and lectures notes on the topic have been neatly collated in one volume, *Hermeneutics: The Handwritten Manuscripts*, edited by Heinz Kimmerle and translated by James Duke and Jack Forstman (1977). A feminist response to Schleiermacher is provided in *Schleiermacher and Feminism: Sources, Evaluations, and Responses*, edited by Iain G. Nicol (1992). Dilthey's major writings on hermeneutics have also been collected together in a single text, *Hermeneutics and the Study of History: Selected Works*, vol. 4 (1996), edited by Rudolf A. Makkreel and Frithjof Rodi. The essays included in this volume span Dilthey's career and can largely be read in conjunction with Schleiermacher's *Hermeneutics*, in particular as a response to the psychological aspect of Schleiermacher's method.

Heidegger's *Being and Time* (John Macquarrie and Edward Robinson, trans., 1962) combined with his subsequent response to and criticism of his own work, *On Time and Being* (Joan Stambaugh, trans., 1972), constitute the starting point for much of contemporary hermeneutical theory. *Poetry, Language, Thought* (Albert Hofstadter, trans., 1971) contains Heidegger's later reflections on the relationship between language, poetry, art, and Dasein. Hans-George Gadamer's monumental *Truth and Method* (Joel Winsheimer and Donald G. Marshall, trans., 1989) revives the German romantic terminology of "hermeneutics" in critical synthesis with Heidegger's notions of "Dasein." An investigation of the normative structure of Gadamer's "ontology" constitutes the focus of Robin Schott's "Whose Home Is it Anyway? A Feminist Response to Gadamer's Hermeneutics," in Hugh J. Silverman, ed., *Gadamer and Hermeneutics* (1991).

Paul Ricoeur's engagement with Gadamer and the hermeneutical tradition can be found in his *Hermeneutics and the Human Sciences* (John B. Thompson, ed., 1981), which includes one of the most clear and succinct accounts of historical hermeneutics, "The Task of Hermeneutics" (pp. 43–62). Eloise A. Buker addresses Ricoeur's engagement with Gadamer in "Feminist Social Theory and Hermeneutics: An Empowering Dialectic?" *Social Epistemology* 4, no. 1 (1990), pp. 23–39. Jürgen Habermas's critical reception of Gadamer is encapsulated in his *Knowledge and Human Interests* (Jeremy Shapiro, trans., 1971).

Diverse "post-structural" hermeneutic methods can be found in Jacques Derrida's *Of Grammatology* (Gayatri Chakravorty Spivak, ed. and trans., 1976) and Julia Kristeva's *Revolution in Poetic Language* (Leon S. Roudiez, trans., 1984). *Derrida and Feminism: Recasting the Question of Woman* (1997), edited by Ellen K. Feder, Mary Rawlinson, and Emily Zakin, offers a critical appraisal of Derrida's method in relation to feminist theory. A helpful feminist analysis of Julia Kristeva's work is contained in Kelly Oliver's *Reading Kristeva: Unraveling the Double-Bind* (1993).

KATHLEEN O'GRADY

Feminist Hermeneutics

Feminist hermeneutics is concerned with theories of interpreting the relationship of women and the Bible. How did women make sense of the Bible in various religious and cultural traditions? How are women to read the Bible today? What are the best or most appropriate interpretive methods and disciplinary approaches to the question of biblical women? How should women readers approach legal and historical materials in biblical texts? How should they read informational gaps and absences of women? Feminist hermeneutics deals with questions of specific interpretations of narratives about women, as well as with the theoretical issue of how to interpret these women's presentations and contributions to the biblical story and to biblical history. The field is devoted to making explicit the androcentric assumptions of translators and traditional interpreters; it rejects the possibility of objective, neutral, or value-free interpretation.

As a young and still emerging field in biblical studies, it is indebted both to literary and historical criticism on the one hand and to women's studies, notably feminist religious studies, on the other. Spurred by the critique in such ground-breaking works as Mary Daly's *Beyond God the Father* (1973) and Rosemary Radford Ruether's collection *Religion and Sexism* (1974), feminist interpreters were faced with the daunting task of rereading the Bible as women. The first responses to the biblical text sought to "depatriarchalize" the Bible, or to strip it of centuries of distortive translations and interpretations. In *God and the Rhetoric of Sexuality* (1978), Phyllis Trible used the methods of rhetorical criticism, offering a close reading of the biblical text. By focusing on the text itself, Trible showed that Eve is presented in less condemnatory terms than is traditionally believed. Furthermore, the disturbing lack of equality between Adam and Eve introduced in Genesis was understood to be "redeemed" in the Song of Songs. Trible suggested that the Bible includes female "countervoices" distinct from the patriarchal and androcentric perspective of much of the biblical text. Whereas interpreters of the Hebrew Bible tended to focus on the text itself, New Testament interpreters tended to use historical-critical methods going behind and beyond the text to the historical and social context in search of clues as to the actual contributions of women to the early church. The move from the text to what Elisabeth Schüssler Fiorenza called a "feminist life center" was effected by a combination of liberation theology—the attempt to liberate a life-affirming message from the patriarchal context shaping the Bible—and historical-critical methods placing women at the center of Christian life and theology. In *In Memory of Her* (1983), Schüssler Fiorenza combined a feminist hermeneutics of suspicion and a hermeneutics of remembrance, the one focusing on the androcentric biblical text and the latter focusing on the lives of women in the history of Jesus' early disciples. The biblical text was approached as offering clues and hints as to the real-life accomplishments of women in the early Jesus movement, and historical reconstruction was used to fill out a picture only partially presented in the biblical text. Another attempt to articulate the challenges of a Christian feminist hermeneutics was made by Mary Ann Tolbert *The Bible and Feminist Hermeneutics* (1983). Tolbert identified two feminist approaches: an "ascendancy position," which pursues a radical response of revolution and separatism, and an "equality position," which aims for reconciliation and the full humanity of women. In *Bread Not Stone* (1984) Schüssler Fiorenza argued for reclaiming the Bible as a feminist heritage and resource while at the same time subjecting the Bible to critical evaluations. The method of historical reconstruction was to serve a liberating reading, while a feminist consciousness was to serve the critical rejection of women's subordination. A similar synthesis from a literary-textual perspective was offered by Phyllis Trible in *Texts of Terror* (1984).

In *Lethal Love* (1987) Mieke Bal argued for narrative theory as a hermeneutic tool, elaborating on narratological concepts of focalization, characterization, analogy, and chronology and combining them with gender ideologies to explore male–female pairs in the biblical narrative. In *Death and Dissymmetry* (1988), Bal continues her critique of traditional biblical criticism, with special focus on historical scholarship. Using deconstructionist, psychoanalytic, and feminist literary frameworks, Bal challenges some of the most influential scholarship on the book of Judges by focusing on the repressed woman in the text.

The 1990s attest to a growing diversity in political, theoretical, and religious perspectives and demonstrate an interest in hermeneutic inclusiveness. Neither the humanities nor the social sciences will dominate this exciting field; debate and heterogeneity will determine its development for some time to come.

BIBLIOGRAPHY

Brenner, Athalya, ed. *A Feminist Companion to Genesis.* 1993.

Briggs, Sheila. " 'Buried With Christ': The Politics of Identity and the Poverty of Interpretation." In *The Book and the Text: The Bible and Literary Theory.* Edited by Regina Schwartz. 1990.

Collins, Adela Yarbro, ed. *Feminist Perspectives on Biblical Scholarship.* 1985. Showcases the methodological diversity and theoretical plurality within the field.

Fish, Stanley. *Is There a Text in This Class? The Authority of Interpretive Communities.* 1980.

Foucault, Michel. *Power/Knowledge: Selected Interviews and Other Writings, 1972–1977.* Edited by Colin Gordon. 1972.

Fuchs, Esther. "The Literary Characterization of Mothers and Sexual Politics in the Hebrew Bible." In *Feminist Perspectives on Biblical Scholarship.* Edited by A. Y. Collins. 1985. The first ideological critique of biblical narrative.

———. "Who Is Hiding the Truth? Deceptive Women and Biblical Androcentrism." In *Feminist Perspectives on Biblical Scholarship.* Edited by A. Y. Collins. 1985.

Mitchell, W. J. T., ed. *The Politics of Interpretation.* 1982.

Newsom, Carol A., and Sharon H. Ringe, eds. *The Women's Bible Commentary.* 1992.

Osiek, Carolyn. "Feminist and the Bible: Hermeneutic Alternatives." In *Feminist Perspectives on Biblical Scholarship.* Edited by A. Y. Collins. 1985. The first methodological taxonomy of feminist hermeneutics.

Reagan, Charles E., and David Stewart, eds. *The Philosophy of Paul Ricoeur: An Anthology of His Work.* 1978.

Russell, Letty M. *Feminist Interpretation of the Bible.* 1985. Includes the first articulations of black feminist and Jewish feminist interpretations.

Schüssler Fiorenza, Elisabeth. *But She Said: Feminist Practices of Biblical Interpretation.* 1992.

ESTHER FUCHS

Hestia and Vesta

Hestia was the ancient Greek goddess associated with the hearth and hearthfire, the Greek counterpart of Roman Vesta. The child of Rhea and Kronos (Hesiod,

Theogony 453–454), Hestia disliked the "works of Aphrodite," swore an oath to remain a virgin, and was granted by Zeus a "great honor instead of marriage": to sit at the heart of the household and receive offerings (*Homeric Hymn to Aphrodite* 5.21–32; see also *Homeric Hymn to Hestia* 29). Rooted in and identified with this immovable locus of domestic and civic life (her name was synonymous with the word for hearth), Hestia was unable to venture forth, much less to take part in the procession of the gods (Plato, *Phaedrus* 247a). The development of myth and cult associated with her is thus conspicuously constricted for a divinity of the Greek pantheon. Hestia was depicted infrequently in Greek art, but when she appears it is as a mature woman, veiled and draped.

From earliest times the hearth was the symbolic center of life in civic and private contexts. It was where foreign dignitaries were entertained and suppliants sought refuge. In historical times this political center was located in the office of the city magistrates, within which the sacred fire was maintained. Colonists likely took fire from there to the civic hearth of their new colony. At Delphi the hearth was sometimes regarded as communal for all of Greece (Plutarch, *Aristides* 20.4). Newcomers (brides, slaves, and newborns) were introduced to each household by rituals connected with the hearth. Hestia often received first offerings and was first addressed in prayers and oaths (Pindar, *Nemean Ode* 11.1–7; Aristophanes, *Birds* 865–866). That Plato retained Hestia as one of only three gods for his utopia attests to the importance of this deity in Greek tradition (*Laws* 745b, 848b).

The worship of Vesta was originally a private cult connected to the family but in historical times developed into a state cult that expressed and guaranteed the continuity of the Roman people. Tradition connects the origin of her cult with legendary kings, Romulus and Numa, near the time of Rome's founding, 753 B.C.E. (Livy, *Histories* I.20.3; Dionysius of Halicarnassus, *Roman Antiquities* II.64.5–65.4; Varro, *De Lingua Latina* 5.74). The circular shrine to Vesta in the Roman Forum contained no cult statue but housed her eternal fire, sacred things, and the *fascinum* (an apotropaic, erect phallus) (Ovid, *Fasti* VI.295–298).

The only female priesthood in Rome attended Vesta. The six Vestal Virgins were primarily chosen from senatorial families; they maintained strict chastity during their thirty-year minimum service to the goddess. A Vestal convicted of any sexual breach of her vow of chastity was sentenced to burial alive (Pliny, *Epistle* 4.11; Plutarch, *Numa* 10.4–7). Though they could marry after their term, few did, and bad luck was associated with such unions (Dionysius of Halicarnassus, *Roman Antiquities* II.67.2; Plutarch, *Numa* X.1–2). Upon en-

Vesta, Roman sculpture, third to fourth centuries C.E. (Charles & Josette Lenars/Corbis)

tering the religious order, they left their father's control without having to enter the tutelage of another male; this constituted a unique status and enabled special privileges, including the right to bequeath property (Aulus Gellius, *Attic Nights* I.12.9).

BIBLIOGRAPHY

Beard, Mary. "The Sexual Status of Vestal Virgins." *Journal of Roman Studies* 70 (1980): 12–27.

Dumézil, Georges. *Archaic Roman Religion.* Translated by Philip Krapp. 1970. Pp. 311–326.

Farnell, Lewis Richard. *The Cults of the Greek States.* Vol. 5. 1909. Pp. 345–373.

Fischer-Hansen, Tobias. "Vesta." In *Lexicon Iconigraphicum Mythologiae Classicae* V. 1990. Pp. 412–420.

Hommel, H. "Vesta." In *Aufstieg und Niedergang der römischen Welt.* Vol. 5, pt. 2. 1972. Pp. 397–420.

Malkin, Irad. *Religion and Colonization in Ancient Greece.* 1987. Pp. 114–134.

Sarian, Haiganuch. "Hestia." In *Lexicon Iconigraph-icum Mythologiae Classicae.* Vol. 5. 1990. Pp. 407–412.

Vernant, Jean-Pierre. *Myth and Thought among the Greeks.* 1983. Pp. 127–175.

See also Home.

G. M. SOTER

Heterodoxy and Orthodoxy

The concepts underlying the terms *heterodoxy* and *orthodoxy*, both derived from Greek, are found in debates over teaching and doctrine in all major world religions. Orthodoxy literally means right opinion or sound doctrine. In usage it denotes what is in accord with authoritatively established practice. Heterodoxy, by contrast, is teaching that dissents from what is generally recognized as normative.

The context of orthodoxy is the consequence of historical and theological processes during which varying doctrines and practices are reconciled or rejected. Heterodoxy can only appear once orthodox criteria have been established. Orthodoxy looks back to the beginnings of the religion for its authority and claims to be in continuity with the original foundation. Heterodoxy appears when the original teachings are unclear or disputed.

While heterodox teachings can continue to survive on the fringes of a religious system, over time such teachings may achieve the recognition of a reform movement within a religious community. Conservative Judaism is one illustration. Alternatively, teachings may be labeled heretical and discarded by self-defining orthodoxy; the repudiated gnostic Christianities of the second and third centuries are examples.

At the close of the twentieth century academics are questioning the assumptions of the Enlightenment regarding the usefulness of the categories of heterodox, orthodox, and heretical. The distinctions are less clear than previously claimed. Scholars are less confident that pure reason and objectivity are possible in the study of religion, with its consequent simplistic distinctions among heterodox, orthodox, and heretical.

Orthodoxy in nonliterate religious communities is defined and expressed through myth and ritual. Myth provides the core content, while ritual reinforces corporate identity through performance. Social organizations regulate interactions within the group, for example in regard to sexuality. Departures threaten the stability of the community and may result in exclusion from group society. The possibility of reintegration is sometimes offered through rituals whereby the offender is again made eligible for group membership.

In literate communities, as a religion moves from an oral tradition to a written one, certain elements are intentionally excluded or they drop out of the transmission of the tradition, while other teachings are singled out for greater attention. When the written tradition is reduced to a recognized canon, further refinement of teaching and doctrine occurs. Heterodoxy arises when there is dissent over decisions of inclusion or exclusion. If the orthodox position is sustained through political or legal means, heterodoxy may represent opposition to the enforced position. Feminist critics point out that in religions relying on canonical traditions, texts that are omitted frequently contain powerful female symbolism. With greater literacy and access to scripture, women may develop interest in divergent traditions where these texts are in circulation, particularly if the writings offer greater opportunities for female expression.

Scholars such as Roger Gryson, Carol Christ, and Elaine Pagels note that women historically have been attracted to movements that have been labeled heterodox or heretical. The implication, either stated or implied, is that heterodox movements allowed women greater voice and potential for leadership than was possible among orthodox groups. This position has been challenged by Shannon McSheffrey in her *Gender and Heresy* (1995). McSheffrey argues that heterodoxy does not necessarily lead to gender equality, nor to questioning patriarchal gender categories. Greater sensitivity to factors that influence the construction of women's identity is leading scholars into more nuanced interpretations of the relationship between gender and heterodoxy. For instance, Buddhism and Jainism, which were initially understood as heterodox movements in the sixth century B.C.E., attracted women in large numbers, as did heterodox movements within Hinduism, such as Bhakti. Some of these women left a legacy of poems describing their religious accomplishments as well as the opposition they experienced from male counterparts.

In many cases, texts concerning nonorthodox religious movements have come down in documents written mainly by their opponents. These cannot always be relied on to give fair or accurate descriptions of women's attraction to heterodox religions. Materials on women are scattered in numerous sources, and for some historical periods and traditions precious little literature has survived.

Among early Christians, heterodox groups such as the second-century Montanists, with its emphasis on ecstatic prophecy, attracted many women. Ascetic communities afforded early medieval Christian women a refuge where their own spirituality could be explored.

Women counted among the supporters of the sixteenth-century Reformers, while in the nineteenth century movements such as the Seventh Day Adventists and the Christian Scientists provided new potential for women's religious expression in worship and in leadership.

Historically, Jewish religious orthodoxy marginalized women by restricting the closeness of the divine relationship to that between God and men, as descendants of Adam. Women's religious experience centered on domestic activities and their performance in accordance with Jewish teachings. In the medieval period Jewish women, like their Muslim sisters, found mysticism a satisfying religious experience that offered an intimate relationship with God. In the twentieth century Reform and Reconstructionist movements within Judaism have appealed to women, particularly those in the United States, seeking a greater voice within the community at large. However, these reformation movements remain unrecognized as Judaism by the Israeli rabbinate. Judith Plaskow (1990) suggests that to the degree that the Jewish community is willing to reinterpret change not as a break with the past, but as representing continuity with tradition, the impact of feminism on women's religious participation will be consolidated.

Within the Muslim world women's opportunities for religious participation have been largely in the mystical movement known as Sufism. The writings of the early Sufis suggest its attraction lay with the independence and autonomy women found. Celebrated as a female model is the ninth-century mystic Rabi'a al-'Adawiyya. Stories about her tell of her undercutting the formalism and literalism of orthodox religion, even to the degree of teaching men in spiritual matters. However, no Muslim female mystic has founded or been in charge of any main Sufi order. Twentieth century Muslim women often display their religious involvement through devotion to particular saints, ritualized through prayers, gifts, and visits to shrines. In Morocco female groups associated with the Jilaliyyat, a Sufi order, gather for weekly prayer over a basketful of stones called the stones of the ancestors. Each year these women also move a pile of sacred rocks to see what is hidden within and to make predictions, particularly with regard to the weather, based on what emerges. In Egypt supernatural forces are appealed to through performance of *zars* or seances. The *zar* is found among many social classes and functions as an exorcising ceremony for both women and men, although the ceremonies are separate. In Nubia the practitioners of *zars* are women, but in other locations, such as Iraq, women assist the men conducting the ceremonies.

BIBLIOGRAPHY

For women in Buddhism see:

Gross, Rita M. *Buddhism after Patriarchy: A Feminist History, Analysis and Reconstruction of Buddhism.* 1993.

Lang, Karen Christina. "Lord Death's Snare: Gender-Related Imagery in the Teragāthā and the Therīgāthā." *Journal of Feminist Studies in Religion* 2, no. 2 (1986):63–79.

Paul, Diana Y. *Women in Buddhism: Images of the Feminine in the Mahāyāna Tradition.* 2d ed. 1985.

For women in Judaism see:

Koltun, Elizabeth, ed. *The Jewish Woman: New Perspectives.* 1976.

Plaskow, Judith. *Standing Again at Sinai: Judaism from a Feminist Perspective.* 1990.

For women in Christianity see:

Burrus, Virginia. "The Heretical Woman as Symbol in Alexander, Athanasius, Epiphanius, and Jerome." *Harvard Theological Review.* 84, no. 3 (1991): 229–248.

Christ, Carol. "Heretics and Outsiders: The Struggle Over Female Power in Western Religions." In *Border Religions of Faith.* Edited by Kenneth Aman. 1987.

Massumi, Brian. *Heterologies: Discourse on the Other.* 1986.

McNamara, Jo Ann. "The Rhetoric of Orthodoxy: Clerical Authority and Female Innovation in the Struggle with Heresy." In *Maps of Flesh and Light: The Religious Experience of Medieval Women Mystics.* Edited by Ulrike Wiesthaus. 1993.

For women in Islam see:

Ahmed, Leila. "Early Islam and the Position of Women: The Problem of Interpretation." In *Women in Middle Eastern History: Shifting Boundaries in Sex and Gender.* Edited by Nikki R. Keddie and Beth Baron. 1991.

Gürsoy-Naskali, Emine. "Women Mystics in Islam." In *Women in Islamic Societies: Social Attitudes and Historical Perspectives.* Edited by Bo Utas. Scandinavian Institute of Asian Studies. 1983.

Keddie, Nikki R., ed. *Scholars, Saints and Sufis: Muslim Religious Institutions Since 1500.* 1978.

DIANE TREACY-COLE

Heterosexism

Heterosexism refers to the structural oppression produced by cultural institutions and practices that privilege or require heterosexuality. Heterosexism as a category of analysis was initially articulated by North American feminists who called attention to the fact that most contemporary cultural formations, including religion, define heterosexuality as the only legal, normal, natural, god-given form of sexual identity.

Although the term *heterosexism* is relatively recent, the systematic critique of heterosexuality and its impact on women's lives emerged in the 1970s as a facet of second-wave feminism: the Cohambee River Collective, a black feminist group, and the Furies, a white lesbian feminist group, were among the first to insist that cultural privileging of heterosexuality can be theorized as a form of oppression that interacts with but is not encompassed by other forms of oppression such as racism, sexism, and classism (for the 1977 statement of the Cohambee River Collective, see Hull, Scott, and Smith, 1982; for the 1971 statement of the Furies, see Myron and Bunch, 1975). In 1980, Adrienne Rich coined the phrase "compulsory heterosexuality" to describe the implicit and explicit pressures placed on women to conform to heterosexual social and sexual practices (Rich, 1980; see also Daly, 1978; Lorde, 1984).

Heterosexism constitutes one of the many intersecting forms of oppression that affect women's (and men's) lives; as such, scholarly examinations of heterosexism most properly belong within analyses of systems of domination. The concept of heterosexism makes it possible to move from a discussion of the experiences of individual women to theoretical explanations that illuminate the systemic dynamics that unite a diverse range of experiences.

An analysis of heterosexism presupposes that heterosexuality is a culturally and historically specific construct that cannot be presumed to be a universal timeless category (specifically on this topic, see Katz, 1996; Richardson, 1996; and Boyarin, 1997). Exposing heterosexuality as a historically and culturally specific construct does not in itself ensure any transformation in religious or other cultural formations (Butler, 1993); nevertheless, it does allow one to question the universality and necessity of compulsory heterosexuality.

Within the study of religion, explicit analysis of heterosexism has remained confined to feminist scholarship and, to a lesser extent, scholarship by gay men. By identifying heterosexism as a particular form of structural oppression, feminist scholars of religion can reveal both how religious traditions themselves may be shaped by heterosexism and how they participate in or challenge it. Jewish, Christian, and post-Christian lesbian feminists in particular have contributed to a growing awareness of how many religious traditions and most scholarship on religion promote or reinforce het-

Adam and Eve, the primordial heterosexual couple of Western monotheism, are depicted in a tenth-century Coptic fresco painting (Gianni Dagli Orti/Corbis).

erosexism. In keeping with the political character of feminism, those who theorize heterosexism and reveal its operations in religious communities seek to dismantle it (Daly, 1978; Beck, 1982; Schüssler Fiorenza, 1993; Heyward and Hunt, 1986; Heyward, 1989; Hunt, 1989; Ruether, 1989; Mollenkott, 1991, 1994; Alpert, 1992; Hill, 1993; Jung and Smith, 1993; see also the periodical *Beyond Heterosexism*).

HETEROSEXIST METHODS AND THE STUDY OF WOMEN'S RELIGIOUS LIVES

Heterosexism—concretely manifested in contemporary American society by the effects of legal and religious norms and homophobia—operates as a limiting lens in the study of women's religious lives across cultural and historical boundaries. Heterosexist scholarship presumes that gender depends largely upon heterosexual erotic identification (Butler), that the heterosexual bond is fundamental to the maintenance of culture, and that only heteroerotic identification has divine approval.

As a consequence of these assumptions, heterosexist scholarship explains the interrelationship between religion and sexual behavior solely in terms of heterosexuality (e.g., celibacy as exceptional; female homoeroticism as bad). These assumptions have resulted in a dearth of scholarship in two areas: the religious lives of women who do not conform to heterosexual norms, and systemic analysis of the relationship between sexuality and religion.

Within Judaism and Christianity, heterosexism can be illustrated using the biblical account of the creation of humanity in Genesis 2–3. This narrative is notorious for its role as a proof text for religiously sanctioned assertions that cultural expressions of male dominance and female subordination have their roots in and justification through God's own actions. But even those who would challenge sexist readings of this text generally interpret it as a foundation text for the naturalness, if not rightness, of heterosexual sexual pairing and marriage, thereby grafting heterosexism onto dominant Jewish and Christian understandings of human origins (Edwards in Hasbany, 1989–90).

APPROACHES TO HETEROSEXISM

Although little scholarship exists to date that takes heterosexism in religion as its primary focus (but see Jung and Smith), a growing variety of scholarship contributes to its analysis. Some scholarship that addresses heterosexism and religion does so by examining the impact of heterosexism on the lives of women, especially lesbians, within particular religious traditions (Judaism: Beck; Balka and Rose, 1989; Alpert, 1992; Christianity: Heyward and Hunt; Hunt; Ruether; Mollenkott, 1991, 1994; Martin, 1995). This impact includes the effects of religiously inspired homophobia, which can range from refusal to accept open lesbians as religious leaders, to lack of recognition of lesbian partnerships, to support of violence against lesbians (Blaney, 1987; Hasbany).

Alternatively, scholars may contribute to an analysis of heterosexism by analyzing nonheterosexual sexual identities and practices or forms of resistance to heterosexuality (Buddhism in China: Sankar, 1985; Mormonism: Schow, Schow, and Raynes, 1991; "world religions": Swidler, 1993; Christianity: Brooten, 1996; Matter, 1986). Yet another type of study explores the connections between the construction of gender, sexuality, family, religion, and state (Islam: Combs-Schilling, 1989; Moghadam in Parker et al., 1992; Buddhism: Cabezón, 1992; Chinese studies: Zito and Barlow, 1994; Jainism: Zwilling and Sweet, 1996; Hinduism: Katrak, in Parker et al., 1992). A final example of scholarship that indirectly challenges heterosexism exposes heterosexuality and gender dimorphism as a cultural and historical construct through an examination of religiously significant individuals who defy analysis through heterosexist

lenses (Hinduism: Nanda, 1990; Goldman, 1993; Cohen, 1995; Native American traditions: Williams, 1986; Roscoe, 1991; Jainism: Zwilling and Sweet, 1996; cross-cultural: Herdt, 1994).

Heterosexism remains one of the most underanalyzed structures of oppression in the study of all religions, and homophobia largely remains a socially tolerated and religiously sanctioned stance; thus, not even all feminist scholars of religion attend to heterosexism in their critiques of religious traditions and scholarship or in their articulations of strategies to overcome oppression. The homophobia of scholars of all sexual and theoretical orientations partly accounts for this lack; a more fundamental obstacle, however, is the heterosexism that inheres in academic programs of study, which determine the norms for methodological inquiry (Pippin and Henking, 1996).

BIBLIOGRAPHY

Alpert, Rebecca T. "Challenging Male/Female Complementarity: Jewish Lesbians and the Jewish Tradition." In *People of the Body: Jews and Judaism from an Embodied Perspective.* Edited by Howard Eilberg-Schwartz. 1992.

Balka, Christine, and Andy Rose, eds. *Twice Blessed: On Being Lesbian or Gay and Jewish.* 1989.

Beck, Evelyn Torton, ed. *Nice Jewish Girls: A Lesbian Anthology.* 1982.

Beyond Heterosexism. Boulder, Co.: AlterVisions, 1992–.

Blaney, R. "Homophobia/Heterosexism and Lesbian/Gay Experience: An Annotated Bibliography." In *The Annual of the Society of Christian Ethics.* Edited by Diane M. Yeager. 1987.

Boyarin, Daniel. *Unheroic Conduct: The Rise of Heterosexuality and the Invention of the Jewish Man.* 1997.

Brooten, Bernadette. *Love between Women: Early Christian Responses to Female Homoeroticism.* 1996.

Butler, Judith. *Bodies that Matter: The Discursive Limits of "Sex."* 1993.

Cabezón, José Ignacio, ed. *Buddhism, Sexuality, and Gender.* 1992.

Cohen, Lawrence. "The Pleasure of Castration: The Postoperative Status of Hijras, Jankhas, and Academics." In *Sexual Nature, Sexual Culture.* Edited by Paul R. Abramson and Steven D. Pinkerton. 1995.

Combs-Schilling, M. Elaine. *Sacred Performances: Islam, Sexuality, and Sacrifice.* 1989.

Daly, Mary. *Gyn/Ecology: The Metaethics of Radical Feminism.* 1978.

Goldman, Robert. "Transsexualism, Gender, and Anxiety in Traditional India." *Journal of the American Oriental Society* 113 (1993): 374–401.

Hasbany, Richard, ed. "Homosexuality and Religion." Special issue of the *Journal of Homosexuality* 18 (1989–90): 1–231.

Herdt, Gilbert, ed. *Third Sex, Third Gender: Beyond Sexual Dimorphism in Culture and History.* 1994.

Heyward, Carter. *Touching Our Strength: The Erotic as Power and the Love of God.* 1989.

Heyward, Carter, and Mary E. Hunt. "Roundtable Discussion: Lesbianism and Feminist Theology." *Journal of Feminist Studies in Religion* 2 (1986): 95–106.

Hill, Renee L. "Who Are We for Each Other? Sexism, Sexuality, and Womanist Theology." In *Black Theology: A Documentary History.* Vol. 2, *1980–1992.* Edited by James H. Cone and Gayraud S. Wilmore. 1993.

Hull, Gloria T., Patricia Bell Scott, and Barbara Smith, eds. *All the Women are White, All the Blacks are Men, But Some of Us are Brave: Black Women's Studies.* 1982.

Hunt, Mary E. "On Religious Lesbians: Contradictions and Challenges." In *Homosexuality, Which Homosexuality? International Conference on Gay and Lesbian Studies.* Edited by Dennis Altman et al. 1989.

Jung, Patricia Beattie, and Ralph F. Smith. *Heterosexism: An Ethical Challenge.* 1993.

Katz, Jonathan. *The Invention of Heterosexuality.* 1996.

Lorde, Audre. *Sister Outsider: Essays and Speeches.* 1984.

Martin, Dale B. "Heterosexism and the Interpretation of Romans 1:18–32." *Biblical Interpretation* 3 (1995): 332–355.

Matter, E. Ann. "My Sister, My Spouse: Woman-Identified Women in Medieval Christianity." *Journal of Feminist Studies in Religion* 2 (1986): 81–93.

Mollenkott, Virginia Ramey. "Heterosexism: A Challenge to Ecumenical Solidarity." In *Women and Church: The Challenge to Ecumenical Solidarity in an Age of Alienation.* Edited by Melanie A. May. 1991.

———. "Overcoming Heterosexism—To Benefit Everyone." In *Homosexuality in the Church: Both Sides of the Debate.* Edited by Jeffrey S. Siker. 1994.

Myron, Nancy, and Charlotte Bunch, eds. *Lesbianism and the Women's Movement.* 1975.

Nanda, Serena. *Neither Man nor Woman: The Hijras of India.* 1990.

Parker, Andrew, Mary Russo, Doris Sommer, and Patricia Yaeger, eds. *Nationalisms and Sexualities.* 1992.

Pippin, Tina, and Susan Henking, eds. "Alter(ed) Sexualities: Bringing Lesbian and Gay Studies to the Religion Classroom." *Spotlight on Teaching* 4, no. 2 (Nov. 1996). Insert in *Religious Studies News* 11, no. 4 (Nov. 1996).

Rich, Adrienne. "Compulsory Heterosexuality and Lesbian Existence." *Signs* 5 (1980): 631–660. Reprinted in *Blood, Bread, and Poetry: Selected Prose, 1979–1985.* 1986.

Richardson, Diane, ed. *Theorising Heterosexuality: Telling It Straight.* 1996.

Roscoe, Will. *The Zuni Man-Woman.* 1991.

Ruether, Rosemary Radford. "Homophobia, Heterosexism, and Pastoral Practice." In *Homosexuality in the Priesthood and the Religious Life.* Edited by Jeannine Gramick. 1989.

Sankar, Andrea. "Sisters and Brothers, Lovers and Enemies: Marriage Resistance in Southern Kwantung." *Journal of Homosexuality* 11 (1985): 69–81.

Schow, Ron, Wayne Schow, and Marybeth Raynes, eds. *Peculiar People: Mormons and Same-Sex Orientation.* 1991.

Schüssler Fiorenza, Elisabeth. *Discipleship of Equals: A Critical Feminist Ekklesia-ology of Liberation.* 1993.

Sears, James T., and Walter Williams, eds. *Overcoming Heterosexism and Homophobia: Strategies that Work.* 1997.

Swidler, Arlene, ed. *Homosexuality and World Religions.* 1993.

Williams, Walter. *The Spirit and the Flesh: Sexual Diversity in American Indian Culture.* 1986.

Wittig, Monique. *The Straight Mind and Other Essays.* 1992.

Zito, Angela, and Tani E. Barlow, eds. *Body, Subject, and Power in China.* 1994.

Zwilling, Leonard, and Michael Sweet. " 'Like a City Ablaze': The Third Sex and the Creation of Sexuality in Jain Religious Literature." *Journal of the History of Sexuality* 6 (1996): 359–384.

See also **Queer Theory.**

DENISE KIMBER BUELL

Hierarchy

In a hierarchical system, elements are ranked in relation to one another with reference to a transcendent principle or model. The assignment of value is central to hierarchy; differences between culturally constructed categories are evaluated, with some categories esteemed more than others. Hierarchy involves the creation of boundaries between constituent parts; the destruction of these boundaries is a transgression that threatens the stability of the entire order. In a hierarchical society, socially constructed boundaries separate different social classes, the most common division being that between men and women. The universal ranking of men above women, based upon an absolute distinction between gender domains, is the most widespread form of social hierarchy. To threaten this gender distinction is to threaten the social order; powerful sanctions are enacted to enforce it.

The behaviors and activities regulated by a person's place within a hierarchy may include: occupation, marriage options, religious practices, styles of dress, eating practices, residence area, and so on. Looking at one such example, the ritual of marriage, serves well to highlight the contours of a hierarchical society. Restrictions upon marriage practices must be in place in order to assure the maintenance of a hierarchical order. Endogamy (marriage within one's group) is a common prescription in hierarchical societies, serving to maintain the boundaries between groups. However, hypergamy, a form of marriage in which a woman is married to a man of higher status, is also a common feature of hierarchical societies. While it serves to confirm the superiority of higher classes (who receive the daughters of lower classes, but do not offer their own daughters in exchange), it also highlights the fact that men rank higher than women. Attention to who marries whom, who makes arrangements for a marriage, and what criteria they use, also serve to outline power relations within a hierarchical order, both between classes and between men and women.

In many societies the high-ranking religious roles are reserved for men, sometimes taking the form of a male-only hierarchy alongside the social hierarchy, such as the Roman Catholic line of apostolic succession, as described by Nancy Jay, or the Hawaiian royal sacrificial cult, as described by Valerio Valeri. While religion frequently serves to tie women to devalued social positions, it sometimes offers a means for women to alter their station in life. Caroline Walker Bynum argues that medieval women who pursued religious vocations could escape to large degree kinship and marriage ties. In other religious systems women take on roles as religious specialists within systems dominated by men, as in the case of Buddhist nuns or Rome's Vestal Virgins.

Louis Dumont, in his study of the Indian caste system, argues that the polar tension between purity and impurity is the linchpin upon which hierarchical ideologies rely, though it might be more accurate to say that hierarchical ideology relies upon acceptance of a certain model of order, and an eschewal of behaviors that are defined as "impure" to the extent to which they threaten that order. Thus, impurity does not necessarily inhere to members of a particular group but may correspond to behaviors that threaten the social structure as a whole. However, the strata in a hierarchy are constructed as functionally specialized, component parts that together make up a larger organic whole; to be born into a particular stratum is to be born into a specific function that has clearly defined relationships to other strata. The cultural logic of hierarchy tends to efface the labor basis of the social structure, insisting that those ranked lowest perform more material forms of production, including biological reproduction, while those ranked highest carry out cultural forms of production, such as creation and transmission of values and texts. Classical India's Laws of Manu and ancient Greece's *Republic* of Plato are just two of many examples that classify women along with the lower classes. However, within the same system, women are also ranked with the class into which they were born or married.

Complicating our understanding of hierarchy is the fact that several hierarchical systems may be in operation at once, such as those of class, caste, sex, and age. As a result, the same person might occupy varying positions depending on the most relevant ranking system for the context at hand. For example, in relation to her husband, an upper-class woman might be devalued, but she will be ranked higher than another woman of lower class; while a lower-class man might rank far below an upper-class man, he has the compensation of ranking above a woman of his own class. Such interpenetrating hierarchical systems tend to reinforce the larger social structure of which they are a part, benefiting most drastically those who are at the apex of all of the component systems, usually an adult, upper-class male. According to the ideology of hierarchy, high ranks subsume lower ranks, and men are understood to encompass the entire human species. This is the view from the apex, viewing the totality below through the lens of hierarchical values defined as transcendent, ignoring history and context, in which different interpretations abound. When we accept such a view, we completely overlook those who challenge the unity of the system.

BIBLIOGRAPHY

Béteille, André. *The Idea of Natural Inequality and Other Essays.* 1983. See especially the title essay and "Homo Hierarchicus, Homo Equalis."

Bloch, Maurice. *Ritual, History and Power: Selected Papers in Anthropology.* 1989. See especially "Contradiction in Representations of Women and Kinship."

Bynum, Caroline Walker. *Holy Feast and Holy Fast: The Religious Significance of Food to Medieval Women.* 1987.

Dumont, Louis. *Homo Hierarchicus: The Caste System and Its Implications.* Complete revised English edition. 1980.

Jay, Nancy. *Throughout Your Generations Forever: Sacrifice, Religion, and Paternity.* 1992.

Smith, Brian K. *Classifying the Universe: The Ancient Indian* Varna *System and the Origins of Caste.* 1994.

Valeri, Valerio. *Kingship and Sacrifice: Ritual and Society in Ancient Hawaii.* Translated by Paula Wissing. 1985.

LAURA S. DESMOND

Hildegard of Bingen

Hildegard of Bingen (1098–1179), prophet and visionary, was a Benedictine abbess who founded a monastic community at Bingen, Germany. Given by her parents to the service of God at the age of eight, Hildegard had visions for years but only revealed them when she was in her forties and already an abbess. Although the most prominent, Hildegard was one of several female visionaries who were members of the powerful and elite Rhineland monastic communities during the twelfth century.

A prolific writer, she wrote on a wide variety of subjects, among them theology and doctrine, medicine, mystical visions, poetry, music and letters, all in excellent Latin. Hildegard's great work, *Scivias* (Know the ways), contains visions, theology, and poetry. *Scivias* met with the pope's approval. She continued these visionary and doctrinal instructions in the *Book of Life's Merits* and in her unfinished *Book of Divine Works.* In addition to the liturgical music collected in her *Symphonia,* and the musical *Play of Virtues,* Hildegard wrote scientific and medical treatises demonstrating a considerable knowledge of the natural world, which are included in the *Book of Simple Medicine* and *Causes and Cures.* Much of her autobiographical writings is contained in her *Vita,* composed toward the end of her life.

Hildegard's visions provide the focal point for a divine discourse on the object of the visions. In the *Scivias* Hildegard does not speak to God or for God in the third person, rather God speaks directly through her, commenting on the world and explaining complex theological issues. Her writings reflect her understanding of God's interaction with the ordering of the natural world, and with humans, both body and soul, and provide a call to action and renewal in the tradition of the Hebrew prophets. She was aided by the monk Volmar, her confessor and secretary, who helped her record much of her work.

Manuscript illumination of Universal Man from Hildegard of Bingen's *Scivias,* **c. 1200** (Gianni Dagli Orti/ Corbis)

Called the Sibyl of the Rhine for her clear and commanding gift of prophecy, Hildegard corresponded with and advised the leaders of her day, among them popes and kings. She made preaching tours and gave sermons to bishops, priests, and lay people. Her many accomplishments contradicted her statements claiming a lack of power and poor education. Hildegard argued that, while she was humble and weak, she was authorized to reveal the direct words of God spoken to her in her visions. Such power occasionally brought her into conflict with the religious establishment, which she frequently critiqued. Often the victor in these contests, she remained prominent and persuasive until her death. Among others, she counseled the younger visionary Elisabeth of Schönau, whose work reflects this influence. Hildegard illustrates the considerable religious and intellectual achievements possible for some well-educated, elite women in twelfth-century monastic communities.

BIBLIOGRAPHY

A good introduction and translation is Hildegard of Bingen, *Scivias,* translated by Columbia Hart and Jane Bishop (1990). Hildegard's music is discussed in Barbara Newman, ed., *Symphonia armonie celestium revelationum* (1988).

Two surveys of medieval women's writing include excellent sections on Hildegard: Peter Dronke, *Women Writers of the Middle Ages* (1984), and Elizabeth Alvilda Petroff, *Medieval Women's Visionary Literature* (1986).

For her theology and historical context see Barbara Newman, *Sister of Wisdom: St. Hildegard's Theology of the Feminine* (1987), and Sabina Flanagan, *Hildegard of Bingen, 1098–1179: A Visionary Life* (1989).

ERICA C. GELSER

Himalayan Religions

Stretching 1,500 miles from the highlands of Burma to northern Pakistan, the Himalayan region is a kaleidoscope of ethnic communities whose religious practices variously reflect the plains culture of northern India, the political and social institutions of Tibet, and Hindu and Buddhist textual traditions, as well as observances centered on local deities, clan ancestors, and shamanic curing rites linked with indigenous, nonliterate societies.

The religious landscape of the Himalaya has been influenced by two processes. Isolation, rugged terrain, and remoteness from urban state centers led to an elaboration of local and regional cultural patterns, while migrations, pilgrimage, and trade networks created a hybrid borderland between the Indian subcontinent and the Tibetan plateau, leading to the ethnographic and religious diversity we see today.

EASTERN HIMALAYA

Eastern Himalaya, one of the most culturally diverse and least studied regions of the Himalaya, includes the Indian states of Sikkim, Assam, Arunachal Pradesh, and the Buddhist kingdom of Bhutan. In Sikkim economic opportunities and wage labor under British colonial rule drew migrants from eastern Nepal during the first half of this century. Today Nepali-speaking groups outnumber the indigenous Lepcha in Sikkim. In Arunachal Pradesh and Assam, the incursion of Hindu and Muslim Bengali settlers and Christian missionaries into tribal territories has led to ethnic conflict.

Compared to the rich ethnographic record from Nepal and north India, scholarship about women and religion in this region is sketchy. However, we do find some references to women as ritual experts: the shaman's role was open to Lepcha women; and among the Khasi, a matrilineal and matrilocal group (property in inherited through female relatives and men reside with their wives' kin), women served as priestesses and presided over domestic and community rituals.

Tribal pantheons included male and female deities; a divine couple, Doni-Su, linked with the sun and the earth, figured centrally in the religious traditions of several tribes, suggesting a certain symmetry between gender symbolism, religious ideologies, and gender relations in these small-scale egalitarian communities. Although political instability and two decades of travel restrictions have limited new scholarship, as the area opens, the study of women's moral perspectives and ritual traditions will be welcome additions to our understanding of South Asian women's subjectivities and agency.

WESTERN HIMALAYA

In the Indian states of Himachal Pradesh and Uttar Pradesh, religious practices in the lowlands (below 2,500 ft.) reflect a syncretism of Hindu, Muslim, and Sikh traditions, while in the foothills the religious observances of Pahari or hill people include the worship of Vishnu, Śiva, Devī; the performance of life-cycle rites (*saṃskāras*) by brahmin priests; caste hierarchy and a concern with ritual purity and pollution; and the celebration of major Hindu festivals such as Tij, Holi, Diwali (Tihar), and Dashara (Dasain). Although these features are similar to the cultural patterns of the north Indian plains and the middle hills of Nepal, especially among the Bahun, Thakuri, and Chetri upper castes, the Hindu tradition is not monolithic—it contains a divergent range of individual, class, caste, and gendered perspectives.

In recent years feminist scholars have critiqued Western-biased and orientalist constructions that depict Hindu women as subordinate, submissive subjects who have completely internalized and accepted the patriarchal ideologies of orthodox Hinduism. In contrast, anthropologists Kirin Narayan and Gloria Goodwin Raheja, who conducted fieldwork in Himachal and Uttar Pradesh, found that women's wedding songs and personal narratives expressed dissonant views that challenged and ridiculed male, brahminical structures of authority. Through their ritual practices and popular performances, at weddings and other life-cycle events, illiterate women provided critical commentaries on orthodox Hindu rites and demonstrated that they were capable of constructing their own identity through alternative systems of meaning that did not devalue women or their sexuality.

Androcentric scholarship that focused on brahminical rituals and Sanskrit texts often overlooked the role of women as knowledge bearers and moral agents or, conversely, depicted them as mindless bearers of unchanging tradition. In contrast, Narayan's (1995) study of upper-caste women's ritual practices in Kangra showed that women's interpretations and rites surrounding the annual worship of the sacred *tulsi* (basil) plant varied greatly among households. This ritual knowledge (the *tulsi* plant represents a goddess who marries an incarnation of Vishnu) is transmitted orally among female relatives and female in-laws outside the literary, orthodox realm of brahmin priests.

NEPAL

Nepal's syncretistic and multifaceted religions stem from the hegemony of state-sponsored Hinduism that dates to the thirteenth-century Malla dynasty; the influx of Indian Pahari hill groups, who brought brahminical ritualism and social norms to the Terai (lowlands) and middle-hill region of Nepal in the twelfth century; the Tibetanization and spread of Buddhist traditions across the northern highlands, a process that began in the seventh century; and the coexistence of Hinduism and Buddhism in the Kathmandu valley during the Licchavi period (400–800 C.E.), a time when both religions received royal patronage and elements of the Hindu and Buddhist pantheon merged and also incorporated local cults.

In the middle ranges of Nepal, Tibeto-Burman communities like the Newar, Gurung, and Thakali have strategically adopted some aspects of Hindu ritual and caste practices; others, like the Tamang and Nyeshangba, follow Tibetan Buddhism. Many of these groups also retain their ancestral traditions, which include shamans who mediate between the human and divine realms and cure illnesses; the propitiation of local forest, mountain, and river spirits; agricultural rites and exorcisms; and yearly homage to clan and lineage ancestors. Among the Nyeshangba of north central Nepal, senior women of the household play a central role in domestic and clan rituals: daily they burn juniper to purify the house, and monthly they offer food and beer to their ancestral clan deities, represented by an elder sister and her three younger brothers (Watkins, 1996).

Women's symbolic association with shamanism is discussed by anthropologist David Holmberg (1983) in his study of Tamang ritual specialists. Elsewhere in Nepal, case studies of women as shamans and mediums include Ellen Coon's (1989) ethnographic study of Newar female mediums who have a popular following in the Kathmandu valley, and Vivienne Kondos's (1990) study of a high-caste Hindu woman in Kathmandu who becomes possessed by the goddess Kālī and offers diag-

Hindu women perform a ritual for Tij Brata, a women-only festival, Kathmandu, Nepal (Alison Wright/Corbis).

noses and treatments to men and women who attend her biweekly sessions.

Strengthened by their association with the goddess Devī, these illiterate women operate outside the structures of patriarchal religious authority. As moral agents they wield power and influence decisions in their households and community. Subverting the roles of deferential wife and submissive daughter-in-law, female mediums are respected by their families. In an inversion of orthodox practices, their husbands perform *puja* (give offerings) to them, the women are served first at meals, and are freed from household chores.

Like ethnicity, religion in Nepal is fluid and hinges on the politics of identity. The maintenance of local tradition, the adoption of some facets of Hindu or Buddhist orthodoxy, and the rejection of others reflect human agency and political expediency. In the wake of the 1990 democracy movement, the *janajati* (people's movement) has contested the domination and rule of Nepalese society by high-caste, Bahun-Chetri elites, leading to a decline in Hindu fundamentalism in some quarters and a revitalization of Buddhism in others.

BIBLIOGRAPHY

Bennett, Lynn. *Dangerous Wives and Sacred Sisters: Social and Symbolic Roles of High Caste Women in Nepal.* 1983.

Coon, Ellen. "Possessing Power: Ajima and Her Medium." *Himalayan Research Bulletin* 9, no. 1 (1989): 1–10.

Furer-Haimendorf, Christoph von. *Highlanders of Arunchal Pradesh.* 1982.

Gray, John. "Chetri Women in Domestic Groups and Rituals." In *Women in India and Nepal.* Edited by Michael Allen and S. Mukherjee. 1990.

Holland, Dorothy, and Debra Skinner. "Contested Ritual, Contested Femininities: (Re)Forming Self and Society in a Nepali Women's Festival." *American Ethnologist* 22, no. 2 (1995): 279–305.

Holmberg, David. "Shamanic Soundings: Femaleness in the Tamang Ritual Structure." *Signs: Journal of Women in Culture and Society* 9, no. 1 (1983): 40–58.

Kondos, Vivienne. "Constructing a Hindu Healing Practice: The Case of a Kali-possessed Woman." *Kailash: A Journal of Himalayan Studies* 16 (1990): 27–70.

———. "Images of the Fierce Goddess and Portrayals of Hindu Women." *Contributions to Indian Sociology* 20, no. 2 (1986): 173–197.

Narayan, Kirin. "Birds on a Branch: Girlfriends and Wedding Songs in Kangra." *Ethnos* 14 (1986): 47–75.

———. "How a Girl Became a Sacred Plant." In *Religions of India in Practice.* Edited by Donald S. Lopez, Jr. 1995.

Raheja, Gloria Goodwin, and Ann Grodzin Gold. *Listen to the Heron's Words: Reimagining Gender and Kinship in Northern India.* 1994.

Sax, William S. *Mountain Goddess: Gender and Politics in a Himalayan Pilgrimage.* 1991.

Thompson, Julia. "Speaking of Dissent, Speaking of Consent: Ritual and Resistance among High-Caste Hindu Women in Kathmandu." *Contributions to Nepalese Studies* 2, no. 1 (1993): 47–56.

Watkins, Joanne C. *Spirited Women: Gender, Religion and Cultural Identity in the Nepal Himalaya.* 1996.

See also **Buddhism: Himalayan Buddhism; Hinduism: An Overview; Shamans; Tantra.**

JOANNE C. WATKINS

Hina

Throughout the islands of Polynesia, Hina (or Sina, or Ina) is a mythic woman who lived in the earliest times. Her activities reveal and establish women's nature and roles—as when, on Tahiti and some other islands, she is said to have gone up to the moon, where she may be seen now, seated under a great banyan tree and industriously beating her tapa cloth. In much of Polynesia this activity is one of the most laborious and important of women's tasks.

Where lovers are concerned, two very different stories are told. Often Hina falls in love with a handsome, powerful chief, Tinirau (or Sinilau), who lives on a distant island. Undaunted, Hina runs away from her family and swims far across the ocean, or sometimes rides on the back of a turtle or shark. She finds Tinirau and marries him, and they live together happily.

In other stories, though, Hina is seduced by Tuna (Eel), a phallic eel, while bathing. In this version it is often the trickster hero Māui who discovers what is happening and kills the eel. Hina buries her lover's head, and it grows into the first coconut palm—an acquisition of the greatest value to Polynesian peoples. (The "truth" of this story is revealed by the coconut's three holes, which are representative of the eel's eyes and mouth.) But in New Zealand (Aotearoa), where it is too cold for coconuts to grow, the story changed. Chopped to pieces, Tuna becomes the different species of eel.

Hina's association with the moon no doubt reflects the common belief that the moon controls menstrual cycles. (The Maori of New Zealand believed that the moon was the real husband of all women.) The association of women with the ocean is in accord with Polynesian patterns of imagery. The stories about Hina's lovers reflect an obvious ambivalence about women: when she marries Tinirau she is a "good wife," while in her encounters with the eel (once again, in water), her dangerous sexuality has to be controlled. This last episode, however, does present Hina as a benefactor who gives her people a much-valued resource.

BIBLIOGRAPHY

Beckwith, Martha. *Hawaiian Mythology.* 1940. Reprint, 1970.

Kirtley, Bacil F. "The Slain Eel-god and the Origin of the Coconut, with Satellite Themes, in Polynesian Mythology." In *Folklore International: Essays in Traditional Literature, Belief, and Custom in Honor of Wayland Debs Hand.* 1967.

Luomala, Katharine. *Voices on the Wind: Polynesian Myths and Chants.* 1955.

MARGARET ORBELL

Hinduism

An Overview

In the rich variety of myth, ritual, art, and philosophy that is Hinduism, gender is a critical and complex marker. Both as a religious category for all followers and as a category that speaks directly to the lives of women, the feminine is a significant feature of South Asian culture. Until the past few decades, scholars have focused primarily on the texts of a male-dominated legacy for what understanding there was of the role and status of women. Since the 1980s, however, new work in a broad range of the social sciences, in alternate archival resources, in archaeological and art historical materials, and in fresh approaches to extant texts has allowed silent voices of the tradition to emerge, illuminating women's intricately interwoven worlds.

WOMAN'S BODY AND BODY IMAGE

Reflecting a long tradition, Tryambaka's eighteenth-century *Strīdharmapaddhati,* a guide to the religious duties of women, suggests that the key to a woman's nature (*strīsvabhāva*) lies in understanding the body. Since all bodies are thought to be the result of the working out of past actions (karma), the peculiar features of a woman's body are attributed to past weaknesses, reflected presently in a system of purity and pollution. Temporary and individual pollution (e.g., from menstruation, sexual activity, or childbirth) may be addressed by certain rituals, while permanent and corporate pollution (e.g., of a prostitute or a midwife) may be reconciled only by the soul taking on a new body in rebirth.

While the standards of pure and impure may devalue women, those defining the concepts auspicious and inauspicious illuminate women as the creators of life and as the wellsprings of prosperity. Because a man's fulfillment of the four aims of life (wealth, enjoyment, duty, and liberation) depends in great part upon the woman as enabler, her *śakti,* or female energy, ties her to all other women and to the facilitating power of goddesses like Lakṣmī. Woman's auspiciousness is also tied to a reverence for the sacred land of India. Paralleling the female body as a spiritually powerful field, the religious geography of India maps out the sacred as a goddess herself. Indeed, it is this conviction that underlies the modern cult of Bhārat Mātā, or "mother India," in which Hindus become the children of India and are expected to protect the mother at any cost.

The spatial mapping of the sacred is also manifest in the Hindu body image. The special prominence of the pure head is signified by a woman's attention to hair care and to her adornment with cosmetics, oils, perfumes, flowers, jewelry, and headcover. The location of impurity in the feet is reflected in the reverent bowing before them or the touching of the ground on which they stand. The pure right hand is reserved for eating and giving, and the impure left for cleaning the body below the navel.

The description of a woman's body is often patterned after nature. In Jayadeva's *Gītagovinda,* a poem from the twelfth century C.E., the cowherdess Rādhā is said to have a face like a lotus, eyes of a doe, lips like red berries, breasts like palm fruits, and arms like flowering creepers. Such patterning, coupled with extensive erotic imagery, celebrates female sexuality and reflects the sensuality of daily life often attested in contemporary studies of village households. Clothes and ornaments add to the expression of the body, for not only can dress highlight certain bodily features by color, design, placement, and movement, but it can also mediate the tension between revealing and concealing: what is shown and what is not are part of a complex play of social relations and status markers.

RELIGION AND THE CONSTRUCTION OF THE LIFE CYCLE

Rules (dharma) for the lives of Hindu women are discussed at length in texts, but because they usually reflect the ideals of men they cannot, except with careful scrutiny, betray the social and religious realities of women. What they do reveal, however, is that the tradition undergoes change over time, often with significant developments for women, and that from the orthodox point of view the only rite of passage (*samskāra*) that is particularly marked for women is marriage.

The preference for sons is based on the need to perform a father's funeral rites, to perpetuate the family name, and to provide protection for the family. Daughters signify the loss of wealth and property in dowry at the time of marriage, and the loss of a worker from the family household. There is evidence for female infanticide from the medieval period onward—death through strangulation, poison, drowning, and neglect—even though such murder would bring karmic demerit to its perpetrators. In modern times, the availability of amniocentesis in India has led to the rise of sex-selective abortions to ensure the birth of sons. When a girl is born, *samskāra* rituals are traditionally unavailable and the family celebration is markedly smaller and more

The magnificent temple complex dedicated to Vishnu at Angkor Wat, Cambodia, c. 1100–1150 C.E. (The Stock Market)

private. Nevertheless, literature suggests that much love and care is bestowed upon girls, and that their adoption, as that of Kuntī by Kuntibhoja in the epic Mahābhārata, even took place.

A young girl's maidenhood would normally be the time for formal education. Vedic sources indicate that *upanayana*, or initiation into Vedic studies, was available for young women and the Upanishads attest to learned, philosophically ambitious women like Maitreyī and Gārgī Vācaknavī. From Pānini, a grammarian of the fourth-century B.C.E., there is evidence of women teachers (*ācaryā*) and women preceptors (*upādhyayā*), and heterodox traditions like Jainism and Buddhism allow for education and spiritual advancement for women religious. As a girl's age for betrothal and marriage declined, and as marriage became the female *upanayana*, greater restrictions on formal education for women were established.

Thus, in traditional Hinduism, education for a girl normally takes place in the home and is oriented around the duties she will perform as wife, mother, and contributor to the household. In modern times women's education has been a central issue, and reforms in missionary, British, and Hindu institutions as well as changing attitudes in the larger culture have created a positive climate for women's learning.

Traditionally, a woman's life moves toward her marriage (*vivāha*) and toward the time when, together with her husband, she will become *dampatī*, one of the two masters of the house. A married couple is viewed as a single unit, such that the wife is half of the whole. Because, according to Vedic tradition, the husband cannot fulfill his religious duties without his wife, her presence completes the unit and makes it ritually effective; the wife then is a *sahadharminī*, someone who shares in the husband's duties. For the wife, in turn, marriage is her only traditional rite of passage, and the expectation of marriage for women is nearly universal.

In marriage the woman becomes a *pativratā*, one who is devoted to her husband as lord and whose obedient service to him is her primary duty. The purpose of marriage, is twofold: *prajā*, the bearing of offspring, particularly sons, and *rati*, pleasure. The successful expression of these two ideals within the marriage, and the consequent maturation of an honorable household, bring marital felicity or *saubhāgya*.

The mythology of goddesses provide models for Hindu wives. Following the marriage hymn (10.85), of the oldest Hindu text, the *Ṛgveda*, which portrays the alliance of Sūryā and Soma, the most noted model is Sītā, the wife of Rāma, king of Ayodhyā. Daughter of the earth and King Janaka of Videha, Sītā represents the wifely ideals of purity, devotion, and faithfulness to her husband. Other goddess models include Sāvitrī, whose clever and heroic efforts bring her husband back from the dead; Satī, who sacrifices her own life rather than hear her father reproach her husband; Lakṣmī, whose correct dharmic behavior brings prosperity to her marriage with the god Vishnu, and Parvatī, whose marriage to the god Śiva is blissful and calm. New studies, however, highlight the aggressive and independent behavior that underlies these myths: Sītā's firm insistence on accompanying Rāma into exile and her final repudiation of him as she returns to her mother Earth, and Draupadī's anger at her husbands' behavior during the dice match and her final adamant reliance upon her own resources, for example. In highlighting the contradictory complexities of goddess mythologies, these studies successfully illuminate the social realities of Hindu women.

In most Hindu marriages, the bride is accompanied by a dowry. This process upholds the honor of the woman and her family and provides a range of needed household items as well as personal holdings. Negotiations over the dowry can be extensive and, although attempts have been made to curb or abolish dowry, the system remains. Recently, the phenomenon of "dowry death" has appeared in which extortion for more dowry reaches its limit and the bride is found dead, purportedly by accident, but usually as the result of an intentional kitchen fire. Although the groom is then free to remarry (and collect more dowry), he faces prosecution as do other members of his family.

A wife's ultimate status is generally achieved by bearing a son, but for every child elaborate child-care rituals are performed with the elder women of the family and the midwife acting as tutors for the mother. Extensive use of hands and handling is a feature of Hindu mothering, which eschews an intimate one-on-one relationship between mother and child and favors instead child care by the group. While rapid urbanization and greater contact with non-Hindu influences have altered the traditional family structure, mothering retains great value within Hindu culture.

On the death of a husband, a woman is normally prohibited from remarriage, although one finds vigorous debate in the early legal texts on this question with regard to young widows. Equally debated is the practice of levirate (*niyoga*) by which a widow can have children with a brother-in-law.

Lakṣmī, the Hindu goddess of Prosperity, is depicted here in a statue (Craig Lovell/Corbis).

The practice of sati, in which a wife willingly cremates herself on the funeral pyre of her dead husband, is said to be an ideal expression of the perfect wife (*pativratā*) in union with her mate. Evidence for the practice can be found as early as epic times with Madrī as the prototypical sati, and thereafter instances dot the record. Mughal rulers prohibited the practice, and it was declared illegal in 1829 with the Suttee Regulation Act. Cases still occur, however, and that of Roop Kanwar in 1987 has become a touchstone for strong debate among a number of groups. According to tradition, the sati becomes a goddess and the site of her death becomes a focal point for pilgrimage.

A woman who decides to remain in the world without her husband assumes traditional widowhood: undyed dress, absence of ornamentation, and short or shaved hair. Although the widow retains the right to economic maintenance by her husband's family, this is dependent upon her continued celibacy. As she is now unlucky and inauspicious, she must live an ascetic life ritually aimed at reunion with her husband in the next life.

ECONOMIC LIFE

The household that a wife enters is a network of kin ties as well as an economic unit regulated by legal texts. At marriage certain materials are designated *strīdhana,* or the separate property of the wife. While the exact constitution of *strīdhana* and the wife's dominion over it depend on the source of the property, the woman's status at the time of acquisition, and the school of law under which she falls, the range of *strīdhana* was enlarged with time to include all property obtained by a woman as a maiden, in marriage, or after marriage—excluding immovable property given by the husband.

The economic maintenance of a virtuous wife is guaranteed by Hindu law, and a husband is expected to provide the resources by which a wife carries out her household tasks. Because of the identification of the wife with the household and because of the *dampatī* ideal, joint ownership of household property pertains, at least in theory. Vedic texts declare that the woman is the manager of the household goods, and economic responsibility for household affairs devolves upon the wife, or upon the wife's agreement as representative of the household. The question of property is one of control over use, and, as a greater emphasis on the individual has taken place in modern times, that control has expanded.

Disposal of property by Hindu women normally falls into three categories: hospitable service to guests, gift giving, and inheritance. Casting a woman as the economic representative of the household, *śrauta* (solemn) ritual affirms a woman's centrality in attending to guests. Not only are guests honored by the laws of hospitality but their accessibility to the material offering of a household is assumed, and is mediated by the wife. Special household wealth reserved for religious donations (*dāna*) by women is noted in the legal texts as wealth that must be spent in full. Religious donations by Hindu women are recorded in texts and inscriptions, and the number of widows giving is proportionally high. Finally, disposal of property to heirs by a woman pertains primarily to her *strīdhana,* and the general rule for devolution of *strīdhana,* is upon daughters, under the argument that sons inherit from fathers. Thus, sons traditionally inherit land while daughters receive dowry goods and jewelry.

PUBLIC LIFE

Public life for a Hindu woman was historically curtailed by the practices of seclusion and veiling. Although there is evidence for seclusion, especially by high-caste families, as early as the epic period, it was strengthened in time by the practice of *purdah* among Muslims. A woman's covering of her head is governed by kin relations, with the use of a veil normally occurring only after marriage and in the context of the husband's male relatives. Because the religious rationale for seclusion and veiling underscores the status and honor of a family, expression of the practice varies by caste and group.

In spite of such ideals, historical evidence indicates that girls in ruling families sometimes received military training and occasionally engaged in warfare. Women were also important as queens, ruling as regents on behalf of their youthful sons from early times onward, or occasionally in their own right. At the local level, Vedic women were encouraged to speak at public assemblies, but this feature is not evidenced again fully until the recent influx of women into Indian political life.

RELIGIOUS LIFE

A woman's religious goals reflect the great variety that is Hinduism. Although the orthodox view is that these goals are circumscribed by her duties as wife, the range of spiritual possibilities for women parallels that of men. This is not to say that women have not experienced discrimination in their religious pursuits but, as evidenced by the strong representation of feminine ideals in the Hindu pantheon, modeling for women is substantial.

New work in Indus Valley sites suggests a complex tradition containing significant female symbolism and central roles for women as participants. Some note the existence of fertility cults in which priestesses and animals figured, and in which bangles betokened procreation and motherhood. The worship of a goddess, possibly a protoform of Durgā, is posited with ties to an astral system of divinities, a contest motif, and a cult involving the fig tree and attendant figures reminiscent of the later seven Matṛkas or mothers. Finally, there is evidence of fish symbolism tied to the star Rohiṇī as well as to women's forehead marks.

In the Vedic period, women authored hymns or parts of hymns. Women as *brahmavādinīs* (traditional commentators) were known, and discourses of philosophical women like Maitreyī and Gārgī are preserved in the Upanishads. Later roles for women include ascetic and renunciant possibilities in which there is full devaluation of householdership and the rejection of *strīdharma.* A recent classification of nonhouseholder possibilities includes the renunciatory ascetic (*saṃnyāsinī*), the celibate (*brahmacāriṇī*), and the tantric (*yoginī, tāntrika, sādhikā, siddhā*). Transcending householder spirituality, these women are impelled toward the goals of *mokṣa,* or release from the cycle of samsara.

Participation in ritual was circumscribed for women in the early *śrauta* system. Although her presence was necessary and her mediational role crucial at moments when sexuality and fertility, and hospitality and giftgiving were highlighted, the *patnī* was not the sacrificer, only the sacrificer's wife. Women were given other roles such as almsgiving in the domestic manuals, but it was in the arena of *vratas,* or vowed observances such as fasting, where they achieved full ritual posture. A *vrata* brings about the strīdharmic goal of *saubhāgya,* or marital felicity, through offspring, prosperity, or long life. Thus, while the observance is of and by women, the beneficiaries are members of the whole household. *Vratas* vary greatly among regions in India and often entail four elements: performance of rites, use of verses, drawing of rice-powder diagrams, and recitation of stories.

In addition to *vratas,* domestic practice for a woman includes assisting her husband in worshiping, her own *pūjā* or worship before a household shrine (using water, flowers, ornaments and food), and devotional singing. Religious fairs and seasonal festivals take women outside the home, as do visits to local temples or shrines and pilgrimages. An increased role for women as religious functionaries is evident in modern times among, for example, *pūjāriṇīs,* female temple attendants, and *kīrtanīyās,* professional women devotional singers, though *devadāsīs* as ritual temple dancers and women possessed by the goddess have long been features of the tradition.

The *bhaktimārga* or path of devotion has traditionally been an important rubric for women's spirituality. Historically, bhakti has linked protest against male domination to protest against caste domination, and its universal appeal promises salvation to women, children, and members of lower castes. Although women's spirituality is not synonymous with goddess worship, goddesses do serve a range of functions for women as behavioral models, intercessors for specific requests, and objects of profound devotion.

Goddesses prominent in women's devotions include sister-daughter goddesses, such as Rādhā, the consort of Krishna married to another (*parakīyā*); wife-goddesses, such as Sītalā, the goddess of smallpox; Śerāṅvālī, who possesses her female devotees; Māriyamman, of villages in South India; and wife-goddesses, such as Parvatī, Lakṣmī, and Sītā. Goddesses continue to manifest anew as the films *Devī* (Satyajit Ray, 1960) and *Jai Santoshi Ma* (Vijay Sharma, 1975) demonstrate, and some goddesses like Kālī have become significant as international phenomena.

Women saints have figured prominently in the history of Hindu devotionalism. Among Vaiṣṇava followers are the ninth-century Āṇṭāḷ of the Tamil Ālvār tradition, the sixteenth-century Mirabai of Rajasthan

A woman prepares flower alms for Hindu pilgrims coming to bathe in the Ganges, Varanasi, Uttar Pradesh, India, 1988 (Brian Vikander/Corbis).

devoted to Krishna, and Bahinā Bāī of Maharashtra, who was greatly influenced by the seventeenth-century saint Tukārām. Among Śaivite followers are the sixth-century forest-living Kāraikkāl Ammaiyār of the Tamils, the twelfth-century naked-wandering Akkā Mahādevī of Karnataka, and the brahman Lallā Dēd of Kashmir who followed a tantric practice. The lives of these women saints were often marked by an early dedication to god, defiance of marriage and other social norms, spiritual initiation, and mystical communion with god.

Contemporary practice of Hinduism by women and current efforts to better women's lives in India are not always coterminous. While Hindu practice may still be based in traditional *strīdharma* for modern women, other efforts continue to confront what is seen as violence against women and to ensure proper health care, access to jobs, and decent wages. The views of Hindu women today on such issues as population control, family planning, education, arranged marriage, occupations, and styles of leadership are as varied as the religion itself, but it is clear that there is a rich array of female models within the Hindu tradition. Not insignificant are the wealth of new vehicles used to carry these images: film, television, radio, novels, magazines, comic books, posters, and the internet, each offering new ways of transforming the tradition to speak significantly to women. While the message may not be univocal, it may certainly be consistently Hindu.

BIBLIOGRAPHY

Good comprehensive discussions of women and Hinduism can be found in A.S. Altekar's *The Position of Women in Hindu Civilization, From Prehistoric Times to the Present Day* (1938; 2d ed., 1973); Pandurang Vaman Kane's five-volume, seven-part classic *History of Dharmaśāstra* (1930–1962) under critical topics such as marriage and *strīdhana;* Frédérique Apffel Marglin's "Female Sexuality in the Hindu World," in *Immaculate and Powerful: The Female in Sacred Image and Social Reality,* edited by Clarissa W. Atkinson, Constance H. Buchanan, and Margaret R. Miles (1987); I. Julia Leslie's *The Perfect Wife: The Orthodox Hindu Woman According to the Strīdharmapaddhati of Tryambakayajvan* (1989); and in Leslie's *Roles and Rituals for Hindu Women* (1991), an excellent collection of articles by noted scholars covering a wide range of myth and practice.

While original texts are cited in most references noted here, two good collections of pertinent sources are edited volumes by Serinity Young, *An Anthology of Sacred Texts By and About Women* (1993), and by Donald S. Lopez Jr., *Religions of India in Practice* (1995). Other edited collections which have useful articles in them are Yvonne Yazbeck Haddad and Ellison Banks Findly, *Women, Religion and Social Change* (1985) (see articles by Ellison Banks Findly, Sandra P. Robinson, Donna Marie Wulff, and Lou Ratté); and Nancy Auer Falk and Rita M. Gross, *Unspoken Worlds: Women's Religious Lives* (1989) (see articles by Charles S. J. White, Doranne Jacobson, Susan S. Wadley, and James M. Freeman).

Contributions on the goddess tradition and women's relationships to it include Lawrence A. Babb's *The Divine Hierarchy: Popular Hinduism in Central India* (1975); David Kinsley's *Hindu Goddesses: Visions of the Divine Feminine in the Hindu Tradition* (1986); Sally J. Sutherland's "Sītā and Draupadī: Aggressive Behavior and Female Role-Models in the Sanskrit Epics," *Journal of the American Oriental Society,* 109, no. 1 (1989): 63–79; Thomas B. Coburn's *Encountering the Goddess: A Translation of the Devī-Māhātmya* (1991);

Stanley N. Kurtz's excellent *All the Mothers Are One: Hindu India and the Cultural Reshaping of Psychoanalysis* (1992); and the edited collection of John Stratton Hawley and Donna Marie Wulff, *Devī: Goddess of India* (1966).

Regional studies of women and Hindu culture include Manisha Roy's *Bengali Women* (1972, 1992); Susan S. Wadley's edited collection *The Powers of Tamil Women* (1980); Lynn Bennett's *Dangerous Wives and Sacred Sisters: Social and Symbolic Roles of High-Caste Women in Nepal* (1983); William P. Harman's *The Sacred Marriage of a Hindu Goddess* (1989); Lindsey Harlan's *Religion and Rajput Women: The Ethic of Protection in Contemporary Narratives* (1992); Kathleen M. Erndl's *Victory to the Mother: The Hindu Goddess of Northwest India in Myth, Ritual, and Symbol* (1993); Gloria Goodwin Raheja and Ann Grodzins Gold's *Listen to the Heron's Words: Reimagining Gender and Kinship in North India* (1994); and Anne Mackenzie Pearson's *"Because It Gives Me Peace of Mind": Ritual Fasts in the Religious Lives of Hindu Women* (1996).

Contributions that focus on special issues of Hindu marriage include S. J. Tambiah's "Dowry and Bridewealth and the Property Rights of Women in South Asia," in *Bridewealth and Dowry,* edited by Jack Goody and S. J. Tambiah (1973); Dorothy Stein's "Burning Widows, Burning Brides: The Perils of Daughterhood in India," *Pacific Affairs* 61, no. 3 (Fall 1988): 465–485; John Stratton Hawley's edited collection *Sati, The Blessing and the Curse: The Burning of Wives in India* (1994); and Lindsey Harlan and Paul B. Courtright's edited collection *From the Margins of Hindu Marriage: Essays on Gender, Religion, and Culture* (1995).

For works on women religious, see A. K. Ramanujan's "On Women Saints," in *The Divine Consort: Rādhā and the Goddesses of India,* edited by John Stratton Hawley and Donna Marie Wulff (1982); Frédérique Apffel Marglin's *Wives of the God-King: The Rituals of the Devadasis of Puri* (1985); and Linda Johnsen's *Daughters of the Goddess: The Women Saints of India* (1994).

For studies on aspects of Hindu women in the modern period, see Gail Omvedt's *We Will Smash This Prison! Indian Women in Struggle* (1980); Rehana Ghadially's edited collection *Women in Indian Society: A Reader* (1988); Kumkum Sangari and Sudesh Vaid's edited collection *Recasting Women: Essays in Colonial History* (1989); Elisabeth Bumiller's *May You Be the Mother of A Hundred Sons: A Journey Among the Women of India* (1990); and Leigh Minturn's *Sita's Daughters: Coming Out of Purdah; The Rajput Women of Khalapur Revisited* (1993).

For examples and discussions of women and Indian art, see Heinz Mode's *The Women in Indian Art* (1970);

Barbara Stoler Miller's *Exploring India's Sacred Art: Selected Writings of Stella Kramrisch* (1983); and Stephen P. Huyler's *Painted Prayers: Women's Art in Village India* (1994).

ELLISON BANKS FINDLY

Religious Rites and Practices

From the earliest times for which we have evidence, the religious activities of women in South Asia have been more prominent in the domestic than in the public realm. The wife of the sacrificer was a necessary but generally silent partner of her husband in the Vedic *śrauta* sacrifices; in the few actions she was called on to perform, she appears most often to have stood for sexuality and fertility. The most—indeed, the only—dramatic example of this is the point at which the queen of the patron of a Horse Sacrifice (*aśvamedha*) is required to lie with the dead horse under a cover in its grave. In the domestic (*gṛhya*) sacrifices, the wife played more active roles, and she had the primary responsibility for giving alms and providing hospitality on behalf of her household.

Throughout the history of the Hindu tradition and into the present time, women's religious practices have continued to focus on the household. Very few women have remained unmarried as adults or have led an ascetic life outside of a domestic context. The contrast between a girl's relatively free existence in her parental home and her many responsibilities once she moves to her in-laws' house has in many cases been a stark one and forms the basis for much folklore and literary imagery. Within their new home married women sometimes carry out the daily worship (*pūjā*) of the gods in the household shrine; generally, though, women's primary religious activities have centered on the preparation and serving of food, the birth and survival of children, the pleasure and comfort of the husband, and the general welfare of the family. A woman's god is said to be her husband, and a young bride's mother-in-law socializes her into the service of the husband and the other domestic rituals of the household.

Many of these domestic rituals center on food. Numerous festival occasions are marked by the cooking and consumption of special dishes, many of them quite complicated and time-consuming to prepare. Food offerings to the ancestors must also be prepared and presented at special times. On many other occasions women, especially high-caste women, and sometimes men practice fasting, avoiding grains and other foods considered normal, and eating fruits and foods prepared from certain root-vegetables. Such a fast is generally performed as part of a *vrata*, or vow. Even on a normal day, the choice, preparation, and serving of food, includ-

Ni Made Suri performs her daily Me Sai Ban ritual, making many small offerings of rice in order to ensure that the local volcano remains quiet, Batuan, Bali, Indonesia (Roger Ressmeyer/© Corbis).

ing its placement on the plate, is highly ritualized, especially in high-caste and wealthy households.

A *vrata*, which generally also involves some other rituals besides a special diet, is most often undertaken as a regular observance for the welfare of the husband and children. Childless couples, especially the wives, engage in a wide variety of religious activities aimed at increasing their own fertility, including rituals to placate beings (water spirits, serpents, and so on) understood to prevent a woman from becoming pregnant or to cause her children to be sickly or die young. Often women and their husbands or other relatives make a promise to deities held to have a positive effect on fertility, conditional on fulfillment of their desire for healthy children. They promise, for example, to go on pilgrimage with the child, once it has reached a certain age, to the temple of the god or goddess; to have the child's hair cut for the first time at the temple and to offer it to the god or goddess; or to make some other, often quite elaborate, offering.

Women are held to be responsible for the health and welfare of their husbands. A woman is to carry out this duty not only by cooking and managing the household in concert with her mother-in-law and her husband's brothers' wives but also by carrying out *vratas* for her husband's long life and prosperity. The ideal of the *pativratā*, the woman totally dedicated to the service of her husband, finds its culmination in the sati, the woman who immolates herself on her husband's funeral pyre so as not to become a widow. Very few women have ever become satis. As many castes do not allow widows to remarry, most women whose husbands predecease them are expected to dedicate themselves to devotional and ascetic activities directed toward other gods.

In some castes and families, a woman who is menstruating receives a "vacation" from most household chores. She does not cook or clean, and in some cases she remains outside the house, on a verandah or in the yard.

In general, the lower a woman's caste, the greater her religious role outside the home. Women (especially older women and young girls) frequently, though less often than men, serve as priests in the temples of non-Brahmanical deities in cities and in the countryside. Somewhat more often than men, women become possessed by goddesses who speak through them, answering the questions of people suffering from unexplained maladies or other difficulties. Women travel with men to distant and nearby holy places, participate in local and pilgrimage festivals, and make offerings in temples of local and pilgrimage deities. At least as often as men, women become possessed by ghosts and travel with their families to individuals or places reputed to cure such conditions.

In the context of urban bhakti religion, too, women play public roles. They participate in the group singing of *bhajans*, devotional songs, in temple halls and in one another's homes, and a few women have become performers of *kīrtans*, song-and-sermon performances. There are also specifically feminine folklore genres, some performed in the home but others outside it. In traditional royal temple contexts, women's primary performance role has been as *devadāsīs*, temple dancers. Such women are married to the god of a major temple and serve him by dancing and performing other ritual actions in the temple.

BIBLIOGRAPHY

Flueckiger, Joyce Burkhalter. *Gender and Genre in the Folklore of Middle India*. 1996.

Harlan, Lindsey. *Religion and Rajput Women: The Ethic of Protection in Contemporary Narratives*. 1992.

Jamison, Stephenie W. *Sacrificed Wife/Sacrificer's Wife*. 1996.

Leslie, Julia, ed. *Roles and Rituals for Hindu Women*. 1991.

Marglin, Frédérique Apffel. *Wives of the God-King: The Rituals of the Devadasis of Puri*. 1985.

McGee, Mary. "Feasting and Fasting: The Vrata Tradition and Its Significance for Hindu Women." Ph.D. diss., Harvard University, 1987.

Pearson, Anne Mackenzie. *"Because It Gives Me Peace of Mind": Ritual Fasts in the Religious Lives of Hindu Women*. 1996.

See also **Devadāsīs**.

ANNE FELDHAUS

Modern Movements

The eighteenth-century British conquerors of India were not concerned with Indian women or gender relations. They were interested in religion and social customs but rarely regarded women as victims of Hinduism. In the case of sati (the immolation of a wife with her husband's corpse before she technically becomes a widow), some British observers wrote admiringly of these women for their loyalty and courage. Female infanticide was interpreted as a departure from scriptural dictates, and *devadāsīs* (female servants of the gods, often temple dancers) were exoticized and eroticized.

Early in the nineteenth century British officials adopted a new attitude toward Hinduism and its gender ideology. James Mill, in his influential History of British India (1826), argued that women's position was an indicator of society's advancement; by that measure, India was backward. Missionaries concurred. Armed with the moral righteousness of their "civilizing mission," the British denounced Indian religions for oppressing women.

These ideas influenced members of the Bengali intelligentsia and then spread to other metropolitan areas. Employing foreign ideas and indigenous concepts, the intellectuals proclaimed the importance of social reform and modifying gender relations. In their discussions, women were constructed as victims or heroines but the reactions and responses of real women were not recorded.

Rammohun Roy (1772–1833), who denounced sati, is usually listed first among reformers concerned with improving women's status. By the second half of the century there were reformers in all parts of British India. In Bengal, Iswar Chandra Vidyasagar championed female education and led campaigns to legalize widow remarriage and prohibit polygyny. Keshub Chandra Sen, a leader of the Brahmo Samaj, envisioned new roles for women and set up schools, prayer meetings, and experimental living arrangements. In northern India Swami Dayananda Saraswati, the founder of the Arya Samaj, encouraged female education and condemned marriages between partners of unequal ages, dowry, and polygyny. In western India Mahadev Govind Ranade founded the National Social Conference to focus attention on social reforms, and the Parsi journalist Behramji Malabari wrote heart-rending articles on the evils of child marriage and the tragedy of enforced widowhood for young women. In southern India R. Venkata Ratnam Naidu opposed the devadāsī system, and Virasalingam Pantulu worked for marriage reform. Individually and through organizations, these men focused attention on deleterious customs and encouraged female education.

Traditionally, education involved learning to read sacred literature and excluded both women and Sudras. Christian missionaries opened the first girls' schools but their institutions were regarded with suspicion. It was not until Indian reformers turned their attention to female education, in the second half of the century, that the movement gained momentum. Members of the Brahmo Samaj led the movement in eastern India, while in Madras it was the Theosophical Society and in the north the Arya Samaj. As women became educated, they also set up schools. For example, Pandita Ramabai (1858–1922), awarded the title Pandita in recognition of her great learning, worked with reformers in western India to educate women through the Arya Mahila Samaj (Aryan's Women's Society). In Calcutta Mataji Maharani Tapaswini founded the Mahakali Pathshala (Great Mother Kali School) to promote female education in harmony with Hindu religious and moral principles. And in Madras "Sister" Subbalakshmi (1886–1969) established a school for young high-caste widows in 1912.

By the turn of the century interest in women's issues had waned as the intelligentsia turned to nationalist issues. However, "new women," educated and socially conscious, were forming their own associations to define women's problems. At first they were tutored by men; for example, in Bombay members of the Parthana Samaj helped Pandita Ramabai Saraswati set up the Arya Mahila Samaj, and Justice Ranade's wife Ramabai ran the organization. The Bharata Mahila Parishad (Ladies Social Conference), of the National Social Conference, had its first meeting in 1905 and focused attention on female education, the plight of widows, early marriage, dowry, and child welfare. Only a few years later Saraladevi Chaudhurani, critical of male patronage, began a women's organization for women only, Bharat Stree Mahamandal (The Large Circle of Indian Women). These women reformers identified key issues: female education, child marriage, the observance of purdah, and women's status in the family as interrelated and intertwined. Privileged by class and social status, they had little impact on poor and rural women.

After World War I these women and their successors created three national women's organizations: the Women's Indian Association, the National Council of Women in India, and the All India Women's Conference to present women's demands for education, the franchise, and legal reform.

In nationalist ideology, mother-goddess became a sign for the nation. Novels and songs extolled the Motherland, and the self-sacrificing woman was welcomed into the political arena. At early meetings of the Indian National Congress, women attended as delegates and appeared on stage singing in praise of Mother India. When the British partitioned the province of Bengal in 1905, women joined men in boycotting foreign goods and buying only swadeshi (country-made) goods.

Soon after Mohandas K. Gandhi (1869–1948) returned to Indian in 1915, he worked with women leaders to develop a role for women in his nonviolent movement. Indian needed, Gandhi said, women like the ancient heroines: Sita, Damayanti, and Draupadi. Sita, heroine of the Rāmāyaṇa, went into exile with her husband, withstood the advances of the demon Rāvaṇa, and proved her fidelity through the test of fire. Damayanti, the faithful and long-suffering wife of Nala, was able to recognize her husband in any guise. Draupadī, wife of the five Pandava brothers in the Mahābhārata, was wagered and lost in a dice game but saved from dishonor by the god Krishna. Gandhi urged women to emulate these heroines in their domestic and political lives. Because he insisted women first ask the permission of their guardians, his call to action did not threaten the patriarchal family. Yet he empowered women who, for the first time, heard they counted.

By 1921 women were forming women's political organizations, joining street demonstrations, and courting arrest. For example, Sarojini Naidu inaugurated the Rashtriya Stree Sangha in Bombay while in Calcutta Basanti Devi was arrested for selling khaddar (homespun cloth) in the street. In 1930 the Civil Disobedience movement was in full swing, and throughout British India women took primary responsibility for the foreign cloth boycott. Mimicking Hindu rites, women took swadeshi vows to spin thread, wear khaddar, and boycott foreign cloth.

To mobilize women, leaders made use of Hindu legends and symbols. Latika Ghosh, the Oxford-educated

Mohandas Gandhi, called Mahatma, leaves his Simla residence for Wardah, helped by his doctor, Sheila Nayyar (right), and Susila Ben (left), 16 July 1945 (Hulton-Deutsch Collection/Corbis).

founder of the Mahila Rashtriya Sangha in Bengal, recalled the battles between the *devīs* (goddesses) and *asuras* (demons) and told women they were the *shaktis* (principle of female energy) of the nation. Satyavati Devi, a north Indian leader, composed a song in prison with these lines: "Jump into the burning fire,/ And stand firm in the holy war,/ Do not retreat from the battle." The call was heard all over India, and women responded by joining demonstrations, courting arrest, and willingly serving time in jail.

After independence in 1947 women were "rewarded" for their role in the freedom struggle with a statement of gender equality in the Indian Constitution, the right to vote, and the Hindu Code Bill (separate acts rewriting for Hindus the laws of marriage and divorce, adoption, and inheritance). Twenty-five years later the women's movement accused the state of ignoring issues of gender justice and equality. Identifying the key problems as sexual assault and domestic violence, the autonomous women's movement united women across class, regional, and religious lines. However, much of the symbolism employed to construct the new non-Western feminist image was borrowed from Hinduism but as cultural idioms rather than religious symbols.

The 1990s has witnessed a new use of these symbols and notions of female empowerment by Hindu militants. To the chagrin of Indian feminists, Shiv Sena (a communal party in Bombay) urged women to be modern Durgās and avenge the wrongs against Hinduism. Women belonging to the Rashtra Sevika Samiti, the women's wing of the Hindu right, have been at the forefront of attacks on Muslims. Uma Bharati and Sadhvi Rithambara, two important leaders of Hindutva

skilled at inciting crowds to violence, are educated and unmarried young women not unlike their liberal counterparts. Appropriating the rhetoric of the feminist movement of the 1980s, the Bharatiya Janata Party has made violence against women its rallying call but given the issue a communal twist in accusing Muslim men of raping Hindu women. The new visibility of women in the right-wing movement has had a dampening effect on the women's movement that was so buoyant and optimistic in the 1980s. Opposing this movement has been an important issue for women formerly involved in issues of gender justice.

BIBLIOGRAPHY

There are two comprehensive studies of reform in colonial India: Charles H. Heimsath's *Indian Nationalism and Hindu Social Reform*, (1964) and Kenneth W. Jones' *Socio-Religious Reform Movements in British India* (1989). David Kopf's *The Brahmo Samaj and the Shaping of the Modern Indian Mind* (1979) is a thorough analysis of the Brahmo Samaj, while Meredith Borthwick's *The Changing Role of Women in Bengal, 1849–1905* (1985) and Ghulam Murshid, *Reluctant Dubutante: Response of Bengali Women to Modernization, 1849–1905* (1983) focus on women and gender issues in the Samaj.

Lata Mani's "Contentious Traditions: The Debate on Sati in Colonial India," in *Recasting Women, Essays in Colonial History,* edited by Kumkum Sangari and Sudesh Vaid (1989), focused attention on the discourse of reform and argued women themselves became the battleground. L. S. Vishwanath, in "Efforts of Colonial State to Suppress Female Infanticide: Use of Sacred Tests, Generation of Knowledge," *Economic and Political Weekly,* 33, no. 19 (1998), pp. 1104–1112, charts the shifting tactics of a colonial government trying to eliminate female infanticide.

In *The Nation and its Fragments: Colonial and Postcolonial Histories* (1993) Partha Chatterjee discusses the resolution of the woman question by nationalists within a home-world dichotomy. In "Hindu Conjugality and Nationalism in Late Nineteenth Century Bengal," in *Indian Women: Myth and Reality,* edited by Jasodhara Bagchi (1995), Tanika Sarkar traces the development of the nationalist ideology of the family and the rewoven myth of the pure woman who plays a redemptive role inside that family. Equally useful for conceptualizing this period is Mrinalini Sinha's *Colonial Masculinity: The 'Manly Englishman' and the 'Effeminate Bengali' in the Late Nineteenth Century* (1995).

For an understanding of women's reaction and response to these reforms, see Rosalind O'Hanlon, *Tarabai Shinde: A Comparison Between Women and*

Men (1994), Pandita Ramabai's *The High-Caste Hindu Woman* (1887), Parvati Athavale, *My Story: The Autobiography of a Hindu Widow*, translated by Rev. Justin E. Abbott (1930), and Monica Felton, *A Child Widow's Story* (London, 1966). Meera Kosambi's essays on social reform in western India have been collected in *At the Intersection of Gender Reform and Religious Belief* (1993).

For the nationalist period there are Gandhi's letters to women in the ashram: M. K. Gandhi, *To the Women* (1941), and collected essays and speeches on women: *M. K. Gandhi: Women and Social Justice* (1954). The best single essay on Gandhi and women is Madhu Kishwar, "Women and Gandhi," *Economic and Political Weekly*, 20, no. 40 (1985), pp. 1691–1702 and 20, no. 41 (1985), pp. 1753–1758. Sujata Patel's "Construction and Reconstruction of Woman in Gandhi," *Economic and Political Weekly*, 23, no. 8 (1988), pp. 377–388 examines Gandhi's ideology of gender difference.

There are a number of autobiographies of women who joined the nationalist movement, for example, Manmohini Zutshi Sahgal, *An Indian Freedom Fighter Recalls Her Life* (1994), Muthulakshmi Reddy, *Autobiography of Dr. (Mrs.) Muthulakshmi Reddy* (1964), and Kamaladev Chattopadhyay, *Inner Recesses, Outer Spaces: Memoirs* (1986).

Two recent books on women in colonial and postcolonial India are Radha Kumar's *The History of Doing: An Illustrated Account of Movements for Women's Rights and Feminism in India, 1800–1990* (1993), and Geraldine Forbes' *Women in Modern India* (1996).

Key works for understanding the women's movement from the 1970s to the 1990s are: *Toward Equality: Report Of The Committee On The Status Of Women In India* (1974); Gail Omvedt's *We Will Smash This Prison!* (1980); *In Search of Answers*, edited by Madhu Kishwar and Ruth Vanita (1984); and Flavia Agnes' "Protecting Women Against Violence? Review of a Decade of Legislation, 1980–1989," *Economic and Political Weekly*, 27, no. 17 (1992), pp. WS19–WS33. John Stratton Hawley, ed., *Sati: The Blessing and the Curse: The Burning of Wives in India* (1994) includes articles that examine sati as a living tradition.

One of the first volumes on women and Hindutva was Amrita Basu, ed., "Women and Religious Nationalism in India," *Bulletin of Concerned Asian Scholars*, special issue, 25, no. 3 (1993). The more recent *Women and Right-Wing Movements: Indian Experiences*, edited by Tanika Sarkar and Urvashi Butalia (1995), includes excellent articles on this topic. Purnima Mankekar's "Television Tales and a Woman's Rage: A Nationalist Recasting of Draupadi's 'Disrobing,'" *Public Culture*, 5 (1993), pp. 469–492, examines how women understood a spe-

cific episode in Indian television's many hours of Hindu legends. Mankekar suggests that programs designed to reinscribe traditional roles may unwittingly encourage female solidarity and a feminist critique of society.

See also **Devadāsīs**; **Durgā and Kālī**.

GERALDINE FORBES

In the West

Hindu immigrants arrived in the Caribbean as workers in the nineteenth century, but it was in the late twentieth century that hundreds of thousands of Hindus settled in Western Europe (primarily England), Canada, and the United States. The patterns of immigration have been different in each country; Hindus settled in England after being ejected by repressive rule in some African countries. After the loosening of immigration laws in the 1960s, it was initially men who came to the United States for professional education and then settled as immigrants.

TEMPLE HINDUISM

With the increasing numbers of Hindu families came the need for houses of worship. Although the first Hindu worship center was the Vedanta Temple built in 1906 in San Francisco, the first immigrant temples in the United States were built in Pittsburgh and New York in the 1970s. The temples have large community halls and place heavy emphasis on cultural activities. Music and dance, long considered to be paths to salvation within the Hindu traditions, are taught in many temples, and many performances are held in these centers. Temple priests are generally males of the brahmin caste, but women are involved in temple administration at various levels, with some holding prominent leadership position in the larger temples in the United States.

The temples house many deities; most popular are various forms of Vishnu, including Venkatśvara, Rāma, and Krishna. The goddesses Lakṣmt (Lakshmi) and Durgā are prominent in many Hindu temples in the west. Although the goddess Kālī is worshiped by many Hindus, and is popular among Western feminists, in the Hindu temples in America she is generally conspicuous by her absence. There are very few shrines for her, and when represented, it is usually in the form of a calendar picture. Unlike in India, where sectarian temples are popular, temples in the West have many deities, most of whom have pan-Indian recognition.

Local goddesses and rituals are generally not imported into the United States, and animal sacrifice is not seen in Hindu temples of South Asian origin. In

Young Indian girls perform a traditional dance at a celebration of the Hindu festival Diwali in Seattle, Washington, 1995 (Dean Wong/Corbis).

some local shrines and domestic rituals in India, and in temples where Hindus from the Caribbean worship, women dance under possession. Possession by the goddess in such ritual occasions is seldom seen in Hindu temples of South Asian origin in the West.

Although women do not generally officiate as priests in these temples, there are a few exceptions. Women have also innovated new ritual functions; for instance, in some temples, like the Venkateśvara Temple of Atlanta, women regularly carry the image of the goddess in procession. In India this is done only by men.

Menstruation is considered to be polluting by the so called high-caste textual and brahminical traditions in Hinduism. Menstruating women do not go to a temple in India; but in the diaspora the patterns seem to have changed. Because the temples serve as community centers and learning institutions—"Sunday schools" that teach religion to children—and because many women are in administrative roles in temple organization, rules of purity and pollution associated with menstruation are apparently left to the worshiper's discretion.

DOMESTIC RITUALS

Many of the rituals traditionally performed at home in India are now done in temples. The *varalakṣmī vrata*, for instance, a domestic ritual dedicated by south Indian women to the goddess Lakṣmī in late July or early August, is a home ritual in India but regularly done in temples in Canada and the United States.

The fall festival of Navaratri (Nine Nights) celebrated in honor of the goddesses Lakṣmī, Durgā, and Sarasvatī in many parts of India is celebrated in different ways in the diaspora. Women from Tamilnadu, South India, celebrate this festival at home with huge displays of religious and secular dolls. People go from house to house, singing classical songs in the Carnatic musical style. Popular in south India, these festivities are seen in a grand way among the Tamil and Telugu-speaking diaspora population all over the United States.

People from Gujarat dance the nights away during Navaratri. The *garbha* (womb or creative energies) dance is a circular one in praise of the mother goddess Durgā. The *dandiya raas*, a dance with sticks, celebrates the dance of Lord Krishna and the cowherd girls. These dances are performed by Gujarati emigres in large numbers; thousands of worshipers attend the dance in large community centers in the large metropolitan areas of England, Canada, and the United States. Festivals such as Holi, a colorful springtime ritual, and Diwali, the fall festival of lights, are also celebrated by Hindus in the diaspora.

In the West, unlike in India, marriages are not arranged on a regular basis. Caste and diet restrictions are also relaxed considerably, except when it comes to ritual duties in temples.

SPIRITUAL TEACHERS

Spiritual teachers, or gurus, belonging to the many Hindu traditions as well as new, charismatic leaders periodically tour foreign countries, meeting devotees, giving discourses, training children in summer camps, inaugurating temples, and participating in public functions. Notable are the highly respected (male) leaders of Swaminarayan movement and Chinmaya mission. Women gurus like Ma Amritanandamayi (Ammachi) periodically tour parts of the world in summer; other women gurus have set up organizations in the West.

The Ramakrishna Mission became popular in the United States through the efforts of Swami Vivekananda toward the end of the nineteenth century and still has monasteries and philosophical centers in parts of the Western world. Recent women's monastic movements such as the Sarada Ashram in Michigan have a fair number of devotees of West European descent. Sectarian movements such as the International Society for Krishna Consciousness (ISKCON; more popularly known as the Hare Krishna movement) have a considerable number of women devotees, but not many in leadership roles.

The Internet has thousands of sites that portray the importance of religious leaders, advertise their visits to Western countries, and list pilgrimage sites in India; temple home pages, pictures of deities, and discourses of gurus abound. Other lists serve as discussion forums for the various Hindu traditions and for people from various parts of India. In the absence of real temples, some home pages are constructed as Internet shrines for goddesses such as Kālī. Perhaps the greatest change in the Hindu traditions in the twentieth century is this explosion of information and the accessibility of materials through the electronic media. In religious traditions where salvific knowledge was kept to the privileged elite, this accessibility of information to men and women of all sectors and castes of society marks a phenomenal change.

BIBLIOGRAPHY

Eck, Diana. "On Common Ground: World Religions in America." CD-ROM that explores the history, beliefs, and current practices of fifteen religious traditions in the United States. New York: Columbia University Press. 1997.

Leonard, Karen Isaksen. *The South Asian Americans.* 1997.

Narayanan, Vasudha. "Creating the South Indian 'Hindu' Experience in the United States." In *A Sacred Thread: Modern Transmissions of Hindu Traditions in India and Abroad.* Edited by Raymond Williams. 1992.

ON-LINE RESOURCES

The Ganesha temple of New York (with links to other temples in the United States)
<http://www.indianet.com/ganash>
"The Hindu Universe"
<http://hindunet.org/home.shtml>
The South Asian Women's Network
<http://www.umiacs.umd.edu:80/users/sawweb/sawnet/>
Official Home page of Ma Amritanandamayi
<http://www.ammachi.org/>

See also **Durgā and Kālī**; **Lakṣmī**; **Sarasvatī**.

VASUDHA NARAYANAN

History of Study

Although anecdotal knowledge about the Indian subcontinent has circulated in the West since at least the time of Herodotus, the Greek historian of the fifth century B.C.E., it was the wave of exploration, trade, and conquest begun by Europeans in the late fifteenth century that led to the systematic study of Indian civilization by Westerners. By the middle of the eighteenth century, when European rivalries focused attention on India, the codification of Western knowledge about Indian religions was well under way. The term *Hindu* came to be used by Westerners in the late eighteenth century as a designation for all indigenous, non-Muslim religiosity in India. Originally a geographic term designating the Indus River and, by extension, the inhabi-

tants of the Indian subcontinent, *Hindu* has no precise equivalent in any Indic language. The term *Hinduism* is often used today to refer to any Indian religious tradition rooted in the Vedas, an ancient body of hymns and commentaries (portions of which date back to 1200 B.C.E.). But the term has also been used in a more restricted sense to denote the living tradition of iconic worship focusing on personal deities that grew out of the earlier aniconic sacrificial tradition of the Vedas.

The British had compelling utilitarian reasons for promoting the study of Hindu religious life. The British East India Company, having in 1772 assumed responsibility for the administration of civil justice in Bengal, encouraged the study of Sanskrit, the language of the Vedas, and commissioned studies of Hindu law. Called upon to judge cases to be decided according to Hindu law, British administrators naturally felt that if they were to govern in accordance with Hindu legal codes, they ought to know what these codes were. One of the most influential British scholar-administrators of this period was Sir William Jones (1746–1794). A lawyer and a linguist specializing in Persian (the official diplomatic language of India until 1835), Jones arrived in Bengal in 1783 as a Supreme Court judge and in 1784 founded the Asiatic Society of Bengal, the first society for the study of Indian culture. Jones established the importance of Sanskrit in the science of philology and made it his task to prove the affinity of Sanskrit, Greek, and Latin as "siblings" in the Indo-European family of languages, thus revealing undreamed-of resemblances among what were then considered disparate languages and cultures.

Despite the ground-breaking role played by Jones in the creation of Indology as a discipline of study, it was James Mill (1773–1836), the Utilitarian philosopher and journalist, who wrote the period's most influential Western history of India. Mill completed his monumental *The History of the British in India* in 1817 without ever visiting India. Whereas the accounts by Jones and his colleagues saw the Hindus as a people with a glorious past whose high culture was now in a state of decline, Mill judged the culture to be degraded from the start. The hegemony of the priestly class and the low status of Hindu women were, for Mill, indications of the barbarity of Hindu culture. Mill's history had a decisive influence not only on British views of India (it was required reading at Haileybury College, where civil servants of the East India Company were trained until 1855) but also on European Indology. The German philosopher Georg Wilhelm Friedrich Hegel (1770–1831), for example, relied on Mill's work in his reconstruction of world history. Codifying the long-held Western belief in the dreamlike, irrational quality of Indian thought, Hegel located Indian civilization at a low level in the evolutionary scheme of things—a point just prior to the awakening of subjective reason in human history.

HINDU WOMEN AND THE POLITICS OF IMPERIALISM

In the cultural and ideological encounter between England and India that provided the major impetus for the development of Indology, the status of Hindu women came to occupy a significant place. Where the early years of British rule were characterized by a laissez-faire style of tolerance for Indian ways of life (a large number of the early East India Company officials, for example, married Indian women and observed Indian customs and religious practices), by the early nineteenth century the British began to be more openly critical of Indian gender politics and more actively involved in legislating women's rights in India. Although these efforts may have been fueled in part by altruism, self-serving motives were undoubtedly at work as well. Behind the Indian "woman question" lay the pressing issue of whether Indians were capable of governing themselves in a "civilized" fashion. Fighting against the oppression of women in India served the British as an indication of the moral superiority of Western culture and hence as a justification of British rule in India. In 1829 the British policy of nonintervention in Hindu custom and ritual practice was challenged by the Act of Abolition, which outlawed sati, the immolation of widows on their deceased husbands' funeral pyres, and set the stage for other interventions in the area of religious custom concerning women, such as child marriage and temple prostitution.

Fueled by ambivalent motives, British reforms had mixed effects. Joanna Liddle and Rama Joshi have argued that some early British reform efforts had an adverse effect on lower-caste women. Such women lost rights they had enjoyed—divorce, widow-remarriage, and female inheritance, for example—when British law made Hindu laws pertaining to brahmin women binding for all castes. The record on temple courtesans or *devadāsīs* is also ambivalent. Frédérique Apffel Marglin and Kay Jordan have argued that efforts to outlaw *devadāsīs* overlooked the ways in which the *devadasi* institution benefited women by offering them unparalleled opportunities for education, property ownership, and personal autonomy.

Western women played significant roles in the framing of the Indian "woman question" in the colonial era. Some resisted the imperialist stance of the dominant discourse on women in India; others were complicitous in it. The U.S. journalist Katherine Mayo stands as a prime example of the empire-boosting powers of imperial feminism. In 1927 Mayo published *Mother India*, a graphic account of life in India highlighting the plight of Hindu women. Mayo's highly polemical book drove home the need to fight the home-rule movement, arguing that British colonial rule was needed as a source of moral reform in this benighted part of the globe. Margaret Noble (known by her Hindu religious name, Sister Nivedita) and Margaret Gillespie Cousins stand as examples of feminist reformers more sympathetic to Indian nationalist aspirations and more apt to be critical of imperial rhetoric. Both played an active role in founding organizations to involve Indian women in public life, such as the All India Women's Conference.

BIBLIOGRAPHY

Altekar, Anant Sadashiv. *The Position of Women in Hindu Civilization.* 1978.

Chaudhuri, Nupur, and Margaret Strobel. *Western Women and Imperialism: Complicity and Resistance.* 1992.

Cohn, Bernard S. *Colonialism and Its Forms of Knowledge: The British in India.* 1996.

Courtright, Paul. *The Goddess and the Dreadful Practice.* Forthcoming.

Das, R. M. *Women in Manu and His Seven Commentators.* 1962.

Hawley, John Stratton, ed. *Sati, the Blessing and the Curse: The Burning of Wives in India.* 1994.

Hawley, John Stratton, and Donna Marie Wulff, eds. *The Divine Consort: Radha and the Goddesses of India.* 1986.

Jordan, Kay K. "Devadasi Reform: Driving the Priestesses or the Prostitutes Out of Hindu Temples?" In *Religion and Law in Independent India.* Edited by Robert Baird. 1993.

Liddle, Joanna, and Rama Joshi. "Gender and Imperialism in British India." *South Asia Research.* 1985.

MacMillan, Margaret. *Women of the Raj.* 1988.

Mani, Lata. "Contentious Traditions: The Debate on Sati in Colonial India." In *Recasting Women: Essays in Colonial History.* Edited by Kumkum Sangari and Sudesh Vaid. 1989.

Marglin, Frédérique Apffel. *Wives of the God-King: The Rituals of the Devadasis of Puri.* 1985.

Marshall, P. J. *The British Discovery of Hinduism in the Eighteenth Century.* 1968.

Masters, Alfred. "The Influence of Sir William Jones upon Sanskrit Studies." *Bulletin of the School of Oriental and African Studies* 11 (1943–1946): 798–806.

Mayo, Katherine. *Mother India.* 1927. Reprint, 1930.

Mill, James. *The History of British India.* 1817. Reprint, 1972.

Mukherjee, S. N. *Sir William Jones: A Study in Eighteenth-Century Attitudes to India.* 1968.

Nandy, Ashis. *The Intimate Enemy: Loss and Recovery of Self under Colonialism.* 1983.

Rajan, Rajeswari Sunder. *Real and Imagined Women: Gender, Culture, and Postcolonialism.* 1993.

Said, Edward. *Orientalism.* 1978.

Sangari, Kumkum, and Sudesh Vaid. *Recasting Women: Essays in Colonial History.* 1986.

Spivak, Gayatri. "Can the Subaltern Speak? Speculations on Widow-Sacrifice." *Wedge* 7, no. 8 (1985): 120–130.

Tharu, Susie, and K. Lalitha, eds. *Women Writing in India.* 1991.

Wadley, Susan S., ed. *The Powers of Tamil Women.* 1980.

Wilson, Liz. "Who Is Authorized to Speak? Katherine Mayo and the Politics of Imperial Feminism in British India." *Journal of Indian Philosophy* 25, no. 2 (1997): 139–151.

LIZ WILSON

History

The study of history, derived from the Greek word *histor* (knowing; inquiry), provides substance, texture, and depth to our knowledge of the past and of ourselves in relation to that past. A clear distinction should be made between an understanding of history as continuous event, the totality of human experience and activity down through the ages, and history as recorded account, the apprehension and interpretation of past events by historians. The earliest Greco-Roman models of history writing, as exemplified by works of Herodotus (c. 484–425 B.C.E.) and Livy (59 B.C.E.–17 C.E.), consisted primarily of the documentation of political and military vicissitudes. Until the twentieth century the dominant focus of recorded history has remained the fate of empires and nations, foregrounding male achievements in public structures of power. The twentieth century has witnessed a vast expansion in definitions of historical subject matter and a corresponding fragmentation of the field into a number of subdisciplines. Marxist history, "third world" history, the history of science, women's history, religious history, and many others now have their own discrete sources and methodologies. Development of this new and animated pluralism has been enhanced by postmodern theory, notably the retreat from a belief in the possibility of a unified, impartial account of the past and recognition of the inescapable ideological subjectivity of the historian

at work. The emergent definition of history is that of an infinitely diverse contested series of discourses imputing nuanced meanings to the past.

In its depiction of human history as the primary arena of divine action, the historiography of monotheistic religions has been characterized by the construction of narratives which portray the purposeful triumph of good over evil. Christian patristic historical writing combined eschatology (a study of the doctrines of death and judgment, heaven and hell), with an ecclesiological emphasis concomitant with the institutionalization of the early church. Since Eusebius of Caesarea's fourth-century volume *Ecclesiastical History,* European and North American religious historical scholarship has produced a systematic examination of the development of ecclesiastical structures, doctrinal purity, theological reforms, and the clerical officialdom that implemented such changes. Recently, a more broadly defined social history of religion has redirected scholarly focus away from the narrow confines of the church's formal administration and its male elites to a recovery of the spiritual beliefs and values of the laity.

WOMEN'S HISTORY

Consideration of women's distinctive religious experiences as a significant analytical category has been virtually nonexistent in mainstream studies of ecclesiastical politics or popular religiosity. Stimulated by the feminist movement of the 1960s, the advent of women's history introduced a radical paradigm shift in history writing, attributing equal recognition to female agency in the building of human civilization. In *The Majority Finds Its Past* (1979), American historian Gerda Lerner outlined the methodological challenge first enunciated by Mary Beard in 1946, that in falsely universalizing male experience, establishment history had presented a distorted androcentric account that was responsible for the systematic exclusion of more than half the human race. The retrieval of women previously marginalized or *Hidden from History,* as British historian Sheila Rowbotham's important 1973 text described it, and the discernment of female social, economic, political, and religious participation in every era constitutes the fundamental rationale of women's history. Just how such a past should be reconstructed continues to provoke lively theoretical debate. The compensatory quest for individual heroines, a centuries-old literary genre, has brought forth many hagiographies of pious queens, abbesses, saints, and mystics. Sensible of the discrepancies posed by the recovery of exceptional women for the daily lives of the majority and influenced by social history's desire to write "history from below," contemporary feminists have redefined the parameters of the

An image that carries many historical overtones; women accused as witches are being burned alive in this woodcut print from a German broadside, c. 1555 (Stock Montage, Inc./Historical Pictures Collection).

historical enterprise, asserting the dynamics of the private familial sphere as an equally valid area of historical investigation.

Because female cultures throughout history have been so intricately interwoven with the life of the church, synagogue, or temple, the retrieval of women's religious visibility is of huge significance in restoring women to their past. In conjunction with the dual force of Christianity as both oppressor and liberator of women's lives, feminists have assessed the historical response of the church to the female presence in terms of two basic historiographical types: 1) A deconstruction of clerical misogyny and corresponding analysis of theological justifications for female subordination. 2) A positive emphasis on reclaiming women's obliterated contributions to the life of the church. Spanning these approaches is an examination of the tension between dominant prescriptive ideologies of femininity as espoused by institutional religious teaching and the reality of women's religious experience —what women actually did. Within this broad framework historians have investigated a range of themes relating to women's spiritual practices and beliefs. The following summary highlights some of the key texts and approaches in women's religious history to arise since the 1960s.

FEMINIST REVISIONS OF RELIGIOUS HISTORY

Feminist writing on early Christian history and late antiquity has encompassed a variety of approaches in its reconstruction of female spirituality in the ancient world. Elisabeth Schüssler Fiorenza's pioneering study *In Memory of Her* (1983) enlarged our understanding of active female leadership in the nascent Christian communities and alerted readers to the exclusionary poli-

tics of the canonization process. Deborah Sawyer's *Women and Religion in the First Christian Centuries* (1996) emphasizes the pluralistic context of early Christianity and its relationship to Greco-Roman culture and Jewish religion, providing a comparative analysis of divergent female religious imagery and customs. Other historians have investigated the gendered dimensions of martyrdom, asceticism, and heresiology.

Medieval scholarship on women and religion has been characterized by an emphasis on life in the convent and the richness of female devotional writing. This is amply attested in numerous studies of women mystics such as Julian of Norwich and Hildegard of Bingen, whose texts affirmed the sacrality of the female and expressed the feminine side of the divine. Caroline Walker Bynum's outstanding contribution to medieval historiography has been to illuminate the graphic physicality of much female piety. She demonstrates the way in which women mystics recast what may now be perceived by feminists as highly ambiguous metaphors of suffering and self-sacrifice into symbols of real female empowerment.

Early modernists like Merry Wiesner have paid particular attention to the impact of the Reformation and Counter-Reformation on women's everyday religious and family life in the sixteenth century, cautioning against an exaggeration of the alleged benefits of Protestantism for European women. Protestant ideals of marriage, it is argued, upheld rather than challenged patriarchal authority while denying women the feminine element so prevalent in Catholic worship. The combined significance of religion and gender has been assessed in the European witchcrazes of the sixteenth and seventeenth centuries. According to historians Lyndal Roper and Christina Larner, socially vulnerable women suffered horrifying consequences of Christian misogyny, underscored by new theological and legal theories of demonology.

The scholarship on modern women's religious history is impressive and continues to flourish. Texts such as *Women and Religion in America*, edited by Rosemary Radford Ruether and Rosemary Keller (3 vols., 1981), and *Religion in the Lives of English Women, 1760–1930*, edited by Gail Malmgreen (1986), have uncovered an abundance of women's roles in Jewish and Christian spiritual traditions as missionaries, fundraisers, preachers, moral reformers, and nuns. The feminization of religion, understood in terms of women's numerical, organizational, and theological influence in the churches, has received sophisticated treatment by American historians Barbara Welter and Ann Douglas. As Gerda Lerner shows in *The Creation of Feminist Consciousness* (1993), it is possible to locate instances of female resistance to patriarchal religious authority in every historical period. It was the nineteenth century, however, that witnessed the emergence of an organized form of Anglo-American religious feminism dominated by the debate over women's equal access to ministerial leadership. Feminist Biblical criticism, often appropriated in the cause of women's right to preach, also came of age. Nineteenth-century American feminists Sarah Grimke, Matilda Joslyn Gage, and Elizabeth Cady Stanton produced scathing critiques of patriarchal Biblical religion and its debilitating effect on women's status. As the collection of essays *Searching the Scriptures,* edited by Elisabeth Schüssler Fiorenza (2 vols., 1993, 1994), shows, these critiques provide a fitting historical prototype of subsequent feminist religious scholarship.

THEORETICAL CONSIDERATIONS

Restoring women to the past means reshaping and expanding the distorted, male-specific landscape of traditional religious history to construct narratives that accommodate the experiences of both sexes. From the women warriors of the pre-Islamic era to the medieval Sufi women who dwelt in the rare female *ribāṭ*s (fortresses); from women's political participation in the life of ancient Israel to the economic initiatives of the early modern Jewish wife and mother; from nineteenth-century English Catholic nuns to African-American female holiness preachers, historians have become increasingly sensitive to the impact of race, class, and ethnic tradition on the myriad representations of women's religious historical experience. Such research may deepen understanding of existing accounts, introduce new concerns, or compel reexamination of assumed categories and explanations. Joan Kelly's groundbreaking exposition of periodization has shown, for example, that gauging the expansion and diminution of female activity may well provide a chronology of religious change entirely different from that determined by male interests. Womanist theology and goddess religion have challenged history at its deepest level, redefining traditional sources and questioning the nature of historical evidence. African-American scholars have created a new historical canon in retrieving their spiritual foremothers, drawing upon slave narratives, poetry, and spiritual autobiographies. As Jacquelyn Grant has argued, confronted with a history of acute objectification and disempowerment, the unearthing of black women's traditions of spiritual and political resistance is a major factor in creating a transformative womanist theology. Spiritual or goddess feminists reconstruct their ancient foremothers from archaeological evidence, denoting the existence of prepatriarchal, matrifocal, and possibly goddess-worshiping or matriarchal societies. Despite vigorous feminist debate regarding the lack of straightforward evidence and veracity of sources, the work of archaeologist Marija Gimbutas and others challenges history defined as an exclusively literary account of the past, alerting scholars to the creative possibilities of prehistoric accounts of women and religion.

Given the range of themes and approaches encompassed by the history of women and religion, theoretical clarification is essential. Feminist disputation surrounding the various interpretive frameworks of women's history, feminist history, and gender history have important ramifications for the development of the field in terms of the types of projects undertaken, subjects of study, and conclusions drawn. Is the retrieval by women's history of historiographical areas of omission responsible for providing a merely supplementary narrative that fails to challenge existing male-defined categories? Does a focus on female oppression or patriarchy deny women full historical agency? To what extent did religious women collude in as well as struggle against ecclesiastical hierarchical structures? How might this illuminate the tensions between religious women of various ethnic and class statuses? Does the more inclusive paradigm of gender history, with its emphasis on female-male relations, threaten to decenter the study of women once again?

The recovery of women as makers of their own spiritual histories rather than passive recipients of an imposed patriarchal order can be vital in the affirmation of contemporary feminist intellectual and political strategies. The historian aims to understand the past both on its own terms and through the prism of the present, providing insights of relevance through responsible historical scholarship. Thus, scholars of women and religion have warned against uncritical affirmations of our spiritual foremothers, contending that we cannot plunder the religious symbols of the past without acknowledging the importance of the spiritual-historical milieu in which they were articulated. Bynum's work is particularly instructive here. Her insistence on historical specificity compels the realization that religious women of the past must be allowed to emerge as historical actors in their own right with their own concerns, even when these conflict with current feminist analyses and interests. Women have been central, not marginal, to the founding and shaping of many of the world's religious traditions. The task ahead for the history of women and religion is the development of multiple narratives that document a full, inclusive historical vision of the significance of the female presence.

BIBLIOGRAPHY

Beard, Mary. *Woman as Force in History: A Study in Traditions and Realities.* 1946.

Bynum, Caroline Walker. *Fragmentation and Redemption.* 1992.

———. *Holy Feast and Holy Fast.* 1987.

Douglas, Ann. *The Feminization of American Culture.* 1977.

Gimbutas, Marija. *The Language of the Goddess.* 1989.

Grant, Jacquelyn. *White Women's Christ and Black Women's Jesus.* 1989.

Kelly, Joan. "Did Women Have a Renaissance?" In *Becoming Visible: Women in European History.* Edited by R. Bridenthal, C. Koonz, and S. Stuard. 1987.

Larner, Christina. *Witchcraft and Religion: The Politics of Popular Belief.* 1984.

Roper, Lyndal. *Oedipus and the Devil, Witchcraft, Sexuality and Religion in Early Modern Europe.* 1994.

Rowbotham, Sheila. *Hidden from History: 300 Years of Women's Oppression and the Fight Against It.* London, 1973.

Welter, Barbara. "The Feminization of American Religion: 1800–1860." In *Clio's Consciousness Raised: New Perspectives on the History of Women.* Edited by Mary Hartmann and Lois Banner. 1974.

Wiesner, Merry. *Women and Gender in Early Modern Europe.* 1993.

See also **Gage**, **Matilda Joslyn**; **Goddess**; **Womanist Traditions**.

SUE MORGAN

History of Religions

The independent study of religions, free from the tutelage of Christian theology, has come into its own since the late nineteenth century as a nontheological, nonnormative way of studying religions by using historical, phenomenological, and comparative methods. This large field of inquiry is often called *history of religions* in a wider sense, or described by the German term *Religionswissenschaft.* The term *religious studies* has come to be used, whereas older scholarly works tended to refer to the field as *comparative religion* (see the scholars and textual selections included in Waardenburg, 1973, and the history of comparative religion given by Sharpe, 1986).

The study of religion has an ancient pedigree, but its pursuit on a cross-cultural basis is a modern development that began with the German comparative philologist Max Müller (1823–1900). During the late nineteenth century a comparative methodology for the study of religions was developed on a systematic basis and led to the creation of a new scholarly discipline, often called *science of religion.* European scholars wrote histories of

particular religions or established comparisons of particular religious phenomena (such as mysticism or prayer, for example) across different religions, or developed systematic typologies and classifications of religions.

The first four chairs in the history of religions were founded in the Netherlands after the reform of the theological faculties in 1876, followed by the creation of a chair at the Collège de France in Paris and several chairs at universities in Switzerland, Britain (Manchester and London), Scandinavia, the United States (Harvard and Chicago), and other universities of the Western world. International history of religions congresses, devoted to the study of many religions and methodological issues, have been regularly held in Europe since 1900, and out of these grew the International Association for the History of Religions, founded in 1950 in Amsterdam, which meets every five years in a different country of the world.

During the late twentieth century the study of religions has developed as a comparative, cross-cultural, and global field of studies, pursued in many universities and colleges around the world. The term *history of religions* can now be used in a narrow sense, where history is the descriptive study of the human past, primarily concerned with factual and descriptive matters, or it can refer to a more comprehensive historical-comparative enterprise concerned with important issues of hermeneutical interpretation and the meaning of past religious history for people living in the present.

The German-American historian of religions Joachim Wach (1898–1955) established the science of religion in Chicago and is the founder of the so-called Chicago school in the history of religions. His successor, the Romanian scholar Mircea Eliade (1908–1986), who emigrated to the United States after World War II, gave the history of religions his own emphasis, based on a particular hermeneutic, which is evident from his books and the journal *History of Religions,* founded in 1961. Eliade strongly affirms the importance of the history of religions through its provision of a critical, interpretive method, a "creative hermeneutics" for contemporary culture, programmatically announced as "A New Humanism" in the first number of his journal. Many scholars have criticized Eliade's extension of the meaning of the history of religions—which, for him, ultimately assumes a soteriological function—as inappropriate.

Eliade's particular hermeneutical and phenomenological approach has provided the framework for *The Encyclopedia of Religion,* edited by him with the help of many international collaborators, and published in 1987. But this widely used reference work also provides abundant factual evidence of how much the study of religion is still deeply rooted in an androcentric framework, largely left unquestioned. The data and theories gathered in the sixteen volumes of *The Encyclopedia* provide visible evidence for the continuing marginality and invisibility of women in most men's scholarship, still unaffected by critical gender perspectives and unaware of their restrictive understanding of *homo religiosus*. Almost every article in the *Encyclopedia* provides an instructive example of what has been called the "malestream" nature of established scholarship. Ugo Bianchi's entry "History of Religions" presents a widely accepted understanding of the development, theories, concepts, and classifications of this field, yet lacks any acknowledgment of the contributions of earlier or contemporary women scholars, or the new questions raised by women's studies. This is also true of Eric Sharpe's widely used textbook *Comparative Religion,* whose second, updated edition of 1986 contains a new chapter, "From Comparative Religion to Religious Studies," surveying the new intellectual and organizational developments that have influenced the study of religion since the 1970s. There is no mention whatsoever of the growth of women's studies in religion.

A similar "sexism by omission" marks most of the articles of *The Encyclopedia of Religion.* Surprisingly, this large reference work does not even include an entry on either patriarchy or matriarchy, though it contains articles titled "Androcentrism" and "Women's Studies" in religion. Women as religious practitioners, active in larger numbers than men, and women as religious specialists are largely ignored in the *Encyclopedia.* For example, it describes only four women scholars (Ruth Benedict, Barbara G. Meyerhoff, Jane E. Harrison, and Evelyn Underhill) among the 142 significant scholars of religion to whom a separate entry is devoted.

The growth of women's studies and feminist theory since the late 1960s has increasingly led to a fundamental reorientation or paradigm shift in the study of religions that affects all data, theories, and methodological discussions, as is evident from the perceptive methodological observations and criticisms of the traditional history of religions by Rita Gross (1974, 1977). Once the presence and voices of women are rediscovered and made accessible to us today, women are inspired to ask new questions and feel challenged by a very different past. Women have been the object of studies in the history of religions, as pursued by male scholars, but now women are themselves the subjects of such studies, formulating questions on the basis of their own experience and insight. Studies by women scholars in the history of religions are providing important new data in hitherto unresearched areas; their questions and methodological concerns will produce more gender-inclu-

sive scholarship and create a more balanced, global history of religions.

Feminist theory has provided trenchant critiques of patriarchy, sexism, and androcentrism. Androcentrism in particular, with its implicit assumption that male experience is the universal human norm and can express the generic human point of view without taking into account the experience and perspective of women, permeates thought, language, and texts. Women scholars in response have developed a sophisticated "hermeneutics of suspicion" with which they approach sacred texts, religious institutions, and teachings, as well as previous scholarship on religion. What was once considered universal validity and truth in previous writings undergoes a thorough deconstruction and reform. New knowledge about women in world religions, as documented in many separate studies on women in various religious traditions, is poised to become fully integrated into mainstream scholarship about religion.

One of the first studies presenting women's religious lives in non-Western cultures was the volume edited by Nancy Falk and Rita Gross, *Unspoken Worlds* (1980), followed by a study of the everyday religious experiences of ordinary women edited by Pat Holden (1983). To a large extent we know more about the experiences of exceptional women in the past who diverged from traditional, socially prescribed female roles—and thereby attracted the attention of their contemporaries—than we know about the religious beliefs and practices of ordinary women. As Rita Gross (1983) has pointed out with regard to the study of the past, the "single greatest barrier to scholarship on the topic of women's lives and experiences, apart from androcentric consciousness, is that it is much more difficult to find the data in historical than in contemporary situations because fieldwork is more likely than texts to contain the potential information" (pp. 588–589).

Much fieldwork is being carried out today with regard to women inside and outside the mainstream religious traditions, and also within new religious movements. What do the sacred scriptures, the theological and spiritual writings, teach about women, and how far have women's voices helped to shape them (Young, 1994)? How do different religions draw on feminine images and symbols, especially in speaking about ultimate reality and transcendence? To what extent do women take part in general ritual and religious practice, and how far have they developed their own? How far do women hold authority in particular religions? To what extent are they free to follow a special religious calling through becoming ascetics, monastics, or mystics? How far is asceticism through its inherent dualism of body and spirit, sexuality and spirituality, linked with misogyny and antifeminism? All these questions are of decisive significance to contemporary women scholars in the history of religions.

Also important is the problem of historiography: how are the emergence and growth of the history of religions or religious studies as an academic discipline described, and which topics of investigation, theories, achievements, and scholars are considered most significant? Is there any acknowledgment of the pioneering work of earlier women scholars who contributed to the development of the study and representation of religion as a field of intellectual and comparative inquiry? Such women scholars existed in the past, but their achievements have gone largely unacknowledged (King, 1993, 1995b). Much greater efforts at retrieval are required to give women scholars the visibility they deserve in the official accounts of the history of religions.

To a considerable extent the boundaries of the history of religions are organizationally mapped by scholars grouped together in the International Association for the History of Religions (IAHR), which holds quinquennial congresses and publishes the journal *Numen*. Women have always participated in considerable numbers in these congresses, but it was only at the fourteenth congress, in 1980, that a section called "Femininity and Religion" was included for the first time. This was not continued at the 1985 congress, but the 1990 and 1995 congresses included a section on "Religion and Gender" (King, 1995a). The American Academy of Religion has included a "Women and Religion" section since 1972. The American-based *Journal of Feminist Studies in Religion*, published since 1985, has presented many articles offering alternative visions of feminist methodology and feminist religious scholarship (see especially the roundtable discussions of vol. 1, no. 2 [1985]; vol. 3, no. 1 [1987]; and vol. 11, no. 1 [1995]).

Today the history of religions is marked by a pluralism of traditions, content, and methods and a dialogue among disciplines, cultures, and international scholars—including a growing number of women—from various regions of the world. Many of these women, though not all, use feminist theories and methods of research, contributing to the transformation of history of religions as a field of intellectual inquiry and systematic study. In practice, however, a strong gender imbalance remains, with a preponderance of male scholars shaping the field. It is also dominated by Western scholars and viewpoints in the contemporary study of religions. Because of Western origins and ideas, the history of religions means in many places in practice still the study of religions other than Judaism and Christianity, whereas the comparative study of religions is understood by

some as the theology of other religions, constructed from a specific Christian theological perspective. However, the rise and growing recognition of religious pluralism in all societies around the globe encourages interreligious encounter and dialogue in a more neutral and open-ended way, without the dominance or subordination of any one religion, but the concerns of contemporary women remain a largely missing dimension in the public representations, activities, and studies of interreligious dialogue.

BIBLIOGRAPHY

Bianchi, Ugo. "History of Religions." In *The Encyclopedia of Religion.* Vol. 6. Edited by Mircea Eliade. 1987.

Buchanan, Constance H. "Women's Studies." In *The Encyclopedia of Religion.* Vol. 15. Edited by Mircea Eliade. 1987.

Christ, Carol P. "Mircea Eliade and the Feminist Paradigm Shift." *Journal of Feminist Studies in Religion* 7, no. 2 (1991): 75–94. A perceptive critique of Eliade's approach to the goddess material in ancient religions. See also Carol P. Christ, *Rebirth of the Goddess*, 1977, pp. 80–86.

Christ, Carol P., and Judith Plaskow, eds. *Womanspirit Rising: A Feminist Reader in Religion.* 1979; rev. ed., 1992. A pioneering and influential collection of essays providing feminist interpretations of religion. Its primary focus is the challenge of feminism and women's experience to religion as traditionally practiced, the reconstruction of tradition and creation of new traditions, not the history of religions or methodological concerns.

Cooey, Paula M., William R. Eakin, and Jay B. McDaniel, eds. *After Patriarchy: Feminist Transformations of the World Religions.* 1991. Focuses on particular themes in various religions rather than on treating religious traditions in their entirety.

Falk, Nancy A, and Rita M. Gross, eds. *Unspoken Worlds: Women's Religious Lives in Non-Western Cultures.* 1980.

Gross, Rita M. "Androcentrism and Androgyny in the Methodology of History of Religions." In *Beyond Androcentrism: New Essays on Women and Religion.* 1977.

———. *Buddhism After Patriarchy: A Feminist History, Analysis, and Reconstruction of Buddhism.* 1993. Here a wide spectrum of the Buddhist tradition is analyzed, with a focus on Indian and Tibetan Buddhism (Mahayana and Vajrayana), but not Theravada Buddhism. For the history of religions, see especially the two valuable "Methodological Appendices": "Here I Stand: Feminism as Academic

Method and as Social Vision" and "Religious Experience and the Study of Religion: The History of Religions."

———. *Feminism and Religion: An Introduction* 1996. A wide-ranging, accessible study that provides a helpful introduction to the entire field and reiterates important methodological points. See especially chap. 1, "Defining Feminism, Religion, and the Study of Religion," and chap. 2, "Feminism's Impact on Religion and Religious Studies: A Brief History."

———. "Methodological Remarks on the Study of Women in Religion: Review, Criticism and Redefinition." In *Women and Religion*. Edited by J. Plaskow and J. A. Romero. 1974.

———. "Women's Studies in Religion: The State of the Art 1980." In *Traditions in Contact and Change: Selected Proceedings of the XIVth Congress of the International Association for the History of Religions*. Edited by Peter Slater and Donald Wiebe. 1983.

Holden, Pat, ed. *Women's Religious Experience: Cross-Cultural Perspectives.* 1983.

King, Ursula. "Feminism: The Missing Dimension in the Dialogue of Religions." In *Pluralism and the Religions*. Edited by John May. 1998. Discusses the mutual challenge of feminism and interreligious dialogue.

———. "Historical and Phenomenological Approaches to the Study of Religion: Some Major Developments and Issues Under Debate Since 1950." In *Theory and Method in Religious Studies: Contemporary Approaches to the Study of Religion*. Edited by Frank Whaling. 1984; rev. ed., 1995[a]. Provides a survey of the methodological discussions in the history of religions 1950–1980, but does not deal with the feminist critique of the study of religions.

———. "A Question of Identity: Women Scholars and the Study of Religion." In *Religion and Gender*. Edited by Ursula King. 1995[b]. The article examines the relationship between women and the historiography of the study of religion with reference to the development of the International Association for the History of Religions, the articles in the *Encyclopedia of Religion*, and the contribution of several women pioneers to the modern study of religion.

———. "Rediscovering Women's Voices at the World's Parliament of Religions." In *A Museum of Faiths: Histories and Legacies of the 1893 World's Parliament of Religions*. Edited by E. Ziolkowski. 1993. Examines the defective historiography of the World's Parliament of Religions with regard to the presence and contribution of women. An effort at historical retrieval that opens up avenues for further research.

———. "Women Scholars and the *Encyclopedia of Religion.*" In *Method and Theory in the Study of Religion* 2, no. 1 (1990): 91–97. Looks at the silences of the *Encyclopedia* regarding the work of women scholars in religion.

Sharma, Arvind, ed. *Women in World Religions*. 1987. A helpful collection of essays dealing with women in various religious traditions, but mostly descriptive rather than analytical.

Sharma, Arvind, and Katherine K. Young, eds. *The Annual Review of Women in World Religions*. Regularly published since 1991, these volumes provide many insightful articles on women past and present.

Sharpe, Eric J. *Comparative Religion: A History.* 1975; 2d ed., 1986. A well-known, widely used textbook lacking any recognition of women's work in the study of religions.

Waardenburg, Jacques, ed. *Classical Approaches to the Study of Religion: Aims, Methods and Theories of Research*. Vol. 1, *Introduction and Anthology*. 1973. A classic reference work that includes a survey of a hundred years' study of religion and substantial extracts from the most influential scholars in the history of religions up to 1950 (no women are included).

Young, Serinity, ed. *An Anthology of Sacred Texts By and About Women*. 1994. A valuable sourcebook that includes a rich selection of historical and contemporary texts ranging from Judaism, Christianity, and Islam to the Ancient Near East, Greece, Rome, Northern European paganism, shamanism, tribal religions, Hinduism, Buddhism, Confucianism, Taoism, and Alternative Religious Movements. Even this wide-ranging collection cannot be fully comprehensive; discerning readers will notice that there are no entries on Jainism, Zoroastrianism, or Sikhism, for example, nor on contemporary new religious movements. The large volume also contains a systematic introduction on several genres of sacred literature and several cross-cultural themes associated with women in various religious traditions.

See also **Eliade, Mircea.**

URSULA KING

Home

Home as a religious symbol is found in cultural traditions all over the world. Its prevalence and importance derive primarily from humans' physical need to construct shelter from the elements. But the religious symbol of home signifies much more than mere protection from cold, wind, and rain. What transforms a dwelling into a home is precisely the distinctive pattern of meanings and values, drawn largely from religious resources, that people incorporate into the physical structure of a cave, tent, hut, house, or apartment building: home reproduces the religiously sanctioned order of existence.

Most commonly home symbolizes a space of stability, wholeness, and repose. People in many different cultures strive to create homes that reflect the same ordering principles governing the cosmos as a whole. For example, each home (*hosh*) of the Hofriyati of northern Sudan, in accordance with their broader cultural concerns, contains carefully guarded enclosures: the men enter their quarters through a separate entrance in the front, and the women enter their quarters through a rear entrance. The architecture of the *hosh* thus reminds all household members of the supreme importance in religious, social, and physical affairs of protecting precious interiors from the polluting effects of dangerous exteriors.

Many cultures attend carefully to providing homes not just for the living but for the dead as well. The pyramids of ancient Egypt are only the most prominent examples of this widespread concern for giving a home to the deceased person's spirit or soul. The whole web of rites and beliefs surrounding graves, burials, and ancestors may be seen as outgrowths of the desire to ensure that the dead have homes every bit as secure and orderly as those of the living.

In some cultures home is regarded symbolically as a religious goal, for example the final destination of a wandering hero. The long journey of Odysseus is motivated by an unshakeable desire to return to the island of Ithaca, where his wife, Penelope, has been trying to protect the integrity of their home from rapacious suitors. In this sense, home is religiously meaningful in symbolizing the end of heroic trials, dangers, and battles; home, and the women who occupy it, symbolize the longed-for rest, comfort, and security that male heroes struggle to regain.

As the examples mentioned above suggest, the religious symbolism of the home is intimately connected to the construction and maintenance of gender differences. Although both men and women live within the home, it is almost universally regarded as the distinctive sphere of women. Within the home women are charged with the tasks of cooking, cleaning, weaving, child-rearing, and generally preserving the orderliness of the space. To the extent that home is a religious symbol, the work of women within the home may be accorded a high degree of religious value. However, in many cultures the religious worth of women's work is tempered by the fact that the household's male members remain the ultimate authorities. The lofty idealization of the religious influence of Puritan women in eighteenth and nineteenth century New England on their families did not change the fact that these women

A young woman prepares to light joss sticks at her home Buddhist shrine, Taichung, Taiwan, 1991 (Kevin R. Morris/Corbis).

were strictly limited in their out-of-home activities. In cases such as this domestic tasks have religious value insofar as they allow women to serve men and satisfy men's needs for a peaceful, well-ordered sanctuary. Home is a religious place for both women and men, but in very different ways: for women, it is where they live, work, and serve; for men, it is where they return to, rest, and rule.

As the massive transformations wrought by industrial and postindustrial modes of production have swept across the planet, the symbolism of home has taken on new importance. Very frequently home is regarded as a privileged sanctuary against the dehumanizing, secularizing, antitraditional effects of modernization. In the contemporary North American context, homes, and the women who run them, have been assigned the specific task of morally and religiously educating society's children. Because the culture at large is seen as having failed in this task, it is left to homebound mothers to teach the "family values" of love, compassion, self-restraint, and mutual service. By contrast, some sociologists and theologians assert that this emphasis on home as an institution of moral and religious instruction is too extreme and actually stunts the full development of children by widening the gap between private and public spheres of life. This intensifying debate over the proper role of the home in contemporary society only underscores its pervasive symbolic resonance and its continuing relevance as a topic of comparative religious inquiry.

BIBLIOGRAPHY

Good comparative studies of the religious significance and symbolism of home are Colin Duly's *The House of Mankind* (1979), Mircea Eliade's *The Sacred and the Profane* (1968), and Kathryn Allen Rabuzzi's *The Sacred and the Feminine: Toward a Theology of Housework* (1982). More detailed studies include Janice Boddy's *Wombs and Alien Spirits: Women, Men, and the Zar Cult in Northern Sudan* (1989), Nancy Cott's *The Bonds of Womanhood: "Woman's Sphere" in New England, 1780–1835* (1977), and Lila Abu-Lughod's *Veiled Sentiments: Honor and Poetry in a Bedouin Society* (1986). Important studies of home, gender, and contemporary society are Christopher Lasch's *Haven in a Heartless World: The Family Besieged* (1977) and Bonnie Miller-McLemore's *Also a Mother: Work and Family as Theological Dilemma* (1994).

See also Architecture; Domestic Rites; Space, Sacred.

KELLY BULKELEY

Hospitality

The act of providing hospitality or of being a host (from Latin *hoste* or *hoiste*) generally implies a sharing of substance with the *hostis*, the stranger or foreigner, the guest who arrives from afar at the house. Charity, by contrast, occurs with the giver going to the needy person and providing resources of cash or kind. Though being hospitable may involve receiving and entertaining equals or superiors at home, hospitality to the disenfranchised or the homeless sojourner has been acclaimed as a religious virtue. In the lore of different religions, providing for a stranger who chances upon one's doorstep is often rewarded with transcendent abundance. These accounts describe a divine reward that is not of human computation or substance for men and women, especially those who are not affluent, who display hospitality.

Many instances of altruistic giving or hospitality have been particularly associated with women. In the biblical story of the aged widow of Zarephath, the lone woman and her son experience dire poverty during a period of drought. At the time when they were resigned to eating their last meal and then to wait to die, Elijah appeared at their door and requested some water and bread. They provided their last nourishment to the guest. Their reward was an ultimate plentitude; the jar of meal and cruse of oil remained sufficient to sustain them until the rains appeared (1 Kings 17:8–16). Narratives of such selfless generosity are cherished as reflections of the biblical edict whereby a welcoming hospitality toward the stranger, *ger*, is sanctified: "for you were strangers in a strange land" (Lev. 19:34, Ex. 12: 49). Hence the importance of hospitality in the Judaic tradition; institutions for the relief of the sick, poor, and needy are an important part of community life.

In Christianity, hospitality is regarded as a cherished act in keeping with the example of Jesus, who said: "I was a stranger and you took me in" (Matt. 25:35). At the Last Supper, he demonstrates his role as host by washing the feet of his disciples and providing them with food. Many Christian orders take on the mission of feeding the poor and tending to the sick as a definitive context of their lives. Historically, monks and nuns focused on the ideal of caring for the disenfranchised and attempted to ameliorate their lives with the provision of shelter, food, and other services. Mother Teresa of Calcutta became part of an example that includes the twelfth-century Hospital Sisters of St. Augustine of Paris. The Catholic Worker Houses of Hospitality, instituted by Dorothy Day, the order of the Sisters of Mercy, and the Sisters of St. Dominic of Amityville all reflect this devotion to the mission of hospitality and caring.

In the Muslim tradition, the act of "giving" is directed in the Qur'an as a principal merit; thus people are commanded: "O! you who are faithful, give of the good things that you have earned" (2.267). The generosity of the Prophet Muhammad and his companions is projected as an indubitable ideal of human behavior. Hadith accounts celebrate the gracious hospitality displayed by men and women in the early community toward the stranger or the pauper who arrived at the door to share a meal or to find a place to rest. The Prophet's daughter, Fatimah, and her husband, ʿAlī ibn Alī Ṭālib, once ended up fasting for three consecutive days as a result of their hospitality. Each evening, as they were about to eat their meager fare, an indigent person chanced upon their door. They gave away their portion and subsisted on water. Similarly, the Prophet's wife, Zaynab, has been remembered as "she with the long reach or arm" for her generosity. Again, when the Muslims migrated from Mecca to Medina, the Prophet created a bond of brotherhood between them and the local Medinians, who would be responsible for their subsistence in a new place. These Medinians, referred to as Ansar (helpers), opened their homes to the needy Meccans. In an anecdote associated with the eighth-century Muslim saint Rabi'ah al-'Adawiyyah, the hospitality theme is revived with a certain drama. When two guests arrive, she gives her last two loaves to a beggar who also comes to her door. Subsequently, by Divine Providence she is rewarded with twenty fresh loaves, which she then provides to her guests.

The classical restrictions of caste and the associated notions of pollution in the Hindu tradition limit the rendition of hospitality to specific conditions. While the Brahmin or the *samnyasin* at the door will be granted food by the *dvija* (twice born, i.e., *brahmin, ksatriya, vaishya*) householder, hospitality may not be provided impromptu to the stranger who appears seeking refuge or assistance. Within this general framework, women are primary agents of generosity. In Hindi creed, the divine power associated with wealth and abundance is personified as a female deity, Lakṣmī. According to lore, Princess Gandhari, daughter of King Subala and wife of King Dhitarashtra, provided hospitality to the sage Vyasa and received a boon whereby she asked for a hundred sons who were thus granted to her. In the story of Rāma and Sītā, when Sītā is commanded not to leave the hut while Rama is away, she is confronted with a predicament: should she give something to the beggar on her doorstep or remain inside her hut? She decides to do both: keeping one foot inside the threshold, with the other foot she steps out to give food to the beggar, who happens to be a demon in disguise. Her impulse to be charitable is tempered by her duty to be obedient.

Hospitality is important in the Buddhist tradition and women are specifically prominent for their generous actions. The bowl of porridge that supplied nourishment to the Buddha just before his enlightenment was placed under the tree for a tree-spirit by a young maiden. The original begging bowl of the Buddha that provided food for him and his followers is associated with a virtuous woman, Amrita Surabhi. Concealed in a lake, the meritorious bowl emerges annually on the Buddha's birthday and rises towards Manimekhalai, a paragon of virtue. This righteous woman then takes it to areas where people are destitute due to drought and disease. Upon her arrival, the deity Indra immediately feeds the hungry and the ailing are healed by touching the bowl.

Among Native Americans hospitality is an essential focus of community life. Their hospitable welcome to the early Europeans enabled the first Euroamerican communities to survive. This generosity is celebrated in the United States as Thanksgiving Day, a national holiday when people give thanks to God and share a meal with relatives as well as outsiders.

BIBLIOGRAPHY

Attar, Farid al-din. *Muslim Saints and Mystics: Episodes from the Tadhkirat al-Auliya.* 1990.

Bonet-Maury, Amy-Gaston, "Hospitality (Christian)." In *Encyclopaedia of Religion and Ethics.* Edited by James Hastings. 1908–1926.

Butler, L. "Hospitallers and Hospital Sisters." In *New Catholic Encyclopaedia.* 1989.

Coomaraswamy, Ananda K., and Sister Nivedita, eds. *Myths of the Hindus and Buddhists.* 1967.

Day, Dorothy. *The Long Loneliness: The Autobiography of Dorothy Day.* 1989.

Khan, Ebrahim. *Anecdotes from Islam.* 1960.

Knappert, Jan. *Indian Mythology: An Encyclopedia of Myth and Legend.* 1991.

Koenig, John. *New Testament Hospitality: Partnership with Strangers as Promise and Mission.* 1985.

Mercier, Charles Arthur. *Leper Houses and Medieval Hospitals.* 1915.

Murray, Harry. *Do Not Neglect Hospitality: The Catholic Worker and the Homeless.* 1990.

O'Flaherty, Wendy Doniger, ed. and trans. *Hindu Myths: A Sourcebook.* 1975.

Ogletree, Thomas W. *Hospitality to the Stranger: Dimensions of Moral Understanding.* 1985.

Singer, Charles Joseph, and E. Asworth Underwood. *A Short History of Medicine.* 1962.

Young, Serinity, ed. *An Anthology of Sacred Texts by and About Women.* 1993.

HABIBEH RAHIM

Hulda

According to the Bible, Hulda is the prophet to whom King Josiah (c. 640–609 B.C.E.) sends inquiries concerning the great book of the law that was found in the temple by the high priest Hilkiah. In 2 Kings 22:15–20, Hulda confirms that the book, which was probably some form of what we now know as Deuteronomy, contains God's decrees of doom for a sinful Israel. Yet because Josiah has harkened to the words of the book and subsequently undertakes a series of great reforms based upon its commandments, Hulda's otherwise doleful prophecy rewards him with a promise that he will die in peace before God's wrath is served.

Although other woman prophets are mentioned in the Bible (Deborah, Miriam, the wife of Isaiah, and Noadiah), only two, Hulda and the wife of Isaiah, are active during the classical period of Israelite prophecy (the eighth through sixth centuries B.C.E.). Of these two, moreover, only Hulda performs the typical prophetic role of advising the king. Why only Hulda fulfills this function is unclear. Although some have argued that her authority is secondary, derived from her marriage to Shallum, the keeper of the king's wardrobe, it is more likely that Hulda's ability to serve as prophet stems from the fact that she lives in an age of social upheaval and instability. According to sociologists, it is in precisely such periods that women are able to break through traditional gender barriers to assume positions of political and religious power.

BIBLIOGRAPHY

Ackerman, Susan. "Isaiah." In *The Women's Bible Commentary.* Edited by C. A. Newsom and S. H. Ringe. 1992.

Camp, Claudia V. "1 and 2 Kings." In *The Women's Bible Commentary.* Edited by C. A. Newsom and S. H. Ringe. 1992.

Hackett, Jo Ann. "In the Days of Jael: Reclaiming the History of Women in Ancient Israel." In *Immaculate and Powerful: The Female in Sacred Image and Social Reality.* Edited by C. W. Atkinson, C. H. Buchanan, and M. R. Miles. 1985.

SUSAN ACKERMAN

Humor

Humor exposes that which is ordinarily denied—that mores and norms are regularly broken, that some suffering cannot be resolved, that dogmatic claims can be deflated. It can be provoked against absolutism of any kind, and thus finds religion a favorite target. In addition to absolutism, religions have critical, transcendent, ecstatic, and antinomian impulses, and in these respects a more positive affinity with humor may also obtain. Sacred-comic traditions are present in the popular expressions of most religions and in more formal contexts as well.

Women's comic expressions are restricted within patriarchal religion and society. Cross-cultural studies indicate that comic forms typical of males—for example, joking, horseplay, slapstick, ritual insults and pranks—are not typical of women (Apte, 1985). Psychological studies, though not as broadly cross-cultural, have shown that as children learn sex roles, girls' performance of public humor decreases significantly in relation to that of boys (McGhee, 1979). In adulthood, female comic forms flourish best in women-centered spaces, where they contribute to the construction of women as a distinct and self-conscious group. In the presence of men, women must often dissimulate what they find funny. For this reason, male interpretations of humor should not be assumed applicable to women. Instead, the distinctive responses of women must be sought through empirical research and imaginative reexaminations of existing materials.

Feminist scholarship does not stop at the male-defined borders of religion when exploring women's spirituality; the same procedure should be followed when investigating women's sacred-comic expressions. This is necessitated especially where secularization has removed humor, along with women and sex, even farther from the realm of the sacred. For religious feminists, the sacred is understood as that which is culturally sacralized and that which is humanly liberative. Wherever women's humor occurs, it provides clues to where the sacred, in both these senses, may be found: humor can unmask the pretensions of male sacrality, while providing women with critical insight and forbidden pleasures.

Women's sacred-comic or analogous expressions can be discerned in five settings.

WOMEN-CENTERED OR WOMEN-ONLY RELIGIOUS TRADITIONS

According to Susan Starr Sered (1994), several extant woman-dominated religions involve spirit possession. These include Korean shamanism, Burmese Nat cults, Afro-Brazilian religions, the spirit cults of northern Thailand, Ryukyu Island religion, Black Carib religion, and the *zar* religion of Islamic North Africa and the Middle East. Although these traditions do not emphasize comic forms as such, it could be argued that spirit possession parallels the sacred-comic—for example, social hierarchies may be symbolically inverted, and ritual license may be given to cross-gender masquerade, vulgarity, drunkenness, sexual burlesque, or obscenity. In effect, sex-role transgression is simultaneously permitted and contained, transferring responsibility from the woman performers to supernatural beings and ritual-aesthetic forms.

WOMEN AS COMIC PERFORMERS IN MIXED SETTINGS AND IN MALE-DOMINATED RELIGIONS

In some parts of India, during the Holi festival, low-caste women beat men with sticks in a mock battle; in the wedding rituals of northern and central India, women of the bride's side may sing bawdy songs and ritually abuse the groom's male kin. Other religions permit similar comic license to women when acting collectively during special events. In vodou, women possessed by the trickster Gede can enact comic forms more individually. However, aside from occasional sightings of a female version (Gedelia), Gede remains emphatically male (Brown, 1991). Women are among the Christians who have followed Paul's advice and become "fools for Christ" (1 Cor. 4:10), simulating madness for the sake of spiritual growth. In Eastern monasticism, "Holy Fool" became an honorific term akin to "virgin" or "martyr" and in its feminine form has been occasionally conferred on nuns (Saward, 1980). Women also took part in the widespread Western tradition of carnival, though the specific parameters and meanings of these forms for women have received little scholarly attention (Davis, 1965).

WOMEN'S DISTINCT RECEPTIONS OF MALE SACRED-COMIC TRADITIONS

A number of religions include male-dominated traditions of ritual humor, which women experience as audience and butts. Men play all roles in the elaborate comic rituals that belong to the Christian traditions of indigenous peoples in Mexico's Highland Chiapas; the ridicule of women for breach of sex-roles is a central theme (Bricker, 1973). In the Purim plays of Eastern European Judaism, men traditionally played every role, including that of the wily and seductive Queen Esther. In a much-studied healing ritual of (Theravada) Buddhist Sri Lanka, male exorcists perform comic enactments of demons in order to heal possessed individuals, who are almost always female.

In these and similar rituals, women have a distinct reception position. In the Sri Lankan case, for example, it may be significant that demonic possession makes a single woman unmarriageable and, for a married woman, permits expressions of aggression that would otherwise be unthinkable. Further, the comic and ritual efficacy of these events may be differently understood by women than by men. When women laugh, they may do so for reasons of their own, and the spiritual forces that men aim to exorcise, women may aim to integrate (see Saiving, 1976).

In their sense of the ironic as well, women interpret religious traditions from subject positions that differ from men's. Irony, like humor, is a response to contradiction, although in irony there is a greater emphasis on the cognitive element and the comic pleasure may decay into bitter insight. Idealized motherhood, for example, lends itself easily to irony. An illustration within the Hebrew Bible in Yael (Judges 4:17–22 and 5:24–27), who mothers the warrior Sisera to death, feeding him milk and then driving a tent peg through his skull (Bal, 1988). In Sanskrit comic literature of the eleventh century (*Kṣemendra, Samayamātrka*), there is the figure Kaṅkālī, "the Mother of Harlots," a cagey old crone who is a comic rendition of the laughing Goddess Kālī (Siegel, 1987). Kaṅkālī cares only about money not about sex, thus achieving a kind of detachment and clarity that eludes her male customers. Like Marilyn Monroe in *Gentlemen Prefer Blondes* (1953), she knows that "diamonds are a girl's best friend."

In androcentric readings, such figures are typically taken to reveal the truth beneath an appearance—in this case, the "true," corrupt, and destructive nature of woman that lies beneath the appearance of her sexual allure or motherly compassion. For women who must live in this double bind, however, the irony may be that both its sides are true: the oversexualization that comprises "woman" as a patriarchal ideal is at the same time the basis of her demonization. The woman who is brazenly "good" at being "bad" can therefore be a source of defiant delight and practical wisdom.

PROFANATION OF MALE SACRALITY AND PRIVILEGE IN NONRELIGIOUS SETTINGS

According to one scholarly account, the chief entertainment among Muslim women in an Iraqi village was to ridicule men in their absence (Fernea, 1965). From a feminist critical viewpoint, this could be viewed as a delegitimation of certain male prerogatives. In a different world, rock star Madonna desacralizes male-defined spirituality by incorporating the virgin versus whore dichotomy into a single campy representation. Attached like a mask, femininity can then be seen as a "put on," a performance with roots in ancient traditions of sacred-comic transvestism.

WOMEN'S COMIC PERFORMANCE IN EMERGING WOMEN-CENTERED SPIRITUALITY

There is abundant anecdotal evidence of new comic sensibilities and forms in women's spirituality groups, for example, a neopagan ritual group dresses in clerical collars and Groucho masks to demonstrate at a priestly ordination; a Jewish Rosh Hodesh (New Moon) group, largely lesbian, performs a Purim play in reversed "butch-femme" roles. Some feminist theologians have also reappropriated humor or laughter. For Carol P. Christ, the laughter of Aphrodite illuminates eros as sacred mystery; for Mary Daly, women Laughing Out Loud can exorcise the power of patriarchal religion.

As women's religious voices are proclaimed, the world resounds with renewed laughter. Some may find that laughter heretical, and their God may shrink in its presence. But it carries the insights and delights that have always sustained women, and for many people, women and men, that deserves to be called sacred.

BIBLIOGRAPHY

Apte, Mahadev. *Humor and Laughter: An Anthropological Approach.* 1985. Summary and analysis of cross-cultural data on humor, including a chapter on religion and another on humor and gender inequality.

Bal, Mieke. *Death and Dissymmetry: The Politics of Coherence in the Book of Judges.* 1988. Feminist literary analysis of the biblical book of Judges, exploring the dissymmetry of power relations as enacted in military and domestic violence.

Bricker, Victoria. *Ritual Humor in the Highland Chiapas.* 1973. Detailed anthropological analysis of the sacred-comic traditions of the Highland Chiapas, but insufficiently attentive to women's reception-positions.

Brown, Karen McCarthy. *Mama Lola: A Vodou Priestess in Brooklyn.* 1991. Detailed anthropological study of a Vodou community, with a focus on women's leadership and experience, and a section devoted to the trickster Gede.

Christ, Carol P. *Laughter of Aphrodite: Reflections on a Journey to the Goddess.* 1987. Thealogical essays recounting a gradual rejection of patriarchal religion and discovery of laughter and eros as sacred via the Greek goddesses.

Daly, Mary, with Jane Caputi. *Webster's First New Intergalactic Dictionary of the English Language.* 1987. Radical feminist wordplay, remorselessly attacking the minions of patriarchy.

Davis, Natalie Zemon. "Women on Top." In *Society and Culture in Early Modern France.* 1965; repr. 1975. A rare historical analysis of medieval comic traditions in their sexual symbology, arguing that these traditions served socially transformative as well as conservative purposes.

Fernea, Elizabeth. *Guests of the Sheikh: An Ethnography of an Iraqi Village.* 1965; repr. 1969. Ethnographical account of life in an Iraqi village, including the ridicule of men in women-only contexts.

Kapferer, Bruce. "Entertaining Demons: Comedy, Interaction and Meaning in a Sinhalese Healing Ritual." *Social Analysis* 1 (1979): 108–151. Anthropological study of a Sri Lankan exorcism, in which the possessed is a newly betrothed girl. Excellent source for details of the ritual, but wanting in feminist critical insight.

Lefkovitz, Lori Hope. "Eavesdropping on Angels and Laughing at God." In *Gender and Judaism: The Transformation of Tradition.* Edited by T. M. Rudavsky. 1995. Beginning with the enigmatic laughter of Sarah, argues that women's laughter promises a more fluid and body-centered Judaism. Draws on the French feminists Catherine Clement and Hélène Cixous.

McGhee, Paul. "The Role of Laughter and Humor in Growing Up Female." In *Becoming Female: Perspectives on Development.* Edited by Claire B. Kopp. 1979. A summary of existing psychological studies on humor and sex role development, by a leading researcher in the psychology of humor.

Saiving, Valerie. "Androcentrism in Religious Studies." *The Journal of Religion* 56, no. 2 (1976): 177–197. A feminist methodological critique of androcentrism in the work of Mircea Eliade. Very applicable to feminist interpretations of male-centered comic and exorcism rites.

Sands, Kathleen M. "Ifs, Ands, and Butts: Theological Reflections on Humor." *Journal of the American Academy of Religion* 64, no. 3 (1996): 499–523. Theoretical exploration of humor as a theme for religious reflection in a postmodern context, with queer humor as an illustration.

Saward, John. *Perfect Fools: Folly for Christ's Sake in Catholic and Orthodox Spirituality.* 1980. A historical and theological interpretation of long-standing tradition of mystical lunacy within Christianity. Predominantly composed of male examples.

Sered, Susan Starr. *Priestess, Mother, Sacred Sister: Religions Dominated by Women.* 1994. A rigorous and insightful study of twelve woman-dominated religions, of which nine centrally involve spirit-possession and permit behaviors akin to the sacred-comic.

Siegel, Lee. *Laughing Matters: Comic Tradition in India.* 1987. A witty and comprehensive study of Sanskrit comic literature by an Indologist and scholar of religion, though largely devoid of feminist analysis.

See also **Possession**; **Rites of Passage**; **Spirits**; **Tricksters**.

KATHLEEN M. SANDS

Hurston, Zora Neale

Zora Neale Hurston (1891–1960) was the most prolific African-American woman writer in the United States from 1930 to 1950. She wrote four novels—*Jonah's Gourd Vine* (1934), *Their Eyes Were Watching God* (1937), *Moses, Man of the Mountain* (1939), *Seraph on the Suwanee* (1948); two books of folklore, *Mules and Men* (1935) and *Tell My Horse* (1938); an autobiography, *Dust Tracks on a Road* (1942); eight plays; and more than fifty short stories and essays. Though Hurston was not, at least in the traditional sense, a religious writer, contestable ethical issues and religious imagery pervade her work. Hurston's texts preserve, like forms embedded in prehistoric ore, traces of her upbringing in Florida as the daughter of a black Baptist preacher.

Hurston possessed a sharp accuracy in reporting the positive sense of self that exists among poor, marginal blacks, "the Negro farthest down." The primary impetus for her writings was to capture the density of simple values inherent in the provincialism of African-Americans who worked on railroads, lived in sawmill camps, and toiled in phosphate mines, earning their keep as common laborers.

Working both as a collector and systematizer, Hurston included explicit religious materials in her writings, ranging from full-length sermons, prayers, and proverbs to the passing acknowledgment of biblical people and sacred places. Hurston's extreme closeness to the sensibilities of her unlettered characters, along with her meticulous collection of folklore, legends, superstitions, music, and dance of the common people, enabled her work to serve as a rich repository of resources that help us understand the religious vernacular which dominated African-American Christian culture during the first half of the twentieth century.

BIBLIOGRAPHY

Hemenway, Robert. *Zora Neale Hurston, A Literary Biography.* 1977.

Gates, Henry Louis, Jr., and K. A. Appiah, eds. *Zora Neale Hurston: Critical Perspectives Past and Present.* 1993.

Walker, Alice, ed. *I Love Myself When I Am Laughing . . . & Then Again When I am Looking Mean & Impressive: A Zora Neale Hurston Reader.* 1979.

Wall, Cheryl A., ed. *Zora Neale Hurston: Folklore, Memoirs, & Other Writings.* 1995.

———. *Zora Neale Hurston: Novels and Stories.* 1995.

KATIE G. CANNON

Hypatia

Hypatia was born in Alexandria, Egypt, about 370 C.E. All evidence indicates that she spent her entire life in this city with her father, Theon, a mathematician and philosopher. Hypatia commanded respect and in some circles provoked controversy. Occasionally, she participated in the political activities of Alexandria, serving as an esteemed advisor on current issues. She possessed great moral authority; all the sources agree that she was

Hypatia, an undated modern illustration (Corbis-Bettmann)

a model of courage, righteousness, civic devotion, and intellectual prowess. The virtue most honored by her contemporaries was her *sophrosyne,* which manifested itself in sexual abstinence with men, modest dress, moderate living, and a dignified attitude toward her students.

Hypatia became the head of the Platonist school at Alexandria. She came to symbolize learning and science, which the early Christians identified with paganism. All of Hypatia's work is lost, except for titles and some references to it—none to purely philosophical work, only to work in mathematics and astronomy. Hypatia wrote commentaries on Diophantus's *Arithmetica,* on Apollonius's *Conics,* and Ptolemy's astronomical works.

In 412 Cyril became bishop of Alexandria; a few years later, about 415, men in Cyril's employment assassinated Hypatia. It was a political murder provoked by long-standing conflicts in Alexandria.

Most of what we know about Hypatia's life comes from the biography done by Synesius, her favorite student. Some letters of Synesius to Hypatia exist; these ask her advice on the construction of an astrolabe and a hydroscope.

BIBLIOGRAPHY

Alic, M. *Hypatia's Heritage: A History of Women in Science from Antiquity through the Nineteenth Century.* 1986.

Bernal, Martin. *Black Athena: The Afro-Asiatic Roots of Classical Civilization.* 1987.

Dzielska, Maria. *Hypatia of Alexandria.* Translated by F. Lyra. 1995.

Snyder, Jane MacIntosh. *The Woman and the Lyre: Women Writers in Classical Greece and Rome.* 1989. See esp. pp. 113–121 for Hypatia.

SHELLEY P. HALEY

Iconography

In the East

Centuries of overland and maritime contact spread Hinduism, Buddhism, Islam and Christianity across vast areas of Asia. As each interacted with localized religious and cultural traditions, such as Sikhism and Jainism in the South Asian subcontinent, Bon in Tibet, Shinto in Japan, and Taoism and Confucian thought in China, the iconographic diversity and overlapping visual traditions that mark Asian religious imagery evolved.

Two main factors underlay the enormous proliferation of goddess images in the South Asian Hindu traditions: the role of the visual in the apprehension of the divine and the overlap and sharing between local, regional, and brahmanic traditions. The goddess, ultimately a manifestation of supreme energy, takes many forms. Although her forms have evolved and shifted over centuries within various Hindu sectarian traditions, artists' manuals and ritual verses contain standard iconographic formulas and descriptions. The major Hindu goddesses are classified as benign or terrifying: Benign goddesses, such as Pārvatī, are depicted as beautiful, often royal, women; their bodies are constructed according to an aesthetic tradition in which poetic similes (e.g., lotus-eyes), rather than mimetic naturalism, convey ideal form. Their voluptuous bodies are the antithesis of the emaciated, fierce goddesses, such as Kālī and the Mahāvidyas, whose prominent ribs, gaping mouths, and pendulous breasts signal insatiable hunger. The emaciated body may also evoke the ascetic, as it does for Karraikal Ammaiyar, a Tamil saint whose flesh melted away to facilitate unwavering devotion to the god Siva. Worship of goddess images within home and temple is a daily practice for devout Hindu men and women. Many rituals that concern family protection are gendered female. One such is the creation of protective diagrams at domestic thresholds. Traditionally made from rice powder and renewed daily, these linear, geometric patterns may contain auspicious symbols such as the lotus or swastika.

In the earliest Buddhist visual programs from first-century B.C.E. North India, female nature-spirits, drawn from pre-Buddhist traditions, adorn sacred sites. Iconographically similar to the nature-spirits, Gandharan images (third–fifth centuries C.E.) of Queen Māyā giving birth to the Buddha serve as an example of the transformation of a general motif into a purely Buddhist narrative. As Buddhism evolved and spread across Asia, its pantheon became more complex; Buddha and bodhi-

Relief sculpture depicting a reclining Queen Māyā with servants illustrates the conception and birth of the Buddha, Java, Indonesia (Dean Conger/Corbis).

sattva (enlightened being) images were used for both meditation and worship. Tārā, a female bodhisattva of pure wisdom and a savior goddess, became popular first in North India, then in Nepal and Tibet. A unique form of the goddess within Tibetan Buddhism is her personification as wisdom in sexual union with the male as compassion; the intertwined couple represents the nonpolarized state of enlightenment. These images were made for initiates only. In China the modification of the Buddhist canon after contact with local traditions is most strikingly evidenced in the transformation of the male bodhisattva of compassion, Avalokiteśvara, into the female deity Kuan Yin, goddess of mercy and bestower of children. Variously represented as a sexually alluring maiden, aged female, or fisherwoman, Kuan Yin often wears white robes, symbolic of purity, and is accompanied by a pilgrim or young children.

The Visitation depicts Mary visiting her cousin Elizabeth (Francis G. Mayer/Corbis).

BIBLIOGRAPHY

Dehejia, Vidya. *Devi: The Great Goddess.* Exhibition catalogue, Smithsonian Institution, Sackler Gallery. Forthcoming.

Dehejia, Vidya, ed. *Representing the Body: Gender Issues in Indian Art.* New Delhi, 1997.

Hawley, John S., and Donna M. Wulf, eds. *Devi: Goddesses of India.* 1996.

Klein, Anne C. "Nondualism and the Great Bliss Queen: A Study in Tibetan Buddhist Ontology and Symbolism." *Journal of Feminist Studies in Religion* 1 (1985).

Willis, Janice. "Female Patronage in Indian Buddhism." In *The Powers of Art.* Edited by Barbara Stoler Miller and Richard Eaton. 1992.

Yü, Chün-fang. "Guanyin: The Chinese Transformation of Avalokitesvara." In *Latter Days of the Law: Images of Chinese Buddhism, 850–1850.* Edited by Marsha Weidner. 1994.

See also **Durgā and Kālī**; **Kuan Yin (Kannon)**; **Maya**; **Pārvatī**; **Tārā**.

DEBRA DIAMOND

In the West

In Europe women have produced, consumed, and commissioned a wide range of religious and devotional objects, many of which characterize a gendered form of religious piety. Scholars have begun recuperating women's accomplishments and imagery, especially those of aristocratic women and nuns during the period of the late Middle Ages.

Medieval cloistered women used images that directed devotional exercises. These images often demanded tender responses, such as ornate, miniature cradles in which a small Christ doll could be rocked (Metropolitan Museum of Art, New York). Nuns and Beguines also made various types of handiwork, especially embroidery (not tapestries, as has been thought), and baked Eucharist wafers, which often bore images. These devotional objects, part of women's realms of food and domestic labor, have not yet received much scholarly attention.

The subject of women's devotional images is often a relationship—for example, the Visitation (the relationship between the pregnant cousins Elizabeth and the Virgin Mary), or the Pietà (the relationship between the Virgin and her dead son). Ziegler (1992) argues that Beguines' Pietà sculptures compel a sensual response on the part of the viewer. A manuscript with illustrated prayers to St. Anne centered on various flowers (Royal Library, the Hague) demands an olfactory response, the "Talking Crucifix" at the Poor Clare's Convent of San Damiano in Assisi an auditory response.

During the Renaissance women continued to commission religious painting. In the Dominican Cloister of St. Katherine at Nuremberg, for example, nuns worked in a wide range of artistic forms, such as panel paintings and manuscripts, in which they depicted themselves as cultural producers (Schraut, 1991). In the fifteenth century the cloistered nuns at the Benedictine abbey of St. Walburg in Eichstatt and the Dominican nuns in Pisa invented unique forms of iconography that can legitimately be called "women's images" (Hamburger, 1997; Roberts, 1994).

Laywomen made use of other devotional objects in addition to pictures, such as rosary beads. After the inception of the Rosary Devotion (fifteenth century), which had a strongly gendered character, women frequently commissioned images of themselves with their beads, an attribute of their piety. This devotional exercise had an adamantly visual component and drove the production of cheap printed and more expensive painted visual guides for prayer. Women also ordered illustrated prayer books, often books of hours, with portraits of themselves shown in devotional postures and an emphasis on female saints.

In Christian iconography female saints appear as subjects in all manner and form of imagery. The Virgin Mary, in her various guises (intercessor, *sedes sapientiae*, model of compassion, miracle worker, protectoress) is the most common subject matter of Western art. Women saints, including Barbara, Margaret, and other virgin martyrs, frequently appear defending—or dying for—their chastity.

BIBLIOGRAPHY

Hamburger, Jeffrey. *Nuns as Artists: The Visual Culture of a Medieval Convent*. 1997.

Roberts, Anne. "Chiara Gambacorta of Pisa as Patroness of the Arts." In *Creative Women in Medieval and Early Modern Italy*. Edited by E. Ann Matter and John Coakley. 1994.

Schraut, Elisabeth. "Kunst im Frauenkloster: Überlegungen zu den Möglichkeiten der Frauen im mittelalterlichen Kunstbetrieb am Beispiel Nürnberg." In *Auf der Suche nach der Frau im Mittelalter: Fragen, Quellen, Antworten*. Edited by Bea Lundt. 1991.

Wood, Jeryldene. *Women, Art, and Spirituality: The Poor Clares of Early Modern Italy*. 1996.

Ziegler, Joanna. *Sculpture of Compassion: The Pietà and the Beguines in the Southern Low Countries*. 1992.

KATHRYN RUDY

Identity

Identity means sameness: the opposite of difference. Yet identity also stands for a sense of self—of unity, continuity, and permanence. It can be attributed to an individual or a group, functioning as a concrete and a general category. By definition, religion means something that binds. Religions bind persons together, internally and externally, singularly and corporately. As such religion can give identity, creating personal and communal unities.

Augustine's *Confessions* contains a classical, theistic expression of personal identity: how can the 'I' who continually undergoes change and struggles with the ravages of his own inconstancy continue to be myself? Augustine's answer is to find his identity in a personal, all-powerful being who remains changeless and eternal in sustaining paternal love. So divine constancy preserves personal identity despite human inconstancy.

Belief in a personal deity can also be a condition for communal identity. Religious symbols and ritual practices are equally important for this identity. Symbols both constitute and are constituted by the individual and corporate experiences of the sacred. Rituals should reflect the experiences of human subjects, both male and female. But the identity constituted by religious practices often conceals the sexually specific differences of subjects.

The manner of achieving identity remains an issue. A seeming neutrality can mask an exclusive unity. Personal deities conceived as masculine and patriarchal by theistic religions have given men a sense of self, unity, and privilege, as well as social and economic power from which women are excluded. As patriarchal forms of Christianity, Islam, and Judaism have failed to unite women, so too have historic forms of Buddhism, Confucianism, and Hinduism failed to create a coherent cultural identity for women.

Catholicism offers its myth of Mary the mother of God as a model. Seeking to identify with the contradictory ideal of a virgin mother exposes human mothers to constant frustration and oppression. Protestantism, to which this impossible representation of motherhood is less central, is no better in having Jesus serve as the model for human identity, in relation to a Father and a mother. He is the model man-son; he offers a vision of the world that constitutes the parameters of individual, social, and cultural identity. But this is inadequate for the identity of women. Even if Jesus interacts with women, a religious community united by belief in his identity offers women no mother–daughter genealogy, no adequate representation of women's relation to nature, to the universe, to each other, and to others.

Feminist scholars have insisted that women simply lack identity. Matriarchal religions could and possibly did give women that missing sense. Feminist philosopher-theologian Mary Daly articulates a communal identity that aims to unite women with the cosmic dimensions of their world. But Daly's account excludes men. Instead of reversing sexism, alternative accounts of sexual difference aim to recognize the identities of both sexes, preventing a narcissistic and imperialistic inflation of sameness. And giving space to sexual difference exposes the human limitations that provide an opening for the divine.

However, the African-American writer bell hooks raises the crucial question for the end of this century. *Ain't I a Woman?* records the intertwining of racism and sexism. Women theologians and scholars in religion have to realize the ways in which their own accounts of female identity may exclude those who are different from them in terms of race, ethnicity, or class. The Muslim sociologist Fatima Mernissi admits that one of her greatest lessons about Muslim identity came from listening to a narrative of female resistance told by an illiterate, seventy-nine-year-old Arab woman. This Arab woman challenged the educated, feminist assumption that uneducated, religious women are merely submissive to patriarchal control. In listening, Mernissi heard the tales exchanged by Muslim women about their subtle means to subvert male power.

Beneath the dominant histories of world religion are hidden resources for women who seek to subvert the hierarchy created by patriarchal identity. Biased configurations of religion eclipse the histories of resistance, rebellion, and dissenting devotion; the task is to reconfigure identity out of the memory of saints and dissenters. Two examples, one from Islam and the other from Hinduism, illustrate the ground for a liberating memory in world religion.

First, Mernissi elucidates the paradox of present memory, which has forgotten the preeminence of women on the political stage in the first decades of Islam. Early Muslim women triumphed in the political world as mothers and queens. But the Muslim narratives that gave enormous importance to female disciples, the mothers of believers, the wives of prophets and kings are suppressed by later forms of Islam, which insist that women obey only, not lead. Those who contest women's entitlement to political rights in the name of Islam select the figure of the slave woman (*jariya*) from a period of absolutism. This piece of history has lost its memory in excluding the free woman's identity.

Second, social historian Parita Mukta also charts the distortion of religious history by powerful patriarchs. To regain lost memory, Mukta listens to the narratives of literate and illiterate women, especially to the poetry of the legendary Mirabai. Mira, the medieval poetess and saint, gave up a princely life to practice Hindu devotion (bhakti), joining a marginalized community that sang devotion to Krishna. The particular communities, which still sing the *bhajans* of Mirabai, resist the dominant form of religion. The identity of Mirabai endures

through the people who bind themselves to her liberating memory and despite another memory that eclipses her subversive message.

Thus identity is found and lost, sought and rejected, freely chosen and imposed, celebrated and mourned. Women embrace identity to be empowered, though identity also disempowers. Perhaps once identity involves agency and memory within a changing context of relationships, it will move us beyond paradox. What must be remembered are those women and men whose solidarity in religious devotion make it possible to resist the exclusive identity of sex-biased power. This memory creates the unifying ground for mutual recognition of sexual difference and for the emergence of our materially specific identities.

BIBLIOGRAPHY

Augustine. *The Confessions.* Translated by P. S. Pine-Coffin. 1961. Esp. Books X, XI. Though patriarchal, still the most important classical account of identity formation in relation to a personal deity.

Bynum, Caroline Walker, Stevan Harrell, and Paula Richman, eds. *Gender and Religion: On the Complexity of Symbols.* 1986. With an important introduction.

Cixous, Hélène. "We Who are Free, Are We Free?" In *Freedom and Interpretation: The Oxford Amnesty Lectures 1992.* Edited by Barbara Johnson. 1993. Presents a Jewish woman's poetic and critical reflection on free identity within a complex tapestry of voices expressing dissent as an epic of memory.

Daly, Mary. *Beyond God the Father: Toward a Philosophy of Women's Liberation.* 1973; 2d ed. with an Original Reintroduction, 1985. Contains a landmark critique of patriarchal religion with detailed analyses of women's oppression, proposing sisterhood as the basis for women's liberation and identity.

Griffiths, Morwenna. *Feminisms and the Self: The Web of Identity.* 1995. Presents a methodological and reflective engagement with interdisciplinary questions of self-identity.

hooks, bell. *Ain't I a Woman? Black Women and Feminism.* 1981. Examines black women's experience of racism from the seventeenth century to the present, and decisively challenges the exclusive identity of women assumed by white, middle-class feminism.

———. *Yearning: Race, Gender and Cultural Politics.* 1990. Includes essays that take further her earlier confrontation of racism and sexism.

King, Ursula. "Introduction: Gender and the Study of Religion" and "A Question of Identity: Women Scholars and the Study of Religion." In *Religion and Gender.* Edited by Ursula King. 1995. A gender studies approach to world religion, both empirical and theoretical.

Ricoeur, Paul. "Self as Ipse." In *Freedom and Interpretation: The Oxford Amnesty Lectures 1992.* Edited by Barbara Johnson. 1993. Offers a significant account of personal and narrative identity to which are attached agency, continuity, and the responsibility that supports a new concept of rights.

Mernissi, Fatima. *The Forgotten Queens of Islam.* Translated by Mary Jo Lakeland. 1993. Gives greater historical background on women in the first decades of Islam.

———. *Women's Rebellion and Islamic Memory.* 1996. Contains analyses of women's identity in Islam from ten years of research.

Mukta, Parita. *Upholding the Common Life: The Community of Mirabai.* 1994. Contains a moving, first-hand account of steps taken to retrieve the history and memory of the poetess-saint Mirabai.

Warner, Marina. *Alone of All Her Sex: The Myth and Cult of the Virgin Mary.* 1985. An important study of the origin and growth of the Virgin's cult, as well as the continuing appeal of the contradictory images of the Virgin Mary in Catholic teachings, art, fantasies, and fables.

PAMELA SUE ANDERSON

Ideology

Ideology emerged as the science of ideas, proposed by the eighteenth-century French thinker Comte Destutt de Tracy. Originally understood as an effort to develop a philosophy of mind or ideas as distinct from metaphysics, ideology soon became a pejorative term, first with Napoleon, then continuing in the social theory of Karl Marx (1818–1883). In *The German Ideology* (1845–46), Marx states that the "first premise of all human history" is survival, maintained in the production and reproduction of conditions necessary to sustain human material existence. The ideas or "consciousness" of an era reflect all the concrete conditions of human life in that specific context. Human history and consciousness are the products of work undertaken by individuals in society, and most often the prevailing ideas and values of a given epoch are the ideas of the "ruling class." In societies where masculinity is the accepted standard of normative humanity, women will always be perceived and treated as inferior beings to males. Marx's understanding is thus valuable for most feminist theories, as it locates all cultural images, ideas, ethical norms, and worldviews within the concrete social, political, and economic arrangements of any given society. From this perspective, women are able to identify the material interests of sexism, identifying further how men and certain sections of society benefit from the widespread subordination of women. In the field of religious studies, feminists are able to expose the underlying relations of power that favor male domination concealed within the ideological cloak of theological doctrines and religious practices. A Marxian critique of ideology demystifies the sacred aura of religious beliefs, thereby revealing the ways in which specific groups of males are privileged by the domination of women. The entire range of feminist theory may be understood as a form of ideology critique applied to a particular discipline. In the field of religion, ideology critique is as yet mainly implicit, although it is central to feminist critiques of religion.

BIBLIOGRAPHY

Hewitt, Marsha Aileen. *From Theology to Social Theory: Juan Luis Segundo and the Theology of Liberation.* Bern, 1990. Chapter 1.

Marx, Karl, and Friedrich Engels. *Collected Works.* Vol. 5. 1976.

See also Critical Theory; Marxism; Postmodernism.

MARSHA AILEEN HEWITT

Images of Women

Literary Images of Human and Divine Women

In her groundbreaking 1928 essay, *A Room of One's Own*, British feminist and novelist Virginia Woolf analyzed the images of women in European literature to conclude that, while in actuality women were being "locked up, beaten and flung about the room" by their fathers, brothers, and husbands, in literature by those same men they are praised as quasi-divine paragons of beauty, moral perfection, and power. Disturbed by this dichotomy, Woolf envisioned a world in which women have genuine authority, including the authority of authorship. Only then, Woolf suggested, will their literary images reflect reality.

It is too soon to know if Woolf's hypothesis is correct, for women have just begun to write in sufficient numbers to offset centuries of male domination. The new writing by women unfolds a range of female roles: one finds less idealization, more true divinity. In Woolf's own fiction, women such as Mrs. Ramsay in *To the Lighthouse* and Clarissa in *Mrs. Dalloway* are imperfect and distinctly human, yet elicit awed worship from friends and family whom they lead into communion with the continuity and transience of life.

Literary images of human and divine women vary widely within and among cultures. Male and female writers work both for and against dominant religious and cultural traditions, sometimes reinforcing, sometimes challenging conventional notions of divinity and female excellence. The primary factor that affects literary images of women is the degree to which the divine is regarded as immanent or transcendent; because women are almost universally regarded as more allied to nature than are men, the representation of human and divine women is typically a function of the writer's view of nature and its relationship to divinity. As thorough study of the multitude of images of women in global literature would require volumes, this article sketches significant representations of goddesses and mortal women in the works of Western writers only. For discussion of images of women in non-Western traditions see the bibliography.

In the earliest extant body of European literature—the epic and lyric poems of ancient Greece—the boundaries between the exemplary human and the divine are permeable, and females as well as males move freely between the realms. For example, in the *Iliad* and the *Odyssey* (eighth century B.C.E.), Homer gives mortal women such as Penelope or Arete divine beauty, intelligence, and wisdom while goddesses such as Athena or Aphrodite are characterized as looking and speaking and at times even thinking like mortals. Both the goddesses and the exemplary human women are superhuman. Yet, paradoxically, the ideal of human existence is acceptance of its limitations; only in that acceptance can one become truly godlike. Thus Odysseus rejects the embrace of a goddess in order to return to Penelope, his mortal wife. And Penelope, faithful to this flawed man, acquires the attributes of an earth-goddess, awaiting the return of the sun.

Sappho's lyric poetry (seventh century B.C.E.) suggests an even more fluid boundary between the human and the divine. In gynocentric poems that focus on emotion rather than action, Sappho invokes Aphrodite and the Muses, inviting them to join her circle of women on earth. The divine feminine in Sappho is gracious, generous, abundant—celebrating the sensuous richness of earthly life. A mortal approaches divinity by being a lover or a poet: with the help of Aphrodite, one is "like a god," adored by one's beloved; with the help of the Muses, one transforms experience into exquisite song that grants immortality to the singer. Because Sappho is both lover and poet, multiply blessed by the goddesses to whom she is devoted, she herself becomes like a divinity, celebrated by Plato and others as the tenth Muse.

By the time of the Athenian tragedians' appearance in the fifth century B.C.E., the distance between humanity and divinity has increased; now the gods are distinct from all humans, and from females in particular. (An important exception is Euripides' Dionysus, an am-biguously human and feminine god who claims women as his ecstatic worshipers in *The Bacchae*.) Mortal women in the tragedies by Aeschylus, Sophocles, and Euripides are rarely exemplary; instead they are deeply flawed characters who find themselves in impossibly difficult situations. Perhaps the only truly admirable women are Sophocles' Antigone and, in Euripides' *The Trojan Women,* Hecuba, who, after refusing to assent to a belief in the gods as explanations for human suffering, injustice, or weakness, accepts exile and slavery with calm dignity.

Clytemnestra, in Aeschylus's *Oresteia*, is politically assertive and sexually aggressive, affirming the primacy of the mother-daughter bond. But because Aeschylus's trilogy ritually enacts the triumph of patriarchy, Clytemnestra is sacrificed. The new feminine ideal becomes submission to patriarchal order. Female divinities in the *Oresteia* are split into two extremes: the coolly rational Athena, identified with Apollo and her father Zeus, and the fiercely irrational Furies who call on their ancient "Mother Night." The stern, armor-clad Athena who acts as judge in the *Oresteia* bears little resemblance to the playful goddess of the *Odyssey*. And the Furies of Aeschylus are a far more negative version of the dangerous feminine than are Homer's divine seductresses, Calypso and Circe. This splitting of the divine (and human) feminine into extreme positive and negative attributes is characteristic of patriarchal thought, and has persisted into the Christian era with the portrayal of human women as either idealized virgins or demonic whores.

In contrast to the early Greek conception of divinity as perfected humanity of both genders, within early Christianity (and partly due to the influence of Platonism and Neoplatonism), divinity is defined largely in opposition to humanity and nature, and particularly to women. God is singular (even as a Trinity), male, and—except insofar as He is incarnate in Jesus—disembodied. Because the flesh in the early Church is regarded as corrupt, women, more identified with body than are men, are largely characterized as temptresses. And, strictly speaking, there is no goddess—no female aspect to divinity—within Christianity. The only exemplary women are saints, mortifying their flesh in imitation of Christ.

Yet, during the late Middle Ages, the cult of the Virgin Mary opened the way for an extraordinary and influential literary movement: the Provencal courtly love tradition, with its idealization of an inaccessible woman, devotion to whom served to civilize men. The epitome of this tradition is Dante's Beatrice, a Florentine woman enshrined in his thirteenth-century *Vita Nuova* and *The Divine Comedy*. Identified with the Trinity and praised for the saving grace bestowed by her eyes and lips, Beatrice serves as Dante's gateway

world. Madonna-like in her femininity and virginity, Nell is also identified with Christ, in a bold effort, characteristic of nineteenth-century literature, to reconnect the feminine with the divine.

Yet in sharp contrast to figures like Nell and the domestic angel, Elizabeth Barrett Browning, in her 1856 epic poem *Aurora Leigh*, portrays a heavenly women who is neither virginal, idealized, nor dead. Not so much an angel in the house as a goddess in the woods, Barrett Browning's poet-heroine Aurora is an intensely human, sexual woman, identified with earth, who claims to speak with God's voice as she affirms a feminist theology of immanence.

Barrett Browning's epic, while articulating a growing trend in nineteenth-century literature, in fact anticipates the themes and values that have emerged in twentieth-century feminist literature: a return of a fully embodied goddess, a theology of immanence, and a higher valuation of all aspects of mortal women. This movement has been fueled by the infusion into Western literature of writers drawing on indigenous traditions that see divinity, the earth, and women as inseparable. Women such as Gloria Naylor and Louise Erdrich are among many African-American and Native American writers creating female characters allied to animals and the forces of nature, possessing elemental power and embodying divinity even as they embrace their full humanity.

In her *Aurora Leigh* Elizabeth Barrett Browning (1806–1861) portrayed a heavenly woman who was neither virginal, idealized, nor dead (Corbis-Bettmann)

into divinity. Although many feminist critics have found the impersonal Beatrice (who acquires her greatest virtues after her death) to be an oppressive and unrealistic feminine ideal, she can be understood as an apparition of the divine feminine, the goddess manifesting herself in the guise of a mortal woman and within the limits of Christian doctrine.

By the nineteenth century in England and North America, Dante's exalted vision of the divine feminine has been domesticated; instead of an unattainable lady who does not even greet her worshiper, one encounters the heroine of Coventry Patmore's 1847 *Angel in the House*, a wife and mother whose function is to lead her husband and children upward, away from the corruptions of the world toward spiritual values. Patmore's poem gives name to a type prevalent in nineteenth-century literature—woman as domestic angel. An extreme version of this figure is Little Nell, the central character in Charles Dickens's immensely popular 1840 novel, *The Old Curiosity Shop*. A severely abused fourteen-year-old virgin, Nell dies to save a fallen

BIBLIOGRAPHY

Allen, Paula Gunn. *Spider Woman's Granddaughters: Traditional Tales and Contemporary Writing by American Women.* 1989.

Auerbach, Nina. *Woman and the Demon: The Life of a Victorian Myth.* 1982.

Benko, Stephen. *The Virgin Goddess: Studies in the Pagan and Christian Roots of Mariology.* 1993.

Bogin, Meg. *The Woman Troubadors.* 1976.

Christ, Carol. "Victorian Masculinity and the Angel in the House." In *A Widening Sphere: Changing Roles of Victorian Women.* Edited by Martha Vicinus. 1977.

Christ, Carol P. *Diving Deep and Surfacing: Women Writers on Spiritual Quest.* 1980.

DeJean, Joan. *Fictions of Sappho, 1546–1937.* 1989.

Donovan, Josephine. *After the Fall: The Demeter-Persephone Myth in Wharton, Cather, and Glasgow.* 1989.

Edwards, Carolyn McVickar. *The Storyteller's Goddess: Tales of the Goddess and Her Wisdom from around the World.* 1991.

Elm, Susanna. *Virgins of God: The Making of Asceticism in Late Antiquity.* 1994.

Fabella, Virginia, and Mercy Amba Oduyoye, eds. *With Passion and Compassion: Third World Women Doing Theology.* 1989.

Fabella, Virginia, and Sun Ai Lee Park, eds. *We Dare to Dream: Doing Theology as Asian Women.* 1990.

Gatta, John. *American Madonna: Images of the Divine Woman in American Literary Culture.* 1997.

Gilbert, Sandra, and Susan Gubar. *The Madwoman in the Attic: The Woman Writer and the Nineteenth-Century Literary Imagination.* 1979.

Gleason, Judith. *Oya: In Praise of an African Goddess.* 1992.

Gottner-Abendroth, Heidi. *The Dancing Goddess: Principles of a Matriarchal Aesthetic.* 1991.

Griffin, Susan. *Woman and Nature: The Roaring Inside Her.* 1978.

Hoehler-Fatton, Cynthia. *Women of Fire and Spirit: History, Faith, and Gender in Roho Religion in Western Kenya.* 1996.

Holloway, Karla F. C. *New Dimensions of Spirituality: A Biracial and Bicultural Reading of the Novels of Toni Morrison.* 1987.

Jayakar, Pupul. *The Earth Mother: Legends, Goddesses, and Ritual Acts of India.* 1990.

Kaberry, Phyllis. *Aboriginal Woman: Sacred and Profane.* 1939.

Keuls, Eva C. *The Reign of the Phallus: Sexual Politics in Ancient Athens.* 1985.

Kinsley, David. *The Goddesses' Mirror: Visions of the Divine from East and West.* 1989.

Klein, Anne Carolyn. *Meeting the Great Bliss Queen: Buddhists, Feminists, and the Art of the Self.* 1994.

Kyung, Chung Hyun. *Struggle to Be the Sun Again: Introducing Asian Women's Theology.* 1990.

Lauter, Estella. *Women as Myth-Makers: Poetry and Visual Art of Twentieth-Century Women.* 1984.

Mernissi, Fatima. *Women and Islam: A Historical and Theological Enquiry.* 1991.

Mullett, G. M. *Spider Woman Stories: Legends of the Hopi Indians.* 1979.

Paul, Diana Y., ed. *Women in Buddhism: Images of the Feminine in Mahayana Tradition.* 1985.

Pratt, Annis. *Dancing with Goddesses: Archetypes, Poetry, and Empowerment.* 1997.

Petroff, Elizabeth Alvida, ed. *Medieval Women's Visionary Literature.* 1986.

———. *Body and Soul: Essays on Medieval Women and Mysticism.* 1994.

Russell, Letty, Kowk Pui-lan, et al. *Inheriting our Mother's Gardens: Feminist Theology in Third World Perspective.* 1988.

Sabbah, Fatna A. *Woman in the Muslim Unconscious.* 1984.

Showalter, Elaine. *A Literature of Their Own: British Women Novelists from Bronte to Lessing.* 1977.

Stone, Merlin. *Ancient Mirrors of Womanhood: Goddess and Heroine Tales from Around the World.* 1984.

Tavard, George Henri. *Juana Ines de la Cruz and the Theology of Beauty: The First Mexican Theology.* 1991.

Watkins, Joanne C. *Spirited Women: Gender, Religion, and Cultural Identity in the Nepal Himalaya.* 1996.

JOYCE ZONANA

Visual Images of Human and Divine Women

Images of women are a continuous theme in the art of humankind. In prehistoric art the female body is represented much more frequently than the male body, as a whole or in parts (eyes, breasts, vulva), as well as by way of an ornamentally stylized sign language. In the earliest prehistoric representations it is often difficult to determine whether the represented figure is a woman (priestess, ancestor), a goddess, or the sacred feminine as nature and creative force. The first goddesses with distinct features appear in the early advanced civilizations, perhaps for the first time in Catal Hüyük (Anatolia). These goddesses embody fertility, the forces of life and death, of light and darkness, and they also tell us something of the ways to relate to untamed nature and to culture. In the course of history goddesses and divine women assume human features. The Virgin Mary, for instance, is shown at times as human and humble, simple and earthy, at other times as celestial, courtly and princesslike. Women in high social positions have often lent their features to celestial women: Agnes Sorel, the mistress of King Charles VII of France, had herself portrayed as the Virgin Mary, and the Khmer queen Jayarajadevi, wife of Jayavarman VII, as the Buddhist goddess Tara. In modern art it is often an important woman in the artist's life who is immortalized as Divine Woman with cosmic references—for example, *Portrait of the Artist's Wife* by the Russian Ivan Kliun (1910) or *My Nanny and I* by the Mexican Frida Kahlo (1937).

THE BODY OF WOMAN

The feminine body as a whole is a powerful image of the wonders and secrets of life and its transformations. It is the place of birth, rebirth, and change; nourishing, sheltering, devouring, the powers of life and death all come together in the body of woman. The child experiences the mother's body so early and overwhelmingly that its image of it even later in life remains often more tactile and sensorial than visual. Thus many partial images in early cultures evoke the goddess through her vulva, breasts, or eyes. On the other hand, the maternal body is experienced as the boundless, all-encompassing space, without beginning or end, as Mother Earth herself or as the sky. Temples, tombs, or initiation caves are represented as the devouring and regenerative body of the goddess. To this day the sanctum sanctorum in the Hindu temple is called Garbha-Grha (womb chamber). In many cultures the dwelling is imagined as a holy, living, feminine body. Respect for this holy maternal body regulates the behavior of the inhabitants of the house down to the smallest details.

In the Christian Middle Ages, Mother Earth was thought of as alive. An eleventh-century manuscript of Monte Cassino shows living creatures drinking from the breasts of the earth, and trees, rivers, and animals growing out of the earth's body. This nourishing Mother Nature, as Sapientia (Wisdom) or Philosophia, becomes the Alma Mater of wise men, taking bearded philosophers to her breast. The double aspect of physical fertility and wisdom reveals itself in many representations of the feminine body. In such images Mother Nature (Matter and Matrix) and Transcendent Wisdom (the wisdom gained from the transformation in the dark) often appear as one; for example, in the *Vierges Ouvrantes* from the fifteenth century—wooden statues of the Virgin Mary reverenced especially in France that reveal God the Father and Christ inside her body when a double door is opened. In this image, declared heretical and banned by the church in the same century, the comprehensive feminine body symbolizes Sophia, the feminine divine wisdom or the Holy Spirit, which, together with Father and Son contained inside her, forms the Holy Trinity.

WOMAN RECLINING

Images of reclining women, although not too common in early and primitive art, are nevertheless full of meaning. In an Indian stone relief of a lotus-headed goddess lying on the ground with bent legs, showing her vulva (Hyderabad, 600 B.C.E.), giving birth is represented as an act of creation. More frequently, though, the reclining pose points not to the birth process but to a condition of quiet surrender, of spiritual receptivity and trance. Already in the late Magdalenian (17,000–10,000 B.C.E.), reliefs of slender feminine bodies in completely relaxed, resting postures can be found on the uneven walls of a cave entrance. Nearby, engraved images of bison and wild horses suggest that the faceless women are shamans or else priestesses of the Mistress of the Animals in a state of profound trance and communion with the world of the spirits. The famous little terracotta figures of sleeping women in Malta (3800–3600 B.C.E.) seem to have something in common with these priestesses from the Magdalenian. The Hypogeum temple of Malta was at the same time tomb, oracle, healing center, and place of rebirth, and the two identical figures found in the Hypogeum itself show women sleeping on a platform. The statuettes have been interpreted as priestesses in charge of dream incubation and healing.

Christian art has its reclining women, particularly Anne (after giving birth to her daughter Mary) and the Virgin Mary herself, who is represented lying prone twice: after the birth of Jesus and again in the moment of her death. It is significant in Christian art that it is not the act of the divine birth that is shown but the state of fulfillment and quiet marvel following it. The prone position of Mary expresses calm, a pause in between times, the zero hour. (One is reminded of the Indian God Vishnu resting in the nothing, in the primal ocean between two creations.) Images of the death of Mary in the Middle Ages were a visual instruction of good death. Mary is represented as an aged woman lying in bed, holding a lighted candle and surrounded by Christ's disciples. Above her in heaven Christ appears, receiving the soul of his mother, represented as a little girl in his arms. The prone position of the dying Mary expresses trust, surrender, the leaving behind of matter, of a body that is no longer needed.

WOMAN SITTING OR ENTHRONED

In the Western Hemisphere the throne has always been a symbol of the highest spiritual and worldly authority. In fact, sitting on chairs was at one time only for the privileged few. In ancient (e.g., Egyptian) art, working people are represented standing or sitting cross-legged. In the West African culture of the Ashanti, the Golden Stool, a throne no one ever sits on, embodies the divine power of the king. The Bible mentions the throne of God, and in early Christian art the empty throne becomes a symbol of the divine presence. Much older than these images of male spiritual authority, however, is the connection between woman and throne, which is documented for the earliest advanced cultures. In Catal Hüyük (6000 B.C.E. in Anatolia) the goddess sits on a throne in the moment of giving birth, supporting herself on two lionesses. The early goddesses often seem to be inextricably linked with their throne. Indeed, the name of the Egyptian goddess Isis means throne, and her emblem is the throne she carries on her head. She became the most powerful goddess of antiquity in the Hellenistic period, and, once in decline, passed her throne on to Mary, who is herself referred to as the seat of wisdom (Sedes Sapientiae). In the Romanesque period the enthroned Mother of God, holding her son in her lap, takes the place of earlier representations of Divine Wisdom through an empty throne. The body of Mary becomes the matrix on which the divine Logos reposes and incarnates itself: the mother as the throne of God.

WOMAN STANDING

If the sitting woman figure hints at calm, relaxed authority, in the standing figure the emphasis is on the

Isis, pictured here seated on a throne, became the most powerful goddess of antiquity. Her name means throne, and the throne has always been a symbol of the highest spiritual and worldly authority (Roger Wood/© Corbis).

control of the universe. The feminine figure in upright position commands the forces of life and death, ruling actively. Her position in the center of the cosmos is often emphasized by two wild animals flanking her, identifying her as Mistress of the Animals. Sometimes a pillar substitutes for the central image of the divine mistress. The tree of life, as an image of her creation perpetually renewing itself, or a wooden post driven deep into the ground can also represent her upright figure. As mistress of the world, the divine woman (Hettithian mother goddess as well as certain representations of the Virgin Mary of the late Middle Ages) sometimes stands on a lion or upon a world sphere around which a dragon winds, or on a moon sickle, while her head is surrounded by stars and the sun radiates from their womb (Mary identified with the Woman of Revelation). On the other hand, the Indian goddess Kālī steps firmly on her male partner Siva, whose immobility stops her destructive movement.

As mistress of the earth the goddess needs to touch the ground or to be rooted to it. If, however, the empha-

sis is upon her celestial, otherwordly aspects, her wings are often more important than her feet. She stands in the clouds, floats down, appears in front of the moon disk (the Buddhist Tārā, Kuan Yin). As celestial woman she embodies the other, transcendent dimension of existence and attracts the beings up to herself. Or she protects them all under her cloak. The cosmic and celestial queen does not need a child on her arm to be identified as the merciful mother of all beings: she is the center of all beings, equally accessible to all her children. Subtle changes in the posture of this centered, upright woman-figure, such as an inclination of the head or a slight bending at the waist, indicate that the goddess moves out of the center of the cosmos and refers to another presence: In the motherly inclination toward the child, Mary moves her son into the foreground, and with a humble inclination of the head bows to a higher authority. With a dainty move of the body, the Indian goddess Pārvatī draws attention to her Lord, Siva. Through an elegant, playful mode of representation, the female images of many advanced cultures become models of feminine beauty and charm, while at the same time letting go of spiritual authority.

WOMAN IN MOTION

Goddesses who are dancing, driving carts, or riding animals embody the incessant activity of creation, which is interpreted in India as a feminine force, that of *shakti*. A small terra-cotta statue from predynastic Egypt (fourth millennium B.C.E.) represents a woman in motion with lifted arms—is she a cosmic dancer keeping the dance of creation in motion? Cybele, the Middle Eastern mother goddess, whose image reached Rome at the end of the third century B.C.E., rides through the universe on a chariot drawn by lions. Many goddesses ride on the animal that emblematizes their strength. A whole army of Indian mother goddesses, riding on peacocks, tigers, crocodiles, and other unusual mounts, protects their children from the insolence of the demons. The most famous of these belligerent goddesses is Durgā, "the Inaccessible," who storms into battle upon a lion to restore order in the world. But then an even fiercer destroyer of demons is the black goddess Kālī, an emanation of Durgā's wrath. She is the essence of unbounded feminine destructive energy, rushing over the battlefield on foot.

Some divine women occasionally travel by boat, most famously Isis, Mary, and the Buddhist Tārā. All three are associated with the origin of the far shore because they have absorbed features of ancient star goddesses, who from afar guide the sailor across the sea. Their task is to guide the movements of all beings through the storms of existence. They are at the same time far and near, unalterable light in the sky and reliable vehicle, taking their children to the other shore.

BIBLIOGRAPHY

Dalmia, Yashodhara. *The Painted World of the Warlis: Art and Ritual of the Warli Tribes of Maharashtra.* New Delhi, 1988.

Devi-mahatmya. *The Glorification of the Great Goddess.* Edited and translated by Vasudeva S. Agrawala. Varanasi, 1963.

Ibbitson Jessup, Helen, and Thierry Zephir, eds. *Sculpture of Angkor and Ancient Cambodia: Millenium of Glory.* 1997.

Forsyth, Ilene H. *The Throne of Wisdom: Wood Sculpture of the Madonna in Romanesque France.* 1972.

Gadon, Elinor W. *The Once and Future Goddess: A Sweeping Visual Chronicle of the Sacred Female and Her Reemergence in the Cultural Mythology of Our Time.* 1989.

Getty, Adele. *Goddess: Mother of Living Nature.* 1990.

Gold, Penny Schine. *The Lady and the Virgin: Image, Attitude and Experience in Twelfth-Century France.* 1985.

Kinsley, David. *The Goddesses' Mirror: Visions of the Divine from East and West.* 1989.

Les Miracles de Notre-Dame de Rocamadour au XIIe siècle: Textes et traductions d'après les manuscrits de la Bibliothèque Nationale. Toulouse, 1996.

Mookerjee, Ajit. *Ritual Art of India.* London, 1985.

Neumann, Erich. *The Great Mother.* 1963.

Schiller, Gertrud. *Ikonographie der christlichen Kunst.* Vol. 4, 2, *Maria.* Gütersloh, 1980.

CORNELIA VOGELSANGER

Myths and Symbols

Myth and symbol are deeply interconnected. Neither are found in pure form in the world of the senses, although both arise from it. Even when fantastically altered, both myth and symbol arise from a reality that can be seen, heard, touched, smelled, tasted; in return, each object or story that we experience partakes of, but does not exhaust, the symbol or myth it evokes. Although symbol has a static quality as compared to myth's narrative structure, myths form their action around symbols, and the interpretation of symbol is by reference to myth.

Symbol is sometimes connected to, but more often differentiated from, abstraction. Abstractions are simplifications of forms and objects found in nature; the circle, for instance, is found in visual art from ancient to contemporary times but is never found in nature. Benoit Mandelbrot's fractal geometry has shown that Euclid did not express nature but abstracted it. The full

moon is not a circle, except at a great distance. At closer scale, the moon is discovered to have an irregular shape, just as the sun's outline is not a simple round but a layered sequence of flaring forms. Mountains are not triangles, plains are not straight lines, stars are never pentagrams.

When an abstraction serves as a symbol, it does so by making reference to myth, as when the rayed vehicle that carries the Japanese sun goddess is abstracted into the simple circle seen on that nation's flag. But more often the abstraction is a glyph, a kind of shorthand writing that points to a quality, energy, or cosmic force often embodied in myth. Such is the case among North American Plains Indians, for whom the circle indicates the totality of creation, or in Hindu thought, in which the mandala-circle is a visual expression of the otherwise inexpressible spiritual meaning of a mantra or chant.

In literary theory symbol is defined by its difference from such figurative speech as image, allegory, and metaphor. An image is the physical form of a symbol, with its latent mythic reference only implied (or ironically played against). Metaphor, which is essentially a linguistic equation, uses objects as illustrations of qualities and ideas, as opposed to embodying those ideas as a symbol does. Most interestingly, literary critics have traditionally differentiated allegory from symbol in that allegory equates a physical object to its corollary in the nonphysical world so as to evoke and support a specific worldview, whereas symbol is alleged to evoke some "permanent objective value" (Holman, 1972, p. 519). Yet symbols are hardly free of the freight of cultural meaning.

JUNG'S ARCHETYPAL THEORY

The psychologist Carl Jung argued that there are realities—for which he coined the term archetypes—that find their way into myth and symbol. Such archetypes are larger, more complex, and more self-contradictory than the stories and objects that express them—to wit, for Jung, "the feminine," an inexhaustible source of such mythic characters as Aphrodite and Demeter and Hera, who each express a different aspect of the overarching archetype. The archetype of the feminine can express itself, Jung and his followers claim, in such nonpersonified symbols as the shell, the shoe, the unopened lock.

Archetypes, which are like patterns of possibility, reside in a hypothesized collective unconscious. The symbol, according to Jung, is the doorway to that collective unconscious. "As the mind explores the symbol," he said, "it is led to ideas that lie beyond the grasp of reason" (1964, p. 21). Such symbols and narratives sur-

A hanging scroll by Kobayashi Eitaku (1843–1890) depicts the goddess Izanami with Izanagi creating the Japanese islands (Museum of Fine Arts, Boston).

rounding them appear spontaneously in dreams, more consciously in myth and art.

Jung believed that archetypes are beyond culture and therefore have no proscriptive value. In fact, he stressed that "archetypes are not determined as regards their content, but only as regards their form" (1971, p. xxxi). Yet as defined by his writings and those of his fol-

lowers, "the feminine," rendered as passive, connected to the fluctuating moon and the chaotic unconscious, carries definite proscriptive force. Of the problematic parts of Jung's work, none is more so than his articulation of the concepts of anima and animus, the first being the feminine within the male soul, the latter being the masculine within the female. Here Jung uses a word that means "soul" to refer to something which, by his definition, only men can possess. Many of his comments on the subject seem weighted with uneasiness about the feminine. "Woman has no anima, no soul, but she has an animus" (1971, p. 174), he says in *Marriage as a Psychological Relationship.* Writing at a time when European and American women were leaving the home to enter previously male professions, Jung referred with concern to "the growing masculinization of the white woman," which he suspected to be "connected with the loss of her natural wholeness (*shamba*, children, livestock, house of her own, hearth fire)" and worried whether "the feminizing of the white man is not a further consequence" (1989, p. 263). When the feminine is seen as symbolized by a lock and the masculine as a key, it seems astonishing that anyone could dismiss the implications that correct sexual behavior entails the woman awaiting the opening entry of the man rather than, say, pursuing her own pleasure.

To understand such use of symbolism, and its connection to the cultural content of myth, let us explore a typical symbol: the apple. In the world of the senses, the apple is a roundish fruit that bears numerous small seeds within a nourishing, sweet or tart flesh under a thin, colorful (often red) skin. In the realm of symbolism, the apple's meaning is established in reference to the myths in which it figures. Thus Cirlot (1962) defines the apple as "symbolic of earthly desires, or of indulgence in such desires." This meaning derives from the Hebraic myth of the Garden of Eden, wherein a fruit (commonly described as an apple) is offered to Eve, the weak-willed female ancestor of humanity, by the serpent who opposes the creator-God. Secondarily, the apple is seen as a symbol of potential discord, from the Greek myth of Eris, who threw the golden apple that started the Trojan War. Or it appears as a symbol of danger, from the European fairy tale in which a jealous witch-mother offers the innocent Snow White a poisoned apple that sends her into a dreamless sleep.

When the symbol is understood by reference to the myths it evokes, its every appearance comes laden with cultural meanings. In the case of the apple, the Eden reference is often evoked in European art. When a woman is shown with an apple, the symbolic meaning is that she is tempting the male viewer to leave safety and security behind, to follow her out of Eden into a sexualized or dangerous wilderness. Such is the case with twentieth-century American painter Edward Hopper's *Table for Ladies,* in which the bowing waitress's carelessly exposed breasts echo the fruit she offers. Even a still life in which an apple is prominent calls forth the Eden reference, as in *Fruit Bowl, Glass and Apples,* one of many by French painter Paul Cézanne (1830–1906), in which the fruit is arrayed as temptingly as an odalisque.

The apple has other mythic meanings that have been lost or discounted as the Eden narrative has become predominant. Among the Balts, for instance, the apple represents the sun goddess Saule, who is described as each evening settling her round, red self into an apple tree in the West; it is to this apple tree that the souls of the dead fly, to join the goddess and await rebirth. A similar idea may underlie the Celtic conception of Avalon, the isle of apples where heroes reside in a time-out-of-time. A Greek myth, of the golden apples of the Hesperides, describes a similar orchard in the West where a dragon guards the fruit of the magical tree. These golden apples, associated in late Greek myth with trouble-making Eris and the initiation of the war on Troy, originally belonged to the women's goddess Hera, a gift from her mother when she moved from maidenhood to sexual maturity. These are not, however, the apples that naturally arise in the minds of typical viewers of the paintings described above, embedded as they are in the culture of Eve and Eden.

SEMIOTIC INTERPRETATIONS OF SYMBOL

The meanings we grant to a symbol carry a great deal of cultural direction. It is significant in this regard that the word itself is connected to the Latin *symbolus,* "baptismal creed," for symbols are used by societies to define the limitations of human life within them, as well as to describe their possibilities. The field of semiotics—other than archetypal theory, the major approach to examining symbolism—offers a structure for understanding the connection of myth and social context. Following the work of philosopher Ferdinand de Saussure, semiotics describes a symbol as a kind of sign, made up of two parts: the signifier, which is the form (visual or aural) the sign takes, and the signified, which is the concept or meaning the sign indicates. The connection between the form of the sign and its meaning is admitted to be culturally and historically defined, rather than being somehow "universal," in the way an archetype is proposed to be.

Semiotics and the related theories of structuralism and deconstructionism view myth as a series of signs whose interconnections reveal its meanings. Thus symbol is a kind of sign that carries the cultural (and often political) meaning of the myth, not only within itself, but in its relation to other symbols or signs in the mythic structure.

Just as feminist scholars have questioned the ways in which myth is used to proscribe and prescribe behavior, so they have challenged conventional interpretation of symbolism. The work of Marija Gimbutas is especially important in this regard, for she worked with Paleolithic and Neolithic symbols for which the attendant mythic structures have been lost. By comparing and contrasting the varying ways in which symbols were used on ancient artifacts, Gimbutas not only established a vocabulary of symbolism but proposed a likely social structure (gylandic, or woman-centered) that such a vocabulary would express.

CHAOS AS SYMBOL: A CASE STUDY

As an example of the way a symbol can be interpreted to support and uphold a worldview, let us examine the case of chaos. As typically defined, chaos is a formless void, a fluid mixing of elements, an undifferentiated mass of potentiality. As such, according to Cirlot, it is associated with the unconscious. He stops short of connecting chaos with femininity, although Jung typically spoke of the unconscious as feminine, while the masculine was connected with consciousness and reason. (Tellingly, both chaos and the feminine are also connected with darkness and even connected with evil, as we see in the definition of Gnostic dualism in Hasting's *Encyclopedia of Religion.*) Barbara Walker (1988) goes further, defining chaos as a quintessentially feminine symbol, "the stage of the Great Goddess." In European culture, Katherine Hayles (1990) has pointed out, chaos typically appears as "the other," against the ordered world of the self, and in patriarchal thought "the other" has been defined as feminine.

This linking of chaos and femininity has deep roots. It first appears in European thought in the *Theogony* of Hesiod, who proposed a vision of chaos "giving birth"—clearly a feminine act. This juxtaposes chaos, as a feminine force, with some unexpressed opposite—apparently, masculine order. Yet not only is chaos of neuter gender in ancient Greek, but the myth itself shows that the primal ordering figure is Gaia, a goddess who is the first to rise out of Chaos.

This Greek myth echoes many other myths in which chaos is a genderless void from which emerges an ordering feminine principle. Tuli, the Polynesian primal bird-goddess, flew across the primal waters, forming land wherever she perched to rest. The Hawaiian Lai-l'ai, similarly the first creature to emerge from chaos, was the creator of humanity. The Japanese Izanami, with her mate Izanagi, stirred the soup of chaos so as to create form. Thus primal goddesses create form, rather than embody chaos.

Late-twentieth-century science has begun to challenge the dualistic thinking that has opposed chaos and order as symbols of the feminine and the masculine. Science has for centuries divided male from female, mind from body, self from world. Yet the science of dynamical systems, also known as chaos or complexity studies, has forced a reconsideration of these simplistic, if neat, divisions. Chaos is revealed as the seedbed of order, rather than its polar opposite. As Katherine Hayles observes, there is still significant resistance to seeing this new philosophical and scientific schema as a challenge to normative views of masculinity and femininity.

BIBLIOGRAPHY

Briggs, John, and F. David Peat. *Turbulent Mirror: An Illustrated Guide to Chaos Theory and the Science of Wholeness.* 1989.

Child, Heather, and Dorothy Colles. *Christian Symbols, Ancient and Modern: A Handbook for Students.* 1972.

Cirlot, J. E. *A Dictionary of Symbols.* 1962.

de Man, Paul. *Blindness and Insight.* 1983.

de Saussure, Ferdinand. *Course in General Linguistics.* 1978.

Douglas, Mary. *Natural Symbols: Explorations in Cosmology.* 1970.

Eagleton, Terry. *Literary Theory: An Introduction.* 1983.

Gimbutas, Marija. *Language of the Goddess.* 1993.

Griffin, Susan. *Woman and Nature: The Roaring Inside Her.* 1978.

Hayles, N. Katherine. *Chaos Bound: Orderly Disorder in Contemporary Literature and Science.* 1990.

Holman, C. Hugh. *A Handbook to Literature.* 1972.

Janson, H. W. *History of Art.* 1963.

Jung, Carl. *Memories, Dreams, Reflections.* Recorded and edited by Aniela Jaffee. 1989.

———. *The Portable Jung.* Edited and with an introduction by Joseph Campbell. 1971.

Jung, Carl, et al. *Man and His Symbols.* 1964.

Lasswell, Harold Dwight. *The Comparative Study of Symbols: An Introduction.* 1952.

Leeds-Herwitz, Wendy. *Semiotics and Communication: Signs, Codes, Cultures.* 1993.

Mandelbrot, Benoit B. *The Fractal Geometry of Nature.* 1982.

Merleau-Ponty, Maurice. *Signs.* 1964.

Pierce, Charles Sanders. *Reasoning and the Logic of Things.* 1992.

Prigogine, Ilya. *The End of Certainty: Time, Chaos and the New Laws of Nature.* 1997.

Sebok, Thomas Albert. *Signs: An Introduction to Semiotics.* 1994.

Tiefenbrun, Susan W. *Signs of the Hidden: Semiotic Studies.* Amsterdam, 1980.

Walker, Barbara. *Women's Dictionary of Symbols and Sacred Objects.* 1988.

PATRICIA MONAGHAN

In the Hebrew Bible

As in surrounding cultures, the Hebrew Bible portrays women primarily in terms of their relationships to men: mother, lover, wife, widow, daughter, sister, servant, queen. Portraits vary depending on the form of literature under consideration: in law codes, women are most visible when they are perceived to be out of place or in moments of transition from the control of one male (father) to that of another (husband). In narrative, women play active roles in the direction, management, and protection of their families. In the poetry of wisdom literature, they form a literary trope that emphasizes patriarchal society's ambivalence toward women, simultaneously praised as wives and abhorred as dangers. In prophetic literature, the people Israel are portrayed as a faithless wife and mother who must be punished and rehabilitated by God the husband (Hos. 2, Isa. 54; a standard shaming technique that assaults male honor by assigning female roles to men). Because of emphasis on family stories from the tribal and pretribal period (as compared to the annalistic or mythological survivals from neighboring cultures), the images presented provide a more rounded, well-developed view of women's roles, primarily those in the home, than might otherwise occur. Even so, patriarchal ideology, which valorizes the male as the primary focus of the national god's concerns, ensures that women remain clearly secondary characters and citizens, whether of the literary or the social world.

A dominant image is that of the special mother, whose longed-for child, usually destined to become a national hero, is obtained only with difficulty, often including divine intervention or annunciation of the birth (Sarah, Hagar, Rebecca, Rachel, the mothering of Moses, Samson's mother, Hannah, Ruth and Naomi). A prominent motif in regional folklore, this complication augurs an important role for a child and a special relationship with the deity. Often ancestor stories in Genesis emphasize the role of the mother in securing the divine blessing and promise for the proper offspring, even against the expressed intentions of the patriarchal father (Gen. 21:27). The presence of such stories may suggest a muted female voice of genuine women's experience, which has been modified and absorbed into the

ably talkative character: not only does she have little sense of shame or wrongdoing (Prov. 5, 6, 7, 9), but in some narratives her positive qualities may be praised and used by God on behalf of the nation (Rahab, innkeeper and perhaps harlot of Joshua 2). Evil queens like Jezebel (1 Kgs. 16, 18, 21; 2 Kgs. 9), Athalya (2 Kgs. 11), or the foreign wives who turn aside the hearts of God-fearing kings (1 Kgs. 11), are held up as horrors who deserve their punishments.

Archaeological evidence as well as textual studies allow the outline of some of the public and informal roles women might play. The role of the queen mother (*gebûrâ*) probably extended from court roles to some ritual behaviors (2 Kgs. 11). Women served as midwives and nurses (Gen. 35, 38; Exod. 1; Ezek. 16) and their negative equivalents, sorceresses and diviners (Exod. 22, Lev. 20, Deut. 18, 1 Sam. 28 [the medium of Endor], 2 Chron. 33). These roles might be acquired through general housewifely duties, and practitioners were probably trained by their female relatives. A woman known for her language skills in counseling might become known to her village as a wise woman (2 Sam. 14, 20). Such designations also cover full or part-time skilled occupations such as ritual mourner (Jer. 9, 2 Chron. 35, Ezek. 32), and other "women's work" requiring specialized training, such as weaving (Exod. 35:25–26). In the realm of religion and cult, women served occasionally as prophetesses (Exod. 15, Judg. 4, 2 Kgs. 22, Isa. 8) and one female judge is mentioned (Judg. 4 5). Women weavers for the goddess Asherah were housed in the Jerusalem temple (2 Kgs. 23:7), and some assert, on the basis of biblical polemics, a widespread cult of ritual prostitution (Hos. 2, etc.). Mothers are portrayed as officiating in household goddess cults in Jeremiah 13. Women are especially associated with the playing of hand-drums and were probably regular performers of cult and secular songs (Exod. 15, Judg. 11, Ps. 68), with special connections as authors and performers of victory songs (1 Sam. 18). In other areas of authorship, the queen mother of King Lemuel is credited with making an "Instruction" for her son (Prov. 31); Queen Jezebel wrote letters showing her knowledge of Israelite legal customs (1 Kgs. 21), and Queen Esther is also associated with the creation of documents (Est. 9).

Although portrayal of the Israelite god relies heavily on male-defined social roles (king, judge, shepherd, redeemer, etc.), a number of texts depict this god with traits considered female. Both male and female humans are said to be made in *his* image in Genesis 1:27. God's behavior is often that of a household manager: *he* clothes the miscreant human pair in Genesis 3:21; in Deuteronomy 32 and Proverbs 8, *he* gives birth to Israel and Lady Wisdom, respectively; in Hosea, *he* is the

An engraving of Rebecca and Eliezer by Gustave Doré (Chris Heller/Corbis)

national story, whose priorities are male heroism and its special place in God's plans for the people. Both implicitly and explicitly, it is clear that the role of wife is only a preliminary step on the path to motherhood (a notable exception is the Beloved of the Song of Songs), where a woman is thought to experience her greatest fulfillment, achieve honor among her group, and secure her future well-being (Ruth 1, 4). God, as the opener of wombs and protector of children, fills an important function in women's personal stories, since a mother's successful delivery is equivalent to a warrior's victory in battle (1 Sam. 2): both are attributed to the intervention of the Hebrew god.

Negative corollaries exist for every positive example: protective mothers are juxtaposed with female cannibalism and prospective child abuse (1 Kgs. 3; 2 Kgs. 6:25–31). Exemplary wives like the one praised in Proverbs 31 are balanced by nagging, quarrelsome, adulterous, and vain ones (Prov. 11, 12, 14, 19, 21, 25). Adulteresses are strongly condemned, and rituals like the *sotah* in Numbers 5 suggest that male fears might be projected onto wives without any particular occasion of negative behavior on their part. The adulteress, the foreign, loose woman, or the prostitute is a remark-

mother of Ephraim; and in Isaiah, *he* suffers over the people's wickedness like a woman in labor (Isa. 42). Functions normally performed by ancient Near Eastern goddesses are routinely transferred to the Israelite god or his surrogates. The remarkable figure of Lady Wisdom (Prov. 1–9) may be a survival of an Israelite scribal, mother, or personal goddess, existing only in literary dress, but still speaking with a voice of divine authority.

BIBLIOGRAPHY

Brenner, A., and F. van Dijk-Hemmes. *On Gendering Texts: Female and Male Voices in the Hebrew Bible.* Leiden, 1993.

Fewell, Danna N., and David M. Gunn. *Gender, Power, and Promise: The Subject of the Bible's First Story.* 1993.

Fontaine, Carole R. "The Social Roles of Women in the World of Wisdom." In *A Feminist Companion to Wisdom Literature.* Edited by Athalya Brenner. Vol. 9. Sheffield, U.K., 1995.

Maier, Christl. *Die "fremde Frau" in Proverbien 1–9: Eine exegetische und sozialgeschichtliche Studie. Orbis Biblicus et Orientalis,* 144. Göttingen, 1995.

Meyers, Carol L. "Of Drums and Damsels: Women's Performance in Ancient Israel." *Biblical Archaeologist* 54 (1991): 16–27.

CAROLE R. FONTAINE

In the New Testament

Analyzing the images of women in the New Testament is, in certain ways, an artificial enterprise. The books in the New Testament represent only a portion of the writings composed by Christians from the mid-first century to the early second century C.E. To inquire about the images of women in this collection, which does not reach its present canonical form until probably the late fourth century C.E., is thus, from a historical perspective, to investigate early Christian images through fourth-century lenses. Nevertheless, such inquiry is warranted precisely because the books of the New Testament come to occupy a privileged central place within Christianity, and their images of women loom large in Western tradition.

Within the canon, the presence of women actors fluctuates and their images vary. At least thirty-six individual women are named in the New Testament (not including women from the Hebrew Bible). Numerous others are anonymous. Virtually half the named women come from a single author—the writer of the two-part work, the Gospel of Luke and the Acts of the Apostles. Twelve women are explicitly named in four of the seven letters universally agreed to have been written by Paul. Luke and Paul between them thus mention thirty-two of the named women. Fifteen books in the New Testa-

ment name no individual women; nine contain no explicit mention of individual women, either named or anonymous (again, not including women from the Hebrew Bible).

Women are less likely to be portrayed within family contexts than is the case in the Hebrew Bible. Virtually half the named women are not identified by familial connections to men. Seven of the twelve women named in the synoptic Gospels (Mark, Matthew, and Luke) are identified by familial connections to men. But of the twelve women named in the undisputed Pauline epistles, nine appear with no male relatives or spouses.

Women who are represented with family ties (confined almost entirely to the gospels) are most often represented as wives or mothers (about a dozen each). In the Gospels, all the named mothers have adult sons, while unnamed mothers are equally likely to have either sons or daughters.

Interestingly, even when women are identified by their male relations, fathers and husbands are often conspicuous by their absence. Only two women named in the Gospels Mary, the mother of Jesus, and Elizabeth, the mother of John the Baptist, have husbands who appear in the narratives, and John's parents appear only in Luke.

Women explicitly identified as widows figure regularly in the narratives of Luke. But they are rare elsewhere in the Gospels and absent in the genuine Pauline epistles. Otherwise, widows appear only in the pseudo-Pauline 1 Timothy, where the word designates an order of women as well as a woman whose husband has died. Several women appear independent of male control (the Gentile mother of the demon-possessed daughter in the region of Tyre [Mark 7:24–30; Matthew 15:21–28]; Susanna [Luke 8:3], Salome [Mark, 16:1], and Mary of Magdala [Luke 8:3 and elsewhere]).

Women are rarely identified by their fathers, or mothers, for that matter (Luke's description of the four prophesying daughters of Philip being a notable exception [Acts 21:9]). While New Testament writers do not share the Hebrew Bible's interest in filiation, adult men in the gospels are occasionally known as their fathers' sons.

Most women in the New Testament appear as free persons and occasionally even as elites, but female slaves and servants appear sporadically [e.g. Acts 12:13, 16:16–18]. Some may be members of the Jesus movement, but others are cast as peripheral players in the larger drama.

In the Gospels generally, women are primarily seen within the framework of ordinary rural and urban life. In Jesus parables they appear engaged in domestic tasks such as grinding grain, baking bread, and sweeping their houses. In the narratives, women are present in the crowds, at synagogues, and at festivals in Jerusalem. They are depicted as actors: dining with Jesus, financing the Jesus movement, providing hospitality, anointing or intending to anoint Jesus both before and after his death. They are depicted sometimes as recipients of Jesus' healing miracles, or of his teachings, sitting at his feet in the classic position of a disciple. They are the discoverers of his empty tomb and witnesses to his resurrection.

When compared with the Hebrew Bible, though, women in the gospels are disproportionately imaged as ill, possessed, widowed, bereft of beloved children, poverty-stricken, and otherwise disadvantaged. In the Gospel of John, an adulterous woman and a Samaritan with a seemingly unsavory sexual history figure prominently. Portraits of mature women surrounded by devoted husbands and healthy children are virtually nonexistent.

In Luke's second volume, the range of images of women widens, as does the geographic scope of the narrative. Numerous aristocratic women appear, Jewish and non-Jewish, joining the nascent Christian movement or offering their tacit support. Priscilla teaches [Acts 18:2–3, 18–19, 24–26]. Luke shows us occasional images of women engaged in commerce (Lydia of Thyatira [Acts 16:14–15]), and even a congregation of women assembled for Sabbath worship (Acts 16:11–13), as well as the four unmarried women prophets, the daughters of Philip.

The sources of the New Testament's images may be as diverse as the images themselves. Some New Testament writers appropriate images of women from Hebrew Bible narratives and paradigms. The image of the "special mother," so prominent in the Hebrew Bible, appears in the New Testament in the Matthean and Lukan birth narratives. The widow of Nain (Luke 7:11–17) is closely modeled on a story about Elijah (1 Kgs. 17:8–24). Paul makes explicit use of the biblical story of Sarah and Hagar for his own interpretation of the children of Abraham.

Yet in general it might seem that the images of women in the Gospels, in Acts, and in at least some of Paul's letters, correlate reasonably well with ancient social experience. Several scholars have recently suggested that Luke's plentiful portrait of women nevertheless seeks to counter concerns that Christian women were not, in fact, in sufficient conformity with ancient expectations of appropriate gendered behavior. The role played by such ancient understandings of gender becomes more visible in some of Paul's letters and in certain other New Testament writings. While Paul names numerous women as leaders and co-workers in the Jesus movement, women also appear in his letters generically, as problems to be solved (for example, the

behavior of the Corinthian women prophets, 1 Cor. 11:3–16 and perhaps also 1 Cor. 14:33b–36, although many scholars believe this to be a later interpolation). For Paul gender is visible as a fundamental category of divine order, even if this creates a tension with his dictum in Galatians 3:28 that there is no male and female in Christ Jesus. Such concerns about gender may also lie behind the representation of women's speech in the New Testament generally. Women's speech is a subject of anxiety for some New Testament authors: female characters in the New Testament rarely speak, and when they do, their lines are few.

In the remainder of the corpus attributed to Paul, images of women shift even further. The Pastoral Epistles are stereotypic in their explicit denigration of women as weak, ignorant, lacking in discernment and self-control, and easily prone to sexual and theological error. Sharing with a number of other New Testament epistles (for example, Colossians, Ephesians and 1 Peter) a concern for conformity to ancient norms of appropriate behavior for women and men that reflects a pervasive gendered hierarchy, these epistles represent "good" women as those who conform to such norms and "bad" women as those who do not.

Feminine imagery for the divine in the New Testament is generally limited, with the possible exception of the representation of Jesus as Sophia (Wisdom). Only Revelation makes substantial use of feminine imagery, not for the divine, but for both the church and her opponents. In casting the church as virtuous mother and bride (Rev. 12; 19:7–9; 21:2; 21:9) and the opponents of the church as sexually immoral (depicting Rome as "the whore of Babylon" [Rev. 17–18] and an unknown female prophet as the idolatrous biblical Jezebel [Rev. 2:18–29]) the writer of Revelation affirms gender as a fundamental category of order and disorder.

As in the Hebrew Bible, women in the New Testament are represented as either agents of evil or agents of redemption. The pernicious plotting of Herodias and her daughter in the death of John the Baptist, the wiles of the latter-day Thyatiran "Jezebel," and even the dangerous false teachings accepted by the weak and ignorant women in 1 Timothy are contrasted with the virtuous actions and the faithful discipleship of women such as Mary the mother of Jesus, Elizabeth the mother of John, Mary of Magdala, and the various women witnesses to the resurrection.

BIBLIOGRAPHY

D'Angelo, Mary Rose. "Women in Luke-Acts: A Redactional View." *Journal of Biblical Literature* 109, no. 4 (1990): 441–461.

Fiorenza, Elisabeth Schüssler, ed. *Searching the Scriptures: A Feminist Commentary.* 2 vols. 1993–1994.

Kraemer, Ross S., and Mary Rose D'Angelo, eds. *Women and Christian Origins: A Reader.* 1998.

Newsom, Carol A., and Sharon Ringe, eds. *The Women's Bible Commentary.* 1992.

Schottroff, Luise. *Lydia's Impatient Sisters: A Feminist Social History of Early Christianity.* Translated by Barbara and Martin Rumscheidt. 1995.

Seim, Turid Karlsen. *The Double Message: Patterns of Gender in Luke-Acts.* 1994.

ROSS S. KRAEMER

In the Apocrypha

The so-called Apocrypha are Jewish religious books or additions to books not found in the Hebrew Bible. With the exception of 2 Esdras (which is found in Old Latin translations), all are included in the Greek version of the Hebrew Bible (Septuagint). In the sixteenth century these books were separated from the canon by the Protestant reformers but accepted by the Roman church (Council of Trent, 1546). Protestant and Jewish canons exclude these works, but all Catholic, Greek Orthodox, and Slavonic Orthodox Old Testaments include them as Deuterocanonical books. What to call these writings is problematic. Recent terminology like "The Late Writings of the Old Testament" misleadingly suggests they are later than the Hebrew Bible, which is not always the case.

Like other parts of the Bible, the Apocrypha or Deuterocanonical books contain positive and negative images of women (for the worst see Sir. 22:3; 25:24; 42:14). The content and context of these eighteen books (see the listing in the New Revised Standard Version of the Bible) is androcentric, yet in prayers and relationship with God, women like Sarah (in Tobit), Judith, Esther, Susanna, and the unnamed martyred mother in 2 and 4 Maccabees achieve a measure of transformative independence from patriarchal societal norms. Three books are titled by the names of courageous Jewish women who model covenant faithfulness in times of crisis: Judith, Esther, and Susanna (compared to Ruth and Esther in the Hebrew Bible and no New Testament book).

Sixteen female characters are named. The most fully developed are faithful Jewish wives, mothers, daughters, or widows. Passing references cite women from the Hebrew Bible and also non-Jewish women, most of whom have royal associations. Judith and Susanna are the only named women in their eponymous books. Tobit includes four Jewish female characters: Deborah (1:8), Anna (1:20 ff.), Sarah (3:7ff.), and Edna (7:2ff.), and refers in a prayer to Genesis' Eve (8:6). Baruch mentions Hagar (3:23), another woman from Genesis. In addition to the Jewish woman Esther (see esp. Add.

Esth. 14:1–15:16), the Book of Esther names three non-Jewish women: Vashti (1:9–22), Zosara (5:10–14; Zeresh in Esth. 5:10ff.), and in the postscript, Cleopatra (likely Cleopatria II, 11:1). 1 Maccabees names and makes reference to another Cleopatra (Cleopatra Thea, 10:57–58; cf. 11:9–12). 2 Maccabees mentions one woman, Antiochis, the king's concubine (4:30). 3 Maccabees tells of Arsinoë, Philopator's courageous sister (1:1, 4); and 1 Esdras cites two women: Agia, daughter of Bartzillai and wife of Jaddus, whose sons returned from the exile to claim the priesthood (5:38; she is not mentioned in the parallel lists of Ezra 2:61 and Neh 7:63), and Apame, who is the daughter of the illustrious Bartacus and exercises powerful control over the king as his concubine (4:29–31).

Unnamed women, some of whom are significant characters, appear throughout the Apocrypha (except in Prayer of Azariah, Prayer of Manasseh, and Psalm 151) as community members, brides, widows, wives, mothers, daughters, nurses, servants, prostitutes, and worshipers. Most notable of these unnamed women is the steadfast, courageous mother martyred with her seven sons (see esp. 2 Macc. 7:1–42 and 4 Macc. 14:11– 18:24). She is recognized for her noble words to each of her sons that evidence a "woman's reasoning and man's courage" (2 Macc. 7:21) and praised for her love for her children (4 Macc. 14:13ff). In an unforgettable passage, it is said that "because of their birth pangs" mothers "have deeper sympathy toward their offspring than do the fathers. Considering that mothers are the weaker sex and give birth to many, they are more devoted to their children" (4 Macc 15:4–5). The conclusion is intended as high praise, "If, then, a woman advanced in years and mother of seven sons, endured seeing her children tortured to death, it must be admitted that devout reason is sovereign over the emotions" (4 Macc. 16:1).

Female representations appear in five of the books. Wisdom is personified as a woman (Wisd. Sol. 6:12–21ff.; Sir. 4:11; 6:18; 14:20–21; 15:2–4; 51:13ff.; Bar. 3:9–4:4). God is personified as a mother (2 Esd. 1:28; 2:2), nurse (2 Esd. 1:28), and hen (2 Esd. 1:30). Earth (2 Esd. 7:54, 62), Zion (2 Esd. 9:38–10:54), Babylon and Asia (2 Esd. 15:46–63), and righteousness and iniquity (2 Esd. 16:49–52) are personified as females. One goddess, Nanea, is cited and it is in her Persian temple that Antiochus IV (Epiphanes) is stoned and decapitated (2 Macc. 1:13–16).

BIBLIOGRAPHY

Bellis, Alice Ogden. *Helpmates, Harlots, and Heroes: Women's Stories in the Hebrew Bible.* 1994.

Dictionary of Women in Scripture: Named and Unnamed Women in the Hebrew Bible,

Apocryphal/Deuterocanonical Books, and New Testament. Edited by Carol Meyers, Toni Craven, and Ross Kraemer. Forthcoming.

TONI CRAVEN

Immanence and Transcendence

Immanence and *transcendence* are terms that were designed to represent opposite ends of a spectrum within Western theologies, and indeed they successfully describe an ongoing tension found in Western religions. Generally applied to a deity, though occasionally to more amorphous concepts like "the sacred," these terms map out the relationship between human beings and the divine: principally, how far apart they are, and how they might most effectively encounter one another. At the extreme of immanence, God is in us and around us, and is at no time distant from us. At the extreme of transcendence, God is "totally Other," a being separated from us by an immeasurably huge gulf.

Reformers in various religious traditions have sought to move their coreligionists in one direction or another along the immanent-transcendent spectrum of belief. Certainly Christianity, to take but one example, has had theologians like Friedrich Schleiermacher arguing for a radical immanence, that the world is in God, and others, like Karl Barth, insisting that any attempts to bring God into human understanding is doomed to failure, since it ignores God's complete transcendence of human experience. And yet most religions do not in practice adhere to any strict placement of the divine at one end or the other of the immanent-transcendent spectrum. The two concepts—God as immanent, God as transcendent—seem almost inseparable. Even when the theological rhetoric strongly favors a single side of the dichotomy, one can usually detect evidence of the opposite position in the form of a subtext, an opposing tension. This is perhaps to be expected: If a deity is not somehow larger, greater, or more encompassing than humans, that deity does not seem truly godlike; deity becomes an unnecessary postulate if one could as easily talk about "the world" or "the universe." On the other hand, if a deity completely transcends human life and communication between human and divine becomes difficult or impossible, such a deity is rendered nearly useless for human purposes. Clearly, as virtually all religions have shown, the interesting territory is in the middle ground between immanence and transcendence.

Theoreticians and theologians of immanence and transcendence have been predominantly male across Western religious traditions. This raises the interesting

A mid-life portrait of Mary Baker Eddy (1821–1910), the founder of the Church of Christ, Scientist (Corbis-Bettmann)

question of how the concepts of immanence and transcendence are handled by women: do women find this a meaningful distinction, and if so, where do they wish to see the religions placed along the continuum these terms describe?

Like all such questions, this one does not admit of a straightforward answer. Yet within the religious history of the United States at least, the argument has often been made that women, given the freedom to create and describe their own religious views, will hold to immanentist views of deities and the divine. There is excellent support for this argument: When and where American women have emerged as religious leaders (generally outside of mainstream religions, within which their leadership has traditionally been restricted), they have often stressed experiential interaction with the divine, and a sense that God can be found either within the self, or very close to home. Mary Baker Eddy, founder of Christian Science, Emma Curtis Hopkins, founder of the New Thought metaphysical traditions, and numerous other nineteenth-century religious women emphasized the ease with which one can know and experience the divine, present within one's own Soul or Mind. Contemporary parallels can be found in the work of feminist theologians and religious practitioners who also insist on God(dess)'s immanence. The Women-Church movement focuses on the divine's immanence, as does the feminist spirituality movement, which often contrasts its own belief that Goddess is present in women and nature with Christianity, which it lambasts for placing God in a transcendent realm. As American women have become acquainted with the other world religions, they—like the men who have usually preceded them—have applied the concepts of immanence and transcendence to them (no matter how bad the fit from the point of view of the religions' original practitioners). Women have frequently taken these religions in a more immanentist direction or adopted only those portions of the religion that focus on God's nearness. For example, the Hindu concept of atman, with all its metaphysical openness to the divine within and around one, has been far more popular on the American scene than has devotion to Vishnu (or even Shakti). And as American women are admitted into the clergy of more established religious traditions such as Conservative and Reform Judaism and Protestantism, they often emphasize the immanentist side of these traditions and downplay doctrines of transcendence.

Those women who promote an immanent view of the divine are often explicit about the gendered nature of their choice. They see this as a uniquely feminine way of relating to God. God is found within the domestic world to which women have at times been restricted; God is in the whisperings of our hearts, more like the intimate conversation of women than the public oratory of men. The metaphor of motherhood is especially common in arguments on behalf of God's immanence: the divine is said to contain us as mothers contain their children, and to relate to us out of this close biological identity, similarity, or interdependence. Transcendence, in contrast, is often thought to be a "male" theology based on authority and hierarchy, with God sitting at the top of the organizational chart of the universe.

The relationship of women to immanentist theologies is clearly part of a generalized ideological construct having to do with stereotypes of maleness and femaleness that women, men, and religious researchers hold in common. Because these stereotypes work at the level of ideology, they are culturally "true" to a degree: that is women, when self-consciously acting as women are expected to act, promote the "feminine" values of relationality, nurturance, and mutuality. They impute these values to the divine and call it immanence. And

yet there are factors that cut the other way: For example, many men have also promoted immanence as a religious value, from American empiricism forward, and have done so without conceptualizing immanence as "feminine." Additionally, there are a great many women today who champion God's transcendence from within fundamentalist or orthodox Christian or Jewish groups, sometimes suggesting that their devotion to a transcendent male God should stand as the model for all human beings, who—male and female alike—are "feminine" in relationship to God's "masculinity."

In sum, in spite of a suggestive correlation between women and immanent theologies, there is little reason to believe that this is an unchanging feature of the religious landscape, even in the West where these terms were coined and frequently given a gendered gloss.

BIBLIOGRAPHY

Eller, Cynthia. "Immanence and Transcendence in Women's Thea/ologies." *1998 Annual Review of Women in World Religions.* Forthcoming.

Plaskow, Judith, and Carol P. Christ. *Weaving the Visions: New Patterns in Feminist Spirituality.* 1989.

Ruether, Rosemary Radford. *Sexism and God-Talk: Toward a Feminist Theology.* 1993.

Sered, Susan Starr. *Priestess, Mother, Sacred Sister: Religions Dominated by Women.* 1994.

Starhawk. *The Spiral Dance: A Rebirth of the Ancient Religion of the Great Goddess.* 10th annv. ed. 1989.

Wessinger, Catherine, ed. *Women's Leadership in Marginal Religions: Explorations Outside the Mainstream.* 1993.

See also **Women's Contemporary Spirituality Movement.**

CYNTHIA ELLER

Inanna

During the second half of the third and early part of the second millennia B.C.E., the Sumerian goddess Inanna was worshiped in seven cities of southern Mesopotamia (among them Zabala, Agade, and Kish), but principally in her temple Eana at Uruk. Her name may mean "Lady (of) Heaven." The cuneiform sign conveying her name (*mùš*) represents a ring-post with streamers, but the implication is obscure. By the third millennium B.C.E. she was linked to the Semitic goddess Ishtar, making it difficult to distinguish her own characteristics. Inanna has many avatars, among them Nanaya and Annunitum.

The literature about Inanna, mostly preserved by scribes of later periods, can be divided into three categories. The first, myth, is best represented by narratives, hymns, and laments in a cycle in which Inanna seeks to expand her power, which can be termed "Inanna and Dumuzi." This includes "Inanna's Descent into the Netherworld" and "Inanna and Bilulu," narratives that, among other goals, explain the seasonal cycle; when Inanna enters the netherworld in a move to control it, Dumuzi, her husband, is forced to stay there, separated from Inanna for half a year. During the other half, however, his sister Geshtinanna takes his place in the netherworld (ruled by Inanna's sister Ereshkigal), thus allowing yearly renewal of fecundity on earth. A number of hymns were composed in honor of rulers (such as Shulgi of Ur and Iddin-Dagan of Isin), who personified Dumuzi when undergoing a ritual celebrating a sacred marriage with Inanna.

Also in the category of myth is "Inanna and Enki," in which Inanna appropriates from Enki, god of Eridu, the *me*, "divinely set norms," which give harmony to the cosmos, and brings them to her city, Uruk. Less well understood are her visits to Kur, the netherworld ("Inanna and Shukatelluda" and "Inanna and Utu").

The second literary category includes a number of poems that center around the exploits of Uruk rulers (Gilgamesh, Enmerkar, Lugalbanda), with colophons to label them as praise for Inanna. In these poems, Uruk rulers are challenged for supremacy by leaders from other city-states (Aratta, Kish), a positive outcome decided for those states that receive Inanna's favor.

The third category includes hymns honoring Inanna, some of which are generally assigned (correctly or not) to the family of Sargon of Agade (Akkad). They include a collection of temple hymns, "Inanna and Ebikh," "Inni-shagurra," and "Ninmesharra" (often cited as the "Exaltation of Inanna"). Such hymns were the earliest literary creations assigned an author—in this case Enkheduanna, Sargon's daughter, who lived in the twenty-third century B.C.E.

Judging from this literature, Inanna's powers are manifold. She embodies the drive to unite sexually, implying fecundity, but rarely the drive to mother and never to nurture. Inanna exudes life-force. Whether Inanna originally displayed the martial characteristics that are readily associated with Ishtar cannot be ascertained. The planet Venus is often connected with Inanna.

Although Inanna deeply affected the poetic imagination in Mesopotamia, her place in the pantheon may have depended on the status of the city-state where each poem was first created: richer and more powerful locales were able to keep a larger pantheon and re-shape her role to suit the condition. Occasionally she is the daughter of An, head of the pantheon, and has Utu (sun-god) and Nanna (moon-god) as siblings. But she is also said to have had Enki (sweet-water and wisdom-god), Enlil (executor of divine will), and even Nanna as father. Her mother is said to be Ningal. Some historians of art identify—though not always convincingly—deities in sexual poses with Inanna.

BIBLIOGRAPHY

Balz-Cochois, Helgard. *Inanna: Wesensbild und Kult einer unmütterlichen Göttin.* 1992.

Bottéro, J., and S. N. Kramer. *Lorsque les dieux faisaient l'homme: Mythologies mésopotamiennes.* 1989.

Bruschweiler, Françoise. *Inanna: La déesse triomphante et vaincue dans la cosmologie sumérienne.* 1987.

Hallo, William W., and J. J. van Dijk. *The Exaltation of Inanna.* 1978.

Jacobsen, Thorkild. *The Harps That Once . . . Sumerian Poetry in Translation.* 1987.

Sasson, J. M., et al, ed. *Civilizations of the Ancient Near East.* 4 vols. 1995. See the chapters on Sumerian literature and religion.

See also **Ishtar and Anat; Mesopotamian Religions.**

JACK M. SASSON

Incest

Sexual relations or marriage between members of the same nuclear family or between close relations of the extended family are not subject to a universal taboo, as is often claimed. In *The Original Sin: Incest and Its Meaning* (1986), W. Arens disputes previous scholarship that held that the proscription against incest is a universal cultural creation, indeed paradigmatic of the very emergence of culture; he asserts instead that humans have an innate aversion to incest and that it is the practice, not the prohibition, of incest that is the cultural creation in need of explication. To demonstrate the practice, Arens cites well-documented incestuous marriage patterns of royal families viewed as incarnating divinity in ancient Egypt, Thailand, Hawaii, and Peru, as well as recent ethnographic observations on rituals of incest among the Shilluk, Lovedu, and Azande societies in Africa in which the incest rituals form part of the installation rites for new kings or queens, or are used by the rulers in response to social calamities as a means of restoring social well-being. These rituals are religious in nature, being imitations of goddesses and gods whose incestuous behaviors in myth are emblematic of their own nonhuman divine status. They confer an analogous status of divinity on royalty in the installation rite or, through the shattering of normal human kinship relations at a time of great social stress, they symbolize a radical rupture with the old order that enables the creation of a new one. Arens's examples can be supplemented by others similarly drawn from religious ritual. In *Sex in the World's Religions* (1980), Geoffrey Parrinder mentions the ritualized incest that Buddhist adepts are encouraged to incorporate in the practice of tantristic sex. Classicists and ancient Near Eastern scholars often refer to sacred sexual rites found in cultures of the third to the first millennium B.C.E., some being orgiastic in form, meaning all normal kinship ties were temporarily suspended, thus allowing incest to occur. The practice of incest, then, is found not infrequently in a religious ritual form.

The sacred myths of the ancient Egyptians abound with incestuous relations among the gods and goddesses, such as the sister-brother couple of Isis and Osiris, whose son, Horus, was believed to be reincarnated in each succeeding pharaoh. A great many polytheistic religious traditions around the world exhibit variations on the incestuous mythic theme, especially in their creation myths. The Greek account in Hesiod's *Theogony* (seventh century B.C.E.), for example, relates that Gaia, the Earth, was the first deity. She bore a son by herself, through parthenogenesis, and subsequently mated with him to conceive the next generation of gods. The sibling pair, Rhea and Kronos, were parents to the third generation, including the god who became the dominant deity in the Greek pantheon, Zeus, and his sister-wife, Hera. It is the ubiquity of similar mother-son or sibling incest myths in polytheistic traditions globally that inspires psychoanalytic approaches to the study of religious myths, such as the Freudian explanation that religious myths embody psychological projections onto the gods and goddesses of repressed, unconscious incestuous desires felt by humans. Significantly, father-daughter incest, though noticeably rare as a form of this mythic incest pattern, is not entirely absent, as for example in the case of the ancient Indic god Prajapati's intercourse with his daughter in the *Ṛgveda* (10.61) around 1200 B.C.E.

Implicit in the foregoing is the idea that, while permitted for divinities or in certain restricted ritual contexts, incest is not viewed in polytheistic traditions as normally acceptable behavior for humans. The major monotheistic traditions of Judaism, Christianity, and Islam share this aversion, as expressed in the Qur'an's list of prohibited marriages (4.23) and in the prohibited sexual relations specified in the biblical passages of Leviticus 18 and 1 Corinthians 5. However, the incidence of incestuous behavior—not in ritual form, but in the form of incestuous sexual abuse of children, mostly girls—has been recognized as far from uncommon in contemporary Jewish, Christian, and Islamic societies. Research on the problem, conducted primarily by Jewish and Christian feminists, consistently implicates patriarchal religion as a factor contributing to incestuous sexual abuse of girls and as an impediment to recovery from the psychological and spiritual harm the incest causes. Such feminist analysis characterizes father-daughter incest in particular as a way of inculcating female obedience and acceptance of sexual victimization, and thus as a tool for perpetuating certain social constructions of patriarchal gender relations.

BIBLIOGRAPHY

Adams, Carol J., and Marie M. Fortune, eds. *Violence Against Women and Children: A Christian Theological Sourcebook.* 1995. Several articles dealing with incestuous abuse of girls are usefully combined with articles on other forms of sexual violence against females in Christian culture, revealing the scope and contours of the theological problem of which incest is but one manifestation. Collectively, the notes and works cited comprise a rich and current resource for scholarly and pastoral purposes.

Cohn Spiegel, Marcia. "Spirituality for Survival: Jewish Women Healing Themselves." *Journal of Feminist Studies in Religion* 12, no. 1 (1996): 121–137. Illustrates the tendency by Jewish victims of incest and other forms of violence against women to protect the Jewish community before themselves by remaining silent about their abuse, but also shows how women's creative reforms within the tradition make it possible for victims to retain their Jewish identity and ritual practice while in the process of recovery.

Herman, Judith Lewis, and Lisa Hirschman. *Father-Daughter Incest.* 1981. A classic in the field, with some of the earliest evidence linking prevalence of the problem with conservative religious families, and offering preliminary analysis of Christian roots of the problematic patterns of male supremacy, despotic paternal rule, rigid sex roles, and a sexual double standard.

Martens, Tony. *The Spirit Weeps: Characteristics and Dynamics of Incest and Child Sexual Abuse.* 1988. One of the few sources to concentrate on the incest problem in the aboriginal communities where the legacy of sexual abuse experienced in Christian-run boarding schools has produced soaring rates of incest along with other social problems such as alcoholism.

Ochshorn, Judith. "Ishtar and Her Cult." In *The Book of the Goddess: Past and Present.* Edited by Carl Olson. 1986. One of several scholarly publications on ancient goddess worship that typically tend to acknowledge the frequency of the mother-son and sister-brother mythic incest motifs without critically and directly addressing the incest issue itself. This is clearly an area in need of further analysis.

Rank, Otto. *The Incest Theme in Literature and Legend: Fundamentals of a Psychology of Literary Creation* [1912]. Translated by Gregory C. Richter. 1992. Presents an early Freudian analysis but is still a useful source for scholarship on incest in ancient myths and rituals along with literature and legend. A chapter devoted to father-daughter incest includes press reports of this crime at the time of first publication in support of the author's acknowledgment of it as the most frequent sexual crime in fact, if not in myth.

Redmond, Sheila Ann. "The Father God and Traditional Christian Interpretation of Suffering, Guilt, Anger and Forgiveness as Impediments to Recovery from Father-Daughter Incest." Ph.D. diss., University of Ottawa. 1993. Presents a comprehensive analysis of relevant theological, pastoral, psychoanalytic, and feminist scholarship on the subject, and leads to a wholesale indictment of the Christian tradition.

Rush, Florence. *The Best Kept Secret: Sexual Abuse of Children.* 1980. Contains one of the first critical discussions of the religious roots of the problem; argues that the Bible and the Talmud encourage sex between men and very young girls.

Russell, Diana E. H. Russell. *The Secret Trauma: Incest in the Lives of Girls and Women.* 1986. A statistical study including the information that Protestant and Roman Catholic women who were incest victims as girls have defected from their religious upbringing at significantly higher rates than Christian women who were not victims, the second group proportionately more so than the first. Also shows the defection rate for Jewish victims to be much lower than for either Christian denomination.

See also **Isis.**

MARYMAY DOWNING

Indo-European Religions

The notion of Indo-European religions—or "Indo-European" anything—is a hypothetical construct, predicated on the discoveries of the eighteenth and nineteenth centuries, showing broad phonologic and morphologic similarities within the Indic, Iranian, Armenian, Anatolian, Baltic, Slavic, Greek, Italic, Germanic, and Celtic language families. To explain these resemblances most experts posit a common ancestral language, "Proto-Indo-European," to which these others are related, much as Romance languages are related to Latin. Other explanations are possible, including slow processes of diffusion (Trubetzkoy, 1939) or an original lingua franca that developed with long-distance trade (Crevatin, 1979). These, however, have gained less acceptance than the genetic model, which, though it has much to recommend it, also raises serious problems.

The genetic model implies the existence of a primordial community of people who spoke the ancestral language, a group that has borne several different names. "Proto-Indo-Europeans" is now most favored, but until the end of World War II, they were usually known as "Aryans," a term that endures in racist discourse. Racism, indeed, often figures in the discipline of Indo-European studies, sometimes flagrantly and sometimes in more subtextual fashion. In general, it follows from a line of speculation that moves from linguistic resemblances to a proto-language, spoken by a proto-community, living in an original homeland, which for various reasons (many specious) is frequently imagined to be in northern Europe. The expansion of language and community throughout Eurasia is then theorized as a process of conquest made possible by the community's inherent superiority over others. Finally, intermarriage with conquered populations is said to have produced decadence, with the result that those who believe they remain pure of blood (or DNA, in updated versions) urge strenuous measures designed to reverse such mongrelization (Poliakov, 1974; Olender, 1992; von See, 1994).

EVOLVING THEORIES

Variants of this narrative were accepted by leading scholars of the nineteenth century (Ernest Renan, Friedrich Max Müller) and popularized by major cultural figures (the comte de Gobineau, Richard Wagner). In this century the Nazi party and state enthusiastically adopted racial theories of this sort which provided the ideological basis for the Holocaust. Since 1945 such racial theories have not been acceptable in polite scholarship or society, and discourse about "the Indo-Europeans" has changed accordingly. In late-twentieth-century scholarship, two major variants enjoy significant support, although both have drawn serious criticism.

The first, advanced by Marija Gimbutas, identifies the primordial community with the Kurgan culture of the south Russian steppes, known from archaeological

Bronze Age Hittite funerary stele of a scribe depicted as a child standing on his mother's lap, Anatolia, eighth century B.C.E. (Gianni Dagli Orti/Corbis)

sites in which large burial mounds (*kurgans*) are a salient feature. In her view, the material remains of these people correspond closely to the reconstructed vocabulary of the Indo-European language family. The chief aspects she stresses are patriarchal authority; social stratification; a warrior elite; metal weaponry; crude, unembellished ceramics; an economy with limited agriculture, but based on transient pastoralism; and a pantheon focused on celestial males. Beyond this, Gimbutas draws a schematic contrast to the culture area she calls Old Europe (roughly, Mitteleuropa from the Baltic to the Balkans), which she understands to have been matrifocal, peaceful, artistically creative, given to settled agriculture, and possessed of a religion that emphasized chthonic female figures associated with fertility and nurture. This quasi-paradisal world, however, was overrun by a series of Indo-European invasions. Some contest her interpretation of archaeological data, however, and argue that "Indo-European" expansion was part of the gradual process that brought agriculture into Old Europe from Anatolia and the Ancient Near East (Renfrew, 1987). Others see her dualistic schema as an inversion of the old story, through which it is made to serve the purposes of a romantic

feminist and Lithuanian nationalist. Thus, "Indo-Europeans" appear as Russian, rather than German, invaders, and their triumphs are thematized in tragic, rather than heroic, mode.

A second theory, more immediately concerned with religion than with origin and expansion, is that developed by Georges Dumézil, who maintained that Indo-Europeans were set apart from all others not only by their language but also by an understanding of reality that found expression in such diverse areas as theology, mythology, epic literature, ritual, law, medicine, and pattern of social organization. In all these domains he perceived a taxonomy that divided things into three hierarchically differentiated "functions": 1) sovereign power, which had both magical and legal-juridical aspects; 2) force, chiefly military violence; 3) production, reproduction, and all that contributes to well-being, abundance, and pleasure (agriculture, herding, trade, sexuality, fertility, etc.). In scores of books and hundreds of articles, Dumézil adduced impressive evidence, and his theories have met with wide acceptance (Littleton, 1982; Puhvel, 1987; Sergent, 1995). In the eighties and nineties, however, critics have argued that he managed to rewrite the story of Indo-European triumphalism, such that the system of "three functions" now plays the role that "blood" once played—that is, the distinguishing feature that made world conquest possible. More disquieting still, critics note the resemblance of that system to others idealized by the European right, particularly the "integral nationalism" of Charles Maurras, founder of the Action Française and chief ideologist of the Vichy regime (Momigliano, 1994; Lincoln, 1991; Grottanelli, 1993).

LINGUISTIC DATA

If one renounces the desire for master narratives and focuses solely on linguistic data, a few points can be made about "Indo-European" understandings of women and religion. First, a certain ambivalence is evident in the semantics of the word for woman, *k^wen-* (the asterisk denotes a hypothetical reconstruction, based on comparison of Greek *gynē*, Sanskrit *jā́ni*, Avestan *jaini*, Old High German *quena*, English *queen*, and others). As in English, these words can convey profound respect (as in "Her majesty the Queen") or equally strong contempt (as in "drag queen"), but rarely middle ground, since women are not something toward which the presumed male subject harbors neutral feelings. Second, parental roles were gendered in prejudicial fashion. Thus, *$p^hH t^h$er-* (Sanskrit *pitár*, Greek *patḗr*, Latin *pater*, Old Irish *athir*, Gothic *fadar*) was a term that could be used for human beings only, since fatherhood was a social relation that involved dignity and authority, while *maHtʰer-* (Sanskrit *mātár,* Armenian *mayr,* Greek *métēr,* Latin *māter,* Old High German *muoter*) could be used for animals as well as people, since motherhood was construed as a relation more biological than social. This division of linguistic labor encoded the understanding that father gave children cultural goods— name, status, and moral knowledge—while mothers gave them the natural gifts of their bodies and food.

Linguistic comparisons indicate that goddesses were roughly as numerous as gods, although less important, the authority of the paramount deity being underscored by his designation as *t'yeus* pʰHtʰer- (Greek *Zeús páter,* Latin *Jiu-piter,* Vedic *Dyáuṣ pitắ*). Among the goddesses we can reconstruct are personified natural phenomena (Dawn, Moon, Earth, Death and Decay), along with others that embody important aspects of culture (Voice, Hearth, Intoxication). Typological comparisons suggest that female deities were also associated with sovereignty, the fertility of the land and herds, the passage of time, and the weaving of fate. This last item holds particular interest, since a prime economic activity for women was the production of cloth, and the only specialized religious role women played was that of seeress or sibyl. Here also a certain ambivalence is evident, for the knowledge and speech of women was not correlated with a capacity for action. As in the classic case of Cassandra, women foresaw catastrophes about which they could do nothing; the men to whom their speech was directed often were unwilling to listen or unable to comprehend, as a result of which they were doomed to suffer disaster, while learning things the hard way.

BIBLIOGRAPHY

Bader, Françoise. *La langue des dieux ou l'hermétisme des poètes indo-européens.* Pisa, 1989.

Benveniste, Emile. *Indo-European Language and Society.* Translated by Elizabeth Palmer. 1973.

Crevatin, Franco. *Ricerche sull' antichità indoeuropea.* Trieste, 1979.

Dumézil, Georges. *L'Idèologie tripartie des indo-européens.* Brussels, 1958.

Gamkrelidze, Thomas V., and Vjacheslav V. Ivanov. *Indo-european and the Indo-europeans: A Reconstruction and Historical Analysis of a Proto-language and a Proto-culture.* Translated by Johanna Nichols. Berlin, 1995.

Gimbutas, Marija. *The Goddesses and Gods of Old Europe, 6500–3500 B.C.* 1982.

Grottanelli, Cristiano. *Ideologie miti massacri: Indoeuropei di Georges Dumézil.* Palermo, 1993.

Lincoln, Bruce. *Death, War, and Sacrifice: Studies in Ideology and Practice.* 1991. Pp. 231–268.

Littleton, C. Scott. *The New Comparative Mythology: An Anthropological Assessment of the Theories of Georges Dumézil,* 3d ed., 1982.

Mallory, James. *In Search of the Indo-Europeans: Language, Archaeology, and Myth.* London, 1989.

Momigliano, Arnaldo. *A. D. Momigliano: Studies on Modern Scholarship.* Edited by G. W. Bowersock and T. J. Cornell. 1994.

Olender, Maurice. *The Languages of Paradise: Race, Religion, and Philology in the Nineteenth Century.* 1992.

Poliakov, Leon. *The Aryan Myth: A History of Racist and Nationalist Ideas in Europe.* 1974.

Puhvel, Jaan. *Comparative Mythology.* 1987.

Renfrew, Colin. *Archaeology and Language: The Puzzle of Indo-European Origins.* London, 1987.

See, Klaus von. *Barbar, Germane, Arier: Die Suche nach der Identität der Deutschen.* Heidelberg, 1994.

Sergent, Bernard. *Les indo-européens: Histoire, langues, mythes.* Paris, 1995.

Trubetzkoy, N. "Gendankin über das Indogermanenproblem." *Acta Linguistica* 1 (1939): 81–89.

BRUCE LINCOLN

Infanticide

Infanticide, the deliberate killing of infants, is ubiquitously condemned in the religions of the world because life is considered sacred and children a divine gift. For instance, it is forbidden in the laws given to Moses— "You shall not give any of your children to devote them by fire to Moloch, and so profane the name of your God" (Lev. 18:21); and by the Qur'an—"Kill not your children for fear of want: We provide sustenance for them as well as for you. Verily the killing of them is a mighty transgression" (17.31). Both these commands point to preexisting practices such as the child sacrifices that were made to the deity Moloch in the ancient Middle East and the frequent killing of baby girls by pre-Islamic Arabs. Historically, in some tribal rituals, though a child or young virgin would be sacrificed, the killing would not be regarded as infanticide but as an auspicious sacred offering. Such religious offering of children does not appear to be a current practice.

As a social practice, however, infanticide appears to have persisted, especially of female infants. Historically, some Rajput tribes of Gujrat in India were notorious for their female infanticide. Into the late 1800s, other societies, too, have been guilty of direct infanticide or deliberate neglect resulting in death. In Europe until the nineteenth century the abandonment of new-

The Holy Family during their flight into Egypt to escape Herod's decree to kill all babies born in Bethlehem (Richard List/Corbis)

born babies was common. As a result, foundling homes emerged to care for these babies. Still, because of the trauma of abandonment suffered during the first few hours after birth, these babies had a very high mortality rate. The low rate of population growth among Japanese peasants during the Tokugawa period has been in part attributed to the possible prevalence of abortion and infanticide. In China reports of infanticide, especially as affecting female babies, have surfaced since medieval times, particularly during times of adversity such as famine or flood. In the twentieth century, stringent population planning requirements have led to abortions as a means of birth control. Disproportionate male-to-female birth ratios reported in contemporary China are attributed to underreporting of female infants or to infanticide or fetal abortion when the determination of gender is possible through technology. In part of India, as well, in adverse situations such as famines, infant mortality has been enormous. Among others, Amartya Sen has worked extensively on poverty, dislocation, and the increased risk for the survival of children.

Legends, religious and quasireligious, from many parts of the world delineate the theme of the slaughter of innocent babies by tyrannical fathers or rulers. Associated with this theme is the leitmotif of the royal or divine child who, saved from infanticide, is raised by foster parents frequently oblivious to his distinguished personality. In the biblical narrative of Moses, to avoid the fulfillment of the prediction of doom and to protect himself from the possibility of harm, the Pharaoh ordered that all first-born of Israel be killed. As a result of his mother's quick wits, the baby Moses was put in a basket that drifted down the river. Providentially, the baby was found and brought up by the daughter of the

Pharaoh. Moses indeed redeems his community and foils the Pharaoh's evil. In the New Testament, the Gospel of Matthew provides a similar narrative with regard to the birth of the baby Jesus. Herod was forewarned of a redeemer and had all the babies slain in Bethlehem and the coastal areas. Meanwhile, Joseph was guided by an angel to take refuge in Egypt with Mary and Jesus. After the crisis was over, Joseph was divinely directed to return to the land of Israel and eventually resided in Nazareth, where Jesus grew up.

This theme reverberates in Hindu lore, albeit with a more complicated structure, as there are multiple births and mothers. In the narrative of the birth of the lord Krishna, Kamsa, the king, seeks to protect his power and thwart the prophecy of a child who will be responsible for his death. Eight children are to be born to Devaki and her husband Vasudeva, with the youngest having the power to exterminate the king. Kamsa has Devaki and Vasudeva imprisoned and each child killed upon birth. But the eighth child, the baby Krishna, is miraculously switched with the female infant born at the same time to Yasoda; Krishna is safely transferred to Yasoda's home, and the girl baby is killed instead. Krishna, an incarnation of the supreme lord Vishnu, lives, restores goodness, and eradicates evil.

In ancient Greek sacred lore, the tale of Rhea and Kronos has a similar plot. To thwart a prediction that one of his own children will be the cause of his destruction, Kronos swallows Hestia, Demeter, Hera, Hades, and Poseidon, all born to Rhea. When Zeus is born, Rhea hides the baby in a cave in Crete and tricks Kronos into swallowing a stone. In time, Zeus fights and defeats his father, then forces him to disgorge the other children. In all the above infanticide narratives divine providence is seen to triumph over human tyranny.

BIBLIOGRAPHY

Clark, Alice. "Limitations on Female Life Chances in Rural Central Gujarat." *The Indian Economic and Social History Review* 20, no. 1 (March 1983): 1–26.

Dreze, Jean, and Amartya Sen., eds. *Indian Development: Selected Regional Perspectives.* 1997.

Goodrich, Norma Lorre. *Ancient Myths.* 1960.

———. *Medieval Myths.* 1958.

Hull, Terence H. "Recent Trends in Sex-ratios at Birth in China." *Population and Development Review* 16, no. 1 (March 1990): 63–83.

Kertzer, David I., and Michael J. White. "Cheating the Angel-Makers: Surviving Infant Abandonment in Nineteenth-century Italy." *Continuity and Change* 9, no. 3 (1994): 451–480.

Lee, James, Wang Feng, and Cameron Campbell. "Infant and Child Mortality among the Qing Nobility:

Implications for Two Types of Positive Check." *Population Studies* 48 (1994): 395–411.

Li, Lillian M. "Life and Death in a Chinese Famine: Infanticide as a Demographic Consequence of the 1935 Yellow River Flood." *Society for Comparative Study of Society and History* (1991): 466–510.

Mosher, S. W. "Why Are Baby Girls Being Killed in China?" *Wall Street Journal,* July 25, 1983.

O'Flaherty, Wendy Doniger. *Hindu Myths.* 1975.

Osamo, Saito. "Infanticide, Fertility and 'Population Stagnation': The State of Tokugawa Historical Demography." *Japan Forum* 4, no. 2 (October 1992): 369–380.

Sen, Amartya Kumar. *On Ethics and Economics.* 1987.

———. *Poverty and Famines: An Essay on Entitlement and Deprivation.* 1981.

Siu-lun, Wong. "Consequences of China's New Population Policy." *The China Quarterly* 98 (1984): 220–240.

Tien, H. Yuan. "Abortion in China: Incidence and Implications." *Modern China* 13, no. 4 (1987): 441–468.

HABIBEH RAHIM

Initiation

Initiation is the practice through which adult female being is produced for each successive initiate at the same time it is reproduced as a cultural ideal. Interpreted on its own terms, and in comparison to parallel ceremonies for males, rituals of initiation let one perceive just which aspects of female existence a given society acknowledges, cultivates, seeks to control, or invests with value, as well as the contradictory demands the group makes on women. Thus, a group that celebrates the emergence of a woman's sexuality and fertility may simultaneously insist she adopt attitudes of modesty and shame, just as one that emphasizes her strength and capacity for work may also urge her to become selfless, reticent, and unassertive.

Initiation rituals of the Yangoru Boiken, who live on the middle Sepik River in Papua New Guinea, offer a convenient example (Roscoe, in Lutkehaus and Roscoe, 1995, pp. 55–82). Upon her first menstruation, a girl is placed in seclusion, where she remains for four days, eating nothing and being vigorously washed each day. During this time she is celebrated with honorific songs, introduced to the spirits of her clan, and in the past her body was scarified. On the fifth and culminating day of the ceremony, she is brought before her kin and community, adorned with elaborate decorations and objects of value. Finally, a respected female relative sits in front of her, puts money in her hands, then wipes sweat from

An initiation ritual of a Bwiti cult in Cameroon involves the use of the psychotropic drug iboga and represents a journey to the land of the dead (Daniel Laine/Corbis).

her own underarms and proffers it to the initiate, who licks it from her fingers. This done, the older woman takes back the money, distributes it to other kin, and feeds the initiate a piece of twine, ash from a cooking fire, then taro (the staple crop) and a sweet coconut soup.

The process begun by the natural event of menarche is thus completed by cultural acts, which transform the girl who is the initial object of the proceedings into the woman who is their final product. Those who stage the ritual use seclusion, fasting, and washing to deconstruct her previous social and biological person, then reconstruct her as an adult by having her ingest—and thereby incorporate in the most literal fashion—three material representations of industrious and diligent labor: the sweat of an ideal woman; twine, useful in many tasks and known for its durability; and the fire at which women work to feed their husbands, children, and others.

Initiation reorganizes the initiate's body and consciousness according to the demands of local aesthetic and ethical preferences. Her body is magnified—made (to seem) larger and more grand—by the ornaments heaped on it. Each of these indexes some specific value; collectively, they make the woman an ambulatory sign of all that is idealized in womanhood, and all that will make her an object of others' desire. Decked out with these, she is described as *narandauwa*, "a woman whom people come and look at": a perfected object of beauty, whose availability for marriage is announced in this moment. In the sequence of gestures where money is given, then taken from her, the ritual also constructs her as a person who will attract and produce wealth, but who will circulate it to others, rather than keeping it for herself. Finally, the taro and coconut she eats remove her from the liminal state that commenced with her fast and seclusion. Tasting these sweet and nourishing foods, she resumes normal life, her social, ontological, and moral status having been profoundly transformed.

Rituals of initiation vary widely from one society to another, but usually display the three-step rhythm described by van Gennep (1960) as separation-liminality-reincorporation, and by Lincoln (1991) as enclosure-metamorphosis-emergence. In contrast to men's rituals, those performed for women are more likely to be performed for individuals rather than groups; to be triggered by the physical onset of puberty rather than a calendric schedule; and to concern themselves more with cultivating capacities for biological reproduction than with forging age-and-sex group solidarity or establishing the basis for political advancement.

Some ceremonies celebrate emergent sexuality, while others—including those that involve extreme forms of genital surgery—seek to suppress or contain it. Some are concerned primarily with the transition from child to adult; others also focus on the issue of gender, undertaking to create a female out of a previously androgynous or asexual being. Physical and emotional aspects of the proceedings are also infinitely variable. The initiate may be nurtured and honored, subjected to violence, terror, and degradation, or she may have experiences of both sorts at different moments of the proceedings. But whatever their differences, initiation rites consistently work to construct women according to their society's hegemonic standards and for the benefit of the group as a whole—or at least that of its dominant fractions.

BIBLIOGRAPHY

Gennep, Arnold van. *The Rites of Passage.* Translated by Monika Vizedom and Gabrielle Caffee. 1960.

Kratz, Corinne. *Affecting Performance: Meaning, Movement, and Experience in Okiek Women's Initiation.* 1994.

La Fontaine, J. S. *Initiation: Ritual Drama and Secret Knowledge across the World.* 1985.

Lincoln, Bruce. *Emerging from the Chrysalis: Rituals of Women's Initiation.* 1991.

Lutkehaus, Nancy, and Paul Roscoe, eds. *Gender Rituals: Female Initiation in Melanesia.* 1995.

Paige, Karen, and Jeffrey Paige. *The Politics of Reproductive Ritual.* 1981.

Richards, Audrey. *Chisungu: A Girl's Initiation Ceremony among the Bemba of Zambia.* 1956.

See also Genital Mutilation; Rites of Passage; Ritual.

BRUCE LINCOLN

Inner Asian Religions of Nomadic Peoples

It was within Inner Asia—that immense landmass occupied by innumerable tribes and surrounded by China, India, Persia, Greece, and Rome—that the Amazons and Kingdoms of Women first appeared and were registered in ancient histories. A law among the Amazons prevented them from marrying until they had killed an enemy; they were called "man-killers." Those men who were allowed into their midst were unable to learn their language. The Massagetae, who lived east of the Caspian Sea, were ruled by a queen named Tomyris. According to Herodotus, the ancient Greek historian (c. 480–425 B.C.E.), Tomyris refused a marriage alliance with the Persian ruler Cyrus (557–530 B.C.E.) and later took part in the battle where Cyrus was defeated and killed. The Massagetae worshiped the sun and sacrificed horses, but the role of the queen in religious ceremony was not revealed. Arguably a part of myth or folk belief, in reality there were women warriors and rulers among the various tribes or clans of Inner Asian peoples, especially among the Sauromatians (sixth to fourth century B.C.E.) of the lower Volga region and south of the Urals.

Although early Inner Asian peoples were accused of having no religion by historians of the civilizations surrounding the region of Inner Asia, nothing could be further from the truth. The religions of these early peoples have begun to surface from tombs and from the very sands of Inner Asia, revealing a rich religious mosaic. When archaeologists excavated Neolithic graves in former Sauromatian regions during the twentieth century, a few rich burials for women were found, some containing sacrificial altars. Such archaeological evidence, in addition to written accounts, opened a controversy over the possibility of matriarchal societies (Jacobson, 1987). Hierarchy in prehistoric and ancient Inner Asian society seems to have been determined more by class than gender.

During the ancient and early Medieval periods, the nomadic peoples of historic Inner Asia, primarily Turkic and Mongolian tribes or mixed confederacies, claimed not only a religious pluralism but a religious tolerance that permitted a selected syncretism of major systems of belief—Buddhism, Islam, Judaism, Manichaeism, and Christianity—as these religious philosophies were spread via the vast Silk Road network across Eurasia. At the same time, the indigenous religions of Inner Asia developed along two lines. The popular or folk religions were unorganized systems of beliefs held by the common people; the imperial religions, more organized and connected with aristocracy, were at times in conflict with the popular religion of the people. Although specific aspects of the indigenous religions could vary from tribe to tribe, among clans, or even by geographic location, there were many common features throughout Inner Asia.

The popular religions were characterized by shamanistic practices, totemism, polytheism, animism; the focus was of a practical nature, borne out of the necessities of everyday life. A shaman could be either a man or a woman called upon to intercede on behalf of man, woman or child, or even animal herds, with the spirit world for good or evil. They had power over the weather, forecast the future, and cured diseases of people and animals. Fertility rites, divination, scapulimancy (predictions made by using the shoulder blades of sheep), and geomancy (predictions made according to features of the land) were all practiced by various peoples. Sacred lands and waters (Turkic: *iduq yer sub*), zoomorphic and anthropomorphic idols, often referred to by their Mongol name (*ongons* or totems), were of primary importance. Cults grew up around natural phenomena, and especially around mountains (by Turkic and Mongol peoples) and trees (by the Huns), animals (most notably the wolf among the Turk and the horse among the Mongols), elements such as fire, and astral bodies such as the sun, moon, and star complexes. Among the Mongols, for example, in some places fire ceremonies were performed exclusively by women, in others only by men. Seasonal ceremonies protected both the people and their livestock. Spirits or powers resided everywhere and, as such, were taken into consideration before any action, however simple, from road travel to preparations for hunting or war, from birth to marriage to death.

After the Mongols conquered China, the imperial religion tended to oppose shamanism and totemism; it was centered more upon myths of origin—often with divine births and superhuman qualities present for the founder of the tribe—and ancestor cults developed, sometimes for both male and female personages. This heritage, passed down through rulers and their clans, as well as the ceremonies surrounding their burial and the preservation of their memory, became part of the tribal identity, infused in its religious tradition, and an indicator of political legitimacy. Early nomadic steppe tribes, including confederacies such as the Xiong-nu on the western and northern borders of China (c. third century B.C.E. to the end of the fourth century C.E.) practiced human sacrifice, burying officials, servants, wives, and consorts at the death of a ruler. (The Xiong-nu

are often equated with the Huns of the west.) Mongol women performed spring offerings to the ancestors. Although women could gather mare's milk for ceremonies, during the thirteenth and fourteenth centuries after the conquest of China, when the "Golden Tombs' Mare Milking" ceremony was performed for deceased Mongol emperors, male nobles of the court took over the entire process. The imperial religion was more monotheistic, centered around the all-powerful sky-god Tengri, supported by the supreme female earth goddess, Umay, and later by an underworld.

The role of women in Inner Asian religion was an intricate part of everyday life and custom that followed a number of tendencies. Women were more independent in nomadic tribes than among settled peoples. Noble women could be warriors or rulers (among Mongolian peoples and pre-Islamic Turkic tribes) and after death be worshiped in ancestor cults, particularly the mothers or wives of major Mongol khans. (But this did not make them equal, only powerful.)

In both Mongolian and Turkic regions, women among the common people assumed less public roles in religion: sewing clothes for religious ceremonies, making domestic idols and amulets, preparing food offerings. Through their role of raising children, women preserved the religious traditions, taboos, and customs of a people, often controlling the rate of religious change. Sometimes these changes are even reflected in their language.

Female deities, especially the earth-mother goddess, were an important part of the religious pantheon(s). Women could act as intermediaries between the spirit world and everyday life, participating in and at times conducting the rituals of passage. The detailed role of women in the religious life of nomadic Inner Asia remains an area for further investigation.

BIBLIOGRAPHY

Dankoff, Robert. "Kāšġarī on the Beliefs and Superstitions of the Turks." *Journal of the American Oriental Society* 95 (1975): 68–80.

Franke, Herbert. "Women under the Dynasties of Conquest." In *La donna nella Cina imperiale e nella Cina repubblicana.* Edited by Lionello Lanciotti. 1980. Reprinted in Herbert Franke, *China under Mongol Rule.* 1994.

Heissig, Walther. *The Religions of Mongolia.* 1970, 1980.

Jacobson, Esther. *Burial Ritual, Gender and Status in South Siberia in the Late Bronze–Early Iron Age.* Papers on Inner Asia, no. 7. Indiana University Research Institute for Inner Asian Studies. 1987.

Meserve, Ruth I. "Inner Asian Religion." In *The Encyclopedia of Religion.* Edited by Mircea Eliade. 1987.

Ratchnevsky, Paul. "La condition de la femme mongole au 12e/13e siècle." In *Tractata Altaica.* Edited by Walther Heissig, John R. Krueger, Felix Oinas, and Edmond Schütz. 1976.

Róna-Tas, A. "Dream, Magic Power and Divination in the Altaic World." *Acta Orientalia* (Hungary) 25 (1972): 227–236.

Rossabi, Morris. "Khubilai Khan and the Women in His Family." In *Studia Sino-Mongolica: Festschrift für Herbert Franke.* Edited by Wolfgang Bauer. 1979.

Roux, Jean-Paul. "Turkic Religions." In *The Encyclopedia of Religion.* Edited by Mircea Eliade. 1987.

Sinor, Denis. "Hun Religion." In *The Encyclopedia of Religion.* Edited by Mircea Eliade. 1987.

———. "'Umay': A Mongol Spirit Honored by the Türks." *Proceedings of International Conference on China Border Area Studies.* 1987.

See also Amazons; Amulets; Animals.

RUTH I. MESERVE

Inspiration

From the first verbal record of human religious life, women, human and divine, have both served as and experienced inspiration. Inspiration is related to many other elements of religious behavior, such as possession and mystical experience; the focus here is on its simplest meaning, "breathing into," giving life through breath. Breath is also traditionally associated with speech. Inspiration so understood did not always take the form of a goddess per se, but it did take the form of a feminine principle. For purposes of space I will focus solely on the five major world religions, acknowledging the link between women and inspiration in Native American and African traditions as well.

In the Indian tradition the goddess Vac, or speech, creates the world and inspires the brahmin priest with eloquence so that he may sacrifice more effectively and keep the world running on its traditional course. Speech also mates with breath so as to make the first principles of grammar in early Indian mythology. In later texts she consorts with the creator god Prajapati; without her inspiration the world cannot come into being. In classical Hinduism this function is taken over by Sarasvatī and Śrī as goddesses of the arts and learning.

In the related Buddhist tradition, inspiration comes in the form of *prajñāpāramitā*, the perfection of wisdom. *Prajñāpāramitā* begins as a philosophical princi-

The Hindu god depicted in this sculpture is Sarasvatī, wife of Brahma and goddess of the earth (Charles & Josette Lenars/Corbis).

ple that later becomes a female goddess who acts as a kind of impetus for analytical thought. In Tibetan Buddhism green Tārā and white Tārā are both goddesses associated with compassion and discriminating wisdom—the wisdom to tell the difference between reality and illusion. The female bodhisattva Kuan Yin also acts to inspire and enliven the downtrodden in this particular way in some Chinese Buddhist myths.

In the Jewish and Christian traditions, inspiration and wisdom have also been associated with a female principle, or with femininity. Hebrew Ḥokhmah, or wisdom, is a figure that moves between humans and God; she is mentioned in the book of Job and elaborately presented in the book of Proverbs. There, she acts as God's playmate and inspiration for creation. Jewish gnostics, like the Indian poets, see wisdom as endowing creation with image and spirit and sending the prophets. Although Ḥokhmah did not become a full-fledged deity, later Judaism developed the idea of the Shekhinah—originally a noun that meant the "indwelling" of God. The Shekhinah becomes more and more personified in midrashic literature, communicating with Moses and attracted to aesthetic and ethical qualities in humans; the Shekhinah reaches her fullest shape in the medieval mystical movements of the Kabbalah.

In the Christian tradition, the Holy Spirit also has a feminine aspect. Christians read *ruach*, "the spirit" that moves over the face of the waters in Genesis 1, as nothing less than the Holy Spirit, or breath itself. Because of the common Biblical reference to Ḥokhmah, in the Christian tradition Ḥokhmah becomes Sophia who acts as God's consort or daughter. In early Christian texts, especially Syriac ones, trinities occur of Father-Son and Holy Spirit-Mother. In the Gospel of the Hebrews, Jesus refers to the Holy Spirit as mother, and in other Syriac writings the Holy Spirit is a maternal power that broods over the waters of baptism. Deaconesses in the early church may also have been representatives of the Holy Spirit and associated with female prophets. Thus, the Holy Spirit could be Christ in female form, Sophia, or Wisdom, or Ecclesia, the bride of Christ. The feminine Holy Spirit was also associated with Mary in both medieval and modern theologies of the Catholic and Orthodox churches.

Although Islam's radical monotheism prevents the tradition from having any theology of the feminine divine, both Qur'anic and hadith traditions contain wise women who were inspirations to the prophet Muhammad. These include 'A'ishah, who was consulted on theological and juridical subjects; Fāṭimah, the prophet's daughter, who in the Shiite tradition is a virgin who embodies all that is divine in womanhood; and Khadija, his merchant-wife, who provided moral support and inspiration during the troubling time of the prophet's first visions.

In other mythological traditions, mention should be made of two figures: in Greek myth, in addition to the semidivine Muses, Athena acts as the goddess of intelligence and the inspiration of arts, crafts, and civilization. From the Celtic tradition, the goddess Brid acted as inspiration for druids and poets, and her Christian counterpart, St. Brigid, was the matron saint of poetry and the arts.

The discussion above reveals three important elements in the relationship between feminine force and inspiration. First, the feminine power of speech and the creative principle of wisdom are linked in many cultures. Second, the wisdom of the female is frequently mediated by the purity and power of virginity. Third, the consort figure and the wise counselor figure, inspir-

ing the Hero-God, frequently merge into one and the same woman.

BIBLIOGRAPHY

PRIMARY SOURCES

Charlesworth, J. H., ed and trans. *Odes of Solomon.* 1973.

Conze, Edward, trans. *The Perfection of Wisdom in Eight Thousand Lines.* 1973.

Doniger, Wendy, trans. *Ṛg Veda.* 1981.

Dimmitt, Cornelia, and Van Buitenen, A. B. *Classical Hindu Myth.* 1978.

Evelyn-White, Hugh, trans. *Hesiod, The Homeric Hymns, and Homerica.* 1920.

Meeks, Wayne, et al., eds. *HarperCollins Study Bible* (New Revised Standard Version). 1989.

O'Hanlon, John. *Lives of Irish Saints.* 1875–1903.

Tanakh: New Translation of the Holy Scriptures According to the Traditional Hebrew Text. 1985.

Wilson, Martin, ed and trans. *In Praise of Tara: Songs to the Saviouress: Source Texts from India and Tibet on Buddhism's Great Goddess.* 1986.

SECONDARY SOURCES

Beyer, Stephan. *The Cult of Tara.* 1973.

Blofeld, John. *Bodhisattva of Compassion.* 1977.

Condren, Mary. *The Serpent and the Goddess.* 1989.

Kinsley, David. *The Goddesses' Mirror.* 1989.

Newman, Barbara. *From Virile Woman to WomanChrist.* 1995.

———. *Sister of Wisdom.* 1987.

Patai, Raphael. *The Hebrew Goddess.* 1978.

Paul, Diana. *Women in Buddhism.* 1985.

Pickthall, Muhammad. *The Meaning of the Glorious Quran.* 1996.

Powell, Benjamin. *Athenian Mythology.* 1976.

Schimmel, Annemarie. *My Soul is a Woman: The Feminine in Islam.* Translated by Susan H. Ray. 1997.

See also: **'A'ishah; Athena (Minerva); Fāṭimah; Khadija; Kuan Yin; Muses; Sarasvatī; Speech; Sophia; Tārā; Virgin Mary; Wisdom.**

LAURIE LOUISE PATTON

Interreligious Dialogue

Religions have been in contact with one another throughout history, but interreligious dialogue, or the interfaith movement, is a modern development, first emerging in the late nineteenth century and continuing through the initiative of several Christians in the West.

The precise start is often taken to be the World's Parliament of Religions (1893), held in Chicago in the wake of the World Columbian Exposition. The centennial of this event was celebrated in the same city, resulting in an important proclamation, *A Global Ethic* (1993). The end of the twentieth century has seen a flourishing of interfaith organizations, dialogue groups, conferences, and publications, including influential initiatives from the World Council of Churches and the Roman Catholic Church (see the detailed survey, *Pilgrimage of Hope: One Hundred Years of Global Interfaith Dialogue,* by Marcus Braybrooke [1992]).

A critical study of interreligious dialogue shows that, historically, the process of dialogue is closely linked to earlier colonial and missionary activities of Western people in non-Western parts of the world. Today, interreligious dialogue is a global phenomenon carried out by people of various faiths in the East and West, South and North. However, few dialogue practitioners appear to understand that interreligious dialogue is strongly imbedded in the patriarchal structures of the existing religions and includes many exclusive sexist practices and deeply androcentric ways of thinking.

So far, relatively little work has been done on interreligious dialogue from the perspective of women's studies and critical theory. Religious feminists have only begun to address this topic. Further research should attend to the impact of gender variables on the practice and theology of dialogue.

Although women have participated in interreligious dialogue since the 1893 World's Parliament of Religions, their presence and participation have been largely left unrecorded in standard historical accounts. In our time women from all faiths are active in dialogue groups at local, regional, national, and international levels, but women's voices are rarely heard in public as the officially organized dialogue meetings are male-dominated and mostly represented by "spokesmen." This situation is directly connected with issues of religious leadership, so far a male prerogative; religious identity and representation; and the historiographical and theological accounts given of interreligious dialogue.

Contemporary women's experience and the theoretical perspectives of women's research in religion, theology, philosophy, epistemology, hermeneutics, and ethics raise fundamental questions about interreligious dialogue, as Maura O'Neill, in her pioneering study *Women Speaking, Women Listening: Women in Interreligious Dialogue* (1990), and others since then, have shown. The challenge of gender may be the most difficult one for men in positions of religious leadership; while it is already difficult to accept the "other faith" in a dialogue situation, such faith is, at least, usually encountered through another man. Thus woman is doubly other—of another faith and another gender—in interreligious dialogue. More and more, women of faith around the world share their experience of faith and spirituality through dialogue with each other.

Women's dialogue is not only of significance for the future shape of all interreligious dialogue but also raises questions for women themselves. Some of these concern whether feminist insights have universal application or possess only a limited sociocultural relevance, and to what extent religions are a liberating or an oppressive force in women's lives. A complicating factor is that some women consider their own faith mainly as liberating but view other religious traditions as mostly oppressive.

Gender perspectives have hardly yet entered the academic discussions about religious pluralism, dialogue, and the theology of religions. The positions of exclusivism, inclusivism, and pluralism, distinguished by Christian theologians as different attitudes to other faiths, remain deeply embedded in androcentric perspectives. Much of the dialogue among women of faith has occurred at the level of shared stories and experience, of experiments with worship and descriptive accounts, but without the necessary comparative analysis or accompanying critical theological reflection. While men's dialogue has not yet dialogically appropriated the insights of women's own dialogue, the interreligious dialogue among women has not yet sufficiently called into question the androcentrism and exclusiveness of male dialogue. Thus the two different forms of dialogue provide a mutual challenge for each other in the light of greater gender awareness.

BIBLIOGRAPHY

Abraham, Dulcie, Sun Ai Lee Park, and Yvonne Dahlin, eds. *Faith Renewed: A Report On the First Asian Women's Consultation on Interfaith Dialogue.* 1989. Organized by Christian women, this meeting featured Buddhist, Christian, Hindu, Jewish, and Muslim women participants, as well as women from the indigenous traditions. Participants examined the liberative and oppressive aspects of their religion and looked at the practical, social, legal, and economic effects of religious and sociocultural discrimination against women.

Hewitt Suchoki, Marjorie. "In Search of Justice." In *The Myth of Christian Uniqueness: Toward a Pluralistic Theology of Religions.* Edited by John Hick and Paul Knitter. 1989. Provides a critical discussion of the connections between justice, religious pluralism, and a feminist perspective which "must radically affirm religious pluralism."

King, Ursula. "Feminism: The Missing Dimension in the Dialogue of Religions." In *Pluralism and the Reli-*

gions. Edited by John May. 1998. Examines the challenge of feminism for interreligious dialogue and for the structures and institutions concerned with dialogue; also considers the challenge interreligious dialogue poses for contemporary feminism.

———. "Rediscovering Women's Voices at the World's Parliament of Religions." In *A Museum of Faiths: Histories and Legacies of the 1893 World's Parliament of Religions.* Edited by E. J. Ziolkowski. 1993. Presents the discovery that many women were plenary speakers at the World's Parliament of Religions and what they had to say—in some cases still of significance today.

Küng, Hans, and Karl-Josef, Kuschel, eds. *A Global Ethic: The Declaration of the Parliament of the World's Religions.* 1993. A small, impressive document, widely debated and of historical significance in its attempt to launch the development of a commonly agreed global ethic among the different religions. Though not written from a specifically gender-aware perspective, the last of its four directives expresses a clear commitment to "a culture of equal rights and partnership between men and women."

McCarthy, Kate. "Women's Experience as a Hermeneutical Key to a Christian Theology of Religions." *Studies in Interreligious Dialogue* 6, no. 2 (1996): 163–173. Argues persuasively that Christian feminist theology offers considerable resources for a new approach to a Christian theology of religions; author does not explicitly analyze the androcentric and exclusive character of this theology, nor does she engage with the work of the few other feminist writers on religious pluralism.

O'Neill, Maura. *Women Speaking, Women Listening, Women in Interreligious Dialogue.* 1990. The first critical study of interreligious dialogue from a feminist philosophical and theological perspective. Based on contemporary women's experience, it clarifies some important perspectives of dialogue and examines whether Jewish, Christian, Muslim, Hindu, or Buddhist images and concepts of ultimate Reality are neutral, inclusive, or exclusive with regard to gender. Discusses substantive issues with lucidity and concision; its ideas have influenced further discussion about women and interreligious dialogue.

Ramey Mollenkott, Virginia, ed. *Women of Faith in Dialogue.* 1988. Describes the experiences of women of various faiths. Presents a multifaceted dialogue concerning women's struggles within their own religious communities, their dialogue on working together for justice in the world, and their celebration of an interreligious service of worship.

URSULA KING

Intoxicants and Hallucinogens

Intoxicants and hallucinogenic substances derived from plants or other sources have been used by human beings for thousands of years, mainly as facilitators for religious ecstasy and to permit individuals to come into firsthand contact with spirit or divinity. For most of human prehistory, hallucinogens were associated with nomadic hunter-gatherer societies where women did not hunt but were relegated to the private domain. Male hunters used intoxicants and hallucinogens in shamanistic religious rituals to divine the future and to know where to seek out animals.

Excluded from the hunt because of the odors associated with menstrual blood, lactation, and other reproductive processes, women were kept away from hunting implements and often made to obey strict taboos during their menses. Direct ingestion of psychedelic plants among women in the prehistoric period appears to have been quite incidental and not seen as appropriate gender behavior. Evidence from contemporary hunting and gathering societies suggests, however, that once a woman reached menopause, the nonordinary states of consciousness attainable through the use of intoxicants and hallucinogens would occasionally occur. Contemporary examples of hunter-gatherers include the Australian Aborigines, who utilized the plant hallucinogen Pituri (various *Duboisia* spp.) in male initiation rituals to diminish the pain of genital operations on the youths and to pay the elders performing these operations (Dobkin de Rios and Grob, 1994).

With the domestication of plants and animals about ten to twelve thousand years ago, changes occurred in the use of intoxicants and hallucinogens. African societies such as the Tsonga of Mozambique used *Datura fatuosa* in a girls' school to promote fertility, to stimulate a culturally stereotypic vision of the god believed to ensure offspring. Contemporary ethnographic studies from South America illustrate that women seek out traditional healers who employ powerful hallucinogens, such as San Pedro (*Trichocereus pachanoi*) that allow both the healer and client to experience a visionary state so as to identify the source of witchcraft that is believed responsible for the client's illness or misfortune (Dobkin de Rios, 1968, 1973). In the tropical rain forest cultures of Peru and Brazil, consisting of both tribal peoples and mestizos, plant hallucinogens are used mostly by men. In curing rituals, intoxicants and hallucinogens allow the user to contact supernatural entities, control them, and make them do their bidding. Contemporary South American women of the Peruvian rain forest often seek out hallucinogenic visions to solve personal and marital problems but personally play a

A Borra Indian woman processes coca leaves for use as an intoxicant, a common practice among indigenous peoples in Amazonian Peru (Wolfgang Kaehler/ Corbis).

minor role in ritual performance, except occasionally after menopause.

Pregnant women are sometimes excluded from active roles in hallucinogenic rituals because a substance's purgative effects (diarrhea and vomiting) might provoke premature labor. Occasionally a family member, seeking to find out who has bewitched the woman, will take the hallucinogen in the place of a pregnant patient. However, studies of members of the spiritualist church Uniao do Vegetal who use *ayahuasca* show that women are actually given a tea made of the hallucinogen during their pregnancy and labor to enhance their health (Grob et al., 1996).

A totally different pattern of women's use of hallucinogens characterizes the Kuma peoples of the Mount Hagen region of New Guinea (Reay, 1960). Both men and women ingest wild mushrooms (*pandanus, boletus,* and *psilocybe*) as condiments, and at one time of the

year a combative frenzy is caused by these plants. Although women do not exhibit the characteristic behavior of the men, who chase up and down the mountain in a dance formation, they do dance, whistle, sing, giggle and laugh, let out loud yells, and experience an intoxication that lasts several days. As reported by Maria Reay, intoxicated women become delirious and irresponsible, and their sons decorate them in their best feathers and give them weapons to hold. At this time, married women are permitted to dance in formation in ways that only men and unmarried girls do. Women return to their houses and boast of real or imaginary sexual adventures. Sometimes these hallucinogenic experiences are so embarrassing to the women that they plunge into a nearby river to stop the hallucinations from occurring. No ritual preparation or activity accompanies these hallucinogenic experiences of women, nor are they stigmatized or do they achieve any prestige by this behavior. This behavior may symbolically counter the traditional low status of women through a rite of rebellion and illustrate the widespread sexual antagonism that exists between men and women in many New Guinea societies.

In all the societies for which we have data, women's role in intoxicant and hallucinogenic ritual performance is minimal. In shamanic cultures, there are no salvational goals to achieve by using intoxicants and hallucinogens, and the chief focus is on power and its exercise by religious practitioners, who are mainly men. Since women do not hunt, they do not fulfill the virtues of the religious tradition, and only after menopause while in a liminal state are women seen to transcend gender limitations. There are occasional supernatural beings such as the fertility god of the Tsonga who are sought after through hallucinogenic vision, but most often a multiplicity of spirit forces, often named and mythic, rather than any concept of a high or solitary god. Scholars pay little attention to women and hallucinogens since there seems to be relatively little participation of women in religious activities connected to these substances, except in modern times, as clients utilizing the visionary states for healing or seeking to understand the supernatural causation of illness.

BIBLIOGRAPHY

Dobkin de Rios, Marlene. "Folk Curing with a Psychedelic Cactus in Northern Peru." *International Journal of Social Psychiatry* 15 (1968): 23–32.

———. *Hallucinogens: Cross-cultural Perspective.* 1996.

———. "Peruvian Hallucinogenic Folk Healing: An Overview." In *Psychiatry: Proceedings of the Fifth World Congress of Psychiatry.* Edited by R. de la Fuente and M. Weisman. Vol. 2. 1973.

————. "Twenty-Five Years of Hallucinogenic Studies in Cross-cultural Perspective." *Anthropology of Consciousness* 4, no. 1 (1993): 1–8.

————. *Visionary Vine: Hallucinogenic Healing in the Peruvian Amazon.* 1984.

Dobkin de Rios, Marlene, and Charles Grob. "Hallucinogens, Suggestibility and Adolescence." In *Yearbook for Ethnomedicine and the Study of Consciousness.* Edited by Christian Ratsch and John R. Baker. 1994.

Grob, Charles, et al. "Human Pharmacology of Hoasca." *Journal of Nervous and Mental Diseases* 184, no. 2 (1996): 85–94.

Grob, Charles, and Marlene Dobkin de Rios. "Adolescent Drug Use in Cross-cultural Perspective." *Journal of Drug Issues* 22, 1 (1992): 121–138.

Johnston, Thomas F. "Datura Use in a Tsonga Girls' Puberty School." *Economic Botany* 26, no. 4 (1972): 340–351.

Reay, Maria. "Mushroom Madness in the New Guinea Highlands." *Oceania* 31, no. 3 (1960): 137–139.

MARLENE DOBKIN DE RIOS

Inversion

Symbolic inversion has been broadly defined as "any act of expressive behavior which inverts, contradicts, abrogates, or in some fashion presents an alternative to commonly held cultural codes, values, and norms be they linguistic, literary or artistic, religious, or social and political" (Babcock, 1978, p. 14). Such "counteractive patterns of culture" are those "elements of a culture's own negation" that provide "metasocial commentary" and are indispensable to its functioning (Geertz, 1966, p. 65).

Since the early Renaissance at least, the word *inversion* has been used to mean a turning upside down or a reversal of position, order, sequence, or relation. The concept, however, is even older than the word; the topos of the world upside down, *mundus inversus,* which grows out of the stringing together of *impossibilia,* is as old as Greek parody of the Homeric journey to Hades (Curtius, 1963; Donaldson, 1970). Inversion is an ancient and primary principle of ritual and of comedy: "a sudden, comic switching of expected roles: prisoner reprimands judge, child rebukes parent, wife rules husband, pupil instructs teacher, master obeys servant" (Donaldson, 1970, pp. 5–6). The stringing together of such *impossibilia,* most explicitly in early European broadsheets (Kunzle, 1978), may mistakenly lead one to regard all inversions as equivalent and as

natural, which they surely are not (Stallybrass, 1991). Neither are their effects equivalent; the same inverted set could just as easily be subversive and oppositional as containing and reinforcing of the system in question. The most universal primal form of difference, of binary opposition, and of role reversal is between male and female.

And why not? For "gender differences have always been fundamental to how cultures understand and organize themselves" (Ochshorn, 1996, p. 62). Some scholars, such as feminist philosopher Luce Irigaray (1985), would argue not only that all binaries are implicitly gendered, but that male–female is the primary, underlying opposition. While the terms of all binaries are asymmetrical and differently valued, male and female are especially so. The positive and more stable term of the binary (e.g., order and rationality) is always male; woman is disorderly and irrational by definition, "undecidable" (Derrida, 1978). Given this logic, it is not surprising that men in play, ritual, or revolt frequently cross-dress, as do those who elect a spiritual vocation (Davis, 1978; Mack, 1986; Bynum, 1984, 1986).

In late-twentieth-century academic discourse, male poststructuralist critics have themselves engaged in "critical cross-dressing," using the language of the feminine and the topos of the disorderly woman as a "model" for their deconstructive analyses, in which the first move is inversion, the second displacement. Feminist theorists Teresa de Lauretis and Gayatri Spivak have analyzed the violence of this rhetoric, pointing out that the representation of violence is inseparable from the notion of gender; when "you reverse the direction of a binary opposition . . . you discover the violence" (Spivak, 1990, p. 8). These and other poststructural feminist "unaligned voices" have reclaimed deconstructive strategies for themselves to "talk back," to write "reverse discourse" (Weedon, 1987), arguing that the "unlearning of institutionalized language" is a necessary step to "the unsaying of what has been said and congealed" (Trinh, 1987, pp. 3, 13).

From Bergson's observation in "The Idea of 'Nothing' " (1913) that there are no negatives in nature, Kenneth Burke developed his thesis on the negative as a function peculiar to symbol systems, anticipating later structural and poststructural discussions of the necessity of the negative and the inevitability of binary oppositions. Following Hegel and Nietzsche, Burke argued that religion is perhaps the most explicitly negativistic of all symbol systems. Religions, moreover, are frequently constructed in opposition to other social structures and discourses, and religion is characterized by a *via negationis,* or what has become known as "negative theology": God is defined in terms of what he is not (Burke, 1968, p. 437).

A gender reversal is, as Caroline Bynum (1986, pp. 268–273) has remarked, an image of the transformation of the ordinary to the extraordinary, of the mundane to the sacred. To become the opposite gender is an "obvious image of renunciation and conversion." "Reversal and renunciation" are, therefore, "at the heart of religious dedication, of purification and elevation." Not surprisingly, Christian women have assumed male attire (e.g. Joan of Arc); male religious leaders, be they Gandhi, Jesus Christ, St. Francis, or a Pueblo Indian *cacique*, are addressed and regarded as "mother" (Bynum, 1982; Mack, 1986) and not infrequently wear skirts. Storyteller Isak Dinesen, herself a cross-dresser, once remarked regarding the power of inversion that "Moses in trousers could never have brought forth water from a rock." And Victor Turner has remarked, "in male-dominated societies, *communitas* may wear a skirt," confirming that the figure of woman who is socially peripheral is symbolically central and, like all inversions, constitutes a necessary "cultural subjunctive" (1978, p. 289).

BIBLIOGRAPHY

Babcock, Barbara A. *The Reversible World: Symbolic Inversion in Art and Society.* 1978.

Bergson, Henri. "The Idea of 'Nothing.' " In *Creative Evolution.* Translated by Arthur Mitchell. 1911.

Butler, Judith. *Gender Trouble: Feminism and the Subversion of Identity.* 1990.

Burke, Kenneth. "A Dramatistic View of the Origins of Language and Postscripts on the Negative." In *Language as Symbolic Action: Essays on Life, Literature, and Method.* 1968.

———. *The Rhetoric of Religion: Studies in Logology.* 1961.

Bynum, Caroline Walker. *Jesus as Mother: Studies in the Spirituality of the High Middle Ages.* 1982.

———. "Women's Stories, Women's Symbols: A Critique of Victor Turner's Theory of Liminality." In *Anthropology and the Study of Religion.* Edited by Robert L. Moore and Frank E. Reynolds. 1984.

———. " '. . . And Woman His Humanity': Female Imagery in the Religious Writing of the Later Middle Ages." In *Gender and Religion: On the Complexity of Symbols.* Edited by Caroline Walker Bynum, Stevan Harrell, and Paula Richman. 1986.

Curtius, Ernst Robert. *European Literature and the Latin Middle Ages.* Translated by Willard R. Trask. 1963.

Davis, Natalie Zemon. "Women on Top: Symbolic Sexual Inversion and Political Disorder in Early Modern Europe." In *The Reversible World: Symbolic Inversion in Art and Society.* Edited by Barbara A. Babcock. 1978.

De Lauretis, Teresa. "The Violence of Rhetoric: Considerations on Representation and Gender." *Semiotica* 54, nos. 1–2 (1985): 11–31.

Derrida, Jacques. *Spurs: Nietzsche's Styles.* Translated by Barbara Harlow. 1979.

Donaldson, Ian. *The World Upside Down: Comedy from Jonson to Fielding.* 1970.

Foucault, Michel. *The History of Sexuality.* Vol. 1. 1978.

Geertz, Clifford. *Person, Time, and Conduct in Bali: An Essay in Cultural Analysis.* 1966.

Hegel, G.W.F. *The Phenomenology of Mind.* Translated, with an introduction and notes, by J. B. Baillie. 1964.

Irigaray, Luce. *Speculum of the Other Woman.* Translated by Gillian C. Gill, 1985.

Kunzle, David. "World Upside Down: The Iconography of a European Broadsheet Type." In *The Reversible World: Symbolic Inversion in Art and Society.* Edited by Barbara A. Babcock. 1978.

Lloyd, Genevieve. *The Man of Reason: 'Male' and 'Female' in Western Philosophy.* 1984.

Mack, Phyllis. "Feminine Behavior and Radical Action: Franciscans, Quakers, and the Followers of Gandhi." *Signs* 11, no. 3 (1986): 457–477.

Marx, Karl. *Capital.* Vol. 1. Translated by Ben Fowkes. 1976.

Minh-ha, Trinh T., ed. "She, the Inappropriated Other." *Discourse* 8 (1987).

Ochshorn, Judith. "Sumer: Gender, Gender Roles, Gender Role Reversals." In *Gender Reversals and Gender Cultures: Anthropological and Historical Perspectives.* Edited by Sabrina Petra Ramet. 1996.

Pateman, Carole. *The Disorder of Women: Democracy, Feminism and Political Theory.* 1989.

Ramet, Sabrina Petra. *Gender Reversals and Gender Cultures: Anthropological and Historical Perspectives.* 1996.

Riley, Denise. "Does a Sex Have a History: 'Woman' and Feminism." *New Formations* 1 (1987): 35–45.

Spivak, Gayatri. *The Post-colonial Critic: Interviews, Strategies, Dialogues.* 1990.

Stallybrass, Peter. "The World Turned Upside Down: Inversion, Gender and the State." In *The Matter of Difference: Materialist Feminist Criticism of Shakespeare.* Edited by Valerie Wayne. 1991.

Turner, Victor. "Comments and Conclusions." In *The Reversible World: Symbolic Inversion in Art and Society.* Edited by Barbara A. Babcock. 1978.

Weedon, Chris. *Feminist Practice and Poststructuralist Theory.* 1987.

See also Deconstruction; Ritual; Structuralism.

BARBARA A. BABCOCK

Iranian Religions

Traditional Iranian religion, also known as Persian religion (c. 1200 B.C.E.–seventh century C.E.), is a multilayered structure that encompasses a pantheon of Indo-Iranian deities (some of whom find their counterparts among Hindu divinities) whose cult and ritual formed the foundation of all subsequent religious ideology; the ethical dualism of Zoroastrianism, which was constructed upon the base of that earlier belief; and, finally, various Semitic religious traditions that made their way into Persian religion with the growth of the Persian empire, which at its height extended from Asia Minor to India.

Information about earliest Persian religion (c. 1200 B.C.E.–600 B.C.E.) is scant, but it would seem that the gods of the oldest pantheon were personifications of aspects of nature and the elements that were later seen to embody the ethical ideals of a warrior culture; their attributes are described in a collection of twenty-four hymns, the *Yashts*, later incorporated into the *Avesta*, the sacred text of Zoroastrianism and the main source for information of the earliest period.

The only significant female deity in traditional Persian religion was Ardvi Sura Anahita, the strong undefiled waters, source of all waters on earth, and of the cosmic ocean. Ahura Mazda, the creator of all, has entrusted her with watching over his work. From her comes all fertility, for she "purifies the seed of males and the womb and milk of females" and "extends her powers of life to all living creatures" (*Yasht* v. 5). Described as radiant, beautiful, and nobly born, full of strength and courageous nobility, Anahita "advances on a four-horsed chariot and crushes the demons, the tyrants, all hurtful beings." Portrayed wearing a golden mantle and necklace and a golden crown decorated with the rays of the sun and a hundred stars, she is "a slender maiden with noble bearing . . . who has a very trim waist, ample breasts, and white arms adorned with bracelets."

In the Achamenid period (sixth and fifth centuries B.C.E.), her worship was widespread, with temples and shrines throughout the Persian empire; and she seems to have been identified with many local goddesses and their cults. According to the Greek historian Strabo (first century B.C.E.), the daughters of noble families were compelled to serve as prostitutes in her temples in Anatolia before they might marry, although this story is historically dubious since it is a practice ascribed earlier by Herodotus to the Babylonian worship of Ishtar. Anahita's origins are obscure, and it has been suggested that she is not Persian; she has variously been identified as the Canaanite Anat, the Anatolian Anaitis, and the Mesopotamian Ishtar.

A relief sculpture depicting Ahura Mazda. The chief Zoroastrian deity stands in the ruins of Persepolis in Takht-i Jamshid, Iran (Charles & Josette Lenars/Corbis).

The religious reforms of the sixth-century B.C.E. prophet Zoroaster (Zarathustra) had a profound effect on traditional Persian religion. Zoroaster is represented in Persian thought as a mystic and a prophet who assumed for himself a special relationship with the supreme deity. Reinterpreting most of the traditional divinities, he recast them in an ethical light; thus, the old gods became abstractions of spiritual qualities. Zoroastrianism is marked by a profound dualism: the world is engaged in a never-ending struggle between Truth and Lie, Order and Disorder. Evil is not merely the absence of Good; it is a real, substantial force, and the opposition of good and evil is the basis of all Zoroastrian teaching. Even the gods are locked into this combat.

Leading the forces of good is Ahura Mazda or Ohrmazd, the Wise Lord, the source of all that is good. Humans can share in his being through participation in the seven aspects of his character, the Amesha Spenta (Bountiful Immortal Ones), called the sons and daughters of Ahura Mazda: Truth, the Desired Kingdom, Devotion, Integrity, Obedience, Immortality, Good Mind. It is thought that these figures are grounded in older divinities, but they have been utterly transformed by Zoroastrian teaching into abstract ethical ideals.

Three of the Amesha Spenta are conceived of as feminine: Devotion (Armaiti), Integrity (Haurvatat), and Immortality (Ameretat). Armaiti, described as presiding over the earth and as the giver of pasture to cattle, embodies the ethical principles of faithful obedience, religious harmony, and worship. Haurvatat and Ameretat, who are often mentioned in the texts, represent the ideals of vigor and are the sources of life and growth.

Below the Seven Immortals are the Worshipful Ones (Yazatas), who are the guardian spirits of the heavenly bodies (e.g., Mithra as the sun) and spirits of nature (including Anahita), but also includes Haoma (the life-giving sap of the sacred plant) and Atar (Fire). Fire is the visible sign of Ahura Mazda's presence, the path to the gods, the mediator between heaven and earth, the purifier.

Locked in a struggle to the death with the heavenly world is the parallel world of evil spirits, ruled over by Angra Manyu or Ahriman, who dwells in an abyss of darkness, and whose aim is the ruin and destruction of the world. All that is evil is the work of Ahriman and his seven emanations (Wrath, Discord, Apostasy, Anarchy, Presumption, Hunger, and Thirst), whose aim is to bring suffering and death to the good creation. But at the end of time evil will be defeated and destroyed with the help of humans, who must join the forces of Ahura Mazda. All will be renovated and purified in a great consuming fire.

Zoroastrianism became the official religion of the Persian kings in the sixth century B.C.E., but the spread of Islam in Persia in the seventh century C.E. led to its almost total disappearance; small communities still survive in Iran and India (where they are called Parsis).

Given the imagery of battle that pervades the liturgy, Zoroastrianism emphasizes the masculine. In the first through third centuries C.E., a transformed version of the cult of Mithra, Mithraism, spread through the Roman world; with its emphasis on the virtues of courage, bravery and integrity, it became extremely popular among the Roman army. Often described as a rival to Christianity, its refusal to allow the initiation of women was one of the major causes of its eventual disappearance.

BIBLIOGRAPHY

Bailey, H. W. "The Second Stratum of the Indo-Iranian Gods." In *Mithraic Studies.* Edited by John R. Hinnells. 1975.

Boyce, Mary. "A History of Zoroastrianism." In *Handbuch der Orientalistik* 7, nos. 1–5 (1975).

Dutchesne-Guillemin, Jacques. *The Hymns of Zarathustra.* Translated from the French by M. Henning. London, 1952. Reprint, 1992.

Dresden, M. J. "Mythology of Ancient Iran." In *Mythologies of the Ancient World.* Edited by N. S. Kramer. 1963.

Frye, Richard Nelson. *The Heritage of Persia.* 1962.

Gershevitch, Ilya, ed. *The Cambridge History of Iran,* vol. 2. *The Median and Achaemenian Periods.* 1983.

Ghirshman, Roman. *Iran from the Earliest Times to the Islamic Conquest.* 1954. Reprint, 1978.

Meyer, Marvin W., ed. *The Ancient Mysteries: A Sourcebook.* 1987.

Sethna, Tehmurasp Rustamji, ed. *Yashts in Roman Script with Translation.* Karachi, 1976.

Vermaseren, Maarten Jozef. *Mithras: The Secret God.* 1963.

Yarshater, Ehsan, ed. *The Cambridge History of Iran,* vol. 3. *The Seleucid, Parthian and Sasanian Periods.* 1983.

Zaehner, Robert Charles. *The Dawn and Twilight of Zoroastrianism.* 1961.

TAMARA M. GREEN

Irrationality

Irrationality, like its correlatives reason or rationality, is imprecise as a concept and therefore difficult to define. It can and, at times, does mean many different things, ranging from the ravages of dementia to the madness of Eros to the ecstasy of creative genius. There is no single agreed-upon norm for determining irrationality or its opposite. Furthermore, since irrationality's meaning is merely derivative, it includes anything and everything that is thought to be not rational. Irrationality can perhaps best be understood in the private sense of the failure to grasp, understand, or reason. One is irrational, then, when one is without the faculty of or not endowed with reason; temporarily without the faculty of reason, deprived of reason; without or deprived of sound judgment; not in accordance with reason, utterly illogical. Woman, for example, is held to be irrational in so far as her thoughts and behaviors are not in accord with principles of male-based reason or are absurd by patriarchal societal standards.

Irrationality is used here particularly as it applies to philosophy, ontology, epistemology, psychology, ethics, and religion. In the histories of all these fields, one characteristic of irrationality has been agreed on under patriarchy throughout the ages and across many cultures: irrationality is categorically attributable to all women and small children. By definition of their gender, women as a race or a class traditionally have been held to be irrational, as well as childlike, emotional, and prone to hysteria (an exclusively female diagnosis; the word's etymological root being the Greek word for uterus).

In many Western cultures the paradigm of humanity is the rational man. In Biblically based traditions, the Genesis story of the Fall is sometimes interpreted to indicate that man's original ability to reason was somewhat diminished or darkened by his eating of the Garden's forbidden apple. According to this same narrative, women are believed to be twice-fallen, first because of their sinful succumbing to Satan and second because of their role in tempting Adam to sin. Furthermore, as derivative creatures, women are often held to have only subordinate abilities.

In Greek tradition men were believed to be inherently rational, and rationality was the expected standard for male behavior. Yet, Socrates, in particular, saw that great blessings came to male society by way of madness. Four types of madness in men were thought to be divinely provided to induce societal change: prophetic, ritual, poetic, and erotic. However, where women were concerned in Greek society, irrationality or madness was a different matter. Women were thought to be inherently irrational. Aristotle, for example, taught that females, as defective and misbegotten males, were incapable of the normal state of rationality. He further believed that nature allowed for and even intended the production of defective males, that is, females, for the purpose of the regeneration. As the nineteenth-century English philosopher Herbert Spencer saw it, humans possessed a finite quantity of nerve force. However, though they had the same amount of the essential force, women, because they had to use virtually all of their "nerve force" to support the bodily functions of their sex (such as menstruation, pregnancy, etc.) remain irrational whereas males, by reason of their physiology, are able to devote most, if not all, of theirs to rational thinking.

Centuries later the Christian theologian and synthesizer Thomas Aquinas followed Aristotle's line of thought, elaborating further on women's natural subordination to men and confirming females' inability to function rationally.

In the era of the scientific revolution, so-called objectivity could have helped change the assessment of women as inherently irrational; yet many patriarchal philosophers and theologians of the Enlightenment extended the male line of self-aggrandizement in terms of the perfection of the power of intellection. René Descartes perpetuated a dichotomy in which rationality was assigned to the male and irrationality to the fe-

male. The eighteenth-century philosopher Immanuel Kant believed that morality in women was based irrationally on feelings, whereas men lived by reason and made their ethical decisions based on logic. In the nineteenth century Arthur Schopenhauer, speaking of the maturity of male reasoning powers and mental facilities, stated that females may attain a reason of a sort, but that it is "very niggardly in its dimensions." That is why, he believed, women remain children throughout their lives, tend toward extravagance, and carry their unbridled inclinations to lengths that border on madness.

For twentieth-century French psychoanalytic theorist Luce Irigaray women have a specificity that sets them apart from men. She takes on Plato's and Freud's definitions of women as irrational and invisible, imperfect or castrated males, and maintains that women caught in a male-centered world have no way of knowing, expressing, or symbolizing themselves. Phyllis Chessler, among other feminist scholars, has suggested the direct correlation between the male ethic of mental health and women's need to adapt their behaviors and to adjust their emotional, intuitive, imaginative, and intellectual experiences to the patriarchal requirements for female "normalcy." Women have long refused to split reality into bipolar categories such as irrationality and rationality, body and soul, and so on.

Honored in women's wisdom traditions across cultures, irrationality is related to chaos, intuitive knowing, ancient spiritual and creative energy, and the power of shamans and healers. It celebrates dualities such as the sun and the moon, light and darkness, natural cycles and rhythms, and diverse ways of living and being in the world. The women's wisdom traditions that underlie all cultural traditions include living in the present (read by patriarchy as failure to reason about the value of the past and the hopes for the future); honoring mystery, not just objective reality, and supporting the integrity of the whole. It embraces the patriarchally defined and rejected figures of the bag lady, the madwoman, the lesbian, the wild woman, the spinster, the witch, and the crone. Many of its elements are being reclaimed from mythology, fairy tales, and women's oral traditions. Key figures emerge such as Medea, Cassandra, Artemis, Inanna, Hathor, Kālī, Osun, the Ice Queen, and the Sybil, etc. Taken together, they embody the paradox of creation and destruction. Notions of lunacy, madwomen, and wild women are nearly universal. The radical meaning of their irrationality holds a revelatory message for women's transformation into wholeness.

BIBLIOGRAPHY

Agonito, Rosemary. *History of Ideas on Women.* 1977.

Awiakta, Marilou. *Selu: Seeking the Corn-Mother's Wisdom.* 1993.

Belensky, Mary Field, et al. *Women's Ways of Knowing: The Development of Self, Voice, and Mind.* 1969.

Chessler, Phyllis. *Women and Madness.* 1973.

Daly, Mary. *Outercourse: The Be-dazzling Voyage.* 1992.

Dodds, E. R. *The Greeks and the Irrational.* 1951.

Eisler, Rianne. *The Chalice and the Blade.* 1985.

Gilbert, Sandra M., and Susan Gubar. *The Madwoman in the Attic: The Woman Writer and the Nineteenth-Century Literary Imagination.* 1984.

Gilman, Charlotte Perkins. *The Yellow Wallpaper.* 1890.

Hewitt, Marsha Aileen. *Critical Theory of Religion.* 1993.

Irigaray, Luce. *Speculum of the Other Woman.* 1974; 1985.

Leonard, Linda Schierse. *Meeting the Madwoman: Empowering the Feminine Spirit.* 1994.

Lerner, Gerda. *The Creation of Patriarchy.* 1986.

Millett, Kate. *The Looney Bin Trip.* 1990.

Piercy, Marge. *Woman on the Edge of Time.* 1976.

Roberts, Jane. *Psychic Politics.* 1976.

Showalter, Elaine. *A Literature of Their Own: British Women Novelists from Bronte to Lessing.* 1977.

Spender, Dale. *Mothers of the Novel.* 1986.

Tan, Amy. *The Hundred Secret Senses.* 1995.

Tavris, Carol. *Mismeasure of Woman.* 1992.

See also **Shamans**.

LORINE M. GETZ

Ishtar and Anat

Anat is a major Northwest Semitic goddess in the pantheon of the ancient city of Ugarit in modern northern Syria. She is the sister of the fertility god Baal and daughter of the chief god El. Anat was worshiped widely across Mesopotamia and in Egypt as well as in Syria, Israel, and Anatolia. References to Anat in the literature of Mari and Ugarit date from as early as the second millennium B.C.E. In the Hebrew Bible she is never mentioned as a goddess, though her name occurs in the personal name of the Israelite judge Shamgar son of Anat (Judges 3:31) and in several place names.

Although the root meaning of her name is in dispute among scholars of Semitic languages, in Arabic the word connotes sexuality, force, violence, aggression, belligerency, obstinacy, and zealousness—characteristics of the Anat of myth and legend. She is often known by the epithet *btlt 'nt,* "Nubile Anat," and sometimes as *rḥm 'nt,* "Womanly Anat." Renowned for her loveliness and grace, she is the epitome of beauty to whom women in Ugaritic legends are compared.

Anat takes an active role in the legends concerning her brother, Baal. A goddess of great courage and ferocity, she bathes her feet in the blood of those she has slain. When Mot, the god of the unsown wilderness, causes an extended drought by swallowing Baal, the god of fertility, Anat avenges her brother. She seizes Mot, cleaves him in two, winnows him, burns him, grinds him in a hand-mill, and sows him in the field where birds eat his remains. Her zealous actions appear to revivify her brother, whose return heralds renewed fertility.

Anat shares a dwelling with Asherah, who is a minor goddess of fertility in Ugaritic myth. Asherah is a consort of the chief god, El, and her most frequent epithets are *'aṯrt ym,* "Lady of the Sea," and *qnyt 'ilm,* "Creator of the Gods." Like Anat, Asherah is also associated with hunting and horses and with Baal in his adventures against his enemies. She intervenes in his battle against his mortal adversary Prince Yamm, and she also encourages El to permit Baal to build the palace he desires. Although she is a separate divinity in Ugaritic tradition, Asherah's identity is merged with Anat's in some Egyptian, Greek, and Roman accounts. In Egypt, Anat/Asherah is regarded as a major deity, a forceful goddess of war. Her name occurs as part of several Hyksos names, and some New Kingdom rulers were her devotees as well.

Anat, in her role as warrior and lover, is also identified with other divine figures in antiquity, most notably the classical goddess Athena. At least one equation of Anat with Athena occurs in a fourth-century B.C.E. inscription from Cyprus inscribed in both Phoenician and Greek. It is also possible that the goddess represented in Northwest Semitic art and statues as an armed, winged goddess is Anat. Athena is depicted in this way in classical mythology.

Like Anat and Asherah, Astarte of Ugarit, the Akkadian Ishtar, is a goddess of fertility and is also identified with war and sexuality. In some accounts, the distinctions among these three goddesses are obscured, and they are treated as a single divinity. Ashtoret, a plural feminine form of the Northwest Semitic name Ashtart/Astarte/Ashteret, is the generic term for "goddess" in the Hebrew Bible. The word is based on the Ugaritic goddess whose Biblical name is deliberately corrupted by vocalizing it using the vowels of the Hebrew word *boshet,* meaning "shame," as part of the Israelite condemnation of all pagan idolatry. In the Hebrew Bible, her worship is associated with the Phoenician city of

Sidon (1 Kings 11:5, 2 Kings 23:13). The monk Eusebius, who wrote in the fourth century C.E., equates a goddess known as Ashtarte with Aphrodite.

In both her Northwest Semitic and Mesopotamian guises, Astarte/Ishtar is a celestial divinity, often associated with the evening star. As Ishtar, she is the primary goddess of Mesopotamia and bears the epithet "Queen of Heaven." Like her Sumerian predecessor, Inanna, Ishtar is also identified with the planet Venus. Other goddesses were probably clustered into the mythic complex of Ishtar/Inanna. Ishtar has a reputation for passion, sexuality, and ambition. She has many consorts but is most closely associated with the shepherd Tammuz (Sumerian Dumuzi). The sacred marriage ritualized the relationship between Ishtar/Inanna and Tammuz/Dumuzi, expressed in the mating of a Mesopotamian king with a sacred prostitute to renew fertility of earth and herd.

In parallel Akkadian and Sumerian myths, Tammuz/Dumuzi is forced to spend half the year in the underworld as a substitute for Ishtar/Inanna, whose ill-advised descent into the nether regions threatens to end in disaster for both the goddess and for the fertility she governs. The annual cycle of agriculture is mirrored in these two myths, fertility returning when Tammuz/Dumuzi ascends from the netherworld to mate with his consort goddess, and disappearing with him upon his descent during the second half of the year. In the Hebrew Bible, Israelite prophets specifically condemn rituals associated with Ishtar/Inanna and her consort. Families baking cakes for the Queen of Heaven (Jer. 7:18, 44:17–19, 25), and women weeping for Tammuz in the Temple courtyard (Ezek. 8:14) are Biblical reflections of the pervasive power of these myths.

BIBLIOGRAPHY

Frymer-Kensky, Tikva. "Inanna—The Quintessential Femme Fatale." *Biblical Archaeology Review.* September/October 1984: 62–64.

———. "Goddesses: Biblical Echoes." In *Feminist Approaches to the Bible.* Edited by Herschel Shanks. 1995.

Leeming, D., and J. Page. *Goddess: Myths of the Female Divine.* 1994.

Olson, Carl, ed. *The Book of the Goddess Past and Present: An Introduction to Her Religion.* 1989.

Patai, R. *The Hebrew Goddess.* 3d enl. ed. Foreword by M. Stone. 1990.

Walker, B. G. *The Woman's Encyclopedia of Myths and Secrets.* 1983.

See also **Inanna.**

DIANE M. SHARON

Isis

The ancient Egyptian goddess Isis has a long history that developed from rather modest beginnings. Always a beneficent deity, her earliest attested appearances come with the Pyramid Texts beginning about 2350 B.C.E., in which she and her sister Nephthys play a major role in the rebirth and revival of the deceased king. Only a few of these texts depict her as the sister-wife of Osiris, sovereign of the realm of the dead, and mother of Horus, the royal god, roles for which she becomes extremely well known in later times.

Before the Pyramid Texts, several other goddesses played prominent roles, most notably Neith and Hathor. Neith, a creator deity, dates to earliest times, while Hathor rose to prominence in the middle of the third millennium. Both deities bore special relationships to the king and queen.

Over time, Isis, the daughter of the sky goddess Nut and the earth god Geb, born on the fourth epagomenal day of the year, who initially appeared virtually only in mortuary contexts, expanded her sphere of influence, due largely to her increasing prominence as mother of

Bronze statue of the goddess Isis nursing the Pharaoh, c. 350–600 C.E. (Gianni Dagli Orti/Corbis).

the Horus-king. Having conceived her son on Osiris, her deceased brother-husband, after he was killed by his brother Seth, she describes her action as follows:

> I have acted as a man although I was a woman,
> In order to make [Osiris's] name survive on earth
> (P. Louvre 3079 I, col. 110,11. 20–22).

This remarkable act contributed to her reputation as universal mother and goddess of magic, roles that began to be fairly prominent in the New Kingdom, as attested by various tales and magical spells or incantations. During this time, too, the goddess, previously identified by the throne sign on her head, began to appropriate the insignia of other goddesses, most notably the cow horns and sun disk of Hathor. Similarly, her cult, virtually nonexistent before the Middle Kingdom, only began to rise to prominence in the New Kingdom. Contemporaneously she began to collect a series of epithets, such as "Oldest of the old," "Goddess from whom all Becoming arose," "the great Lady—Mistress of the Two Lands of Egypt," "Mistress of Shelter, Mistress of Heaven," "Mistress of the House of Life," "Mistress of the Word of God," and "the Unique." These descriptive phrases appear in profusion during the first millennium B.C.E. and later, most notably in the hymns from her Ptolemaic temple at Philae.

During the Ptolemaic period, she assumed the role of savior in the Aegean world and eventually became a focus of mystery religions, such as that evidenced in Apuleius: but within the native Egyptian world, she continued to appear within the Osirian ritual assisting the deceased in rebirth and renewal with the help of her sister Nephthys, as hymned in the "Lamentations of Isis and Nephthys." Thus one finds in Isis a very complex deity who is not easily described and, in fact, cannot truly be comprehended apart from her development—not her role, because that was not static—in the religion of ancient Egypt.

BIBLIOGRAPHY

Virtually no studies exist currently that address ancient Egyptian goddesses including Isis beyond describing and discussing them in the context of Egyptian history, religion, or literature. Thus the first two of the following few sources represent significant discussion about the goddess, and the third presents translations of important primary sources accompanied by a fine contextual discussion.

Egan, Rory B. "Isis: Goddess of the Oikoumene." In *Goddesses in Religions and Modern Debate*. Edited by Larry Hurtado. 1990.

Münster, Maria. *Untersuchungen zur Göttin Isis vom Alten Reich bis zum Ende des Neuens Reiches.* 1968.

Zabkar, Louis V. *Hymns to Isis in Her Temple at Philae.* 1988.

See also **Mystery Religions.**

SUSAN TOWER HOLLIS

Islam

An Overview

Islam means submission to the will of God, which Muslims believe has been revealed clearly in the Qur'an, the Islamic sacred scripture. God's will is that humanity create a just society, one that reflects the equality of all human beings share in the eyes of their Creator. Thus, justice is a dominant paradigm in the Qur'an. Among the most often quoted verses of this fourteen-chapter (sura) text is the following:

> O Believers, establish justice, be witnesses for God, even if it goes against yourselves, or your parents, or relatives, whether rich or poor; God is closer than either. (sura 4:134)

Muslims believe that the Qur'an is the final message in a series of messages that God (Allah) has delivered to humanity. They believe Islam is the culmination of the monotheistic tradition that began some 4,000 years ago with Abraham's encounter with God. Judaism and Christianity are part of Islamic history; Jews and Christians are among the communities to whom earlier revelations were sent, and their stories are recounted in the Qur'an. Although some of these "people of the Book" are pious, according to the Qur'an, the majority have gone astray. Prophet Muhammad was sent by God to seventh-century Arabia as the "seal of the prophets" (sura 33:40). His mission was to reveal the complete message of God and correct the errors into which earlier communities had fallen.

Among the major signs of corruption in the earlier messages, according to the Qur'an, was the injustice and oppression that prevailed in the region. The Qur'an therefore emphasizes social reforms. Central to its message of reform is the dignity of women and their inclusion in teachings of human equality, although that did not always translate into social reality.

SCRIPTURAL BACKGROUND

Women are considered more extensively in the Qur'an than in any other religious scripture, and that consideration stresses women's substantial equality with men:

> Men who submit [to God] and women who submit [to God], believing men and believing women, obedient

men and obedient women, truthful men and truthful women, steadfast men and steadfast women, humble men and humble women, men who give charity and women who give charity, men who fast and women who fast, men who guard their chastity and women who guard their chastity, men and women who remember God often—God has prepared for them forgiveness and great reward. (sura 33:35; cf. 4:125)

The Qur'an reflects an awareness of the low status of women in the Arabian peninsula of the seventh century. It sharply criticizes those who denigrate the value of women, and it condemns female infanticide (sura 16:59–60; cf. 81:8). Other abuses of women prevalent in pre-Islamic society are also addressed. Men are prohibited from inheriting wives from their fathers (sura 4:20). Women are not to be exchanged for a dower (*mahr*). Rather than doing away with the practice outright, however, the Qur'an insists that women (rather than their families) be given their dower as a source of economic independence (sura 4:4; cf. 4:25), which is another theme in its treatment of women. Women must be allowed to keep whatever they earn (sura 4:3). The Qur'an also requires that, unlike any other religion at that time, females receive inheritance (sura 4:7–12). This includes wives, mothers, daughters, and sisters. The fact that daughters (and sisters) receive half of what sons (and brothers) receive is considered by many to be a reflection of the reality that most women get married and that their husbands are responsible for their maintenance.

Many Muslims believe the practice of forced marriage is prohibited by a verse in the Qur'an that calls for divorced women to be able to marry whom they choose "if they agree between themselves in the proper way" (sura 2:233). All Muslims agree that the Qur'an insists that the marriage relationship be sustained by feelings of love and tenderness. A loving marriage is considered one of the "signs" of God (sura 30:22). Wives are "as garments" to their husbands, just as husbands are to their wives (sura 2:188). Arbitrary divorce is forbidden. Instead, the Qur'an requires efforts at reconciliation between couples, which can be initiated by women (sura 4:129). The reconciliation process is carefully detailed, requiring representatives from both the husband's and the wife's family and trial separations (sura 4:36). If reconciliation cannot be achieved the divorce is granted, but husbands are required to allow their former wives to keep any gifts they have given them and to treat them humanely, which includes supporting them until it is clear that there is no pregnancy (the completion of three menstrual cycles), or until the birth of the baby.

Because the Qur'an gives women these unprecedented rights, Muslims believe that it inaugurated rev-

An ancient Qur'an is displayed for a religious festival. Women are considered more extensively in the Qur'an than in any other religious scripture (Earl Kowall/Corbis).

olutionary reforms in the rights and status of women. Yet the Qur'an does distinguish among the responsibilities of women and men. In a discussion of marriage it says that women "have rights similar to those [of men], but men are a degree above them" (sura 2:229). That distinction is further emphasized, for example, when it explains that men are in charge of women because "God has favored some of them over others and because they spend of their wealth" (sura 4:35). Therefore, although women have certain rights, they are supposed to be obedient. Wives are described as being like "tilled land" for their husbands, "so approach your tilth when and how you like" (sura 2:224).

This distinction in status is also reflected in the Qur'an's position on polygyny. Women are required to be strictly monogamous, whereas men are allowed to marry up to four wives (sura 4:3; cf. sura 24:33). But these stipulations, too, are believed to have been liberating in their historical context. Women are given economic independence, while men are required to support their wives. Furthermore, before Islam there was unlimited polygyny. That, combined with the proviso that polygyny is permissible only if the wives are treated equally, renders the limitation to four wives an improvement in women's status. Moreover, the permission to marry up to four wives was granted in the historical context of wartime, when there was an abundance of orphans and widows who needed support. Many Muslims believe that this extenuating circumstance further limits the permission for polygyny. Finally, the Qur'an claims that "you cannot do justice among [multiple] wives, however much you may desire to" (sura 4:130), implying that it favors monogamy.

Although women and men are not equal in social status in the Qur'an, women are on a spiritual and moral par with men. In addition to the verses promising equal reward for equal virtues, the Qur'an emphasizes people's moral equality in its telling of the story of humankind's fall from the Garden of Eden. The Qur'an does not give the name of Adam's female counterpart or describe the circumstances of her creation, but she plays a role similar to that of Adam. God warns Adam that the devil is his and his wife's enemy (sura 20:117). In one telling the devil tempts Adam, and it is Adam who "disobeyed his Lord and went astray" (sura 20:121). In another, the devil whispers to Adam and his partner (sura 7:20–22), and both disobeyed (sura 20:121 and 7:22). Either way, unlike the Christian telling, this version does not hold the woman responsible for the fall of humanity. Furthermore, the Qur'an claims that both the man and the woman asked for forgiveness and, in response, they were together granted "a garment of righteousness" (sura 7:26).

Islamic teaching presents numerous examples of pious women who serve as "examples to the believers," such as stories about the women in the life of the patriarch Abraham (Ibrahim). As with Adam's wife, the Qur'an does not mention the name of either Abraham's wife or his consort. But in oral tradition (collectively known as hadith literature), the latter is named Hagar, and she is portrayed as a righteous person chosen to play an essential role in the establishment of true religion, Islam. Her enormous perseverance, having been exiled with her son Ishmael (Isma'il) to Arabia, allowed her son to survive and the religion to thrive. Her desperate search for water near the sacred shrine in Mecca, the Kaaba, is commemorated annually in the pilgrimage (hajj) ritual.

The women in the life of Moses (Musa) are also instructive. The Qur'an relates God speaking to Moses and telling him that He "revealed to your mother a revelation" to put the child Moses into an ark and put it in the river so that Moses could be saved and live to be a great prophet. Thus, the Qur'an allows women to receive revelation. The pharaoh's wife is also presented as a righteous woman who participated in the divine plane for Moses, praying, "Deliver me from the oppressors" (sura 66:12).

Among the women most often referred to in the Qur'an is Mary (Maryam), the mother of Jesus ('Issa), with an entire chapter named after her. Like the mother of Moses, she received a message from God: she would conceive a "righteous son" by miraculous means. Her role in the fulfillment of the divine plan is likewise praised, and in her obedience and chastity she is presented as another example to believers (sura 66:12).

The wives of Prophet Muhammad are accorded special status in the Qur'an. The Qur'an says they "are not like any [other] women" (sura 3:33). Nevertheless, many scholars trace the introduction of seclusion for women to a verse requiring people to make their requests of favors from the Prophet's wives "from behind a curtain" (sura 33:54). Others trace the requirement for modest dress—a kind of seclusion—to the Qur'an's requirement that women cover themselves with their cloaks so that their dignity may be recognized (sura 33:56; cf. 24:32) and to verse where modesty rules are more specifically spelled out. In the latter, women are required to cover their private parts and hide their beauty from all men except close relatives and to refrain from looking at men and trying to attract their attention in the way they walk (sura 24:32). Significantly the latter verse is preceded by one making the same requirements of men.

Thus, while the Qur'an distinguishes between the roles and social status of men and women, it does not distinguish between their moral responsibility. It presents models of obedience and submission displayed by both sexes. The ideal of obedient submission that came to be associated with women, in fact, is presented in the Qur'an as applying to all human beings. Obedience and submission are to the will of God, not to men. The women discussed are presented as examples for all believers, not for women alone.

THE EXPANSION AND INSTITUTIONALIZATION OF ISLAM

After the death of Prophet Muhammad (632 C.E.), his followers built one of the most vibrant civilizations in the world, spreading nearly halfway around the globe within a century. By the tenth century C.E. Islamic civilization had spread from the Middle East across North Africa into Spain and into Anatolia, Central Asia, and the Indian subcontinent. Bringing together the ancient heritages of Africa, Greece, Persia, and India, it developed the most sophisticated culture known to the Western world. Responsible for the revival of classical learning and the development of advanced mathematics, science, technology, and the arts, medieval Islamic civilization bequeathed to Europe much of the learning on which the latter would base its own Renaissance.

Such accomplishments were based on an elaborate administrative structure and, most importantly, a highly developed legal structure. Islam's legal structure, developed essentially in the seventh through ninth centuries, consists of five major schools of law and a vast body of diverse codes. It incorporates not only Qur'anic teachings, but a good deal of customary practice in the various regions it came to serve, including vestiges of Roman and Persian legal codes. (The generic name for Islamic law is *Shari'a,* although the specific legal codes are more properly called *fiqh,* legal knowledge. Shari'a is considered to be of divine origin, actually a reflection of God's will for humanity, and therefore immutable. *Fiqh,* on the other hand, reflects human efforts to codify God's will for practical implementation. As such, it must remain flexible and open to adjustment.

The basic inspiration for Islamic law is the written scripture, the Qur'an. But the Qur'an is augmented by a large body of oral traditions (hadith literature), believed to embody the living example of Islam given by Prophet Muhammad (the sunna). The oral reports collected, authenticated, codified, and committed to writing by the third century of Islam—came to be considered of revelatory power second only to the Qur'an.

In hadith literature, as well as in the accompanying scriptural commentary (*tafsir*) based on it, distinctions in the moral responsibility of women and men begin to appear. Al-Tabari (d. 923), for example, wrote a hadith-based commentary in which he names Adam's wife (Hawwa', or Eve) and ascribed to her much of the same characteristics described in Christian teaching. He wrote that it was she who was responsible for tricking Adam into disobedience. More importantly, she felt no remorse afterward, thereby demonstrating her moral inferiority to Adam. God therefore cursed both snakes and women. Snakes would have to slither on the ground, and women would have to bleed regularly and have unwanted and difficult pregnancies. Men were not cursed by God, but they had to share in the curse God leveled against the earth, so that they would have to work harder in order to make a living.

Such elaborations on scripture became the source for a good deal of Islamic legislation and its rationale. For example, the Qur'an stipulates that when people make business deals, they should write them down and have them witnessed by two men or one man and two women (sura 2:283). This verse was interpreted in Islamic law as a general statement that the testimony of a woman is worth half that of a man and that women's testimony is generally valid only in cases involving "women's issues," such as childbirth. This disparity in the credibility of people's testimony is explained by way of women's mental and moral deficiencies, determined from the extra-Qur'anic explanations of the story of Eden. The verse was also used to explain that recompense for the murder or injury of a woman (blood money, *tha'r*) is half that of a man.

The issue of ritual purity also affects women's status in Islamic law. The Qur'an places great emphasis on spiritual or moral purity, stipulating that believers must wash before prayer. There are elaborate regulations for appropriate cleansing that are based on various levels and sources of impurity. These range from simple ablutions (*wudu*) to a full bath (*ghusl*), with allowances made for dry ablutions (*tayammum*) in case water is not available. This provision points to the largely symbolic nature of the cleansing ritual. Yet the Qur'an also displays a concern with menstrual blood, which is not symbolic (sura 2:223). Interpreted in extra-Qur'anic lore, women's lesser moral status is partially explained by the impurity resulting from their menstrual and postpartum bleeding. Women are prohibited from praying or touching a Qur'an, much less spending time in a mosque, during times of bleeding. To regain a state of purity, a full bath is required.

The bath is also required to regain a state of purity after contact with sexual fluids for both women and men (although in some schools of Islamic law, impurity results only if the emissions are accompanied by sexual pleasure). However, sexual emission for men is not associated with general moral deficiency, as is women's blood. This discrepancy is explained by the founder of one of Islam's major schools of legal thought, ash-Shāfi'ī (d. 820). Ash-Shāfi'ī says that even though purification by washing with water is required of all believers, simple washing is not sufficient to purify a menstruating woman. It is only effective upon the cessation of menstruation. Ash-Shāfi'ī concludes that women are excused from praying while menstruating because the impurity is not something resulting from willful disobedience but from a natural bodily function. Therefore, the lack of prayer during menstruation is not considered neglect of religious duty.

The extra-Qur'anic explanations of women's moral and mental deficiency are also reflected in Islamic laws requiring women to have male guardians who are responsible for all major decisions in their lives, including appropriate marriage partners. Accordingly, a Muslim man may marry a Muslim, a Jew, and/or a Christian, that is, anyone to whom a scripture considered valid by Muslims has been revealed. A Muslim woman may only marry a Muslim man; it would be considered unwise to entrust her or the children that they would produce to the guardianship of a non-Muslim. Women's inferiority is likewise reflected in laws concerning apostasy. Male apostates are subject to capital punishment in Islam, but if a Muslim woman rejects the religion, because of her inherent incapacities she is not subjected to the full extent of the law. Instead she is to be forced (under threat of physical punishment or imprisonment, if necessary) to return to the religion. This despite a Qur'anic verse stating categorically, "There is no compulsion in religion" (sura 2:257).

Despite their moral and mental deficiencies, women are considered extremely powerful and downright dangerous in some extra-Qur'anic traditions and commentaries. According to a hadith report women have a power similar to Satan's to distract men from their otherwise virtuous activities. Women are therefore the greatest source of *fitna,* moral chaos. For this reason, women must be kept under control, and one way of doing this is by covering them and keeping them out of public view.

Hadith literature also contains positive statements about women's virtues, but its statements concerning women's weaknesses are the ones that found their way into law and practice. For example, justification for the practice of female circumcision is found in hadith. This practice was never widespread in Islam nor did it become a requirement in Islamic law; however, it is acceptable in all but one of the major schools of law and, for those communities that do practice it (primarily in sub-Saharan Africa), justification is found in hadith materials.

THE END OF ISLAMIC UNITY AND THE RISE OF COLONIALISM

The Islamic legal system provided the basis for cultural unity in the Muslim empire even in its farthest reaches. The legal system, however, was not sufficient to maintain the empire's political unity. As early as the fourteenth century the Muslim world was being fragmented into a series of autonomous or semi-autonomous principalities. In addition to regional power struggles, the Middle East had suffered attacks and occupation by the European crusaders and the Mongols. Within a few centuries, European entrepreneurs had made inroads into the Muslim world, gaining control of valuable trade routes in the Middle East and establishing lucrative business relationships throughout the Islamic world.

Eighteenth- and nineteenth-century Muslim reformers from Africa to the Indian subcontinent tended to focus on the decline in educational standards, scientific research, entrepreneurship, political dynamism, and overall social solidarity that had allowed the Europeans to gain dominance. An increasing number of reformers attributed the problems to deviation from Islamic standards. They argued that a society that truly adhered to Islamic principles would be characterized by vibrant intellectual, artistic, social, economic, and political culture.

By the twentieth century Europe's exploitation of resources and markets had become overwhelming. France had taken control of Algeria and Tunisia and was well ensconced in Syria; Italy had established a presence in Libya; Britain had taken control of Egypt and the major ports on the Persian Gulf, with clear designs on Iraq; Russia was threatening the Ottoman Empire from the north; and France, Britain, and Russia were competing for dominance in Palestine. Opposition to Europe, therefore, joined Islamic self-critique and heightened Islamic consciousness as characteristics of twentieth-century Islamic discourse.

MODERN INTERPRETATIONS AND LEGAL REFORMS

In this context Islamic reform came to include calls for reform in the status of women. One of the earliest Islamic modernists was Qasim Amin (d. 1908), an Egyptian intellectual who attributed the decline in Islamic society to its deviation from Islamic standards, especially in its treatment of women. Women are the nurturers and teachers of young Muslims, he proclaimed. Without the freedom and dignity the Qur'an had prescribed for them, they produced an Islamic society too weak to defend itself from colonial aggressors. Similarly, Egyptian reformer Muhammad 'Abduh (d. 1905) argued that the health of Islamic society depended upon education and that education must be universal. He was particularly critical of polygyny and arbitrary divorce, which he saw as sources of social decadence.

Women established organizations early in the twentieth century to help secure their rights in the Muslim world. Some organizations were secular, such as the Union of Egyptian Women, founded in 1923 and affiliated with the International Alliance for Women's Suffrage. Others were specifically religious, such as Egypt's Muslim Women's Association, founded in 1936 by Zaynab al-Ghazali. Al-Ghazali had been associated with the Union of Egyptian Women but found its approach foreign. She insisted that it was not necessary to go beyond Islam to remedy the pitiable condition into which Islamic society, its women included, had fallen. The Qur'an and the example set by Prophet Muhammad had provided women full freedom in both the private and public spheres, including social, economic, and political rights. Women's primary task is motherhood, al-

Ghazali taught, but if that is attended to, they may enter any sphere of life where their skills are needed.

This religious orientation is distinctive in the movement to elevate the status of Muslim women. Rather than finding the source of disparity in the treatment of women in the religion, Islamic reformers (often called Islamists) find it in deviations from Islam. Thus there is a tendency to consider the medieval religious sources of discrimination to be inauthentic. Some see the medieval interpretations as resulting from non-Islamic sources, specifically Jewish and Christian sources. Sayyid Qutb (d. 1966), for example, the major ideologue of Egypt's Muslim Brotherhood, believed that women are not responsible for men's moral weakness. He stressed the equality of women and men, both soldiers in the struggle against injustice.

Similarly, popular Egyptian television preacher Sheikh Muhammad Metwali al-Sha'rawi emphasizes the moral equality of the sexes in Islam and the complementary nature of women's and men's make-up. Women, having been shown in the Qur'an to play important religious roles, obviously have abilities equal to those of men. But women's primary roles are domestic, caring for their husbands and children, which thus are essential religious roles.

Efforts to improve the lot of women in Muslim countries have been complicated by postcolonial political problems, particularly the growing hostility between Muslim countries and the secular West. Secularism is seen by many in Muslim countries as the source of the moral decadence, which is epitomized by the West's colonial atrocities, its materialism, and its exploitation of women. Stressing the uniqueness of Islamic identity and morality has become increasingly popular. The widespread trend of "Islamic dress" for women—wearing modest clothes and a headscarf—is the most obvious manifestation of this effort to establish a unique identity based on moral superiority. To many Muslim women, the new "veil" represents not their subservience to men but their empowerment to participate actively in public life without fear of unwanted sexual overtures.

In the legislative sphere, heightened Islamist awareness has resulted in reevaluation of some reforms made on behalf of women earlier in the century. Efforts to curtail polygyny, for example, have met with resistance from the spokespeople of Islamic propriety. In fact some progressive legislation has been reversed in the name of Islamic identity. For example, in Iran the Pahlavi shahs (1926–1979) had sought legitimacy independent of the traditionally powerful clerics by introducing legislation without regard for Islamic validation. Thus, wearing the veil was banned and coeducation was encouraged. When the shah was overthrown in the 1979 Islamic revolution, the Iranian legal structure was revised in generally traditional Islamic terms, which meant a return to the veil and to the segregation of the sexes. Iranian women continued to play a public role and participate in Iran's political life; supporters of Islamist legislation claim that was because of the veil, opponents say it was despite the veil. In Pakistan in the 1960s women were guaranteed the basic rights accorded to them by Islam. Progressive interpretations were also incorporated into legislation, such as giving women's testimony equal weight with that of men. In the late 1970s and the 1980s, however, following the secularist regime of Zulfikar Ali Bhutto, Zia al-Haq's military regime sought religious legitimization, allowing the reversal of some progressive measures. Since that time, other heads of governments, including a twice-elected female prime minister, have refrained from outspoken support for women's legal equality for fear of losing Islamist support.

Under current circumstances then—Muslim countries striving for political and economic development and cultural independence from the dominant Euroamerican "West"—more traditional interpretations of women's social roles have taken precedence over the progressive interpretations popular in the early and mid-twentieth century. Whether this trend is permanent or a result of specific and changing circumstances remains to be seen. In either case, the strong scriptural foundation for discourse on women indicates that the subject cannot be ignored.

BIBLIOGRAPHY

Ahmed, Leila. *Women and Gender in Islam.* 1992.

Badran, Margot. *Feminists, Islam, and Nation: Gender and the Making of Modern Egypt.* 1994.

Esposito, John L. *Women in Muslim Family Law.* 1982.

Fernea, Elizabeth Warnock, ed. *Women and the Family in the Middle East: New Voices of Change.* 1985.

Haddad, Yvonne Yazbeck, and John L. Esposito, eds. *Islam, Gender, and Social Change.* 1998.

Haddad, Yvonne Yazbeck, and Ellison Banks Findly, eds. *Women, Religion, and Social Change.* 1982.

Hoffman Ladd, Valerie J. "Women's Religious Observances." In *The Oxford Encyclopedia of the Modern Islamic World.* Edited by John L. Esposito. Vol. 4. 1995.

Keddie, Nikki, and Lois Beck, eds. *Women in the Muslim World.* 1978.

Mernissi, Fatima. *Beyond the Veil.* 1985.

Stowasser, Barbara Freyer. *Women in the Qur'an: Traditions and Interpretations.* 1994.

Toubia, Nahid, ed. *Women of the Arab World: The Coming Challenge.* 1988.

Wadud-Muhsin, Amina. *Woman and Qur'an.* 1992.

FILMS

Gaunt, Marilyn. "A Veiled Revolution." Icarus Films. 1982.

———. "Women Under Siege." Icarus Films. 1982.

"Not Without My Veil: Amongst the Women of Oman." Filmakers Library. 1993.

"Paradise Lies at the Feet of the Mother." Ambrose Video Publishing. 1993.

"Sudan: The Harsher Face of Islam." Filmakers Library. 1996.

"Women and Islam." Films for the Humanities and Sciences. 1994.

TAMARA SONN

Religious Rites and Practices

Because of gender segregation and social restrictions, Muslim women's ways of expressing their religious beliefs often differ from Muslim men's. The lack of any single religious institution, combined with the religion's spread in many cultures and societies and its many adherents (nearly one billion at the end of the twentieth century), does not permit the description of any single pattern of Islamic belief and practice. The religious activities of women in Islam can be viewed as their attempts to mold a universal faith to their own perceptions of the world. Such expressions provide for women's special circumstances and define the steps that aid them in attaining status, as individuals and Muslims, in the ways their own cultures and societies define.

The five pillars are the explicitly prescribed devotional duties of Muslim women and men: profession of faith (*shahada*, testimony about God's oneness and Muhammad's prophecy), daily prayers (*salat*), fasting (*sawm*) during the month of Ramadan, alms giving (*zakat*), and the pilgrimage to Mecca (*hajj*). Notions of personal ritual purity, achieved through proper ablutions and intentions, are central to these and other religious acts.

Muslim women are less apt than men to pray five times daily and to fast, although in some societies women are devout in these duties. Women may regard themselves as being as pious as men but may feel restricted by family and household obligations. Most homes contain prayer paraphernalia, sometimes including a woman's head covering used especially for prayer. The annual giving of alms is primarily men's duty, who usually control family finances, but women donate food and other household resources to the needy out of their own notions of charity. The pilgrimage to Mecca in Saudi Arabia is stipulated only if personal, financial, and family circumstances warrant it. Many more men than women perform this pilgrimage.

Often active in other Islamic rites and practices, women regard participation as highly meritorious. Religious activities are often their primary opportunities for life outside the home and domestic responsibilities. Because women perform many rituals collectively, female solidarity results. Women are empowered by these actions and interactions.

For religious rituals performed at home, women have the responsibility of cleaning, preparing, and serving food, and welcoming guests. No specific religious significance adheres to these acts of preparation and service other than general, not explicitly Islamic, notions of cleanliness and hospitality. The home itself and spaces within it are not sanctified and purified. Preparation, consumption, and distribution of food play a part in religious ritual, but the food itself is not regarded as sacred or pure.

Islamic calendrical rites are important for Muslim women. The Feast of Sacrifice ('Id al-Adha, 'Id al-Kabir), commemorating Ibrahim's (Abraham's) willingness to sacrifice his son and coinciding with the annual pilgrimage to Mecca, features animal sacrifice (performed only by men), distribution of meat to the poor, and a communal meal. The feast ('Id al-Fitr) at the end of Ramadan, the month of fasting, features family celebration and visiting among kin.

For Shia Muslims, the month of Muharram commemorates the martyrdom in 680 C.E. of Imam Husayn (third Shia imam, son of the prophet Muhammad's daughter Fatimah). Women gather to mourn his death, wail, and utter prayers for his intercession in this life and the hereafter. In all-female gatherings, women religious practitioners recite from the Qur'an and recount the tragic tale of Husayn. Having their own personal and family problems, women relate to Husayn's suffering. Shia women also attend performances of passion plays (*ta'ziyah*) that reenact the battle where Husayn was martyred. Men play women's parts in these dramas.

Some Sufi mystical orders and religious brotherhoods are exclusively female; others have female members. Devotees venerate and supplicate saintly persons, living and dead, who are believed to have spiritual power (*baraka*). Remembrance rituals (*dhikr*) include prayers, ecstatic chanting and dancing, drumming, and Qur'anic recitals. Males and females perform these rituals separately or, in some places, together.

Women make pilgrimages to local saints' tombs and places where miracles are said to have occurred. They travel with their families or in all-female groups, bring food to share, and make donations to religious personnel there. Some shrines have both male and female caretakers, the latter tending to women and children and keeping the shrine clean and comfortable.

Everywhere Muslim women gather to mourn the deaths of family and community members. Sometimes these funerals and memorial gatherings occur at mosques, ritually dedicated spaces where women are usually separated physically from male mourners. Women also meet at cemeteries for memorials, often on the third, seventh, and fortieth days after a death, on the one-year anniversary, and on subsequent anniversaries. On Thursday or Friday afternoons, they meet at graveyards to wail, utter prayers, and share food that they have purchased or prepared.

In some places the prophet Muhammad's birthday (*maulid al-nabi*) provides a day for family gatherings. In many places women collectively commemorate the birth and death days of saints, who are figures known widely or only locally. Women holding commemorative gatherings invite local religious practitioners, sometimes females, who recite from the Qur'an and organize prayers. After prayers women eat together and return home with extra food for their families.

Curing and spirit-possession cults of various kinds are found in many Muslim areas. The majority of participants are females; spirit possession is often said to be primarily a symptom of women, and the individuals who are skilled in exorcism are often women. These and other collective rites give women a means of addressing and solving problems that other realms of their lives may not provide.

Vows and prayers are important in the religious lives of many Muslim women, who offer promises to perform a task or make a donation if their requested wish is granted. Women sponsor gatherings in their homes in order to make and fulfill vows. At shrines and wayside places where miracles have occurred, padlocks, personal mementos, bits of knotted cloth, and piles of stones indicate vows. Men are sometimes said to be reluctant to interfere with women's attempts to contact supernatural forces.

Women place protective amulets on their children, especially vulnerable infants and the ill. Blue beads, packets holding Qur'anic passages, the five-fingered "hand of Fatimah," and other amulets contain Islamic symbols and meanings.

Life-cycle events—birth, female initiation, marriage, divorce, and death—usually include Islam-related rituals. Where clitoridectomy is performed (always at the hands of female specialists), women often claim (erroneously) that the genital operation is mandated by Islam.

Some other aspects of ritual life, such as fortune telling, divining, dream interpreting, and spell casting, cross over into what some scholars define as magic. Many Muslim women, however, consider any and all of

Muslim women pray at the Dome of the Rock, Jerusalem, 1995 (Annie Griffiths Belt/Corbis).

these ritual activities as part of their religious participation as Muslims. Other scholars argue that ritual is "Islamic" if practicing Muslims declare that it is.

Through these many rites and practices, women define Islam in terms that allow their active participation and empowerment. Often discouraged from attending the mosque, women seek out other places of sanctity and worship, such as shrines. Because they may be excluded from men's community-based acts of worship, they create their own, more private, gatherings for prayer, mourning, and curing. Specific women's issues, especially fertility and child mortality, prompt them to seek solutions through pilgrimages, appeals to holy persons, curing sessions, amulets, and vows.

Many Muslim women's lives are structured by such principles and patterns of social organization as patriarchy, patrilineality, patrilocality, child marriage, polygyny, sudden repudiation, seclusion, and male domination of economic and political systems. Religious expression allows women some degree of personal control. Offering many of them perhaps their only legitimate arena for activities outside the home, religious ritual mitigates the isolating effects of seclusion and gender segregation. Links among women are created, which often cut across and override the barriers of kin and status. As a powerful social force, female solidarity in societies that ordain the segregation and seclusion of women is one way of enhancing their position and decreasing their dependence on men.

Local religious practices link women with more universally accepted Islamic rituals. Through religious ritual, women turn an abstract faith into a pragmatic one. They embroider on the foundations of Islam by employing its symbols and metaphors in unique and personal ways. In creating an individual and less formal system of belief and practice, women enhance the appeal of Islam, which is, for them, a living faith.

BIBLIOGRAPHY

Even in this era of increased sensitivity to issues of gender, most general publications on Islam still ignore or underreport the role of women in religious ritual and practice. Many scholars of Islam regard women's rituals as unworthy of representing this great and historically significant religious tradition. Others, although perhaps interested but lacking access, have been unable to observe women's religious practices. Ethnographic accounts of Muslim women offer documentation of the many diverse ways they practice their religion.

Beck, Lois. "The Religious Lives of Muslim Women." In *Women in Contemporary Muslim Societies.* Edited by Jane I. Smith. 1980.

Betteridge, Anne. "The Controversial Vows of Urban Muslim Women in Iran." In *Unspoken Worlds: Women's Religious Lives.* Edited by Nancy Falk and Rita Gross. 1989.

Bowen, Donna Lee, and Evelyn Early, eds. *Everyday Life in the Muslim Middle East.* 1993.

Bringa, Tone. *Being Muslim the Bosnian Way: Identity and Community in a Central Bosnian Village.* 1995.

Combs-Schilling, M. E. *Sacred Performances: Islam, Sexuality, and Sacrifice.* 1989.

Dwyer, Daisy. "Women, Sufism, and Decision-Making in Moroccan Islam." In *Women in the Muslim World.* Edited by Lois Beck and Nikki Keddie. 1978.

Fernea, Elizabeth. *Guests of the Sheik: An Ethnography of an Iraqi Village.* 1965.

Fernea, Robert, and Elizabeth Fernea. "Variations in Religious Observance among Islamic Women." In *Scholars, Saints, and Sufis: Muslim Religious Institutions in the Middle East Since 1500.* Edited by Nikki Keddie. 1972.

Friedl, Erika. "Islam and Tribal Women in a Village in Iran." In *Unspoken Worlds: Women's Religious Lives.* Edited by Nancy Falk and Rita Gross. 1989.

———. *Women of Deh Koh: Lives in an Iranian Village.* 1989.

Hooglund [Hegland], Mary. "Religious Ritual and Political Struggle in an Iranian Village." *MERIP Reports* 12 (1982): 10–17, 23.

Mernissi, Fatima. "Women, Saints, and Sanctuaries." *Signs* 3 (1977): 101–112.

Tapper, Nancy. "Ziyaret: Gender, Movement, and Exchange in a Turkish Community." In *Muslim Travellers: Pilgrimage, Migration, and the Religious Imagination.* Edited by Dale Eickelman and James Piscatori. 1990.

Tapper, Nancy, and Richard Tapper. "The Birth of the Prophet: Ritual and Gender in Turkish Islam." *Man* (n.s.) 21 (1987): 69–92.

LOIS BECK

In the Arab Middle East

The Qur'an, Islamic sacred scripture believed to have been delivered by the Prophet Muhammad in seventh-century Arabia, shows significant concern for human dignity and equality. Central to its message of social reform is the status and security of women. The Islamic legal structure, however, codified by the tenth century, maintained male legal superiority and control by men over women. All the major schools of law allowed men to marry four wives, without enforcing the Qur'an's stipulation that allows polygyny under specific circumstances or the requirement that wives be treated equally and equitably. Men were given the right to divorce at will, without being required to attempt the arbitration and trial separations stipulated by the Qur'an, and women's right to divorce was severely limited. Women were prohibited from engaging in business without the permission of, or traveling without being accompanied by, a male guardian. Islamic law stipulated that women must obey their husbands and submit to punishment in cases of disobedience. Similarly, Qur'anic requirements for modesty were interpreted as requiring women's segregation from all but close family members and being hidden from public view by veils. Women's roles were strictly domestic, requiring little or no education. Although women were generally allowed to go to the mosque, where they could pray in segregated quarters (except during their menstrual periods), the more common practice was for women to pray at home.

The disparity between the Qur'anic ideals of human equality and women's status in Islamic law and custom has resulted in a broad range of reformist critiques over the past century or more. Egyptian Rifa'ah Rafi' al-Tahtawi (d. 1873), for example, argued the need for women's education for the sake of harmonious marriages and the well-being of the family. Another Egyptian, Qasim Amin (d. 1908), insisted that the very health of the nation depended upon elevation of the status of women. Muhammad 'Abduh (d. 1905) taught that Muslims had strayed from their commitment to reason and high culture, resulting in Europe's ascendancy. He therefore advocated education for all Muslims, women included, and agreed with Amin that polygyny was not in keeping with Qur'anic teachings concerning women's equality.

Muslim women in Middle Eastern cities such as Cairo and Beirut agitated for reforms as early as the 1920s, insisting on their social, economic, private (family), and political rights. Numerous women's organizations sprang up demanding the right to education and rejecting segregation, symbolized by the veil. These organizations included religious reformers as well as secularists.

Opponents of equal rights for women supported their positions with traditionalist interpretations of the Qur'an, based on oral tradition (hadith) and medieval Qur'anic commentary (*tafsir*), according to which women are considered both mentally and morally inferior to men. Many modern Muslim reformers believe the traditional materials in question are not authentically Islamic, merely customary. These reformers stress the moral equality of the sexes in Islam and the complementarity, if not equality, of women's and men's natures. They claim that the verses stressing the dignity of women must be taken as normative.

The results of reform efforts have been varied in the Arab world. As would be expected, they have been more successful among the educated classes in urban centers than in rural areas. A number of other factors have played significant roles in efforts to elevate the status of women in the Arab countries. One of them is the nature of the country's political structure. Jordan, for example, was created as a state after World War I, with a monarchical government imposed on a tribal and predominantly rural society. Its 1991 National Charter specifies that females and males are legally equal. Nevertheless, the government has tended to rely on the support of tribal leaders, thereby strengthening their characteristic patriarchy. As a result, few specific legal reforms have been made concerning the status of women. They remain subject to the guardianship of men, including in matters related to travel and citizenship. For example, women were given the right to vote in 1974, but they may only do so through proper registration in a "family book," which is the sole province of males. The government has supported educational initiatives and has devoted portions of its planning programs to advancement of women's vocational training. As a result, literacy is increasing for both females and males, but the rate of women's illiteracy remains nearly twice that of men.

Another major factor influencing the status of women in the Arab world is the association of concern for women's rights with the West (Europe and the United States) and its colonial legacy. Algeria, for example, was colonized by France beginning in 1830 and brutally subjugated. After eight years of war, which claimed

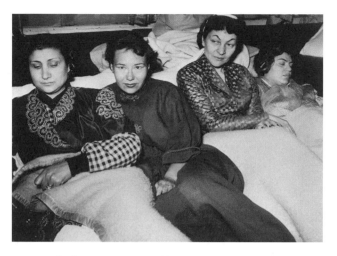

Doria Shafi, Egyptian suffrage leader (second from right), and other women suffrage activists promised to fast until their native country allowed privileges they demanded, Cairo, 21 March 1954 (UPI/Corbis-Bettmann).

nearly a million Algerian lives, Algeria received its independence in 1962. Since that time it has been under secular rule with a constitution that guarantees women's legal equality with men. Yet the bitter colonial legacy resulted in the abolition of French colonial law in 1975, including some laws improving women's status, and the reinstatement of elements considered essential to Islamic law. In 1984 a new "family code" was passed stipulating that women must have male legal guardians and protecting polygyny.

Related to the rejection of imposed Western laws is the growing popularity of political Islam, or Islamism, a grassroots movement in existence since the 1920s, determined to purge the Muslim world of decadent foreign influences and restore an authentically Islamic framework. The first specifically Islamic women's organization was the Muslim Women's Association, founded in 1936 in Egypt by Zaynab al-Ghazali, in association with the Muslim Brotherhood, founded in 1928. Al-Ghazali rejects Western models of women's liberation and insists that Islam guarantees women's rights, including education and participation in public life. But women's primary role is in the family, a role for which they must be properly educated. The Islamist trend became dominant following the defeat of Arab forces by Israel in 1967, which represented to many the bankruptcy of Western values. The Islamist approach to women's rights stresses its superiority over other models and its uniqueness, symbolized by "Islamic dress" for women—wearing modest clothes and a headscarf.

Although to earlier generations of reformers the veil symbolized subjugation, in recent decades wearing the headscarf has become a popular symbol of Islamic identity.

The increasing popularity of Islamism has influenced legislation, as well. Egyptian women, for example, among the Arab world's most vocal reformers, were guaranteed education and labor rights and given protection against child marriages in the 1920s. Women were given the right to vote in 1956. In 1979 marriage and divorce laws were revised to protect women from arbitrary divorce and polygyny, and seats were reserved for them in parliament and provincial councils. However, opposition to President Anwar Sadat's pro-West policies tainted these reforms in the eyes of Islamists. The 1979 legislation was repealed in 1985 on constitutional grounds and protections for polygyny and men's right to divorce were reinstated.

Nevertheless, the dominant trends in Arab society are increasing urbanization, improved literacy rates, and agitation for democratic reforms. As they have elsewhere in the world, these factors will undoubtedly result in greater autonomy for women, as will heightened awareness of Qur'anic teaching about the dignity of women.

BIBLIOGRAPHY

Ahmed, Leila. *Women and Gender in Islam: Historical Roots of a Modern Debate.* 1992.

Amin, Qasim. *Al-A'mal al-Kamilah li Qasim Amin.* Edited by Muhammad Amara. 1976. The complete works of the leading turn-of-the-century Egyptian advocate of the emancipation of women.

Fernea, Elizabeth W., and Basima Q. Bezirgan, eds. *Middle Eastern Muslim Women Speak.* 1977. Voices of contemporary Arab Muslim women, including both religious and secularist viewpoints.

Haddad, Yvonne Y., and John L. Esposito, eds. *Islam, Gender, and Social Change.* 1998. Discusses the impact of Islamic resurgence on the status of women.

Hoffman, Valerie. "An Islamic Activist: Zaynab al-Ghazali." In *Women and the Family in the Middle East.* Edited by E. W. Fernea. 1985. Interview with leading Egyptian Islamist advocate of women's empowerment.

Mernissi, Fatima. *Beyond the Veil: Male-Female Dynamics in a Modern Muslim Society.* 1976.

———. *Women and Islam: An Historical and Theological Enquiry.* Translated by Mary Jo Lakeland. 1991. Interpretation by leading Moroccan feminist sociologist, considered secularist by Islamists.

Smith, Jane I., ed. *Women in Contemporary Muslim Society.* 1980.

Zuhur, Sherifa. *Revealing Revealing: Islamist Gender Ideology in Contemporary Egypt.* 1992.

See also **Islamist Modern Movements.**

TAMARA SONN

In Iran and Turkey

The impact of Islam on women and women's relationship to Islam in Turkey and Iran is shaped by specific histories of Islam, particular Islamic thinkers, and varying traditions in local areas, as well as each state's position on religious matters. Sunni Islam (primarily the Hanafi legal tradition), which does not approve of *mut'a* (temporary) marriage, predominates in Turkey, whereas Shiite Islam (the Jafari school of legal tradition), which does allow for *mut'a* marriage, predominates in Iran. However, minority sects of Islam, particularly the Alevi, are sizable in eastern Turkey and also, apparently, in western Iran. In Iran and among the Alevi, the Nahjul Balagha (collected sermons and writings of the Prophet's son-in-law Ali) is an important religious source; and the *sayyed* distinction (as a descendant of the Prophet Muhammad) carries status even for women. The Turkish state has had a noticeably greater emphasis on secularism, whereas the Iranian state (under the Islamic Republic) has more actively promulgated implementation of religious law (such as insistence on *hejab*, or female covering) and increased religious instruction in Iranian schools. In Iran there is also more participation by women in debates about women and religious law.

Historically, explication of women's theological and social status in Islam has been drawn mainly from readings of prominent religious texts like the Qur'an or hadith; from male interpreters of religious law; and even, occasionally, from travel accounts by Europeans. An interest in recuperating women's perspectives has led to reassessments of texts and new attention to women's participation in social practice and ritual life; several studies examine the ambiguity of women's position, changing religious interpretations regarding their obligations and legal rights in divorce, marriage and property control, and their ability to influence the application of codified religious law (Sonbol, 1996; Haeri, 1986; Tabari and Yeganeh, 1982).

Women are obliged to fulfill the basic duties or five pillars of Islam (including *namaz*, or ritual prayers) and are considered equal in the eyes of God. Yet, in the popular view, their religious rites and position are generally considered inferior to those of men, and they can expect different receptions in the afterlife. This is due partly to the importance placed on purity concerns in worship; women's bodily impurities can negate the merit of their acts of devotion and necessitate ritual purification (*ghosl* in Iran; *aptes* in Turkey). In some cases women are expected to be more faithful in observance, as in keeping the fast, because their assigned tasks and relegation to the household are said to allow them this "luxury." Traditionally women have had less access to literacy, formal religious schooling, mosque activities, and, most important, to making *tafsir* (legal opinions and interpretations). Women do often preside at women's religious meetings, celebrations, or Qur'an classes as teachers, readers, or preachers and can achieve religious status (like Mashhadi, Haci, Haji) for completing pilgrimages to important shrine cities, but they have had little access to positions of formal religious authority. Women occasionally have gained unofficial recognition in Turkey as mullahs (low-ranking religious clerics) and in Iran as *mojtahed*s (high-ranking religious clerics) by giving and writing legal opinions; but they are not allowed to accumulate followers, which is important to achieving individual prominence. Other female religious specialists, like healers or those who prepare amulets, hold an especially ambiguous status on the margins of Islam.

Women are central to many community ritual occasions, making arrangements and preparing foods for weddings or during the Shiite Ashura ritual enactment of Hossein's martyrdom (*taziyeh* or *shabih*s in western Iran), although they are usually only observers in the public celebrations surrounding the latter events. Because many women's religious practices are conducted privately in the home and designated as less formal than men's, many of the references to women in Islam are found in general texts on social life. Wishes or desires (*niyet, niyat* in parts of Iran; *dilek* in Turkey) for specific favors such as passing an exam or finding a husband and religious vows (*nazr* in Iran; *adak* in Turkey) often result in hosting *sofreh* (ritual meals) or *rowzeh* or *mersiyeh* (recitations of the martyrdom of Imam Hossein) in Iran and *mevlud, mevlüt* (recitation of the narrative of Muhammad's life) in Turkey; these practices can involve ritual crying and are usually but not always sex segregated. Women in both countries seek religious merit (*sevab, savab*) through pilgrimage to local shrines (*zayarat, ziaret*). Although there is a major Shiite shrine dedicated to the sister of the eighth Imam Reza, Ma'sumeh does not become as important a hagiographical source for emulation as do other Islamic women like, in Iran, Fatima, Zeynab, and Khadija, and, in Turkey, Ayse.

Women's access to and engagement with religious knowledge depends on class, urban or rural residence, personal religiosity, and sectarian differences. For example, *Mevlud* is recited for funerals in Turkish villages

Two Iranian women in traditional black veils visit the Jame Mosque in Yazd, Iran (Nazima Kowall/Corbis).

(Delaney, 1991) but wider uses are reported at marriages, circumcisions, and festivals (Olson, 1994; Tapper, 1983). *Sofreh* are often secular in provincial Iran (Jamzadeh and Mills, 1986) but predominantly religious in urban areas (Betteridge, 1993). Although observances such as fasting and prayers have been infrequent in nomadic groups like the Shahsavan and Shiite Qashqa'i, among whom women do not inherit property, women exercise control over rituals associated with life cycle events and persist in alms-giving and pilgrimage activities (Tapper, 1978; Beck, 1978). There are indications that women may also enjoy more social integration with men in the religious practices of some Sufi groups. In addition, the Islamic revival of the late twentieth century has had a decided impact on women's social and religious lives, generating significant controversy over women's behaviors (Acre, 1991; Haeri, 1993).

BIBLIOGRAPHY

Acre, Feride. "Women in the Ideology of Islamic Revivalism in Turkey: Three Islamic Women's Journals." In *Islam in Modern Turkey, Religion, Politics and Literature in a Secular State.* Edited by Richard Tapper. 1991.

Bauer, Janet. "Sexuality and the Moral 'Construction' of Women in an Islamic Society." *Anthropological Quarterly* 58 (1985): 120–129.

Beck, Lois. "Women among Qashqa'i Nomadic Pastoralists in Iran." In *Women in the Muslim World.* Edited by Lois Beck and Nikki Keddie. 1978.

Betteridge, Ann. "Women and Shrines in Shiraz." In *Everyday Life in the Muslim Middle East.* Edited by Donna Bowen and Evelyn Early. 1993.

Delaney, Carol. *The Seed and the Soil: Gender and Cosomology in Turkish Village Society.* 1991.

Ferdows, Adele, and Amir Ferdows. "Women in Shi'i Fiqh: Images through the Hadith." In *Women and Revolution in Iran.* Edited by Guity Nashat. 1983.

Friedl, Erika. "Ideal Womanhood in Postrevolutionary Iran." In *Mixed Blessings: Gender and Religious Fundamentalism Cross Culturally.* Edited by Judy Brink and Joan Mencher. 1996.

Good, Mary-Jo DelVecchio. "A Comparative Perspective on Women in Provincial Iran and Turkey." In *Women in the Muslim World.* Edited by Lois Beck and Nekki Keddie. 1978.

Haeri, Shala. "Obedience versus Autonomy: Women and Fundamentalism in Iran and Pakistan." In *Fundamentalisms and Society.* Edited by Martin Marty and R. Scott Appleby. 1993.

Kadioglu, Ayce. "Women's Subordination in Turkey: Is Islam Really the Villain?" *The Middle East Journal* 48 (Fall 1994): 645–660.

Kamalkhani, Zahra. "Women's Everyday Religious Discourse in Iran." In *Women in the Middle East: Perceptions, Realities, and Struggles for Liberation.* Edited by Haleh Afshar. 1993.

Mahdavi, Shireen. "The Position of Women in Shi'a Iran: Views of the 'Ulama." In *Women and the Family in the Middle East: New Voices of Change.* Edited by Elizabeth Fernea. 1985.

Marcus, Julie. *A World of Difference: Islam and Gender Hierarchy in Turkey.* 1992.

Mir-Hosseini, Ziba. "Women and Politics in Post-Khomeini Iran: Divorce, Veiling and Emerging Feminist Voices." In *Women and Politics in the Third World.* Edited by Haleh Afshar. 1996.

Olson, Emelie. "The Use of Religious Symbol Systems and Ritual in Turkey: Women's Activities at Muslim Saints' Shrines." *The Muslim World* 84 (July–October, 1994): 202–216.

Tabari, A., and N. Yeganeh. *Women in the Shadow of Islam: The Women's Movement in Iran.* 1982.

Tapper, Nancy. "Gender and Religion in a Turkish Town: A Comparison of Two Types of Formal Women's Gatherings." In *Women's Religious Experience: Cross-Cultural Perspectives.* Edited by Nancy Falk and Rita Gross. 1983.

———. "The Women's Subsociety among the Shahsevan Nomads of Iran." In *Women in the Muslim World.* Edited by Lois Beck and Nikki Keddie. 1978.

Tapper, Nancy, and Richard Tapper. "The Birth of the Prophet: Ritual and Gender in Turkish Islam." *Man* 22 (March, 1987): 78–92.

———. "Religion, Education and Continuity in a Provincial Town." In *Islam in Modern Turkey.* Edited by Richard Tapper. 1991.

Sonbol, Amira El Azhary. "Introduction." In *Women, the Family and Divorce Laws in Islamic History.* Edited by Amira Sonbol. 1996.

JANET L. BAUER

In Africa

This article explores the topic of women and Islamic religious traditions in Africa historically and culturally. Since Islam as locally received produced an enormous range of compromises with preexisting customs, beliefs, institutions, and practices, generalizations for the entire continent are somewhat perilous. The historical timing of Islam's appearance and methods of implantation in new regions influenced women's access to religious hierarchies, sacred knowledge, and socioreligious life in general. African women carved out considerable spaces for themselves in the realms of Sufism (i.e., Islamic mysticism) and saint cults not only as participants but also as religious exemplars and patrons. Some pious women became the focal points of local or trans-local collective rites to honor the very special living and dead; this was true, and is still true, in Africa north of the Sahara, West Africa, in the Sudan, and East Africa. For example, in the eastern Sudan today, the tomb-shrine of Sitt Maryam (d. 1952) in Sinkat is a principal pilgrimage center for followers, male and female, of the Sudanese Khatmiyya Sufi order. Finally, various late twentieth-century movements of Islamic revival and reform, often erroneously labeled "Fundamentalism," have also influenced African women's access to religious traditions, both negatively and positively.

Africa's initial contact with Islam as a conquering force came in 639 when Arab Muslim armies conquered northern Egypt from Arabia; by 700 the area from Morocco to Egypt was under Islamic rule, and Islamization of the Nile Valley began. Nevertheless, Judaism, Christianity, and local cults continued to be practiced by many inhabitants of northern Africa long after the conquests or the accompanying migrations. In the twelfth and thirteenth centuries, conversions in Nubia and the Sudanic belt to the south were effected by intermarriage between Arab bedouin immigrants and local women whose offspring inherited chieftainships through matrilineal succession. Due to East Africa's proximity to Arabia, with its holy cities of Mecca and Medina, the northern Swahili coast also boasted a Muslim merchant community from the ninth century on. In Somalia, local women played a role similar to that of the Sudan, hastening conversion and cultural-religious syncretism through marriage with Arab traders who had settled there. Before 1,000 Islam was established in sub-Saharan and West Africa—signifi-

A little girl reads the Qur'an as her fellow pupils watch in Ibadan, Nigeria (Paul Almasy/© Corbis).

cant conversions had occurred at Takrur by the late ninth century and in Goa on the Niger River by the next century. By the thirteenth century, Muslim kingdoms or statelets appeared throughout West Africa, but Islam constituted the religion of courts, warriors, and literate elites; the peasantry and countryside remained faithful to pre-Islamic African religious traditions and spiritual systems as well as inheritance customs that were usually matrilineal.

By the eighteenth century, Islamic communities and states stretched south of the Sahara from the Atlantic to the Red Sea. Until the eighteenth century, Islam was mainly introduced to sub-Saharan Africa by missionaries—often itinerant Sufis or scholars and teachers—as well as traders and merchants working the trans-Saharan trade or the east African-Arabian Sea commerce. Pilgrimage across Africa to Mecca also brought conversions since pilgrims often proselytized along their journey. Finally, the disorders accompanying the establishment of various forms of European colonial rule from the late eighteenth century on also hastened Islamization, as did numerous holy wars undertaken by Muslim scholars cum militant reformers in roughly the same period. In the late twentieth century, Islam is

the fastest-growing African religion, outpacing Christianity.

During the earliest politicomilitary conquests of Mediterranean Africa, Islam came in direct, sustained contact with Christianity and Judaism; both had strong patriarchal traditions according women subordinate status within the community of believers; descent was normally reckoned by the patrilineal principle, and most inheritance rights were accorded to males. However, in sub-Saharan Africa, where conversion occurred later, the bearers of Islam, mainly traveling teachers or merchants, often accommodated local sacra-spiritual systems as well as marriage customs and rites; this in turn shaped women's participation in communal religious observances. Conversion to Islam was frequently accomplished in stages; initial contact with the new religion meant that Africans accepted specific elements of Islamic culture and practice—dress, including various forms of veiling, food and the observance of dietary restrictions, the use of amulets, and some religious concepts. Final stages effected considerable sociolegal changes, which might entail shifts from matrilineal to patrilineal organization and communal to private ownership of property. Since women in sub-Saharan Africa have historically been the most active members of many communities in both agricultural production and trade, conversion to Islam had to accommodate that tradition. Indeed, today Muslim women in Sudanic Africa remain the most active traders and entrepreneurs.

Thus across the African continent, enormous syncretism obtained so that matrilineal succession, marriage rites, and even spirit cults—for example, the Zar cult of northern Sudan—persisted and were woven into local understandings of Islam. Freedoms accorded to women and their access to public spaces varied considerably, often in accordance with local politics. For example, Old Nubia (i.e., the lands bordering the Nile between Egypt and Ethiopia) enjoyed well-developed pre-Islamic traditions of women exercising power, which persisted into the Islamic periods. Many queens were either recognized rulers or the true powers behind the throne, and matrilineal inheritance and succession remained in force even after the wide-spread acceptance of Islam. The question of female seclusion and veiling in newly converted African communities is also exceedingly complex, and local adaptations to Islamic norms of modesty and gender roles varied considerably. For instance, in early nineteenth-century central Sudanic Africa, a political struggle erupted between different Muslim groups that placed women at the center of the debate. The Muslim king of Gobir (in northwestern Nigeria) forbade veiling since it represented an emblem of puritanical Islamic reformers politically opposed to his rule. When power passed to these reformers, they objected to women's attending public preaching at the mosque and enforced veiling. Thus, depending upon region, ethnicity, and class, conversion to Islam could bring heightened sexual segregation and differing definitions of appropriate access for females in public space, which consequently might limit formal access to some communal religious celebrations.

Thus, Islam imposed socially-constructed behavior, the most visible being the segregation of male and female spaces and the high sociomoral value placed upon female modesty and chastity. While varying in time and space, Islamic norms of conduct meant that women fulfilled some duties differently from men. For example, women are required to perform five daily prayers. However, due to Islam's insistence on strict sexual segregation, females are either barred from communal services at congregational mosques, performing prayers at home instead, or participate in specially-designated spaces within the mosque.

There is no ordained clergy in Islam; however, all religious roles and functions are normally exclusive male preserves. The personnel of law courts and other religiolegal institutions can only be men. An important consequence of Islam's spread in Africa was expanded literacy, a result of the establishment of mosques, courts, and theological schools. Until the modern era, education and literacy were largely the preserve of the Muslim male hierarchy, although imparting the fundamentals of Islamic learning to elite women was not uncommon. In some African societies, upper-class women were tutored at home, where they memorized the Qur'an and mastered Islamic texts. Women, excluded from formal enrollment in theological colleges and mosque-schools, nevertheless attained advanced levels of erudition. One striking example was the sister of a Muslim ruler in northern Nigeria, Nana Asma'u (1793–1865), who composed a huge corpus of religious works although she was schooled at home. The movement to reform and modernize Islam, particularly in regard to female status and rights, came in the late nineteenth century. Formal education became a high priority, with the goal of instructing women in Islamic knowledge and values so that they would be better mothers and citizens.

In this regard, there exist compelling female exemplars, especially from the prophet Muhammad's era (570–632). Muhammad's daughter, Fāṭima, is exalted by all Muslims as a pious virgin and the perfect embodiment of womanhood. Biographical collections, an extensive literature composed by male scholars from the ninth century on, contain scattered references to female erudites, Sufis, and saints. Related to and overlap-

ping with biographical literature is hagiography, which principally celebrated saintly men but contained scattered references to pious women. However, perhaps the most beloved holy person from medieval Tunisia is the thirteenth-century female saint Lalla 'Aisha Manoubia (d. 1267), regarded as one of the patron saints of the city of Tunis and to whom are attributed numerous miracles recorded in written hagiographic works as well as transmitted through oral legends. Sitt Nasra 'Adlan (1800?–c. 1860) of Sinnar in Nilotic Sudan remains alive today in folk memory for her wise administration and her compelling political presence, which challenged both the British and Egyptian conquerors of the Muslim Funj Kingdom after 1820.

Until the present, African Muslim women's religiosity has found the greatest expression in "popular" observances and festivals preserved chiefly, but not exclusively, in oral traditions. The most visible articulation of these beliefs was the saint's shrine or Sufi lodge, whether in the village or urban quarter. Some Sufi orders admitted females as disciples, although participation was normally subject to sexual segregation. From the mid-nineteenth century on, Senegalese branches of the Tijaniyya Sufi order counted numerous female members, some of whom were accorded positions of spiritual authority within the Sufi hierarchy. The complex relationship of Muslim women to Sufism and saint veneration is illustrated by the biography of a nineteenth-century Algerian holy woman, Lalla Zaynab (1850?–1904), one of the most striking examples of a woman who was not only a member of a Sufi order but also succeeded her father as its regional leader. Zaynab enjoyed an elevated sociospiritual position due to a number of factors: she was from a saintly lineage claiming descent from the Prophet; she had achieved advanced learning; she was viewed as an exceptionally virtuous, pious woman; and finally, Zaynab's devotees, male and female, believed in her miracle-working powers. Lalla Zaynab also had access to another external source of socioreligious empowerment; she successfully defied French colonial authorities in the Sahara in a bitter dispute over her father's succession in 1897. She was revered in her lifetime as a living saint, spiritual patron, and mystic by the faithful, male and female. With her death in 1904, Zaynab's tomb-shrine became the object of collective pilgrimage and still is today. While Zaynab's story appears somewhat unusual, this may be attributable to the relative lack of research devoted to women in African Islam during the past. Nevertheless, Zaynab's biography, and those of others like her, indicates that women as much as men played a determining role in how Islam was locally interpreted and lived throughout the African continent.

BIBLIOGRAPHY

Ahmed, Leila. *Women and Gender in Islam.* 1992.

Boyd, Jean. *The Caliph's Sister: Nana Asma'u, 1793–1865: Teacher, Poet, and Islamic Leader.* 1989.

———. *The Works of Nana Asma'u (1792–1865).* 1983.

Badron, Margot. *Feminists, Islam, and Nation: Gender and the Making of Modern Egypt.* 1995.

Beck, Lois, and Nikki R. Keddie, eds. *Women in the Muslim World.* 1978.

Berkey, Jonathan. *The Transmission of Knowledge in Medieval Cairo.* 1992.

Boddy, Janice Patricia. *Wombs and Alien Spirits: Women, Men, and the Zar Cult in Northern Sudan.* 1989.

Callaway, Barbara, and Lucy Creevey. *The Heritage of Islam: Women, Religion, and Politics in West Africa.* 1994.

Clancy-Smith, Julia. "The House of Zainab: Female Authority and Saintly Succession in Colonial Algeria." In *Women in Middle Eastern History: Shifting Boundaries in Sex and Gender.* Edited by Nikki R. Keddie and Beth Baron. 1991.

Hambly, Gavin R. C., ed. *Women in the Medieval Islamic World: Power, Patronage, and Piety.* 1998.

Kenyon, Susan M. *Five Women of Sennar.* 1991.

Mernissi, Fatima. *Beyond the Veil: Male-Female Dynamics in Modern Muslim Society.* 1987.

———. "Women, Saints, and Sanctuaries." *Signs* 3 (1977): 101–112.

Ruete, Emily. *Memoirs of an Arabian Princess from Zanzibar.* Introduction by Patricia W. Romero. 1996.

Roded, Ruth. *Women in Islamic Biographical Collections From Ibn Sa'd to Who's Who.* 1992.

Rosander, Eva Evers, and David Westerlund, eds. *African Islam and Islam in Africa.* 1997.

Strobel, Margaret. *Muslim Women in Mombasa, 1890–1975.* 1979.

Tucker, Judith. *Women in Nineteenth-Century Egypt.* 1985.

Zuhur, Sherifa. *Revealing Reveiling: Islamist Gender Ideology in Contemporary Egypt.* 1992.

JULIA CLANCY-SMITH

In Asia

More adherents of Islam live in Asia than in any other part of the world. With its origin in seventh-century Arabia, Islam spread through Asia, appearing in South and Central Asia in about the tenth century and in Southeast Asia in the fifteenth century. Asian Islam experienced several forms of colonialism, including British in South Asia, Russian and Chinese in Central Asia, and British and Dutch in Southeast Asia, with independence throughout ensuing in the twentieth century. Today Muslims predominate in the nations of Afghanistan, Pakistan, Bangladesh, Indonesia, and Malaysia and represent substantial populations in India and former Soviet Central Asia (including Kazakhstan, Turkmenistan, Kirgizstan, and Uzbetistan), as well as minority groups in China, Taiwan, and the Philippines.

The impact of Islam on Asian women depends on the histories of the conversions of various populations, the preexisting religious traditions, and the dominant forms of social organization, economic production, and related sexual divisions of labor. Religious backdrops to conversion to Islam provide syncretistic possibilities and have included Hinduism and Buddhism in South Asia, shamanism and animism in Central Asia, and Hinduism and animism in Southeast Asia. While Islam has encouraged or mandated female seclusion and sexual segregation, reliance on female participation in agricultural, trading, and other activities, particularly in Southeast Asia, have compromised this important religio-cultural practice.

The importation of Shari'a, or religious law, into Asia and its intersection with indigenous customary law has shaped the civil and religious status of women; so, too, has the dissemination of a social construct of women, an important communal symbol of religious and social ethics in Muslim society. These issues have been addressed in various legal reform movements pertaining to personal and family status law of great significance to women throughout colonial, and now independent Asian Islamic states. In this century women have been at the center of debate between secularism and Islamization and play a pivotal role in the dual crises of the identity of an Islamic society and the legitimacy of competing political discourses. Some confusion in gender relations has resulted from the competition between the gender imagery and social contract contained in the Qur'an and the norms of changing civil society.

There is no single pattern of Islamic belief and practice for Muslim women in Asia. Significant to the assimilation of Islam throughout Asia were missionary activities dominated by Sufism, a more personalistic and less legalistic aspect of Islam emphasizing, for example, saints' cults and pilgrimage. For the most part, women have been restricted from advanced formal religious education and participation in formal religious institutions. Ritual exclusion of women stems from both patterns of sexual segregation and laws of ritual impurity. However, segregation provides the opportunity for women among themselves to engage in life-cycle ceremonies, participate in Sufi organizations, lead prayer gatherings and readings of the Qur'an, engage in spirit

Girls practice aerobics in the courtyard of their Muslim madrasa school in the Menteng area of Jakarta, Indonesia, 1995 (Sergio Dorantes/© Corbis).

healing, and go on pilgrimages to saints' tombs and shrines. To the extent that women engage in relatively unregulated religious activities, they have been able to acquire sacred authority. Restrictions on religious literacy have not precluded Muslim women from constructing meaningful religious lives, although salvation and virtue have been linked to stereotypical gender roles that stipulate different ethical capabilities of men and women. These restrictions, however, exist in conjunction with pragmatic issues, such as the need for female labor outside the home, and in tandem with indigenous custom that can either reinforce or question the stereotypes. In South Asia, compared with Southeast Asia, the concept of separate sexual spheres has prevailed more forcefully, with a moral division of labor relegating women to the domestic or private sphere and defining them according to their kinship connections with men. In Southeast Asia indigenous custom as well as a higher female participation of women in secular education has somewhat eroded traditional Islamic gender stereotypes.

Recent periods of rapid social change throughout Muslim Asia highlight the discourse about women and the relationship between codes of behavior derived from Islamic goals and principles and those from secular goals. The issue of veiling has become a focus and complex aspect of debate among women and between men and women, and makes central the role of religious ideology in the mesh of personal and political concerns. In all Muslim Asian societies religiously defined modesty and clothing for women sends unmistakable messages. For many women the adoption of Islamic dress and affiliation with Islamism can represent the affirmation of meaningful ethical and cultural customs under conditions of rapid social change. Thus, Western models of modernity are challenged with a so-called resurgence of veiling, particularly among middle-class women. In Indonesia, veiling represents a new historical consciousness in which women try to forge meaningful modern lives in non-Western terms. In Malaysia, Islamic ways of dress for middle-class women are borrowed from Middle Eastern traditions and represent a form of religious nationalism and assertion of class interests.

In all Muslim countries questions of male and female identity, of family roles, and of the place of women in society are grappled with both on an individual level and at the intersection of state, religion, and society. A small movement of educated, professional women in Malaysia, the Sisters in Islam, is concerned with male bias in family law courts and questions historic male hegemony in the interpretation of the Qur'an. In Pakistan and Afghanistan, previous legal reforms significant to female status, such as divorce rights and legitimate age for marriage, have been rescinded under Islamization pressures. In Bangladesh, women are a pivotal issue in the assessment of Islamic versus Bengali values in determining national identity. Likewise in India, Muslim women have become crucial symbols of communal identity in the face of the majority Hindu population. Here, as elsewhere, the religious justification of male control over women becomes part of a wider political agenda.

Throughout Muslim Asia, there is a tension between Islam as an expression of a global, noncommunal identity versus the expression of either minority or majority nationalistic identity. Women are at the core of this tension at all levels, from the local to the national, between Islam (of varying degrees of strictness) and local custom and between religious and secular discourses about the capacities and rights of women. How this tension plays out in various Asian locales demonstrates both the power of Islamic gender ideology and the possibility of malleability in the context of different cultural backgrounds and religio-political agendas. As in the Muslim Middle East, women in Muslim Asia remain a source of debate between competing political factions about access to religious and secular arenas. Women's participation in this debate is varied, but necessary, if they are to articulate for themselves spiritual and otherwise meaningful Islamic paradigms.

BIBLIOGRAPHY

Jeffrey, Patricia. *Frogs in a Well: Indian Women in Purdah*. 1979.

Jones, Gavin W. *Marriage and Divorce in Islamic South-East Asia*. 1994.

Kandiyoti, Deniz, ed. *Women, Islam and the State.* 1991.

Mandelbaum, David G. *Women's Seclusion and Men's Honor: Sex Roles in North India, Bangladesh, and Pakistan.* 1988.

Nagata, Judith. "How to Be Islamic Without Being an Islamic State: Contested Models of Development in Malaysia." In *Islam, Globalization and Postmodernity.* Edited by Akbar S. Ahmed and Hastings Donnar. 1994.

Ong, Aihwa, and Michael Peletz. *Bewitching Women, Pious Men: Gender and Body Politics in Southeast Asia.* 1995.

Papanek, Hanna, and Gail Minault, eds. *Separate Worlds: Studies of Purdah in South Asia.* 1982.

Pillsbury, Barbara L. K. "Being Female in a Muslim Minority in China." In *Women in the Muslim World.* Edited by Lois Beck and Nikki Keddie. 1988.

Wazir, Jahan Karim. *Women and Culture: Between Malay Adat and Islam.* 1992.

CARROLL McC. LEWIN

In Europe

Muslims in Europe represent a range of background and national identities. Their numbers have been growing steadily over the course of this century and now form significant populations in a number of European countries.

The first small immigrant Muslim communities emerged in Ruthia and Poland in the fourteenth century (Tatars), then Moguls arrived in the eighteenth century, mainly as soldiers in the Prussian army in the 1730s and in France and Austria. Later immigrants came from the former colonies: Maghrebians to France after 1920, Indo-Muslims to Britain, and Indonesians to the Netherlands after World War II. Since the late 1950s nearly two million Turks have come to Germany, where they have worked primarily in industries recovering from the war. Sizable groups of immigrants, mainly laborers, reside in several Western and middle European countries. Political turmoil in various parts of the Muslim world has resulted in greatly increased immigration to Western Europe, specifically the Iranian revolution of 1979, the first Gulf War in 1980, and growing political pressures in various Arab countries. The end of the twentieth century has seen Muslims leaving Pakistan, Afghanistan, Bosnia, and Albania. Whereas most of the Iranian and Arab immigrants from the fifties on were atheistic intellectuals, those coming later have tended to be shaped more directly by the Sunni or Shiite Islam of their home countries.

Many Muslim immigrants are adopting measures to ensure that their customs and their rights are preserved in a non-Muslim Western culture. One of the most visible measures is the insistence of some that women and girls wear head-scarves in school and in public places to symbolize their adherence to Islam. Some Europeans oppose this requirement on the grounds that it is oppressive to women, and others because they see it as opposed to the secular foundation of the state. Nearly every Western European country has had its head-scarf controversy. For many Muslims the head-scarf both protects the dignity of Muslim women and allows them to participate in the public sphere, and also symbolizes the range of issues of concern to Muslim women in European society, among the most important of which is education.

Greater opportunity for education exists for immigrant women now than for earlier generations. At the same time many are insisting on such issues as separate education for girls, appropriate dress for athletic activities, and the refusal to study certain subjects that they feel attack Muslim values of modesty. Some are bringing their grievances to courts of law. Islamic education usually takes place in supplementary lessons at mosques or in private settings on evenings and weekends. Not all Muslims agree on what is essential for girls and women in the public sphere, with tensions among different immigrant groups or even among members of a single Muslim community sometimes as evident as those between Muslims and non-Muslim Europeans. Those among the younger generation who decide to maintain orthodox Islamic observances often stress cultural identity over and against a growing local rejection of "the foreign." Others try to forge a new European Islam by reclaiming the principle of "independent judgment" as a right of every Muslim.

Normally every ethnic (and linguistic) Muslim community has its own socioreligious life. Women unite in groups for sociocultural and religious identity and support. Many express their convictions through participation in religious activities particularly designed for women, such as feasts and special sessions for Qur'an readings. Some play active roles in helping to interpret Islam to an often hostile European society. Growing economic problems contribute to anti-Muslim feelings, and often Islam is particularly criticized for its treatment of women as a result of such media presentations as the film "Not Without My Daughter," which intensified an anti-Islamic position on women's issues in many parts of Western Europe. At the same time many Muslim youth, born and raised in Europe and having lost ties to the home countries of their parents, resist specific identification with Islam as a hindrance to assimilation into European culture.

Muslim communities have existed in many parts of eastern Europe since Ottoman domination from 1470 on, in countries such as Albania, Bosnia, Macedonia, Romania, Bulgaria, and Poland. Until the overthrow of Communist governments in the 1990s, religious life was restricted and sometimes, as in Bulgaria, suppressed. It appears that older women played important roles in preserving Islamic traditions in those countries, traditions that are now being actively revived. Muslims have formed significant communities in European sections of the former Soviet Union. Studies about the religious life and roles of Muslim women in the Soviet period are lacking, although there are reports by the Soviet press of educational and professional paths followed by women of Muslim origin (educated, of course, as atheists).

Female European converts to Islam represent a small but committed group. These are frequently, but not exclusively, women who are married to Muslim men and feel affiliated with their husbands' ethnic, cultural, and religious identities. Several Islamic organizations, most of them Sunni, are working for the propagation of Islam in many Western European countries, especially since the late 1980s, but women are underrepresented in the movement.

Several of the teachers in the Chicago Moslem School come from Islamic countries (Hulton-Deutsch Collection/Corbis).

BIBLIOGRAPHY

Djait, Hisham. *Europe and Islam: Cultures and Modernity.* 1985.

Gerholm, T., and Y. G. Lithman, eds. *The New Islamic Presence in Europe.* 1988.

Lewis, Bernard. *Muslims in Europe.* 1994.

Nielsen, Jorgen S. *Muslims in Western Europe.* 1992.

Shaded, W. A. R., and P. S. van Koningsveld. *The Integration of Islam and Hinduism in Western Europe.* 1991.

WIEBKE WALTHER

In North America

The Muslim community in the United States and Canada is composed of members of a wide range of ethnic, national, and cultural groups. Including African Americans, immigrants from numerous countries, and white converts, it is the most diverse Muslim population in the world. Muslim women in the North American context thus have to contend with issues of identity relating to culture and ethnic origin as well as religion and gender.

As they affirm their affiliation with Islam, some North American Muslim women espouse a more conservative or traditional understanding of their roles and obligations. Others attempt to interpret scripture and tradition so as to be able to assume the full participation in family and society that they believe is legitimately theirs under the Islamic system. Those who identify themselves as feminists are clear that their understanding of the term does not necessarily coincide with that of many Western feminist thinkers.

The multicultural nature of Islam in North America has been celebrated as proof of the uniting force of the religion. In certain cases, however, diversity can complicate efforts to create an integrated Muslim community. Culture and religion are close-knit, and immigrants sometimes have felt that their particular interpretation of Islam in terms of dress or custom is more authentic than that of others. New Muslims, such as some of the African American women who have opted out of mainline U.S. culture, have found Islam appealing because of its promise of equality to all believers. Although they are generally well accepted by their immigrant sisters, occasionally they find that cultural affiliations override commonality.

Muslim women as well as men are increasingly vocal about their dismay at the way in which their religion is portrayed in the media, fostering what they see as the innate prejudice most North Americans have against Islam. They have initiated efforts to counter this through education, public presentations, community information sessions, and other means in an attempt to put forth what they believe to be a more accurate portrayal of Islam. Increased attention to working within the national educational system has resulted in some opportunities for Muslim children and their parents to talk about their religion or to be allowed to celebrate their holidays.

Increasing numbers of North American Muslim women are engaged in the workforce, although some struggle with concerns over whether it is appropriate for women to be employed outside the home and what occupations are most suitable. Many feel that engagement in the public realm in which close interaction with men is often necessary is acceptable if women wear appropriately modest dress. Yet this can lead to discrimination by employers or others. Within the Muslim community itself there is a wide range of opinion as to whether wearing Islamic dress is mandatory, desirable, or unnecessary, and in what contexts it should be adopted. In general, both men and women allow these determinations to be made by individual women themselves.

A number of the specific issues faced by North American Muslim women are related to their participation in the family structure. They generally resist non-Muslim patterns of dating. Some seek husbands through the services of Muslim journals or organizations. Abortion is forbidden in Islam, but there is a range of opinion concerning birth control. The disparity between divorce laws in North America and those that obtain according to Islamic law in some other countries often causes tensions, as do the regulations and expectations concerning child custody after divorce. Because women are the primary care providers for the elderly, serious problems arise for nuclear families in which both husband and wife are employed.

Muslim women in North America have played important roles in the religious life of their respective communities throughout this century and continue to participate significantly as these communities grow, take on trained leaders, and increasingly enjoy new facilities. Many serve as the primary instructors in the faith and practice of Islam for the children of their families and congregations as well as for other women, and some are engaged in home schooling. As Islam continues to grow in North America, it appears that women will be active in helping to define the community, including expectations of all of its members, relationships between different elements of its constituency, and its presence as a visible part of the North American religious scene.

BIBLIOGRAPHY

al Faruqi, Lamya. *Women, Muslim Society and Islam.* 1988.
Haddad, Yvonne Y., ed. *The Muslims of America.* 1994.
Haddad, Yvonne Y., and Jane I. Smith, eds. *Muslim Communities in America.* 1994.
Wauge, Earle H., Sharon McIrvin Abu-Laban, and Regula Qureshi, eds. *Muslim Families in North America.* 1991.

JANE I. SMITH
YVONNE Y. HADDAD

Islamist Modern Movements

Early Western analyses described social and political movements that drew their inspiration from conservative Islam as "Islamic revival," "Islamic resurgence," "militant Islam," and "Islamic fundamentalism." They highlighted Western views of Islam as a religion: its violent nature, traditional lifestyle, and its inability to adjust to the challenges of the modern world. They also overlooked Islam's important role in the modernizing and developmental policies of the 1950s and the 1960s. This partisan view neglected mention of the many progressive interpretations of the religion utilized by different states to amend Muslim personal status laws (marriage and divorce laws) to outlaw polygyny in Tunisia and restrict the practice in Iraq, Syria, and the former South Yemen. In all these states, women were also given the equal right to file for divorce. New interpretations of the religion in socialist Egypt were used to support women's reproductive rights.

The debate on the various interpretations of Islam and the divergent political roles they played in the immediate past and present of Arab states substituted the early prominent religious emphasis with the political. This switch was reflected in the coining of the concept of Islamism now widely used to discuss these groups and their commitments. In addition to representing how these groups or movements defined themselves, Islamism established an important distinction between "official" and "oppositional" Islam. Islamism took the latter as its focus of analysis and explored the political and economic conditions that led to its rise in the 1970s and the 1980s.

Generally speaking, the students of contemporary Islamisms suggested that Islamisms were a response to the recent developmental and legitimacy crises in the region. In Egypt, Algeria, and Tunisia, they represented the diminishing ability of centrally planned economies to deliver promised economic growth, employment, and social services, which affected the prospects of the younger members of the middle classes who had been the primary beneficiaries of these regimes. Increased corruption among the ruling elites contributed to further state delegitimation. In Lebanon and in Syria, Islamism represented protest movements to the exclusion of the Shia and Sunni (the major religious division within Islam) majorities, respectively, from political power.

A young Muslim woman wears concealing black veils, Lamu, Kenya, 1974 (Owen Franken/Corbis).

Finally, state Islamization policies were used in Pakistan to distinguish the regime of General Zia ul-Haq from that of his predecessor. In Malaysia, the inclusion of Islamist activists in cabinet level positions was designed to mobilize popular support. The exclusion of Islamists from political power in many states including Indonesia, Algeria, and Tunisia, led them to serve as a voice there for opposition.

In the Persian Gulf oil producing states, the decline in oil prices along with the first (1979–1986) and second Gulf wars (1991) undermined the rising expectations of the middle classes and their confidence in the ruling elites. In response, Islamist challengers in Saudi Arabia and Kuwait launched powerful critiques of states that in theory claimed to rule in the name of Islam, but which were described as corrupt and wasteful.

The above crisis disproportionately affected the college educated young men and women of the middle classes. Unemployment, housing shortages, the decline and rising costs of medical care and education have also affected their financial ability to support families. This explained why they emerged as the earliest supporters of Islamism.

In many ways, the Islamist movements offered some women new social standards of respectability. While many within these movements supported women's right to education, they disagreed on the type of education to be pursued. Many Islamists left the nature and choice of education wide open to women. Others insisted that women's education should be connected to their primary role as caretakers. This represented a return to gender-specific education that restricted women's choices, level, and type of education.

On the question of women's work, the Islamist discourse emphasized the importance of women's domestic responsibilities. They highlighted the divinely ordained character of these roles. Most supported women's work outside of the home only in cases of "necessity," which was taken to mean economic need. Some disagreed with this view and voiced a public need for women teachers and doctors who would service other women. Finally, there were those opposed to women's public work under any condition.

The above debate encouraged young unemployed women to return to domesticity. Higher levels of unemployment among young middle-class women than among the men of this class, and women's dependence on their families due to late marriage or on husbands after marriage rationalized the status quo. Because many women continued to go to school and to work, there was considerable discussion of how to make these settings Islamically correct. Some insisted on the strict sexual segregation of men and women in places of study and work. Others emphasized the observance of modesty and Islamic modes of dress as sufficient in mixed work settings. The result was an informal separation of the sexes and an uneven change in the relations between men and women in the educational and work arenas.

Islamist women within the middle class did not share the polemical view that Islam was opposed to women's rights. They stressed that before Islam women had no rights and that Islam gave them an independent legal standing and the right—even if an unequal one—to inheritance. They justified this inequality by pointing to the fact that women have no financial responsibility for the family, which under Islamic rules was a male obligation. These women have played a variety of important roles in Islamist movements. The Egyptian Zaynab al-Ghazali was a founding member of the Muslim Brotherhood. Both she and the Brotherhood played key social and political roles in the power struggles of the 1970s and the 1980s. In Sudan, Islamist women represented the National Islamic Front in parliament. The political visibility of Islamist women in Egypt and Sudan aside, most women, who participated in these movements, served as foot soldiers. On campuses, in Islamic clinics, and in social gatherings, they have actively recruited other women into the movement by suggesting the desirability of the Islamic mode of dress and learning more about Islam. In electoral campaigns, they have distributed leaflets, campaigned for Islamist candidates among women, and cast their votes in their support.

Finally, women's widespread adoption of the Islamic mode of dress, instead of Western-style clothing, in the major cities of these states served as a visible symbol of their acceptance of Islamist social prescriptions. Since rural and urban working-class women had never abandoned their traditional clothing styles, the women who donned the new Islamic dress were largely from the middle class. They pressured older middle and upper-class women to follow the new modes of dress that became identified with religiosity and social respectability.

While the Islamic mode of dress was often misidentified as veiling, it did not require the covering of the face. Instead, it required the covering of the head and body so that only the face and the hands remain uncovered. There were some among that group who insisted on covering the face and the hands as a marker of a greater level of religiosity, but they represented a small minority. Even though there was not much discussion in the literature of the Islamic mode of dress for men, many middle class men have also replaced Western style clothing with the traditional *thob* or *Jilbab,* some type of head cover, and beards.

These new forms of dress for men and women represented new levels of religiosity in contemporary Islamic societies and the desire to adhere to religious prescriptions in one's daily life. Women's attendance at mosques (including prayers and religious discussions) rose dramatically in many states. In Egypt, some section of big mosques were designated for women. Some women have become the sheikhs of women's mosques in Jordan. In Algeria proselytizing on behalf of the Islamists was one of the few public activities in which all women could be legitimately engaged. The Egyptian state recruited women for these paying jobs.

Finally, secular feminist women reacted to the successful inroads that Islamism has made among middle-class women by developing an interest in Islamic history, religious debates, writings, and views regarding women's role within the family and society. The result were feminist interpretations of the Qur'an and hadith that were often used to support gender equality and feminist views of the history of the religion.

BIBLIOGRAPHY

Batatu, Hanna. "Syria's Muslim Brethren." *Merip Reports* no. 110 (1982): 12–20.

Bouatta, Cherifa, and Doria Cherifati-Merabtine. "The Social Representation of Women in Algeria's Islamist Movement." In *Identity Politics and Women.* Edited by Valentine M. Moghadam. 1994.

Burgat, François, and William Dowell. *The Islamic Movement in North Africa.* 1993.

Charrad, Mounira. "Repudiation Versus Divorce: Responses to State Policy in Tunisia." In *Women, the Family and Policy: A Global Perspective.* Edited by Esther N. Chow and Catherine Berheide. 1994.

Cudsi, Alexander Cudsi, and Ali E. Hillal Dessouki, eds. *Islam and Power.* 1980.

Dekmjian, R. Hrair. "The Rise of Political Islam in Saudi Arabia." *Middle East Journal* 4 (1994): 629–631.

Entellis, John P. "Islam, Democracy and the State: The Reemergence of Authoritarian Politics in Algeria." In *Islamism and Secularism in North Africa.* Edited by John Ruedy. 1996.

Esposito, John L. *The Islamic Threat.* 1995.

Esposito, John L., ed. *Islam and Development: Religion and Sociopolitical Change.* 1980.

Hale, Sondra. "Gender, Religious Identity and Political Mobilization in the Sudan." In *Identity Politics and Women.* Edited by Valentine M. Moghadam. 1994.

Hatem, Mervat F. "Egyptian Discourses on Gender and Political Liberalization: Do Secularist and Islamist Views Really Differ?" *Middle East Journal* 4 (1994): 661–676.

———. "Privatization and the Demise of State Feminism in Egypt." In *Mortgaging Women's Lives.* Edited by Pamela Sparr. 1994.

Hermassi, Abdel Baki. "The Political and the Religious in the Modern History of the Maghrib." In *Islamism and Secularism in North Africa.* Edited by John Ruedy. 1996.

Macleod, Arlene Elowe. *Accommodating Protest: Working Women, the New Veiling and Change in Cairo.* 1991.

Mernissi, Fatima. *The Veil and the Male Elite.* 1991.

Molyneux, Maxine. "Women's Rights and Political Contingency: The Case of Yemen, 1990–1994." *Middle East Journal* 3 (1995): 418–431.

Piscatori, James P., ed. *Islam in the Political Process.* 1983.

Tetreault, Mary Ann, and Haya al-Mughni. "Modernization and its Discontents: State and Gender in Kuwait," *Middle East Journal* 3 (1995): 403–417.

Wright, Robin. *Sacred Rage: The Wrath of Militant Islam.* 1995.

See also **Ghazali, Zaynab al-; Islamic Law.**

MERVAT F. HATEM

History of Study

The study of Islam began in earnest in Europe when medieval Christianity gradually lost its fear of Islam. Until the Enlightenment this study was seen as part of the discipline of theology. It was the province of men until the mid-1930s. From early on the intellectual study of Islam was closely associated with the efforts of Christian missionaries who were usually, though not always, predisposed to extremely negative interpretations.

The study of Islam has always been closely connected with the study of oriental languages, especially Arabic. After 1085 Toledo became the headquarters of the Spanish Catholic Church and for decades was a center for translation of texts from Arabic into Latin. Here in 1143 the first Latin rendering of the Qur'an was commissioned by Peter the Venerable, Abbot of Cluny, and carried out by the Benedictine astronomer Robert of Ketton. This translation was printed in Basel in 1543 by the Calvinist theologian Bibliander. The Arabic-speaking philosopher and mystic Raymond Lull found a language school for Franciscan missionaries in Majorca in 1276. During the thirteenth and fourteenth centuries a flood of anti-Islamic polemic appeared in which Islam was described as a false religion of violence and self-indulgence, with Muhammad portrayed as the Anti-Christ.

Scholarly interest in translations of Arabic scientific and philosophical works, however, continued until the sixteenth century. The Crusades and the Kingdom of Jerusalem provided an opportunity for Franks to learn first hand about Muslims, their religion, and their culture, which was in many ways clearly superior to that of the West. This occasioned several relatively objective works about the Prophet and his faith, such as Godfrey of Viterbo's twelfth-century *Universal Chronicle*. Toledan Archbishop Don Rodrigo Jimenez de Rada (1170–1247) dedicated his *Historia Arabum* to Arabic history in Spain.

With the emergence of the Ottoman Empire after the fall of Constantinople in 1453, and the renaissance and rise of humanism, Europe's thirst for knowledge about Islam increased. During the sixteenth and seventeenth centuries Arabic printing presses were set up in Rome, Venice, Paris, Leiden, and Breslau to print religious texts for Arab Christians. The first chairs for the study of Arabic and other oriental languages were established in countries with trading interest in the Near East such as England (Oxford) and the Netherlands (Leiden). With the Enlightenment, open-mindedness toward other religions increased. After the gradual decline of Ottoman power Arabic and Islamic studies gradually became separated from theology, and more objective and tolerant depictions of Islam and Muhammad appeared. Europe began to develop a fascination for things Oriental, fostered by Antoine Galland's adaptation of the *Arabian Nights* in the early eighteenth century. Islam began to be portrayed as eminently rational and tolerant. Some, such as the French Henri Boulanvilles (1658–1722) even characterized Muhammad as a heroic figure, while the German philosopher Leibniz (1646–1716) portrayed Islam as a "natural" religion.

French and British authors such as Voltaire, Montesquieu, Diderot, Hamilton, and Beckford, among others, wrote pseudo-Oriental novels that were actually intended to satirize European upper classes. It was with the growth of an objective travel literature (e.g., Tavernier, Volnay) that Islam began to be better known to the European public and that female voices were added to the descriptions of Muslims and their faith. Lady Mary Wortley Montagu, who accompanied her husband to Turkey in 1716–1718, was the first recognized woman traveler in the Near East. In her letters to real and fictive addresses, published posthumously in 1763, she gave impassioned depictions of Turkish upper-class harems, describing the amiability and happiness of their inhabitants. Following her model a number of vivid depictions of women's travel in the Middle East and the lives of Muslim women came from the pens of authors such as Hester Stanhope, Anne Blunt, Gertrude Bell, Freya Stark, and Isabelle Eberhard.

In 1795 the first chair of Arabic was instituted at the School of Living Oriental Languages in Paris under Professor Silvestre de Sacy, under whom Orientalists from many European nations studied. Russia's colonial interests in Central Asia led to the founding of the Faculty of Oriental Studies in St. Petersburg in 1850. By the nineteenth century, then, Islamic studies had become accepted as a formal scholarly discipline. Arabic grammars and dictionaries were published, numerous manuscripts were edited and printed, and a variety of Oriental societies were founded in places such as Paris, London, and Leipzig. The developing colonialism facilitated access to Islamic countries, and as more source materials became available in print in Arabic, Persian, and Turkish, Islam began to be studied as a sociocultural phenomenon.

The study of Islam as a field of science of religion began with the work of the Hungarian Ignaz Goldziher (1850–1921) and the Dutch Arendt J. Wensinck (1882–1939). Numerous scholars from a range of countries and disciplines contributed to the first edition of the *Encyclopedia of Islam* (1913–1942), whose second edition, begun in 1960, features an even greater range of contributors. Before World War I European and American Orientalists were interested primarily in classical Islam and philology. After World War II, encouraged by the growing political and economic importance of the Middle East and other Muslim countries, the range of study has broadened greatly and includes many more sociological and anthropological investigations, as well as works on Sufism and popular religion, including a variety of studies on women's religious roles and practices and their role in social and cultural history.

Women emerged as serious scholars of Islam after their admission to university study became possible. Else Reitemeyer of Germany began to learn Arabic as a guest at Rome University after traveling in the Near East in the late 1800s. She published her first book about Arab geographers in 1903 and finished her Ph.D. in Heidelberg in 1912. Hilma Grinquist of Finland in the 1920s was the first scholar to do systematic ethnographic research among Palestinian women and children. In the next decade two German Jewish emigrants, Sara Kohn of Leiden and Gertrude Stern of London, published their doctoral work on gender studies. Ilse Lichtenstädter, who after 1960 taught classical Arabic literature at Harvard University, finished her German doctorate on old Arabic love poetry in 1931. One of the best known of women scholars writing about women in Muslim history was the Iraqi Christian Nabia Abbott, professor of Islamic Studies at the University of Chicago from 1949 to 1963.

Over the last half of the twentieth century, and particularly from the 1970s through the 1990s, the study of Islam by women and of women in Islam by both males and females has virtually exploded. A range of women scholars are studying various aspects of Islam, from Annemarie Schimmel on piety and mysticism to Ana Lambton on Persian history to Laura Veccia Vaglieri on Shiite Islam to Yvonne Haddad on political Islam to Jane Dammen McAuliffe and Barbara Stowasser on Qur'an and hadith to name only a few. Many women, and some men, both Muslim and non-Muslim are investigating issues related specifically to women in Islam. Their works deal with women in Qur'an and hadith and in Islamic history, with the particular circumstances of women in a variety of Muslim contexts, with theory and practice, with politics and social movements, and with the religious practices that have been particular to women since the earliest days. These studies cover a range of disciplines, many of them reflecting new contextual work in the field of social anthropology. Increasingly, Muslim women themselves are taking the lead in analyzing issues of culture, politics, and women's rights, as well as writing polemical literature in defense of the faith. A few, such as Zaynab al-Ghazali from Egypt, Riffat Hasan, Amina Wadud, and Aziza al-Hibri, are interpreting Qur'an and tradition from an Islamic feminist perspective.

BIBLIOGRAPHY

HISTORY OF ISLAMIC AND ORIENTAL STUDIES

Fück, Johann W. *Die arabischen Studien in Europa bis in den Anfang des 20, Jahrhunderts.* 1955.
Hourani, Albert. *Islam in European Thought.* 1991.

Rodinson, Maxime. *Europe and the Mystique of Islam* ("La Fascination de l'Islam" [1980]). Translated by Roger Veinus. 1987.
Waardenburg, Jacques D. *Mustashriḳūn* ("Orientalists"). In *The Encyclopaedia of Islam.* Vol. 7. 1992..
Watt, W. Montgomery. *The Influence of Islam on Medieval Europe.* 1972.

On women's travelogues, see:

Melman, Billie. *Women's Orients: English Women and the Middle East, 1718–1918: Sexuality, Religion and Work.* 1992.

No work on women's scholarship in the field of Islamic or Oriental studies has been published. Important works by women include:

Abbott, Nabia. *'Ā'ishah the Beloved of Muḥammad.* 1942. Reprint, 1972.
———. *Two Queens of Baghdad: Mother and Wife of Hārūn al-Rashīd.* 1946. Reprint, 1974.
———. "Women and the State in Early Islam." *Journal of Near Eastern Studies* 1 (1942): 106–126, 341–368.
Granquist, Hilma. *Birth and Childhood in a Palestinian Village.* 1947.
———. *Child Problems among the Arabs.* 1950.
———. *Marriage Conditions in a Palestinian Village.* 2 vols. 1931, 1935.
———. *Muslim Death and Burial: Customs and Traditions Studied in a Village in Jordan.* 1965.
Kohn, Sara. *Die Eheschließung im Koran.* 1934.
Lichtenstädter, Ilse. "Das Nasīb in der altarabischen Qaside." *Islamica* 5 (1932): 17–96.
Reitemeyer, Else. *Beiträge zur arabisch-islamischen Geographie. Nachdruck ihrer Schriften aus den Jahren 1903, 1912 und 1932.* Edited by Fuat Sezgin. 1988.
Stern, Gertrude. *Marriage in Early Islam.* 1939.

BIOGRAPHICAL ARTICLES

Gabrieli, Francesco. "Laura Veccia Vaglieri, 1893–1989." *Orientalisti del Novecento.* 1993. Pp. 173–178.
———. "Victoria Vacca di Bosis, 1891–1988." *Orientalisti del Novecento.* 1993. Pp. 167–172.
Mahdi, Muhsin. "Nabia Abbott." *Journal of Near Eastern Studies* 40 (1981): 163–172. Includes a bibliography of her works by M. Krek, completed some months before her death.
Schimmel, Annemarie. "Ilse Lichtenstädter, 1901–1991." *Die Welt des Islams.* 1992.

WIEBKE WALTHER

Islamic Law

Islamic law is one of several ancient Near Eastern "theocratic" legal systems in which law is an integral component of a religious system disclosed by a deity to a prophet, whose revelations are later written down and edited as a sacred scripture containing the word of God. Theocratic law is highly resistant to modification or repeal because of the dogma that only God, and not man, can abrogate God's laws.

Muslims believe that the doctrines and practices of Islam were revealed by God to the prophet Muhammad in the Qur'an. Religious scholars called *'ulamā'* (sages) and *fuqahā'* (jurists) formulate laws based on interpretations of the Qur'an and the *sunna* (the Prophet's practice); judges with the title of *qāḍī* (decisor) administer the body of Islamic law known as Shari'a in special religious courts. It is noteworthy that Islamic law evolved in a process virtually identical to its closest historical cousin, Talmudic law. The striking similarity in structure and content reflects cultural interaction among Arabs and Jews in pre-Islamic times as well as the fact that both systems developed predominantly in the same milieu, namely Iraq—Jewish law from the third to sixth centuries and Islamic law from the eighth to tenth centuries. Both systems were subsequently further elaborated by generations of scholars in a process that continues to this day (Wegner, 1982b).

Four important schools of Islamic jurisprudence have survived with some variations in the laws, and the penetration of Islam into non-Arab regions led to the incorporation of some indigenous customs. The rules thus vary somewhat from place to place. A significant aspect of any culture's worldview is its perception of women and their social role. Like all legal systems, the Shari'a mirrors the social realities of the society in which it emerged. Except where explicitly changed by Qur'anic texts and interpretations, women's rights continued largely to reflect the legal status of women in sixth-century pre-Islamic Arabian culture, but in medieval times, Muslim women became progressively more confined by law and custom to the seclusion of the home (Coulson, 1964; Smith, 1985).

THE PRIVATE DOMAIN

Most Western countries (even those with an official state religion) practice separation of church and state and do not compel their citizens to follow religious laws of marriage and divorce, but most Muslim countries (even those with Western-style civil and criminal codes) still retain Islamic law in matters affecting personal status. Shari'a laws governing women deal mainly with marriage, divorce, and related topics like child custody, women's inheritance rights, and regulations about veiling or seclusion; contemporary Muslim feminists interpret the Qur'an's veiling provisions (sura 24:31) less rigorously, claiming that these practices were not indigenous to Arabia but entered Islam through foreign influence (Mernissi, 1987, 1991; Ahmed, 1992).

The Shari'a defines and restricts the status of women in both the private and public cultural domains. Like all known legal systems prior to the late twentieth century, Islamic law is patriarchal in its stance, viewing women as most appropriately confined to the private sphere of home and family and defining their status by reference to men who are their legal guardians (sura 4:2). A girl begins life as her father's daughter (if he dies, she becomes the ward of a close male relative). The father or guardian must approve her marriage partner and often arranges her marriage to a man of his choice, though her consent is required in principle. The nuptials take place pursuant to a marriage settlement drawn up by her father and the bridegroom, who agree on a specified sum as brideprice, the *mahr*.

From a formal, legal perspective, the Muslim bride (like the Jewish bride) is treated as an object of acquisition: "nothing so resembles a sale as does marriage" (Malik, medieval founder of the Maliki School of Jurisprudence, cited in D. Santilla, *Istituzioni di Diritto Musulmano Malichita*, vol. 1 [1926], p. 214. Cf. the Jewish mishnaic rules for acquiring a wife and other property in Mishnah Qiddushin 1:1–4). This is why Islamic divorce (like Jewish divorce) is effected by a unilateral act of release by the husband (Wegner, 1982a). The Muslim husband must recite a prescribed formula, the *ṭalāq* (often translated "repudiation" but literally meaning "release"), on three separate occasions (sura 2:229) to preclude an impulsive divorce that he may later regret. In the late twentieth century, some Muslim countries placed additional curbs on arbitrary divorce by interpreting the Qur'anic prescription to "let her go with kindness" (sura 2:231) as requiring the husband to pay his divorcée a sum at least equivalent to a year's maintenance. Child custody rules vary from place to place, but generally favor the husband, since Islamic law treats children as the father's (and not the mother's) property.

The Qur'an permits polygyny (though not polyandry), allowing a maximum of four wives, plus any concubines recruited from among a man's slaves (sura 4:3). Today, slavery has been abolished in most Muslim countries and concubinage is rare. Polygyny, though permitted, is not a religious requirement; because (sura 4:3) forbids a man to take more wives than he can reasonably support, or to take more than one unless he can treat all his wives with fairness and equality, the practice has become the exception rather than the norm. After gaining independence from colonial powers in midcentury, some Islamic states (Algeria, Egypt, Iraq, Jordan, Morocco, Syria, Tunisia), enacted reforms based on reinterpretation of Qur'anic rules; and the power to decide such questions now often resides with the *qāḍī* in a Shari'a court rather than with the husband (Esposito, 1982; Coulson, 1964; Coulson and Hinchcliffe, 1978). Also, some schools permit a first wife to stipulate that the husband will take no other wife without her consent, but illiterate Muslim women do not know of this right and thus rarely exercise it.

It is clear that in principle Islamic law treats women as persons and not mere chattel. However, in Islam (as in all legal systems prior to the twentieth century) men enjoy more rights and powers and therefore a higher status than women (sura 2:228; 4:34). Muslim women, whether or not subject to a husband, possess both rights and responsibilities. Within marriage, a wife's rights are clearly defined—most notably, she is entitled to her *mahr* in return for dedicating her sexual and reproductive function exclusively to her husband's use, and also to *nafaqa* (maintenance by the husband) in return for accepting the status of *iḥtibās* (custody, restraint). Interestingly, as in other ancient Near Eastern laws (and in striking contrast to Western legal systems prior to the nineteenth century), a wife retains ownership of any property she brings to the marriage or later inherits from her parents. By Qur'anic law (sura 4:11), daughters inherit half as much as do sons.

A woman "released" by widowhood or divorce from subjection to a husband has a higher level of personhood; she can legally manage her own property, transact business, make contracts, and make her own decisions concerning remarriage. Rich widows could be found even in pre-Islamic Arabia (for instance, the Prophet's first and only wife until her death after a twenty-five year marriage was the wealthy widow Khadija, fifteen years his senior).

THE PUBLIC DOMAIN

No matter what rights and powers a woman may possess in the private domain of Islamic law, her status in the public cultural domain is virtually that of nonentity. By some interpretations, she may not even leave the house without her husband's permission, express or implied; if she does go out, in most Muslim countries she must either veil or cloak herself in accordance with varying interpretations of the Qur'anic law on this topic (sura 24:31, 60). At the end of the twentieth century, veiling and other restrictions on women were most severe in Iran, Pakistan, and Afghanistan—none of which,

incidentally, is an Arab state; thus the interpretation of Islamic law in those countries may well reflect other cultural concerns besides those of Islam.

In matters of religious observance, women are bound to observe those four of the five main duties ("pillars") of Islam which can be performed in the privacy of the home: declaration of Muslim faith, daily prayer (sura 2:43), almsgiving (sura 2:43), and fasting (sura 2:183–185). The fifth pillar, hajj (pilgrimage), incumbent on men (sura 2:196), is not obligatory for women, since it entails traveling in the public domain, thus requiring the husband's consent and the company of a suitable chaperone. Similarly, women are not required, or even expected, to attend Friday communal worship in the mosque; in some countries, such as Pakistan, this is discouraged or even proscribed by custom. As in other traditional or conservative religions (such as Catholicism, Mormonism, evangelical Christianity, and Orthodox Judaism), a Muslim woman's opportunities for participation in the public religious domain of communal worship or study of sacred texts are severely curtailed, where they exist at all. Despite traditions of women's leadership in early Islam, law and custom bar women from public religious and lay leadership roles. However, the latter rule has occasionally been relaxed in some non-Arab Muslim countries (for instance, in the election of Benazir Bhutto as Prime Minister of Pakistan).

The status of women in some Muslim countries improved during the quarter century following World War II. The rise of modern Muslim feminism, which coincided with a worldwide swing of the pendulum toward fundamentalism, generated a backlash, and the pace of Muslim women's progress slowed during the last quarter of the twentieth century. It is difficult to predict what lies ahead for Muslim women engaged in the struggle for more rights, greater freedom, and a higher level of personhood within their religious culture.

BIBLIOGRAPHY

Ahmed, Leila. *Women and Gender in Islam.* 1992.
Coulson, N. J. *A History of Islamic Law.* 1964.
Coulson, Noel, and Doreen Hinchcliffe. "Women and Law Reform in Contemporary Islam." In *Women in the Muslim World.* Edited by Lois Beck and Nikki Keddie. 1978.
Esposito, John L. *Women in Muslim Family Law.* 1982.
Mernissi, Fatima. *Beyond the Veil: Male-Female Dynamics in Modern Muslim Society.* 1987.
———. *The Veil and the Male Elite: A Feminist Interpretation of Women's Rights in Islam.* 1991.
Smith, Jane I. "Women, Religion and Social Change in Early Islam." In *Women, Religion and Social Change.* Edited by Yvonne Haddad and Ellison Findly. 1985.

Wegner, Judith Romney. "Jewish and Islamic Marriage and Divorce Law." *Harvard Women's Law Journal* 5 (1982a): 1–33. Documents the extensive degree of correspondence between classical Jewish Talmudic and Islamic laws governing women.

———. "Talmudic and Islamic Jurisprudence: The Four Roots of Islamic Law and Their Talmudic Counterparts." *American Journal of Legal History* 26 (1982b): 25–72.

"The Veiled Revolution." Directed by Marilyn Gaunt. Produced by Elizabeth Fernea. Icarus Films. 1982. An excellent short video that documents how Egyptian women use veiling to facilitate Muslim feminist groups.

JUDITH ROMNEY WEGNER

Israelite Religion

Pre-Monarchical Israelite Religion and Ancient Israel under the Monarchs, Prophets, and Priests

Scholars have increasingly come to agree that the ethnic and, eventually, national entity we know as ancient Israel emerged in c. 1200 B.C.E. out of the context of Canaanite society. This means we should expect striking similarities between Canaanite and early Israelite culture, and indeed we do find them: Hebrew, the language of Israel, is a Canaanite dialect; the material remains of early Israelite sites, and in particular the pottery remains, show clear continuities with Canaanite pottery types; and the early Israelite artistic repertoire, both literary and iconographic, is in large part derived from older Canaanite paradigms. Yet at the same time early Israel is different from Canaan. The Canaanites tended to live in large, urban settlements located in flat or nearly flat regions such as the Esdraelon Plain and the Jezreel Valley, whereas Israelite settlement was concentrated in small villages in the Samaritan Hills. The Canaanite economy was based on relatively large-scale manufacture and trade, whereas the Israelite economy was primarily agrarian with only a minimum of small-scale cottage industry. Canaanite architectural remains include several palaces and other administrative-type buildings, suggesting a relatively stratified and bureaucratized social order, in contrast to a virtual absence of monumental buildings at early Israelite sites and, by implication, a relatively undifferentiated and nonhierarchical Israelite social order.

This general presentation of early Israelite culture as being both continuous with and differentiated from its Canaanite antecedent describes as well the more specific case of early Israelite religion. At one level, early Israelite religion was Canaanite. For example, the God of Israel, whose proper name was Yahweh, is imagined in early Israelite tradition as being very much like El and Baal, the major gods of the Canaanite pantheon. Like the head of the Canaanite pantheon El Yahweh can be envisioned as "creator," both of the cosmos and of humans, as the "father" of humanity, and as lawgiver and judge. Yahweh and El moreover can both be called "Bull," and probably both can be represented by a bull image in the cult. Further, Yahweh's roles as king and warrior are derived from El imagery, as well as from Canaanite descriptions of the god Baal. This is particularly obvious in texts where Yahweh goes to war on Israel's behalf using the weapons of rain, lightning, and thunder, as it is Baal in Canaanite religion who is associated with the storm.

Exodus 15:1–18, which many scholars would claim is the earliest text we find in the Hebrew Bible (c. 1150 B.C.E.), illustrates vividly the way early Israelite tradition drew on older language of the storm-warrior god Baal to describe Yahweh. A hymn in genre, Exodus 15 celebrates Yahweh's victory over Pharaoh's Egyptian forces at the Reed (Red) Sea by recounting how a mighty tempest aroused by Yahweh so churned the sea that it capsized the boats on which the Egyptians traveled and tossed Pharaoh's soldiers into a watery grave. This poem's larger narrative structure suggests Israel's dependence on older Canaanite traditions. The Exodus 15 account of a conflict involving storm and sea, followed by descriptions of the mountain-top sanctuary that Yahweh established after the victory (v. 17) and of the people's proclamation of Yahweh as king (v. 18), parallels in multiple respects a Canaanite myth that tells of a fight between Baal and a god named "Sea." After the storm god triumphs, this myth recounts how the other Canaanite gods proclaim Baal as king and build a palace-temple (the word is the same in the Canaanite language) from which Baal can rule.

Yet at the same time that a hymn like Exodus 15 can derive both its descriptions of its divine hero and its larger narrative structure from Canaanite antecedents, there is still much about this poem that is distinctively Israelite. Unlike the Canaanite tale, for example, which is set exclusively in cosmic or other-worldly space and takes place in primordial time, the Israelite rendition posits an earthly location (somewhere on the waters of the Reed Sea) and a setting in historical time (most probably some point in the mid-thirteenth century B.C.E.). In Israelite tradition the Canaanite story has been "brought down to earth," or, as some scholars have described it, the genre that was originally Canaanite "myth" has become in Israelite religion "epic." As "myth" has become "epic" moreover certain attributes of the narrative's actors have changed: in the Israelite presentation, the exclusively divine characters of Canaanite tradition have, except for Yahweh, become human (the Egyptian soldiers, the redeemed Israelites), or, like "sea," they have become natural forces under Yahweh's control. "Polytheism," to put the matter another way, has become "monotheism." The movement from polytheism to henotheism—the confession that while many gods exist, there is only one God (Yahweh) whom Israel should worship—and other distinctively Israelite revisions of older Canaanite traditions have manifold implications for the place of women in Israelite religion. For example, the movement from a Canaanite pantheon of deities to the Israelite worship of only one God, and the worship of a God, moreover, who was definitely imagined as male (see, e.g., Exod. 15:3), means that the goddess figures of the older Canaanite pantheon in large part disappear. Yet attributes of certain Canaanite goddesses come to be assigned to the Israelite God. In Deuteronomy 32, for example, the Israelite God is described as the one who writhed in labor pains to give birth to the Israelite people. This sort of female-specific language might well be derived from traditions regarding the Canaanite mother goddess Asherah. More speculative, but also possible, are the arguments of Mark S. Smith and some kindred scholars who see Asherah language as underlying a text found in Genesis 49:25 (c. 1000 B.C.E.) that associates Yahweh with breasts and the womb.

Divine attributes of goddesses are also reinterpreted as human characteristics and used to describe some of the Bible's women actors. In Judges 5, Yahweh has human allies in his victory in battle: these include Deborah, who arises to lead her people in their time of crisis and may even participate in the fighting herself. Also of note is Jael, who, after the battle is over and all but the enemy war leader defeated, offers him hospitality at her tent and then, while he eats and drinks unsuspectingly, kills him by smashing his head. These depictions of female warriors who fight side-by-side with Yahweh, the male storm god, are highly reminiscent of the Canaanite myth of Baal and the god of death, Mot, who is defeated by the storm god's fighting in concert with his sister-consort Anat. There is, moreover, another Canaanite myth of Anat (the Epic of Aqhat) that describes how this warrior goddess defeats one of her foes by luring him into a tent to eat and drink peaceably and then shatters his skull when he is off-guard. The parallels to the Judges 5's description of Jael are unmistakable.

What does the survival of goddess imagery in some early Israelite poetry mean for the religious experi-

ences of actual women during this period? Studies of the role of goddess imagery in other religious traditions have shown that there is no necessary correlation between powerful female figures in a culture's religious literature and the existence of powerful women members of society. On the other hand, the early Israelite impulse to reinterpret the goddesses of Canaanite myth by ascribing their attributes to human females may imply a larger cultural acceptance in early Israel of the notion that real women are capable of the exploits described for literary characters like Deborah and Jael. The archaeological evidence suggesting that earliest Israel was a fairly nonhierarchical society argues for this as well, since JoAnn Hackett has demonstrated that the less institutionalization and bureaucratization there is in a society, the more possibilities there are for women to play powerful (and public) roles in the society's functioning. In less institutionalized societies, women can be deeply involved in their household and village economies, assume primary and even exclusive responsibility for education and socialization of the young, participate in judicial affairs, contribute to military efforts, and, of greatest interest to us here, serve as religious functionaries. And the Biblical evidence, although sketchy, suggests two major religious responsibilities women could assume in Israel's early history: they could be ritual musicians at certain times of pilgrimage and other cultic celebrations and hold the office of prophet. Some texts describe women's musical performances at the time of Israel's annual vineyard festival. Judges 21:21 recounts how at this feast, which was held at Shiloh, the young women of the town came forth to dance. First Samuel 2:1–10, the so-called Song of Hannah, also presents music performed by a woman that is purportedly associated with the Shiloh festival.

The hymns of Exodus 15:1–18 and Judges 5, which commemorate a victory secured by Yahweh over some enemy nation, were sung by women as part of a cultic celebration. Exodus 15:1–18, although placed in the mouth of Moses, was much more likely to have originally been ascribed to Moses' sister, Miriam. Indeed, in Exodus 15:20–21, the ascription of the hymn to Miriam is made explicit. Similarly, while Judges 5:1 assigns the victory hymn (2–31) to both Deborah and her associate Barak, the original ascription most likely identified Deborah alone as the singer, since the verb used for the singing is in the feminine singular. Women's special role as the musicians who celebrate victories in war is further attested in Exodus 15:20, where the women of Israel join Miriam in singing and dancing; in Judges 11:34, where the daughter of Jephthah greets her father with dancing and the music of a hand-drum after he returns home victorious from battle; and in 1 Samuel

18:6–7, where the women of Israel serenade Israel's first king, Saul, with dancing, hand-drums, and a victory hymn as he marches back from doing battle against the Philistines.

Exodus 15:1–18 and 20–21 and Judges 5 also both present their women musicians as prophets. Whereas Miriam is labeled a prophet (Exod. 15:20), Deborah (Judg. 5) is not assigned the title explicitly, although intimations of her prophetic stance abound: she assumes the typical role of the prophetic intermediary by making clear that the war that Judges 5 describes was waged with the approval of Yahweh; also, like some of the Bible's prophets, she assumes the responsibility for determining the Israelite army's composition. Indeed, so clear is Deborah's prophetic role in Judges 5 that a later Israelite interpreter of the hymn, the author of Judges 4, does assign her the actual title "prophet" (Judg. 4:4).

The title "prophet" is assigned to only three other women in the next six hundred years of Israelite history: the wife of Isaiah (Isa. 8:3); Huldah (2 Kgs. 22:14); and Noadiah (Neh. 6:14). The wife of Isaiah, moreover, is probably called prophet only as an honorific, a title derived from her marriage to her husband. This means that after a monarchical form of government was inaugurated in Israel (c. 1050 B.C.E.), women prophets virtually disappeared (although the institution of prophecy generally thrived).

If opportunities for women to hold significant and public positions of power are present in societies where institutionalization and bureaucratization are at a minimum, then, conversely, in societies showing significant degrees of these characteristics, and also centralization, the opportunities for women to wield power are relatively sparse. Throughout most of the period from 1050 B.C.E. to 450 B.C.E., Israel was such a society. Certainly in the religious sphere this was the case. Beginning in c. 1000, Jerusalem became the religious center of the nation, and a large temple dedicated to Yahweh was built there. A hereditary and all-male priesthood that traced its ancestry to Moses and his brother Aaron became well established and was placed under royal patronage. Although other religious functionaries, most notably the prophets, did not have as rigid an organizational structure, they nevertheless assembled into bands that were, with only one possible exception (see Ezek. 13:17–23), made up of men.

For many women, this exclusion from the public practice of Israelite religion seems to have had the effect of relocating their religious devotions into the private or domestic sphere. The main type of female musical performance attested for the monarchical period is associated with the more private experience of death, with women serving as ritual mourners and singers of lamentation. It is also likely that women of this period helped tend the sorts of small, household shrines now well attested in the archaeological record. Worship at these home-based sanctuaries most probably centered around the offering of daily sacrifices; ancient Israelite women, like women in cultures the world over, had primary responsibility for the management and distribution of their households' food supplies. Two texts in Jeremiah, 7:16–20 and 44:15–28, describe a scene of domestic devotion in which the children gather wood, the fathers kindle fires, and the women knead dough to make offering cakes for a goddess called the Queen of Heaven.

But the Queen of Heaven is obviously not Yahweh, and this datum suggests a second way in which women worshipers responded to their exclusion from public participation in the Yahweh cult: they turned to the worship of other gods, either in addition to or instead of the worship of Yahweh. For example, women are described in Ezekiel 8:14 as mourning the death of the Babylonian fertility god Tammuz, recalling in ritual the laments that, according to Mesopotamian myth, were performed by Tammuz's female relatives and bride. First Kings 15:13 and 18:19 identify two royal women, Maacah, the queen mother of King Asa, and Jezebel, the wife of King Ahab, as devotees of the cult of the goddess Asherah, and according to 2 Kings 23:7 there was also a cadre of women stationed in the temple in Jerusalem who served Asherah by weaving garments to be draped over her cult statue.

The participation of royal women in the cult of Asherah, however, along with the presence of Asherah cult functionaries within the walls of Yahweh's temple, suggests that the worship of Asherah was a special phenomenon in Israelite religion, not limited to just women and just the private or domestic sphere. The almost forty Biblical texts mentioning Asherah or her cult icon, a sacred tree or pole called the *asherah*, as well as archaeological remains (most notably the thousands of female figurines, now believed by many to represent Asherah, that have been found in all sorts of contexts in ancient Israel, including cultic and funerary), also seem to indicate that worship of Asherah was a widespread phenomenon. The popularity of this cult can be explained by developments in the "genealogy" of Yahweh, whereby Israel's earliest descriptions of the character of its God were derived from older depictions of Canaanite deities. In the monarchical period, this practice continued in some respects, but the impulse to use Baal language to describe Yahweh abated, due to fears that a too close identification of Yahweh with Baal would lead Yahweh worshipers away from the cult of the former and into the quite vibrant cult of the latter. The use of El language to describe Yahweh, conversely, was viewed to hold little or no threat; there was no particularly vital cult of El into which Yahweh worshipers might disappear. Because El was paired with a consort, Asherah in Canaanite religion, as the Israelites more and more embraced the use of El imagery to describe Yahweh, some associated El's consort with Yahweh, including, as noted above, members of the royal house (queen mothers, in particular, seem to have a special relationship to the cult of Asherah) and, as 2 Kings 23:7 implies, at least some within the temple hierarchy.

A look at the context of 2 Kings 23 reveals that this text's central concern is to describe an attempt by King Josiah in c. 625 B.C.E. to remove Asherah's cult servants from the temple in Jerusalem and, more generally, to remove all traces of Asherah worship from Yahweh's abode (the cult statue of the goddess [23:6]and the vessels used to offer sacrifice to her [23:4]). Other texts from this same period similarly speak out against the worship of other gods. During Israel's exilic period, c. 586–537 B.C.E., this sort of monotheistic dictum becomes more and more the norm. Also, several exilic and postexilic texts speak out against those who continue to worship Yahweh but do so through participation in rituals that the Bible's priestly and prophetic authors regard as inappropriate. In Isaiah 57:3–13 and 65:1–7, for example, which date from c. 535–520 B.C.E., there are condemnations of those who include in their devotions to Yahweh the sacrifice of children, offerings to the dead, fertility rites, and participation in incubation and necromantic rituals. The language of Isaiah 57:3–13, moreover, proposes an association between these allegedly apostate behaviors and women by personifying Jerusalem as a sorceress, an adulteress, and a harlot and accusing her of cultic deviancy. The polemic is unrelenting and serves to bring to the fore a tendency that is found only sporadically in pre-exilic materials: to single out women as responsible for religious behaviors that deviate from the prescribed worship of Yahweh (see, e.g., 1 Sam. 28:3–25, where a woman is cited as a practitioner of necromancy, even though this rite is said to be forbidden in Yahwistic tradition; also, Isa. 1:21–23, 3:16–24, 4:1, 32:9–14; Hos. 1–3, 4:13; and Amos 4:1–3).

By the time of the exile, then, women have in many respects become the "villains" of Israelite religion. Only in isolated outposts does positive female imagery remain. Papyri from a fifth-century B.C.E. Jewish colony located in Elephantine, in southern Egypt, for example, evoke the divine names Anatyahu and Anatbethel, which perhaps combine the name of the ancient Canaanite goddess Anat with, respectively, the name (Yahu) and a designation (Bethel) of the Israelite God.

BIBLIOGRAPHY

Ackerman, Susan. "Isaiah." In *The Women's Bible Commentary.* Edited by C. A. Newsom and S. H. Ringe. 1992.

———. "The Queen Mother and the Cult in Ancient Israel." *Journal of Biblical Literature* 112 (1993): 385–401.

———. *Under Every Green Tree: Popular Religion in Sixth-Century Judah.* 1992.

Ahlström, Gösta W. *Aspects of Syncretism in Israelite Religion.* 1963.

Albertz, Rainer. *A History of Israelite Religion in the Old Testament Period.* 1994.

Albright, William F. *Yahweh and the Gods of Canaan: A Historical Analysis of Two Contrasting Faiths.* 1968.

Bird, Phyllis. "Israelite Religion and the Faith of Israel's Daughters: Reflections on Gender and Religious Definition." In *The Bible and the Politics of Exegesis: Essays in Honor of Norman K. Gottwald on His Sixty-Fifth Birthday.* Edited by D. Jobling, P. L. Day, and G. T. Sheppard. 1991.

———. "The Place of Women in the Israelite Cultus." In *Ancient Israelite Religion: Essays in Honor of Frank Moore Cross.* Edited by P. D. Miller, P. D. Hanson, and S. D. McBride. 1987.

———. "Women's Religion in Ancient Israel." In *Women's Earliest Records From Ancient Egypt and Western Asia.* Edited by B. S. Lesko. 1989.

Burns, Rita J. *Has the Lord Indeed Spoken Only Through Moses? A Study of the Biblical Portrait of Miriam.* 1987.

Coogan, Michael D. "Canaanite Origins and Lineage: Reflections on the Religion of Ancient Israel." In *Ancient Israelite Religion: Essays in Honor of Frank Moore Cross.* Edited by P. D. Miller, P. D. Hanson, and S. D. McBride. 1987.

Craigie, Peter C. "Deborah and Anat: A Study of Poetic Imagery." *Zeitschrift für die alttestamentliche Wissenschaft* 90 (1978): 374–381.

Cross, Frank M. *Canaanite Myth and Hebrew Epic: Essays in the History of the Religion of Israel.* 1973.

Dempster, Stephen G. "Mythology and History in the Song of Deborah." *Westminster Theological Journal* 41 (1978): 33–53.

Dever, William G. "The Contribution of Archaeology to the Study of Canaanite and Early Israelite Religion." In *Ancient Israelite Religion: Essays in Honor of Frank Moore Cross.* Edited by P. D. Miller, P. D. Hanson, and S. D. McBride. 1987.

———. "Material Remains and the Cult in Ancient Israel: An Essay in Archaeological Systematics." In *The Word of the Lord Shall Go Forth: Essays in*

Honor of David Noel Freedman in Celebration of his Sixtieth Birthday. Edited by C. L. Meyers and M. O'Connor. 1983.

————. *Recent Archaeological Discoveries and Biblical Research.* 1990.

Fohrer, Georg. *History of Israelite Religion.* 1972.

Goitein, S. D. "Women as Creators of Biblical Genres." *Prooftexts* 8 (1988): 1–33.

Gruber, Mayer I. "Women in the Cult According to the Priestly Code." *Judaic Perspectives on Ancient Israel.* Edited by J. Neusner, B. A. Levine, and E. S. Frerichs. 1987.

Hackett, Jo Ann. "In the Days of Jael: Reclaiming the History of Women in Ancient Israel." In *Immaculate and Powerful: The Female in Sacred Image and Social Reality.* Edited by C. W. Atkinson, C. H. Buchanan, and M. R. Miles. 1985.

————. "Women's Studies and the Hebrew Bible." In *The Future of Biblical Studies: The Hebrew Scriptures.* Edited by R. E. Friedman and H. G. M. Williamson. 1987.

Meyers, Carol. *Discovering Eve: Ancient Israelite Women in Context.* 1988.

————. "Of Drums and Damsels: Women's Performance in Ancient Israel." *Biblical Archaeologist* 54 (1991): 16–27.

Miller, Patrick D. "Israelite Religion." In *The Hebrew Bible and Its Modern Interpreters.* Edited by D. A. Knight and G. M. Tucker. 1985.

Niditch, Susan. *Ancient Israelite Religion.* 1997.

Olyan, Saul M. *Asherah and the Cult of Yahweh in Israel.* 1988.

Patai, Raphael. *The Hebrew Goddess.* 1967.

Poethig, Edith B. *The Victory Song Tradition of the Women of Israel.* Ph.D. diss., Union Theological Seminary, 1985.

Smith, Mark S. *The Early History of God: Yahweh and the Other Deities in Israel.* 1990.

Tigay, Jeffrey. *You Shall Have No Other Gods: Israelite Religion in the Light of Hebrew Inscriptions.* 1986.

Trible, Phyllis. "Bringing Miriam out of the Shadows." *Bible Review* 5, no. 1 (February 1989): 14–25, 34.

————. *God and the Rhetoric of Sexuality.* 1978.

Vawter, Bruce. "The Canaanite Background of Genesis 49." *Catholic Biblical Quarterly* 17 (1955): 1–18.

Vos, Clarence J. *Woman in Old Testament Worship.* Delft, 1968.

Winter, Urs. *Frau und Göttin: Exegetische und ikonographische Studien zum weiblichen Gottesbild im Alten Israel und in dessen Umwelt.* Freiburg, 1983.

See also **Asherah; Deborah; Goddess; Hebrew Bible: God in the Hebrew Bible; Prophecy.**

SUSAN ACKERMAN

Jackson, Rebecca Cox

Rebecca Cox Jackson (1795–1871), black visionary and Shaker eldress, lived most of her life in Philadelphia. She worked as a seamstress and married a man named Samuel S. Jackson but had no children. Her *Autobiography* has left a vivid account of her religious awakening, visionary experiences, preaching tours, and eventual organization of a black Shaker community in Philadelphia.

Jackson's early religious formation was in the African Methodist Episcopal Church, a denomination established in Philadelphia since the eighteenth century. After a dramatic, literal awakening in terror during a thunderstorm, her visions centered on learning to hear and obey the voice of God. A covenant of sanctification led her to ascetic practices, including celibacy, against the "carnality" of the established churches. In 1837 she was accused of heresy and subjected to a trial led by clergy of various black Presbyterian and Methodist churches. This marked her split from mainstream Christianity.

Jackson was attracted to the intense asceticism, fervent millenarianism, and feminist theology of the Shakers from 1843 on; between 1847 and 1851 she and a follower, Rebecca Perot, were members of the South Family of the Shaker Community at Watervliet, near Albany, New York. Jackson and Perot returned to Philadelphia and established an independent black Shaker community, which survived Jackson by forty years.

A renowned preacher, Jackson never traveled as far as her contemporary, Jarena Lee, but was well known in the middle Atlantic states and southern New England. Throughout her adult life she was the recipient of vivid, blinding revelations of God's power and the necessity of self-denial and obedience. These are reminiscent of the visions of such earlier Christian women as Hildegard of Bingen and Teresa of Avila.

BIBLIOGRAPHY

Duclow, Geraldine. "The Shaker Family of Philadelphia," *The Shaker Messenger* 13 (1991): 5–7. A thoughtful discussion focusing on the Philadelphia Shaker Community during and after Jackson's death.

Humez, Jean McMahon. *Gifts of Power: The Writings of Rebecca Jackson, Black Visionary and Shaker Eldress.* 1981. This is the main study of Jackson to date. It includes a lengthy introduction, an edition of the *Autobiography,* related documents on Shaker doctrine and A.M.E. female preaching, photographs, and letters.

Walker, Alice. "Gifts of Power: The Writings of Rebecca Jackson." In *In Search of Our Mother's Gardens: Womanist Prose.* Edited by Alice Walker. 1983.

Williams, Richard E. *Called and Chosen: The Story of Mother Rebecca Jackson and the Philadelphia Shakers.* 1981. Includes selections from Jackson's works.

E. ANN MATTER

Jainism

One of the world's oldest religious traditions, Jainism is still the faith of about three and a half million followers in India and in countries where Jains are settled (mainly United Kingdom, United States, Canada, and some African countries). The status of women is a crucial issue in the history of the tradition, being one of the main points of the oldest sectarian division between the Śvetāmbaras and the Digambaras.

The historical beginnings of Jainism date back to the sixth–fifth centuries B.C.E., when Mahāvīra, the main expounder of the doctrine, structured the community. This community, known as the fourfold *saṅgha*, included women as two of its components: laywomen (*śrāvikā*) and nuns (*sādhvī*), alongside laymen and monks. In contradistinction to the Buddhist tradition, there is no Jain record indicating that the creation of the nun's order was problematic. In fact, when the size of the religious communities is given, nuns usually outnumber monks, at least among Śvetāmbaras even today. The names of respected women appear in early sources and are depicted in the narrative literature as ideal types of virtue and generosity. This is all the more worthy of notice since women's voices have seldom been handed down directly: Jain sources are prevailingly ascribed to men or are male-oriented. Though it is true that a few highly charismatic nuns have been in a position to express themselves through their autobiographies (Jñānamati, 1990) or through the redaction of religious pamphlets, no breakthrough dogmatical treatise is known to have been composed by any woman of the tradition.

The high number of nuns in the Jain orders over the course of time has not had a great impact on their rank within these orders. This is shown by the specific texts devoted to the exposition of the monastic code developed by the Śvetāmbaras as a part of their canon. Although no statement seems to record any fundamental inequality between monks and nuns, the redaction of this code points in a different direction and rests on the underlying thought that a woman, being unsteady by nature, needs to be under greater control. General rules applying to monks and nuns are largely similar, but there are additional and stricter rules meant to restrict options open to nuns in activities connected with their daily routine, and especially with food regulations. Furthermore, their independence and freedom are limited by a general subordination to the monks: (1) even when having a long religious life they may be under the authority of junior monks; (2) they need more years than their male colleagues to reach high positions in the religious hierarchy; (3) nuns have their own religious titles which imply a rank inferior to those of monks (see *Kalpasūtra*). This last point is best exemplified in the organization of the Terāpantha movement, a modern subsect of the Śvetāmbaras mostly active in Rajasthan. When it originated (in the eighteenth century) a single teacher (*ācārya*) was the head of both monks and nuns; the regular increase of nuns resulted in the institution of a female head (*pramukhā*) who commands smaller units. However, her role is that of a coordinator meant for practical purposes; she is not considered the female counterpart of the *ācārya*, who is the decision-making authority, but rather remains subordinate to him.

As far as access to sacred scriptures is concerned, there is again no theoretical avowed distinction between nuns and monks. On the contrary, Jainism (like Buddhism) basically admits access for all and differs, in this respect, from the orthodox Hindu tradition, where women are refused access to the Vedas. However, the nuns' educational level is very difficult to assess, and hardly any nun's name stands out for her intellectual achievements. Today, nuns' and more broadly women's education is a crucial issue, for instance among Jain subsects of the Śvetāmbara group. While some Terāpanthins and Sthānakvāsins claim that monks and nuns can study all texts, others (part of the Mūrtipūjaks) state that the nuns are of lesser ability and prevent them from being in a position to study certain difficult or controversial canonical texts, especially those connected with the monastic code. The efforts of some prominent nuns who try to use their prestige and influence to promote women's education must, however, be underlined. They profess that before religious initiation, young girls must undergo a probational period during which they will be given at least basic instruction not only in Jainism but also in grammar or literature. Promoting women's education is also an important point of the Terāpanthin subsect. It is implemented through a special category of nuns who are officially free from certain rules restricting their movement and who can visit distant institutions in India or abroad in order to pursue academic research. Although nuns are allowed to give public sermons, not many do so. More often, they are seen surrounding the preaching monk and carefully listening to him.

As for Jain laywomen, their book knowledge of the tradition varies according to their social environment. From time to time, resolutions are passed by various Jain conferences to encourage women's education (Cort, 1995). In fact, their knowledge and place in the community are mostly practically oriented toward the two areas where the prevalent gender hierarchy is reversed: preparation of food and performance of rituals, for which men are completely dependent on them. In a tradition such as Jainism, food is far from being a minor question. The observance of specific dietary rules is one of the clearest means to ensure sectarian identity. Thus the woman at home functions as a guardian or a modifier of the tradition through the various roles ascribed to her: it is she who offers alms to the begging Jain mendicants who come to her door, which implies

An eleventh century Jainist statue of Tīrthankara
(Angelo Hornak/Corbis)

that she masters a minute sequence of actions and rules; and it is she who prepares the meals for the family and decides whether a rule like the one that forbids eating after sunset will be observed, and knows which type of food must be cooked depending on the day (festival or ordinary, etc.). Finally, it is she who has a full command of the complicated calendar and typology of fasts that regulate the Jains' lives. Fasting is actually the true women's penance and a way for them to gain a high reputation for religiosity (Reynell, 1991; Laidlaw, 1995).

Also in women's control is the reproduction of the community. Women handle marriages and impart basic teachings to the younger generations. This latter task is done mainly through the telling of Jain legends and stories, the old stock of which is kept alive thanks to new versions available to women through modern translations in small and inexpensive booklets, or by listening to the daily sermons of the monks and nuns, which they normally attend in large crowds. Religious hymns form another category of literature in which women are

quite proficient. Chanting and reciting are two manifestations of feminine religiosity at work in domestic as well as in temple rituals.

Differences exist among subsects as to whether women are to be allotted the same rights as men in worshiping images. Fundamentalists hold that they should never be allowed to enter the innermost temple sanctuary or to touch the idols because they can never reach the indispensable degree of purity to do so; others allow direct contact under certain circumstances, and restrict it for reasons of temporary impurity only. Nonidolatrous Jains, however, lay more stress on internal worship and they have more egalitarian conceptions. Recent studies have shown that women have the real authority as far as conduct and performance of ritual itself are concerned (Kelting, 1995).

The two main sects of Jainism—the Digambaras and the Śvetāmbaras—have debated for centuries women's ability to gain salvation (Jaini, 1991). The Digambaras, whose name means "sky-clad," believe that nudity is essential for Emancipation, and that it is a mendicant's symbol of perfect detachment from everything, whether material possession or moral defilement. Since it is not acceptable for women to be naked, a woman's body is an impediment to Emancipation. The prerequisite for a woman's salvation lies in being reborn as a man. The Śvetāmbaras, or "white-clads," on the other hand, focus on a more internal approach; provided an individual is able to fulfill "right faith, right knowledge, and right behavior," which are the only necessary conditions for attaining the goal, gender does not matter. From the beginning of the Christian era to the end of the twentieth century, this debate about female religiosity has been continuously sustained in many texts, all written by male ascetics. Authors from the two groups have done their best to provide logical arguments and close analysis in favor of their respective opinions, trying to go beyond mere postulates. Some, for instance, have drawn a fine distinction between the notion of gender and that of sex by way of a Sanskrit term (*veda*) meaning in fact libido and transcending the physiological sex distinction.

Theological debates on women and Emancipation are mirrored in the construction of gender in myth. Basically atheistic, the mythology of the Jain tradition centers around the lives of its "ford-builders" (*Tīrthaṃkaras* or *Jinas*), who number twenty-four. Like other humans, the Jinas are beings who have gone through the world of transmigration and have been born under different shapes among gods, animals, or human beings. In their last incarnation, they are human beings who soon leave the worldly life and become religious mendicants in order to devote themselves entirely to the practice of asceticism, which results in perfect knowledge (*kevala-jñāna*) and, finally, Emancipation. Accounts of the Jinas' biographies are an important part of the literary tradition. Both Śvetāmbaras and Digambaras agree that twenty-three out of these twenty-four Jinas are men but they disagree about Number 19, named Malli. The Digambaras unanimously say that Malli (or Mallinātha) was a boy who lived the ordinary career of a Jina, and consider the absence of any feminine representation as a proof that Malli is masculine; their rivals state that Malli became a Jina during her last birth as a woman. The Śvetāmbara narrative enhances the ambivalence of woman's status as seen by this religious group: Malli had to be a woman as a kind of atonement for some act of deception committed in a former existence, but at the same time she was deemed able to lead the same life as the other twenty-three Masters' and to reach equality with them through Emancipation. This could explain why (except for an uncertain instance, see *The Peaceful Liberators*, No. 26, p. 139) no representation of Malli with any feminine sexual characteristic is available: all Jinas are pure emancipated souls. The fact that the Śvetāmbaras include in their canon a specific text narrating the life of Malli, whereas not all Jinas are provided with a full-fledged individual biography in this literary stratum, surely indicates their desire to stress their sectarian specificity on this point.

The two groups again disagree on the place occupied by women in the life of the twenty-fourth Jina, Mahāvīra. The Digambaras' position admits no compromise: women are a threat to all, especially as they may prevent the monks from strictly observing the vow of chastity, which is everywhere said to be the most difficult to comply with. Hence, even talking with women (or about them) is rendered (under the catchword *itthī-kahā*) as negative. Under these circumstances, it seems impossible to conceive of Mahāvīra as being subjected to these temptations in any way. Albeit the young handsome son of a princely family, he renounces the world in perfect chastity and never surrenders to the delights of love, thus embodying the perfect ascetic. On the contrary, several features of this Jina's biography as told by the Śvetāmbaras underline the key role of women: 1) although reluctant to do so, Vardhamāna (Mahāvīra) accepts his parents' command to get married; 2) he fathers a daughter, who moreover becomes the wife of his nephew, and the couple is responsible for an important schism in the community. This intentional stress on feminine lineage may be a part of a strategy meant to underline sectarian identity against the Digambaras (and perhaps also against the Buddhists, since Siddhārtha Gautama is said to have fathered a son). The de-

sire to describe Mahāvīra as a perfect householder before he renounces the world is perhaps a way to bring the ideal he represents closer to the ordinary man; this less extremist view is more in accordance with accepted social patterns.

Like other Indian traditions, Jainism exhibits a continuous tension between a negative image of woman and a tendency to extol certain women figures viewed as worthy of worship because of their spiritual achievements or because they represent protective entities and are equated with benevolent motherly characters. Iconography testifies to a fairly ancient cult rendered to the mothers of the Jinas, and especially to Marudevī, the mother of the first one, who is said to have been the first emancipated soul. Knowledge, a cardinal concept in the Jain doctrine, takes shape in figures that are all feminine. This applies to the goddess Sarasvatī, who is as important for the Jains as she is for other Indians; to the so-called *vidyādevīs*, who are representations of various sciences; and to the "eight mothers" (*mātṛkās*), a group of eight basic notions of Jain ethics. The main feminine deities of the Jain tradition, however, are the female attendants (*yakṣiṇīs*) attached to the main Jinas. Among them, Cakreśvarī, Padmāvatī, and Ambikā have gradually become independent figures and occupy an outstanding place, invoked by devotees who seek their protection on specific occasions of their daily lives (Cort, 1987). While the Jinas appear as distant spiritual ideals, these female deities are nearer to the human world and its difficulties.

Although the Jain tradition is not devoid of some of the usual prejudices against women, it undoubtedly gives them some place in its general ethical project. Using Alan Sponberg's classification of attitudes toward women, we can say about Jainism that at a soteriological level, women are fully included in the Śvetāmbara pattern, only partly in the Digambara pattern; that at an institutional level, it is man-centered; that ascetic misogyny is also evidenced; and finally, that soteriological androgyny is illustrated by the idea that any individual of either sex can have both masculine and feminine characteristics. The construction of gender is a complicated process, constantly hesitating between two extremes.

BIBLIOGRAPHY

Babb, Lawrence A. *Absent Lord: Ascetics and Kings in a Jain Ritual Culture.* 1996. Contains data on the place of women in the Jain tradition, especially in the late twentieth century.

Balbir, Nalini. "Women in Jainism." In *Religion and Women.* Edited by Arvind Sharma. 1993. A survey of the main issues concerning the place of women in the Jain tradition in history and in the modern world.

Cort, John E. *Defining Jainism: Reform in the Jain Tradition.* The 1994 Roop Lal Jain Lecture. 1995.

———. "Medieval Jain Goddess Traditions." *Numen* 34, no. 2 (1987): 235–255.

Das Kalpa-sūtra. Die alte Sammlung jinistischer Mönchsvorschriften. 1905. English translation by May S. Burgess in *The Indian Antiquary* 39 (1910): 257–267. One of the oldest and most basic texts setting out monastic regulations.

Dineś, Muni. *Sādhvīratna Puṣpavatījī Abhinandan Granth.* 1987. See esp. pp. 237–300. A Felicitation Volume published in honor of a nun from the Sthānakvāsī (nonidolatrous) subsect containing a collection of articles in Hindi largely written by women.

Dundas, Paul. *The Jains.* 1992. The most up-to-date handbook on the subject, with comments on the place of women in the community.

Jaini, Padmanabh S. *Gender and Salvation: Jaina Debates on the Spiritual Liberation of Women.* 1991. Fundamental in-depth study with translations and analyses of the main Jain texts related to this crucial issue, including one of the most important indigenous texts, Śakaṭāyana's *Strīnirvāṇa-prakaraṇa.*

Jñānamati, Āryikā. *Merī smṛtiyām.* 1990. Autobiography of a prominent Digambar Jain nun written in Hindi. Interesting evocations of her personal reactions to the faith and firsthand information about aspects of the monastic daily life.

Kelting, Mary Whitney. "Who's Running the *Puja?* A Jaina Women's Mandal and the Rituals of Performance." Paper read at the International Conference on Approaches to Jaina Studies: Philosophy, Logic, Rituals and Symbols. March 31–April 2, 1995. Fieldwork investigation (in Poona) of how women assess their power against the male sponsors during the rituals.

Laidlaw, James. *Riches and Renunciation: Religion, Economy, and Society among the Jains.* 1995. Study based on intensive fieldwork in Jaipur (Rajasthan), with a wealth of firsthand information on contemporary practice.

Mahias, Marie-Claude. *Délivrance et convivialité: Le système culinaire des Jaina.* 1985. Study of the place and role of food habits in the dogmatic system of the Jain tradition. Based on fieldwork conducted in Delhi.

Mallī-Jñāta. Das achte Kapitel des Nāyādhammakahāo im sechsten Aṅga des Śvetāmbara Jainakanons. 1983. The canonical biography of the nineteenth Jina as told by the Śvetāmbaras.

The Peaceful Liberators: Jain Art from India. Edited by Pratapaditya Pal et al. 1995. Richly illustrated catalogue of a fundamental exhibition of Jain art shown in the United States and England, along with independent chapters on issues connected with Jain ethics and practice.

Reynell, Josephine. "Women and the Reproduction of the Jain Community." In *The Assembly of Listeners.* Edited by Michael Carrithers and Caroline Humphrey. 1991.

Shântâ, N. *La voie jaina: Histoire, spiritualité, vie des ascètes pèlerines de l'Inde.* Paris, 1985. Informative study about the lives of Jain nuns in the past and in the present with reference to all types of sources.

Sponberg, Alan. "Women in Early Buddhism." In *Buddhism, Sexuality and Gender.* 1992.

NALINI BALBIR

Joan of Arc

Joan of Arc (1412–1431), a French peasant girl, became a national heroine and saint. Popularly known as "the Maid" (*la Pucelle*), Joan led the French troops as standard-bearer in the Hundred Years' War against the English. Joan claimed to have received visions from angels and saints, including Michael, Catherine, and Margaret, who directed her to request support from the French dauphin Charles for her military mission. At age seventeen in 1429, Joan secretly left her parents' home, put on men's clothing, and procured an audience with Charles, who sent her to undergo weeks of questioning by an ecclesiastical panel in Poitiers. While the textual record of that panel has not survived, a clerical member, Seguin de Seguin, later stated that the panel had found "nothing but good in her" and had advised Charles that there would be nothing to lose by making use of her. A group of noble women in Poitiers performed a physical examination also and confirmed Joan's claim to virginity. Charles provided Joan with the military support she needed and on 8 May 1429, Joan and her armies successfully lifted the English siege on Orléans. Joan entered battle directly on a horse, carrying a standard on which was painted the Lord holding the world flanked by two angels on a field of fleur-de-lis, the symbol of the French monarchy. Joan later claimed that she also carried a sword but never killed anyone, using the weapon only to defend against attacks on her person. The sword itself, Joan said, had been miraculously provided to her by heaven. After victory in Orléans, Joan was popularly acclaimed as God's emissary to the French people. Joan then escorted Charles to his coronation at the cathedral in Rheims in July of that same year.

A year and a half later, however, Joan's fortunes took a downward turn. While she continued to wage war

Saint Joan of Arc, a French national heroine, depicted dressed in armor (Corbis-Bettmann).

against English strongholds in France, she was wounded and captured in battle at Compiègne, then brought to ecclesiastical trial in Rouen for heresy by political enemies. Joan was condemned as a relapsed heretic for charges that included lying, sorcery, schismatism, bloodthirstiness, and wearing men's clothing. Her mystical companions were denounced as Satan's emissaries. Joan was burnt at the stake before a large crowd on 31 May 1431, and her ashes buried in the Seine. Twenty-five years after her execution, the "Rehabilitation" or "Nullification" Trial of 1456 overturned the condemnation verdict and justified her role as leader of French liberation. This second ecclesiastical trial was conducted by Joan's French supporters ostensibly in service to the pope. The Hundred Years' War had by that time ended and Joan's political cause been vindicated. Her mystical experience was defended as authentic and her mission as divine. Joan of Arc was beatified in 1908 and canonized in 1920 by the Roman Catholic Church. Joan's "afterlife" has included a prominent role in centuries of European art, music, and literature. Of particular note are Christine de Pizan's fifteenth-century poem *Ditié de Jehanne D'Arc*, Carl Theodore Dreyer's

silent film "La passion de Jeanne d'Arc" (1927–28), Mark Twain's novel, *Personal Recollections of Joan of Arc* (1899), and George Bernard Shaw's play, *Saint Joan* (1924)

BIBLIOGRAPHY

Duparc, Pierre, ed. *Procès en nullité de la condamnation de Jeanne d'Arc.* 5 vols. Paris, 1977–1988.

Margolis, Nadia. *Joan of Arc in History, Literature, and Film: A Select, Annotated Bibliography.* 1990.

Pernoud, Régine. *Joan of Arc by Herself and Her Witnesses.* Translated by Edward Hyams. 1982.

Quicherat, Jules, ed. *Procès de condamnation et de réhabilitation de Jeanne d'Arc.* 5 vols. Paris, 1841–1849.

Tisset, Pierre, ed., with Yvonne Lanhers. *Procès de condamnation de Jeanne d'Arc.* 3 vols. Paris, 1960–1971.

Warner, Marina. *Joan of Arc: The Image of Female Heroism.* 1981.

Wheeler, Bonnie, and Charles T. Wood, eds. *Fresh Verdicts on Joan of Arc.* 1996.

See also **Cross-dressing**.

JANE MARIE PINZINO

Jonas, Regina

Regina Jonas (1902–1944) was the first woman to be ordained as a rabbi. Born in Berlin, she was raised in a poor, religious home. She completed rabbinical studies at the Hochschule für die Wissenschaft des Judentums in Berlin with a thesis entitled "Can women perform the rabbinical appointment?" Jonas concluded that, "except for prejudice and novelty . . . hardly anything" stood against it. In July 1930 she passed her final oral examinations administered by some of the leading rabbis and scholars of liberal Judaism in Germany, including Leo Baeck, Julius Guttmann, Ismar Elbogen, and Eduard Baneth. The latter had marked her thesis as "Good" and probably intended to agree to her ordination. After his sudden death in the summer of 1930, however, Jonas was not ordained but given a certificate as an "academically approved teacher of religion." Finally, on 27 December 1935 Jonas was ordained privately by the liberal rabbi of Offenbach, Max Dienemann.

Following her ordination, the Jewish community of Berlin employed Jonas, but only as a religion teacher. She was also allowed to take over the "rabbinical-pastoral care" at the Jewish old-age home, hospital, and public institutions. Jonas was considered a gifted preacher and pastor. She often lectured about religious, biblical, and historical topics and about the status of women in Judaism.

In her writings Jonas insisted on the traditional Jewish separation of men and women in synagogues and stressed the Jewish principle of chastity. She also believed that the responsibilities of motherhood meant that only unmarried women should be rabbis.

Jonas was deported by the Nazis to the Theresienstadt concentration camp on 6 November 1942 where she continued her pastoral work as a rabbi among the inmates. On 12 October 1944, she was deported to the Auschwitz death camps and murdered.

BIBLIOGRAPHY

Herweg, Rachel Monika. " 'Mein Name ist Frau Regina Jonas. Ich bin nicht die Frau eines Rabbiners. Ich bin Rabbinerin. Was kann ich für Sie tun?' Die Rabbinerin Regina Jonas (Berlin 1902–Auschwitz 1944)." In *Frauen in pädagogischen Berufen*. Vol. 1. Edited by Elke Kleinau. Bad Heilbrunn, 1996.

Kellenbach, Katharina von. " 'God Does Not Oppress Any Human Being.' The Life and Thought of Rabbi Regina Jonas." In *Leo Baeck Institute Year Book*. Vol. 39. 1994.

RACHEL MONIKA HERWEG

Juana Inés de la Cruz

Juana Inés de la Cruz (1648 or 1651–1695), feminist poet, scholar, and nun, was born Juana Ramírez de Azbaje in Nepantla, near Puebla, in colonial New Spain. She was the illegitimate daughter of a Spanish-born father and an American-born mother of Spanish descent (*criolla*). Juana's intellectual precocity brought her to the attention of the viceregal court of the Marquis of Mancera in Mexico City, where she served from 1661 until 1667. In 1669 she took the veil at the convent of San Jerónimo. Her personal library was renowned as the most extensive in the Americas; the learned and powerful corresponded with her, commissioned courtly secular poems, and visited her convent salon for literary and philosophical discussions.

Beginning in 1676 Juana was commissioned to compose *villancicos* (carols) for feast days in the cathedrals of Mexico and Puebla. Her last series, composed in 1692 for the cathedral of Oaxaca, praises the wisdom and learning of Catherine of Alexandria, and it figures among the most defiantly feminist texts written for performance in the context of the Catholic liturgy. The best-known example of her dramatizations of Catholic doctrine is *El divino Narciso* (1690), an *auto sacramental* that illustrates the cultural syncretism of European and indigenous religious traditions in colonial Spanish America and dramatizes the conflict between the violence of the Conquest and its religious justification. Sor Juana's secular play *Los empeños de una casa* ("The Trials of a Household") has autobiographical elements.

In 1690 Sor Juana's *Carta Atenagórica* (Athenagoric Letter), a critique of a sermon by a Portuguese cleric, Antonio Vieyra, was published, apparently without her knowledge or permission. A male cleric using the feminine pseudonym "Sister Philothea" (probably Manuel Fernández de Santa Cruz, the bishop of Puebla), reprimanded Sor Juana for venturing into the exclusively masculine field of theology. Sor Juana's place as "first feminist of the Americas" is firmly established by her reply, the *Respuesta a Sor Filotea* (1691), a defense of her intellectual freedom and a challenge to the exclusion of women like herself from higher education. Nonetheless, in 1693 she signed a general confession and in 1694 a renewal of her vows, in blood, renouncing humanistic studies. She was also forced to give up her library and her scientific and musical instruments to be sold for charity. There is some new evidence, however, that she continued her literary and scholarly activities. She died during an epidemic while caring for her sisters in the convent.

Juana's secular verse is considered the culmination of Baroque lyric in the Spanish language. Her friendships with two vicereines, Leonor Carreto, Marquise of Mancera; and María Luisa Manrique de Lara, Countess of Paredes and Marquise of la Laguna, whose husbands served as viceroys from 1664 to 1674 and 1680 to 1688 respectively, inspired many of her poems. Her best-known verses, "Hombres necios que acusáis" (You foolish and unreasoning men), and her sonnet on the theme of carpe diem, "Este que ves, engaño colorido" (This object which you see, a painted snare), expose the fallacies of patriarchal moral standards and Renaissance poetic conventions. Her long philosophical poem in *silvas* (a Spanish version of free verse), the *Primero sueño* (First Dream), is an exploration of the methods of human knowledge. Sor Juana was known during her lifetime as the "Tenth Muse," and her poetry was published in Spain with the help of the Countess of Paredes in three parts, *Inundación castálida* (1689), *Obras* (1692), and *Fama y obras pósthumas* (1700).

BIBLIOGRAPHY

WORKS BY SOR JUANA

The Answer/La respuesta. Translated by Electa Arenal and Amanda Powell. 1994. Includes a general introduction, an anthology of poetry, and a bibliography.

Obras completas. 4 vols. Edited by Alfonso Méndez Plancarte (vols. 1–3) and Alberto G. Salcedo (vol. 4). Mexico, 1951–1957.

Poems, Protest, and a Dream: Selected Writings. Translated and edited by Margaret Sayers Peden with an introduction by Ilan Stavans. 1977.

A Sor Juana Anthology. Translated by Alan S. True-blood. 1988.

Sor Juana's Dream. Translated and with an introduction by Luis Harss. 1986.

WORKS ON SOR JUANA

Bénassy-Berling, Marie-Cécile. *Humanisme et religion chez Sor Juana Inés de la Cruz: La femme et la culture au XVIIe siècle.* Paris, 1982. (Spanish trans. by Laura López de Belair. *Humanismo y religión en Sor Juana Inés de la Cruz.* Mexico, 1983.)

Franco, Jean. "Sor Juana Explores Space." In *Plotting Women: Gender and Representation in Mexico.* 1989.

Martínez-San Miguel, Yolanda. "Engendrando el sujeto femenino del saber o las estrategias para la construcció de una conciencia epistemologica colonial en sor Juana." *Revista de Crítica Literaria Latinoamericana* 20, no. 40 (1994): 259–280.

Merrim, Stephanie, ed. *Feminist Perspectives on Sor Juana Inés de la Cruz.* 1991. Includes Josefina Ludmer's essay on the *Respuesta,* "Tricks of the Weak."

Myers, Kathleen. "Sor Juana's *Respuesta:* Rewriting the Vitae." *Revista Canadiense de Estudios Hispánicos* 14, no. 3 (1990): 423–431.

Paz, Octavio. *Sor Juana o las trampas de la fe.* Barcelona, 1982. (English trans. by Margaret Sayers Peden. *Sor Juana, or, The Traps of Faith.* 1988.)

Poot-Herrera, Sara, and Elena Urrutia, eds. *Y diversa de mí misma entre vuestras plumas ando: Homenaje internacional a Sor Juana Inés de la Cruz.* México, 1993.

Sabat-Rivers, Georgina. *Estudios de literatura hispanoamericana: Sor Juana Inés de la Cruz y otros poetas barrocos de la colonia.* Barcelona, 1992.

Scott, Nina M. " 'La gran turba de las que merecieron nombres': Sor Juana's Foremothers in *La respuesta a Sor Filotea.*" In *Coded Encounters: Race, Gender and Ethnicity in Colonial Latin America.* Edited by Javier Cevallos-Candau. 1994.

See also Monasticism: In the West.

EMILIE L. BERGMANN

Judaism

An Overview

Judaism has existed for most of its life as a minority religion under the governance of other religions. Shaped by exilic experiences, Jews have generally considered themselves members of both a religion and an ethnic community. Yet Judaism is open to new members through ritual conversion and includes members of societies from all continents.

Although Judaism is often regarded as one of the most patriarchal of religions, because exclusionary practices have long marked its central features, women in certain eras have also played key roles in private and public Jewish life. Prior to the modern period, women were generally excluded from the formulation of Jewish law, from leading public worship, and from the study of sacred texts. Yet women are never described in Jewish literature as having been absent from the collective revelation at Mount Sinai when God, in traditional Jewish belief, revealed the Torah. At that revelation, according to rabbinic literature, both the Biblical text and an oral tradition were transmitted, with the latter subsequently recorded in the Talmud, a massive collection of Jewish legal and theological teachings compiled in Palestine and Babylonia during antiquity. Yet that revelation, which stands at the heart of Judaism, consisted of texts revealed by a God who is usually imaged as male to a male leader, Moses, and enshrined women's position as inferior in status to men.

Central to Jewish belief are the mitzvot, the divine commandments, which include a range of ritual and ethical obligations through which Jews fulfill their side of the covenant with God. According to that covenant, ratified in the Bible, God, creator of the universe, responds to the mitzvot with concern and care for the Jewish people. Ultimately, that divine concern will culminate, according to Jewish belief, in redemption, at which time God will send a messiah who will bring peace and tranquility to all humanity, as well as to nature.

God and the messiah are traditionally described in Jewish texts as male figures, and only men are obliged to observe all of the mitzvot, leaving women as secondary figures in Jewish religious life. Yet feminist scholars toward the end of the twentieth century have revealed that women actually played a far more active role in shaping Judaism through the centuries than is conventionally assumed. Scholarship has made it clear that the Bible and Talmud were not the sole and absolute guiding forces in Jewish history but existed alongside other traditions that often contradicted their rules. For example, analysis of archaeological evidence has challenged conventional Jewish assumptions that monotheism was widely accepted by the eighth century B.C.E. with evidence that syncretistic worship continued long after, including worship of goddess figures and pagan deities alongside the God of Israel. Although women in ancient Israel could not serve as priests in the Temple, women were accepted as charismatic leaders, judges, and prophets and wielded power as monarchs during the First and Second Commonwealths (c. 1000–586 B.C.E. and c. 515 B.C.E.–70 C.E.). Women also functioned in the cult as ritual musicians, singing victory songs to God after triumphs in war and serving as professional mourners during times of lamentation. And while the Talmud's divorce law permits only a man to divorce his wife, never vice versa, ancient papyri found at Elephantine (island in Nile River in Upper Egypt) from the sixth century B.C.E. reveal that women, too, took the initiative and divorced their husbands.

While some scholars, such as Ross Kraemer (1992), have argued for a decline in women's religious status during the period of the Babylonian exile after 586 B.C.E., as Judaism came under the increasing control of the male priestly leadership, others, such as Tamara Cohn Eskenazi (1992), disagree. Eskenazi notes that the Persian administration of Elephantine gave women broad legal powers and suggests that women in Judah, which was also under Persian administration, most likely had similar legal rights, despite priestly control of the cult.

In Palestine during the Second Commonwealth (Second Temple) period a multitude of Jewish religious practices developed, while the Jewish Diaspora expanded to include much of the Greco-Roman empire as well as Babylonia and Palestine. Women were excluded from leadership of the Sadducees, the hereditary priesthood that ran the Temple cult, and from membership in the Essenes at Qumran, a group of monastic Jewish men living near the Dead Sea who denounced the corruption of the priesthood and believed in the imminent messianic era. On the other hand, some women achieved prominence among the Pharisees, scribes who interpreted Biblical Judaism for application to everyday religious practice; and the teachings of the women are recorded in the canonical texts of the Pharisees, the Mishnah and Talmud. Women also formed their own monastic community in Egypt, the Therapeutae. Jewish women were also active in the guerrilla rebellions against Roman rule in Palestine and in the movements that formed around the many messianic figures of the period, including Jesus. Some of those charismatic and apocalyptic movements seem to have granted women leadership roles, and Judaism began to acquire numerous female converts, the most famous of whom is Queen Helena of Adiabene.

Following the destruction of the Jerusalem Temple in 70 C.E., which was both a religious and political devastation, Jews were forced to abandon the sacrificial worship of the Temple and turn exclusively to a religion practiced not in a national shrine but at home and in communal institutions, namely, ritual baths, synagogues, and rabbinic academies. Biblical and Talmudic purity laws that had demanded immersion in water as a purification from sin prior to entering the Temple were no longer applicable. Instead, purity laws were reduced to women's immersion in a ritual bath seven days after the cessation of menstrual bleeding, with abstention from sexual relations during the "unclean" two weeks. Women as well as men attended communal religious worship services, particularly on the Sabbath and holidays, but women were not under obligation to pray three times a day. Instead, their religious influence increasingly revolved around the home, the site of holiday celebrations over festive meals. Study of religious texts and their commentaries became the nearly exclusive domain of Jewish men, who composed a vast literature of Biblical commentaries, interpretations of Jewish law, and works of philosophy and mysticism. If women also wrote learned texts in the Middle Ages, they have not been preserved.

Women also served as leaders of the domestic sphere of communal life, often supervising collection and distribution of charity. Jewish women in medieval Europe also worked frequently as midwives and healers, serving both Jews and Christians. Leniency in Jewish law regarding practice of birth control gave Jewish women greater independence than their Christian neighbors, which sometimes stimulated anti-Jewish resentments. The tendency of Jews to adapt to their surrounding culture, on the other hand, meant that Jewish women were generally confined by the strictures of the larger, non-Jewish society. Although they were able to travel and operated independently as businesswomen in Christian Europe, Jewish women of North Africa and other Muslim lands more often lived within a demarcated domestic sphere.

Feminist scholars have criticized the exclusion of women from study and public worship, their relegation to household duties, and their association with forces of impurity; yet they have also uncovered a lively Jewish religious life practiced by women within patriarchal strictures. Some Jewish women in the Middle Ages became learned figures of religious authority, explicating the Biblical teachings to other women in the synagogue. Recently uncovered prayerbooks for women reveal that they imbued their domestic responsibilities with religious significance, for example, viewing their baking of challah, braided bread for the holidays, as a priestly act.

Feminist scholars, including Rachel Adler, Miriam Peskowitz, Chana Safrai, Tal Ilan, Judith Wegner, and others, are also reinterpreting classical rabbinic texts.

Female Jewish rabbi, Leeza Taylor, reads the words of the Torah (© Bill Aron/PhotoEdit).

For example, the Talmud prohibits women from reading the Torah in the synagogue, stating, "a woman should not read from the Torah because of the honor of the congregation." Yet the very existence of the prohibition may be evidence that women did read from the Torah, or the prohibition would not be necessary.

By bringing forth hidden aspects of Jewish history, feminist scholarship decenters the dominant, privileged position of rabbinic literature, which has for too long been held up as "normative." The results suggest broader definitions of Judaism, as well as women's roles within it. For example, the separation of women from men during synagogue services became the rabbinic rule that governs Orthodox synagogues to this day, although archaeological data from ancient Israel gives no evidence that women sat separately from men in the ancient synagogue. On the contrary, evidence indicates that women served in a variety of important leadership positions in at least some ancient Jewish communities. Scholars have yet to determine when and why the sepa-

ration of women from men in the synagogue first became customary.

Feminist scholarship by Renée C. Levine, Ada Rapoport-Alpert, and Chava Weissler, among others, also has uncovered forgotten aspects of Jewish women's history. For example, although women were excluded from composing the major textual traditions of Jewish mystical literature, they developed their own spiritual practices and prayers. And whereas the major non-Orthodox denominations of Judaism did not officially approve the ordination of women rabbis until recent years, a seventeenth-century Jewish woman in Kurdistan was called a rabbi; a Hasidic woman, the Maid of Ludmir, briefly served as spiritual leader of her community until her marriage, which allegedly spoiled her spiritual gifts; and a German-Jewish woman, Regina Jonas, was ordained privately as a Reform rabbi in 1935—only to be murdered by the Nazis at Auschwitz in 1944.

The modern period brought new opportunities for Jewish women, not only to enter the secular spheres of society but also to become more deeply engaged in Jewish religious practice. The Reform movement, which developed in Europe during the nineteenth century, granted girls as well as boys a confirmation ceremony and provided opportunities for women to study Jewish religious texts at the non-Orthodox rabbinical schools they established. By the twentieth century women and men began to sit together in non-Orthodox synagogues, and women are now ordained rabbis in the Reform, Conservative, and Reconstructionist branches of Judaism. Within Orthodox Judaism, which still mandates separate seating in its synagogues, schools now exist to train women in classical rabbinic texts, and all-women prayer groups have formed. Some Orthodox synagogues now have women serving as assistant rabbis, with responsibilities for teaching, preaching, and counseling. Jewish feminists from all the denominations have been active since the early 1970s in composing feminist commentaries on the Bible, new prayers and rituals, and theological formulations that are increasingly becoming part of mainstream Jewish life and that will change the face of Judaism forever.

BIBLIOGRAPHY

Adler, Rachel. *Engendering Judaism: An Inclusive Theology and Ethics.* 1998.

Brooten, Bernadette. *Women Leaders in the Ancient Synagogue.* 1982.

Eskenazi, Tamara Cohn. "Ezra-Nehemiah." In *Women's Bible Commentary.* Edited by Carol A. Newsom and Sharon H. Ringe. 1992.

Grossman, Susan, and Rivka Haut, eds. *Daughters of the King: Women and the Synagogue: A Survey of*

History, Halakhah, and Contemporary Realities. 1992.

Hauptman, Judith. *Rereading the Rabbis: A Woman's Voice.* 1998.

Ilan, Tal. *Jewish Women in Greco-Roman Palestine.* 1996.

————. *Mine and Yours Are Hers: Retrieving Women's History from Rabbinic Literature.* 1997.

Kraemer, Ross Shepard. *Her Share of the Blessings: Women's Religions among Pagans, Jews, and Christians in the Greco-Roman World.* 1992.

Levine, Renée C. "Women in Spanish Crypto-Judaism, 1492–1520." Ph.D. diss., Brandeis University, 1982.

Peskowitz, Miriam B. *Spinning Fantasies: Rabbis, Gender, and History.* 1997.

Rapoport-Alpert, Ada. "On Women and Hasidism: S. A. Horodecky and the Maid of Ludmir Tradition." In *Jewish History: Essays in Honor of Chimen Abramsky.* Edited by Ada Rapoport-Alpert and S. J. Zipperstein. 1988.

Sabar, Yona, trans. and ed. *The Folk Literature of the Kurdistani Jews: An Anthology.* 1982.

Taitz, Emily. "Women's Voices, Women's Prayers: The European Synagogues of the Middle Ages." In *Daughters of the King: Women and the Synagogue.* Edited by Susan Grossman and Rivka Haut.

Wegner, Judith Romney. *Chattel or Person?: The Status of Women in the Mishnah.* 1988.

Weissler, Chava. "Prayers in Yiddish and the Religious World of Ashkenazic Women." In *Jewish Women in Historical Perspective.* Edited by Judith Baskin. 1991.

————. "The Traditional Piety of Ashkenazic Women." In *Jewish Spirituality.* Vol. 2. Edited by Arthur Green. 1987.

See also **Jonas, Regina.**

SUSANNAH HESCHEL

Religious Rites and Practices

Judaism, like other religions, provides an individual with meaning and structure in life. It emphasizes acts, both rituals and deeds of loving-kindness. Jewish beliefs underlie the acts but play a secondary role. Judaism holds that not only do such acts have intrinsic value but, ultimately, will bring the one who performs them to a state of perfect faith.

The Jewish way of life is laid out in the Torah, the first five books of the Bible. A combination of historical narrative and prescriptive law, these volumes present the principles and practices of Judaism in outline form.

The ten commandments, addressed to men, and through men to women, make reference to the theological and moral foundations of Jewish life: the belief in one God, who created the world and intervened in Jewish history, and the requirement to respect the integrity of other men's life, wife, and property. At Sinai the Jewish people entered into a covenant with God, pledging loyalty to God and steadfast observance of the commandments in exchange for freedom, prosperity, health, long life, progeny, and entrance into Israel, the promised land.

Ever since Sinai, Jews have been studying the Bible, in particular the Torah, and trying to develop a system of thought and action. The period following the destruction of the cultic center in Jerusalem in 70 C.E. was especially productive. In an attempt to transform Judaism into a home-based rather than a Temple-based religion, and in response to the spread of the Jewish community beyond the boundaries of Israel, a class of individuals called rabbis or sages produced the Talmud, a vast compendium of law and ethics. It is hard to know whether these men read their conclusions into the verses or derived them from the verses. But it matters little, because by the end of the rabbinic period, about 700 C.E., Jewish practice had assumed the shape that it still has today. For example: the Bible requires sanctification of the Sabbath and cessation of all work, but little else. The rabbis of the Talmud first defined, in detail, the different kinds of prohibited labor, and then infused the day with a sense of holiness. They required a Jew to light candles on Friday night, the onset of the Sabbath; recite sanctification blessings over a cup of wine; eat a festive meal in festive dress; say Sabbath prayers; and devote time to the study of sacred text. All of these actions, not alluded to in the Bible, and not likely to have been part of the Biblical way of life, made it possible for every Jew, man and woman alike, to experience Judaism in a unified manner.

THE CHANGING STATUS OF WOMEN IN RELIGIOUS RITES

Biblical Judaism is patriarchal. A man takes a woman to be his wife by paying a sum of money to her father and may dismiss her at will by giving her a bill of divorce. She may not take him in marriage nor divorce him. He, but not she, may have more than one spouse at the same time. Sons, but not daughters, inherit from fathers. A father or husband may cancel a daughter's or wife's religious vows. A woman cannot do the same to a man. Such rules describe a social and religious configuration in which men are dominant and women subordinate.

This patriarchal structure, although never repudiated, grew weaker over time. There is extensive evidence of a modification in outlook, a growing rabbinic recognition of and discomfort with patriarchal privilege. Though no one sought to grant women equality under the law, nonetheless significant improvements were made. A survey of marriage and divorce law, as well as synagogue practices, provides evidence of such a trend.

Marriage

By the end of the Talmudic period, the abolition of the bride price, the requirement of securing the bride's consent, and the institution of the *ketubah*, a document that guaranteed a married woman certain basic rights or protections, transformed marriage to such an extent that it could not longer be described as a purchase but as a negotiated relationship entered into by a woman and a man. A further important change was made by Rabbenu Gershom, a tenth-century Franco-German rabbi, who threatened excommunication for any man who took more than one wife, effectively ending the dying practice of polygamy.

Divorce

Divorce legislation changed less. According to the Bible, and later the Talmud, the power to divorce lay almost exclusively in a man's hands. A wife could neither resist divorce nor initiate it, except in a small number of cases, such as denial of support. This extreme imbalance disabled Jewish women over the centuries, allowing men to take their wives hostage and extort moneys from them in consideration of granting a divorce, or else, out of spite, not to release the first wife but still take a second. A woman who is tied to a man she does not live with, but whom she is not free to divorce, is called an *agunah*, an anchored woman.

In the late twentieth century a variety of solutions to this divorce problem have been proposed by rabbis, mostly male, who recognize the injustice of this situation. For example, one version of a prenuptial agreement states that should a couple civilly divorce and the husband then refuse to give his wife a Jewish bill of divorce, their marriage may be annulled by a Jewish court of law, thereby freeing a woman to remarry without obtaining a divorce document from her first husband.

Synagogue Practice

Radical changes have also taken place in the synagogue, mainly in the 1980s and 1990s. Until that time, the synagogue was a male-dominated institution. Only men could serve as rabbi and prayer leader, count in the *minyan*, the quorum of ten needed for communal prayer, read from the Torah in public, and so on; women came to pray on Sabbaths and holidays but never to lead services. The technical reason for women's exclusion was the principle that only those who are obligated to pray may join the quorum, lead it in prayer, and discharge thereby the prayer obligations of others. Although true, the underlying question is what accounts for this differentiation in men's and women's ritual obligations. The answer is that symbolic acts, like eating matzoh on Passover, mark Jewish time and history and are, therefore, the essential rituals of Judaism. Their performance is assigned to men, the full-fledged members of the Jewish community. Women are not prohibited from performing them, however, but rather exempted.

In the 1990s, many synagogues adopted an egalitarian stance and offered women the same opportunities for participation in public prayer ritual as men. Many communities have also begun to alter the liturgy, to call upon the foremothers of the Jewish people and not just the forefathers, to refer to God as Sovereign and not King. Orthodox synagogues, as a rule, eschew such changes. They seat men and women separately and erect a *mehitzah*, a partition, between the two sections of the synagogue, to eliminate the possibility of sexual distraction.

OVERVIEW OF RABBINIC LITERATURE

The basis of Jewish practice today is the Talmud, the literary and legal legacy of the rabbis who lived in the first five or six centuries C.E. These men developed an extensive elaboration and expansion of the Torah, producing a detailed set of instructions for how to live a religiously observant and morally upright life. Interspersed among the paragraphs of legal analysis are aggadic statements, short homilies on subjects as diverse as the importance of having a good breakfast and marrying off one's children while they are still young.

The Talmud is composed of two major parts: the Mishna, the sixty-volume code of law produced by the rabbis of the first two centuries C.E., tightly organized by topic and legally dense, and the Gemara, the wide-ranging analysis of Mishna that uncovers the scriptural origins of ritual requirements, debates the precise meaning of Mishnaic phrases, and accommodates earlier laws to later developments. The Talmud is more interested in process than in product; its love of intricate logical analysis is legendary. It is characterized by discussion and dispute, with the minority opinion recorded alongside of the majority. A Jew who wants to find out how a matter under discussion was resolved has to consult one of the later codes, the best known and most authoritative being the *Shulhan Arukh*, "the set table," published in the mid-sixteenth century.

One of the central requirements of Judaism is to spend time studying ancient, sacred texts, like the

Torah and the Talmud. This is considered so important that many men choose to spend all their time in study at an academy called a yeshivah, rather than be gainfully employed.

Women do not study in these institutions. Ever since the time of the Mishna there has been a ban on teaching women sacred texts, or at least a negative attitude to doing so. Men viewed women as not especially interested in intellectual pursuits and not capable of serious study. This situation, too, is changing. Women of different Jewish denominations now study Jewish texts and even, like men, can be ordained as rabbis. Making it possible for women to acquire Jewish knowledge and occupy positions of authority is the key to restoring gender balance and ethical consistency to Judaism.

RITES OF PASSAGE

Rites of passage, an essential part of Jewish practice, provide an opportunity for the community to be advised of critical changes in the lives of its members, of milestones they have reached, and to celebrate or grieve with them. Each celebratory ceremony, aside from a funeral, includes blessings, ritual acts, and a festive, communal meal. It used to be true that only the birth of a boy was formally recognized, with his circumcision the occasion for a party. Today, "naming" ceremonies for girls, marking their formal entrance into the community, are almost as common. Also today, a girl's coming of age is as likely to be celebrated as a boy's. In recognition of his becoming bar mitzvah, and her becoming bat mitzvah, each is invited to read a portion aloud from the Torah and Prophets and to present a learned discourse on the reading. Weddings, which mark publicly the promise of two individuals to care for each other and build a Jewish home together, do not discriminate between bride and groom, except that a woman's traditional silence during the ceremony is now being replaced by her active involvement. Judaism does not distinguish between death rites for men and for women. Kaddish yatom, the prayer for the deceased, is now being recited daily by female relatives as well as male. All of these changes paint a new portrait of Judaism, one which values its female and male members equally.

DOMESTIC PRACTICES

Because a woman in the past usually worked in the home, assuming responsibility for child-rearing and all domestic labor, many of the Jewish rituals of the home came under her purview. She maintained the dietary laws in the kitchen, prepared the special Sabbath and holiday foods, provided the holiday clothing, and, probably most important, imparted basic Jewish knowledge

A girl's coming of age is celebrated at a bat mitzvah—where she is invited to read aloud from the Torah (Richard T. Nowitz/Corbis).

to her young children. She was responsible for shaping their Jewish behavior and developing in them an appreciation of and love for Jewish ritual and values. It is true that formal Jewish education for boys and girls began at a young age, but the critical contribution of mothers in shaping Jewish souls is well-established. Today, for the most part, both parents are actively involved in raising their children and creating a Jewish home.

BIBLIOGRAPHY

Biale, Rachel. *Women and Jewish Law: An Exploration of Women's Issues in Halakhic Sources.* 1984.

Geffen, Rela. *Celebration and Renewal: Rites of Passage in Judaism.* 1993.

Grossman, Susan, and Rivka Haut, eds. *Daughters of the King: Women and the Synagogue.* 1992.

Hauptman, Judith. *Rereading the Rabbis: A Woman's Voice.* 1997.

Klein, Isaac. *A Guide to Jewish Practice.* 1979.

Siegel, Richard, Michael Strassfeld, and Sharon Strassfeld, eds. *The Jewish Catalog.* 3 vols. 1976.

See also **Buddhism: Religious Rites and Practices; Christianity: Religious Rites and Practices; East Asian Religions: Religious Rites and Practices; Hinduism: Religious Rites and Practices; Islam: Religious Rites and Practices; Ordination: In Judaism.**

JUDITH HAUPTMAN

From the Babylonian Exile Through the Second Temple

In 539 B.C.E. the Persian ruler Cyrus defeated the Babylonians, becoming ruler over much of the ancient Near Eastern world. According to biblical narratives,

Cyrus (called God's anointed, or Messiah [Isa. 45.1]) authorized Judeans living in exile in Babylon to return to the land of their ancestors and rebuild their ancestral temple to the God of Israel in the city of Jerusalem (see, e.g., Ezra 1:1–4, 7–8; 2 Chron. 36:23; see also Neh. 2:1–8).

The composite biblical narrative Ezra-Nehemiah describes the reconstitution of the people of Israel as a pure community dedicated to the observance of God's commandments and the reinstitution of the sacrificial cult in Jerusalem. Each book emphasizes different aspects of that reconstitution, with intriguing implications for women. Ezra emphasizes the reestablishment of the male priestly sacrificial system and the certification of priestly lineages back through Aaron, the brother of Moses. Nehemiah focuses more on the rebuilding of Jerusalem and on a communal reaffirmation of the Mosaic covenant.

Ezra identifies intermarriage between Judean men and foreign women as a primary cause of the Babylonian exile and a central problem in the identity of the current Judean community (Ezra 9). It urges the returning exiles to avoid the sins of their ancestors by abandoning both their foreign wives and the offspring of those marriages. Ezra ends with the household of Israel purged of (idolatrous) foreigners.

In Nehemiah intermarriage appears as only one of many boundary issues, and the exile is portrayed as the consequence of communal failure to keep the commandments. Nehemiah repeatedly details the presence of women and men in the covenantal community. Women are present at the inaugural covenant ceremonies on the first day of the seventh month (Neh. 8:2–3) and at the oath to keep the commandments on the twenty-fourth day of that same month (Neh. 10:28–29).

The apparent presence or absence of women as active participants in narratives of the late-sixth-century covenant community may be shaped by existing traditions about women. Nehemiah's explicit inclusion of women in the covenant ceremonies accords with Deuteronomy (e.g., 29:10). Ezra's failure to include women explicitly is more consistent with Exodus (esp. 19:15 where Moses instructs the "people" not "to go near a woman" in preparation for receiving the Law). Ezra and Nehemiah may reflect debate over the limits of women's authority and prestige in the (re)constituted covenant community. Women who had remained in Israel might have attained increased authority, power, and prestige, thus posing significant challenges to those attempting to reinstitute the priestly system. Further, as Tamara Eskenazi (1992) points out, when the identity and boundaries of a community are perceived to be

at risk, concern about intermarriage often intensifies in connection with the protection of land rights. Such circumstances might account for Ezra's heightened emphasis on men who marry foreign women rather than on women who marry foreign men. Noting that papyri from Elephantine, a Judean settlement in Egypt, document (Judean) women inheriting from fathers and husbands, Eskenazi suggests that such practices may have been common in late-sixth-century Yehud (the Persian name for this region) as well. If so, marriage to "foreign" women would have posed a significant problem to those attempting to solidify land holdings within the new covenant community. The compulsory expulsion of foreign wives would instantly increase the number of eligible men, which may have been severely diminished as a consequence of the exile. The book of Ruth, in which a Moabite woman ultimately becomes the grandmother of King David, may have been composed as a counterweight to the stance of Ezra-Nehemiah.

Although the dating of the law codes in Exodus, Leviticus, Numbers, and Deuteronomy lies outside the scope of this article, it is noteworthy that many biblical laws pertaining specifically to women serve as antidotes to precisely the issues perceptible in Ezra (and to a lesser degree in Nehemiah). The Mosaic law allows daughters to inherit from their fathers only when no brothers survive and effectively makes it possible for wives to inherit from their husbands (Num. 27:8–11); outlaws intermarriage; allows polygyny but not polyandry; and apparently authorizes only men, but not women, to initiate divorce. If we were to take the Elephantine papyri as a more reliable reflection of sixth-century B.C.E. Judean "law" and practice, we might wonder whether biblical "laws" on these subjects could represent relatively late formulations fashioned precisely as responses to these situations.

In the late fourth century B.C.E., Alexander the Great conquered the entire region and began a systematic program to suffuse the ancient Mediterranean with Greek culture. Less than a century after Alexander's death, Jewish scriptures began to be translated into Greek, reflecting the reality that the many Jews living outside the land of Israel, particularly in Egypt and eventually elsewhere, knew Greek as their primary language. Yet Hellenization caused severe conflict among Jews in the land of Israel over just how much accommodation to Greek culture was acceptable. In 164 B.C.E., or thereabouts, a relatively small band of anti-Hellenists, known as the Maccabees, wrested control of Jerusalem from its Seleucid rulers, reinstituting the Temple sacrificial system. The Maccabees and their successors ruled independently for about a century and then entered into an increasingly uneasy alliance with

Rome that erupted in the Jewish revolt of 66 C.E., culminating in the destruction of the Temple in 70 C.E. A vast number of Jews in the land of Israel died during the revolt, and thousands more were enslaved or exiled to Rome; they ultimately formed the basis of a large Jewish community that existed in Rome from the second to at least the fourth centuries.

The historical sources for Jews and Judaism(s) from the Maccabean conflict to the destruction of the Temple focus primarily on men and male experience. While several elements of Jewish observance, including sabbath observance and abstinence from pork, figure prominently in the sources, the Maccabean conflict itself is often expressed in terms of an exclusively male symbol, circumcision. Nevertheless, glimpses of Jewish women's lives and concerns are visible.

A raft of Jewish fiction dating to the Hellenistic period uses the gendering of Israel as female to express and explore issues of Jewish identity, particularly the circumstances of those many Jews who lived outside the land of Israel in regions ranging from Persia to Egypt to Asia Minor. These works include the book of Esther, contained in the Tanakh, and the books of Judith, Susannah, and perhaps Tobit, all transmitted as part of Greek Jewish scripture, conventionally known as the Septuagint. A Greek translation of the Hebrew Esther contains substantial additions that exhibit particular concern for issues of gender.

Scholars such as A. J. Levine debate how much any of these stories reflect the experiences of Jewish women. All these works are set in "the past," and none is presented as contemporaneous with the experiences of its authors (with perhaps the exception of Esther). Feminist scholarship has become particularly skeptical of the utility of these texts as historically reliable evidence and has increasingly focused on how ideas about gender might have been used to debate the realities of ancient Jewish life.

In the aftermath of the Maccabean conflict, a number of significant Jewish factions appear to have emerged in the land of Israel, including those identified by the first-century Jewish historian Flavius Josephus as the Pharises, the Sadducees, the Essenes, and the Sicarii. Though scholarly and popular treatments, influenced by the prevalence of the Pharisees and Sadducees in the New Testament, give the impression that many people would have identified with one or another of these labels, figures provided by both Josephus and the first-century C.E. Alexandrian Jewish philosopher Philo suggest that only a few thousand persons identified themselves as members of these groups. Their influence appears confined almost exclusively to Roman Palestine, and there is little evidence that such divi-

sions applied to the large Jewish diaspora communities in Egypt, Asia Minor (modern Turkey), Rome, and Babylonia.

Ancient sources use the terms Pharisee, Sadducee, and Essene as categories of male identity. Philo of Alexandria, for instance, said that Essenes do not take wives, a statement that both defines the Essenes as male and excludes women from their community. By contrast, he is explicit about the presence of women among a monastic philosophical community, called the Therapeutae, living a life of asceticism and contemplation outside Alexandria. But Josephus, writing several decades after Philo, knows both of Essenes who do not marry and those who do.

Whether women were Essenes in their own right, apart perhaps from being the wives or blood relatives of male Essenes, is difficult to determine. The Dead Sea Scrolls (thought by most, though not all, scholars, to come from an Essene community) contain a few references that may support the view that at least some women were active participants in the Essene life, but none of these is unambiguous. Graves from a cemetery at Qumran, near the caves where the scrolls were found, have yielded a few skeletons of adult women and children. Because these were found in areas considered by many scholars to be "secondary" from the main burial site, and the total number of opened graves is so small, it is difficult to draw any definitive conclusions.

Whether women understood themselves as Sadducees or Pharisees is again a difficult question. No contemporaneous evidence points to women active in Sadducean circles. Josephus chronicles the support of a few powerful women for the Pharisees, including Alexandra Salome, who ruled as queen from 76–67 B.C.E. after the death of her husband Alexander, but this is hardly evidence for women Pharisees. Tal Ilan (1995) has argued that the Pharisees garnered their allegiance because they were, in reality, an opposition group during the Second Temple Period, and opposition groups were more likely to attract the patronage of aristocratic women. Even if this were true, it would not materially alter the perception that these divisions were largely if not entirely male alliances.

Several sources suggest Jewish women's participation in the various anti-Roman and messianic movements in the first century C.E. Feminist scholarship has illuminated the significant presence of women in the Reign of God movement centered on Jesus of Nazareth. In a little-noticed passage, Josephus remarks that the revolutionary Simon bar Giora was accompanied by a following of women, including bar Giora's wife. Interestingly, just as Jesus is often thought to have abrogated the kosher laws and Jewish purity regulations, Josephus claims that Simon abandoned the kosher laws and Jewish laws of ritual purity.

Some scholars have argued that the appeal of the Jesus movement to Jewish women lay particularly in its renunciation of Jewish purity laws governing menstruation and heterosexual intercourse, but their arguments rest on flawed readings of both Jewish sources and the Gospels (Kraemer, 1998). Women's actual observance of menstrual purity regulations in this period is difficult to determine. While women in Pharisaic families, for instance, may well have adhered to the kinds of rules later found in rabbinic sources, women "of the land" and those living far from the temple in Jerusalem may not have done so.

Focusing on the presence of women among these relatively small groups may inhibit better inquiries. The vast majority of first-century Jews living in the land of Israel are known, in later rabbinic sources, as the *am ha'aretz,* the people of the land. While the rabbis portray them almost exclusively as male, they were, of course, equally female. Various sources, including later rabbinic writings, suggest that these "ordinary" people, women and men, were much less concerned than the rabbis with religious observances, ritual purity, and so forth.

The writings of Josephus, on the other hand, recount the extensive involvement of elite Jewish women in the affairs of the first century. Josephus, and his modern interpreters after him, have tended to judge these women by their conformity to standards of gender-appropriate behavior. Approaching these women from a critical feminist perspective may revise our thinking about many Jewish women in the Greco-Roman period.

It is also worth reflecting on how meaningful a traditional periodization of Jewish history is for women. As has been suggested, the "return" and the rebuilding of the Temple, traditionally viewed as evidence of God's mercy and forgiveness toward the people, Israel, may be seen to disenfranchise women. Nehemiah might then represent an effort to compensate in some way by stressing the incorporation of Judahite women, who bind themselves to the covenant on their own. In traditional paradigms of Jewish history, Hellenization is coded negatively, and some scholars have tended to blame Hellenization for increasing restrictions on Jewish women. In fact, Hellenization generally increased alternatives for women and weakened traditional gender distinctions in the ancient Mediterranean, allowing women greater access to public life. The evidence from diaspora Jewish communities, themselves often viewed as departing from "authentic" mainstream Judaism, suggests that women played greater public roles in the lives of those communities than they did in communities governed by rabbinic regulations.

BIBLIOGRAPHY

Brenner, Athalya, ed. *A Feminist Companion to the Bible.* A series of multi-author volumes on the books of the Hebrew Bible. 1993.

Eskenazi, Tamara. "Ezra-Nehemiah." In *The Women's Bible Commentary.* Edited by Carol A. Newsom and Sharon H. Ringe. 1992.

Grabbe, Lester. *Judaism from Cyrus to Hadrian.* 2 vols. 1992.

Ilan, Tal. "The Attraction of Aristocratic Women to Pharisaic Judaism During the Second Temple Period." *Harvard Theological Review* 88 (1995): 1–33.

———. *Jewish Women in Greco-Roman Palestine: An Inquiry into Image and Status.* Tübingen, 1995.

Kraemer, Ross S. "Jewish Women in the Diaspora World of Late Antiquity." In *Jewish Women in Historical Perspective.* Edited by Judith Baskin. 1991. 2d ed. forthcoming.

———. "Jewish Women and Women's Judaisms at the Beginnings of Christianity." In *Women and Christian Origins: A Reader.* Edited by Ross S. Kraemer and Mary Rose D'Angelo. 1998.

———. "Monastic Jewish Women in Greco-Roman Egypt: Philo on the Therapeutrides." *Signs: Journal of Women in Culture and Society* 14, no. 1 (1989): 342–370.

Meyers, Carol. *Rediscovering Eve: Ancient Israelite Women in Context.* 1988.

Meyers, Carol, ed., with Toni Craven and Ross S. Kraemer. *A Dictionary of Women in Scripture.* Forthcoming.

Newsom, Carol A., and Sharon H. Ringe, eds. *The Women's Bible Commentary.* 1992.

Niditch, Susan. "Portrayals of Women in the Hebrew Bible." In *Jewish Women in Historical Perspective.* Edited by Judith Baskin. 1991.

ROSS S. KRAEMER

Roman, Byzantine, and Sassanian Judaism

THE ROMANS IN PALESTINE

During the Hellenistic era, women occasionally served as rulers of the Ptolemaic and Seleucid empires, whose domains had extended to Palestine in the third and second centuries B.C.E., respectively. These rulers included the ill-fated Cleopatra VII (69–30 B.C.E.), whose efforts to ally herself with Rome's leadership, first as Caesar's mistress and later as Mark Antony's wife, proved to be futile in halting both Rome's conquest of the Ptolemaic lands and the demise of the dynasty.

In the years immediately preceding Cleopatra's birth, Palestine was briefly ruled by a woman as well—the

Jewish Queen Salome Alexandria, wife of and successor to the Hasmonean king Alexander Janneus. According to the first-century Jewish historian Josephus, Salome Alexandra followed her husband's advice and made peace with his opponents, the Pharisees. However, she was less successful in insuring a peaceful succession following her reign (76–67 B.C.E.). Her sons, Aristobulus II and Hyrcanus II, vied for the kingship, and each turned to Rome for assistance. The Roman General Pompey, who, consistent with Rome's expansionist policies, was already in Syria, would take advantage of the dynastic dispute. By 63 B.C.E. Palestine was in Roman hands. The Romans remained for roughly seven hundred years. Thus, with the exception of the histories of the Parthian and Sassanian Jewish communities farther east, Jewish history and the history of Judaism, including Jewish women's histories, from the first century B.C.E. through the seventh century C.E., must be studied against the backdrop of Roman political, legal, social, and economic history.

Not long after Pompey's conquest of Palestine, Herod, best-known for his large-scale building projects including his massive renovation of the Jerusalem Temple, supplanted the Hasmoneans with Roman support. He ruled as their client king from 37–4 B.C.E. To augment his standing within the Jewish community and to further legitimate his claims to the throne, he married Mariamne, the granddaughter of Hyrcanus II. However, in 29 B.C.E., fearing that she was plotting against him, he had her assassinated. Later, he also had additional members of the Hasmonean family killed.

Members of Herod's family ruled in Palestine, with varying degrees of authority, through most of the first century; but in the aftermath of Herod's death, political power rested primarily with the procurators sent by Rome to govern the region. The policies and practices of many of the procurators, social and economic divisions within Palestinian Jewry, and, especially, the growing militant messianic religious-nationalist aspirations of segments of Palestinian Jewry, culminated in the Roman-Jewish War of 66–73/74 C.E. In 70 the Roman Army destroyed the Jerusalem Temple, thereby bringing to an end the ancient Israelite system of sacrifice and atonement and with it those varieties of Judaism that were Temple-centered.

THE SEPARATION OF JUDAISM AND CHRISTIANITY

Both pharisaic-rabbinic Judaism and Christianity survived the profound upheavals of the first century, at least in part because of characteristics shared by these non-Temple-centered kinds of Judaism. The process of separation between Judaism and Christianity would oc-

cur gradually. It is important to remember that earliest Christianity, the Jesus Movement, was a first-century Palestinian Jewish apocalyptic movement. Jesus, a holy man, teacher, and healer, admonished people to repent because the arrival of the Kingdom of God was imminent. He was crucified by the Romans during the procuratorship of Pontius Pilate (26–36) probably because they mistakenly believed him to be a political revolutionary. The followers of Jesus believed that he had been resurrected and would return as the Messiah.

Although the Jesus Movement originated in Palestine, not long after his death missionaries endeavored to bring it to both Jews and, for example, in the case of Paul, non-Jews in the larger Mediterranean world. Paul differed from those members of the Jesus Movement who continued to follow Jewish law. He argued that the Law was no longer a vehicle for right relationship with God and personal salvation. However, even as he preached, wrote letters, sought converts, and endeavored to promulgate his beliefs concerning the status of Jewish Law and the significance of the resurrection of Jesus, Paul understood himself to be a Jew. Like the earliest followers of Jesus, Paul also believed that the end-time process had begun. Indeed, he expected Jesus to soon return, probably in his own lifetime.

The New Testament Gospels of Mark, Matthew, and Luke, each of which reflects a distinct voice within emerging Christianity, present diverse, theologically driven interpretations of disputes among various Jewish groups—Pharisees, Sadducees, the followers of Jesus, and so on. It is only the Gospel of John, the latest among the four, written at the close of the first or at the beginning of the second century, that uses the term "the Jews" as a multipurpose designation for Jesus' adversaries. The language of John may reflect the anger and the pain of the Jewish Christian Johannine community as it became separate, "divorced," from the larger Jewish community; it may also reflect the community's attempt to develop an identity in contrast to this "other" Judaism in an empire that, while it had recognized Judaism as a legal religion at least since the days of Julius Caesar, was often hostile to new religions and associations. The Roman government feared that such new groups might pose a political threat to Roman rule, or might undermine the religious and social fabric on which the well-being of the Empire was dependent.

Like the Gospel of John, the correspondence between the Roman Emperor Trajan and Pliny the Younger, Governor of Bithynia in Asia Minor, is a significant marker in the process of separation between Judaism and Christianity. Pliny asked Trajan to review the governor's policy toward Christians. The correspondence

(c. 111–113) indicates that the Roman government now viewed Christians as a group separate from Jews, and unlike the Jews, as an illegal association whose members, under certain circumstances, could be subject to execution.

To be sure, various Jewish Christian groups, which continued to practice Jewish law and regard Jesus as the resurrected Messiah, seem to have persisted in areas of Syria and Palestine as late as the fifth century. As boundary blurrers, they were condemned in the writings of both the Church Fathers and the Rabbis. Throughout the early centuries of Christianity, the Church Fathers also condemned what they perceived as Judaizing tendencies among their adherents, as they endeavored to erect secure boundaries between Judaism and Christianity. However, the process of separation was largely completed by the early second century.

WOMEN IN JUDAISM

Interestingly, the New Testament is one of the major sources for gleaning data concerning women in first-century Judaism. Although the roles of women in earliest Christianity have sometimes been presented as illustrative of the greater opportunities offered to women in Christianity relative to Judaism, in fact, they are indicative of the opportunities available to at least some Jewish women. The Gospels suggest that Jesus' followers included women, even among his innermost circle. The letters of Paul and the Book of Acts depict women in a variety of important activities, including preaching and prophesying, and serving as missionaries, deacons, and patrons of house churches.

The leadership opportunities for women in the church declined significantly in the succeeding centuries. This is reflected in the "household codes" of some of the latest New Testament documents that espouse a subordinate role for women. Perhaps the important roles for women in earliest Christianity can be likened to the "Rosie the Riveter" phenomenon of World War II, in which a situation of profound instability and upheaval yielded greater opportunities for women. During periods of increasing stability, which often follow times of crises, opportunities for women frequently contract.

It is also important to recall that the earliest rabbinic document, the Mishnah, is roughly a century later in date than the latest books of the New Testament. Indeed, the formative documents of rabbinic Judaism, the Mishnah, Tosefta, Palestinian and Babylonian Talmuds, and the Biblical commentaries known as Midrashim, were completed between the third and seventh centuries in the rabbinic academies of Roman Palestine and Sassanian Babylonia. Thus, although they signifi-

cantly postdate the New Testament, they are contemporary with the writings of the Church Fathers.

Similar images of the "ideal" woman are found in the "household codes" of the New Testament, the later literature of the rabbis and the Church Fathers, and in many genres of pagan Roman literature. An epitaph of a Roman housewife of the first century B.C.E. is illustrative. The husband of the deceased describes his wife as "best and most beautiful, a worker in wool, pious, chaste, thrifty, faithful, a stayer-at-home" (ILS 8402).

However, just as this epitaph must be evaluated in the context of the sources that describe Roman women functioning in a broad range of activities and occupations outside of the home, so, too, the depictions of women in rabbinic literature must be evaluated in the context of other literary and nonliterary sources. Rabbinic literature reflects the interests and concerns of the rabbis—a male scholarly elite of late antique holymen who may have evolved out of the older scribal Pharisaic community. For the rabbis, holiness was achieved through the study of Torah and the performance of commandments (*mitzvot*). Women were exempted, indeed discouraged, from pursuing the former, and were also exempted from most positive and time-bound *mitzvot*. Thus women were excluded from the rabbinic hierarchies of achievement.

As Jacob Neusner (1980) has observed, rabbinic interest in women focused on her capacity as a purveyor of uncleannesses during her menses and on those occasions when a woman and her property had to be transferred from the domain of her father to that of her husband and sometimes back again. As a mother, wife, and daughter operating within the confines of rabbinic law, a woman was to be praised and treated well. However, the abstract female, functioning outside of the constraints of rabbinic teaching, was a source of chaos and danger.

Nevertheless, just as rabbinic literature is not seamless and requires that each document be studied on its own terms, so, too, the rabbinic treatment of women is not seamless both within and among rabbinic texts. For example, the Mishnah, as Judith Wegner (1988) has observed, distinguishes between dependent and autonomous women. Widows, divorcees, and unmarried adult daughters, unlike their dependent counterparts, could control and dispose of their property and could also arrange their own marriages.

The rabbis created in their documents, as Neusner (1980) reminds us, an orderly and sanctified universe. For example, the majority of the Mishnah is concerned with Temple practice, although at the time of the Mishnah's editing, the Temple had not been standing for more than a century. Thus, rabbinic literature yields far more information on the roles of women as envisioned by the rabbis than it does on the flesh and blood women of Roman Palestine or Sassanian Babylonia. It is also by no means clear to what degree the rabbis were authoritative outside of their academies in the formative centuries of rabbinic Judaism. As Shaye Cohen (in Shanks, 1992) has noted, Diaspora Jewry appears to have celebrated the Jewish holidays, worshiped God, and so on, in the absence of significant rabbinic influence.

Nevertheless, it is significant that rabbinic literature, despite the legal disadvantages accorded to women, provides a framework in which some women could accrue wealth and control their property. Inscriptions from the Roman Diaspora provide evidence of such women. Some were donors and occupied important positions of communal leadership, participating, like their pagan and Christian counterparts, in the Roman practice of euergetism or benefactions. Bernadette Brooten's (1982) study of synagogal inscriptions also makes clear that some Jewish women held synagogal leadership positions, including that of the *archisynagoge*, the head of the synagogue. To be sure, these women were atypical in that most men and women lived in poverty. Socioeconomic status was generally more likely than religious identity, or at times even than gender, to have affected the opportunities available to an individual.

Although some women held leadership positions in Jewish communal institutions, women's religious practices were heavily focused on the domestic or private sphere. They included lighting the Sabbath candles in the home and following the religiously mandated rituals and behaviors associated with food preparation and with women during their menses.

The ancient literary and nonliterary sources do not enable historians to ascertain precisely the religious beliefs of Jewish women or men, whether in Palestine, Babylonia, or the Roman Diaspora, during the formative centuries of rabbinic Judaism. However, it is possible to outline a core set of beliefs. These included the belief in God and God's giving of the Torah to Moses at Mount Sinai. The Torah provided a framework for right relationship with God and eternal salvation. Rabbinic Judaism would develop the belief that the later teachings of the rabbis, embodied in their formative documents, were also Torah. Indeed, at Mount Sinai God had given to Moses the Dual Torah—both the Written Torah and the Oral Torah. The Written Torah had been given to all of Israel while the Oral Torah had been transmitted from one generation of (male) sages to the next.

Jewish eschatological speculations were varied. However, many eschatological texts include the beliefs that at the end-time a messiah (or messiahs) would appear and be instrumental in a process that would ultimately include the resurrection of the dead, a final judgment, and, eventually, the establishment of the kingdom of God. As noted above, the Roman Army had destroyed the Jerusalem Temple in 70. In the aftermath of the disastrous anti-Roman War of Bar Kochba (132–135), the Roman Emperor Hadrian banned Jews from Jerusalem (although the duration of this policy, and the degree to which it was enforced, are unclear). The city was transformed into pagan Aelia Capitolina. It is therefore not surprising that Jerusalem occupied a central place in Jewish eschatological hopes and expectations. Many texts envision the rebuilding of the Temple and the renewal of the entire city. In some texts, the now perfected earthly Jerusalem ascends to heaven; in other texts, a heavenly Jerusalem descends to earth.

Nonrabbinic sources for Palestinian Jewish women's history are very few in number. Thus, for example, one cannot determine how Palestinian Jewish women negotiated divorces from their husbands. Whereas Roman law enabled either a man or a woman to initiate divorce proceedings, rabbinic law dictated that only a man might do so. It is also worth recalling that from 212, with the promulgation of Emperor Caracalla's "Constitutio Antoniana," all free inhabitants of the Roman Empire were granted citizenship. Yet, in reading rabbinic documents, one is barely aware of the presence of the Roman courts.

The second-century archive of Babata, a young widow from the village of Mazoa on the Dead Sea, makes clear that at least some Jewish women made use of the Roman courts. Babata's cache, consisting of thirty-five documents in Greek, Nabataean, and Aramaic, includes marriage documents, property deeds, and documents concerning litigation about property matters and procuring the guardianship of her deceased husband's son. Her legal affairs brought her into contact with the Roman provincial courts at Petra and at Rabbat Moab.

Historians cannot determine the degree to which Babata was typical. However, it is important to note that throughout the Roman and Byzantine periods, Jews lived among non-Jews. Even in Palestine, most major Jewish centers of population had mixed populations. Thus, Jewish women's history must be considered in the dynamic context of the complex relationships between the Jewish communities and the larger communities of which they were a part—and, at the same time, in which they were in some ways distinct.

Byzantine Palestine, the period of the fourth to seventh centuries, saw both the Christianization of the region and the legal deterioration of the status of Jews and Judaism. Christianity had entered the fourth century as an illegal and persecuted faith; it would exit the century as the state religion. Christian Rome would promulgate legislation to limit the spread of Judaism, and increasingly to remove Jews from most offices in the imperial bureaucracy. It is not clear to what degree such legislation was enforced, nor what its impact was on the lives of Jewish men and women. However, in the seventh century, Jews and Judaism would have to respond to a new set of challenges and opportunities engendered by the Islamic conquest of both the Sassanian Empire and much of the Eastern Roman Empire.

BIBLIOGRAPHY

Brooten, Bernadette. *Women Leaders in the Ancient Synagogue: Inscriptional Evidence and Background Issues.* 1982.

Cohen, Shaye J. D. *From the Maccabees to the Mishnah.* 1987.

Gager, John. *The Origins of Anti-Semitism: Attitudes toward Judaism in Pagan and Christian Antiquity.* 1985.

Geller, Barbara. "Epilogue: Transitions and Trajectories: Jews and Christians in the Roman Empire." In *The Oxford History of the Biblical World.* Edited by Michael Coogan. Forthcoming.

Grabbe, Lester L. *Judaism from Cyrus to Hadrian.* Vol. 2, *The Roman Period.* 1992.

Hauptman, Judith. *Rereading the Rabbis: A Woman's Voice.* 1998.

Ilan, Tal. *Jewish Women in Greco-Roman Palestine: An Inquiry into Image and Status.* 1995.

Jagersma, Henk. *A History of Israel from Alexander the Great to Bar Kochba.* 1986.

Kraemer, Ross Shepard. *Her Share of the Blessings: Women's Religion among Pagans, Jews and Christians in the Greco-Roman World.* 1992.

————, ed. *Maenads, Martyrs, Matrons, Monastics: A Sourcebook on Women's Religions in the Greco-Roman World.* 1988.

Nathanson, Barbara Geller. "Toward a Multicultural Ecumenical History of Women in the First Century/ies C.E." In *Searching the Scriptures: A Feminist Introduction.* Edited by Elisabeth Schüssler Fiorenza. 1993.

Neusner, Jacob. *A History of the Mishnaic Law of Women.* Pt. 5, *The Mishnaic System of Women.* 1980.

————. *Rabbinic Judaism: Structure and System.* 1995.

Peskowitz, Miriam. *Spinning Fantasies: Rabbis, Gender, and History.* 1997.

Saldarini, Anthony. "Babatha's Story." *Biblical Archaeological Review* 24, no. 2 (March/April 1998): 28–33, 36–37, 72–74.

Schüssler Fiorenza, Elisabeth. *In Memory of Her: A Feminist Theological Reconstruction of Christian Origins.* 1983.

Segal, Alan A. F. *Rebecca's Children: Judaism and Christianity in the Roman World.* 1986.

Shanks, Hershel, ed. *Christianity and Rabbinic Judaism: A Parallel History of Their Origins and Early Development.* 1992.

Wegner, Judith. *Chattel or Person? The Status of Women in the Mishnah.* 1988.

See also **Patronage**.

BARBARA GELLER

In the Middle Ages

In medieval times most Jews lived outside the land of Israel, with significant populations in the Muslim worlds of North Africa, the Middle East, western Asia, and Spain; smaller numbers of Jews lived in Christian Europe. Jewish communities generally governed themselves by the Babylonian Talmud, which regularized family, business, community, and religious norms, although divergence from various aspects of rabbinic legislation affecting women's lives was not uncommon. The major intellectual endeavor of medieval Judaism was the continuation of the Talmudic enterprise through collections of rabbinic answers to legal questions (responsa literature), the production of legal codes, and Biblical and Talmudic commentaries. The Karaites, a schismatic sect of the Middle Ages that rejected the entire body of Talmudic legislation in favor of a return to personal study of the Hebrew Bible, mounted the only significant challenge to rabbinic authority, but the group's missionary activities among the Rabbanites had all but ceased by the end of the eleventh century. Medieval Judaism is also distinguished for its achievements in religious philosophy and mysticism.

Medieval rabbinic Judaism ordained separate gender roles and religious obligations, relegating females to secondary, enabling positions. However, norms and customs of local environments were also factors in how Jewish social life developed, since Jews assumed the language, dress, and many of the mores of their gentile neighbors, including cultural attitudes toward appropriate female behavior. Recovering Jewish women's personal or spiritual aspirations, or their feelings about the expectations imposed upon them, is all but impossible since virtually no documents written by medieval Jewish women survive.

According to sources ranging from the eighth to the twelfth centuries, Jewish social life in urban centers of the Muslim world such as Baghdad and Cairo was strongly influenced by Islamic customs, and polygyny was not uncommon. Though Jewish women of prosperous families were not literally isolated in women's quarters, community norms dictated that women remain out of the public eye. Women, who married quite young, were often protected by social safeguards written into their marriage contracts altering Jewish laws and practices unfavorable to women, particularly in the areas of divorce, ordinarily a solely male prerogative, and desertion. Some Jews in the land of Israel never adopted the unilateral marriage contract (*ketubah*), issued in the husband's name, that was mandated by the Babylonian Talmud. The Cairo Genizah, a major source of documents pertaining to medieval Jewish life, has preserved tenth- and eleventh-century contracts from the land of Israel defining marriage as a partnership and that permit wives the right to initiate divorce proceedings.

Although education of boys in both religious and secular subjects was common, Jewish women were rarely literate. Genizah documents report that women, who had no obligation to worship communally, were pious in observing home-based laws incumbent upon them. Women who chose to attend synogogue prayed in a gallery separated from male worshipers. Prosperous women often donated Torah scrolls or left legacies for the upkeep of the synagogue; these actions reflect women's strategies for asserting themselves in a realm of communal activity from which they were otherwise excluded.

The small Jewish communities of medieval Christian Europe lived in an atmosphere of religious suspicion and legal disability. Following the Crusades, Jews were barred from virtually any source of livelihood but moneylending. They were often compelled to wear distinctive clothing and badges; toward the end of the Middle Ages, Jews were either expelled from areas where they had long lived (including England in 1290 and Spain in 1492) or forced to live in crowded ghettos. Despite their political insecurity, Jews enjoyed a high standard of living and were significantly acculturated. Women's status was higher than in the Islamic milieu as indicated by large dowries, significant freedom of movement, and eleventh-century rabbinic ruling forbidding polygyny for Jews in Christian countries, attributed to Rabbi Gershom ben Judah, who also ruled that no woman could be divorced against her will. Jewish women were active participants in the economic survival of their families; wives of rabbinic leaders, such as the twelfth-century Dolce of Worms, sometimes supported their households through moneylending activities. Such independent businesswomen, including widows in control of significant resources, possessed property and appeared in court on their own

The expulsion of the Jews from Spain in 1492 by command of the Inquisition is depicted in this engraving (Corbis-Bettmann).

behalf, despite Talmudic regulations to the contrary. According to notarial documents from Spain, some husbands evaded Jewish inheritance laws disadvantaging women by filing Latin wills with Christian courts.

Women's involvement in business required literacy in the vernacular and bookkeeping skills, but training in Hebrew and the study of Jewish texts were rare for girls; such study was limited to a few women from elite families. Such learned women, including Dolce, and the thirteenth-century Urania, also of Worms, often led prayers for women in their communities. From the male point of view, however, learned Jewish women were irrelevant to Jewish scholarship and communal life. Women's testimony on legal or religious matters was considered only if they were regarded as reliable witnesses to the practices of distinguished fathers or husbands. Ordinary women were taught laws and liturgy essential to their domestic lives and religious obligations; for married women these would include regular immersion in the ritual bath (*mikvah*).

Medieval Jewish family life in Christian Europe was based on ideals of mutuality between spouses, including in sexual relations. Birth control, through women's use of a contraceptive barrier (*mokh*), was permitted by numerous rabbinic authorities (perhaps to the envy of Jewish women's Christian neighbors). Religious leaders in this milieu were also united in their total opposition to wife beating, insisting that an abusing husband not only be severely penalized but also be compelled to grant his wife a divorce, if this was her wish. Authorities elsewhere in the Jewish world were not so stringent; some, such as the twelfth-century physician and philosopher Moses Maimonides, permitted husbands to beat wives who did not fulfil their domestic obligations.

Religious and secular medieval Jewish literatures represent women as untrustworthy, sources of sexual temptation, and demonic; negative attitudes already present in Talmudic tradition are often intensified. The thirteenth-century German *Book of the Pious* (*Sefer Hasidim*) associates women with sorcery and witchcraft and assumes that even the most pious woman has the potential, however unwitting, to tempt a man to sin or sinful thoughts. Customary law concerning the menstruating woman (*niddah*) became more exclusionary, particularly in the Christian sphere. According to the sixth- or seventh-century *Baraita de Niddah*, the menstruant is forbidden to enter a synagogue, to come into contact with sacred books, to pray, or to recite God's name. Although rabbinic authorities objected to these exclusions, stating that ritual impurity does not bar any person from holding a Torah scroll or engaging in prayer and study, observance of these restrictions became standard components of female popular piety in Central and East Europe.

In the gender imagery that pervades medieval Jewish mystical writings (Kabbalah), the male, created in the divine image, is the dominant, primary sex, while females are passive and secondary. In sexual union female distinctiveness, and by analogy the feminine aspect of the divine, the Shekhinah, is effaced and absorbed by the preeminent male entity from which she was originally derived. While the Shekhinah as bride is a positive symbol, pointing to divine unity, the Shekhinah alone, sometimes represented as a menstruant (*niddah*), is dangerous, since the unconstrained female and her menstrual blood are linked to the demonic forces responsible for evil in the world.

BIBLIOGRAPHY

Baskin, Judith R. "From Separation to Displacement: Perceptions of Women in *Sefer Hasidim*." *Association for Jewish Studies Review* 19, no. 1 (1994): 1–10.

———. "Jewish Women in the Middle Ages." In *Jewish Women in Historical Perspective*. Edited by Judith R. Baskin. 1991.

Cohen, Shaye J. D. "Purity and Piety: The Separation of Menstruants from the Sancta." In *Daughters of the King: Women and the Synagogue*. Edited by Susan Grossman and Rivka Haut. 1992.

Dishon, Judith. "Images of Women in Medieval Hebrew Literature." In *Women of the Word: Jewish Women and Jewish Writing*. Edited by Judith R. Baskin. 1994.

Friedman, Mordechai. "Marriage as an Institution: Jewry under Islam." In *The Jewish Family: Metaphor and Memory*. Edited by David Kraemer. 1989.

Goitein, S. D. *A Mediterranean Society*. 5 vols. 1967–1988.

Grossman, Avraham. "Medieval Rabbinic Views on Wife-Beating, 800–1300." *Jewish History* 5 (1991): 53–62.

Koren, Sharon F. "Mysticism and Menstruation: The Significance of Female Impurity in Medieval Jewish Spirituality." Ph.D. diss., Yale University. 1997.

Melammed, Renée Levine. "Sephardi Women in the Medieval and Early Modern Periods." In *Jewish Women in Historical Perspective*. Edited by Judith R. Baskin. 1991.

Stow, Kenneth R. *Alienated Minority: The Jews of Medieval Latin Europe*. 1992.

Wolfson, Elliot R. *Circle in the Square: Studies in the Use of Gender in Kabbalistic Symbolism*. 1995.

JUDITH R. BASKIN

Early Modern Era (1492–1789)

Much of our knowledge of the accomplishments of Jewish women in the early modern era derives from the writings of those who tried to contain women's activities. When early modern Jewish women enjoyed economic, religious, social, or intellectual opportunities, it was often for the benefit of their families and not without the objections of rabbinic leaders. The period offers richer literary, archival, and published materials about Jewish women, particularly named women, than those available from the medieval period, but this more detailed picture should not lead us to accept the mistaken notion—repeated in general and in Jewish historiography—that the Renaissance and the Reformation offered true equality.

During the early modern period rabbis tried to make the boundaries between Jewish men and women more distinct by removing ambiguities in Jewish law that may have benefited Jewish women. For example, the law allowed women to wear tefillin straps at prayer; to be called to the Torah; to be counted for prayers; to say

Kaddish for a deceased father; to participate in the service when menstruating; to testify in court; to initiate divorce, especially in Muslim countries; to inherit, bequeath, buy, and sell property; and to serve as ritual slaughterers of animals. How widely women engaged in these activities cannot be determined. There is, however, evidence of educated women, as late as the early modern period, slaughtering and preparing kosher meat, praying in Hebrew (one began her morning blessings by reciting praise that God 'had made me a woman and not a man"), teaching, working as scribes and printers, and holding the title *rabit* or *rabanit*, found in classical rabbinic literature for a woman who participated in rabbinic discussions. Scholarly women included Fioretta (Bat Sheva) Modena, who knew Torah, Mishna, Talmud, Midrash, Jewish law (especially Maimonides), and kabbalistic literature such as the Zohar, and her sister, Diana Rieti. Modena set out to live in Safed, a community of mystics in Palestine, but died en route. Debora Ascarelli of Rome gained recognition for her rhymed Italian translations of Hebrew liturgical poetry, completed about 1537 and published in Venice in 1601, becoming perhaps the first published work by a Jewish woman. Madama Europa di Rossi worked as a professional musician in sixteenth century Mantua. Sarra Copia Sullam (1592–1641) of Venice gathered a salon of men of letters and published a polemical *Manifesto* in 1622. The first Jewish woman to write an autobiography, Glückl of Hameln (1645–1719), despite her success in business, measured her accomplishments by the men in her life and her children.

Women adopted ascetic practices such as daily fasting, prayer, placing ashes on their heads, wearing sackcloth, and denying themselves. Even though Rabbi Abraham Yagel (1553–1623) admitted that the intentions of these pious women were good and holy, he declared that their single-minded devotion to God constituted a dereliction of their duties to their husbands and their homes. Other rabbis expressed great ambivalence toward the education of Jewish women beyond the literacy that was necessary for domestic management, for fear that it would inflame their passions and endanger their honor. When on one occasion women made their grievances public by stopping the prayer service, loudly cursing those men who had done them wrong and asking for vengeance, one rabbi expressed the view, "over his women, every man shall be ruler in his house and rebuke his wife"—although the situation in itself contradicted him.

New parameters of behavior developed for Jewish women in Spain and Portugal during the Inquisition, which, established by Catholic rulers and the church at the end of the fifteenth century, fostered the emigration of crypto-Jews (those who continued to practice Judaism in secret) and destabilized rabbinic authority. Without their traditional perquisites men displayed weakening loyalty to Judaism. Inquisitorial dossiers tell how women maintained Jewish survival by teaching crypto-Jewish practices, sometimes without the knowledge of their husbands. Around some young crypto-Jewish women visionaries gathered small messianic movements. Crypto-Jewish women also controlled vast fortunes and powerful commercial and political networks. The widow and former Portuguese New Christian Doña Gracia Nasi (1510–1569), controlled her family's financial and charitable enterprises, devoting resources to resettle crypto-Jews. Gradually she took her family across Europe to the Ottoman Empire.

Jewish women in the Ottoman Empire—including Bula Iqshati, one or more women with the name Esther who held the position of Kyra (or lady) at the court, and Esperanza Malchi—gained access to power by serving the women of the Sultan's harem and providing medical, diplomatic, and commercial services to the court. Benvenida Abravanel (b. 1473), a former New Christian from Lisbon, settled in Italy, where she taught Leonora, the daughter of the Spanish viceroy, who became the Duchess of Tuscany and wife of Cosimo de'Medici.

As the exercise of royal prerogatives among Christian women throughout Europe produced a backlash, so too among Jews. Not only did a polemical literature about the nature of women emerge, showing many similarities with the Christian *querelle des femmes* tractates, but the early modern rabbis tried to limit women's access to power. For example, Joseph Caro (1488–1575) displayed a zeal for wifely obedience that extended beyond the mandate he could find in tradition. In his *Beit Yosef* and *Shulkhan Arukh*, by quoting selectively from medieval rabbinical decisions that had actually ruled in favor of women seeking divorce from their violent husbands, he undermined that right. Moses Isserles (1520–1572), an Ashkenazic commentator on Caro, downgraded the sin of wife-beating to the level of hitting another man, in contradiction to the medieval rabbis' assertion that striking women was a greater offense. Other writers of early modern literary, ethical, devotional, and religious texts, basing their work on traditional rabbinic, medieval kabbalistic, and later Hebrew texts, considered physical chastisement of one's wife a necessary aspect of Jewish marriage, despite attempts to limit it in matters connected with sexual intercourse. Their works received mass printed in the various Jewish vernaculars, including Yiddish and Judeo-Italian.

Joseph Caro was also a kabbalist, a mystic. He recorded in *Maggid Mesharim*, his conversations with a heavenly, female voice involving vivid sexual imagery of male and female union and the union of God with the

Shekhinah, God's female presence; he also told of his attempt to make intercourse an act of ascetic religious devotion rather than of physical intimacy. Judging from Caro's work female imagery of the divine does not reflect any positive change in the legal standing of women or emotional attitudes toward them.

The devotional literature of eastern European Jewish women, *tekhines,* reflected the realm of the religious life of women: menstrual purity, childbirth, Sabbath candle-lighting, and challah-baking; visits to the cemetery; and daily, Sabbath, high-holy-day, and fast-day prayer. These prayers, authored by both women and men, capture the voice of women but not always their own actual words. In reading the Hebrew versions, *tekhinot,* many women were enabled to pray for the birth of sons.

"The Jewish woman was given complete equality in the emotional, mystical, religious life of Beshtian Hasidism." So wrote Samuel A. Horodezky (1871–1957) in 1923. Most reports of women having equality among the pietistic Hasidim who followed Israel ben Eliezer (c. 1700–1760), known as the Baal Shem Tov (the Besht), during the early eighteenth century can be traced back to this statement. It could also be argued that Hasidism drew men away from their families, created an all-male realm around the *tzaddik,* the pious leader, and ignored women as an audience. There are few documented comments about women Hasidic leaders. It is telling that in 1909 Horodezky had already written about the "modest, passive" role of women among Hasidim. When he wrote of their "complete equality" with men in 1923, it was not because he had made new historical discoveries: after leaving the Ukraine for Berlin in 1907, Horodezky had in fact come under the influence of German Jewish feminism and the Zionist movement and therefore wanted to find role models for the new Jewish settlement in Palestine. According to Horodezky, Hannah Rachel Verbermacher, the Maid of Ludmir (b.c. 1815) attracted attention for her beauty, piety, and knowledge of Hebrew. She broke off an engagement and adopted a regiment of piety, acquiring a reputation for miracle working, saintliness (being a female *tzaddik*), and attracting a following. but she was repudiated by male *tzaddikim* and pressured into marriage. After two unsuccessful marriages ended her career as *tzaddik,* she spent the remainder of her life in the Holy Land. The story of the Maid of Ludmir itself repudiates the claim of women's equality in the Hasidic movement: her success as a religious leader was an unresolved conflict with her womanhood.

The real impetus for greater and freer activity by Jewish women in the public, communal, and religious spheres was simply the normal give and take between traditional rabbinic texts and the changing needs of Jewish families; depending on the conditions, women could bow to tradition, adapt it to their needs, or defy it. Although attempts were made to limit the power of Jewish women, some individuals enjoyed more success than others. Some historians, out of a desire to find paradigms for change in the position of Jewish women during their own day, have claimed to see in the early modern era the rise of new values, a new status in the Jewish community, or the liberation of women. Others, studying the same period, have sought to bolster traditional ways by pointing to the satisfactory position of women in Jewish tradition. That a few women enjoyed certain benefits, usually on behalf of their extended families, does not prove that substantive changes had come for all. Those changes were yet to come.

BIBLIOGRAPHY

Both primary and secondary writings about Jewish women during the early modern period are still very diffuse. Articles by Renee Levine Melammed on Sephardic women, Chava Weisler on eastern Europe, and Howard Adelman on Italy are available in Judith Baskin, ed., *Jewish Women in Historical Perspective* (1991); for extensive, updated citations, see the revised edition of 1997. For a survey of the major works on Jewish history of this period, many of which have sections on Jewish women, see Howard Adelman, "Early Modern Jewish History, 1450–1750," *American Historical Association's Guide to Historical Literature* (1995). The definitive history of the Jews up to the early modern period is Salo W. Baron, *A Social and Religious History of the Jews* (1960–1993), which has been completely indexed (1995). For an extensive Hebrew study of the Jewish woman in the Middle East, see Ruth Lamdan, *'Am bi-fene 'atsman: nashim Yehudiyot be-Erets-Yisrael Suryah u-Mitsrayim ba-meah h-shesh-'esreh* (Separate People: Jewish Women in Palestine, Syria, and Egypt in the Sixteenth Century; Tel Aviv, 1996). To follow up specific themes from this article, see also Howard Adelman, "Wife-Beating Among Early Modern Italian Jews, 1400–1700," *Proceedings of the Eleventh World Congress of Jewish Studies* (Jerusalem: The World Union of Jewish Studies, 1994): BI, 135–142; Amnon Cohen, *Jewish Life under Islam: Jerusalem in the Sixteenth Century* (1984), pp. 127–137; Ada Rapoport-Albert, "On Women in Hasidism, S. A. Horodezky and the Maid of Ludmir Tradition," in *Jewish History: Essays in Honour of Chimen Abramsky,* edited by Ada Rapoport-Albert and Steven J. Zipperstein. See also Libby Garshowitz, "Gracia Mendes: Power, Influence, and Image," in *Power of the Weak: Studies on Medieval Women,* edited by Jennifer Carpenter and Sally-Beth MacLean

(1995); Don Harran, "Doubly Tainted, Doubly Talented: Jewish Poet Sara Lapio (d. 1641) as a Heroic Singer," in *Musica Franca,* edited by Irene Alm, Alyson McLamore, and Colleen Reardon (1996), and "Madama Europa, Jewish Singer," in *Festa Musicologica,* edited by Thomas J. Mathiesen and Benito V. Rivera (1995).

See also Gluckl of Hameln.

HOWARD ADELMAN

Modern Era

Modern Judaism shattered the "sacred canopy" of religious belief and practice that characterized premodern Jewish religious life. In the modern age, Jews have enjoyed a plurality of religious and secular expressions of Jewish identity, with new opportunities for women for study, religious observance, and communal leadership. While the beginnings of the modern period are debated by historians, most identify it with the political emancipation of the Jews following the French Revolution. Emancipation granted Jews civic status as citizens of the state, marking a crucial transition of Jews from their semiautonomous corporate status as a group to individual standing in relation to the state and society. In western Europe the process occurred gradually from 1789 to 1871, and in eastern Europe the process took even longer, achieving completion only with the Bolshevik Revolution in 1917. In the course of the nineteenth century, Jews were increasingly able to enter a secular realm, free from religious coercion, making the degree of their religious observance of Judaism or any other religion a matter of free choice. Being Jewish could be a matter of faith or ethnicity.

Because of that freedom, being Jewish in the modern period has entailed options for religious and ethnic identities. Jews were free to abandon religious observance, marry non-Jews, and even convert to other religions, and growing numbers of Jews did so. The authority of Jewish law and rabbis could no longer be enforced upon all Jews; it could now be voluntarily accepted or rejected. Both extreme piety and assimilation into Christian culture became matters of choice rather than imposition.

Modernity brought radical reforms of Jewish religious life and the emergence of denominational distinctions along the lines of observance and belief. Reform Judaism began in the early nineteenth century when individual families, dissatisfied with synagogue services, initiated their own worship services in private homes. Prayers were recited in the European vernacular instead of Hebrew, music was played on the organ, and edifying sermons were delivered weekly. Those re-

forms eventually entered the synagogues, particularly in urban areas, and became the predominant forms of Jewish religious expression. They were complemented by a rapid decline in Jewish observance of private religious commandments, such as daily prayer and dietary regulations. Despite Reform Judaism's willingness to radically change the liturgy, it did not initially grant women equal rights. By the mid-nineteenth century, teenaged girls were given ceremonies of confirmation along with the boys, but women still sat separately from men in the Reform synagogues. Mixed seating was introduced in the United States in 1851 in Albany and in 1854 at Temple Emanu-El in New York; it became common by 1869 when many new post–Civil War synagogues opened.

During the course of the nineteenth century, Reform Judaism spread throughout Europe and the United States, generating an offshoot—Conservative Judaism—which took root in the early twentieth century primarily among East European immigrants living in the United States and situated itself as a moderate force between Orthodox and Reform Judaism. The Conservative movement was the slowest to grant women some rights in the synagogue services, and even today its seminary still refuses rabbinical ordination to lesbians and gay men. Reconstructionist Judaism, an offshoot of the Conservative movement, began in the United States during the 1930s with a distinct religious philosophy based on the writings of Mordecai Kaplan and became a pioneer in granting equality to women in matters of Jewish law and observance. Its seminary was the first to welcome gay and lesbian students for the rabbinate.

Within Orthodox Judaism, which adheres strictly to rabbinic law, women suffer the greatest disadvantages. Men have control over marriage and divorce, women sit separately at synagogue services and are not counted in the quorum for communal prayer, and heterosexual marriage is the required norm. Homosexuality is condemned as a sin. Still, modernity has brought some changes in women's status even within Orthodox communities. In part, fear of secular influences motivated the creation of schools for Orthodox girls, both in Europe and the United States, to inculcate traditional learning as well as secular subjects within a pious framework. Orthodox women also formed organizations to promote Zionist and social-service causes through fund raising and volunteer work. Within the ultra-Orthodox community women's studies of biblical texts are encouraged not for the sake of educating and empowering but for maintaining women's ignorance and dependence on men, as Tamar El-Or (1994) has argued.

In the political arena emancipation arrived differently for Jewish women than for Jewish men. Jewish women had to await the emancipation of all women, which did not happen until the twentieth century. Caught in the bourgeois expectations of middle-class European life, many Jewish women of the modern era were not able to take advantage of the new opportunities for education and careers. Moreover, they faced the double prejudices of antisemitism and sexism. Still, Jewish women were afforded new opportunities for education, careers, and religious leadership. Classical Jewish texts, particularly the Talmud, which had been the exclusive domain of men, were increasingly taught to Jewish women as well, and reforms undertaken by the synagogues began to open some avenues for women's participation. The emergence of secular Jewish literature also brought opportunities for women's Jewish self-expression through belles lettres.

Even as the religious and secular realms presented new possibilities for women's equality and leadership, they also maintained older forms of discrimination. In the name of equality, for example, distinct spheres of women's traditional expression of Judaism were minimized or eliminated by non-Orthodox Jews, such as mikveh observance (immersion in the ritual bath following menstruation and childbirth), which declined radically in the modern era. Certain secular movements, including Zionism, while proclaiming adherence to the equality of men and women, nevertheless kept positions of leadership firmly in men's hands.

Within the small Jewish population of the United States prior to the 1880s, women received only minimal Jewish education and were not voting members of the community. The demography quickly shifted at the turn of the century, as over two million Jews from eastern Europe immigrated to the United States between 1881 and 1924. They included women who had been exposed to political organizing and analysis, and who soon became major forces in the nascent labor, socialist, anarchist, and communist movements in New York and other cities in the early years of the twentieth century. However, once those movements were institutionalized—as labor unions and political parties—women were removed from leadership positions.

Similarly, during the early years of the Zionist movement, particularly during the early waves of immigration to Palestine prior to statehood, women worked alongside men in the cultivation of farmland. Yet with the establishment of the State of Israel, women were not granted proportional roles of power within the government. Instead a myth of gender equality within the State was promoted, which covered up the reality of women's subservience. For example, while women are drafted into the Israeli army, they are assigned subordinate tasks and kept from combat duty.

A young woman and man attend a Reform Yom Kippur service (Ted Spiegel/Corbis).

Throughout the modern era women managed to retain some influence on social service charities within the Jewish communities of the United States and Europe, collecting and distributing funds and goods, and running schools and vocational training programs. Those activities, a central feature of maintaining Jewish communal cohesion, became the basis for modern women's organizations, such as Hadassah, National Council of Jewish Women, and Women's American ORT (Organization for Rehabilitation and Training), which became wealthy and powerful institutions during the course of the twentieth century. With the growth of assimilation, as Marion Kaplan (1979) has shown, women have been generally more reluctant than men to abandon religious traditions and Jewish identification. Paula Hyman's (1980) description of a strike in 1902 by New York immigrant women against a sudden rise in the cost of kosher meat captures both the commitment of these housewives to maintaining Jewish traditions and the power they were able to exert in subverting the price rise.

Despite the increased opportunities for women's leadership in modern Jewish life, discussions of Jewish identity continue to be predicated on the male Jewish experience. Few women writing modern Hebrew or Yiddish literature were accorded the same recognition for their work as their male colleagues by a literary establishment dominated by men. Jewish literature in all languages remains overwhelmingly preoccupied with the male experience as the vehicle for exploring Jewish identity.

Similarly, modern Jewish theology also defines Jewish experience in male terms. Often written in apologetic terms for a wider Christian readership, Jewish theology defends the traditional role of women as an expression of respect for femininity. Jewish theologians from Moritz Lazarus to Emanuel Levinas proclaim the moral superiority of Jewish law but disregard the inferior status it grants to women. Likewise, Jewish history, which began to be written in the nineteenth century, has been almost exclusively about men's experiences.

The Jewish Women's Organization in Germany, founded in 1904, was the first organizational effort to promote women's rights within the European Jewish community. Among its achievements were winning women's right to vote in Jewish communal elections and establishing alliances with the wider German feminist movement. Its fight against white slavery within the Jewish community was less successful, and its ties to German Christian feminists were broken with Hitler's rise to power in 1933.

Antisemitism became a central feature of Jewish life in the modern era, affecting religious as well as political decisions. Although Jews hoped the tolerance brought by modernity would overcome the Christian anti-Judaism that had led to periods of religious persecution during the Middle Ages, the rise of racial theory in the nineteenth century transformed theological prejudice into a secular Judeophobia. Heightened during periods of economic or social unrest, antisemitism became a central element within the political and social landscapes of Europe, the Soviet Union, and the United States, reaching its zenith with the rise of National Socialism and the Nazi genocide of the Jews during World War II.

Modern antisemitism has often drawn on gendered stereotypes that have marked Jewish men either as emasculated or as potential sexual aggressors, as Sander Gilman (1991) has delineated. Jews were considered abnormal for a variety of reasons, ranging from their lack of an independent state to their alleged sexual degeneracy. Antisemites have sometimes pointed to the

inequality accorded Jewish women under Jewish religious law as a sign of Jewish sexual perversity. At the outset of emancipation antisemites called for the thorough assimilation of Jews into Christian society, but by the 1870s they denounced the alleged danger of assimilated Jews whose identity was not immediately apparent. Antisemites further denounced the supposed threat posed by Jews to Christian society, complaining that Europe was in danger of being "Judaized." By the early twentieth century, Jews were compared to bacilli, vermin, and rodents, and calls for their extermination were expressed long before the Nazis began their annihilation of six million European Jews, which brought a virtual end to European Judaism.

Jewish responses to modern antisemitism varied and included calls for further assimilation, efforts to prosecute authors of defamatory anti-Semitic literature, and published defenses of Judaism. Antisemitism, particularly in Russia, spurred mass emigration of Jews to the United States and also inspired many Jews to become active in political movements, particularly socialism and communism, that promised to end the social and economic conditions allegedly responsible for anti-Semitic sentiments. Early Zionism was also motivated in large measure by anti-Semitic movements in Europe, with the belief that antisemitism could never be overcome in Europe, which meant that the only solution was to leave. Zionists called for the renewal of Jewish culture by establishing a homeland and for a Jewish state that would meet other nations on equal footing.

Even as Zionism sought to overcome antisemitism and inaugurate a new era in Jewish history, it mimicked certain aspects of the gender stereotyping found in anti-Semitic writings. For example, as Michael Berkowitz (1993) has pointed out, Zionism sought the creation of a new, "muscular" Jewish man while denigrating traditional Judaism and Diaspora Jewish history as effeminate and emasculating. The equating of the Jew with the male and masculinity left no apparent place for Jewish women, as Jewish feminists such as Myra Glazer (1981) have pointed out.

Efforts by women to win ordination as rabbis were initiated in the United States and Germany during the early twentieth century. Henrietta Szold was granted permission in 1903 to study at Conservative Judaism's Jewish Theological Seminary in New York, but only on condition that she not request ordination; Martha Neumark was permitted to study at Reform Judaism's Hebrew Union College in Cincinnati, but its Board of Governors decided in 1922 that women should not be ordained. Regina Jonas, who completed her studies and examinations at the liberal seminar in Berlin in 1930, was denied ordination. Ultimately, Jonas became the first woman rabbi by receiving private ordination in Germany in December 1935, but it was not until the rise of the Jewish feminist movement in the 1970s that ordination of women rabbis and equality of women in non-Orthodox synagogues became the norm. Sally Priesand was ordained at Hebrew Union College in 1972, the Reconstructionist Rabbinical College ordained Sandy Sasso a rabbi in 1974, and the Jewish Theological Seminary ordained its first woman rabbi, Amy Eilberg, in 1984.

BIBLIOGRAPHY

Baum, Charlotte, Paula Hyman, and Sonya Michel. *The Jewish Woman in America*. 1976.

Berkowitz, Michael. *Zionist Culture and West European Jewry before the First World War*. 1993.

El-Or, Tamar. *Educated and Ignorant: Ultraorthodox Jewish Women and Their World*. Translated by Haim Watzman. 1994.

Gilman, Sander. *The Jew's Body*. 1991.

Glazer, Myra. *Burning Air and a Clear Mind: Contemporary Israeli Women Poets*. 1981.

Hyman, Paula. *Gender and Assimilation in Modern Jewish History: The Roles and Representations of Women*. 1995.

———. "Immigrant Women and Consumer Protest: The New York City Kosher Meat Boycott of 1902." *American Jewish History* 70 (September 1980): 91–105.

Hyman, Paula, and Deborah Dash Moore, eds. *Jewish Women in America: An Historical Encyclopedia*. 1998.

Kaplan, Marion A. *The Jewish Feminist Movement in Germany: The Campaigns of the Jüdischer Frauenbund, 1904–1938*. 1979.

See also **Jonas, Regina; Szold, Henrietta.**

SUSANNAH HESCHEL

The Holocaust

The term *Holocaust*, from the Greek for "a burned offering," has been used since the 1960s to refer to the murder of approximately six million European Jews by Nazi Germans and their collaborators during World War II (1939–1945). The Hebrew word *Shoah*—catastrophe—is now used as a synonym.

Hatred of Jews was the center of Nazi ideology. Hitler and his associates preached what the scholar Saul Friedländer calls "redemptive antisemitism": the belief that Jews were the root of all evil and Germany could be saved from collapse only by total removal of Jews and Jewish influence (*Nazi Germany and the Jews*, vol. 1, 1997). Religious prejudices were only one element in Nazi antisemitism, with its pseudoscientific notions of blood and race and its paranoia about international conspiracies; but old habits of Christian anti-Judaism helped normalize the new strain of hatred for Christians in Germany and throughout Europe.

Debate continues over whether the label *Holocaust* includes persecuted groups other than Jews. Jews were the main target of Nazi genocide; it was against Jews that National Socialist Germany mobilized all its resources—bureaucratic, military, legal, scientific, intellectual, and religious. But the Nazi state also initiated systematic mass killing of people deemed handicapped—the so-called Euthanasia Program—and against European Gypsies (Sinti and Roma). These programs shared with the genocide of the Jews personnel, methods of killing, and goals of so-called racial purification. Only in these cases—Jews, Gypsies, the handicapped—did the perpetrators seek out children for killing, an indication that the intention toward the group was total annihilation.

National Socialist Germany also persecuted, incarcerated, and killed Communists, homosexual men, Jehovah's Witnesses, and Afro-Germans, as well as many Polish gentiles and Soviet prisoners of war. Members of these groups shared some of the torments heaped on Jews, Gypsies, and the handicapped. But these cases are not usually included under the term *Holocaust;* they were either less massive in scope and total in intention than the Jewish genocide—for example, about two thousand Jehovah's Witnesses were killed in German camps—or, as in the case of millions of Soviet POWs, those killed did not include children.

It is difficult to determine when the Holocaust began because it was a series of steps that culminated in the slaughters Nazi jargon labeled the "Final Solution" to the "Jewish problem." In January 1933 Adolf Hitler was appointed chancellor of Germany. Within months his new regime introduced measures to crush Communists, exclude Jews from public life, and sterilize supposed bearers of hereditary diseases; Hitler also began preparing for war in search of *Lebensraum*—living space in eastern Europe for the allegedly superior "Aryan race." Only 37 percent of Germans ever voted for Hitler's National Socialist German Workers' Party, and in 1933 many Germans had misgivings. However, Hitler proved masterful at engineering foreign policy successes and organizing shows of public support that generated enthusiasm. Moreover, key elites—Protestant church leaders and many top Catholics, conservatives, university professors, and civil servants—welcomed the new regime. They applauded its hard line against "godless Bolshevism" and praised its pledge to send women back to the home, promote the values of

Several women stand in row as victims of war after being taken during the destruction of the Warsaw Ghetto in Poland in 1943 (The National Archives/Corbis).

blood and soil, and break the supposed stranglehold on cultural life of Jews and "degenerates," homosexuals, feminists, and liberals. The first religious group outlawed in 1933 was the unpopular Jehovah's Witnesses. In March 1933 the Nazi government opened the first concentration camp at Dachau, near Munich. Other camps followed, including one at Ravensbrück, for women.

By 1935 Nazi legislation put forth definitions of Jews and, by opposition, "Aryans," a necessary step toward isolating, expropriating, and murdering Jews in the German Reich and the areas it controlled. Although Nazi ideologues insisted Jewishness was racial, their legal definition relied on religious distinctions. Germans with three or four grandparents of the Jewish faith counted as "non-Aryans"—that is, as Jews, regardless of their own or their parents' affiliations and beliefs. The laws also created categories for *Mischlinge,* Germans of "mixed blood." Both official German churches, Roman Catholic and Protestant, cooperated by provid-

ing the baptismal certificates on which proof of "Aryan blood" depended.

The November Pogrom of 1938, commonly called Kristallnacht, or Night of Broken Glass, was the first violent, public attack on Jews and Jewish property in the Third Reich, which by late 1938 included Austria and part of Czechoslovakia. Groups of Nazi thugs—Stormtroopers, Hitler Youth, party elites—attacked synagogues, smashed windows of Jewish shops, plundered Jewish homes, and assaulted Jewish women and men. Other Germans joined in the looting; some looked on or grumbled about disruption of public order. One focus of Kristallnacht was the physical manifestations of Judaism: perpetrators torched hundreds of synagogues and desecrated Torah scrolls. German police arrested twenty thousand Jewish men and sent them to concentration camps. In the wake of the pogrom, many Jews fled. Between 1933 and 1939 the Jewish population of Germany dropped from around five hundred thousand (about 1 percent of the population), to between two and three hundred thousand. Many sought refuge elsewhere in Europe—France, Poland, the Netherlands—where they fell into German hands again during the war.

It was not Jews but those deemed handicapped who became targets of the first mass killing program in Nazi Germany. Beginning in 1939 with an initiative to murder children, the "Euthanasia" or T-4 Program involved doctors, nurses, bureaucrats, and social workers, as well as administrators of mental hospitals and other institutions, many of them church-run, in the slaughter of seventy to eighty thousand Germans considered "lives unworthy of living." Despite efforts at secrecy, information leaked out. Public protests peaked in 1941 when prominent churchmen and private citizens denounced the murders. Hitler ordered the program stopped, although killings continued under cover, often outside Germany.

In September 1939 Germany invaded Poland. The Holocaust was inextricably linked to the war. National Socialist goals of racial purification and spatial expansion made war not only necessary but desirable in the minds of Hitler and Nazi "true believers." War delivered into German hands the large Jewish populations of eastern Europe—Poland, Ukraine, Romania, Hungary—as well as the Jews of the West: France, Belgium, the Netherlands. War hardened the perpetrators and numbed onlookers.

With the war, Nazi persecution expanded and accelerated; ghettoization of Jews in Poland began in 1939; by June 1941, with the invasion of the Soviet Union, Nazi perpetrators began implementing total annihilation. Mobile killing squads, the Einsatzgruppen, accompanied regular German military into Soviet territory. Their orders were to shoot high-ranking Communists and Jews. In the killing fields of southern Ukraine, the ravine of Babi Yar outside Kiev, the death pits of Latvia and Lithuania, the Einsatzgruppen shot over one million Jews. They also murdered Gypsies and patients from mental hospitals. The killers sought more efficient methods, and by late 1941 innovators had begun experimenting with poison gases used in the T-4 Program. By 1942 the Nazi death camps of Belzec, Chelmno, Treblinka, Sobibor, Majdanek, and Auschwitz-Birkenau were in full operation. German transports moved Jewish women, children, and men from all over Europe to those sites for killing.

The Nazis did not restrict attacks to religious Jews; they included Christians who had converted from Judaism as well as children and grandchildren of converts. Sometimes Nazi perpetrators singled out Orthodox and observant Jews for particular tortures. They often scheduled assaults for Jewish holidays and sought to prevent expressions of religious devotion in the camps. Jewish religious responses differed; some survivors record despair at hearing the prayers of pious fellow inmates; others report that faith and tradition gave strength and sparked spiritual resistance.

Women's and men's experiences in the Holocaust converged and diverged in significant ways, summed up in the phrase "different horrors, same hell" (Myrna Goldenberg, "Different Horrors, Same Hell: Women Remembering the Holocaust," in *Thinking the Unthinkable*, edited by Roger S. Gottlieb [1990]). Jewish men were more likely to be killed in labor camps in Poland from 1939 to 1941, but more women were among the groups "selected" from the ghettos in 1942 and 1943 for transport to death camps. At the camps men had a better chance of being chosen for slave labor; SS authorities regularly consigned women, particularly if pregnant or with small children, directly to the gas. Social conventions of gender shaped techniques of hiding, forms of resistance, even the way experiences are remembered and narrated.

In 1944 and 1945, as Allied forces closed in, SS Reich leader Heinrich (Himmler) ordered the death camps evacuated and the remaining inmates killed or relocated to German-held territories. Death tolls of the resulting "death marches" were high; "liberation" came too late for many. Those Jews who survived found themselves without homes, families, or communities. As they struggled to begin new lives—in the displaced person camps of Germany, in Palestine and later Israel, in the United States, Canada, Australia, South Africa, and Latin America—some tried to put the past behind them. Others remained committed to remembering.

Religious responses are equally hard to generalize. Some Jewish survivors abandoned their religious tradition; others emerged more devoted than ever.

The Holocaust remains a burning issue for Jewish thinkers, theologians, and philosophers. Does the Holocaust demand that humanity adopt a relentless position of questioning toward God, as Elie Wiesel suggests? Does it call for rejection of ideas of "covenant" and "chosen people," as Richard Rubenstein asserts? Is the Holocaust a challenge to affirm Judaism so as not to hand Hitler a "posthumous victory," as Emil Fackenheim argues? Is it, as Emmanuel Levinas writes, about "loving the Torah more than God," experiencing the force of a God who hides his face through the intermediary of a teaching, the Torah?

Some Christian theologians, such as Franklin Littell, have also wrestled with the legacy of the Holocaust. However, the most important Christian responses have been expressed not in scholarly discourse but in the words and sometimes silences in public statements about the past. The Stuttgart Declaration of Guilt, issued by the German Protestant church in 1946, included only vague allusions to Christian complicity. The 1997 Apology of the French Catholic bishops, in contrast, repented for the Catholic Church's silence in the face of Nazi persecution, and begged forgiveness from the Jews of France for teaching contempt for Jews.

BIBLIOGRAPHY

The standard work on the Holocaust remains Raul Hilberg, *The Destruction of the European Jews*, 3 vols. (rev. ed., 1985). See also the excellent account by Leni Yahil, *The Holocaust: The Fate of European Jewry* (1987), which, unlike Hilberg's study, incorporates Jewish sources. Indispensable on the Holocaust specifically as experienced and recorded by women is the volume by Carol Rittner and John K. Roth, eds., *Different Voices: Women and the Holocaust* (1993). Rittner and Roth include excerpts from a number of women's memoirs, as well as groundbreaking essays by Vera Laska, Gisela Bock, Marion A. Kaplan, Sybil Milton, Claudia Koonz, and Joan Ringelheim. Also essential are two collections that helped establish the study of women's history of the Holocaust: Esther Katz and Joan Miriam Ringelheim, eds., *Women Surviving the Holocaust: Proceedings of the Conference* (1983); and Renate Bridenthal, Atina Grossmann, and Marion Kaplan, eds., *When Biology Became Destiny: Women in Weimar and Nazi Germany* (1984). For newer contributions see *Women and the Holocaust*, a special issue of the journal *Contemporary Jewry*, 17 (1996). A fine example of women's biography of the Holocaust is Mary Lowenthal Felstiner, *To Paint Her Life: Charlotte Salomon in the Nazi Era* (1994). On gender-specific issues related to hiding, see the documentary film by Mira Reym Binford, "Diamonds in the Snow" (1994). An intriguing case study of Jewish resistance that pays attention to issues of gender is Nechama Tec, *Defiance: The Bielski Partisans* (1993). For an examination of the perpetrators that is sensitive to women and gender, see Gitta Sereny, *Into That Darkness: An Examination of Conscience* (1983). Religious responses to the Holocaust from within Hasidic tradition are presented in Yaffa Eliach, *Hasidic Tales of the Holocaust* (1982); Eliach includes women's stories as well as men's. Useful for its excerpts from standard writings on the Holocaust is John K. Roth and Michael Berenbaum, eds., *Holocaust: Religious and Philosophical Implications* (1989). Only one of the twenty-four pieces in the book was authored by a woman.

DORIS BERGEN

Contemporary Jewish Life

The pattern of women's roles in Jewish religious life since World War II has varied in different national contexts. Although the domination of Orthodox religiosity in Europe and Israel has limited the elaboration of roles available to women in public worship, many of the most significant developments in world Judaism today revolve around changing possibilities for women in the areas of religious leadership and participation.

UNITED STATES

These issues have been particularly definitive of the postwar era in the United States, where Jewish institutions have responded to the expectation that women should find as much opportunity in public religious life as they began to find in other arenas of public life during this period. The dedication and energy that women brought to burgeoning congregational life in the 1950s contributed to growing expectations that women should be more fully acknowledged within Jewish religious life. The emergence of feminist challenges to traditional religious structures in the late 1960s pushed the American Reform movement to fulfill a longstanding rhetoric of gender equality by ordaining, in 1972, the first American woman rabbi. This momentous innovation was echoed by the Reconstructionist movement in the following year. The American Conservative movement initially resisted the break with tradition associated with female religious leadership even as many Conservative congregations were simultaneously pushing toward increased involvement by female congregants. The Conservative Jewish Theological Seminary's decision to ordain women in 1983 reflected the perception that a vital progressive movement within American

Judaism could not continue to exclude women from positions of religious authority.

Feminist concerns have also brought change to American Orthodox Judaism, although, in keeping with strict interpretations of Jewish religious law, Orthodox leaders have continued to reject the possibility of female rabbinical leadership. Representatives of various Orthodox groups often seek to justify traditional Jewish practices, which some acculturated American Jews reject as demeaning to women, in terms of women's empowerment and autonomy. A vast expansion in educational opportunities and expectations for girls and women across the broad range of American Orthodoxy also indicates a responsiveness to prevailing societal beliefs supporting more prominent roles for women in public and religious life. Growing numbers of Orthodox women who are well educated in Jewish texts are beginning to challenge the notion of a religious world based solely on male religious authority. The introduction in some communities of women's prayer groups represents an attempt to expand women's engagement in public worship within the constraints of traditional interpretations of Jewish religious law. These groups, however, have been declared illegitimate by some Orthodox authorities, on the grounds that such advances push too hard on the boundaries of tradition. Innovations in the late 1990s have included the introduction of female "congregational interns" in a few modern Orthodox congregations and, since 1997, an annual "International Conference on Feminism and Orthodoxy." Although such challenges to the traditional structure of male leadership will certainly continue, it is also clear that such advances will remain a primary source of tension and division within the Orthodox community.

Significant changes in relation to women's roles have marked all the movements of American Jewish life. Indeed, acceptance of the logic of equality, with contemporary challenges to the gendered language of prayer in both Hebrew and English and a general reexamination of patriarchal traditions and theologies, continues to bring forth much creativity and vitality in contemporary American Jewish life.

ISRAEL

The presence of American-based religious movements in Israel has helped to raise questions about the prevailing expectations regarding women's roles in Israeli Jewish life. Notably, the Reform movement began to ordain Israeli women as rabbis in 1992. The official state-sanctioned religious establishment, however, disallows Reform and Conservative religious authority in the Jewish state. Indeed, the presence of women rabbis and the notion of egalitarian inclusion of women in

The Western Wall, divided into a men's and women's section, is an important site for Jews from all around the world, and it is always busy with people coming for prayer (Bojan Brecelj/Corbis).

public worship are prominent among the many practices and beliefs that make progressive versions of Judaism so objectionable to the Israeli religious establishment. Still, the proliferation of serious educational institutions offering traditional training in Jewish classical texts to women, which arose in part to respond to demand from those coming from outside of Israel, now meets an expanding demand among native Israelis as well. The recent creation of a program to train women in Talmudic law so that they might serve as advocates in religious courts for other women facing legal questions in matters of marriage and divorce indicates the growing acknowledgment of women's competence as authority in religious law even by the religious establishment.

In keeping with traditional practice, most Israeli synagogues exclude women from leadership and active participation in public worship and mandate the physical separation of men and women at prayer. The most prominent challenge to this traditional order comes from a group founded in 1989 called Women at the Wall, whose members orchestrate their own group worship, including the reading of Torah, in the women's section at the Western Wall, the venerated remnant of Jerusalem's ancient temple. The group's efforts have been vociferously, sometimes violently, rejected by the Orthodox establishment. The late twentieth-century resurgence of ultra-Orthodoxy in small but influential groups in both the United States and Israel guarantees that the issue of women's proper roles will continue to be a flashpoint in the divide between Orthodox and non-Orthodox Jews, even as this issue animates change and dynamism among both traditional and progressive Jewish groups.

EUROPE

Great Britain's Reform movement ordained its first woman rabbi in 1975. Since then, Britain's minority progressive movements, Liberal and Reform, have openly embraced the principle of gender equality. As in the United States, liberal British Jewish leaders are still struggling with the challenge of adjusting a patriarchal religion to contemporary assumptions about gender and of translating a commitment to equality into true access for women to positions of status and authority as religious leaders. Great Britain's majority traditional Jewish establishment maintains the usual gender distinctions of Orthodox Jewish worship and leadership; yet feminist energy has emerged from within numerous communities in the late 1990s in the form of women's prayer groups. By accepting some restrictions imposed by Britain's Orthodox Chief Rabbi, the prayer groups have become an active mainstream movement and a subject of division only within the extreme right wing of British Judaism.

The legacy of the Holocaust frames the question of women's roles in continental European Judaism just as it frames every question in the much-reduced Jewish communities of Europe. In Eastern Europe and the former Soviet Union, where the native Jewish populations continued to decline under often actively anti-Semitic postwar regimes, the limited public Jewish worship that remains has been conducted principally in traditional Orthodox modes. In these and other continental communities, questions of expanding participation for women have been of little note until the 1990s. Still, with the creation of more liberal congregations within these and many countries in Western Europe, the currents of challenge and change surrounding women's status in Judaism have begun to make themselves felt in a number of continental Jewish communities. In 1998 women rabbis served one liberal community in France and one in Germany. As Jewish communities struggle with the task of reconciling patriarchal traditions with contemporary values, it seems a certainty that the challenge of finding a place for women will continue to define the evolving shape of Judaism around the world.

BIBLIOGRAPHY

Antler, Joyce. *The Journey Home, Jewish Women and the American Century.* 1997.

Beck, Evelyn Torton. *Nice Jewish Girls: A Lesbian Anthology.* 1982. Reprint, 1989.

Bridges: A Journal for Jewish Feminists and Our Friends. 1990–.

Davidman, Lynn. *Tradition in a Rootless World: Women Turn to Orthodox Judaism.* 1991.

El-Or, Tamar. *Educated and Ignorant: Ultraorthodox Jewish Women and Their World.* 1993.

Forward (English). 1990–.

Heschel, Susannah. *On Being a Jewish Feminist: A Reader.* 1983.

Hyman, Paula E., and Deborah Dash Moore, eds., *Jewish Women in America: An Historical Encyclopedia.* 1997.

The Jewish Chronicle. 1844–.

Lilith: The Independent Jewish Women's Magazine. 1976–.

KARLA GOLDMAN

Modern Movements

The political, social, religious, and cultural movements of modern Jewry, at first glance, are conspicuous by virtue of their apparent inclusion of women. To no small extent this accurately reflects the participation and prominence of women in organized Jewish life since the entry of Jews into mainstream European and American societies in the nineteenth century. After all, in socialist parties, relief societies, and trade unions, from the 1880s to the 1940s Jewish women were outspoken and dynamic organizers; there have been a number of significant Jewish women writers, on Jewish and general themes, in most Western languages and national contexts; women provided much of the grassroots support for Zionism, in both Palestine and the Diaspora from World I until decades after the founding of Israel in 1948; since the 1980s women rabbis have emerged as a formidable force in the Conservative, Reform, and Reconstructionist movements; and specifically Jewish feminist movements seem to have had a significant impact on Jewish women's lives and on the shape of feminism writ large from the beginning to the end of the twentieth century. Jewish women, as individuals, have made tremendous inroads in secular education and professions in the West, signified in part by the ascension of attorney Ruth Bader Ginsberg to the Supreme Court of the United States in 1993.

One of the major forces behind Judaism's division into competing currents, and a primary way they continue to be distinguished, emanate from their stance toward women. Varieties of orthodoxy have been tacitly united in keeping women out of the rabbinate and removed from liturgical, ritual, and decision-making roles in synagogue life. Although a sophisticated corpus of apologetics concerning women in traditional Judaism exists, partly fueled by a "return" to fundamentalism among Jews who were not previously observant, there is a significant void between so-called orthodox groups and all of the others, where "nonsexist" language and "egalitarian" services have become a matter of course. On the other hand, it may be argued that as the rabbinate and synagogue duties have become "feminized" in the non-Orthodox spheres, there has been concomitant loss of prestige for leadership in these areas. The religious realm, per se, has lagged behind the "secular" Jewish scholarly community, if one judges by the relative number of women Jewish studies' "chairholders," versus, say, the number of women who are head rabbis of large congregations.

Nevertheless, observers of Jewish women in modern movements would be well-served to heed the prescription of historian and theoretician Joan Wallach Scott in *Gender and the Politics of History* (1988): that it is misleading to identify women's "contributions" to distinct movements and causes as the essence of "women's history." Scott argues that if one rigorously incorporates the history of women in existing historical narratives, the result is not a "addition," but a completely different narrative. To take the Zionist movement as a representative case: it is one thing to talk about women's achievements in Zionism, under the auspices of organizations such as the British-centered Women's International Zionist Organization, and Hadassah, the Women's Zionist Organization of America. According to standard accounts the role of women appears as a fairly straightforward story of ever-increasing accomplishments in certain circumscribed areas, such as education and health care. But if one seeks to actually rewrite the history of Zionism by considering the women's organizations as important components of the movement overall, the entire history of Zionism reads differently—as does the history of women in Zionism. One might, as a consequence, gain a sense of the real and bitter conflicts on the basis of gender in Zionism, and the extent to which men actively worked to assure their dominance of the movement, even by resorting to threats and abuse of the instruments of the organization's governance. Similarly, in the Yishuv, the pre-state Jewish settlement in Palestine, sociologist Deborah Bernstein has convincingly detailed how the efforts of women workers to attain equality with men, though valiant, were largely fruitless. Although the imagery and symbolism of the Zionist movement, even before the famed "Second Aliyah" (1902–1918), stressed the notion that women had an equal status with men, the reality was far from this romanticized egalitarian vision. Golda Meir, who served as prime minister of Israel from 1969 to 1974, was the exception that proved the rule.

Often outstanding individual women are cited to show how hospitable Jewish movements have been to women and women's rights. For example, Henrietta

Golda Meir, who served as prime minister of Israel from 1969–1974, was one woman who achieved equal status in the Zionist Movement (Hulton-Deutsch Collection/Corbis).

Szold was active in both the effort for Jewish cultural revitalization through her participation in the Jewish Publication Society of America, and later, the Hadassah organization. Rose Schneiderman was a leader of the Women's Trade Union League, the campaign for women's suffrage, and the International Ladies Garment Workers Union. Although each of these women are recalled as heroines who worked tirelessly for their political passions, both experienced repeated snubs and intentional stonewalling on the part of the male establishment in trying to carry out their respective programs. In the end, it may be said that both saw great deeds through to their ends: for Szold the firm entrenchment of Hadassah hospitals and the educational institutions in the Jewish national home; for Schneiderman the legislation that helped ensure the protection of women under federal and state laws. But in the realm of either explicitly or implicitly Jewish movements, both women suffered chronic disrespect and grave disappointments. It is not unreasonable to presume that women who mostly confined their activities to social welfare work, such as Lillian Wald of New York and Siddy Wronsky of Vienna, were slightly less frustrated than those like Szold and Schneiderman, who dared to venture into the hurly-burly of "Jewish politics," mostly a man's sport. Analogously, it may be said that the women who focused their efforts on the National Council of Jewish Women suffered fewer indignities than their sisters of Hadassah or of the Women's Trade Union League.

Jewish women did not fare much better in the world of modern Jewish literature, which was often inextricably intermingled with party politics. Even the best-known women writers in Hebrew and Yiddish were barely recognized as leading lights in their fields. Although strong arguments may be made for others, Dvorah Baron was perhaps the most famous female Hebrew writer, and Kadya Molodowsky, a notable (later) Yiddish poet and novelist; neither, however, has a secure place in the canon. Paradoxically, two of the most famous memoirists of early modern to modern Jewry are women: the first is Gluckl of Hameln, whose seventeenth-century memoir was rediscovered by her descendant, Bertha Pappenheim—the founder and moving spirit of the Juedischer Frauenbund, the preeminent Jewish-feminist organization in Central Europe before the Holocaust. The second is Anne Frank, whose adolescent diary remains one of the touchstone works of literature from the darkest horrors of the twentieth century. At best, Jewish women's engagement with modern movements has been fitful and uneven. Despite some evidence of "progress" in the long run, it seems that women have had a greater role in providing a voice for ethical conscience, in the Jewish and larger non-Jewish worlds. In terms of cultural significance this may be seen as exceeding the self-consciously political attempts at the elevation of women's material lives and status, or the integration of Jewish women into the world of men. Yet the fact remains, as historian Susan Glenn has argued, that Jewish women have been remarkably active and visible in seeking both to carve out a political space for themselves as well as to promote agendas they deem worthy for the common well-being of society at large.

BIBLIOGRAPHY

Baskin, Judith R., ed. *Jewish Women in Historical Perspective*. 1991.

Berkowitz, Michael. *Western Jewry and the Zionist Project, 1914–1933*. 1997.

Bernstein, Deborah. *The Struggle for Equality: Urban Women Workers in Pre-State Israeli Society*. 1987.

Galchinsky, Michael. *The Origins of the Modern Jewish Woman Writer*. 1996.

Glenn, Susan. *Daughters of the Shtetl: Life and Labor in the Immigrant Generation.* 1990.

Hyman, Paula. *Gender and Assimilation in Modern Jewish History.* 1995.

Kaplan, Marion. *The Jewish Feminist Movement in Germany: The Campaigns of the Juedischer Frauenbund, 1904–1938.* 1979.

Kuzmack-Gordon, Linda. *Women's Cause: The Jewish Women's Movement in England and the United States, 1881–1933.* 1990.

Rogow, Faith. *Gone to Another Meeting: The National Council of Jewish Women, 1893–1993.* 1993.

Sacks, Maurie, ed. *Active Voices: Women in Jewish Culture.* 1995.

Schneiderman, Rose. *All for One.* 1967.

Shargel, Baila. *Lost Love: The Untold Story of Henrietta Szold.* 1997.

See also Gluckl of Hameln; Pappenheim, Bertha; Szold, Henrietta.

MICHAEL BERKOWITZ

History of Study

The modern historical study of Judaism began in the nineteenth century as part of an effort by Jews to achieve political emancipation in Europe. Jewish studies was intended to undermine assumptions about the historical course of the Christian West, particularly Christianity's superiority to other religions, by examining Western history from the perspective of the Jewish experience. That radical impulse did not initially extend to the study of women. Historians studying Judaism interested themselves from the outset in the history of Jewish men, paying very little attention to Jewish women. Even the very act of historical scholarship was described as a "manly" activity. The rise of the Jewish feminist movement in the 1970s at the same time that Jewish studies took hold in American universities brought the first attention to Jewish women's history and sparked feminist investigation of Judaism.

Scholarship on women and Judaism now extends to all periods, from ancient Israel to the twentieth century. While historians are primarily concerned with revealing forgotten aspects of women's history, feminist scholars are also reconsidering the nature of Judaism in light of women's experience, thereby recapturing the radical impulse present at the outset of Jewish studies. David Biale, Daniel Boyarin, Sander Gilman, and Howard Schwartz have initiated studies of representations of the Jewish body and sexuality that reveal Jewish self-understanding and the perception of Jews by non-Jews.

Modern Jewish Biblical scholarship first developed during the twentieth century, primarily in response to what was perceived as anti-Jewish biases within Protestant Biblical studies. The defensive nature of that scholarship insisted upon an early dating of monotheism, the uniqueness of Israel within the ancient Near East, and the exclusion of fertility cults that granted women equality and positions of leadership. Feminist studies of the Hebrew Bible have reconsidered many of these arguments, especially the early emergence of monotheism and its claim to one male God and the absence of fertility cults in ancient Israel. Archaeological discoveries that pair the male God of the Hebrew Bible with a female consort, Asherah, suggest a place for goddess tradition within ancient Israelite tradition, and, according to Susan Ackerman (1993), a greater place for women worshipers in the cult than that indicated in the Biblical text. Feminist literary analyses of Biblical texts have been wide ranging. Phyllis Trible (1984) has highlighted both the positive depictions of women in texts such as the Song of Songs and the garden of Eden episode and, conversely, the use of language that conjures up images of the subjugation and rape of women such as Hagar (Genesis 16, 21), Dinah (Genesis 34), Jeptha's daughter (Judges 11), and the Levite's concubine (Judges 19). Whereas Cheryl Exum (1993) and Esther Fuchs have argued that even the most prominent female figures in the Pentateuchal narratives and historical books of the Bible participate in a patriarchal agenda, Ilana Pardes (1992) argues that some women in the Bible actively resist patriarchy.

Research on the history of Jewish women has been primarily a task of discovery, which entails looking for remnants of women's lives in male-authored documents and in archaeological and inscriptional data. The laws of the Mishnah, according to the pioneering study of Judith Wegner (1988), permit unmarried, mature women full financial independence, while young women fall under the control of their fathers and married women are controlled by their husbands. Judith Hauptman, among others, has exposed ways in which some women's rights entered the Jewish legal system, even overcoming Biblically based disenfranchisement. Rabbinic texts are sometimes contradicted by archaeological and inscriptional data; for example, Samuel Safrai and Bernadette Brooten (1982) have argued that there is no religious basis for separate seating in the ancient synagogue, and evidence indicates that women sometimes served as religious leaders of their communities, thus contradicting the private role assigned women under Talmudic law.

On the basis of remnants of legal documents and other materials, medieval social historians such as S. D.

Goitein have demonstrated that even married Jewish women, particularly those living under Christian rule, worked in a wide range of professions, such as servants, artisans, shopkeepers, and merchants. In Muslim countries Jewish women generally followed the convention of remaining at home except for visits to the synagogue. In both regions, however, Jewish women were known for their exemplary piety and for resisting forced conversion in periods of severe persecution. Among Jews pressured to convert to Christianity in Spain during the fourteenth and fifteenth centuries women were particularly stalwart in practicing Jewish traditions in secret, under threat of the Inquisition.

In early modern Europe, Jewish women frequently worked in independent business ventures. One eighteenth-century German-Jewish woman, Gluckl of Hameln, wrote an autobiography describing both her family life and her extensive and highly successful European trading business. Jewish women were often figures at the forefront of the transition from piety to secularism. Women from wealthy families were often given secular education in languages, mathematics, music, and art so that they could interact more effectively with the non-Jewish world. During the Enlightenment several prominent Jewish women in Berlin opened salons in their homes in which significant intellectual and cultural exchange took place between Jews and Christians.

In examining the modern period, conventionally marked by historians as a period of Jewish assimilation and declining religious observance, feminist historians such as Marion Kaplan (1991) and Paula Hyman (1995) have argued for a differentiated view of women's experience. Rather than measuring the frequency of activities such as synagogue attendance (which was never encouraged of women), they suggest examining women's spheres of responsibility in the home for creating Sabbath and holiday celebrations, and they conclude that women actually resisted processes of secularization more strongly than did Jewish men. On the basis of women's experiences, the fundamental understanding of modernity should be altered, from how its impact on modernity is measured to understanding the gendered nature of being a Jew.

Scholarship on Judaism in modern times has turned to gender theory for fresh interpretations of Jewish texts and the social functions of Jews. Analyses of Zionism by David Biale and Michael Berkowitz (1993) have described its central preoccupation with creating a "muscular Judaism" and a "new Jewish man." Zionists rejected the image of the Jew in the Diaspora as a pious, studious schlemiel and replaced it with a secular, strong, and militarily accomplished Jew. Studies of modern Jewish literature by Esther Fuchs (1987) and Naomi Seidman (1997) reveal similar patterns of valorizing the masculine Jew and equating Jewish concerns with those of men and their masculinity. The ambiguities presented by a contemporary Jewish valorization of the masculine Jew and the masculine military prowess of the State, coexisting with a self-description of the male Jew as effeminate, in combination with the changing status and roles of women present important issues at the forefront of feminist Jewish scholarship.

BIBLIOGRAPHY

Ackerman, Susan. "The Queen Mother and the Cult in Ancient Israel." *Journal of Biblical Literature* 112, no. 3 (1993): 385–401.

Baskin, Judith, ed. *Jewish Women in Historical Perspective.* 1991.

Berkowitz, Michael. *Zionist Culture and West European Jewry before the First World War.* 1993.

Boyarin, Daniel. *Carnal Israel: Reading Sex in Talmudic Culture.* 1993.

———. *Unheroic Conduct: The Rise of Heterosexuality and the Invention of the Jewish Man.* 1997.

Brooten, Bernadette J. *Women Leaders in the Ancient Synagogue: Inscriptional Evidence and Background Issues.* 1982.

Davidman, Lynn, and Shelly Tenenbaum, eds. *Feminist Perspectives on Jewish Studies.* 1994.

Eilberg-Schwartz, Howard. *People of the Body: Jews and Judaism from an Embodied Perspective.* 1992.

Exum, J. Cheryl. *Fragmented Women: Feminist (Sub)versions of Biblical Narratives.* 1993.

Fuchs, Esther. *Israeli Mythogynies: Women in Contemporary Hebrew Fiction.* 1987.

Gilman, Sander. *The Jew's Body.* 1991.

Goitein, S. D. *A Mediterranean Society: The Jewish Communities of the Arab World as Portrayed in the Documents of the Cairo Geniza.* 1967–1993.

Hyman, Paula. *Gender and Assimilation in Modern Jewish History: Roles and Representations of Women.* 1995.

Kaplan, Marion A. *The Making of the Jewish Middle Class: Women, Family, and Identity in Imperial Germany.* 1991.

Pardes, Ilana. *Countertraditions in the Bible: A Feminist Approach.* 1992.

Safrai, Samuel. *Am Yisrael bi-yeme ha-Bayit ha-sheni.* Tel Aviv, 1970.

Seidman, Naomi. *A Marriage Made in Heaven: The Sexual Politics of Hebrew and Yiddish.* 1997.

Trible, Phyllis. *Texts of Terror: Literary-Feminist Readings of Biblical Narratives.* 1984.

Wegner, Judith Romney. *Chattel or Person?: The Status of Women in the Mishna.* 1988.

See also **Asherah; Gluckl of Hameln.**

SUSANNAH HESCHEL

Julian of Norwich

Julian of Norwich (1343–c. 1416), a fourteenth-century mystic, is the first English woman identified as an author. From at least 1393 or 1394, she was an anchorite, one walled away from the world. The two versions of her *Showings,* also known as *Revelation of Love,* were incited by a visionary experience she had while she lay near death in May 1373 in Norwich, England. As she was being given the last rites on the eighth day of her illness, the crucifix held before her face seemed to come alive as she beheld scenes from the Passion of Christ.

Julian probably composed the original short text of the *Showings,* the earliest account of her revelations, soon after the visionary experience of 1373, but perhaps as late as 1388. Six times the length of the short text, the second version or long text was completed after 1393 when Julian says she received clarification that enabled her to understand the parable of the lord and servant presented to her in Revelation Fourteen. This long text incorporates Julian's reflections on her visionary experience for more than twenty years and develops concepts only hinted at in the short text, such as the solution to the problem of evil that she presents in Revelation Thirteen and the extended discussion of the motherhood of Jesus in Revelation Fourteen. The short text survives in one manuscript of the mid-fifteenth century. Excerpts from the long text are found in the Westminster Anthology produced around 1500, and the entire long text is extant in four manuscripts copied in religious houses on the Continent around 1650.

Although Julian says that she was near the middle of her thirtieth year when the visionary experience occurred, she does not indicate her position in life. Scholars debate whether she was a lay person or a member of a religious order at the time she received the revelations. Bequests in several wills dating from 1393 until 1416 verify that during those years she was an anchorite in the church of St. Julian, whence we derive the name by which she is known today. Margery Kempe, a visionary from nearby King's Lynn, consulted with her about 1413 and reports on their meeting in her autobiographical *Book,* the second known to be composed by an English woman. A scribal note introduces the only extant copy of the short text as the work of a recluse of Norwich named Julian who was still alive in 1413.

Julian's revelations can be loosely grouped into three categories: visions of Christ's suffering during the Passion, auditions about the causes and consequences of evil, and "ghostly" or abstract showings concerned with humankind's essential relationships with the persons of the Trinity. These last two topics are the focus of the substantial additions that she makes to the longer text. Her development of an original theodicy or solution to the problem of evil in Revelation Thirteen and her creative exploration of the concept of Jesus as a mother in Revelation Fourteen attest Julian of Norwich's maturation, over the course of twenty or more years, from a devout visionary to a sophisticated theologian.

BIBLIOGRAPHY

Baker, Denise N. *Julian of Norwich's Showings: From Vision to Book.* 1994.

Bradley, Ritamary. *Julian's Way: A Practical Commentary on Julian of Norwich.* 1992.

Jantzen, Grace. *Julian of Norwich: Mystic and Theologian.* 1988.

Julian of Norwich. *Showings.* Translated by Edmund Colledge, O.S.A., and James Walsh, S.J. 1978.

Nuth, Joan. *Wisdom's Daughter: The Theology of Julian of Norwich.* 1991.

Watson, Nicholas. "The Composition of Julian of Norwich's *Revelation of Love.*" *Speculum* 68 (1993): 637–683.

DENISE N. BAKER

Jung, Carl

Carl Jung (1875–1961) was an influential psychiatrist who, aside from several trips abroad, spent his life in his native Switzerland. After breaking off collaboration with Sigmund Freud in 1913, Jung developed a branch of psychology called "analytic" or "depth psychology." His system posits the existence of archetypes: inherited, partially unconscious forces that profoundly affect imagination and behavior. Central to the theory is "individuation," a complex process of spiritual growth that involves proper psychological alignment with basic archetypes. Unlike Freud, who considered religion detrimental to psychological maturity, Jung believed that the course of maturation he described could be facilitated through religious practice.

Toward the end of his life, Jung said in an interview that he did not have to believe in God because he "knows" (Jung, 1977). Such famed remarks—coupled with theories that track the mysterious archetypes in folklore, mythology, dreams, and religions—have led

Carl Jung is noted for his theories of personality, including the ideas of introversion and extroversion, the existence of archetypes, and the theory of a collective unconscious (Corbis-Bettmann).

some to suggest that Jung's psychology is itself a religion, one that exalts its founder and positions Jungian therapists as spiritual leaders (Noll, 1994, 1997).

Jungian psychology has been interpreted as beneficial for women because the archetype of the anima grants femininity importance and respect. Each man is said to have an anima, a feminine dimension that he must develop to attain psychological and spiritual wholeness. A woman's masculine animus functions in a similar compensatory manner. (Emma Jung, 1957). In *Answer to Job* (1952), Jung's last major work, he gives God an anima by arguing that the Assumption of Mary accords femininity divine status and completes the deity's image.

Some feminists argue that the anima/animus model can perpetuate sexist stereotypes (Goldenberg, 1979; Wehr, 1987). Woman as anima exists chiefly as an enigmatic, inspirational image in men's minds. Man as animus is rational and intellectual, a part of a woman that is supposed to remain secondary to her conscious personality. Thus, women who perform too well in so-called masculine careers might be labeled "animus-ridden"; while men who exhibit traditionally feminine traits could be dismissed as possessed by the anima. According to his critics, Jung elevates prejudice to metaphysics by claiming that quasi-divine archetypes

determine racial and sexual stereotypes (Goldenberg, 1979; 1993).

Women who influenced Jung included his mother, Emilie Preiswerk, who frightened and fascinated him by displaying two personalities as well as psychic abilities; his cousin, Helene Preiswerk, whose skills as a medium inspired his doctoral dissertation; his wife, Emma Rauschenbach, whose resources improved his financial situation; and Toni Wolff, an important confidante with whom he had a long and public affair. The heiress Mary Conover Mellon set up the Bollingen Foundation to publish his writings in English. Several women among his circle of disciples, such as Esther Harding, Jolande Jacobi, and Marie-Louise von Franz, became prominent analysts and authors who disseminated his theories.

BIBLIOGRAPHY

Goldenberg, Naomi. *Changing of the Gods: Feminism and the End of Traditional Religions.* 1979. A critical feminist interpretation of Jung's work.

———. *Resurrecting the Body: Feminism, Religion and Psychoanalysis.* 1993. Reflections on racism and sexism in Jung's theory of archetypes.

Jung, C. G. "Answer to Job." In *The Collected Works of C. G. Jung.* Edited by William McGuire et al. Translated by R. F. C. Hull. 1953–1983. Vol. 2. Pp. 353–470. Jung's interpretation of the meaning of the Catholic doctrine about Mary's assumption into heaven.

———. "The 'Face to Face' Interview," with John Freeman, BBC television, Oct. 22, 1959. In *C. G. Jung Speaking: Interviews and Encounters.* Edited by William McGuire and R. F. C. Hull. 1977. Pp. 424–439. Jung gives a lively account of important themes in his life's work.

———. "The Syzygy: Anima and Animus." In *The Collected Works of C. G. Jung.* Edited by William McGuire et al. Translated by R. F. C. Hull. 1953–1983. Vol. 9. Pp. 11–22. Jung's exposition of his theory about the anima and animus.

Jung, Emma. *Animus and Anima: Two Essays.* 1957. Jung's wife gives an expanded version of her husband's theory about masculinity and femininity.

Lauter, Estella, and Carol Schreier Rupprecht, eds. *Feminist Archetypal Theory: Interdisciplinary Re-Visions of Jungian Thought.* 1985. Feminist modification of key Jungian theories.

McLynn, Frank. *Carl Gustav Jung.* 1996. A balanced account of the life of C. G. Jung.

Noll, Richard. *The Aryan Christ: The Secret Life of Carl Jung.* 1997. Argues that Jung had the grand ambition to found a religion.

———. *The Jung Cult: Origins of a Charismatic Movement.* 1994. Critical interpretation of Jungian psychology as a religion.

Ulanov, Ann Belford. *The Feminine in Jungian Psychology and in Christian Theology.* 1971. Explores parallels between Christianity and Jungian psychology on the subject of femininity.

Wehr, Demaris. *Jung and Feminism: Liberating Archetypes.* 1987. Argues for the usefulness of Jungian theory for women's psychological and spiritual development.

NAOMI R. GOLDENBERG

Juno

The name "Juno" probably comes from the Latin for "a young female creature." The name belonged to an ancient Italian goddess, but every woman and every goddess possessed her own "juno," the kernel of her individuality, her eternally self-renewing youthful fertility, her generativity. Juno was both the femaleness of each woman and a divine source of female power from which all women draw. Preeminently a goddess of women, Juno was associated with all the phases of a woman's life: birth, adolescence, marriage, childbearing. Her association with female rhythms led to her becoming a goddess of the moon.

In later Roman religion Juno was the wife of Jupiter and thus often seen as the equivalent of the Greek Hera. However, there are significant differences. Though Hera, too, was once an all-powerful female deity, in the classical period many of her original powers and attributes had been taken over by other goddesses. Not so with Juno. She remained a warrior goddess, still sexual, associated with the dark time of the new moon and with the underworld. In Virgil's *Aeneid* one can clearly see vestiges of the cosmogonic, all-powerful, multifaceted goddess she once was. His "savage" Juno, who descends to the deepest reaches of the underworld and stirs up its most dreadful creatures to cause havoc and chaos, represents the amorality of a divine world indifferent to justice and human suffering. Juno appears as a frightening embodiment of primal female energy, far more frightening than Hera's domestic fury.

BIBLIOGRAPHY

Kerényi, Carl. *The Religion of the Greeks and Romans.* 1962.

Monaghan, Patricia. *The Book of Goddesses and Heroines.* 1981.

Rose, H. J. *Religion in Greece and Rome.* 1959.

CHRISTINE DOWNING

Kāma

Kāma, desire, appears in ancient Hindu texts (Vedas and Upanishads) as the impulse to create and as attachment to sense objects. The legal treatises (*dharmaśāstras*) identify *kāma* as one of the *puruṣārthas* or "aims of men," the others being *artha* (material well-being), dharma (duty, law, order), and *mokṣa* (liberation). These values are often associated with the four *varṇas* (social classes): liberation with Brahmins, duty with warriors, material success with the farmer-merchant class, and desire with the servant class. Like men of low status, women are frequently represented as especially susceptible to carnal desire and as generally unsuited to ascetic practice.

The *puruṣārtha* schema reveals ambivalence about conjugal union and domestic living. On the one hand, desire and reproduction are essential if men are to repay their debt to their ancestors, who need descendants to offer them ritual meals. On the other, coitus is thought to weaken a man physically and to distract him from the pursuit of liberation. Many myths feature ascetics who have renounced sexual pleasure but are tempted in their forest retreats by lustful nymphs and prostitutes.

One of the most widely known Hindu texts is Vatsyāyana's Kamasutra, a treatise on the proper pursuit, enjoyment, and management of desire. The author recommends the study of *kāma* for both men and women in youth and middle age.

As the god Kama, desire torments Siva, the divine yogi. Shooting arrows of flowers with a bowstring of bees, Kama causes Siva to lust after the goddess Pārvatī. In one myth variant, Siva retaliates by incinerating Kama with a beam from his third eye. Ironically, this

Kāma, c. eleventh century sculpture (Seattle Art Museum/Corbis)

559

makes Kama all the more devastating, for now he is invisible and better prepared to strike.

BIBLIOGRAPHY

Burton, Richard F., trans. *The Kāma Sutra of Vatsyayana.* 1996.

Doniger, Wendy, trans. *The Laws of Manu.* 1991.

O'Flaherty, Wendy Doniger. *Śiva: The Erotic Ascetic.* 1973.

LINDSEY HARLAN

Kāraikkāl Ammaiyār

Kāraikkāl Ammaiyār (The Lady of Kāraikkāl) is one of the sixty-three saints (Nāyanmār) of Śaiva tradition in Tamil south Indian Hinduism. Scholars date her to the mid-sixth century C.E., placing her as one of the earliest Nāyanmār of the tradition. She is a proponent of *Śiva-bhakti,* a religious perspective that encourages active participation in the worship of Siva, through such activities as calling God's name, temple service, and the singing of hymns. Although there are two other women saints among the sixty-three (Mankaiyarkkaraci, the Pandyan Queen; and Icaiñāniyār, the mother of the important author Cuntarar), Kāraikkāl Ammaiyār alone is remembered as a woman author. Three hymns in praise of Siva are attributed to her: the "Tiruvālankāṭṭumūttatirupatikam" (The Sacred Verses on the Form at Tiruvālankāṭṭu), the "Tiruiraṭṭaimaṇimālai" (The Jewel-Garland of Sacred Couplets), and the "Aṟputat-tiruvantāti" (The Holy Antāti Verses on [His] Miracles); they are included in the penultimate eleventh volume of the Śaiva canon, or *Tirumuṟai.*

The hagiographies of all of the Tamil Śaiva saints are written in the *Tiruttontar Purāṇam,* which is attributed to Cēkkiḻār of the twelfth century, and constitutes the twelfth volume of the *Tirumuṟai.* Kāraikkāl Ammaiyār's story appears as the twenty-fourth chapter in this volume. This story tells us that she was once Puṇitavati, a faithful wife living in the coastal town of Kāraikkāl. One day she fed a Śaiva mendicant a mango that her husband had given her. When the husband later asked for the mango, she received another from Siva; this power terrified her husband, who ran away. Subsequently, her husband released her from the marriage, and she asked Siva to release her from her youthful feminine body. Possessing a skeletal, demonic appearance, she journeyed to Siva's kingdom in the Himalayas, then settled in the town of Ālankāṭu in Tamil country, to watch the Lord's dance at a cremation ground. Her hymn, the "Tiruvālankāṭṭumūttatirupati-

kam," is a self-portrait, describing her demonic appearance. This appearance was captured in bronze sculptures of the saint, which have been placed in Siva temples since medieval times.

BIBLIOGRAPHY

Kāraikkāl Ammaiyār's story and selection from her hymns are presented in English in Norman J. Cutler, *Songs of Experience: The Poetics of Tamil Devotion* (1987); and Vidya Dehejia, *Slaves of the Lord: The Path of the Tamil Saints* (1988). Dehejia's book discusses artistic representations; on bronze casting, see also O. C. Gangoly, *South Indian Bronzes* (1915; repr. 1978), which includes a frontispiece photograph of a striking medieval bronze image of Kāraikkāl Ammaiyār, now housed at the William Rockhill Nelson Gallery of Art, Kansas City, Missouri.

See also Bhakti; Saints.

KAREN PECHILIS PRENTISS

Karma

Karma, from the Sanskrit root *kṛ,* "to do, to make," is a concept focal to many spiritual paths born in India. These share the premise that a given karma, or deed, will produce an equivalent outcome, or "fruit," in the doer's future. A "good," that is, a constructive, deed will bring an appropriate benefit to the doer; a "bad," or destructive, deed will do appropriate damage. The connection between deed and fruit is usually believed to be automatic; no supernatural agent appears as rewarder or punisher. Often this teaching of karma is linked to the expectation of reincarnation, the belief that a person on dying will be reborn in a human or other living form, and that this process will recur again and again. One's karma, in this case, determines the shape that rebirth will take. However, effects of karma are not limited to a future life; they may surface at any time.

The precise types of deed entailed in karmic recompense and the mechanism through which this occurs are differently defined in different traditions. For the ancient caste of hereditary intellectuals called brahmins, karma was ritual action, especially fire sacrifice, and its fruits were the worldly benefits and heavenly rebirth said to be the products of a well-done sacrifice. Buddhists understood karma in principally moral terms; what counted most in shaping one's future was whether one had done injury, lied, stolen, misbehaved sexually, and whether one had protected the teachings and used wealth constructively. An important component in Buddhist teachings about karma was the desire that prompted a deed. The force projecting one from life to life was pursuit of unfulfilled desires.

The Jains had perhaps the most distinctive understanding of karma. They portrayed it as a material substance occurring in eight subvarieties that flowed into, and placed limits upon, a being's *jīva*, its basic substratum of life and intelligence. Action of any type attracted karma, but passionate, violent action drew the karma that did its host the greatest damage. Although theorists of other traditions denied such materialist concepts of karma, these surfaced very commonly in popular expectations. Hence even Buddhist lay-disciples spoke of "acquiring" *puṇya karma*, good karma. Hindu writings on popular practice, meanwhile, taught of actions that could cleanse one of *pāpa*, bad karma, such as bathing at sacred *tīrthas*, "crossing places," or activating a *vrata*, one of the optional vow-based rituals that Hindu women often take up.

Karma teachings have held both positive and negative implications for women. On the positive side, expectations that good deeds must bring results offered hope for women bound to household roles. Teachings on karma assured women lay-disciples that even a small deed such as feeding a hungry monk would bring the doer some benefit, whether this entailed increasing her household's prosperity, gaining a better human rebirth, or winning a stretch after death in some happy, though temporary, paradise. On the negative side, karma was often cited to justify women's lot in their present life. If a woman's in-laws abused her, if she suffered in childbirth or became an early widow, if she had little chance to study or to practice spiritual disciplines, this could always be blamed on past karma and treated as something she had to live through, so that an evil karma's effects could be exhausted. Hence religions presupposing the operations of karma had little motivation to ease women's pain or to challenge prevailing social practice.

BIBLIOGRAPHY

Nearly any reputable work on Indian religions will have something to say about karma. One handy source treating classic conceptions of karma across traditions is Bruce R. Reichenbach's *The Law of Karma: a Philosophical Study* (1990). Wendy Doniger O'Flaherty's edited collection *Karma and Rebirth in Classical Indian Traditions* (1980) supplements this with a dozen studies of karma in specific textual traditions. Charles F. Keyes and E. Valentine Daniel's collection, *Karma: An Anthropological Inquiry* (1983), shows how karma concepts function on a popular level, both in India and in Tibet and Southeast Asia. Ronald W. Neufeld's edited *Karma and Rebirth: Post Classical Developments* (1986) takes up constructions of karma in contemporary movements of India and North America, as well as some Buddhist movements of Tibet and East Asia. Writings specifically concerned with the link between women and karma are rare, but readers can consult Susan S. Wadley's *"Vrats:* Transformers of Destiny" in Keyes and Daniel (cited above); also see references to karma in Rita M. Gross, *Buddhism after Patriarchy: A Feminist History, Analysis, and Reconstruction of Buddhism* (1993).

NANCY AUER FALK

Kempe, Margery

Margery Kempe (c. 1373 – c. 1440), the second woman to compose a book in English, dictated her autobiography to a priest in the 1430s. Born into a prominent family in Norfolk, Kempe had her first visionary experience in her early twenties as she suffered from what appears to have been a postpartum psychosis after the birth of her first child. Her religious commitment did not develop, however, until many years later when, after the birth of thirteen other children, she persuaded her husband to make a vow of chastity with her in 1413.

Margery Kempe embarked on a life of devotional practices, visionary experiences, and pilgrimages that made her a controversial figure in her own lifetime. Clarissa Atkinson has demonstrated the similarities between Kempe and continental holy women such as Bridget of Sweden, Mary of Oignies, and Elizabeth of Hungary, who served as her models. Kempe's visionary experience, like theirs, centered on passionate love of Christ. In keeping with the practice of affective meditation, she often envisioned herself as a participant in the events of Christ's life. She also saw herself wedded to the Godhead in the tradition of bridal mysticism. Because of her independent travels (to Canterbury, Santiago de Compostela, Rome, and Jerusalem) and outspoken criticism of clerical vices, such as swearing and lechery, Kempe was several times accused of the English heresy Lollardy, but she was always acquitted of the charges after satisfactorily responding to examination by church officials. Being questioned by the archbishop of York, for example, she was accused of violating Paul's prohibition against women preaching. She not only successfully defended herself against this accusation, but went on to criticize the moral corruption of priests with an exemplum about a defecating bear.

The only extant copy of *The Book of Margery Kempe*, a fifteenth-century manuscript once owned by the Carthusians of Mount Grace Priory, was not recovered until 1934.

BIBLIOGRAPHY

Atkinson, Clarissa. *Mystic and Pilgrim: The Book and the World of Margery Kempe.* 1983.

Kempe, Margery. *Book.* Translated by B. A. Windeatt. 1985.

Lochrie, Karma. *Margery Kempe and Translations of the Flesh.* 1991.

Staley, Lynn. *Margery Kempe's Dissenting Fictions.* 1994.

See also Autobiography and Biography: An Overview; Elizabeth of Hungary; Pilgrimage.

DENISE N. BAKER

Khadija

Khadija, known in the Muslim tradition as "Tahira" (the Pure) and "Kubra" (the Great), was the first and most important wife of Muhammad, who remained monogamous during her lifetime.

Khadija, who was the daughter of Khuwaylid and Fatima, belonged to the clan of Asad of the ruling tribe of Quraysh in Mecca. Prior to her marriage to Muhammad, she had been married twice to men from Arab nobility and had borne children in both marriages. While it is believed that one of her husbands died, leaving her a widow, she was probably divorced from the other husband. The order of her marriages is disputed.

When Muhammad entered Khadija's life, she was a single woman who owned property and engaged in trade. She employed Muhammad to take her merchandise to Syria and was so impressed by how well he executed his commission and by his personality that she offered him marriage. Muhammad accepted the offer. At the time of the marriage he is said to have been twenty-five and Khadija forty, but in the opinion of some scholars both Muhammad and Khadija were younger than what is generally stated.

Khadija bore Muhammad four girls and one or possibly two boys, supported him in every way, and stood by him through the most difficult times of his life. She was the first person to accept the authenticity of his prophetic mission, obtaining confirmation of this also from her relative Waraqa bin Nawfal, a well-known Christian scholar. Her death in 619 C.E. was a great loss to Muhammad, who continued to the end of his life to remember her with the deepest love, respect, and gratitude.

BIBLIOGRAPHY

A useful source of biographical information is the article on Khadija in *The Encyclopedia of Islam*, new ed., edited by E. Van Donzel, B. Lewis, and C. H. Pellat, vol. 4 (1978). Accounts of her life are also given in Bint al-Shati, *The Wives of the Prophet*, translated by Matti Moosa and D. Nicholas Ranson (1971); Hasan Farzana, *The Wives of the Holy Prophet* (1984); and S. M. Mandaniu 'Abbasi, *Family of the Holy Prophet* (1982, repr. 1994).

Articles on Khadija also appear in books containing stories of notable Muslim women, such as Muhammad Saeed Siddiqi, *The Blessed Women of Islam* (1982).

Non-English sources include Inayat 'Arif, "Hazrat Khadijatul Kubra," in *Sharfunnisa'*, vol. 1 (Lahore, 1959); Niaz Fatehpuri, "Ummul Momineen Hazrat Khadijatul Kubra," in *Sahabiyat* (Karachi, 1957); Syed Asghar Hussain, "Hazrat Khadija," in *Naik Bibian* (Karachi, 1968); Aslam Jeerajpuri, "Umm ul Momineen Hazrat Khadija," in *Namwar Musulman Khwateen* (Lahore, 1996); and Mahmood Ahmad Khan, "Hazrat Khadijatul Kubra," in *Umhatul Momineen* (Lahore, 1996).

RIFFAT HASSAN

Knowledge

In the European tradition the term *knowledge* has gender implications because reason, one source of knowledge, has long been associated with masculinity. Aquinas, for instance, describes the relation of husband to wife as a form of qualified justice, in which one party belongs to the other, because reason predominates in men (*Summa theologiae*, 1.92.1, 2–2.57.4). Modern philosophers, beginning with Descartes, have tended to separate reason from the emotions more than did their ancient and medieval predecessors, and women, still considered less rational, came to be associated with the emotions. Some contemporary feminists celebrate women's supposed emotional connectedness and view it as an alternative way of knowing (Ruddick; Belenky et al.) Despite this theory, many traditions portray women as the possessors of valuable knowledge.

Ancient Greek literature includes many such women. In the *Iliad* Achilles' mother, the sea nymph Thetis, knows that early death awaits her son at Troy but tragically cannot convince him to heed her (Bk. I). Similarly, in the *Odyssey*, Apollo gives Cassandra the gift of prophecy but spitefully prevents anyone from believing her. In contrast to Thetis, Ariadne gains the knowledge that does save the hero she loves, Theseus, who volunteered to enter the Labyrinth in Crete to slay the Minotaur. She learns the secret of the labyrinth from its architect, Daedalus, and, after securing a promise of marriage from Theseus, passes it on to him. Theseus kills the Minotaur, but Ariadne dies before she and Theseus can reach Athens and marry.

The Greeks and Romans also consulted prophetesses known as sibyls. The most famous, the Sibyl of Cumae, was believed to have written the Sibylline Books, oracular manuscripts consulted by the Romans to resolve important religious questions. In Virgil's *Aeneid* the Sibyl of Cumae knows the way back from the Underworld, and Aeneas consults her before embarking on his heroic journey to the land of the dead (Bk. VI). To explain the prevalent correlation of female mythological figures with death, some argue that women's ability to confer life associates them imaginatively with death. Similar explanations account for figures like Circe, the *Odyssey*'s beautiful, seductive witch, who employs magical knowledge to harm men.

Plato's *Symposium* offers another example of a woman who possesses extraordinary knowledge. Socrates' culminating speech in praise of love relates his conversation with Diotima, a Mantinean woman who, among other feats, managed to postpone a plague for ten years (202a–212c). Socrates reports that Diotima described for him the highest mysteries of love, which consist in the supreme knowledge of absolute and eternal beauty. He uses a gendered term to describe his relation to knowledge, referring to himself as a midwife because he helps his interlocutors bring forth their innate knowledge. In fact, in many cultures midwives are considered repositories of powerful and esoteric knowledge. The possession of this knowledge does not usually lead to an elevated station. In India, for instance, midwives are untouchable because of their contact with ritually polluting amniotic fluid and blood. Midwives, furthermore, are not uncommonly accused of witchcraft.

In many religions female deities have primarily cognitive functions or attributes. In esoteric tantric Buddhism, for instance, a class of female beings called *ḍākinīs* appear prominently. The Sanskrit feminine noun *ḍākinī* literally means "one who goes in the sky." *Ḍākinīs* are deities that can appear in human form, and their primary role consists in aiding the meditating Buddhist. They bring the liberating and transforming knowledge the meditator seeks. They are sometimes described as consorts because the meditator must unite with the message they bear, but they often appear in gruesome and horrible forms. Ultimately, they come to symbolize the experience of the highest Buddhist insight: emptiness.

The American Shakers, founded by Ann Lee, also associated a female divine figure with knowledge. During the mid-nineteenth century the already charismatic Shakers underwent a period of even more intense ecstatic inspiration. This era became known as Mother Ann's Work, during which Holy Mother Wisdom, the female aspect of the deity who "dwells" with the Father,

A traditional birth attendant helps a mother learn to care for her newborn, Gambia, Africa, 1996 (Liba Taylor/Corbis).

regularly inspired female "instruments" who recorded her messages. Holy Mother Wisdom's distinguishing attribute was divine omniscience. She knew the ways of the world, the state of souls, and the wiles of the devil. Accordingly, she delivered ethical guidance. She also offered apocalyptic prophecies.

In many instances women are associated with a specific type of knowledge. Medieval Christians recognized that the character of the knowledge of God a woman could attain differed from that of many men. Women were generally prevented from studying scripture or learning theology. In addition to the general unwillingness to educate women, this reluctance found sanction in a scriptural dictate that women should keep silent in church (1 Cor. 14:34–35). In sixteenth-century Spain a conflict arose between those who derived their knowledge of God from theological training (*letrados*) and those whose knowledge of God was primarily experiential (*espirituales*). Women mystics, like Teresa of Avila (1515–1582), bereft of formal theological training, were *espirituales* and considered dangerous to orthodoxy. The devil could more easily deceive the weak reason of an uneducated woman.

BIBLIOGRAPHY

Belenky, Mary Field, Blythe McVicker Clinchy, Nancy Rule Goldberger, and Jill Mattuck Tarule. *Women's Ways of Knowing: The Development of Self, Voice, and Mind.* 1986.

Hamilton, Edith. *Mythology.* 1940.

Procter-Smith, Marjorie. *Women in Shaker Community and Worship: A Feminist Analysis of the Uses of Religious Symbolism.* 1985.

Ruddick, Sara. "Maternal Thinking." *Feminist Studies* 6 (1980).

Weber, Alison. *Teresa of Avila and the Rhetoric of Femininity.* 1990.

Willis, Janice D. "Ḍākinī: Some Comments on Its Nature and Meaning." In *Feminine Ground.* Edited by Janice D. Willis. 1987.

See also Ḍākinīs; Lee, Ann; Teresa of Avila; Wisdom.

MATTHEW BAGGER

Kuan Yin (Kannon)

Kuan Yin (Kannon) is the Chinese counterpart of Avalo-kitésvara, a major bodhisattva worshiped throughout the Buddhist world. Known also as Kuan-shih-yin (Kanzeon), meaning "Observer of the Sounds of the World," the deity is mentioned in over eighty scriptures. According to the "Universal Gateway" chapter of the Lotus sutra, which circulated separately since the fourth century as the "Kuan-yin Sutra," Kuan Yin can appear in as many as thirty-three different forms in order to save different types of people. Among these forms, seven are feminine: nun, lay woman, wife of an elder, householder, official, Brahman, and girl (*Scripture of the Lotus Blossom of the Fine Dharma,* 314–315).

Like all great bodhisattvas in Mahayana Buddhism, Kuan Yin cannot be said to possess any gender characteristics, although in India, Southeast Asia, Tibet, and China up until the Tang dynasty (618–907), Kuan Yin is usually depicted as a handsome and princely young man. From about the tenth century, however, the deity began to undergo a process of feminization. By the fourteenth century this process reached completion, and Kuan Yin became a completely sinicized goddess. Under Chinese influence, the Japanese Kannon assumed similar feminine traits. She often wears a hooded white cape and is accompanied by Sudhana and Dragon Girl. Her home is P'u-t'o Island.

Kuan Yin is known for her great compassion. Whoever calls her name for help receives quick response. Miracles about her abound. She saves people from physical dangers and spiritual crises. She grants children to infertile women and escorts the dying faithful to the Pure Land. Aside from calling her name, the most popular ritual is the chanting of the Great Compassion Dharani (*Ta-pai chou*) followed by confession of sins. Many temples are named after her. While especially beloved by women, Kuan Yin's devotees include both monastics and lay people and come from all walks of life. She is indeed the "Goddess of Mercy."

BIBLIOGRAPHY

Scripture of the Lotus Blossom of the Fine Dharma.
Translated from the Chinese of Kumarajiva by Leon Hurvitz. 1976.

Kuan Yin, statue at the Monastery of Solitary Joy, Jixian, China (Dean Conger/Corbis)

Stein, Rolf A. "Avalokitesvara/Kouan-yin, un exemple de transformation d'un dieu en deesse." *Cahiers d'Extreme-Asie* 2 (1986): 17–77.

Tay, C. N. "Kuan-yin: The Cult of Half Asia." *History of Religions.* 16, no. 2 (1976): 147–177.

Yu, Chun-fang. "The Cult of Kuan-yin in Ming-Ch'ing China: A Case of Confucianization of Buddhism?" In *Meeting of the Minds.* Edited by Irene Bloom and Joshua A. Fogel. 1997.

———. *Kuan-yin: The Chinese Transformation of Avalokiteshvara.* Forthcoming.

CHUN-FANG YU

Kuṇḍalinī

Kuṇḍalinī is a Sanskrit word for inner energy, power, or psychic awareness that is visualized in the form of a serpent. This serpent power is referred to as *kuṇḍalinī shakti* and is thought of as female, an ever-present, immanent form of the divine feminine in Hindu and Buddhist Tantrism. In tantric meditation and worship, the adept awakens the *kuṇḍalinī,* which is normally coiled and unconscious in a lower power center (chakra) of the body, and causes her to ascend a central channel in the body. In this ascent, *kuṇḍalinī* passes through six chakras and finally enters the uppermost energy center. The goal of this form of tantric yoga is to experience the shower of great bliss when the *kuṇḍalinī* unites with the deity residing in the uppermost chakra. Various types of meditation and worship may be used to arouse the *kuṇḍalinī* and cause her to ascend the adept's body. The most common type is the recitation of mantras, verbal formulas that embody particular deities. The adept also undertakes other yogic techniques in arousing the *kuṇḍalinī,* such as breath control, assuming proper bodily postures, and meditating on yantras and mandalas (schematic diagrams that are microcosmic representations of the macrocosm). In left-handed tantric practices, the adept sometimes arouses her through sexual intercourse or erotic stimulation. The ascent of the *kuṇḍalinī* through the chakras represents the expansion of consciousness, and her arrival in the topmost chakra symbolizes spiritual awakening or ultimate enlightenment.

BIBLIOGRAPHY

Eliade, Mircea. *Yoga: Immortality and Freedom.* 1958.

Kinsley, David. *Tantric Images of the Divine Feminine.* 1997.

Woodroffe, John. *The Serpent of Power.* 1958.

DAVID KINSLEY